Economics and Public Policy

An Analytical Approach, Sixth Edition

▶ ▶James R. Kearl

Learning Solutions

New York   Boston   San Francisco
London   Toronto   Sydney   Tokyo   Singapore   Madrid
Mexico City   Munich   Paris   Cape Town   Hong Kong   Montreal

Pearson Learning Solutions, 501 Boylston Street, Suite 900, Boston, MA 02116
A Pearson Education Company
www.pearsoned.com

Printed in the United States of America

1 2 3 4 5 6 7 8 9 10 V357 15 14 13 12 11 10

000200010270648217

RR

ISBN 10: 0-558-86084-2
ISBN 13: 978-0-558-86084-4

Contents _____

PART II THE CASE FOR THE GOVERNMENT

CHAPTER 13 Monopoly and Cartels 225

The Great Debate: Markets and the Role of Government

At the heart of this book is a question that has been part of one of the great, ongoing debates of history: When should a community rely on individual decisions mediated through markets to organize activities and when should it rely on collective actions through a government? At times this question has been answered on a large scale and entire economies have been organized around collective action and government control. Russia's economy was once organized this way when it was part of the Soviet Union; the economies of Cuba and North Korea are still organized in this fashion. But even for societies that claim to be organized mostly by private efforts and markets like those in Western Europe, Japan and North America, there are vigorous debates about whether to organize collectively in specific areas. The debate over the government's role in the provision of health care is an example: Should we rely on individual decisions and markets to deliver drugs to the elderly, or should the government intervene and organize the distribution of medication to the elderly? Should we rely on individual decisions and markets with regard to medical insurance and the choice of doctors, medical treatments, and the like, or should there be government insurance or even government, rather than private, provision of medical care? Or should we, for another example, rely on markets and prices to organize the conservation and distribution of water during a drought or should the government intervene, mandate conser-

vation and distribute water without regard to prices and markets?

I live in Utah, a state that in the best of times is arid. During a drought, the problem of too little water is a very serious one. During a recent severe drought, a letter to the editor of a local paper was interesting for what it did not say, as much as for what it said:

> Since moving back to Utah in 1990, I have experienced two droughts in 12 years, with seven of those years under drought conditions. To date I have not seen our leaders take positive, corrective action. Instead of doing nothing, they can implement a statewide water efficiency program that includes:
>
> Implementing a statewide drought-tolerant landscape ordinance, which restricts the amount of water-gulping vegetations in our desert environment.
>
> Instituting an indoor water-efficiency ordinance.
>
> Passing a residential/commercial gray water ordinance.
>
> Requiring builders and developers to save as much water as the anticipated yearly use of a new project before issuing a building permit.
>
> Passing an ordinance that allows the installation of water-free composting toilets in Utah.
>
> Allowing storm water and treated sewage water to be used for industrial cooling and processing, irritating golf courses, and groundwater recharging.

(Passing) a rainwater and snow melt ordinance where water collected from the roof an be used for indoor potable and non-potable requirements, and in irrigating the landscape.

The water we save by implementing this program is equivalent to an expanded water supply.

Note that the writer, who presumably gets his bread from a market and not from the government, who buys gasoline in a market that is organized by private, rather than public interests, and who undoubtedly lives in a home that the government was not involved in building does not even mention prices or markets as a way of solving the problems created by the drought. That is, for water, he is quite willing to abandon the market and rely on some form of collective action. Or more precisely, his initial reaction to drought-created problems is to expand the role for government.

Following the September 11, 2001 terrorist attacks, we faced a choice of whether to continue to rely on privately-provided security screeners at airports or have the government provide security. The question, which led to a short debate in early 2002, was resolved quite quickly by shifting screening and security provided to the government.

These are examples of literally hundreds of current public policy questions where the relative merits of the government versus private activity are at issue. Indeed, day-in and day-out we make decisions to rely more on the government in one area and less in another and, obviously at the same time, to rely less on markets in one area and more in another.

The tension between greater reliance on individual decisions and markets versus greater reliance on collective actions and governments is the overarching theme that ties the specific, detailed materials that follow together. This is the *public policy* part of the title to this book. To sharply focus on this theme, I have divided this book into two parts:

Part I makes the case for relying on markets, rather than government to organize economic and social activities. Or, more precisely, it makes the case for markets as *the* essential mechanisms for organizing economic and social activity with only a minimal role for government. I try to make the case as persuasively as I can that societies and economies can be organized effectively with minimal government and that, moreover, a greater-than-minimal

government is likely to undermine the effective organization of society and the economy. In fact, in the concluding section of Part I, I show that commonly used public policies make the world worse off—that is, that markets "get it right" and that more-than-minimal government activity just messes things up. In short, Part I is "The Case for the Market."

Part II makes the case for relying a more active and expanded role for government. Or, again more precisely, the case against unfettered and unregulated markets and the case for a more expansive role of the government in organizing economic and social activity. It does so in a slightly roundabout way by analyzing those circumstances in which private interests mediated through markets *fail* to effectively organize economic and social activities. That is, Part II outlines market pathologies where unfettered and unregulated markets "get it wrong" and shows that when markets get it wrong there are, in principle, public policies that make things better. Here too, I try to make the case as persuasively as possible. You can think of Part II is "The Case for the Government and Active Public Policy."

In the end, you will have to decide which case is the most persuasive. As will become apparent, it is my view that this is almost certainly tied to particular circumstances. That is, there isn't a neat, simple, global answer to a question about the appropriate role for government. Instead, we will find that in some circumstances markets "get it right" while in others, they don't.

The approach to this public policy debate developed in the following chapters is analytical. You will be a better, more informed, participant in this great debate and in its particular day-by-day, circumstance-by-circumstance playing out in specific public policies, if you understand how markets and market economies work in some deep, rather than, superficial sense. This is the *economics* part of the title. We begin with a simple assumption about human behavior—that individuals are, for the most part, self interested—and a simple assumption about our circumstances—that there is scarcity and, hence, never enough, even in the best of times. We then trace what follows. And what follows lays the foundation for understanding the interplay between markets and the government. With this brief overview, its time to begin. Bon voyage!

Part I ▶ ▶
The Case for Markets

Chapter 1 ▶ ▶
Scarcity, Choices and Costs

We live in a world of scarcity. Food, while reasonably abundant in some areas of the world, is tragically scarce in other areas. Thus, some people have never known hunger, but others are often hungry and still others literally starve. Food is scarce because there are resource constraints: Otherwise fertile land is barren because it lacks water. Sometimes land with adequate water is not productive because it lacks soil nutrients or because the growing season is too short. Land that has both nutrients and adequate water may not be very productive because those farming it lack necessary skills, tools, machines, and other implements.

Even when there is land with adequate water, nutrients, and skilled farmers, the amount of food that can be produced is limited. Land used for residential purposes cannot be simultaneously used for agricultural purposes, and vice versa. Similarly, land used for residential housing cannot be easily put to other uses. For example, land used for university buildings or student apartments, cannot be used for parking lots. As a consequence, there's typically not as much parking close to campus as most college students would prefer.

Scarcity even affects our leisure activities: There are a limited number of front row seats at a rock concert. Consequently, most people will have to watch from farther away than they might prefer. Even seats at the back are limited, so some people who might want to attend a concert are unable to do so. Not everyone can visit Yosemite National Park

and, as a consequence, only a relatively small number of people get to enjoy the vistas.

Examples of scarcity abound, and we bump into limits or constraints of one sort or another all of the time. In fact, **scarcity** dominates our lives, determines our opportunities and shapes our experiences. Because scarcity is pervasive, the consequences of scarcity penetrate virtually every aspect of our lives. **Economics** is a study of these consequences. In this chapter we consider two important consequences: the *problem of allocation* and the *problem of coordination*.

▶ The Problem of Allocation: Choices

Scarcity forces us to make choices. To understand the nature of these choices, suppose that you found yourself apparently alone on an island, as Daniel Defoe's famous character Robinson Crusoe did. The desire to eat, drink, sleep, and to be clothed and sheltered would force you to confront the particular constraints of being alone on an island. What choices would you have to make?

Choices About Leisure and Work

There are only 24 hours in a day. This means that you would have to decide how to divide your time between sleep and relaxing on the beach (activities we will call **leisure**), and gathering food, water, and other materials useful for clothing and shelter (activities that we will call **work**). Because of the limited time in each day, if you choose to sleep or engage in some other leisure activity for an additional hour, you are at the same time choosing to work less. Choosing to work less means that you are choosing to have less to eat or drink or wear or shelter you from the weather and whatever else may lurk on the island. You can either have more of one of these things or more sleep but not more of *both* sleep *and* food, or sleep *and* shelter, or sleep *and* clothing.

Choices About What to Produce and What to Consume

Once you decide how much to work, you then have to decide what particular mix of food, water, clothing, and shelter to produce. Here too, scarcity forces choices: A decision to gather more water is equivalent to a decision to have less food or less clothing or less shelter. If you choose to work eight hours a day and of those eight use one hour searching for water, for example, you cannot at the same time be building shelter or producing clothing.

Choices About Present Versus Future Consumption

Even after you have chosen a particular mix of food, water, clothing, and shelter, other choices remain. For example, you may be nervous about the possibilities that bad weather or illness will keep you from gathering food or water on a particular day. These concerns force you to make another choice: "How much of what I have already gathered should I consume now, and how much should I save for a rainy day?" A decision to consume more today is equivalent to a decision to have less in storage for tomorrow. Having less in storage means that you will have less to consume tomorrow should bad luck strike. Hence, you can be protected from the consequences of sickness or bad luck only if you consume less today and choose to **save** some of what you produce for a rainy day.

You might also decide that if you took some time today to make a tool, such as a fishing pole, it would enhance your ability to get food tomorrow. You cannot gather food and construct a tool at the same time, so the decision to make a tool that will make you more productive tomorrow implies that you must consume less today. Or, viewed in a slightly different way, scarcity means that you can only use a tool to increase your consumption *tomorrow* if you

decrease your consumption *today* and use your time to construct the tool instead of producing things to consume. (Tools of this sort are called **capital**; the production of new capital is called **investment**.)

You are not, of course, stranded on an island, but live in a developed, modern economy. Nevertheless, the effects of scarcity are the same. *Scarcity forces each of us to make choices about how we will allocate our time, what particular mix of things we will consume, how we will divide our consumption between the present and the future, and whether we will sacrifice consumption now to accumulate capital so we can increase our consumption tomorrow.*

▶ The Problem of Allocation: Costs

Choices always have costs. Specifically, the particular thing you choose "costs" you what you did not choose. Thus sitting on a beach rather than working costs you the output that you didn't produce. Or, buying a Coke costs you what you could have purchased with the $.75 if you hadn't bought the Coke.

Opportunity Cost

A measure of the cost of any particular choice is the value to you of the alternatives you could have chosen but did not—the forgone opportunities. When there are several alternatives that are not chosen, it is useful to define the cost associated with a particular choice as the value of the *best* forgone opportunity. That is, *the cost of a choice is the value of the best thing that is given up when the choice was made.* This measure of the cost of a particular choice is called **opportunity cost**.

Constraints and Opportunity Cost

The relationship between scarcity, choices and opportunity cost can be illustrated by returning to the problems you would face if you were stranded on an island. Suppose, for example, that having chosen to devote eight hours of each day to work and sixteen to leisure, you find that if you devote the full eight hours to gathering coconuts, you can gather 100 coconuts. For simplicity, let's ignore the possibility of saving. Then, working eight hours would also allow you to consume 100 coconuts. If you devote your full workday to gathering palm leaves, however, we'll assume that you can gather 200 palm leaves. Consequently, consuming 200 palm leaves is also a possible choice.

If you decided to devote two hours to palm-leaf production and only six hours to coconut production, your production of coconuts would decline from 100 to 75 and your production of palm leaves would increase from 0 to 50. Hence, choosing to produce 50 palm leaves *costs* you 25 coconuts. More generally, we can assume that any reallocation of time from coconut production to palm-leaf production costs you one-half coconut for each additional palm leaf you decide to produce. Or, if you shift your effort from palm leaves to coconuts, you will find that each additional coconut produced costs two palm leaves. Table 1 illustrates a few other production choices you might make.

A Production Possibilities Frontier

Your ability to produce coconuts and palm leaves, and the costs of choosing to increase or decrease the production of each, can be illustrated by plotting the various *maximum* combinations of coconuts and palm leaves that can be produced in an eight-hour work day. These combinations of coconuts and palm leaves that could be produced—for example, 100 coconuts and 0 palm leaves, 50 coconuts and 100 palm leaves, or 25 coconuts and 150 palm leaves—define a frontier of production alternatives or possible production choices. The **production possibilities frontier**, or **PPF**, illustrated in Figure 1 is a boundary between the output choices that can be produced, and hence consumed, and those that cannot be produced. It's a picture, if you will, of scarcity and the choices that you confront.

If you remain alone on the island, your PPF also represents your possible consumption choices. For example, if you choose to produce 50 coconuts and 100 palm leaves, you are at the same time choosing

Table 1
Your Production Possibilities

	Quantity of coconuts produced		Quantity of palm leaves produced
	100	and	0
or	75	and	50
or	50	and	100
or	25	and	150
or	24	and	152
or	23	and	154
or	0	and	200

Figure 1
Your Production Possibilities Frontier

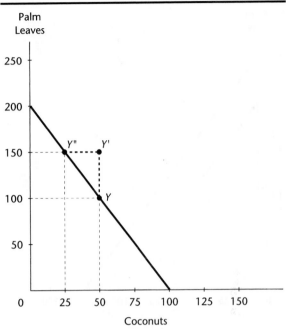

If, in eight hours of working, you can produce 100 coconuts or 200 palm leaves, you can divide your eight-hour workday between the production of each, giving you the PPF illustrated. Because your consumption is limited by the amount you can produce, you can only consume combinations of coconuts and palm leaves that lie along your PPF. You cannot consume Y', for example, because it lies beyond your PPF.

a consumption bundle of 50 coconuts and 100 palm leaves. If you want to consume a different mix of coconuts and palm leaves, you will have to change the way that you allocate work time between coconut and palm-leaf production. Even though this relationship between production possibilities and consumption possibilities may appear trivial, *one of the very important functions of an economy is to allow individuals to consume different bundles of commodities than they produce.* Toward the end of this chapter we will explore the reasons why this is possible.

The effect of different leisure-work choices. Clearly, if you choose a different mixture of leisure and work, devoting more hours to work and fewer to leisure, your PPF will lie farther out: you can produce and consume more coconuts *and* more palm leaves. For example, if you devote an additional two hours to work and are as productive in those two hours as in

Figure 2
The Effect of More Work on PPF

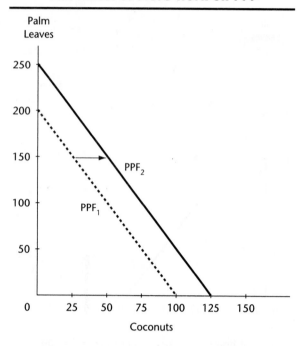

The shift between PPF_1 and PPF_2 illustrates the effect of an increase in the number of hours worked each day.

the previous eight, you could produce 125 coconuts or 250 palm leaves, or some appropriate combination of the two. The new production choices are illustrated in Figure 2. By producing more, of course, you would also enjoy less leisure. Not surprisingly then, leisure-labor choices play an important role in determining how much you actually produce and, more generally, how much an economy actually produces. Note that if you spend more time working and remain as productive as before, producing an additional coconut still has an opportunity cost of two palm leaves. That is, the opportunity costs associated with PPF_1 are exactly the same as the opportunity costs associated with PPF_2. These costs are determined not by the hours devoted to the production of palm leaves or coconuts but by your productive abilities in each activity.

The effect of different skills and resource availabilities. The number of coconuts and the number of palm leaves you can produce depend upon how much time you devote to work, how plentiful palm leaves and coconuts are, and how skillful you are at harvesting each. More generally, the amount that

can be produced depends on both the level and the quality of the **inputs** used in production activities.

For instance, suppose that you decide to consume less on a particular day and construct a tool (perhaps a long hook) that enhances your ability to gather coconuts but not palm leaves. Because of your investment, your production possibilities would change. It might be that by devoting eight hours to coconut production with the tool you can produce 150 instead of 100 coconuts. If the tool did not change your ability to produce palm leaves, however, you could still gather at most 200 palm leaves each day. This new production possibilities frontier is illustrated as PPF_3 in Figure 3.

Notice that if you spent part of a day developing your skills and abilities in coconut production instead of either working or building new capital, it would have much the same effect as the creation of a tool. Thus, capital can be accumulated either in the form of tools or training. Indeed, in an economy like that of the United States, there is a substantial amount of **physical capital** (such as buildings and machines), but there is also a substantial amount of

Figure 3
The Effect of More Capital on PPF

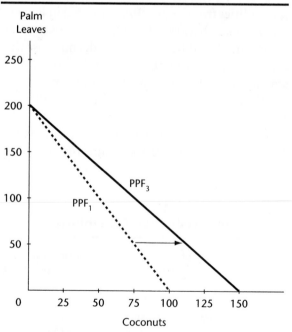

The shift between PPF_1 and PPF_3 illustrates the effect of your building a tool to help you gather coconuts but not palm leaves.

less visible but equally important **human capital** (that is, individuals who have acquired skills, abilities, or education). In either case, scarce resources have to be used to produce capital instead of other things.

If you use the tool you've built, the cost of producing and consuming one additional coconut decreases from two palm leaves for each coconut to 1⅓ palm leaves for each coconut. Coconuts have become less costly. This shouldn't be a surprise because the new tool increases your coconut productivity, and intuitively, you would expect that this increased productivity would lower the cost of producing coconuts. On the other hand, even though you remain as effective at palm-leaf gathering as you were prior to the construction of the tool, palm leaves are now *relatively* more costly. Before you made the investment, one palm leaf cost ½ coconut and now it costs ¾ coconut.

In general, a person's productivity depends on his or her innate skills, skills acquired through training, tools, and the way skills and tools are combined to produce output. How they are combined is determined by what we will call **technology**. In addition, of course, how much a person can produce depends upon how he or she chooses to divide time between leisure and work. Changes in any of these things will change an individual's production possibilities. Opportunity costs, then, are unlikely to remain static for one individual or to be the same for different individuals. For example, a student-athlete who reveals his skills in a year or two of college, will, if offered an opportunity to become a professional, often take it. The reason is that the opportunity cost of remaining in school has changed and, if offered a lot of money to "turn pro," an especially skilled college student-athlete will find continuing to go to school "too costly."

▶ An Aside: The Role of Logical Models

The production-possibilities frontier in Figure 1 is a simplified way of looking at the many choices that you confront. You are, of course, unlikely to be interested in producing either palm leaves or coconuts. "Coconuts" and "palm leaves" are merely symbolic of the kinds of goods that you might choose to produce and consume. Thinking in terms of only two goods is also a considerable simplification because many thousands of goods are produced and con-

sumed in an economy each day. A simplification that uses symbols to stand for other things, is called a **logical model**. A logical model is an abstract way of illustrating the essence of seemingly complex situations by focusing attention on the most important elements.

A logical model is unrealistic in the sense that it is not a complete description of the complexities of the world. However, making simplifying assumptions is important if a model is to cast light on interesting but complex phenomena. Models, even if simple, are useful if they reveal underlying processes that are hidden by the complexities and messiness of the real world.

To simplify and create a model, assumptions have to be made. In the model of opportunity cost and production choices just developed, for example, it was *assumed* that you produce only two goods, coconuts and palm leaves. It was also *assumed* that you work only a fixed number of hours each day and use the rest of your time for leisure activities. In addition, it was *assumed* that you have certain abilities that are reflected in the differing amounts of coconuts and palm leaves you can collect in a given amount of time. Some of these assumptions are more realistic than others, but all are important in eliminating extraneous details that are of less importance. In this case, simplification allowed us to focus on understanding the meaning of opportunity cost. Ultimately, the value of a logical model is its usefulness—it must isolate important aspects of a situation and help us understand and critically and carefully analyze them. Economics is *analytical*. That is, it relies on abstract models and reasoning to understand the world in which we live.

▶ The Problem of Coordination

Suppose that while wandering along the beach one day, you discover a footprint in the sand and find that you're not alone on the island. A second person, let's call him Friday, also lives on the island. Does this discovery affect the constraints you confront, the choices you must make, or the resulting costs? More broadly, does the fact that none of us is an island unto ourselves and that each of us lives in a society with many other individuals affect our constraints, choices, or costs?

Alone or in a society, scarcity forces choices and imposes costs on each of us. Many of the constraints that force you to make choices, however, now confront both you and Friday. There are increased demands on the available resources and, in a sense, some resources become more scarce. For example, your success in gathering coconuts will depend, in part, on the availability of coconuts. Clearly, with Friday on the island, the availability of coconuts will depend in part on Friday's efforts to gather them. It follows that scarcity creates **competition**, which in turn creates a potential for conflict and the need for coordination: Who owns what? Who gets access? How should things be divided and distributed? Who decides? How are disagreements to be settled? Should people cooperate or go their own way?

The task of crossing an intersection in a car illustrates this coordination problem. Space in the middle of the intersection between two busy streets is, obviously, scarce. Just as obvious, if two or more automobiles occupy this scarce space at the same time, serious problems are created—cars are damaged, property destroyed, and lives endangered. Thus, competition for this scarce space needs to be coordinated: Who gets to go first? How is this decided? What are the penalties for failure to yield? Coordination in this case is sometimes accomplished with mechanical devices. A green light allows entry to the intersection; a red light prohibits entry. At other times, simple rules are used to coordinate competing interests, such as "Yield to a car entering the intersection from the right." These are simple arrangements that solve a fairly simple coordination problem. In an economy with millions of individuals and tens of thousands of commodities, many coordination problems are far more complex.

Self-interested Behavior and Incentives

Individuals may want to cooperate; they may want to compete. Some (or all) may simply want to "do their own thing," pursuing self-interested goals; others may be altruistic. Individual motivation may be purposeful or it may be subconsciously programmed by psychological experiences or by genetic expression. These motives are not mutually exclusive, of course. Individuals may want to cooperate in some situations and compete in others. Individuals are undoubtedly both altruistic and self-interested. Individual behavior is likewise undoubtedly both purposeful and subconsciously programmed. Whatever the mix of human motives, competition between

individuals for whom **self-interest** is a *dominant* motive is particularly intense because self-interested individuals pursue options, make decisions, and respond to particular circumstances by examining how the options, decisions, and responses affect themselves, and not how they affect others.

Motives by themselves do not determine the choices that individuals make—these choices are also determined by inducements called **incentives**. Incentives are, in turn, determined by the costs associated with different choices. Thus, costs provide incentives for an individual to respond in particular ways in specific situations. Incentives, as we will see, are enormously important in the organization of economic activity and, consequently, the role of incentives will be an important theme throughout the discussion that follows.

It is important to note that assuming that individuals are primarily self-interested is not the same as assuming that self-interest is correct, moral, or likable. The assumption that behavior is self-interested is not a judgment about the morality of such behavior. It is, rather, a judgment that *most* individual actions are undertaken with a primary concern for how they will affect the individual taking the action. Assuming that self-interest is important is an acknowledgment that, if an economy is to be understood, it must be understood in terms of the interactions among self-interested individuals. Effective coordination of these competing interests is, as we will learn, a matter of getting the incentives right.

Coordination

It is easy to imagine particular methods of social coordination that suppress certain self-interested choices. For example, one person may have power to penalize behavior that is inconsistent with his or her wishes. Authoritarian control of this sort coordinates competing interests by allowing the interests of a very few individuals to dominate while the interests of others are ignored or quashed.

Or, coordination may occur through the power of custom or tradition. In this case, it is the family, clan, or tribe that effectively coordinates individual interests. Self-interested behavior is tempered and competing interests coordinated by allegiance to custom and family or by social habits that receive group approval.

In settings where neither coercion nor custom is the dominant organizing principle, self-interested behavior might be coordinated by appeals for individual sacrifice or the tempering of self-interest for some greater good. Sometimes, for example, calls to rally to a cause are used to offset individual interests—individuals are asked to develop and exhibit public virtue and sacrifice individual interests for some greater interest. Patriotic fervor during a war is an important way of getting people to set aside self-interest and sacrifice. Making people feel that they are part of a team, and that the success of the team depends upon their forgoing self-interest, is also important in securing commitment and effort. Indeed, team or community success is often stressed over individual success as a way of coordinating potentially competing interests.

Notice that in each of these cases there is a coordinator: some person or some group of persons who explicitly coordinates actions using coercion, allegiance, persuasion, or incentives. There is, it turns out, another option in which competing interests are coordinated by competition itself. This may strike you as paradoxical or even circular. After all, it is the competition that scarcity creates that leads to the coordination problem in the first place. In certain circumstances, however, the interaction of self-interested individuals needs no coordinator. Instead, a kind of **spontaneous order** emerges from the interaction of individuals who have what appear to be competing interests. We consider two ways that this might happen, first through exchange, and then through exchange and specialization.

▶ Exchange, Specialization, and the Invisible Hand

Suppose that by chance you find yourself on a very unusual island. When you wake up each morning, there are 200 manna (M) and 20 quail (Q) littering the beach near your shelter. With almost no effort, you can gather all of the manna and quail, which you can then consume over the course of the day.

Preferences

It would appear that your problems are over because you don't have to make choices about how much to work or what mix of manna and quail to produce. However, even though manna and quail appear each morning without any effort on your part, they remain

scarce in the following sense: If 300 manna and 30 quail appeared, you would be better off than with the 200 manna and 20 quail that actually appear, or, it follows if only 150 manna and 17 quail appear, you would be worse off. That is, there is scarcity if you would always prefer to have more manna and quail or, perhaps, more of one commodity but no less of the other.

You might prefer a different mix to the one that appears each morning. Suppose, for example, that you would consider yourself better off with a consumption bundle composed of 210 manna and 17 quail. You like manna and quail, but at the current level of consumption of each, you like manna somewhat more. That is, you would quite willingly give up 3 quail in order to get an additional 10 manna. Put simply, the bundle of (210 M, 17 Q) is preferred to the bundle of (200 M, 20 Q). You would, of course, be even better off if you could get an additional 10 manna without having to give up any quail. More precisely, even though the consumption bundle containing 210 M and 17 Q is preferred to the (200 M, 20 Q) bundle, any bundle with 210 manna and more than 17 quail would be even better.

Nature treats Friday just as well as it does you, and each morning when Friday arises he finds 200 manna and 20 quail at his doorstep. He, like you, is delighted and consumes all of the manna and quail each day. Suppose, however, that even though he very much enjoys the fortunate circumstances, Friday would think himself even better off if he had a slightly different mix of manna and quail. Specifically, suppose that Friday would like some extra quail and would be willing to give up 15 manna for at least 1 quail. That is, Friday prefers (185 M, 21 Q) to (200 M, 20 Q).

A fortuitous interaction. One day, having gathered your daily endowment of quail and manna, you stumble across Friday, who has also just gathered his daily endowment of quail and manna. Suppose that Friday proposes a game of chance in which the two of you put all of your manna and quail into a common container and throw dice to determine a new division. Because you know that manna and quail appear daily near your shelter, you figure that you have nothing to lose and agree to play the game. You roll the dice and win 210 manna and 17 quail. This is terrific! By dumb luck you happen to win a bundle that you prefer to your original bundle of 200 manna and 20 quail. Friday then rolls the dice and wins 185 manna and 21 quail. He, of course, congratulates himself under his breath for his shrewdness because, from his perspective, his winnings are preferable to his original endowment of 200 manna and 20 quail.

You both leave excited by your good fortune. Each of you believes that you won. In fact, each of you did win in the sense that each is better off with the new allocation of manna and quail. Each of you lost a little of something that you valued relatively less and won more of something that you valued relatively more. Note that this game of chance has a very curious outcome: You think that you won. Simultaneously, Friday believes that he won. Both of you probably believe that because you won, the other person must have lost. But this is clearly not the case. Moreover, although both of you feel that you won, you are consuming, in total, *fewer* quail and manna than you were prior to playing the game. That is, at the conclusion of the game, the total consumption for both you and Friday is 395 manna (210 for you and 185 for Friday) and 38 quail (17 for you and 21 for Friday), but the sum of your initial endowments was 400 manna and 40 quail. Thus, each of you left better off, even though five manna and two quail were left behind!

Exchange

Instead of thinking of this as a game, suppose that when you first met Friday had offered to trade 10 manna for 2 quail. You would undoubtedly walk away following such a trade believing that you got the better of the deal, because after the trade you have 210 manna and 18 quail—a consumption bundle that you prefer to your original endowment.[1] In this case, Friday offered a trade in which you would give up quail, which you value relatively less, in exchange for manna, which are relatively more valuable to you.

Friday leaves the trade with 190 manna and 22 quail and thinks that he got the better of the deal. He might even believe that, since he is a winner in the exchange, he must have taken advantage of you and that, as a consequence, you were a loser. Both of you, of course, win in this exchange and neither loses.

Exchanges of this sort have an **invisible hand**, that is, unintended beneficial consequences for others that result from the individual pursuit of self-interest. If an outside observer knew a little about each of your preferences, it would appear to her that you and Friday are cooperating. But of course you aren't. Each of you is interested in your own well-being and not in the well-being of anyone else. Yet in a self-interested effort to make yourself better off, each of you makes the other person better off. Although the example is simple, the consequences of exchanges of this sort are profoundly important for an economy. In fact, this simple example illustrates five important points about economic activity.

1. You and Friday are *individually* better off if you have the opportunity to trade manna and quail than if you are alone on separate sides of the island. That is, a **society** or **economy** composed of you and Friday, in which the two of you trade, improves your well-being as well as Friday's even though neither of you may have an interest in enhancing the well-being of the other person. Self-interest and opportunities for exchange, not a desire to cooperate, bring you together. Yet the outcome is in a real sense "cooperative."

2. The gains from exchange are *real*, not imaginary. Indeed, in the simple game of chance, the gains were at least five manna and two quail. Why? Because when the game was concluded, each person left better off than before the game was played, but 5 manna and 2 quail remained behind, seemingly forgotten. It is the possibility of capturing some of these gains and making themselves better off that provides an incentive for individuals to trade.

3. These gains from exchange exist because you and Friday value manna and quail *differently*. Instead of making coordination more difficult, differences among individuals make spontaneous coordination easier because the differences provide more opportunities for exchanges of the sort just outlined. If I had demonstrated to you that you would be better off in a society of individuals who were just like you, you would dismiss the demonstration as unrealistic and uninteresting. Why? Because you know that the world is filled with people who are different than you

---

[1] If (210 M, 17Q) is preferred to (200 M, 20 Q), then clearly (210 M, 18 Q) is preferred to (200 M, 20 Q).

are. Thus, the fact that there are gains from exchange because individuals are different is extraordinarily important.

4. Exchange is *not* like an athletic contest. That is, you may have thought that because you won at the game, Friday must have lost. In many ways we are conditioned to believe that if there are winners, there must be losers. Exchange, however, produces winners without losers because both you and Friday end up with allocations that are individually preferred over your initial endowments. And, significantly, each of you is better off, even though the total number of quail and manna available has not changed.

5. Even though the amount of quail and manna does not increase, the reallocation through exchange produces something important: *increased individual well-being.* It is tempting to measure economic activity by the amount of goods and services that have been produced: "If more goods and services are produced, the individuals living in an economy must be better off; if no additional goods and services are produced, those living in an economy must not be any better off." This perception of economic activity is wrong. Measurements of the quantity of goods and services an economy produces are only imperfect indicators of what economic activity really produces: individual well-being. Indeed, in this simple example, there is production of well-being through exchange, even though no additional goods are actually produced.

Specialization

Unfortunately, food does not appear at our doorsteps each morning. Instead, we have to work to transform whatever resources are available to us into goods that we would like to consume. Suppose, then, that the island upon which you find yourself has coconuts, which you can eat, or palm leaves, which you can use for shelter and clothing. To get either one, however, you must work. Figure 1 (above) provides a picture of your ability to produce coconuts and palm leaves. Suppose that Friday can produce only 50 palm leaves if he devotes all of his work time to this activity. Friday, however, is very skillful at

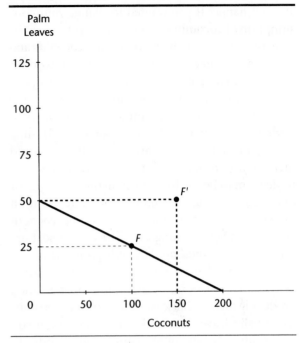

Figure 4
Friday's Production Possibilities Frontier

coconut production, and if he chooses to produce only coconuts, he can produce 200 per day. For Friday, then, one coconut costs ¼ of a palm leaf. Figure 4 illustrates Friday's PPF.

You could, if you wanted to, consume 50 coconuts and 100 palm leaves (point *Y* in Figure 1) and Friday could, if he wanted to, consume 100 coconuts and 25 palm leaves (point *F* in Figure 4). For concreteness, assume that this is what each of you chooses to produce and consume. In this case, someone looking down on the island would find that the total production of coconuts and palm leaves by you and Friday is 150 coconuts and 125 palm leaves, as shown in Table 2.

Table 2
Total Production by You and Friday
When There Is No Exchange

	Number of coconuts	Number of palm leaves
Your production	50	100
Friday's production	100	25
Total production	150	125

Now suppose that you and Friday discover each other. What might you do? Exchange, of course. Why exchange? If you wanted to change your consumption of coconuts or palm leaves, you would be constrained by your ability to produce coconuts and palm leaves, and consuming an additional coconut would cost two palm leaves. Meeting Friday opens new opportunities. Why? You can either produce the additional coconuts you want to consume or try to trade with Friday for additional coconuts. Trading might, in fact, be very attractive. If you could increase your production of palm leaves by two and trade them to Friday for *more* than one coconut, for example, you would certainly be in a better position than if you chose to produce an additional coconut yourself. Indeed, as long as trades of this sort are possible, *you should produce only palm leaves and then trade for whatever number of coconuts you want.* Why? You are better off trading for coconuts than producing them because you can *buy* more coconuts using palm leaves in a trade with Friday than you can produce by giving up palm leaves in order to produce more coconuts along your own PPF. A trade of two palm leaves for more than one coconut would allow you to increase your consumption of *both* palm leaves and coconuts, that is, consume beyond your production possibilities frontier.

Suppose, for example, that Friday was willing to trade one coconut for one palm leaf. In this case, you could produce 200 palm leaves and trade 50 of them for 50 coconuts. Doing so would permit you to consume exactly the same number of coconuts you did at point Y before such a trade became possible and also consume 150 palm leaves. This consumption bundle, point Y' in Figure 1, lies *outside* of your PPF. *By specializing and exchanging, you can now consume more than you could possibly produce by yourself.* This would certainly improve your well-being. But would Friday really be willing to make such a trade?

When Friday is alone, each additional palm leaf he consumes costs him four coconuts (that is, his consumption is determined by his PPF). If you were to offer Friday one palm leaf for only one coconut, he would be delighted. Indeed, Friday would have the incentive to produce only coconuts. Why? With this trading opportunity, Friday can produce coconuts and then trade them for palm leaves at a lower cost (in terms of the number of coconuts he must give up to get a palm leaf) than if he had given up some

coconut production in order to produce palm leaves himself. For example, if you offer Friday 50 palm leaves for 50 coconuts, Friday will specialize in coconut production, producing 200 coconuts. He can then trade 50 coconuts with you for 50 palm leaves. After the exchange, Friday's consumption will be 150 coconuts—the 200 produced minus the 50 traded for palm leaves—and 50 palm leaves, point F' in Figure 4.

Point F' in Figure 4 lies *outside* of Friday's PPF. That is, by specializing and exchanging, Friday can now consume more than he could possibly produce by himself. In a real sense, Friday can "produce" palm leaves less expensively by trading for them than by actually producing them, as long as he can trade one coconut for one palm leaf.

Table 3 summarizes what has happened to you and Friday. Note that trading one coconut for one palm leaf makes *both* you and Friday better off. Because you are better off, you may think that you have taken advantage of a trading partner who wasn't quite as shrewd as you were—you won, therefore, the other person must have lost. Once again, however, we see that each of you won even though there was scarcity and you were competing.

Specialization and productivity. The gains from specialization can be measured directly by considering the total output in this two-person economy. If Friday specializes in the production of coconuts, he will produce 200 coconuts and no palm leaves. If you specialize in palm-leaf production, you will produce no coconuts, but will be able to produce 200 palm leaves. Thus, the total production for the economy will be 200 coconuts and 200 palm leaves. Remember that before you and Friday began to

Table 3
The Change in Consumption Bundles When You and Friday Trade

| | You | | Friday | |
	Coconuts	Palm leaves	Coconuts	Palm leaves
Consumption before trade	50	100	100	25
Consumption after trade	50	150	150	50

exchange coconuts and palm leaves, the total production in the economy was 150 coconuts and 125 palm leaves. Clearly, output in the economy has increased, in this case by 50 coconuts and 75 palm leaves.

This increase in the production of both coconuts and palm leaves means that *both* you and Friday can have *more* coconuts and *more* palm leaves. Note that even though the economy composed of you and Friday is more productive, neither you nor Friday is individually more productive. Each of you continues to produce on your respective original production possibilities frontiers. The gain to the *economy* comes because each of you specializes rather than producing both commodities.

Deciding how to specialize. You might be wondering whether you could specialize in coconut production and do better (or whether Friday could specialize in palm-leaf production and do better). This isn't possible. To see why, suppose that you produce coconuts and offer them to Friday in exchange for palm leaves. In this case, you would have to get at least two palm leaves for every coconut you produced in order to make trading worthwhile. The reason is that, given your PPF, you can always produce two additional palm leaves for each coconut you decide not to produce. Thus, if you received fewer than two palm leaves from Friday in trade for each coconut, you would be worse off trading than going it alone.

Suppose, then, that you offer Friday one coconut in exchange for three palm leaves. Friday would refuse such an offer—if he wanted to give up the consumption of three palm leaves, he could, by moving along his own PPF, increase his consumption of coconuts by 12. Your offer simply isn't good enough. Even if you offer Friday one coconut for two palm leaves, Friday would refuse to trade. Why? Because if he wanted to consume more coconuts, he could decrease his production of palm leaves by two and, by moving along his own PPF, increase his consumption by eight coconuts. This is far more coconuts than you are offering for an equivalent sacrifice in palm-leaf consumption.

Alternatively, suppose that Friday decided to produce palm leaves and trade for coconuts. Friday would have to get at least four coconuts for each palm leaf in trade, because he could always get four for one by moving along his own PPF. Suppose,

then, that Friday offers you one palm leaf for six coconuts. This would be a bad deal for you. If you cut your consumption of coconuts by six, you could, by yourself, produce an additional 12 palm leaves along your own PPF. It follows that you would never be willing to give up six coconuts in consumption for only one palm leaf. Indeed, you wouldn't be willing to give up six coconuts in consumption for fewer than 12 palm leaves. Friday, obviously, would never make you such an offer if he were specialized in palm-leaf production. The conclusion? Seeking out trading opportunities will never lead Friday or you to specialize in that commodity that costs either one of you the most to produce. Put differently, *individuals will specialize so as to minimize their opportunity costs.*

Specialization and relative production costs. Specialization is determined by differences in **relative production costs**, that is, by differences in the costs to individuals of producing one thing versus producing another. To see why note that when you find yourself alone on the island, the cost of producing and consuming a coconut is determined only by your own ability to gather coconuts and palm leaves. There is no sense in which coconuts or palm leaves are relatively expensive; one coconut simply costs two palm leaves. When Friday appears, however, the opportunity cost of consuming additional coconuts is no longer determined by your PPF. Instead, your opportunity cost is determined by trades that Friday is willing to make. Coconuts will cost less in trade than if you produce them yourself, so meeting Friday has made coconut production relatively costly for you. You can minimize those costs by producing only palm leaves and trading for coconuts.

To illustrate this point, suppose that instead of finding Friday on the island, you meet Defoe, whose production possibilities frontier is illustrated in Figure 5. The consumption of an additional coconut costs Defoe five palm leaves or, alternatively, the consumption of an additional palm leaf costs him ⅕th of a coconut. In this case, you can trade coconuts for palm leaves cheaper than you can produce them yourself. For example, if you offer Defoe one coconut for three palm leaves, Defoe will be delighted. (Friday, remember, would refuse such a trade.) For Defoe, consuming an additional coconut by cutting palm-leaf production costs five palm leaves. Therefore, Defoe can get more coconuts by producing

Figure 5
Defoe's Production Possibilities Frontier

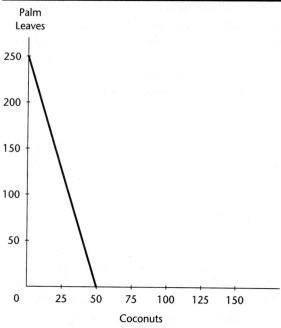

Defoe must give up five palm leaves for every coconut he gathers. Because this is more than you must give up, if you met Defot, you would specialize in gathering coconuts and he would specialize in gathering palm leaves. (Remember, you specialized in gathering palm leaves when you met Friday.) Thus, the activity in which you specialize depends not only on your production costs, but also on the production costs of potential trading partners.

depend upon being better at some activity than anyone with whom one might trade. After all, Friday is absolutely better at producing coconuts than you are (he can produce 200 per day but you can only produce 100), and you are absolutely better at producing palm leaves (you can produce 200 palm leaves per day but Friday can only produce 50). Although specialization appears to depend upon someone's *absolute advantage*, it does not.

To see why, suppose that Friday's production possibilities are illustrated in Figure 6. Friday can produce more coconuts per day than you can (1,000 versus 100), *and* Friday can produce more palm leaves per day than you can (250 versus 200). Friday is *absolutely* better at producing both goods. Notice, however, that when you meet Friday, his opportunity costs are exactly the same as they were when he could only produce 200 coconuts or 50 palm leaves. That is, producing a palm leaf still costs Friday four coconuts along his PPF. However, the opportunity cost for Friday of producing an additional palm leaf is the number of palm leaves he can trade for. You would be willing to trade a palm leaf for anything greater than ½ coconut—far fewer than the four coconuts Friday would have to sacrifice to

Figure 6
Absolute Versus Comparative Advantage

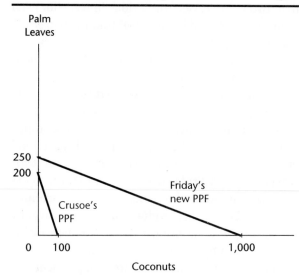

Even though Friday can now produce more coconuts (1,000 versus 100) and more palm leaves (250 versus 200) than you can, his relative costs of producing coconuts and palm leaves have not changed. Therefore, even though he has an absolute advantage in producing both coconuts and palm leaves, he still has a comparative advantage only in producing coconuts.

palm leaves and making trades for coconuts than he can if he tries to produce coconuts himself. Clearly, by trading one coconut for three palm leaves, you can also consume more palm leaves than you can if you produce palm leaves yourself.

If you meet Friday, the differences in your relative production costs are such that you would tend to specialize in palm-leaf production. If you meet Defoe, however, the differences in your relative production costs are such that you would tend to specialize in coconut production. Your ability to produce coconuts and palm leaves hasn't changed. Your opportunity costs, however, are determined by the opportunities to trade, and these change if you meet Defoe rather than Friday.

Comparative versus absolute advantage. It might appear from the examples developed to this point that specialization and the gains from exchange

produce another palm leaf himself. Thus trade would occur, and you and Friday would tend to specialize as before—you, in palm leaves, and Friday, in coconuts even though Friday is a better producer of both coconuts and palm leaves. Thus *specialization depends only on relative production costs, that is, on **comparative advantage**, not on overall productivity or absolute advantage.*

That difference between comparative and absolute advantage is enormously important. It means that you do not have to be better at some activity than anyone else in order to gain from participation in an economy. All that matters is that you be *different* from other participants in your ability to produce goods and services. All of us are different, but few of us are absolutely better. The principle of comparative advantage means, however, that *everyone* can specialize beneficially in some activity. Instead of exchange and specialization benefiting only a few individuals, they benefit all—we may not be the best, but we can be relatively better.

Conversely, comparative advantage implies that even if you were better at everything than other people, you should not try to do everything, but should specialize instead. For example, suppose that you are the best computer programmer in town and a very good lawyer as well. Should you do your own computer programming? The opportunity cost of doing your own programming is the income you could earn if you used the time devoted to computer programming as a lawyer. If you are relatively better at being a lawyer, it always makes sense to hire someone else (less skilled than you, perhaps) to do your computer programming.

The distribution of the gains. How much better off you or Friday will become with specialization and trade depends upon what each of you actually gives up for the good produced by the other person. In the particular model we are considering, this depends upon your bargaining ability.

For example, suppose that you are able to obtain three coconuts for each palm leaf and choose to consume 150 palm leaves. You would then be able to consume 150 coconuts by trading 50 palm leaves for 150 coconuts. If Friday made this trade, he would be able to consume 50 coconuts and 50 palm leaves. Both you and Friday are better off with this trade than you would be without it because you both are able to consume outside of your own production

possibilities frontiers. If Friday drove a tougher bargain, however, and obtained one palm leaf for two coconuts, he could continue to consume 50 coconuts but would have 75 palm leaves. You would then be able to consume 150 coconuts but only 125 palm leaves. Both of you remain better off than you would be if you refused to specialize and trade. Clearly, however, you are not as well off as you were when the exchange was three for one, whereas Friday is better off with the changed trading conditions.

The important point is that the division of the gains from specialization and exchange will depend upon the amount of other goods that can be obtained by giving up some of what you produce—the **exchange ratio** or, as we will come to call it, the **relative price**. If the exchange ratio is high for the good you specialize in producing, your gains are higher than if the exchange ratio is low. If the exchange ratio changes, your gains from specialization will also change, increasing when the exchange ratio increases and decreasing when the exchange ratio decreases. Even though the gains may decrease with a change in the exchange ratio, however, you are still better off specializing and trading than retreating into self-sufficiency. In short: exchange and specialization are the foundations of economic activity and, consequently, for individual well-being.

► Another Aside: Individual Outcomes, Unintended Consequences, and Social Aggregation

A warning: Thinking carefully and critically about the problems of coordination is difficult. One of the reasons is that often what appears to be true for an individual *cannot* be true of a group of individuals. It is quite natural to try to understand the behavior of a group of individuals by examining our own individual experience. This approach of extending, projecting, or extrapolating from our individual experiences to those of a group of individuals can, however, lead to mistakes. For example, in the division of a pie, a single individual can have a larger share, but it is not possible for *everyone* to have a larger share of the same pie. Indeed, one person can have a larger share only if someone else has a smaller share. In this case, what can be true for a particular individual (a larger piece of pie) cannot be true to everyone.

As we have seen, exchange and specialization are not like dividing a pie of fixed size between two individuals. Instead, when you seek out trading opportunities in order to make yourself better off, those with whom you compete (and trade) are made better off as well. Competition among self-interested individuals has *unintended* consequences. You want to increase your well-being, but as you do so your efforts also increase Friday's well-being—something you had not intended.

Sometimes there are adverse unintended consequences. For example, sometimes you might decide that if you go a little early to something, you will avoid long lines and a lengthy delay. This works as long as most people either hold different beliefs about how long the line will be or are indifferent to standing in lines. Obviously, if everyone holds the same beliefs and responds in the same way, a large group of individuals will show up early and create a long line earlier with even lengthier delays—if everyone starts for home at 4:00 P.M. to avoid the 5:00 P.M. rush-hour traffic, rush-hour traffic will simply start one hour earlier. An ugly, brown path across an otherwise attractive lawn is also an example of an unintended consequence. You might think to yourself, quite correctly, that a single person cutting a corner between two paved paths will not create an ugly path in the grass, and therefore you cut the corner rather than remaining on the pavement. Such paths are, of course, created by a large group of individuals, each correctly believing that his or her action alone will not harm the grass. The collective effect, however, is what we see—ugly, brown paths across the grass. Similarly, it can't matter very much if one person throws waste paper on the side of the road, but many people, each thinking that it can't matter, make an unsightly mess of the roadside.

The important point that these examples illustrate is that self-interested behavior need not lead to satisfactory results, collectively or individually, and what seems possible in the individual case need not be possible for a group of individuals. This makes the unintended *beneficial* consequences of exchange and specialization all the more remarkable and important.

▶ Summary

Scarcity, choice, and costs. Something is scarce if we want more than is available and, as a conse-quence, possibilities are limited. Scarcity implies that individuals must make choices. In particular, scarcity forces each of us (1) to choose how we will allocate our time between leisure and work; (2) to choose the mix of things that we will consume; and (3) to choose between consumption now and consumption in the future.

Every choice has an associated opportunity cost. For each choice, the opportunity cost is the value of the best alternative that could have been chosen but was not. Changes in productive abilities, either because a person becomes more skillful or because a person employs the use of a capital good, will often change opportunity costs. Individuals typically make choices that minimize opportunity costs.

Production possibilities. An individual's production possibilities depend upon individual skill, the tools available to the individual, training and acquired skills, work effort, and the technology that combines ability, skills, tools, and resources. Because these differ for different individuals, individuals will typically have different opportunity costs.

The ability to produce, the possible choices, and their costs can be represented by a production possibilities frontier. A PPF indicates the maximum amount that can be produced of any particular mix of goods and services.

Scarcity, competition, and coordination. Scarcity leads to competition among individuals. As a consequence, there is within any economy or society a coordination problem. In this regard, scarcity forces a group of individuals to ask (1) how they will coordinate their possibly competing interests, (2) how they will distribute things among themselves, (3) who will decide, and (4) how disputes will be settled.

Exchange and specialization. If individuals have different preferences, exchanging goods that they value less for goods that they value more increases the well-being of all parties to such exchanges. As long as individuals freely trade, exchange is guided by an *invisible hand*—both parties to the exchange will be better off. Thus, exchange is a way of coordinating competing interests.

Exchange allows individuals to specialize. Specialization depends upon *relative* production costs: the cost to one person of producing something relative to the cost of producing the same thing to someone with whom the person might trade. That is, specialization depends on comparative advantage. An individual has a comparative advantage in the production of a good if his or her relative costs of producing that good are lower than those of someone with whom the individual might trade.

Specialization consistent with comparative advantage will increase the amount of goods and services available to an economy without using additional resources. Hence, specialization coordinates competing interests in a useful and productive way. Moreover, the gains to an individual from specialization do not depend upon being absolutely better at some activity than other individuals. All that matters is that an individual be relatively better or have a comparative advantage. So long as individuals are different from one another, each will have a comparative advantage.

Exchange and specialization lead to a kind of spontaneous order, in which competing interests are coordinated in ways that have the potential to benefit all participants. In *The Wealth of Nations* (1776), Adam Smith first argued that exchange had this property, which he described as follows:

> *As every individual, therefore, endeavors as much as he can . . . He generally, indeed, neither intends to promote the public interest, nor knows how much he is promoting it . . . He intends only his own security; and by directing that industry in such a manner as its produce is in this, as in many other cases, led by an invisible hand to promote an end which was no part of his intention . . . By pursuing his own interest he frequently promotes that of the society more effectually than when he really intends to promote it. I have never known much good done by those who affect to trade for the public good. It is an affectation, in deed, not very common among merchants, and very few words need be employed in dissuading them from it.*

Chapter 2 ▶▶
Organizing an Economy

Just as scarce resources limit the ability of an individual to produce and consume, scarce resources also limit the ability of an economy to produce goods and services. As a consequence, societies as well as individuals must make choices, confront costs, coordinate activities, exchange, and specialize. A nation chooses the fraction of its resources it will allocate to national defense, for example. In doing so it affects the resources available for other purposes, including capital formation and consumption. Moving resources from other activities to national defense has costs: Output must be given up elsewhere in the economy, the distribution of output among individuals within the economy may change, and future production possibilities may be affected. These effects and the possible options a society must choose among can be characterized by thinking of the economy as having an *aggregate* production possibilities frontier that indicates the possible output mixes the economy as a whole might produce if all of its resources were used in the best possible way.

In this chapter, we focus on three broad questions: What determines an economy's production possibilities or potential output? What elements are important in the organization of economic activity if an economy is to produce at its potential? What are the consequences of choosing different output mixes or of changing the economy's output mix?

The Aggregate Production Possibilities Frontier

If you and Friday trade and specialize, the two of you form an economy, albeit a small one. If your individual PPF's are Figure 1 (yours) and Figure 2 (Friday's), the aggregate PPF for your economy might look something like Figure 3. To see why, suppose that your mother organizes the production activities of both you and Friday. If she has both of you specialize in coconut production, total production for the economy will be 300 coconuts and 0 palm leaves. Now, if she wishes to increase palm-leaf production a little and to minimize the costs of doing so, you will be asked to shift from coconut production to palm-leaf production because you are the lowest relative cost producer of palm leaves. That is, relative to Friday, you have a *comparative advantage* in palm-leaf production. For the economy, producing an additional palm leaf has an opportunity cost of ½ coconut. If your mother wants more palm leaves, she will continue to rely on you to produce them until you are completely specialized in palm-leaf production, at which point, the economy's output will be 200 palm leaves and 200 coconuts. Therefore, the production mix of 200 coconuts and 200 palm leaves is on the economy's aggregate PPF.

Once you have specialized in producing palm leaves, the production of any additional palm leaves means that Friday has to shift from coconut production. For the economy, the opportunity cost of doing so is 4 C for each palm leaf produced. Note

Figure 1
Your Production Possibilities
Frontier Revisited

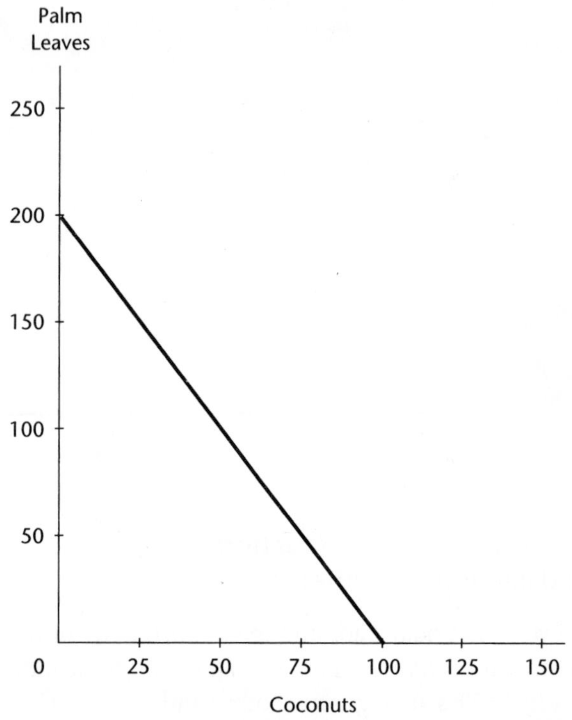

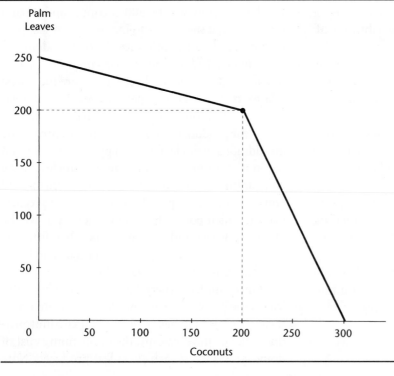

Figure 2
Friday's Production Possibilities
Frontier Revisited

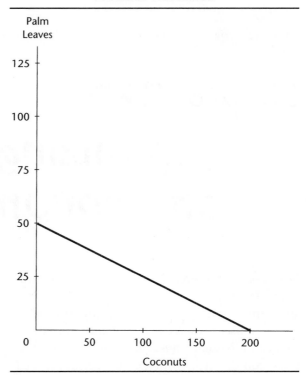

Figure 3
The Production Possibilities Frontier for an Economy of Two People

This graph illustrates the aggregate PPF for an economy consisting of you and Friday. If both of you produce only coconuts, the economy will produce 300 coconuts; if both of you produce only palm leaves, the economy will produce 250 palm leaves. The aggregate PPF is bowed out because the cost of producing coconuts in terms of palm leaves is different for you than it is for Friday.

that, for the economy, the cost of producing palm leaves has *increased*. Further increases in palm-leaf production can be obtained by having Friday give up additional coconut production until Friday is completely specialized in producing palm leaves. When both you and Friday have specialized in palm-leaf production, the economy's output will be 250 palm leaves and 0 coconuts. Figure 3 is, therefore, an **aggregate production possibilities frontier** for the economy when production is organized consistent with comparative advantage.

Suppose Defoe appears. The differing abilities of each person to produce goods and services are illustrated by the production possibility frontiers in Figures 1, 2, and 4. By an argument like the one just presented, the aggregate PPF for this new economy will look like the one illustrated in Figure 5.

Resources and Aggregate Production Possibilities

Note that when Defoe arrives, the economy's aggregate production possibilities are greater than when you and Friday were alone (compare Figures 5 and 3). This shouldn't be surprising: the economy

Figure 4
Defoe's Production Possibilities Frontier Revisited

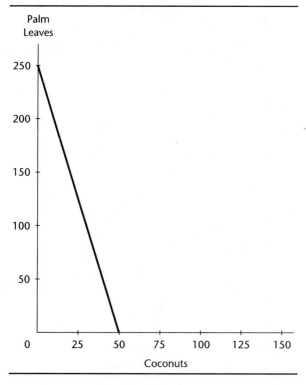

Figure 5
The Production Possibilities Frontier for an Economy of Three People

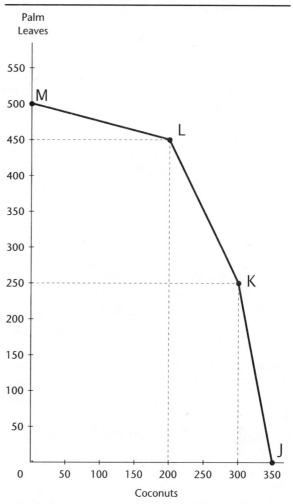

This graph illustrates the aggregate production possibilities frontier for an economy consisting of you, Friday, and Defoe.

now has more workers and, with more resources, will have a greater ability to produce. This idea generalizes: an economy's aggregate production possibilities are determined by its **resources** and its available **technologies**. The resources available to an economy include **natural resources**, such as fertile land, minerals, or water; manmade resources or **capital**, such as machines, factories, homes, roads, or transportation equipment; the effort and willingness to work of those living within the economy, which we will call **labor**; and the skills and abilities of these individuals, which we will call **human capital**. The technologies available to an economy determine the methods that can be used to combine

Table 1
Resources, Technologies, and an Economy's Production Possibilities

Type of resource	Change in resource	Effect on aggregate PPF
Capital	Increase	Outward shift
	Decrease	Inward shift
Human capital	Increase	Outward shift
	Decrease	Inward shift
Natural resources	New discoveries	Outward shift
	Depletion	Inward shift
Labor	Increase	Outward shift
	Decrease	Inward shift
Technological or organizational innovation that enhances the productivity of capital	New discoveries	Outward shift
Technological or organizational innovation that enhances the productivity of labor	New discoveries	Outward shift

labor, capital, and natural resources in order to produce goods and services. In a sense, technology determines the "recipe" for combining the inputs.

Clearly, changes in available resources or technologies will change an economy's aggregate production possibilities. Thus, as noted earlier, when the labor resources available to an economy increase (e.g., Defoe appears), the aggregate PPF shifts outward. By contrast, if natural resources are depleted, the aggregate PPF shifts inward. If technological innovation increases the productivity of existing natural resources, capital, or labor, the aggregate PPF shifts outward. In each case, the economy's *potential output* changes. Table 1 summarizes these and several other possibilities.

The effects of resources on an economy's aggregate production possibilities are seen most dramatically during wars and natural disasters when the available resources change quickly and by a substantial amount. For example, more than two million British men were killed or seriously injured during World War I. This meant that by the end of the war Britain's aggregate production possibilities were below what they would otherwise have been. In a direct way, the senseless destruction of a whole generation of young men in the fields and forests of France imposed costs on all British citizens long after the war ended. Figure 6 illustrates this effect.

At times nature also dramatically changes the resources available to an economy. For example, drought in Africa often decreases, in tragic ways, the resources available to many economies on that continent. In parts of the Soviet Union in the late 1980's, massive earthquakes that destroyed much of the housing and many of the factories also reduced the capital available to the Soviet economy. The decreased production possibilities, illustrated by a shift in the aggregate PPF like that shown in Figure 6, led to widespread famine, starvation, and disease in Africa and further compounded already difficult

Figure 6
The Effect of War on an Economy's Production Possibilities Frontier

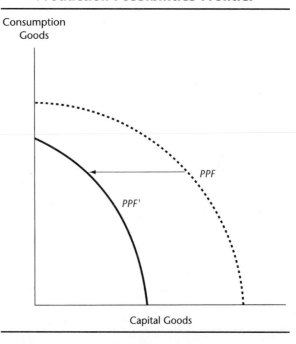

economic circumstances in what was then the Soviet Union.

The Efficient Use of Scarce Resources

When an economy is producing at a point along its aggregate PPF, increases in the production of one commodity cannot occur without decreases in the production of other commodities. That is, economies, like individuals must make choices and, as a consequence, face costs. In addition, because the aggregate PPF represents the *maximum* possible production given an economy's resources, along a PPF, resources must be *fully employed* and *used in the best possible way*. When an economy is producing as much as possible, given its scarce resources and the leisure-labor choices that individuals make, the economy is **efficiently** using its resources. In terms of an aggregate PPF, an *economy is efficiently using its resources when it is not possible to increase the production of one thing without decreasing the production of something else.*

Production within an aggregate PPF is always possible, of course, but such production is not efficient. Resources are either not fully employed or are fully employed but in ineffective ways. In either case, production of one or more commodities can increase without giving up the production of other commodities. For example, an economy with unemployed resources will be at some production point to the interior of the aggregate PPF, such as point *A* in Figure 7. If the economy is producing at *A*, it can move to *B*, producing more of both goods by using resources readily available within the economy that are not currently employed.

▶ Relative Prices and Incentives

It turns out that we don't really need your mother to organize production activities efficiently in a three-person economy. If individuals respond in self-interested ways to **relative prices**, individuals will make choices on their own that organize the economy exactly as your mother would have done.

What is a "relative price?" When you offer Friday 1 coconut for 1 palm leaf, it is useful to think of one coconut as the price of a palm leaf. More generally, the relative price of a commodity is the amount of one good that an individual must give up to get one unit of another good—2 coconuts for 1 palm leaf, for example. Generally, prices are

Figure 7
Inefficient Production

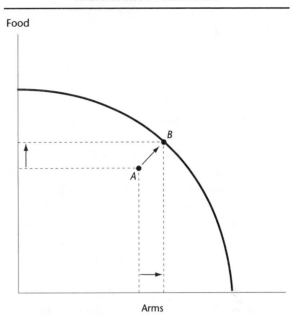

Unemployed (or underutilized) resources lead to production in the interior of the economy's PPF (at point *A*, for example), while fully employed resources lead to production of the PPF (at point *B*, for example). Note that when an economy is producing at *A*, it can increase production of arms without giving up the production of food. Indeed, if it wishes, the economy can increase the production of both arms and food without sacrificing anything.

specified in money terms. In this case, the relative price is implicit rather than explicit. If shirts are priced at $24 each and oranges at $2 per pound, for example, the relative price of a shirt is 12 pounds of oranges or, conversely, the relative price of a pound of oranges is $\frac{1}{12}$th of a shirt. That is, if you purchase one additional shirt, you would have to purchase 12 fewer pounds of oranges, and vice versa. Note that the relative price would be the same if a shirt costs twenty-four Euros and oranges sell for two Euros per pound. That is, relative prices do not depend upon what an economy uses for its money or even if it has money.

Decentralized Organization of Economic Activity

To see why an economy does not need an outsider to organize economic activity, consider the response of each person in the small economy whose fate we have been following to the incentives provided by a specific relative price. In particular, suppose that the relative price is one coconut for four palm leaves (i.e., 1 C for 4 P).

At this price, you would find it advantageous to produce only coconuts and trade for any palm leaves you wished to consume. This is because you can get more palm leaves through trade than you can get by producing them yourself. Friday would also find it advantageous to produce only coconuts and trade for palm leaves for the same reason. Defoe, on the other hand, would find it advantageous to produce only palm leaves and trade for coconuts, because he can purchase coconuts for fewer palm leaves than it would cost him to produce them along his PPF. Thus in response to a relative price of 1 C for 4 P, you and Friday will specialize in coconut production, producing in total 300 coconuts; Defoe will specialize in palm-leaf production, producing 250 palm leaves.

The resulting output—300 coconuts and 250 palm leaves—is on the aggregate PPF. (It's point K in Figure 5.) Thus, decentralized self-interested choices in response to a relative price of 1 C for 4 P will accomplish the specialization necessary to move this economy to its production possibilities frontier. *The economy is spontaneously organized, without the direction of anyone, in response to a particular relative price and the incentives it provides.* Nothing else is needed. This is a remarkable result: the pursuit of self-interest has an invisible hand in two respects. First, exchange makes others better off even as it makes you better off. Second, given a particular relative price, the pursuit of self-interest leads to an efficient organization of production for the economy as a whole and, hence, to an efficient use of scarce resources. That is, given the announced relative price the economy spontaneously organizes itself not in some haphazard way, but so that it's on its PPF.

coconuts cheaper than you can produce them. As a consequence of this change in the relative price, the economy will move from point K to point L in Figure 5. Aggregate production will be 450 palm leaves and 200 coconuts. Thus, *changes in relative prices change the production mix within an economy.* They do so because they provide incentives for individuals to organize production differently.

Note what has happened: As palm leaves become more valuable (as reflected in the increase in the relative price of palm leaves from 1 C for 4 P to 1 C for 1 P—since 1 C buys fewer P, P must have become worth more), the economy *increases* palm-leaf production and *decreases* coconut production. It makes good sense that the economy should respond this way. However, this response does not require direction from anyone. Instead, the incentives provided by the new relative price, self-interest, and the opportunity to exchange and specialize move the economy to produce those things that appear to be of greater value. This is a really stunning result: the economy *spontaneously reorganizes* itself in response to a change in relative price by moving resources to the production of the good that is valued relatively more. It's as if the economy had a brain or was being run by someone, but, of course, all there is is self-interest and a new relative price.

How relative prices are determined. There is nothing in this discussion to suggest how relative prices are determined. In some economies, relative prices are set by governmental decree. In others, relative prices are determined by tradition or convention. In an economy that relies on markets, relative prices are determined by interactions within markets. This is not quite as mysterious as it seems and we will consider in Chapter 4 how it is that markets determine relative prices. Be patient!

The Effect of Changes in Relative Prices on the Output Mix

If the relative price of palm leaves changes from 1 C for 4 P to 1 C for 1 P, Defoe will continue to produce palm leaves and trade for the coconuts he wants to consume. Friday will continue to produce coconuts and trade for the palm leaves he wants to consume. You, however, should respond to the change in relative price by shifting from coconut production to palm-leaf production because you can now trade for

▶ Aggregate Choices and Social Costs

Changing the output mix in an economy is costly: more of one thing can be produced only if less of something else is produced. As we have seen, these costs increase as more and more resources are moved from the production of one thing to the production of something else. Changing the output mix in an economy has subtler costs as well. As the output mix changes, the distribution of output among individuals within the economy might change. This

Table 2
Aggregate Production Possibilities

| Production choice | Aggregate output | | Individual output | | | | | |
| | | | You | | Friday | | Defoe | |
	P	C	P	C	P	C	P	C
J	0	350	0	100	0	200	0	50
K	250	300	0	100	0	200	250	0
L	450	200	200	0	0	200	250	0
M	500	0	200	0	50	0	250	0

means that some individuals may benefit from the change while others may be harmed. In addition, as the output mix changes today, the economy's *future* production possibilities may change.

Increasing relative costs. In general, the aggregate production possibilities frontier for an economy exhibits increasing relative costs. Graphically, this means that the aggregate PPF curves outward. There are several reasons for this, one of which can be easily understood by supposing, once again, that your mother is organizing the economy composed of you, Friday, and Defoe so as to produce as much as possible. If she wants to produce nothing but coconuts, 350 coconuts can be produced—100 from you, 200 from Friday, and 50 from Defoe—as illustrated by point J in Figure 5.

If she wants to produce some palm leaves, she will have to decide who should change from coconut production to palm-leaf production. If you produced palm leaves it would cost your mother ½ coconut for each palm leaf produced. Choosing Friday would cost her four coconuts for each palm leaf produced; choosing Defoe would cost her ⅕th coconut for each palm leaf produced. Clearly, choosing Defoe to produce palm leaves will minimize the costs of switching some resources from coconut to palm-leaf production.

When palm-leaf production increases to 250, Defoe will be completely specialized in palm-leaf production but you and Friday will still be producing only coconuts. At that point, aggregate output will be 250 palm leaves and 300 coconuts. If more palm leaves are desired and your mother wishes to minimize costs, she will have to rely on you to produce any additional palm leaves. Doing so, however, comes at ½ coconut per palm leaf and relative costs

increases as the production of coconuts falls and the production of palm leaves increases.

After you have specialized in palm-leaf production, aggregate output will be 450 palm leaves and 200 coconuts. At this point, additional palm leaves can be produced only by Friday at a cost of 4 C for 1 P. The costs of producing palm leaves have increased further. The production possibilities for the economy of you, Defoe, and Friday are summarized in Table 2, where production choices J, K, L, and M correspond to similarly numbered points in Figure 5. The costs associated with producing these different mixes are summarized in Table 3.

Costs increase because as additional palm leaves are produced, resources that are less effective in producing palm leaves must eventually be devoted to this activity rather than to producing coconuts. This is true for this simple economy; it is also true for the complex economy within which we live. That is, *the more that resources are shifted from one activity to another, the more costly further changes become.*

The Distribution of Output

Changes in relative prices not only change an economy's production mix, they also change the distribution of output or what is generally called **distribution of individual income** among those living within the economy.

Table 3
The Cost of Producing Palm Leaves

Quantity of palm leaves	Cost per palm leaf
0–250	$\frac{1}{5}$ coconut
250–450	$\frac{1}{2}$ coconut
450–500	4 coconuts

The reason for this distributional effect of relative price changes should be apparent. When the relative price of palm leaves increase, Defoe, who is producing palm leaves, is going to be able to trade for *more* coconuts than he could when the relative price of palm leaves was lower. Clearly, Defoe benefits from this change. If, for example, Defoe wants to consume 150 palm leaves and trade the remaining 100 palm leaves for whatever coconuts he can get, when the relative price is 1 C for 4 P, Defoe can trade 100 palm leaves for 25 coconuts. When the relative price is 1 C for 1 P, however, Defoe's consumption of coconuts will increase by 75 coconuts, from 25 to 100, because he can trade 100 palm leaves for 100 coconuts. Defoe is clearly better off when the relative price of palm leaves increases.

When the relative price of coconuts changes from 1 C for 4 P to 1 C for 1 P, Friday will continue to produce coconuts. Coconuts are now *less* valuable because every coconut trades for fewer palm leaves. It shouldn't be surprising, then, that the share of output that Friday receives will fall as a consequence of this relative price change. For example, if Friday consumes 175 of the 200 coconuts he produces and trades the remaining 25 coconuts for whatever palm leaves he can get, when the price is 1 C for 4 P, he can consume 100 palm leaves. When the relative price of coconuts falls to 1 C for 1 P, however, Friday's consumption of palm leaves will fall from 100 to 25. Friday is clearly worse off after the price change. He will continue to specialize, however, because even when each palm leaf costs a coconut, he can trade for palm leaves for less than he can produce them. That is, his consumption of both coconuts and palm leaves is still greater than if he were to go it alone.

It is not clear what happens to your consumption. You avoid the full effect of the decline in relative price of coconuts by switching from coconut production to palm-leaf production. That is, you change what you are doing.

This example illustrates two important points: *First, when relative prices change, the distribution of income also changes.* Those producing goods and services whose relative price has increased find that their incomes increase. Those producing goods and services whose relative price has decreased find, in general, that their incomes decrease. *Second, when relative prices change, the distribution of jobs across an economy also changes, and some individuals will have to move from one job to another job.* Changing jobs is often difficult because individuals have to retrain or move from one location to another.

These distributional consequences are enormously important because they can make economic change politically difficult. Individuals tend to care more about their incomes than they do about larger notions of efficiency. This means that there will often be political pressures within an economy to either change relative prices so as to advantage particular groups of individuals or prevent changes in relative prices so as to forestall a fall in income for particular groups. Consider, for example, efforts in our own economy to protect the US steel industry or US textile industry from the price changes that follow from international trade. Or, for a further example, the efforts by farmers to protect their incomes from declining agricultural prices. This suggests that in analyzing the development of particular public policies, attention should be paid to the distributional effects of the changes in relative prices due to the policies. In particular, you ought to ask yourself the following questions:

1. Who wins when relative prices change?
2. Who loses?
3. How does the political system respond to these gains and losses?

Economic Growth

Economies are dynamic. Choices made about what to produce and consume today will affect what an economy can produce in the future. Generally, an economy with more natural resources or more labor or more capital will be able to produce more. In most cases, however, an economy doesn't choose the stock of natural resources available to it. Nature has either been generous or stingy. Moreover, many natural resources are depleted, rather than increased as time passes. Furthermore, the size of the potential labor force may not be a choice for the economy as a whole because family size is usually (but not always) a private matter. Thus, even though an increase in natural resources or an increase in labor will increase the economy's production possibilities, neither may be a choice that we can make collectively if we wish to increase our ability to produce over time. (We do, of course, make collective choices about whether to permit immigration of additional labor.)

By contrast, the amount of capital available to the economy is something that can be chosen, because capital is itself produced. This means that we can collectively choose to influence the rate of economic growth. However, additional capital can be produced only if resources are transferred from the production of other goods and services. That is, we must collectively consume less than we produce if additional resources are to be made available for capital formation.

This choice between consumption today and economic growth (potentially more consumption in the future) can be illustrated by thinking of the economy as producing capital goods and consumer goods. In Figure 8, if an economy chooses the production mix indicated by point A instead of point B, it will have more capital in the future because it is using resources today to produce capital instead of goods and services for consumption. The position of the aggregate production possibilities frontier is determined, in part, by the amount of capital an economy has, so this production of more capital will increase future production possibilities. This effect is illustrated by an outward shift in the aggregate PPF, from PPF_1 to PPF_2 in Figure 8(a).

By contrast, even though it starts with the same production possibilities as the economy producing at point A, an economy that chooses the production mix at point B will not have the same production possibilities in the future. The reason for the difference is that the economy consumes more now and its production possibilities will have shifted out by less in the future as a consequence. Note, however, that more capital can be produced and potential future output increased only if less is consumed today. Put directly, *capital formation necessary for economic growth requires the sacrifice of current consumption*. We must *save* and then use the resources to produce capital. **Aggregate saving** is the difference between what an economy can produce and what is actually consumed by those living within it.

In general, when aggregate saving is greater, so is the amount of capital produced. For a country like the United States that has the ability to produce lots of commodities, choosing to produce fewer consumption goods and more capital goods is substantially easier than for a desperately poor country like

Figure 8
The Effect of Producing Capital on Economic Growth

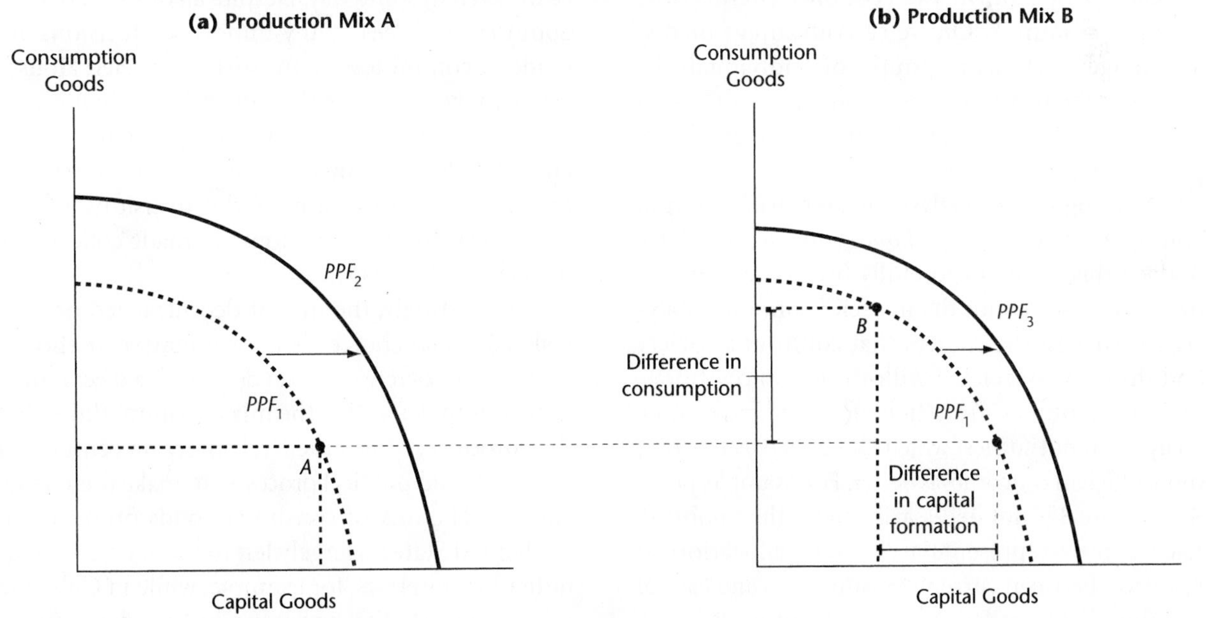

An economy choosing production mix A will have higher economic growth (from PPF_1 to PPF_2) than an economy choosing production mix B (from PPF_1 to PPF_3) because although capital is a productive resource, it can only be obtained by sacrificing current consumption.

Mali where sacrificing some consumption goods to produce more capital goods may lead to starvation. Herein is the dilemma of economic development and growth.

An economy's production possibilities are also determined by technology. To the degree that an economy can stimulate technological innovation, it can also stimulate economic growth. Frankly, however, not much is known about policies that effectively foster technological innovation except, of course, that policies that reward innovative activities are likely to lead to more innovation than policies that do not.

Aggregate Choices

An aggregate PPF is a model of the choices that a society must make and the associated costs. If a society chooses to devote more resources to one activity, it must devote fewer resources to other activities. Thus aggregate choices have costs, just as individual choices do. We can devote more resources to defense or more resources to consumption, but we cannot do both if the economy is efficiently using its resources. Or, we can devote more resources to current consumption or more resources to capital formation and, hence, future consumption, but we cannot do both if the economy is efficiently using its resources. Or, we can advantage or disadvantage particular groups of individuals by changing the mix of output produced or by resisting output mix changes that would occur as relative prices change.

Nothing in our analysis suggests *which* output combination a society *should* choose. We have dodged this issue purposefully because economics has little to say about the matter. Economic analysis can suggest the choices that confront a society and the costs associated with those choices, but as long as resources are efficiently used, economic analysis cannot suggest which choice between two or more efficient outcomes is better. For example, point *A* in Figure 8 is not necessarily better than point *B*. Each simply represents a different allocation of resources between current consumption and capital creation. Economic growth in and of itself is not valuable. It is desirable only because it means that, at some point in the future, individuals will be able to consume more than they could have if there were no economic growth. The appropriate tradeoff

between "more consumption today and less growth" and "less consumption today, more growth and more consumption in the future" is not easily determined. Similarly, the income distribution at point *K* in Figure 5 is not necessarily better than the distribution of income at point *L*. That is, there is no specific distribution that is economically "right."

Collective decision making. Clearly, choices about the mix of output, the amount of capital formation, or even the distribution of output are important. However, we have ignored the question of *how* a group of individuals or a society makes collective or social choices. This, it turns out, is a complex problem. Some collective choices are simply the aggregate outcome of many individual choices. In this case, all of the important elements of social choice are *decentralized*—each individual makes his or her own choice and the social choice is just the sum of these choices. For example, Americans do not vote as a group on the mix of hamburgers and hot dogs or shirts and pants that the economy produces. The social choice is just the sum of individual decisions—on a given day perhaps 500,000 individuals buy hot dogs, 125,000 purchase shirts, and so on. Other social choices, however, are purposefully made by groups of individuals. These choices are *centralized* in some way. Despite all of the bad jokes about committees, many important decisions are made by committees of one sort or another: Households make decisions that affect individual members. Governments make decisions that affect their citizens. Production decisions in firms are not merely the aggregation of the decisions of the employees. Instead, decisions are made collectively by the firms' managers.

Interestingly, the mix of decentralized or centralized social choices is itself a matter of choice. Some societies rely more on decentralized economic processes to determine the mix of commodities that they produce, while others rely more on centralized economic and political processes to make these same choices. The mix of consumer goods produced in the United States is largely left to the aggregation of individual interests, for example, while in Cuba the mix of consumption goods produced is determined, in large part, by a central planning department of the Cuban government.

Either by decentralized individual decisions or purposeful centralized collective decisions, we choose a production mix for an economy. We choose the mix of hamburgers, shirts, restaurants, and vegetables. Not only do we choose the mix of goods to be individually consumed, but we also choose those that we consume jointly with other individuals such as national defense, postal services, national parks and wilderness areas, highways, etc. As we choose a production mix, we also influence the distribution of income across our society. And by making decisions about resources that will be devoted to current consumption as opposed to capital formation, education and research and development, we also influence how fast the economy will grow.

▶ Summary

Aggregate production possibilities. An aggregate production possibilities frontier represents the boundary between what an economy can produce, given its resources and available technologies, and what it simply does not have resources to produce. In this sense, an aggregate PPF represents the *potential* output mixes for an economy when its resources are fully and effectively employed, given the level of technological development of the economy (that is, producing **efficiently**).

Changes in either the resources or technologies available to an economy will change the economy's production possibilities. When more resources are available or when there are technologies that allow for more to be produced with a given level of resources, the economy's production possibilities will increase.

Relative prices and decentralized organization of economic activity. Aggregate economic activity can be efficiently organized through decentralized individual responses to relative prices. That is, production on an aggregate PPF does not necessarily require centralized direction or control. Rather, individual, self-interested responses to relative prices can lead individuals to specialize in such a way that the economy spontaneously organizes itself and produces at its potential. Moreover, individual, self-interested responses to *changes* in relative prices can lead to a spontaneous reorganization of economic activity such that an economy produces at its potential, even though its output mix changes.

Increasing relative costs. Because resources are not equally effective in all uses, increasing the production of one commodity will become increasingly costly. That is, an aggregate PPF is generally characterized by increasing relative costs (bows outward).

Relative prices and distribution. Changes in relative prices lead to changes in an economy's production mix. In addition, however, changes in relative prices often change the distribution of income and jobs within an economy. These changes will matter, as we will see later, in the development of public policies and pose important distributional and adjustment problems with which each society must deal.

The production mix and economic growth. Different production mixes will matter not just in terms of their possible effects on the distribution of income but also because a society can influence its rate of growth by choosing to consume less than it produces (thereby, **saving**), using the remaining resources to build new capital, thereby increasing its aggregate production possibilities through time. The cost of greater potential output in the future is, however, less consumption in the present.

Chapter 3 ▶▶

Minimizing the Effects of Impediments to Exchange and Specialization

This chapter has a simple theme: The gains from exchange and specialization are so enormous that if things stand in the way of fully capturing them, institutional arrangements emerge to reduce or eliminate any impediments to exchanging and specializing. Specifically, we consider the role of property rights, contracts, money, firms and intermediaries in reducing transaction costs and facilitating exchange and specialization.

▶ The Role of Property Rights

Getting to the PPF is not, unfortunately, simply a matter of allowing individuals to make choices given the available resources and prices. Otherwise, a country with abundant resources like Russia or Argentina would not be encountering economic difficulties. Something more is needed. The "something more" includes determining the correct incentives for resource use. Getting the incentives correct, in turn, depends at least in part on **property rights**.

To see why (and to understand the meaning of "property right"), note that while we have focused on the central role of specialization and exchange, we have not been very explicit about exactly *what* is being produced and traded. Coconuts, palm leaves, manna, and quail hardly represent the kinds of commodities that are actually exchanged in a modern economy: shirts, books, Big Macs, medical services, jeans, and so forth. After a particular commodity is identified, you can usually describe in detail what is actually being exchanged. When you purchase a Big Mac, for example, the exchange is your money for meat, catsup, lettuce, pickles, onions, and sesame-seed bun.

Property Rights and Expectations

Consider, however, the following problem. Suppose that there are two separate economies (each, say, on a separate island) populated by individuals who have basically the same likes and dislikes and the same motives. There are automobiles in both economies. In one, economy A, automobile use is governed by the following rules: Any person may purchase an automobile, maintain it as she chooses, and drive it to wherever she wants. When the driver arrives at a particular destination, however, she is required by law to leave the car unlocked with the keys in the ignition. Any person needing transportation is free to use any automobile parked nearby, but this person is also required to leave the car unlocked and the keys in the ignition upon arrival at his destination.

In economy B, automobile use is governed by different rules. Any person may purchase an automobile, maintain it as he chooses, and drive it to wherever he wants. When the driver arrives at a particular destination, he may lock the car and take the keys. Any person needing transportation is free to use his own automobile but is prohibited from using an automobile for which he has no keys, that is, that he did not purchase.

Would you expect any differences in the types of cars in the two economies? What about the maintenance of the cars? Would there be about the same number of cars in each economy, assuming that the population of potential drivers is about the same? How much gasoline would you expect to be in the tank of an average car in economy A compared to economy B?

We would expect, of course, far fewer cars in economy A than in economy B because each individual in economy A would be inclined to let someone else buy a car, using the money that they would have otherwise used for a car for other purposes. Those few who might purchase a car would probably not want an expensive car with lots of accessories. After all, the additional comfort that such accessories might provide could only be enjoyed the first time the car was used since someone else would probably be using the car after the purchaser's first use. In addition, no individual has much incentive to maintain any particular car in economy A. Any effort or money spent on maintenance would only benefit future users. Similarly, no one in economy A would have an incentive to put much more gasoline in the tank than the minimum necessary to travel to their intended destination. Thus, economy A would have a few, low quality, poorly maintained cars, each with little gasoline in its tank.

In economy B, by contrast, accessories that make using the car more enjoyable might be purchased since the purchaser can use the accessories now *and* in the future. Maintenance expenditures benefit the person making them now *and* in the future, as does gasoline added to the tank. Economy B, in contrast to economy A, would undoubtedly have more cars of a greater variety in price and quality. We would expect these cars to be better maintained, on average, each with more gasoline in its tank.

Clearly when we purchase an automobile, we purchase something in addition to a manufactured commodity composed of steel, glass, plastic, and so on. That is, economically valuable commodities are not simply a bundle of physical characteristics that we can see and describe. In addition to whatever physical characteristics commodities may have that are attractive us, commodities are valuable because of what we *expect* to be able to do with them *now and in the future.*

The Common Property Problem

Some additional aspects of these expectations can be understood by considering a simple economy in which each person is paid a wage exactly equal to the value of his or her contribution to the output of the economy, say $40 per day. One day a group of 10 individuals discovers a fishing ground offshore and find that they can sell their catch for $500. They divide the income from fishing evenly among themselves and each has an income of $50 per day.

For each day that these 10 people spend fishing, society loses $400. (Each person's contribution to the output, $40, multiplied by 10.) These losses are more than offset by the $500 value of the fish caught. Giving up $400 to get $500 makes the society wealthier and it makes sense to exploit the fishing ground.

An eleventh person, observing the higher income that fishermen receive, decides to go fishing. Not surprisingly, the total catch increases when there are more fishermen, say from $500 to $506, which, when divided evenly, results in an income of $46 per fisherman.[1] Clearly, the eleventh person is personally better off fishing than working elsewhere in the economy because her income increases from $40 to $46 per day.

What about society? Total output declines by $40 in the rest of the economy when she decides to go fishing. Fishing output increases by only $6, from $500 to $506, however. Thus, even though the eleventh person is better off fishing than working elsewhere in the economy and there is an incentive for her to go fishing, the economy as a whole loses $34. Put differently, it costs society $40 to get $6 when the eleventh person goes fishing. Giving up

---

[1] The equal division rule is unimportant in this example. If the fish are more or less evenly distributed around the fishing ground, when 10 people fish, the average catch would be $50, and when 11 people fish, given the same distribution of fish, the average catch would be $46.

$40 to get $6 is not very sensible, and clearly in this case the pursuit of individual interests by one person undermines the well-being of others.

The problem will only get worse. Each of the 11 fishermen has an income of $46, but those working elsewhere in the economy have incomes of $40. There is an incentive for additional individuals to go fishing even though decisions of this sort will further reduce the total amount of goods and services the economy produces. Indeed, there will be an incentive to shift resources to fishing until those fishing have incomes equal to incomes elsewhere in the economy (i.e., $40 in either place). Up to this point, each individual will personally benefit by changing jobs but by doing so will impose losses on those already fishing and aggregate output for the economy will continue to fall.

This fishery problem is a **common property problem** similar to the automobile problem in economy A. Just as the automobiles in A are available to anyone, no one can be excluded from the fishing ground. The fishing ground is overused as a consequence.

The problem is deeper than simply too many people wanting to fish, however. Because no one can be excluded from the fishing ground, no person *expects* that fish she *does not* catch today will be around tomorrow—any fish not caught by one person today may be caught by someone else. As a consequence, there is an *incentive* for each person to *overfish*.

The incentive for each fisherman to overfish will lead to the depletion of the fish population and perhaps to the extinction of fish. Consider this apparent paradox: No one is particularly concerned about the extinction of beef cattle or pigs or chickens, despite their intensive use for food, whereas there is considerable concern about the extinction of whales, whose use for food is not nearly as widespread. That is, millions of cattle are slaughtered each year without danger of extinction while a few thousand whales are slaughtered each year with great danger of extinction. Shouldn't the chances of depleting the stock of cattle be greater than the changes of depleting the stock of whales, since the former are more intensively used?

The paradox is resolved when we recognize that an important difference between cattle and whales is that those persons who determine whether or not to slaughter and market beef expect that if they do not choose to slaughter today, they will be free to make that choice tomorrow, whereas those persons who may be looking for whales understand that if they do not harvest those they find today, they cannot expect that they will be able to harvest these whales at some future date. This difference in *expectations* means that ranchers will behave differently than whalers even though their basic motives may be the same.

Property Rights and Incentives

Note, however, that while ranchers do not have an incentive to overgraze their own land, they may have an incentive to overgraze public lands where any fodder left for the future will be grazed by someone else's cattle. Forestry users will have an incentive to maintain the lumber productivity of land that will be theirs to use into the future, but they do not have an incentive to be careful with public lands that they will never be able to use again. You probably have a greater incentive to pickup trash around your own property than you do in a public park. Similarly, if you rent and intend to live in the rental unit for only a short time, you have less incentive to take care of things than if you own the place where you live.

What have we learned? For an economy to function well there must be not only relative prices, but a set of arrangements that create appropriate expectations about the future use so that scarce resources are not overused. Without such arrangements, self-interested behavior will be harmful.

Ownership. One way of creating appropriate expectations is to create **property rights** so that individuals own things. Thus, in our earlier example, each person in economy B owns his automobile, whereas no one owns an automobile in economy A. Similarly, individuals own cattle but no individual owns whales.

The role that ownership can play in an economy can be illustrated by returning to the fishing problem. Suppose that the discoverer of the fishing grounds owns the right to go fishing. What does ownership mean in this case? In general, *ownership gives to a particular individual the right, enforceable at law, to exclude others from using a resource without his or her permission.* Hence, if a person owns a fishing ground, she can keep others from fishing if she chooses.

Future interests. When one person owns a fishing ground, she can harvest fish herself or she can hire other people to assist her. Other people will be hired to fish, obviously, only if the increase in the income of the owner is greater than the wage paid to the prospective fisherman. Suppose the owner has hired 10 fishermen and is considering hiring an eleventh. Since the eleventh person increases the value of output in the fishing industry by only $6, this would be the maximum wage an owner of the fishing ground would be willing to pay to have the eleventh person fish. Clearly, at this wage offer, the eleventh person wouldn't want to become a fisherman. Thus, *ownership creates incentives to exploit resources less intensively.* If a resource is owned, additional resources will be applied to its exploitation only if the gain is greater than the opportunity cost of using those resources elsewhere in the economy.

Owners do not have the incentive to overuse automobiles they own, to catch their fish to the point of extinction, to slaughter all of their cattle, to overgraze their land, or to over harvest their timber. That is, *ownership also creates incentives to exploit resources less rapidly.* If a resource is owned and not used now, it can always be used in the future by the owner.

Investments that an owner makes to increase productivity will be to her benefit as long as she can exclude others from exploiting her investment. That is, *ownership also creates incentives to make investments that increase productivity.* Why? Because the future return from this kind of investment belongs to the owner and cannot be appropriated by someone else without the owner's permission.

Restriction on use. In general, restrictions on future uses lower the market value of the resource. As a very simple example, consider what you would be willing to pay for an apple whose use was restricted by a law in the following way: You can exclude others from using your apple, but you can only use it as a decoration; you can't eat it. Would you be willing to pay more or less for an apple whose use is restricted in this way, as compared with the price you would be willing to pay if you could also eat it? The answer must be obvious. The greater the uses to which the apple might be put, the greater will be its value to its owner and the higher would be the amount that someone would be willing to pay for the apple.

Enforcement costs. Creating appropriate expectations about future interests is not costless.[2] Indeed, even though property rights have been established, sometimes the costs of enforcing them are so great that people treat the scarce resource as if it were *not* owned. For example, a copyright is a form of ownership of published ideas and creative efforts. People who write music or publish a book or record a performance expect compensation for what they produce. Copyright laws attempt to provide for this compensation by requiring users to compensate the owners of the copyright. With the widespread use of photocopy machines, recorders of one sort or another and downloading from the World Wide Web, however, published material, records, tapes, and disks can often be used without being purchased from the creators. Unless the government is willing to outlaw the use of these machines or place a policeman at each computer to collect a payment for use, downloading, photocopying and other types of copying will continue. As long as copying continues, the creators will be compensated less than they otherwise would be. Without the expectation of full compensation, certain kinds of creative activities may not be provided in an appropriate way or at an appropriate level.

Sometimes, by contrast, technological innovations lower the costs of the enforcement of ownership. For example, the Great Plains were divided and ownership established by the federal government in the middle part of the nineteenth century. It was, however, very costly to enforce the property rights that people thought they had. An important innovation, barbed wire, dramatically lowered the costs of enforcing property rights and the Great Plains were rapidly fenced later in the century. Only after the Great Plains were fenced did the enormous increase in agricultural productivity occur because only then could the owners of the land easily exclude others from using their resources without compensation.

In sum, the efficient organization of economic activity and use of scarce resources requires that we get the incentives right. However, getting incentives right requires ownership, but creating and enforcing property rights is often costly. When the costs are too high, the resource will either not be provided at all or will be provided, but overused.

---

[2] By now it should be clear that you can talk like an economist by simply invoking the phrase "doing x is not costless, however."

Transferring property rights. Since circumstances change as time passes, resources will be used effectively only if property rights can be transferred to those who come to value them more highly. The importance of a right to transfer can be illustrated by supposing that you own land and have the right to exclude others from using it and the right to use it as you desire. It would appear that with these property rights, there will be appropriate incentives for efficient use of the land. Suppose, however, that there is a law that prohibits the transfer of your land to someone else. In this case, you can use the land but no one else can. Clearly, this law will prevent land from moving to its highest valued use whenever those who would really prefer to exchange it for something more valuable find that they cannot transfer the rights. It follows that in addition to the expectation that one can exclude others from using a resource, and the expectation that one can put a resource to its highest valued use, *an important element of property rights is the expectation that one can sell a resource to others* who may have even higher valued uses for the resource.

▶ Transaction Costs

Transactions, however, take time. For example, it takes time for individuals to find other individuals with whom to make mutually beneficial trades. Devoting time to trading rather than to producing commodities decreases the output that individuals might otherwise produce. Thus, like any other claim on time, trading has an opportunity cost.

Transactions also use up resources that could have been used for other purposes. For example, resources are used to move commodities from one location to another. Using resources in this way means that they cannot be used to produce additional goods and services that individuals might consume. In this case, trading has an opportunity cost in terms of the other uses to which these resources could have been put.

Finally, in certain circumstances, the nature of exchanges may be such that one individual can take advantage of the commitments another individual makes. This makes certain kinds of transactions costly in the sense that anyone who knows that this kind of behavior is possible will be less inclined to transact for fear of being taken advantage of. This hesitancy will limit the kinds of transactions that might otherwise occur, to the detriment of the best use of resources.

For a variety of reasons, then, there are **transaction costs** that may limit the ability of individuals to capture the full gains from exchange and specialization. It follows that *anything that will lower the costs of transacting will increase the output available for other uses.* Human beings are creative, and because the gains from exchange and specialization are potentially so enormous and capturing them so important, we figure out ways to minimize transaction costs. We consider four important arrangements that lower different kinds of transaction costs: contracts, money, firms, and intermediaries.

▶ Opportunistic Behavior and the Role of Contracts

We have not been very explicit about *how* exchanges occur. You might respond that this is a simple matter: a person pays for something and takes it with him. However, many exchanges are more complex than this in that we cannot easily "pay and take it with us." In particular, many exchanges extend over time. As a consequence, it is often the case that one party has to commit and act before a second party does. In cases like this where exchange is not simultaneous, an individual may have an incentive to take advantage of commitments and efforts that another individual makes. **Opportunistic behavior** of this sort makes exchanging and specializing less advantageous and will undermine the ability of an economy to fully exploit its resources and move to its PPF.

For example, if you want to purchase a home, you can simultaneously pay the current owner and obtain title to the home. If, however, you want to have a home built, you cannot simultaneously pay for the home and obtain title because non-simultaneous performance (the home is built before it is paid for or, alternatively, the home is paid for before it is built) creates incentives for one individual to take advantage of the other party to an exchange. If a person agrees to build you a home and then receive payment for it after it is completed, you might be tempted to take advantage of his investment in the partially finished home by asking him to renegotiate the agreed-upon price. It will be costly for him to find another buyer, which gives you some leverage in this renegotiation. On the other hand, suppose that you pay before the house is started. The builder will have an incentive to work on other projects and only work on your home when it is convenient, thus delaying its completion. Even though this will be irritating, it will also be costly to find another builder, so now the builder has leverage.

These kinds of problems can often be overcome by relying on a written agreement or **contract**. As a consequence, when performance isn't simultaneous many exchanges occur only after the parties have specified in a quite formal way their respective obligations or, in other words, negotiated a contract. While negotiations over contract terms are themselves costly—they take time and effort—carefully negotiated contracts reduce the chances of opportunistic behavior and, hence, its cost. The effectiveness of using contracts depends, of course, on a legal system that enforces the terms to which the parties agree.

Reputation

Not every exchange where opportunistic behavior is possible needs the protection of a formal contract. For many exchanges where performance is not simultaneous, the **reputation** of the parties to the exchange will be damaged if they behavior opportunistically and do not perform as they agreed. For example, when you purchase meat from a local butcher, you are willing to pay $3.50 per pound because you believe that you are buying meat of a certain quality. If the butcher only expected to sell to you once, she might have an incentive to behave opportunistically by substituting lower-quality meat. If she expected (and wanted) you to return, however, the effect of this opportunistic behavior on her reputation would matter. As a consequence, she is unlikely to sell you anything but the best because her business will flourish only if she has a good reputation. In an important sense, then, reputation is useful for enforcing agreements in addition to or in lieu of a formal legal system, particularly when the same buyers and sellers interact repeatedly over time.

▶ Coincident Wants and the Role of Money

Virtually every economy develops *something* that is commonly used to trade for almost *all* other commodities. Those willing to give up a good, service, or resource accept this thing as payment and those who want to trade for a good, service, or resource offer this thing as payment. We will refer to this commonly traded thing as **money**. As we will see, money develops because it is less costly to transact using a commonly traded commodity than it is to trade items directly or to **barter**. That is, money develops as a way of reducing certain transaction costs.

Barter is costly. In order to make an exchange, one individual with some commodity, say A, who wants a different commodity, say B, has to find a second individual with B who happens to want A. In an economy with a large number of commodities and a large population of individuals, the matching of **coincident wants** may be difficult and time consuming and, as a consequence, costly. Money eliminates the problem of matching coincident wants because, by definition, money is that thing that is commonly accepted in exchange.

Bartering

To see why money lowers the costs of transacting, suppose that you are a lawyer specializing in helping people write wills who has an acute attack of appendicitis. With barter you must find a physician who wants a will *and* who is willing to exchange an appendectomy for it *and* who is willing to provide the operation now (since your condition will not allow you to wait). How can you find a physician who wants exactly what you have to trade at exactly the time you want to trade it?

A partially completed will won't be recognized by the courts; on the other hand, each person needs only one completed will. What if you find a physician who does want to trade for a completed will but who does not think that a single will is appropriate payment for an appendectomy? For instance, suppose that the physician thinks seven wills would be adequate payment (but, of course, he or she only needs one). This points to an additional problem with barter: how are you to divide this indivisible commodity (a completed will) so as to exchange for commodities that are either relatively inexpensive (a haircut, for example) where a completed will buys too much or commodities that are relatively expensive, where several completed wills would be necessary to complete the exchange (an automobile, for example)?

What if you need the appendectomy *now* and can only offer a completed will *in the future*? How would you make this kind of exchange? On the other hand, what if you wanted to trade legal services *today* for a possible appendectomy delivered some time *in the future*? How would such an exchange be made?

None of these problems is insurmountable. In each case, exchange among many parties, inventories, or special contracts could be used to make the desired trades.[3] It should be clear, however, that problems such as these make transactions costly.

Using Money Instead

The use of money solves many of these problems, thereby lowering the costs of transacting. That is, if there is one thing ("money") that everyone desires to have, all exchanges can be undertaken using this thing ("money"). Thus, when an economy has "money," the problem of coincident wants disappears since if you are a lawyer, you can trade a completed will with whomever wants it for money and then use money to purchase the services of a physician when the need arises.

For money to be useful in lowering transaction costs, it has to be accepted by you as payment for goods sold or services rendered *and* it has to be accepted by others when you want to purchase goods or services. Two characteristics make something money. First, its use in exchanges by *others* must be widespread. That is, something has to be widely used in exchange to be money. Second, there must be an easy way to determine whether what is actually offered to you in an exchange will, in fact, be acceptable to others in future exchanges. That is, it cannot be easy to counterfeit or self-produce. What

this means is that *money is useful in trade and hence valuable because it is useful in trade.* Money is not valuable because it has intrinsic value or is backed by something with intrinsic value. It's valuable because it's useful, that is, because it lowers transaction costs.

Money as a Unit of Account

Once money has developed in an economy to lower transaction costs, however, it can play other useful roles. One of these is its use as a convenient way of measuring or denominating economic activity. That is, in addition to being a **medium of exchange**, money is often used as a **unit of account**. For example, instead of specifying the relative price of some good in terms of what it can be exchanged for ("the relative prices of three coconuts is two palm leaves" or "the relative price of this shirt is ½ pair of shoes"), relative prices can be specified in terms of the money, say dollars: "the price of this shirt is $24." If shirts are priced at $24 and a pair of shoes at $48, then the money price *implicitly* measures the relative price of shoes in terms of shirts—two shirts for one pair of shoes.

An aside: measuring the value of money. A problem with using money as a unit of account is that its value changes if most prices change. That is, the *purchasing power* of money can change. One way of dealing with this problem is to measure the general or aggregate **price level** using a **price index**. Perhaps the best known price index that serves this purpose is the **Consumer Price Index** or **CPI** (less well-known indices include the producer price index (PPI) and the GDP deflator).

Each of these indices is arbitrarily assigned the value 100 in a specific year called the "base year." The index then moves away from 100 depending upon whether money prices, in general, increase or decrease. When the index increases, say from 100 to 120, prices measured in dollars have, on average, increased by 20 percent [(120–100)/100]. Such an increase is commonly referred to as an **inflation**. When an index decreases, say from 200 to 190, prices measured in dollars have, on average, decreased by 5 percent [(200–190)/200]. This decrease is referred to as a **deflation**.

Changes in a price index are useful because they tell us something about the purchasing power of money. Thus, when there is an inflation, $1 buys less

---

[3] In this regard a nineteenth-century economist, Stanley Jevons, related the following account:

> *Mademoiselle Zeile, a singer of the Theatre Lyrique at Paris . . . gave a concert in the Society Islands. In exchange for an aria from Norma and a few other songs, she was to receive a third part of the receipts. When counted, her share was found to consist of three pigs, twenty-three turkeys, forty-four chickens, five thousand cocoa-nuts, besides considerable quantities of bananas, lemons and oranges . . . In Paris . . . this amount of live stock and vegetables might have brought four thousands francs, which would have been good remuneration for five songs. In the Society Islands, however, pieces of money were scarce; and as Mademoiselle could not consume any considerable portion of the receipts herself, it became necessary in the mean time to feed the pigs and poultry with the fruit.*

over time and when there is a deflation, $1 buys more over time.

It is important to note, however, that a change in the overall price level—an increase in the CPI from 100 to 120 for example—does not necessarily affect relative prices or opportunity costs. Thus, the relative price of shirts and hams is unaffected if, because of inflation, the price of shirts increases from $24 to $48 and the price of hams increases from $12 to $24. Similarly, the relative price is unaffected if because of a deflation a shirt that was priced at $24 is now priced at $12 and a ham previously priced at $12 is now $6. In both cases the purchasing power of money changes, but in neither case has the relative price of shirts and hams changed.

A further aside: measuring an economy's output. Using money as a unit of account means that the aggregate output of an economy can also be measured. We could measure the output of an economy by simply listing the production of the various goods: so many shirts, so many cars, and so many apples. This particular way of accounting for the aggregate output of an economy would be extremely cumbersome. In these circumstances money becomes a useful accounting device. Because prices are almost always specified in money terms, a dollar measure of the output in each market can be easily created: add up the dollar value of the production of each good produced by multiplying the number of units produced of each good by its money price. (Example: Apples sell for $1.00 per pound. The economy produces 1,000,000 pounds of apples. Therefore, the dollar value of apple production is $1,000,000.) It may not be possible, as the saying goes, "to add apples and oranges," but it is possible to add the *dollar value* of apple production with the *dollar value* of orange production. The dollar measure obtained by doing this for *all* of the commodities an economy produces is referred to as **aggregate output** or **national income** or, more technically, as **Gross Domestic Product (GDP)**.

▶ Firms

To this point, we have focused on a single individual specializing in the production of some commodity. Individuals can often be more productive if they work together as a group or team to produce commodities through their *joint* rather than individual effort. Organizing production by relying on teams allows individuals to specialize even further. Thus, for example, a shrewd Henry Ford noted that a large number of individuals each producing complete automobiles was not as productive as the same individuals working as a team on an assembly line where each could further specialize in some component of the automobile production process. This idea is not new. Long before Henry Ford decided to produce automobiles using teams working on an assembly line, Adam Smith began his famous treatise, *The Wealth of Nations,* by discussing the enormous productivity gains that accompany the division of labor in a pin factory:

> *The greatest improvement in the productive powers of labour, and the greater part of the skill, dexterity, and judgment with which it is any where directed, or applied, seem to have been the effects of the division of labour . . . To take an example . . . a workman not educated to [pin making] . . . nor acquainted with the use of the machinery employed in it . . . could scarce, perhaps, with his utmost industry, make one pin in a day, and certainly could not make twenty. But in the way in which this business is now carried on . . . [o]ne man draws out the wire, another straights it, a third cuts it, a fourth points it, a fifth grinds it at the top for receiving the head . . . and the important business of making a pin is, in this manner, divided into about eighteen distinct operations . . . I have seen a small manufactory of this kind where ten men only were employed. . . . [t]hese ten persons, . . . could make among them upwards of forty-eight thousand pins in a day. Each person, therefore, making a tenth part of the forty-eight thousand pins, might be considered as making four thousand eight hundred pins in a day. But if they had all wrought separately and independently, . . . they certainly could not each of them have make twenty.*

Smith noted that team efforts of this sort were likely to increase productivity for three reasons: First, the performance of specialized workers improves through practice and repetition; that is, workers learn by doing. Second, specialized workers do not lose time moving from one task to another. Third, Smith argued, specialized production stimulates technological progress because specialized worker, focusing their attention on the details of a production process, are likely to discover more efficient ways of doing particular tasks.

Shirking

Because it leads to further specialization and for the other reasons Adam Smith identified, team production has the potential to dramatically increase the productive capacity of an economy. But it also creates a problem. If the output of the group is greater than the sum of the outputs of its individual members working separately, then it is difficult to identify the contribution of any single team member to the output of the team. For example, if each of five individuals working alone can harvest 20 coconuts for an aggregate harvest of 100 coconuts, but the five individuals working as a team can harvest 200 coconuts, *which* worker produces the additional coconuts? The answer is, in an important sense, that they *all* do. Herein lie two problems.

First, team members have an incentive to work less intensely. Such behavior is called **shirking**. Put differently, if my contribution cannot be determined easily and shirking on my part cannot be detected easily, why should I work hard? Why not take it easy and take advantage of the other team members' hard work? If everyone acts the same way, of course, the team will not be as productive as it otherwise might be.

Second, it is difficult to determine the appropriate level of compensation for each team member. That is, if I am the manager of a firm and I cannot easily measure the contribution of each employee to the output of the firm because they work in teams, on what basis should I determine each person's compensation? The question is important to a firm because if individuals are not provided with incentives that reward their efforts, team activities will, once again, be less productive than they otherwise could be.

Firms exist, in part, to overcome these problems—they exist in order to make teams of workers productive. That is, firms are institutional arrangements that organize teams, deal with shirking and figure out how to compensate specialized workers. Firms do so by having some individuals who specialize in organizing, monitoring, managing, and compensating others who work in teams. It follows that a firm will have a number of people who are not directly engaged in the production of output, but who, rather, facilitate production by others. Thus, firms have **supervisors** and **managers**.

Hierarchical Organization

Managers and supervisors, of course, also have incentives to shirk; they are also part of a team—in this case, the firm—and their contribution often cannot be measured easily. When shirking by managers and supervisors is a serious problem, we would expect to observe *supervisors* of supervisors. Then, perhaps, *supervisors* of supervisors of supervisors. And so on. In this sense, a firm is likely to be organized *hierarchically*, with different levels of management superimposed over the groups of workers who actually produce output. The less serious the shirking problem among production workers or managers, the less hierarchical the firm needs to be. The more serious the shirking problem, the more hierarchical the firm needs to be in order to get the most output from a team of production workers *and* managers.

Transaction Costs

Nothing in this discussion of team production suggests the span of activities a firm might undertake. In this regard, an interesting problem for a firm is the degree to which it should integrate across the various steps necessary to produce its final output. For example, a shoe manufacturer could produce its own heels or it could purchase them in a market for heels. It could also tan its own leather or purchase leather from a separate firm that specializes in tanning. If the shoe-manufacturing firm tans its own leather rather than purchasing tanned leather, or makes its own heels rather than purchasing them, the firm is *integrating* different production activities within its direct control.

Why would a firm integrate across different steps in a production process rather than purchase various inputs, including intermediate goods, in the market? It turns out that certain kinds of market transactions are costly, and integration is a way of lowering transaction costs.

Opportunistic behavior, once again. Firms often need to be able to plan on the availability of resources over a long period in order to make appropriate decision about investment, training of workers, and other matters. Long-term market relationships pose a problem, however, because one or both participants might have an incentive to behave opportunistically, thereby taking advantage of the other party with whom they have the long-term relationship. For example, if I know that you are dependent upon my supplying you with electricity, I may be able, at some point after our initial agreement, to take advantage of your dependence and force you to pay me more for the electricity than you (or I) had originally intended. Opportunistic behavior of this sort makes it difficult to sustain long-term relationships and, as a consequence, makes it difficult to fully capture the gains from specialization.

As we noted earlier in this chapter, this problem is sometimes solved by relying on formal contracts. It is often impossible to specify a response to each contingency that might happen over the course of the contract, however. In addition, because enforcing a contract through legal action is itself costly, individuals may have incentives to renege on their commitments. For either reason, opportunistic behavior sometimes becomes a problem when transactions occur in markets. As a consequence, the use of markets may be costly.

A way of minimizing these costs is to avoid markets and *internalize transactions within an organization that can force various groups to coordinate their activities and not behave opportunistically.* In short, transact *within a firm* instead of transacting with independent parties in markets. A firm may reduce these kinds of transaction costs because firms do not rely on "arms-length" market transactions based on implicit or explicit contracts where others may behave opportunistically. Instead, a firm controls these transactions directly and forcefully by keeping them within one organization.

For example, before 1925, General Motors purchased car bodies in the marketplace from an independent supplier, Fisher Auto Body. Now, however, General Motors produces its own bodies and Fisher Body is part of GM. The move from market transactions to integration within a single firm followed a 1919 market contract between GM and Fisher Auto Body in which both agreed that Fisher would be the sole supplier of bodies to GM, thus insuring that GM would have a supply of bodies and that Fisher could sell the auto bodies it produced. While this looked like a beneficial market transaction, the agreement created some potential problems. GM was dependent on Fisher and would have had very costly production disruptions if Fisher had not delivered bodies on schedule and at competitive prices. On the other side, Fisher was dependent on GM because it was using dies and other equipment specifically designed for GM bodies and would have had costly disruptions if GM had refused to accept the bodies as promised at a price that would return an appropriate profit. Each firm apparently feared that the other party would take advantage of the agreement its dependency and the initial 10-year contract set the price using a carefully specified formula. Shortly after the contract was signed, however, changes in economic circumstances led GM to suspect that it would lose money if it continued to adhere to the contract. Rather than face these problems in the marketplace, or perhaps in the courts, GM decided to internalize the transactions rather than take its chances in a market and it merged with Fisher in 1926, thereby removing the possibility of opportunistic behavior.

The internalization of economic activities (that is, the move of certain transactions from markets to within a firm) explains why firms engage in many different activities rather than focusing on just one. Thus, firms that produce cars may also produce auto bodies and transmissions. In addition, firms that produce cars may also distribute and sell them to consumers. When firms internalize various parts of the production and distribution processes, they are said to be **vertically integrated**. Thus, the GM-Fisher Body merger was a **vertical merger** that created a more vertically integrated firm.

On the other hand, it should be clear that not all activities are integrated within a single firm. Firms that produce cars generally do not produce tires or batteries, but purchase them from independent firms. In addition, firms that produce goods frequently do not market them directly to consumers but sell them to specialized marketing firms for wholesale or retail delivery. Presumably, in those cases where a firm is willing to deal in the marker, rather than integrating the activity within the firm, the problems of opportunistic behavior are minimal.

It is not always possible to predict when economic activities are likely to be organized within a firm rather that through market transactions, but in the following circumstances we would expect more internalization and fewer market transactions:

1. When a buyer contracts with a firm for the production of a custom-made or specialized product, the buyer will not be able to purchase the product elsewhere after the contract has been made. On the other hand, the producer will have a difficult time finding another buyer after the custom-made product has been produced. Thus, buying and selling custom-made products in a market, even with a carefully specified contract, places both buyer and seller in a position where each is exposed to the possibility of opportunistic behavior by the other party. In these circumstances, economic activity is often more effectively organized by having both "buyer" and "producer" be units of the same firm.

2. When the delivery of an input from one firm to another requires specialized capital—that is, capital that cannot be used easily for other purposes—one firm may be able to take advantage of the firm that has already acquired the specialized capital. Why? The capital is essentially worthless unless the firm that acquired it can sell its output to the second firm. For example, if a pipeline has been built in order to deliver crude oil to a refinery, but the refinery has not yet been built, the party that was to have built the refinery can take advantage of the substantial investment of the oil pipeline company by renegotiating a lower price for oil using the threat of not building the refinery at the end of the pipeline. Or, if the refinery is built first, the party that was to have built the pipeline can take advantage of the substantial investment of the refinery company by renegotiating a higher price for oil using the threat of not building the pipeline as a bargaining ploy. In such circumstances, market transactions have costs that can be avoided if the entities acquiring the specialized capital are part of the same firm.

3. If it is difficult for buyers and sellers to foresee future events that would dramatically change the costs and benefits associated with a contract, or if it is difficult for a party to a contract to verify that events which would affect the contract have actually occurred, then contracts that effectively protect each party are difficult to negotiate. For example, efforts to specify pricing formulas for long-term contracts are difficult either because prices and costs can change unpredictably over time or because the buyer is unwilling to take the seller's word about what actually happened to costs. In cases like this, economic activity is frequently better organized by having the two contracting parties be part of the same firm.

Clearly, each firm has to decide what activities it will undertake internally (integrate) and what activities it will contract for in markets (demand). Each firm may make different decisions about when it will integrate and when it will contract. That most firms are vertically integrated to some degree, however, suggests that firms evolved, in part, as an alternative to the market in *governing* potentially opportunistic behavior. Essentially, a firm substitutes direct control for an exchange relationship, using authority instead of negotiation as a way of organizing economic activity.

Scale Economies

Sometimes as firms become larger, the productivity gains are more than proportional to the increase in the size of the firm. For example, it may be that an assembly line's output can be doubled without doubling *all* of the inputs a firm employs. If the technologies associated with a particular firm's production process allows such an adjustment, the firm is said to have **economies of scale**.

Why is there generally more than one firm in an industry? If internalization rather than reliance on the market lowers transaction costs, and if, because of scale economies, larger firms are more productive than smaller firms, why do we generally see many firms in an industry that are not fully integrated instead of one large, fully integrated firm? The answer: At some point, the costs of internalization and direct control exceed the potential efficiency gains from further integration or expansion. Unfortunately, this explanation essentially says that there are many firms because there are many firms. It turns out, however, that firms are necessarily bureaucratic. Bureaucratic organizations have their own difficulties and costs:

1. It is extremely difficult to monitor the productivity of individuals in a bureaucratic organization like a firm when output cannot be directly observed.

2. The interests of individuals in bureaucratic organizations are likely to be at odds with the interests of the owners of the organization.

3. Effective management requires good information about what is happening within a bureaucratic organization. The costs of acquiring this information almost always increase as the size of the firm increases.

Thus, while there are technological reasons why larger firms may be more productive, there are organizational and managerial reasons why, beyond some point, larger firms may be less productive. It follows that the size of a firm will be determined by production technologies which determine the optimal size of teams, the costs of monitoring shirking, the costs of relying on markets rather than within-firm controls, and the costs of organizing and managing. As a consequence, the "optimal" size of a firm is likely to differ from industry to industry.

Curiously, in most markets there are a large number of firms, some small and some large. This suggests that even though scale economies may be important up to some point, beyond that point there may not be much advantage to being larger.

The size of firms is also limited to some degree by the size of the market. Firms tend to be smaller when markets are smaller. When transportation costs are high, for example, firms tend to be smaller and more locally focused. Lower transportation and communication costs mean that firms can be national and even international in scope. Since in these cases, the markets themselves are also larger, the number of firms in many markets may continue to be very large.

The size of firms can also be affected by public policy. Fear of antitrust prosecution, where the government may legally attack firms that grow too large, may limit the size of some firms. On the other hand, government subsidies to producers or legal restrictions on competition or entry may increase the size of firms. These important public policy matters will be considered more fully in other chapters.

▶ Intermediaries

An **intermediary** is someone who specializes in trading. Since specialization typically lowers costs, intermediaries, often called *middlemen*, lower transaction costs. By doing so, they allow for more effective use of resources. If you move to a new city, for example, you can either have a real estate agent show you the homes that are for sale or you can look for a home by yourself. Similarly, a resident who wants to sell a home can either list it with a real estate agent who will show the home to interested buyers or do it himself. Why do most people use intermediaries rather than transacting directly? The short answer: transactions are often costly.

To understand the role that intermediaries might play in lowering transaction costs, consider once again the simple economy where you and Friday received an endowment of manna and quail each morning. Remember that you preferred 210 manna and 17 quail to your endowment of 200 manna and 20 quail while Friday preferred (180 M, 21 Q) to his endowment (200 M, 20 Q).

Suppose that it costs you and Friday something to find and make deals. Assume, to be specific, that it costs Friday 16 M to transact and that the cost to you is 2 Q. These costs reflect output lost because, for example, of the time taken to find a trading partner, negotiate, and actually make an exchange. They might also include the costs of transporting and preparing commodities for exchange. Table 1 sum-

Table 1
The Consequences of Costly Transactions

	Endowment	Preferred position	Transaction costs	Offer net of transaction costs
You	200 M, 20 Q	210 M, 17 Q	2 Q	No more thant 1 Q for 10 M
Friday	200 M, 20 Q	180 M, 21 Q	16 M	No more than 4 M for 1 Q

Table 2
The Consequences of Trading Through an Intermediary

	Endowment	Preferred position	Offer from intermediary	Outcome
You	200 M, 20 Q	210 M, 17 Q	3 Q for 10 M	210 M, 17 Q
Friday	200 M, 20 Q	180 M, 21 Q	20 M for 1 Q	180 M, 21 Q
Intermediary's gains				10 M, 2 Q

marizes the possibilities. Note that transaction costs are so high in this case that there are no beneficial exchanges between you and Friday.

Suppose, however, that there is a third person on the island who specializes in facilitating exchanges, and who can, because he specializes in trading, trade at lower costs. This person might offer you 10 M for 3 Q and then offer Friday 1 Q in exchange for 20 M. Table 2 summarizes the outcome. Here the intermediary transfers manna from Friday to you, keeping 10, and transfers quail from you to Friday, keeping 2. Both you and Friday are better off trading through this intermediary than you are if you can't trade.

The intermediary profits from facilitating the transactions by capturing some of the potential gains that would otherwise be lost. Indeed, it is the possibilities of doing so that creates incentives for firms and individuals to become intermediaries. The intermediary can do this, however, only so long as it is less costly for her to facilitate the exchange between you and Friday than it is for the two of you to trade directly. The point of this example is simply put: *The potential gains from exchange provide an incentive for individuals to trade. When direct trade is costly, these gains also provide a substantial incentive for intermediaries to facilitate trades.*

A very substantial fraction of the jobs available in modern economies are as intermediaries (e.g., real estate agents, stock brokers, certain kinds of lawyers, most retail outlets, etc.). This is indirect, but very good evidence of the enormous gains from exchange and specialization in modern economies. That is, these gains must be so large that a substantial fraction of the work force can derive its income solely from reducing the transaction costs that would otherwise limit exchange and specialization.

Are Intermediaries Productive?

The role of intermediaries or middlemen is viewed with considerable ambivalence. Since no additional output is actually produced by the trading activities in which they are involved, it is tempting to think of intermediaries as unproductive. Economic production, however, is not simply the physical creation of new commodities; it is also the creation of satisfied individuals. As the manna-quail exchange example in Chapter 1 illustrated, the common perception that the only way that individuals within an economy can be made better off is if the output of the economy actually increases, is quite wrong. Measurements of the quantity of goods and services an economy produces (e.g., GDP) are only imperfect indicators of what economic activity really produces: individual well-being. In the example just outlined, the trading services provided by a third party are *economically productive* because both you and Friday are better off after the trade through the intermediary than you would be if no trade occurred. This gain occurs because manna and quail are reallocated even though the third party did not increase the quantity of either available in the economy.

▶ Summary

Property rights and incentives. Economic activity can be effectively organized and the gains from exchange and specialization fully realized only if individuals have both present *and* future interests. Otherwise, resources will be used too intensively and there will be too little investment. Getting incentives right requires property rights, which include the right to exclude, the right to use with minimal restrictions, and the right to transfer.

Contracts. Economic activity can be effectively organized and the gains from exchange and specialization fully realized only if resources can easily move from lower-valued uses to higher-valued uses. Because some trades are complex, however, there is the possibility that the movement of resources from lower-valued to higher-valued uses may be undermined by opportunistic behavior. Hence, an economy has to develop institutional arrangements, rules and enforcement mechanisms that prevent or minimize opportunistic behavior. Chief among these are formal contracts enforceable in a judicial system.

Money. Economic activity can be effectively organized and the gains from exchange and specialization fully realized only if transaction costs, particularly those associated with the problem of coincident wants, are minimized. As a consequence, a commonly traded third commodity, money, has evolved in virtually every economy. Instead of trading goods for goods, individuals trade goods and resources for money and then trade money for goods and resources.

Firms. Teams are often more productive than individuals working alone. However, team production creates opportunities for individual workers to shirk.

Shirking can be reduced, and the substantial gains from team production realized, if some people monitor the work effort of others. Since these monitors have, in turn, incentives to shirk, firms are organized where there is a hierarchy of monitors. Thus, the typical pyramidal organization of a firm evolved to reduce or minimize the shirking problem. Likewise, the rich array of compensation schemes (e.g., wages, salaries, commissions, tips, bonuses, stock options, etc.) evolved as ways to eliminate or reduce the costs of shirking and monitoring.

Intermediaries. Intermediaries are individuals or firms that specialize in facilitating trades between other individuals or firms. Because intermediaries are specialists, the costs of trading through an intermediary are frequently lower than the costs of trading directly. Although intermediaries generally do not produce additional output, they increase individual well-being by lowering the costs of transacting, thereby facilitating the movement of commodities from lower valued to higher valued uses. In this important sense, intermediaries are productive.

Chapter 4 ▶ ▶
Choices and Marginal Analysis _____

In Chapter 1 we learned that scarcity forces individuals to make choices and that because of scarcity, choices have costs. For the most part, individuals appear to be both purposeful and self-interested as they evaluate these costs and make choices. That is, individuals appear to make decisions that advance their own interests. This chapter makes this notion more precise. We first consider the assumption that the process by which individual choices are made is **rational**. We then consider what follows if individuals **maximize** their well-being. The purpose of this chapter is to develop a general set of principles that describe rational, maximizing decisions. In later chapters we will consider specific applications, first for individuals as they choose how much to consume (Chapters 6 and 7), and then for firms as they choose how much to produce (Chapters 8 and 9).

▶ Rational Choices

Choices are inevitable and dominate our lives. Some are trivial; others are momentous. Most are neither, but simply cannot be avoided because we live in a world of scarcity. Sometimes other people or groups of people make choices for us: "Eat your spinach." "Take out the garbage." "Pay your taxes." "Take English 101." "Be at work at 8:00 a.m." Most of the time, however, our choices are our own: "What should I do now?" "Which shirt should I buy?" "Should I study or sleep?" "What flavor do I like best?" "Which courses do I want to take?" "What do I want to major

in?" "Where should I live?" There are, however, several ways by which individuals might make choices.

Traditional Choices. Sometimes we simply do what is familiar to us. If our father has been a farmer, we become farmers. If our family has always lived in Utah, we live in Utah. If people have always worn leaves and walnut shells to weddings, we wear leaves and walnut shells for the occasion. If we have always eaten bean burritos for lunch, then we continue to eat bean burritos for lunch. In short, some choices are determined by tradition or inertia.

Choosing based on tradition implies that choices won't change much over time. However, individuals appear to change their behavior too much for tradition to be the dominant determinant of choices. People change jobs; they wear various clothing styles; they consume different things at different times; they are mobile and move about the country; they look for deals when shopping (sometimes its squash for dinner, at other times its beans, depending on the prices of each at the supermarket).

Random Choices. Sometimes we choose randomly. We don't know why we make particular choices—we have to make a choice and one thing appears as good as another. When there are lots of alternatives about which we know very little, our choices may not have much pattern or consistency. Consider, for example, the problem of selecting what to order on a first visit to a new Chinese restaurant that has a 10-page menu. In situations like this, your choices may very well be random because you don't have any way to decide which items are preferable, but you need to order something if you are to eat.

Choosing randomly implies that there will be little pattern in the choices that individuals make. There are, however, patterns and even predictability in human behavior. In particular, students systematically take courses that move them toward graduation; demanders want to purchase more when the market price is lower; suppliers want to sell more when the market price is higher.

Rational Choices. Often, choices are purposeful. That is, we have objectives or goals and make choices that systematically move us toward these objectives or goals. As a consequence, our choices are patterned and predictable or, in other words, rational. Individuals who are rational will make different choices at different times, but, generally, only when there are changes in the environment within which choices are made. Specifically, behavior is **rational** when those making decisions:

1. make informed comparisons between the options they might choose,

2. are consistent in their comparisons of options they might choose, and

3. choose those options they prefer.

Comparability

Individuals who are rational are able to compare pairs of alternatives. They may make a comparison between different goods such as models of cars, or locations for homes, or types of food, or styles and colors of clothing, or between various services provided by doctors, lawyers, plumbers, or teachers. For the owner of a firm, the comparison might be between alternative energy inputs such as coal, gas, or oil or between using labor or machines. **Comparability** is at the heart of rational behavior. Unless you can say, "For me, this is better than that" or "I like this thing more than that thing" or "This option is likely to have a higher payoff than that option," you cannot make a rational choice. More formally, options that an individual may choose are **comparable** if, given any two options A and B, an individual can say that A is **preferred** to B or that B is **preferred** to A or that A and B are equally good (in

which case the person is said to be **indifferent** between A and B).

Consistency

Individuals who are rational are consistent in their choices. In fact, **consistency** is such a basic requirement of rational behavior that we often speak, loosely, of inconsistent behavior as being irrational. What does it mean to be consistent? Formally, if an individual compares A with B and likes A, and then compares B with C and likes B, then **consistency** requires that the individual will like A more than C. (Decisions that are consistent in this sense are sometimes referred to as **transitive**.)

If individuals can make informed comparisons and if their comparisons are consistent, all options that might be chosen can be ordered from the most desired or most preferred option to the least desired or least preferred option. Thus, if A is preferred to B and B is preferred to C, then there is a **preference ordering** of A over B over C. For example, suppose that you want to buy an ice cream cone at Baskin-Robbins and have already tasted chocolate, pecan, and licorice so that you can make informed comparisons of these flavors. If you have determined that you prefer chocolate to licorice and that you prefer licorice to pecan, then consistency implies that you need not make a comparison between chocolate and pecan—it must be that you prefer chocolate to pecan and to any flavor that you don't like as much as pecan.

Choosing the Best Option

Having made comparisons and ordered the alternatives, rational individuals choose those options that make them better off. That is, they **maximize** their well-being. This means, simply, that individuals try to do the best they can as they confront and deal with scarcity. In doing so, they try to anticipate the consequences of choices that they might make.

Information

Making comparisons between options requires information. If you've never been to a Chinese restaurant and know nothing about the various dishes, you obviously cannot make comparisons between them. Likewise, it would be difficult for you to compare chocolate almond fudge ice cream with wild berry ice cream if you did not know about, or had never tasted, wild berry ice cream. Assuming that individuals can make comparisons *implies* that they are informed about the options that might be chosen.

Clearly we are not always informed about our options. As a consequence, our choices may not always be purposeful or rational. In situations like this, we sometimes rely on tradition to guide us, or we may rely on others to assist us in our choices, or we may simply choose randomly one from among the several options before us. For example, unless you know a lot about the dishes at a particular restaurant, it may not be possible to make a rational choice among menu items. Watching people order in restaurants illustrates and emphasizes this point: Before ordering, people frequently ask others about their intended orders. They may also ask about the specialties of the house or what is recommended. Often no one wants to be the first to order, and everyone defers to someone else in an effort to see what they order. Frequently, after one person has ordered, others will say that her selection sounds good and follow with the same order. Sometimes we simply ask someone else to order for the group.

As we make decisions, we obtain information about the particular choices that we make. This information allows us to choose more rationally when we confront the same options again. A person who frequently eats at Chinese restaurants gains information about typical dishes on the menu and then can rank them, for example. Because of the importance of making rational decisions, we sometimes purposefully search out information about their options: we shop around, we read product reviews in *Consumer Reports,* we surf the web, we look at the ads in the newspaper, and in many other ways seek to become better informed. Searching for information provides indirect evidence that individuals consider rational choices important.

Although it is important to be informed, information is almost always costly to obtain. Because it takes time to shop around or gather information, choices will frequently be made with less than full information and it may be rational to be partially ignorant. Put differently, we must often make decisions and choose options with whatever information is available. For options for which information is incomplete, we have to make guesses about the consequences of a particular choice. Individuals, in this case, have **rational expectations** if they make informed guesses that use *all* the relevant information available to them in a way so as to minimize any possible errors.

If we are partially informed, some of our choices will have unpredicted consequences, and some decisions will turn out to be mistakes. Clearly, a full understanding of how individuals make choices requires an understanding of how individuals obtain information and how they deal with uncertainty when complete information is not readily available. These matters are important; we will deal with them in Chapter 16.

Who Should Choose?

In most societies there is conflict about the boundaries of individual choice. Should certain choices be left to individuals or should they be made collectively? There are few more divisive issues at present than the question of whether a woman should be free to choose an abortion, for example. But conflict on a lesser scale swirls around other questions of individual versus collective choice: Should the government have the right to limit the choice of what individuals may read by censoring certain books or other published materials? If your answer is a firm no, what about child pornography or materials that are blatantly racist? Should the government have the right to prohibit or limit the choice to consume certain kinds of drugs such as heroin, alcohol, or marijuana? Is your answer any different if the use of a particular drug harms no one but the individual user? Should a government be able to restrict a cancer "cure" that is totally harmless but also totally ineffective? Should a government (or an airline company) have the right to prohibit smoking on airlines? Should parents have the right to limit the choices that their children make? If so, until what age? In questions such as these there is widespread disagreement about who should make which choices—individuals, parents, doctors, the government, etc.

These disagreements exist because of fundamental disagreements about whether individuals ought to be able to make mistakes and about who is in a better position to evaluate the consequences of particular decisions. But they also exist because some choices have consequences for others as well as the person making the choice. Drinking alcohol has individual consequences, but it also has other consequences when people who drink then drive. Smoking adversely affects those who are nearby. Thus, individual decisions are not always private matters even if we decide that the individual most directly affected is the best person to make the choice. (We will explore some of these issues further in Chapter 15.)

Economics presumes that, in most cases, individuals are in the best position to choose and ought to be free to do so. This presumption implies that either the consequences of most decisions rest with the individual making the decision or that the individual is in the best position to weigh any effects on others. Since this is clearly not the case for all decisions, this presumption is sometimes at odds with the development and implementation of public policies. Indeed, many of the policy issues that will be discussed in the following chapters are shaped in interesting ways by the tension over who should choose.

▶ Maximization and Marginal Analysis

If individuals have compared the options they might choose and ordered them in a consistent manner, we would expect them to select their most preferred or best option. Surely this is not surprising. There are two things that make selecting the most preferred or best options somewhat more complex, however.

First, not all the options about which an individual has information can be chosen because, as usual, scarcity matters. Put simply, given your income you might not be able to afford the $50,000 automobile of your dreams. Virtually all of us confront the same kinds of constraints: time, prices, our income or wealth, or, if we manage a firm, input prices and the technologies or manufacturing processes available to the firm. The larger social environment within which we make choices and the market structure that aggregates individual choices are also important constraints.

Second, as we make choices, costs and benefits may change. This occurs because of the **law of diminishing marginal returns**.

Diminishing Marginal Returns

People consume ice cream, but they also consume spinach. They consume meat, but also pasta and fish

and bread and many other things. A Baskin-Robbins customer who loves ice cream probably does not spend his entire food budget on ice cream. Indeed, were we to observe his actual consumption of food, we would likely find a rich variety of foods in his daily diet. He may even eat spinach occasionally even though, in the abstract, he greatly prefers ice cream to spinach. Why would his diet include some spinach as well as ice cream?

Firms employ skilled workers, but they also employ workers with fewer skills, and they use machines as well as labor. If highly skilled workers are productive, why doesn't the manager of a firm hire a very large number of these workers to take advantage of their productivity and increase the output of the firm instead of using workers with lower skills? And, if workers are productive, why do firms purchase expensive machines?

To each of these questions you might respond, "Well, if I eat spinach, it must be that I prefer spinach," or "If the firm buys machines when it could have hired more workers, then machines must be more productive." But these responses beg the questions, because we could turn them around: If I really prefer spinach, why do I eat any ice cream, or if machines really are more productive, why does the firm sometimes hire more workers?

The key to answering these questions is the concept of **diminishing marginal returns**: As the amount of one item used or consumed increases relative to the amount of other items that could be used or consumed, the *incremental* or *marginal* value of that item, at some point, will begin to decrease.

The meaning of *marginal*. Marginal refers to the last unit, or the additional unit, or each subsequent unit. For example, the *marginal* ice-cream cone would be the last one purchased and eaten. The *marginal* output of labor would be the additional output produced by the last worker hired or, more generally, the additional output produced with each subsequent worker hired. An additional hour spent studying is the *marginal* study hour.

The meaning of *diminishing marginal returns*. Diminishing marginal returns occurs when the value of the *marginal* choice is less than the value of previous choices. For example, one ice-cream cone per day may be highly satisfying. Your well-being may continue to increase if you eat more than one cone per day. In a situation of diminishing marginal returns, however, each subsequent cone consumed each day adds *less* to your overall satisfaction than does the first cone. Or, to take another example, suppose a firm continues to increase the number of workers it employs but doesn't increase its capital or supervisory personnel. In this case, diminishing marginal returns means that the firm will eventually find that the increases in output from hiring an additional worker become smaller and smaller. In each case, it is important to note, we are assuming that nothing changes except the number of ice-cream cones eaten in a day or the number of workers a firm employs over some given period of time.

Satisfaction for an individual or output for a firm in these examples may, of course, continue to increase as more ice-cream cones are consumed or more workers hired, but because of diminishing marginal returns, each does so at a diminishing or decreasing rate. Tables 1 and 2 illustrate this important idea numerically; Figures 1 and 2 illustrate the point graphically. Note that the principle of diminishing marginal returns is the same for either a firm or an individual.

The consequences of diminishing marginal returns. As a consequence of diminishing marginal returns, even if they prefer ice cream to spinach in the abstract most Baskin-Robbins customers will, at some point, consume spinach rather than an additional ice-cream cone. Put simply, because of

diminishing returns, as you consume more and more ice-cream cones, the last ice-cream cone that you eat will eventually be worth less than a serving of spinach in terms of the additional satisfaction it provides to you. At that point, you may well decide to have some spinach rather than an additional ice-cream cone.

More formally, as more and more of one good is consumed over a fixed period of time, an individual will find that the **marginal satisfaction**, or what economists sometimes call the **marginal utility** of a choice, diminishes. Because of *diminishing* marginal satisfaction or utility, individuals generally consume a mix of goods and services rather than one or only a few goods and services.

Similarly, a plant manager may choose to use other productive inputs rather than hiring another worker because, as more and more workers are employed, the contribution of the last worker employed to the output of the firm will be small—the effect of diminishing marginal returns. Again, more formally, as a firm increases its use of a particular input, it will find that the **marginal product** of that input falls. Because of *diminishing* marginal productivity, then, firms will generally employ a mix of inputs rather than only one or a few.

The last ice-cream cone is not inferior in quality to the first one consumed, and the last worker is not inferior in quality to the first worker hired. They are worth less only because they are the *last* units chosen and being so add less to the well-being of the individual or to the output of the firm. The fifth

Table 1 Total Output and Diminishing Marginal Returns for a Firm		
Number of workers	Output per day (bushels)	Additional (marginal) output (bushels)
		100
10	100	
		90
20	190	
		60
30	250	
		40
40	280	

Table 2 Total Satisfaction and Diminishing Marginal Returns for an Individual		
Ice-cream cones per day	Satisfaction	Additional (marginal) satisfaction
		100
1	100	
		50
2	150	
		20
3	170	
		5
4	175	

Figure 1
Diminishing Marginal Output

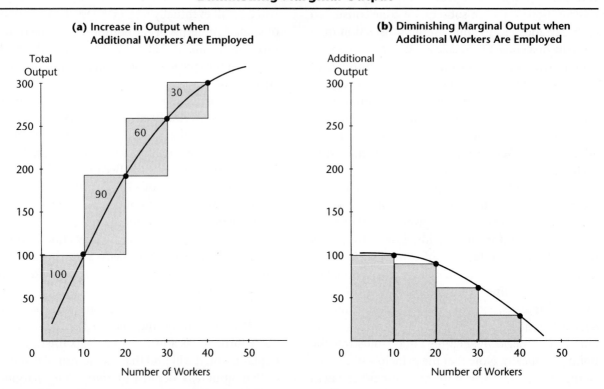

The additional output produced per worker decreases as the number of workers increases, *ceteris paribus*. Part (a) measures the change in total output for a firm; part (b) is derived from part (a) by measuring the change in output per worker as the number of workers changes. Note that the shaded areas in both graphs represent the same amount of additional output.

ice-cream cone eaten in a half hour adds less satisfaction than the first. The tenth ice-cream cone eaten in the same half hour adds even less. Or, for a firm, when lots of workers are already employed, adding one additional worker adds less to output than earlier workers. As a consequence, given a firm's capital stock and other inputs, doubling the number of workers generally will not double a firm's output.[1]

Why diminishing marginal returns? An important characteristic of diminishing marginal returns is something is *fixed*. In the case of the ice-cream consumer, the *amount of time* over which the con-

sumption occurs—a half hour, or an hour, or a day—is fixed. For the manager of a firm, the *number of machines and supervisory personnel* available cannot be quickly changed. In addition, the firm makes its output decisions within a particular production period such as a day, a month, six months, or a year. To find those situations when diminishing marginal returns will be important, look for one element that is unchanging or fixed against which an individual makes choices.

For example, if we are considering how many ice-cream cones a person would like to consume in the next fifteen minutes, the effects of diminishing marginal returns would be far more evident than if we were considering how many cones that person would like to consume in the next year. Or, for example, the diminishing marginal returns associated with hiring additional workers would be more important to a firm with 50 workers but few

[1] In the case of a firm, a certain size workforce may be needed to minimally staff a factory and the first few workers may not have as high a value as subsequent workers. In this case, the effect of diminishing marginal returns occurs eventually, but not necessarily immediately.

Figure 2
Diminishing Marginal Satisfaction

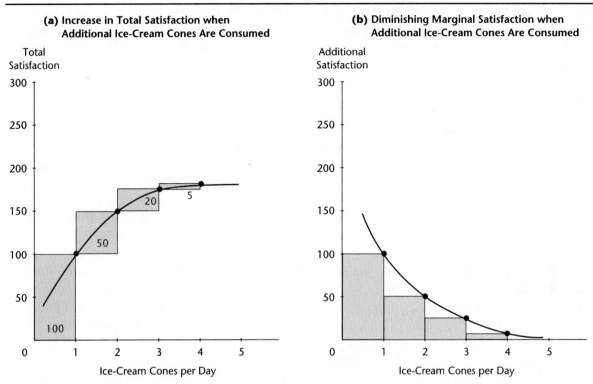

(a) Increase in Total Satisfaction when Additional Ice-Cream Cones Are Consumed

(b) Diminishing Marginal Satisfaction when Additional Ice-Cream Cones Are Consumed

The additional satisfaction from consuming an additional ice-cream cone decreases as the number of ice-cream cones consumed per day increases, *ceteris paribus*.

machines and supervisory personnel than it would be to a firm that had many more machines and supervisory personnel, but the same 50 workers.

Maximization

In order to make best or optimal choices, an individual has to balance *marginal* benefits with *marginal* costs. "But why *marginal* benefits and *marginal* costs rather than total benefits and total costs?" you may ask. Fair question.

Marginal benefits. To answer to this question, consider a tennis player who plays regularly. Because time is scarce, the tennis player is forced to make decisions about the number of times she will play tennis each month. Table 3 characterizes the overall or total satisfaction she obtains from playing different amounts of tennis each month in dollar terms. (If you find attributing dollar values to satisfaction disturbing, you could think of the same example as describing the production decision of a factory

owner or manager. For example, "sets per month" might be equivalent to the number of employees hired to work on a particular task per month, and "total satisfaction" might be equivalent to the dollar value of the output or revenue these workers produced.)

Table 3
The Benefits of Playing Tennis

Number of sets	Total satisfaction
1	$20
2	30
3	38
4	44
5	48
6	50
7	51
8	51

Diminishing marginal returns will be important at some point because the time period in this example is fixed. That is, we're considering the optimal number of sets to play in a one-month period. Indeed, increasing play from two sets to three sets increases satisfaction by $8, but increasing play from four sets to five sets increases satisfaction by only $4. Hence, diminishing marginal returns are evident.

If tennis were free, this player would play no more than eight sets per month if she wished to maximize her overall satisfaction. The best or optimal decision is easy to find in this simple example—simply look for the largest dollar value of total satisfaction, $51, and then note the level of activity, eight sets per month, that is consistent with achieving this level of satisfaction.

Are there any generalizable characteristics associated with this optimal decision that would help us select "best outcomes" in more complex settings or where less information is available? To answer this question, consider what happens to total satisfaction as the number of sets played each month changes (or, if you prefer, what happens to a firm's revenue as the number of employees changes). Table 4 provides a summary.

Marginal satisfaction in this example is the additional satisfaction obtained when an additional set of tennis is played. It can be estimated by calculating the *change* in total satisfaction divided by the *change* in the number of sets played. For example, increasing the level of play from three to four sets per month increases total satisfaction from $38 to $44. The change in total satisfaction is $6, and the change $ in sets played is 1. Thus, marginal satisfaction is $6. (If this table illustrated the revenue for a firm, the marginal revenue the firm obtained when the fourth worker was hired would be $6.)

By examining the column of numbers that represent marginal satisfaction, it should be clear that the eighth set has marginal satisfaction of zero and that, at any level of play less than eight sets per month, the marginal satisfaction from an additional set is positive. Thus, we appear to have a simple rule for maximizing: "Choose that level of play where the marginal benefit of a further increase in the number of sets played per month is just equal to zero."

Does this rule work in all situations? For the data given in Table 4, playing tennis is free, except for the time involved. Does this matter in the determination of the optimal level of play? Or, put more generally: Do optimal decisions change when there are explicit costs as well as benefits? To answer this question, suppose that each set costs $4, as illustrated in Table 5.

Marginal cost. Its easy to see in Table 5 that when tennis costs $4 per set, playing no more than five sets per month maximizes the individual's net benefit. Not surprisingly, the best decision when it costs something to rent the court is different from the best decision when the courts are free. Clearly, it is no longer true that the best option occurs where the

Table 4
The Marginal Benefits of Playing Tennis

Number of sets	Total satisfaction	Marginal satisfaction
		$20
1	$20	
		10
2	30	
		8
3	38	
		6
4	44	
		4
5	48	
		2
6	50	
		1
7	51	
		0
8	51	

Table 5
Marginal Benefits of Playing Tennis When the Court Must Be Rented

Number of sets	Total satisfaction	Total cost	Net benefit
1	$20	$ 4	$16
2	30	8	22
3	38	12	26
4	44	16	28
5	48	20	28
6	50	24	26
7	51	28	23
8	51	32	19

marginal satisfaction is zero. The best or optimal decision must account for the *marginal cost* of playing an additional set of tennis, as well as the marginal satisfaction or marginal benefit obtained from playing an additional set. This point is illustrated in Table 6.

Table 6 includes a column indicating the marginal cost associated with playing each additional set of tennis. **Marginal cost** is the additional cost incurred by the tennis player when an additional set of tennis is played. Marginal cost can be estimated by dividing the *change* in the total cost of playing tennis when an additional set is played by the *change* in the amount of tennis played. For example, playing five sets costs $20, but playing six sets costs $24. Therefore, the one additional set increases costs by $4. This is the marginal cost of playing the sixth set.

We found, by simply looking at the overall costs and benefits of playing tennis, that when tennis costs $4 per set the optimal level of play was five sets per month. What are the characteristics of this *best choice* in terms of marginal satisfaction and marginal cost? If the player decided to increase her activity from four to five sets per month, total satisfaction would increase by $4. Total costs would also increase by $4, because this is what the player must pay for the additional set. Therefore, *at the optimal level of play, the marginal satisfaction from an additional set of tennis is exactly equal to the marginal cost incurred.*

Table 6
The Marginal Benefits and Marginal Costs of Playing Tennis

Number of sets	Total satisfaction	Marginal satisfaction	Total cost	Marginal cost
		$20		$4
1	$20		$ 4	
		10		4
2	30		8	
		8		4
3	38		12	
		6		4
4	44		16	
		4		4
5	48		20	
		2		4
6	50		24	
		1		4
7	51		28	

Note in Table 6 that for any level of play less than the optimal level, the marginal satisfaction exceeds the marginal cost, or in other words, the additional satisfaction from one more set of tennis exceeds the additional cost of renting a court to play the additional set. Conversely, for any level of play greater than that which maximizes net benefit, the marginal cost exceeds the marginal satisfaction. For example, if the player decided to play seven sets per month, the marginal satisfaction would be $1 and the marginal cost $4.

The Best or Optimal Choice

We can now state the general principle: *The optimal or best choice occurs when marginal benefit equals marginal cost.* Thus, to make a best or optimal choice, you would need to separate the costs associated with a decision from the benefits, and then choose the level of activity so that marginal benefit equals marginal cost. It follows that if the marginal costs are greater than the marginal benefits of a particular choice, that choice cannot be best or optimal. Nor can a choice be best if marginal benefits are greater than marginal costs unless increasing the activity level a small amount drives marginal cost above marginal benefit.

A rule for moving toward the best or optimal choice. Suppose that, at your current activity level, marginal benefit exceeds marginal cost. You should increase your activity—"do a little more." If you did, benefits would increase by the marginal benefit; costs would increase by the marginal cost. Since, however, marginal benefits are greater than marginal costs, the net benefit from doing a little more *must* increase and you have to be better off. For example, if the marginal benefit from one scoop of ice cream is $3 and the marginal cost is $1, buying an additional scoop will increase overall benefits by $3 but increase overall costs by only $1. The difference between total benefits and total costs—the net benefit you get from eating ice cream—will increase by $2. Therefore, if at a given level of activity, marginal benefit exceeds marginal cost, the level of activity should be *increased* in order to move toward the optimal choice.

Suppose, on the other hand, that marginal cost exceeds marginal benefit. You should cut back. If you did, costs would decrease by the marginal cost;

benefits would also decrease, but by the marginal benefit. Since marginal costs are greater than marginal benefits, the net benefit from decreasing your activity level a little bit would increase. In this case, for example, the marginal cost of an additional scoop of ice cream might be $1.50 and the marginal benefit only $.75. Buying one fewer scoop of ice cream would reduce your total costs by $1.50 and your total benefits by $.75 and your net benefit would increase by $.75 even though you are eating less ice cream. Therefore, if at a given level of activity, marginal benefit is less than marginal cost, the level of activity should be *decreased* in order to move toward the optimal choice.

Putting these two observations together suggests a simple rule for finding the optimal or best choice: *Increase any level of activity if marginal benefits are greater than marginal costs; decrease any level of activity if marginal benefits are less than marginal costs.* An important feature of such a rule is that a decision maker does not need to know the overall costs or benefits associated with each level of activity that might be chosen. The only information needed for an improvement in one's position is the additional or marginal benefit and the additional or marginal cost of a small change in your current level of activity.[2]

Thus, if the tennis player knew nothing about the total satisfaction she might receive for playing six or seven sets per month, she would be led by this simple rule to increase her activity level from zero sets per month to one set per month, then to two, then to three, then to four, and finally to five sets per month. Why? If she were playing one set per month, she would need to ask only if playing a second set per month was worth more to her (the marginal benefit) than the cost of the additional set (the marginal cost). If it was worth more, she should play a second set each month. Having moved to this level of monthly activity, she would then only need to ask if playing a third set per month was worth more than the third set cost. If so, she should once again increase the number of sets she played per month. This would continue until she found that increasing the level of play per month by one set was worth less to her than the other things she could do with the $4

(and time) it cost to play an additional set. In our example, if she increased her level of play beyond five sets per month, she would find that the additional set was not worth the cost.

In addition, if tennis were initially free and she was playing eight sets per month, when the club began to charge a $4 fee for each set, she would cut back her activity first to seven sets per month and then to six and finally to five sets per month. In this case, she would find that when she had to pay $4 per set, the cost of playing would be greater than the additional satisfaction she received from the eighth set each month and would thus reduce how much she played each month. Similarly, she would find that the seventh set just wasn't worth it at a cost of $4 and would play less. If she cut her activity level below five sets per month, however, she would find that the last set she gave up was really worth more to her than what the tennis club was charging for the use of the court. Thus, she would happily settle for five sets per month, paying $4 for each set.

Even though it costs the same for each set of tennis in this example, as the player changes the number of sets she plays each month, the marginal satisfaction obtained from playing the last set of tennis changes because of diminishing marginal returns. This means that the tennis player can, by changing how much she plays, bring marginal satisfaction into line with marginal cost. More generally, because of diminishing marginal returns, as the level or intensity of an activity changes, marginal benefits or marginal costs will change. This means that increasing or decreasing the level or intensity of an activity will generally move marginal cost and marginal benefit toward each other.

The irrelevance of sunk costs. Individuals seeking the optimal or best decision will ignore costs that cannot be affected by the decision. Put simply, "sunk" costs are irrelevant where **sunk costs** are any unrecoverable expenditure made in the past.

To see why sunk costs don't matter, suppose that the tennis club has a fixed monthly membership fee in addition to a fee for the use of the courts. To make this example specific, suppose that the tennis player, for whatever reason, had *already* paid a fee of $10 to join a tennis club. Would this change her decision about how many sets she should play this month?

Table 7 provides estimates of the marginal costs and marginal benefits for the tennis player when the

---

[2] There is an exception to this generalization when a firm is losing money. In this case it may be the best decision to quit operating. We will explore this possibility in a later chapter.

Table 7
Marginal Benefits and Marginal Costs of Playing Tennis When There Is a Fixed Membership Fee

Number of sets	Total satisfaction	Marginal satisfaction	Total cost	Marginal cost	Net benefit
		$20		$14	
1	$20		$14		$ 6
		10		4	
2	30		18		12
		8		4	
3	38		22		16
		6		4	
4	44		26		18
		4		4	
5	48		30		18
		2		4	
6	50		34		16
		1		4	
7	51		38		11

Table 8
Marginal Benefits and Marginal Costs of Playing Tennis When The Fixed Membership Fee Changes

Number of sets	Total satisfaction	Marginal satisfaction	Total cost	Marginal cost	Net benefit
		$20		$44	
1	$20		$44		−$24
		10		4	
2	30		48		−18
		8		4	
3	38		52		−14
		6		4	
4	44		56		−12
		4		4	
5	48		60		−12
		2		4	
6	50		64		−14
		1		4	
7	51		68		−17

membership fee is included in total costs and the club continues to charge $4 per set played.

If we use the rule we have developed for maximizing—equate marginal cost with marginal benefit—the optimal number of sets to play each month is five. (At this level of activity, marginal satisfaction is just equal to marginal cost.) If Table 7 is compared with Table 6, it is clear that the optimal amount of tennis is *the same* as when there was no fixed membership fee. The fixed membership fee, having already been paid, is irrelevant to the subsequent decisions about how much to play. Indeed, the characteristics of the optimal choice are exactly the same as those derived earlier—net benefit is maximized when marginal cost equals marginal benefit. We get this perhaps surprising outcome because *sunk costs do not affect marginal costs and, therefore, cannot affect the optimal decision.*

If for some reason, for example, the tennis player had already paid a monthly membership fee of $40, such a payment should not affect the optimum level of activity for the month after it has been paid. And it does not, as Table 8 illustrates.

In Table 8, playing five sets per month *minimizes* the loss—any other activity level will lead to higher losses. That is, as the last column indicates, the player

made a mistake by paying the $40 membership fee. Having made this mistake, however, her losses are minimized if she plays five sets per month, where the net benefit at this level of play is −$12.

We have found that the best choice is precisely the same if there is (a) no membership fee, or if (b) a $10 membership fee has been paid, or if (c) a $40 membership fee has been paid. Thus, the decision that maximizes gain or minimizes losses is independent of any fixed fee already paid. To state the conclusion again: maximizing decision makers will disregard all sunk costs. A number of folk aphorisms suggest this idea: "Don't cry over spilt milk." Or, "It's water under the bridge." Each suggests that the past cannot be changed and therefore shouldn't matter.

Another way of thinking about the "sunk costs are irrelevant" rule is to note that the only things that can matter in making choices are those things that the choices can actually affect or change. Things that cannot be affected by a particular choice are irrelevant. In terms of the example we have been considering, the tennis player cannot choose *not* to pay $10 or $40 once the fees have been paid. All the tennis player can choose is how many sets of tennis to play. The sunk costs of the membership fees do not affect this choice. Hence, sunk costs cannot matter. On the other hand, the payment of a rental fee to play an additional set of tennis is affected by the choice to play the additional set. Therefore, this marginal cost will matter.

Note that a fixed membership fee will affect a decision about whether or not to initially join the tennis club. In this particular decision, the membership fee is relevant because the cost is $0 if one doesn't join and $40 if one does. In this case, the membership fee is not yet a sunk cost but is, instead, the cost associated with the current decision to join or not to join. Choosing to join makes sense if the fee is $10. It doesn't make sense if the membership fee is $40, however. *Anticipated* fixed membership fees affect a decision to join because they vary with that particular decision; by contrast, fixed membership fees that have already been paid cannot affect the decision about how much to play because they do not vary with the different levels of play that might be chosen. In short, the only things that can matter in a decision are things that can actually be chosen. If you're thinking about joining a tennis club, then you get to decide whether to pay the monthly membership fee—this decision has not yet been made. If, however, you've already joined, then your only decision is how much to play and that will be affected by, among other things, the cost per game played.

The equi-marginal principle. Individuals consume more than a single good or service, of course. Similarly, firms generally use more than a single input. Indeed, as we noted earlier, because of the diminishing marginal returns to any particular activity, individuals generally choose a collection of different goods and services to consume, and firms generally choose to employ a mix of inputs. We observe tennis players consuming a bundle composed of many things, including tennis, housing, various types of food-stuffs, and different leisure activities, even if tennis is their favorite activity. And we observe firms using a collection of productive inputs, including different kinds of labor, raw materials, machinery, and not just a single productive input like skilled labor.

When there are many choices, a decision to do more of one activity has an opportunity cost in terms of other activities that aren't done. If you spend the time and money to play an additional set of tennis, for example, you have to give up an additional ice-cream cone or some other thing that you could do with your time and money. As a conse-

quence, the marginal cost of a decision needs to be thought of in terms of the *marginal opportunity cost* of the particular choice made. If a dollar spent on one good yields less marginal satisfaction than does a dollar spent on another good, you ought to change your consumption mix, consuming less of the first and more of the second. Similarly, if a dollar spent to hire an additional worker yields less marginal revenue for a firm than does a dollar spent on additional capital, then a firm ought to change its input mix, using less labor and more capital.

This suggests a generalization of the rule for a best or optimal decision: *When there are many things that can be chosen, the best mix is obtained when the marginal benefit per additional dollar cost is the same for all things consumed or all activity levels chosen.* This generalization is called the **equi-marginal principle**.

Suppose, for example, that our tennis player also likes ice cream. (To keep the example simple, assume that these are the only two goods.) Tennis costs $4 per set; ice cream costs $2.00 per half-gallon. Both tennis and ice cream are costly, so if the tennis player has a fixed monthly income, consuming more ice cream means that she will have less money to use for tennis and, conversely, playing more tennis means that she will have less money to use for ice cream. What is the best mix of ice cream and tennis to consume?

If the marginal satisfaction per dollar spent on ice cream exceeds the marginal satisfaction per dollar spent on tennis, the tennis player should consume more ice cream and play less tennis. Conversely, if the marginal satisfaction per dollar spent on tennis exceeds the marginal satisfaction per dollar spent on ice cream, she should consume less ice cream and play more tennis. To see this point, suppose that the marginal satisfaction from playing the last set of tennis is 8 and the marginal satisfaction from eating the last half-gallon of ice cream is 20. If tennis costs $4 per set and ice cream costs $2.00 per half-gallon, then the

additional utility per
dollar spent on tennis

$$\frac{8}{\$4.00} < \frac{20}{\$2.00}$$

additional utility per
dollar spent on ice cream

or, in words, the person gets more satisfaction for an additional dollar spent on ice cream than on tennis.

This means that if expenditures are shifted from tennis to ice cream, for each set of tennis given up, two half-gallons of ice cream can be purchased. Giving up the last set of tennis lowers total satisfaction by 8—the marginal satisfaction obtained from the last set of tennis. However, purchasing another half-gallon of ice cream with part of the $4 increases total satisfaction by 20—the marginal satisfaction obtained from an additional half-gallon of ice cream. Clearly, reallocating expenditures from tennis to ice cream *increases* the well-being of the tennis player and she has $2 remaining to spend on what she wants! Put differently, the consumption mix before the reallocation *cannot* have been the best possible mix because we have found another one that was better.

Diminishing marginal returns now become important: As expenditures are reallocated from tennis to ice cream, the marginal satisfaction obtained from ice cream *decreases* because of diminishing marginal returns (more ice cream is consumed per month). At the same time, the marginal satisfaction obtained from tennis *increases* (less tennis is played per month). If the marginal satisfaction per dollar spent on tennis is still less than the marginal satisfaction per dollar spent on ice cream, a further reallocation of expenditures from tennis to ice cream will produce a better mix. If, however, the marginal utility per dollar that is spent on tennis is greater than the marginal utility per dollar spent on ice cream, than a reallocation from ice cream to tennis will make the individual better off.

When the marginal satisfaction per dollar spent is the same for each good, it is not possible to find a better mix. That is, when

$$\frac{\text{MS of good A}}{\text{dollars spent on A}} = \frac{\text{MS of good B}}{\text{dollars spent on B}} \quad (1)$$

you have found the optimal mix. Or, in words, when an individual has many things from which to choose, *the optimal mix of choices will be found when the marginal benefit per dollar cost is the same for each thing actually chosen.*

Description or Prescription?

Is marginal decision-making descriptive of what people actually do, or does it prescribe what they should do if they want to maximize? In short, is it descriptive or prescriptive? Our analysis to this point has been descriptive of what individuals must be doing if they are maximizing.

For some purposes it may be useful to drop the *assumption* of maximization and think instead of maximization as a goal. In these cases, the characteristics of the maximizing decision lead to two decision rules:

1. Equate the marginal benefit per additional dollar cost for each choice across all possible choices.[3] And,

2. Ignore past expenditures or sunk costs.

These two rules can be descriptive or prescriptive. That is, they describe what individuals who are *assumed* to be maximizing must be doing, or they outline a procedure by which to maximize, *if* maximization is desired. For many public policy questions, for example whether to build a new highway or a new military airplane or a new dam or a new housing project, it may be more appropriate not to assume that maximization will automatically occur but rather to consider maximization *as a goal* to be achieved. For public policy decisions, then, these rules then provide guidance about the information needed and the type of decisions that are required to select the "best" policy: a decision maker needs information on marginal costs and marginal benefits, but can safely ignore sunk costs.[4]

▶ Some Concluding Comments on Rationality and Maximization

It is obvious that individuals are not always rational, even by a notion of rationality as broad as that outlined in this chapter. Our own experiences—as well as those of literary figures such as Albert Camus' Stranger, Richard Wright's Bigger, or Herman Melville's Captain Ahab—show that often irrationality and self-destruction or defeat are part of human nature. These literary figures suggest that irrationality dominates choices. Is this likely? It is also sometimes argued that rationality and maximization require too much of individuals. Is this

---

[3] When the choice is about varying the amount of a single thing that is selected, this rule becomes "equate marginal cost with marginal benefit."

[4] This approach to public policy is sometimes referred to as *cost-benefit analysis.*

true: Do individuals have to be sophisticated or really intelligent or trained in economics to be rational or to maximize? Finally, it is sometimes argued that even if rational, individuals will behave altruistically and not in their self-interest. While it is undoubtedly true that human's have a mix of motives, is altruism or concern for others likely to be the most important?

These criticisms, while interesting, aren't compelling. You don't have to be thinking in precisely the terms used in this chapter nor do you have to take an economics class to learn to behave rationally. When you throw a basketball toward a hoop mounted 10 feet above the ground, for example, you are solving a complicated physics problem. Being very good at basketball does not actually require you to know physics, however. Analogously, you may be able to choose rationally without knowing the language or rules of maximizing just outlined: you need only be able to make consistent comparisons and understand the benefits (to you) and costs (to you) of "small steps." Finally, with regard to the last criticism when you meet a stranger, which is the best assumption: That he will act in his interest or that he will act in your interest? The stranger may, of course, act in your interest or act irrationally but what matters if you want to predict his most likely behavior is how you *think* he will behave. In this setting, most people would expect strangers to behave in their own interest.

Not surprisingly, then, we will *assume* throughout the remainder of this text that individuals are capable of making rational choices and that rational behavior dominates other kinds of behavior. That is, we will assume that individuals order choices in a consistent manner, think about consequences by taking notice of costs and benefits, and make choices consistent with the marginal principles just outlined. It follows that in trying to understand human behavior, *marginal effects* and *incentives* will matter. We will return to these two ideas and their consequences, in one form or another, repeatedly throughout this book.

▶ Summary

Rational choice. While some choices may be based on tradition or others may be random, most choices are assumed to be purposeful or rational. To make rational choices individuals must

> make informed comparisons
> have consistent orderings
> choose the most preferred or best option.

Marginal analysis. The **marginal benefit** associated with a choice is the additional benefit obtained by increasing the activity level a small amount. The **marginal cost** associated with a choice is the additional cost incurred when the activity level is increased by a small amount. Thus, *marginal utility* is the additional satisfaction obtained when consumption of some good or service is increased by a small amount. Similarly, *marginal revenue* is the additional revenue obtained by the sales some output are increased by a small amount.

The best or optimal choices. The best or optimal *level* of activity is where the marginal benefit associated with a particular choice is just equal to the marginal cost of the choice. When there are a number of different activities from which to choose, **marginal opportunity costs** must be considered. In this case, the best or optimal *mix* of choices is the one where the marginal benefit per additional dollar cost is the same over all choices made.

Best or optimal choices are unaffected by sunk costs. That is, the only things that can matter when trying to find the best or optimal choice are those that can actually be affected by the choice. As a consequence, past expenditures cannot matter.

In short, to optimize:

> Equate the marginal benefit per additional dollar cost for each choice across all possible choices.

and

> Ignore past expenditures or sunk costs.

Chapter 5 ▶▶

Markets and Relative Prices _____

Relative prices are enormously important in the organization of economic activity and coordination of competing private interests. Although this was emphasized in Chapters 1 and 2, our discussion to this point has ducked the question of how relative prices are actually determined. This chapter focuses on answering this question, that is, on the determination of relative prices when exchange, specialization, and other interactions among individuals occur within markets.

▶ Markets

Markets are as old as recorded civilization. In earlier times, they were primarily physical locations where people who lived in households scattered across the surrounding countryside would gather periodically to exchange goods and services. Going to market was an important economic and social activity, something akin to going to the mall today. Indeed, it was so important that permanent market locations often developed into the towns and cities that now dot much of the landscape.

Markets are not necessarily specific physical locations where exchanges occur, however. They are, rather, institutional arrangements that tie specific exchanges together. A particular transaction occurs in a specific place, of course, but tens of thousands of similar transactions scattered across a community or a nation or even the world may constitute a market for a particular item. If there is a market for a particular commodity, a person can expect the nature of the transaction to be similar in different locations. For example, we speak of the housing market or the rental market in a city, even though there is no central location where houses are bought and sold or where apartments are offered for rent. Although there may be a few local peculiarities, buying a home in one part of a city is similar to buying a home in another part of a city; indeed, buying a home in one part of the country is similar to buying a home in a different part of the country. Similarly, we may speak of the market for cereal or soft drinks or shirts or jeans or computer software even though each is sold in dozens of different locations in the community and in thousands of different locations throughout an economy. Thus a market need not have a single physical location as long as transactions for a specific good (or service or resource) in one place are related to the transactions for the good (or services or resource) in some other place.

Even when all market transactions actually occur in a specific place, communications networks often allow those living long distances away to participate. For example, the New York Stock Exchange is located on Wall Street in lower Manhattan, but people transact in this market from throughout the United States and, indeed, from throughout much of the world. As a consequence, decisions made in Idaho are related to decisions made in Maine or London or Paris or Tokyo. It follows that in this case, at least, the physical location of the market is irrelevant, and it makes sense to speak of a national and even an international market for what is actually bought and sold in lower Manhattan.

In each of these examples, a **market** is a set of related transactions for a particular thing, be it housing, soft drinks, medical services, or IBM stock.

In an important sense, a market is also an idea. That is, describing something as "a market" is a way of thinking about the consequences of the many transactions that occur for a specific good, service, or resource. Participants in a market may not know or care about such consequences and may not even think of themselves as participating in a particular market. If you want to rent an apartment, for example, you just want a place to stay. How this interest in a place to stay affects the relative price of rental housing, the amount of rental housing that is built, the ability of others to rent housing, or other decisions that others make is likely to be of little concern to you. Your rent and the quality and quantity of apartments available, however, will depend upon the desire for a place to stay expressed by a large number of people like yourself.

There are markets for hundreds of thousands of commodities. Things that satisfy individual wants or desires are frequently referred to as **products**. Product markets are, in turn, divided into markets for tangible products, or **goods**, and markets for intangible **services**. A hamburger is a good, but a doctor's examination is a service. When you buy an automobile you are purchasing a good, but when you have someone adjust the carburetor in your automobile, you are purchasing a service.

There are also markets for commodities that are themselves used to produce goods or services, usually referred to as **resource** or **input** markets. Coal is a resource used in the production of goods and services and sometimes in the production of other resources, such as machinery. Resource markets are often subdivided into three broad categories consistent with our discussion of resources in Chapter 2: markets for natural resources, labor markets, and capital markets.

To keep things simple, we will generally refer to things that are used to satisfy individual desires as **goods** and things used in production as **resources**. When it doesn't matter whether the focus of our analysis is a good or a resource, we will generally use the term **commodity**.

Suppliers and Demanders

People who come to a market because they want to buy are **demanders**. Others, **suppliers**, come to sell. Demanders have money and want commodities; suppliers have commodities and want money. The interaction of demanders and suppliers determines both a market price and the amount actually bought and sold. The market price, in turn, creates incentives for both suppliers and demanders that may affect many other markets.

▶ Market Supply

Generally, suppliers want to sell more when the relative price is higher. That is, there is usually a *positive* relationship between the price at which a commodity sells and the amount that suppliers are willing to provide to the market. Why is more provided when the relative price is higher? When the price for something increases while the prices of other commodities remain unchanged, suppliers will find that their profits increase if they increase the amount they provide to the market. Table 1 illustrates this notion of supply: At a price of $1.00, suppliers are willing to provide up to 10,000 pencils, and at a price of $2.00, suppliers are willing to provide up to 20,000 pencils, and so forth. This list is called a **supply schedule**.

The supply curve. Figure 1, a **supply curve**, is a graph of the supply schedule listed in Table 1. In this graph, price is measured along the vertical axis and the quantity supplied or demanded is measured along the horizontal axis. For example, at a price of $2.00 per pencil (measured along the vertical axis), firms are willing to supply 20,000 pencils per month (measured along the horizontal axis). When the

Table 1
Supply Schedule for Pencils

Price	Maximum amount that suppliers are willing to provide (per month)
$ .50	2,000
.75	7,000
1.00	10,000
2.00	20,000
3.00	25,000

Figure 1
A Supply Curve

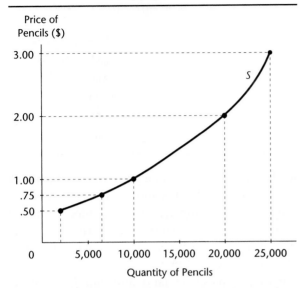

This graph illustrates a market supply curve for pencils, from the supply schedule in Table 1. Producers will supply more pencils to the market when the price of pencils is higher. As a consequence, the supply curve slopes upward and to the right.

price increases to $3.00 per pencil, the amount that suppliers are willing to provide increases to 25,000 per month. Hence, the positive relationship between price and the quantity that suppliers would willingly provide to a market is illustrated visually by an upward-sloping supply curve.

For convenience, we will call the entire supply schedule or supply curve **market supply** or just **supply**. We will refer to the specific amount that suppliers would be willing to provide to the market *at a particular price* as the **quantity supplied**. Quantity supplied corresponds to a single point along a supply curve or a single price-quantity combination in a supply schedule.

Measuring prices. Note that in both Table 1 and Figure 1, the price *p* is measured in terms of dollars per unit. Any change in the dollar price of pencils reflects a change in the *relative price* of pencils as long as the dollar prices of other commodities do not change. That is, when the dollar price increases and no other dollar price changes, for example, pencils sell for more relative to the other things that suppliers might provide to the market.

A caution: When most prices increase (**inflation**) or decrease (**deflation**), a change in the dollar price of a single commodity will not necessarily coincide with a change in a relative price because the dollar prices of other commodities will have also changed. Suppose, for example, that the dollar price of shirts increases from $24 to $30 and that because of inflation most other prices increase as well. The Consumer Price Index (CPI) is a commonly used measure of the "average" of most prices in an economy. Suppose that the CPI increases, say, from 100 to 150, indicating that there has been a 50% inflation. Even though the dollar price has increased, shirts have become relatively cheaper. To see why, divide each dollar price by the price index. When these adjusted prices are compared, $24/100 > $30/150, and the price of shirts has fallen relative to the "average" of other prices in the economy. By contrast, if the price of shirts increases from $24 to $30 and, at the same time, the CPI increases from 100 to 110, the price of shirts relative to the "average" of other prices in the economy increases since $24/100 < $30/110, although not by as much as the dollar price change might suggest. Thus, when the dollar price per unit increases, you need to be careful in jumping to the conclusion that the relative price has increased. Whether it has depends on what has happened to other prices. When will a change in a dollar price be a change in the relative price? Answer: When other prices aren't changing. Therefore, when we draw a picture of a supply curve (and below, a demand curve) with the dollar price along the vertical axis, we are *assuming* that other prices aren't changing.

Measuring quantities. The quantity Q of the commodity that suppliers willingly provide to the market is measured over a specified time period. In the specific example illustrated in Figure 1, Q is the number of pencils that suppliers are willing to provide to the market each month. In other settings, Q could be the number of cars that firms are willing to supply in a year, or the number of hours of work that individuals are willing to supply per day.

A second caution: The quantity that suppliers are willing to provide will almost always change when the time period over which they might provide commodities to a market changes. That is, the quantity that suppliers are willing to provide over a year is undoubtedly larger than the quantity that those same suppliers are willing to supply in the next 24 hours. Hence, it is important in thinking about supply to have clearly in mind the time period over which the supply comes to the market—a day, a month, a year, between August and October, and so on.

► Market Demand

How will demanders respond to higher relative prices? Generally, less is wanted when the relative price is higher. This is because the price of pencils represents the opportunity cost of purchasing pencils rather than something else. When the price of pencils increases, the opportunity cost of purchasing pencils increases as long as the prices of other commodities that demanders might purchase do not change. When the opportunity cost of a choice increases, individuals find other things to purchase or simply do without. As a consequence, there is a *negative* or *inverse relationship* between the price of a commodity and the amount that demanders want to purchase. In Table 2, for example, when the price is $2.00 per pencil, demanders want to purchase no more than 3,500 pencils per month. At $3.00, 2,000 pencils are demanded, and at $1.00, demanders want to purchase no more than 10,000 pencils. A list of the quantity that demanders want to purchase at various possible prices is a **demand schedule**.

A demand curve. A **demand curve** is a graph of a demand schedule. Thus, Figure 2 is the demand curve corresponding to the demand schedule in Table 2.[1] The inverse relationship between price and the quantity that demanders would be willing to purchase is illustrated visually by the demand curve *D*: when the price is $1.00, 10,000 pencils are demanded, but when the price increases from $1.00 to $2.00 the amount that demanders are willing to purchase falls to 3,500 pencils.

Note that on the vertical axis in the demand graph we have the dollar price per unit *p* as a measure of the relative price, as in the supply graph. The quantity *Q* that participants in this market are willing to purchase each month is measured on the horizontal axis. As with market supply, it is important

---

[1] Both the supply curve in Figure 1 and the demand curve in Figure 2 are smooth between the points provided in the respective supply and demand schedules. This is expositionally convenient and doesn't change the analysis in any important way.

Table 2
Demand Schedule for Pencils

Price	Maximum amount demanders are willing to purchase (per month)
$ .50	20,000
.75	13,000
1.00	10,000
2.00	3,500
3.00	2,000

to clearly identify the time period over which *Q* is measured—per day, per month, per year, between August and September, and so on. Indeed, in order to make useful and interesting comparisons between the amount that suppliers would be willing to supply and the amount that demanders would be willing to purchase, demand and supply must be measured over the same time period.

A demand schedule or demand curve illustrates the relationship between price and the quantity demanded *when everything else that may affect the decisions of demanders is unchanged.* Likewise, a supply schedule or supply curve illustrates the relationship between particular relative prices and the quantities supplied *when everything else that may*

Figure 2
A Demand Curve

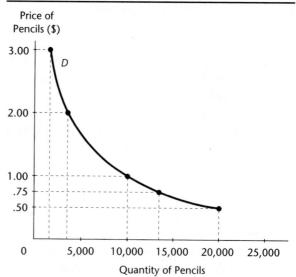

This graph illustrates the market demand curve from the demand schedule in Table 2. Consumers will demand more pencils when the price is lower; hence, the demand curve slopes downward and to the right.

affect the decisions of suppliers is unchanged. This includes, as noted above, the price of other goods. We can get at demand or supply by asking a simple question: "What would happen if only the dollar price changed *and nothing else?*" For demand, the most likely outcome is that the quantity demanded decreases with an increase in the price. For supply, the quantity supplied increases with an increase in the price. The Latin phrase *ceteris paribus,* which means "all else equal" or "everything else unchanged," will be used to indicate that nothing else changes. Thus, the **First Law of Demand** is that there is an inverse relationship between the relative price of a commodity and the quantity demanded, *ceteris paribus.*

▶ A Market

A market is created when demanders and suppliers trade commodities, either directly or for money. In this respect, one can hardly resist overlaying Figures 1 and 2 to obtain Figure 3, a picture of a market. Figure 3 provides a useful way of thinking about what is occurring when some individuals want to sell and others want to buy. No one, of course, actually sees a supply curve or a demand curve when participating in a market. Suppliers and demanders can sense the effects of supply and demand, however. To see why, consider how markets adjust.

Market Adjustment

What if at a particular price, suppliers want to provide more than demanders want to purchase? Or, conversely, what if at a particular price, demanders want more than suppliers are willing to provide? In either case, the market price will *change* and *continue* to change until suppliers bring to market that quantity that demanders wish to purchase. Or, equivalently, the market price will change and continue to change until demanders wish to purchase the quantity that suppliers want to sell. In this way, markets coordinate the different interests of demanders and suppliers. To see how this coordination actually works, consider what happens when the price is too high and then when the price is too low.

Excess Supply. At a price of $2.00 in the market for pencils illustrated in Figure 3, suppliers would like to sell 20,000 pencils while demanders want to purchase only 3,500. The quantity that suppliers want

Figure 3
The Market for Pencils

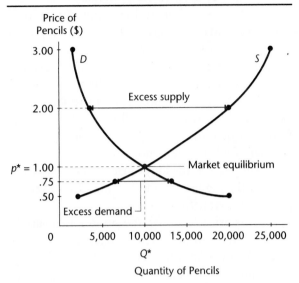

When we overlay the supply curve in Figure 1 and the demand curve in Figure 2, we get a graphical representation of the market for pencils. The point at which the supply and demand curves cross is the market equilibrium. At that point, the quantity that firms willingly provide to the market is equal to the quantity that individuals wish to purchase. When the market price for pencils is greater than $1.00, the quantity supplied is greater than the quantity demanded, resulting in excess supply. Conversely, when the market price is below the equilibrium price, there is excess demand.

to exchange exceeds the quantity that demanders want to purchase. When this occurs, there is *excess supply.* In this market, there will be an excess supply at any price above $1.00 per unit.

Excess Demand. At a price of $.75, suppliers are willing to sell 5,000 pencils but demanders want to purchase 13,000 pencils. The quantity that suppliers are willing to supply is less than the quantity that demanders want to purchase. As a consequence, there is an *excess* demand. Note that for any price below $1.00, there is excess demand in this market.

Eliminating Excess Supply. When there is excess supply, suppliers are frustrated: The quantity they intended to sell is simply not being purchased. As a consequence, suppliers will have to think about doing things differently. In Figure 3, for example, when the price is $2.00 there are 16,500 unsold pencils. From the suppliers' perspective, selling some pencils at a lower price, say $1.50, will be better than not selling any pencils at $2.00. It follows that as a consequence of the excess supply, there is an incentive for some suppliers to lower their price in an effort to get rid of their unsold pencils. As they lower the price, all other suppliers will be forced to lower the price they charge as well (if they don't demanders will switch purchases from the higher-priced suppliers to the now lower-priced suppliers). For example, those who were selling 3,500 pencils at $2.00 (the quantity demanded at this price, remember) will find that demanders will purchase from other suppliers at the lower price rather than from them at the higher price unless they too lower the price they charge for pencils.

As the price decreases, the amount that suppliers are willing to provide also decreases—selling pencils is now relatively less profitable. This decrease in the amount that suppliers are willing to provide, "the quantity supplied" for short, is illustrated by distance B in Figure 4.

Figure 4
Market Adjustment When the Price Is Above the Equilibrium Price

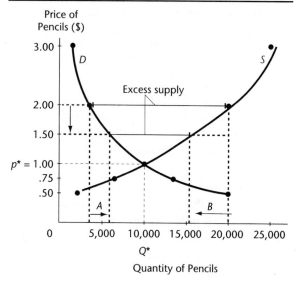

Quantity of Pencils

At a price of $2.00, the quantity of pencils supplied exceeds the quantity demanded. Suppliers will try to get rid of their excess pencils by lowering the price. If they lower the price to $1.50, the quantity demanded will increase by distance A and the quantity supplied will decrease by B. There is still an excess supply at this price, however, so the price will continue to fall until it reaches $1.00, at which point, the quantity supplied and the quantity demanded are equal. That is, when the price is $1.00, suppliers can sell the amount of pencils that they intended to sell.

On the demand side, as the relative price decreases, the amount of the commodity that demanders want to purchase increases. This increase in "the quantity demanded" is illustrated by distance A in Figure 4.

If the price is $1.50, there will still be an excess supply, but the excess supply is now less than it was when the price was $2.00. That is, the market has adjusted to decrease the excess supply. Since an excess supply remains, however, suppliers will still hold unsold pencils. It follows that there will continue to be downward pressure on the price of pencils. As the price falls, the quantity supplied decreases and the quantity demanded increases. This adjustment will eventually eliminate the excess supply. In particular, when the relative price falls to $1.00 in the Figure 3 market, there will no longer be an excess supply. Thus, *if the market price is free to decrease when there is excess supply, the excess supply will be eliminated by market forces.*

Eliminating Excess Demand. If, by contrast, the price is below $1.00, there will be excess demand. For example, suppose the price is $.50 per pencil. At this price, demanders want to purchase more pencils than suppliers are willing to provide to the market. As a consequence, demanders will be frustrated and unhappy. Some frustrated demanders may offer to pay a higher price—at the current price they get nothing but if they offer a higher price, suppliers will have an incentive to sell to them rather than to someone else. If some demanders are willing to pay a higher price, others also will be forced to pay a higher price. That is, the suppliers now selling 2,000 pencils at $.50 will divert sales to those offering higher prices.

When the price increases, say to $.75, two things happen. First, the increase in price makes suppliers more willing to provide pencils to the market. That is, "the quantity supplied" increases. This increase is illustrated by distance F in Figure 5. Second, the higher price decreases the amount of pencils that demanders want to purchase. That is, "the quantity demanded" decreases by G in Figure 5. Although some demanders are willing to pay the higher price, others decide pencils aren't worth the increased price and reduce the quantity they demand or drop out of the market entirely.

When the price increases, the responses of suppliers and demanders are such that the excess

Figure 5
Market Adjustment When the Price Is Below the Equilibrium Price

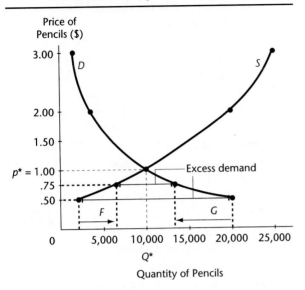

At a price of $.50, the quantity of pencils demanded exceeds the quantity supplied. Demanders competing to purchase pencils will bid the price up. If the price increases to $.75, the quantity demanded will decrease by distance *G* and the quantity supplied will increase by distance *F*. There is still an excess demand at this price, however, so the price will continue to increase until it reaches $1.00, the equilibrium price, where the quantity demanded equals the quantity supplied. That is, when the price is $1.00, demanders will be able to purchase the amount of pencils that they intended to purchase.

demand decreases. As this kind of adjustment continues, the price will increase until it reaches $1.00. At $1.00, there is no excess demand and, consequently, no incentive for the price to increase further. Thus, *if the market price is free to increase when there is excess demand, the excess demand will be eliminated by market forces.*

Predictability. If there is excess supply or excess demand, market prices will change in predictable ways: When there is excess supply, the price will decrease. If, on the other hand, there is excess demand, the price will increase. These kinds of changes will eliminate the excess supply or excess demand. Thus, in the market for pencils illustrated in Figures 4 and 5, when the price fell from $2.00 toward $1.00 because of excess supply, the excess supply was eliminated. When the relative price increased from $.50 toward $1.00 in response to excess demand, the excess demand was eliminated.

Table 3 summarizes these adjustments for the supply and demand schedules illustrated in Tables 1 and 2.

Equilibrium

In the market for pencils, excess demand or excess supply pushes the price toward $1.00. What's so special about a market price of $1.00? At $1.00, suppliers *willingly* provide 10,000 pencils to the market and demanders *willingly* purchase them. Since neither demanders nor suppliers are frustrated, there will be no pressure for the price to either increase or decrease. The market is in **equilibrium**.

Put in a slightly different way, at a market price of $1.00, what demanders want to purchase coincides exactly with what suppliers want to sell. Demanders do not, at this price, desire to consume more (or fewer) than 10,000 pencils; suppliers do not, at this price, desire to supply more (or fewer) than 10,000 pencils. Thus there is no reason for the quantity supplied or the quantity demanded or the relative price to change. (In Figures 3, 4, and 5, p^* and Q^* are the market equilibrium price and quantity respectively.)

Table 3
Market Adjustment in the Market for Pencils

Price	Quantity supplied	Quantity demanded	Outcome	Effects on price
$ .50	2,000	20,000	Excess demand of 18,000	Increases
.75	5,000	13,000	Excess demand of 8,000	Increases
1.00	10,000	10,000	Equilibrium	No change
2.00	20,000	3,500	Excess supply of 16,500	Decreases
3.00	25,000	2,000	Excess supply of 23,000	Decreases

At a market equilibrium, the interests of both suppliers and demanders are coordinated. It is not necessary for either demanders or suppliers to seek the market equilibrium or even care whether or not the market reaches equilibrium. Nor do they need to coordinate their activities so as to move the market toward equilibrium. That is, demanders do not need to know anything about suppliers, nor do suppliers need to know anything about demanders. Each group simply responds to the same relative price as it chooses. When the separate responses coincide, however, there is no pressure for the relative price to change; if the separate responses do not coincide, the market cannot be in equilibrium and there will be pressure for the price to change. Coordination is as simple as that!

It is important to understand what equilibrium does *not* mean. It does not mean that demanders would not like to have more of the good; they would, but only at a price that is *lower* than the equilibrium price. It does not mean that suppliers would not like to sell more of the good; they would, but only at a price that is *higher* than the equilibrium price. It does not mean that suppliers and demanders have the same motives. In general, they will be quite different: suppliers want to provide the commodity for money with the intent of making profits, while demanders are willing to exchange money for the commodity with the intent of improving their well-being. Finally, market equilibrium does not mean that demanders would not prefer a lower price or that suppliers would not prefer a higher price. Demanders always want lower prices; suppliers always want higher prices. If the price is anything but that one associated with the market equilibrium, however, some demanders or some suppliers will be frustrated and there will be pressures for the price to change. The importance of the equilibrium price is that it is the *only* price at which the interests of demanders happen to coincide precisely with the interests of suppliers.

If prices are free to increase or decrease, markets can effectively coordinate competing interests. The world around us is full of changes and surprises, however. Markets are useful and interesting ways of organizing economic activities if they not only coordinate competing interests but also respond in effective ways to such changes and surprises. Consider, then, how markets respond to changes.

▶ A Shift in Demand

Suppose that the drinking age is lowered from 21 to 18. What will happen to the demand for beer? How will suppliers respond?

If the drinking-age restriction has been effectively enforced against individuals below the age of 21 who would, but for the restriction, like to drink, the demand for beer will increase as more individuals enter the market. This increase is illustrated in Figure 6 by the shift of the demand curve to the right, from D to D'. For example, at $1.50 per six-pack, 100 six-packs are demanded each day prior to the change in the law, but 200 are demanded at the same price following the change in the law.

At the original equilibrium price of $1.50 per pack there will now be excess demand. Clearly, $1.50 can no longer be an equilibrium price. Indeed, there will be pressure for the price to increase. As the price increases, suppliers increase the quantity of beer they provide to the market. This response by suppliers is illustrated by a movement along the original supply curve S.

Figure 6
The Effect of an Increase in Demand

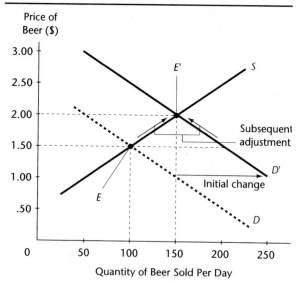

Lowering the drinking age increases the demand for beer, as illustrated by the shift of the demand curve from D to D', thus creating excess demand and putting upward pressure on the original equilibrium price of $1.50. The market then moves toward a new equilibrium at $2.00. Note that when demand increases, both the market price and the quantity sold are higher than they were at the original equilibrium price.

Table 4
Adjustment to an Increase in Demand for Beer

Price	Quantity supplied	Quantity demanded before change in law	Quantity demanded after change in law	Consequence
$1.50	100	100	200	Excess demand
2.00	150	50	150	New equilibrium

Even though at each price more beer is demanded following the change in the law, there remains an inverse relationship between the relative price and the quantity demanded. Therefore, as the price increases because of the market adjustment to the excess demand at p*, individuals will want to purchase less. This effect is illustrated by a movement along the new demand curve D' toward E'.

The new equilibrium price is $2.00. Demanders want to purchase 150 six-packs at this price; suppliers willingly provide 150 six-packs to the market at this price. As a consequence of the lower drinking age, then, the market equilibrium price is higher; as a consequence of the increase in demand *and* the higher price, more beer is provided to the market. Table 4 illustrates this adjustment numerically.

This kind of adjustment can occur in any market when demand increases. It follows that for most markets *an increase in demand will lead to a higher equilibrium market price, with more of the commodity being both bought and sold in the market,* ceteris paribus.

▶ A Shift in Supply

Suppose that instead of a change in the law regulating the drinking age, the costs of brewing beer increase. What will happen to supply? What will demanders do?

Higher costs will make beer suppliers less willing to supply what they once did at the current market price because profits will fall. Supply will decrease as a consequence. This change in the willingness of suppliers to provide beer to the market is illustrated by a shift in supply from S to S' in Figure 7. For example, at $1.50 per six-pack, firms were willing to supply 100 six-packs per day to the market prior to the increase in costs, but are now unwilling to do so. Clearly, $1.50 can no longer be an equilibrium price since there is now excess demand for beer. As a consequence, there will be upward pressure on the market price. As the price increases, demanders will

purchase less beer. This effect is illustrated as a movement along the *original demand curve* from E toward E'.

Suppliers, even though they are now unwilling to provide the same quantity to the market at each price (because their costs have increased), will want to increase the quantity supplied somewhat, because the market price has increased. This change in quantity supplied is illustrated as a movement along the *new supply curve.* When this adjustment is completed, the market will produce a new equilibrium price, $2.00, that is higher than the old equilibrium price, $1.50, and the quantity of beer bought and

Figure 7
The Effect of a Decrease in Supply

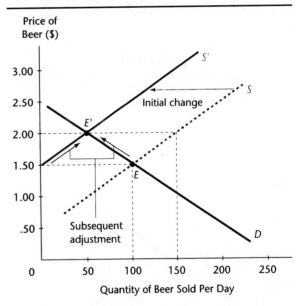

When the costs of brewing beer increase, suppliers are not as willing to supply it as they had been previously. This decrease in supply is illustrated by a leftward shift of the supply curve, from *S* to *S'*. At the original equilibrium price of $1.50, there will be excess demand, putting upward pressure on the market price. The market will move toward a new equilibrium price of $2.00. Note that when supply decreases, the market price increases, but the quantity sold decreases.

Table 5
Adjustment to an Increase in the Cost of Brewing Beer

Price	Quantity demanded	Quantity supplied before increase in costs	Quantity supplied after increase in costs	Consequence
$1.50	100	100	0	Excess demand
2.00	50	150	50	New equilibrium

sold will have decreased. Table 5 illustrates this adjustment.

This kind of adjustment can occur in any market when the supply decreases. Thus, for most markets *a decrease in supply will lead to a higher equilibrium market price, with less of the commodity being both bought and sold in the market,* ceteris paribus.

▶ Some Other Possibilities

Two other possible adjustments are illustrated in Figures 8 and 9. In Figure 8, demand falls (perhaps because of an increase in the legal drinking age from 19 to 21). As a consequence, there is excess supply at

the original equilibrium-relative price. You should carefully work through the adjustment process, examining what happens to suppliers and then to demanders as the relative price changes in response to this excess supply. As you do, you will find that when demand decreases, equilibrium is reestablished with a lower equilibrium price and with less being exchanged in the market. It follows that for most markets, *a decrease in demand, if nothing else changes, will lead to a lower equilibrium market price with less of the commodity being both bought and sold,* ceteris paribus.

In Figure 9, supply increases (perhaps the cost of brewing beer decreased for all suppliers). In this case, there will be excess supply at the original equi-

Figure 8
The Effect of a Decrease in Demand

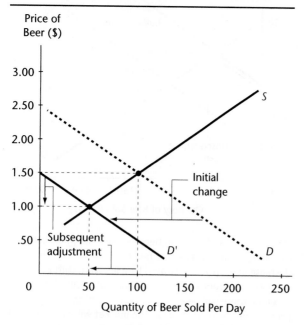

After a decrease in demand, both price and quantity sold fall, from D to D'.

Figure 9
The Effect of an Increase in Supply

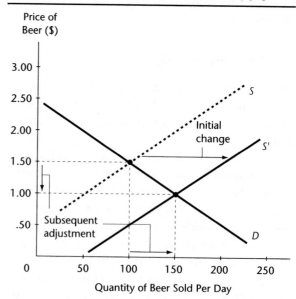

After an increase in supply, from S to S', the quantity sold increases and the equilibrium price falls.

librium price. You should carefully think through the adjustment process that ensues, examining what happens to suppliers and demanders as the relative price changes in response to this excess supply. You will find that when supply increases, equilibrium is reestablished with a lower equilibrium price and with more being exchanged in the market. For most markets, *an increase in supply will lead to a lower equilibrium market price with more of the commodity being both bought and sold,* ceteris paribus.

There are, of course, other possible changes in the world that will affect supply, demand, or both supply and demand. We will explore many of these in the coming chapters as we examine more carefully the roles of prices and profits in an economy and the effects—intended or otherwise—that government policies have on markets.

A Caution

The discussion to this point suggests that all markets are alike in the way that they adjust. This is not so. In some markets, prices adjust freely and quickly. In other kinds of markets, however, prices adjust slowly. When they do, excess supply or excess demand will persist for a longer period of time, which may create problems. For example, unemployment is excess supply in the labor market. Because labor markets do not appear to quickly adjust to changes in the economy, some individuals will find themselves unable to find work for weeks or even months. In still other markets, public policies limit the adjustment of market prices, and excess demand or excess supply appears and persists. For example, a law that prohibits transactions at prices above a specified level will create problems if the market equilibrium price is above the legal limit because with this law it will be impossible for the market price to bring the interests of suppliers into line with those of demanders. (We will explore the problems that follow public policies that limit price movements in Chapter 12.)

Moreover, we have glossed over *exactly* what puts downward pressure on relative prices when there is excess supply and upward pressure on relative prices when there is excess demand. It turns out that this is a difficult problem. When there is excess supply, suppliers will be unhappy that they cannot sell all that they wish to and some may begin to offer lower prices for what they wish to sell. After all, selling something

at a lower price will be better than selling nothing at a higher price. Similarly, when there is excess demand, demanders will be frustrated and some will offer higher prices in order to make sure that they get the good. Paying a higher price and actually getting the good may be better than going without at a lower price. While this argument may seem convincing, economics does not yet have rigorous explanations or theories about what triggers these kinds of adjustments or even if they occur in this way.

Change in Demand Versus Change in Quantity Demanded

Graphs of demand and supply force us to think carefully about what is happening in a market: Will the equilibrium market price tend to increase or decrease because of a change in the interests of demanders? Will the equilibrium market quantity tend to increase or decrease in response to a change in the interests of suppliers?

To answer these kinds of questions, it is important to distinguish the responses of demanders and suppliers to *changes in the market or relative price* from responses to *changes in factors other than the market or relative price.* For example, if the price of beer increases, demanders will generally want to purchase less beer at the higher price. If the drinking age is increased to 24, by contrast, there will be less demand for beer at every possible price. These two sentences describe quite different situations.

By convention, economists refer to responses by demanders to a change in the relative price *alone* as a **change in the quantity demanded**. This change is always illustrated by a *movement along* a demand curve and not by a shift of a demand curve. Similarly, the response by suppliers to a change in the relative price *alone* is a **change in the quantity supplied**. A change in the quantity supplied is always illustrated by a *movement along* a supply curve.

If, at all possible relative prices, demanders want to increase the amount that they are willing to purchase because of some change that is not directly related to the price itself, demand has increased. When demanders want to decrease the amount they purchase at each market price, demand has decreased. These changes are illustrated by a *shift* of the demand curve and not by a movement along a given demand curve. Thus, demand changes when something other than the market price changes—a change in the price of some other commodity or a change in the incomes of demanders, for example. An **increase in demand** is represented by an outward or rightward shift. A **decrease in demand** is represented by an inward or leftward shift.

Similarly, if at all possible market prices, suppliers want to increase (or decrease) the amount that they are willing to provide to the market, supply has changed. This is always illustrated by a *shift* of the supply curve. Supply changes when something other than the relative price changes—a change in the cost of an input or a change in the technology of producing or distributing the commodity, for example. An **increase in supply** corresponds to an outward or rightward shift in *S;* a **decrease in supply** corresponds to an inward or leftward shift in *S.*

What Leads to Changes in Demand?

Demand will change whenever there are changes that affect demanders' decisions *other than* changes in the price of the commodity itself. Table 6 indicates some of the most important changes that affect market demand.

For example, the demand for new cars will increase if consumers' incomes, on average, increase. But the demand for new cars might decrease if the price of gasoline, a related commodity, increases. In addition, the demand for new cars will decrease if demanders suddenly decide they prefer public rather than private transportation. The demand for new cars will also decrease if the transaction costs involved in purchasing a new car increase or if there are restrictions on property rights that make cars less useful. The demand for new cars today might also increase if individuals thought the price of new cars would be higher next week.

In addition to these changes, each of which may affect the decisions of individual demanders, changes in the number of participants in the market will also change market demand. When the population increases there will, in general, be more individuals who wish to drive. Hence, demand for cars will increase. Figure 10 illustrates each of these possibilities.

What Leads to Changes in Supply?

Supply will change whenever there are changes that affect suppliers' decisions *other than* the price of the product itself. Table 7 lists the most important possibilities.

For example, when the price of steel increases, fewer new cars will be supplied to the market at each possible market price. By contrast, if there are technological innovations that lower production costs (such as computer-aided robots that weld car bodies), we should expect the supply of new cars to increase. Similarly, if there are organizational innovations like the development of the assembly line, supply will increase. If the price of trucks increases relative to cars, however, firms producing cars might shift from car to truck production and the supply of cars will decline. And if firms believe that prices will be higher a week from now than they are today, the supply of new cars today will decline, at least until next week. Of course, if it costs a firm more to market new cars, this increase in transaction costs will decrease market supply.

In addition to these changes that directly affect the decisions of individual suppliers, changes in the number of suppliers will also change market supply. Thus, if existing suppliers expand or if new suppliers begin producing the goods, market supply will increase. Figure 11 provides a supply-demand illustration for each of these possibilities.

**Table 6
Some Causes of Changes
in Market Demand**

Changes in the incomes of demanders
Changes in the prices of other, related commodities
Changes in transaction costs
Changes in property rights
Changes in expectations about the future
Changes in preferences

**Table 7
Some Causes of Changes
in Market Supply**

Changes in the prices of inputs
Technological innovations
Organizational innovations
Changes in the prices of other, related outputs
Changes in transaction costs
Changes in expectations about the future

Figure 10
The Effects of Changes in Demand on the Market for New Cars

(a) Personal income in the United States increases (income of demanders changes)

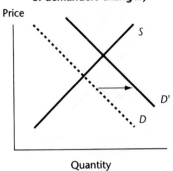

(b) The price of gasoline increases (price of a related commodity changes)

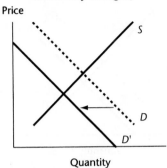

(c) Licensing becomes more difficult (change in transaction costs)

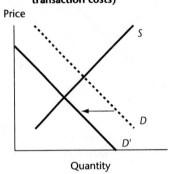

(d) Restrictions on resale are imposed (change in property rights)

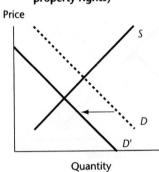

(e) Price is expected to increase next week (change in expectations about future prices)

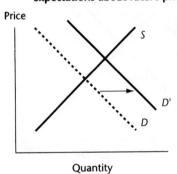

(f) Commuters are persuaded to use public transportation (change in tastes)

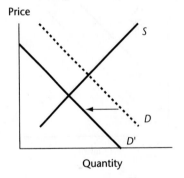

(g) Population increases (change in number of participants in the market)

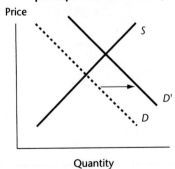

Figure 11
The Effects of Changes in Supply on the Market for New Cars

(a) Price of steel increases (price of input changes)

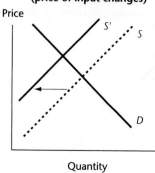

(b) Robotic welders are developed (technological innovation)

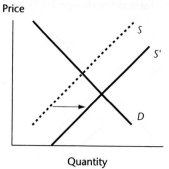

(c) Assembly lines are developed (organizational innovation)

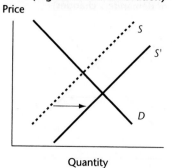

(d) The price of pick-up trucks increases (price of a related product changes)

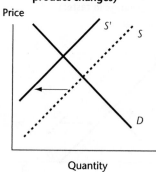

(e) Costs of transporting cars increase (change in transaction costs)

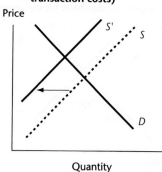

(f) Price is expected to increase next week (change in expectations about future prices)

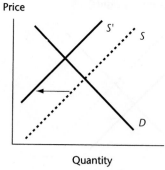

(g) Market entry by new suppliers (change in number of participants in the market)

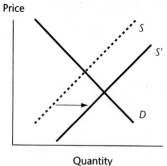

▶ Summary

Markets. Some individuals have money that they wish to exchange for goods, services, or resources; others have goods, services, or resources that they wish to exchange for money. The former are **demanders**; the latter, **suppliers**. A market is created when suppliers exchange with demanders. More formally, a market is a set of related transactions for a specific commodity, usually using money as a medium of exchange.

Demand. Demanders, in general, will purchase more if the price is lower. The maximum amount that demanders wish to purchase at all possible market prices is the **market demand**. The **quantity demanded**, by contrast, is the amount that demanders are willing to purchase at a *specific* market price. Quantity demanded is inversely related to the relative price, *ceteris paribus.* This relationship is often called the First Law of Demand.

Supply. Suppliers, in general, will provide more to a market if the price is higher. The maximum amount that suppliers wish to sell at all possible market prices is the **market supply**. The **quantity supplied** is the amount that suppliers will provide to the market at a specific market price. Quantity supplied is directly or positively related to the relative price, *ceteris paribus.*

Demand, supply, and equilibrium. If the quantity demanded is greater than the quantity supplied at a particular price, there is **excess demand**. If the quantity demanded is less than the quantity supplied at a particular price, however, there is **excess supply**. If the market price increases when there is excess demand, and decreases when there is excess supply, a market coordinates the differing interests of demanders and suppliers. Specifically, the price moves to equate the quantity that suppliers willingly provide to the market with the quantity that demanders want to purchase. When the price is such that there is neither excess demand nor excess supply, the amount that demanders wish to purchase will be equal to the amount that suppliers wish to sell: the market is in equilibrium at that price.

Changes in the desires of either suppliers or demanders will lead to predictable changes in price:

1. An increase in demand, if nothing else happens, will lead to an increase in the market price.

2. An increase in supply, if nothing else happens, will lead to a decrease in the market price.

3. A decrease in demand, if nothing else happens, will lead to a decrease in the market price.

4. A decrease in supply, if nothing else happens, will lead to an increase in the market price.

Demand will change with changes in the following:
The incomes of demanders
The prices of other, related commodities
Transaction costs
Property rights
Expectations about the future
Population, and
Demanders' preferences.

Supply will change with the following:
Changes in the prices of inputs
Technological innovations
Organizational innovations
Changes in the prices of other, related outputs
Changes in transaction costs
Changes in expectations about the future, and
Changes in the number or size of firms.

Chapter 6 ▶ ▶
The Demand for Goods and Services _____

The most important concept in economics, and the most widely applied, is the simple idea that when the relative price of something increases, demanders will want less of it. Or, conversely, that when the relative price decreases, demanders will want more. Nothing characterizes "thinking like an economist" or "using economics" more than the widespread and sometimes relentless application of this idea. It has been applied to the "demand for crime" in an effort to understand the effect of the death penalty on the murder rate; to the "demand for children" in studies of the effects of market opportunities for women on the size of families; to the "demand for legislation" in analyzing the political process; to the "demand for accidents" in investigating the effects of lawsuits on safety; and, of course, to the "demand for commodities" when focusing on traditional market activities. In each of these areas and many more, the inverse relationship between price, appropriately defined, and quantity demanded is a powerful concept for understanding how individuals and groups of individuals behave. *The* central idea embedded in demand is that individuals *substitute*. That is, we respond in a predictable way to changes in prices by *substituting* things that are relatively inexpensive for things that are relatively dear. Indeed, a demand curve can be thought of as a picture of substitution.

▶ Individual Demand

Goods are good, as are services. That is, they yield satisfaction and enhance well-being when used or consumed. Eating an apple makes you feel better. So does driving a new car or wearing new clothes. As a consequence, goods and services are desired and valued. Our preferences determine what we would like to consume. However, we confront constraints that determine what we are able to consume. Constraints change. Your income will be greater after you graduate. It may grow through time or it may fall dramatically if you become unemployed. The prices you pay fluctuate. Transactions are sometimes more, sometimes less, costly. As each of these constraints changes, we adjust and make different choices. The central question in this chapter, and in much of economics, is whether and in what sense are these adjustments predictable?

Individual Choices When Relative Prices Change

We begin our analysis of this question by considering the effect of price changes on the decisions that individuals make. Consider the decisions of the tennis player whose maximizing behavior we analyzed in Chapter 4. Table 1 provides a description of the satisfaction or utility she obtained from various amounts of play each month.

Table 1
The Benefits of Playing Tennis

Sets per month	Total satisfaction	Marginal satisfaction
		$20
1	$20	
		10
2	30	
		8
3	38	
		6
4	44	
		4
5	48	
		2
6	50	
		1
7	51	
		0
8	51	

Table 2
An Individual Demand Schedule

Possible price ($)	Desired quantity at that price (number of sets)
$ 0	8
1	7
2	6
4	5
6	4
8	3
10	2
20	1
>20	0

The optimal level of play will depend, remember, on *marginal cost* and *marginal benefit*. For consumers, the marginal benefit is the additional or marginal satisfaction obtained from playing one more set of tennis. Marginal satisfaction can be estimated by:

$$\frac{\Delta \text{ total satisfaction}}{\Delta \text{ sets per month}}$$

where Δ indicates the change in quantity.[1] Estimates of marginal satisfaction are provided in the third column in Table 1. Because of diminishing marginal returns, a demander's marginal satisfaction will, at some point, begin to fall as the amount consumed in a given time period increases.

If market price is $2 per set, playing an additional set costs $2. Hence, from the individual's perspective, $2 is the marginal cost of playing a set of tennis. In general, from a demander's perspective, *the market price is the marginal cost of consuming an additional unit of a particular commodity.*

Best or optimal decisions require that an individual make adjustments in the amount consumed until marginal benefit is equal to marginal cost. Hence, the tennis player whose preferences are illustrated in Table 1 will select that level of play that

brings her marginal satisfaction into line with the market price. When the market price is $2, the best decision is to play six sets per month. If the price decreases to $1, however, she will choose to play seven sets per month. On the other hand, if the market price increases to $4, she will play five sets each month. At a price of $6 per set, she will play four sets, at a price of $8, three sets, and at a price of $10, two sets. If the price increases to $20 per set, her best response is to play one set of tennis and, at any price greater than $20, to play no tennis. These combinations of market price and *desired* level of play are the individual's **demand schedule,** which is summarized in Table 2.

This individual demand schedule summarizes the tennis player's *best* response to each price. Clearly, a best (or "optimal") response is to play less tennis when the price of tennis is higher. Note that the best decision depends on both the market price and an individual's preferences. The *direction* of response to any change in the price, however, depends only on the price and follows directly from the assumption of diminishing marginal returns introduced in Chapter 3. An individual **demand curve** corresponding to this demand schedule is plotted in Figure 1.

Substitution

Substitution is the key to understanding demand. More precisely, there is an inverse relationship

[1] The Greek letter Δ will be used throughout the text to indicate "change" or "difference." Thus, if $x_1 = 10$ and $x_2 = 12$, $\Delta x = (12-10) = 2$.

Figure 1
An Individual's Demand for Tennis

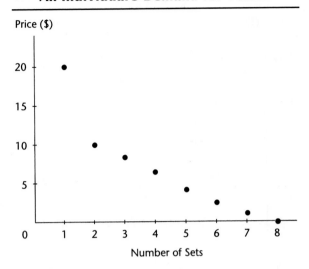

This individual desires a greater amount of tennis when the price per set is lower. Her individual demand schedule is provided in Table 2.

between price and quantity demanded because individuals *substitute* relatively inexpensive things for relatively expensive things as prices change. A change in one price will *always* make some things relatively less expensive and other things relatively more expensive. We have to give up more of other things to purchase the same amount of a commodity whose price has increased, for example. When the opportunity cost increases, demanders have an incentive to find other commodities or activities, now relatively less expensive, which substitute in providing satisfaction.

This does not mean that one commodity substitutes perfectly for another, or that all commodities substitute equally well for each other, or that substitution is necessarily easy. Some things are better substitutes than others. An orange is probably a better substitute for an apple in providing a juicy snack than is a hamburger or french fries. Moreover, substitution is, at times, difficult. If you have appendicitis, there is no really good substitute for an appendectomy. As long as individuals can substitute one thing for another, however, there will be an inverse relationship between market price and the quantity demanded. Conversely, an inverse relationship between price and quantity implies that substitution is occurring.

The concept of *substitution* is easily understood by considering what you would have to give up if you continued to purchase exactly the same quantity of some good, say an apartment, when the price doubles and your income does not change. Suppose, for instance, that your income is $1,000 and you spend $250 for rent. If the rent doubles, it will take $500 to remain in the same apartment. If you decide to stay put and pay the additional rent, you will have less money to spend on other things. ($500 instead of $750). Clearly, your consumption of other things will have to decline. In this sense, an apartment and other things you might buy substitute for one another. We do not simply cut our consumption of other things when the price of one thing increases, of course. Instead, when the price of something doubles, *desired* purchases of that thing decrease. A higher price provides incentives for individuals to seek less costly, even if imperfect, substitutes for the higher-priced commodity; conversely, lower prices encourage individuals to substitute the now relatively less costly commodity for other things. Thus, in an important sense, the inverse relationship between price and desired consumption is just a way of depicting substitution.

Substitution and Maximization

To see the idea of substitution in a slightly different way, suppose that you consume only two commodities, apples, A, and bananas, B, with dollar prices p_A and p_B and relative price, p_A/p_B. From Chapter 3 we know that if you are rational, you will consider the marginal opportunity cost in making decisions and the equi-marginal rule must hold. This means that the marginal satisfaction obtained from consuming the last apple, per dollar spent on apples, must be equal to the marginal satisfaction obtained from consuming the last banana per dollar spent on bananas, or

$$\frac{MS_A}{p_A} = \frac{MS_B}{p_B}$$

where the MS_A and MS_B are the marginal satisfaction obtained from consuming an additional apple and an additional banana respectively.

Allocating your income between A and B will lead to the consumption of a certain amount of A and a certain amount of B (the actual amounts of

A and B consumed will be determined by your preferences). Suppose we observe you purchasing 10 apples when the price of apples is $1 (point y in Figure 2). What happens when the price of apples falls to $.50? The marginal satisfaction per dollar spent on apples will be greater than the marginal satisfaction per dollar spent on bananas,

$$\frac{MS_A}{p_{Anew}} > \frac{MS_B}{p_B}$$

and the current consumption mix of A and B can no longer be the best mix. Why not? After all, the change in the price of apples by itself cannot affect the satisfaction you get from eating additional apples or bananas—MS_A and MS_B have not changed since they depend only on the quantities of A and B that you consume. Although MS_A, MS_B, and p_B have not changed, p_A has fallen to p_{Anew}, and, as a consequence, the additional or marginal satisfaction *per dollar spent* on A is greater than the additional or marginal satisfaction per dollar spent on B. Thus, even though your enjoyment of apples and bananas hasn't changed, when the price of apples changes, you get more satisfaction *for each dollar spent* on apples than you do for each dollar spent on bananas. In this case, the only thing that makes sense is for you to substitute apples for bananas. It's as simple as that. Thus at $.50 per apple, your desired consumption of apples might increase to 20, point z in Figure 2.

Diminishing marginal satisfaction. Substituting apples for bananas obviously changes the mix of apples and bananas that you consume. As the consumption of A increases, the marginal satisfaction of A falls because of diminishing marginal returns; as the consumption of B decreases, the marginal satisfaction of B increases, again because of diminishing marginal returns. This means that the marginal satisfaction per dollar spent on A declines, and the marginal satisfaction per dollar spent on B increases as you substitute A for B. The substitution of A for B continues until the marginal satisfaction per dollar spent on each commodity is once again equal.

If the abstractions using MS_A, MS_B, p_A, and p_B are confusing, you might think of this problem in the following way. Suppose that the price of apples is $1.00 and the price of bananas is also $1.00. If the marginal satisfaction from consuming an additional

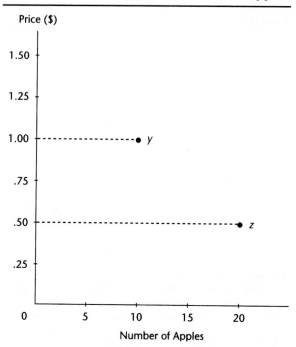

Figure 2
The Effect of a Change in the Price of Apples

If the price of apples falls, the marginal satisfaction per dollar spent on apples will exceed that for other goods, such as bananas. Consequently, a consumer will substitute apples for bananas until the marginal satisfaction per dollar spent on both goods is equal. Thus, the quantity of apples demanded is greater at the low price of $.50 than at the higher price of $1.00.

apple is 2, then by the equi-marginal rule, the marginal satisfaction from consuming an additional banana must also be 2. (If it's not equal to 2, the mix of apples and bananas is not optimal). Therefore,

$$\frac{2}{\$1.00} = \frac{2}{\$1.00}$$

When the price of apples falls from $1.00 to $.50,

$$\frac{2}{\$.50} > \frac{2}{\$1.00} \text{ or } 4 > 2$$

Because of the decline in price of apples, you get "more bang for the buck" in consuming apples than with bananas. It follows that you will substitute apples for bananas. Spending $1.00 less on bananas would decrease your satisfaction by about 2. Spending an additional $.50 on apples would increase your satisfaction by about 2. Therefore, a dollar could purchase more satisfaction if reallocated from bananas to apples. That is, for each $1.00 transferred from banana purchases to apple purchases, you lose about 2 units of satisfaction from fewer bananas but you gain about 4 units of satisfaction from consuming more apples because each dollar buys two apples.

As more of one commodity and less of the other is consumed, however, the effect of diminishing marginal returns becomes important. In particular, as more apples are consumed, the marginal satisfaction from apple consumption will decrease, say, from 2 to 1.5. On the other hand, as fewer bananas are consumed, the marginal satisfaction from banana consumption will increase, say from 2 to 3 (again, because of diminishing returns). After the substitution of apples for bananas,

$$\frac{1.5}{\$.50} = \frac{3}{\$1.00} \text{ or } 3 = 3$$

and the marginal satisfaction per dollar spent is the same for each commodity. You are now making a best or optimal decision, *given* your income and the prices of apples ($.50) and bananas ($1.00). To get there you had to *substitute* apples for bananas in response to the price change.

Willingness to Pay

While the demand schedule is a pairing of market prices and the quantity an individual wishes to purchase, it is also a reflection of how much an individual is willing to pay for any *additional* consumption of a particular commodity. That is, individuals adjust the quantity they wish to purchase until the marginal satisfaction obtained from purchasing the last unit is just equal to the market price. This means, for example, that if Figure 2 illustrates your demand for apples, you would be willing to pay no more than $1.00 for an additional apple if you were currently purchasing 10 apples and no more than $.50 for an additional apple if you were currently purchasing 20 apples.

Hence, the individual demand schedule can be thought of in two ways.

1. It is the quantity an individual wishes to purchase *at each price.*

2. It is the amount of money that an individual is willing to pay for a small additional amount *at each level of consumption.*

The inverse relationship between relative price and quantity demanded implies, then, that there is an inverse relationship between willingness-to-pay for additional consumption and the level of desired consumption. This means that individuals will be willing to pay more per unit for a commodity if they have less of it and less per unit if they have more of it. This isn't very surprising since most of us would be willing to pay far more for a drink of water in a desert than we are willing to pay for a drink of water when we have easy access to lots of water.

▶ Market Demand

The **market demand** is the sum of the quantity that all demanders wish to purchase at each price. At a particular relative price, some individuals will want to consume a lot of a particular commodity; other individuals will want to consume less; still others may not want to consume any. For example, at $2 per set the tennis player whose demand is illustrated in Table 2 and Figure 1 wants to play six sets of tennis per month. Suppose that another individual, with different opportunities perhaps, wants to play 10 sets per month when the price is $2 and a third would like to play five sets. Each of these individuals will be attempting to rent courts during the month. Therefore, at $2 per set, the market demand is 21 sets per month.

It follows that the quantity demanded in the market at any particular price is simply the sum of the quantity that each individual wishes to purchase at that price. This relationship between individual demand and the market demand is illustrated by the market demand schedule in Table 3. The corresponding individual and market demand curves are shown in Figure 3. Again, both exhibit an inverse relationship between price and quantity demanded.

The First Law of Demand

The inverse relationship between the market price and the quantity that participants in a market wish to purchase is often referred to as the First Law of Demand, as was noted in Chapter 4. This inverse relationship occurs for two reasons:

1. For each individual currently in the market there is generally an inverse relationship between the market price and desired consumption.

Table 3
Market Demand

Possible price	Individual demand (sets per month)			Market demand (sets per month)
	Tennis Player 1	*Tennis Player 2*	*Tennis Player 3*	
$ 1	7	11	8	26
2	6	10	5	21
4	5	9	3	17
6	4	8	2	14
8	3	7	1	11
10	2	6	0	8
20	1	2	0	3
23	0	1	0	1
>23	0	0	0	0

2. As the market price decreases, additional demanders enter the market and, as the market price increases, demanders leave the market.

In Figure 3, for example, when the market price is $23 per set, only one person wants to play tennis. When the price falls to $20, this person would like to play *more* tennis, substituting tennis for other activities, *and* a second person would like to play as well. As the market price continues to decrease, both of these people would like to substitute *more* tennis for other activities and the quantity demanded increases. A third player enters the market when the price falls to $8. When the market price is above $8, this person has other things to do with his time and money and, as a consequence, his interests in tennis are not reflected in the market demand. At a market price of $8 or below, however, the market demand will be affected by his desire to play tennis.

Figure 3
Individual and Market Demands

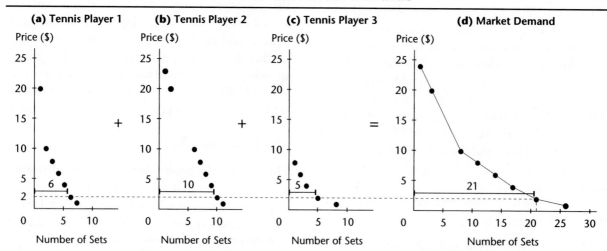

Each individual in an economy has a different demand schedule. The market demand curve is simply the summation of all individual demand curves, as illustrated here. As the market price falls, individuals already in the market purchase more and new ones enter the market. Thus, at a price of $20 per set, only players 1 and 2 will play any tennis. If the price falls to $8, however, players 1 and 2 will play more tennis and player 3 will also play.

Evidence?

Sophisticated statistical analyses of a very large number of markets studied by economists over the years have invariably found an inverse relationship between the amount purchased in the market and the market price. That human behavior is consistent with downward sloping demand curves is an extraordinarily robust empirical fact.

In addition, however, there is a good deal of simple evidence with which you are familiar. Fruit and vegetables are less expensive in the late summer and early fall than at other times of the year. Typically they are harvested in larger amounts during this season. Because fruits and vegetables are perishable, the greater quantity that comes to the market can only be sold if prices are lower. In other words, a lower price is necessary to entice sufficient demand. Presumably, farmers would sell their produce at higher prices if they could. They accept lower prices only because that is all that demanders will pay for additional amounts when there are lots of fruits and vegetables around. Similarly, businesses selling clothing would prefer higher prices. But sales are common. Why? Suppliers announce sales and discounts because they believe that they can get more people to buy their goods only if they lower the price. You undoubtedly shop around. Why? Presumably because your decision to buy is affected by the market price and you want to find the best deal.

Public Policy and "Wants"

In policy debates, in surveys of consumer interest, or in casual conversation, it is often asserted that "no one wants" a particular product or that some commodity "is in great demand" without specifying at what price "no one wants anything" or "demand is great." This is a serious error. *How many* people are interested in something and *how much* they are interested is not independent of the price. At lower relative prices, more people will be interested and each person's interest will be greater, *ceteris paribus;* at higher relative prices, fewer people will be interested and each person's interest will be less, *ceteris paribus.* It does little good to speculate whether I want a new sports car independent of price, for example. If a new car were only $10,000, I might very well go out and buy one, but at $60,000, I will probably think twice about making the purchase. Asking whether or not I *want* a new car is quite different from asking if I *am willing* to actually purchase one at the current market price.

This point is worth emphasizing: How many people want something, and how much each person wants, cannot be determined without specifying a price. This is commonly misunderstood. For example, newspapers often report surveys with headlines like "BYU Students Want More Parking." The articles often make no sense because the surveys are conducted without specifying a price. Put simply, at a price of $1000 per month per parking place, BYU students will want less parking and there will probably be more than enough on-campus parking; at a price of $0 per month, however, everyone will drive their car to the center of campus and there probably won't be enough on-campus parking. The number of parking places available is the same in either case. How much students want changes with the price, however. Clearly, there is a price at which there will be plenty of parking.

Willingness to Pay

Market demand is the sum of the quantities that demanders individually wish to purchase when each must pay the same market price. Therefore, market demand can be interpreted in terms of the *quantity* that individuals, in aggregate, wish to purchase *given the price,* or in terms of the *willingness* of individuals, in aggregate, to pay for additional output, *given the amount that they are currently purchasing.* For instance, in Figure 3, when 17 sets of tennis are demanded, each individual is willing to pay no more than $4.00 for an additional set of tennis. Thus, the market price tells us something about individuals. We cannot determine from the market demand how much tennis any individual would like to play, but we can determine the maximum price that each individual is willing to pay to play *additional* tennis, whatever his or her current level of play. Thus, if 21 sets of tennis were supplied to the market, consumers would individually be willing to pay no more than $2 for an additional set of tennis; if 11 sets were supplied, consumers would, individually, be willing to pay no more than $8 for an additional set and so forth.

Willingness to pay is not the same as *ability* to pay. There is considerable confusion about this matter in public policy discussions. It is frequently argued, for example, that when prices increase, the rich will get the goods and the not-so-rich will have to find substitutes or go without. This argument would suggest that unless the preferences of different income groups are quite different, the best of everything would go to the rich. However, the market doesn't distribute new automobiles to the rich first and to the not-so-rich later. It distributes them to those willing to pay for automobiles. As a consequence, expensive automobiles are purchased by a broad cross-section of the population, both the rich and not-so-rich. To test this, if you surveyed the cars in a parking lot by age, model, and brand, would the higher-priced cars be owned solely by the rich and the lower-priced cars owned solely by the not-so-rich? Probably not.

People with higher incomes do have a command over more goods than do people with lower incomes. The poor cannot consume as the rich do. This is a distributional issue of considerable importance. In any particular market, however, the allocation of goods is not completely determined by the ability to pay. All that we can say for sure is that, when market prices increase, commodities are rationed to those willing to pay more, and those willing to pay less leave the market.

► Changes in Market Demand When Other Prices Change

There are many things besides the market price that may affect your consumption decisions—your income, perhaps your wealth, certainly the prices of other goods, what's the "in" thing, and so forth. As these things change, the decisions you make will also change. For example, decisions about the amount of tennis you play will be affected by the prices of tennis racquets, tennis balls, clothing, the prices of other leisure activities such as swimming, racquetball, movies, as well as the prices of other things that could be done with the time and money devoted to tennis. Each of these, *in addition to the price of tennis itself*, may affect your demand for tennis.

Along a demand curve, we assume that all those things that might possibly affect the decision about how much tennis to play *except* the price of tennis do not change. Specifically, we assume that the prices of tennis balls, movies, and swimming all stay the same; we assume that your income stays the same; we assume that the temperature outside stays the same. Thus, along a demand curve, we consider the

effect of a change in the quantity demanded when the price changes, *ceteris paribus*. (*Ceteris paribus* means, remember, "everything else the same.") But of course, everything else does not remain the same; things change.

Some commodities tend to be consumed together or jointly. For example, tennis and tennis balls, tennis and tennis racquets, bread and butter, coffee and cream, automobiles and gasoline, CD players and compact discs are consumed jointly. Commodities of this sort are **complements**. Other commodities tend to be interchangeable in consumption. These are called **substitutes**. Some examples of substitutes might be tennis and racquetball or tennis and swimming, or rice and bread, or rice and potatoes; different brands of clothing, different ways of getting to work, and so forth. Still other commodities that substitute for each other may not appear to have much relationship to one another except that, as the price of one increases and income remains the same, consumption must fall. For example, an economics textbook doesn't have any obvious relationship to gasoline or ice cream, but spending part of your income on a textbook will affect your ability to purchase gasoline and ice cream.

Complements

When the price of tennis balls increases, individuals will substitute other things for tennis balls, moving back along the demand curve for tennis balls. One of the things that an individual may do is to substitute old balls for new balls, using each ball for a longer period of time. The increase in the price of tennis balls also makes playing tennis relatively more costly, however, and individuals will substitute other activities that do not require tennis balls. Thus, even though the dollar price of a set of tennis may not change, when the price of tennis balls increases tennis become more costly at *every* dollar price per set. Consequently, the number of sets individuals wish to play each month will decrease, say, from point x to point y in Figure 4. However, tennis becomes more costly at *every* dollar price per set. Put simply, if two commodities are complements and the price of one increases, the demand for the other commodity will decrease. As a consequence, the entire demand curve will shift to the left, from D to D' in Figure 5.

Figure 4
The Effect of an Increase in the Price of Tennis Balls on the Quantity of Tennis Demanded

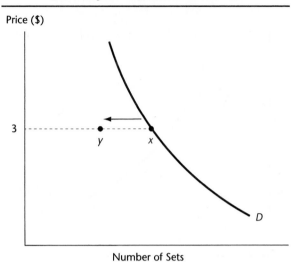

When the price of tennis balls increases, the price of playing tennis also increases. As a consequence, individuals will generally play less tennis, even if the price of a set of tennis itself does not change. In this figure, the amount of tennis that individuals wish to play at the market price of $3 per set might fall from x to y.

Figure 5
The Effect of an Increase in the Price of a Complement on Demand

Demand for a good decreases at every price when the price of its complement increases, as illustrated by the leftward shift of the demand curve, from D to D'.

On the other hand, if the price of tennis balls falls, tennis is relatively less expensive to play than it once was, even though the price per set hasn't changed. We would expect that the number of sets played each month would increase. This effect would be illustrated by a shift of the demand curve outward (or to the right). Consumers will be willing to pay more to play each set of tennis since the total cost of playing tennis has decreased somewhat with the decrease in the price of tennis balls. More generally, if two commodities are complements and the price of one decreases, the demand for the other commodity will increase. This change is represented by a rightward shift in the market demand curve. Since demand can be thought of in terms of willingness to pay, demanders will be willing to pay more for a commodity when the price of a complement falls, and less when it increases.

It is important to remember that *along* the demand curve, substitution occurs when the market price changes. Hence the demand curve in Figure 5 slopes downward to the right. The demand curve itself shifts only when something *other than the price of the commodity* changes, that is, when something

changes affecting the quantity demanded at every price.

Substitutes

Suppose that the price of tennis is $7 per set, but the price of a game of racquetball increases. People will play less racquetball as a consequence of the change in price and substitute other activities for racquetball. One of these activities may be tennis. Thus, even though the dollar price of tennis is unchanged, tennis has become *relatively less costly* with the increase in the price of racquetball and is, as a consequence, more attractive. If tennis and racquetball are substitutes, we would expect people to play more tennis at the current price of tennis because of the change in the price of racquetball. This change is illustrated by the movement from point x to point y in Figure 6.

Tennis is, of course, more attractive at every price per set when the price of racquetball increases. Hence, at each price, the quantity of tennis demanded will increase. This is illustrated by the shift from D to D' in Figure 7. If two goods are

Figure 6
The Effect of a Decrease in the
Price of a Complement on Demand

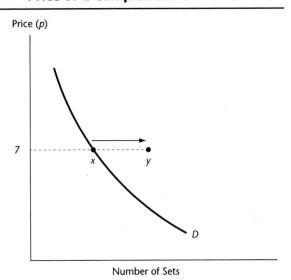

When the price of racquetball increases, individuals will find that their marginal satisfaction per dollar spent on tennis exceeds that for racquetball. They will therefore substitute tennis for racquetball, thus playing more tennis, even though the price of tennis has not changed. Thus, the quantity of tennis demanded at a price of $7 per set increases, as illustrated by the movement from *x* to *y*.

Figure 7
The Effect of an Increase in the
Price of a Substitute on Demand

Demand for a good increases at every price when the price of its complement decreases, as illustrated by the rightward shift of the demand curve, from *D* to *D''*.

substitutes, the demand curve for one will shift to the right, (*D* to *D'* in Figure 7) when the price of a substitute increases. The demand curve will shift to the left when the price of a substitute declines. Put differently, when the price of a commodity increases, individuals will be willing to pay more for substitute commodities, and when the price of a commodity declines, individuals will be willing to pay less for substitute commodities.

▶ Changes in Market Demand When Income Changes

You might suppose that the effect of income on demand would be straightforward because, if you have more money, you will be able to consume more goods. This is obviously true. However, you may not *want* to consume more of a particular good when your income increases. Remember, ability to pay is not the same as willingness to pay.

Normal Commodities

If the demand for a good increases when individual incomes increase, the good is a **normal commodity**.

Thus it might be that when a tennis player's income increases from $400 to $450 per week, she will want to increase her level of activity from three sets per month to four sets per month when the price is $7 per set, as illustrated in Figure 8. If income had this positive effect on desired consumption at $7 per set, it is likely that it would have a similar effect at any other price and that the demand curve would shift (from *D* to *D'* in Figure 9). Similar increases in income for most demanders of tennis would shift the market demand curve in a comparable manner. For example, with higher incomes, people tend to live in larger homes and eat in restaurants more frequently. Both larger homes and food prepared outside the home are normal commodities. That is, as incomes have increased in the US, so have the average size of a house and the number of meals eaten in restaurants.

Inferior Commodities

Changes in income can result in a quite different consumption pattern, however. Sometimes, when income increases, *less* of some commodity is consumed and the demand curve shifts to the left (from *D* to *D''* in Figure 10). Such commodities are called

Figure 8
The Effect of a Increase in an Individual's
Income on the Quantity Demanded

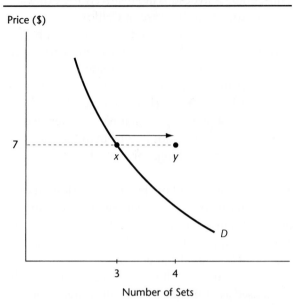

If tennis is a normal good, then individuals want to play more tennis when their incomes increase, even if the price of tennis does not change. This is shown by the movement from *x* to *y* when the price of tennis is $7 per set.

Figure 9
The Effect of an Increase in Income
on the Demand for a Normal Good

When their incomes increase, individuals purchase more normal goods at each price, as shown by the rightward shift of the demand curve, from *D* to *D'*.

Figure 10
The Effect of an Increase in Income
on the Demand for a Inferior Good

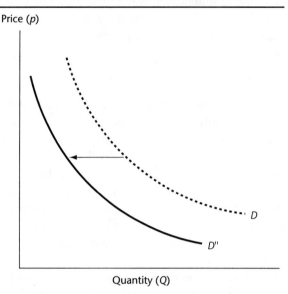

When their incomes increase, individuals purchase fewer inferior goods at each price, as shown by the leftward shift of the demand curve, from *D* to *D''*.

inferior commodities. Examples might include tuna fish or peanut butter sandwiches. When living on a student budget you consume a lot of tuna fish and peanut butter sandwiches. When your income increases you may switch from sandwiches to steak. The decision to buy a new or used car is also affected by income. At a lower income you may find used cars more attractive than you would if your income were higher. As people's incomes increase, fewer used cars and more new cars might be purchased. If this were generally true, used cars would be inferior commodities.

It is important to remember that in each comparison, we are assuming that the relative prices of sandwiches and steak or used cars and new cars are not changing. Of course changes in relative prices—for example, an increase in the price of peanut butter while the price of steak remains the same, or a decrease in the price of used cars while the price of new cars remains the same—will lead to changes in the quantity demanded (represented by movements *along* existing demand curves). In contrast, income changes cause a shift in the entire demand curve.

▶ Other Effects on Market Demand

Prices may change in subtle ways when transactions are costly. Expectations about the future, particularly about future prices, will also affect market demand. In addition, because market demands sum up the demands of individuals, when there are more individuals, there is likely to be a greater market demand. Finally, tastes and preferences do change.

Changes in Transaction Costs

If it costs you more to transact, your demand is likely to be less. Waiting in lines, traveling long distances, having to shop around, being charged a sales tax, or generally being inconvenienced will make a difference in how much you want to purchase. Increases in transaction costs *for everyone* will lower demand, shifting the demand curve to the left. If everyone has to wait in line for tickets to a rock concert for most of a day, for example, demand will be less than it otherwise would be. Decreases in transaction costs for everyone in a market will increase demand, shifting the demand curve to the right. For example, better transportation systems that make it easier to get to shopping areas will increase demand in those areas. Although neither of these effects is surprising, there are some interesting examples in which transaction costs differ for different individuals. When this happens, individuals will face *different* relative prices and will, if demand theory is correct, make *predictably different* choices. Consider the following examples.

Transportation costs. Suppose that it costs as much to ship a grade A avocado from California to New York as it does to ship a grade B avocado. What difference will this make? Both grade A and grade B avocados will cost less in California than in New York because of the shipping costs. We would therefore expect Californians to consume more avocados of both grades than New Yorkers. We would also expect that New Yorkers would consume a higher percentage of grade A avocados relative to grade B avocados than do Californians, however. To see why, consider a specific case.

Suppose that it costs $.10 to ship an avocado from California to New York and that grade A and grade B avocados sell for $.50 and $.25, respectively, in California. The relative price of grade A to grade B avocados is 2 in California ($.50/$.25). Avocados purchased at these prices in California and then shipped east would cost $.60 for grade A avocados and $.35 for grade B avocados by the time they

reached New York. The relative price of grade A to grade B would be 1.71 in New York ($.60/$.35). Thus, grade A avocados are relatively *less* expensive in New York than they are in California, and New Yorkers should be expected to consume a higher percentage of grade A avocados and a relatively lower percentage of grade B avocados, substituting higher quality for lower quality. Avocados are *more* expensive in New York relative to other things, however, so we should expect that New Yorkers would consume fewer avocados in total than Californians, substituting other things for avocados.

Taxes. A similar kind of change in the desired consumption mix occurs when a dollar tax is imposed on close substitutes with different prices. For example, suppose that a $2,000 tax is imposed on the sale of both used and new cars. The price of both new and used cars will increase. Fewer cars will be purchased as individuals substitute other things for the purchase of new or used cars. The mix between used and new cars purchased will also change, however. New cars will have a lower price relative to used cars after the tax than they did before the tax, even though both used and new cars have higher prices relative to other goods. Therefore, such a tax will distort the consumption mix toward new cars.

Again, to be specific, suppose that new cars are priced at $20,000 before the tax and $22,000 after the tax and that used cars are priced at $4,000 before the tax and $6,000 after the tax. The relative price of new versus used cars prior to the tax is 5 ($20,000/$4,000) but it declines to 3.7 ($22,000/$6,000) after the tax is imposed—relative to used cars, new cars are *less* expensive. This change in relative prices will change the mix of new and used cars purchased in a predictable way: The proportion of new cars among all cars sold will increase.

What is "price?" When there are transaction costs, in a real sense "price" is different from the easily observed dollar price. That is, transaction costs change opportunity costs without necessarily changing dollar prices. For example, if a ticket to a rock concert is priced at $15 but you have to stand in line for two hours to purchase it, the "full" price is a lot more than $15. What an individual is willing to pay is a combination of the dollar price plus time. Does the relative price change if the dollar price remains at $15 but the waiting time increases to three hours?

Of course it does: it increases. Moreover, willingness to pay in dollars may be quite different from willingness to pay in time. Therefore, because of this particular kind of transaction cost, tickets will be allocated differently than they would with a change in the dollar price equal to the value of time spent waiting.

More generally, to describe the full price requires careful consideration of opportunity costs. For example, it is well known that couples living in economies with high per capita income have, on average, smaller families than couples living in economies with low per capita income. This may seem a bit odd. After all, parents living in wealthy economies can afford to have more children, whereas parents living in poor economies can ill afford to spread their meager incomes across a large number of children. One possibility is that the relative prices of having children are different. It turns out that they probably are: In an economy with well-developed market opportunities for both men and women, the possible market income for women is larger than in economies without such opportunities. Raising children is a time-intensive activity, particularly for mothers. It follows that the greater the possible market income available to women, the greater the opportunity cost of having each child. Thus, women in economies with high incomes would be expected to have fewer children than those in economies with low incomes, *ceteris paribus*.

Changes in Expectations

If everyone thought that the relative price of some commodity would be higher next week than it is today, then demand would increase today as a consequence. That is, a *change in expectations* about the future will make a difference *today*. For example, if the government announces a forthcoming new tax on something that you could purchase either now or later, you will probably purchase it now to avoid the tax you expect to pay in the future. As everyone responds in the same way, market demand will increase now and so will the price. Or, for example, if a large business announces that it plans to build a new factory in a small town, the demand for land will increase *now* in expectation of the effect that the influx of people will have on the price and availability of land in the *future*.

Changes in Population

As indicated earlier, market demand is the sum or aggregation of individual demands for a particular commodity. Therefore, as the number of individuals in an economy changes, market demand will also change. Generally, increases in population will increase demand, shifting market demand curves to the right. For example, as a consequence of the increase in population in the US, there is greater demand for land in rural areas of the country as well as in New York City. Consequently, land prices are substantially higher today than they were a generation ago. Similarly, the demand for land in China continues to increase with the increasing population. By contrast, during the fourteenth century, when the bubonic plague swept through Europe killing a large fraction of the population, the demand for land decreased and there was a dramatic decline in land rents as a consequence.

It follows, of course, that when an economy has more households, there will generally be a greater demand for good, services, and resources. Hence the demand for bread is greater in the United States than it is in Norway or Switzerland. Similarly, the demand for housing is greater in New York City than it is in River Heights, Utah. (The effects of these differences in demand upon the market price will, of course, also depend upon supply.)

Changes in Tastes and Preferences

For the most part, economists look first for changes in relative prices or incomes in explaining changes in behavior, but tastes and preferences do change and these changes affect demand. A person may decide that jogging is more enjoyable than tennis or that the sedentary life is really better than a life filled with sweat and effort. Hula-hoops are the "in" thing for one generation but not for another. Skateboards have gone through several cycles of being "in," then "out," then "in" again. Roller blades are now the rage. Clothing fashions change. When tastes and values change, the best decisions for households are likely to change as well. For "in" things, demand increases; when they go "out," demand falls.

Why are some things "in" and then "out," or vice versa? About all that can be said is that the "in" things are "in." There has been a long and interesting debate as to the source and frequency of such changes in values and tastes. Perhaps we are just fickle about some preferences. Perhaps our tastes are influenced by others. Perhaps we are manipulated. For example, it has been argued by some that our tastes are products of advertising and easily changed to favor particular products. This argument suggests that our market demands are really creations of polling and advertising firms. At its extreme, this view suggests that free individual choice is a myth and that choices are, instead, created and manipulated. On the other hand, others argue that information about many commodities is costly to acquire, and, consequently we are all ignorant to various degrees when we make choices. In this case, advertising is viewed as a method of reducing the costs of acquiring information. Thus, tastes, values, and resulting choices are not manipulated but are, rather, informed by advertising.

Relying on the First Law of Demand as the *principal* explanation of behavior (that is, assuming that changes in prices or, more generally, opportunity costs, are the most important reason for changes in behavior and that differences in prices or opportunity costs are the most important explanation for differences in behavior among individuals) implies that tastes and values are relatively stable. That is, we are less interested in why individuals buy a specific good, apples, than, say, why the level of apple consumption changes from its current level.

Do tastes differ among individuals and change through time? Surely. Does culture matter? Of course. But the possible role of tastes and culture can be best understood, an economist would argue, by first deciding how much of the observed differences among groups of people or the observed changes through time for any particular group can be explained by considering relative price and income differences or changes. *It is this reliance on relative prices as the important element in explaining behavior that characterizes the economic approach to problems.*

Substitution and Income Effects

Relative price changes also change *real* income, and income changes may, as we have seen, either increase or decrease demand depending upon whether a commodity is a normal commodity or an inferior one. This poses a problem for our analysis of demand: Suppose that you consume only three commodities, apples, bananas, and oranges (A, B and O respectively). If p_A, p_B and p_O represent the prices of apples, bananas, and oranges and y is your income then,

$$(p_A \times A) + (p_B \times B) + (p_O \times O) = y \qquad (1)$$

Don't be frightened by the symbols. All Equation (1) says is that, if you spend all of your income, the amount you spend on apples plus the amount you spend on bananas plus your expenditures on oranges must be equal to your total income.

If you are making consumption choices so as to maximize your well-being, given your tastes, income, and the prices of the three commodities, then the equi-marginal rule implies that

$$\frac{MS_A}{p_A} = \frac{MS_B}{p_B} = \frac{MS_O}{p_O} \qquad (2)$$

will determine how you divide your income among the three commodities. (MS_A is the marginal satisfaction from consuming apples, MS_B the marginal satisfaction obtained from bananas, and MS_O the marginal satisfaction from consuming oranges.)

What happens if the price of apples decreases? You will no longer be making the best decision about the mix of apples, oranges and bananas. In terms of Equation (2),

$$\frac{MS_A}{p_{Anew}} > \frac{MS_B}{p_B} = \frac{MS_O}{p_O}$$

That is, the marginal satisfaction per dollar spent on apples will now be greater than will the marginal satisfaction per dollar spent on either bananas or oranges. The relative price of A is lower, so therefore you will tend to substitute A for O and B, cutting your consumption of bananas and oranges and increasing your consumption of apples.

So far, so good. Now to the problem: When the price of A falls and the dollar prices of O and B do not change, the total amount that you can purchase with your income will increase. That is, the fall in the price of apples means that your dollars can now buy more of everything. It is as if you have more income. We learned earlier that income changes may *either increase or decrease* demand depending upon whether a commodity is normal or inferior. Consequently, the overall effect of the price change on the quantity demanded is not clear.

For example, suppose that you were spending one half of your monthly income of $100 on apples (purchasing 50 pounds) and the price of apples fell by one half, from $1.00 per pound to $.50 per pound. At the new price you could continue to purchase exactly the same amount of bananas and oranges as you did before and exactly the same amount of apples as well. If you did this, the 50 pounds of apples you were consuming would now cost $25 rather than $50 and the oranges and bananas would together still cost $50. Having bought exactly the same number of A, B, and O as you did previously, you would have $25 left over to spend as you wished. Thus, even though your *dollar or nominal income* has not changed, the decline in the price of A makes your income go further and your *real income* has increased. When the price of apples falls and no other dollar price changes, it is as if someone gave you $25 (akin to increasing your income from $100 to $125 when the price of apples was still $1.00). The conclusion: The change in the price of A, while inducing substitution of A for other commodities, also changes other things that may affect the decisions you make.

Presumably, you would treat this change in real income like any other change in income and allocate it across *all* of the commodities you consume, consistent with whether they are normal or inferior. If A is a normal commodity, this **income effect** will push in the same direction as the **substitution effect** of the relative price change. Both effects mean that the lower price motivates an increase in the quantity of A demanded—the lower relative price for apples will induce you to substitute apples for other things and your higher real income will also induce you to purchase more apples.

On the other hand, if A is an inferior commodity, this income effect will push in the opposite direction from the substitution effect. That is, if apples are an inferior commodity, you will want to purchase *more* of A because its relative price has declined but *less* of A because your real income is higher. In this case, the demand for A will be inversely related to the price of A *only if* the substitution effect is greater than the income effect that occurs when the relative price changes.[2]

To tell which of two possible outcomes will occur, we have to examine how individuals actually behave in market settings. That is, whether there is

an inverse relationship between market prices and the quantity demanded in a market is an *empirical* issue. There will be an inverse relationship between relative prices and the quantity demanded only if the income effect for inferior goods is small, relative to the substitution effect. This means that when we rely on the First Law of Demand, we assume, based on substantial evidence, that substitution dominates any other adjustments that individuals might make in response to relative price changes.

► Summary

Price and quantity demanded. When the price of a commodity or activity increases, less will be demanded because individuals will substitute other commodities or activities for the one whose price has increased; conversely, when the price of a commodity or activity decreases, more will be demanded because individuals will substitute this commodity or activity for other things that have become relatively more expensive. Thus, there is an inverse relationship between relative price and quantity demanded. This is known as the First Law of Demand.

Substitution. Central to the inverse relationship between relative price and quantity demanded is the ability to substitute. Identifying some goods as substitutes may be obvious: Pepsi is a substitute for Coke, and vice versa. Some substitutes may be not as obvious: time devoted to planning shopping trips when the price of gasoline increases is a substitute for higher-priced gasoline. Or, perhaps, even more subtle: if expenditures on a wide variety of commodities are cut back when the price of a good that is more necessary increases in price, it implies that individuals are substituting as well.

Two interpretations of demand. A demand schedule or demand curve can be interpreted in two ways. First, it represents the maximum quantity that demanders wish to purchase at each price. Second, it represents the maximum amount of money that individuals would be willing to pay for any additional amounts, given the current level of purchases.

Effects of changes other than price. Anything that changes the environment within which individuals make decisions will also affect market demand. These include changes in individual incomes,

---

[2] If the income effect is greater than the substitution effect, quantity demanded will be *positively* related to price. Goods for which this is true are called *Giffen goods*.

changes in the prices of other goods, changes in the number of persons desiring to purchase some commodity, changes in transaction costs, changes in expectations, and changes in tastes or preferences. These changes will increase or decrease demand, shifting the demand curve either to the right or the left. Table 4 summarizes the possibilities.

Substitution and income effects of a price change. A change in the relative price also changes the real income of consumers. For normal commodities,

the substitution effect of a price change and the income effect of the real income change reinforce each other, leading to an inverse relationship between price and quantity demanded. For inferior commodities, however, the substitution effect and the income effect go in opposite directions. Thus, there will be an inverse relationship between price and quantity demanded for inferior goods only if the substitution effect is more important than the income effect. Empirical evidence suggests that this is so.

Table 4
Effects on Demand

Change	Effect on demand	Direction of shift in D	Type of commodity
Increase in income	Increase	Rightward	Normal
Decrease in income	Decrease	Leftward	Normal
Increase in income	Decrease	Leftward	Inferior
Decrease in income	Increase	Rightward	Inferior
Increase in price of another good	Increase	Rightward	Substitute
Decrease in price of another good	Decrease	Leftward	Substitute
Increase in price of another good	Decrease	Leftward	Complement
Decrease in price of another good	Increase	Rightward	Complement
Expectation of an increase in price in the future	Increase	Rightward	
Expectation of an decrease in price in the future	Decrease	Leftward	
Increase in transaction costs	Decrease	Leftward	
Decrease in transaction costs	Increase	Rightward	
Increase in fashionability	Increase	Rightward	
Decrease in fashionability	Decrease	Leftward	

Chapter 7 ▶ ▶

Substitution and Elasticity

The essence of demand is substitution. Because we substitute, behavior is predictable: an increase in price will reduce the quantity demanded; a decrease in price increases the quantity demanded. It is often important to know not just that demanders substitute, however, but whether they substitute "a lot" or "a little" when the market price changes. Put somewhat differently, will the quantity that demanders wish to purchase fall by a small amount or a large amount when the market price increases by a small amount? Business decisions and public policies turn on the answer to this question. For example, in the early 1980's, the New York City Opera cut ticket prices by 20 percent in an effort to attract more patrons and eliminate losses. At almost the same time, the New York City Transit Authority raised subway fares in an effort to reduce its growing deficit. These very different responses to deficit problems aren't necessarily contradictory. As we will see, in some circumstances revenues will increase with an increase in price, while in others, revenues will fall. However, as we will also see, a government policy that simultaneously tries to increase government tax revenues and substantially discourage smoking by increasing the tax on cigarettes is contradictory. To understand the reasons why, we need to explore measures of the *responsiveness* of demand to price changes.

▶ Responsiveness to Price Changes

Consider the two markets illustrated in Figure 1. Since demand curves aren't actually seen, at the initial equilibrium the two markets will look identical to the participants. In particular, the initial equilibrium price is the same in each market, say, $1.00. In each market, the size of the increase in supply is also assumed to be the same. After the supply shift, however, the markets look quite different. If the market demand looks like that in Figure 1(a), the relative price adjustment is larger and the quantity adjustment is smaller than if the market demand looks like the one illustrated in Figure 1(a). Why? Because the quantity demanded in part (b) is *less* responsive to a price change than is the quantity demanded in part (a). As a consequence, the market price has to decline much further in part (b) to coax out an increase in quantity demanded sufficient to bring the market into equilibrium after the supply shift. Thus, *how much* the market price has to change to bring the market to a new equilibrium when supply changes will depend upon *how responsive* the quantity demanded is to a price change.

An Aside. If you tugged a little on a rubber band and it stretched a lot, you might think of the rubber band as being very elastic. Conversely, if the same tug on a different rubber band didn't stretch it much, you might think of this rubber band as being *in*elastic.

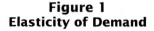

Figure 1
Elasticity of Demand

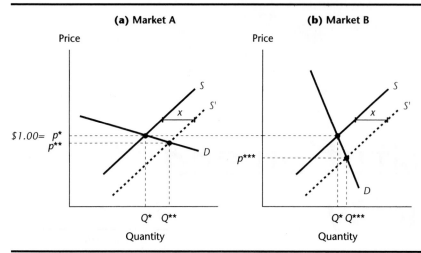

Demand at point p^* is more responsive to a change in price in market A than in market B. As a consequence, an increase in supply results in a larger change in the amount sold in the first market (from Q^* to Q^{**}) than in the second (from Q^* to Q^{***}), even though the shift in supply is the same in both markets (distance x). Thus demand at p^* in market A is more elastic than it is in market B. Note that this comparison must be made from the same initial p and Q because the elasticity cannot be determined from the slope of the demand curve.

Back to economics. Economists have adopted this language: If the quantity demanded is sensitive to small changes in relative prices, demand is said to be **elastic** or, more precisely, **price elastic.** If, on the other hand, the quantity demanded is relatively insensitive to small changes in relative prices, we will speak of demand as being **inelastic** or **price inelastic.**

The demand curve in Figure 1(b) is price inelastic—the quantity demanded does not change much with changes in the market price. If the demand for subway rides looked like this, an increase in fares would increase revenues for the transit authority. If, however, the demand for cigarettes looked like this, a tax-induced increase in price wouldn't reduce smoking by much. By contrast, the demand curve in Figure 1(a) is price elastic at the original fare of $1.00, and a small change in the relative price induces very large changes in the quantity demanded. If the demand for subway rides looked like this, an increase in fares would most likely lead to a larger, not smaller, deficit.[1] If the demand for cigarettes looked like this, however, the government could more successfully deter smoking by pushing the price of cigarettes up.

These differences in the responsiveness of demand to a change in the market price are extraordinarily important. For example, if the demand for

agricultural products is like the demand illustrated in Figure 1(b), then a larger-than-normal harvest will substantially affect the market price, but if the demand is like Figure 1(a), a larger-than-normal harvest will not affect the price by much. Thus, whether demand for agricultural products is relatively responsive to price or relatively unresponsive to price will make a substantial difference to farmers. Why? If the supply increases but the market price does not decrease much, farmers' incomes will increase. If, however, the supply increases but the market price decreases substantially, farmers' incomes may actually fall even though the harvest is abundant.

▶ Price Elasticity of Demand

Formally, the **price elasticity of demand,** e_d, is defined as

$$e_d = \frac{\text{percentage change in quantity demanded}}{\text{percentage change in price}} \quad (1)$$

The price elasticity is also called **own-price elasticity of demand** or, more commonly, the **elasticity of demand** because the percentage changes in price and quantity in Equation (1) both refer to the *same* good.

If the numerator in Equation (1) is *large* relative to the denominator, then the quantity demanded is responsive to small changes in relative prices and the elasticity of demand will be greater than 1.0. (We are using the absolute value here.) If, on the other

---

[1] A linear demand curve is not solely elastic or inelastic. Instead, the elasticity of demand will vary along the demand curve. At the initial fare of $1.00, the demand curve in Figure 1(a) is certainly more elastic than the demand curve in Figure 1(b). Whether demand is actually elastic at $1.00 will depend upon the change in quantity relative to the initial quantity demanded.

Table 1
Possible Effects of Price on Quantity Demanded

Initial price	Price after change	Change in price	Initial quantity	Quantity after price change	Percentage change in quantity
$10	$11	10%	100	98	− 2%
10	11	10	100	75	−25

hand, the numerator in Equation (1) is *small* relative to the denominator, then the quantity demanded does not change much in response to small relative price changes and the elasticity of demand will be less than 1.0. An elasticity of demand of −2 means that a 1 percent decline in price will increase the quantity that demanders desire to purchase by 2 percent, or that a 1 percent increase in price will decrease the quantity demanded by 2 percent. Or, an elasticity of demand of −0.5 means that a 1 percent change in price will lead to a 0.5 percent change in quantity demanded.

Demand is **elastic** if the absolute value of the measured elasticity is greater than 1. Demand is **inelastic** if the absolute value of the measured elasticity is less than 1. If the percentage change in quantity demanded is the same as the percentage change in price, the absolute value of the ratio in Equation (1) is equal to 1.0 and is **unitary elastic.** Consider, for example, Table 1. Demand would be inelastic in the first case ($|{-}2\%/10\%| < 1$) and elastic in the second case ($|{-}25\%/10\%| > 1$).

Table 2 provides some estimates of actual price elasticities of demand for a number of commonly purchased goods. For example, the quantity of butter demanded is very responsive to price—the measured elasticity is 1.40. This means that a 10 percent increase in the price of butter decreases the

Table 2
Some Estimates of Elasticities of Demand*

Commodity	Absolute value of elasticity	Commodity	Absolute value of elasticity	Commodity	Absolute value of elasticity
Cottonseed oil	6.92	Alcohol	0.92	Auto repair	0.36
Tomatoes	4.60	Beef	0.92	Medical insurance	0.31
Green peas	2.80	Telephone service	0.89	Margarine	0.30
Legal gambling	1.91	Sports equipment	0.88	Potatoes	0.30
Lamb	1.90	Movies	0.87	Sugar	0.30
Restaurant meals	1.63	Flowers	0.82	Coffee	0.25
Marijuana	1.51	Citrus fruit	0.80	Eggs	0.23
Peaches	1.50	Bus travel	0.77	Spectator sports	0.21
Butter	1.40	Air travel	0.70	Water	0.20
Automobiles	1.35	Shoes	0.70	Theater, opera	0.18
China and crystal	1.34	Household appliances	0.67	Natural gas (residential)	0.15
Apples	1.30	Legal services	0.61	Gasoline and oil	0.15
Charitable giving	1.29	Clothing	0.60	Milk	0.15
Taxi services	1.24	Physicians' services	0.58	Electricity (residential)	0.13
Cable TV	1.20	Train travel	0.54	Newspapers, magazines	0.10
Chicken	1.20	Jewelry, watches	0.54	Mail	0.05
Radios, TV sets	1.19	Cigarettes	0.51		
Beer	1.13	Radio, TV repair	0.47		
Furniture	1.01	Toilet articles	0.44		
Housing	1.00	Cabbage	0.40		

*The estimates in Tables 2, 3, 4, and 5 are drawn from a large number of empirical studies on market demand.

quantity demanded by about 14.0 percent. This relationship can be calculated in the following way.

$$-1.40 = \frac{\text{percentage change in quantity}}{\text{percentage change in price}}$$

Therefore,

$$1.40 \times \text{percentage change in price} = -\text{percentage change in quantity}$$

and

$$1.40 \times 10\% = -14.0\%$$

A price elasticity of this size means that small changes in the price of butter will lead to relatively large changes in the quantity demanded. The demand for butter must look more like Figure 1(a) than 1(b).

On the other hand, for some commodities a small change in the price produces an even smaller change in the quantity demanded. It should be no surprise that the elasticity of demand for water is quite low (0.20), as is the elasticity of demand for electricity (0.13) and medical insurance (0.31). For each of these commodities, the quantity demanded is not very responsive to a change in the price of the commodity. That is, when the price changes, individuals simply do not change the quantity of water or electricity demanded by very much; the demand for water or elasticity must look more like Figure 1(b) than 1(a).

Because there is an inverse relationship between relative price and quantity demanded along a demand curve, either the numerator or denominator in Equation (1) will be negative. Thus, a price elasticity will have a negative sign, although often the absolute value of e_d is reported and the elasticity of demand is quoted as a positive number.

Elasticity of Demand and Market Adjustment

The elasticity of demand is important because it determines how much variation in price is necessary to bring about adjustment in a particular market when supply changes. For example, in the early 1970s a group of oil-producing countries (OPEC) agreed to reduce the quantity of oil supplied to the world oil market. The demand for gasoline is quite inelastic over short periods of time: it has been esti-

mated to be about −0.2. As a consequence, for every 10 percent decrease in the amount of gasoline supplied to the market, the market price will increase by 50 percent. This change in market price can be calculated in the following way:

$$\text{Elasticity} = \frac{\text{percentage change in quantity}}{\text{percentage change in price}}$$
$$= -0.2 \left(\text{as estimated statistically}\right)$$

Given this estimated elasticity, if the quantity decreases by 10 percent, then

$$\text{percentage change in price} = (-0.10)/(-0.2)$$
$$= 0.50$$

or a 50 percent increase in price.

Since demand for gasoline is quite inelastic, only a large change in price would cause the quantity demanded to fall by enough to bring the market for gasoline into equilibrium with the decrease in supply. As a consequence, a modest change in the quantity of oil OPEC supplied to the world market caused a very large increase in the equilibrium price of crude oil and its derivatives such as gasoline and heating oil. By contrast, if the elasticity of demand for gasoline had been high, then the effort by OPEC to restrict the amount of oil supplied to the world market would not have changed the price of gasoline by very much.

Estimating the Elasticity of Demand

Since the elasticity of demand measures how demanders actually behave, Equation (1) must be estimated using data from actual markets. There are different estimates of (1) that depend upon what kind of information is available:

1. arc elasticity estimate: requires information on two price-quantity combinations

2. point elasticity estimate: requires information on one price-quantity combination and the slope of the demand curve

3. total expenditure estimate: requires information on changes in total expenditures and the direction of a price change

4. degree of substitution estimate: requires information on the range of substitutes

Arc elasticity estimate. The elasticity of demand can be approximated with observations on at least two price-quantity combinations along a demand curve. If at p_1, demanders desire to purchase q_1, and at p_2, they desire to purchase q_2, then the elasticity can be approximated with the following calculations:

$$\text{percentage change in quantity} = \frac{(q_2 - q_1)}{(q_2 + q_1)/2} \quad (2)$$

$$\text{percentage change in price} = \frac{(p_2 - p_1)}{(p_2 + p_1)/2} \quad (3)$$

therefore,

$$\text{arc elasticity} = \frac{(q_2 - q_1)/(q_2 + q_1)/2}{(p_2 - p_1)/(p_2 + p_1)/2} \quad (4)$$

This undoubtedly looks very messy and difficult to remember. If you'll think about the concept that we are trying to measure, it makes sense: we want an estimate of the *percentage change in quantity* and the *percentage change in price*. The numerator in (2) and (3) is the change in quantity and price, respectively. To create a percentage, we need to measure these changes relative to starting point. We could measure it from the initial price and quantity (that is, from p_1, q_1) or from the final price and quantity (p_2, q_2). Or, we could measure it from some point between (p_1, q_1) and (p_2, q_2).[2] To avoid the ambiguity, we just need to be consistent. By general agreement, economists measure the percentage from the point halfway between (p_1, q_1) and (p_2, q_2), that is, at ($p_2 + p_1$)/2 and ($q_2 + q_1$)/2. Hence, you can think of Equation (4) as measuring the percentage changes in price and quantity from the *average* price and *average* quantity, respectively.

If at a price of $40, the demand for purple sneakers is 35,000 pairs and at a price of $50 people want to purchase only 25,000 pairs, for example, the estimated elasticity of demand can be calculated as follows:

$$\%\Delta \text{ in quantity} = \frac{25,000 - 35,000}{30,000} = -0.33$$

$$\%\Delta \text{ in price} = \frac{50 - 40}{45} = 0.22$$

and

$$\text{arc elasticity} = \frac{-0.33}{0.22} = -1.50$$

The absolute value is 1.50 and demand is elastic between these two price-quantity combinations.

Point elasticity estimate. We can derive the formula for the second method of estimating elasticity by noting that for small changes in p and q, the

$$\text{percentage change in q} = (\Delta q)/q$$

and,

$$\text{percentage change in p} = (\Delta p)/p$$

Since the elasticity of demand is the percentage change in quantity divided by the percentage in price,

$$e_d = \frac{(\Delta q)/q}{(\Delta p)/p}$$

Rearranging, we have

$$e_d = \Delta q/\Delta p \times p/q.$$

$\Delta p/\Delta q$ is the slope of the demand curve at (p, q). Therefore,

$$e_d = p/q \times 1/\text{slope}$$

Using this formula, the **point elasticity** can be estimated if we know the slope of the demand curve and any point (that is, any p, q combination) along it. Each of the elasticities in Table 2 is calculated in this way using statistical techniques to estimate the slope of the different demand curves and then estimating elasticity at the market equilibrium price.

While it may not be obvious, if you look at the point elasticity of demand formula for a moment, it should be clear that *elasticity is not the slope of the demand curve, although it is related to the slope.* Thus, in Figure 2, D_1 is more elastic than D_2 but it

---

[2] If you are asked to measure the percentage change between, for example, 100 and 200, the change is 200−100 = 100, which is a 100% change if you measure from 100, and a 50% change if you measure from 200. Or, it's a 75% change if measured from the mid-point between 100 and 200. Percentage changes *always* have this ambiguity.

Figure 2
Elasticity Versus Slope

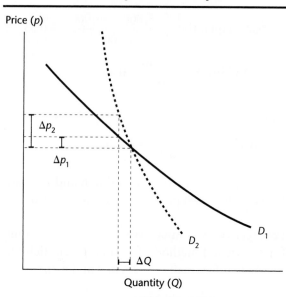

Curve D_1 is more elastic than D_2 at the intersection of D_1 and D_2. It is not possible to know whether D_1 or D_2 are elastic or inelastic, however, because elasticity is not equivalent to slope.

Figure 3
Comparing Elasticities

(a) Both D_1 and D_2 Are Inelastic

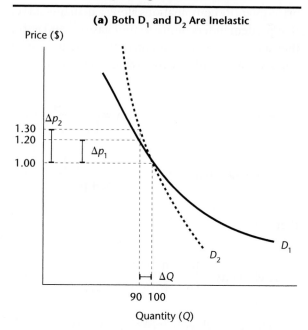

(b) D_1 Is Elastic, But D_2 Is Inelastic

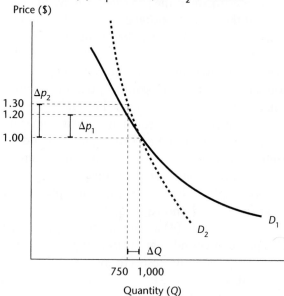

In both parts (a) and (b), D_1 is more elastic than D_2 at p=1.00. (a) Both demand curves are inelastic. The change in quantity demanded is about 10 percent, with a change in price along D_1 of about 20 percent and along D_2 of about 30 percent. (b) By contrast, D_1 is elastic, but D_2 is inelastic. The change in quantity demanded is about 25 percent, but the change in price along D_1 is about 20 percent while along D_2 it's about 30 percent.

is not possible to say that D_1 is actually elastic and D_2 inelastic at Q. To see why, compare part (a) in Figure 3 with part (b).[3]

Total Expenditures Estimate. If we ignore sales taxes, the dollar amount that households spend in a market for a particular commodity is equal to the total revenues suppliers receive. That is, total expenditure and hence, total revenue will be equal to the amount sold multiplied by the market price or,

$$TE = TR = p \times Q$$

---

[3] The elasticity of demand varies along a linear demand curve. This can be understood by considering the point elasticity formula just developed. Along a linear demand curve, slope is constant. Therefore, (1/slope) is constant. However, along a linear demand curve, p/Q will vary as illustrated for three points along the linear demand curve Q = 1000−200p:

p ($)	Q	p/Q
1.00	800	1/800
2.00	600	2/600
3.00	400	3/400

Since 1/slope is −200, the demand curve has elasticity of −0.25 at a price of $1.00, −0.67 at a price of $2.00, and −1.5 at a price of $3.00. Thus, a linear demand curve is elastic at one end and inelastic at the other—at a higher price more substitution occurs.

Total expenditure (or total revenue) can be illustrated on a graph of demand and supply since the price (p) is along one axis and the quantity (Q) is along the other. It's the shaded area in Figure 4. Along a demand curve, price and quantity move in opposite directions. As a consequence, total expenditure can either increase or decrease when the market price increases. That is,

$$\uparrow p \times \downarrow Q \rightarrow \uparrow \text{ or } \downarrow \text{ in total expenditure}$$

$$\text{or} \downarrow p \times \uparrow Q \rightarrow \uparrow \text{ or } \downarrow \text{ in total expenditure}$$

Is there a way to tell what will actually happen to total expenditure or total revenue? The answer to this question is closely related to the price elasticity of demand. If demand is elastic, then the percentage change in quantity is larger than the percentage change in price. That is,

$$\text{If } e_d > 1, \text{ then } \% \Delta Q > \% \Delta p$$

This means that a small decrease in the price will lead to an increase in total expenditures by demanders and hence to an increase in total revenues for suppliers (Q increases more than p falls). Or, con-

versely, a small increase in the price will lead to a decrease in total expenditures or total revenues (Q falls more than p increases). Therefore, if demand is elastic, total expenditures or revenues will move in a direction *opposite* to the price change. This relationship is illustrated in Figure 5. The effect on total revenue can be seen by comparing the two shaded areas. Area A represents the increase in revenue resulting from the increase in the amount sold. Area B represents the decrease in revenue because of the decrease in price. Because A is greater than B, revenues have increased.

If demand is inelastic then the percentage change in quantity is smaller than the percentage change in price. That is,

$$\text{If } e_d < 1, \text{ then } \% \Delta Q < \% \Delta p$$

In this case, a small decrease in the price will lead to a decrease in total expenditures by demanders and hence to an decrease in total revenues for suppliers (Q increases less than p falls). Or, conversely, a small increase in the price will lead to an increase in total

Figure 4
Total Expenditures

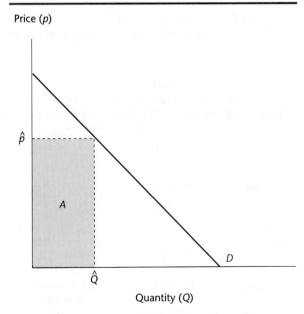

If the market price is $\hat{p}$ and the amount purchased at this price is $\hat{Q}$, then total expenditures equal area A.

Figure 5
The Effect of a Decrease in Price on Total Expenditures

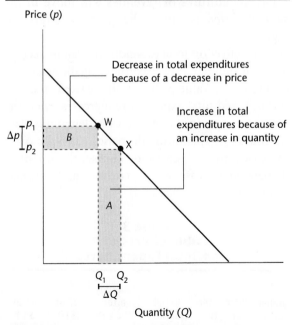

When demand is elastic, a decrease in price leads to an increase in total expenditures because the decrease in price is offset by an increase in quantity sold.

Figure 6
The Effect of a Decrease in Price on Total Expenditures

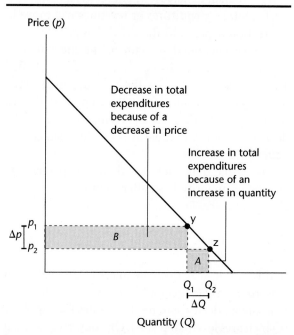

When demand is inelastic, a decrease in price also leads to a decrease in total expenditures.

expenditures or total revenues (Q falls less than p increases). Therefore, if demand is inelastic, total expenditures or revenues will move *in the same direction* as a price change, as illustrated in Figure 6.

The effect on total expenditures can be seen in a slightly different way by considering the extension of Table 1 in Table 3. In the first case demand is inelastic and total expenditure increases when the price increases. In the second case, demand is elastic and total expenditure decreases when the price increases. In both cases, of course, the quantity demanded decreases as the price increases (because of the First Law of Demand).

Table 3
Possible Effects of Price on Total Expenditures

Initial price	Price after change	Initial quantity	Quantity after change	TE at $10	TE at $11
$10	$11	100	98	$1,000	$1,078
10	11	100	75	1,000	825

Why does total expenditure sometimes fall when the price increases and at other times increase when the price increases? When demand is elastic, there are good substitutes available. After all, the own-price elasticity is a measure of substitution. If there are good substitutes, then when the price increases, the quantity demanded will fall by a large amount because demanders will readily substitute. Thus, total expenditure will decrease. By contrast, when demand is inelastic, there aren't particularly good substitutes available. When there are few substitutes and the price increases, the quantity demanded will fall only a little because demanders cannot easily minimize the effect of the price increase by moving to other goods. It follows that total expenditure will increase as a consequence.

This relationship between price elasticity of demand and total expenditures or total revenues implies, of course, that if you cannot estimate the elasticity using either the arc or point-slope approaches but observe that when the price falls, total expenditures increase, you know that the elasticity has to be greater than 1.0. And if when the price falls, total expenditures decrease, the elasticity has to be less than 1.0. This approach does not give a numerical estimate of the elasticity, but does tell us whether demand is elastic or inelastic. Table 4 summarizes this point.

Changes in Elasticity of Demand Along a Demand Curve. Because elasticity is not the same as slope, the elasticity of demand may very well be different

Table 4
Relationship Between Total Expenditures and Elasticity of Demand

Change in p	Change in TE or TR	Implied Value of e_d
Decrease	Increase	> 1.0
Increase	Increase	< 1.0
Increase	No change	= 1.0

Value of e_d	Change in p	Effect on TE or TR
> 1.0	Decrease	Increase
	Increase	Decrease
< 1.0	Decrease	Decrease
	Increase	Increase
= 1.0	Increase or decrease	No change

at different points along a demand curve. This can be seen by examining the relationship between elasticity of demand and total expenditure. In Figure 4, total expenditure is the area of the rectangle A (total expenditure is $p \times Q$, remember). Now compare Figure 5 with Figure 6. In both diagrams, the demand curve is the same and the size of the price change is the same. In Figure 5 the decline in price leads to an overall increase in total expenditures, however, whereas in Figure 6 the decline in price leads to an overall decrease in total expenditures. Hence, demand must be elastic between points w and x in Figure 5 and inelastic between points y and z in Figure 6. (This confirms that a linear demand curve is generally elastic at the top, inelastic at the bottom, and unitary elastic at the midpoint.)

Two exceptions to this observation are illustrated in Figures 7 and 8. The demand curve in Figure 7 is said to be perfectly inelastic; the demand curve in Figure 8 is said to be perfectly elastic. Perfectly inelastic demand means that no matter how high the price goes, demanders will still want to purchase the same quantity. Perfectly elastic demand implies that if the relative price increases at all, demanders will stop buying the product altogether.

Figure 9 illustrates a demand curve that has an elasticity of 1.0 at every point. In this case, firms

Figure 8
Perfectly Elastic Demand

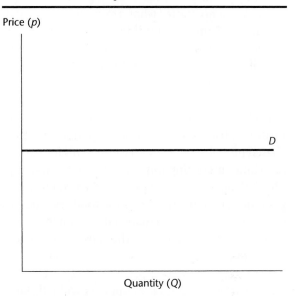

Demand is perfectly elastic if consumers are willing to buy any amount of a good at the market price, but will buy nothing if the price increases.

Figure 9
A Unitary Elastic Demand Curve

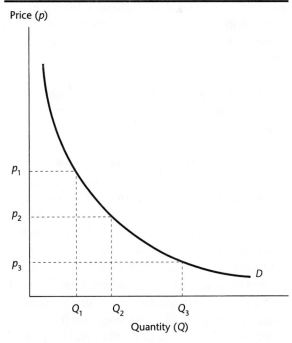

Along a unitary elastic demand curve, every point has an elasticity of demand equal to 1. This means that the total revenue that a firm receives will be the same, no matter what quantity of output it sells.

Figure 7
Perfectly Inelastic Demand

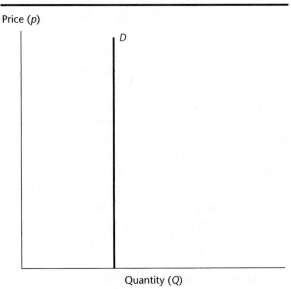

Demand is perfectly inelastic if the quantity demanded does not change at all when the price changes.

will earn the same amount in total revenue no matter what quantity they sell (that is, p × Q will always be the same no matter what p you pick). Note that the demand curve is not linear; instead it is a *rectangular hyperbola*, so named because a rectangle inscribed anywhere below the curve will always have the same area.

The demand for insulin probably looks more like Figure 7 than Figure 8. Even if the price of insulin substantially increases, the quantity purchased probably changes very little. This inelasticity has some interesting implications for insulin suppliers. If supply falls, the price is likely to increase a good deal, thereby increasing the total revenues for suppliers. However, a demand curve with this shape is a two-edged sword. If the supply of insulin increases (because, for example, new suppliers enter the market), the market price will decrease "a lot" and the total revenues for suppliers will fall. More generally, if the demand for medical care is inelastic, an increase in the supply of doctors or medication lowers the total expenditures on medical care, resulting in lower total revenues for doctors and pharmaceutical firms.

The demand for many farm products is also price inelastic. This means that crop fluctuations generally lead to large price changes. When there is a crop failure, prices increase substantially, but a bumper crop leads to a substantial decrease in the price. As a consequence of this low elasticity of demand, the market produces the unusual result that total farm revenues tend to increase when there is a poor harvest. When there is a good harvest, however, total farm revenues decline.

Degree of substitution "estimate." As noted earlier, substitution is the essence of demand and a demand curve is a "picture" of substitution. The elasticity of demand is a way of measuring whether substitution is easy or difficult. If Coca-Cola and Pepsi are close substitutes, that is, if it's easy for consumers to substitute one for the other, then a small increase in the price of Coke will lead to a large change in the quantity of Pepsi purchased. Other soft drinks may also be good substitutes. Thus, some of your friends may switch to 7-Up or Sprite or Dr. Pepper. The quantity of Coke demanded would, as a consequence, have a high price elasticity of demand. On the other hand, if Pepsi and other soft drinks are poor substitutes for Coke, then a small increase in the price of Coke

is unlikely to change the quantity of Coke demanded by much and Coke will have a lower price elasticity. *Thus, measuring the elasticity of demand is a way of measuring how substitutable one good is for other goods that individuals consume.*

Making educated guesses about the size of the elasticity of demand. While precise measures of elasticities are useful, because the price elasticity of demand measures substitutability, it's possible to make educated guesses as to whether the measured elasticity is likely to be relatively large or small by thinking about the available substitutes. For example, there are clearly few good or easy substitutes for an operation to remove an appendix that is about to rupture. So we could expect the elasticity of demand for appendectomies to be quite low, or inelastic. Coca-Cola, however, would appear to have many substitutes, so we would expect the demand for Coca-Cola to be quite elastic.

The demand for Coca-Cola would also probably be far more elastic than the demand for soft drinks in general. Why? There are several close substitutes for Coke—Pepsi, 7-Up, Dr. Pepper. As a consequence, if the price of Coke increases very much, we could expect many Coke drinkers to switch to one of these other soft drinks. But if the prices of *all* soft drinks increase, other drinks like hot chocolate or orange juice aren't likely to substitute as well for soft drinks as one soft drink substitutes for another soft drink. Thus, we would expect the demand for soft drinks in general to be *less* elastic than the demand for just Coke.

Similarly, the elasticity of demand for a particular brand of salt is likely to be considerably greater than the elasticity of demand for salt itself. Why? All other brands of salt are almost certainly very good substitutes for any particular brand of salt, but MSG or pepper or paprika are not very good substitutes for salt. Indeed, in this case, one might expect the demand for salt in general to be inelastic (few good substitutes), but the demand for a particular brand of salt to be quite elastic (lots of other brands). As a general rule, then, *the more narrowly defined the product, the more elastic the demand.*

Budget shares and price elasticity of demand. Ease of substitution is determined by a number of things. In part, it is a matter of preferences. If no one can tell the difference between Coke and Pepsi or between

Bumblebee and Carnation tuna, then substitution should be easy and the measured elasticity will be large.

Setting this effect aside for a moment, a second factor affecting the price elasticity of demand is the amount of a person's income typically spent on the commodity. If a large percentage of each person's budget is spent on a particular commodity, it is likely that the person will be more price conscious and hence more sensitive to small price changes—a *small* percentage change in the price of a commodity on which a *large* percentage of everyone's income is spent is likely to be more important than a very large percentage change in the price of a commodity that takes only a small fraction of each person's income. This suggests that demand will be more elastic if the fraction of demanders' budgets devoted to the commodity is larger. For example, demanders are likely to be far more sensitive to changes in the prices of automobiles than they are to the price of nutmeg and, consequently, the elasticity of demand for automobiles is probably greater than the elasticity of the demand for nutmeg. That is, a 50 percent increase in the price of nutmeg will not affect the quantity of nutmeg demanded as much as a 50 percent increase in the price of automobiles will affect the quantity of automobiles demanded because the nutmeg price increase will have a trivial effect on household budgets whereas the automobile price increase will have a very substantial effect on those same budgets.

▶ The Second Law of Demand

For the most part, the notion of choice only makes sense if different commodities can replace each other in the decisions made by individuals and firms. Making choices may be difficult, however, because alternatives are not perfectly interchangeable, it's often costly to substitute, and substitution requires information not always immediately available to the decision maker.

Obtaining information and then making adjustments and changes is not easy, but it is likely to be easier if you have longer to gather the information and make the adjustments and changes. Imagine, for example, your immediate response to a doubling of your rent, tuition, or the price of gasoline. Will this immediate response differ from your response

after several months? After one year? After several years?

Generally, the answers to the latter three questions are "yes," "yes," and "yes." That is, in general, individuals are able to make *more and larger adjustments* to price changes the *longer* they have to adjust. This observation leads to what is sometimes called the **Second Law of Demand**, which states that *the price elasticity of demand will increase with time.* That is, over longer and longer periods of time, more things become substitutes and more substitution occurs in response to a relative price change. Table 5 provides some estimates of short-term and long-term price elasticities of demand. These estimates are derived from actual market data, that is, from the choices that individuals actually make.

Notice that in every case the long-term elasticity is greater than the short-term elasticity. For example, the short-term elasticity of demand for water is 0.20 while the long-term elasticity of demand is 0.44. Both short- and long-term demands are inelastic, but the long-term elasticity is twice as large as that for the short term. In contrast, the short-term demands for owner-occupied housing, foreign travel, and electricity are all inelastic, while

Table 5
Long- and Short-Term Price Elasticities of Demand

Good	Short-term elasticity	Long-term elasticity
Tobacco products	0.46	1.89
Jewelry	0.41	0.67
Toilet articles	0.20	3.04
Owner-occupied housing	0.04	1.22
China and glassware	1.55	2.55
Electricity	0.13	1.89
Water	0.20	0.44
Medical care and hospitalization	0.31	0.92
Tires	0.86	1.19
Auto repairs	0.40	1.38
Durable recreation equipment	0.88	2.39
Motion pictures	0.88	3.69
Foreign travel	0.14	1.77
Gasoline	0.15	0.78

the long-term demands are elastic. There are, apparently, not many immediate substitutes for these goods, but there are lots of substitutes when individuals are given time to find them and to make the necessary adjustments.

The energy problems of the past 20 years are an important illustration of the difference between the ability to substitute in the short term versus the ability to substitute in the long term. The United States is dependent upon imported oil as a source of energy. Substantial short-term price changes, such as those experienced during the early and mid-1970's, are unlikely to affect the quantity demanded by very much because the short-term costs of substituting other things for oil are quite large. In fact, the short-term price elasticity for gasoline is less than 0.2. But in response to the higher relative prices, people began driving less and using less electricity. Because the relative price remained high over time, people found more and more substitutes and changed their habits so that demand slowly became much more sensitive to the price. We moved, not instantaneously, but dramatically just the same, toward lighter cars with more fuel-efficient engines, *substituting* small size and better technology for gasoline and hence for crude oil. We also began to build homes with better insulation, *substituting* insulation for oil. We changed the way that electrical generating plants burned fuel, *substituting* coal for oil. None of these efforts occurred the moment the price of oil increased, but they did occur over the months and years following the price increase. Consequently, the long-term elasticity is more than four times the short-term elasticity. (Compare 0.78, gasoline's long-term elasticity of demand, with 0.15, its short-term elasticity of demand.)

The effect of this kind of change is illustrated in Figures 10 and 11. Because demand was inelastic in the short term, the OPEC reduction in supply moved the market equilibrium from E to E′ in Figure 10, with prices increasing dramatically and quantity demanded falling, but not by very much. Further adjustments occurred over time as consumers continued to find substitutes, however, and the market equilibrium moved to E″. The market price fell from its short-term level even as the quantity of OPEC oil purchased continued to decline. The nature of this adjustment can be seen in Figure 11—price increased initially and then decreased with time.

Figure 10
The Long-Run Elasticity of Demand

Demand is more elastic in the long run than in the short run because, in the long run, individuals have more time to find substitutes after a price increase. This can be represented by the rotation of D to D′ at point E. Thus, if there is a decrease in supply (from S to S′), the short-run effect on price is larger than the long-run effect is.

Figure 11
Market Adjustments Over Time After a Decrease in Supply

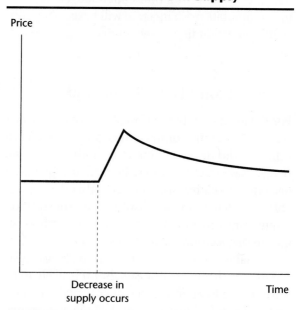

Because the elasticity of demand increases with time, a decrease in supply causes a larger increase in price immediately than it will over a longer period of time.

Over the past few years those countries producing oil have become acutely aware of this increasing ability of oil-consumers to substitute. This substitution means that the ability of oil producers to continually increase the price of oil is limited. As a consequence, for example, the price of crude oil peaked in dollar terms in 1979 and has decreased since that time. The price adjusted for inflation has decreased even more dramatically.

▶ Other Demand Elasticities

The discussion in Chapter 6 outlined several things that affect demand in addition to the market price, including income and the price of other commodities. It is possible to use the general idea of elasticity to actually measure the responsiveness of demand to these things as well.

Elasticity in General

In general, elasticity can be thought of as a measure of the responsiveness of the quantity demanded to changes in *anything* that might affect demand. Formally, a general elasticity (e) would be measured by

$$e = \frac{\text{percentage change in quantity demanded}}{\text{percentage change in } anything \text{ that affects quantity demanded}}$$

Income Elasticity of Demand

A measure corresponding to our earlier discussion of the effect of income changes on demand is the **income elasticity of demand** (e_i),

$$e_i = \frac{\text{percentage change in quantity demanded}}{\text{percentage change in income}}$$

For a normal commodity, this measure will be *positive*, indicating that as income increases, demand increases, *ceteris paribus*. That is, the demand curve shifts to the right as individual incomes increase. If this increase in demand is less than the percentage increase in income, the estimated elasticity will be less than 1.0, and the commodity will be normal, but income inelastic. Commodities with positive income elasticities less than 1.0 require a decreasing percentage of an individual's income as income increases. Food is an example.

If the income elasticity is positive and greater than 1.0, the commodity will be normal and income

elastic. As individual incomes increase, the percentage of income devoted to this commodity also increases. Commodities of this sort are sometimes referred to as *luxuries*. Foreign travel and expensive, high-end cars are examples.

Inferior commodities have a *negative* measured income elasticity of demand—as income increases, demand decreases, *ceteris paribus*. That is, the demand curve shifts to the left as individual incomes increase.

Income elasticity of demand	Commodity description
$e_i > 1$	The commodity is a normal good and a luxury item.
$0 < e_i < 1$	The commodity is a normal good.
$e_i < 0$	The commodity is an inferior good.

Table 6 provides estimates of income elasticities of demand from studies of various markets, while the above table summarizes our discussion of the income elasticity of demand. For example, because the income elasticity is –0.20, pig products are inferior goods; as income increases, the demand for pig products decreases. In fact, given this estimate of the income elasticity, when income increases by 10 percent, the demand for pig products, *ceteris paribus*, decreases by 2 percent. This can be calculated in the following way:

$$-0.20 = \frac{\text{percentage change in the demand for pig products}}{\text{percentage change in income}}$$

therefore

$-0.20 \times \text{percentage change in income}$
  $= \text{percentage change in the demand for pig products}$

and

$$-0.20 \times 10\% = -2\%$$

Cable television, however, is a normal commodity although the demand is income inelastic—the estimated income elasticity is .83. This means that a 10 percent increase in income will increase the demand for cable TV by about 8 percent. Furniture is a normal commodity that is income elastic; a 10 percent increase in income will increase demand by about 15 percent.

Table 6
Estimates of Income Elasticities of Demand in the United States

Good	Elasticity	Good	Elasticity
Automobiles	2.46	Charitable donations	0.70
Alcohol	1.54	Mail (letters)	0.65
Housing, owner-occupied	1.49	Tobacco	0.64
Furniture	1.48	Gasoline, oil	0.48
Books	1.48	Housing, rental	0.43
Dental services	1.42	Butter	0.42
Restaurant meals	1.40	Eggs	0.37
Shoes	1.10	Meat	0.35
Clothing	1.02	Electricity	0.20
Water	1.02	Coffee	0.00
Medical insurance	0.92	Margarine	−0.20
Cable TV	0.83	Starchy roots	−0.20
Telephone calls	0.83	Pig products	−0.20
Physicians' services	0.75	Flour	−0.36
Fruits and berries	0.70	Whole milk	−0.50

Since a change in income changes demand (that is, shifts the demand curve), the income elasticity measures the *size of the shift in the demand curve* when income changes by a small amount. This is illustrated in Figure 12. Notice that the shape of the demand curve has nothing to do with the income elasticity of demand: it could be flat or steep and still have the same income elasticity.

Earlier we noted that the demands for many farm products food were price inelastic. It turns out that demands for most farm products are also income inelastic. As a consequence, as incomes increase in an economy, the demand for agricultural products increases, but not by as much as the increase in income. As a consequence, over a long period of time, the relative size of the farm sector declines. We see this clearly in the history of the United States. More agricultural commodities are produced in the U.S. today than 100 years ago, but the fraction of the total output of the economy produced by the agricultural sector has declined dramatically. A century ago, more than 50 percent of the work force was employed in agriculture. By 1910, this number was reduced to about 35 percent. Today, less than 4 percent of the population is employed in the agricultural sector of the economy. These changes are related, in part, to the low income

Figure 12
The Income Elasticity of Demand

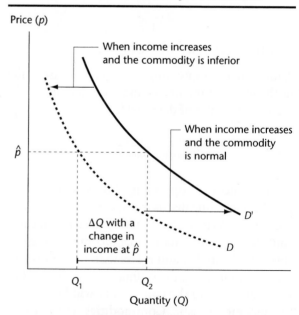

The income elasticity of demand measures the shift in demand that occurs when income changes by a small amount. The income elasticity of demand for a normal commodity is positive, and for an inferior commodity, it is negative. (ΔQ is that change in quantity demanded at the price indicated when income changes.)

elasticity, and also to massive technological advances that have increased the supply much more rapidly than population growth has increased demand.

Cross-Price Elasticity of Demand

The elasticity measure corresponding to our discussion of the effects of changes in the prices of other commodities in Chapter 6 is the **cross-price elasticity of demand** (e_x). It is defined as:

$$e_x = \frac{\text{percentage change in the quantity of A demanded}}{\text{percentage change in the price of B}}$$

If the cross-price elasticity between goods A and B is *positive*, A and B are *substitutes*. An increase in the price of one will lead to an increase in demand for the other. If the cross-price elasticity is *negative*, A and B are *complements*. An increase in the price of one will lead to a decrease in demand for the other. Substitutes and complements can be cross-price elastic or cross-price inelastic, depending upon whether the absolute value of the measured elasticity is greater than or less than one.

Table 7 provides some estimates of actual cross-price elasticities of demand. Notice, for example, that travel by train (Amtrak) and travel by air are substitutes—the cross-price elasticity is 0.60. This means that a 10 percent increase in the price of airline tickets increases the demand for train travel by about 6 percent. Train travel and bus travel are much better substitutes, however; a 10 percent increase in the price of bus tickets increases the demand for train travel by almost 13 percent.

Because the estimated cross-price elasticity for clothing and footwear is negative, they are complements. Apparently, when the price of shoes increases and the quantity demanded decreases, the demand for clothing also decreases, although not by much. The estimated cross-price elasticity is –0.01. Cheese and butter are complements as well. A 10 percent increase in the price of butter decreases the demand for cheese by 6 percent.

The cross-price elasticities in Table 7 are measures of changes in demand like those illustrated in Figure 13. Because a change in the price of either a complement or a substitute changes demand (i.e., shifts the market demand curve), the cross-price elasticity is a measure of the *size of the shift in the demand curve* when the price of one of these commodities changes by a small amount.

Table 7
Estimates of Cross-Price Elasticities of Demand in the United States

Good changing in quantity	Good changing in price	Cross-price elasticity
Florida interior oranges	Florida Indian River oranges	+1.56
Amtrak Railways	Bus travel	+1.29
Amtrak Railways	Air travel	+0.60
Margarine	Butter	+0.81
Butter	Margarine	+0.67
Natural gas	Fuel oil	+0.44
Beef	Pork	+0.28
Groceries	Dairy products	+0.28
Electricity	Natural gas	+0.20
Pork	Beef	+0.14
California oranges	Florida interior oranges	+0.14
Confectionery	Tobacco products	+0.12
Tobacco products	Drinks	+0.09
Confectionery	Drinks	+0.07
Dairy products	Fish	+0.05
Household articles	Other durables	+0.05
Clothing	Footwear	−0.01
Groceries	Meat products	−0.12
Dairy products	Meat and meat products	−0.15
Fruits	Sugar	−0.28
Cheese	Butter	−0.61

► Summary

Elasticity of demand. The elasticity of demand is defined as the percentage change in quantity demanded divided by the percentage change in price. If the percentage change in quantity demanded is small relative to the percentage change in price, this ratio will be less than one and demand is said to be inelastic. If the percentage change in quantity demanded is large relative to the percentage change in price, the ratio will be greater than one and demand is said to be elastic.

Substitution. The price elasticity of demand reflects the responsiveness of quantity demanded to a change

Figure 13
Cross-Price Elasticity of Demand

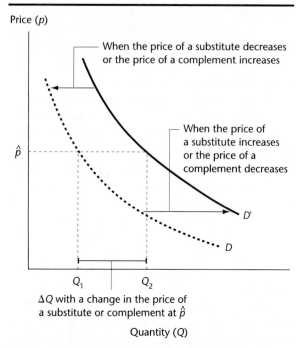

Price (p)

When the price of a substitute decreases or the price of a complement increases

When the price of a substitute increases or the price of a complement decreases

$\hat{p}$

D'

D

Q_1 Q_2

ΔQ with a change in the price of a substitute or complement at $\hat{p}$

Quantity (Q)

The cross-price elasticity of demand measures the shift in demand caused by a small change in the price of another good. The cross-price elasticity of demand for substitute goods is positive, and for complementary goods, it is negative. (ΔQ is the change in quantity demanded at the price indicated when the price of another good changes.)

in the market price. Or, in other words, it reflects the ease of substitution of other things for the commodity whose price has changed. A high elasticity of demand indicates that there are many substitutes for a particular commodity; a low elasticity of demand indicates that substitution is more difficult.

Elasticity of demand and total expenditures. Total expenditures are equal to the market price multi-

plied by the amount bought and sold in the market. Changes in total expenditures when the market price changes are closely related to the elasticity of demand: if demand is elastic, total expenditures will increase when the price decreases and total expenditures will decrease when the price increases. If, however, demand is inelastic, total expenditures will move with the price change. If demand is elastic for a particular commodity, that is, $|e_d| > 1$, total expenditures will move in a direction opposite to a price change. On the other hand, if demand is inelastic, that is, $|e_d| < 1$, total expenditures will move in the same directions as a price change.

The size of the price elasticity. The "size" of the elasticity of demand depends upon three things: (1) the ease of substitution, (2) the proportion of a typical person's income spent on the commodity, and (3) the period of time since the price change. The elasticity of demand will be higher when substitution is easier; when expenditures on a particular commodity represent a larger fraction of a person's income; and when the period of adjustment to the price change is longer (the **Second Law of Demand**).

Income elasticity and cross-price elasticity. The concept of elasticity can be used to measure the responsiveness of demand to the change of anything that affects consumers' decisions. We considered two changes that affect consumers' decisions: (1) changes in income and (2) changes in the prices of other commodities. The elasticity associated with the latter is called the cross-price elasticity of demand and for the former, the income elasticity of demand. A positive cross-price elasticity indicates that two commodities are substitutes; a negative cross-price elasticity indicates that two commodities are complements. The income elasticity of demand is positive for normal commodities and negative for inferior commodities.

Chapter 8 ▶▶
Short-Run Competitive Supply _____

Under what circumstances will suppliers be willing to provide more to a market if the relative price of a commodity increases? Why might they provide less when the relative price decreases? What does a positive relationship between relative price and quantity supplied imply about the way markets allocate resources or adjust to changes in costs or demand? In this chapter we begin a two-part analysis of these, and related, questions.

In an important sense, our analysis of supply will not be essentially different from our analysis of demand. *Both* suppliers and demanders confront constraints, face tradeoffs, and must make choices. For both, best or optimal choices will reflect a comparison of marginal benefits with marginal costs. Economizing principles are the same in either case. Different institutional arrangements make the context within which suppliers make decisions a bit different from that within which demanders make their decisions, however. In particular, our analysis of market supply is based on two very important assumptions—first, that a firm is constrained in its production decisions by its *existing* capital stock, and second, that a firm makes its production decisions acting as if these decisions will *not* affect the price at which it can sell its output. The first assumption limits our analysis to the **short run**; the second limits our analysis to **perfectly competitive markets**.

Some situations are neither short-run nor competitive. In the next chapter we will consider situations in which firms can change the amount of capital they have available (long-run competitive

supply). Later we will consider situations in which firms know they can affect the price at which they sell their output (monopoly and monopoly-like behavior).

▶ Short Run and Long Run Decisions

Firms, of course, decide what to produce. They also decide how much to produce. Closely associated is the decision about how many inputs to employ. Firms decide on not only the number of inputs, however, but also the proportion of one input to another. They decide on compensation schemes. Firms also decide how to finance production activities. Finally, firms decide which technologies and organizational structures to adopt.

Organizing Production

Firms use inputs to produce outputs. These inputs include labor, capital, intermediate goods purchased from other firms, natural resources, and so forth. A firm determines how to combine these inputs by adopting a particular technology. Thus, for example, a farmer combines labor, land, seed, water, fertilizer, pesticides, herbicides, and equipment to produce crops. How these resources are combined, and in what proportions, depend upon the technologies that are used. Using more equipment may reduce the need for labor, or using an herbicide to control weeds may require certain kinds of machinery but reduce the need for other kinds of machinery and labor.

Production periods. It is useful to think of a firm as having two production periods—a short-run period and a long-run period. The **short run** is a period during which *some* inputs are fixed while others may vary. The **long run** is a period over which *all* inputs may vary. Often, the amount of capital a firm has available cannot be easily or quickly changed and in the short run the firm can vary its output *only* by changing the amount of labor and natural resources it uses, whereas in the long run the firm can vary its output by changing *any* productive resource including labor, natural resources, and capital. Capital is the important element in distinguishing short-run and long-run decisions since it takes time to create and install new capital, particularly plant and certain kinds of equipment.

Capital provides services that are used in producing commodities, but the capital itself depreciates only slowly through time.[1] Thus, at any moment of time, a steel mill will have a particular amount of fixed capital in buildings, blast furnaces, coke ovens, and so forth. Its furnaces and ovens, moreover, embody the steel-making technology that was current when they were built. Although a firm may make decisions that will eventually lead to more or less capital at some point in the future, it cannot *quickly* increase or decrease its output by adding a new blast furnace.

A firm's capital stock changes over time. It slowly wears out, or **depreciates**, or it becomes obsolete as new technologies are developed. It may also be scrapped or sold for other uses. Firms also **invest**, thereby increasing the amount of capital available for production, but such additions also only occur slowly over time and cannot change a firm's level of production immediately.

Diminishing marginal returns. Even though a firm cannot quickly change how much capital it has, it can use its existing capital more intensively or less intensively by changing the amount of labor that it employs with its fixed capital. Hiring additional workers and adding a swing shift from 4 P.M. to midnight or a graveyard shift from midnight to 8 A.M. are common ways for firms to increase the

intensity with which they use their capital. Overtime is also a way of increasing the use of fixed capital, in this case by employing workers for more than eight hours each day or on weekends using the same plant and equipment. On the other hand, firms can use capital less intensively by shutting down one of several production lines or one of several furnaces or not using one of several trucks. In doing so, firms will employ less labor.

Why is this distinction between the short run and long run important? A firm will encounter diminishing marginal returns as it varies the labor that it employs with its *fixed* stock of machines, equipment, and buildings. As a consequence, output per worker will eventually *decline as additional workers are employed and capital is used more intensively*, or output per worker will *rise at some point if fewer workers are employed and capital is used less* intensively. These effects will matter to a firm as it makes decisions about how much to supply to the market. In the long run, by contrast, a firm can change the amount of capital it has and so diminishing marginal returns may not be important. It follows that diminishing returns will not affect long run decisions.

Short-run production decisions. The output for a firm that produces tennis balls using labor and capital is illustrated in Table 1. Note that in the short run, the amount of capital does not change. Hence, the firm can increase the amount produced each day only by employing additional workers.

Table 1
Production of Tennis Balls per Hour

Capital (number of factories)	Labor (number of workers)	Output
1	0	0
1	15	75
1	20	100
1	25	150
1	30	225
1	35	275
1	40	315
1	45	345
1	50	365
1	55	380
1	60	390
1	65	395

---

[1] **Capital**, remember, is any commodity that is produced but then used to produce other commodities rather than being consumed directly by individuals. **Investment** is the acquisition of new capital. **Depreciation** is the wearing out of capital.

Figure 1
Production of Tennis Balls When Capital Is Fixed

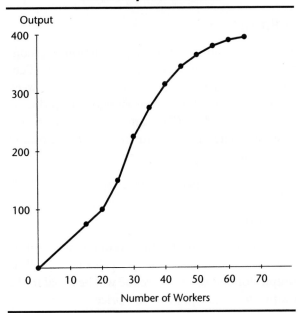

Table 2
Production of Tennis Balls per Hour

Capital (number of factories)	Labor (number of workers)	Output	Marginal product of labor
1	0	0	
			5
1	15	75	
			5
1	20	100	
			10
1	25	150	
			15
1	30	225	
			10
1	35	275	
			8
1	40	315	
			6
1	45	345	
			4
1	50	365	
			3
1	55	380	
			2
1	60	390	
			1
1	65	395	

This relationship, illustrated graphically in Figure 1, is the firm's **total product**. The firm's **marginal product** for any input, in this case labor, is the *change* in total product when the use of input *changes by a small amount*. Thus, the **marginal product of labor** is the change in output when the number of workers employed is changed.

Formally,

$$\text{Marginal product (MP)} = \frac{\text{change in total product}}{\text{change in quantity of an input}}$$

Table 2 provides estimates of the firm's marginal product of labor, which are graphed, in turn, in Figure 2. Thus, for example, when the firm increases the number of workers employed from 25 to 30, output increases from 150 to 225 tennis balls per hour. The marginal product of labor is calculated as follows:

$$\Delta \text{ in output} = 225 - 150 = 75$$
$$\Delta \text{ in input} = 30 - 25 = 5$$

and therefore

$$\text{MP} = 75/5 = 15$$

For this firm, the marginal product of labor at first increases, perhaps because of the advantages of team production. That is, increasing employment

Figure 2
Additional Output Produced When Additional Workers Are Hired

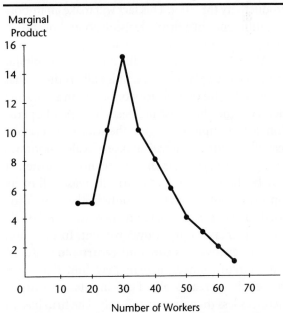

The marginal product of labor is determined by dividing the change in output produced when additional workers are hired by the change in the number of workers hired.

by 5 workers from 20 to 25 increases output by 50 units, and increasing in employment by 5 workers from 25 to 30 increases output by 75 units—the marginal product of labor is 10 units and 15 units, respectively. Further increases in employment exhibit diminishing marginal returns, however. Increasing employment from 40 to 45 workers increases output by 30 units but an additional 5 workers from 45 to 50 increases output by only 20 units. In these cases, the marginal product of labor is 6 units and 4 units, respectively. The marginal product of labor decreases because the fixed capital stock is used more intensively as additional workers are employed. More generally, *as a firm uses more of a variable input when at least one other input doesn't change (is "fixed"), the marginal product of the variable input eventually falls.*

Long-run production decisions. Production decisions in the long run are not, in any fundamental way, different from those in the short run—a firm employs inputs in order to produce outputs. In the long run, however, a firm is free to acquire or sell its fixed resource. Often this fixed resource is capital. Thus, over longer periods of time output can be increased either by using capital more intensively or by acquiring additional capital. When *all* inputs are changed, there may not be diminishing marginal productivity for labor. This fact will make an important difference in a firm's decision about how much to supply to the market in the long run.

When a firm increases the amount of capital it uses, it changes its **scale**. A tennis ball producer that doubles the size of its factory or builds an additional factory somewhere else increases its scale of operation, for example. Changing the scale of operation may allow a firm to take advantage of **scale economies** or **increasing returns to scale** as noted earlier. It may be, however, that as a firm increases all of its inputs, its output increases only in the same proportion. That is, a 5 percent increase in *all* of its inputs increases output by 5 percent. In this case, the firm encounters **constant returns to scale**. In some circumstances, a firm may find that even though it increases all of its inputs, its output increases less than proportionately. The firm has, in this case, encountered **decreasing returns to scale**. Hence, when *all* inputs are changed there may not be diminishing marginal productivity for labor. This fact will make an important difference in a firm's

decision about how much to supply to a market in the long run.

▶ Profits

Firms are assumed to make production decisions with the intent of maximizing their profits. **Economic profits** are equal to the difference between the total revenues a firm receives from producing and selling output (TR), and the total economic costs associated with producing and selling output (TC).[2] *That is,*

$$\text{Profits} = TR - TC$$

Revenues

The determination of **total revenue** is straightforward—the firm gets whatever price it can sell its output for and its total revenue will be equal to the output sold multiplied by this price, or,

$$TR = p \times q$$

where p is the market price and q is the quantity a firm produces and sells.

Costs

Total cost is the sum of *all* of the costs associated with production. Thus, the tennis-ball firm in Table 1, would have the short-run total costs illustrated in Table 3 if the cost-per-hour of using capital was $100 and it paid $5 per hour for each worker it employed. The total cost to produce 100 balls per hour, for example, is $200—the cost of capital is $100 and the cost of labor is $100 (20 workers at a $5 wage).

Some of this firm's costs are fixed, notably the cost for capital. Total cost can be divided into corresponding components: **Fixed cost** is the amount that the firm must pay for its fixed inputs. Other costs, in this example the cost of labor, are variable. **Variable cost** is the amount that the firm must pay for its variable inputs.

Although it appears that calculating Total Cost is straightforward, it isn't. Economic costs include the payments that the firm makes to factors of production, including wages, rents, interest payments,

---

[2] Some differences between economic costs and accounting costs will be explained later in this chapter.

Table 3
Production Decisions and Short-Run Costs

Capital (number of factories)	Capital cost ($)	Labor (number of workers)	Wage ($)	Labor cost ($)	Total cost ($)	Total output (number of balls)
1	$100	0	$5	$ 0	$100	0
1	100	15	5	75	175	75
1	100	20	5	100	200	100
1	100	25	5	125	225	150
1	100	30	5	150	250	225
1	100	35	5	175	275	275
1	100	40	5	200	300	315
1	100	45	5	225	325	345
1	100	50	5	250	350	365
1	100	55	5	275	375	380
1	100	60	5	300	400	390
1	100	65	5	325	425	395

and compensation for other inputs it purchases. These are *explicit costs* from the firm's perspective. It has to make out checks to pay the owners of the inputs when it uses them. In addition, however, the cost of producing output includes *implicit costs.* These are the opportunity costs of previously purchased inputs used in current production, the value of the depreciation of capital, and the payments to the owners of the firm that would be necessary to keep them from transferring their capital and other resources to other activities or uses.

Opportunity cost of inputs. Total cost includes the price of inputs at the current market price, *not* the invoice or historical price. For example, as we learned earlier the cost to a jeweler of using gold purchased a month ago for $300 per ounce is the current market price of gold, not the original purchase price.

An important opportunity cost arises when a firm owns a productive input that it can easily sell or rent. For example, owning a building creates an opportunity cost for a firm. If a firm can rent the building to someone else for $10,000 per month, then its opportunity cost of using the building itself to produce output is $10,000 per month. If the firm cannot earn enough when using the building itself to pay itself a rent equal to $10,000 per month, then its use of the building is not profitable. As the firm calculates its costs, it similarly must value *each* input at its most profitable alternative use.

Value of depreciation. Total cost includes the value of the depreciation of a firm's capital. Even though a firm does not actually pay anyone for the depreciation, it must either invest to offset the depreciation and maintain its capital stock or find itself with less capital in the future.

Opportunity costs for owners. Finally, total cost includes an implicit return to the owners for their contributions to the firm. This return is the opportunity cost associated with owners providing resources to this firm rather than some other business. The implicit return is usually measured by the **normal rate of return** or **normal profits**, whereas the actual rate of return is the dollar payout each year to an owner as a fraction of his or her dollar contribution to the firm. That is, if an owner provides $1,000 to a firm and receives payments of $60 per year, then the rate of return to the owner is 6 percent ($60/$1,000). The normal rate of return is the amount the owner could have expected to earn, on average, had he or she used the $1,000 elsewhere in the economy.

Economic Profits and Economic Losses

Economic profits (or simply "profits") are the difference between the revenues a firm receives and economic costs, which include a normal return for the owners of the firm's capital. **Economic losses**

("losses") occur when the total revenues do not cover all the economic costs.

Appropriately priced input costs and depreciation are sometimes called **accounting costs** because the implicit return to owners is generally not included in a firm's traditional cost accounting. By this definition, a firm's revenues may very well cover accounting costs but fall short of providing a normal return on the capital investment of its owners. If so, the firm is incurring losses even though it is making accounting profits. In addition, a firm is *not* making profits if its revenues exceed accounting costs by exactly the amount necessary to keep owners from moving capital elsewhere. In this case, the firm is just breaking even. A firm makes profits only if revenues exceed *all* costs, explicit and implicit, including the opportunity costs for resources provided by its owners. To see why this distinction important, consider the following example:

Suppose that you left a job paying $30,000 per year in order to start your own firm. If, at the end of your first year in business, the total revenues minus all accounting costs equaled $24,000, your income would be the accounting profit of $24,000. However, your firm (that is, you) actually lost $6,000 because your "profit" fell short of what the job you left would have paid. In other words, the total economic costs for the firm include your opportunity costs of $30,000. Thus, even though your firm made accounting profits of $24,000, it was not profitable. You would probably want to return to your old job because of this economic loss.

The use of economic rather than accounting costs implies that economic profits are determined, in part, by the return on financial resources *elsewhere* in the economy, that is, on the normal rate of return. A firm making economic profits provides to its owners a rate of return on their capital that is *greater than* the normal rate of return. A firm making losses provides its owners a rate of return on their capital that is *less than* the normal rate of return. A firm makes no economic profits (breaks even) when its revenues are just *equal to* its costs, including the owners' opportunity costs. Such a firm earns the normal rate of return on its owners' contributions.

The normal rate of return may differ from one industry to another, depending upon how uncertain the revenues and costs are for the industry as a whole. In general, firms in industries with greater uncertainties or risks have higher normal rates of return on average than do firms in industries with less risk.

You might, justifiably, ask yourself, "Why such emphasis on *economic* profits?" The reason is that incentives matter. Owners of firms who are not doing as well as they might do in other activities have an incentive to change. If, however, they can do no better elsewhere in the economy, they have no incentive to change.

▶ Perfectly Competitive Markets

The market structure within which firms interact determines the relationship between the market price and the decisions a firm makes. There are a number of different possible market structures, each with different implications for economic behavior. Two are particularly well understood: a **perfectly competitive market** structure and a **monopolistic market** structure. Monopolistic firms have control over the price at which they sell their output and will be considered in detail in later chapters. By contrast, a market structure is perfectly competitive if a firm *cannot* affect the market price by any decision it might make. In a perfectly competitive market, a firm is a *price taker*. That is, in a competitive market, a firm observes the market price and decides whether to increase or decrease its production, *given* the observed or expected price. In a perfectly competitive market, a firm cannot affect the price at which it sells its output by changing the amount that it produces or the way that it markets its output. Moreover, in a competitive market, suppliers learn everything they need to know about the demand side from the market price. The reasons why this is so follow.

▶ Perfectly Competitive Markets and a Firm's Demand Schedule

In a perfectly competitive market, each firm acts as if the demand for its own output is perfectly elastic at the current market price. This relationship between the firm and the market for its product is illustrated in Figure 3. A demand curve of this sort implies that there is *perfect* substitutability between the good the firm produces and some other good a consumer might purchase. If substitutability is perfect, *any* change in the price the firm asks for its output will lead to immediate substitution by con-

Figure 3
The Demand for a Perfectly Competitive Firm's Output

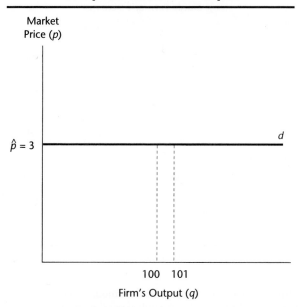

If the goods produced by different firms are perfect substitutes, then each firm has a perfectly elastic demand curve. It will be able to sell all that it wants at the current market price, but if it attempts to raise its price, consumers will immediately and completely substitute other goods.

sumers. This means, of course, that substitutes must be readily available to consumers.

A firm might face this demand if there are many firms supplying virtually identical goods to a market. Consumers in such a market can easily substitute the output from any one firm for another. A wheat farmer, for example, produces a commodity that is the same as that produced by any other wheat farmer. If that wheat farmer attempts to charge a higher price than any of the neighboring farmers, people who purchase wheat will simply buy from the neighboring farmers because *any other* farmer's wheat is a perfect substitute for *this* farmer's wheat. As a consequence, the wheat farmer who is attempting to raise his price will sell very little.

It is important to note that the market demand for wheat may have a typical downward slope even though the demand faced by any single farmer is perfectly elastic at the market price. Why? The market demand reflects the ability of consumers to substitute *other things* for wheat, but the demand for a particular farmer's output reflects the ability of consumers to substitute *other farmers' wheat* for his or her wheat. When the market price of wheat changes, substituting other things for wheat is more difficult than substituting one farmer's wheat for another farmer's higher-priced wheat. Therefore, a firm's demand can be perfectly elastic, even though the market demand is not.

To summarize, a market is perfectly competitive when each firm in the market acts as if its demand is perfectly elastic, even though it understands that the market demand—that is, the demand for the total production of all similar firms—is not. Figure 4 illustrates the relationship between a single farmer's demand and the market demand when the market price of wheat is $3.00 per bushel.

The elasticity of demand for a firm's output in a competitive market. How can a firm behave as a price taker—that is, as if the market price is fixed or, equivalently, as if its demand curve is perfectly elastic—when it knows that the market demand is inversely related to the market price?

Consider the market demand schedule for tennis racquets illustrated in Table 4. The price elasticity of demand is approximately 1 along this demand schedule. That is, if a single firm produces all of the tennis racquets for this market, for each 1 percent that it lowers its price, the quantity demanded increases by 1 percent and its total revenues for tennis-racquet sales remains around $1 million per

Table 4
The Market Demand for Tennis Racquets

Price per racquet ($)	Quantity of racquets demanded
$10.00	100,000
9.90	101,000
9.80	102,000
9.71	103,000
9.62	104,000
9.52	105,000
9.43	106,000
9.35	107,000
9.26	108,000
9.17	109,000
9.09	110,000

Figure 4
Market Price and a Competitive Firm's Demand

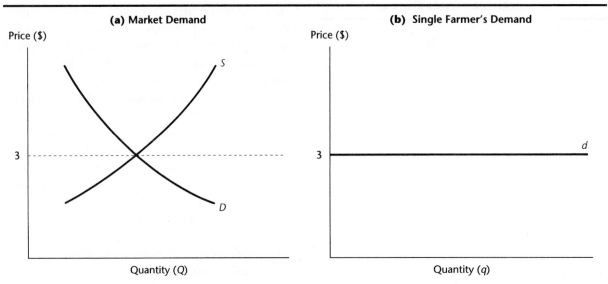

A market is competitive when individual firms act as if they have perfectly elastic demand curves, even though the market demand curve is not perfectly elastic. Note the difference in the quantity scales for the individual farmer (*q*) and the market (*Q*). *q* might be measured in thousands of bushels, for example, while *Q* might be measured in millions of bushels.

month. For example, if this firm increases its output from 100,000 units per month to 110,000 units per month, it can sell the additional racquets only if it lowers its price from $10 per unit to $9.09 per unit. Because the decline in price along the demand curve is about the same percentage as the increase in output, the firm will find that its total revenue changes very little (100,000 × 10 is approximately the same as 110,000 × 9.09).

Suppose that instead of one firm producing all of the racquets, there were 100 firms in this industry, each producing 1,000 racquets. Each would find that it could sell its output for $10 per racquet. If one firm decided to *double* its output but no other firm changed the amount that it produced, the market price would fall to $9.90 per racquet. To see this, note that the total number of racquets delivered to the market would be 101,000—99,000 from the 99 firms that did not change their production plus 2,000 from the firm that doubled its production. Given the market demand schedule, when 101,000 racquets are supplied to the market, the market price falls to $9.90.

The firm that doubled its output would find that its very large change in production (a 100 percent change) had a relatively *small* impact on the price at which it sold its racquets (a less than 1 per-

cent change). Hence, even though the market price elasticity is about 1, this one firm will find that *its* price elasticity is about 67, because the elasticity of demand for one firm's output

$$= \frac{-(2,000-1,000)/1,500}{(\$9.9.-\$10)/\$9.95}$$

$$= .67/.01 = 67$$

Even though the firm might know that the *market demand* had an elasticity of 1, the manager's experience would indicate that, *for the firm,* the elasticity of demand was well above 50! Market demand may, of course, be quite elastic or quite inelastic, depending upon the substitutes for the particular commodity being traded in the market. However, a very large number of firms producing the same or very similar commodity will each confront an individual demand curve with very high elasticity, even if the market demand curve is inelastic.

▶ Profit Maximization

If you were the manager of a firm in a perfectly competitive market, what decisions would you have to make? Since you would be constrained by the fact that you cannot change your firm's capital stock quickly or affect the product's market price in the short run, your strategy would be simple: Choose a level of output that maximizes profits at the given market price. Additional output is produced, of course, by employing more inputs. (To keep the discussion as simple as possible, we will assume that labor is the firm's only variable input and capital is its only fixed input.)

General Rule: Marginal Revenue Equals Marginal Cost

Revenues are the benefits to firms from producing and selling goods and services. The expenditures on inputs, including appropriate consideration of the opportunity costs of the owners, are the costs associated with such production decisions. As we noted at some length in the chapter on marginal analysis, the *best* production decision will be one in which the marginal benefit associated with the level of output produced just equals the marginal cost of producing that level of output. For the firm, then, profits are maximized when the **marginal cost** (MC) associated with varying the amount of labor employed to produce one additional unit of output, *q*, is *exactly equal* to the **marginal revenue** (MR) that the firm earns from selling the last unit of output produced. Or, profits are maximized when the level of production is adjusted until

$$MR = MC$$

Why does this lead to maximum profits? Suppose that a firm thought it was maximizing profits, but the cost of producing one additional unit was \$.50 (its marginal cost) and the additional revenue from selling this unit was \$1.00 (its marginal revenue). If the firm produced only one more unit of output, its costs would increase by \$.50 and its revenues increase by \$1.00. Because profits are the difference between revenues and costs, and revenues increase by more than costs, profits would increase by \$.50. Therefore, the firm is *not* maximizing its profits when MR is greater than MC.

On the other hand, if the firm thought that it was maximizing its profits but its marginal cost was \$1.00 and its marginal revenue was \$.50, then when the firm produced one fewer unit of output, its revenues would fall by \$.50 (because it would now have

less to sell). Its costs would fall by \$1.00, however, because this is the cost of producing the last unit of output. By producing less, the firm's costs would fall by more than revenues (\$1.00 versus \$.50). Its profits would therefore increase. Put simply, the firm is *not* maximizing profits when MC is less than MR. This argument is illustrated in Figure 5.

This argument shows that if marginal costs are *greater* than marginal revenues, profits can be increased if the firm *decreases* its production. Or, if marginal costs are *less* than marginal revenues, profits can be increased if the firm *increases* its production. Thus, profits can be maximized only when a firm chooses a level of production such that marginal revenue is exactly equal to marginal cost.

Marginal Revenue for a Firm in a Competitive Market Equals Market Price

"So what?" you must have been thinking to yourself as you read along earlier. "Why does it matter if the demand for a firm's output is perfectly elastic?" The answer: *If the demand for a firm's output is perfectly elastic, marginal revenue for the firm will be the same as the market price at which it sells its output.* To see this, note that total revenue is determined by the market price and amount of the good that the firm actually sells,

$$TR = p \times q$$

Marginal revenue is defined as the change in total revenue when the firm sells one additional unit of output,

$$MR = \Delta TR / \Delta q \qquad (1)$$

If the demand for a firm's output is perfectly elastic, the price at which it can sell its output does *not* vary with its own production decisions. Thus, when a firm changes its production,

$$\Delta TR = p^* \times \Delta q$$

Rearranging, we have

$$\Delta TR / \Delta q = p^*$$

which is identical to our definition of marginal revenue in Equation 1. This means that in a perfectly competitive market, marginal revenue must be equal to the market price,

$$MR = p^*$$

Figure 5
When Marginal Costs Do Not Equal Marginal Revenue

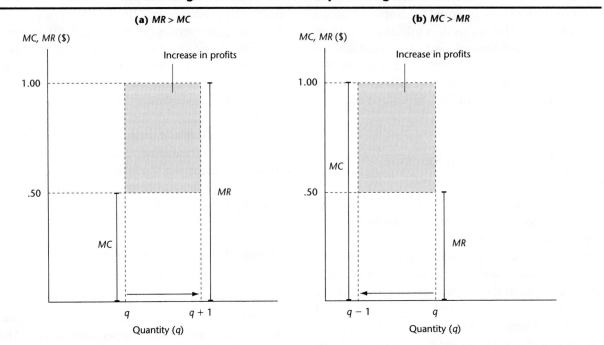

(a) When *MR* is greater than *MC*, increasing output from q to $q + 1$ would increase profits by $.50—the difference between *MR* and *MC*. (b) When *MC* is greater than *MR*, decreasing output from q to $q - 1$ would increase profits by $.50—the difference between *MC* and *MR*.

For example, in Figure 6, if the firm is producing 100 units, it can sell them for $3 each. If it does, its total revenue will be $300. If the firm decides to produce one additional unit, increasing production to 101 units, it can continue to sell its output for $3 per unit and its total revenue will be $303. Clearly, total revenue has increased by $3 when the output increased by 1. Therefore, marginal revenue must equal $3. Of course, $3 is also the market price. For a firm in a competitive environment, then, *marginal revenue is equal to the market price.*

This discussion of marginal revenue gives us one of the pieces of information necessary to determine a firm's profit maximizing decisions. The other necessary piece of information is marginal cost.

Short-Run Marginal Costs for a Competitive Firm

Just as you have wondered about the relevance of distinguishing between the market demand and the demand for a competitive firm's output, you may also be thinking, "Who cares whether a firm's capital stock is fixed in the short run? What difference

Figure 6
Marginal Revenue and Market Price in a Perfectly Competitive Market

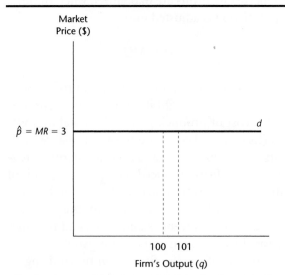

If a firm in a perfectly competitive market increases its output, say, from 100 to 101 units, it will sell the additional unit at the same price as the original 100. Therefore, the additional production increases the firm's revenues by $3. It follows that $3—the market price— is the competitive firm's marginal revenue.

does it make?" The answer: *If a firm's capital stock is fixed, marginal cost will increase as a firm increases its level of output.* That is, as a firm uses its existing capital more intensively by increasing the rate of production, the cost of producing each additional unit of output will increase. Why?

In the short run, a competitive firm can vary its output only by varying the amount of labor it employs with its fixed capital. But as a firm varies the amount of labor it employs, it will encounter diminishing marginal returns. For example, as the tennis-ball firm we considered earlier increased the number of workers that it employed, given its fixed capital stock, the output per worker eventually fell. Because the quantity of capital is fixed, a firm's fixed costs do not change as it changes its level of output. If the firm pays the same wage for each worker hired, however, the cost of producing each additional unit of output—that is, the firm's marginal cost—*must* eventually increase.

Table 5 illustrates this point. The data are plotted in Figure 7. The more general relationship between marginal cost and output is illustrated in Figure 8.

Table 5
Production Decisions and Marginal Costs for a Firm Producing Tennis Balls

Output per hour	Total cost ($)	Marginal cost ($)
100	$200	—
		$ .50
150	225	
		.33
225	250	
		.50
275	275	
		.63
315	300	
		.83
345	325	
		1.25
365	350	
		1.67
380	375	
		2.50
390	400	
		5.00
395	425	

Figure 7
Marginal Costs

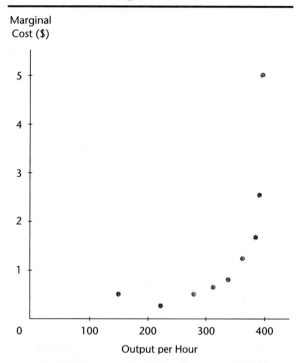

As shown in Table 5, as the firm expands production, its marginal cost decreases at first but then increases because its capital is fixed in the short run. The reason why is that as more labor is employed, the marginal product of labor eventually falls.

Marginal cost increases *not* because of increases in wages or capital costs—neither of these change—but, instead, marginal cost increases because of *diminishing marginal productivity*. That is, when additional workers are hired, the output per worker eventually declines because the capital stock is fixed. Because each worker continues to be paid the same wage and because output per worker must eventually decline, marginal costs must eventually increase.

Because the effect of diminishing returns is likely to be more dramatic as a firm uses its existing capital *more intensively*, a firm's marginal costs are determined by the *rate of production*. The more quickly a firm attempts to produce its output, the greater its marginal costs will be.

A Firm's Competitive Supply

We now have both pieces of information necessary for profit maximization: marginal revenue and

Figure 8
The Short-Run Marginal Cost Curve for a Typical Firm

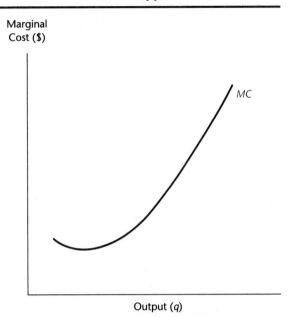

Marginal Cost ($)

MC

Output (q)

As a firm's output increases—that is, as it produces more rapidly and uses its capital more intensively— marginal cost increases.

marginal cost. To see this, refer to Table 6. Suppose, for example, that the market prices at which this firm could sell its output is $.63 per tennis ball. It would respond by hiring 40 workers and producing 315 tennis balls per hour because, if it did, its marginal cost would be $.63 and it would be maximizing profits. If the competitive market price increases to $.83

per tennis ball, the firm finds that at its old level of production, marginal cost ($.63) is well below marginal revenue ($.83—the new market price). Therefore, the firm has an incentive to increase production. In the short run, it can only increase production by hiring more workers, however. If five additional workers are hired, output will increase and marginal costs will also increase to $.83. More importantly, however, the firm's profits will also increase. Once this adjustment has occurred, the firm has no incentive to make further adjustments. If the market price remains at $.83, its profits are maximized when 345 tennis balls per hour are produced.

Suppose, however, that the market price further increased to $1.67. The firm would respond once again by hiring more workers—using its capital more intensively—in order to increase its output because the marginal cost of increasing output a small amount is $.83 but the marginal revenue to be obtained from selling any increased production is $1.67 (the new market price). As the firm increases its output by hiring more workers, marginal costs once again increases because of diminishing marginal returns. When the firm employs 55 workers, however, it will find that it cannot increase its production and still increase its profits any further because its marginal costs are now $1.67.

It appears from this discussion that the marginal costs schedule is the competitive firm supply schedule. As it turns out, this is basically correct. At each market price, the marginal cost schedule gives the firm's profit-maximizing response or its best

Table 6
Production Decisions and Profits

Output	Total cost ($)	Fixed cost ($)	Marginal cost ($)	Total revenue*	Profit or loss ($)
150	$225	$100	$ .50	$ 75.00	−$ 150.00
225	250	100	.33	75.00	−175.00
275	275	100	.50	137.50	−137.50
315	300	100	.63	196.88	−103.12
345	325	100	.83	287.39	−37.61
365	350	100	1.25	456.25	+100.25
380	375	100	1.67	694.60	+319.60
390	400	100	2.50	975.00	+575.00
395	425	100	5.00	1,975.00	+1,550.00

* When price equals marginal cost.

production decision, q^*. Thinking of the firm's marginal costs schedule (or curve) as its supply schedule (or curve) is almost, but not quite, correct, however.

To Produce or Not To Produce?

A firm in competitive market must actually make two decisions: First, "Should *anything* be produced?" Second, if it decides to produce, "How *much* should be produced?" We have an answer to the second question: produce the level of output that maximizes profits, that is, the level of output where MC = p*.

It is possible, however, that profits are maximized—or losses minimized—when a firm does not produce at all. Suppose, for example, that tennis balls sell at a very low market price, so no matter how many the firm decides to produce, it will have losses greater than $100. If the firm chose not to produce anything, its costs would be $100 because it has to pay for its capital. (The firm's fixed costs are $100.) If this amount is less than the losses incurred when the firm produces tennis balls, it would be better off not producing than it would be producing and selling at the low market price. By shutting down, the firm would minimize its losses. It follows that a firm would only choose to produce if its losses, *when it was producing,* were less than $100. In our tennis-ball example, the firm would only choose to produce if the market price was at least $.83, as shown in Table 6. For example, if the market price were $.50, the firm would have to adjust its output to 275 units in order to make the marginal cost equal the market price. If it did so, it would incur a loss of $137.50. If it produced *nothing,* however, its loss would be $100—its fixed cost. As a consequence, a firm that is profit-maximizing (in this case, loss-minimizing) would choose *not* to produce when the market prices was $.50. A similar argument holds for any price less than $.83.

For any price greater than $.83, by contrast, the firm will either lose less than $100, break even, or make a profit. A loss of less than $100 is better than a loss of $100 (and a positive profit is better still!), so the firm will certainly choose to produce and sell its output when the price is $.83 or more per unit. For this firm, choosing when to produce and then how much to produce would lead to the output decisions indicated in Table 7.

Table 7
A Firm's Supply Decision

Market price ($)	Actual profit or loss ($)	Actual output
$ .50	−$ 100.00	0
.33	−100.00	0
.50	−100.00	0
.63	−100.00	0
.83	−37.61	345
1.25	+100.25	365
1.67	+319.60	380
2.50	+575.00	390
5.00	+1,550.00	395

The "actual output" column is the firm's **supply schedule**. Notice that a firm may produce even though it is losing money if it would lose *more* money by shutting down. You may have noticed from news reports that there are firms which report losses for several months or even years, yet they continue to operate. This is the reason.

Fixed costs and the decision to shut down. The decision to produce or not to produce can be illustrated in a slightly different way by considering a firm's fixed and variable costs. Total costs are equal to fixed costs plus variable costs:

$$TC = FC + VC$$

Profits equal revenues minus total costs:

$$\text{Profits} = TR - TC$$

Therefore,

$$\text{Profits} = TR - (VC + FC)$$

Or

$$\text{Profits} = (TR - VC) - FC$$

If the firm does not produce anything, *both* its revenues and its variable costs will be zero, thus:

$$TR - VC = 0$$

And its losses will be equal to its fixed costs:

$$\text{Losses (negative profits)} = -FC$$

But if by producing output, its total revenue is greater than its variable costs, the firm's losses will be less than its fixed costs. That is, if

$$(TR - VC) > 0$$

then by operating,

$$losses < FC.$$

However, if by producing, the firm finds that its revenues are less than variable costs,

$$(TR - VC) < 0$$

it will *increase* its losses by producing.

This argument is illustrated for the tennis-ball firm in Table 8. Note that once again, the firm's supply schedule starts at zero, but jumps to 345 when revenues are sufficient to cover variable costs. Supply then increases with price.

Average costs, marginal costs, and the decision to produce. This argument can be illustrated in a slightly different way by considering the per unit cost, or average cost, of producing output. Average total cost, for example, is just total cost divided by a firm's output:

$$\text{Average total cost (ATC)} = \frac{\text{total cost}}{\text{total output}}$$

Likewise,

$$\text{Average variable cost (AVC)} = \frac{\text{variable cost}}{\text{total output}}$$

and

$$\text{Average fixed cost (AFC)} = \frac{\text{fixed cost}}{\text{total output}}$$

Note that because

$$TC = VC + FC$$

It must be that

$$TC/q = VC/q + FC/q$$

or, in other terms,

$$ATC = AVC + AFC.$$

As we have just seen, a firm will choose to produce as long as its total revenue is larger than its variable costs, that is, if

$$(TR - VC) > 0.$$

Thus it will choose to produce as long as

$$TR/q - VC/q > 0$$

where TR/q is a firm's average revenue. But this is just the market price, because

$$TR = p \times q \quad \text{and} \quad \frac{p \times q}{q} = p$$

Of course, VC/q is average variable cost (AVC).

What have we learned? The argument above demonstrates that a firm will choose to produce whenever total revenue is greater than variable cost

Table 8
Production Decisions and Costs

Possible output	Labor (number of workers)	Wage ($)	Variable costs ($)	Total revenue ($)	Actual output
150	25	$5	$125	$ 75.00	0
225	30	5	150	125.00	0
275	35	5	175	137.50	0
315	40	5	200	196.88	0
345	45	5	225	287.39	345
365	50	5	250	456.25	365
380	55	5	275	694.60	380
390	60	5	300	975.00	390
395	65	5	325	1,975.00	395

which is equivalent to a decision to produce whenever

$$p - AVC > 0$$

or, rearranging slightly, whenever the market price is greater than average variable cost,

$$p > AVC$$

A firm in a perfectly competitive market maximizes profits by adjusting its output until its marginal cost is just equal to the market price. Therefore,

$$MC = p > AVC$$

and the firm will provide output to the market as long as

$$MC > AVC.$$

Don't get overwhelmed with the symbols. We are trying, remember, to think through the decision process of a firm that has marginal costs, MC, average variable costs, AVC, and faces a market price, p. This decision process can be seen both numerically and graphically by considering the tennis-ball firm once again. Table 9 summarizes average cost calculations for this firm. The general relationship between average costs is illustrated in Figure 9.

Table 10 compares the firm's supply decision from Table 6 with average variable cost from Table 9. Note that the firm provides output to the market whenever the market price is greater than average

Table 9
Average Costs

Output	Average total cost ($)	Average variable cost ($)	Average fixed cost ($)
0	—	—	—
75	$2.33	$1.00	$1.33
100	2.00	1.00	1.00
150	1.50	.83	.67
225	1.11	.67	.44
275	1.00	.64	.36
315	.95	.63	.32
345	.94	.64	.29
365	.97	.68	.27
380	.99	.71	.26
390	1.03	.76	.26
395	1.08	.82	.25

Figure 9
The Short-Run Average Cost Curves for a Typical Firm

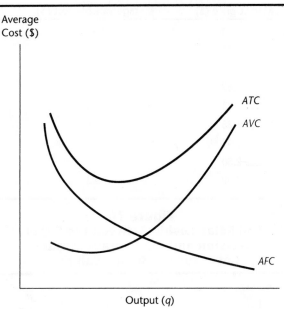

Average total cost is the sum of the average variable cost and the average fixed cost. Thus, in a graph of this sort, the distance between *ATC* and *AVC* must equal the distance between *AFC* and the horizontal axis. Note that *ATC* must be the highest curve.

variable cost. Note in addition that marginal costs is greater than average variable cost when output is 345 tennis balls or more per day. Therefore, the firm should produce whenever marginal cost is greater than average variable cost. This is the firm's supply. Figure 10 illustrates this point using the data in Table 10. Figure 11 shows the general relationship between marginal cost, average variable cost, and the firm's supply curve.

▶ Short-Run Market Supply

Market supply is obtained by adding the output produced and delivered to a market by all the firms at each possible market price. At a particular market price, some firms may choose to supply a little. Still others may choose not to produce anything, shutting down in order to minimize their losses.

Suppose, for example, that the three firms illustrated in Table 11 supply the market with tennis balls. At a market price of $.63, the first firm would choose to produce nothing, the second firms, 220 units, and the third firm, 150 units. Thus, when the

Table 10
Production Decisions and Marginal Costs

Market price ($)	Average variable cost ($)	Supply decision	Total cost ($)	Marginal cost ($)
$ .50	$.83	0	$100	$ 0
.33	.67	0	100	0
.50	.64	0	100	0
.63	.63	0	100	0
.83	.64	345	325	.83
1.25	.68	365	350	1.25
1.67	.71	380	375	1.67
2.50	.76	390	400	2.50
5.00	.82	395	425	5.00

Figure 10
The Relationship Between the Supply Decision and the Average Variable Costs for the Tennis-Ball Firm

Cost ($)

5

4

3

2

1

0   100   200   300   400

Output

MC

AVC

To maximize profits, a firm must choose a level of production such that the marginal cost equals the market price, and the market price is above the average variable cost. Thus the firm will supply tennis balls to the market along the solid section of its marginal cost curve.

market price is $.63, the total market supply would be 370 tennis balls. At a higher market price, each firm would want to increase its production and provide more to the market. At a lower market price,

Figure 11
The Relationship Between Supply and Average Variable Cost for a Typical Firm

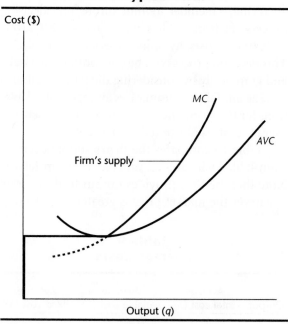

Cost ($)

Firm's supply

MC

AVC

Output (q)

Table 11
Short-Run Market Supply

Possible price ($)	Supply of firm 1	Supply of firm 2	Supply of firm 3	Market supply
$0.63	0	220	150	370
0.83	345	280	170	795
1.25	365	330	185	880
1.67	380	370	195	945
2.50	390	400	200	990
5.00	395	420	203	1,018

Figure 12
Individual Firms and Market Supply

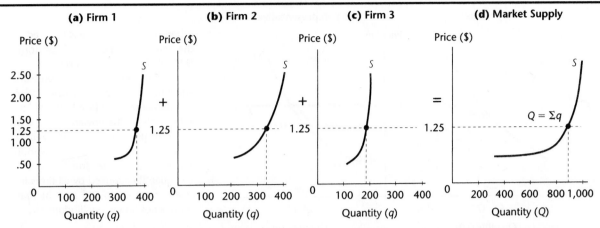

The market supply curve is the sum of the quantity that each firm is willing to produce at a given market price.

each firm would want to decrease its production and provide less to the market. The ability of each firm to do so is constrained by diminishing marginal productivity. This market supply curve is illustrated in Figure 12.

In the short run, market supply is positively related to the relative price for two important reasons:

1. As the market price increases, each firm uses its capital more intensively, thereby increasing output but also increasing marginal cost.

2. As the market price increases, firms that were previously providing output but had ceased production in order to minimize losses will find it profitable to begin production again, using capital that had previously been left idle.

Two Interpretations of Market Supply

One way to think about market supply is that it is the total amount provided to the market *at each possible market price.*

Supply can also be thought of as the marginal cost of providing additional output to the market, *given existing firms' current production decisions.* Why does supply have this second interpretation? Because in a competitive market, each firm adjusts its output until its marginal cost is just equal to the market price. Hence, the marginal cost of producing a small amount of additional output is the market price. Although different firms might have very different total costs because of their organization, technolo-

gies, or available capital, their *marginal* costs of supplying output to the market will be exactly the *same:* each firm adjusts its production in response to the same market price, equating *its* marginal cost of production to the common market price. This does not mean that each firm will produce the same amount. Some firms will supply a little, while others supply a lot in response to a particular market price. The additional cost of producing one additional unit of output will be the *same* for all firms, however.

Market Adjustment and Equilibrium, Once Again

In Chapter 5, we first discussed the important ideas of *equilibrium* and *market adjustment*. Now that you have a better understanding of demand and short-run supply, we can revisit some examples we considered in that chapter.

A market is in equilibrium when the quantity that consumers wish to purchase at a particular price is exactly equal to the production that firms wish to sell at that same price. This concept is illustrated in terms of supply and demand in Figure 13. The equilibrium quantity exchanged in the market, Q^*, is the sum of the equilibrium outputs, q^*, of each of the competitive firms. In addition to the typical supply-demand diagram, Figure 13 also shows a representative competitive firm. The scale on the horizontal axis for the market will be quite different from the scale along the horizontal axis for the representative firm. For example, Q (the quantity in the

Figure 13
Market and Firm Adjustment to an Increase in Demand

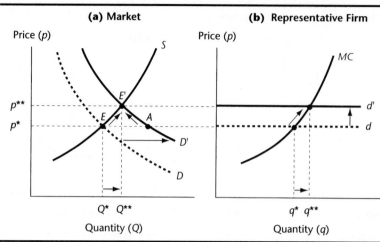

(a) Market

(b) Representative Firm

When the drinking age is lowered, the demand for beer increases from D to D'. At p*, there is excess demand, thus putting upward pressure equal to (A − E) on the market price. The demand curve faced by individual firms also shifts upward (from d to d'). In response to higher market prices, the quantity supplied by individual firms increases from q* to q**. The quantity supplied by all firms increases from Q* to Q** and the market reaches a new equilibrium at E'.

market) might be measured in the thousands or millions and q (the quantity produced by a single firm) in hundreds.

An increase in demand. How does lowering the drinking age affect firms producing beer? Demand increases, as illustrated by the shift from D to D' in Figure 13. At p* there is now excess demand. When there is excess demand, the market price increases. Two things happen:

First, some individuals begin to substitute other goods for beer because beer's relative price has increased. This substitution is reflected by a movement along the *new* demand curve, D', from point A toward point E'. Substitution continues until the marginal satisfaction per dollar spent is the same for beer as it is for any other good the consumers might purchase. That is, substitution continues until consumers are just willing to pay p**, and no more, for beer.

Second, as the market price increases, beer producers find that q* is no longer the best level of production because marginal revenue is now greater than marginal cost. They will begin to employ more workers in order to increase their production. A brewery may add a swing shift, for instance. As production increases, marginal costs increase because each brewery's capital is being used more intensively. As long as marginal costs are less than the market price, however, it makes sense for each firm to increase the use of its capital in this way. Output will increase until each firm's marginal cost is just equal

to p**. Consequently, output will increase from q* to q** for each firm. The amount supplied to the market by all firms therefore increases from Q* to Q**.

At the new equilibrium, E', the quantity of beer demanded by individuals is once again exactly equal to the total production that firms willingly provide to the market. That is, the price that individuals are willing to pay for Q** is just equal to the amount that firms must receive in order to provide Q** to the market.

A decrease in demand. If instead of lowering the drinking age, the drinking age were increased, demand would decline. This change is illustrated by a shift from D to D″ in Figure 14. At p* there is excess supply, so the market price will decline. Two things then happen:

First, as the market price declines, individuals will have the incentive to substitute beer for other goods. This substitution is visually illustrated by the movement down the new demand curve from point A toward E'. Substitution will continue until the marginal satisfaction per dollar spent is the same for beer as it is for any other good the consumers might purchase. That is, substitution continues until consumers are just willing to pay p**.

Second, as the market price begins to fall breweries find that marginal cost is greater than the price at which they can sell their beer. Each firm has an incentive to cut its production, thereby reducing the impact of the price change on its prof-

Figure 14
Market and Firm Adjustment to a Decrease in Demand

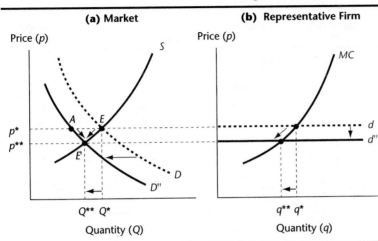

(a) Market

(b) Representative Firm

When the drinking age is raised, the demand for beer decreases from *D* to *D''*. At *p**, there is excess supply, thus putting downward pressure equal to (*E − A*) on the market price. The demand curve faced by individual firms also shifts downward (from *d* to *d''*). In response to lower market prices, the quantity supplied by individual firms decreases from *q** to *q***. The quantity supplied by all firms decreases from *Q** to *Q*** and the market reaches a new equilibrium at *E'*.

its. In the short run, they can only do this by decreasing the amount of labor they use, either by laying off workers or by using all workers for fewer hours each day. Capital will be used less intensively and marginal costs decrease. This decrease is visually illustrated by the movement down the supply curve from point E toward point E'. Firms will individually decrease production from q* to q**, moving down their own supply/marginal cost curve.

At the new equilibrium, E', the quantity of beer demanded by individuals is once again exactly equal to the total production that firms willingly provide to the market. Individuals are willing to pay no more than p** for the Q** delivered to the market; firms

are collectively willing to supply no more than Q** when they receive p**.

A decrease in supply. If all brewery workers negotiate a higher wage, each firm producing beer will find that its costs will increase. The amount of beer supplied to the marker will decrease. This change is illustrated by the shift from S to S' in Figure 15.

In this case, the increase in wages shifts the marginal cost curve for each firm from MC to MC'. To see why, consider the firm whose costs are summarized in Table 12. Because each firm must pay the higher wage, each will find the its variable costs increase. Workers are no more productive than they were before the wage increase and the firm's capital

Figure 15
The Effect of an Increase in Wages on the Market and Competitive Firms

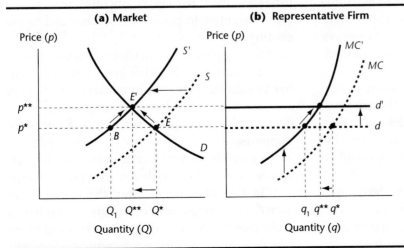

(a) Market

(b) Representative Firm

An increase in wages shifts each firm's marginal cost curve to the left (from *MC* to *MC'*), resulting in a decrease in market supply (from *S* to *S'*). At *p**, firms are only willing to supply *q₁* to the market, causing the market supply to fall from *Q** to *Q₁*. But this causes excess demand at *p** equal to (*E − B*), putting upward pressure on the market price, thus inducing firms to increase production (moving along their new marginal cost curve) from *q₁* to *q***. The total output supplied to the market by all firms increases from *Q₁* to *Q***.

Table 12
Production Decisions and Short-Run Costs

Capital	Capital cost ($)	Labor	Labor cost ($)	Total cost ($)	Total output	Marginal cost ($)
			When wage = $5			
1	$100	40	$200	$300	315	
1	100	45	225	325	345	$ .83
1	100	50	250	350	365	1.25
1	100	55	275	375	380	1.67
1	100	60	300	400	390	2.50
1	100	65	325	425	395	5.00
			When wage = $8			
1	100	40	320	420	315	
1	100	45	360	460	345	1.33
1	100	50	400	500	365	2.00
1	100	55	440	540	380	2.67
1	100	60	480	580	390	4.00
1	100	65	520	620	395	8.00

stock is the same, so the marginal product for labor will not change. This means that the firms marginal costs increase, as illustrated in the last column.

Because of the increase in costs, at p^* each firm finds it profitable to produce only q_1, thus supplying the market with only Q_1. Clearly, because of the change in costs, p^* is no longer the equilibrium price. Indeed, at p^* there is excess demand. The market price will begin to increase. As it does, consumers will substitute other things for beer. This substitution is illustrated by the movement along D from E toward E'. Once again, substitution continues until the marginal satisfaction per dollar spent is the same for beer as it is for any other good that consumers might purchase. That is, substitution continues until consumers are just willing to pay p^{**}.

As the market price increases, however, each firm finds that the new price is above the marginal cost of producing q_1. This means that there is a profit incentive for each firm to increase output by employing labor more intensively that it would at q_1. Marginal cost will be higher and firms increase the quantity supplied until they are producing q^{**} along MC'. This is illustrated by the movement along S' from B toward E'. At E', marginal cost (now higher because of the increase in wages) is equal to

p^{**} so no firm has an incentive to make any further changes in its output decision. At p^{**}, consumers no longer have an incentive to substitute. Therefore, p^{**} is a new market equilibrium price.

Just the reverse occurs if each firm in a competitive industry finds that its costs—such as the price of hops, an important ingredient in beer—decreases. You should work through the adjustments.

Incentives to adjust. The important characteristic of these adjustments is that when the market price increases, *ceteris paribus*, competitive firms have a profit incentive to employ more labor and to use existing capital more intensively. When they do, the quantity supplied to the market increases. Individual consumers, on the other hand, have an incentive to substitute away from markets where prices are increasing, thereby decreasing the quantity demanded. Thus, quite different self-interested responses—maximizing profits for firms and maximizing well-being for individuals—move the market toward equilibrium when market prices change.

On the other hand, when the market price decreases, *ceteris paribus*, competitive firms have a profit incentive to employ fewer workers and to use capital less intensively, thereby decreasing the quantity supplied to the market. Individual consumers have an incentive to substitute toward this market, thereby increasing the quantity demanded. Again, quite different self-interested responses to the decreased market price move the market toward equilibrium.

Markets adjust in predictable ways and toward equilibrium, then, because of the self-interested behavior of the various participants. Self-interest does not lead to chaos or lack of coordination. Even though no single individual determines the price, the *market price both coordinates behavior and is itself the outcome of that coordinated behavior*. An increase in the market price rations goods among demanders, encouraging those who can most easily substitute to do so. It also signals firms to increase production in response to the increase in demand and the increased potential for profits. A decrease in the market price entices demanders to purchase more. It also signals firms to decrease production in response to the decrease in demand and the lowered potential for profits.

Price Elasticity of Supply

The size of the effect on price and quantity of an increase or decrease in demand will depend, not surprisingly, upon the responsiveness of the quantity supplied to changes in relative prices. Loosely, how large the relative price and quantity adjustments are when the demand curve shifts depends, in part, on what the supply curve looks like at a particular price. Compare the two markets illustrated in Figure 16. An identical change in demand leads to very different market outcomes. In both cases, relative prices and quantities fall, but the change in price is relatively less in part (a) than in part (b), while the change in quantity is relatively greater in part (a) than in part (b). The different equilibrium in these markets result from differences in the elasticity of supply.[3]

In the market illustrated in part (a), a small decline in the relative price leads to a large change in quantity supplied; that is, supply is elastic. In the market illustrated in part (b), a larger decline in relative price leads to a smaller change in quantity supplied.

In this market, supply is inelastic and the market price has to decrease by a larger amount in order to coordinate the competing interests of suppliers and demanders and eliminate any excess supply.

$$\text{elasticity of supply} = \%\Delta \text{ in quantity supplied} / \%\Delta \text{ in price}$$

This formula is similar to the one used to calculate elasticity of demand. The only difference is that to estimate elasticity of supply, we measure quantity along a supply curve rather than along a demand curve. The interpretation of this estimate is analogous to what we learned when calculating the elasticity of demand: supply is **elastic** if the measured elasticity is greater than 1; it is **inelastic** if the measured elasticity is less than 1; if the percentage change in quantity supplied is the same as the percentage change in price, the elasticity of supply is **unitary**. Thus, for example, a supply elasticity of 2 would mean that a 1 percent increase in the price of a commodity would lead to a 2 percent increase in the quantity suppliers would be willing to provide to the market. Or if the elasticity of supply were 0.5, a 1 percent increase in the price of a commodity would lead to a 0.5 percent increase in the quantity supplied to the market.

Elasticity of supply and market adjustment. The elasticity of supply is important because it indicates how much variation in price is necessary to bring about adjustment in a particular market when demand changes. For example, if the college you are attending suddenly increases the size of its freshman class, there will be an increase in the demand for rental housing near the college. Rents will increase. If the supply of rental housing is elastic, your rent will not change by much. If the supply of rental housing is inelastic, however, your college's decision to admit more students will increase your rent substantially.

▶ Summary

Short run. A firm must often make short-run decisions about production without being able to change its capital stock. Because the capital stock in these circumstances is fixed, the firm finds that its marginal costs increase as it increases production and decrease as it decreases production.

---

[3] Once again, elasticity will vary along a linear curve, in this case the supply curve. As a consequence, it is not possible to say that one supply curve in Figure 16 is elastic and the other inelastic. All that can be said is that, at the initial market price, one is *more* elastic than the other (or, if you wish, less inelastic).

Figure 16
Elasticity of Supply

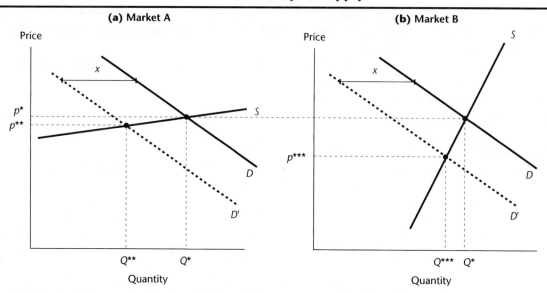

Supply at point p^* is more responsive to a change in price in market A than in market B. As a consequence, a decrease in demand results in a larger change in the amount sold in the first market (from Q^* to Q^{**}) than in the second (from Q^* to Q^{***}), even though the shift in demand is the same in both markets (distance x). Thus supply at p^* in market A is more elastic than it is in market B. Once again, note that this type of comparison must be made from the same initial price and quantity because, in general, the elasticity of supply cannot be determined from the slope of the supply curve.

Profits. Profits are total revenues minus total costs, where revenues are equal to the amount sold multiplied by the market price. Total costs are equal to the explicit and implicit costs of production, including the explicit costs associated with payments to input owners, the implicit costs associated with the use of previously purchased intermediate goods and resources, the value of depreciation, and the normal rate of return to the owners of the firm.

Perfectly competitive market. If a firm sells its output in a perfectly competitive market, then it will find that no decision it makes about how much to produce will affect the price at which it can sell its output.

Short-run competitive supply for a firm. When a firm finds its capital is fixed and that it sells in a competitive market, the marginal cost schedule (or curve) for the firm becomes the firm's short-run competitive supply schedule (or curve) as long as the market price is greater than average variable cost. If the market price is below the firm's average variable cost, the firm will shut down.

The output provided to the market (market supply) is the sum of the amount each competitive firm is willing to produce at each possible market price. Short-run competitive market supply is positively related to the market price—sloping upward to the right—because in the short run each firm will find that, as it attempts to increase production in response to higher market prices, marginal cost increases. Short-run market supply is also positively related to the market price because as the market price increases, firms that chose not to produce when the market price was below their average variable cost and left their capital idle, now find that it is once again profitable to use their capital. In doing so, they reenter the market.

Chapter 9 ▶▶
Long-Run Competitive Supply

The themes in this chapter are simple: First, a short-run competitive market equilibrium cannot persist for long if, at the market equilibrium price, firms are making either economic profits or incurring losses. Economic profits entice new firms to enter a market and provide incentives for existing firms to expand. Economic losses drive existing firms from a market and provide incentives for remaining firms to reduce fixed costs, a task that is often accomplished by selling part of their capital and contracting. Entry or exit (or expansion or contraction) changes the market supply. As a consequence, the market price moves away from its short-run equilibrium level.

Second, a market equilibrium can persist only when economic profits are expected to be zero because only then will there be no incentive for suppliers to enter or exit. Hence, only when economic profits are expected to be zero will a competitive market be in both short-run *and* long-run equilibrium, that is, at an equilibrium where there are no incentives for further changes in prices or in the amount produced, bought, and sold.

▶ Profits and Losses

Consider first the long-run consequences for competitive markets of profits and losses:

The Long-Run Consequences of Short-Run Economic Profits

Economic profits provide an incentive for new firms to enter a market. To see why, let's think about what happens if demand suddenly increases, for example, suppose that consumers suddenly develop a taste for bagels. The demand for bagels will increase. As the demand for bagels increases, the market price will increase. Firms already in the market will respond to the higher price in the short run by using *existing* capital *more intensively*. That is, they will employ more workers and other inputs they can easily vary. As a consequence, the quantity supplied to the market will increase somewhat. This outcome is illustrated in Figure 1 by the movement toward the new equilibrium E'. At E', the quantity supplied is equal to the quantity demanded and the market price is p^{**}. The short-run increase in production by an existing representative firm (through more intensive use of capital) is illustrated by the distance labeled $1b$; the increase in quantity supplied to the market by *all* firms is illustrated by the distance labeled $1a$.

If the firms currently in the market were earning a normal rate of return at the original market price, then at this new, higher price, those same firms will now be making economic profits for reasons we will explore more carefully later. It follows that the owners of the firms will earn a higher than normal rate of return on the resources they have provided to this industry.

There are two possible responses. First, profitable firms may want to acquire more capital, thereby expanding. Second, outsiders will want to enter the market by starting new firms. Thus, there will be **entry** and **expansion** and, as a consequence,

Figure 1
Long-Run Adjustment When Profits Are Positive

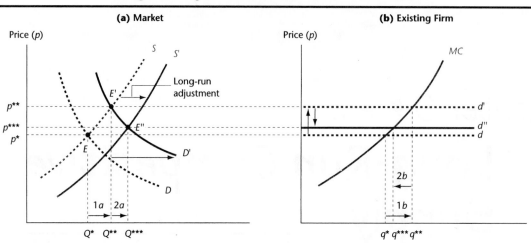

In the short run, an increase in demand (from D to D') leads to an increase in the market price (from p^* to p^{**}). In response, existing firms increase production from q^* to q^{**}, thus moving the market to a short-run equilibrium at E'. Because of the higher market price, existing firms will then be making economic profits. New firms will enter the market, pushing the supply curve out (from S to S'), moving the market from the short-run equilibrium at E' to a long-run equilibrium at E''.

there will be more and, perhaps, larger firms supplying the market.

Entry by new firms will increase the quantity provided to the market *at every possible market price.* That is, market supply increases. As a consequence, the market price will fall from its short-run equilibrium level. This long-run response to short-run profits is illustrated by the rightward shift of the supply curve from S to S'.

In sum, *when there are economic profits, there will be further market adjustments: the number and, perhaps, size of firms will increase; market supply will increase; the market price will decrease; and the quantity bought and sold will increase.*

The Long-Run Consequences of Short-Run Economic Losses

While the possibilities of economic profits stimulate entry, sustained losses drive firms from a market. To see why, let's trace the effects of a sudden decrease in demand, for example, suppose that rock music suddenly became less popular. The demand for rock recordings would decrease. As demand decreased, the market price would also decrease. Recording firms would respond in the short run by using their *existing* capital *less intensively.* Firms use capital less

intensively by laying off workers and reducing the use of other inputs that can be easily adjusted. Output would decrease somewhat as a consequence. The lower market price would move the market toward a new equilibrium. This response is illustrated in Figure 2 by the movement toward E'. At E', the quantity supplied is equal to the quantity demanded and the market price is p^{**}. Hence, E' is an equilibrium. In this case, the decrease in production by an existing representative firm is illustrated by the distance labeled 1*b*; the decrease in quantity supplied by all firms is represented by distance 1*a*.

If the recording companies were originally earning a normal rate of return, then at the new equilibrium price they will be incurring economic losses. As a consequence, the return on the capital that the owners have provided will be less than the return elsewhere in the economy. Firms will want to reduce their fixed costs. They can do so by reducing the amount of capital they have or, in some cases, by leaving the market altogether. Thus, there will be **contraction** and **exit** and, as a consequence, there will be fewer and, perhaps, smaller firms supplying the market.

As firms leave the market, the quantity supplied decreases *at every market price.* That is, market supply decreases. The market moves toward a new equilibrium for which the market price is higher. This

Figure 2
Long-Run Adjustment with Losses

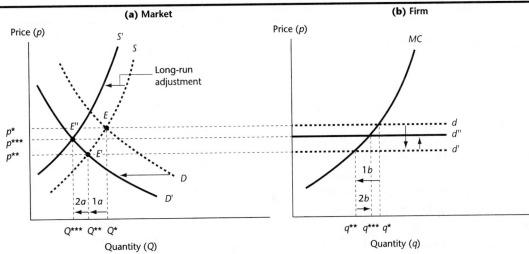

If demand suddenly falls from D to D', the market price also falls, from p* to p**. Firms then cut production from q* to q**, but they will incur economic losses because of the lower market price. In response to these losses, some firms will exit the market, shifting the market supply curve from S to S'. The market will then move from a short-run equilibrium at E' to a long-run equilibrium at E''. The market price will then be higher than it was in the short run, but the quantity sold will be smaller.

long-run response is illustrated by the leftward shift of the supply curve, from S to S'.

In sum, *when there are economic losses, there will be further market adjustments: the number and, perhaps, size of firms will decrease; the market supply will decrease; the market price will increase; and the quantity bought and sold will decrease.*

The Long-Run Consequences of Zero Economic Profits

It should be clear that the only time there will be no incentive for firms either to enter or exit is when the economic profits that they can expect to earn are equal to zero. In other words, a market will be in **long-run equilibrium** only when the rate of return on capital that new or existing firms might expect to earn is equal to the normal rate of return in *other,* comparable activities elsewhere in the economy.

▶ Profits and Costs

As we learned in Chapter 8, profits are maximized when the level of production is chosen such that *marginal cost* is equal to *marginal revenue* (where marginal revenue is the market price for firms in competitive markets, remember). At this level of

production, however, *total cost* may be greater than, or less than, or just equal to *total revenue.* Thus, adjusting production decisions until marginal cost is just equal to market price is the best a firm can do in its pursuit of profits, but it does not necessarily mean that a firm will actually make economic profits. Sometimes the best a firm can do is minimize its losses. At other times, the best a firm can do is earn the normal rate of return on its capital. And, at still other times, the best a firm can do results in economic profits. Each is a possible profit-maximizing outcome.

Whether a firm makes economic profits, earns a normal rate of return, or incurs losses depends upon at least some circumstances that are beyond its control. Specifically, some costs, notably those associated with inputs that are fixed in the short run, are beyond the immediate control of the firm. If a firm spends a lot of money on new capital, those costs cannot be changed later. In addition, in a competitive market, no single firm can affect the market price at which it can sell what it produces. Given these constraints, the firm makes its best output decision. Once this decision is made, the market price and the costs from earlier decisions then determine, in part, the firm's actual profits. Thus, losses or profits are not necessarily the outcome of bad or good choices by a firm or the results of bad or good management. Often, they are simply a consequence of changes in the market price.

Short-Run Average Total Cost and Profits or Losses

To see why the best a firm can do may not always lead to economic profits or even a normal rate of return, we compare the market price at which a firm sells its output with the *average total cost* that the firm incurs as it produces that output. When the market price is *greater* than the average total cost of producing output, the firm earns an above normal rate of return. When the market price is *less* than the average total cost, however, the firm incurs economic losses and earns a below normal rate of return. A firm will earn a normal rate of return only when the market price at which it sells its output is equal to the average cost at which it produces the output.

Consider, for example, the costs for the tennis ball firm detailed in Table 1. The marginal cost schedule is the firm's short-run supply schedule, as long as the market price is greater than average variable cost. Table 2 indicates the resulting profits for the firm when marginal cost is equal to the market price. For any market price up to $.83, losses will be $100—the firm's fixed costs. At prices equal to or greater than $.83, the firm will choose to operate.

Table 1
Production Decisions and Short-Run Costs

Fixed cost ($)	Variable cost ($)	Total cost ($)	Output	ATC	AVC	MC
$100	$ 0	$100	0	—	—	—
100	75	175	75	$2.33	$1.00	$1.00
100	100	200	100	2.00	1.00	1.00
100	125	225	150	1.50	.83	.50
100	150	250	225	1.11	.67	.33
100	175	275	275	1.00	.64	.50
100	200	300	315	.95	.63	.63
100	225	325	345	.94	.65	.83
100	250	350	365	.96	.68	1.25
100	275	375	380	.99	.72	1.67
100	300	400	390	1.03	.77	2.50
100	325	425	395	1.08	.82	5.00

Table 2
Production Decisions and Short-Run Average Total Costs

Output	Total cost ($)	ATC ($)	MC ($)	Profits ($) (when MC = p)
0	$100	$2.00	—	—
0	100	1.50	$ .50	−$100.00
0	100	1.11	.33	−100.00
0	100	1.00	.50	−100.00
315	300	.95	.63	−100.00
345	325	.94	.83	−38.65
365	350	.96	1.25	+106.25
380	375	.99	1.67	+259.60
390	400	1.03	2.50	+575.00
395	425	1.08	5.00	+1,550.00

For example, if the market price is $1.25, the firm will choose to produce 365 units of output because, when it does, its marginal cost is $1.25. Should the market price increase to $2.50, the firm will respond by increasing its output to 390 because, when it produces at this level, its marginal cost will also be $2.50. At any market price, then, the firm adjusts its output to market changes so as to bring its marginal cost (column 4 of Table 2) into line with that market price.

By comparing column 3 in Table 2 with column 4 and then looking at the corresponding profit in column 5, we can see that profits are negative whenever the entry in column 3 is greater than the entry in column 4 and positive whenever the entry in column 3 is less than the entry in column 4.

Average Total Cost, Marginal Cost, and Profits. Several relationships are of interest in Table 1 and 2. First, when the market price is *less* than average total cost, the firm incurs losses. By contrast, when the market price is *greater* than the average total cost, the firm makes economic profits. For example, when the price is $.83, average total cost is $.94 and profits are −$38.65 (see Table 2, row 6). When the price is $1.67, however, average total cost is $.99 and the firm's profits are $259.60 (see Table 2, row 8).[1]

It is important to understand what this means. The firm is trying to make as much profit as it can, but when the market price is $.83, it loses $38.65. Losing $38.65 is the best that it can do! On the other hand, if the market price increases to $1.67, the firm makes a profit of $259.60—the best that it can do at *this* market price. A competitive firm cannot choose its market price; it simply responds to whatever price the market determines and then takes its losses or profits.

The second interesting relationship to note in Table 2 is that when marginal cost is *less* than average total cost, average total costs are *decreasing*, and when marginal cost is *greater* than average total cost, average total costs are *increasing*. For example, at a marginal cost of $.63, average total cost falls from $.95 to $.94 when output increases, but at a marginal cost of $1.25, average total cost increases from $.96 to $.99 when output increases.

Finally, when average total costs are near their minimum, economic profits are near zero. This can also be seen in Table 2: when output is between 345 and 365, *ATC* is at its minimum and profits are near zero.

Average total cost, marginal cost, and profits, more generally. The observed numerical relationships in Table 2 are not unique to this particular example. The general principles can be developed as follows:

Point 1. If average total cost is less than market price, profits must be positive, and if average total cost is greater than market price, the firm must be making losses.

To see this, note that by definition

$$ATC = TC/q.$$

It follows, obviously, that

$$TC = ATC \times q.$$

Total revenue is equal to the market price multiplied by the number of units that the firm sells, *q*:

$$TR = p \times q$$

Look carefully at both of these equations. Since the firm's output, *q*, is the same in both equations, *if ATC is less than p, TC must be less than TR*. (If *ATC*

= $1.00 and *p* = $2.00, for example, then $q \times \$1.00$ is certainly less than $q \times \$2.00$.) If total cost is less than total revenue, however, then the firm must be making economic profits. That is,

$$\text{Total profit} = \underset{\text{TR}}{p \times q} - \underset{\text{TC}}{ATC \times q}$$

Hence, if total profit > 0, then it must be that $p \times q > ATC \times q$, and, therefore, $p > ATC$.

On the other hand, if *ATC* is greater than *p*, *TC* must be greater than *TR*. When total cost is greater than total revenue, the firm must be making economic losses. Once again,

$$\text{Total profit} = \underset{\text{TR}}{p \times q} - \underset{\text{TC}}{ATC \times q}$$

And in this case, if total profit < 0, then it must be that $p \times q < ATC \times q$, and, therefore, $p < ATC$.

And, of course, if *ATC* just equals *p*, total cost just equals total revenue and the firm earns a normal rate of return on the owners' resources since

$$\text{Total profit} = \underset{\text{TR}}{p \times q} - \underset{\text{TC}}{ATC \times q}$$

If total profit = 0, then it must be that $p \times q = ATC \times q$, and, therefore, $p = ATC$.

To summarize, we have developed a checklist for determining whether a firm is making economic profits:

1. find the optimal (profit maximizing) level of production by choosing q so that MC is equal to the market price, p*

2. at that level of production, q*, determine the ATC

3. compare ATC at q* with the market price, p* and
   if ATC > p*, the firm is incurring economic losses
   if ATC = p*, the firm has zero economic profits
   if ATC < p*, the firm is making economic profits

Point 2. When marginal cost is below average total cost, average total costs will fall, but when marginal cost is above average total cost, average total costs will increase.

---

[1] Remember that profit maximizing behavior implies that p = MC; therefore, the numbers in the column headed "MC" can also be read to be the market price, p.

To explain this difficult but important point, consider some quite different examples that illustrate the relationship between "average" and "marginal": Suppose that a baseball player has 20 hits in 60 times at bat. His batting average would be .333 (20 divided by 60). If he goes 4 for 5 today, his "batting marginal"—the effect of the last game he played—is .800 (4 divided by 5). If his average was .333 but in his most recent game he hit .800, intuition would suggest that his batting average would increase. It does. That is, before his last game he had a .333 average, but after his last game he has 24 hits in 65 times at bat, for a batting average of .369, which is indeed greater than .333. His average increased because the marginal was greater than the previous average. On the other hand, if he goes 1 for 5 today, his batting "marginal" is .200 and you would guess that his batting average would fall. In fact, it falls from .333 to .323 because he now has 21 hits out of 65 times at bat.

For a second example, consider that tender but important average, your grade-point average (GPA). Suppose that your GPA on a four-point scale is 3.0. If you get a 4.0 *this* term (the last or marginal term), you know that your grade-point average will increase. On the other hand, if you get a 2.0 this term, your marginal is below your average and, not surprisingly, you new grade-point average will be below 3.0.

Thus, *a marginal below the average pulls the average down while a marginal above the average pulls the average up.* As a consequence, even though the actual dollar value of average cost depends upon a wide variety of things (including wage rates, interest rates, rental rates, the technology the firm employs, and how efficient the firm is), the *qualitative* relationship between a firm's average costs and its marginal costs must be like that illustrated in Figure 3.

If the marginal is below the average, the average falls; if the marginal is above the average, the average increases. Therefore, *marginal cost will always equal average total cost at the minimum of average total cost.* That is, if your grade point average is 3.0 and last semester you also earned a 3.0, then your GPA will not change. Similarly, if a baseball player is batting .333 and has 2 hits in 6 times at bat in his last game, his batting average will not change either.

Point 3. Economic profits are zero when the market price is equal to the minimum average total cost of producing output.

To see why, consider the firm illustrated in Figure 3. The market equilibrium price is p^*. To maximize its profits in the short run, the firm must adjust its output so that marginal cost is equal to this price. The firm will choose to produce q^*. At q^*, average total cost is greater than marginal cost by the amount indicated by the distance A. It follows that average total cost is also greater than the market price. Since p^* < ATC, the firm is incurring losses. Indeed, these losses are equal to the area of the rectangle indicated in Figure 3.

Figure 3
The Effect When Price Is Less Than Average Total Cost

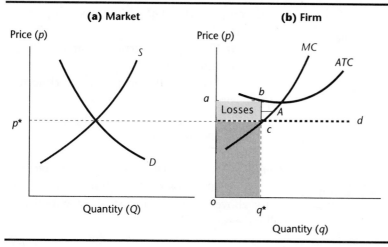

(a) Market   **(b) Firm**

If the market price is p^*, firms will produce q^*, where price equals marginal cost. But at this level of production, the market price is below the average total cost to the firm. The firm receives revenues equal to the area op^*cq^*, but costs equal area $oabq^*$. The firm will therefore be making losses equal to the lighter red area.

Figure 4
The Effect When Price Is Greater Than Average Total Cost

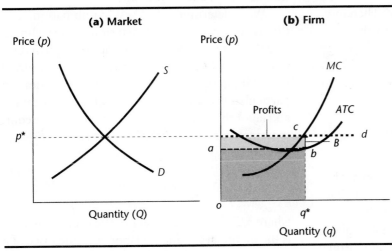

(a) Market

Price (*p*)

Quantity (*Q*)

(b) Firm

Price (*p*)

MC

Profits

ATC

c

a

B

b

d

o

q*

Quantity (*q*)

If the market price is *p**, firms will produce *q**, where price equals marginal cost. But at this level of production, average total cost is below the market price. Revenues to the firm equal area *op*cq**, but costs only equal area *oabq**. The firm will therefore earn positive economic profits equal to the lighter red area.

Why? Losses are the difference between a firm's revenues and its costs. The area of any rectangle is the height multiplied by the base, so *p** (height) x *q** (base) is the firm's total revenue. This is illustrated by the area outlined by *op*cq**. Because total cost is equal to *ATC* x *q**, the firm's total cost in Figure 3 is the rectangle with base *q** and height *ATC*—the area outlined by *oabq**. Losses are equal to the difference between total revenue and total cost, so those losses can be represented by the difference between these two rectangles and losses are equal to the rectangle *p*abc*.

Figure 4 tells a different story about the plight of the firm. If the market price is *p**, this firm will choose to produce *q**, thereby equating marginal

cost with the market price. At *q**, average total cost is less than marginal cost and, therefore, less than the market price by the distance *B*. Average total cost in this case is *oa* (or *q*b*) whereas marginal cost is *op** (or *q*c*). The total cost of producing *q** is *q** × *ATC*, which is indicated by the area *oabq**. The total revenue obtained when *q** is sold at the competitive market price of *p** is *q** × *p**, which can be measured by the area *op*cq**. In this case, profits are positive and equal to the area of the rectangle indicated in Figure 4.

Finally, Figure 5 tells yet another story. In this case, if the market price is *p**, the firm will choose to produce *q**. At *q**, marginal cost and average cost are exactly the same and average cost is at its

Figure 5
The Effect When Price Equals Average Total Cost

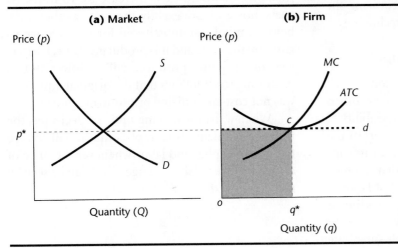

(a) Market

Price (*p*)

S

p*

D

Quantity (*Q*)

(b) Firm

Price (*p*)

MC

ATC

c

d

o

q*

Quantity (*q*)

If the market price is *p**, firms will produce *q**, where price equals marginal cost. At this point, price also equals average total cost. This means that both revenues and total costs equal area *op*cq**. The firm will therefore earn zero economic profits when the price equals the average total cost.

minimum. Marginal and average cost are, in this case, measured by q^*c (or op^*). Total cost will be op^*cq^*; total revenues will also be op^*cq^*. Therefore, profits will be zero. When profits are zero, the market price is just equal to the minimum of average total costs. This means that when profits are zero, a competitive market provides commodities to demanders at the *lowest technically possible* cost.

▶ Long-Run Average Cost and Long-Run Market Supply

In the long run, a firm can vary all of its inputs. This means that a firm can determine *both* how much to produce and how to go about producing. That is, in the long run, it can choose the mix of capital, labor, and other resources it wishes to use, *substituting* one input for another.

A firm can also choose the scale of its activity. Sometimes, if the firm expects to earn profits, it makes sense to expand an existing plant. At other times, it makes sense to build additional plants. Of course, a new firm can choose any combination of inputs it wishes, as long as they are consistent with the technologies available, and it can choose whether to organize those inputs in a single plant or in several plants.

When a firm acquires new capital, it may also adopt new technologies, particularly when a technology is embedded in a particular kind of capital. For example, when you buy a computer, you buy a particular configuration of memory, hard disk, and processing speed (that is, a particular technology). Even though it is still possible to purchase older, slower machines, if you added capital today (rather than five years ago), you have the option of acquiring a faster new machine. Thus, by acquiring the new capital, you also acquire the new technology.

Substitutability and Choice of Inputs

A supplier's demand for inputs, like a consumer's demand for goods and services, is very much affected by substitution, in this case, by the ability of a firm to substitute one input for another. In the short run, of course, the firm cannot substitute capital for labor (or labor for capital, for that matter), but may be able to substitute one kind of labor—say highly skilled workers—for another kind of labor—workers with lower skills—or vice versa. In the long run, however, the firm can freely substitute

and will choose the "best" or "optimal" combination of capital and labor.

What determines the "best" combination? Two things: technology (which determines the technical way that inputs substitute for one another) and input prices (which determine the profit-maximizing mix of inputs given these technical possibilities). In particular, firms will choose the amount of capital and labor they wish to use consistent with the equimarginal rule for maximizing profits:

$$\frac{MP_K}{p_K} = \frac{MP_L}{p_L} \tag{1}$$

where MP_K is the marginal product of capital, MP_L is the marginal product of labor, p_K is the price of a unit of capital, and p_L is the price of a unit of labor. The **marginal product of capital** is the amount by which a firm's output increases when a firm adds a small amount of capital; the **marginal product of labor** is the amount by which a firm's output increases when a firm hires additional workers.

To see why this profit-maximizing rule corresponds to a best or optimal long-run mix of inputs, suppose that the relationship does not hold. To make the argument specific, suppose that a unit of capital costs $2.00 and adds 10 units of output to the firm's production, whereas the last unit of labor hired costs $1.00 and adds three units of output. This combination of capital and labor is not optimal. Specifically, the firm could employ two fewer units of labor. If it did, its output would fall by about six units. But its costs would also fall (by $2.00). The firm could then employ an additional unit of capital. Its cost would go back up (by $2.00). If it did this, output would then increase by 10 units. Its costs, however, are exactly the same as they were before capital was substituted for labor. Since its costs are the same and it is producing more, its average costs per unit produced will be lower and its profits higher. It follows that the original input mix was not cost-minimizing or profit-maximizing.

When a firm is making optimal decisions, the profit-maximizing rule implies that it will change the mix of capital and labor whenever the price of capital relative to labor changes. This can be seen by rearranging Equation (1) so that

$$\frac{MP_K}{MP_L} = \frac{p_K}{p_L} \tag{2}$$

If the price of capital relative to labor increases, firms will adopt technologies that are less capital-intensive; if the price of capital relative to labor falls, firms will adopt technologies that are more capital-intensive. That is, in Equation (2), when p_K increases, the equality will only be reestablished if the ratio of MP_K / MP_L increases. This ratio can only increase if the amount of capital relative to labor decreases so that the marginal product of capital increases and the marginal product of labor decreases. Thus, when making long-run input decisions, firms will behave in much the same way as consumers when they respond to changing market prices. Specifically, in the long run, firms substitute lower-cost inputs for higher-cost inputs, *ceteris paribus*.

Average Total Cost When the Optimal Combination of Inputs Is Chosen

Given that a firm can substitute labor and capital in the long run but cannot do so in the short run (that is, can only use capital more or less intensively), we need to distinguish between *short-run average total cost* and *long-run average total cost*. With regard to long-run average cost, there are three possibilities:

1. Increasing returns to scale
2. Constant returns to scale
3. Decreasing returns to scale

Increasing returns to scale. When a firm increases all of its inputs, its potential output may increase more than proportionally to the increase in its inputs. That is, doubling inputs may *more* than double output. This effect is called **increasing returns to scale** or **economies of scale**.

There are a number of reasons why a firm might encounter economies of scale. A firm may be able to break its production into more steps, thereby using its labor inputs in more specialized tasks as it grows. With this further specialization, its output might increase by an amount that is greater than the increases in its inputs. A larger firm may also be able to utilize more highly specialized and expensive machines that increase output by an amount more than proportional to the increase in capital and labor used but which are only cost-effective to acquire when the volume of output is high. Think, for example, of the different equipment a farmer might employ if he or she framed a few acres rather than several hundred acres or several thousand acres. There may also be highly specialized tasks requiring costly training and that are, as a consequence, only viable when a firm can spread those costs over a large output. Set-up costs and management personnel costs might not vary with output, so that the larger the firm and the greater the output, the smaller the set-up costs per unit. For example, a firm may not need to double its marketing personnel in order to sell twice as much output, or it may not need to double the number of managers or supervisors when it doubles the number of machines. Multi-product firms may be able to lengthen production runs for each product, thereby lowering per unit costs. In addition, there are generally economies of scale associated with holding inventories or stocks of spare parts. That is, as a firm gets larger, it generally does not need to increase proportionally its stock of inventory, spare parts, or other service-related items. Finally, there may be a gain in efficiency because a firm is able to adopt new technologies as it acquires new capital.

In any of these cases, a firm's average costs decrease as it expands, as seen in Figure 6. Clearly, **decreasing long-run average costs** result directly from increasing returns to scale.

Economies of scope. Firms can grow by expanding their capacity to produce a single output. When they do so, economies of scale are possible. In addition, however, firms can grow by producing more than a single kind of output. If, as sometimes happens, it is cheaper to produce two or more products jointly than it is to produce them separately, there are **economies of scope**. For example, one firm could raise and slaughter cattle only for their hides and another could raise and slaughter them only for their meat, but there are clearly advantages for a single firm to produce both hides and meat at the same time. As a consequence, the costs of producing both meat and hides will be lower than if they were produced by separate firms. Meat and hide production has an economy of scope. More generally, economies of scope are usually possible when a single input can be used simultaneously to produce more than one kind of output.

Constant returns to scale. It may be that output changes in proportion to any change in inputs. For example, an existing firm can always replicate its

Figure 6
Economies of Scale

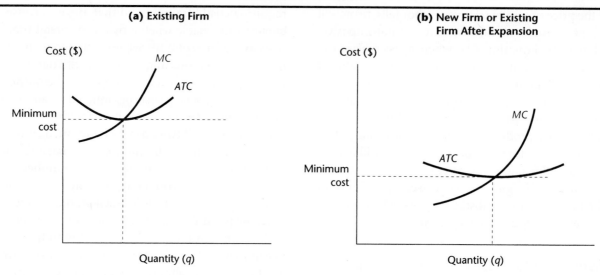

(a) Existing Firm

Cost ($)

MC

ATC

Minimum cost

Quantity (q)

(b) New Firm or Existing Firm After Expansion

Cost ($)

MC

ATC

Minimum cost

Quantity (q)

When there are economies of scale, new firms or old firms that expand have lower minimum average total costs than existing firms. In this case, larger firms have lower costs than smaller ones.

current plant in a separate plant and, it would appear, double its output by doubling its inputs. If it could, its production would have **constant returns to scale**. In this case there are no efficiency gains from becoming larger; average costs *at their minimum* will be the same for a larger or smaller firm as illustrated in Figure 7. A firm encountering constant returns to scale will have **constant long-run average costs**.

Decreasing returns to scale. If a firm increases all inputs, but output does not increase proportionally to the increase in inputs—that is, a doubling of inputs results in less than double output—the firm confronts **decreasing returns to scale or diseconomies of scale**. In this case, the minimum average cost associated with the optimal combination of inputs increases as the firm increases its size and the firm has **increasing long-run average costs**.

Figure 7
Constant Returns to Scale

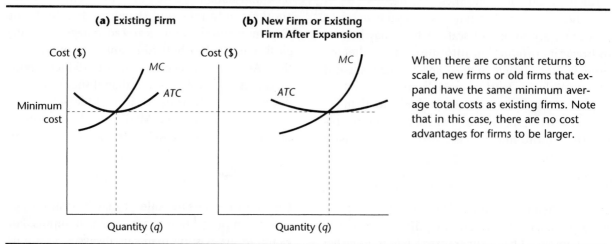

(a) Existing Firm

Cost ($)

MC

ATC

Minimum cost

Quantity (q)

(b) New Firm or Existing Firm After Expansion

Cost ($)

MC

ATC

Quantity (q)

When there are constant returns to scale, new firms or old firms that expand have the same minimum average total costs as existing firms. Note that in this case, there are no cost advantages for firms to be larger.

Why might a firm encounter decreasing returns? It may be that as firms increase in size, the management and control of specialized production or marketing activities becomes more difficult, thereby increasing costs. That is, monitoring costs might increase. The transportation costs necessary to service a larger market might also increase, although this problem can be quite easily overcome by having several plants instead of one. Or, it may be that some input simply cannot be acquired in additional amounts, for example, a particularly attractive location or a highly skilled manager, and, hence, beyond some point, average costs increase because less attractive locations or less skilled managers must be used.

The difference between diminishing returns and decreasing returns. A caution: diminishing returns and decreasing returns to scale are sometimes confused. They are, however, quite different concepts.

Diminishing returns occur when a firm increases the amount of *one* input used, while the amount of other inputs used, such as capital or land, does not change. As a consequence of the more intensive use of the fixed input, increases in output become smaller and smaller as more of the variable input is used. Thus, employing more and more workers in the same factory or to farm the same land leads to diminishing returns to labor, or what we have termed slightly differently, to the *diminishing marginal product of labor.*

Decreasing returns to scale occur when a firm increases *all* inputs, but increases in its output are *less* than proportional to the increase in the inputs. Decreasing returns are not a consequence of diminishing returns.

The concepts are different, so it shouldn't be surprising that the consequences are different as well. Diminishing returns means that at some point, in the short run, as the amount produced increases, marginal cost will also increase. Decreasing returns, by contrast, means that as a firm gets larger in the long run, average total costs will increase even when the firm chooses the optimal input mix.

Short-Run and Long-Run Average Costs

Once a firm has determined the best combination of capital, labor, and other resources, it will be able to minimize costs only if it actually produces the intended output. In the short run, however, the demand for the firm's output might not be equal to the amount that it planned to produce. Indeed, as we explored in some detail in Chapter 8, a firm may have opportunities to increase its profits if it uses its capital more intensively than originally planned by increasing the use of labor. Conversely, a firm may find that it can minimize losses if it uses its capital less intensively than originally planned by decreasing its use of labor. In either case, short-run average costs will always be *greater* than long-run average costs because the **long-run average cost curve** represents the lowest possible cost of producing each possible level of output when the firm can freely adjust both capital and labor. In the short run the best that a firm can do is live with its earlier decisions about how much capital to acquire and adjust the only thing that it can: its use of labor. In the long run, by contrast, not only can the firm adjust its labor or other variable inputs, it can also vary the amount of capital it employs.

Thus, as Figure 8 illustrates, a firm can choose to move along the long-run average cost curve *only in the long run*, that is, only by optimally adjusting capital, labor, and any other necessary inputs (essentially picking one of the short-run average cost curves illustrated in the figure). In the short run, the firm's choices are constrained by the amount of capital it acquired earlier and it can only move along its short-run average cost curve as it changes its output in response to changes in the market price. For example, the firm in Figure 9 has planned to produce at q. Market conditions, however, are such that it sells only q^*. As a consequence, its average costs are higher than they would have been at the optimum level of output. Its average costs are also higher than they would have been had the firm known it was only going to be able to sell q^*. Had it known, it would have acquired less capital and operated at a smaller scale, as illustrated by $SRAC_2$. It chose to acquire more capital, however, and is stuck with $SRAC_1$, at least in the short run.

Long-Run Market Adjustment When There Is Entry and Exit

It is important to remember that the *expected* economic profits for any firm that might enter an industry must be zero or else the market cannot be in long-run equilibrium. If a firm expects to be able to earn economic profits, it will enter the market,

Figure 8
A Long-Run Average Cost Curve

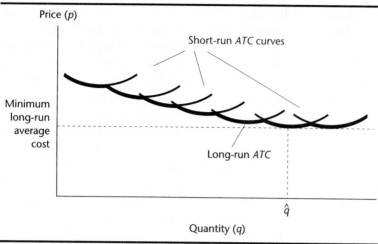

In the long run, a firm can choose different mixes of capital and labor, thus taking advantage of economies of scale when they are available. In this case, as the firm expands, it moves along a long-run average cost curve as indicated. Its average production costs lessen as it expands, until it reaches the scale indicated by $\hat{q}$. At this point, average total costs will not fall with further expansion.

thus increasing supply and the market price will fall from its short-run level. But how far will it fall? The short answer: It depends on the shape of the long-run average cost curve the firm faces. The longer answer follows:

Constant long-run average costs. Suppose that the industry has a constant long-run average cost technology. Any new firms and existing firms will be similar in that their minimum average cost of producing commodities will be the same. A representative existing firm and a new entering firm are illustrated in Figure 10.

Suppose demand increases. The market price increases and existing firms earn economic profits

because, at E', the market price is now above average total cost. A market will obtain a new long-run equilibrium when the expected profits for *entering* firms are zero. If minimum average total costs for the potential new firm are the same as for old firms, in the long run, the market will have to adjust until the market price returns to p^*, its original level. Why? At any price greater the p^*, potential new entrants have positive expected profits. At any price less than p^*, existing firms have losses. A market will only obtain a long-run equilibrium when there is no incentive for either entry or exit, that is, when expected economic profits for new entrants and existing firms are zero. This will only occur when entry has shifted the supply curve to the right so

Figure 9
Optimal Production Scale

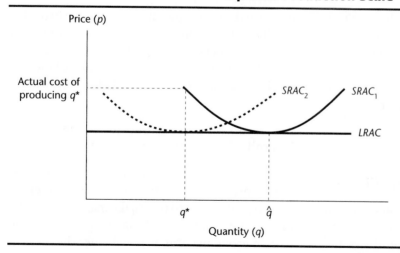

In this example, the firm chooses its input mix by assuming that it will produce $\hat{q}$. A change in market conditions, however, means that, given its capital stock, its optimal short-run output is q^*. If q^* is the most that it can sell in the long run, its costs will fall along $SRAC_1$. In this case, it would have been better off planning to produce less, to make its costs fall along $SRAC_2$. That is, in the long run, $SRAC_2$ is optimal if the firm plans to produce q^*, but $SRAC_1$ is optimal if it plans to produce $\hat{q}$.

Figure 10
Long-Run Adjustment in a Constant-Cost Industry

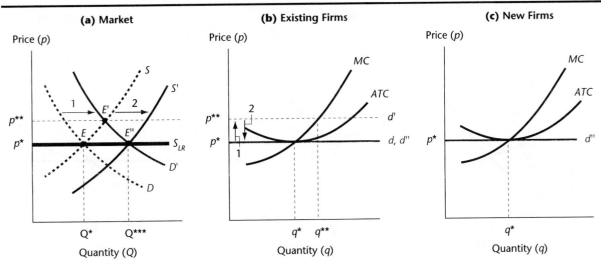

If demand increases from D to D' in a constant-cost industry, the market moves from its original equilibrium at E to a new short-run equilibrium at E' as existing firms increase production from q^* to q^{**} in response to the higher market price of p^{**}. Because they see an opportunity for profits, new firms will enter the market, causing supply to increase. If these firms have the same costs as existing ones, supply shifts from S to S', at which point the market price at the new equilibrium, E'', is the same as the market price at the original equilibrium, E. The long-run supply curve is a horizontal line that connects the two long-run equilibria, E and E''. Note that Q^* equals the sum of the quantities q^* produced by the existing firms and Q^{***} equals the sum of the quantities q^* produced by existing firms plus entering firms.

that the market price is p^*. In this case, the **long-run competitive supply curve** is flat and, over the long run, the market price will neither increase nor decrease.

Decreasing long-run average costs. An industry characterized by decreasing costs has a quite different long-run supply curve. In this case, new firms enter with average costs below those of old firms, or old firms can lower costs by expanding. This effect on the market is illustrated in Figure 11.

Suppose that demand increases from D to D' as shown in Figure 11. The market price increases; existing firms get economic profits as a consequence. These profits provide an incentive for new firms to enter or existing firms to expand. With decreasing long-run average costs, entry and expansion will continue, and, hence, will continue to shift the supply curve to the right until the market price declines from its short-run level, p^{**}, to the price at which entering firms can no longer expect to make positive

profits, p^{***}. As illustrated, the long-run equilibrium price when the industry is larger will be lower than the long-run equilibrium price when the industry is smaller.

In this case, old firms that do not expand will incur losses once the market price has fallen below p^*. These firms will either have to exit or expand. If an industry has increasing returns to scale, the **long-run competitive supply curve** will slope downward and over the long run as the industry grows larger, the market price will decrease.[2]

Increasing long-run average costs. If, instead of constant or increasing returns to scale, the industry is characterized by diseconomies of scale, new firms will have higher average costs than old, smaller

---

[2] In certain cases, decreasing returns to scale may be inconsistent with perfect competition. As we will see in Chapter 13, if costs continue to fall as firms grow, a few firms or even one firm may come to dominate the market.

Figure 11
Long-Run Adjustment in a Decreasing-Cost Industry

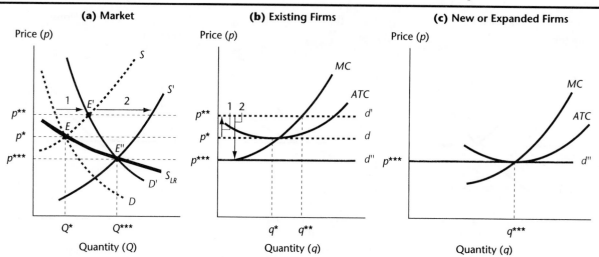

If demand increases from D to D', but the long-run costs are decreasing, the market moves from its original equilibrium at E to a new short-run equilibrium at E' as existing firms increase production from q^* to q^{**} in response to the higher market price of p^{**}. Because they see an opportunity for profits, new firms will enter the market and existing firms will expand. Because these larger firms have lower costs than the original, smaller ones, the potential for profits still exists, even when the market price falls below the original equilibrium price of p^*. Therefore, supply continues to increase from S to S' until the price falls to p^{***}, at which point, there is no incentive for additional entry or expansion. Note that Q^* equals the sum of the quantities q^* produced by the existing firms and Q^{***} equals the sum of the quantities q^{***} produced by existing firms that expand plus entering firms.

firms. If demand increases, thus increasing the market price, economic profits will be positive.

As always, entry will continue as long as expected profits for *entering* firms are positive. Thus, a long-run equilibrium cannot be obtained until the market price decreases to p^{***} in Figure 12 from its short-run position at p^{**}. At any price greater than p^{***}, entry will continue to occur and new capital will move to this market. At any price less than p^{***}, however, potential entering firms cannot expect to make profits and entry will cease. Notice the curious result that at price p^{***}, new firms can expect no economic profits, but old firms will earn positive economic profits because their average total cost is below the market price p^{***}.

Even though old firms are making positive economic profits, new firms will not enter because, for whatever reason, their costs are higher than those of the old firms. In this case, the **long-run competitive supply curve** will slope upward, and, in the long run, prices will increase as demand increases and the industry becomes larger.

Empirical Evidence on Long-Run Costs

Without detailed cost data for a specific industry, it is not possible to predict whether a new entrant or an expanding firm in a particular market will find economies of scale, diseconomies of scale, or constant returns to scale. Thus, if there is a large increase in the demand for bagels, *in the long run*, the price of bagels may be lower than it is today, higher than it is today, or about the same as it is today, even though *in the short run*, the price will certainly increase from its present level. The long-run price effect that follows an increase in demand depends upon the technology or cost structure available as new or expanded bagel producers respond to the profitable opportunities provided by the increase in demand. Similarly, when firms exit from the recording business in response to a large decrease in demand for rock music, in the long run the price of CDs may rise, fall, or stay about the same as the current price, even though in the short run, the price will certainly decrease. Put directly, *it is not possible*

Figure 12
Long-Run Adjustment in an Increasing-Cost Industry

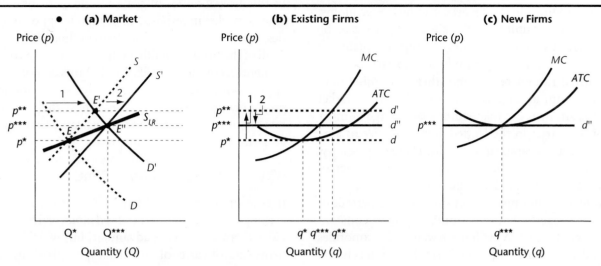

If demand increases from *D* to *D'* in an increasing-cost industry, the market moves from its original equilibrium at *E* to a new short-run equilibrium at *E'*, as existing firms increase production from q^* to q^{**} in response to the higher market price of p^{**}. Because they see an opportunity for profits, new firms will enter the market, causing supply to increase. But because the new firms have higher costs than the existing ones, they will stop entering once the supply has increased from *S* to *S'* and the market price has fallen to p^{***}. Therefore, at the new equilibrium, *E''*, the market price is higher than it was at the original equilibrium, *E*. At the new price of p^{***}, the old firms will produce q^{***} and their average costs will be below the market price. Because they have lower costs, the old firms will make economic profits or rents, while the new firms will make zero economic profits. Note that Q^* equals the sum of the quantities q^* produced by the existing firms and Q^{***} equals the sum of the quantities q^{***} produced by existing firms plus entering firms.

to predict precisely what will happen to the long-run market price when entry or exit occurs. Economic theory tells us, however, that with entry, market prices will fall from their short-run level and, with exit, market prices will increase from their short-run level. Thus, good economics sometimes requires an answer that begins: "I don't know because. . . ."

Efforts to directly estimate the average total cost curve when all production costs are included find that for many industries, the long-run average cost curve looks something like that illustrated in Figure 13. Average costs fall dramatically as very small-scale firms become somewhat larger but, beyond a certain point, average costs do not change greatly with changes in scale.

The point at which costs no longer fall when output increases is called the **minimum efficient scale**. With some important exceptions to be discussed later, the minimum efficient scale is small relative to the size of the market, generally 2 to 3

Figure 13
Long-Run Costs

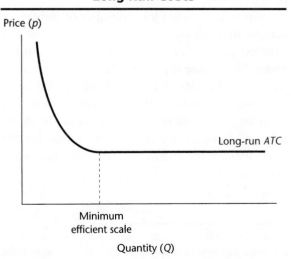

Empirical estimates suggest that long-run costs fall dramatically as the size of very small firms increases, but after a certain point, these costs do not change further.

percent of the market. This means that, in principle, there can be a large number of more or less equally efficient firms in most markets in the U.S. economy.

The possibilities of scale economies can be inferred by considering survivorship. Any plant size that survives for long must be able to earn at least a normal rate of return and, therefore, must have minimum average costs at or below the market price. It turns out that within a fairly large number of industries in the United States, the size of surviving firms varies substantially. There may be a few large firms, but there is also a large number of smaller firms supplying the same market. The persistence of this mix of firm sizes for long periods of time suggests that these industries have constant returns to scale. Why? If there were scale economies or diseconomies, the mix of firm sizes would change over time. In particular, if there were scale economies, a small firm would have to become larger over time in order to survive since with economies of scale larger firms are more profitable at current market prices. If, on the other hand, there were diseconomies of scale, larger firms would be less profitable at current market prices and we would see large firms becoming smaller over time. If the mix of smaller and larger firms persists with little change over time, this implies that each firm is earning at least a normal rate of return and more or less equally cost-effective. But this could only be true for both large and small firms if average costs were about the same, that is, if these firms faced constant returns to scale.[3]

Empirical studies for a number of industries suggest that the share of output produced by the smallest firms has fallen over time in the United States. These same studies indicate that the share of output produced by the largest firms has also fallen over time. For most of these industries, there is a fairly large variance in the size of the firms "in the middle." Hence, these studies imply that for the many firms in the middle, size does not affect average cost.

---

[3] It may be that there are scale economies but that the price is above the minimum average costs of a large firm because the large firm has market power and provides an umbrella for the small firms. This possibility is explored in a later chapter when we discuss monopoly.

▶ Economic Rents

In the diseconomies of scale case, new firms can enter a market in response to profitable opportunities, but only with costs higher than those of some or all of the firms currently in the industry. As a consequence, economic profits for old firms do not disappear with the entry of new firms. Economic profits or, more generally, returns above the normal rate of return that persist for some firms even in the long run are called **economic rents**.

Why Are There Economic Rents?

If entering firms have higher costs, it is because existing firms use some *specialized input*, which provides them with a cost advantage, but which new firms cannot easily obtain. This specialized input might be, for example, a particularly skillful manager who is much better than any other manager who could be hired. If this manager is really much better than any new managers, while a new firm may be able to choose the optimal amount of capital, labor, and other resources, it cannot employ the same manager (or one with equal skill) as another firm is already using. Anyone can open an automobile factory, for example, but not everyone can open one managed by Henry Ford.

The specialized input might be a particularly attractive location. In this case, a new firm can enter a market with the optimal combination of capital and labor, but it cannot be located in exactly the same place as an existing firm. Anyone can open a pizza restaurant, for example, but since a limited amount of land is available, a late comer might not be able to locate right next to a college campus.

The specialized input might be a worker with a unique skill. In this case, a new firm might not be able to find employees as skilled as those employed by the existing firms even though it can do everything else an existing firm can do. A new basketball team can be formed in Los Angeles, for example, but Shaq and Kobe Bryant play for the Lakers, and it may be difficult to find two players as talented to play for the new team.

In each of these examples, a new entrant is at a disadvantage when compared with one or more existing firms. This disadvantage will be reflected in higher costs for entering firms and existing firms will get economic rents.

Who Receives the Economic Rent?

The owner of the unique input may also be the owner of the firm. Often, however, someone other than the owner of the firm owns the unique input. Firms, both old and new, can often compete for the unique input. When they do, rents will end up going to the actual owner of the unique input and not necessarily to the firm currently using the unique input.

If one firm has a particularly skillful manager and consequently lower production costs, for example, other firms can enter the market with higher costs because they are not as well managed or they can try to persuade the manager to leave her current job and work for them. As other firms make this manager higher salary offers, her current employer must respond with a higher salary offer as well or else she is likely to leave. The value of the manager to any firm is the rent she produces for her employer. Therefore both the new and the old firms should be willing to pay *an amount up to the rent* to have the manager work in their firm.

The outcome? Competition eventually moves the rent from the firm employing the unique input to the owner of the unique resource. The costs for the firm that initially employed the unique input increase, either because it has to pay its especially skillful manager more or because its manager moves to another firm and it's no longer as well managed. The firm that hires the especially skillful manager finds, however, that its costs do not decrease much even though it now employs the unique input because competition forced it to pay its new manager a salary equal to the rent she creates. As a consequence, what was originally a rent for a particular firm becomes a cost to whomever employs the especially skillful manager—all firms end up with approximately the same costs, and the especially skillful manager ends up with a high income.

In the case of the LA Lakers, for example, Kobe is a unique input. Teams will compete within the rules established by the National Basketball Association for his services. As they do, the Lakers will have to increase what they pay Kobe to keep him from moving to another team. An analogous argument suggests that the owner of land in a particularly attractive location will capture most of the rent associated with the location as firms compete with each other for right to use the land. Thus, if a fast-food store has a particularly attractive location near a campus, a new entrant can either build in a less attractive place or it can try to purchase or rent the property where the competing, more profitable firm is located. This means that whoever owns the property will get the rent that reflects the locational advantage.

Do Economic Rents Serve Any Socially Useful Purpose?

Typically, higher input prices increase the supply of inputs. Thus, if the incomes of engineers increase, more students will choose to become engineers. Economic rents occur, however, when inputs are unique and, therefore, where it's difficult or impossible to increase supply. As a consequence, it might appear that economic rents serve no useful purpose in an economy. As we have learned, rents occur because of competition for the unique input. In doing so, they provide an incentive for unique inputs to be used in the firm where they have the highest value. It follows that economic rents are important in allocating unique input among competing uses. Kobe Bryant, for example, will end up playing for the team to whom he is the most valuable. In this case, he gets the rent (and becomes a wealthy young man), but the rent plays an important role in allocating Kobe's services between basketball and other activities and among basketball teams.

Demands and Costs

Kobe's unique talents matter, of course, because lots of people want to see him play. Because demand drives up Kobe's worth and thus the salary that the Lakers must pay, the Lakers' costs in this case are determined in part by the demand to see Kobe play. Owners of professional sports teams often argue, however, that high salaries for players lead to high ticket prices because the team is "only passing along the outrageous salaries the market has forced it to pay." This isn't necessarily so.

Higher salaries are often a consequence of higher ticket prices, not vice versa. Ticket prices are high because fans demand seats at basketball games. Similarly, advertising time for televised professional football games is costly because people want to watch these games on TV. Because entry by new teams with equally talented players is difficult, these demands for seats and advertising time create rents for the current owners of professional teams. With competition among teams for talented players, however, the rents move from the team owners to the players in the form of high salaries. Thus, high ticket prices and high advertising time prices lead to high salaries not vice versa.

If this argument seems wrong, consider the low salaries of soccer players, gymnasts, swimmers, or chess players. Are they less talented than football and basketball players? Or is it that soccer, gymnastics, swimming, and chess simply are less popular spectator sports? It should be apparent that because these activities are not wildly popular spectator activities, demand is low, ticket prices are low and, hence, salaries are low. This suggests that not all unique inputs will earn rents. Rents will occur only when there are unique resources *and* when there is substantial or increasing demand for the good or service produced using these scarce and unique resources.

▶ Summary

Profits, losses, and incentives. If all firms in an industry earn economic profits, there will be an incentive for new firms to enter the market and for existing firms to expand. Entry or expansion brings new capital to the market. If, on the other hand, most firms in an industry incur economic losses, there will be an incentive for existing firms to leave the market or to contract. Exit or contraction moves capital away from the market and toward other activities.

Long-run equilibrium. A market is in long-run equilibrium when the profits that any potential entering firm expects to earn are zero and when firms within the industry can expect to earn a normal rate of return. This means that a perfectly competitive market cannot be in long-run equilibrium unless any existing firm earns profits equal to what the owners of the firm's capital might earn if they used their capital elsewhere in the economy.

The effects of exit and entry. As firms exit or enter, the market supply changes. With entry and expansion, market supply increases, and the market price falls from its short-run level. With exit and contraction, market supply decreases, and the market price increases from its short-run level.

Long-run supply. The long-run supply curve is perfectly elastic if there are constant long-run costs; it slopes downward if there are decreasing long-run costs; and it slopes upward if there are increasing long-run costs. These correspond to constant returns to scale, increasing returns to scale, and decreasing returns to scale, respectively. What the long-run supply curve for any particular industry looks like is an empirical matter that depends on the specific characteristics of that industry.

The importance of long-run adjustments. The important point of this chapter is that the market price can adjust so that the quantity supplied to the market is exactly equal to the quantity demanded—a short-run equilibrium—yet market adjustments continue. This is because profits and losses create incentives for additional market adjustments. If, at a short-run equilibrium, both old and new firms can expect to make profits, entry will occur and the market price will decline. Or if at a short-run equilibrium firms are incurring losses, they will exit as soon as they can dispose of their capital and the market price will increase. Thus, market prices will no longer change only when both the quantity supplied is exactly equal to the quantity demanded *and* expected profits are zero for any firm that enters or leaves the market. That is, a market is in long-run equilibrium only when supply is equal to demand and profits are zero.

Economic rents. If there are unique, scarce inputs whose supply cannot be easily increased and if there is competition for the use of these inputs, economic rents will be created. Generally, competition among firms employing these inputs will mean that the economic rents will go to the owners of the unique inputs.

Chapter 10 ▶▶
Competitive Markets and Efficiency

We live in an economy that relies mostly on markets, and therefore on prices and profits, to coordinate private interests. Even so, there has been a long and vigorous debate about the appropriate balance between markets and other ways of coordinating competing interests. Thus, even within economies that already rely extensively on markets, direct governmental regulation is often thought to be an attractive alternative for accommodating competing interests. Debates in the United States about health care or agricultural policy or environmental policy or the role of public schooling often pit greater reliance on the government against greater reliance on markets.

This chapter makes the case for markets. Chapter 12 furthers this argument by outlining the problems that are often created when a government intervenes in market economic activity. By contrast, the remainder of the book (the chapters beyond 12) outlines in some detail the reasons why markets may not work. In a sense, these chapters make the case for appropriate government intervention. Thus, this is the first chapter in a series whose purpose is to engage you in the larger public policy debate about whether or when to rely relatively more or relatively less on markets.

A way of framing this important debate is to ask what an economic system ought to do. Posing a question about how an economic system *ought* to work is quite different from analyzing *how* an economic system actually works. Describing how markets work and predicting responses to incentives is sometimes called **positive analysis**. Evaluating market outcomes as consistent or inconsistent with what ought to be is called **normative analysis**. The term *normative* means that judgments are made about whether markets do things right or well. In order to make normative judgments, there must be a standard or norm against which to evaluate outcomes. The standard or norm most frequently used in economics is *economic efficiency*. (Efficiency will be defined more fully later in this chapter. For now, think of the efficiency norm in terms of whether markets coordinated activities so as to allocate goods, services, and resources in the best possible way.)

Although economic efficiency is an important norm, it is not the only standard against which we might want to judge the performance of markets. There is a second standard against which market economies are frequently judged—the standard of *fairness* or, if you prefer, *equity*. Other norms may matter as well. For example, some have argued that preventing the centralization of political power and fostering individual freedom are norms against which markets, perfect or imperfect, ought to be judged. The evaluation of markets against these norms is left for you to explore in other courses or on your own.

Choosing a particular norm implies that pursuit of that norm is a good thing. That is, if efficiency or equity or decentralization or freedom are norms, they are also "goods," not "bads." Evaluating an outcome against a norm of efficiency, for example, means that arrangements or outcomes that are less efficient are also less attractive, whereas arrangements or outcomes that are more efficient are better, *ceteris paribus*. The problem of how a society might come to choose one or more norms is challenging and interesting; it is, alas, also a matter that is also left for you to explore on your own. For the remainder of the text, we will simply assume that efficiency ought to matter to a society as it decides whether to collectively intervene in economic activity or rely more on markets.

▶ Prices and Profits

Are perfectly competitive markets efficient? Yes . . . but to understand this answer fully, we need to come at it in a somewhat roundabout way by first considering more carefully the roles that prices and profits play in a market economy.

Incentives

In the short run, market adjustments are constrained by the inability of firms producing particular commodities to change the amount of capital they have. As a consequence, market prices fluctuate with changes in demand or supply so as **to ration** what is produced among demanders and **to provide incentives** for firms to vary the intensity with which they use their capital. That is, prices allocate the amount produced among competing users or uses and, at the same time, provide incentives to increase or decrease the amount produced. Economic profits play a slightly different role. When they differ from zero, they provide an incentive **to** either **enter** or **exit.** Entry or exit (or expansion or contraction) changes the amount of capital available in a particular market. Thus, economic profits allocate capital across an economy.

The following examples, each of which you have already seen in other contexts, focus on the roles of prices and profits. You should pay particular attention to way competitive markets adjust and coordinate competing interests.

An increase in demand. When demand for something increases, its market price increases. Analytically this can be thought of as a rightward shift in a demand curve and a movement toward a new equilibrium price, as illustrated in Figure 1. The higher market price plays two important roles: it rations and it stimulates production.

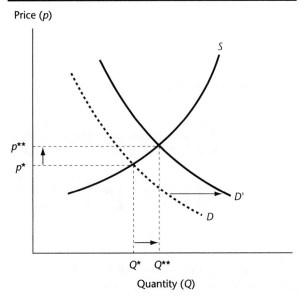

Figure 1
The Short-Run Consequences of an Increase in Demand

Price (*p*)

In the short run, an increase in demand shifts the demand curve to the right (from *D* to *D'*), increasing both the market price and the quantity traded in the market.

1. The higher market price has a rationing function. The amount of additional output that can be produced in the short run is limited by the available resources, particularly the amount of capital. In general, the output that can be produced in the short run will not be sufficient to satisfy the increased demand at the current market price. Competition among demanders will increase the market price. Even though individuals want more—that is, demand has increased—the higher price provides an incentive for some individuals to find suitable substitutes. Those who are less willing or, perhaps, less able to substitute pay the higher price. Thus, the higher market price rations what the market is capable of producing to those willing to pay the most for it. In this rationing function, a market price will increase until those willing to pay at least the current market price are able to purchase available output. Those unwilling to pay the higher market price for the quantity they are currently consuming purchase less or, in some cases, simply do without. In this way, the available output is rationed.

2. The higher market price stimulates production. As the market price increases, producers have an incentive to use their existing plant and equipment more intensively by employing additional resources, primarily labor, so as to increase the production of the now more-desired commodity. This incentive effect makes sense. After all, an increase in demand means that consumers want more produced. The market responds by squeezing more out of the currently available capital. Labor and other resources are reallocated from other markets to those markets where demand has increased.

There are still further effects. A short-run increase in the market price will generally mean that firms currently supplying the market will earn economic profits. That is, firms that happen to produce something consumers suddenly want more of will be rewarded with economic profits for being in the right place. Profits are not simply the rewards for good judgment or, perhaps, good luck, however. Profits also provide an incentive for additional resources, primarily capital, to move from other uses in the economy to the production of those items whose demand has increased. This profit effect takes more time than the more immediate price effects just outlined. As capital moves with the entry of new firms or the expansion of existing firms, however, output increases beyond the short run increase. That is, in the long run, more is provided to the market to satisfy the increased demand. Analytically, this is represented by a rightward shift in the supply curve, as illustrated in Figure 2.

The effect of this movement of capital and increase in output is to lower both the market price and profits. The lower price provides an incentive for demanders to increase the quantity purchased. While it may appear unfair that the market price increases in the short run so as to push lower-valued demanders out of the market and particularly unfair that "lucky" firms earn economic profits, the subsequent movement of resources in response to the higher profits ultimately drives the market price back down. More output becomes available in the market in the long run. As new firms enter the market in the long run and existing firms expand, the price decreases and economic profits are eliminated.

Figure 2
The Long-Run Consequences of an Increase in Demand

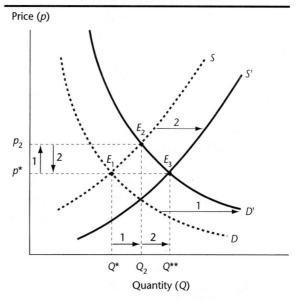

In the short run, an increase in demand increases both the market price and the quantity supplied (from E_1 to E_2). In the long run, the higher market price creates positive economic profits, which induces new firms to enter the market and old firms to expand production. Supply increases (from S to S'), causing the price to fall, but the quantity supplied to the market increases further.

In a sense, prices are like shock absorbers on a car—they move quickly to accommodate a change in demand or supply. In this particular case, when demand increases, prices increase to ration and to encourage more intensive use of capital. They then fall as the market responds in the longer run with an increase in supply. By contrast, profits allocate capital and other resources across markets. When they increase, they entice capital and other resources to move, but fall to zero as entry and expansion occur. Note that the market price *increases* in the short run (Figure 1) and then *decreases* in the long run (Figure 2), but the quantity supplied to the market *increases* in the short run (Figure 1) and then *increases further* in the long run (Figure 2). Whether the new long-run market price is higher or lower than the original long-run equilibrium price depends upon scale economies and long-run costs, as noted in Chapter 9. The long-run effect on the quantity provided to the market is clear, however. That is, market output increases somewhat in the short run and then increases further in the long run.

A decrease in demand. On the other hand, if consumers decide that they want to purchase less of a particular commodity at the current price, the market price will fall. Analytically, this effect is represented as the leftward shift in the demand curve and decrease in the market price shown in Figure 3. A lower market price has two effects.

1. The lower price encourages consumers to substitute this commodity for other commodities *even though demand has declined.* This effect is important because the scarce resources tied to the production of a particular commodity, primarily capital, cannot be transferred immediately to other uses. It makes sense to use these resources when possible. As a consequence of the substitution following a decrease in the market price, the economy continues to make effective use of these scarce and productive resources until they can be shifted to other uses.

2. The lower price encourages firms to cut production and use their existing plant and equipment less intensively. This immediately frees some resources, primarily labor, for use elsewhere in the economy. This response is important because resources that can easily move to other activities should do so. After all, demand has fallen. Once again, lower relative prices indirectly lead to the reallocation of labor and other resources. In this case, resources are moved away from the production of goods that consumers are less interested in purchasing.

Once again, there are further effects. A short-run decrease in the market price generally results in lower profits and, at times, in economic losses for those firms currently supplying the market. Firms that happen to produce something that consumers suddenly find less desirable are penalized for being in the wrong place. Lower profits encourage the reallocation of capital to other uses in the economy. The profit effect takes more time than the more immediate price effect. As capital moves with the exit of firms, however, the output provided to the market decreases beyond the short-run decrease. Fewer and fewer goods are supplied to the market, precisely the result that consumers signaled they wanted when they chose to consume less. These long-run consequences are illustrated in Figure 4. The movement of capital from a market with decreased demand serves to increase both the market price and the profits for the remaining firms, however.

Thus like shock absorbers on a car, prices decrease with a fall in demand and then increase as resources move away. Once again, we see that profits allocate capital and other resources across markets. In this case, lower-than-anticipated profits or actual losses provide an incentive for capital to move toward other markets and away from a market where demand has declined. As this movement of capital occurs, the market price increases and profits for the remaining firms increase until they earn a normal rate of return. Note that the market price *decreases* in the short run (Figure 3) and then *increases* in the long run (Figure 4), but the quantity supplied to the market *decreases* in the short run (Figure 3) and then *decreases further* in the long run (Figure 4). Whether the new long-run market price is below or above the original long-run equilibrium price depends upon scale economies and long-run costs, as noted in Chapter 9. The long-run effect on the market price depends upon the specific characteristics of each industry, but the overall effect on quantity is clear—market output decreases

Figure 3
The Short-Run Consequences
of a Decrease in Demand

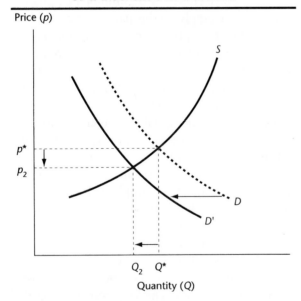

In the short run, a decrease in demand shifts the demand curve to the left (from D to D'), decreasing both the market price and the quantity traded in the market.

Figure 4
The Long-Run Consequences of a Decrease in Demand

Price (*p*)

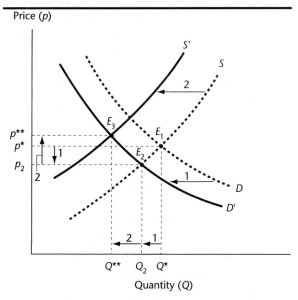

In the short run, a decrease in demand decreases both the market price and the quantity supplied (from E_1 to E_2). In the long run, the lower market price creates economic losses for firms, who then either cut back supply or exit the market. This decreases supply from (S to S'), causing prices to increase, but the quantity supplied to the market to decrease further.

in the short run and then decreases further in the long run.

An increase in production costs. To see the effects of increased costs of production, consider a third example. When input or resource prices increase, firms find that their costs increase and, at each market price, they will want to provide less to the market. For example, if wage rates increase for *all* firms in a particular industry, market supply decreases. A decrease in market supply results in a higher market price. The higher price encourages consumers to find substitutes. Put differently, the higher market price provides an incentive for individuals to purchase less of those commodities whose production costs increase and more of those commodities whose production costs have not changed. The higher price also partially or fully offsets the higher costs of producing the commodity.

If the price change *fully offsets* the increase in costs, then existing firms will continue to operate and there will be no movement of resources from

this market. If the increased costs are *not fully offset*, however, firms will incur losses and some will exit. In this case, capital will move from this market to other markets. As the supply falls further, the market price increases further.

Substitution is not static. The more time individuals have to find substitutes, the more substitution there will be. Hence, when prices increase because of increases in production costs, demanders will, with time, find additional substitutes for the commodity whose price has increased. This additional substitution increases the elasticity of demand for this commodity and puts pressure on firms to look for ways to lower costs. Over the long run, therefore, firms often choose a different mix of capital and labor. Hence, once again, prices act as shock absorbers, initially increasing with the higher production costs and then, perhaps, decreasing as consumers find additional substitutes over time.

Possible long-run consequences are illustrated in Figure 5. Note that in this case, the market price *increases*, whereas the quantity supplied to the market *decreases* in the short run and then *decreases*

Figure 5
The Long-Run Consequences of an Increase in Production Costs

Price (*p*)

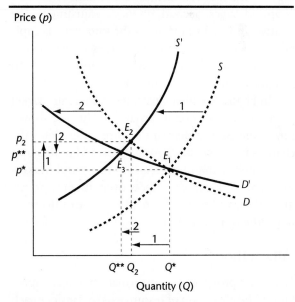

In the short run, an increase in production costs increases the market price and decreases the supply (from S to S'). In the long run, as consumers have time to find substitutes, demand falls (from D to D'), lowering the market price and further decreasing the quantity supplied.

further in the long run. An increase in production costs in a particular market leads to a decrease in the resources devoted to that market and to a corresponding decrease in the output provided. Once again, the net effect on output is clear. Quantity decreases in both the short and long run. The net effect on the price, however, is unclear because it depends, among other things, on the degree to which demanders can substitute, both in the short and in the long run.[1]

Price vs. quantity adjustments. We use abstractions such as "demand" or "supply" and "the short run" or "the long run" to concisely sum up the concrete day-by-day decisions of individuals who actually do substitute, decide to increase or decrease production, decide to make new investments or to close a business, and in other ways determine how they will respond to the incentives that prices and profits provide. The abstractions are useful because they impose order on our thinking. It is important to remember, however, that these abstractions only describe what individuals and firms are actually doing. In this regard, we have learned two facts about market behavior: First, price fluctuations are relatively more important in the short run, absorbing the initial effects of market demand or market supply changes. Second, quantity adjustments are relatively more important in the long run, as capital and other productive resources move toward activities that are more profitable and away from activities that are less profitable.

In Figure 6, which illustrates changes in market prices over time, quantities and profits are shown for an increase in demand. Figure 7 illustrates the changes in market prices, quantities, and profits over time when demand decreases. (You should take a moment to sketch the effects over time on prices, quantities, and profits from an increase or decrease in production costs.)

Information

Prices and profits convey information that is important in the allocation of resources. We consider each in turn:

Figure 6
Prices, Quantities, and Profits Over Time Following an Increase in Demand

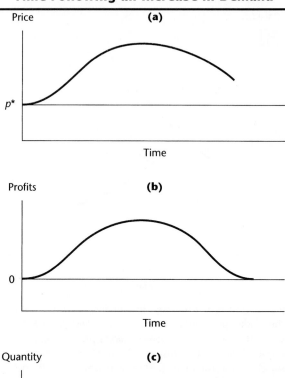

When demand increases, prices increase in the short run, then decrease in the long run. Profits also increase initially, but then return to zero over time. The quantity supplied, however, increases in the short run, and then further increases in the long run.

The role of prices. If the demand for a specific good increases, in a sense, the good is relatively scarcer. The market price increases. Consumers respond *as if they knew* that there was excess demand. That is, they respond to higher market prices by adjusting consumption patterns. No one has to announce that the good is relatively more scarce and that adjustments will have to occur. Demanders simply respond to the higher market price by finding substitutes as if they had been given this information. Consumers would generally prefer not to look for substitutes, but they do.

---

[1] A decrease in cost would have the opposite effects. (Take a moment and think through the adjustments.)

Figure 7
Prices, Quantities, and Profits Over Time Following an Decrease in Demand

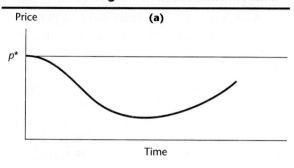

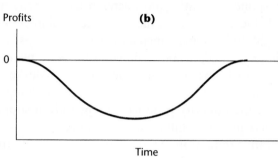

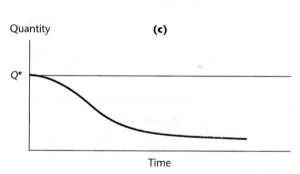

When demand decreases, prices fall in the short run, but increase in the long run. Profits follow a similar pattern, falling in the short run but returning to zero in the long run. Quantity, however, decreases in the short run and then decreases even further in the long run.

When firms observe the market price increasing, they behave *as if they knew* that demanders wanted more resources devoted to the production of this particular good. Again, no one needs to poll demanders and then announce that they would like to purchase more and hence wish that resources would be reallocated so as to increase production. Firms simply respond in a self-interested way to the higher market price by employing more labor and using capital more intensively.

If production costs increase, supply will decrease and prices will begin to increase. In this case,

demanders will respond *as if they knew* that the costs had increased by substituting other commodities for this commodity, thereby reducing the amount demanded. They do so even though they are unlikely to know anything about the firms that produce the commodities they purchase or about the costs of producing those commodities. The increase in price conveys this information about the increase in costs. On the other hand, when production costs decrease, supply will increase and prices will begin to decrease. Demanders will respond *as if they knew* that the costs had decreased by substituting this commodity for other commodities even though they are unlikely to really know anything about the costs of producing this commodity.

In each of these cases, the market price conveys information from consumers to firms and from firms to consumers even though there is, in fact, no effort by one to inform the other. As a consequence, each time a price is determined, it becomes a valuable piece of information about the available opportunities to buy, to sell, to produce, and so forth. Information of this sort about what others are willing to do is essential if economic coordination is to occur. The aggregation and transmission of this kind of information is a truly remarkable property of markets.

To see just how remarkable it is, imagine that market pries do not exist and that you have the responsibility to allocate resources among several possible uses and then distribute the goods and services produced among several different users. Should you allocate more labor to beer or bread production? To the production of paper or electricity? To the production of clothing or cars? Should more bread be allocated to your neighbor or to a person across town or to someone in another state? These are tough decisions. To make them requires a great deal of information, information that would be very costly and difficult to acquire. Yet literally millions of allocational decisions just like these are made every day by markets. Market prices gather and transmit the necessary information without anyone's really thinking about it. Resources are then allocated as individuals recognize opportunities and respond to the incentives that prices provide.

Role of profits. Profits and losses also convey information. When demand increases, for example, in the long run the market responds by reallocating capital from other activities to the activity where demand has increased. The increase in demand means that consumers want more produced, so the owners of capital respond *as if they knew* what consumers wanted by expanding the productive capacity in *that* particular market. This information about how consumers would like productive resources to be allocated across the economy is not directly gathered by firms nor is it directly communicated by consumers. Instead, the effect of consumer decisions, in the form of profits or losses, conveys the information from consumers to the owners of capital.

The importance and subtlety of this informational aspect of profits can be illustrated as follows: Suppose that you knew nothing about the distribution of economic profits across the economy but had the responsibility of deciding how capital should be allocated across the various production activities. Should more capital be allocated to shirt production or to paper production? If more should be allocated to shirt production, how much more? How would you decide when to move capital from one activity to another? Where to move capital? How much capital to move? Once again, these are extraordinarily difficult questions to answer in that sensible answers require a great deal of information. Markets gather and convey this information in the form of economic profits or economic losses. Self-interested individuals then respond to profitable and unprofitable opportunities. No one actually gathers the information about where to allocate capital for the economy as a whole and no one needs to centrally direct the allocation or reallocation of capital across the economy. Instead, self-interested pursuit of profits leads to reallocations from markets where demanders want less produced to markets where demanders want more produced.

Linkages

Prices and profits also link markets together. This linkage occurs because changes in prices induce substitution, meaning that one good or resource is being used in place of another. In addition, profits or losses reallocate capital and other resources among markets. It is often surprising how far these linkages can extend. For example, anchovies caught near the South American coast are used as a source of protein in feed for cattle. Occasionally, the

anchovies fail to arrive off the South America in their usual numbers. As a consequence, the same fishing effort leads to a much smaller catch, resulting in an increase in the marginal cost per ton of anchovies (see Figure 8). As the price of anchovies increases, users of anchovies substitute other protein sources in cattle feed and elsewhere.

Soybeans are a substitute source of protein. Hence, the failure of the anchovies to appear and the resulting increase in price increases the demand for soybeans (see Figure 9). If the demand increase occurs early in the agricultural year, farmers can respond by planting more acres in soybeans so supply increases. That is, the supply curve shifts to the right. If the demand increase occurs after crops have been planted, farmers will work the acres planted with soybeans more intensively by using additional fertilizers and by more careful harvesting techniques and the quantity produced along a given supply curve increases. Either devoting more acres to soybean production or devoting more time and resources to soybean production results in fewer acres or in less time and other resources being devoted to other crops. As a consequence, the supply of, say, wheat declines. Thus, the failure of anchovies to appear off the South American coast

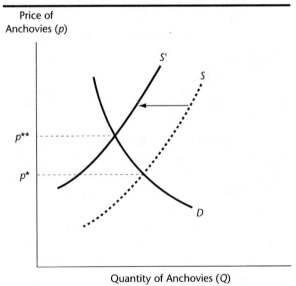

**Figure 8
The Price of Anchovies with an
Unexpected Decrease in Supply**

In the short run, an unexpected decrease in the supply of anchovies leads to a higher market price.

**Figure 9
The Price of Soybeans After an
Increase in the Price of Anchovies**

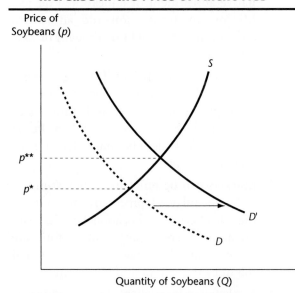

Anchovies and soybeans are substitute sources of protein, so an increase in the price of anchovies increases
the demand for soybeans, thus increasing their price.

**Figure 10
The Price of Wheat Following an
Increase in the Price of Soybeans**

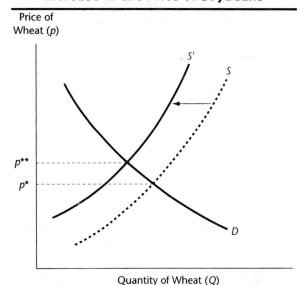

If the price of soybeans increases, farmers will plant
more soybeans and less wheat. This decreases the supply of wheat, and consequently, its price increases.

has now led to higher prices for bread and other
foods using wheat (see Figure 10).

The higher prices for anchovies (because of the
decrease in supply) and higher prices for alternative
protein feed supplements (because of the increase
in demand) increase the costs of feeding beef cattle
(see Figure 11). Thus, the failure of anchovies to
appear off South America also leads to higher prices
for beef and other meats where anchovies are used
as part of the feed. This in turn increases the
demand for substitutes such as pork and chicken.
Hence, the prices of pork and chicken increase
because of the increased costs for feed for cattle.

The decrease in anchovies leads to changes in a
large number of markets because of the substitution that accompanies price changes. Costs increase
in the anchovy, beef, and wheat markets but the
higher demand in the soybean, chicken, and pork
markets yields profits. This increase in profits provides an incentive for entry. Entry, however, will
depend on whether the price of anchovies is expected to remain high. That is, the profits currently
accruing to soybean producers may be reduced by
the competitive entry of *either* new soybean producers or old anchovy producers, should the fish
appear the next season.

**Figure 11
The Price of Beef Following an
Increase in the Price of Feed**

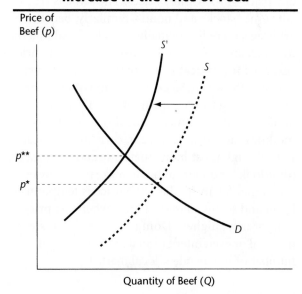

Increases in the prices of anchovies and soybeans, both
used as sources of protein in cattle feed, decrease the
supply of beef and increase its price.

Arbitrage. For the most part, the linkages illustrated in this example are not direct, but occur because of substitution by the individuals and firms who look for profitable alternatives in response to price changes. Sometimes, however, individuals and firms create direct cross-market linkages by specializing in moving commodities between markets in response to profitable differences in prices and rates of return. This activity is called **arbitrage**. For example, if some assets in a particular financial market offer a much higher return than do other assets, individuals will move financial resources from lower-return activities to the higher-return activity. This action tends to equalize the rates of return across financial assets.

Or, for example, some individuals specialize in buying used automobiles at a lower price in one area and transporting them to areas where the prices are expected to be higher. Prices increase in the former area and decrease in the latter area as a consequence. This kind of activity tends to link what were separate markets, creating a single market spread across a large geographical area, even though most individuals buy and sell only locally.

As a consequence of arbitrage, there is a national market in financial instruments. U.S. government bonds, for example, sell for the same price virtually any place in the United States. The same is true of corporate stocks and bonds. Similarly, because of arbitrage, there is essentially a single global market for gold, and gold sells for virtually the same price (except for physical transportation costs) everywhere in the world. So do dollars and other currencies in foreign exchange markets. There are also national and even international markets for commodities such as wheat, sugar, corn, and soybeans. Even though most individuals buy and sell locally, some look for opportunities to make money by buying in market areas where the price is temporarily lower and selling in market areas where the price is temporarily higher. Doing so creates a single national or even international market rather than a number of independent local markets.

▶ Efficiency

There are at least four important ways that markets can be considered efficient:

1. Markets can be efficient if price changes and profit-induced capital movements can accommodate changes in the economy more rapidly and with less disruption than alternative adjustment or allocational devices. Minimizing transaction and adjustment costs in this way might be thought of as an *adjustment efficiency.*

2. Markets can be efficient if they gather and transmit the information necessary to make appropriate allocations and adjustments more rapidly and with less cost than alternatives can. This might be considered an *informational efficiency.*

3. Markets can be efficient if they stimulate technological development to a greater degree than do alternative allocational mechanisms, facilitate changes and innovation, and respond quickly to new opportunities. This might be thought of as *dynamic efficiency.*

4. Markets can be efficient if commodities are allocated to the highest valued uses and if resources are used in the most productive ways. This is **allocative efficiency**.

For the most part, economists have focused on allocative efficiency because, when markets fail to allocate goods, services, or resources efficiently, scarce and valuable resources are wasted and, as a consequence, many individuals have lower incomes than would otherwise be the case. The claim that competitive markets are allocatively efficient also implies that *no* alternative allocational mechanism or form of economic organization can allocate resources better than competitive markets can. The allocative efficiency of competitive markets is, in fact, Adam Smith's claim that individuals pursuing their own interests are guided, in a market economy, "as if by an invisible hand" to increase the well-being of others.

The other three notions of efficiency that have been outlined are also important norms, however. Indeed, the increased interest in the role of markets in the late 1980s and 1990s in Eastern Europe, Russia, and elsewhere occurred not just because of the enormous difficulties these economies encountered in making centralized allocational decisions, but also because of problems associated with incentives for individuals to engage in productive activities, to economize, to quickly adapt to changing circumstances, and to innovate and create.

Allocative Efficiency in General

Sometimes "efficiency" is interpreted in a purely technical way: an activity that uses fewer resources must be more efficient than a different activity that uses more of the same resources. This interpretation of efficiency won't do, however—producing something (say "widgets") that no one wants, even if widgets are produced in the least costly way, is hardly an efficient use of scarce resources. Clearly, *efficiency has to be related in some way to what we use, consume, and hence value.* In this regard, a particular allocation of commodities is allocatively efficient if it is not possible to reallocate any commodities to make at least one person better off without making anyone else worse off.

A simple test for allocative efficiency is: Does the use of an additional dollar's worth of scarce resources produces at least an additional dollar's worth of satisfaction? Or, in more technical terms: Does the marginal cost of producing an extra unit of output equal the amount that individuals are willing to pay for any additional production?

This notion has an intuitive appeal. Using resources valued at $1 to produce something for which consumers are only willing to pay $.50 is clearly not an efficient use of scarce resources. The converse might not be quite so evident, but we will see that it also holds: Using resources valued at $.50 to produce something for which consumers are willing to pay $1.00 is also not an efficient use of scarce resources.

With this introduction, the remainder of this chapter evaluates the following claim: *Competitive markets allocate scarce resources efficiently if they are competitive, if there are no externalities, and if markets clear.* The "proof" of this claim follows. Before proceeding with the proof, however, it is important to note that many times markets are not competitive, that externalities exist, and that markets do not always clear quickly. We will consider these problems and their consequences beginning with Chapter 13.

Allocative efficiency and competitive markets. To evaluate this claim, consider a competitive market in long-run equilibrium (Figure 12). What do we know about such a market outcome?

1. It is an equilibrium. That is, the quantity suppliers willingly provide to the market at the equilibrium price is exactly equal to the quantity demanders willingly purchase at the same equilibrium price. In this sense, the competing interests of households and firms are accommodated.

2. Economic profits are zero. Thus, there is no incentive for either entry or exit.

3. *Each* person purchasing some of this commodity pays the *same* market price

4. *Each* firm producing some of this commodity sells it for the *same* market price.

5. The price that individuals pay for the commodity is the *same* price that firms receive when they sell the commodity.

Figure 12
A Market with Allocational Efficiency in Long-Run Equilibrium

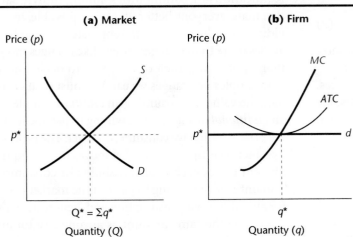

(a) Market

Price (p)

p^*

$Q^* = \Sigma q^*$

Quantity (Q)

(b) Firm

Price (p)

MC

ATC

p^*

d

q^*

Quantity (q)

When a market is in long-run equilibrium, four conditions are satisfied: (1) the quantity of the commodity supplied just equals the quantity demanded at the market price and the firms in the market make zero economic profits; (2) each consumer purchasing the good pays the same price; (3) each firm selling the commodity receives the same price; and (4) firms receive the same price that individuals pay.

Taken together, these properties imply that the market outcome is allocatively efficient. To see why, we consider each in turn.

Equilibrium market price for all consumers. At a market equilibrium, the maximum amount that each consumer would be willing to pay for *additional* production is exactly equal to the price that he or she actually pays. Because *all* individuals in a market make choices confronting the *same* market price, however, the amount that an individual is willing to pay for additional output is the same as the amount that every other individual in the market is willing to pay for additional output. Thus, the gains from exchange noted in Chapter 1 are fully exploited by competitive markets. To see why, suppose that p_A is the market price for commodity A (apples). Any rational consumer of A, say Jane, will adjust the amount that she purchases until the marginal satisfaction is exactly equal to the market price or,

$$MS_A \text{ for Jane} = p_A \tag{1}$$

where MS_A is Jane's marginal satisfaction or, more fully, the satisfaction obtained from consuming an additional apple. (Remember that marginal satisfaction is measured in terms of a dollar's worth of *other* goods that could be purchased.) Diminishing marginal returns implies that whatever the market price, marginal satisfaction (and hence willingness to pay for additional output) eventually declines as consumption increases. Thus, individuals need only increase purchases from the market until the satisfaction obtained from consuming a bit more is just equal to the amount they must pay.

This is also true for Dick, who will adjust the amount of A he consumes until

$$MS_A \text{ for Dick} = p_A \tag{2}$$

Indeed, it is true for all individuals who maximize their well-being and consume commodity A.

Each individual makes his or her own choices. However, *at the competitive market equilibrium, the price of commodity A is the same for each individual,* so it follows that,

$$MS_A = MS_A = MS_A \tag{3}$$
$$\text{For} \quad \text{For} \quad \text{For anyone}$$
$$\text{Jane} \quad \text{Dick} \quad \text{purchasing A}$$

If everyone is willing to pay exactly the same amount for any additional production, it is not possible to reallocate some of the production of commodity A among its consumers in a way that increases the well-being of one person without making someone else worse off. Recall that mutually beneficial trades between Crusoe and Friday were possible because their preferences were different. Loosely, when everyone faces the same price, everyone's preferences *at the margin* are the same. Therefore, the gains from exchange are being fully exploited.

Conversely, if individuals value the same commodity *differently*, the gains from exchange are *not* being fully exploited. To see why, suppose that Jane would be willing to pay \$.50 for an additional apple but that Dick would be willing to pay no more than \$.20 for an additional apple. If Jane and Dick were to trade, apples would move from Dick to Jane and money from Jane to Dick. That is, Jane would be better off if she could purchase an additional apple at any price below \$.50 per apple. But, at any price greater than \$.20, Dick would be better off if he sold one or more of his apples, because an apple is worth at most \$.20 to him. He could then use the money obtained from the sale to purchase something else worth more to him. Therefore, a reallocation of apples from Dick to Jane and of money from Jane to Dick will make both better off as long as the price of apples is greater than \$.20 but less than \$.50. Clearly, the only time when a deal like this is not possible is when both Dick and Jane pay the same price for apples. When they do, the amount that one gains from obtaining one more apple is the same as the amount that the other gains from selling one more apple, and a deal that reallocates apples and money isn't possible. This point is illustrated in Figure 13.

Thus, competitive markets find outcomes where reallocations of commodities among individuals that make everyone better off are *not* possible. Individuals may have very different tastes—some like apples more than oranges, others like oranges more than apples, and each of us is free to decide how many apples or oranges we eat. We must each evaluate the value of consuming an *additional* apple or an *additional* orange and be willing to pay the market price for what we consume, however. The process by which a competitive market moves toward equilibrium forces each of us to adjust our consumption until we are willing to pay just the market price for any additional consumption and, hence, are willing to pay the same amount as anyone else for an additional apple or orange. Because each person

Figure 13
Prices for Consumers in Efficient Markets

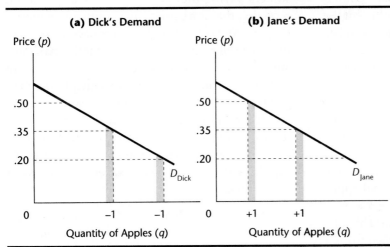

(a) Dick's Demand

Price (*p*)

.50
.35
.20

D_{Dick}

0   −1   −1

Quantity of Apples (*q*)

(b) Jane's Demand

Price (*p*)

.50
.35
.20

D_{Jane}

0   +1   +1

Quantity of Apples (*q*)

When Dick pays $.20 and Jane pays $.50 for an apple, Dick values an additional apple less than Jane does. Hence, moving apples from Dick to Jane results in a more efficient allocation. A competitive market brings about precisely this kind of reallocation. That is, at the market equilibrium ($.35), Jane is willing to pay less for an additional apple than the value that Dick places on giving up an additional apple. In efficient markets, *all* consumers pay the same price.

adjusts his or her consumption *given the same market price*, the gains from exchange are being fully exploited and, equivalently, apples are being allocated to the highest-valued users.

Equilibrium market price for all producers. At a competitive market equilibrium, each profit-maximizing firm will have adjusted its production until its marginal production cost is exactly equal to the market price. As long as input prices fully reflect the opportunity cost to society of using scarce resources in one activity rather than another, the marginal cost of producing each commodity accurately reflects the true cost to society of using scarce resources. That is, profit maximization leads each firm producing apples to adjust its output until

$$MC_A \text{ for firm } 1 = p_A \quad (4)$$

where MC_A is the marginal cost of producing apples and p_A is the market price. This happens, once again, because diminishing marginal returns implies that as a firm increases its output in the short run, marginal cost increases. Thus, given the market price, a firm wishing to maximize profits increases its level of production until the cost of producing any additional output is just equal to the market price.

This is also true for firm 2,

$$MC_A \text{ for firm } 2 = p_A \quad (5)$$

Indeed, this will be true for every firm that is producing commodity A as long as each firm is attempting to maximize profits.

Each firm faces the same market price, p_A, so the cost of increasing the production of A by the first firm will be exactly equal to the marginal cost of producing A by the second firm, and so forth. That is,

$$MC_A = MC_A = MC_A \quad (6)$$
For   For   For any firm
firm 1   firm 2   producing A

What is the significance of (6)? If the marginal cost of producing A is the same for all the producers, *then it is not possible to reallocate scarce resources among the firms producing apples to increase the production of A*. As a consequence, the gains from specialization are being fully exploited and apples are being produced by the least-cost suppliers.

For example, suppose that apples are priced at $.35 each and each firm producing apples has adjusted its production until its marginal cost is equal to the market price. If firm 1 decreased its production by one apple, its costs would fall by $.35. If firm 2 were then encouraged to increase its production by one apple, its costs would increase by $.35. Thus, firm 2 could never bid resources away from A to lower the costs to society of producing and providing apples to the market.

If, however, firms have different marginal costs of producing the same good or service, the allocation of resources among the firms cannot be efficient. For example, suppose that to produce a particular quantity of apples firm 2 has marginal cost of $.60 and firm 1 has marginal cost of $.20. That is, the cost in terms of real resources used is $.60 if firm 2 produces another apple while it's $.20 if firm 1 produces another one. Even though each firm may be minimizing its own costs, this cannot be an efficient use of resources. Why not? Resources could be taken from firm 2 sufficient to reduce its production by one apple. Doing so would save the economy $.60 in scarce resources. Production of apples would, of course, decrease. If some of these resources were given to firm 1, however, the production of apples would increase, but at a cost of only $.20 per apple. The economy would have the same number of apples *and* it would have $.40 worth of resources that could be conserved or used to produce additional apples or other things. It follows that reallocating resources lowers costs and, perhaps, increases output. This kind of reallocation is clearly not possible when firms 1 and 2 have exactly the same marginal production costs. Thus, when marginal production costs are equal, the gains from specialization are fully realized and output is produced by the least-cost producers. This argument is illustrated in Figure 14.

Competitive markets find allocations where reallocations of this sort are not possible. In a competitive market each firm sells its output at the same market price and, therefore, the marginal cost for all firms producing a particular commodity is the same. Firms may have different overall costs. They may be organized differently. Some may be small, others large. At the margin, however, the cost of producing an additional unit of output is the same for all firms producing a particular commodity as long as all firms face the same market price.

Equilibrium market prices. In addition to all consumers paying the same price and all producers receiving the same price, in a competitive market *the price that consumers pay is the same as the price that the firms receive.* This means that the maximum amount that consumers are willing to pay for any additional production is exactly equal to the marginal cost to society of using more resources in this activity. In short, a dollar's worth of scarce resources results in at least a dollar's worth of satisfaction.

As we have learned, because all demanders and suppliers in a particular market face the same market price,

$$
\underset{\substack{\text{For}\\ \text{Dick}}}{MS_A} = \underset{\substack{\text{For}\\ \text{Jane}}}{MS_A} = \underset{\substack{\text{For anyone}\\ \text{purchasing } A}}{MS_A} = p_A
$$

and

$$
\underset{\substack{\text{For}\\ \text{firm 1}}}{MC_A} = \underset{\substack{\text{For}\\ \text{firm 2}}}{MC_A} = \underset{\substack{\text{For any firm}\\ \text{producing } A}}{C_A} = p_A
$$

It follows that

$$
\underset{\substack{\text{For anyone}\\ \text{purchasing } A}}{MS_A} = \underset{\substack{\text{For any firm}\\ \text{producing } A}}{MC_A} \qquad (7)
$$

In words, the amount of money that individuals are willing to pay to increase their consumption of apples by a small amount is exactly equal to the cost to firms of increasing the production of apples by the same amount. Hence, competitive markets are efficient.

Figure 14
Marginal Costs for Firms in Efficient Markets

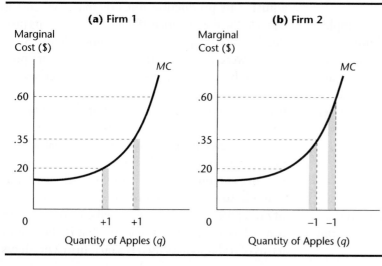

If firm 2 produces at a marginal cost of $.60 and firm 1 produces at a marginal cost of $.20, the total cost of production to society can be lowered by transferring some resources from firm 2 to firm 1. When both firms produce at a marginal cost of $.35, it is impossible to reallocate resources between them to lower the cost of production further. In efficient markets, *all* firms produce with the same marginal costs.

Another look at allocative efficiency. There is a slightly different approach to explaining why competitive markets are efficient that, although it may be less intuitive, also suggests the importance of substitution. The argument is as follows:

If the price of commodity A relative to commodity B is p_A / p_B, each consumer adjusts consumption so that

$$MS_A / MS_B = p_A / p_B \qquad (8)$$

(The equi-marginal rule implies that each individual maximizing his or her own well-being adjusts consumption of A and B so that $MS_A / p_A = MS_B / p_B$.) The ratio MS_A / MS_B is referred to as the **marginal rate of substitution in consumption**.

All consumers pay the same prices, so Equation (8) must hold for all consumers of A and B. This means that, *at the margin*, all consumers *substitute* additional consumption of A for additional consumption of B in the same proportion.

Profit-maximizing firms producing A adjust production so that

$$p_A = MC_A \qquad (9)$$

and profit-maximizing firms producing B adjust production so that

$$p_B = MC_B \qquad (10)$$

Therefore,

$$p_A / p_B = MC_A / MC_B \qquad (11)$$

That is, even though A and B will generally be produced by different firms, the market price of A relative to the market price of B reflects the marginal cost of producing A relative to the marginal cost of producing B. The ratio MC_A / MC_B is called the **marginal rate of transformation in production**.

Two things equal to the same thing are equal to each other. In a competitive market, if

$$MC_A / MC_B = p_A / p_B \qquad (12)$$

and if

$$MS_A / MS_B = p_A / p_B \qquad (13)$$

then it must be that

$$MC_A / MC_B = MS_A / MS_B \qquad (14)$$

Thus, in competitive markets, the *marginal rate of substitution* in consumption is equal to the *marginal rate of transformation* in production. Why is this

important? The term to the right of Equation (14) indicates how consumers *substitute* a little more A for a little less B. The term to the left indicates the *relative costs* of producing A and B—that is, the additional amount of A that can be produced if the production of B is reduced a little. Put differently, MC_A / MC_B indicates how A and B substitute along a production possibilities frontier. Taken together, these mean that in competitive markets, the opportunity cost of increasing the production of A by moving additional resources from the production of B—that is, substituting A for B in production—for *all* firms is exactly equal to the rate at which *all* individuals value and substitute additional A for B in consumption.

A simple example illustrates the point. Suppose that the marginal cost of producing bread is $1.50 per loaf and the marginal cost of producing apples is $.50 per pound. This means that if an economy wants to increase the production of bread and decrease the production of apples, it must give up three pounds of apples for each additional loaf of bread produced. Suppose, however, that consumers are willing to trade six loaves of bread for an additional pound of apples. The economy *cannot* be producing the efficient mix of bread and apples. To see why, note that if one individual cut her consumption of bread by six loaves, thereby freeing resources for the production of apples, this person could be fully compensated for her loss of bread by receiving an additional pound of apples. (Remember, we are assuming that consumers are willing to substitute six loaves of bread for one pound of apples.) Giving up the production of six loaves of bread would, however, allow 18 pounds of apples to be produced *using no additional* resources because the marginal cost of producing bread is $1.50 per loaf and the marginal cost of producing apples is $.50 per pound. Thus, this person could have made a better deal than she expected. She could have received 18 pounds of apples for her sacrifice of six loaves of bread. As a result of this reallocation from bread production to apple production, no other individual is harmed and this individual is better off. Therefore, the economy could not have been using its resources efficiently.

In sum, there are three aspects of allocative efficiency:

1. Commodities must be distributed among consumers so as to exploit all potential gains

from exchange. This distribution occurs when each individual pays the same market price as does every other individual who consumes the commodity.

2. Productive resources must be used in the least-cost way so as to exploit all potential gains from specialization. This usage occurs when each firm producing a particular commodity bases its production decisions on the *same* market price as every other firm producing the same commodity.

3. Firms have to produce the right mix of commodities so that the opportunity cost to society of moving resources from one production activity to another is equal to the rate at which individuals substitute one commodity for another in satisfying their own well-being. Put simple, $1 in production costs must produce at least $1 in satisfaction. This equivalency occurs when the price that individuals are willing to pay for additional output is the *same* price that firms respond to when they make their production decisions.

A TEST FOR EFFICIENCY: An allocation is efficient only if the price that consumers are willing to pay for additional output is equal to its marginal production cost. This suggests a simple test: At a given market outcome, it must be that MWTP (marginal willingness to pay) is equal to MC (marginal cost). Alternatively, a given market outcome cannot be efficient if MWTP > MC or MWTP < MC.

Least-Cost Production

In the long run, there is yet another sense in which markets are efficient. As exit and entry push a market moves toward a long-run equilibrium, suppliers adjust their output so that market price is equal to marginal cost. With entry and exit the market price adjusts, in turn, until expected profits for any entering firms are zero. When profits are zero, however, marginal cost is equal to the *minimum* of average total costs. This means that the *market price is also equal to the minimum of average total costs.* Hence, in the long run, a competitive market produces output in the most technically efficient way. In the long run, a competitive market selects the most efficient technology, minimizes the resources devoted to the production of commodities, and then sets a price that reflects the full costs of producing the commodity.

In the short run, however, the efficient market outcome is *not necessarily* the least-cost outcome. The market does the best that it can *given the short-run constraints*, but the market price need not be equal to the minimum of the average total costs. If economic profits are positive, the market price is above the minimum average total cost; if there are economic losses, the market price is below the minimum average total cost. Put differently, the market does not necessarily select the technologically most efficient level of production in the short run because to do so would be economically inefficient.

Incentives to adopt new technologies. It might appear that firms in a competitive industry have little incentive to look for, develop, or adopt new technologies because in the long run each earns only a normal rate of return by using the most technically efficient technology currently available. This is not the case. Firms in a perfectly competitive market cannot increase the price at which they sell what they produce. Therefore, the only way that they can increase profits is by lowering costs. As a consequence, each firm in a perfectly competitive market will be looking for some technological or organizational innovation that will lower *its* costs so that it will be able to earn economic profits.

Robert H. Frank, an economist at Cornell University, has noted an interesting example. Wind deflectors on the top of the cabs of large tractor-trailer trucks lower costs because they reduce drag as the large, generally square, trailer pushes through the air. It has been estimated that using a deflector reduces diesel fuel consumption by about 15 percent. Looking for a competitive advantage—that is, for economic profits—truckers experimented with different ways of reducing costs. A few put deflectors on the cabs of their trucks. When they started doing so, few trucks had wind deflectors. Saving diesel fuel meant that these truckers were more profitable. This spurred adoption of the innovation by other truckers. As more and more truckers adopted the innovation, however, the cost saving came to be reflected in the market price. This meant that truckers could no longer earn above-normal profits by installing such a device. It also meant that virtually all truckers now had to have a wind deflector in order to have costs that were the same as those of other truckers.

Figure 15
Relationship Between Consumers' Marginal Satisfaction
and Firms' Marginal Costs in Efficient Markets

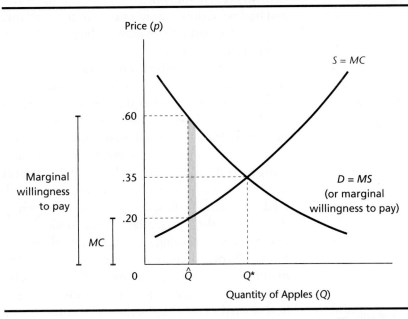

If production is limited to $\hat{Q}$, consumers' willingness to pay for additional apples ($.60) exceeds the marginal cost of producing additional apples ($.20). Both firms and individuals would be better off if production increased to Q^*, where individual willingness to pay just equals the marginal cost of production. In efficient markets, consumers' marginal satisfaction equals the firms' marginal costs.

Thus, because the new technology had a payoff for those willing to innovate and change, it was adopted. Because it lowered costs, however, it came to be adopted by everyone and the market moved to a new least-cost production level.

Some Implications of Allocative Efficiency

Clearly, market prices play a very important role in achieving efficiency. Each person in a competitive market buys at the *same* price; each firm in a competitive market sells at the *same* price; both individuals and firms buy and sell at the *same* price. Thus, if you observe (1) different people paying different prices or (2) different firms selling at different prices or (3) the price individuals pay differing from the price that firms actually receive, it's a good initial guess that there is some kind of inefficiency. (It's only an initial guess, however, because there are some exceptions to this simple rule, but it's not a bad place to start.) The following examples illustrate this point.

If the output is held below the market equilibrium production level, the outcome is inefficient. Figure 15 illustrates this point. When the production of apples is limited to $\hat{Q}$, consumers would be willing to pay at least $.60 for an additional pound of apples; the marginal cost to society of producing an additional

pound would be only $.20. Therefore, this limitation is inefficient—the amount that consumers are willing to pay for additional production is greater than the cost to society of increasing production a small amount (i.e., MWTP > MC).

If transaction costs decrease, there will be efficiency gains for the economy. Figure 16 illustrates this point. When transaction costs are equal to $.25 for each pound of apples purchased, firms receive only $.25 per pound when consumers pay, in market price and transaction costs, $.50. Clearly, consumers are willing to pay more for additional apples than the costs to society of actually producing apples (i.e., MWTP > MC). Thus if transaction costs can be lowered, say to $.10 per pound, more apples will be produced *and* consumed. Everyone is better off and the economy is more efficient because the marginal cost of producing apples is closer to the amount that consumers are willing to pay for additional apple production.

Prices, not some abstract notion of physical efficiency, are important in determining efficient allocations. Is shipping by train more efficient than shipping by truck? The answer depends, in part, upon the price of train service compared with the price of truck service. These will differ with different input prices. Is a diesel locomotive more efficient than a coal locomotive? The answer depends,

Figure 16
The Effects of Transactions Costs

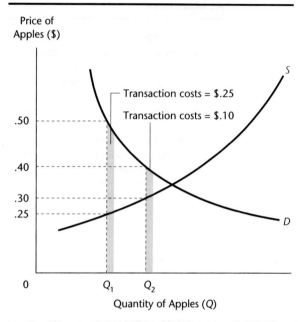

If transactions costs equal $.25., firms receive only $.25 when the price to consumers is $.50 ($Q_1$). In this case, willingness to pay exceeds the marginal cost of producing additional apples. If transactions costs can be lowered, say to $.10, more apples will be consumed (Q_2), and willingness to pay ($.40) will be closer to the marginal cost ($.30).

the widespread use of oxen and horses instead of tractors, or the use of people instead of machinery in many areas of the world indicates how inefficient and backward the economies are. *Given* the relative prices of resources, these may be the most efficient methods of organizing economic activity.

If you find this reliance on prices rather than on some notion of absolute physical or technical efficiency puzzling remember that ships driven by the wind, which is free, are *less* economically efficient than ships driven by fuel oil, which is costly. The full marginal costs of using wind power exceed those of using fuel oil when time-in-transit and the number of people required to manage the ship are considered. Similarly, heating from solar sources, where the energy is also free, is often *less* economically efficient than heating using natural gas, fuel oil, or electricity, all of which cost money. Why? The full marginal cost of using solar power often exceeds the cost of using natural gas or other costly sources of heat when the cost of the solar equipment, back-up systems, and other factors are considered. In each case, market prices and marginal costs matter.

Consumer and Producer Surplus

Consumer surplus is the difference between what individuals *would be willing to pay* for what they are currently consuming and the amount they *actually have to pay*. These two amounts frequently differ because of an important property of the market equilibrium price: The equilibrium market price is a measure of the amount that individuals would be willing to pay for the *last* unit purchased and individuals are often willing to pay much more for the first, or *inframarginal*, unit consumed than they are for the last, or *marginal*, unit consumed.

These distinctions—between marginal and inframarginal, and between what individuals would be willing to pay and what they actually pay—can be understood by considering a market where each individual purchases only one unit of the commodity. Examples might include markets for refrigerators or stoves or dishwashers or, perhaps, television sets. Consider, then, a simple market where a new television set is brought into your classroom and sold to the highest bidder. If the auction is run well, the television set will be sold to the person willing to pay the most for it. To make the example concrete, suppose that the TV is sold for

in part, on the prices of diesel oil and coal. Even though locomotives may get more useful energy from burning diesel oil than from burning coal, allocative efficiency depends upon the price of diesel fuel relative to the price of coal. If the price of diesel fuel were high enough and the price of coal were low enough, it would be allocatively efficient to return to coal-powered trains, just as it was efficient for some power plants to return to coal for electrical power generation when the price of fuel oil increased in the 1970s.

Is using a large number of people to farm by planting and harvesting by hand, for instance, less efficient than replacing people with machines? Or, is using an ox or horse to pull a plow less efficient than using a gasoline-powered tractor? The answer depends, in part, on the price of tractors relative to the wage of farm workers and the price of oxen or horses. If gasoline is sufficiently expensive relative to the costs of maintaining an ox, using oxen will be economically efficient, even though oxen are much slower than tractors. Hence, it is simply not true that

$400. Following the auction, the person who values a TV the most, as measured by his or her willingness to pay, now has a TV. We don't know how much the person who walks off with the TV was truly willing to pay, except that it was at least $400. We do know, however, that the value the losing bidder places on the TV is just a little bit below $400. Why? If the second-highest bidder valued it more than $400, the bid price would have been higher; conversely, if the second-highest bidder valued it less than $400, the bid price would have been lower.

Suppose, at this point, that a second new TV is brought into the room and offered for sale to the highest bidder. It should be clear that the price will be less than $400. Why? If anyone in the room had been willing to pay more than $400, he or she would have bid a higher price for the first TV. Suppose that the price is $360. This bid is just a little bit above the value of the TV to the losing, or third, bidder because, if the losing bidder valued it more, the winning bidder would have had to bid more and, if the losing bidder had valued it less, he or she would not have pushed the bid price up to $360.

Following the auction of the second TV set, a third is brought into the room and sold to the highest bidder. By an argument similar to that noted above, the final bid price would have to be below $360, say $340. We could continue this auction until a number of TVs had been sold. If we did, we might find a price schedule that looked something like that illustrated in Table 1.

The schedule in Table 1 looks a lot like a demand curve. In fact, it is. Remember that market demand is simply the sum of the demands of each

of the participants in the market. In this case, each person has a simple demand: the first person demands one TV at $400; the second person demands one TV at $360; and so on. The market demand is illustrated in Figure 17.

Now suppose that instead of auctioning each of the TVs to the highest bidder in sequence, TVs were offered to your class at a price of $250 each. How many would be sold? Six. Why? Only six individuals were willing to pay at least $250 for TVs when they were sold individually. If six TVs are sold at $250, however, the second person who was willing to pay just a little less than $400 now pays $150 less than this amount. In a very real sense, the difference between the market price and what the individual was willing to pay is a surplus. Similarly, the third individual who was willing to pay just a little less than $360, now pays only $250. Thus, she has a surplus of a little less than $110. Clearly, when six TVs are sold for $250 each, every person except for the

Table 1
Prices for Television Sets

Quantity of TVs	Final bid price
1	$400
2	360
3	340
4	300
5	275
6	250
7	200
8	190

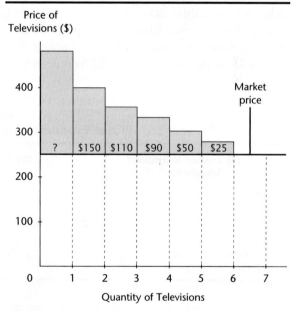

Figure 17
Consumer Surplus

Although everyone who purchases a television set in this market pays $250, some individuals would have been willing to pay more. For example, one person would have been willing to pay $400, but actually paid only $250 ($150 less). The difference between what consumers actually pay and what they would have been willing to pay is the consumer surplus, as indicated by the shaded area.

sixth pays something less than he or she would actually have been willing to pay to purchase a TV. In this simple example, then,

consumer surplus
$$> \$150 + \$110 + \$90 + \$50 + \$25 + \$0$$
$$> \$425$$

Consumer surplus is actually greater than $425 because we haven't added in the amount the first person would have been willing to pay since it isn't revealed by the auction (the first person only has to pay a little more than the maximum amount the second person is willing to pay). While we don't know the maximum she would have been willing to pay, we do know that she was willing to pay at least $400 and, therefore, has a gain of least $150. Hence, consumer surplus is at least $575. Notice that this amount is shown as the area between the demand curve in Figure 17 and the market price of $250.

This idea extends readily to the more common case where consumers purchase more than one item. For example, suppose that an individual wishing to take some friends to the Super Bowl would be willing to pay $100 for one ticket, $75 for a second ticket, $50 for a third ticket, $40 for a fourth ticket, and $25 for a fifth ticket, but is able to purchase tickets for $25 each. She will purchase five tickets. The total amount the individual would have been will-

ing to pay for five tickets is $100 + $75 + $50 + $40 + $25 = $290. In the market, however, the consumer pays only 5 × $25 = $125. Therefore, there is consumer surplus equal to $165. The reason this is so is that consumers adjust the amount they consume until the maximum amount they are willing to pay for the *last* unit is just equal to the market price. This means, in general, that they would be willing to pay much more for all but the last unit purchased.

Thus, a more typical demand curve, as illustrated in Figure 18, also reflects consumer surplus. Consumer surplus in this case is represented by the area between the demand curve and the market price. In Figure 18, area A ($p^* \times Q^*$) is the total amount that consumers actually pay in the market for the good. Area A plus area B equals the total amount that individuals would have been willing to pay for the good. Hence, the difference (area B) is equal to consumer surplus.

We can, through an argument similar to that for consumer surplus, develop a measure of **producer surplus,** defined as the difference between what firms *actually sell* their output for and what they *would have been willing to receive for the same* output. Recall that a firm maximizes its profits (or minimizes its losses) if the price it receives is just equal to the marginal production cost. Consider, then, the marginal cost curve illustrated in Figure 19. If the price is $100, the firm chooses to produce 50 units.

Figure 18
Total Expenditures and Consumer Surplus

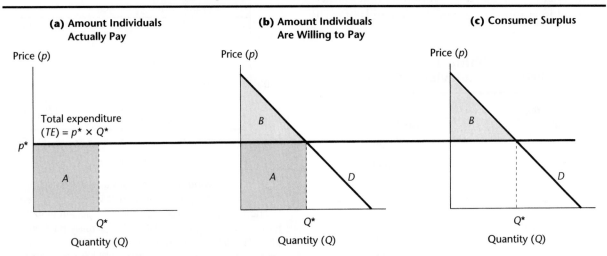

When D is the market demand, A is the amount that consumers actually pay (their total expenditure), A + B is the amount that they would have been willing to pay, and B is the consumer surplus.

Thus, the firm's revenues are $5,000. If the price had been $40, however, the firm would have been willing to produce 20 units—the marginal cost per unit is $40. If the price had been $75, the firm would have been willing to sell an additional 20 units—the marginal cost per unit for the last 20 units produced is $75. Therefore, when the firm sells *all* of its output for $100, it receives a surplus of $60 per unit on the first 20 units produced and $25 per unit on the next 20 units produced, but no surplus for the last 10 units produced. The firm's surplus is $1,200 plus $500, or $1,700 as represented by the gray area between the marginal cost curve and the market price curve in Figure 19.

This surplus can be seen in a slightly different way by noting that each of the first 20 units costs $40 to produce. The total variable cost of producing the first 20 units is $800. By a similar argument, the total variable cost of producing the next 20 units is $1,500 (20 × $75) and for the final 10 units it is $1,000 (10 × $100). The firm's total revenue is $5,000 (50 × $100), and so the firm's surplus, which as noted above is $1,700, is the difference between total revenue and total variable cost.

Using the market supply curve (which reflects, remember, the marginal production costs for each firm in the market), we can obtain the producer surplus generated in a market as illustrated in part (c) of Figure 20.

Figure 19
Producer Surplus

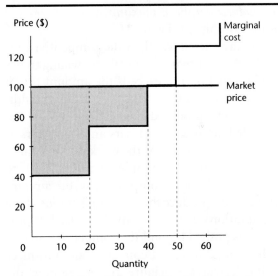

This firm would be willing to sell 20 units at a price of $40, those 20 units plus an additional 20 at a price of $75, and those 40 units plus an additional 10 at a price of $100. If it sells all 50 units for $100, then it receives a producer surplus equal to the shaded area.

Allocative Efficiency, Competitive Markets, and Surplus

We learned earlier that the equilibrium in a competitive market is allocatively efficient. At the competitive equilibrium, the sum of consumer and

Figure 20
Total Revenues and Producer Surplus

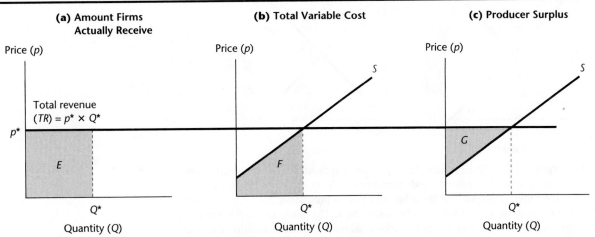

When S is the market supply, E is the amount that consumers actually pay (the firms' total revenue), and F is the total variable cost (remember that S reflects the marginal cost curves of each firm in the market), then G is the producer surplus.

producer surplus is maximized. Thus, *allocative efficiency occurs at the point where the sum of consumer and producer surplus is maximized.* To understand this relationship, see Figure 21.

For any output less than the competitive output, the amount that individuals are willing to pay for additional output exceeds the amount that it costs to produce additional output. Thus, if additional output is produced, there is a surplus that can be divided between consumers and producers as illustrated in Figure 21. At the market equilibrium, however, the amount that individuals are willing to pay for any additional output equals the amount that it costs to produce the additional output; there is no additional surplus to divide. Indeed, if production is pushed beyond the competitive market equilibrium, the sum of consumer and producer surplus decreases. In Figure 21, for example, the additional cost of producing Q_2 is greater than the additional benefit consumers receive. Hence, the sum of consumer plus producer surplus is lower than at the competitive equilibrium. Therefore, a perfectly competitive market maximizes the sum of producer plus consumer surplus.

ANOTHER TEST FOR EFFICIENCY: An allocation is efficient only if the sum of consumer surplus and producer surplus is at its maximum. Alternatively, an allocation cannot be efficient if the sum of consumer surplus and producer surplus can be increased by producing either more or less than the current level of production. This is a common test for efficiency that is widely used in the analysis of public policies.

The Marginal Use or the Marginal Buyer Determines the Market Price

We can use the example developed earlier in this section to illustrate a very important point about the way that markets work. Suppose that instead of being willing to pay $250, the 6th person would only have been willing to pay $200 for a TV (and that all other consumers valued TVs at less than $200). If six TVs are brought into the room, the market clearing price would now be $200 per TV, not $250. If the 6th person was only willing to pay $100 (and all other consumers valued TVs at less than $100), then the market clearing price would be $100. Note that the

Figure 21
The Relationship Between Consumer Surplus and Producer Surplus at the Competitive Market Equilibrium

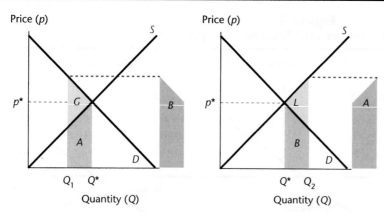

(a) If output is below Q^* (for example, Q_1), increasing production increases the surplus to be divided between producers and consumers by G because consumers are willing to pay B for additional output, but the additional cost of producing the additional output is A. (b) If, however, output increases (for example, to Q_2), a loss of L will occur because consumers are willing to pay B', for the additional output, but the additional cost of producing the additional output is A'. Because A' is greater than B', the sum of producer and consumer surpluses falls. This sum is greatest at the competitive market equilibrium.

amount that the person who values a TV the most (at least $400) and is, therefore, willing to pay the most, *does not* determine the market clearing price! Instead, the market price is determined by the value that the marginal buyer puts on the item being sold.

▶ Summary

Prices and profits. Prices ration scarce commodities among competing interests. Prices convey information. Prices and profits provide incentives to move or reallocate resources from activities of lesser value to activities of greater value, where value is determined by the willingness of individuals to pay. Prices and profit also link markets together through substitution and arbitrage.

Prices and profits coordinate competing interests so as to allow an economy to capture the gains from specialization and exchange. In particular, competitive markets allocate goods and services to the highest-valued users and resources to their most productive use.

Allocative efficiency. A market is allocatively efficient when the maximum amount that individuals are willing to pay for any additional production is equal to the marginal cost of producing any additional goods. Alternatively, a market is allocatively efficient when the sum of consumer plus producer surplus is maximized. Competitive markets are allocatively efficient.

Other notions of efficiency. Three additional notions of efficiency are important: adjustment efficiency, informational efficiency, and dynamic efficiency. For the first, the important question is whether markets adjust to changes and shocks more quickly than can alternatives. For the second, the important question is whether markets gather and transmit information about demands and supplies more quickly than can alternatives. For the third, the important question is whether markets stimulate and reward individual initiative to change and innovate.

Consumer and producer surplus. Consumer surplus is the difference between the amount that individuals are willing to pay for what they currently purchase minus the amount that they actually have to pay. Because the market price is determined by the amount that individuals are willing to pay for the last or marginal unit purchased, markets create a consumer surplus.

Producer surplus is the difference between what firms receive for producing a certain output and what they would have been willing to receive and still make the same production decision. Because the market price is determined by the minimum price that firms must receive to produce the last or marginal unit provided to the market, markets create a producers' surplus as well.

Competitive markets maximize the sum of consumer surplus plus producer surplus. Thus, given scarce resources, competitive markets make consumers and producers, taken together, as well off as possible.

Chapter 11 ▶▶
International Trade and Domestic Markets

Sony Walkman's, VW Passats, mangos, bananas—the availability of these and countless other things produced outside of the United States makes it obvious that exchange and specialization transcend national boundaries. In this chapter we focus on the reasons for international trade as well as on the effects of international trade on US markets. While we won't directly deal with the current debate about the merits of "globalization," understanding the reasons for the increased movement of goods, services and even people across national boundaries is critical to any evaluation of the consequences—good or not-so-good—of greater integration of the economies around the world.

▶ Why Trade?

In Chapter 1 we considered exchange and specialization among individuals within an economy. The key element in stimulating specialization was the difference in the *relative* production costs between you and Friday or between you and Defoe. From the incentives for individuals to exchange and specialize emerged an economy and it follows that within any economy there is extensive trade among individuals and highly specialized production as well. Each of us shares, in varying degrees to be sure, in the wealth created.

Suppose that we replaced "you" in any of the previous discussions of exchange and specialization with "the United States," and replaced "Friday" with "Japan." Would the argument that there are gains from exchange and specialization change? The short

answer: No. To see why, consider the two economies illustrated in Figures 1 and 2. Figure 1 is a copy of Figure 1 in Chapter 1 except that parts have been relabeled to show the ability of the United States to produce automobiles and rice rather than your ability to produce coconuts and palm leaves. Figure 2 is the same as Figure 4 in Chapter 1, except that it represents Japan's ability to produce automobiles and rice instead of Friday's ability to produce coconut and palm leaves.

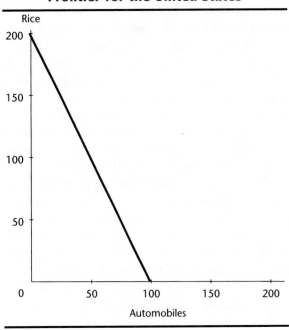

**Figure 1
The Production Possibilities
Frontier for the United States**

Figure 2
The Production Possibilities Frontier for Japan

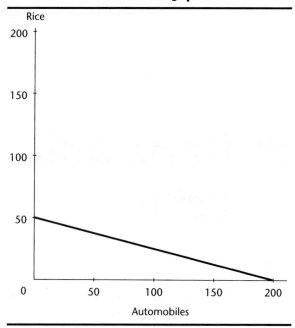

Comparative Advantage in International Trade

Given these two production possibility frontiers, the opportunity cost of producing fewer automobiles and more rice in the United States is one automobile for two tons of rice (that is, 1 A for 2 R). The opportunity cost for Japan of producing fewer automobiles and more rice is eight automobiles for two tons of rice (8 A for 2 R). Since the opportunity cost of producing rice is less in the United States than it is in Japan, the United States has a **comparative advantage** in rice production. Conversely, since the opportunity cost of producing automobiles is less in Japan than it is in the United States, Japan has a comparative advantage in automobile production. These differences in relative production costs *within each economy* provide powerful incentives to open trade between two economies just as similar relative cost differences among individuals provide powerful incentives to trade within an economy.

If there is no international trade, each economy's ability to produce determines its consumption possibilities. If the United States chooses to specialize in rice production, however, it can trade some of the rice it produces with Japan for automobiles, purchasing automobiles for *fewer* tons of

rice per automobile than it would cost to produce automobiles in the United States. Similarly, if Japan chooses to specialize in automobile production, it can trade some of the automobiles it produces for rice and purchase rice for *fewer* automobiles per ton of rice than it would cost to produce rice in Japan. Each country has an incentive to specialize consistent with comparative advantage—the US in rice and Japan in automobiles. With international trade both countries benefit because each is able to consume *more* rice and *more* automobiles than would otherwise be possible.

This argument is, of course, virtually identical to the argument demonstrating the substantial gains from specialization and exchange within an economy developed in Chapter 1. Only the labels have changed. If you reread Chapter 1 substituting "the United States" for "you" and "Japan" for "Friday," the discussion is the classic argument for free trade that has been understood for more than 200 years. Briefly recapping:

- Individuals trade because they can purchase some commodities from others more cheaply than they can produce these goods themselves. Similarly, if nations respond to the incentives provided by relative cost differences, they will also trade because some goods can be purchased from other nations more cheaply than they can be produced within the economy.

- Specialization for individuals is determined by comparative advantage within a domestic economy. Similarly, specialization in international trade will be determined by comparative advantage within a worldwide or global "economy."

- In the same way that individuals have a comparative advantage with respect to other individuals as long as they have different abilities to produce commodities, nations with different abilities to produce commodities *must* have a comparative advantage relative to other nations.

- Hence, just as *absolute* advantage does not matter in determining your opportunities to advantageously participate in an economy (that is, you don't have to be absolutely better than anyone in order to gain from specializing), absolute advantage is irrelevant in determining whether a nation should choose to trade. If other countries might be better at producing everything than the United States, the U.S. economy still gains from international trade. Even if other countries have cheaper labor or more abundant natural resources or superior technologies or more capital, the U.S. (or *any* other economy) benefits from international trade and greater domestic specialization whenever there are different relative costs of producing the same commodities among different nations.

- Whatever the distribution of gains from exchange and individuals among individuals, exchange and specialization tend to maximize the value of production within an economy. Similarly, if nations trade consistent with comparative advantage, the value of worldwide or global production will be maximized.

- Finally, the fact that individuals differ one from another means that an individual will always have a comparative advantage in producing something. Similarly, as long as our economy differs from other economies, the U.S. economy will *always* have a comparative advantage in some production activities and a comparative disadvantage in others, even if we do not have an absolute advantage in any single activity or even if we have an absolute advantage in every activity. Likewise, our trading partners will have a comparative advantage in some production activities and a comparative disadvantage in others, whatever the resources available to them.

▶ International Trade and Domestic Markets

We can be more precise about the effects of international trade on domestic markets and explore what happens within the U.S. when changes occur elsewhere in the world by considering the effects of imports and exports on specific markets.

Imports and Domestic Markets

In Figure 3, the equilibrium domestic market (relative) price is above the world price. If imports were

**Figure 3
The Effects of Imports on
Domestic Markets**

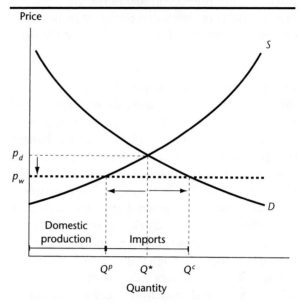

Without international trade, the domestic price, P_d, prevails: domestic suppliers will supply Q^* to the market and domestic consumers will demand the same amount. With international trade, however, the world price, p_w, prevails. At this price, domestic consumption is Q^c, but domestic production is only Q^p. The difference will be imported from abroad.

not allowed to enter the economy, domestic firms would produce and sell Q^*. When individuals can purchase abroad at a price that is below the domestic price, however, the domestic market cannot be in equilibrium at Q^* and p_d. Indeed, consumers within the economy will buy from foreign producers rather than domestic producers as long as domestic producers attempt to charge a price greater than p_w. This ability to import will push the domestic market price down and toward the world price.

As the price within the US economy falls, quantity demanded increases. In the market illustrated in Figure 3, the quantity demanded increases from Q^* to Q^c as long as domestic consumers are free to purchase from either foreign firms or domestic firms at the world price p_w. Domestic producers, by contrast, will decrease production as prices fall. Specifically, in Figure 3 domestic firms are willing to supply only Q^p when the world price is p_w. Following these adjustments by both consumers and producers within the United States, a new market equilibrium is reached where domestic firms produce Q^p and consumers purchase Q^c. The difference, $Q^c - Q^p$, is **imported** from foreign producers. This domestic market is now fully integrated in the international market and consumers can purchase from either domestic producers or foreign producers at the same price.

Effects of changes in the world price. *Changes* in the world price will affect domestic markets as illustrated in Figure 4. For example, if the world price decreases from p_w to p'_w and there are no changes in either domestic demand or domestic production costs, more will be imported and less will be produced domestically. The amount that consumers purchase, however, increases. Figure 4(a) illustrates these effects. As the world price decreases, domestic production decreases while domestic consumption increases. Hence, if foreign producers become more efficient, U.S. consumers will benefit. At the same time, resources will move from this domestic industry to other areas of the economy where the US has a comparative advantage.

If, instead, the world price increases, say from p_w to p''_w in Figure 4(b), demanders will purchase less and more will be produced domestically. Imports will decrease as a consequence. When the world price for an imported good increases, domestic firms that compete with imports are made better off because they can sell more and at a higher price. US consumers are, however, made worse off because they must pay higher prices and find suitable substitutes.

Gains from trade. The concepts of consumer and producer surplus introduced in Chapter 10 can be used to measure the gains from trade. These gains are area B in Figure 5. Why? When the world price is below the domestic price, consumers purchase some of what they consume from abroad rather than from domestic producers. Domestic consumption increases from Q^* to Q^c, *while domestic production decreases from Q^* to Q^p*. Firms lose area A in producer surplus; consumers gain area $A + B$ in consumer surplus. Hence, the net effect of trade on the domestic economy is a gain of B. Notice that there are *both gains and losses*. Consumers gain, but domestic producers in this market lose. Not surprisingly, then, some people within an economy support free international trade, while others oppose it. However, since the gains always exceed the losses,

Figure 4
The Effect of Changes in the World Price on Domestic Markets with Imports

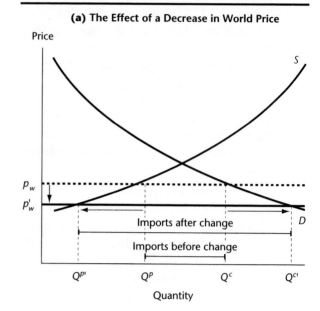

(a) The Effect of a Decrease in World Price

(b) The Effect of an Increase in World Price

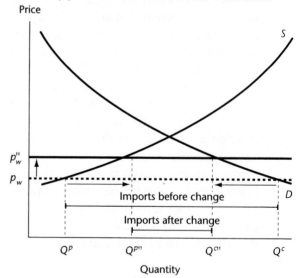

(a) A decrease in the world price (from p_w to p'_w) increases the quantity demanded from Q^c to $Q^{c'}$ but decreases the quantity produced domestically from Q^p to $Q^{p'}$. An increase in imports makes up the difference between domestic supply and demand. (b) An increase in the world price from p_w to p'_w decreases the quantity demanded from Q^c to $Q^{c''}$ but increases the quantity produced domestically from Q^p to $Q^{p''}$. Exports fall as well.

as illustrated, and there are always net gains to international trade. That is, the economy as a whole is better off with trade.

Figure 5
The Effect of Imports on Allocational Efficiency

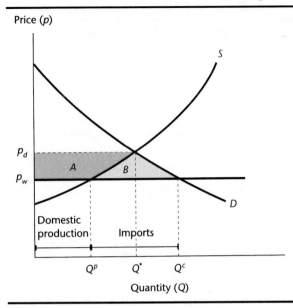

If the domestic price, p_d, is greater than the world price, p_w, then foreign producers can supply additional output at a lower cost than domestic producers can, and domestic consumers are willing to pay more for additional output than foreign consumers are. A more efficient allocation of resources can be achieved if domestic consumers import goods from foreign markets. At the world price, domestic production falls, causing domestic producers to lose producer surplus equal to area A, but domestic consumption increases, so consumers gain additional consumer surplus equal to area A + B. The net gain in total surplus because of world trade is equal to area B. Therefore, in this case, imports increase allocational efficiency.

Exports and Domestic Markets

If the world price is above the domestic price, domestic firms have an incentive to export some or all of their production. In Figure 6, for example, the domestic price is p_d when there is no trade. If the world price is p_w, foreigners will want to purchase from U.S. firms rather than from their own firms. (**Exports** from the United States must be equal to **imports** for one or more other countries.) Presumably domestic firms would prefer to export their production and sell in foreign markets at the higher world price instead of domestic markets at the lower domestic price. As a consequence, the domestic price will increase. As the domestic price increases, the quantity demanded in domestic markets falls, from Q^* to Q^c in Figure 6. As the price at which firms can sell their output increases, however, the quantity that domestic firms produce increases from Q^* to Q^p. The difference between domestic consumption and domestic production, $Q^p - Q^c$, is **exported.**

Effects of changes in the world price. Not surprisingly, when an economy is integrated in international markets, changes in prices elsewhere in the world will affect domestic markets. When a country is exporting a particular commodity and its world price increases, for example, domestic producers are made better off because they sell more and at a

Figure 6
The Effect of Exports on Domestic Markets

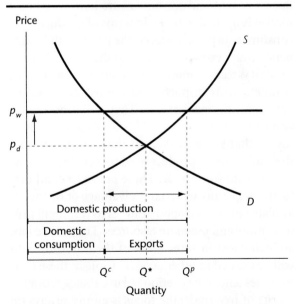

When the domestic price, p_d, is below the world price, p_w, domestic firms would rather sell their products abroad at the higher world price. Because of this increase in price, domestic consumption is lower than it would be without international trade (Q^c instead of Q^*), while supply is greater (Q^p rather than Q^*). The difference between domestic supply and demand is exported to other countries.

higher price. Domestic consumers, however, are made worse off in the sense that as the world price increases, they must either pay the higher price or find substitutes. (This point is illustrated in Figure 7(a). The effects of a decrease in the world price when domestic firms supply both the domestic market and export to other markets are illustrated in Figure 7(b).)

▶ The Distributional Effects of International Trade

As we have just learned, trade between economies changes relative prices *within* an economy. In Chapter 2 we learned that changes in relative prices often lead to changes in the distribution of income. It follows that opening an economy to international trade (or, once open, any changes in world prices) will have income distributional effects. In general, when the world price of a particular commodity is below the domestic price, consumers benefit and domestic producers are harmed when the market is opened to trade. Conversely, when the world price of a commodity is above the domestic price, domestic producers benefit and consumers are harmed when a market is opened to trade. In terms of producer *plus* consumer surplus, however, the gains to the "winners" always exceed the losses to the "losers."

Put directly, some domestic suppliers who must compete with imports will almost certainly be adversely affected by trade. They will produce less and user fewer resources. This is just a nice way of saying that some workers at these firms will lose their jobs. Those producers who export will, however, benefit from trade. These producers and new firms that spring up to take advantage of the newly available profitable opportunities to trade will produce more and use more resources. Thus, while jobs are being lost in some areas of the economy, jobs will be created in other areas. Curiously, these beneficiaries tend to be overlooked in debates about the merits of free trade; the focus is almost always on jobs lost in import-competing industries and almost never on jobs created in the expanding exporting industries. The benefits to consumers of the lower prices and greater variety available when they are free to purchase goods from abroad are also often overlooked. While there are winners and losers, because specialization increases output and permits an economy to consume output combinations that

Figure 7
The Effects of Changes in the World Price on Domestic Markets with Exports

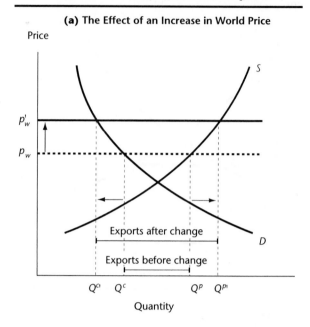

(a) The Effect of an Increase in World Price

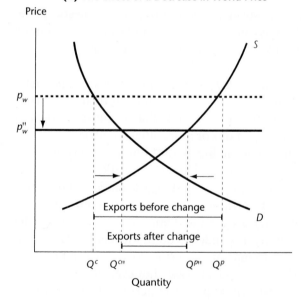

(b) The Effect of a Decrease in World Price

(a) An increase in world price from p_w to p'_w decreases domestic quantity demanded from Q^c to $Q^{c'}$ and increases the quantity produced domestically from Q^p to $Q^{p'}$. Thus the total quantity available for export increases. (b) A decrease in world price from p_w to p''_w increases the quantity demanded domestically from Q^c to $Q^{c''}$ but decreases the quantity produced domestically from Q^p to $Q^{p''}$. Thus the total quantity available for export decreases.

lie beyond its production possibilities frontier, *the gains to the economy as a whole from free trade must be greater than the losses.*

▶ Money in International Trade

International trade is a little more complex than trade within an economy because unlike trade within an economy where all suppliers and demanders use the same money, each economy typically has its own money. This means that when goods are imported, the foreign firms selling the good and the domestic consumers purchasing the good must agree on the price *denominated in a particular country's money.* For example, if US consumers are purchasing French cheese, there must be an agreement on the price either in Euros (the European money) or dollars (the US money). In addition, since there is no "international money," there must also be an agreement on the money that will be used in the transaction. That is, either US consumers will have to pay in Euros or French farmers will have to accept dollars. If US consumers agree to pay in Euros, they must get Euros. If, however, French farmers agree to accept dollars, they will generally want to exchange them for Euros. As a consequence, the efforts of consumers and firms to buy or sell products abroad create two kinds of international markets: one for commodities and, at the same time, one for foreign currencies.

Foreign Exchange Markets

International markets for currencies (where, to continue with our example, US consumers can purchase Euros and/or French farmers can sell US dollars) are called **foreign exchange markets**. Because some foreigners want to import US goods and need dollars and because some foreigners accept US dollars in exchange for goods they export to the U.S., there is a foreign exchange market for the US dollar. In this market, citizens of the United Kingdom, Japan, Germany and other countries can buy US dollars with their own currencies or sell US dollars that they might have accepted as payments for goods they shipped to the U.S. Similarly, there is a foreign exchange market for the Japanese yen where the citizens of the United Kingdom, the United States, Germany and other countries can purchase yen with Euros, dollars or other currencies.

Relative prices in these markets are called **exchange rates**. The euro-dollar exchange rate is,

for example, the number of euros it takes to purchase one US dollar.[1] Because there are a large number of different economies in the world, most of which use different domestic currencies, there are also a large number of foreign exchange markets and exchange rates (the dollar-pound rate, the euro-dollar rate, the yen-dollar rate, the euro-yen rate, etc.)

Exchange-rates and the "Price" of Imports and Exports

The exchange rate determines the price of a country's exports *in terms of the importing country's money.* For example, if an automobile produced and exported from Japan sells for 2,600,000 yen and the exchange rate is 130 yen per dollar, it would cost

$$\frac{2,600,000 \text{ yen}}{130 \text{ yen}/\text{dollar}} = \$20,000 \qquad (1)$$

when imported into the United States. Note that *from the perspective of an American consumer* the price of a Japanese automobile can change either because the price in Japan changes (the numerator in equation 1) or because the exchange rate changes (the denominator). For example, if the dollar falls in value relative to the yen from 130 yen/dollar to 120 yen per dollar, then an automobile that remains priced at 2,600,000 yen in Japan would cost $21,667 in the United States—an increase of a little more than 8 percent. By contrast, the price in Japan could increase, say from 2,600,000 yen to 2,808,000 yen and if the value of the dollar relative to the yen remained at 130 yen per dollar, the price in the United States would also be $21,667.

As a consequence, a fall in the value of the dollar relative to foreign currencies (called a **depreciation** of the dollar) makes foreign-produced commodities more expensive *in US-dollar terms* and, hence, for US consumers. This same change also makes US exports less expensive *in foreign currency terms.* If US soybeans sell for $5.00 a bushel, for example, the

---

[1] Exchange rates can be quoted either in terms of the foreign currency required to purchase one US dollar or the number of US dollars required to purchase one unit of a foreign currency. Except for the US dollar-British pound exchange rate (which is quoted in newspapers in terms of the number of dollars required to purchase a pound—for example, $1.65 per pound), most exchange rates are quoted in terms of the amount of foreign currency required to purchase one dollar—for example, 130 yen per dollar.

price in Japan is 650 yen when the exchange rate is 130 yen per dollar, but only 600 yen when the exchange rate is 120 yen per dollar. ($5.00 × 130 yen/dollar = 650 yen; $5.00 × 120 yen/dollar = 600 yen).

Conversely, an increase in the value of the dollar relative to foreign currencies (an **appreciation** of the dollar) makes foreign-produced commodities less expensive in US-dollar terms and, therefore, cheaper for US consumers. At the same time, this increase makes US exports more expensive in foreign currency terms and, therefore, more costly for foreign consumers.

Clearly, when an economy is open to trade, the value of its currency in foreign exchange markets will affect how the "world prices" of particular commodities are perceived within the economy. Changes in "perceived world prices" because of changes in the value of a nation's money in foreign exchange markets will change how much is imported and, *simultaneously*, how much is exported even if prices within an economy do not change. That is, if US dollar prices within the U.S. do not change and Euro prices within Europe do not change the perceived costs of European exports to the United States and US exports to Europe will change if the Euro/US dollar exchange rate changes. Hence, foreign exchange markets are important when economies are open to trade.

The demand for foreign exchange. Suppose that American importers of Toyotas agree to pay for them with yen. Because yen do not circulate within the US economy, US importers must purchase yen using dollars. This creates a demand for yen. In addition, some Japanese exporters may agree to accept dollars in payment for the goods they sell to US buyers. Since dollars do not circulate in Japan, these exporters will want yen rather than dollars. This also creates a demand for yen. Note that those who demand yen, simultaneously supply dollars. Some US citizens may also want to purchase stocks or bonds in the Tokyo stock exchange or purchase part of a Japanese firm. In order to do so, these people—who have dollars—must purchase yen. In general, the demand for a country's currency in foreign exchange markets is derived from the demand for its exports as well as for its assets (stocks, bonds, land, etc.).

The supply of foreign exchange. Who might be willing to sell yen? Suppliers in foreign exchange markets are individuals who now hold yen but who want dollars. For example, Japanese importers of Boeing commercial jets might have agreed to pay for the planes with dollars. To do so, these importers must purchase dollars using their yen in foreign exchange markets. Clearly, a demand for dollars creates a supply of yen. There may also be US firms who have agreed to accept yen in payment for what they exported to Japan. These American exporters are suppliers of yen because US firms will typically want to get out of yen and into dollars since they operate primarily within the US economy. Some Japanese citizens may also want to purchase stocks or bonds in the New York stock market or purchase part of a U.S. firm or even purchase U.S. real estate. Since all of these transactions within the US occur in dollars, any Japanese wishing to do so must exchange their yen for dollars. They become suppliers of yen in the foreign exchange market. Notice that *anyone who supplies yen must also be a demander of a different currency*—in this example, dollars. In general, the supply of a country's currency in foreign exchange markets is derived from its demand for imports from abroad and the desire of its citizens to make foreign investments.

Exchange-rate determination. Figure 8 illustrates a foreign exchange market for yen. The quantity of foreign exchange supplied or demanded—in this case yen—is measured on the horizontal axis. The relative price or **exchange rate**—in this case the dollar price of each yen—is measured along the vertical axis. To keep this straight, think of yen as a commodity like apples. In a supply-demand diagram illustrating the apple market, of course, the quantity of apples is along the horizontal axis; the relative price of apples measured in dollars, that is, the amount of dollars needed to purchase a pound of apples, is measured along the vertical axis. The same idea is used in Figure 8. Yen are being bought and sold as if they were "apples." Hence, it is the amount of dollars needed to purchase one yen that is the relative price on the vertical axis. In a market for apples, the demanders are people who have dollars who want apples. In the market for yen, the demanders are people who have dollars who want yen. In a market for apples, the suppliers are people who have apples who want dollars. In the market for yen, the suppliers are people who have yen who want dollars.

The equilibrium price, e^*_y, is the dollar price that must be paid for each yen when Q^* yen are will-

Figure 8
Foreign Exchange Market for Yen

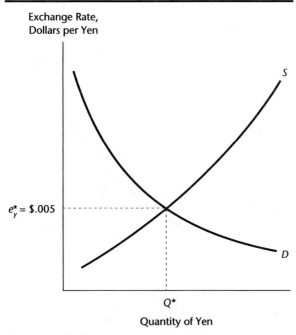

In the foreign exchange market for yen, *D* is the demand for yen by those holding dollars and *S* is the supply of yen. In this market, the equilibrium price of yen is $.005 for each yen. In other words, one dollar buys 200 yen.

ingly supplied and demanded in the dollar-yen foreign exchange market. If e^*_y is $.005 per yen, for example, each yen costs one-half cent and a person can purchase 200 yen for each dollar. Looked at slightly differently, suppliers of yen must give up 200 yen to receive a dollar. The dollar price of yen ($.005) is the **exchange rate**.

When the amount of dollars required to purchase a yen increases, the yen is said to **appreciate**. Anything priced in yen (such as video cameras exported from Japan to the US) will cost more to someone with dollars and the quantity demanded by those holding dollars will be less. That is, the demand for yen slopes downward like a typical market demand curve because, in part, the demand for imports is inversely related to the dollar price imports. Note, by contrast, that when the yen appreciates anyone supplying yen gets more dollars per yen and anything priced in dollars (such as Boeing 777s exported from the US to Japan) will cost less to someone with yen. The quantity of jets demand will increase. But this means that the supply curve of yen

has the usual shape since more yen will then be supplied to the market.

A currency that decreases in value relative to another currency is said to **depreciate**. When a currency depreciates, a unit of the currency buys less of a second currency. For example, if a dollar purchases 1.2 Euro one day but only 1 Euro the next, the dollar has depreciated in value relative to the Euro. Anything priced in Euros (a vacation in France, for example) will now be more costly to holders of dollars; anything priced in dollars (US wheat, for example) will now be less costly to holders of Euros.

The exchange rate is a relative price, so if one currency appreciates in value relative to another currency, the other currency *must* depreciate in value relative to the first. That is, if it takes more dollars to buy one yen (the yen has **appreciated**), the converse must be true: it takes fewer yen to buy one dollar (the dollar has **depreciated**).

Not all currencies are traded in foreign exchange markets, but many are. Because of the large number of different currencies that are traded, the array of exchange rates is large: dollar-pound, dollar-Euro, dollar-peso, US dollar-Canadian dollar, Euro-peso and so forth. Because there are many foreign exchange markets for a particular currency, a currency may appreciate in one foreign exchange market and, at the same time, depreciate in a different foreign exchange market. For example, the dollar price per yen may increase from $.005 per yen to $.008 per yen (a depreciation of the dollar relative to the yen) while, on the same day, the dollar price per Argentine peso may go from $.75 to $.50 (an appreciation of the dollar relative to the peso). In general, however, over a given period of time, a currency will tend to either appreciate or depreciate relative to most foreign currencies.

Foreign exchange market adjustments. A currency appreciates or depreciates because of changes in demand or supply in the foreign exchange market for that currency. If the supply of yen increases, for example, the dollar price per yen must decrease, *ceteris paribus*. (The supply of yen might increase because of an increase in Japanese demand for US exports, for example.) This change is illustrated by a shift from S to S' in Figure 9. In this case, the dollar has *increased* in value relative to the yen because it now takes *fewer* dollars to purchase the *same* amount

Figure 9
An Increase in the Supply of Yen

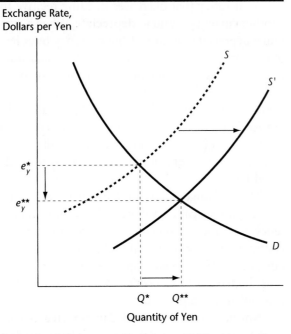

When the supply of yen increases, the price of yen will fall. When the dollar price of yen falls, the yen is said to have depreciated and the dollar to have appreciated in value.

Figure 10
An Increase in the Demand for Yen

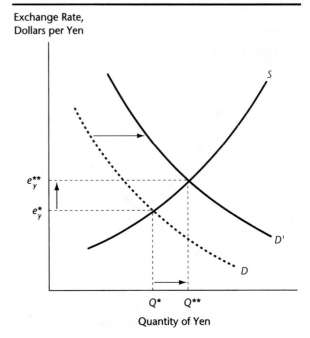

When the demand for yen increases, the price of yen will increase as well. When the price of yen increases, the yen appreciates and the dollar depreciates in value.

of yen. That is, the dollar has appreciated. For example, if e^*_y falls from $.005 per yen to $.004 per yen, this means that 100 yen, which used to cost $.50, now costs $.40 or that a person can now purchase 250 yen for each dollar whereas, before the price change, he or she could purchase only 200 yen. Clearly, a decrease in the demand for yen also leads to an appreciation of the dollar.[2]

The dollar will depreciate if there is an increase in demand for Japanese exports by US consumers, *ceteris paribus*. This change in the foreign exchange value of the dollar is illustrated in Figure 10. The effects of these kinds of changes in supply and demand in foreign exchange markets is summarized in Table 1.

A caution. An appreciation or depreciation of a currency in foreign exchange markets does not neces-

sarily affect the purchasing power of the money *within* an economy. That is, appreciation and depreciation should not be confused with inflation and deflation. The latter refers to changes in the purchasing power of money within an economy; the former to changes in the price of money in foreign exchange markets.

▶ Trade Imbalances

One of the consequences of using money to facilitate trade (rather than trading goods for goods) is that at any moment of time, the value of a country's exports need not be equal to the value of its imports. The value of a country's exports might exceed the value of its imports. In which case, the country is running a **trade surplus**. Alternatively, the value of a country's imports might exceed the value of its exports and it will be running a **trade deficit**. The size of a deficit or surplus can be measured by **net exports**:

$$\text{net exports} = \text{value of exports (X)} - \text{value of imports (M)}$$

---

[2] Exchange-rate changes are always a little confusing. You can keep these changes sorted out by remembering that the currency you are holding is appreciating if less is needed to buy the same amount of a foreign currency and that the currency you are holding is depreciating if more is need to buy the same amount of a foreign currency.

Table 1
Effects of Changes in Supply and Demand on Exchange Rates

Change in market	Equivalent change	Effect on exchange rate (dollars per yen)	Effect on dollar
Increase in supply of yen	Increase in demand for dollars	Decrease	Appreciation
Decrease in supply of yen	Decrease in demand for dollars	Increase	Depreciation
Increase in demand for yen	Increase in supply of dollars	Increase	Depreciation
Decrease in demand for yen	Decrease in supply of dollars	Decrease	Appreciation

Generally, a country cannot run either a trade deficit or trade surplus for an extended period of time. To understand why, suppose that imports increase and the United States begins to run a trade deficit (net exports are negative). In this case, the U.S. would be importing more goods and services than it was exporting. If the foreigners who earn dollars for their exports to the US are initially unwilling to use those dollars to purchase US goods and services <u>and</u> unwilling to hold the dollars, this change in net exports will lead to an increase in the supply of dollars in foreign exchange markets. As we have just learned, this is equivalent to an increase in the demand for foreign currencies. An increase in the demand for a foreign currency will, *ceteris paribus*, increase the price of the foreign currency in terms of US dollars. (Equivalently, the increase in supply of dollars will decrease the price of U.S. dollars in terms of foreign currency.) In other words, the US dollar will depreciate in foreign exchange markets.

If the demand for imports from Japan by US consumers increases, for example, the demand for yen will increase (or, equivalently, the supply of dollars will increase), the price of yen will increase, and more dollars will be needed in order to purchase exactly the same number of yen. This change in the foreign exchange value of the dollar affects both imports and exports. Since fewer yen can be purchased with each dollar, Japanese exports to the US are more expensive for US consumers. Since more dollars can be purchased with each yen, US exports to Japan are cheaper for Japanese consumers. As a consequence, the quantity of US imports will decrease and the quantity of US exports will increase. This adjustment tends to eliminate the trade deficit that occurred when net exports fell. More generally, *when a country has a trade deficit and foreigners do not want to hold the currency or assets of that coun-*

try, the exchange rate will change (the currency of the country with the trade deficit will depreciate) so as to bring the value of exports into line with the value of imports, thereby moving the economy toward a trade balance.

Is an appreciation better than a depreciation? It may appear that there are advantages if the dollar appreciates because foreign goods, in terms of US dollars, become less expensive. Although this is an obvious benefit to people who buy imports, it hurts US exporters. Because an appreciation in the dollar is the same as a depreciation of the currency of a trading partner, commodities produced within the U.S. will become more expensive to foreigners. This will make it more difficult for US manufacturers and farmers to sell their goods abroad; it will also make competition between domestic and foreign producers within the United States more intense. On the other hand, a depreciation of the dollar that increases US exports also makes imports more expensive and reduces competition between domestic and foreign producers in US markets. Domestic prices might also increase as a consequence. In short, an appreciation of a currency benefits domestic consumers and hurts domestic exporters, but a depreciation of a currency benefits exporters and hurts consumers.

A recap. We can summarize these adjustments to a trade imbalance as follows:[3]
A US trade deficit leads to an

   -> accumulation of dollars by foreigners, an
      -> increase in supply of dollars on foreign exchange markets, a
         -> depreciation of the dollar, a

---

[3] You could, of course, substitute any other country for the "U.S." in this description.

-> decrease in the price of US goods to foreigners and an increase in the price of foreign goods in the U.S., an
    -> increase in US exports and a decrease in US imports.
        -> The trade deficit is reduced or eliminated.

Or, U.S. trade surplus leads to an
  -> accumulation of foreign currencies held by US citizens, a
    -> decrease in supply of dollars on foreign exchange markets, an
      -> appreciation of the dollar, an
        -> increase in the price of US goods to foreigners and a decrease in the price of foreign goods in the United States, a
          -> decrease in US exports and an increase in US imports
            -> The trade surplus is reduced or eliminated.

An exception. Will trade deficits and trade surpluses always disappear? Not necessarily. If you reread the above description of the adjustments that a trade deficit or surplus kick off, you will note that the adjustments in foreign exchange markets occur *if foreigners do not want to hold U.S. dollars when the U.S. is running a trade deficit* or *if US citizens do not want to hold foreign currencies when the United States is running a trade surplus*. If, however, foreigners want to hold US dollars (or things like US stocks or bonds or real estate), then the dollars that they accumulate when the U.S. runs a trade deficit will not show up in the foreign exchange markets and the dollar's foreign exchange value won't change. If the dollar doesn't depreciate when the U.S. is running a trade deficit, for example, then there will be no adjustments in imports or exports and the trade deficit can persist. This means that the United States can run a trade deficit, but only as long as foreigners are willing to hold US dollars or US-dollar assets. Put differently, but equivalently, Japan can run a trade surplus with the United States but only if the Japanese are willing to hold US dollars or US-dollar assets. A consequence of this important exception is that governments sometimes try to manipulate the foreign exchange value of their currencies in order to sustain a trade deficit or surplus. It has been argued, for example, that the Japanese government has purposefully kept the value of the yen low in foreign exchange markets in order to maintain a trade surplus with the United States and Europe.

Other Determinants of Net Exports

Aggregate or national income also affects net exports. Imports tend to increase when incomes within an economy increase, and fall when incomes fall. As a consequence, U.S. net exports typically increase when incomes increase more rapidly abroad than within the US; they tend to decrease when incomes increase more rapidly within the US than abroad. For example, one of the contributors to the large US trade deficit of the past several years has been the decade long period recession in Japan—Japanese incomes have not grown much since the early 1990s and, as a consequence, Japanese demand for imports, including imports from the United States, has fallen. Robust economic growth in the United States during the 1990s, however, led to a substantial increase in the demand by US consumers for imports from Japan. Hence, the large US trade deficit with Japan.

▶ Summary

Specialization and comparative advantage. If the price of a commodity is higher outside of an economy than inside, domestic firms have an incentive to export part or all of what they produce. Conversely, if the world price for a commodity is lower than the domestic price, individuals have an incentive to import part or all of what they consume. Responding to differences in prices will lead nations to specialize consistent with comparative advantage. International trade and domestic specialization between economies consistent with comparative advantage increases the overall level of output available to each economy. These gains do not come without consequences, however. International trade and domestic specialization imply interdependence and integration in an international or global economy. In addition, since changes in relative prices sometimes alter the distribution of economic rewards within an economy and the allocation of jobs across an economy, international trade and domestic specialization will also have income distributional effects.

Exports and imports. Sales abroad by domestic firms are **exports**. Purchases abroad by domestic firms or individuals are **imports**. Exports from one country are imports to other countries with whom they trade. For a single economy, **net exports** are the difference between the value of its exports and the value of its imports. In symbols, net exports = x – m (where x is the "value of exports" and m is the "value of imports").

Markets for foreign currencies. Because there is not a single currency that is accepted for transactions everywhere in the world, trade between nations leads to markets for **foreign exchange** in which individuals and firms buy and sell the currencies of other countries. The **exchange rate** is the price of one currency in terms of another currency. Exchange rates are determined by interactions of supply and demand in foreign exchange markets, although governments sometimes intervene to manipulate the foreign exchange value of their currencies.

Changes in the foreign exchange value of a currency change the price of imports from the perspective of domestic importers. Changes in the exchange rate also change the price of exports from the perspective of foreigners. More precisely, if the dollar appreciates relative to the yen, each dollar will purchase more yen. The prices of imports from Japan to the United States decrease from the perspective of US consumers and the prices of exports from the United States to Japan increase from the perspective of Japanese consumers. If the dollar purchases fewer yen (the dollar depreciates), the opposite occurs.

Changes in net exports. An appreciation of an economy's currency in foreign exchange markets will make its exports appear more costly to foreigners and, generally, its exports will fall. Also, as just noted, an appreciation also makes imports from abroad appear less costly to domestic citizens, and, as a consequence, imports will increase. The combined effect of an appreciation, then, is that net exports will fall. If a country has balanced trade—that is, net exports are zero—then it will find itself with a trade deficit (net exports will be less than zero). If a country has a trade surplus—that is, its net exports are positive—the effect of the appreciation will be to reduce the size of the surplus.

A depreciation of an economy's currency in foreign exchange markets will have the opposite effect: net exports will increase. In this case, an economy with balanced trade will find that now has a trade surplus; one with a trade deficit will find that the deficit falls or is eliminated.

It follows that if a country's currency appreciates when it is running a trade surplus, the appreciation will tend to eliminate the surplus and if depreciation occurs when there is a trade deficit, the depreciation will tend to eliminate the deficit. For this reason, net exports can be *persistently* different from zero (e.g., negative) only if individuals in one economy choose to hold the currency or assets of another economy.

Chapter 12 ▶▶
Public Policy and Competitive Markets: Market Distortions

This chapter focuses on public policies that alter otherwise efficient market outcomes. The policies considered include **commodity taxes, market subsidies, price ceilings, price floors, restrictions on entry or exit, prohibited markets, and tariffs and quotas.** These policies may alter competitive market outcomes either because they undermine the ability of the otherwise competitive market to coordinate competing interests or because they prevent a competitive market from efficiently allocating goods, services, or resources.

It is important to keep in mind that markets may not always coordinate activities effectively or achieve efficient outcomes on their own. When they fail to do so, one or more of the public policies explored in this chapter may be useful in moving a market toward, rather than away, from a more efficient allocation of resources. We consider the possibilities of "market failure" and possible public policy responses in the remaining chapters in this book. For the purpose of discussion in this chapter, however, we assume that the market outcome in each case would be efficient *but for* the government's intervention.

This raises the question of why a government would want to distort otherwise efficient outcomes. Although sometimes distortions come about inadvertently, often the purpose of a policy is to distort the market outcome. Some specific reasons why a government might wish to distort an otherwise efficient market outcome will become evident as we consider each policy. At this point, however, we note two general reasons. First, allocative efficiency may be only one of several goals that a society chooses to pursue and, as a consequence, a society may be willing to give up something in terms of efficiency in order to achieve some other goal more effectively. For example, a society may be willing to give up some efficiency gains in pursuit of fairness. Second, it may be in the private interest of a particular group to alter an otherwise efficient market outcome because its members gain more from the distorted market outcome than they do from an efficient one. Governmental policy generally creates winners who benefit from the distortion, and losers who would be better off if the market were free to allocate resources efficiently. The public policy process, for whatever reason, favors these winners over the losers. Hence, to understand why market outcomes are sometimes purposefully distorted, you should ask yourself who wins and who loses when the government intervenes.

▶ Commodity Taxes

Taxes alter or distort market outcomes. This is particularly true when governments tax the sale of a specific commodity. There are two types of commodity taxes: taxes that are a percentage of the sales price, called **ad valorem commodity taxes**, and **specific commodity taxes** that are fixed in dollar terms. Most states impose ad valorem taxes on retail sales in the 4-to-9-percent range. When there is a 7 percent sales tax, for example, a consumer has to pay $1.07 at the check-out stand for an item marked with a price of $1.00. By contrast, the federal excise tax on cigarettes is a specific tax, currently $.16 per pack, regardless of the price of cigarettes.

A tax on a particular commodity, whether ad valorem or specific, generally changes the market price and, as a consequence, the amount bought and sold. It is often supposed that if the government imposes a tax, say of $1.00 per item, the market price will increase by $1.00, as firms simply pass the tax along to consumers. This isn't necessarily so, however. To see why, suppose that the government requires the firms producing a particular good to collect a specific sales tax of t (for example, a $ .05 tax on each unit sold). From a firm's perspective, the tax would be viewed as part of the cost of producing and selling the good. For example, if the firm had previously been willing to supply 1,000 units at an untaxed price of $.50, then with a $.05 tax, it would be willing to supply 1,000 units only for a total price of $.55. In fact, at every level of production, firms must receive a price that is $.05 higher to induce them to produce at that level. Graphically, this is equivalent to a $.05 upward vertical shift in this firm's supply schedule. Because each firm in the market is required to collect the tax, the market supply falls. This effect is illustrated by a leftward shift in the supply curve in Figure 1.

▶ Market Effects of a Commodity Tax

Because of this tax, the market price increases from p^* to a new equilibrium price of p^{**}. As the price increases, consumers have an incentive to find substitutes and consume less. As a consequence, in the case illustrated in Figure 1 the market price does not increase by the full amount of the tax. Because it doesn't, firms have an incentive to produce less— for them the net-of-tax price has fallen, not increased. That is, as illustrated in Figure 1, p^{**} is the price that consumers pay whereas p_f is the price that firms get to keep. Note that the price that firms receive (p_f) is *less* than the price that consumers pay (p^{**}). Therefore, the amount firms wish to produce *and* the

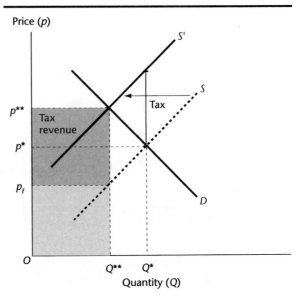

Figure 1
The Effect of a Tax on a Market

When firms must collect a tax, they supply less at each market price because some of the revenues collected must be paid to the government as the tax. This shifts the supply curve to the left (from S to S'). The market price increases from p^* to p^{**}, but firms only receive p_f for each good sold. The quantity purchased also falls from Q^* to Q^{**}. The tax is equal to $p^{**} - p_f$. Total tax revenue is shown by the darker shaded area; revenues to the firm by the lighter shaded area.

amount that individuals wish to consume falls from Q^* to Q^{**}. The difference between the price consumers pay and the net-of-tax price firms receive, $p^{**} - p_f$, is the tax per unit that the firm collects and remits to the government.

The Government's Tax Revenue. The government chooses a tax level or tax rate, t. The government's tax revenue is this tax rate multiplied by the quantity that is actually bought and sold, Q^{**}, after the tax is imposed:

$$\text{Tax revenue} = t \times Q^{**} \qquad (1)$$

where t is a specific tax, or it is

$$\text{Tax revenue} = t \times (p \times Q^{**})$$

when t is an *ad valorem* tax rate.

Since the tax pushes the market price up to p^{**}, total expenditure by all consumers is $p^{**} \times Q^{**}$, which is represented by the area of the large rectangle in Figure 1 (0p** on one side; 0Q** on the other). On the other hand, since the tax pushes down the net-of-tax price that firms receive, the total revenue for firms, *net of the taxes they remit to the government*, is $p_f \times Q^{**}$, the lighter-shaded rectangle. The darker-sided rectangle represents tax revenues paid to the government, $t \times Q^{**}$.

The response of demanders to the higher price affects the tax revenue that the government receives because substitution changes the quantity that is bought and sold *as a consequence of the tax itself*. This means that while the government gets to choose t, it doesn't get to choose its tax revenue because, as is clear in (1), Q^{**} is determined by the market and not by the government. This point is evident in Figure 2. Demand in one market is perfectly inelastic and demand in the other is perfectly elastic. In the market with perfectly inelastic demand, the amount sold does not change when the tax is imposed; in the market with elastic demand, the amount sold changes quite dramatically when the tax is imposed. Clearly, the government's tax revenue will be different even if a tax of the same amount is imposed in each market. If the before-tax equilibrium price and quantity are the same in both markets, the government's tax revenue as measured by the shaded rectangle in each case is much larger when demand is less elastic than it is when demand is more elastic. The reason for this difference is that demanders can avoid paying a sales tax by finding substitutes that are not taxed, when pos-

sible. When substitutes are readily available, demand is more elastic; when it is more difficult to find substitutes, demand is less elastic.

If the purpose of a tax is to generate revenue for the government, public policy should be directed toward taxing commodities without good substitutes. That is, the government should impose commodity taxes in markets where demand is relatively inelastic, as illustrated in part (a) of Figure 2. For this reason, taxes on salt and bread were important sources of revenue for governments in the nineteenth century and before. During that same period, the Russian government also taxed vodka. Good substitutes, in each of these cases, were difficult to find.

If, on the other hand, a government's primary purpose is to change consumption patterns rather than generate tax revenues, it can most successfully alter consumer choices when there are good, non-taxed substitutes for whatever is being taxed. A tax on margarine is likely to yield little revenue, for example, but it will increase the demand for butter because butter and margarine are good substitutes. An increase in the price of butter would, of course, increase the income for dairy farmers, a possible reason for such a tax-induced market distortion.

Inefficiency: Too Little Is Produced

When a commodity tax is imposed on an otherwise competitive market, resources are inefficiently allocated. The reason is simple. There are two prices in the market—one for consumers and one for

Figure 2
The Effect of a Tax Depends on the Elasticity of Demand

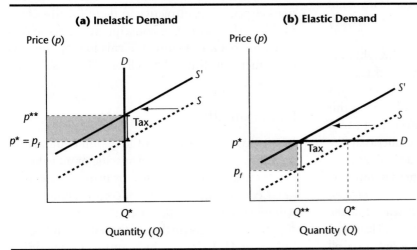

(a) Inelastic Demand

Price (p)

p^{**}

$p^* = p_f$

Tax

Q^*

Quantity (Q)

(b) Elastic Demand

Price (p)

p^*

p_f

Tax

Q^{**} Q^*

Quantity (Q)

If demand is perfectly inelastic, the quantity traded in the market does not change after a tax is imposed, and the price received by the firm after the tax, p_f, equals the before-tax market price, p^*. In contrast, when demand is perfectly elastic, the quantity traded drops dramatically (from Q^* to Q^{**}) after a tax is imposed; the market price does not change, but the price that firms receive falls by the full amount of the tax. The shaded areas are the government's tax revenue.

producers. As a consequence, the amount that individuals are willing to pay for additional output differs from the cost of producing additional output. This inefficiency can be seen in Figure 1. When Q^{**} is purchased, demanders are willing to pay p^{**} for any additional production. The marginal cost of producing the good, however, is only p_f. Hence, because of the tax, the marginal cost of additional output is less than the amount that consumers are willing to pay for this additional production (in terms of the test for efficiency suggested in Chapter 10, MWTP>MC). The inefficiency associated with a commodity tax is that *too few resources will be devoted to this market and too little will be produced and consumed.*

A measure of inefficiency: the deadweight burden.
Changes in consumer and producer surplus can be used to measure the size of this inefficiency in a particular market. In the market illustrated in Figure 3, for example, a commodity tax lowers output from Q^* to Q^{**} and increases the market price that consumers pay from p^* to p^{**}. Consumers lose because the price they pay increases (to p_c in Figure 3) and the quantity purchased decreases. Firms lose because the price, net of taxes, that they receive decreases (to p_f in Figure 3) and the quantity sold decreases as well. The *loss* in consumer surplus is A + a; the *loss* in producer surplus is B + b. These losses are partially offset because the government gains A + B in tax revenue. Unfortunately, the offset is only partial because part of the consumer surplus loss (*a*) and part of the producer surplus loss (*b*) are not transferred to the government as tax revenues. As a consequence, the tax imposes a **deadweight burden** on the economy equal to *a + b*. The deadweight burden is a quantitative measure of the inefficiency created by the tax.

In what sense is area (*a + b*) a "deadweight burden" or loss to the economy? To answer this question, suppose that the government divides its tax revenue between consumers and producers in this market such that consumers receive payments of *A* and producers, payments of *B*. Remember that A + B equals the government's tax revenue *T*. Following this redistribution of the government's tax revenue, consumers and producers would *still be worse off than they were before the tax was imposed*, while the government would be no better off. It is clear why the government is not better off—it has disbursed all

Figure 3
The Deadweight Burden of a Tax

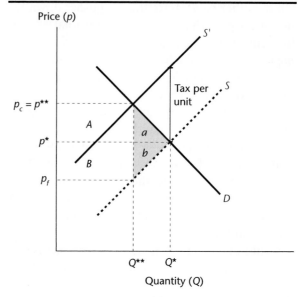

When a tax is imposed, consumers lose area A + a in consumer surplus and producers lose area B + b in producer surplus. The government gains area A + B as tax revenue, but the economy loses area a + b. This area, a + b, is the deadweight burden or efficiency loss created by the tax.

the revenue obtained from the tax. It is, perhaps, a bit puzzling why individuals and firms are worse off. After all, the full amount of the tax they paid has been returned to them. The return of the tax revenue collected from consumers and producers simply cannot fully compensate consumers and producers who paid it, however, because the tax itself *changes the market price*. This change is the reason for the deadweight burden. Consumers substitute other commodities that were, at the original market price, less attractive to them for this commodity. They lose as a consequence. This loss is equal to area *a* in Figure 3. Firms lose because, as consumers substitute, they sell less. This loss is equal to area *b*.

Long-Run Effects

In general, if a market is in long-run equilibrium prior to the imposition of a specific or ad valorem tax, the tax will create losses for firms. As a consequence, some firms will exit or contract and capital will move away from this market. As firms exit the supply curve shifts further to the left (from S' to S" in Figure 4). Exit continues until the remaining

Figure 4
The Long-Run Effect of a Tax

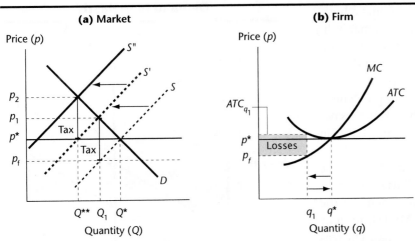

In the short run, firms incur losses after a tax is imposed because the price they receive, p_f, is below their average costs. Some firms then exit from the market, shifting the supply curve to the left (from S' to S''). In a constant-cost industry, firms continue to exit until the after-tax price that they receive is equal to the original equilibrium price, p^*. At this point, consumers bear the full burden of the tax—that is, the price they pay, p_2, equals $p^* + t$ in the long run. Note that the shift from q^* to q_1 shown in part (b), which occurs after the tax is imposed, corresponds to the shift from S to S' in part (a). Similarly, the shift from q_1 to q^* in part (b) that occurs after firms exit because of losses corresponds to the shift from S' to S'' in part (a).

firms no longer incur losses. If, for example, the industry has constant long-run costs, the firms remaining in the market will only earn normal rates of return when the net-of-tax price is at the pretax market price level (p^*). At this point, the tax has been passed fully along to the consumer, but not in the direct sense of firms simply charging a higher price when the tax is imposed. The higher price comes only as firms exit and resources move to other markets. Firms exit, of course, because they can't easily pass along the full amount of the tax. Clearly, the deadweight burden increase further as, in the long run, additional resources move from activities that are taxed to other activities. (This can be confirmed by observing that the triangle representing the deadweight burden increases in size as the amount actually bought and sold moves further away from Q^*.) Tax revenue is, of course, generated for use by the government.

Who Pays a Tax?

Because taxes alter decisions, it is not obvious who actually pays the tax. Indeed, as we will see, the division of the tax burden among individuals generally

will not be what the government intended. As a consequence, an important issue in the design of a tax system is to ascertain the true **tax incidence**—in other words, to determine who really pays a particular tax.

The government does get to determine various aspects of a tax system, including tax rates and who has to actually remit the tax revenue. However, government *does not* get to decide who will actually pay a particular tax. Instead, markets, not the government, determine who actually pays a tax.

The government often acts, of course, as if it got to decide who actually pays the tax. Indeed, those who write tax laws expend substantial effort in devising complex tax systems because they believe that by doing so they can determine who actually pays the taxes they impose. In recent tax reform efforts, for example, considerable and often heated debate focused on whether to tax corporations or individuals, with a number of politicians and commentators arguing that "business must pay its fair share." In the end, Congress lowered personal income tax rates while increasing corporate income tax rates. This was done because at least some member of Congress believed that they could shift the burden of the tax from individuals to corporations. But you ought to ask yourself: "What does it really mean to say that Congress intends to make businesses pay their fair share?" Does it mean that individuals pay less in overall taxes? Of course not. Corporations are legal entities owned by individuals and collecting more taxes from corporations and fewer taxes directly from individuals simply changes the group of individuals who pay the tax. It does not shift the tax from individuals to some other entity in the economy—such a shift isn't possible.

Understanding that the government can, in the end, only tax individuals doesn't tell us which individuals pay the tax. Can the government decide which individuals pay the tax? No. Markets limit its ability to determine *which* individuals pay. The reason for this limitation can be illustrated most easily by considering the incidence of the commodity taxes we have been studying.

Assume that the government imposes a sales tax, and collects it from firms. Each firm will view the per unit tax as an increase in its marginal costs and, as a consequence, will provide less to the market at any given price (or, equivalently, will demand a higher price for each level of output). In supply-demand terms, the market supply shifts upward as indicated in Figure 5. Even though each firm in a competitive market is a price taker, the aggregate effect of each firm's response to the tax will be to shift market supply by the full amount of the tax. That is, from the market's perspective, it is as if each firm tried to pass along the full amount of the tax to the demanders through higher prices.

Whether firms can actually pass the tax along to consumers or consumers can avoid the tax so that firms must pay it depends, in part, on how easily consumers can substitute other things for the taxed good or service. That is, the incidence of an excise tax depends, in part, on the elasticity of demand. If demand is perfectly inelastic as in Figure 5, consumers, or, more generally, demanders, will bear the full tax, even in the short run. Before the tax is imposed, consumers pay p^* for each unit purchased while firms receive p^* for each unit sold. After the tax is imposed, consumers pay p^{**}. Each firm collects p^{**} per unit sold from each consumer, but each firm then pays t, the per unit tax, to the government. The price that firms receive, net-of-taxes, is p_f (where $p_f = p^{**} - t$). When demand is perfectly inelastic, p_f will be equal to the per unit price that firms received

Figure 5
The Burden of a Tax When Demand Is Inelastic

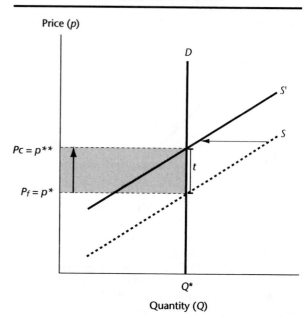

In a market where demand is perfectly inelastic, consumers will bear the full burden of a tax. Before the tax, consumers pay p^* and firms receive p^*. After the tax, consumers pay p^{**}, which is equal to $p^* + t$, but firms still receive p^*. The tax drives a wedge equal to t, the tax rate, between the price that consumers pay and the price that firms receive.

before the tax was imposed, p^*. We can conclude that when demand is perfectly inelastic, demanders, not suppliers (and hence, not those individuals who own or work for suppliers), will pay the *full* amount of the excise tax. The reason is simple: suppliers attempt to pass the tax along; as the price increases, demanders cannot find substitutes; therefore, they cannot avoid paying the tax by substituting other goods or services for the taxed one; therefore, they pay all of the tax.

If demand is perfectly elastic, by contrast, the firms that supply the market in the short run, and thus those individuals who either own or work for the firm, will pay the excise tax. This point is illustrated in Figure 6. After the tax is imposed, households pay p^*, the same price that they paid before the good was taxed. Because for each unit sold firms receive p^* but must pay t to the government, the net-of-tax price the firms actually receive is p_f, which is below p^* (the price that the firms received before the tax was imposed), by exactly t (the per unit tax).

Figure 6
The Effect of a Sales Tax
When Demand Is Elastic

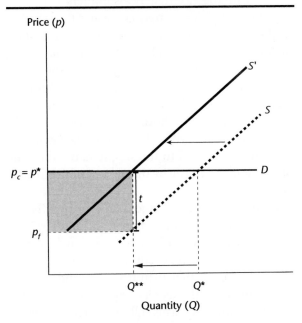

In the short run, firms will bear the full burden of a tax if demand is perfectly elastic because any increase in price will lead consumers to completely substitute other goods for the one being taxed. Once again, the tax drives a wedge equal to t, the tax rate, between the price that consumers pay and the price that firms receive. When demand is perfectly elastic, however, the price consumers are willing to pay does not increase, so the price that firms receive falls by the full amount of the tax. As a consequence, the amount provided to the market falls from Q^* to Q^{**}.

Figure 7
The Burden of a Tax When Demand
Is Not Perfectly Elastic

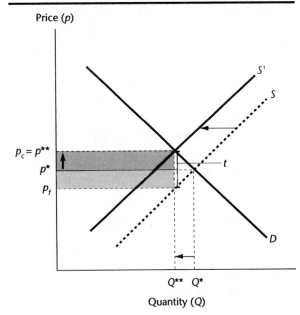

When demand is neither perfectly elastic nor perfectly inelastic, the burden of a tax will be shared by consumers and firms. The darker area is the burden paid by consumers because of the increase in market price—it increases, however, by less than the full amount of the tax, t. The lighter area is the burden paid by firms because of the decrease in price they receive—it decreases by less than the full amount of the tax, t. Once again, the tax drives a wedge equal to the tax rate t, between the price consumers pay and the price firms receive. The price consumers pay increases by a fraction of the tax rate because they substitute somewhat as the price increases. The price firms receive decreases by the remaining fraction of the tax rate because the market price consumers pay does not increase by the full amount of the tax.

In this case, demanders avoid the tax completely by substituting other goods so easily that the market price cannot be pushed up. That is, while suppliers would like to pass the tax to demanders, any attempt to increase the price in this market is met by immediate substitution by demanders. After the tax is imposed and a new market equilibrium reached, households purchase less—the quantity demanded has fallen—but because other things are perfect substitutes (the demand curve in Figure 6 is perfectly elastic), it can't really matter to them. As a consequence, suppliers pay the full tax.

In the typical market illustrated in Figure 7, suppliers and demanders *share the tax burden*. This happens because demanders substitute to some degree, but because no untaxed *perfect* substitutes are available, the market price increases somewhat with the tax. Because there are *some* substitutes available,

however, the market price does not increase by the full amount of the tax. The government *always* collects t for each unit of the good that is sold, so the difference between what demanders pay and suppliers receive is t. Because the price that consumers pay increases, but not by the full amount of the tax, the net-of-tax price that a firm receives must be below the before-tax equilibrium price, p^*. Hence, when demand is neither perfectly inelastic nor perfectly elastic, suppliers (firms) and demanders (consumers) each pay part of an excise or commodity tax.

These three examples illustrate that the tax burden on firms and consumers—the tax incidence—depends upon the elasticity of demand in the market on which the tax is imposed. The higher the elasticity of demand, the less demanders pay, *ceteris paribus*. Or, put differently, the more elastic the market demand, the more the burden of an excise or commodity tax falls on suppliers. The elasticity of demand for a particular commodity depends, of course, on demanders' abilities to substitute. In some markets, substitutes are readily available so demand is elastic at the current market equilibrium and suppliers bear more of the burden of the tax. In other markets, substitution is not as easy, demand is less elastic or even inelastic at the current market equilibrium and demanders bear more of the burden of the tax.

Effect of differing supply elasticities. The division of tax between demanders and suppliers also depends upon the elasticity of supply. This point is illustrated in Figure 8, where two markets with identical demand curves are represented. The supply curve is less elastic in part (b) than in part (a) at the initial market price, however. As a consequence, a specific excise tax of exactly the same dollar amount will increase the price by less in part (b) than it will in part (a). That is, *the more inelastic the supply, the more the burden of a tax falls on suppliers.*

In summary, the more elastic the demand curve and the less elastic the supply curve, the greater the fraction of the tax that the suppliers will bear; the more elastic the supply curve and the less elastic the demand curve, the greater the fraction of the tax that demanders will bear. When demanders are individuals or households, the incidence of at least some fraction of a tax that affects the market price is clear. When suppliers are firms, however, the incidence of the fraction borne by the firm cannot be established clearly without knowing whether the tax is shifted backward to the suppliers of labor and other inputs or borne by the owners of the firms.

Does tax incidence change if an excise tax is collected from demanders rather than suppliers? The short answer: No. (Although there may be differences in the resources required to collect the tax from suppliers rather than from demanders.) The longer answer, with detailed explanation, follows:

If a commodity tax is collected directly from the consumer, then because any point along the demand curve indicates the maximum price that consumers are willing to pay for any additional output, market demand will shift until the market price plus the tax equals the maximum amount that individuals were

Figure 8
The Burden of a Tax and the Elasticity of Supply

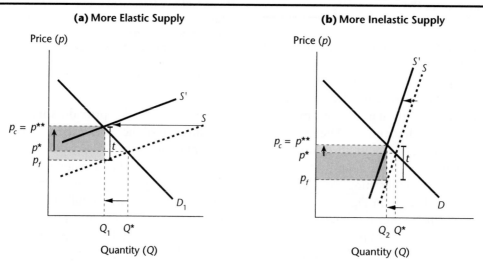

When supply is more elastic, consumers will bear more of the burden of a tax, as shown by the darker shaded area in part (a) while firms will bear relatively little, as shown by the lighter shaded area in part (a). When supply is less elastic, however, most of the tax burden will fall on firms. Compare, for example, the lighter area with the darker area in part (b).

willing to pay for additional output at each point along the initial demand curve. For example, if a consumer must pay $1.00 plus a tax of $.10, quantity demanded will be whatever it would have been if the price was $1.10 *when there was no tax.* Put simply, consumers care about the full price they must pay, not about how the price might be divided between payments to the government and payments to firms.

On the other hand, if the tax is collected from producers, then whereas the marginal cost curve indicates the net amount that the firm must receive at each level of production in order to provide output to the market, market supply will shift until the market price less the tax equals the full marginal cost along the original supply curve. That is, if the producer receives $1.10 per unit sold but must pay $.10 to the government, the net-of-tax price to the firm is $1.00 and the firm will supply the quantity that it would have been willing to provide when there was no tax and the market price was $1.00. Like consumers, firms care about the amount of money they actually receive for each good sold, not the amount that individuals happen to pay, some of which must be passed along to the government.

Because the maximum that demanders are willing to pay for additional output and minimum that firms must receive for additional output are independent of from whom the government actually collects the tax, the incidence of a commodity or excise tax is independent of who actually writes a check to the government for the tax. Figure 9 illustrates this argument graphically. An identical excise tax is collected from demanders in part (b) and from suppliers in part (a). In each part of the figure, supply and demand are the same and, hence, the before-tax equilibrium (p^*, Q^*) is the same in each panel. It should be clear that the tax incidence is the *same* in both panels. *Because the government cannot determine how the tax is divided between suppliers and demanders, it cannot change the tax incidence by shifting the collection of the tax from consumers to firms or vice versa.* Put differently, the government gets to decide from whom it will collect the tax, that is, who will have to remit tax payments to the government. It does not get to decide who actually pays the tax.

Despite this conclusion, legislative debates often center on whether a tax should be imposed on consumers or producers. As we've just learned, if markets are competitive, this debate is fruitless. First,

Figure 9
Incidence Is Independent of from Whom an Excise Tax Is Collected

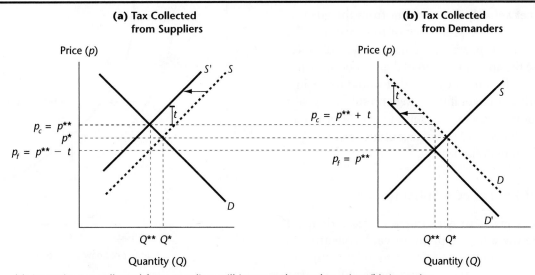

(a) An excise tax collected from suppliers will increase the market price. (b) An excise tax collected from demanders will decrease the market price. In either case, however, the price that firms actually receive will be the same, as you can see by comparing p_f in part (a) with p_f in part (b). Likewise, in either case, the price that demanders actually pay will be the same, as can be seen by comparing p_c in part (a) with p_c in part (b). The difference between p_f and p_c is the per unit tax.

the government cannot impose a tax on consumers alone or on producers alone. Rather, it imposes a tax on a market transaction. The market then determines the incidence of the tax. Second, the government cannot change the market-created tax incidence by determining from whom it will collect the tax because the incidence of tax is independent of whether consumers collect and remit the tax or producers collect and remit the tax.

A caution. This analysis has considered the effects of taxes in a *single* market (something economists call *partial equilibrium analysis*). Because individuals respond to tax-induced changes in market prices by substituting across markets, and because firms respond to tax-induced changes in prices by adjusting their demand for inputs, taxes imposed on a single market almost always affect many different markets. Chapter 10 discussed an example of how a change in one market cascades through a number of other markets. Because markets are linked together, the overall effects of a tax may extend far beyond those determined by focusing on a single market alone. (A consideration of the overall effects, which is generally difficult to do, is part of what economists call *general equilibrium analysis*.)

▶ Market Subsidies

A **market subsidy** is a payment from the government to firms for producing or to consumers for purchasing a particular commodity. Subsidies increase the amount of a good that is produced and consumed beyond the levels that would occur in a competitive market if there were no subsidy. Like a commodity tax, a market subsidy may be either ad valorem (based on a percentage of the price) or specific (fixed in dollar terms).

Market Effects of a Subsidy

Subsidies given to consumers increase demand because the effective price for each consumer is lower with the subsidy. In terms of the supply-demand picture, the demand curve shifts to the right. Subsidies given to suppliers increase supply because the return to a firm from producing the subsidized commodity increases. This effect can be illustrated by a rightward shift of a supply curve. Examples of each type of subsidy follow.

Subsidizing consumers directly. Food stamps are a subsidy provided directly to consumers. In the food-stamp program, a needy person buys a stamp for less than a dollar, and then uses it like money to purchase one dollar's worth of food. To make the example more specific, suppose that needy people can purchase food stamps with purchasing power of $1.00 for $.50 per stamp. This means that everything in the local market that is priced $1.00 has an *effective* price of $.50 for those with food stamps. For the owner of the store, however, each $1.00 food stamp is redeemed by the government for $1.00. Suppose, to keep the example simple, that food stamps are available to all consumers in a particular market. If without food stamps, 100 loaves of bread were demanded at a price of $1.00 per loaf, or, 150 loaves were demanded at a price of $.50 per loaf, then, with food stamps, 150 loaves would be demanded. That is, demand increases because of the subsidy, as illustrated in Figure 10.

The market effect of this increase in demand is evident in Figure 11—the market price increases from p^* to p^{**} and the quantity bought and sold

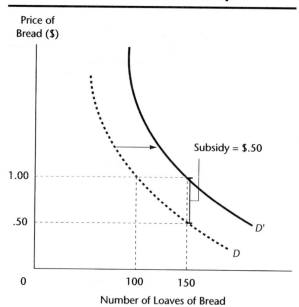

**Figure 10
The Effect of Food Stamps**

Without food stamps, consumers demand 100 loaves of bread at a price of $1.00 and 150 loaves at a price of $.50. If food stamps worth $.50 are given to everyone, the demand for bread increases from D to D' and consumers then demand 150 loaves of bread at a market price of $1.00.

Figure 11
The Effect of a Consumption Subsidy

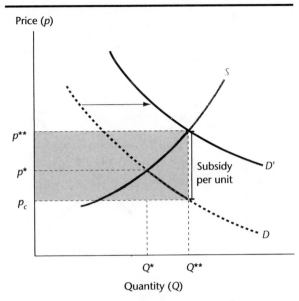

A subsidy provided to consumers increases demand (from D to D') and increases both the quantity sold (from Q^* to Q^{**}) and the market price (from p^* to p^{**}), which is also the price that firms receive. The price that consumers actually pay, p_c, however, is below the equilibrium price because of the subsidy. The shaded area indicates the total subsidy paid by the government.

Figure 12
A Subsidy for Oil Production

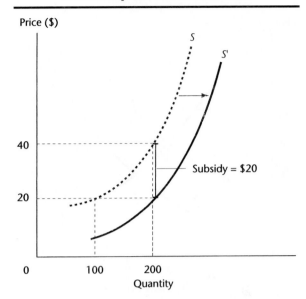

Without a subsidy, producers supply 100 barrels of oil to the market at a price of $20 per barrel and 200 barrels at a price of $40 per barrel. If producers are given a subsidy of $20 for each barrel of oil produced, the supply of oil increases from S to S'. In this case, producers would supply 200 barrels of oil at a market price of only $20.

also increases from Q^* to Q^{**}. That is, a subsidy given to consumers changes *both* production and consumption decisions. The government pays the difference between the price that consumers actually pay, p_c, and the price that firms receive, p^{**}.

Subsidizing producers directly. If production rather than consumption is subsidized, firms will increase their output at every market price. Suppose, for example, that each firm producing oil from oil shale was willing to produce 100 barrels per day if the price of oil was $20 and 200 barrels per day if the price of oil was $40. If, when the price of oil is $20, the government offers a subsidy of $20 for each barrel produced, the firms producing shale oil will increase their output to 200 barrels, as illustrated in Figure 12.

A subsidy provided directly to producers decreases the market price. For example, in Figure 13, the market price falls from p^* to p^{**} with a subsidy, while the quantity bought and sold increases from Q^* to Q^{**}. Hence, a subsidy changes both production and consumption decisions. The subsidy provided by the government is the difference between

the market price, p^{**}, and the amount that firms receive from producing the commodity, p_f.

Notice that when the subsidy is provided directly to consumers, market prices increase, but when the subsidy is provided directly to firms, market prices decrease. The firm doesn't care who receives the subsidy because the effective price it receives *after* the subsidy *increases* by the same amount *in either case*. Similarly, the consumers don't care because the effective price they pay *after* the subsidy *decreases* by the same amount *in either case*.

Inefficiency: Too Much Is Produced

A subsidy drives a wedge between the price that firms actually receive and the price that households actually pay. Any time there are two prices in a market, an inefficiency is likely. In this particular case, the marginal cost of producing additional output at the new equilibrium is *greater* than the amount that consumers would have been willing to pay for any additional output in the absence of a subsidy (MC> MWTP). Therefore, society uses *more* than a dollar's

Figure 13
The Effect of a Production Subsidy

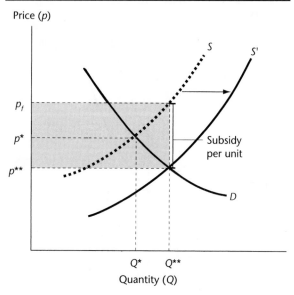

A subsidy provided to firms increases supply (from S to S'), increasing the quantity sold (from Q^* to Q^{**}) but decreasing the market price (from p^* to p^{**}). The price that firms receive, however, exceeds the market price (p_f). The shaded area represents the total subsidy paid by the government.

Figure 14
The Deadweight Burden of a Subsidy

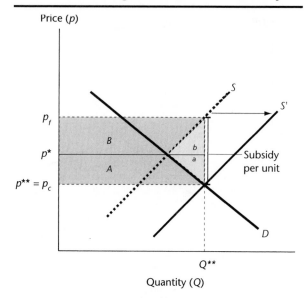

When the government provides a subsidy, consumers gain area A in consumer surplus and firms gain area B in producer surplus. But the subsidy costs the government $A + a + B + b$ (subsidy per unit, $s \times Q^{**}$). The total subsidy is greater than the sum of the gains in consumer and producer surplus by $a + b$. Therefore, a subsidy imposes a deadweight loss or efficiency burden on the economy equal to $a + b$.

worth of resources to get an additional dollar's worth of satisfaction. *A subsidized market outcome is inefficient because too much is produced and consumed.*

The size of inefficiency can be estimated by considering the deadweight burden the subsidy imposes on the economy. In Figure 14, a subsidy of s provided to firms lowers the market price consumers pay from p^* to p_c. As a consequence of the lower price, the quantity demanded increases and, as a further consequence, consumer surplus increases by A. Firms receive p_f, and because they sell additional output at a higher price, producer surplus increases by B. Thus, *both* consumers and producers gain. The government has to provide a subsidy of $s \times Q^{**}$, however, which is equal to the area $(A + a) + (B + b)$. In order to gain the necessary revenue to provide the subsidy, the government must levy taxes elsewhere in the economy. The amount of the subsidy, and therefore the tax, is *greater* than the sum of the increase in consumer and producer surplus $(A + B)$ by the amount $(a + b)$. It follows that the subsidy imposes a deadweight loss on society equal to $(a + b)$.

Long-Run Effects

Unless short-run supply is perfectly elastic, subsidies provided to consumers initially increase market prices. Higher prices, with no other changes in the market, lead to greater profits, and greater profits induce entry. Entry increases the supply. This effect is represented by a shift from S to S' in Figure 15. With entry, the economic profits that the original firms received because of the subsidy-induced price increase are competed away. Entry further distorts the economy—the subsidy encourages the reallocation of capital toward this market and away from other activities. Remember that, from an efficiency perspective, the additional goods produced are worth *less* to consumers than the cost of producing them. Entry makes this inefficiency get worse over time.

Figure 15
The Long-Run Effect of a Consumption Subsidy

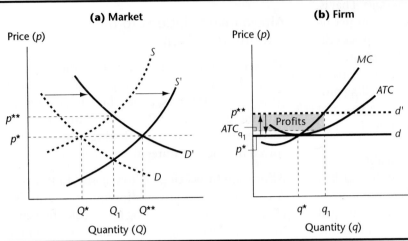

(a) Market

(b) Firm

In the short run, a subsidy that increases demand from D to D' [part (a)] creates positive economic profits for firms [part (b)] as the price that they receive increases from p^* to p^{**}. In the long run, more firms will enter the market until profits again equal zero, thus increasing supply from S to S'. This increases the economic inefficiency of the subsidy by moving more resources into the subsidized market.

▶ Price Ceilings

Governments sometimes pass laws directing that the market price of a commodity can be no *higher* than some specified level $\tilde{p}$. This quantity $\tilde{p}$ is referred to as the **price ceiling** or **maximum legal price**. If the law is enforced and if $\tilde{p}$ is below the market equilibrium price, the price ceiling creates excess demand. Figure 16 illustrates this outcome. Without the price ceiling, the equilibrium price would be p^*. Because the market equilibrium price p^* is greater than the ceiling price $\tilde{p}$, however, it is *illegal* to trade at what would have been the equilibrium price.

Examples of price ceilings include: rent controls on apartments, where the equilibrium rent might be $800 per month and the government regulates rents so that no landlord can charge more than $400 per month; price controls on gasoline, where the equilibrium price might be $1.00 per gallon and the government mandates that the price charged cannot exceed $.40 per gallon; price controls on oil, where the p^* might be $20 per barrel and $\tilde{p}$ is $10 per barrel; ceilings on deposit interest rates, where the equilibrium interest rate might be 8 percent, but banks are prohibited from paying more than 5 percent; controls on exchange rates, where the equilibrium exchange rate might be 10 pesos per dollar, but the government sets the exchange rate at 4 pesos per dollar.

Market Effects of a Price Ceiling

What happens if a government establishes a price ceiling? Consider the market pictured in Figure 16. At $\tilde{p}$, consumers want to purchase Q_1. When the price is $\tilde{p}$, however, firms are only willing to supply

Figure 16
The Effect of a Price Ceiling

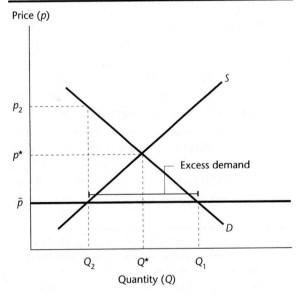

When a price ceiling, $\tilde{p}$, is set below the market price, p^*, there is a shortage. At $\tilde{p}$, consumers demand Q_1, but firms are only willing to supply Q_2. The difference, $Q_1 - Q_2$, is the amount of excess demand created by the price ceiling.

Q_2. This means that $(Q_1 - Q_2)$ consumers are not able to purchase what they wish at the announced price, $\tilde{p}$.[1] *The price ceiling creates a shortage.* That is, the market no longer coordinates the competing interests of demanders and suppliers. The price ceiling invites individuals to substitute this commodity for other commodities because the price is relatively low. At the same time, however, the price ceiling provides an incentive for firms to produce less, not more, because the price firms receive is also relatively low.

Some of the consumers who are unable to purchase the commodity at $\tilde{p}$ are new to the market. Indeed, when the law is passed and enforced, $(Q_1 - Q^*)$ new consumers enter the market, encouraged by the apparently lower relative price to substitute this commodity for others. This means that the problems associated with price ceilings *do not* turn on the production disincentives alone. Indeed, even if production did not change, dictating a legal price that is below the equilibrium price creates excess demand, that is, a shortage occurs when there is a price ceiling even when market supply is perfectly inelastic. (You should draw the relevant diagram to demonstrate to yourself that this is so.) This means, for example, that even though the quantity of housing does not change when rent controls are imposed, rent controls still create a shortage of housing.

The rationing problem. Scarcity implies that commodities must be rationed. Prices ration commodities on the basis of willingness to pay: those who are willing to pay more get the commodity; those who are only willing to pay less do not. When a price ceiling is imposed, prices no longer serve this socially useful function. That is, the market price no longer rations the amount provided to the market (Q_2, in Figure 16) among the competing consumers (Q_1, in Figure 16). Therefore, an *alternative* rationing device that does not depend upon the price must be

devised. Price ceilings create—they do not solve—coordination problems.

Alternative Solutions to the Rationing Problem

There is simply no way around the rationing problem. When a government imposes and enforces a price ceiling, it forces, either directly or indirectly, the emergence of a different kind of allocational mechanism to solve the rationing problem that is solved by prices in unregulated markets.

Allocation by waiting or "first come, first served." A common alternative rationing procedure is to allocate the goods according to the rule "first come, first served." By using this procedure, Q_2, the amount that firms are willing to produce at $\tilde{p}$, will be sold at price $\tilde{p}$ to the *first Q_2* people who show up. Because there is excess demand, however, some people who would like to purchase the commodity at $\tilde{p}$ will be unable to do so. As a consequence, rationing by the rule of first come, first served *always* creates queues or lines. Those willing to wait the longest—that is, those who can most easily adjust their schedules to show up at suppliers earlier—will be at the front of the line. Those who are unwilling or unable to wait in line will be unable to purchase the commodity at the ceiling price. This rationing procedure substitutes *time* for *money* as a pricing mechanism.

Clearly, when consumers are forced to wait in lines in order to purchase a commodity, the ceiling price is not really the price that they pay. Instead, the full price is the ceiling price ($\tilde{p}$) *plus* the opportunity cost of using their time waiting instead of doing other things. If a person pays $1.00 for a ticket but waits in line for one hour, for example, the full price is $1.00 *plus* the opportunity cost of the one-hour wait. Unfortunately, even though consumers pay a *full price* that is greater than the ceiling price, producers receive only the ceiling price. Thus, the higher *full price* does not provide incentives to increase production. As a consequence, shortages persist.

Consumers who are willing to pay the most *dollars* for a commodity are not always the ones who are willing to pay the most *time*. That is, some individuals find that their time is worth less than the difference between the amount of money that they would have had to pay at the market equilibrium and the amount of money that they pay at the price ceiling. Others, of course, have a higher opportu-

---

[1] Note that we are supposing that each consumer purchases one unit of a commodity, so that along a demand curve the quantity demanded is also an indication of how many consumers want the commodity at a particular price. The usual case, where consumers purchase varying amounts of a commodity depending upon the relative price, is more cumbersome to describe but does not differ in any important way from the following analysis. Equating a change in the quantity purchased or sold with a change in the number of consumers is merely expositionally convenient.

nity cost of time. Hence, it is likely that Q_2 will be allocated by waiting to a different group of individuals than it would be if price were allowed to ration it. Essentially, the rule of first come, first served rations goods and services to those with a low value of time who are, as a consequence, willing and able to wait in a line in order to purchase the commodity at a money price of $\tilde{p}$.

If the government imposes and rigorously enforces a price ceiling but does not become directly involved in determining how the resulting production should be allocated, rationing-by-waiting virtually always emerges as the rationing mechanism. It is in a sense, the default option. For example, the U.S. government imposed price ceilings on gasoline in response to the 1973 oil embargo, but did not impose an alternative rationing procedure. As a consequence, people had to wait in long lines to purchase gasoline.

Allocation by lottery. The government could allocate the Q_2 goods among the Q_1 consumers using a lottery, thereby randomly allocating the commodity among those who desire to purchase it at the ceiling price. Using this scheme, commodities are allocated to those who are willing to pay at least p and who are lucky. It is, of course, highly unlikely that a lottery will allocate Q_2 to those who would be willing to pay p_2, or even p^*, in either money or time. Consequently, random allocations differ from time or price allocations.

Allocations by coupon. The government could also use coupons to ration. For example, suppose the government imposed a price ceiling on bread and only 400 loaves are produced but 200 individuals each want five loaves of bread at the ceiling price. The government could give each individual a coupon that could be used to purchase two loaves of bread. This rationing procedure allocates commodities equally among all the individuals who are willing to pay $\tilde{p}$.[2]

During World War II, the U.S. government imposed price ceilings using a coupon-rationing scheme. Sugar, gasoline, and a number of other commodities could not be purchased without a coupon, even at the ceiling price. The government decided how many pounds of sugar, gallons of gasoline, and so forth could be used for private consumption and made that many coupons for each commodity. These coupons were then allocated without regard to willingness to pay for the restricted supplies.

Allocation by fiat or bureaucratic process. Sometimes the law imposing the price ceiling either determines the specific allocation or gives the power to allocate to a particular person or governmental agency. In this case, administrative direction and political forces rather than market forces determine who gets what. Frequently, those who mandate direct allocation intend that the price-controlled commodity be allocated to those who "need" it. Who decides what constitutes need? On what basis? Personalizing the allocation in this way frequently allows friendship, favors, or even bribes to determine the allocation. The excess demand that accompanies price ceilings places those who make the decisions in a position of substantial economic and political power. They are put in a position to extract favors from those who want the commodity. Whom you know or who knows you replaces willingness to pay or waiting time or luck as a method for allocating the commodity. It shouldn't be surprising that corruption of one sort or another often accompanies price ceilings when direct allocation is used.

Countries wishing to control the behavior of their citizens can use price ceilings deliberately to *create* shortages.[3] The state can then allocate goods on the basis of "appropriate" behavior. For example, the excess demand for apartments in Moscow because of rent controls and governmental allocation meant that Soviet authorities could—and did—demand certain kinds of behavior from those who wanted apartments in the city. Dissidents had a difficult time finding housing and therefore, in this sense, dissident behavior was policed by excess demand.

---

[2] This scheme will only work if the commodity affected by the price ceiling is divisible. That is, if there are 200 people who would each like to buy a car when only 100 are produced, it is not very practical to give each a coupon for half a car. The government could still allocate the cars with coupons if it printed 100 coupons and distributed these to 100 consumers, but then the government would have to decide how to allocate the coupons. This decisions, however, is no different from the original problem of deciding how to allocate the cars.

[3] This argument was first advanced by Evsey Domar of MIT.

Allocation based on historical use. If market supply is quite inelastic, a commodity can be rationed by *initially* allocating it to those who were purchasing it prior to the imposition of the price ceiling.[4] When the short-run supply is perfectly inelastic, for example, the commodity may be rationed to the *original* Q^* purchasers. This rationing device is common when rent controls are imposed in a city. Current renters are generally allowed to continue to occupy their apartments when the rent ceiling is imposed and pay the new, reduced controlled rents. As a consequence, of course, newcomers are excluded from the rental housing market. Or, for example, at one time the FCC priced broadcast licenses well below what individuals or firms were willing to pay for the right to broadcast and then allocated licenses without considering willingness to pay. Hence, individuals initially seeking a license had to "be nice" to the FCC. Once allocated, however, license renewals were usually routine and licenses were, as a consequence, allocated to those already occupying the licensing positions.

Reallocation

Because none of the alternatives just described allocate on the basis of willingness to pay, **reallocation** is common. Scalping tickets is an example. As a consequence of scalping, tickets move from lowered-valued users to higher-valued users even after the firm has sold all of its tickets. People who really want to see a football game or a rock concert can almost always find someone willing to resell tickets they purchased earlier. Tickets to the Super Bowl that initially cost $50 might sell for $500 or more. (Note that scalping does not necessarily result from government-imposed price ceilings but sometimes from ticket prices that were originally set too low.)

The reason that reallocation occurs can be easily seen in Figure 16. Note that Q_2, the amount produced, is worth p_2 to demanders.[5] In fact, if only Q_2 was delivered to the market and there was no price

ceiling, the market price would *increase* to p_2. Note also that each of the alternative rationing procedures *replaces willingness to pay with some other criteria for making allocations.* Taken together, these two observations imply that price ceilings will frequently be accompanied by resale or black markets.

To see this point, suppose that resale was legal and that Q_2 in Figure 16 had been randomly allocated among demanders. Because random allocation is unlikely to coincide with willingness to pay, some individuals who would have been willing to pay p_2 do not get any of the commodity. On the other hand, some individuals who do get some of the commodity would have been willing to pay no more than $\tilde{p}$. Because $\tilde{p}$ is well below p_2, if these individuals can find each other, a beneficial trade can occur. Those willing to pay more are demanders in the resale market; those who would not have been willing to pay the equilibrium price (p_2) but who "won" in the alternative allocational scheme are suppliers. As a consequence, unless transaction costs are high, a commodity whose price is controlled by the government eventually goes to the Q_2 people willing to pay at least p_2 for it. Clearly, after this reallocation takes place, the actual allocation of commodities is exactly what would have been produced by the market if Q_2 had been produced and sold without a ceiling on the market price! Thus, if the government doesn't prohibit resale, the allocation of the commodity across the economy will be unaffected by the price ceiling except, importantly, that less will be available.

Black markets. If the government prohibits resale when it imposes the price ceiling, a **black market** often emerges. In a black market, resale occurs anyway, but illegally, in settings that make detection difficult. For example, many countries impose ceilings on the price at which people within the country can exchange foreign currency for domestic currency. (For instance, the official exchange rate might be four pesos for one dollar when the market rate would be eight pesos per dollar.) In the black market, transactions for currencies occur on the street rather than in banks or other financial institutions. These transactions are much more difficult for a government to monitor and police than are transactions in banks. Not surprisingly, the black-market exchange rate is often very different from the officially imposed ceiling. (The black-market price might be twelve pesos for one dollar.)

---

[4] Supply must be quite inelastic for those who have been purchasing the commodity to continue to do so. Otherwise, allocation by historical use won't work.

[5] If the price increases to p_2, there is no rationing problem; p_2 rations the amount actually produced among the competing consumers. But p_2 is an illegal price and allocation by willingness to pay is precisely the approach that a price ceiling is supposed to avoid.

The problem with resale. The problem with resale when there is a price ceiling, whether the resale is legal or illegal, is that the revenue goes to those who *initially* purchased the commodity and not to those who actually produce and distribute it. As a consequence, resale prices ration the commodity based on willingness to pay in the resale market, but they do not provide production incentives. Unless consumers purchase directly from producers or from intermediaries who purchase directly from producers, higher prices in the resale market have no effect on production decisions.

Innovations Around Price Ceilings

Because producers who sell at the ceiling or maximum legal price do not benefit from the higher prices that their consumers are able to obtain in legal or illegal resale markets, there is an incentive to look for innovative or creative ways to skirt the price ceiling legally.

Tied sales. One way for a firm to get around a price ceiling is to tie the sale of the price-controlled commodity to another commodity whose price is *not* regulated and then raise the price of the second commodity to compensate for the below-market controlled price. Suppose that a price ceiling of $1.00 is imposed on commodity A, for example, but some consumers would be willing to pay $2.00 for the resulting production of A ($1.00 corresponds to $\tilde{p}$ in Figure 16 and $2.00 corresponds to p_2). Commodity B whose price is not controlled, also produced by the firms that produce A, ordinarily sells for $1.50. Thus a firm can sell A for $1.00, the ceiling price, and B for $1.50. However, a clever firm might sell A for $1.00 only if a buyer also purchases B for $2.50. That is, to purchase A, you must purchase B. The price for the package of A and B is $3.50, equivalent to $1.50 for B and $2.00 for A, even though A is invoiced at the legal maximum of $1.00.

During the gasoline shortage that accompanied price controls in the early 1970s, gasoline was often allocated to those who were regular customers of a service station or who were willing to purchase tires, batteries, or services such as a lube job or an oil change. Each of these linkages could be part of a tied sale. Sometimes when there is rent control, landlords will only rent furnished apartments. Prospective renters can then rent the apartment at the ceiling price only if they are willing to rent the furnishings. Since the rent on furnishings isn't regulated, landlords can recover the lost rent on apartments in higher rents for furnishings. In a more troubling example, the legal purchase price for adoptive babies is zero, but you generally cannot adopt without purchasing the assistance of lawyers, adoption agencies, and perhaps paying for the medical services associated with the delivery of the baby. In this case there is still a positive price for adoptive children, whether we like it or not, but intermediaries, not the biological parents, receive most of the revenue. In this case, adoption is tied to the purchase of "adoption services."

Producing close substitutes. Another way to get around a price ceiling is to shift production to a close substitute whose price is not controlled. For example, for a short time during World War II, the prices of new cars were regulated but the prices of used cars were not. Used car prices were above the ceiling price imposed on new car prices, providing an incentive to "produce" used cars from new cars. Sellers might drive their new cars around the block, perhaps scratch the paint in a place or two, and put the newly made used cars for sale in the used car lot. Similarly, a price ceiling on apartment rents creates an incentive to produce condominiums, a close substitute for an apartment, by selling apartments rather than renting them

Lowering quality. If the quality of the price-regulated commodity can be changed reasonably easily, firms can also get around the price ceiling by lowering the quality of what they produce, thereby lowering their production costs. Thus, a price ceiling on ice cream is likely to quickly result in ice cream that uses less cream and more inexpensive ingredients that substitute for cream. Rent controls slowly but surely lead to apartments of lower quality because landlords no longer have the same incentive to maintain their property. In addition, renters often have to provide their own maintenance such as painting or replacement of light bulbs or assume such services as garbage disposal and cleaning that may have been provided by the landlord before the rent ceiling was imposed. During the price controls on gasoline in the early 1970s, the first thing to disappear was someone who washed your car windows, checked tire pressures and insured that the radiator had enough water while gasoline was being pumped into your car.

Making in-kind payments. Demanders can also circumvent price ceilings by offering to pay amounts beyond the ceiling price, not in cash, but in-kind. Curiously, these in-kind payments are often not illegal, even when paying a higher cash price is. For example, when ceilings are set on interest rates that banks can pay in their efforts to attract deposits, they often respond by making payments of the maximum interest rate and then offering gifts to depositors. ("A one year deposit of $1,000 pays 5 percent interest *plus* a new camera.")

In Sum. Clearly, as each of these examples illustrates, *it is not enough to simply declare a maximum legal price. If the government does so, it must be willing to enforce the price ceiling and be ready to respond to the adjustments and innovations that occur in the market as a consequence of the ceiling price.*

Long-Run Effects

In the long run, the rationing problems get worse, not better. For example, if the market is in long-run equilibrium before the price ceiling is imposed, the price ceiling results in losses for firms, denoted by the shaded area in Figure 17. Firms respond to losses by exit. This shifts the supply from S to S'. The number of consumers desiring to purchase the com-

modity at p does not decrease because the apparent price has not changed. Therefore, as the output provided to the market falls from Q_2 to Q_3, the rationing problem becomes increasingly difficult. Clearly, in the long run, a price ceiling creates *larger and larger* shortages and *increases* rather than decreases the full price in terms of waiting time, resale price, transaction costs, and so on. In Chapter 10 we found that profits move resources to markets where demand is high. Price ceilings completely undermine this important function. Indeed, when there are price ceilings, the lack of profits moves resources *away* from markets where demand is high.

Inefficiency: Too Little Is Produced

Price ceilings create inefficiencies. The explanation is simple: The full price that consumers pay is greater than the price that firms actually receive. Different prices for consumers and producers in the same market, remember, usually mean that there is inefficiency. Or, more precisely, because the opportunity cost to an economy of using resources to produce additional output is lower than the amount that consumers would be willing to pay for the increased output, resources are not allocated to highest-valued uses (MC < MWTP). As a consequence, from an efficiency perspective, *too little is produced.* This argument is illustrated in Figure 16. Consumers would be willing to pay p_2 for additional production beyond Q_2. The marginal cost of producing additional output is only $\tilde{p}$, however.

Figure 17
The Long-Run Effect of a Price Ceiling

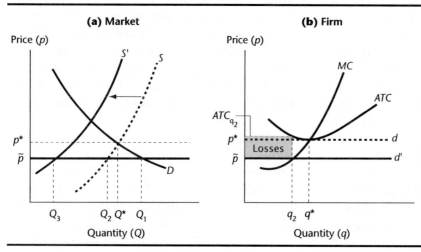

In the short run, a price ceiling leads to excess demand of Q_1 – Q_2, as firms cut production from q^* to q_2 in response to the lower price. As a result, the market supply falls to Q_2. At the ceiling price, firms make economic losses. Some firms exit the market, shifting the supply curve to the left (from S to S'). In the long run, excess demand equals Q_1 – Q_3.

In addition, innovations by firms (such as tied sales, the production of substitutes, and quality changes) and reallocations by consumers through resale or black-market transactions *increase* transaction costs. Increased transaction costs impose real—and frequently substantial—losses on society. When prices are allowed to move freely in response to demand and supply, they minimize the costs of rationing and conveying the information necessary to encourage appropriate future production. The extensive bureaucracies or the long lines that spring into existence with price ceilings are clear evidence of the rationing or allocational costs that are actually saved.

"Efficiency be damned," you respond. "Price controls are designed to help the poor." The poor might be willing to purchase a commodity at the market price but cannot because of income constraints. If they can manage to obtain the commodity through some alternative rationing mechanism, they indeed benefit. However, none of the rationing schemes associated with price ceilings *necessarily* allocates a commodity to the poor:

- Are the poor more likely to get commodities by standing in line? The poor would have an advantage only if they have lower opportunity cost of time than the rich. However, many of the rich have more flexibility in the use of their time than the poor do. Those with flexibility can usually arrange to be the first to come, and hence first to be served. The wealthy can also afford to pay others to stand in line for them.

- Are the poor more likely to get commodities by a random allocation? Poor people will benefit from random allocation only if they are luckier than rich people.

- Are the poor more likely to get coupons than the rich? Perhaps.

- Are the poor more likely to have friends in important places who can allocate by fiat? Unlikely.

- Are the poor more likely to have an historical claim than the rich? Not always.

The point is, of course, that alternative rationing mechanisms are often no more likely to allocate scarce goods and services to the poor than prices and, in many cases, are less likely to do so. More-

over, price ceilings allow those who make the decisions regarding the rationed commodity to indulge their preferences. Markets really don't care about the skin color or socioeconomic class of potential renters; landlords with increased power to *arbitrarily* allocate because of rent control may.

Deadweight burden. Firms always lose when there are price ceilings unless they can easily innovate around the price through tied sales or quality changes. This loss can be measured by the change in producer surplus, equal to area $(B + b)$, in Figure 18. The effect on consumers depends on the method used to allocate the amount produced (Q_2) among the competing demands (Q_1). For example, if those willing to pay at least p_c can purchase the commodity at the ceiling price, they gain consumer surplus equal to B. Because less is produced, however, other consumers who would have been willing to pay at least p^* do without. The loss in consumer surplus for these consumers is equal to a. In this case, the deadweight burden is at least $(a + b)$. In the best of circumstances, the gain to some consumers may be larger than the loss to other consumers (that is, $B > a$). If demand is inelastic, however, there is always a net loss in consumer surplus. In addition, because it is highly unlikely that those willing to pay p_c actually get the commodities when an alternative rationing mechanism is adopted, the deadweight burden of $(a + b)$ is almost certainly a lower bound on the actual efficiency loss.

► Price Floors

Governments sometimes pass laws directing that the market price of a commodity can be no *lower* than some specified level, say $\hat{p}$, or more directly, prohibiting the sale of a commodity at a price *below* $\hat{p}$. This quantity $\hat{p}$ is referred to as the **price floor** or **minimum legal price**. If the law is enforced and if $\hat{p}$ is above the equilibrium price, there will be excess supply. This effect is illustrated in Figure 19. Because the market equilibrium price p^* is less than the price floor $\hat{p}$, it is illegal to trade at what would have been the equilibrium price.

Examples of price floors include minimum wage laws (where the equilibrium wage might be $4.00 per hour, but the law dictates that employers must pay at least $5.25 per hour) and agricultural price supports (where the equilibrium price of milk

Figure 18
The Deadweight Loss of a Price Ceiling

**(a) Deadweight Burden
of a Price Ceiling**

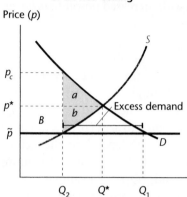

(b) In Aggregate, Consumers Lose

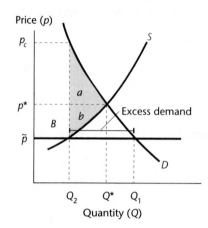

When there is a price ceiling, firms lose $B + b$ in producer surplus because of the lower price. If Q_2 is allocated to those willing to pay p_c but who only have to pay $\tilde{p}$, they gain B. Those consumers who would have been willing to pay at least p^* but cannot purchase anything lose a. The deadweight burden is the difference, $(B - a) - (B + b)$ $= -(a + b)$. Although it appears that consumers benefit, as part (b) indicates, this isn't necessarily so—if demand is inelastic at what would be the price ceiling, a is greater than B, so consumers, in aggregate, lose. Note that the measure of deadweight loss is the lower bound on the loss—it does not include the increased transaction costs that occur because of waiting in line, or of transacting in resale or black markets.

might be \$.80 per gallon, but the government makes it illegal to sell milk for less than \$1.40 per gallon, or where the equilibrium price of wheat might be \$3.00 per bushel, but the minimum legal price is \$4.00 per bushel).

Market Effects of a Price Floor

Imposing a legal minimum price does two things. First, the apparently higher relative price encourages firms to produce more. This change is illustrated by the movement along the supply curve from Q^* to Q_2 in Figure 19. Second, the higher price encourages buyers to buy less, substituting other commodities for this commodity. This change is illustrated by a movement along the demand curve from Q^* to Q_1. The result of these separate decisions is that a price floor creates a surplus or excess supply. The surplus is equal to $Q_2 - Q_1$.

Note that when a minimum price is legally imposed, the resulting production, Q_2 in Figure 19, is worth only p_2 to consumers. That is, if firms produced what they would like to produce at $\hat{p}$ but were forced to sell it at a price that cleared the market,

the market price would fall to p_2, which is the amount that demanders are willing to pay for additional output when they are able to buy Q_2 units. Without a price floor, of course, production would decrease and the price would increase to p^*. Both p^* and p_2 are illegal prices, however, and, moreover, firms cannot profitably produce Q_2 and sell it for p_2.

Surpluses and the Disposal Problem

There is no rationing problem when a price floor is imposed. The new price allocates part of the production among those individuals who want to purchase the good or service at the regulated price. Instead, too much is produced and firms end up with unsold inventory which they want to dump into the market. If they were allowed to do so, the price would fall below the minimum legal price—in Figure 19, if the additional production were dumped into the market, the market price would fall to p_2. This means that *effective* enforcement of the price floor requires the government to devise methods for disposing of the surplus in such a way that the market price does not fall.

Figure 19
The Effect of a Price Floor

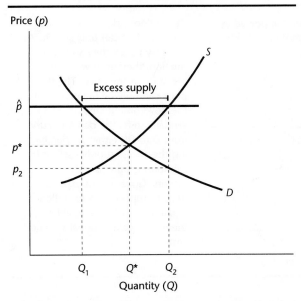

When the government sets a price floor, $\hat{p}$, higher than the market equilibrium price, the result is excess supply. Because the price is higher, firms are willing to supply Q_2 instead of Q^* to the market, but consumers are only willing to purchase Q_1. There is therefore an excess supply equal to $Q_2 - Q_1$.

This *disposal problem* arises not only because the quantity demanded decreases when the price floor is imposed, but also because production increases. Hence, even if the quantity demanded did not decrease because of the higher price, the market will still have excess supply. (You should draw a diagram and demonstrate this point to yourself.) What can the government do to solve its disposal problem?

Allow the surplus to be wasted. One method of dealing with the excess supply is to rigorously enforce the minimum price law and allow the resulting surplus to be wasted. For example, workers who cannot find jobs at the minimum wage are simply unemployed and their productive labor is wasted. Those who can find jobs at the minimum wage gain from the price floor; those who cannot find jobs lose. More generally, suppliers—either workers or firms—who *are able to sell* their output at the minimum price, benefit by the price floor. At the same time, the output of those who *cannot sell* at the minimum price is simply wasted, and as a result, these suppliers lose. Even though this may seem an odd

way of dealing with surplus, it is precisely the option that the government has selected in the labor market. Figure 20 illustrates this outcome.

Government purchase of the surplus. A second method for dealing with the disposal problem is for the government to purchase the excess supply. When it does, demand increases, as illustrated by a movement from D to D' in Figure 21(a). The total market demand, D', includes both the private demand by individuals and the demand by the government.

The government *cannot* resell the surplus. If it did, the market price would fall below $\hat{p}$. The government's only options are to store the surplus, destroy it, or give it away—but only to those *who would not have been willing to purchase it at $\hat{p}$*, provided that the government can figure out who they are. (If the government just gave the surplus away to anyone, private demand falls because some demanders who would have been willing to pay $\hat{p}$ now get the commodity for free and the government would have to purchase an even larger surplus. The U.S.

Figure 20
The Effect of a Minimum Wage

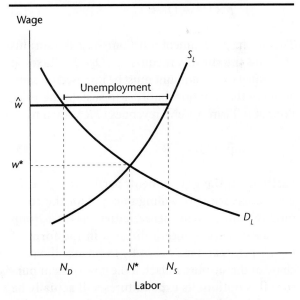

When the government sets a minimum wage, $\hat{w}$, above the equilibrium wage, w^*, the result is unemployment. Because firms demand fewer workers at a higher wage, $N^* - N_D$ employees will lose their jobs. An additional $N_S - N^*$ people will decide they would like to work because wages are higher, but will be unable to find a job. Total unemployment, then, equals $N_S - N_D$.

Figure 21
The Effect of a Price Floor Supported by the Government

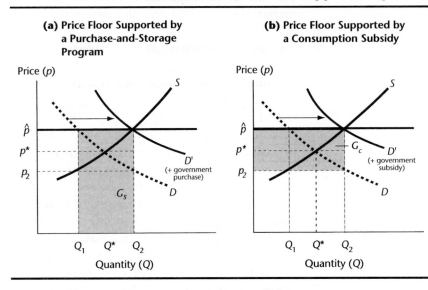

(a) Price Floor Supported by a Purchase-and-Storage Program

Price (p)

(b) Price Floor Supported by a Consumption Subsidy

Price (p)

At the floor price, $\hat{p}$, firms produce Q_2, but can only sell Q_1. As firms try to sell their surplus production, there is downward pressure on the price. The floor price can only be maintained if the government steps in and essentially shifts the demand curve from D to D', either by purchasing the excess supply itself or by subsidizing purchases by consumers. Government expenditures to support the price floor equal the shaded area, although there may be additional storage costs.

government tried to avoid this problem by distributing surplus cheese it purchased to support dairy-product price floors through food banks in poor areas, for example).

In Figure 21(a), total governmental expenditures for the purchase of the surplus, G_S, is

$$\hat{p} \times (Q_2 - Q_1) = G_S \qquad (2)$$

That is, the government must purchase the surplus at $\hat{p}$ and the surplus is equal to (Q_2-Q_1). Taxes at least equal to this amount must be imposed on *some group* in the economy in order to sustain the price floor at $\hat{p}$. Firms receive revenues (*TR*) equal to

$$\hat{p} \times Q_2 = TR \qquad (3)$$

partly from the government, partly from the Q_1 individuals who are willing to pay $\hat{p}$ for the commodity. Note that, in a sense, individuals as a group are taxed twice—once indirectly, in the form of higher prices and once directly to finance the purchase of the surplus. In fact, if the government pursues this option, its expenditures will actually be *greater* than those required to purchase the surplus because it must store or dispose of the surplus and both storage and disposal are also costly. As consequence, if the government solves its disposal problem this way, the cost to taxpayers *exceeds* the additional revenue that producers receive from the price floor.

Subsidize consumption. A third method of supporting the price floor is for the government to purchase all of the output at $\hat{p}$ and then sell it at the appropriate market price. At $\hat{p}$, firms produce Q_2. Therefore, the government is forced to sell the output at p_2. Essentially, in order to maintain $\hat{p}$, the government subsidizes the consumption of this commodity by the difference between $\hat{p}$ and p_2.

This option also requires tax-financed expenditures by the government. If the government purchases all the output produced at $\hat{p}$ in Figure 21(b), for example, it pays $(\hat{p} \times Q_2)$ which, of course, is also the revenue for suppliers. When the government resells the good, its revenues are $(p_2 \times Q_2)$. Because there are no additional long-term storage costs associated with this option, the total cost to the government (G_C) is

$$Q_2 \times (\hat{p} - p_2) = G_C \qquad (4)$$

that is, the difference between the price consumers are willing to pay for Q_2 and the support or minimum price the government pays for Q_2 multiplied by the amount the government actually purchases. Government expenditures in this case are illustrated by the shaded area in Figure 21(b).

Limit production. A fourth policy option for maintaining $\hat{p}$ is for the government to restrict production. The effect of this policy is illustrated in Figure 22 by a shift in supply from S to S'. The resulting

Figure 22
The Effect of a Price Floor Supported by Restricting Production

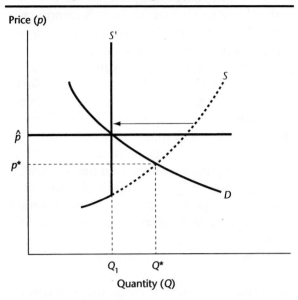

If the government does not want to purchase the surplus production created by a price floor, it can simply restrict production to Q_1, the amount that can be sold at the floor price, as illustrated by the shift in supply from S to S'. Note that this is not a voluntary reduction in supply brought about by economic losses, rather, it is an artificial restriction on how much firms can produce.

market output is Q_1 and the market price after the production restriction is $\hat{p}$. There are several different ways that the government might try to restrict production.

1. The government could pay producers not to produce.

2. The government could purchase the inputs necessary for production from producers, thereby limiting their ability to produce.

3. The government could directly limit production, prohibiting production by some potential producers and penalizing existing producers who produce more than their allotted amount.

To maintain minimum agricultural prices, for example, farmers are sometimes paid to leave land fallow, thereby taking it out of production. Or, for another example, the Federal government once offered to purchase from farmers dairy herds that it then slaughtered in order to decrease the production of milk. Agricultural acreage allotments, essentially

a restriction on how much land can be farmed, are also used to limit agricultural production. In this case, the government specifies a reduced number of acres that can be planted with a certain crop; it then allocates shares of this amount as allotments to certain farmers who then have the right to plant the crop. Similarly, net and boat sizes and limitations on hours at sea are ways of limiting the catch in the fishing industry.

Innovations Around Price Floors

Just as in the case of price ceilings, setting minimum legal prices creates incentives for illegal transactions or legal innovations for getting around the regulations. Thus, it is not enough to simply declare the price in a market must be above the prevailing equilibrium price. The government has to be prepared to enforce the minimum price and respond to the adjustments the market makes.

Purchasing substitutes. One way around minimum legal prices is for individuals or firms to purchase substitutes whose price is not controlled. For example, with minimum wage laws, firms can avoid paying the higher regulated wage by substituting capital for labor, where possible, or by hiring only persons who are more skilled and whose wages would be above the minimum wage anyway. This common response to the minimum wage law means that the resulting unemployment—that is, the surplus associated with the minimum wage—fall disproportionately on young, unskilled, or inexperienced workers.

Using inputs more intensively. If the price floor is supported by a restriction on the use of inputs such as an acreage allotment, suppliers can get around the restriction by farming the remaining land more intensively, thereby substituting other inputs for land. As a consequence of this response, even when the government tries to reduce supply by limiting inputs, it finds itself with surpluses and a costly disposal problem. (One of the unintended and unfortunate consequences of limiting the amount of land that can be farmed is that it leads to environmental degradation: land is farmed too intensively, with too much use of fertilizers, pesticides, and the like.)

Tied sales. Another way of getting around the regulated minimum price is to provide some other commodity or service free when a consumer purchases the price-controlled commodity at the minimum price. For example, a producer might offer free services with the purchase of a commodity at the minimum price. If the free services are valuable to consumers, then this is a way of lowering the *full price* of the commodity.

Changing quality. Yet another way around a price floor is to *increase* the quality of what is provided. For example, there was a price floor on airline ticket prices prior to 1978. Airlines got around the price floor by selling not just a flight from one city to another city, but by offering additional services with the flight such as fancy food and drink, wide seats, special baggage handling, free newspapers, free flight bags, and so on. One airline, prior to deregulation in the mid-1970s, used to advertise "champagne" flights; another airline offered "steak and lobster." Put simply, the price floor induced **nonprice competition**, rather than price competition. Most nonprice competition quickly disappeared when the market price was deregulated and fares fell.

Long-Run Effects

In the long run, the problem of disposing of the surplus gets worse. The higher prices create profits and make activities with price floors more attractive to enter than other activities. Resources move toward these attractive activities as time passes, increasing

supply. For example, in Figure 23, if the government is willing to purchase the surplus or subsidize consumption, firms have the expected profits indicated by the shaded area in part (b). This effect encourages entry, shifting the supply curve to the right from S to S'', further increasing the surplus.

Because of the higher price, consumers also find more substitutes over the long run and the elasticity of demand increases. For example, a minimum price for butter encourages an increase over time in the demand for butter substitutes such as margarine. Similarly, a minimum price for milk encourages consumers to find substitutes over time for milk. A minimum wage may not immediately cause firms to substitute capital for labor, but in the long run it does encourage such substitution, exacerbating the unemployment problem.

High domestic prices because of price floors also encourage foreign firms to export to the United States. This will tend to increase supply unless the entry by these firms into the US market is restricted. Hence, price floors often lead to trade barriers that protect the domestic market from foreign suppliers (trade barriers are discussed later in this chapter). Moreover, higher domestic prices put US exporters at a disadvantage in international markets. For example, the U.S. has traditionally been a major exporter of agricultural products. Within the US economy the demand for agricultural commodities is quite inelastic. Hence, output restrictions of the sort outlined above substantially increase agricultural

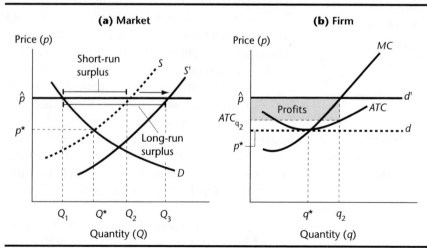

Figure 23
The Long-Run Effect of a Price Floor

When the government supports a price floor, firms make economic profits. Because the industry is profitable, more firms will enter the market, shifting the supply curve to the right (from S to S'). In the long run, surplus production increases from $Q_2 - Q_1$ to $Q_3 - Q_1$. This further increases the government expenditures required to support the price floor.

prices. (You should diagram this argument to convince yourself that this is so.) Within the world economy, however, the demand for agricultural products *from the United States* is far more elastic because other countries also produce agricultural commodities. As a consequence, price supports in the United States reduce the total demand for US agricultural commodities by encouraging foreign demanders to look elsewhere.

Inefficiency: Too Much Is Produced

Minimum prices lead to the inefficient use of resources because the marginal cost of producing the output actually delivered to the market is greater than the amount that individuals would be willing to pay for any additional production (MC > MWTP). For example, at the production level Q_2 in Figure 19, the marginal cost to society of using resources in this market rather than in other productive activities is $\hat{p}$. (The supply curve also measures marginal costs, remember.) Consumers would only be willing to pay p_2 for this level of production, however. Put simply, a dollar's worth of scarce resources is being used to produce additional output for which consumers are not willing to pay a dollar. Indeed, because it is difficult for consumers or firms to be forced to pay more than they want to for a commodity or resource, a surplus develops. In terms of the efficient allocation of resources, *too much is produced.*

▶ Restrictions on Entry

Governmental **restrictions on entry**—that is, limitations on who can sell in a particular market—are one of the most pervasive and least visible ways to affect market outcomes. Such restrictions do not cause the kind of problems created by price ceilings (the rationing problem) and price floors (the disposal problem), but restrictions undermine market *adjustment* and, hence, undermine efficiency.

Effects of a Restriction on Entry

The reasons for and effects of restrictions on entry are easy to analyze. Suppose that demand shifts to the right, from D to D' in Figure 24. Existing firms will make economic profits as a consequence. Profits provide an incentive for entry and, with entry, the profits that existing firms were making disappear. If entry by new firms can be prevented, however, economic profits for existing firms will persist. Not surprisingly, then, existing firms have an incentive to pursue public policy actions that prevent entry by new firms. If entry can be prevented, p^{**} represents the new *long-run* equilibrium price and economic profits will not be competed away. In short, firms that are in the market prior to the demand shift have an incentive to try to block entry by new firms in response to the demand shift.

A restriction of this sort creates a "barrier-to-entry" rent. That is, the barrier to entry is worth

Figure 24
The Incentive for Restrictions on Entry

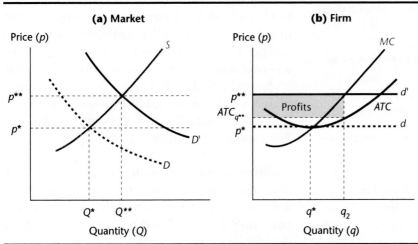

(a) Market

Price (p)

p^{**}

p^*

S

D'

D

Q^* Q^{**}

Quantity (Q)

(b) Firm

Price (p)

MC

p^{**}

$ATC_{q^{**}}$ Profits ATC d'

p^* d

q^* q_2

Quantity (q)

When demand increases (from D to D'), firms make economic profits in the short run. If new firms are free to enter the market, these profits are eroded away by entry until, in the long run, firms no longer make economic profits. But if there are restrictions on entry, the short-run equilibrium price of p^{**} is maintained and existing firms continue making economic profits in the long run.

something: the expected profits that accrue as a consequence of the barrier itself. As we will see in later chapters, there may be competition for this rent and, consequently, a waste of resources that would otherwise be used to produce goods and services.

Methods of Limiting Entry

There are a number of different ways that public policies can be designed to limit entry, including licensing, limiting access to training, and limiting substitution.

Licensing. In response to increased demand and possible entry, existing firms often persuade the government that special qualifications are needed in order to provide a particular service or particular good and only those who meet certain qualifications should receive the state's approval to sell. That is, only those with state-issued licenses can be suppliers. After all, the argument goes, without state scrutiny, unscrupulous individuals may enter this market. Because of arguments like this, state governments now license, or require private agencies to license, hundreds of activities, including fishing, insurance sales, taxi services, and activities of doctors, lawyers, barbers and hairdressers. In addition, the Federal government licenses a large number of activities, including television and radio broadcasting, trucking and shipping, and agricultural production. In virtually every case, the license limits to some degree the ability of new persons or firms to enter in response to market incentives. The restrictions protect those already engaged in providing a service or producing a commodity from the adjustments that accompany demand shifts and profits.

Licensing by itself does not limit entry. Licensing can be used to restrict entry, however, if they are costly to acquire or fewer are issued than the number of firms that would freely enter in the long run. There are a variety of ways to limit the number of licensed suppliers: direct restriction, selecting only "qualified" applicants, or increasing licensing costs.

- The number of licenses can be directly restricted. For example, entry into farming is sometimes limited by directly limiting the number of acres that can be planted in a particular crop. Without an acreage allotment from the government, which can be viewed as a license to produce, a farmer cannot plant, or in some cases, sell certain products and, obviously, cannot enter a market (peanut production is limited in this way, as is tobacco production). It is also illegal, for another example, to operate a taxi in some cities without a government medallion or license.

- Licenses can be limited to those who can demonstrate that they are capable of providing the service. Often these demonstrations require an examination. Limiting the number of people who pass the examination is then an indirect way of limiting entry, even when the licenses themselves are not directly limited.

- Making it costly to prepare for and take an examination limits entry to some degree. Sometimes it is argued that appropriate preparation for a licensing examination requires a certain level of formal education. Because formal education is costly, this cost may be an effective but subtle limit on entry.

Becoming a lawyer provides an interesting illustration of how restriction by licensing works. A person cannot practice law without a bar association license. At one time people could go to work for lawyers and when they had learned a sufficient amount about the law, they could hang out their shingles and practice law (this was how Abraham Lincoln became a lawyer). People could also go to specialized law schools for the same purpose. However, over time various states were persuaded that only those who passed an examination should be allowed to practice law. People could still prepare for this bar examination by apprenticing or going to a law school. Later, the rules were changed so that qualifying to take the bar examination required completion of formal law school training. However, a person could enter law school without a college undergraduate degree. The barrier to obtaining a license was then increased further when law schools were not permitted to admit anyone who had not first completed an undergraduate degree.

Limiting access to training. Similar patterns have developed in medicine and other professions. Medical doctors have been particularly adept at limiting new entry through limitations on medical school slots for new entrants, limiting how many persons can enter certain specialties at the national level, and limiting how many persons can practice in a particular specialty at the local level. One consequence of these barriers is that many prospective entrants have gone to foreign or offshore medical schools located in the Caribbean or Mexico. In an effort to limit entry of this sort, some in the medical profession have sought Congressional passage of laws that would require doctors trained in offshore medical schools to partially retrain in US schools.

Limiting substitution. When firms cannot directly enter a market because of restrictions, they often try to produce close substitutes for which entry is not restricted. As a consequence, effective restrictions on entry may also require regulation of potential substitutes. For example, margarine is a substitute for butter. Margarine is naturally white, however, and must be dyed to look like butter. At one time butter producers sought to make margarine a less attractive substitute by persuading states to prohibit manufacturers from dying it yellow—you could spread something white on your bread or you could spread yellow butter. (Margarine producers responded by selling margarine with a package of dye that a consumer could use to turn white margarine into a yellow butter substitute—the producers weren't violating the law by dying their margarine yellow, they simply provided a way for consumers to dye the margarine themselves.) In another example, railroads were licensed and entry restricted in the late 1800s. The predictable result

was higher prices for hauling freight. Trucks were good substitutes for railroads in freight hauling. So in order to support the initial regulation of railroads, entry into trucking had to be regulated. Both railroads and interstate trucking were eventually regulated by the Interstate Commerce Commission (ICC).

Inefficiency: Too Little Entry Occurs

Limiting entry creates a deadweight burden. In this case, however, it is not because of a wedge between the price that demanders pay and the price that suppliers receive. Instead, the inefficiency occurs because the market equilibrium price is above minimum long-run production cost. The deadweight burden in this case is illustrated in Figure 25.

▶ Prohibited Markets

As a society, we sometimes judge some kinds of market activities to be undesirable, unsafe, or socially inappropriate. In such cases, entry of *any kind* is made illegal. For example, we prohibit markets for sex, child pornography, and drugs such as cocaine, heroin, and marijuana. In the 1920s the sale of alcoholic beverages was made illegal by Constitutional amendment. After the repeal of the amendment, most states continued to prohibit the sale of alcoholic beverages to teenagers.

The government also prohibits markets for commodities found to be unsafe. For example, the Federal Drug Administration (FDA) prohibits the

Figure 25
The Deadweight Loss from a Barrier to Entry

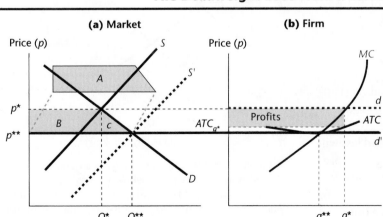

Even in a competitive industry (that is, when market price equals marginal cost), if entry is prevented, there is a deadweight loss because, with entry, supply would increase to S', but is prevented from doing so. Consumers lose the consumer surplus associated with the difference between $p^* - p^{**}$ (p^{**} would have been the long-run equilibrium price) or A. Firms gain producer surplus equal to B. The losses exceed the gains by c.

use of food additives that pose potential health problems. In addition, the government prohibits the sale of certain goods or services where there are substantial uncertainties about the risks involved. For instance, market transactions in untested new drugs and untested new medical procedures are illegal.

We often ban markets for certain goods because there is a broad feeling that some things should simply not be bought and sold. We prohibit markets for adoptive children, for example. We find markets for slaves reprehensible. We are uneasy about markets where blood is bought and sold and rely, instead, primarily on donations. We prohibit markets for body organs and, as a consequence, people can donate—but not sell—their hearts, lungs, eyes, and livers. We don't let people sell their votes. Curiously, we are even uneasy with certain kinds of resale markets where there were no qualms associated with the original sale. So, for example, scalping tickets is sometimes illegal but the original sale of tickets is not.

Finally, market activity is sometimes prohibited for no obvious reason. For instance, the government has decided that markets for the airwaves necessary for broadcasting radio and television signals as well as markets for slots (landing times) at major airports are inappropriate and allocated each of these directly rather than permitting them to be privately bought and sold.

Unless there is almost universal acceptance of the prohibition, the government cannot simply declare some market activity illegal; it has to enforce its declaration. There are three enforcement options: aggressively pursue suppliers of the prohibited commodity; aggressively enforce the law against demanders of the prohibited commodity; or enforce against both suppliers *and* demanders of the prohibited commodity.

Penalizing Suppliers

Because fines or jail terms are costs, penalizing suppliers will shift the market supply as illustrated by the movement from S to S' in Figure 26. Fewer resources will be devoted to the activity and less will be produced and consumed. This change is represented by the movement from Q to Q^{**}. The effect of a "supply-side" policy is to drive up the illegal or *black-market* price. This increase creates a potential problem for society: If there are few substitutes for the illegal commodity, demand will be inelastic.

When it is, the total amount spent on the prohibited commodity will *increase* as the illegal or black-market price increases, making entry into this market very attractive for those willing to operate illegally. For example, the demand for drugs appears to be inelastic. If this is so, prohibiting their use and enforcing this prohibition against suppliers makes participation in the drug market more attractive for some sellers because it *increases* expected revenues.

Penalizing Demanders

Because fines or jail terms are costs, penalizing demanders will increase the full price of buying a prohibited good or service and shift the market demand to the left, from D to D' in Figure 27. The effect on the quantity produced and consumed is the same as when suppliers are penalized: fewer resources are devoted to the activity and less is produced and consumed. In this case, however, the effect of a "demand-side" policy is to drive down the illegal or *black-market* price. Because *both* price and quantity decrease, total expenditure will decline and

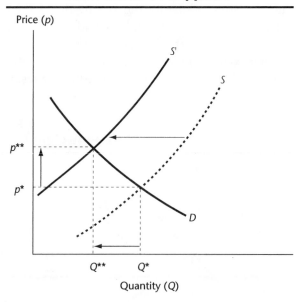

Figure 26
The Effect of Enforcing a Market Prohibition on Suppliers

If suppliers are punished for supplying a good to the market, supply shifts to the left (from S to S'). The quantity exchanged falls from Q^* to Q^{**} and the market price increases from p^* to p^{**}. Total expenditures on the prohibited good may either increase or decrease, depending on the elasticity of demand.

Figure 27
The Effect of Enforcing a Market Prohibition on Demanders

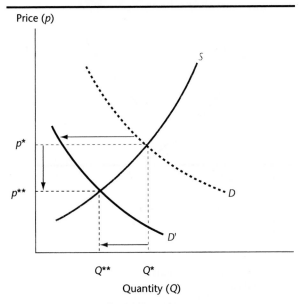

If demanders are punished for purchasing an illegal commodity, the demand curve shifts from D to D'. The quantity traded drops from Q^* to Q^{**} and the market price falls from p^* to p^{**}. Total expenditure on the good falls.

the activity will become less attractive for potential suppliers. This outcome is obviously very different than that which occurs when suppliers are penalized even though in both cases the amount bought

and sold decreases. This poses a difficult public-policy dilemma: enforcing against demanders may be more difficult and less politically feasible, while enforcing against suppliers provides this perverse incentive for entry (that is, greater illegal activity). There is generally less sympathy for drug pushers than for drug users, for example, but enforcing against pushers actually makes drug dealing very lucrative if a supplier can avoid the penalties.

Penalizing Both Suppliers and Demanders

The government could, of course, enforce the prohibition against both suppliers and demanders. If it did, both demand and supply will shift to the left, as illustrated in Figure 28. The quantity actually bought and sold will decrease. In this sense, enforcement against both suppliers and demanders is not different from enforcement against one or the other. The effect on price and, hence, on the total expenditures in the prohibited market is uncertain, however. For example, in part (a) of Figure 28, the price increases because the effect of the enforcement is somewhat greater against suppliers than demanders. On the other hand, if the effect of the enforcement is somewhat greater against demanders than suppliers, as illustrated in part (b), the market price declines. Clearly, the effect on price cannot be determined without carefully examining what happens in the market where the enforcement is occurring.

Figure 28
The Effect of Enforcement on Both Demanders and Suppliers

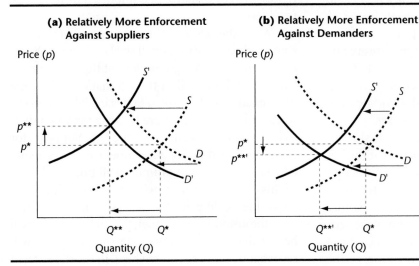

When both demanders and suppliers are punished for participating in illegal markets, both the supply and demand curves shift to the left. The quantity traded in the market falls unambiguously, but the market price may either increase or decrease. (a) If supply falls a great deal but demand does not change much, the market price increases. (b) If, on the other hand, demand falls a great deal but supply does not change much, the market price falls.

▶ Barriers to International Trade

In each case that we have considered to this point, the government directly intervenes in market activities within an economy. For a very long time, however, governments have intervened *indirectly* in domestic markets by pursuing policies known as **trade** or **commercial policies**, which affect the movement of goods, services, and resources across national borders. As a consequence, despite the case for free trade advanced in Chapter 11, international trade has seldom been unencumbered. Although a number of arguments rationalizing such encumbrances have been advanced, policies that interfere with the free movement of commodities among nations are simply a roundabout or less visible way of intervening in domestic markets. To see why this is so, we consider some of the ways that governments have chosen to limit in the flow of commodities from abroad.

Tariffs

A tax imposed on imports from another economy, but *not* imposed on the same good or service produced within the domestic economy, is called a **tariff** or sometimes a **duty**. **Specific tariffs**, like specific sales taxes, are fixed in dollar terms, for example, $1.00 per bushel of foreign-raised wheat. **Ad valorem tariffs**, like ad valorem sales taxes, are set as a percentage of the value of the imported good, for example, a 10 percent tariff on the value of foreign-made television sets.

Imposing a tariff initially increases the price of goods produced abroad relative to those produced domestically. That is, anyone importing a particular commodity on which a tariff has been imposed must pay the tax (the duty), while purchases from domestic producers of the same commodity are not taxed. As a consequence, the amount imported falls and the price for domestic production increases until the price for both imports and domestic production is the same *in the domestic market.*

To see why, consider Figure 29. To make the example specific, suppose this is a picture of the US market for steel. Prior to the imposition of the tariff, consumers are free to purchase either steel produced abroad or steel produced by US firms. Because steel produced abroad is an almost perfect substitute for steel produced domestically, US producers will not be able to price above the world

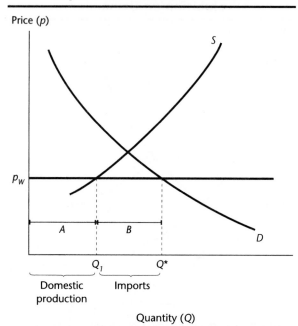

Figure 29
Imports in a Domestic Market

In a market with international trade, consumers can purchase goods from both domestic and foreign firms. In the market illustrated here, domestic demanders can purchase whatever they want at the world price, p_w. At p_w, domestic demanders will purchase Q^*. Of this, Q_1 will be produced by domestic firms and $(Q^* - Q_1)$ will be imported from abroad.

price. As a consequence, the domestic price and the world price will be the same (p_w in Figure 29). When the price is p_w, consumers in the United States purchase Q^*. Of this, Q_1 represented by distance A, is supplied by domestic producers while $(Q^* - Q_1)$, represented by distance B, is imported from foreign producers.

When the U.S. government imposes a tariff, foreign producers (who can sell steel in their own markets or in other foreign markets at the world price) will be willing to sell in the US market only if the price of steel in the United States is higher than the world price since they have to pay a tax when their steel crosses the border into the U.S. Suppose, for example, that the U.S. government imposes a specific tariff of $.25 per pound on all imported steel. In this case, the US price will have to be at least $.25 above the world price for steel (see Figure 30). If it isn't, the amount that foreign producers receive will be less than the world price. In this case, they will sell what they produce elsewhere. In short, the tariff

Figure 30
Effect of a Tariff on Imports

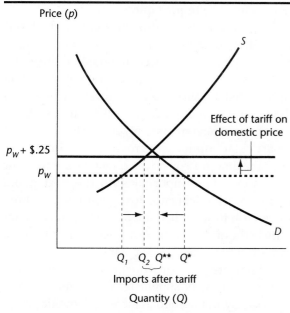

A $.25 tariff increases the price of imports. As a consequence, the amount imported decreases, and the amount purchased from domestic producers increases.

Effects on the allocation of capital across the economy. In the long run, the tariff creates an additional distortion: The higher domestic price creates profits for domestic steel producers. These profits provide an incentive for capital to move from other areas of the economy to steel production (or more generally, to the protected market). Hence a tariff not only distorts production decisions, it also distorts the allocation of capital within the domestic economy because that allocation is determined, in part, by the now-more-profitable opportunities in the protected market. (You should graphically trace these effects to persuade yourself that this is so.)

Effects on the efficient use of resources. Tariffs lead to an inefficient use of scarce resources. This can be seen in Figure 31. When the world price is p_w, the

drives a wedge between the domestic price and the price at which steel is sold elsewhere in the world.

Effects on consumers and domestic producers. As a consequence of the higher domestic price following the imposition of a tariff, consumers will choose to purchase less. It follows that the amount bought and sold decreases from Q^* to Q^{**} in Figure 30. *Consumers are clearly worse off as a consequence of the tariff*—fewer goods are available and the market price has increased.

For domestic producers, however, the outcome is quite different. Although the quantity of steel consumed in the U.S. *falls*, the amount that U.S. producers are able to sell *increases*, from Q_1 to Q_2 in Figure 30. *Domestic steel producers clearly benefit from the tariff.* Essentially, the output of foreign firms is a substitute for the production of domestic firms; the tariff makes the substitute more costly; consumers substitute domestic production for foreign production as a consequence. This distorts the allocation of labor across markets within the economy because domestic output in the protected market increases.

Figure 31
The Deadweight Loss of a Tariff

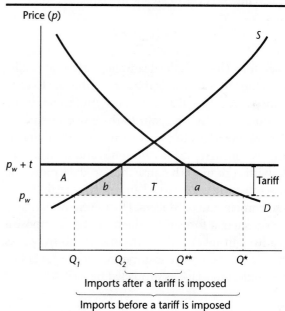

When a tariff increases the price in the domestic market from p_w to $(p_w + t)$, consumers lose $(A + b + T + a)$ in consumer surplus because of the higher price and the fall in consumption. The government gains T in revenue from the tariff. [The amount T equals tariff rate multiplied by the amount imported: $t \times (Q^{**} - Q_2)$]. Firms gain A in producer surplus because the price is higher. The net efficiency or deadweight loss to society, therefore, is equal to area $(a + b)$.

domestic price will be $(p_w + t)$ after a specific tariff is imposed. As a consequence of the higher domestic price, less is consumed. That is, consumption falls from Q^* to Q^{**}. Domestic production, however, increases from Q_1 to Q_2. Therefore, producer surplus *increases* by an amount represented by area A, while consumer surplus *decreases* by area $(A + b + T + a)$. Too much is produced domestically; that is, the gains from specialization are not fully exploited because of the distortion resulting from the tariff. Too little is consumed domestically and the gains from exchange are not fully exploited between the U.S. and other economies. This confirms what was noted earlier: consumers lose and domestic producers gain from a tariff.

The government gains because it receives tariff revenues equal to the tariff rate multiplied by the amount imported—for example, $.25 per pound of imported steel multiplied by the number of pounds actually imported. Since the amount imported is $(Q^{**} - Q_2)$ and the tariff is t, the government's tariff revenue is equal to area T in Figure 31, where

$$T = t \times (Q^{**} - Q_2).$$

Therefore, $(b + a)$ is the deadweight loss that results from the tariff. $(b + a)$ is the sum of the loss to consumers, $(A + b + T + a)$, less the gain to domestic producers, A, less the gain to the government, T.[6] Despite the gains to the government from a tariff because of increased tax revenues and the gains to domestic producers because they produce more, the losses to consumers exceed any *combined* gain to the government and producers. Thus, even though they are directed at foreign production, tariffs impose a deadweight loss on the domestic economy, a loss that falls directly on consumers or, more generally, demanders in markets protected by tariffs.

Quotas

A tariff limits imports by initially increasing the price of foreign-produced commodities relative to the price of domestically produced ones, thereby providing an incentive for consumers to choose domestically produced goods over those that are foreign-produced. A direct way of achieving exactly

the same result is to limit the quantity of imports that can enter the domestic market. Such a limitation is called an **import quota**.

Import quotas are sometimes enforced by issuing licenses to importers equal to the quota amount. For example, if a quota were imposed on shirts and enforced by an import license, to import shirts you would need a license from the government. If you didn't have one, importing shirts would be illegal. Or, a government may simply count the amount of a particular commodity crossing its borders and after the amount equals the quota, refuse to allow any more to be imported until the next quota period. As a consequence, foreign producers sometimes rush to send their goods to the United States early in the quota year because latecomers often have to wait until the next quota year.

What are the consequences of limiting the amount that can be supplied to the US market? Not surprisingly, import quotas increase domestic prices. For example, if the government restricts imports to the quantity indicated in Figure 32, the amount available in the domestic market is the domestic supply plus the *fixed* import quota. Given this supply, the domestic market determines the equilibrium price. Since the amount provided by foreign producers is less than they would be willing to provide at the world price, the short-run effects are higher domestic prices, fewer goods being consumed (because consumers substitute in response to the higher prices), *but* greater sales for domestic firms. Profits will be higher for domestic producers as well. The effect on the domestic market is exactly the same as if an appropriate tariff had been imposed. A quota also eventually leads to a reallocation of capital in the economy and an increase in domestic supply provided to the market in which it has been imposed.

The effects for tariffs and quotas on the domestic price, then, appear to be very much the same. There is one important difference. With a tariff, the government obtains revenue whereas, if the government chooses to use a quota to limit international trade, although it generally does not get any revenue. "But," you may ask, "if imposing a quota has the same effect on the domestic price as imposing an appropriate tariff, who receives the revenues that would have gone to the government had a tariff been imposed instead?" The answer is that the holders of import licenses receive the revenues—

---

[6] This calculation ignores losses imposed on foreign producers.

Figure 32
The Effect of an Import
Quota on a Domestic Market

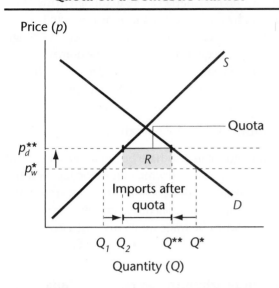

When an economy imposes a quota, it restricts the number of foreign goods that can be imported. The effect is much the same as a tariff. The domestic price increases from p_w to p_d and the quantity demanded in the domestic market decreases from Q^* to Q^{**}. Area R represents the quota rents that go to those who hold import licenses, allowing them to purchase at the lower world price and sell at the higher domestic price.

they are able to purchase the import covered by the quota outside of the U.S. *at the world price,* which is lower than the domestic price, and then sell in the US market *at the higher domestic price.* Put bluntly, if the government imposes a quota on shirts and you can get a license from the government to import shirts, you get to collect some of the revenues that would have gone to the government had it imposed a tariff instead. These revenues are called **quota rents** and are equal to area R in Figure 32.

Effects on the efficient use of resources. Ignoring the distribution of the quota rents for a moment, the gains to domestic producers from a quota are the same as those from a tariff that leads to an equivalent level of imports. The losses to consumers with a quota are also the same as those a tariff creates because, if the level of imports is the same under either a tariff or a quota, the domestic price increases by the same amount. The quota rent is simply a redistribution from consumers to whomever is fortunate enough to be issued one of the import licenses. Hence, Figure 31 can be used to illustrate

the efficiency losses from a quota as well as from a tariff. (T now represents the quota rent rather than the government's tariff revenue.) Both tariffs and quotas, then, impose a deadweight loss on an economy.[7]

A Comparison of Tariffs and Quotas

If a quota and a suitably chosen tariff have the same effect on the domestic market, does it matter which policy is pursued? You might expect the government to prefer a tariff because it is a source of revenue. Those who believe that they will be issued import licenses, however, prefer quotas because they receive the quota rents. The use of quotas may encourage those importers who believe they can get licenses and, hence, get a share of the quota rent, to join with producers in urging the government to restrict imports via quotas. That is, quotas differ from tariffs in that they create interested third parties who seek to obtain the quota rents.

The government *could* collect the quota rent if it wanted to by auctioning import licenses to the highest bidders. In general, bidders would be willing to pay up to the quota rent per unit imported for the privilege of importing at the world price (p_w) and selling in the domestic market at the now-higher domestic price (p_d). If the amount bid for the right to import equals the rent, the government gets the same revenue it would with a tariff if the same amount is imported with a tariff and a quota.[8] As a consequence, economists have argued that if the government wants to use quotas, the least it can do is to capture the quota rent by auctioning the quota licenses to the highest bidder rather than giving them away, and then use the rents for public purposes.

Even if the government auctions import licenses so that importers don't directly benefit by receiving the quota rents, domestic producers may prefer quotas to tariffs. The reason is that with a tariff, foreign producers can increase their share of a domestic

---

[7] Sometimes quotas are combined with tariffs. One possibility is a *tariff-rate quota,* where the tariff increases with the quantity that is imported. For example, the first 100,000 tons of steel may incur a tariff of 10 percent, the next 100,000 tons incur a tariff of 20 percent, and so on.

[8] T is the government's revenue when there is a tariff, it is also the government's revenue in an auction for quota licenses if the government sells the licenses in a competitive auction rather than giving them away.

market if they can lower their production costs and, hence, the world price. With a quota, however, the quantity imported is fixed and therefore unaffected by any cost reductions by foreign producers. This difference between tariffs and quotas is illustrated in Figure 33. When the world price is p_w, a specific tariff of t and an import quota of M have exactly the same effect—imports are M and the domestic price is $p_w + t$. If the world price falls to p'_w because foreign producers lower costs (because of a technological innovation, for example), and if the tariff remained at t, imports would increase from M to M'. As a consequence, the domestic price would fall to $p'_w + t$ and the amount that domestic producers could sell would fall (from Q_2 to Q_1). Thus, even if a tariff had been imposed on imports, lower pro-

duction costs abroad would result in a lower price in the domestic market. As a consequence, domestic firms would lose market share to foreign firms. With a quota, by contrast, the amount imported is unaffected by a decrease in production costs by foreign firms. As consequence, the price in the domestic market will not change. For domestic producers, then, a quota provides a more certain level of protection.

Voluntary Export Restraints

Recently, governments have begun to use a different kind of quota, one in which an *exporting* country, almost always under pressure from an importing country, imposes a quota on *exports* by its firms. This contrasts with the trade quota just discussed, where

Figure 33
A Comparison of the Effects of a Tariff and a Quota When the World Price Falls

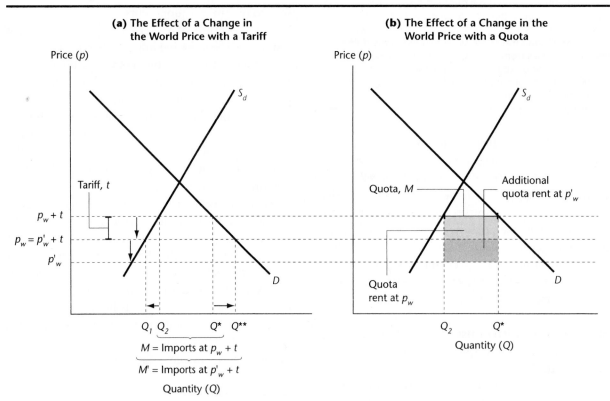

Initially, the amount imported when there is a tariff of t is equal to M, the size of the quota [shown in part (b)]. When the world price falls from p_w to p'_w, the domestic price falls when there is a tariff, from ($p_w + t$) to ($p'_w + t$) and imports increase. The quota is not affected by changes in the world price, however, so imports do not increase when the domestic market is protected by a quota. Only the quota rent increases. Hence, domestic producers are likely to favor quotas so as to render foreign-producer efficiencies irrelevant; persons obtaining quota licenses also favor quotas because they receive part or all of the quota rent.

an *importing* country imposes a quota on *imports* supplied by foreign firms. These new arrangements are referred to as **voluntary export restraints (VERs)** or, sometimes, *voluntary restraint agreements* (VRAs). A closely related restriction is called an *orderly marketing agreement,* (OMA). In 1981, for example, the U.S. government persuaded the government of Japan to limit the export to the United States of automobiles produced in Japan to 1.6 million cars per year.[9] The U.S. government could have imposed an import quota on automobiles coming from Japan but chose, instead, to persuade the Japanese to "voluntarily" limit shipments to the United States.

From an economic perspective, a voluntary export restraint works exactly like an import quota, except that the "license" to import is given to a foreign government, which then determines the share of the quota available to each of its firms. Because a VER limits the goods coming to the United States, the amount available in the domestic market falls and the domestic price increases. The domestic government is not taxing imports, so it gets no revenue from the restricted access to the domestic market. Indeed, what would have been government revenue under a tariff or the quota rent for domestic importers under a quota now becomes a rent *that is transferred to foreign producers.* To see why, note that with a trade quota, US importers purchase at the lower world price and sell in the United States at the higher US price. With a VER, however, foreign producers can sell either directly in the U.S. or through US importers at the higher US price. This means that foreign producers can sell their output at one price, the world price, everywhere except in the United States and also sell in the U.S. at the higher US domestic price. Thus, although foreign firms might prefer to sell more in the United States, if access to the US market is restricted, they would generally prefer a VER over a quota or tariff because they receive some of the rents.

Voluntary export restraints may be solicited from more than one country. For example, a multilateral agreement that covers textiles and apparel, called the Multifiber Agreement (MFA), limits exports of textiles and clothing to the United States and Europe from virtually all textile-producing countries in the world. A similar arrangement was in operation until 1992 for various kinds of steel exported to the United States: the governments of Korea, Germany, France, Great Britain, Spain, Mexico, and Brazil agreed with the U.S. government that they would limit the quantity of steel they allowed their domestic producers to export to the U.S. One of the curious things about these multi-country voluntary export restraints is that the U.S. government has essentially persuaded foreign governments to create and police international cartels *against U.S. consumers.*

The Costs of Protectionism in the United States

The deadweight losses created by tariffs, quotas and other nontariff barriers are substantial. Table 1 provides estimates of these losses for selected industries based on trade patterns and U.S. trade policies in the early 1980s.

Note that in every case, the effect of the particular restriction on trade is to increase the U.S. price, sometimes a little (for example, the price of benzenoid products is estimated to have increased 4.5 percent), sometimes a lot (for example, the price of maritime shipping is estimated to have increased by 60 percent and the sugar quota has increased the domestic price of sugar by 200 to 400 percent). In every case where protective restrictions were in place, domestic output increased, as reflected in the increase in number of individuals employed in the domestic industry. These individuals would generally have been employed elsewhere in the economy, if not for the protectionist policy. In general, the increased expenditures for domestic production because of the higher prices are reflected in the cost per job saved; the deadweight loss is the efficiency loss of the protectionist measure. Note that the deadweight losses per job saved in the protected industries are, in many cases, extraordinarily high (for example, over $1 million per job saved in the specialty steel industry) and that in almost every case, the cost per job saved is probably greater than the average income for those employed in the industry.

Fostering More Open International

Because of the inefficiencies created by trade barriers, nations would almost always be better off if they could mutually agree to lower existing barriers. Since World War II there have been a series of broad-based

---

[9] The voluntary export restraint was later increased to 1.8 million cars per year.

Table 1
Costs of Protectionism for Selected Industries

Industry	Period of restriction	Increase in price (%)	Increase in employment (number of jobs per year)	Cost per job saved ($ per year)	Efficiency loss (millions of $ per year)
Maritime services	1789–	60.0	11,000	270,000	1,000
Book manufacturing	1891–	12.0	5,000	100,000	29
Benzenoid chemicals	1922–1986	4.5	300	>1,000,000	14
Glassware	1922–	12.0	1,000	200,000	13
Rubber footwear	1930–	21.0	7,800	30,000	33
Ceramic articles	1930–	7.0	2,000	47,500	6
Ceramic tiles	1930–	17.3	850	135,000	11
Orange juice	1930–	35.0	2,200	240,000	130
Sugar	1934–	300.0	15,300	60,000	130
Canned tuna	1951–	10.0	1,200	76,000	4
Dairy products	1953–	40.0	25,000	220,000	1,370
Peanuts	1953–	28.0	170,000*	1,000†	14
Textiles and apparel	1957–	24.0	640,000	42,000	4,850
Lead and zinc	1958–1965	9.5	2,200	30,000	5
Petroleum	1959–1973	96.0	43,000	160,000	3,000
Meat	1965–	7.0	11,000	160,000	145
Carbon steel	1969–	12.0	9,000	750,000	330
Ball bearings	1974–1978	2.4	500	90,000	‡
Specialty steel	1976–1986	15.0	500	>1,000,000	30
Fish	1977–	10.0	27,000	21,000	15
Footwear	1977–1981	5.5	12,700	55,000	16
Color TVs	1977–1982	6.0	1,000	420,000	7
CB radios	1978–1981	21.0	600	93,000	5
Bolts, nuts, and screws	1979–1982	6.0	200	550,000	1
Mushrooms	1980–1983	10.0	300	117,000	0.8
Automobiles	1981–	4.4	55,000	105,000	200
Motorcycles	1983–1988	15.0	700	150,000	17

SOURCE: Gary Hufbauer, Diane Berliner, Kimberly Elliott, *Trade Protection in the United States* (Washington, D.C.: Institute for International Economics, 1986), Tables 1.1 and 1.2.

* Acres

† Per acre

‡ Negligible effect

trade negotiations designed to move toward freer trade throughout the world economy. These negotiations were sponsored under the auspices of an international agreement made at the end of the war called the **General Agreement on Tariffs and Trade (GATT)**. This agreement committed the signers, which included the United States, to work toward a more open trading system. The agreement outlined rules for these negotiations and for the way that domestic trade policy would be conducted by the industrialized economies. Over the years, the membership in GATT increased to include most of the world's economies. In the mid-1990s, a GATT-sponsored negotiation led to the creation of an international organization, the **World Trade Organization (WTO)** that would, it was hoped, continue to foster negotiations that opened markets to trade, but that would also provide incentives for countries to abide by the general trade policy rules to which they had agreed.

Preferential trading arrangements. Sometimes a smaller group of nations will negotiate an agreement that lowers tariffs or other barriers among themselves while maintaining trade barriers against other nations. The European Community (EC) began with such an agreement to lower tariffs among the 12 nations collectively called the European Economic Community (EEC), for example. The 12 member nations had no tariffs or explicit quotas for intra-community trade, although non-tariff, non-quota barriers persisted in some cases. The fully integrated economic community established in 1992 finally eliminated these barriers. In addition, however, the 12 member nations adopted *common* tariffs and quotas against all nonmembers. Agreements of this sort are called **customs unions**.[10] Other preferential trading agreements are called **common markets** or **free-trade areas**. In the mid-1990s, for example, the United States joined with Canada and Mexico in a free-trade agreement for selected commodities called NAFTA (for North American Free Trade Area). Negotiations are currently underway to expand NAFTA to include Latin American economies.

Trade diversion or trade creation? It might be assumed that from an economic perspective, lower trade barriers should *always* be better than higher

barriers. Unfortunately, this isn't necessarily so. This is because lower barriers against some, but not all, trading partners have two effects. First, *efficiency may be enhanced* because there is more trade and greater specialization consistent with comparative advantage. Second, *efficiency may be undermined* because trade is diverted from those nations outside of the agreement that have a comparative advantage based on actual costs to those nations within the agreement who have a "comparative advantage" only because of the differences in tariffs or other barriers.

Suppose, for example, that the United States is trading with Malaysia and Mexico and has a common tariff for the same commodity, say, palm oil, coming from each country. Suppose further that Malaysia produces palm oil for $1.00 per pound while Mexico produces it for $1.50 per pound. Finally, suppose there is a 100 percent tariff on imports of palm oil. The cost of oil in the United States will be $2.00 per pound from Malaysia and $3.00 per pound from Mexico. Because the tariff is the same for both exporters, the United States will import palm oil from the lowest cost producer (although it will import less than the efficient amount because of the tariff). Now suppose that the United States signs a free-trade agreement with Mexico so there is no tariff on palm oil imported from Mexico. Mexican palm oil would now cost $1.50 in the United States, while Malaysian palm oil would cost $2.00, as before. Instead of importing from the lowest-cost producer, Malaysia, the United States would begin to import from the higher-cost producer who has a "comparative advantage" only because of the preferential tariff treatment. US consumers would be better off because they would be able to purchase palm oil at a lower price (because of the *trade creation*), but worse off than if tariffs on imports from Malaysia had been lowered by an equivalent amount (because of the *trade diversion*). So, anything less than a global agreement to lower trade barriers may not be the best policy to pursue.

▶ Summary

Commodity tax. A commodity tax is an amount of money per unit bought or sold that must be paid to the government. With a commodity tax, the price that demanders pay is greater than the amount that suppliers can keep. The difference is the per-unit tax that must be given to the government. With the tax,

---

[10] A common external tariff rate prevents the lowest-rate nation in a customs union from collecting all the tariff revenue for goods destined for the entire union.

the quantity bought and sold decreases. In terms of the efficient use of scarce resources, a commodity tax imposed on an otherwise competitive market leads to too little production. There is, as a consequence, a deadweight burden or loss to society.

Market subsidy. A market subsidy is an amount of money per unit bought or sold that is given by the government to either demanders or suppliers. With a market subsidy, the price that demanders actually pay is less than the amount that suppliers receive. The difference is the per unit subsidy provided by the government. With the subsidy, the quantity bought and sold increases. In terms of the efficient use of scarce resources, a subsidy provided in an otherwise competitive market leads to too much production. As a consequence, there is a deadweight burden or loss to society.

Price ceiling. A price ceiling is a limit above which a market price may not legally move. Price ceilings below the market equilibrium price create excess demand because the market price no longer rations the amount produced among those willing to pay the most to purchase it. As a consequence, imposing a price ceiling means that the government must choose an alternative method for rationing, one that does not rely on willingness to pay. Put differently, since with a price ceiling, market prices are no longer permitted to coordinate competing interests, alternative methods for coordinating interests must be devised. The government faces a rationing problem. In terms of the efficient use of scarce resources, too little is produced when there is a price ceiling imposed on an otherwise competitive market. Once again, this means that there is a deadweight burden or loss imposed on society.

Price floor. A price floor is a limit below which a market price may not legally move. Price floors above the market equilibrium price create excess supply. In this case, the government must choose some method for disposing of the surplus, one that will keep the price at or above the legal minimum. The government faces a disposal problem. In terms of the efficient use of scarce resources, too much is produced when a price floor is imposed on an otherwise competitive market, and there is a resulting deadweight burden or loss to society.

Restriction on entry. A restriction on entry is any governmental limitation on market participation by suppliers. Entry restrictions limit market adjustment. As a consequence, the market price is higher than would otherwise be the case. Suppliers currently in a market where entry has been limited, earn returns that are greater than the normal rate of return elsewhere in the economy at least for a while. Entry restrictions in otherwise competitive markets create a deadweight loss to society as a result of the difference between the actual market price and the lower market price that would have been possible without the restriction.

Prohibited market. A prohibited market is one where the government has made transactions at any price illegal. The government must enforce the prohibition (1) against suppliers, in which case the market price increases and the quantity bought and sold decreases; (2) against demanders, in which case the market price decreases but the quantity bought and sold also decreases; or (3) against suppliers and demanders. If the government enforces simultaneously against both suppliers and demanders, the quantity bought and sold decreases but the effect on the market price is uncertain.

Barriers in international trade. A government can indirectly affect domestic markets by limiting imports or exports. There are a number of different ways that a government can interfere with imports. The most common are tariffs, quotas and voluntary exports restraints. A tariff is a tax on an imported good that is not imposed on the same good when it is produced domestically. A tariff increases the price that domestic demanders must pay above the world price, reduces the quantity demanded, and increases domestic production. A quota is a quantitative limit on the amount of imports. If the quota is less than what would be freely imported at the world price, the domestic price will increase, thereby benefiting domestic producers and hurting domestic consumers. A voluntary export restraint is a quantitative limit on the amount of exports one country sends to another country. If the VER is less than what the importing country would choose to purchase at the world price, the VER will increase the domestic price, benefiting domestic producers and hurting domestic consumers.

Part II ▶▶
The Case for the Government

Chapter 13 ▶▶
Monopoly and Cartels ___

Competitive markets are important because they organize activity so that individuals and firms can fully exploit the gains from specialization and exchange. That is, competitive markets allocate resources efficiently. They also coordinate competing interests without coercive governmental or societal intervention. Indeed, as we have just learned, public policies that interfere with otherwise competitive markets create inefficiencies and undermine the ability of competitive markets to coordinate competing interests. But what if a market is not competitive? Will scarce resources be used efficiently? Will competing interests be accommodated and coordinated in appropriate ways? Will public policies foster or undermine efficiency and coordination?

The theme of this chapter is simple: if there is a single producer whose production decisions directly affect the market price at which it can sell its output, it will, in the pursuit of profits, produce less than it would have if the market were competitive. By doing so, this firm can charge a price higher than the competitive price. In this case, the market structure is *monopolistic*, rather than *perfectly competitive*. In terms of Figure 1, if a competitive market has equilibrium output Q^* and price p^*, that same market, if monopolized, would have a lower output and a higher price, say q_m and p_m. Clearly, when a market fails to be competitive, the outcome is quite different from what would have occurred in a competitive market. Because of this difference, markets that are monopolized do not allocate scarce resources efficiently. This chapter explains why this is so, explores

Figure 1
The Effect of a Monopoly on a Market

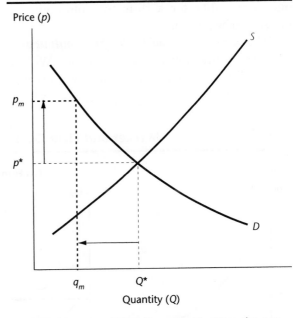

With perfect competition, firms provide Q^* to the market at price p^*. But a monopolist with market power produces less, q_m, and charges a higher price, p_m. Because a monopolist is the sole supplier in a market, the market demand equals the firm's demand. As a consequence, if the firm wishes to increase production, it must also lower its price or, conversely, if the firm decreases production, the market price increases.

the consequences of these differences between perfectly competitive and monopolistic markets, and outlines possible public policy responses.

▶ Market Power

A firm that can affect the market price for its output has **market power.** Technically, a firm has market power if the demand curve for its output slopes downward, that is, if there is an inverse relationship between market price and quantity demanded *for what the firm produces.* In considering whether a firm has market power, then, it is important to distinguish between the demand for firm's output and market demand.

Market demand is, of course, always inversely related to the market price (the First Law of Demand). That is, if the market price changes, the quantity demanded also changes. Or, conversely, if the quantity provided to the market changes, the market price also changes. The degree to which price changes when quantity changes or that quantity changes when price changes is determined by the ability of demanders to substitute. Substitution of one commodity for a different commodity is unlikely to be perfect.

The *demand for a particular firm's output* generally is not the same as *market demand.* While a commodity bought and sold in one market is unlikely to have perfect substitutes from other markets, however, the output produced by one firm within a competitive market is likely to be a near-perfect substitute for the output produced by another firm in the same market. Wheat may not be a particularly good substitute for corn, for example, but the wheat produced by one farmer is a very good, if not perfect, substitute for the wheat produced by any other farmer. Thus although the market demand for wheat is not perfectly elastic, the demand for a particular farmer's output, reflecting the near-perfect substitution *within* the wheat market, is almost perfectly elastic.

Figure 2 illustrates this point. The market demand for the product is less than perfectly elastic but the demand for a competitive firm's output is perfectly elastic. Thus, the market price changes if there is change in total market output, but there is no effect on price when the market output produced by a single firm changes. It follows that no firm in a perfectly competitive market has market power.

If, by contrast, only one firm provides a good or service to a market, the *market demand* and the *demand for the firm's output* will be the same. This lone market supplier is called a **monopoly** or a

Figure 2
Market and Firm Demand in a Competitive Market

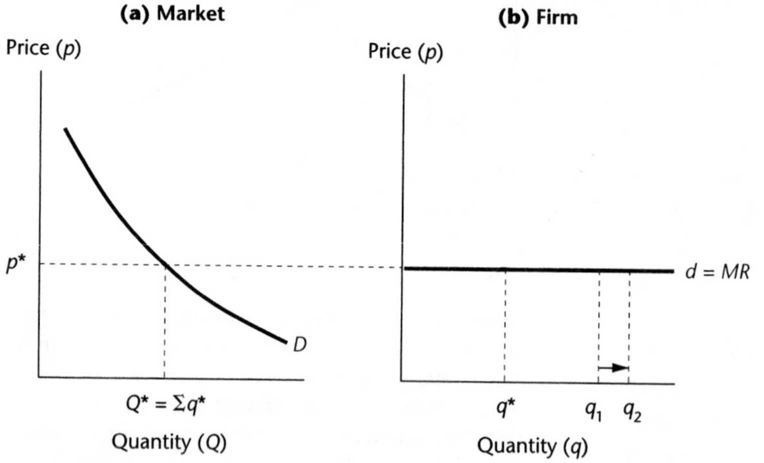

In a perfectly competitive market, the demand for a firm's output is perfectly elastic, even if the market demand for a particular good is not, because products in a perfectly competitive market are homogeneous—any firm's output is a perfect substitute for any other firm's output. Changes in one firm's output also has no effect on the market price. [It is important to remember that the scale for the firm (q) is different from the scale for the market (Q); for example, the scale for the market might be in millions of bushels of wheat, but the scale for the firm might be in thousands of bushels of wheat.]

monopolist. Clearly, the nature of the demand for monopolist's output, Figure 1, is very different from that for a competitive firm, in Figure 2(b). In a competitive market, when a single firm adjusts its output, the market price remains the same (there is no effect on the market price when a single firm's output changes from q_1 to q_2 in Figure 2(b)). By contrast, in a monopolistic market, when the only firm supplying the market adjusts its output—from Q^* to q_m in Figure 1—the market price changes. This difference in the relationship between a single firm's decisions about how much to produce and the market price at which it sells its output is at the heart of the difference between competitive and monopolistic markets. To understand the nature and consequence of this difference, we need to determine how a profit-maximizing monopolist behaves. We will find that its behavior is determined by the marginal revenue it receives when it produces and sells additional output.

▶ Marginal Revenue and Market Price

For a competitive firm, marginal revenue is *equal* to the market price at which the firm can sell its output; for a monopolist, by contrast, marginal revenue is *below* the market price. The reasons why follow.

Marginal Revenue Equals Market Price for a Competitive Firm

A firm, competitive or monopolistic, maximizes its profits by changing the amount that it produces until the additional revenue it receives from producing and selling additional output—its *marginal revenue*—is equal to the additional cost it incurs—its *marginal cost.*[1]

A firm in a competitive market can change the amount it produces but *cannot* expect that its production decisions will affect the market price because it does not have market power. Each additional unit of output produced by a single firm in a competitive market can be sold at essentially the same market price. This means that a firm in a competitive market can expect its revenues to increase by the current market price for each additional unit of output produced and sold. Hence, for each firm in a competitive market, *marginal revenue is the same as the market price.* In these circumstances, a firm wishing to maximize profits chooses a level of production such that marginal cost is just equal to the market price. That is, profit maximization implies that

$$MC = MR.$$

In a competitive market, however,

$$MR = \text{equilibrium market price.}$$

Therefore, a competitive firm will adjust its output until

$$MC = \text{equilibrium market price.} \tag{1}$$

In Figure 2, a profit-maximizing competitive will adjust its output until its marginal cost is just equal to p^*.

Marginal Revenue Is Less than Market Price for a Monopolist

Because the demand for a monopolist's output slopes downward, by contrast, any change in the amount that it produces changes the market price. If the monopolist sells all of its output at the same market price, the monopolist's *marginal revenue will change with these changes in the market price.* Moreover, for a monopolist *marginal revenue will always be less than market price.* The latter point is a somewhat subtle, but particularly important, difference between monopolistic and competitive markets. Understanding this point is important enough that four different ways of explaining the difference follow (pick the one that best helps you to understand this concept).

Marginal revenue is below market price for a monopolist: a numerical illustration. Table 1 is a market demand schedule. It is also the demand schedule for a monopolist (by definition, the sole supplier to the market).

If the firm produces 100,000 units, it can sell its output at $10.00 per unit. If it does, its revenues will be $1,000,000 (100,000 units sold × $10.00). If the monopolist decides to increase its output to 130,000,

---

[1] Recall that **marginal cost** is the *change* in a firm's total costs when it *changes* the quantity that it produces. **Marginal revenue** is the *change* in a firm's total revenues when it *changes* the quantity that it produces and sells.

Table 1
Market Demand and the Demand for a Monopolist's Output

Market price	Total demand
$10.00	100,000
9.50	130,000
9.00	150,000

the market price will fall to $9.50. At this level of output, its total revenue will be $1,235,000 (130,000 × $9.50). Total revenue increases by $235,000 when output increases by 30,000 and the market price decreases by $.50. These calculations are summarized in Table 2.

Notice that in Table 2 the marginal revenue from the decision to increase output from 100,000 units to 130,000 units is approximately $7.83. Why? The change in total revenues when production changes is $235,000; the change in production is 30,000 units. Marginal revenue is defined as the *change* in total revenue from a decision to *change* production. Hence, marginal revenue is approximately $235,000 / 30,000 = $7.83. Clearly, marginal revenue, $7.83, is well *below* the market price, $9.50.

If we try the calculation at a different point on the demand curve, we get a similar result. For example, if the firm increases its output from 130,000 to 150,000, the market price falls to $9.00. Total revenue is $1,350,000 (150,000 units sold × $9.00). The change in total revenue is $115,000 ($1,350,000 − $1,235,000). The change in output is 20,000 (150,000 − 130,000). Therefore, marginal revenue is approximately $5.75 ($115,000 / 20,000). Marginal revenue, $5.75, is well *below* market price, $9.00. In addition, note that marginal revenue *decreases* as the market price decreases.

This difference between marginal revenue and market price occurs because *a monopolist both gains and loses from an increase in production.* A monopolist *gains* revenue from producing and selling *additional output* at the new price determined by the demand for its output. It *loses* revenue, however, because an increase in output can only be sold if the market price falls and when the market price falls, the firm sells *all* of its output—its initial level of production plus its additional production—at the lower price. We can conclude that for a monopolist, marginal revenue is always below the market price, in symbols, MR < p_m.

Marginal revenue is below market price for a monopolist: a geometric approach. Suppose that a monopolist produces q_1 in Figure 3. Given the market demand, it can sell this output for p_1. If the monopolist decides to increase its output by a small amount, say from q_1 to q_2, the market price falls from p_1 to p_2. *The monopolist's total revenue before the production change is the rectangle* op$_1$Aq$_1$, that is, market price, p_1, multiplied by the quantity sold, q_1. Its total revenue after the production change is the rectangle op_2Bq_2. That is, $p_2 × q_2$. The difference between these two rectangles is the change in revenue caused by increasing output from q_1 to q_2. Note that the additional revenue is less than $p_2 × (q_2 - q_1)$. Clearly, for the *last* unit produced (think of $(q_2 - q_1)$ as equal to 1), the additional or marginal revenue is less than the market price p_2.

Why? The reason is that the monopolist confronts a downward sloping demand curve. The additional output $(q_2 - q_1)$ sells for the new lower price p_2, *but so does all of the previous output (q_1)* for which the firm used to receive p_1. Therefore, a monopolist both gains and loses when it increases output. A monopolist gains because it can sell more output, thereby increasing its revenues, as illustrated by the

Table 2
Total Revenue and Marginal Revenue for a Monopolist

Market price	Total demand	Total revenue	Change in total revenue	Marginal revenue
$10.00	100,000	$1,000,000		
			$235,000	$7.83
9.50	130,000	1,235,000		
			115,000	5.75
9.00	150,000	1,350,000		

Figure 3
The Demand for a Monopolist's Output

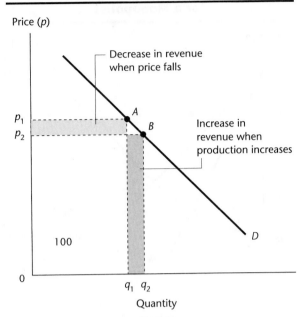

When a monopolist increases production from q_1 to q_2, the price at which it sells its output falls from p_1 to p_2. Because the price falls, the monopoly loses revenues as indicated by the lighter shaded area; because the production increases, it gains revenues as indicated by the gray area. As a consequence, marginal revenue for each level of output is less than the market price.

dark area in Figure 3. The monopolist loses because by increasing its production, the price at which it sells *all* of its output falls, decreasing its revenues, as indicated by the light area in Figure 3.

What follows from this argument? For a monopolist—or any firm with market power—the marginal revenue obtained from any additional output must be below the market price at which it sells the output. This means that whenever a monopolist considers possible changes in its current level of production, it must balance the gains (greater sales) against the losses (lower prices).

Marginal revenue is below market price for a monopolist: an algebraic approach. The relationship between market price and marginal revenue for a monopolist can be illustrated in still another way.

Marginal revenue (*MR*) is defined as the change in total revenue (*TR*) when the firm's output (*q*) changes:

$$MR = \frac{\Delta TR}{\Delta q}$$

When the firm increases its output from q_1 to q_2 in Figure 3, total revenue increases because more is produced and sold. The change in total revenue (ΔTR_1) is equal to

$$\Delta TR_1 = (q_2 - q_1) \times p_2$$

which is illustrated by the darker area. Total revenue decreases because the increased production leads to a lower market price for *all* of the firm's output, however. This decrease is equal to

$$\Delta TR_2 = q_1 \times (p_1 - p_2)$$

which is illustrated by the lighter area. The additional revenue the firm receives from increasing its output is the difference between these gains and losses:

$$\Delta TR = \underset{Gain}{(q_2 - q_1)p_2} - \underset{Loss}{q_1(p_1 - p_2)} \qquad (1)$$

If production is increased by only one unit (that is, $q_2 - q_1 = 1$), then Equation (1) describes marginal revenue,

$$MR = \underset{Gain}{p_2} - \underset{Loss}{[q_1 \times (p_1 - p_2)]} \qquad (2)$$

and the marginal revenue *must be* less than the market price at which the monopolist sells its output,

$$MR < p_2$$
market price

because $[q_1 \times (p_1 - p_2)]$ is a *positive* dollar amount (for example, if q_1 is 1000, $p_1 = \$10$ and $p_2 = \$9$, this expression equals \$1000 which is certainly a number greater than 0).

The first term in Equation (1) is the amount that revenues increase when output increases one unit; the second term is the amount that revenues decrease because the new price, p_2, is lower than the original price, p_1. Clearly, marginal revenue is lower than p_2—the market price—and also lower than the market price at which it was previously selling its output, p_1.

By contrast, if a competitive firm increases its output by one unit, (p_1-p_2) would be zero—a competitive firm has no market power and, hence, the market price does not change when it changes its output. That a competitive firm's marginal revenue is equal to the market price can be confirmed by substituting this 0 price effect in Equation 2:

$$MR = \underset{Gain}{p_1} - \underset{Loss}{(q_1 \times 0)} = \underset{market\ price}{p_1}$$

Marginal revenue is below market price for a monopolist: a mechanical explanation. In Chapter 9 we learned that if an average is falling, the marginal value must be below the average value.[2] The market price is a firm's **average revenue**. To see this, recall that

$$Total\ revenue = q \times p$$

and, by definition,

$$Average\ revenue = \frac{Total\ revenue}{q}$$

Hence, it follows that

$$Average\ revenue = \frac{(q \times p)}{q} = \underset{market\ price}{p}$$

Along a demand curve the market price decreases as the amount delivered to the market increases. Hence, as the quantity provided to a market by a monopolist increases, its average revenue *decreases*. But if an "average" is falling, it must be that the corresponding "marginal" is less than the average. In this case, because average revenue for a monopolist falls when output increases, the monopolist's marginal revenue must be less than the average revenue, or, again in symbols, MR < p_m. This relationship is illustrated in Figure 4.

---

[2] If your grade-point average at the end of the last academic year was 3.5 but your grade-point average at the end of the first semester of this academic year is 3.0, your performance over the past semester—your *marginal* grade-point—must have been well below 3.5 and, indeed, well below 3.0.

Figure 4
Demand and Marginal Revenue for a Monopolist

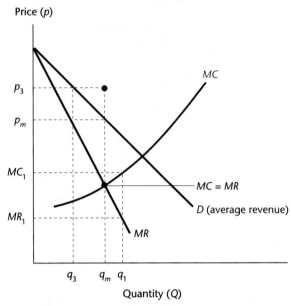

A monopolist produces q_m because, at that level of output, marginal cost equals marginal revenue. If it produces more than q_m, marginal cost is greater than marginal revenue, so the monopolist can increase profits by cutting production. Conversely, if it produces less than q_m, marginal cost is less than marginal revenue, so the monopolist can increase profits by increasing production. At output level q_m, the monopolist charges price p_m—the price that consumers are willing to pay for q_m. This price is above the firm's marginal cost of producing q_m.

▶ Production and Pricing Decisions

A profit-maximizing firm will adjust its output so that marginal cost is equal to marginal revenue. Consequently, the monopolist illustrated in Figure 4 should choose to produce q_m. Any other production decision does not maximize profits. For example, if the monopolist produces q_1, its marginal cost, MC_1, is greater than its marginal revenue, MR_1. Clearly, if the monopolist cuts its production, its profits would increase so it cannot be maximizing profits. On the other side, if the monopolist produces q_3, its marginal cost, MC, is less than its marginal revenue, MR. In this case, the monopolist can increase its profits by increasing its level of production somewhat. Hence, producing q_m maximizes profits. This relationship between output and profits is illustrated in Figure 5.

Figure 5
Profit-Maximizing Output for a Monopolist

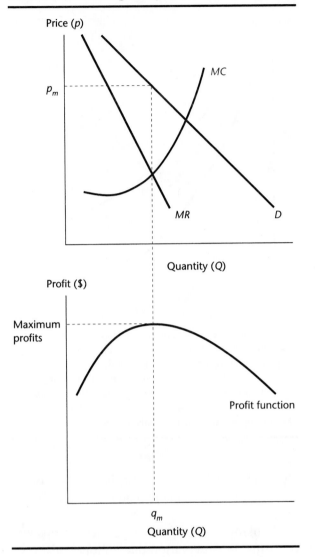

lower its selling price. It follows that if a monopolist produces q_m, the corresponding price on the demand curve, p_m, is the equilibrium market price.

Notice in Figures 4 and 5 that the equilibrium market price that a monopolist receives is always greater than its marginal cost. This is a consequence of the fact that the market price is always greater than a monopolist's marginal revenue. Indeed, we can conclude that if a firm has market power, it can price above its marginal cost. Conversely, if a firm can price above its marginal cost, it must have market power.

▶ The Problem with a Monopoly

In a competitive market, profit-maximizing behavior by firms leads to production for which marginal cost is *equal* to the market price. In a monopolistic market, profit maximizing leads to production for which marginal cost is *less* than the market price. For example, suppose that the marginal cost curve from Figure 4, reproduced in Figure 6, is the summation of the marginal cost curves of a group of competitive firms. That is, assume that the marginal cost curve in Figure 6 is the *competitive market supply*. If this were

Figure 6
Comparing the Competitive Market and Monopoly Outcomes

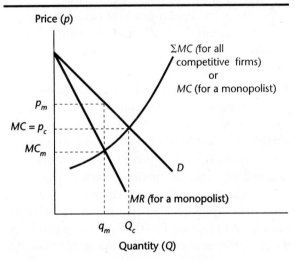

Firms in a competitive market provide Q_c to the market at price p_c because they produce at a level where marginal cost equals both the marginal revenue and the market price. For a monopolist, however, marginal revenue is less than the market price. It therefore produces q_m (where marginal cost equals marginal revenue) and charges p_m.

When q_m is delivered to the market shown in Figure 4, consumers will be willing to pay no more than p_m. That is, after a monopolist has decided how much to produce, *market demand determines the market price*. The monopolist cannot dictate just any market price for q_m. The monopolist cannot, for example, price q_m at p_3. If it did, quantity demanded would fall to q_3 and the monopolist would be unable to sell all that it produced. It would have to lower its price. Market demand—what consumers want and how easily they can find substitutes—constrains the monopolist. If the monopolist wishes to charge a higher price, it must decrease its production; or, if the monopolist increases it production, it must

the case, the competitive market price would be Q_c and the equilibrium market price would be p_C.

"So what!" you think. Compare Figure 6 with Figure 4. It should be clear that if the industry cost structure and the market demand are *exactly the same* for a monopolist and a group of competitive firms, the monopolist will choose to produce *less* than the group of competitive firms will. Because the monopolist produces less, the price in the monopolized market will be *higher* than the competitive price, as can be seen by comparing p_m with p^*.

Inefficiency: Too Little Is Produced

A monopolized market fails to allocate resources efficiently. The reason? In any market—competitive or monopolistic—the equilibrium market price is equal to the amount that consumers are willing to pay for any additional production. The market price at which a monopolist sells its output is above the marginal cost of producing additional output, however. Therefore, at the market equilibrium price, consumers would be willing to pay *more* for any additional output than it costs the monopolist, and society, to produce the additional output (MWTP>MC). This can be seen in Figure 6 by comparing the price at which the monopolist sells q_m with the marginal cost of producing q_m. As a consequence, in terms of the efficient use of scarce resources, *a monopolist produces too little.* You can see the nature of this inefficiency by comparing the difference between q_m and Q_c in Figure 6.

The deadweight burden of a monopoly. Not surprisingly, because a monopolized market allocates resources inefficiently, a monopoly imposes a measurable deadweight burden on society. In Figure 7, the market price when there is a monopoly is p_m rather than p_c, the competitive market price. Consumers lose consumer surplus equal to area $(A + a)$. Producer surplus equal to area b is lost because the monopolist produces less than would be produced if the market were competitive (q_m rather than Q_c). The monopolist gains A, however, because it sells its output, q_m, at the higher monopoly price, p_m. If we ignore any consequences associated with the redistribution of A from consumers to the monopolist, thereby treating the gain of A by the monopolist as equivalent in value to the loss of A by the consumers, there is still a net loss because of the monop-

Figure 7
The Deadweight Loss of a Monopoly

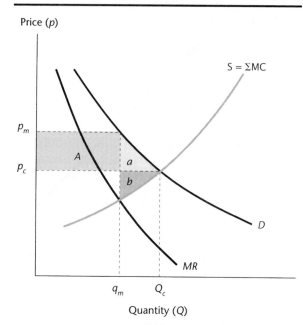

When a monopolist produces q_m rather than Q_c and charges p_c, rather than p_c, consumers lose consumer surplus equal to $A + a$. The monopolist loses area b in producer surplus because of decreased production, but gains area A because of the higher price. The net loss of consumer and producer surplus to society because of the monopoly, therefore, equals area $a + b$.

oly of area $(a + b)$. This quantity is a measure of the deadweight burden on the economy created by the monopolist.

Looking at the efficiency problem in this way confirms the observation that a monopolist produces too little. Any increase in production would decrease the deadweight burden, that is, make area $(a + b)$ smaller. A monopolist would not voluntarily increase production, however, because doing so would lower its profits.

Motives and structure. It might appear that if a monopolist makes a different production decision than a group of competitive firms would when facing exactly the same market demand, the monopolist must have different motives. That is, you might assume that the monopolist has "bad" motives and wears a black hat while the competitive firms (with white hats, of course) have "good" motives. The differences between the monopolist and the competitive firms are not a result of different behavioral motives, however. *Both* the competitive firms and monopolist attempt to maximize profits. *Both* face increasing marginal costs in the short run because of diminishing returns. A monopolist produces less and charges a higher price than does a group of competitive firms because of differences in the market structure within which decisions are made. Simply put, in a competitive environment, production decisions by a single firm will have no affect on the market price; in a monopolistic environment, production decisions by the single firm will have a substantial effect on the market price. These differences in market structures, not differences in motives, lead to the different market outcomes.

Deciding Whether a Market Is Monopolized

A firm cannot be a monopolist unless it has market power. In designing public policies to deal with the monopoly problem effectively, therefore, it is important to determine precisely when a firm does or does not have market power. It turns out that this is a difficult problem. It is sometimes argued that the existence of profits is evidence of market power. At other times, it is argued that the lack of substitutes must lead to a monopoly. Unfortunately, neither of these criteria is a reliable guide to the existence of a monopoly.

Are economic profits evidence of a monopoly? No. First, unfortunately economic profits are often difficult to measure accurately because the presence of rents makes some opportunity costs hard to estimate. Second, as discussed in Chapter 10, a group of competitive firms may, in some circumstances, earn profits in the short run. This means that the existence of economic profits in itself does not distinguish between a competitive market and one that is monopolized.

In competitive markets, entry in response to profits leads to supply changes such that in the long run, potential entrants cannot expect to earn economic profits. Perhaps, then, you might say that any firm that earns economic profits in the long run is a monopolist. Unfortunately, this isn't true either. It is possible, as we also learned in Chapter 10, for certain unique and scarce factors to earn economic rents in competitive markets in the long run. From an outsiders perspective, these rents (just money going to the owners of the unique inputs) are indis-

tinguishable from monopoly profits (also just money going to the owner of a firm).

Economic rent is just a term for returns in excess of the normal rate of return that are not dissipated by entry. For example, if a farmer owns a particularly productive section of land, she may very well earn substantial economic profits as commonly measured. This possibility of economic rents in competitive markets is illustrated in Figure 8. Even though some of the farmers earn economic rent, there is no entry because potential entrants expect profits of zero. If the farmers with the exceptionally productive land sell to other farmers, the price of the land will reflect the economic rent. In that case, the rent becomes a cost for any subsequent purchaser of the land (who will then earn only a normal rate of return). Thus, while the existence of rents need not imply a greater-than-normal rate of return, it is possible that the original owner will earn returns greater than normal even though he or she produces and sells within a competitive market. The important conclusion is that the existence of measurable economic returns in excess of the normal rate of return—in this case, economic rent—even in the long run is not *necessarily* evidence of market power.

Is a low elasticity of demand evidence of a monopoly? No. We know that at least in some regions, the demand for a monopolist must be less than perfectly elastic or it wouldn't have any exploitable market power. We also know that the demand for a competitive firm is almost perfectly elastic. It would appear, then, that differences in elasticity of demand could be used to distinguish a monopoly from a competitive firm. This approach, alas, doesn't work either: a monopolist that is maximizing profits always produces in that section of its demand curve where the demand for its output is elastic (that is, the elasticity of demand for a monopolist is always greater than 1.0 *at the profit maximizing level of production*). And, by contrast, the *market* demand for a group of competitive firms may not be elastic even when the demand for a particular competitive firm's output is infinitely elastic. This means that measuring the elasticity of market demand at the current equilibrium price cannot help determine whether a market is monopolized.

Why is the measured elasticity of demand for a monopolist always elastic? If a monopolist cuts its

Figure 8
Long-Run Profits in a Competitive Industry

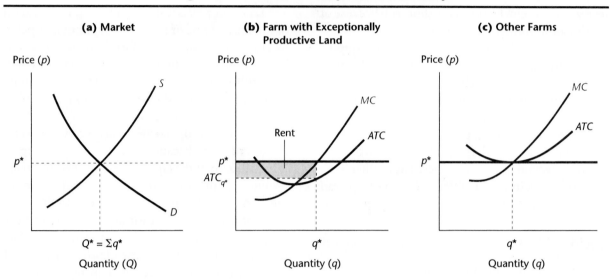

If a farm has exceptionally productive land, making its costs lower than those of other farms, it earns economic rents that cannot be dissipated by entry.

production its costs fall because it is using fewer resources. Its revenues, however, could increase or fall depending upon the elasticity of demand—the monopoly price (p_m) increases with a cut in production and quantity sold (q_m) decreases. Therefore, revenue ($p_m \times q_m$) could either increase or decrease. However, it should be clear that a *profit-maximizing* monopolist would always reduce its production if when it did, its revenue increase because, with cost decreasing and revenue increasing, profits must be increasing. But remember, *revenue increases with a decrease in output and a corresponding increase in price only when demand is inelastic.* Therefore, it never makes sense for a monopolist to choose a level of production in the inelastic portion of its demand curve and, it follows, the elasticity of demand for a monopolist is *always at least 1.0.* That is, for any firm you suspected might be a monopolist, you would always find that the demand for its output was elastic at the market price. In a sense, by driving up the market price a monopolist always creates substitutes for what it's producing. The reason is that if it finds that demanders aren't substituting, it will increase its price, and it will continue to increase its price until doing so isn't profitable. But it will not be profitable to do so only if there is a substantial amount of lost sales in response to a higher price, that is, only if demanders substitute.

Not being able to determine easily whether a market is monopolized is a bit discouraging. It means that any public policy responses to the inefficiencies caused by monopolies will be hotly debated because the existence of each monopoly itself will be at issue, not just the appropriate public policy. (The matter is less discouraging, of course, for those lawyers and economists who, because of this difficulty, have become modestly wealthy in legal disputes that turn on whether a particular firm is a monopoly or, more generally, has market power.)

▶ Barriers to Entry

A monopoly can make economic profits that persist through time only if there are **barriers** that prevent entry by other firms. The monopolist illustrated in Figure 9 earns economic profits equal to the shaded area. These profits make the monopolist's position precarious because they provide substantial incentive for entry by other firms. If entry occurs, the demand for the monopolist's output will no longer be the same as the market demand (there will now be more than one firm supplying the market). The former monopolist will find that the price at which it can sell its output is lower than before the entry occurred, and it will find its profits are lower

Figure 9
Monopoly Profits Create Incentives to Enter

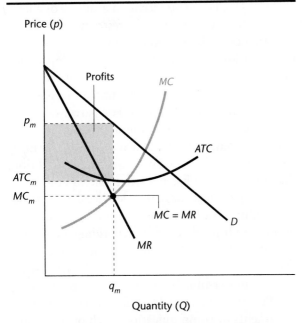

If the monopolist earns positive economic profits by cutting production and increasing prices, other firms have an incentive to enter the market.

as well. The former monopolist may still have market power but, in a sense, it has less market power than it did before entry occurred. As additional firms enter, the former monopolist finds that it has less and less market power and earns smaller and smaller economic profits.

It would appear, then, that monopoly is only a short-run phenomenon and that any monopoly will be systematically undermined by the entry of new firms seeking economic profits. This observation suggests, in turn, that a *monopoly (and monopoly profits) can persist for extended periods of time only if there are barriers that prevent entry by rival firms.*

A **barrier to entry** is any condition that prevents new firms from entering a market in response to the economic profits of existing firms or that disadvantages new entrants relative to firms already in a market. A barrier to entry may result from (1) the exclusive ownership of a scarce resource, (2) specialized knowledge or information not available to other firms, (3) legal restrictions that limit entry by new firms, (4) business practices of an existing firm that makes entry by new firms unattractive, or (5) cost advantages for a single firm over a scale

comparable to the size of the market. Each is considered in turn in the next sections.

Exclusive Ownership of a Natural Resource

Generally, there are a large number of owners of any particular resource. In addition, many resources substitute quite easily for other resources as inputs. When a single firm owns a resource for which there are not very good substitutes, however, it has a monopoly in the market for that resource. For example, International Nickel of Canada owns virtually all of the world's nickel; DeBeers of South Africa owns much of the land on which gem-grade diamonds are easily mined; most of the supply of molybdenum is controlled by the America Metal Climax Corporation. Similarly, at one time, virtually all of the bauxite in the United States was owned by the Aluminum Company of America (Alcoa). Exclusive or near-exclusive ownership of a scarce resource in each of these cases is a barrier to entry. Any firm that relies on one of these resources as an input, but has no ready supply, cannot compete with the firm that owns most or all of the resource. This exclusion from the market, therefore, creates and perpetuates a monopoly.

Specialized Knowledge or Information

Sometimes firms have specialized knowledge or information that is not readily available to potential rivals. This information might allow a firm to produce a new or better product. Or a firm might have knowledge of production techniques that allows it to produce at lower costs than any potential rivals. If no other firm has access to this information, the firm with the information faces a downward-sloping demand curve for its output. Its output is considered new and better and, with lower costs, the old-and-not-as-good output is no longer as good a substitute. At least in the short run, the firm can take advantage of the resulting market power.

Suppose, for example, that all potential rivals have marginal cost curves MC_o in Figure 10 and the firm with specialized knowledge has the marginal cost curve MC_m. No firm can price for long below p_o without losing money except the firm with the specialized knowledge. This means that at a price below p_o the firm with the specialized knowledge confronts

Figure 10
The Effect of Specialized Information

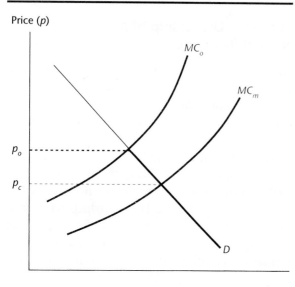

If a firm has specialized information or technologies that allow it to produce at a lower cost than other firms, it has market power at any price below p_o. Why? At any price below p_o, other firms make losses. As long as the firm charges a price above p_c and below p_o, it can exert market power. In this case, it faces a kinked demand curve.

a downward-sloping demand curve and has market power. As a consequence, this firm can charge a price above marginal cost but, obviously, cannot charge a price above p_o.

Legal Restrictions and Franchises

Legal barriers to entry distort market adjustments (see Chapter 12), but they need not create a monopoly. For example, if a market has a large number of competitors and entry is restricted, the barrier to entry does not, in and of itself, change the competitive structure within the market. Firms will adjust output until marginal cost equals price. In this case, the barrier does not create market power for any single firm.

If, however, the legal restriction on entry occurs when there is a single firm (or if the legal restriction on entry reduces the number of firms in the market to one), that firm will become a monopolist and, not surprisingly, choose a level of output where the market price is greater than marginal cost. In this

case, the legal barrier to entry either sustains or creates market power.

The U.S. Postal Service is an example of a legal monopoly that is sustained by restrictions on entry. No other entity is allowed to deliver first-class mail. Competition to the Postal Service is simply prohibited by law. Postage rates are also regulated, however, so that the Postal Service cannot price precisely the way a monopolist would. For parcels, by contrast, the government has allowed entry. In this market, Federal Express, UPS and many other firms compete with the U.S. Postal Service. In addition, the Postal Service has not been able to enforce its monopoly against messenger services. As a consequence, in most large cities there is active competition from firms that hire bicycle-riding messengers to make deliveries. Moreover, recent technological developments—the fax machine and email—have further undermined the monopoly position of the Postal Service, at least for certain kinds of documents or communication. Each of these various forms of entry has put pressure on the Postal Service, which has had to respond with better service, including overnight delivery, special handling, etc.

Patents and copyrights. In addition to exclusive legal franchises or exclusive governmental licenses, both of which are commonly used to restrict entry, governments also issue patents and copyrights. These are legal protections against a particular form of entry: copying the invention, idea, or creative work of someone else. There are numerous examples of American monopolies based at one time or another on patents, including monopolies in aluminum, ethyl gasoline, rayon, cellophane, cellophane tape, safety razors, numerous pharmaceutical drugs, sulfur extraction, and, recently, artificial sweeteners (Nutrasweet, whose patent protection expired in 1993).

A firm granted a patent or copyright is able to exercise monopoly power, however, only if good substitutes for the protected invention or idea do not exist. When an inventor patents or copyrights a new product or production process, other firms often find alternatives that serve the same purpose. As a consequence, patents do not necessarily create monopolies. Even when they do, as we shall see in Chapter 16, a government is caught between conflicting goals—fostering creative effort and allocating resources efficiently.

Pricing Strategies and Business Practices

A monopolist might be able to choose pricing policies that discourage entry. For example, a monopolist may decide to lower its profits by increasing production somewhat and lowering the market price, thus discouraging entry and the *larger* erosion of its profits that would result over time from entry. This kind of behavior is called **limit pricing**.

A monopolist may threaten to always price below its potential competitors so as to drive them from the market should they enter. Or a firm with some market power may attempt to price below the costs of rivals in order to encourage exit on their part. If potential rivals refused to enter the market because of the threat of such actions by the monopolist, or if current rivals left the market because of such pricing policies by a potential monopolist, then the monopoly position would be secure. Such behavior is called **predatory pricing**.

Finally, a monopolist may also pursue business practices that disadvantage its competition, either in the way that it markets its output or in the way it organizes itself. For example, it may try to ensure that any new entrant will have higher marketing costs than it does. Or, for another example, a monopolist may engage in any of a large number of activities that can make entry less attractive, including the vertical integration of production by combining wholesale, distribution, and retailing functions; setting the price at which a retailer can sell a producer's output; tying the purchase of one commodity to the purchase of a second commodity; restricting the distribution of its output by wholesalers or retailers; refusing to deal with firms that deal with its rivals; or pursuing actions that raise rivals' costs.

These practices pose a challenge for public policy. It is extraordinarily difficult to know whether either limit pricing or predatory pricing is, in fact, occurring. (The nature of competition, after all, is that more efficient firms under price less efficient firms.) And, it is even more difficult to know whether the indicated business practices enhance or undermine competition. In other words, we cannot easily discern whether the quantity provided to the market increases, decreases, or stays the same when a firm pursues one of these practices. Unfortunately, the empirical evidence on most of these issues is inadequate. Moreover, there are economic reasons why these business practices might not be sensible for a monopolist to pursue or, on the other hand, might be sensible for any firm, competitive or monopolistic, to adopt. If they are not sensible for a monopolist, then they are unlikely to be practiced. If they are sensible for *any* kind of firm, then they cannot be used as evidence of monopolization.

Some problems. Suggesting that a firm might obtain or retain monopoly power through pricing or organizational strategies has been a recurrent and appealing argument in public policy discussions. As a practical matter, however, proving that a firm is pursuing these strategies is difficult.

For example, both limit pricing and predatory pricing imply that the monopolist's price is "too low." More effective and cost-efficient producers can always price below less effective and higher-cost producers, however. Thus, if a firm sells at a lower price than rival firms, it may simply have lower costs. Of course, it may be using limit pricing to drive new entrants from the market. The price that a firm actually charges tells us little about which of these alternatives is true.

Moreover, a monopolist can adversely affect an entering firm by limit or predatory pricing only if it *increases* its own costs or *lowers* the price at which it currently sells its output. That is, to increase an entrant's costs, a monopolist or potential monopolist must increase its own costs; to lower the price an entrant receives, it must lower the price that it receives. As a consequence, to create barriers to entry using these techniques, a monopolist must *actually* inflict some economic pain on itself in the form of lower profits (akin to shooting itself in the foot), in order to *threaten* to inflict economic pain on a potential entrant. Is a monopolist willing to accept lower profits *for sure now* in order to either forestall the *possibility* of lower profits or enhance the *possibility* of higher profits *at some future time*?

Unless there are other kinds of barriers to entry, such pricing strategies appear to be very risky because when the monopolist increases its prices to make up for its losses, firms that may have been reluctant to enter when the prices were low will be delighted to enter under the monopolist's umbrella of high prices. Framing the argument in this way has led a number of economists to conclude that this kind of alleged pricing behavior by a monopolist is highly unlikely, but, frankly the empirical

Figure 11
Predatory PRicing

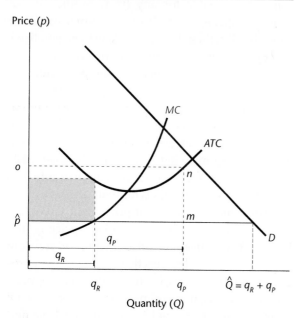

If a predator chooses $\hat{p}$, its rival can minimize losses by choosing to produce q_R. The predator must supply the difference between the quantity demanded at $\hat{p}$ (that is, $\hat{Q}$) and the amount provided by its rival (q_R). The rival incurs the losses indicated by the colored rectangle; the predator incurs the much larger losses indicated by the rectangle $\hat{p}mno$. Hence, a firm engaged in predatory pricing must hurt itself in order to hurt other firms.

consequence, many firms that are clearly *not* monopolists are vertically integrated. The fact that vertical integration occurs in virtually every kind of market suggests that it does not necessarily lead to monopoly power or prevent entry. More generally, it is extraordinarily difficult to know which organizational choices enhance market power and which are important in effectively organizing the production and marketing of a firm's output. Moreover, any practice that increases the amount available in the market is efficiency enhancing.

Scale Economies

If a single firm can supply *all* of the demand in a market at a *lower* cost than can a group of competitive firms, a monopoly naturally arises. In Chapter 9 we noted that entry or expansion could sometimes realize scale economies. In particular, **increasing returns to scale** implies that larger firms have lower costs than smaller firms and, in the long run, as a consequence, smaller firms will be replaced by larger firms. But economies of scale do not necessarily create market power. If the minimum efficient scale is small relative to the market, competition persists even if firms are larger. (These firms, while large, are still small relative to the size of the market.) However, if costs continue to decline with a single firm's expansion until the optimal size for a single firm is very large relative to the market demand, then this firm will come to have market power. In this case, this firm is said to be a **natural monopoly**.

This relationship between declining long-run average costs for a single firm and market demand is illustrated in Figure 12. Lower prices always increase the quantity demanded (the First Law of Demand), but in this market as the firm expands in response to profits by acquiring additional capital, its average production costs decrease. As a consequence, only this firm will survive competitive entry; it will be a monopolist. As such, it will choose to produce q_m and sell its output for p_m. Doing so will allow the firm to make the profits indicated in Figure 12.

You might guess that profits will stimulate entry and undermine the position of the natural monopolist. Any new entrant, however, must be *very* large. To see why, suppose a new entrant started by producing q_e. This firm would have average production costs of ATC_e. It could never compete with the exist-

evidence is inconclusive.[3] The problem for a firm contemplating pricing predatorily is illustrated in Figure 11.

Can the organizational choices of a dominant firm or monopolist make it difficult for new firms to enter? It is sometimes argued, for example, that vertical integration can be used to create a monopoly or exploit monopoly power. Vertical integration, as we learned in Chapter 2, may be a way for firms to minimize the costs associated with using markets. As a

---

[3] It is commonly believed that John D. Rockefeller's original Standard Oil Company, which was broken into several smaller firms in a famous antitrust case in 1911, achieved market power by merging with smaller firms, using the threat of predatory pricing. An economist, John McGee, argued that this wasn't so. Standard Oil, McGee found, rarely engaged in price wars. Instead, it apparently bought out competitors at quite favorable terms to the owners. It may have been possible to do this because of the profits it expected to earn when it became a monopolist.

Figure 12
A Natural Monopoly

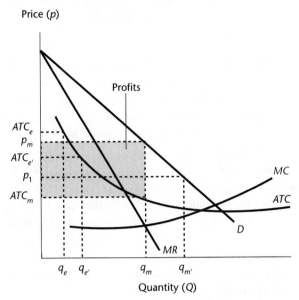

A firm has a natural monopoly if its average costs decline over the relevant range of the market demand curve. When this is the case, the firm is not threatened by entry because it can underprice any potential competitors and still earn a profit. To see why, suppose a new firm enters, producing q_e. At this level of production, the new firm can only make losses because its costs are above the market price, p_m, and well above the monopolist's costs, ATC_m. Even at a higher level of production, $q_{e'}$, when the new firm's costs are below the old market price, they are still above the monopolist's costs. The monopolist can easily price below ATC_e, and still make a profit, while forcing losses on the new firm.

ing monopolist because its costs are greater than the monopoly price, p_m. *As a consequence, the entering firm might start by producing* $q_{e'}$. Its production costs ($ATC_{e'}$) are below the monopoly price, so this might seem sensible. The natural monopolist, however, has even lower costs, ATC_m, and can *always* under-price this new entrant without incurring any losses. That is, if the monopolist increased its production a little in response to the challenge of the entrant, the resulting market price might be p_1. But p_1 is less than the costs of the entering firm but above the costs of the monopolist, and the entering firm makes losses while the monopolist makes profits.

Alternatively, the monopolist might respond passively to the new entrant and continue to produce q_m. If a new entrant produces q_e, the total

amount supplied to the market lowers the price to $\hat{p}$, as illustrated in Figure 13. In this case, the monopolist continues to make profits, although they are not as great as they were before the new firm entered. The entering firm incurs losses, however, and will eventually exit, leaving a single firm producing q_m.

It may be, of course, that the new firm enters at the same scale as the existing firm, that is, by producing q_m. In this case, both firms lose because the market price decreases below their average costs. Either the new entrant or the monopoly will exit; both cannot survive in the market. And, yet again, the market is left with a single producer.

As a consequence of increasing returns to scale, then, the *expected profits* from entry may be very low or even negative, so there is little incentive to enter even though the natural monopolist is making economic profits. In this sense, technology, which is the reason for the decreasing average production costs, creates a barrier to entry.

Utilities such as electrical power, local telephone service, water, natural gas, and sewage disposal

Figure 13
The Problem Faced by a New Entrant
in a Decreasing Cost Industry

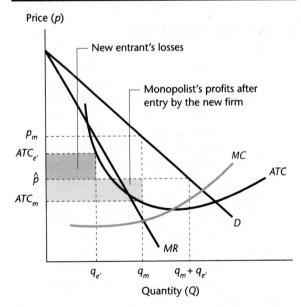

When a new firm tries to enter a decreasing cost industry, the increased quantity provided to the market lowers the market price, from p_m to $\hat{p}$. Thus, even if the new firm could have made profits at the old monopoly price, it now incurs losses and the original monopolist continues to make profits.

companies are generally thought to be natural monopolists. To see why, suppose that one supplier of natural gas or water or sewer services has a pipe down the middle of the road to provide service to all of the homes on the road. This firm can service an additional customer at a much lower cost than a new entrant can because the existing utility would only need to provide a line from its existing pipe in the street to the new home whereas a new entrant would need to provide not only this line but also a central pipe down the street. The firm with the existing distribution system has a substantial cost advantage over any potential entrant in servicing new customers. In addition, the greater the number of homes on that are hooked to the same pipe down the middle of the street, the lower the cost per home of providing the service. (The costs associated with putting a large pipe down the street are the same for a firm with many customers as for a firm with a single customer.) It appears, then, that the technologies that distribute gas, water, electricity, telephone service or sewage disposal are such that a *single* distribution system has lower costs per consumer served than a series of competing distributional systems would. The owner of this distribution system would, of course, have a monopoly.

▶ Collusion and Merger

People of the same trade seldom meet together, even for merriment and diversion, but the conversation ends in a conspiracy against the public, or in some contrivance to raise prices. It is impossible indeed to prevent such meetings, by any law which either could be executed, or would be consistent with liberty and justice. But though the law cannot hinder people of the same trade from sometimes assembling together, it ought to do nothing to facilitate such assemblies; much less to render them necessary.

Adam Smith, from *An Inquiry into the Nature and Causes of the Wealth of Nations*

Market power and, perhaps, a monopoly may be created in two other ways:

1. A group of firms may **explicitly collude**, as Adam Smith observed, in an effort to restrict production and entry, and thereby *jointly* act

like a monopolist. A group of firms that does so is known as a **cartel**.

2. A group of otherwise competitive firms may **merge** into a single firm that has market power.

The possibilities of earning economic profits provide substantial incentives for otherwise competitive firms to collude and attempt to organize themselves to obtain the economic advantages of a monopolist. In the market illustrated in Figure 14, for example, competition among firms results in Q^* being supplied to the market. No firm makes economic profits, as each produces q^*, a small fraction of the total output. If the firms could agree to coordinate their production decisions and cut the total amount provided to the market from Q^* to Q_m, the market price would increase. Each firm might then make economic profits because the price would be well above p^*.

Potential monopoly profits also provide an incentive for otherwise competitive firms without market power to merge to a single firm with market power. For example, prior to a merger, each firm would act as if d^* in Figure 14 was the demand for its output and p^* was its marginal revenue. After the merger, however, the market demand and the demand for the new firm's output are the same. The monopoly created by merger would respond by cutting its output, thereby increasing the price that it received and its profits.

A well-known example of collusion occurred in the 1970s when a group of oil producing nations, OPEC, agreed to restrict output in order to increase the world price of oil. The price of oil increased by about 400 percent within a short period in 1973 as a consequence of this action and then again by about 300 percent in a short period of time in 1979. In the nineteenth century, a number of different industries made comparable agreements—the sugar, whiskey, lead, cottonseed oil, and linseed oil trusts. In each of these cases, a *group* of otherwise competitive firms agreed to limit the total production supplied to the market in order to increase the market price. More recently, Archer-Daniels-Midlands (ADM) and certain Japanese producers of chemicals used in agriculture were found to have formed a cartel.

It is less clear whether any merger has been large enough to move the newly created firm into a monopoly position. Perhaps the closest a merger

Figure 14
The Advantage of Forming a Cartel

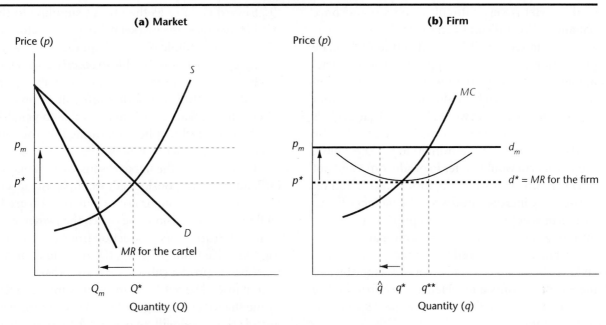

In a competitive market, when the price is p^* and each firm is producing q^* (collectively providing Q^* to the market), all firms make zero economic profits. If the firms form a cartel, they can all earn economic profits if each cuts its production to $\hat{q}$, thus supplying quantity Q_m to the market. But as the market price increases to p_m, each firm has an incentive to increase its individual profits by cheating on the agreement and producing q^{**} instead of $\hat{q}$. If all firms do this, the market output increases and the price falls until all firms once again make zero economic profits.

came to creating a monopoly was the creation of the U.S. Steel Corporation (now USX) from about 1,000 small steel companies at the turn of the century. Because of a series of comparable mergers and firm growth, by the end of the nineteenth century very large firms dominated a number of industries, as indicated in the first column of Table 3. Note that in virtually every case, the "monopoly" position has eroded over time. (**Market share** is the fraction of the market output produced by a single firm.)

Market Forces and the Survival of a Cartel

Cartels are not viewed as a long-term threat to competition because they are inherently unstable. That is, the coordinated behavior of a cartel is almost always undermined by self-interested responses of its members or by new entry into the market. To see why, note first that in order to increase profits, a cartel has to cut production, for example from Q^* to Q_m in Figure 14. This means that *each* member of the cartel has to cut its production from q^* to some

Table 3
Market Share

Company	Year	Market share (%)	Year	Market share (%)
Standard Oil	1899	88%	1909	67%
American Sugar Refining	1892	95	1917	28
American Strawboard	1889	85	1919	33
National Starch Mfg.	1890	70	1899	45
Glucose Sugar Refining	1897	85	1901	45
International Paper	1898	66	1928	14
American Tin Plate	1899	95	1912	54
American Writing Paper	1899	75	1952	5
American Tobacco	1899	93	1903	76
American Can	1901	90	1903	60
U.S. Steel	1901	66	1934	33
International Harvester	1902	85	1948	23
American Smelting	1902	85	1937	31
Corn Products Refining	1906	90	1914	59

point less than q^*. An agreement about how to divide these production cuts among the members of the cartel is very difficult to obtain and once obtained, very difficult to enforce.

You can see why it is so difficult to coordinate production decisions by supposing that the cartel has agreed that each firm will cut its production from q^* to $\hat{q}$. If each firm did this, the total amount supplied to the market would be Q_m. (That is, Q_m is the sum of $\hat{q}$ over all the firms in the cartel.) The market price will increase from p^* to p_m. At p_m, however, *each* firm would prefer to produce q** and not $\hat{q}$. This means that while the cartel's restriction on output may increase profits for the member firms, each firm is not producing at its profit-maximizing output, *given the cartel price*—both marginal cost and average cost are well below the market price, and each firm could increase its output a little bit and increase its profits a lot. Hence, *each firm has an incentive to cheat on the cartel agreement by increasing its output beyond $\hat{q}$.*

This incentive to cheat on the cartel production agreement leads some (or all) firms to produce more than they had originally agreed to produce. As they do, the output supplied to the market increases from Q_m toward Q^*. But as the output supplied to the market increases, the market price decreases toward p^* and the economic profits disappear. Thus, to be effective, a cartel must be able to *observe* and *penalize* cheating on the production agreement. Put somewhat differently, if it is either difficult to observe when a firm cheats or it is not possible to penalize cheaters, a cartel will be undermined by the self-interest of the cartel members.

For essentially the same reasons, a cartel may be difficult to form. Consider, for example, the incentives for a firm to join or not to join. If in Figure 15 all firms except one join the cartel, then when each firm in the cartel cuts production from q^* to $\hat{q}$, raising the price from p^* to p_m, the outside firm can increase its profits substantially by expanding its output to $\tilde{q}$. (The outside firm's profits are illustrated by the shaded area in Figure 15(c).) Clearly any firm *outside* the cartel will be better off than any firm *inside* the cartel. This makes it difficult to get *all* firms to agree to join the cartel because each firm

Figure 15
The Advantage of Being Outside a Cartel

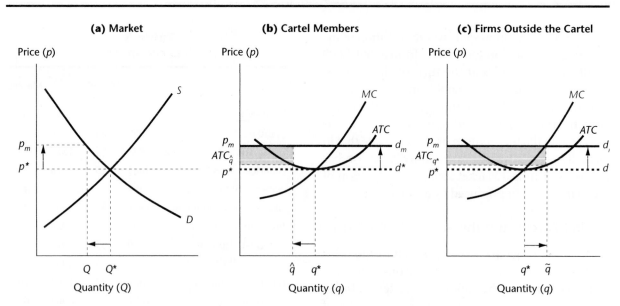

Because there are advantages to being outside it, a cartel may be difficult to form. If the cartel successfully cuts production and increases the market price, cartel members produce $\hat{q}$ and make profits as indicated by the shaded area in part (b). But because firms outside the cartel do not have production restrictions, they produce $\tilde{q}$ at the higher market price and make profits as indicated by the shaded area in part (c). These profits are significantly greater than those made by the firms that are in the cartel.

wants an effective cartel to form, but every firm also wants to be an outsider. Even if agreements among existing firms to restrict output can be enforced, it is generally impossible for them to be enforced against new entrants. New entrants, just like the outside firm in Figure 15, are especially profitable in the short run.

The refusal of some existing firms to join and the entry by new firms will prevent a cartel from raising the price at which its members can sell their output. In addition, the incentives to cheat within the cartel either prevent a cartel from forming, limit its market power once formed, or completely undermine it. As a consequence, simply relying on market forces may be an appropriate public policy for dealing with collusive cartel agreements. These possibilities will be explored further in Chapter 14.

Public Actions and Survivable Cartels

Because policing the agreement among the otherwise competing firms is necessary if a cartel is to survive, otherwise rival firms have an incentive to use the government's power to create and enforce their cartel agreements. Virtually every where a cartel has survived for an extended period of time the government has legally restricted entry, production, or prices. The enforcement powers of private firms are usually limited, but the government can use its power to police cheating effectively.

U.S. government agricultural policies are frequently designed to enforce cartels among otherwise competitive farmers. These agricultural cartels are often created through the use of marketing orders where a group of farmers of a particular crop, such as citrus fruits, are allowed to *collectively determine* how much can be brought to the market. At one time, the U.S. government enforced a cartel in air transportation through the Civil Aeronautics Board that limited competition, barred entry, and set common fares among rival airlines. In international trade, the U.S. government has often pursued policies that encourage foreign governments to limit the amount that their firms sell in the United States through *voluntary export restraints*. Under certain circumstances, these restrictions create a cartel of foreign producers against US consumers.

► Price Discrimination

To this point we have assumed that a monopoly charges all of its customers the same price. A monopoly may, however, be able to charge different customers different prices for the same commodity even though the costs of servicing the different customers do not differ. Doing so is called **price discrimination**. That is, price discrimination occurs when a firm charges *different* individuals *different* prices for essentially the same good or service. Price discrimination also occurs when a firm charges the *same* individual *different* prices for the same good when he or she consumes various amounts.

The incentives to price discriminate are substantial. When a monopoly increases its production, remember, it both loses and gains. In particular, it loses because the additional output lowers the market price for *all* that it produces. A monopolist would obviously have higher profits if it could avoid the losses from lowering the price on units previously sold. It can do so if it can sell its output at different prices to different people.

For example, if a monopolist is producing q_m in Figure 16 and selling to all consumers at the same price, the "uniform" market price is p_m. (For simplicity, cost curves have been omitted in this figure.) *If the monopolist increases its output to q_2*, the market price falls to p_2. Because of this decline in price, the monopolist would not choose to produce the additional output. (In other words, producing q_2 is not profit-maximizing.) If the monopolist could charge p_m to those willing to pay at least p_m for q_m, however, and, *at the same time*, charge p_2 for the additional output, q_2-q_m, to those who would only be willing to purchase this additional output at a price below p_m, it would increase its profits. It would also, of course, produce more than q_m. A monopolist can do this only if it can discriminate among buyers, that is, if it can charge p_m to those purchasing q_m, and then charge p_2 to those purchasing the additional (q_2-q_m).

Necessary Conditions for Price Discrimination

To price discriminate:

1. A firm must have market power. That is, a firm wishing to price discriminate must be able to manipulate the price at which it sells

Figure 16
Price Discrimination

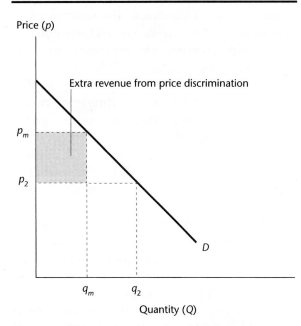

Price discrimination occurs when a firm charges different customers different prices. For example, a firm may charge p_m to the first group of customers and p_2 to the next group. Price discrimination transfers some of the consumer surplus to the producer. It may also provide incentives for a monopoly to increase production to the economically efficient level.

its output by changing the amount it provides to the market.

2. A firm *with market power* must also be able to prevent resale. In this regard, price discrimination is not a simple matter. For example, when the firm illustrated in Figure 16 sells part of its output, q_m, for a higher price, p_m, and part of its output, (q_2-q_m), for a lower price, p_2, it creates the possibility of exchange between the two groups of consumers. That is, those who are willing to pay only p_2 would always be willing to resell the good at some price greater than p_2 while those who paid p_m would always find it attractive to get exactly the same good for some price below p_m. Hence, there is an incentive for those who can buy from the firm at p_2 to resell at some price below p_m to those customers to whom the firm is attempting to charge p_m. If such trades occur, the firm will find that it sells a lot of its out-

put at price p_2 but very little at price p_m. This is hardly what it wants!

Because of these resale possibilities, price discrimination more often occurs in markets for services than it does in markets for goods. In markets for services, what is purchased is consumed almost immediately after purchase. Once it is consumed, it cannot be resold. You can't resell a haircut, for example. Thus, if a barber charges you one price and another customer a different price, the barber's efforts to price-discriminate will not be undercut by one of you reselling your haircut to the other person.

3. A firm *with market power that can prevent resale* must be able to determine which consumers are willing to pay p_m and which are only willing to pay no more than p_2. That is, the firm has to devise a scheme to get consumers to reveal their willingness to pay for its output.

Price Discrimination by Monopolists

Natural monopolies like utility companies often price discriminate. For example, natural gas distribution firms commonly charge one price for the first one-thousand cubic feet of gas that a consumer purchases, a lower price for the next thousand cubic feet purchased, a still lower price for the next thousand cubic feet, and so on. Figure 17 has four different prices plotted for blocks of natural gas: $3.00 per cubic foot up to 1,000 cubic feet, $2.50 per cubic foot for the second thousand cubic feet, $2.00 per cubic foot for the third thousand cubic feet, and $1.50 per cubic foot for usage beyond 3,000 cubic feet.

The plot of these prices looks suspiciously like a demand curve. In a sense, it is. The firm obviously prefers to charge higher prices rather than lower prices, so it must be that the firm is offering lower prices because it's the only way it can induce customers to substitute gas for other commodities and further increase their consumption. The firm could, of course, have induced substitution by charging $1.50 per cubic foot for all gas consumed but it would have lost the revenue illustrated by the shaded area. Hence, the lower price for the last one-thousand cubic feet consumed induces consumers to substitute gas for other resources of energy in more

Figure 17
Declining Block Pricing for Natural Gas

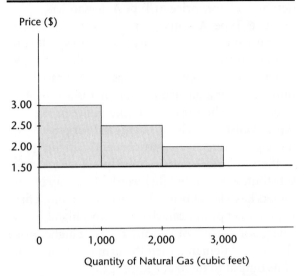

Declining block pricing is an example of price discrimination. In this case, the natural gas company charges $3 per cubic foot for the first 1,000 cubic feet and $2.50 for the next 1,000 cubic feet, and so on. By doing so, the firm gains extra revenues as represented by the shaded area.

marginal uses while the higher price for the first thousand cubic feet consumed takes advantage of consumers' unwillingness to substitute other sources of energy completely for natural gas. Resale is prevented because a customer cannot get the second thousand cubic feet of gas at a lower price without having consumed the first thousand. This kind of arrangement is called **declining block pricing**.

There are a number of other examples of this kind of price discrimination: Electric companies often charge less of the last kilowatt-hour of power used by a single customer than for the first. Similarly, telephone companies almost always charge less for long-distance time beyond the first two or three minutes.[4]

---

[4] Declining block pricing schemes of this sort are good evidence that there is, in fact, an inverse relationship between quantity demanded and the relative price. Otherwise, gas distributors would simply charge $3.00 per cubic foot for all gas consumed. Since they frequently charge a lower price for *additional* consumption by the same consumer, however, the distributors must *believe* that individual demand curve slopes downward, thereby confirming a fundamental insight of microeconomics.

Price Discrimination by Nonmonopolists

Interestingly, price discrimination is not limited to monopolized markets. Indeed, as long as a firm has a little market power, resale can be prevented, and differences between individual customers can easily be ascertained, virtually any firm, however small, can price discriminate. Some examples:

Theaters often charge one price for children under twelve, a different price for students with student-activity cards, a third price for most adults, and a fourth price for adults over sixty-five. Because the higher-priced tickets do not generally guarantee better seats, the theater is essentially selling the same service at different prices to different people. Theater owners must assume that children have a lower willingness to pay (or that parents have a lower willingness to pay for their children than for themselves), that students and senior citizens have a lower willingness to pay than other adults, and that the remaining individuals are the least sensitive to the price of the ticket. (Their demand may be elastic but simply less elastic than that of seniors, students, or children.) Theater owners also price admission differently for those who plan ahead by offering discount coupons that must be purchased before showing up at the theater at a location other than the theater. (Those who just show up at the theater pay a higher price than those who plan ahead and purchase discount coupons.) Resale is generally prevented because the ticket is sold as the person enters the theater. Thus, it is difficult for a ten-year-old to resell his ticket to a thirty-year-old without the theater management noticing. And, frequently, tickets for the different groups are different colors. Again, this allows the theater to easily determine whether a 30-year-old is using a ticket purchased from a 12-year-old.

Airlines engage in a similar form of price discrimination. Most airlines have a complex rate schedule for service between two cities. Children accompanying their parents may pay a "child's price" even though children occupy the same kind of seat as adults. Discounts are often available for people who stay for an extended period of time or who stay over a weekend or who purchase their tickets weeks or months in advance. Business travelers, who often cannot plan very far ahead, stay for shorter periods of time, and want to return home for the weekend, generally pay higher prices than individuals who are able to schedule a trip ahead of time, stay for a longer time, or are willing to stay over a weekend. In this case, airlines must believe that those going for short stays or those who purchase tickets at the last moment are willing to pay the most, and those going for longer stays or those willing to stay over a weekend are willing to pay less. Customers reveal their willingness to pay to the airline by when they purchase tickets and how long or over what days they are willing to stay. Resale is prevented because tickets are checked against picture IDs just before boarding the plane. Thus, for example, a child's ticket cannot be used by an adult nor can a two-week stay be changed to a shorter mid-week trip without having the fares recalculated.

Elasticity of Demand and Price Discrimination

Another way of looking at the differences among individuals that allow a firm to price discriminate is to consider possible differences in elasticities of demand. For example, Figure 18 shows two different kinds of customers for a single firm's output. (To make things simple, we assume that the firm's marginal costs are constant and represent this assumption by a flat marginal cost curve, *MC*.) If a firm with market power adjusts how much it supplies to each group of customers until the marginal

revenue for each group is equal to its marginal cost, the firm will charge a higher price to Type B demanders and a lower price to Type A demanders.

The Type A consumers are generally more responsive to price changes than the Type B consumers are at each price along their respective demand curves. Hence, as long as the firm can determine whether a particular customer is a Type A or Type B and then prevent resale between the two types of customers, it can charge a lower price to the more price-sensitive customers and a higher price to the less-price sensitive customers who cannot substitute as easily. In other words, if a group of customers has a lower price elasticity of demand, a firm with market power can charge them a higher price, whereas if a group of customers have a higher price elasticity of demand, then the firm must offer part of its output to them at a lower price.

Price discrimination in international markets. Differences in elasticity of demand become important in pricing decisions between countries. Frequently, for example, a foreign firm may sell its output at a lower price in the US market than it does in its own domestic market. Doing so is called, pejoratively, **dumping.** It is often argued that a foreign firm that dumps is selling at a price below its costs of production or that its sales in the United States are being subsidized. Either of these may be possible, of course,

Figure 18
Charging a Different Price in Different Markets

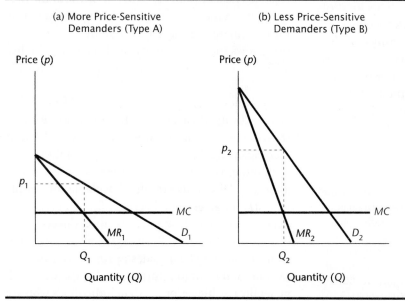

(a) More Price-Sensitive Demanders (Type A)

(b) Less Price-Sensitive Demanders (Type B)

If a firm can separate its customers into two distinct groups (for example, domestic and foreign) where one group is more responsive to price than the other, then the firm can price discriminate successfully. (a) In this market, consumers are more responsive to price; consequently, the firm must charge a lower price. (b) In this market, consumers are less sensitive to price, and thus the firm can charge a higher price.

but the firm could also simply be responding rationally to differences in demand between its own domestic market and the US market. That is, it is more likely to be price discriminating and not selling below cost or at a subsidized price.

If, for example, a Japanese automobile manufacturer has more competition in the US market than it does in the Japanese market, then the demand for its output in the US market is more elastic than the demand for its output in the Japanese market. In this case, Figure 18 provides an explanation of why the firm would rationally price differently in the two markets. Part (a) in this figure represents the demand in the United States, which is more elastic at each price than is demand in Japan, represented by part (b), because there are more substitutes available in the United States for the Japanese firm's output. As a consequence, the price in the United States will be lower than the price in Japan; yet the Japanese producer is neither selling below cost nor being subsidized.

Dumping is almost always considered to be an unfair form of international competition. This is puzzling, however, because dumping Japanese cars, for example, cannot be considered harmful to US consumers who, after all, purchase the same cars that Japanese consumers do, but at a lower price. Despite this, U.S. trade law prohibits dumping. The primary effect of this policy is to raise the price of imported goods in the United States.

It is, of course, possible that the elasticity of demand abroad is less than it is in the domestic market. In this case, a firm would want to charge a higher price for exports than it charges in its domestic market. Pricing in this way is referred to as **reverse dumping**. An interesting example occurred in 1984 and 1985, when luxury automobiles such as BMW and Mercedes-Benz sold for higher prices in the United States than they did in Europe. At one point, a Mercedes cost 40 percent less in Europe than in the United States. (Cost differences like shipping costs can also explain why the price of a commodity abroad is higher than the price of the commodity in the domestic market although it is clear than in the BMW and Mercedes cases, reverse dumping was occurring.)

Is Price Discrimination a Bad Thing?

Price discrimination is clear evidence of at least some market power. Presumably because it is evidence of some market power, certain forms of price discrimination have been condemned by U.S. anti-trust laws (see Chapter 14). Making price discrimination illegal is a mistake, however. The monopoly inefficiency, remember, is that too little is provided to the market. But a firm that can price discriminate generally produces *more* than it would otherwise.

▶ Summary

Market power. A firm has market power if it can affect the market price by changing the amount that it produces. A firm that is large relative to the market for what it produces, in general, has market power. If a firm has market power, its marginal revenue is less than the price at which it can sell its output.

Monopoly. If the output to a market is provided by a single firm, that firm is a monopoly. A monopoly has market power. When a monopolist adjusts its production to maximize profits, the price at which it can sell its output is greater than its marginal cost. A monopolist produces less than a group of competitive firms would produce when confronting exactly the same market demand. It follows that the price in a monopolized market is higher than the competitive price would be.

The inefficiency of a monopolized market. The important difference between a competitive market and a monopoly market is that marginal revenue for a monopolist is *less* than the market price whereas for a competitive firm, the marginal revenue is equal to the market price. This means that at the monopoly market price, the consumer's willingness to pay for additional output is greater than the marginal cost to society of providing the commodity. This is a market failure in the sense that the monopoly outcome is inefficient. A monopolist produces too little relative to the efficient competitive market outcome and, as a consequence, charges too high a price. That is, a monopoly imposes a deadweight burden on society.

Barriers to entry. Market forces tend to undermine a monopoly. In particular, entry in response to monopoly profits reduces a monopoly's market power. This means that a monopoly can persist for a long time only if there is some barrier to the entry of new firms. A barrier to entry is a condition that prevents new firms from entering a market in response to the economic profits that existing firms are making. Barriers to entry include economies of scale, limited ownership of natural resources, and legal restrictions limiting competition and entry. In addition, a monopolist can make entry less attractive for potential rivals by limit pricing, predatory pricing, and making organizational choices that may raise the cost of entry by rival firms.

Cartels and mergers. The profits to be gained from monopoly pricing are an incentive for otherwise competitive firms to collude, thus creating a cartel or, when possible, to merge into a single firm. Market forces tend to undermine cartels. In particular, the higher prices following an effective cartel's restrictions on output provide substantially higher profits for any firm that cheats on the cartel agreement, refuses to enter the cartel agreement, or enters the market after the creation of the cartel but stays outside the cartel. As a consequence, cartels are unstable—they can persist only if they can effectively prevent cheating or entry. Often this means that long-lived cartels are either organized or policed by a government.

Price discrimination. Price discrimination occurs when a firm charges different customers different prices for the same commodity, or charges the same customer different prices for the same commodity as his or her consumption increases. In order to price discriminate, a firm must (1) have market power, (2) be able to prevent resale between customers, and (3) be able to easily determine who is willing to pay a higher price for a commodity and who is not. Price discrimination is evidence of market power, but it is not evidence of monopoly. Even though monopolies frequently price-discriminate, price discrimination is pervasive and provides interesting evidence that firms with even a little market power base their pricing policies on the assumption that quantity demanded is inversely related to price. With price discrimination, the output of a firm with market power generally increases, thereby moving toward the firm's output toward that which would be provided in a perfectly competitive market. In this important sense, price discrimination may partially offset the market failure that would otherwise occur because of market power.

Chapter 14 ▶ ▶
Market Power and Public Policy

A monopoly or cartel that is able to exploit its market power imposes a deadweight loss on the economy. In terms of the efficient use of scarce resources, too little is produced. This means that any policy response to less-than-competitive market outcomes must, in one way or another, increase the output supplied in the affected market. Given this broad policy guideline, what might be done? There are four general policy responses:

1. A government can rely primarily on market pressures to undermine monopolies or collusive behavior among a group of firms.

2. A government can penalize firms that collude or whose behavior leads to or exploits market power.

3. A government can regulate the pricing and production decisions of firms with market power.

4. A government can undertake the activities of a monopolist as a public rather than a private firm.

▶ Substitution and Entry

Markets tend to undermine market power through substitution by demanders and entry by new firms.

Substitution

Monopoly prices encourage substitution, which in turn, limits market power. This substitution effect becomes more important with the passage of time (due to the Second Law of Demand). That is, over time as more and more substitutes are found, the demand for a firm or group of firms exploiting its market power becomes increasingly sensitive to price. As demand becomes more elastic, the allocative inefficiency becomes smaller—the monopoly price moves toward the competitive price and output increases. This effect is illustrated in Figure 1. This effect is likely to be modest, however, and will likely not completely undermine a monopolist.

Even so, substitution is an important constraint on the exercise of market power. For example, a single supplier of natural gas considering an increase in its price must be concerned about consumers moving to alternative sources of energy, such as electricity, fuel oil, coal, propane, wood, or solar power. The more the supplier of natural gas tries to exploit its apparent monopoly position by increasing the market price, the greater will be the incentive for consumers to look for substitutes for natural gas. Over the long term, substitution becomes easier. In the end, even though consumers are unlikely to find perfect substitutes and a single supplier of natural gas is likely to continue to have market power, its market power will be limited to some degree.

A government can indirectly attack the inefficiency that results from market power by implementing fewer policies that limit substitution or make it more difficult to substitute. For example, a tax on steel, but not on aluminum, may increase the market power of the few aluminum producers in

Figure 1
The Effect of an Increase in the Elasticity of Demand on Monopoly Price

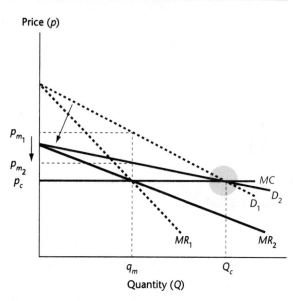

When the elasticity of demand increases (D_2 is more elastic than D_1 at points within the circle), the difference between the monopoly price and the competitive price decreases. (Here, p_m is the monopoly price; p_c is the competitive price; and, to simplify matters, marginal cost, MC, is assumed to be contrast.)

the United States because the tax makes alternatives to aluminum more costly. Similarly, legal rules that limit the substitution of steel for aluminum in, for example, making automobiles would have the same effect.

Entry

Monopoly profits stimulate entry. Entry tends to undermine a monopoly or cartel, or force changes in strategies pursued by firms in markets where tacit collusion might be important. Entering firms do not necessarily have to produce precisely the same good as the firm or group of firms trying to exploit its collective market power. Producing close substitutes, where possible, is almost equivalent to entering a monopolized market. For example, McDonald's might have had market power, but Wendy's and Burger King produce very close substitutes for a McDonald's hamburger. Other fast foods, from tacos to pizzas, are almost as good, or perhaps better, substitutes. In the end, whatever market power McDonald's may have once had has disappeared

with the myriad of rivals who have entered the fast food market.

The possibilities of entry mean that a monopoly like the Postal Service must be concerned about new firms in the message delivery market who offer overnight mail and messenger services. Particularly intense competition has come with the recent development of fax machines, which transmit letters and documents over telephone wires, and, of course email, which transmits messages without a $.37 stamp. Telephones, fax machines, overnight mail, messenger services and email are not quite the same as mail service; but they all substitute for mail service and represent entry into the message-delivery market.

Consequently, a government can indirectly attack the inefficiency associated with market power by eliminating legal restrictions that limit or bar entry. Eliminating such restrictions allows market forces to undermine any market power and associated monopoly-like behavior of firms that had been protected from competition. Deregulating long-distance telephone service, for example, stimulated entry by a large number of new firms. You can now purchase your long-distance service from MCI, AT&T, Sprint, or any of a number of other companies. Whereas AT&T was once viewed as having a near-monopoly in long-distance telephone communication, today no one seriously argues that it has a monopoly. Similarly, deregulation of airfares and lifting legal limitations on entry by new airlines in the late 1970s led to both vigorous price competition and entry. Before 1979, the U.S. government had supported a legal cartel among the airlines and fares were high. When it no longer limited entry or in other ways aided the cartel, fares fell dramatically.[1]

▶ Antitrust Policy

Entry and substitution take time. Likewise, cheating on an agreement to fix production or prices may not immediately undermine a cartel. As a consequence, in some industries market pressures may take a long time to undermine monopoly power or

---

[1] The U.S. government, having supported a legal cartel in trucking and railroads for nearly a century, deregulated both beginning in the late 1970s with similar effects on the costs of shipping.

collusion. In the meantime, the inefficiencies associated with monopoly-like behavior persist. For this reason, and also because of its general concern with bigness, the U.S. government has responded with legal policies for dealing with firms that attempt to create or exploit market power:

1. Explicit collusion is illegal. The U.S. government can, as a consequence, impose substantial penalties on firms that explicitly agree to coordinate production or pricing decisions.

2. The U.S. government has the legal authority to challenge and limit mergers. This means that mergers that might create a monopoly or a market structure dominated by a few large firms can be blocked.

3. The U.S. government has the legal power to break up a firm that has been shown to have monopolized a market. If successful, these efforts can increase competition by creating rivals where there were very few or none.

4. There are legal rules prohibiting certain kinds of behavior by firms that might make entry by potential competitors difficult.

This collection of legal rules, their interpretation by courts, and the government enforcement efforts at federal and state levels are called **antitrust policy**.

Per Se and Rule-of-Reason Approaches

Antitrust policies make economic sense only if they move the economy toward a more efficient use of scarce resources, that is, toward the competitive market outcome (where the level of output is such that market price equals marginal cost). Sensible antitrust policies, therefore, must provide incentives for the output provided to a market to increase, not decrease.

When a firm or group of firms can take an *unambiguously* harmful action—that is, under any circumstances, the market price would increase and the amount provided to the market would decrease—then simply prohibiting the action makes good economic sense. Legal rules that simply prohibit an activity as described in a law or court decision are referred to as *per se* **rules**. More particularly, in a *per se* **approach** to antitrust policy, legality or illegality is determined by a general rule, not by par-

ticular circumstances—the court or enforcement agency simply looks to the action itself, not to its consequences.

Unfortunately for antitrust policy-makers, actions that firms might take cannot always be cleanly divided into those that lead to efficiency and those that undermine efficiency. Frequently, an action could harm economic efficiency, *but at the same time*, it could also promote efficiency. For example, consider the problem for antitrust policy posed in Figure 2.

If the industry is initially competitive, the equilibrium market price is p^* with corresponding output Q^*. At this output, the market price is equal to marginal cost for each firm. Suppose that if all firms in the industry merged, production costs for the new firm would be substantially lower because of scale economies, say, MC_m. The merger would

Figure 2
When a Monopoly Has Lower Costs

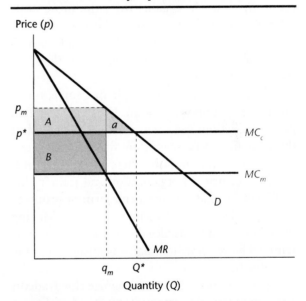

If the firms in a competitive market have marginal costs MC_c, they can produce Q^* at price p^*. By merging to form a single firm, they can lower costs to MC_m. However, the single firm resulting from the merger has market power and will produce only q_m and charge p_m. Although output falls because the monopoly exploits its market power, there is a net social gain in consumer and producer surplus from the merger. Consumers lose $A + a$ in consumer surplus, but A is transferred to the firm, not lost to society. In addition, there is a gain of area B in producer surplus because the monopolist has lower costs. Thus, the net effect is $B - a$. Clearly, if the cost differences are large, B is greater than a, resulting in a net social gain.

create a firm with market power. (Remember that market power is the ability to profitably restrict output.) Because of its market power, the newly formed monopolist would choose output q_m and price p_m.

The merger makes consumers worse off because consumer surplus falls by $(A + a)$ in Figure 2. The amount A is transferred from consumers to the monopolist (in the form of higher prices), who sees it as part of its profit. The amount a, however, is a deadweight loss to the economy. That is, the loss of a to consumers is not offset by a gain to the monopolist, or anyone else. There is, however, a gain in producer surplus of B (in the form of lower costs), which the monopolist also sees as profit. (The monopolist's profits are equal to $B + A$ because, if marginal cost is constant, marginal cost equals average cost.) The gain results from the reduction in production costs. Production costs fall because the monopoly takes advantage of scale economies and, as a consequence, uses fewer scarce resources. The economy as a whole gains from the more cost-effective use of scarce resources. Because area B is larger than area a in this particular example, *there is a net social gain from the merger, even though a monopoly is created.*

This is an extreme example of course, but it illustrates an important point. Namely, that often particular actions can create market power, and, at the same time, a more efficient firm. This suggests that in some circumstances there will be a tradeoff of the efficiencies of organization and scale for the inefficiencies that follow when a firm or group of firms is able to exploit its market power. Making these kinds of actions illegal only makes economic sense when the potential harm is greater than the potential benefit.

Antitrust policies that recognize this tradeoff between potential harms and potential benefits are referred to as **rule-of-reason approaches**. In a rule-of-reason approach, the question of the legality of an action as described in a legal rule or court decision is determined by weighing the potential harm against the potential benefit. It is not based solely on the action itself. Put simply, legality is determined by particular circumstances, not by a general rule and the court or enforcement agency looks at the consequences of an action, not just at the action itself.

The Sherman, Clayton, and FTC Acts

Table 1 provides a brief overview of the important provisions in the major antitrust laws for the United States. The first of these laws, the Sherman Antitrust Act, was enacted in 1890 in response to concern about the growth in the size of firms in the latter part of the nineteenth century. One firm in particular, Standard Oil, caught the attention of the government. By 1879 Standard Oil and its subsidiaries produced 90 percent of the refined oil in the United States and controlled 100 percent of the nation's pipeline capacity. In 1882 the Standard Oil Trust was formed, which concentrated the decision-making power of the firm and its subsidiaries in the hands of nine persons. The trustees proceeded to shut down more than half of Standard Oil's plants, cut output, and raise prices. The Sherman Antitrust Act followed.

Section 1 of the Sherman Act prohibits "every contract, combination in the form of trust or otherwise, or conspiracy, in restraint of trade." Section 2 makes it illegal for any person or entity to "monopolize, or attempt to monopolize, or combine or conspire with any other person or persons, to monopolize." Although the language of the Sherman Act is strong, it is also vague. Therefore, the meaning of the law has developed only as the government or private entities have pursued anti-trust actions against particular firms in the courts, particularly in the Supreme Court.

The second major antitrust law, the Clayton Antitrust Act, was enacted in 1914 in response to concerns about Supreme Court interpretations of the Sherman Act. The Clayton Act was intended to strike at potentially anti-competitive practices in their incipiency. As a consequence, the Clayton Act identifies certain practices as illegal where, in the words of the act, "the effect . . . may be substantially to lessen competition." The Clayton Act limits price discrimination, exclusive dealing and tying contracts, and acquiring stock in a competing company. In addition, the Clayton Act specifically exempts labor unions and collective bargaining agreements from the provisions of the antitrust laws.

While the Clayton Act made it illegal to take control of another firm by purchasing its stock, it did not prohibit obtaining control of a firm by purchasing its physical capital and other tangible assets.

Table 1
The Basis of U.S. Antitrust Law

Act	Year enacted	Key points
Sherman Antitrust Act	1890	*Section 1.* Every contract, combination in the form of trust or otherwise, or conspiracy, in restraint of trade or commerce among the several States, or with foreign nations, is declared to be illegal. *Section 2.* Every person who shall monopolize, or attempt to monopolize, or combine or conspire with any other person or persons, to monopolize any part of the trade or commerce among the several States, or with foreign nations, shall be deemed guilty of a felony.
Clayton Antitrust Act	1914	*Section 2.* (as amended by the Robinson–Patman Act, 1948). It shall be unlawful . . . to discriminate in price between different purchasers of commodities of like grade and quality . . . where the effect of such discrimination may be substantially to lessen competition or tend to create a monopoly in any line of commerce . . . nothing herein contained shall prevent differentials which make only due allowances for differentials in the cost.
		Section 3. It shall be unlawful . . . on the condition, agreement, or understanding that the lessee or purchaser thereof shall not use or deal in the . . . commodities of a competitor . . . where the effect . . . may be to substantially lessen competition or tend to create a monopoly in any line of commerce.
		Section 4. Any person . . . injured in his business or property by reason of anything forbidden in the antitrust laws may sue . . . and shall recover threefold the damages by him sustained, and the cost of the suit, including reasonable attorney's fee.
		Section 7. (as amended by the Celler–Kefauver Act, 1950). No (firm) . . . shall acquire . . . the whole or any part . . . of another (firm) . . . where . . . the effect of such acquisition may be substantially to lessen competition, or to tend to create a monopoly.
Federal Trade Commission Act	1914	*Section 5.* Unfair methods of competition . . . and unfair or deceptive acts or practices . . . are declared unlawful.

In 1950 this loophole was closed by the Celler-Kefauver Act, which applied the Clayton Act's provisions for stock purchases to tangible asset purchases.

The Federal Trade Commission Act, enacted in the same year as the Clayton Act, prohibits "unfair methods of competition" as well as "deceptive acts or practices in or affecting commerce." In addition, the act created an enforcement agency, the Federal Trade Commission (FTC). (The Antitrust Division of the Department of Justice, established in 1907, also has enforcement powers for the government in antitrust matters.)

The courts, particularly the Supreme Court, have had an enormous influence on the development of antitrust policy. In 1911 the Supreme Court, relying on the Sherman Antitrust Act, forced Standard Oil and the American Tobacco Company to divest themselves of a large share of their holdings in other companies. In doing so, however, the Court announced that only *unreasonable* combinations in restraint would be held in violation of antitrust law. This narrow interpretation of the Sherman Act meant that in 1920, U.S. Steel was found not to have violated antitrust laws. Even though the court found that U.S. Steel had intended to monopolize the steel industry, it also found that U. S. Steel hadn't succeeded in achieving a monopoly despite its best efforts. Because it had tried but failed, in the view of the court it had not violated the antitrust laws.

Antitrust policy changed substantially when the Supreme Court developed and announced a *per se* rule against price fixing in a series of legal cases, beginning in 1927 with *United States v. Trenton Potteries* and ending in 1940 with *United States v. Socony-Vacuum Oil Co.* The Court's *per se* approach to price fixing meant that when a combination of firms attempted to fix prices, a test of reasonableness would not be applied. The action itself was illegal, whatever its consequences.

Moreover, in 1945, in *Aluminum Company of America*, the Court reversed its U.S. Steel finding and found Alcoa to be an illegal monopoly, even though it had not engaged in unreasonable behavior. That is, the court's ruling implied that, beyond a certain point, controlling an overwhelming share of a market alone would be an offense if the firm had not done everything possible to avoid obtaining its substantial market share. Although the Court has partially retreated from this position since then, it has not moved back to its earlier position in *U.S. Steel*.

Price fixing is *per se* illegal, but not all agreements among competitors have been ruled illegal by the Supreme Court. In particular, the Court has recognized that in some circumstances, cooperative agreements among firms may enhance, rather than undermine, competition. In *Broadcast Music, Inc. v. Columbia Broadcasting System* (1979), the court ruled that organizations that bring together music copyright holders and collect revenues on their behalf are necessary in order to lower the transaction costs of purchasing the rights to perform a particular composition. The court ruled: "A bulk license of some type is a necessary consequence of the integration to achieve these efficiencies . . ." In *NCAA v. University of Oklahoma* (1984), the court again recognized that cooperation among competitors is required to produce some products. Therefore, the Court ruled that restrictions among competitors that are tied to such cooperation must be considered under a rule-of-reason approach—they are not *per se* illegal. Applying a rule of reason approach in the *NCAA* case, however, the court found that the *NCAA*'s restrictions on television contracts between colleges and TV networks or local stations were not necessary for the successful production of *NCAA* football. That is, the NCAA was violating the antitrust laws. More recently, the government has implicitly allowed agreements between US computer companies and high tech ventures that enhance the worldwide competitiveness of the US computer industry, even though a few years ago, these actions would have been deemed a serious challenge to antitrust policy.

In a series of cases heard in the 1950s, the Court allowed the government to challenge mergers among large firms. The Court's implicit assumption appeared to be that mergers among large firms are not an appropriate way to achieve economies of scale. It went beyond this rationale in *Von's Grocery* (1965), however, when the merger of two supermarkets in California was ruled illegal, even though the merged firm would have had only a 7.5 percent share of the Los Angeles market. Similarly, a merger between the Brown Shoe Company and the Kinney retail store chain was found to be illegal, even though Kinney's share of the national shoe market was less than 2 percent and it bought only 8 percent of its shoes from Brown. More recently, the government has challenged fewer mergers and the Court has had less say in merger activity. In the 1980s, in particular, the Reagan administration was willing to tolerate mergers of large firms that would almost certainly have been challenged by the government in earlier decades. Since then, there has been more scrutiny of mergers by the FTC and DOJ (Microsoft was not permitted to purchase Quicken, for example), but both agencies have been willing to consider the role that efficiencies play and, importantly, the competition that comes from international trade. (A merger of Boeing and McDonald Douglas was permitted even though it resulted in only one U.S. firm producing commercial jet aircraft—competition with Airbus was considered to be enough to limit Boeing's market power.)

Does the antitrust policy determined by these court cases make economic sense? Consider the following arguments about market outcomes under various conditions.

Price Fixing

Price fixing among otherwise competitive firms is almost always unambiguously harmful. An agreement among rivals to fix prices cannot enhance efficiency because no cost-saving integration among the firms occurs when members of the cartel coordinate only their pricing or production decisions. That is, because a cartel is not a single firm, it cannot take advantage of possible organizational or scale economies. As illustrated in Figure 2, because a group of firms by forming a cartel cannot lower the costs from MC_c to MC_m, the cartel imposes a deadweight loss of *a* on the economy and transfers *A* from consumers to producers *without any compensating gain in producer surplus*.

Based on the distinction between *per se* and rule-of-reason approaches to antitrust policy suggested earlier, actions taken to form cartels should be *per se* illegal. They are, at least in the United States. Put simply, private agreements among competing firms to restrict production cannot be enforced by legal means. When discovered, agreements of this sort carry heavy legal penalties, including jail terms for the responsible corporate officers. Courts do not ask whether price fixing is potentially beneficial or successful, just whether an attempt to fix prices occurred. More precisely, because firms that compete in the same market are related horizontally, **horizontal price-fixing** is *per se* illegal under U.S. antitrust law.

A *per se* rule against price fixing makes it difficult for otherwise competitive firms to publicly negotiate and enforce collusive agreements. As a consequence, any collusive agreements among rivals must be made and enforced in secret. Secret agreements are both more difficult to monitor and to enforce against cheaters. Hence, a *per se* rule against horizontal price-fixing reinforces the market pressures that make cartels unstable and short-lived. Moreover, since 1940, these laws have been imposed whether or not the effort to set prices succeeds. Merely the *attempt* to fix prices is a violation of the antitrust laws. There is little question that these laws successfully reduced *overt* price-fixing efforts. Trusts and formal cartels are virtually nonexistent in the United States, whereas they continue to flourish in economies that do not prohibit explicit price-fixing or explicit collusion of other sorts. The antitrust enforcement agencies continue to uncover and, through the courts, penalize secret efforts to fix prices, however. This has led some to conclude that Adam Smith was correct. Business people rarely get together, even in 2006, but they are tempted to conspire to set prices.

Curiously, at times, the government has pursued other policies that conflict with its antitrust policies that make it easier for firms to enforce collusive agreements. For example, bidding procedures on government contracts have probably helped cartels to enforce price-fixing agreements. Specifically, a common practice of keeping all bids secret helps to stabilize a cartel among bidders because cheating by one firm is less obvious to the others. Government policies that restrict entry by new firms also make it easier for cartels to enforce secret price-fixing agreements because cartel members do not need to worry about new firms stealing their business as they fix the market price at a higher-than-

competitive level. In the agricultural area, the government actually facilitates price fixing by allowing producers to use marketing orders to collectively limit the amount of certain kinds of fruits and nuts, for example, which can come to the market. International trade policies that limit imports also limit a kind of entry and competition by foreign suppliers that would, with free trade, undermine market power within the United States and make it more difficult for US firms to collude.

Merger

Forming a cartel is unambiguously harmful because it creates market power, and hence raises prices, without having the potential to create the organizational or scale economies that might lead to lower prices. Coordinating production or pricing decisions among otherwise competitive firms is not the only way of achieving market power, however. Several otherwise rival firms can achieve market power through a merger. Obviously, if two rival firms merge, their pricing and production decisions will be coordinated. In addition, however, their activities will also be integrated because they then form a single firm that may be able to take advantage of organizational or scale economies.

Because of the potential for economic harm from these actions, the U.S. antitrust laws give the government the power to control mergers. Because there are potential benefits as well as potential harms, however, horizontal mergers are considered under a rule-of-reason approach.

Merger to monopoly. When it became clear that trusts would become illegal after the Sherman Antitrust Act was passed in 1890, almost all of the competing firms in several markets where there were trusts merged! For example, the merger of nearly one thousand separate steel producers created the U.S. Steel Corporation, which then dominated the market. By 1904, however, the antitrust laws were also being used successfully to prevent mergers of this sort. As a consequence, it is now simply impossible for all, or even for a large fraction, of the firms in a market to merge and thus avoid the problems of forming and policing a cartel. Hence, both explicit price-fixing and merger-to-monopoly by competing firms have been successfully thwarted by antitrust laws.

Merger to something less than a monopoly. The problem for antitrust policy is that even though it is easy to prevent a merger of all or most of the firms in an industry, frowning on mergers that do not create monopolies only makes sense if scale economies are not possible. If scale economies are possible, however, such mergers may lower production costs because the post-merger firm is larger and, therefore, has lower costs. In this case, a merger that lowers production costs may lead to lower market prices and more output provided to the market. Put simply, a merger among rivals may enhance, rather than undermine, competition.

On the other hand, a merger among rivals *always* decreases the number of firms within a market. Therefore, a merger *always* makes it possible to create a firm with market power or a market structure where tacit collusion among rivals is more likely. Whether or not the larger firm has lower production costs, inefficiencies may develop if the new firm or group of firms in the merger-changed market takes advantage of its market power, thus reducing the output provided to the market and increasing market prices.

In Figure 3, for example, each of two firms produces q_1 at a cost of ATC_1. A merger of the two firms could take advantage of the decreasing cost technology by producing q_2 at a lower cost of ATC_2 ($q_2 = 2 \times q_1$). The danger, of course, is that a firm of this size might have market power and, exploiting its newly created market power, might increase the price.[2] This possibility was illustrated in Figure 2. Or, the merger might create a market structure where collusion among rivals is more likely, even if no single firm has much market power after the merger.[3]

Thus, it is not clear whether prices will go up or down following the merger, although even if prices increase, a net social gain may occur for the reasons noted in our discussion of Figure 2. Clearly, if efficiency matters, we would want a court or other enforcement agency to balance the potential for social gains (either because of lower prices or lower costs due to scale economies) with the potential for higher prices and less output (because of market power or the market structure that the merger created).

---

[2] In antitrust practice, this is called the **unilateral effects** problem.
[3] This is called the **coordinated effects** problem.

Figure 3
The Effect of a Merger

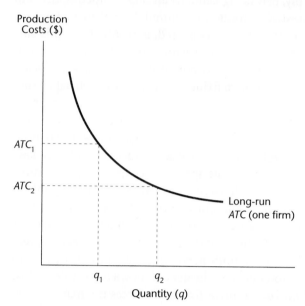

In an industry with decreasing long-run average costs, if two firms each produce q_1, they do so at a higher cost than if one firm produces q_2. In this case, a merger may be warranted because it would reduce production costs. However, because the firm after the merger would be large and there would be fewer firms in the industry, allowing the merger might create a firm with market power or a market structure where tacit collusion is more likely.

On the other hand, where scale economies are possible, firms will grow *without merging* because larger firms have lower costs than smaller firms. Thus, a strict anti-merger policy does not necessarily mean that firms will not be able to take full advantage of scale economies. Indeed, internal growth has an advantage over growth-through-merger because scale economies are actually realized—they are not merely hypothetical possibilities. Larger firms do not necessarily have lower costs than smaller firms, of course. Because scale economies are sometimes difficult to predict ahead of time, firms will almost always claim that costs will fall after the merger in order to justify a merger whose real purpose is securing market power or facilitating collusion. Moreover, internal growth does not necessarily lead to increased concentration, whereas a merger always changes the market structure. That is, there are always fewer firms after the merger than there were prior to it. Whether internal growth leads to greater concentration, however, depends upon whether the quantity demanded increases faster than the optimal firm size. If it does, the market ends up with a larger number of larger firms, each with a smaller fraction of the market.

A merger, then, is not the only way that firms can adopt more efficient technologies or expand to the efficient size. Unless growth within a firm takes a good deal longer than a merger between smaller firms, it may make sense for antitrust policies to be skeptical of mergers. And in fact, current application of the US antitrust laws appears to be somewhat biased toward relying on internal firm growth as a way of adopting more efficient technologies if any exist, and away from mergers as a possible method of obtaining a more efficient-sized firm. Although the U.S. Department of Justice can challenge any mergers that it wishes, it frowns upon mergers between two or more large firms but it has a much more liberal policy for mergers among several smaller firms or among moderately large and small firms.

Merger policy and market structure. Traditionally, merger policy has focused on the possibilities of creating a firm with market power or enhancing the market power already held by a firm. Equally serious, however, is the possibility of creating a **market structure** that facilitates tacit or explicit collusion among firms, each of which has limited market power. To see why, suppose that a market has 40 firms of equal size and that everyone agrees that the market is essentially competitive. If 10 of the firms wish to merge into a single firm, 30 smaller firms would still be competing with the larger firm, so the market would probably remain competitive. Now, if an additional 10 merge, there would be 20 smaller firms and two larger firms. Perhaps the market would remain competitive because it would still be difficult for the 22 firms to collude. Should we be concerned about a third merger among another 10 small firms? Tough question. Tacit collusion is more likely among 13 firms, three of which are large, than among 22 or 40 firms. Even if we aren't concerned about this merger, we certainly ought to be concerned if the last 10 firms merge, because then there would be only four firms, and collusion would become a distinct possibility.

In each case, 10 small firms merge. Whether a potential problem is created depends less on the size of these firms than on the structure of the market *at the time of the proposed merger*. It follows that sensible merger policy ought to be concerned with mergers that create market structures where collusion is more likely, as well as with mergers that create large firms.

The Herfindahl-Hirschman Index and the Department of Justice/Federal Trade Commission Guidelines. Firms need to know whether the government will challenge possible mergers. In response to this need, the Department of Justice (DOJ) and Federal Trade Commission (FTC) issue merger guidelines from time to time.

The most recent guidelines, issued in 1994, detail when the DOJ/FTC will oppose a merger in the courts under Section 7 of the Clayton Act or under power granted to the FTC under the Federal Trade Commission Act. For the reasons just discussed, the guidelines are based on a market's structure both before and after the proposed merger. To determine the market structure, the boundaries of the market itself must first be defined, then market share must be determined, and finally, effects of the merger on the market structure evaluated.

The merger guidelines outline methods for determining a **relevant market** and **market share**, as well as the effects of the merger on the **market structure**. The relevant market is defined, in part, by the probable responses of consumers and existing and potential producers to "small but significant" price changes. Market structure is determined by the **Herfindahl-Hirschman index (HHI)**. The effects on the market structure due to a merger are determined by a comparison of pre- and post-merger HHI values.

Determining the **relevant market** is difficult. Although McDonald's has a 100 percent share of the market of McDonald's hamburgers, it has a much lower share of the "market for hamburgers." It has an even lower share of the "market for fast food" and a trivial share of the "market for food." Similarly, a particular McDonald's outlet has a 100 percent share of the "market" for McDonald's hamburgers in its own immediate locality. It has a lower share of the "market" for hamburgers in a town or city, an even lower share of the "market" for hamburgers in a state or region, and a trivial share of the "market" for hamburgers nationwide. Of course, a hamburger place in New York City doesn't really compete with one sold in Logan, Utah, but a hamburger place in one part of Logan competes with hamburger places elsewhere in Logan, as well as in the surrounding communities. And for some commodities such as brokerage services, a firm in New York does compete with one in Logan.

The point is, of course, that there is no single, obvious way to define a **relevant market**. Should it be defined geographically? Should it be defined in terms of a particular product? How much substitution among sellers spread geographically is to be considered enough? Similarly, how much substitution among products that differ somewhat, but not a lot, is to be considered enough? These questions occur because consumers, not firms or the government, define markets by what they choose to consume and how they substitute. The DOJ/FTC Merger Guidelines attempt to get at consumer substitution by asking whether a price increase for a particular product or group of very similar products that would increase profits for the suppliers can be sustained over time.[4] If it can, the DOJ or FTC assumes that it makes sense to speak of "a market" for this product(s). If it cannot, the DOJ or FTC assumes that there is not a separate market for the product(s).

Once the relevant market has been determined, calculating market share and the pre- and post-merger effects on the market structure using the HHI is straightforward. The HHI is the sum of the square of each firm's market share,

$$HHI = \text{sum over n firms of } (x_i/T)^2$$

where x_i is the absolute size of the ith individual firm, T is the size of the market, and there are n firms in the relevant antitrust market. Put differently,

$$HHI = \text{sum over n firms of } (s_i)^2$$

Where s_i is a firm's share of the total market sales.

This index seeks to measure market concentration in a way that accounts for both the absolute level of concentration and the degree to which larger firms dominate the market. For example, suppose that there are four firms in a market with total sales of $1,000 per week—the largest firm has sales of $500 per week; the second largest firm, $350 per week; the third, $100 per week and the fourth, $50 per week. Shares are calculated by dividing each firm's sales by the total sales in the market. Thus, for example, the share of the largest firm is

$$\$500|\$1000 = .50$$

The HHI for the industry with four firms, where each firm's market share is calculated similarly, is

$$0.50^2 + 0.35^2 + 0.10^2 + 0.05^2 = 0.3850$$

By convention, this number is multiplied by 10,000 and the HHI is said to be 3,850 in this case. Table 2 summarizes the DOJ/FTC guidelines for when either would challenge a merger.

Using these guidelines (first issued in 1984), the Federal Trade Commission challenged proposed mergers between Coca-Cola and Dr. Pepper and between Pepsi-Cola and Seven-Up in 1986. Microsoft's proposed acquisition of Quicken was challenged. Later the merger between OfficeMax and Staples was also challenged. Dozens of less-well-known mergers have been similarly challenged by either the DOJ or the FTC. In fact, the use of the DOJ/FTC merger guidelines now dominates the federal government's policies toward mergers.

Bigness

While antitrust policy appears to tilt slightly toward internal growth rather than merger to achieve scale efficiencies, growth may also create problems

---

[4] Essentially, in the DOJ/FTC approach a "market" is a product or group of products that could be successfully monopolized, that is, that if there was a single supplier of the product(s), it would increase the product's price by a non-trivial amount.

Table 2
Department of Justice Merger Guidelines

Post-merger value of the Herfindahl index	Department of Justice's reaction
< 1,000	Will not challenge merger
1,000–1,800	Will challenge merger that increases the Herfindahl index by at least 100 points
> 1,800	Will challenge merger that increases the Herfindahl index by at least 50 points

because a larger firm may develop market power if demand does not grow as rapidly as does the largest firm supplying the market. With the possible exception of the *Alcoa* decision, US antitrust laws have never made bigness *per se* illegal. Under current law, in fact, *it is not illegal for a firm to be a monopoly.* Likewise, *having market power is not illegal.* Taking advantage of a monopoly position or market power in certain specific ways—what the law calls "monopolization"—is illegal, however.

One of the most controversial areas of antitrust policy is the use of the Sherman and Clayton Acts to split firms that become too large and engage in activities that are judged to be monopolization, into smaller, possibly competing, firms. Standard Oil was split into several smaller firms in the early 1900s, for example. At about the same time, the American Tobacco Company was deemed too large and behaving "badly." It was also divided into smaller, presumable competing firms. In the early 1980s, the DOJ forced the break-up of American Telephone and Telegraph into a group of smaller local-service telephone companies and a single long-distance carrier. More recently, the DOJ pursued antitrust actions against Microsoft and when a federal judge found that Microsoft had "monopolized" the operating systems for PCs market, the government asked the court to force Microsoft to be split into smaller, competing firms. (The government later retreated from this drastic remedy.) A firm doesn't have to be large in some absolute sense to attract antitrust scrutiny. In 2002, for example, the FTC successfully forced the MSC Corporation, a supplier of specialized engineering software to essentially create competing firms because, the FTC claimed, MSC was large relative to the market where it had competed and had behaved "badly."

Dividing a large firm into smaller firms may make sense if there are no scale or organizational economies, but such action *imposes costs* on society if scale or organizational economies are important. That is, when there are *no* scale economies, smaller firms have the same minimum average costs as larger firms. If smaller firms have less efficient ways of organizing and using resources, however, costs (and perhaps prices) *increase* rather than decrease when a larger firm is split. On the other hand, if a large firm did not come to its position because of scale economies, splitting it into smaller firms will foster competition and reduce prices. This need for

balancing the possible costs and benefits suggests that a rule-of-reason approach would be appropriate. Generally, this is the approach that is used in monopolization cases.

Tacit Collusion

Whenever each of a small number of firms has some market power, there are possibilities of tacit collusion. That is, of the firms coordinating their actions without actually directly talking about doing so. The problem for antitrust policy is that market concentration is not evidence *in and of itself* that each of a small number of firms has market power or that tacit collusion among these firms is likely to occur. As a consequence, whether tacit collusion occurs in any particular market is an extraordinarily difficult question to determine. Moreover, if tacit collusion does occur, it may be difficult to find legal ways to force the firms in a market to behave in ways that may not be individually rational or profit-maximizing.

Even though the threshold in concentration beyond which tacit collusion is likely to occur is extraordinarily difficult to determine, it becomes less likely when markets are less concentrated. This suggests two possible antitrust-policy responses to the possibility of tacit collusion:

> First, the government could pursue a policy to prevent mergers that would make the market substantially more concentrated. This is the policy that has been pursued by the U.S. government for a number of years.
>
> Second, the government could pursue a policy of breaking up large firms—even though they may not have much individual market power—to reduce concentration and, thus, the likelihood of tacit collusion. This is not currently U.S. government policy.

Monopolistic Behavior

Our discussion to this point has considered possible legal remedies for actions—coordinating pricing decisions, merging, tacitly colluding—undertaken by two or more rival firms. A single firm may also pursue actions intended to create or enhance its market power. For example, a firm could use predatory or limit pricing to make entry unattractive. Or it might choose to organize itself so as to make it more difficult for rivals to enter its market. It has been argued that integrating vertically, or dealing with suppliers or sellers through particular kinds of exclusive contracts, for examples, may inhibit entry.

Predatory pricing. Predatory pricing occurs when a firm lowers its prices, perhaps below its production costs, in order to drive rival firms from the market. Lowering prices to make entry unattractive imposes costs on the firm, in addition to any costs the predatory pricing might impose on other firms. Thus, before a firm takes this action, it must balance the *certain losses* in the present against the *uncertain gains* in the future from having fewer rivals in the market. Such predatory actions are not impossible, but they seem improbable. Nevertheless, predatory pricing is *per se* illegal.

But there is an evidentiary problem: How can an enforcement agency or court distinguish between a firm that sells at a lower price because it has lower production costs and a firm that sells at a lower price because it is trying to drive rivals from the market through predatory actions? A court cannot blindly accept evidence from the firm claiming injury because all firms would prefer their rivals to charge higher, rather than lower, prices (because they could then increase their prices). Thus, a firm claiming injury is unlikely to be completely forthright about its actual costs. Even if it was, a price offered by a rival below an "injured" firm's production costs *isn't necessarily below the rival's production costs.* The rival may simply be more efficient. If predatory pricing is defined relative to the production costs of the firm claiming injury, the market price would increase to the level charged by the least efficient firm in an industry. Moreover, to make the evidentiary issue even more difficult, in the short-run, firms sometimes rationally price below average total cost as we learned in Chapter 8.

Clearly, predation is easily confused with competition. Allegations of predatory pricing are almost always brought by rivals of particularly aggressive firms who have an interest in reducing competition and raising prices. The nature of competition means that more efficient firms drive the market price below the costs of less efficient firms, thus inflicting losses on them. An antitrust policy that allowed these losers to win predatory-pricing lawsuits would undermine competition and hurt consumers.

In 1986, the *Matsushita Electric Industries v. Zenith Radio Corporation, et al.,* the Supreme Court made it clear that, although it would not completely rule out the possibility of predatory pricing, it would not accept arguments that a firm had engaged in predatory activities for *extended* periods of time. In *Matsushita v. Zenith,* Zenith and some other U.S. firms claimed that Japanese firms had conspired for 20 years to sell consumer electronic products in the United States at prices below production costs, in order to drive the US firms from the US market. The Supreme Court noted that it simply didn't make sense to believe that a firm would inflict losses on itself for 20 years in order to drive other firms from a market. The more sensible interpretation of what happened, the Court suggested, was that the Japanese firm offered lower prices because it had lower production costs.

Resale price maintenance. There are at least two problems that arise when a producer markets its output through a distributor:

1. A distributor that has market power may restrict the amount that it sells in order to increase its profits. However, the producer has an interest in lower, rather than higher, prices at the distribution level—once it sets its price, it wants to sell as much of its output at that price as possible. To keep distributors from reducing the demand for the producer's product, the producer would want to set a *maximum* resale price and encourage distributors to compete in other ways.

2. Some distributors may not do their share in advertising or servicing or otherwise promoting the sale of a producer's product. A producer can overcome some of these difficulties by specifying sales territories for distributors, by requiring that its distributors not sell competing products, or by setting a *minimum* resale price.

A producer can sometimes create an incentive for a distributor to advertise, service, or in other ways promote the sale of its good by setting an **exclusive territory** within which only a single distributor can sell. This works because the distributor gains from its efforts to make sales and provide service. Similarly, a producer can sometimes create an incentive for distributors to provide service by setting a minimum resale price (doing so is called

price resale maintenance), thus giving distributors an incentive to compete in non-price ways—for example, by providing service, warranty repairs, or information about the good and its characteristics. Consumers benefit from these activities on the part of distributors. Without fixed resale prices, however, discount stores might enter the market and, because they can lower their costs by *not providing the services*, sell the product at a lower price. Put simply: consumers go to the full-service store for information, make the purchase at the discount store, and, then perhaps, take the product to the full-service store for warranty repairs or service. For example, an individual wishing to purchase a camera could go to a full-service store for information about different cameras, and then purchase the camera from a discount store that doesn't devote any effort to providing information. The full-service store receives nothing for its efforts. The discount store has lower costs because it doesn't even make the effort. This tends to drive full-service stores from the market. As a consequence, consumers have less information about different products. This hurts the overall sales of the camera manufacturer. Resale price maintenance prevents this because retailers cannot discount—they must compete with each other on the basis of the information and services provided.

While these arguments suggest that vertical arrangements are either benign or beneficial, vertical restrictions can in some circumstances undermine competition. A group of otherwise competitive distributors that wish to collude may be able to use a producer to enforce their collusive agreement against cheating or entry. For example, exclusive territories place a limit on competition among distributors. Dividing a market so that each supplier has "local" market power is just another way of creating a sustainable cartel. So, in addition to encouraging vigorous sales efforts on each distributor's part, the territorial division may also create market power in each territory thereby allowing each distributor to take advantage of its position. Or, having a producer specify the retail price may make it easier for members of a retail cartel to prevent cheating.[5]

The fact that there are potential benefits as well as potential costs means that vertical restrictions either ought to be legal or ought to be considered under a rule-of-reason approach. To the chagrin of many economists, the Supreme Court has held resale price maintenance (sometimes called *vertical price-fixing*) to be *per se* illegal. Moreover, the Supreme Court has been unwilling to consider a rule-of-reason approach to this practice. In a 1984 challenge to the *per se* rule against resale price maintenance by a private party (*Monsanto v. Spray-Rite*), the DOJ intended to join in the argument against the *per se* rule, but it was prevented from doing so by the Congress. Opponents of resale price maintenance contracts, primarily discount stores, persuaded Congress to pass a law forbidding the DOJ's participation in the lawsuit. In its decision, the Supreme Court refused to acknowledge that resale price maintenance might be beneficial in some circumstances and hence legal. Thus, resale price maintenance continues to be *per se* illegal. (This is why you see "recommended price" stamped on products.)

Tie-in sale. A **tie-in sale** occurs when a demander must purchase at least two commodities that are bundled together, for example, a computer and a software package, an automobile and tires, or shoes and shoelaces. Courts have bounced around from rule-of-reason to *per se* approaches in their dealings with tie-in sales.

If the central question in determining whether a firm is a monopolist or has market power is: "What is a market?" The central question in determining whether a tie-in sale poses problems is: "What is a product?" Is a pair of shoes two products (shoes and shoelaces) or a single product (shoes with shoelaces)? Or, is a new car two products (a body and tires) or a single product (a body with tires)?

Tie-in sales occur because transaction costs are lower if consumers can purchase shoes with laces in a single transaction rather than have to shop for shoes and then for shoelaces. Most of the goods that we commonly buy are composed of many separate products. Even though we could purchase each product separately and assemble them ourselves, most of us prefer to purchase an assembled product. Tie-in sales can be used to increase monopoly profits in some circumstances, however. In particular, they can be used to price discriminate. In this case, even though tie-in sales increase the return to

---

[5] Creating and exploiting market power at the distribution level isn't in the interest of a producer because the resulting higher prices reduce the demand for the producer's output. This observation has made many economists skeptical of arguments of the sort just advanced that rely on a producer facilitating a cartel among its distributors.

being a monopolist or having market power, they do not necessarily create greater inefficiencies or deadweight losses. With price discrimination, remember, output provided to a market may actually increase. If it does, the inefficiency associated with market power is reduced because the problem with a monopoly is that too little is produced.

It has been difficult to clearly identify costs of tie-in sales, but the benefits are evident. As a consequence, many economists have argued that tie-in sales ought to be ignored or, at the very least, treated under a rule-of-reason approach. Antitrust law, however, has not been disposed to treat tie-in sales favorably. Thus, a section of the Clayton Antitrust Act makes tie-in sales that reduce competition illegal. In 1917, barely three years after the passage of the Clayton Act, the Supreme Court in *Motion Picture Patents v. Universal Film Manufacturing Co.*, prohibited tie-in sales. In *Northern Pacific* (1958), the Court ruled that a tying arrangement was *per se* illegal. In *Jefferson Parish Hospital v. Hyde* (1984) the Court ruled that "(i)t is far too late in the history of our antitrust jurisprudence to question the proposition that certain tying arrangements pose an unacceptable risk of stifling competition."

The argument the courts seem to have accepted is that tie-in sales, exclusive dealerships, and similar arrangements can be used to extend market power from one market to a second market or that they can be used to foreclose competition. Thus, so the argument goes, if a firm that manufactures a duplicator has market power because of a patent, it can extend this power into the market for ink by requiring customers to purchase both the duplicator and the ink. Or it is argued that, at the very least, requiring a person to purchase ink from the company that sells the duplicator forecloses competition for his or her business from other ink manufacturers.

Most economists are skeptical about this argument for the following reason: If a firm has a monopoly in one market, it doesn't need to leverage into another market in order to obtain monopoly profits. Its market power in the market where it has a monopoly allows it to obtain monopoly profits in that market. Perhaps, you might respond, the monopolist can increase its monopoly profits by extending its market power into another market. In order to do so, however, it would have to increase the price in the second market. But this would make the bundled commodity more expensive and individu-

als would purchase less. A monopoly, remember, is constrained by the demand for what it produces—when price increases, individuals purchase less. Thus, if the firm prices the monopolized product at the profit-maximizing level, increasing the price for the tie-in product only decreases the monopoly's sales and, hence, its profits in the first market.

Should these vertical arrangements be a matter of antitrust concern? Some economists, but not all, have argued that they should not. Their position is that while horizontal arrangements have the *potential* for anticompetitive effects, vertical arrangements do not. Therefore, these economists would argue, horizontal activities are properly the business of antitrust laws, *per se* or rule-of-reason, but vertical activities are not and should be ignored. This is not the position of the US antitrust laws, which scrutinize both horizontal and vertical arrangements. An interesting consequence of this scrutiny is that US antitrust policy encourages firms to grow larger than they otherwise might by integrating vertically. This is because vertical arrangements between independent firms are subject to antitrust scrutiny but vertically integrated firms doing exactly the same thing are not.

Market versus Legal Responses

A society must choose whether it will rely more heavily on market forces or on intervention through legal means to undermine monopoly-like behavior. No one mechanism is likely to be effective in dealing with all the ways in which a firm or group of firms might try to undermine the efficient competitive outcome. Hence, it probably makes sense to rely on both approaches rather than solely on one or the other. Recently, however, legal approaches in some cases have become so complex, difficult, and lengthy that market forces, slow as they may be, undermine the monopoly-like behavior long before the legal system can deal effectively with the problem. For example, the U.S. government brought a suit against IBM in the late 1960s. By the early 1980s, the suit was still being heard in a federal court. Over the intervening period, the computer market changed so dramatically that the data in the case against IBM no longer described the market. IBM may have behaved like a monopoly in the late 1960s or early 1970s, but no one seriously believed that IBM had a monopoly by the mid-1980s, even though this was precisely what the suit was about. Market forces, of the sort described at the beginning of this chapter, had undermined IBM's market power long before the legal system could deal with any problems this market power may have created. Thus, whether a society should choose legal remedies depends not just on whether a legal remedy works in principle, but whether the remedy can be implemented more rapidly than market forces undermine the underlying market power.

The debate about whether to rely on legal remedies is made more complex because there are two quite different interpretations of the purposes of the US antitrust laws. One interpretation is that antitrust laws should prevent monopolization and collusion. That is, antitrust laws should protect and foster competition and provide for competitive markets as much as possible. A second interpretation is that antitrust laws should protect small, independent firms from large, corporate firms. In fact, there is a long series of antitrust rulings by the Supreme Court that reflect the second purpose. In *Chicago Board of Trade* (1918), the Court did not find illegal agreements that restricted price competition in certain circumstances among otherwise competitive brokers; in *Appalachian Coals* (1933), output restrictions that prevented price-cutting by small coal producers were allowed. The merger in *Von's Grocery* noted earlier was deemed illegal in order to protect the corner grocery store from more intense competition by grocery store chains. The Robinson-Patman Act, passed in the middle of the Great Depression (1936), reflects the general tenor of these decisions. This act prohibits (1) discriminatory concessions and discounts to favored buyers, (2) geographic price differentials intended to drive local firms out of business, and (3) quantity discounts that may substantially lessen competition, unless those discounts reflect cost differences or efforts to match pricing decisions of rivals. In a sense, the Robinson-Patman Act is designed to limit or restrain competition while the Sherman Act was designed, at least in part, to encourage competition. Critics have argued that, as a consequence of these apparently conflicting goals, antitrust policy has confused *protecting competition* with *protecting competitors* and, in fact, has at times protected competitors (think of mom-and-pop stores) to the detriment of competition (from large discount stores, for example).

Direct Regulation

Direct regulation of prices—setting a price ceiling below the monopoly price, for example—can be used to remedy market failures caused by monopoly. This may seem a bit paradoxical because, as Chapter 12 demonstrated, regulating prices seriously distorts otherwise competitive markets, creating shortages and their attendant problems. However, the effects of price ceilings are very different when there is a monopoly.

To see why, consider the regulated monopolist illustrated in Figure 4. p_m is the monopoly price. Suppose p_1 is the maximum price a regulatory body will allow the monopolist to charge. That is, the regulated monopolist cannot charge p_m if it produces q_m. Instead, the monopolist has to maximize its profits subject to a price constraint created by the regulatory body. Clearly, for any level of output between

Figure 4
Price Regulation for a Monopolist

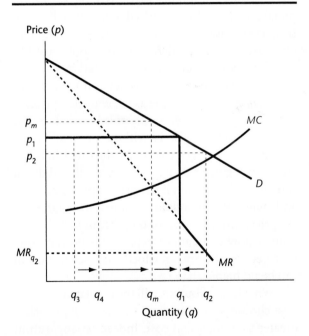

If the government sets a price ceiling below the price that the monopolist is currently charging, production will increase. With a price ceiling at p_1, the monopolist's marginal revenue will be constant (rather than declining) for all levels of production up to q_1. The monopolist will find that, at the old production level of q_m, marginal revenue exceeds marginal cost. It will therefore increase production to q_1, where marginal revenue and marginal cost are again equal.

0 and q_1, the monopolist is constrained by the price ceiling. If the monopolist produces more than q_1, however, its price will be determined by market demand because output greater than q_1 can only be sold at a price below the ceiling of p_1.

Because of the price regulation, the monopolist has the peculiarly shaped marginal revenue curve illustrated in Figure 4. As a consequence, a profit-maximizing regulated monopolist will *increase* its output even though the regulated price is *below* the unregulated monopoly price. (This result holds as long as the regulated price is also above marginal cost.) This is a puzzling result—a price ceiling leads to more, not less, being produced. How can this be?

For any level of output between 0 and q_1, the monopolist receives the *same price* for each additional unit of output it produces. For example, if it chooses to produce q_3, it receives p_1 per unit sold. Everything it produces will sell because, at the regulated price, the quantity demanded is greater than q_3. If the firm then increases its production to q_4, it also receives p_1 per unit. Because the price does not change when output changes as long as output remains below q_1, the regulated monopolist is essentially a price taker. That is, from the regulated monopolist's perspective, its demand curve looks just like one faced by a firm in a competitive market. As a consequence, the monopolist will act as if its marginal revenue is exactly the same as the regulated price.

As long as the firm's output is less than q_1, the regulated monopolist is without market power because of the price ceiling. On the other hand, at any output greater than q_1, the firm will find that it can only sell its output if the market price decreases and, hence, that marginal revenue is less than market price. Therefore, beyond q_1 the monopolist has market power. It cannot exploit this power, however, because the price at which it can sell its output can be no higher than p_1.

What level of output will the regulated monopolist choose? At q_3 marginal revenue is p_1, which is greater than marginal cost. Indeed, at any output below q_1, marginal revenue (that is, p_1) is greater than marginal cost. Thus, profit maximization leads the monopolist to increase its output from q_3 to q_4 to q_m to q_1. In every case, these increases in production increase revenues more than they do costs. That is, MR is greater than MC for any output below q_1. The regulated monopolist, then, will produce at least q_1.

Will it produce at a level beyond q_1? No. If the firm increases its output beyond q_1 to, say q_2, marginal revenue will be MR_{q2}, which is below marginal cost. Consequently, an increase in production beyond q_1 will lower profits from the level obtained by producing q_1. Clearly, at any output less than q_1, marginal revenue is greater than marginal cost, but at any output greater than q_1, marginal revenue is less than marginal cost. This means that the profit-maximizing decision for the firm, *given the price regulation*, is q_1. Setting a price ceiling on a monopoly increases rather than decreases the quantity provided to the market! Moreover, as long as the regulated price is greater than the regulated firm's marginal cost, the market will be in equilibrium in the sense that there will be no excess demand even though there is a price ceiling. In contrast with the effects of a price ceiling on a competitive market, the market price still plays its important role in rationing the amount produced among demanders. Indeed, the regulated monopolist has a profit incentive to increase output, as illustrated in Figure 5. Note, in addition, that as the regulated price decreases, equilibrium output increases. In Figure 6, when the regulated price decreases from p_1 to p_2 to p_3, output increases from q_1 to q_2 to q_3.

There is a limit to the gains from regulating the price that a monopoly can charge, however. If, for example, the regulated price falls to p_4 in Figure 6, the firm will choose to produce *less*, not more, because marginal cost will be equal to marginal revenue (the regulated price, p_4, remember) only when the firm chooses to produce q_4. But now there is excess demand and a rationing problem since at p_4, the quantity demanded is q_5.

Efficiency

For at least a range of possible ceiling prices, a regulated monopolist's output is greater than it would have been in the absence of regulation. Thus, regulating monopoly prices can be efficiency-enhancing. Consider, for example, the measures of deadweight loss illustrated in Figure 7. If a monopolist is free to maximize its profits, it will choose to produce where marginal cost is just equal to marginal revenue—q_m in Figure 7. The output q_m will be sold for p_m, leading to a deadweight loss measured by triangle ABC. With a price ceiling at p_r, however, the same monopolist will choose to produce q_r and the deadweight

Figure 5
The Effect of Price Regulation on a Monopolist's Output Decision and Profits

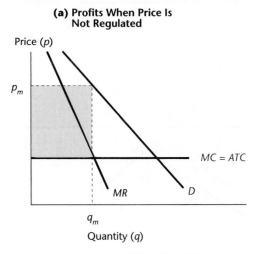

(a) Profits When Price Is Not Regulated

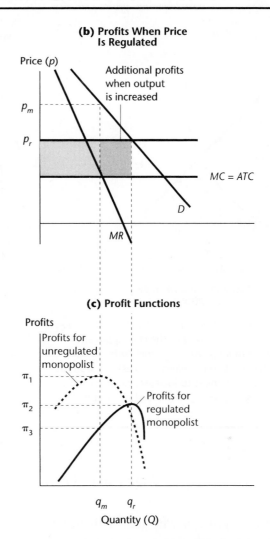

(b) Profits When Price Is Regulated

Additional profits when output is increased

(c) Profit Functions

Profits for unregulated monopolist

Profits for regulated monopolist

This figure provides a simple way of looking at the argument provided in Figure 4. That is, in certain circumstances, if the price at which a monopolist can sell its output is set below the monopoly price, the actual result will be an increase in output. In this case, to keep things simple, MC is constant (and, hence, equal to ATC). The price regulation cuts the monopolist's profits in half if it continues to produce at q_m, which is represented by the lighter area in part (b) and π_3 in part (c). The monopolist, however, can increase its profits from this level by increasing its output to q_r, the gray areas in part (b) and π_2 in part (c). Note that although the regulated monopolist can increase its profits by increasing its output, its profits under regulation are less than they would be if there were no regulation.

loss will fall to aBc. Clearly, if the regulatory body could set the ceiling price just equal to the monopolist's marginal cost (that is, equal to p_c), the deadweight loss, except for the costs of running the regulatory body itself, would be eliminated.

Using regulation to achieve the efficient outcome where marginal cost is exactly equal to market price, however, may be difficult. The regulated price might overshoot (for example, p_4 in Figure 6) or undershoot (for example, p_2 in Figure 6) the price that would lead to the most efficient use of resources (p_3 in Figure 6 or p_c in Figure 7). Indeed, the regulated price may even be above the monopoly price (p_m), in which case, regulation does not move the

economy toward a more efficient use of resources at all.

These quite different outcomes are possible because those regulating the monopolist are unlikely to know the monopolist's marginal cost schedule. This does not mean that a regulatory body cannot increase the monopolist's output in the way that we have just discussed. Rather, it means that it may be unable to increase the output to precisely that point that would be consistent with the efficient use of resources, that is, where $p_r = mc$. In a sense, the regulatory body is groping around in the dark as it attempts to set the maximum price the monopoly can charge. Regulating the price a monopolist can

Figure 6
The Effect of a Price Ceiling on a Monopoply

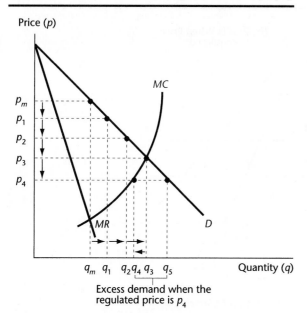

Lowering a price ceiling will continue to increase a monopolist's production, as long as the ceiling price remains above the monopolist's marginal costs. As the price ceiling for this firm is lowered successively from p_m to p_3, production continues to increase. However, if the ceiling price drops below p_3, it will lead to a cut in production.

Figure 7
Lowering the Deadweight Loss of a Monopoly through Regulation

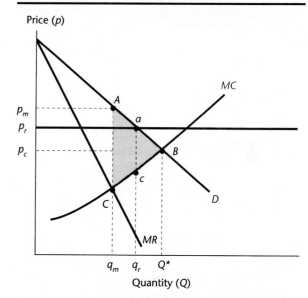

When a monopolist in an unregulated market chooses to produce q_m, the deadweight loss to society is equal to the area *ABC*. If the government sets a price ceiling below p_m, such as p_r, this loss can be reduced to *aBc*. And indeed, if the government knew the monopolist's costs and could set the ceiling price just equal to its marginal cost, at p_c, the deadweight efficiency loss of a monopoly could be eliminated completely.

charge can, as a consequence, have one of four results:

1. The ceiling price may be greater than the unregulated monopoly price. In this case, the ceiling price will not affect the firm's decisions or, obviously, the deadweight burden. (See Figure 8(a).)

2. The ceiling price may be less than the unregulated monopoly price but greater than the competitive price (marginal cost). In this case, the monopolist will increase its output, and the deadweight loss associated with the monopoly will decline. (See Figure 8(b).)

3. The ceiling price may be just equal to the competitive price (that is, to marginal cost). In this case, the monopolist will increase its output as long as its marginal cost is greater than its average total cost, and the deadweight loss associated with the monopoly will be zero, as illustrated in Figure 8(c).

4. The ceiling price may be below marginal cost. In this case, the quantity demanded will be greater than the quantity supplied and a shortage will occur. The deadweight loss may be greater or less than if the price was unregulated. Figure 8(d), illustrates the possibility that regulation may actually increase the deadweight loss, for example.

Natural Monopolies

Regulators seeking efficiency confront an additional problem when the regulated firm is a natural monopoly. A natural monopoly, remember, occurs when the technology is such that there are decreasing average costs throughout the market output range. In this case, setting the regulated price equal to marginal cost may not be possible because *marginal cost for the firm may be less than average cost at all levels of output*. This means that for a natural monopolist, any regulation that moves the price

Figure 8
Possible Efficiency Gains or Losses Associated with Price Regulation

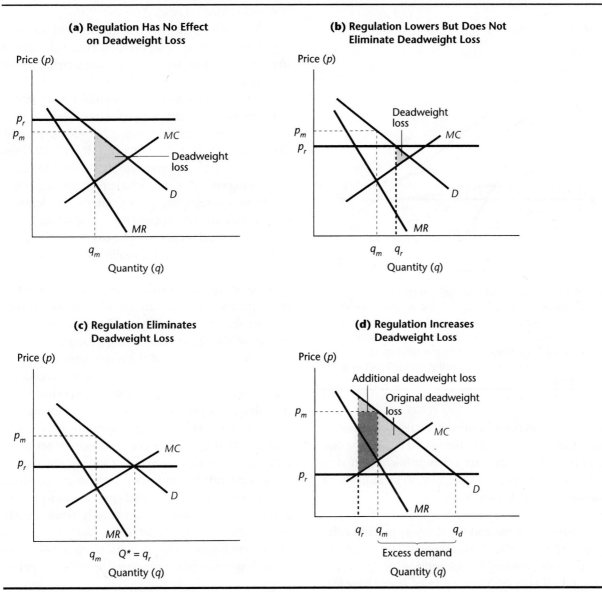

(a) Regulation Has No Effect on Deadweight Loss

(b) Regulation Lowers But Does Not Eliminate Deadweight Loss

(c) Regulation Eliminates Deadweight Loss

(d) Regulation Increases Deadweight Loss

toward marginal cost will, at some point, select a price that is *below* average cost. At that point, the private monopolist will incur losses and not be willing to produce in the long run. As a consequence, a regulatory body will not be able to obtain the efficient outcome by regulating prices.

This problem is illustrated in Figure 9. If the regulatory body sets the regulated price equal to marginal cost in order to obtain the efficient outcome, the regulated price will be below average cost. Thus, the regulation will impose losses on the monopolist equal to the shaded area. The monopoly will choose to leave the market, and output will

fall to zero. The best that a regulatory body can do in this case is to set the regulated price equal to the firm's *average total costs*, p_{ATC}. Note that the regulatory body can't even force the monopolist to achieve technical efficiency where it would produce at the level of output that minimizes average cost. Instead, the regulated monopolist will have excess capacity— its costs would be lower if it could expand its output. It can't, of course, and still earn a normal rate of return.

The only way to achieve efficiency in this case is to subsidize the production of the monopolist! If its production were subsidized, the regulated price

Figure 9
Regulating a Natural Monopoly

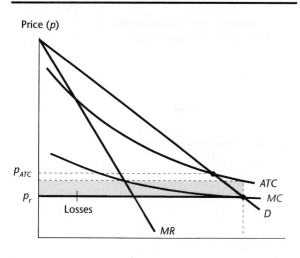

When a firm is a natural monopoly, setting the price equal to marginal cost, a requirement for allocative efficiency, may not be a viable alternative for the government because, at this level of production, the firm's average costs are greater than its marginal costs. The firm will be making economic losses and will exit as a consequence.

would be set at p_r and a subsidy equal to the shaded area would be provided to the firm. This may be one reason public utilities are often publicly owned—public ownership allows the firm to be subsidized through general tax revenues.

Multiproduct firms and the Ramsey pricing rule. Frequently, a regulated monopoly will produce several products, not one. For example, AT&T provided local as well as long-distance service. As we have just seen, if the regulated monopoly has decreasing costs because of economies of scale or scope, a regulatory body will have to set the regulated price above marginal cost. The problem with setting prices above marginal cost is that the output actually produced is less than the optimal or allocatively efficient output. For a regulatory body seeking a close-to-efficient outcome, the smaller the distortion in the quantity demand (resulting from the price being greater than marginal cost), the better. The effect of a particular price on the amount purchased depends upon the elasticity of demand, however. Therefore, in terms of allocative efficiency, when a price must be set at some level greater than marginal cost, it is

better to set higher prices where demand is inelastic and to set prices closer to marginal cost where demand is more elastic.

The reason is that when demand is inelastic, setting the price above marginal cost affects the quantity demanded by less than setting a price above marginal cost does when demand is elastic. This means that a regulatory body should *not* set prices that a monopolist can charge for its different products based on a uniform spread between price and marginal cost. If it does, it will distort outcomes unnecessarily. The appropriate rule, called the **Ramsey pricing rule**, is to make the spread between marginal cost and regulated price greater when demand is less elastic and smaller when demand is more elastic. Some spread is necessary, of course, to allow the regulated but private monopolist to break even.

Service and quality. In our earlier discussion of the consequences of price ceilings when markets were competitive, we found that a firm can lower the quality of the commodity being produced or provide less service to avoid the restrictions of a price ceiling. A regulated monopolist can get around a maximum price in exactly the same way. Thus, even though a monopoly differs from a competitive market in that a maximum price does not necessarily lead to a shortage, other consequences of setting a maximum price are similar. Put simply, unless regulation extends beyond price, consumers may find that they get lower (regulated) prices, but that they also get lower quality. Put differently, price regulation may lead to side effects that hurt consumers unless regulatory bodies pay attention to the quality of the output being produced as well as its price.

The Debate Over Regulation

As we have just learned, regulation can in principle serve the public interest. There is considerable skepticism, however, about whether regulation as a practical matter does serve the public interest.

Why the skepticism? Regulated firms spend enormous sums of money on lobbying activities in order to influence the course of regulation, but they almost never lobby for deregulation. This suggests, quite directly, that regulated firms benefit from the regulations. In fact, it has been argued that some industries really want to be regulated so that they can "capture" the regulators or regulatory process, thereby creating and protecting monopoly or cartels. Why might regulatory bodies be captured and regulations that favor those who are regulated be pursued?

1. Regulatory bodies need to be staffed by experts on the industry that is being regulated. Very often these experts are former employees of the firms that are being regulated, because, obviously, they are likely to know a good deal more about the nature of these firms than outsiders would.

2. Regulated industries often provide attractive job opportunities for the employees of regulatory bodies, again, for the obvious reason that the regulated firms want employees who understand the nature of the regulatory environment within which they work. Who better to serve in such positions than the former regulators?

3. Because regulatory bodies have limited financial resources, they must often rely on the regulated firms to provide the information that is important in making regulatory decisions. This means that the regulatory body comes to rely on the regulated firms in very important ways and not just the other way around.

Because of the importance of substitution and entry, it is difficult to limit regulation to one particular industry. For example, the decision to regulate railroads led quickly to a decision to regulate trucking. Why? When the railroads captured the regulatory body, shipping rates began to increase. Trucking proved to be an attractive and viable substitute. Because unregulated trucking would undermine the position of regulated railroading, regulation had to be extended beyond the railroads to trucking. In the 1930s, for example, Texas and Louisiana placed a 7,000 pound payload limit on trucks that hauled freight between two or more cities served by railroads and a 14,000 pound payload limit on trucks that served only a single station area. At first glance, these seem like odd regulations. Note, however, that in the first case, trucks would have been competing directly with railroads, whereas in the second they would not.

Regulation is a governmental activity, so it always depends on political processes for its cre-ation and governance. The political interests and processes that create regulation are likely to be diverse and many; the purposes that regulation is intended to serve are also likely to be diverse and many. As a consequence, regulation has evolved for a number of different reasons and not necessarily in response to market failure. These include changing the redistribution of income, paternalism, concern for small business or the family farm, and concern about accumulations of economic power. This diversity should be evident when our previous discussion of regulatory distortions in Chapter 12 is contrasted with our discussion in this chapter. Thus, the debate about the appropriate level of direct regulation extends beyond purely economic considerations.

▶ Summary

Entry and substitution. Entry by new firms and substitution by demanders both undermine market power and limit the strategies that firms might pursue as they seek to exploit their market power. This means that the reliance on market forces is a policy option for dealing with monopolies or firms that collude explicitly or tacitly.

Per Se **and rule-of-reason approaches.** The first of the two approaches to antitrust rules, *per se*, defines an action or activity as illegal. The second, the rule of reason, allows a court or enforcement agency to weigh the potential benefits against the potential harms of an action or activity. These different approaches to antitrust policy can be rationalized because some activities or actions that create market power are unambiguously harmful, but others can provide the benefits of lower costs through scale and other economies while possibly creating market power. Thus, sensible public policy should require that courts and enforcement agencies consider both potential harms and potential benefits.

Price fixing. An agreement among otherwise competitive firms to fix prices, called horizontal price-fixing, generally does not allow for economic integration; thus collusion cannot lead to scale economies. Therefore, it makes sense to have a *per se* rule forbidding such an activity and, in fact, the courts have adopted a *per se* rule against horizontal price fixing.

Mergers. Mergers provide potential benefits as well as harm and are scrutinized under a rule-of-reason approach. The enforcement of the antitrust laws, however, frowns on mergers of firms that are large relative to their market, as a way of obtaining potential economies of scale. Growth within the firm can also obtain economies of scale.

Firms that are too large. Dealing with firms that have become too large is more problematic. The antitrust laws do not make bigness or even monopoly illegal, but rather consider the illegal actions ("monopolization") that might follow from bigness or monopoly. Efforts to split large firms into small firms remain controversial, in part because such efforts require lengthy and costly legal procedures.

Tacit collusion. Antitrust policy has been much less successful in dealing with tacit collusion because it is, by nature, difficult to detect. Moreover, even if it could be shown with reasonable certainty that firms were tacitly colluding, prohibiting rational, profit-maximizing *individual* actions of firms is problematic.

Monopolistic behavior. Some kinds of individual strategies the firms might adopt to enhance or maintain market power also pose problems for antitrust policy. In examining predatory pricing it is difficult to know when lower prices result from lower costs and competition, rather than one firm's attempts to drive others from the market or prevent entry by pricing below cost.

Vertical relationships. Most vertical relationships among independent firms are considered by courts under a rule-or-reason approach, balancing potential harms and benefits. An exception is vertical price-fixing (better known as resale price maintenance), which is *per se* illegal. Tie-in sales have sometimes been ruled *per se* illegal and sometimes been considered under a rule-of-reason approach.

Markets versus laws. The use of antitrust laws has been surrounded with controversy from their inception. Some critics argue that most of the problems associated with market power are better solved by relying on market forces. Others argue that the laws have the wrong mix of *per se* and rule-of-reason approaches, and debate vigorously about the kinds of potential harms and benefits that ought to be considered in a rule-of-reason approach. Still other critics are concerned with whether antitrust laws protect competitors, thereby reducing, rather than enhancing, competition. In this regard, there is concern that a firm can use the antitrust laws to get in court what it cannot get in the marketplace. And others argue that there ought to be more vigorous enforcement, even more use of *per se* illegal rules, because the goal is not efficiency alone, but protection of society's interests in fair competition.

Direct regulation. When too little is produced because of a monopoly, the government can provide an incentive for the monopolist to increase its output, thereby moving the market toward the efficient level of output, by regulating the monopolist's prices.

Setting the maximum price that a monopoly can charge below what it would set on its own will force the monopolist to increase its output, as long as the marginal cost curve is below the demand curve. The maximum price will also ration the regulated firm's output among demanders. If, however, the maximum price is set below the point at which the marginal cost curve is equal to the demand curve, a monopolist will decrease its output and the quantity demanded will increase, thus creating a shortage. The efficient outcome can be obtained if the regulated price is set equal to marginal cost, as long as marginal cost is greater than or equal to average total cost.

For a natural monopoly, setting price equal to marginal cost will lead to losses because, in this case, marginal cost is less than average total cost. In this case, a regulatory agency has no choice but to set price at or above average total cost. If the regulated price is set equal to average total cost, a regulated natural monopoly will break even, but will not operate at the efficient scale.

Setting the regulated price equal to either marginal cost or average total cost is, in general, a difficult matter because a regulated firm's costs are not easy to observe.

Chapter 15 ▶ ▶
Externalities _____

Polluted air, acid rain, streams and rivers without fish, garbage deposited along roadsides or trash blowing in the wind, toxic wastes leaking into water supplies—all of these are produced within a market economy. For anyone who claims that self-interested behavior is effectively accommodated by markets, these stand as stark examples of the apparent failure of markets to coordinate competing interests in an appealing way. Do these sorts of problems *inevitably* result in economies that rely on markets? Are they examples not just of the failure of markets but of the failure of economics to provide useful approaches to important contemporary social problems?

This chapter has two purposes: to provide a careful analysis of why such problems occur (the first question), and to illustrate how economic reasoning can illuminate these kinds of problems and suggest possible remedies (the second question). The central theme of the chapter is a simple one. If individuals and firms consider *all* costs and benefits when they make choices, a competitive market will efficiently allocate resources, but if *some* costs or benefits of a decision are not considered, then a competitive market will fail to efficiently allocate resources.

What does it mean for a market to fail in this case? It means simply that if the costs and benefits of consumption decisions by households or production decisions by firms are not fully reflected in the equilibrium market price, the market price will be too "wrong" and either too many "bads" or not

enough "goods" will be produced. Polluted air, acid rain, streams and rivers without fish, garbage deposited along roadsides, trash blowing in the wind, or toxic wastes leaking into water supplies occur because at least some decision makers do not fully account for the costs associated with their choices. The costs are *external* to their decisions and the result is an **externality** (sometimes referred to as a **neighborhood effect**).

An example of a negative externality. Suppose that you own and manage a steel mill that emits particulates such as dust and ash into the air, which fall on an adjoining laundry, soiling the clothing that the laundry cleans. If the price of steel increases, you will probably decide to produce more. This decision benefits you by increasing your profits. It also increases the costs for the neighboring laundry, thereby lowering its profits. As your rate of steel production increases, so does your rate of dust and ash production. When this additional dust and ash falls on the laundry, its costs increase—it has to use additional resources in order to keep things clean. But these costs don't matter to you because you aren't in the laundry business. As a consequence of this relationship between your steel mill and the neighboring laundry, your output decisions cause a detrimental effect: the output of clean laundry decreases when output from your steel mill increases. This effect is an example of a **negative externality**.

It is important to be precise about the nature of the externality. The negative externality does not arise because producing goods also produces by-products such as dust and ash that require disposal—any decision to produce more is virtually always a decision to produce additional by-products. Instead, the problem occurs because the person making the decision to produce more does not consider the costs to *others* of the increase in by-products as long as they can be easily—which is to say freely—dumped in the air or water.

An example of a positive externality. Not all external effects are negative. Suppose that you own bees that gather nectar from apple trees, which are owned by someone else. Even though you produce honey using someone else's apple trees, the orchard owner is undoubtedly delighted, because as your bees gather nectar, they also pollinate the apple trees, thereby producing apples. If the price of honey decreases, you may decide to reduce the number of hives you keep, producing less honey in response to the lower demand. This decision will affect the number of apples that are produced because, with fewer bees, fewer apple blossoms will be pollinated. Since you receive no revenue from selling apples, there is little reason for you to consider the effect of your decision to produce less honey on your neighbor's apple production. In this case, producing honey has benefits—apples—that are not accounted for when you make decisions about how much honey to produce. There is a beneficial effect associated with the production of honey—apple production increases when honey production increases and vice versa—which you do not consider. This side-effect is called a **positive externality.**

The problem does not arise because bees pollinate apple trees at the same time that they gather nectar. The problem occurs because, if you are not compensated for this service, there will be no incentive to consider the value of this service when you decide how many bees to have and how much honey to produce.

▶ "Wrong" Market Prices

When the side effect of a decision is not fully accounted for by the person making the decision, the associated costs or benefits will not be reflected in the market price. Market prices reflect *only* those costs and benefits that decision makers actually consider. When there are side-effects of the sort just

illustrated, the market price will be "wrong"—it will be either too high or too low relative to what the full-cost or full-benefit price would have been. The market outcome will be inefficient. If some costs are external to production decisions, for example, the market price will be too low and too much will be produced. That is, less would be supplied or demanded if producers and consumers had to pay the full costs. If some benefits are external to production decisions, by contrast, too little will be produced. In this case, more would be supplied or demanded if producers and consumers were compensated for the full value of their production or consumption.

These results are not inevitably associated with markets. *Market prices generally force individuals to consider the full costs and benefits of their decisions.* For example, as you eat an apple, you are unlikely to be thinking about the effects your consumption may have on others. Moreover, your neighbor undoubtedly couldn't care less about what you eat, as long as it's not his food. Eating an apple *does* affect your neighbor in one sense, however. Apples are scarce, so when you eat an apple, there will be one fewer apple for others to consume. In this sense, your consumption always affects someone else. Is this an externality? No. The market price that you paid for your apple reflects the cost you impose on others because, in order to consume the apple, you had to be willing to pay *at least* as much as anyone else who wants apples.

Similarly, if a firm employs an additional worker, other firms will be unable to use that particular worker. The effect of this decision is reflected in the market price for labor, the wage rate. As a consequence, each firm is forced to consider the effects of its decisions to use scarce resources on other firms—not directly, but indirectly. If a firm is unwilling to pay at least as much, if not more, for a worker than another firm, the worker will be employed elsewhere.

When the market price is "correct" in the sense that it reflects the *full costs* of producing, and *all of the benefits* of consuming, additional output, a market will employ scarce resources in their highest-valued uses. When the market price is "wrong," scarce resources will not be put to their best or highest-valued uses. Market prices are enormously important because they convey information. Indeed, they are so important that when they convey the wrong information, markets produce the wrong mix of goods and services, and scarce resources are not used in the best or highest-valued manner. However, *market prices only convey correct information if producers and consumers confront the true costs and true benefits of their decisions.* If a person does not consider both the full costs and all of the benefits of a decision, however, he or she will make inappropriate decisions. This result will be that resources that appear to be free, like clean air and clean water, will be wasted. It also means that not enough resources will be allocated to areas where there are external benefits like inoculations against childhood diseases because the market price is below the true social value. Put directly, *if market prices do not incorporate the correct information because of an externality, individuals will be led by the market price to make the wrong decisions.* The challenge for sensible public policy, then, is to get the prices "right."

▶ Negative Externalities

The reasons why negative externalities create problems can be illustrated by considering the fishing problem introduced in Chapter 2.

The Common-Property Problem Reconsidered

The story briefly retold: When a fishing ground is discovered, 10 people go fishing and, on average, catch fish that are sold for $50 each day. Others in the economy are being paid $40, the value of their contribution to total output in activities other than fishing. The difference between $40 and $50 provides an incentive for some of these people to go fishing. An eleventh person goes fishing. At the end of the day, she sells her catch for $46 and is satisfied that she made the right decision to quit her other job and catch fish. Total output *decreases* by $40 in the non-fishing part of the economy because the eleventh person quit her job, but it only *increases* by $6 in the fishing part of the economy even though her income is $46. (Remember that when the eleventh person starts to fish, the total value of the fish caught increases from $500 to $506.)

Her $46 daily wage does not fully account for the effects of her decision on others. There is a negative externality lurking in the fishing ground! In particular, the income of the first 10 fishermen falls from $50 to $46 per day when the eleventh person starts fishing. Since each of the 10 fishermen loses $4, the economy loses $40 in output. The eleventh person gains $6 because her income increases from $40 to $46. The net effect of her decision is a loss to society of $34 even though it's a gain to her of $6.

Clearly, the eleventh person's fishing efforts impose costs on others. These costs are directly measured in this simple example as $4 for each of the 10 fishermen. This is not necessarily a bad thing. The decline in income reflects the diminishing marginal returns due to scarcity and nothing can be done about scarcity—it is simply a fact of life. A problem is created, however, if the eleventh person does not consider the full costs associated with her contribution to diminishing returns when she makes her decision. If she doesn't, the costs are external to her decision—it is the *other* 10 fishermen who bear the costs. Thus, the decision by the eleventh fisherman imposes a negative externality on the economy.

Note that if the eleventh person had to consider the costs her decision to go fishing imposed on others, she would make a different decision. Suppose, for example, that the eleventh person had to compensate the 10 fishermen for their losses. Her income would then be $46 from fishing, less $40 from compensating the fishermen $4 each. Her net income (no pun intended) would be $6 after she paid compensation. Presumably, if she had to pay compensation she would make a different choice when deciding whether to fish or do something else. Put simply, the eleventh person will not fish if she has to give up $40 to make $6, but she will fish if she has to give up $40 to make $46.

Whether the eleventh person fishes or does not fish is not the important issue in this example. The important issue is whether that person considers fully the costs imposed if she chooses to fish. Suppose, to illustrate the point, that the eleventh person was particularly inept at whatever she was doing in the non-fishing sector of the economy and, as a consequence, was paid only $4 per day. Suppose further that the person is much better at fishing. Indeed, she is as good as the 10 people already fishing and, hence, her income in fishing is $46. Since her net income after paying compensation is $6, she would choose to fish. Is there an externality because she decides to go fishing even though she pays compensation? No. If compensation were required, even though the eleventh fisherman's decision would affect other people, there would be no externality, because the net income that the eleventh person receives as a fisherman reflects the effect of her decision on others.

The fact that there is no externality and, hence, no inefficiency, can be seen by noting that in this second example, unlike the earlier example, output in the economy increases rather than decreases when the eleventh person goes fishing. Output falls in the non-fishing sector by $4 when the eleventh person moves to fishing. Because the net contribution of the eleventh person's fishing is $6, however, overall output for the economy increases by $2. This is, of course, quite different from the outcome in the earlier example, where the output for the economy fell by $34 when the eleventh person went fishing.

Additional examples of negative externalities. Almost every industrial activity has by-products that cannot be sold but must be disposed of, including garbage, chemicals, dust, gases, tailings, and so forth. Some of these by-products can easily become mixed with the water used in production; others are easily vented into the air above a plant. As a consequence, air and water frequently become convenient disposal places for industrial by-products. Garbage, chemicals, dust and gases in the air and water are unsightly, degrade the environment, and often create serious health hazards. Put simply, air and water pollution impose costs on those who live or travel near industrial plants. Moreover, wind and water may carry industrial by-products to areas far from the actual source, imposing costs on those living in these areas. There is some evidence, for instance, that acid rain in the northeastern United States and eastern Canada is caused by the by-products of industrial plants in the central United States.

Congestion is also a kind of negative externality. With congestion, each person's participation in an activity adversely affects others' enjoyment of the same activity. For example, each additional driver during rush hour makes the highway more crowded for all other drivers and travel is slower and perhaps less safe. Or, when an additional person drills a well, the water table is lowered for all other wells in the area, making each of them less productive. In an oil field, if oil is pumped rapidly from an underground pool, less oil can be extracted than if it is pumped more slowly. In addition, each new well tapping the same pool lowers the expected share of all other wells tapping the pool. This means that the owner of a well has an incentive to pump rapidly to get the oil before the owner of a neighboring well can. The production of oil from the pool is faster than is optimal and, in certain circumstances, less can be extracted from the pool over its life. Or, when it is already crowded, an additional person makes being at Zion National Park less enjoyable for everyone. Each of these examples is a variant in one way or another of the situation delineated in the fishing problem.

Negative Externalities and Market Outcomes

Figure 1 illustrates the market effect of a negative production externality. In this figure, it is assumed that, although producing the commodity has an associated negative externality, there are no externalities directly associated with consuming it. That is, the willingness to pay for additional output accurately reflects *all* the benefits associated with consuming a good. On the other hand, disposing of by-products without paying for their disposal (by dumping them into the water or into the air) implies that *private* marginal cost (MC_p)—that is, the marginal cost that firms *actually incur*—is less than *social* marginal cost (MC_s)—that is, the *true* marginal cost of producing the commodity from society's perspective. The difference, of course, is the external cost that is imposed on someone in society but that the firms do not have to pay. In symbols,

$$MC_s = MC_p + \text{marginal external cost} \qquad (1)$$

A competitive market will produce Q^* (the horizontal sum of the *private* marginal cost curves over all firms is MC_p—the market supply curve). If Q^* is supplied to the market, the equilibrium price will be p^*. By contrast, if firms actually paid the *true social cost* to dispose of their by-products, the horizontal sum of the true marginal costs over all firms would be MC_s and the market would have an equilibrium output of Q' and an equilibrium price of p'. The market price would be *higher*, and *less* would be both produced and consumed. Notice that the externality is caused by what appears to be a free method for firms to dispose of by-products. Society essentially subsidizes the producers, in this case by the difference between MC_s and MC_p.

Figure 1
The Effect of a Negative Externality

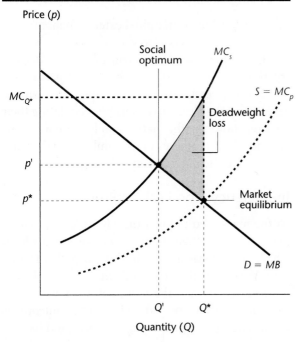

If the actions of firms impose costs on others that the firms do not have to pay, private marginal cost (*MC_p*) is less than the true cost to society (*MC_s*). The market outcome, if all costs were taken fully into account, would be (Q' p'). Because firms do not internalize all of their production costs, however, the market instead reaches an equilibrium at (Q*, p*). Notice that when the economy produces Q*, the marginal cost of additional production (*MC_{Q*}*) is much greater than the amount that consumers are willing to pay for any additional production. As a consequence, there is an inefficiency and an accompanying deadweight loss.

Inefficiency: Too Much Is Produced

If there is a negative externality, the true marginal cost of producing Q* is measured by the distance MC_{Q*}. Consumers pay only p* for this output, however. Clearly, at the market equilibrium, the true marginal cost is *greater* than the market price, and hence, greater than the amount that consumers would be willing to pay for additional output. That is, *consumers are willing to pay less than it costs the economy to produce this additional output*, when *all* costs, both internal and external, are considered (MWTP < true MC at Q*). Put simply, it is as if the economy is using $2.00 in scarce resources in order to produce $1.00 of additional satisfaction or benefit to consumers. It follows that when there is a negative externality, the

economy uses its scarce resources inefficiently: *too many goods are being produced and too many resources are being used in this market.*

Negative consumption externalities. We often think of negative externalities as being primarily associated with production, and hence, with the behavior of firms. Consider, however, persons who disturb their neighbors by playing their stereos loudly or partying noisily, or who smoke in a confined public space, or who litter the beaches or canyons, or who drive polluting automobiles. The noise may interfere with a neighbor's ability to study, work, or sleep. Smoking may create health hazards for those who choose not to smoke. Littering creates visual pollution. Polluting automobiles dispose of potentially unhealthy or in other ways harmful by-products directly into the air. In each of these examples, the negative externality is associated with *consuming* something: music or fun or a cigarette or a candy bar or a can of pop or a drive in an automobile. If consumers are not forced by market prices to consider the external effects of their decisions, they will *overconsume*. That is, there will be too much noise, too much smoke, too much litter, and too much automobile pollution.

▶ Positive Externalities

If you inoculate your child, he or she has a lower chance of contracting a disease. Other children who are not inoculated also have a lower chance of contracting a disease because, with the inoculation of your child, there are fewer potential carriers of disease-causing microbes. In this case, willingness to pay for additional output by an individual does not *fully* reflect the benefits of inoculations because some of the benefits are to others, not to the person getting the inoculation. Instead, a person's willingness to pay only reflects the expected benefits to the individual actually purchasing the inoculation. Similarly, if you spend time creating a beautiful, well-kept yard and home or apartment, you get to enjoy it, but others benefit from your efforts as well. Or, if education makes people less prone to engage in criminal activities or more prone to be good citizens, then the price of an education in a private market would not reflect these positive effects. In each of these examples those who do not pay for the commodity or service receive an *external benefit*.

Positive Externalities and Market Outcomes

In Figure 2, the demand curve, D, summarizes the market participants' individual willingness to pay for additional inoculations—in other words, the private marginal benefit (MB_p) that inoculations provide. (It is the horizontal sum of each individual's willingness to pay for additional output.) However, MB_s, summarizes the true or *social* marginal benefit of inoculations, including the benefit to others when your child is inoculated. The true marginal benefit of an inoculation (MB_s) in Figure 2 is greater than the private benefit (MB_p) because purchasing and consuming the commodity confers a benefit on those who do not purchase the commodity. That is,

the true marginal benefit is equal to the private benefit *plus* the external benefit provided to others:

$$MB_s = MB_p + \text{marginal external benefit} \quad (2)$$

In the presence of this consumption externality, the market equilibrium is Q^* and p^*. If consumers of inoculations were compensated for the service they rendered to others by inoculating their children, however, the market equilibrium would be Q' and p'. The market price would be higher and more would be both consumed and produced.

Inefficiency: Too Little Is Produced

At the market equilibrium in Figure 2, the market price, p^*, is less than the true value of inoculations, which can be measured by the distance MB_{Q^*}. That is, at Q^* the marginal cost of producing additional inoculations is less than the marginal social value that those inoculations provide. The market outcome is inefficient—too little is being produced and too few scarce resources are being devoted to this activity.

Positive production externalities. A positive externality may be associated with a production decision rather than a consumption decision. The honey/apple example discussed earlier is one such example—the production of honey creates a positive externality because it increases the production of apples. Put slightly differently, a positive externality exists because the production of honey lowers the apple grower's cost of producing apples, but the honey producer is not compensated for the service rendered. Because the apple grower does not have to pay for pollination services, there will be too few bees and too few apples. In a sense, what appears to the honey producer to be the marginal cost of producing honey is actually the marginal cost of producing honey *and* pollinated apple blossoms. The private cost is higher than the social cost; the honey producer makes the wrong production decision.

▶ Public Policy Responses That Rely Primarily on Private Interests

We begin our analysis of creating appropriate incentives (or, more precisely, of setting appropriate prices) by considering several remedies that do not depend on government regulatory or tax intervention. These actions include creating markets by

**Figure 2
The Effect of a Positive Externality**

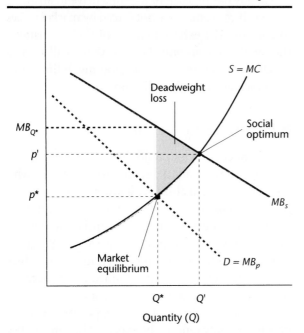

If the consumption of a commodity creates benefits for those who do not purchase it, the marginal social benefit of additional consumption (MB_s) is greater than the marginal private benefit (MB_p) that those who pay for the commodity receive. The market equilibrium is at (Q^*, p^*), but the social optimum is at (Q', p'). Notice that the marginal social benefit from added consumption at Q^* is well above the marginal cost of producing additional output. Hence, there is an inefficiency and an accompanying deadweight loss.

defining and enforcing property rights, forcing uni-tization, facilitating private contracts, and relying on social custom.

Creating Markets

Externalities almost always appear when certain kinds of markets do not develop. For example, firms may be tempted to dump pollution in the air because there is no market in which they must pur-chased air for use in disposing waste. Without such a market, firms do not have to pay to use the air and, as a consequence, are not forced to consider the full opportunity costs associated with their production decisions. Or, a person may be tempted to forgo inoculations, relying on others to be inoculated, because there is no market for the benefits to others of being inoculated. Again, without such a market, individuals cannot recover the full benefits associ-ated with their inoculation decisions. (In this case, they cannot "sell" the benefit they provide and, hence, do not see the full benefit.)

Markets often fail to develop because of prob-lems with property rights. For example, firms dis-pose of by-products in the air because air is common property, just like the fishing ground. Firms do not need to purchase the rights to dump by-products from the owners of the air because there are none. Neighbors who party loudly late at night do not need to purchase rights to propagate noises in the air because, once again, no one owns the air (or more precisely, no one owns the right to a quiet evening). Similarly, cigarette smokers do not need to purchase the right to smoke because no one owns the air in which the by-products of smoking are placed. In each case, the lack of ownership of "air" leads to neg-ative externalities.

Defining property rights. Because lack of owner-ship creates problems, an externality problem can sometimes be solved by establishing ownership of previously unowned resources. Property rights over land, cars, housing, and so forth are easy to define and relatively costless to enforce. In some cases, though, it is very difficult to define and enforce property rights. For example, defining property rights over a fishing ground is relatively easy. Fish migrate from place to place, however. As a result, defining property rights over the fish themselves is almost impossible.

Why does ownership solve the externality prob-lem? Consider, again, the fishing situation. If the fish were owned (for example, think of private owner-ship of a lake rich with fish), the owner would have to hire fishermen at a slightly higher wage than the $40 they were receiving for other kinds of work. Thus, each additional fisherman employed would cost the owner about $40. Clearly, the owner would only hire fishermen who caught more than $40 worth of fish. As a consequence, he would never hire the eleventh fisherman because his income would only increase by $6 by hiring the eleventh person, while his costs would increase by $40. Why? After the effects on the other fishermen are accounted for, the eleventh fisherman produces $6 in additional fish, but the owner of the fishing ground must pay at least $40 in order to persuade her to fish. Being forced to hire people to fish for at least $40 per day forces the owner to consider the effect of the eleventh fisherman on the catch of other fishermen.

Enforcing property rights. This "market" solution is not quite as simple as it seems, however. Property rights can generally be defined quite easily, but it is often much more difficult to enforce a particular property rights arrangement. That is, it is frequently difficult and costly to prevent unauthorized use of a defined property right or to prevent unauthorized transfers from one individual to another. For ex-ample, if a steel mill owns the rights to the air around it, the people living in a neighboring town will typ-ically find it difficult to organize in order to purchase clean air from the mill, even if they were willing to pay for it. Everyone in the community must partic-ipate in the transaction and the process of transact-ing for a single thing ("clean air") with a large number of purchasers is difficult: there is generally an incentive for each person to wait for someone else to buy the clean air because they then benefit with-out having to spend money. On the other hand, if the air right belongs to the community, it may be very difficult for the steel mill to purchase the right to pollute, even if the mill places a greater value on the air for the disposal of some pollution than the citizens of the community place on perfectly clean air. In this case, the steel mill must transact with every person in the community, but some members may hold out for a higher price, knowing that without their permission, the steel mill can't pollute at all because the air space is not divisible. When a single good ("the right to use the air for disposal") must be purchased from a large number of joint owners, transaction costs often undermine any possible trades.

Although in certain circumstances there may be a "natural" way to define the property rights, in many settings it is not clear who should have what rights. Should a firm have the right to use the air for disposal so that individuals must purchase less pollution from the firm? Or, should individuals have the right to clean air so that firms must purchase air for disposal of by-products from individuals? If the answers to these questions strike you as self-evident, consider the problem of smoking in an enclosed space. Should people who do not smoke have the right to clean air, which smokers must purchase to dispose of smoke, or should people who smoke have the right to smoke, so that nonsmokers must purchase clean air? Closer to home, perhaps, should students not yet finished with their finals have the right to a quiet weekday evening so that they can study or should students who have already finished their finals have the right to party and make noise?

In addition, it's not simply a matter of deciding who should have what rights, but *deciding who should decide*. Who should be given the power to determine who has which property rights? The smokers? The nonsmokers? An outsider? Those who want to party? Those who want to study? The dean of students?

Despite these problems, private ownership is pervasive in our society and internalizes many externalities that would otherwise exist. If property rights can be defined and enforced effectively, decision makers are generally forced to consider all of the costs or benefits associated with decisions. That is, ownership internalizes the costs and benefits of decisions. It follows that externalities persist in precisely those areas where creating property rights is likely to be difficult.

Unitizing Ownership

Another solution to the externality problem in some settings is to facilitate single ownership or **unitization** of the separate activities that are connected by the externality. For example, if the beekeeper also owned the orchards that were pollinated by his bees, he would properly consider the effects of his decision to decrease the number of bees because of a

decline in the demand for honey because this decision would affect another source of his income, the production of apples. What was an external benefit (pollination of someone else's apple trees) now is an internal benefit (pollination of his own apple trees). Similarly, if a factory owner also owned all of the land affected by the smoke and other pollutants created as by-products of the factory's production, any increase in by-products would lower the value of the land. Therefore, the owner of both the land and factory would have to consider the effect of a decision to produce more at the factory (that would increase his factory income) on the value of land that he owned (where pollution would tend to decrease the value of the land and the income from land sales or rentals).

An important practical solution to the externality problem with oil pools is for the same firm to own all of the wells pumping from a particular pool. In this case, more rapid extraction by one well simply lowers the ability of other wells owned by the same firm to get as much oil from the ground, directly affecting the firm's revenues. When not all of the oil wells are owned by the same firm, courts will sometimes force the oil field to be exploited *as if* it were owned by a single firm. In cases like this, unitization internalizes what would otherwise be external costs or benefits.

Unitization does pose one problem, however. Creating a single owner for the different activities may create a firm with market power. If so, solving one problem—an externality—creates another problem—a monopoly.

Facilitating Private Contracts

Sometimes it is possible to internalize external costs or benefits through explicit contracts. For example, the positive externality problem described in the honey/apple example has actually been solved by private contracts between honey producers and orchard owners. In these contracts, orchard owners rent pollination services from beekeepers. These rent payments force honey producers to consider the effects on pollination when they make decisions about how many bees to keep in an orchard. That is, any reduction in the number of bees results in lower pollination rents. Clearly these contracts internalize what would have been an externality.

Certain kinds of negative externalities can also be eliminated by private contract. For example, keeping pigs on land in the middle of a nice residential neighborhood creates negative externalities. This kind of potential externality is often internalized by a system of private contracts in which all of the landowners in a certain area jointly agree to restrict the use of their land to specified activities. For example, the owners might restrict the use of land in a particular area to owner-occupied residential housing. This means that no owner could, at some future date, impose an externality on other landowners by keeping pigs, because uses of the land that are prohibited by contracts could be blocked by lawsuits. These kinds of contractual arrangements, known as **restrictive covenants**, are often used for land-use control in new housing developments. Covenants limiting land use for residential purposes, precluding apartments or agricultural uses, are common. Covenants sometimes place restrictions on the architectural design and size of a home, as well as on the kind of landscaping that must be maintained.

Relying on Social Custom

Frequently, externalities are eliminated or controlled by social custom. If two cars occupy the same space in the middle of an intersection, each imposes external costs on the other. "Rules of the road," a form of social custom, often develop: "The first person to the intersection has the right of way." That is, the first person at the intersection has the temporary property right to the scarce space. Or, "if two persons approach an intersection at approximately the same time, the person to the right has the right of way." In this case, the person to the right has the temporary property right to the scarce space in the intersection.

We also have social norms that control, to some degree, when and where it is appropriate to play loud music, smoke, or create other, similar externalities. More generally, we have social norms that suggest how we ought to behave toward our neighbors. Typically, these norms force us to think about the effects of our decisions on others or keep us from making certain kinds of decisions which would violate the social norm and harm others. The importance of these norms is best illustrated by the irritation we feel when someone consistently flouts the norms, imposing costs on others.

▶ Public Policy Responses that Rely Primarily on Governmental Intervention

When transaction costs are high, property rights cannot be effectively defined, transferred from lower-valued uses to higher-valued uses, or enforced against producers of externalities. In such cases, direct legal or regulatory remedies are often pursued. In this section, we consider four forms of direct intervention: taxes, subsidies, private lawsuits, and direct control of output or inputs.

Taxes

Figure 3(b)—taken from Figure 1 in this chapter—compares the market outcome when there is a negative externality with the market outcome when there is an excise tax, shown in part (a)—taken from Figure 1 in Chapter 12. A market with negative production externalities produces too much and the market price is too low. On the other hand, an excise tax distorts a market in the opposite direction, increasing the price and decreasing the amount produced and consumed. Therefore, *if the marginal external cost can be determined accurately,* an excise tax *equal* to the marginal external cost can be imposed on producers, thus distorting the outcome. In this case, however, the distortion is advantageous because it *offsets* the effect of the negative externality and moves the market toward the efficient equilibrium. Consequently, excise taxes, user fees, or effluent taxes, if set equal to the external cost, can be useful policies when negative externalities would otherwise lead to a market failure.

Taxes on pollution, often called **effluent taxes**, are attractive not only because they move a market toward a more efficient equilibrium but because, if they change with changes in the quantity or type of pollution, they provide incentives for polluters to find cost-effective means of lowering pollution. That is, firms that cannot find effective ways of lowering the amount of pollution caused by their production pay the tax, thus increasing their costs while firms that can adopt pollution-reducing techniques have an incentive to do so because they can partially or fully avoid paying the tax. This choice is important because there is no reason to believe that every producer or every production process will be equally good at reducing pollution. It is also important

Figure 3
A Comparison of the Effects of an Excise Tax and a Negative Externality

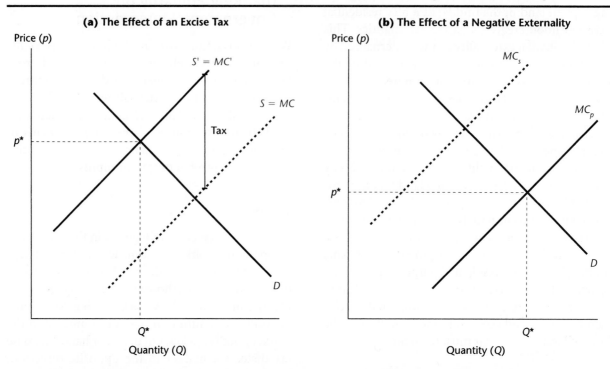

(a) The Effect of an Excise Tax

Price (*p*)

$S' = MC'$

$S = MC$

Tax

*p**

*Q**

Quantity (*Q*)

D

(b) The Effect of a Negative Externality

Price (*p*)

MC_s

MC_p

*p**

D

*Q**

Quantity (*Q*)

The distortions in output created by an excise tax and a negative externality go in opposite directions. As a consequence, an excise tax imposed on suppliers in a market with a negative externality, in principle, can be used to move the market toward the efficient outcome. To achieve the efficient outcome, the excise tax must be equal to the external cost or, in other words, to the difference between the private marginal cost and the social marginal cost.

because it means, obviously, that technologies that reduce pollution will be adopted when it's cost-effective to do so.

In a sense, if firms are taxed on the basis of the pollution that they create, there is a market for pollution. A firm can either buy the right to pollute from the state by paying the tax, or it can avoid the tax by reducing its pollution. If it pays the tax, its costs will increase and it will produce less, including less pollution. Because the phrase "a market for pollution" seems to contradict the goal of internalizing costs, however, effluent taxes or fees have not been particularly popular policy options in the United States.

Subsidies

Figure 4(b)—taken from Figure 2 of this chapter—compares the effect of a positive consumption externality with a consumption subsidy, shown in part (a)—taken from Figure 10 in Chapter 12. A positive consumption externality leads to a market equilibrium where too little is produced and the price is too low. A consumption subsidy distorts a market equilibrium in the opposite direction—too much is produced. *If the value of the positive externality can be determined accurately,* then a subsidy to the purchasers *equal* to this amount will increase both the consumption and production of the activity, and move the economy toward a more efficient use of resources. For example, public health agencies provide inoculations either free or at a much subsidized rate, thus lowering the cost of having your children inoculated and, thereby increasing the number of individuals who will be inoculated. Note that because a positive consumption externality causes an inefficiency where too little is produced, the subsidy could also be provided to the producer as an incentive to increase the amount produced.

Figure 4
A Comparison of the Effects of a Subsidy and a Positive Externality

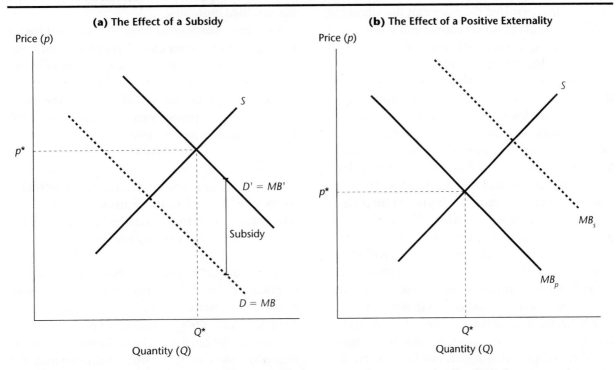

(a) The Effect of a Subsidy

(b) The Effect of a Positive Externality

The distortions in output created by a subsidy and a positive externality go in opposite directions. As a consequence, a subsidy provided to demanders, in principle, can be used to move the market toward the efficient outcome. To achieve the efficient outcome, however, the subsidy must equal the external benefit, which is the difference between the amount that individuals are willing to pay for additional output (the private marginal benefit) and the social marginal benefit.

Tort Law and Liability

If you are in an accident, a lawsuit may result in compensation for the costs imposed on you by someone else's actions. Similarly, if a doctor mistreats you, you may be able to obtain compensation through a lawsuit for the damages imposed by the mistreatment. The body of law that deals with such matters is called **tort law**. *If the liability determined is consistent with the value of the external cost*, tort law can move market activity toward a more efficient use of resources. For example, the negative externality associated with the fishing ground could be internalized if the 10 fishermen could sue the eleventh for damages. If the court accurately measured the damages to the 10 fishermen, the eleventh fisherman would have to pay $40 in damages. Because her catch is worth only $46, her income after paying the damages would be less than her income in other activities, and the externality she imposed on the other 10 would be internalized.

This way of dealing with "individual-specific" externalities is pervasive in the United States. In one famous case, a hotel built an extension that cast a shadow over the pool and beach of an adjoining hotel during the afternoon when people normally enjoy being around the pool or in the ocean. Clearly, the total social costs of the extension were not just the construction costs, but also the decline in value of the adjoining property. The owners of the expanded hotel did not consider all of these costs, however, because some were external to their decision to remodel. The owner of the hotel whose pool and beach were now permanently shadowed brought suit against the neighboring hotel. The court imposed costs on the owners of the expanded hotel (that created the externality) by forcing them to pay damages. In other words, the court decided that the shadowed hotel had a right to sunlight in the afternoon at its pool and beach, and, having decided that the hotel had such a right, the court then forced the owners of the expanded hotel to compensate for the involuntary "transfer" of this right. This increased the costs of the remodeled hotel. It also decreased the price that the adjoining hotel could charge for its rooms and still make a profit because it was now being compensated for the lower value of its pool and beach.

The importance of this kind of lawsuit is that the owners of *another* hotel contemplating an expansion now know that they will have to pay damages for shadowing any adjoining property whose value was in part determined by access to sunshine; knowing this, they will consider this potential "lawsuit" cost of expansion *before* starting construction. The costs will no longer be external to their decisions. That is, if there is a well-established pattern or precedent for making a party with particular characteristics liable for damages from its activities, it is as if property rights were created and costs internalized *for all future interactions of a similar nature.*

It is now well established in US law that negligent behavior makes a person liable to pay damages. Poorly designed or manufactured goods, negligent surgery, negligent driving, and so forth create liabilities that force manufacturers, surgeons, drivers, and anyone else in a situation where negligent behavior might affect others to think about the full costs associated with their activities—they will be subject to lawsuits if their behavior is negligent and imposes costs on others and, as a consequence, negligent behavior will be costly. Another well-developed body of law allows for suits by employees when a workplace is unhealthy or unsafe.

These kinds of lawsuits shift the private marginal cost curve toward the social marginal cost curve by forcing persons involved in activities to consider the costs that they might impose on others. Why? Because they must pay these costs if they are sued and found negligent. As a consequence, individuals and firms are more careful.

Direct Regulation

The discussion to this point has mostly focused on policies that force demanders or suppliers to confront the correct price. If you look at Figure 1 for a moment, however, it is clear that since we know that too much is produced when there is a negative externality, another option would be to limit production to a level below Q^*. Similarly, Figure 2 implies that when there is a positive externality, an option would be to force production above Q^*. Both types of public policies have been pursued, although with limited success. Two examples:

Because automobiles are a major source of urban pollution, some cities have tried to limit the number of cars on city streets. One way of doing this, for example, is to limit the amount of parking. A few years ago, Boston actually reduced the number of public and private parking garages in the city. Doing so made it much more inconvenient to drive a car into the city. The goal was to push people out of cars and onto the (less-polluting) public transportation system. The Environmental Protection Agency (EPA) and state environmental agencies have actually blocked the construction of new roads and the widening of existing roads in some cities in an effort, again, to reduce the number of cars on the road. In addition to worrying about cars as a source of pollution, Los Angeles has the legal authority to close certain factories when pollution levels rise. That is, beyond a trigger amount of pollution in the air, Los Angeles can force selected factories and businesses to close. Doing so reduces pollution from the factories and businesses themselves and also reduces the pollution from automobiles since employees do not have to show up for work.

Forcing people to buy more than they would like (forcing the actual Q to be above Q^* in Figure 2) is very difficult. In the case of inoculations, however, most states have tried to force parents to have their children inoculated by conditioning access to public education on a child being inoculated. Thus, typically, it isn't possible (or at least its very difficult) to enroll a child in the first grade without showing proof of inoculation; in some states, it isn't possible to continue into the fourth grade without proof of additional inoculations beyond those required for enrollment in first grade.

Direct regulation of production techniques. While direct regulation of output is not widely used, the Federal government (typically through the EPA) has often required producers of pollution to employ specific technologies. For example, the Federal government requires all automobiles in the US to have catalytic converters on their exhaust systems. Or, for another example, the EPA specifies in a general way the technologies that power plants and certain factories must employ to scrub pollutants from smokestacks.

Emissions Standards

The EPA and a host of similar state agencies determine specific legal levels for certain kinds of pollution from each source and, hence, determine the amount by which pollution must be reduced. These legal levels are referred to as **emissions standards**. For example, most states have emissions tests for automobiles. Your car has to pass the test annually before you are allowed to use public roads. Analogous kinds of emissions standards are imposed on factories and other identifiable sources of pollution.

Meeting an emissions standard that is below the emissions currently being produced by a firm imposes costs because a firm must take actions to reduce its pollution to the level set by the standard. As a consequence, marginal production costs increase. An increase in private marginal costs moves a market plagued by a negative externality toward the efficient output. Standards are attractive because society can determine precisely how much pollution it wishes to have. Setting standards may also be problematic, however, because if the standard is set too high, it leads to a market outcome in which too little, rather than too much, is produced. By contrast, if the standard is too low, too much, rather than too little, is produced.

The information problem. Taxes equal to the external cost, subsidies equal to the external benefit, output restrictions to hit the efficient level of production, or emissions standards that reduce pollution by the socially optimal amount all require information about the *actual* external costs or benefits. Herein lies an extraordinarily difficult problem for public policy. Consider Figures 1 and 2 again. What is actually observed in both cases is Q* and p*. The social optimum (Q′ and p′) is *not observed*; likewise the actual size of the external cost or external benefit is *not observed*. In fact, the social optimum *cannot* be observed because the externality prevents the market from picking the efficient level of production and corresponding price. So while we know that if there are external costs or benefits the observed market outcome is "wrong," beyond knowing that "too much" is produced when there is a negative externality and "too little" when there is a positive externality, there is absolutely no information about *how much* too much or *how much* too little. Deciding what is the socially correct level of pollution, for example, is a problem fraught with difficulties. Not surprisingly, then, each time a tax, or subsidy, or output restriction, or standard is proposed, there is considerable debate about whether the government has set it at the socially appropriate level. Unfortunately, there is little that can be done to inform the debate.

▶ Cost-Effective Policies

There are, however, actually two problems of interest: First, determining the socially appropriate level of pollution. For the reasons just discussed, this is a very difficult problem and one without easy solutions. And, second, achieving *whatever* level of pollution reduction the government mandates in the most cost-effective way. It turns out that economics has a good deal to say about the second problem.

The second problem is illustrated with the following example: Suppose that there are two polluters. Each can change the amount of pollution it emits, but only by devoting resources to pollution control. Hence, reducing pollution is costly because it uses resources that might have been used for other purposes. Figure 5 suggests one way of thinking about the differing abilities of each firm to reduce pollution. Part (a) of the figure illustrates the marginal cost schedule for pollution reduction by firm 1; part (b) illustrates the marginal cost schedule for pollution reduction by firm 2. For each firm, the marginal cost of reducing pollution increases as pollution is reduced further, showing the now-familiar phenomenon of diminishing marginal returns.

Suppose that the EPA mandates a 20-unit reduction in pollution in a particular area. (For example, the EPA might determine that firms in a particular area should reduce the amount of sulfur dumped into the atmosphere as sulfur dioxide by 20 tons). To explore the problem of minimizing the social cost of achieving this specified target reduction in pollution, the two marginal cost schedules in Figure 5 have been plotted on the same graph in Figure 6. The marginal cost curve for firm 2 has been plotted from the right to the left; for firm 1, MC has been plotted in the familiar fashion, from left to right. If the EPA divided the pollution-reduction quota evenly between the two firms, the marginal cost of reducing pollution by 10 units for firm 1 would be A whereas the marginal cost of reducing pollution by 10 units for firm 2 would be B.

Figure 5
Differences in the Marginal Cost of Reducing Pollution Between Firms

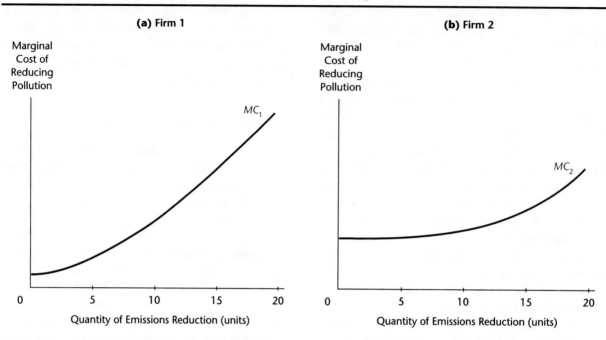

(a) Firm 1

Marginal Cost of Reducing Pollution

MC_1

Quantity of Emissions Reduction (units)

(b) Firm 2

Marginal Cost of Reducing Pollution

MC_2

Quantity of Emissions Reduction (units)

In general, not all firms have the same marginal costs for reducing pollution. For the two firms pictured here, firm 1 has lower initial costs, but these costs escalate very quickly. In contrast, firm 2 has higher initial costs, but the cost of further reductions in pollution increases much more slowly.

Figure 6
Cost-Effective Allocation of a Target Reduction in Pollution

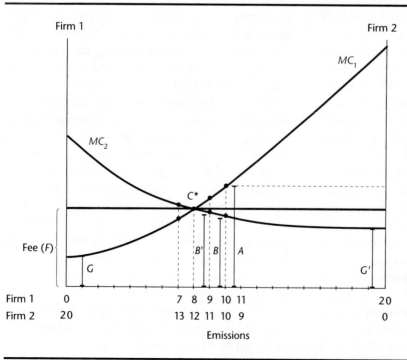

Suppose that we want to reduce the total level of pollution emitted by the two firms shown in Figure 5 by 20 units. Because their costs for reducing pollution are different, dividing the pollution reduction equally between them does not minimize the costs of obtaining a target level of pollution reduction. For example, if each firm is required to reduce pollution by 10 units, the cost to firm 1 is equal to A whereas that for firm 2 is equal to B. It is less costly for firm 2 to reduce pollution further than it is for firm 1. The least-cost reduction to the target level of pollution occurs when the marginal cost of additional reductions by both firms is the same, point c^*—that is, when firm 1 cuts pollution by 8 units and firm 2 cuts pollution by 12.

Dividing the target reduction equally between the two firms clearly is not a cost-effective way of reducing pollution by 20 units. That is, if firm 1 removed only 9 units and firm 2 removed 11 units, the target reduction in pollution could be obtained *at a lower cost to society* because B', the cost to firm 2 of reducing the eleventh unit, is less than A, the cost to firm 1 of reducing the tenth unit. Similarly, if firm 1 removed 8 units and firm 2 removed 12 units, the costs of reducing pollution would again decline. If firm 2 removes 13 units and firm 1 removes 7 units, however, the costs of removing the thirteenth unit by firm 2 would be greater than the cost to firm 1 of increasing its pollution-control activities a small amount (from 7 to 8). Thus, the costs to society from reducing a specified quantity of pollution are minimized when firm 1 removes 8 units and firm 2 removes 12 units. As Figure 6 shows, this coincides with the point at which the marginal cost of further reductions for firm 1 is just equal to the marginal cost of further reductions for firm 2.

This argument can be generalized: The cost of achieving a specific amount of pollution reduction is minimized only when the marginal costs of pollution control are equal for *all* activities that create the pollution. This is a simple, yet effective, rule for deciding how a particular target level of pollution reduction should be allocated among the many producers of pollution to keep the costs of pollution control at a minimum. That is, this criterion can be used to select the most cost-effective pollution-control policy, even when it is not possible to determine whether the target level itself is efficient. (Remember that determining the *efficient* target level of pollution or output requires assessing the benefits of production, the full costs of the externality, and the costs of by-product disposal. It is, as noted earlier, a very difficult problem.)

In general, information about each firm's costs of reducing pollution is not readily available. Is it possible to find a public policy that reduces pollution to some target level in a cost-effective way *even when the enforcing agency does not have information about the differing abilities of firms to reduce pollution?* The answer is yes, in certain circumstances. We consider two different approaches, the use of emission fees or effluent taxes and the use of transferable emission permits.

Emission fees. The use of an effluent tax or fee can minimize the costs of reducing pollution to a spe-

cific level. To see why, suppose that the government selects F in Figure 6 as a per-unit **emission fee**. It costs firm 1 G to reduce pollution by one unit but, if it fails to do so, it must pay F to the government for that unit of pollution. Clearly, firm 1 would choose to reduce pollution by one unit rather than pay the fee. It costs firm 2 G' to reduce pollution by one unit; it would have to pay F to the government if it failed to do so. Firm 2, like firm 1, would choose to reduce pollution by one unit rather than pay the fee or tax.

Each firm, having reduced pollution by one unit, would find that further reductions still cost less than paying the fee, F. Each would continue to reduce the level of emissions. After firm 1 had achieved an 8-unit reduction, however, any further reduction would cost more than paying the fee, F. (For example, for firm 1 to reduce pollution by 10 units would cost A.) Thus, with a fee of F, firm 1 would choose to reduce pollution by 8 units. Firm 2 would choose to reduce pollution by 12 units, but beyond this point, would pay F to pollute rather than further reduce its pollution. Thus, as long as the government chooses the correct per unit fee, F, it can reduce pollution to the desired level, 20 units, at the least cost *without knowing anything about the pollution-control cost structure of either of the firms.*[1]

Even if the government cannot determine the correct per unit fee, as long as the government imposes the same emission fee on each of the many firms that pollute the environment, *each firm will choose a level of pollution reduction such that the marginal cost of reducing pollution equals the emission fee. Therefore, the marginal costs of reducing pollution will be equal across all firms that pollute and pay fees to the government.* And, as we just learned, a particular target is hit with minimum cost if all firms have the same marginal cost of further pollution reduction. Put differently, charging a uniform emission fee to all firms always leads to the minimum-cost allocation of pollution reduction among the various firms. To achieve cost-effective pollution control, the government agency does not need any information about the cost structures of any of the firms on which it imposes the emission fee.

There are two problems with this approach to pollution control. First, even though announcing a

---

[1] We have already noted, however, that as a practical matter, choosing the correct fee is an enormously difficult problem.

specific fee or tax will lead to a cost-effective distribution of pollution reduction across firms as just noted, the government cannot predict precisely the level of pollution reduction it will achieve unless it knows a good deal about the pollution-reduction costs of the firms in the industry. A target reduction in pollution can only be achieved, then, by announcing a fee, seeing how much pollution falls, and then adjusting the fee to move the market toward the desired level of pollution reduction.

Second, as we noted earlier, there is a difference between choosing the cost-minimizing allocation of a given target amount of pollution reduction and choosing the efficient amount of pollution reduction (the optimal target). Imposing an emission fee will allocate a given amount of pollution reduction in the most cost-effective way, but it will not necessarily lead to the most efficient overall reduction in pollution.

An emission fee does have an important advantage over mandating technologies for reducing pollution, however: It stimulates the development and use of technologies that lower the amount of pollution. That is, any technology the firm can use or develop that promises to reduce pollution at less cost per unit than the per unit fee imposed by the government will tend to be adopted because it saves the firm the difference between the cost per unit of pollution reduction of using the technology and the fee the firm would otherwise pay to the government.

Transferable emission permits. A **transferable emission permit** is the legal right to dump a specified amount of pollutants into the environment that can be bought and sold. Any firm wishing to dump pollutants must have a permit equal to or greater than the pollution it emits. Policy makers can set the total quantity of pollution covered by all permits at the level of emissions they wish to allow. A firm without a permit, or with greater emissions than its current permit allows, must either secure a permit from another firm to cover the amount that it wishes to dump or reduce the amount that it dumps. Would this system lead to cost-effective pollution control?

Consider the two firms illustrated in Figure 7. Suppose that each firm has uncontrolled emissions of 20 units and each is given permits to emit only 10 units. Both firms have uncontrolled emissions in excess of their allotment, so both must either reduce their emissions to the specified level or purchase permits from the other firm to emit more than the specified level. Suppose each firm reduces its pollution by 10 units to comply with the number of permits it has. At this level of pollution, the marginal cost of pollution control is higher for firm 1 than it

Figure 7
Selling the Right to Pollute

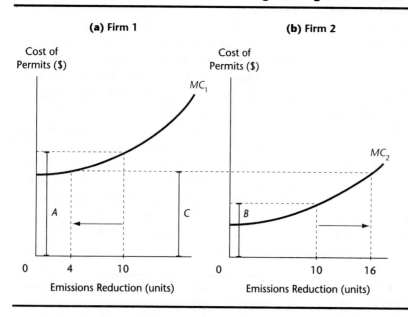

(a) Firm 1

Cost of Permits ($)

MC_1

A

C

0   4   10

Emissions Reduction (units)

(b) Firm 2

Cost of Permits ($)

MC_2

B

0   10   16

Emissions Reduction (units)

If each firm is allowed to emit 10 units of pollution and can sell the permits to other firms, firm 1 will purchase 6 permits from firm 2. Following this transaction, firm 1 reduces pollution by only 4 units, but firm 2 reduces pollution by 16 units. Both firms increase their profits by trading permits in this way and, in addition, pollution is reduced to the target level in the most cost-effective way because the marginal cost of further reductions in pollution is the same for each firm.

is for firm 2 (compare *A* with *B* in Figure 7). As a consequence, each firm values a permit to pollute a little differently and, hence, they have an incentive to trade pollution permits.[2] In particular, firm 1 can lower its costs by purchasing a permit from firm 2 for less than *A*. For example, if it costs firm 1 $20 to reduce pollution from 9 units to 10 units (*A*), but it can purchase a permit for an additional unit of pollution for $15, its costs decrease by $5. But firm 2 can increase its profits by selling a permit to firm 1 for a price higher than *B*. For example, if it costs firm 2 $10 to reduce pollution from 10 units to 11 units (*B*), but it can sell a permit for an additional unit of pollution for $15, its profits increase by $5. Clearly, if firm 2 trades a permit to firm 1 for any price between *A* and *B*, both firms will be better off.

Negotiations between firm 1 and firm 2 will lead to an equilibrium price for permits, illustrated by *C* in Figure 7. At this point, the marginal cost of further reductions in emissions is the same for each firm and equals the price of a permit. When permits sell for *C*, firm 1 reduces emissions by 4 units and purchases 6 permits from firm 2 to add to the 10 allocated to it by the governmental agency. At *C*, firm 2 reduces emissions by 16 units and sells 6 of its permits to firm 1. Pollution is reduced by 20 units, and *the reduction has been achieved in a cost-minimizing way.* That is, the division of the *actual* pollution produced by the two firms is the cost-minimizing division necessary to meet the target set by the government. We can conclude that as long as pollution permits are tradable, the outcome is the same as if an emissions fee had been imposed—the given reduction in pollution is allocated across firms in a way that minimizes cost.

Bubbles and offsets. In an interesting variant of the marketable permit approach to the pollution, the EPA has used **offsets**. The amount of allowable pollution in a particular area is fixed by the government. Old firms can continue to pollute, but the amount of pollution in an area cannot increase. This means that if a new firm enters, it must either adopt technologies that minimize pollution or replace an old firm by purchasing it and its right to pollute. Otherwise, the new firm must choose some other location where pollution is already below the EPA standard. In a particularly creative application of this concept, a firm entering the Los Angeles area was permitted to purchase about 16,000 old, and therefore highly polluting, automobiles from people living in the area. The amount of pollution reduced by destroying these cars was allowed to offset the additional pollution that would be created when the firm entered.

In another variant of this idea, the EPA has created **bubbles**: An imaginary bubble is drawn over a single firm or plant site. The firm can decide to decrease any of the various sources of pollution as long as the total pollution within the bubble is at or below the level determined by the EPA. This encourages firms to allocate pollution among their various activities in the most efficient way by decreasing pollution most from those sources where it is relatively easy to do so, or in other words, where the costs in terms of scarce resources used in pollution control are low. If a firm brings pollution in its bubble below the proscribed amount, it can sell its pollution rights to other firms that have more difficulty meeting the restrictions.

A comparison of fees and transferable permits. If both emission fees and transferable pollution permits lead to a cost-minimizing solution to the pollution-control problem, are there reasons for an environmental policy agency to choose one rather than the other? The answer is "yes," The reasons include:

1. Permits get to the target level immediately; emissions fees only get to the target level over time. The precise fee that will reduce pollution by a target amount can usually be determined only be setting an initial fee, observing the level of emissions, and then increasing or decreasing the fee in order to move the market toward the target. That is, an emission fee scheme requires fee adjustments over time to meet the target—trial and error, if you will. By contrast, in a transferable permit system, the number of permits issued, and hence the target amount of pollution, is determined in the beginning. The price of the permits simply adjusts by the usual market mechanisms until firms balance the

---

[2] We learned in Chapter 1, remember, that if different individuals value something differently, there will be opportunities for mutually beneficial trades between them.

amount of pollution each emits with the costs of emissions control.

2. The two methods differ in how they accommodate new sources of pollution. With permits, additional sources of pollution increase the demand for permits, thereby increasing the permit price. (A new firm would have to purchase permits in the market since it has none.) The quantity of pollution remains the same as long as the number of permits does not change. By contrast, with emission fees, new sources simply purchase the right to pollute at the established fee and the environmental policy agency must undertake specific actions to adjust the fee concurrent with the entry of the new sources. That is, as new sources of pollution emerge, the quantity of pollution increases under an emission fee system, but does not increase under a permit system.

3. The costs of making policy mistakes differ for the two methods. With a permit system, there is no uncertainty about the level of pollution (except for that created by less-than-full enforcement). The price for permits may change as new firms enter, however, making the costs of pollution reduction for firms uncertain. Fees, by contrast, offer more certainty to the firms involved. Their marginal cost of pollution control is more certain because the fee generally does not change from one moment to another. As noted above, however, there is less certainty about the actual amount of pollution that results when a fee or tax is set. Thus, when the quantity of pollution is of greater importance than the marginal costs of pollution control, permits should be preferred. When the costs of policy errors are more closely tied to the marginal costs of pollution control than to the quantity of pollution actually produced, fees should be preferred.

The critical role of transaction costs in externalities: the Coase theorem. When a court or government regulatory agency is faced with conflicts over property rights, it is often left in the uncomfortable position of having to determine the best way to achieve an efficient resolution of the problem. Suppose, for example, that your neighbor wants to build a giant red barn next to your beach house. The barn will block the view of the sun setting across the ocean from your picture window. From an efficiency standpoint, whether or not he should be allowed to build the barn depends on whether you value your scenic view more than he values his red barn. It's easy to see that determining whether the barn is more or less valuable than the view is a difficult matter.

In some circumstances, it is possible to achieve the efficient outcome *even if the court or regulatory agency makes the wrong valuation.* Suppose that you value your view at $1,000 and your neighbor values his barn at $500. The efficient outcome in this case is to prohibit your neighbor from building his barn. Suppose the court or zoning board makes an error and issues a permit to your neighbor to build the barn. In this case, you would be willing to pay up to $1,000 to stop him from doing so. He would be willing to accept any amount greater than $500 not to build. Thus, any payment between $500 and $1,000 will persuade him not to build the barn. Indeed, your neighbor's opportunity cost of building the barn is greater than $500. That is, he can build and use the barn, thereby obtaining $500 worth of satisfaction, or sell the right to build the barn to you for something greater than $500.

Suppose, however, that the view is only worth $100 to you, but the court prevents your neighbor from building the barn. In this case, your neighbor would be willing to pay you up to $500 to buy the right to build the barn. You, on the other hand, would be willing to accept any amount greater than $100 to give up your view. Any payment between $100 and $500 will transfer the right to build the barn from you to your neighbor. Put differently, your opportunity cost for maintaining a view is greater than $100, so you should be willing to give up the view.

This argument suggests that the efficient outcome can be obtained even when the court or regulatory body makes a mistake *as long as trades are allowed after the court or regulatory body has made its decision.* More generally, *as long as property rights can be clearly defined* and *transaction costs are low,* resources will move to their highest-valued use and externalities will be eliminated. This conclusion is known as the **Coase theorem**.

There are two problems with any application of the Coase theorem:

1. If transaction costs are high, resources might not move from lower-valued uses to higher-valued uses, thus creating externalities. For example, if the cost of transacting is more than $500 when your neighbor has the right to build a barn, then he would not sell the right to you. In this case, the barn would be built, even though the efficient outcome is that the view be preserved. Or, if the cost of transacting is more than $400 when you have the right not to have the barn built, then you wouldn't sell the right to your neighbor. The barn would not be built, even though this is the efficient outcome in this case.

2. Even if transaction costs are low, either you or your neighbor might hold out for too much, thereby keeping an exchange from occurring. In general, you wouldn't know the value of the barn to your neighbor. In addition, you would obviously prefer to purchase the right from your neighbor for as little as possible in the first instance and sell it to him for as much as possible in the second. Your neighbor has similar informational problems and interests. Either because you lack information or because you strategically bargain in an effort to get the most from the deal, an exchange that increases efficiency may not occur.

▶ Summary

Externality. If the costs or benefits of a decision to purchase or supply a commodity are not fully and accurately considered by a person or firm making a decision, an externality exists.

Negative externality. When some of the costs of a decision are not considered, there will be a negative externality. That is, one person's decision will detrimentally affect others. The market will not account for these detrimental effects, so it will produce too much. As a consequence, the market outcome is inefficient, and there is a deadweight loss imposed on the economy.

Positive externality. When some of the benefits of a decision are not considered, there will be a positive externality. In this case, one person's decision beneficially affects others. The market will not account for these beneficial effects, so it will produce too little. As a consequence, the market outcome is inefficient, and there is a deadweight loss imposed on the economy.

Externalities and property rights. Positive or negative externalities result when property rights are not clearly defined. One solution to the externality problem, then, is to define and enforce property rights. This is often difficult to accomplish either because these rights are difficult to define, or, if they can be defined, difficult to enforce in ways that encourage market transactions. The costs are simply too high.

Public policies. Taxing activities that create negative externalities and subsidizing activities that create positive externalities move markets toward a more efficient use of scarce resources if the dollar magnitude of the externality can be determined. There is no easy way to gather information about the "true" social costs or social benefits associated with a particular externality, however. As a consequence, governments frequently adopt target quantities for allowable pollution rather than using taxes or fees.

In order to allocate a target reduction in pollution efficiently, firms or other sources with differing marginal costs of pollution reduction must reduce pollution by differing amounts. Both effluent taxes (or emission fees) and transferable pollution permits will allocate a *specified amount* of pollution in a cost-effective way, although their use need not necessarily result in the efficient amount of pollution.

Coase theorem. Externalities arise because property rights are not clearly defined. If transaction costs are low, strategic bargaining problems avoidable, and private valuations accurate, then once property rights are clearly defined, resources will move to the highest-valued use, thus eliminating externalities, regardless of to whom the property rights are assigned. Or, conversely, even when property rights are clearly defined, if transaction costs are high, strategic bargaining problems serious, or private valuations inaccurate, resources might not move to the highest-valued use. In this case, externalities might not be eliminated without more direct public policy responses.

Chapter 16 ▶ ▶
Public Goods, Information, and Uncertainty_____

If you consume an apple, no one else can consume that same apple. Once you've eaten it, it's gone. Similarly, if you spend one hour with your doctor, the doctor cannot provide that same hour's service to another patient. Consumption in each case is *private*. Not all goods are like this—some can be consumed by one person but still be available for consumption by others. For example, you can enjoy the light, color, noise, and excitement of Fourth of July fireworks without affecting the ability of your neighbor to enjoy the *same* fireworks. You can also capture the signal from a television station and use it without hindering anyone else's use of the *same* signal. A ship at sea can use the services of a lighthouse that warns of danger without diminishing the *same* light available for other ships to see. A spraying program that eliminates mosquitoes for you also eliminates mosquitoes for your neighbors. Fire protection for one person's home or apartment often provides fire protection for others in the neighborhood as well. National defense for you is also national defense for me. A clean apartment can be enjoyed by roommates and not just the person who did the cleaning. In contrast with an apple or a doctor's diagnosis (**private goods**), for each of these goods or services consumption is *public*. Not surprisingly, goods and services of this sort are called **public goods** (economists have limited imaginations!).

Public goods pose a serious problem for markets. Markets are organized on the basis of individual decision making, not on the basis of collective decision making, but in an important sense, the provision of public goods requires collective decisions. As a consequence, markets produce too few public goods.

▶ A Pure Public Good

Too little of a public good is produced relative to the efficient level of production because of three characteristics that distinguish public goods from private goods:

1. Consumption of a public good is either non-competitive or non-exhaustive.
2. Consumption of a public good is nonexclusive.
3. Production of a public good is accompanied by positive externalities.

Noncompetitive Consumption

If I consume a public good, the benefit you can obtain from consuming the same good is unaffected. And, conversely, if you consume a public good that is available to me, my benefit is unaffected. As a consequence, consumption of a public good by one

291

individual is said to be **noncompetitive** with the consumption of the public good by another individual. Put in slightly different terms, consumption by one person or many people is **nonexhaustive**—it does not exhaust or destroy the good or service. For example, there is nothing about my watching and enjoying a fireworks display that impairs your ability to watch and enjoy the same display.

Because consumption of a public good is non-competitive, *there is no rationing problem* even though public goods, like private goods, are scarce. An increase in national defense for me does not decrease national defense for you. In fact, it may increase your security. But, of course, national defense requires the use of scarce resources and, therefore, is costly to produce.

Nonexclusive Consumption

If I consume a public good it is difficult, if not impossible, to exclude you from consuming it at the same time. That is, consumption is **nonexclusive**. For example, if I purchase the services of a light-house, I cannot prevent you from using these ser-vices when we are both in the same area. If I purchase the service of the beacon of the lighthouse, it simultaneously provides a beacon to you, even if you didn't purchase the service.

Because consumption is nonexclusive and non-competitive, the cost of producing a given quantity of a public good is the same whether only one per-son or a large number of people consumes it. For example, it costs as much to send a TV signal to your apartment as it does to send it to the entire city where you live. This means that the marginal cost of providing the good or service *to an additional person* is essentially zero, even though the public good itself is costly to produce.

Positive Externalities

It isn't possible to exclude others from consuming a public good, so the purchase or provision of a public good by one person creates a positive exter-nality because others benefit. For example, if I spray for mosquitoes and you live in my neighborhood, you benefit. It follows from our discussion of pos-itive externalities in Chapter 15 that, even if there were a market for public goods, they would be underproduced.

Free Riding

Free riding occurs when a person consumes or uses something that has value without having to pay. Because the consumption of public goods is nonex-clusive and noncompetitive, each of us has an incen-tive to free-ride, that is, to consume public goods and services that *others* have purchased. Because of free-riding, it is often difficult to create a market for a public good, even though everyone values it.

To see why, suppose that someone decided to market television programming. TV programming and the signals necessary to get it to your home are costly to produce. As a consequence, they will not be produced unless a broadcasting firm expects that it can sell its output. If one person purchases a sig-nal that is broadcast through the air, however, oth-ers cannot be kept from using the signal. Thus, even though each of us might be willing to pay for the TV signal if we really had to, we each have an incen-tive to wait for *someone else* to purchase the signal so we can then consume it without paying. That is, to free ride. Because each potential consumer of TV programming has an incentive to free ride, the sig-nal will not be purchased and thus not produced. Put differently, because of effects of free-riding, there will be little or no market demand, even though each of us may value a good or service highly.

A second example: Even though you may want a clean apartment, because cleaning an apartment takes time and effort, you'll wait for a roommate to do it so that you can enjoy the cleanliness without devoting any time or effort to getting it. Each room-mate who understands this will wait in order to free-ride; the apartment becomes dirty and cluttered, even though each roommate would prefer it to be clean.

Free riding and the size of the group. In general, the free-rider problem becomes more serious as the size of the group of potential consumers increases and, as a consequence, the likelihood that the market will provide the public good decreases. For small groups, free-riding can be detected and prevented more eas-ily. For large groups, however, free-riding by any par-ticular individual is detected and prevented less easily. Thus, for example, if only two people live in an apartment, free-riding is easy to detect and perhaps offset. If four people live in an apartment, however, it is more difficult to know exactly who left the dirty dishes. With eight people, it's even more difficult. Hence, we would expect that dirty apartments would be a bigger problem when you have more, rather than fewer, roommates. (It's also true, of course, that larger apartments take more time to clean than smaller apartments do, and that one person's effort seems like a smaller contribution to cleaning the larger one.)

The Market Outcome

As a consequence of free-riding, the demand for a public good understates the true value of the good to a group of individuals. Worse still, the amount that individuals might be willing to pay *in the market* does not reflect how much they value any additional production of the good. This is in stark contrast with a competitive market for private goods, where demand reflects the market participants' willingness to pay.

Figure 1 illustrates the public-good problem. The true, but unobservable, demand is illustrated by D' and the free-riding market demand is D. That is, if we could overcome the free-rider problem and get individuals to reveal how much they actually value the good, the market demand would be D'. There are incentives to free-ride, however, so the demand observed in the market is D. As a consequence, a *market produces less of a public good than a private good,* even if individuals value both in the same way. That is, Q^* is produced when production would be Q' if the good were private. Put somewhat differently, if firms could figure out a way to collect from each individual a payment equal to the value that he or she places on the public good, more of the public good would be produced.

Inefficiency: Too little is produced. If D' in Figure 1 represents individuals' true willingness to pay for additional output—that is, how much they really value the commodity—it must be clear that the market outcome is inefficient. That is, in this market, the cost of producing additional amounts of the public good is less than the amount that individuals would be willing to pay for the additional production, if their *true* preferences could be made known. Thus, public goods lead to a market failure in the sense that *too little is produced* and too few resources are devoted to providing the public goods. An efficient use of scarce resources would, there-

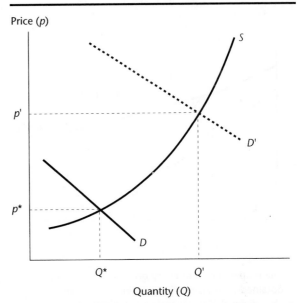

Figure 1
The Market Outcome When There Is a Public Good

In the market for a public good, each individual has an incentive to free-ride on the purchases of others. That is, even though people may value a public good, they will be unwilling to actually purchase it, hoping that others will do so first. Therefore, the demand for the good revealed in the market place, *D*, will be less than the true demand, *D'*, which reflects the value of the good to consumers.

fore, provide more public goods than the market on its own would.

The True Demand for a Public Good

Because consumption is noncompetitive, the "true demand" for a public good (that is, an accurate measure of the benefit that the good provides to consumers) is different from an ordinary market demand. In the markets for apples or bread or tickets or medical services, the quantity demanded at a given price is the sum of the quantities demanded by each individual. For example, if two consumers in the typical market illustrated in Figure 2 have the demands D_1 and D_2, then the market demand, D, is the sum of the quantity demanded along each demand curve for each possible market price. In the market for a private good, the market demand will accurately reflect each individual's willingness to pay for additional output. That is, if individual 1 is willing to pay $\hat{p}$ for Q_1 and individual 2 is willing to pay $\hat{p}$ for Q_2, then the market demand at price $\hat{p}$ would

Figure 2
Market Demand for an Ordinary Good

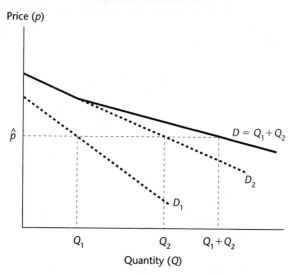

In the market for an ordinary good, the market demand is obtained by horizontally summing the demand of each individual. For this reason the market demand curve reflects each demander's willingness to pay for additional output.

Figure 3
Market Demand for a Public Good

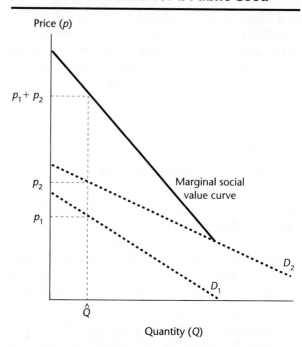

The demand for a public good is obtained by vertically summing the value of the good to each individual.

reflect the sum of these quantities, $Q_1 + Q_2$. Moreover, if $Q_1 + Q_2$ is provided to the market at a marginal cost equal to $\hat{p}$, and if each individual who consumes the commodity pays $\hat{p}$ for his or her share of the output, resources are efficiently used.

In the market for a public good, by contrast, *the value to both individuals of the output provided to the market is the sum of what each would be willing to pay for the same output*. In Figure 3, D_1 and D_2 represent the "true demands" for individuals 1 and 2, that is, what each would be willing to pay for any increase in the production of the public good. The value to the two individuals of the public good is represented by the **marginal social value curve**. That is, if individual 1 would be willing to pay p_1 for $\hat{Q}$ of the public good and individual 2 would be willing to pay p_2 for the same amount of the public good, the value of $\hat{Q}$ to this two-person community would be $p_1 + p_2$. The marginal social value curve can be thought of as the "true demand for the public good."

In terms of public policy, this peculiar demand curve means that if a community wants to provide a public good, it should determine the dollar value of a given amount of the public good to each of its members, add up these dollar values, and, if its pro-

duction costs are less than or equal to this total dollar value, produce or purchase the public good. For example, if each of 1,000 households in a community valued a public park at $100, the public good (the park) would be efficiently provided if it could be built for less than $100,000. (Note again, by contrast, that if each of 1,000 households in a community valued a bicycle at $100, bicycles would be efficiently provided if they could be produced for less than $100 each—bicycles are private, not public, goods.)

▶ Public Policy Options

In many ways, the public-good problem is the quintessential reason for government to play a role in a market economy. In some circumstances, however, it is possible to provide public goods privately. We turn first to these possibilities and then return to public provision.

Make the Public Good Private

The market will provide a public good if its consumption can be made excludable, that is, if some mechanism for excluding non-payers from consuming can be devised. Because public goods have value, consumers and producers may search for ways to make the public good private. For example, suppose TV signals can be scrambled easily, but only unscrambled by means of a device that is activated when payments are made. In this case, TV signals would no longer be a public good. Why aren't such boxes used? The transactions costs associated with installing them, collecting the payments, and policing the system to make sure that hackers don't bypass it are apparently great enough that it's not worth the effort. Moreover, there is a less costly way of making TV a private good: send the signals by cable.

Access to cables can be easily controlled, whereas access to airwaves cannot. You receive the television signal from the cable only if you pay a monthly fee for the right to maintain a hook-up. Moreover, the cable firm can divide the signal that goes to each residence such that sports channels can be marketed separately from movie channels, movie channels can be marketed separately from news channels, and so on. Cable TV is essentially a private—not a public—good.

Although scrambling signals or installing cables around cities are ways of overcoming the problem of nonexclusive consumption of TV programming, these options are inefficient uses of scarce resources if exactly the same programming can be broadcast in another way at a much lower cost. That is, making the good private in this way may overcome the free-riding problem, but only at a substantial cost.

"If broadcast TV signals are public goods," you might ask, "why are they provided at all?" The answer is that another way to make the public good private is to tie it to the provision of a service that requires payment. Broadcasting TV signals is tied to the sale of advertising services. Advertising services are essentially a private good. If a firm does not purchase advertising time, a TV station does not provide the service of airing the firm's advertising. What a broadcast TV station sells, then, is not TV programs to households, but the ability to get viewer attention to advertisers! TV programs are merely a way of delivering advertising services. In a very real sense, we do not consume TV signals, advertisers do. Moreover, *60 Minutes* and *Nightline* are simply the packaging around the advertisements, rather than the other way around.

Because the interests of advertisers may differ substantially from those of consumers, there is no reason to expect that the amount and quality of broadcast TV provided are optimal from a viewer's perspective. This does not mean that there are important market failures in the market for advertising, however. The amount and quality of broadcast TV provided may be optimal from an advertiser's perspective.

Newspapers and magazines have the same properties as TV signals. There are two groups of consumers. For one group, the readers, the paper or magazine is a public good and hence too little would be provided if the firm's only revenues were derived from sales to this group. Readers would really like to be able to free ride by reading the magazines or newspapers that *others* purchased. For the other group, the advertisers, newspapers and magazines are a private good used to deliver advertising. Hence, there are many magazines and newspapers available, but they are filled with ads.

Social Pressure and Social Norms

Some public goods cannot be effectively provided by the government without enormous and costly intrusions into individual lives. Public intervention is not really a useful or viable solution to a dirty apartment problem. In cases such as these, we often use social or peer pressure to overcome the free-rider problem. That is, we try to create a sense of obligation or loyalty in order to encourage individuals to behave in a socially virtuous manner.

In this respect, think about how you and your roommates organize your apartment to keep it clean. You undoubtedly have explicit or implicit agreements about what is appropriate behavior within the apartment. Perhaps you have rules for sharing the workload. There may be occasional disagreements when one person does not abide by the agreements and takes advantage of others (that is, free-rides). You probably try to enforce the rules and minimize the conflict by peer pressure, that is, you shame or shun or in other ways try to make free-riding costly. You may even move in order to find other roommates who either free-ride less or who aren't as nasty when you free ride.

Social norms also play a role in reducing free-riding. Manners, notions of appropriate behavior, pressures to be community-minded, and similar expectations about public behavior that temper free-riding play an important role in our lives. For example, service projects to clean up the areas around highways are a way of producing a public good: attractive highways. That it's difficult to get these kinds of projects organized and that you are tempted to not show up are good evidence of the problems that free-riding create.

Government Provision

Because of the problems of exclusion and appropriate pricing, governmental entities frequently provide public goods. Since the government can tax all of its citizens (and penalize those who refuse to pay), free-riding is difficult; taxing everyone means that everyone has to pay for the public good. In addition, because the government can tax individuals and then subsidize the production of the public good, the pricing problems associated with public goods are also eliminated. With a subsidy, a public good can be provided at a zero price to consumers.

Government intervention to offset the inefficiencies associated with public goods is necessarily coercive, however. That is, you *have* to pay your taxes whether or not you value the public goods provided by the government because, as long as individuals can free-ride on private or governmental provision of a public good, they will not reveal their true preferences for it. The only remedy to this free-riding problem is to force individuals to behave in ways *not* consistent with self-interest. Therefore, if it is determined that a public good should be provided by the government, taxing individuals who benefit from it but who would otherwise free-ride is a coercive but necessary part of the public policy.

The Problem of Information in Public Policy Responses to the Public Good Problem

In developing public policies, we often turn to markets for information about the value that individuals place on particular commodities because, in general, their willingness to pay is reflected in the market price. In the case of public goods, if a government wants to provide a public good *efficiently*, it would first need to determine the dollar value of a particular amount of the public good to each of its citizens—that is, determine each person's willing-

ness to pay for a given quantity—and then add up these dollar values in order to determine how much of the public good the community should produce or purchase. Because of free-riding, unfortunately, the market price is of little use in this exercise and the true demand cannot be estimated accurately using market data. Put simply: economic analysis tells us that too little of a public good is produced by private markets, but nothing in the analysis suggests *how much too little* or how a government would discover what the appropriate level should be. As a consequence, it is possible for the government, like the market, to under produce the public good or, unlike the market, to tax and subsidize too much and overproduce the public good. It is difficult to obtain the efficient outcome precisely because the market fails to produce the necessary information.

The problem of getting the correct information, coupled with the coercive nature of taxation and public provision, means that some individuals who really don't care much about a particular public good (for example, a public park) will be taxed too much and other individuals who really do care about the public good will be taxed too little. This problem occurs because taxes are not based on willingness to pay and devising a tax so that individuals pay a "fair share" is difficult. As a consequence, government provision of public goods almost always unintentionally redistributes income. The lengthy public debates about how much should be spent on national defense or how much should be spent on parks, roads, fire and police protection, and so forth reflect these informational difficulties, as well as the concerns associated with the redistributive effects of the associated taxes.

It is worth noting that the coercion in public good provision is not limited to the government. Peer pressure to provide a fair share often forces individuals to behave in ways that they may not want to. Disagreements about what is appropriate behavior in an apartment or about the peer pressure needed to produce appropriate behavior are evidence of the problems of private coercion.

Unrevealed preferences. Some people argue that if a good is really wanted, the market will provide it and, conversely, that if the market does not provide a good, it must not be worth providing. One of the important implications of this chapter, however, is that when there is a public good, or a good with many of the characteristics of a public good, *even though we would all like to have the good produced,* the market will not provide it. Or, even though we would all like to have more of a good, because of the free-rider problem, the market will provide too little. Put directly, when a good or service has the attributes of a public good, the amount actually demanded and produced in the market does not reflect how we really feel about it. In short, a dirty apartment does not necessarily imply that the occupants prefer a dirty apartment. The public good characteristics of a clean apartment mean that dirty apartments are produced, *even though everyone in the apartment might really prefer a clean apartment to a dirty one and be willing to pay something for a clean apartment.*

▶ Information as a Public Good

Information is enormously important in making decisions. For example, in a geographically dispersed market like the one for groceries, information about prices at competing stores affects the decisions that shoppers make. Similarly, information about the quality of a good or the quality of a potential employee or employer makes a difference in the decisions that individuals and firms make. When you buy a new car, it's important to know if it's a lemon. Or, for example, it would be nice to know the difference between the quality of Del Monte, Dole, and a no-name pineapple sold at a local grocery store. Since this kind of information is valuable, we might expect there to be a market for it—a place where information about the quality of automobiles, stereos, canned and frozen goods, and other commodities could be purchased, or where a firm could purchase information about the quality of potential employees.

Information has many of the characteristics of a public good, however: One person's use of information does not lower the value of the same information to another person. That is, use of information is generally noncompetitive or nonexhaustive. As a consequence, information is unlikely to be produced at an appropriate level in a market economy. To see precisely why, consider the following example:

Information about whether it will freeze tomorrow is valuable. Tomato farmers who know when it will freeze could delay planting to avoid either losses from frost or the costly efforts to save the plants once they were in the ground. A bright entrepreneur might decide to provide this valuable information, assuming that, because it is valuable, it must be profitable to produce and sell.

Suppose that there are 100 farmers and the losses from planting the day before it freezes would be $50 per farmer. An enterprising weather forecaster who understands the nature of these losses, imagines that his revenues from selling an accurate weather forecast would be $5,000. If it costs him $1,000 to produce the forecast, he seems to have ample incentive to produce it and sell the information to the farmers. Will this work out as he expects?

If a farmer purchases the information for $50, he can use the information to avoid losing part of his tomatoes. This is, of course, what the weather forecaster intended. Having purchased the weather forecast, however, the farmer has information that is also valuable to other farmers. His use of this information does not destroy it; nor does it lessen its value to another farmer or to himself. The original weather forecaster, whose cost of producing a weather forecast is $1,000, now has a competitor—the farmer to whom he sold the information. The farmer's cost of producing the weather forecast for other farmers is only $50, however.

The original forecaster is likely to sell far fewer forecasts than he assumed because each sale creates a new competitor with costs lower than his costs. If he sells fewer than 20 forecasts, he loses money. Moreover, he cannot market the forecast to a single farmer at a price that will cover his costs because no farmer will pay $1,000 for it. On the other hand, any farmer who purchases a forecast for no more than $50 cannot lose. The information itself is worth at least $50, and any sales of the information to others are pure profit. Thus, it is highly unlikely that providing the forecast will be privately profitable, even though its value to society ($5,000) exceeds the resources that are used to produce it ($1,000). Hence, it is unlikely that information of this sort will be provided through a "market for the information" itself.

Government Provision of Information

Governments often produce and disseminate information. For example, governments provide weather information. The government also provides information about the effects and risks associated with many other things that we eat, drink, or use: the adverse health effects of smoking or consuming fat and cholesterol, for example.

Governments go beyond merely providing information, however, when they use information about product quality to prohibit the production or use of commodities found to have detrimental effects. Although the public-good problem for information might imply that the government should produce the information, it does not imply that the government should regulate the choices that individuals can make once informed.

Market Provision of Information

Despite the public good nature of information, there are private efforts to produce information for public use. *Consumer Reports* is one such effort. Even here, free-riding surfaces: many of the people who use *Consumer Reports* borrow a copy from a friend or use a library copy. You probably don't subscribe to *Consumer Reports*; few people do. You probably use it occasionally, however. If you use it without purchasing a copy, you are a free rider. That there is substantial free-riding implies that efforts like *Consumer Reports* will not provide as much information as we might wish.

When the Internet was first developed, many people thought that it would be a way of *privately* providing information. Now that you understand the problems with providing public goods—in this case, information—you ought to question whether the Internet can meet this expectation. There is a lot of information on the Internet, but much of it is provided by governments. The Internet is a way of disseminating information at a (substantially) lower cost. This is, of course, a valuable service. Privately produced information is likely to be provided via the Internet, however, only if its in the private interest of the party putting it on the Internet. That is, it's unlikely to be different in kind from the kind of information that has always been provided by firms advertising their wares. Failure to understand the public good aspect of information led, in part, to the Internet bubble in the late 1990s and, as providers came to understand that it would be difficult to recover the costs of privately generating valuable information, to the subsequent failure of most of the so-called "dot coms." The Internet facilitated free-riding; free-riding eventually overwhelmed the private production of information.

Searching as a Way of Producing Information

In many cases, the government simply cannot or does not produce the necessary information, and the free-rider problem overwhelms the private production of information for public dissemination. Information, however, remains valuable. As a consequence, individuals sometimes produce it themselves, most frequently by **searching**, that is, by looking around for the lowest price, the best deal, the highest quality, and so forth.

For example, information about which job pays the most or has the most attractive work environment is valuable. It is unlikely, however, that you would be able to purchase it in a market. As a consequence, when you finish school, you will probably interview with a number of different firms before accepting a job. Interviewing is a form of searching. That is, it is an effort on your part to secure information that you cannot purchase in a market. At the same time, firms want information about the most productive potential employees. This information, which also cannot be purchased in a market, can be obtained, to some degree, by searching among potential employees. This is the reason that firms invite you *and* several other candidates to interviews—they are self-producing information by searching among potential employees. You willingly go to interviews because you want to provide this information *and* because you want information about the job and about potential salaries. Going to a job interview is a way of self-producing such information, that is, a way of searching.

Other examples of searching include shopping around, reading the ads, dating, and attending a few lectures in a course before deciding whether to add or drop. Notice that in each case, you must devote time to the self-production of information. As a consequence, self-production is costly.

Reputation and brand names. Since searching takes time, it is costly. Thus, if we can find ways to minimize the amount of searching that we must undertake, we will have more time for other activities. One particularly important way of minimizing search time is to associate information gathered by searching with some easily identifiable aspect of a commodity or its producer. When individuals do this, particular commodities or firms come to have **reputations**. For example, in order to search over the quality of courses at the beginning of a semester you might rely on information from friends or on your own past experiences with a particular professor. Courses and instructors get reputations and reputations, good or bad, are pieces of information.

Just as a course or instructor develops a reputation that conveys some information about quality, good or bad, **brand names** also convey information about quality, which we obtain by purchasing different brands over time. That is, reputation, based on past searches, is attached to something easily identifiable like a label or logo or brand name. If we find a brand of superior quality at a given price, we no longer need to search for quality. We simply purchase the product with the brand name attached from then on. If later experience proves us wrong (because the quality declines, or the price increases when the quality does not), we will need to search again. Because of the importance of search and reputation, *manufacturers have an incentive to provide goods that are consistently reliable or of relatively constant quality to give their brand name a good reputation.*

McDonald's provides a good example of the importance of search, brand-name identification, and product consistency. No one expects haute cuisine at McDonald's. What McDonald's has come to stand for, instead, is consistency in quality no matter where you go. This predictability is enormously valuable when traveling because you generally have little time to search for the best hamburger in a new city. Indeed, it is so valuable that McDonald's has made a lot of money by selling both hamburgers *and* consistency in quality. As a consequence, information about consistency obtained by searching has become attached to the label "McDonald's"—those golden arches mean something to anyone looking for a quick, *predictable* meal. This reputation is important, but only if McDonald's is easy to identify and if the restaurant maintains consistency. That

is, its reputation is maintained only if the label "McDonald's" represents the same thing in any city in the country or world.

To recap, the costs of searching can be reduced if the information obtained from past searches can be attached to something that is easily identifiable over time so that you don't need to make an extensive search each time you purchase the same thing. For this reason, brand names come to have reputations. The brand name is important because it lowers search costs. Firms can, of course, take advantage of this need to identify previously obtained information with a brand name by differentiating products, thereby creating markets where they have some market power. However, product differentiation occurs not simply because we are persuaded by sometimes-mindless advertising or because a firm wants to create market power, but because we need to be able to clearly attach the information we have obtained to something easily identifiable so that we can make future decisions without devoting additional time to searching.

Warranties. For some goods, information about quality cannot be produced easily even by search because no single individual consumes enough to determine its quality accurately. If, for example, you purchase only one or two dishwashers or automobiles over your lifetime, experience with one dishwasher or car is unlikely to provide useful information for the next purchase. In this case, brand-name reputation plays an important role only if you can obtain reliable information about the brand-name from other individuals. This is difficult. Clearly, an individual who makes infrequent purchases, and thus has little experience, has a serious problem. It might appear that firms could take advantage of your relative ignorance and produce goods of lower quality. However, because firms compete with one another for your purchases and because they want to be in business in the future, they have an incentive to assure you of quality. One common method of doing this is for a producer to offer a warranty, thereby assuming the risk that the product's quality might be something other than what you expected.

Middlemen or intermediaries. As noted in Chapter 3, specialized intermediaries can lower transaction costs.

Searching in order to produce information is, obviously, a particular kind of transaction cost. That is, if you purchase a new car for $20,000, the full purchase price is the $20,000 *plus* the value of your time spent in looking for the best deals on new cars. Intermediaries can sometimes provide this kind of information. In a sense, certain kinds of information *can* be purchased in a market (from intermediaries). For example, information about where the kind of home or apartment you are interested in might be located can be obtained, in some instances, by employing a real estate agent. Should you buy a home or rent an apartment, the agent's commission in part reflects your purchase of this kind of information.

Prices, Quality, and Information

It is sometimes mistakenly argued that markets only work well if *all* consumers have *complete* information. For example, it is often argued that perfect competition requires perfect information. Consumers must know enough to compare products astutely; workers must be aware of all alternative jobs; capitalists must be informed of all competing investment opportunities. Otherwise, it is argued, sellers could charge more than a competitive price and get away with it, and workers could demand more than their services are worth. This kind of argument is based on an incorrect understanding of information and markets.

A particularly important property of markets is that, if *some* individuals search in an effort to produce information for themselves, the market price will come to embody the information learned by those individuals. This means that not everyone needs to be fully informed for competitive markets to work well.

Consider a very simple example. Suppose that there are four stores in a city, each charging a different price for the same good. Information about the low-cost seller is valuable, but it's unlikely that it can be purchased in a market. It can be produced by search, however. That is, as individuals shop at the four stores, they gather information about which one is the most expensive and which is the least expensive. What happens when individuals get this information? Some will cease purchasing in the expensive stores and begin purchasing in the inexpensive stores. If a large enough group searches, this shift will increase the demand in the store with the

lowest prices and decrease the demand in the store with the highest prices. As demand increases at the inexpensive store, so will prices. As demand falls at the expensive store, so will prices. Hence if there are enough searchers, the prices will tend to be the same at each store (assuming that service is about the same in each store). As long as some people engage in this kind of shopping around, however, most individuals only need to go to the most convenient store and can remain completely ignorant of the prices elsewhere.

When there is searching, prices often reflect quality differences. For example, watermelons can be sold either whole or cut. Cut watermelons sell at a higher price per pound because the quality of watermelons is difficult to determine without cutting the melon open. People search for high-quality uncut melons by thumping, sniffing, looking for bee stings, or whatever else they believe will indicate the quality of the melon. Clearly the best way to search is by cutting the melon open. Stores provide this service, but then they have to discard the low-quality melons that would otherwise have been purchased. Cutting the melons also shortens their shelf life. Therefore, the price per pound of cut melon is higher than the price per pound of uncut melon. When you purchase cut melon, you purchase the information about quality, which is visible; when you purchase uncut melon, you take your chances because you cannot easily determine its quality.

Brand names also play an important role in this kind of search. In general, if brand A is, on average, of higher quality than brand B, searching will lead people to purchase more of brand A and less of brand B if A and B are priced the same. Thus the demand for brand A will increase and the demand for brand B will decrease. This will result in a price differential between the two brands—the price of A will increase relative to the price of B. This price difference will persist for as long as the quality differences persist and the brands are easily identifiable. This is one reason why brand name goods usually sell for a higher price and are of higher average quality than no-name or generic goods. Note that prices embody an enormous amount of information, including information obtained when individuals search.

There is a problem with this argument, however. Individuals who don't shop around essentially free-ride on those who do, so the benefit to the market of some people shopping around is a public good and thus may be under produced. It is not clear, then, whether the optimal amount of shopping around does, in fact, occur. Nevertheless, prices convey a lot of information. To see this, suppose that an acquaintance offers you a real deal, "a 2002 Mercedes 300 SEL for only $500 . . . because you're my friend." What would come to mind? Most of us would immediately think that there must be something wrong with the car—it's either hot or it's a lemon. Few of us know the actual price for a 2002 Mercedes 300 SEL, but we do know that the offer is well below what they might be selling for in dealerships. Prices are so important in conveying information that when a price is clearly below the expected range, we respond by thinking that something is wrong with the quality of the good. ("It must be stolen." Or "It must be a lemon." Or "It must have been totaled.")

► Ideas as Public Goods

Ideas are a more specific type of information that also have public-good attributes. That is, the use of an economically valuable idea by one person does not necessarily lessen the value when the idea is used by another person. As a consequence, ideas, like other types of information, will tend to be under produced.

For example, an idea that improves a production process by lowering costs substantially—what we might call a technological innovation—may be costly to produce. If it is, it may be difficult for the inventor or innovator to be fully compensated for its development since others can simply copy the idea once it is developed. If this happens, too few resources will be devoted to developing technological innovations. Or, if it is costly to produce an idea for a work of imaginative writing, musical composition, or artistic merit *and* if it is difficult to prevent others from copying and selling the creation once it has been developed, the creator may not be fully compensated for its development because of free-riding. This will lead to less creative activity than might otherwise occur.

One public policy response to these problems is to create property rights in ideas, particularly when the ideas are embodied in a piece of equipment, written down, or reflected in some other way in a physical product. Specifically, technological

innovations are protected by **patents**; other kinds of ideas in printed or recorded form are protected by **copyrights**. We even protect the information about quality of goods associated with brand names by allowing for legally protected **registered trademarks**.

Patents

With a patent, the government attempts to stimulate innovation by promising to use its policing powers to prevent those who do not compensate the inventor or innovator from using his or her idea. If the idea is a particularly good one—that is, if it lowers costs substantially or brings a new product to the market—an enforceable patent creates a monopoly for the new technology. Thus, as a society we attempt to offset the incentive to produce too few innovations or ideas by promising monopoly profits to innovators. At the same time, however, because a monopoly is created, too little output embodying the new innovation will be produced. There is a tradeoff: the public-good problem must be balanced against the monopoly problem. For this reason, patents are limited to a fixed life (currently 20 years), after which anyone is free to use the idea. (In some countries, patents are only issued if the inventor agrees to license others to develop it. This is not a requirement for a patent in the United States, however.)

If a patented product is not economically viable because few people really want it, of course, no monopoly is created. It is doubtful that the market for a vibrating toilet seat (patent no. 3,244,168, granted in 1966) will ever be very large. Moreover, it is often relatively easy to produce close substitutes for a commodity protected by a patent, sometimes using the materials in the patent application itself. If so, market power for the patented commodity will be limited. As a consequence, many things that might otherwise be patented or copyrighted are simply maintained as **trade secrets**. Whether protected by patents or trade secrets, however, innovations that are "hits" are also "targets" and entry occurs, in this case, by designing and producing close substitutes that are not protected by the original patent.

Copyrights

With a copyright, the government attempts to stimulate innovation by promising to use its policing powers to prevent the dissemination of a creative idea or work of music or art by someone other than the originator. Again, there is a public-policy dilemma. As a society we use the rewards associated with market power as an incentive to produce creative ideas, thus trading off the possibility of creating a monopoly against the possibility of underproduction because of the public-good problem.

The use of policing powers requires real resources, however, and ideas or technological innovations that are easy to copy are often very difficult to protect with modest policing resources. For example, the widespread accessibility of photocopying machines makes copying sheet music or books relatively inexpensive. If buying the sheet music or book that has already been produced costs more than photocopying it does, people will photocopy it rather than purchase it from the producer. That is, users of sheet music or books will free-ride. As a consequence, the market is unlikely to be able to produce these kinds of goods in the appropriate quantity.

A comparable battle has been fought between the producers of software for personal computers and consumers who copy rather than purchase that software. It is not practical to have a policeman at every PC just as it is not practical to have a policeman at every photocopying machine. Firms try to lessen free-riding by trying to make it clear that it is dishonest, thereby appealing to public virtue. In the case of software, they also try to block copying by various technical devices. Here they are trying to make consumption exclusive rather than nonexclusive, and hence to make the software a private good rather than a public good.

Over the past few years, there has also been a tug-of-war between those who produce music and films and people who want to download "free" copies via the Internet. Musicians and filmmakers correctly claim that copying reduces the incentives to produce new music and new films; users correctly claim that for really popular music and films, the producers charge higher prices than it costs them to make copies. If almost free downloading and copying is unabated, however, the production of new music and films will eventually fall.

▶ Rational Ignorance and Uncertainty

Much of the important information that we use is produced only by individual search and producing

information through search is costly, so it is not rational to expect to have complete information about every decision. *Some ignorance is cost-effective.* That is, an individual should search only as long as the expected benefit from searching a little longer (the marginal benefit) is greater than the cost of searching longer (the marginal cost). Since the expected benefit of continuing to search once a good deal of information has been collected is likely to be low while the costs of continuing to search are likely to increase, it's sometimes rational to be partially ignorant. This is illustrated in Figure 4.

Rational Searching and Rational Ignorance

In Figure 4, the degree to which a person is informed is measured along the horizontal axis. The marginal cost and benefit of additional information is measured along the vertical axis. The quantity of information is measured along the horizontal axis—the more information that is gathered by searching, the less ignorant one would be. At some point, a person could become "fully informed." It is likely that the more one searches, the more costly additional searching will be. It is also likely that the more information

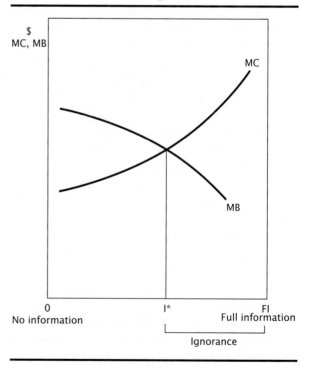

**Figure 4
Rational Ignorance**

one already has, the less valuable will be additional information. Hence, the marginal cost of additional information increases (*MC* slopes upward), while the marginal benefit of additional information decreases (*MB* slopes downward). The optimal amount of information to gather is *I**. Since in Figure 4, *I** is less than *FI* (Full Information), it is *rational to not be fully informed*. That is, if it is costly to search, it is generally *rational to be partially ignorant*.

Uncertainty

Being rationally ignorant means that sometimes mistakes will occur when making decisions. A decision requiring information that is acquired only by individual search, therefore, will have some risk associated with it. That is, the partially-informed decision may have good or bad outcomes. For example, it is often too costly to go to *every* store offering a good in order to find the lowest price. Suppose that, after some shopping around, you purchase the good from the lowest-priced store among those that you sample. It is always possible that a store that you did not sample actually had a lower price. As a consequence, your decision to purchase without searching every store has some uncertainty associated with it about whether you are, in fact, paying the lowest possible price.

Uncertainty does not occur solely because searching is costly. Sometimes information about a particular event simply cannot be produced by any amount of searching (or in any other way); therefore, the associated decisions are always accompanied by uncertainty. For example, marriage is risky because people have only partial information about potential spouses now and absolutely no information about how those individuals may change in the future. Investment is risky for similar reasons: a firm must decide *now* whether or not to build a new machine or a new factory, but the revenues from that new machine will *only accrue in the future* and future demand is unknown. Likewise, choosing a career while in college is risky. You must make the investment in skills *now*, but the demand for those skills may change *in the future*.

Insurance market. Interestingly, there are markets where individuals can exchange certain kinds of risks or the costs of making certain kinds of mistakes. For example, insurance companies gather information about the average automobile accident rate and cost for individuals who are like you. You can then purchase insurance against certain kinds of costs associated with auto accidents. In the same way, the risks associated with illness, other kinds of accidents, or death can be insured. In an **insurance market**, a firm agrees to pay an individual or some other firm a specified sum of money if a bad event happens, and to pay nothing if a bad event does not happen. The market price of this service is called an **insurance premium**.

Futures market. Taking chances in risky situations can sometimes be profitable. As a consequence, some individuals are willing to take chances, essentially buying into risky situations. By doing so, they reduce the risks for others. For example, the size of the wheat harvest in August cannot be known in April. For a farmer, differences in the size of the harvest are an important source of risk. If the harvest is large, the price of wheat will be low; if the harvest is small, the price of wheat will be high. For any farmer, then, there is uncertainty about the price at which his crop will sell when he plants it in April. No amount of searching will produce this information. There are well-developed markets for this kind of risk, however. Farmers can sell the wheat that they *will* harvest in August *before* it's actually harvested it in a **futures market**.

A farmer who wants to insure against price changes that might occur between April and August can sell his yet-to-be harvested wheat in April, promising delivery in August. The price in April for wheat to be delivered in August is the **futures price**. By August, the *then-current* price of wheat (the **spot price**) is likely to be different from the futures price that was agreed upon in April. The actual price of wheat in August may be less than the price was in April. If it is, the person who bought the futures contract from the farmer loses because he or she must take delivery of the wheat from the farmer, rather than buying wheat at the lower price. Or, the actual price of wheat in August may be greater than the price was in April. If it is, the person who bought the futures contract is ahead because the wheat purchased in April can be resold in the market at the higher price. Persons (or firms) willing to take this chance are referred to as **speculators**. Those interested in making their futures less uncertain are referred to as **hedgers**. As long as some people are willing to assume the risk of these kinds of price fluctuations (speculators), those who prefer to have less risk (hedgers) can sell it.

The Economics of Uncertainty

Insurance and futures markets are important because they allow individuals to sell risk to other individuals or firms. That is, if some individuals dislike risk, they will be willing to pay others to assume it. You do not *have* to insure your apartment, your home, or your life. A farmer does not *have* to sell his future wheat harvest in a futures market. Most people do insure against the risk of accidents, fire, theft, or death, however, and many farmers do sell their future production in a futures market. People who prefer secure outcomes to risky ones are said to be **risk-averse**.

Risk aversion explains the demand for insurance. That is, risk averse individuals would be willing to pay some amount of money (an insurance premium, for example) to "buy" a "more secure" outcome when they are faced with risks. A market requires both those willing to pay for a service and those willing to provide the service for a fee, however. Why would anyone be willing or able to supply a more secure outcome (insurance, for example)? That is, why would anyone be willing to *increase* the risk that they face?

One answer is that if some individuals are risk averse and others are tolerant of risk or are willing to speculate, then these speculators would be willing to insure the risks of the risk-averse if they expect a sufficient gain from doing so. In this case, there will be a supply of insurance. Because the essence of risk is that bad events do not *always* happen, a supplier providing insurance often receives the insurance premium without having to pay on the insurance contract. (For instance, you might make payments on your automobile insurance year in and year out without ever having an accident and, therefore, without ever collecting a payment from your insurance company.) Thus, markets that transfer risk will exist when there are risk-averse people on one side and risk-tolerant people on the other.

But what happens if almost everyone is risk-averse? Will there still be a supply of insurance? It turns out that if a supplier can put enough *independent risks* into a pool, it can take advantage of an important law of probability, the **law of large num-**

bers, and in a sense, turn a set of risky situations into a situation with almost no risk. As a consequence, it is sometimes possible for suppliers, even if owned or managed by risk-averse individuals, to insure the risks of risk-averse demanders.

Two phrases in the previous paragraph need further discussion: "independent risks" and "law of large numbers." An **independent risk** is one that when something bad happens to one person, something bad does *not necessarily* happen to another person. Their chances of good and bad events are, instead, *independent* of one another. The **law of large numbers** says, loosely, that if a large number of independent risks, each covered by a separate insurance contract, are pooled, the probability of paying on each insurance contract *at the same time* is *zero*, and the number of contracts on which payments must actually be made equals the *average* of the insured risks.

The law of large numbers. The law of large numbers is a characteristic of a large pool of independent risks such that the chance that bad outcomes will occur *simultaneously* for every risk in the pool is zero. Instead, the number of simultaneous bad outcomes equals the average of the risks of bad outcomes for each of the independent risks, multiplied by the number of independent risks in the pool. The law of large numbers means that the numerical average of the risks displays almost no uncertainty as long as there are a "large" number of independent risks in the pool.

Some intuition about how pooling works can be developed by considering the following example. Suppose that 20 people have an independent chance of losing $100 with probability $\frac{1}{2}$. That is, if you were one of these people, half of the time you would lose $100 and half of the time nothing would happen. (To make the example more explicit, you could imagine that each person has a 1 in 2 chance of getting into an automobile accident with repair bills of $100.) This is clearly a risky situation for each individual. Suppose that a firm offered insurance against the risk. That is, the firm promises that if the bad event actually occurs, it will pay $100 to anyone who buys its insurance. All 20 people sign up. What risk does the firm face?

First, consider the probability that the firm will have to pay on each contract at the same time. This would only occur if each individual *simultaneously* had an accident and lost $100. If the chances of the bad events are independent, the probability of this happening is

½ × ½ × ½ × ½ × ½ × ½ × ½ × (for twenty times) = 1/1,048,576

or about one in a million. This means that if the firm insures the 20 people for $100 each, the probability that it will have to pay on *every* insurance contract at the same time (that is, pay out on the same day 20 × $100 = $2,000) is *essentially zero*. On the other hand, the probability that the firm will not have to pay on *any* of the insurance contracts is also 1/1,048,576. This means that the insurance company will *almost certainly* have to make payments on some contracts.

Clearly, it will be important for an insurance company to know the number of contracts on which it will actually have to make payments. The law of large numbers essentially says that the insurance supplier will *almost certainly* have to pay on one-half of the contracts if the probability of the bad event is ½. That is, a firm insuring each of 20 people against $100 of independent risks will most likely have to make payments to 10 of them. Therefore, the almost-certain cost to the firm of supplying the insurance will be $1,000, plus operating costs.

Of course, an individual either loses or does not lose with probability ½. That is, the cost of the risk for an individual is either $0 or—$100. Therefore, even if the insurance company is risk-averse, its risks are different—*much* lower—than they are for any individual demander. This means that whenever they can pool a sufficiently large number of independent risks, firms will be willing to provide insurance; hence, there will be a supply of insurance.

Portfolio diversification. Changing the nature of the risks associated with decisions by pooling is important in a number of areas outside of formal insurance markets. For example, a common way of lowering the risks associated with holding assets whose future values are uncertain is **portfolio diversification**, which is a kind of pooling of independent risks undertaken by single individuals. Portfolio diversification essentially means "Don't put all your eggs in one basket," an old folk saying

that is sound advice for minimizing certain kinds of risks.

For example, individuals save by purchasing and holding **assets**, such as a stock, a bond, a savings account, real estate, or even money itself. When they do, there is some risk that the asset will change in value before the person can use it to increase his or her consumption. Individuals can lower the risk of losing *all* of their savings by purchasing a **portfolio of assets** in which the risk of any single asset declining in value is independent of the risk of any other single asset declining in value.[1] This makes sense for exactly the same reason as the insurance example outlined earlier. If each of 20 assets has a 1 in 2 chance of being worth nothing and a 1 in 2 chance of being worth $100, then, if spread over these assets, an investment of $2,000 will have virtually a zero chance of being wiped out. Hence, it makes sense not to put all your financial eggs in one basket. In more technical language: portfolio diversification is a way of lowering the risks associated with holding assets whose value changes with time.

Some problems. It appears that even though it may be difficult to produce complete information, the resulting uncertainty of being partially informed can be handled by markets where risks are bought and sold. Unfortunately, this isn't necessarily so. Three problems surface in insurance-type markets that undermine their ability to produce the optimal amount of insurance:

1. The problem of **highly dependent risks**
2. The problem of **moral hazard**
3. The problem of **adverse selection**

Highly dependent risks. If individual risks are highly dependent, a firm cannot lower the risk by pooling. For example, suppose that if *one* person loses $100, *every* person loses $100. In this case, a firm's risk of paying on every contract is ½, exactly the same as the risk that each individual confronts. Put differently, instead of having almost certain costs of $1,000, the insurance company would have costs of

---

[1] The risks don't *need* to be independent. Portfolio diversification will lower the risk of losing all of your money as long as the correlation between the bad events that cause particular assets to lose value is less than 1.00.

$0 one-half of the time and costs of $2,000 the other half of the time.

Insurance against the damage from an earthquake-prone area or from a flood in a flood-prone area is often difficult to purchase precisely because, when the bad event happens to one person, it generally happens to everyone in the area. Therefore, a firm contemplating offering flood insurance cannot take advantage of the law of large numbers by pooling independent risks over many people.

Moral hazard. If the probability of a bad event depends on the choices that individuals can make *after they are insured,* markets for insurance will encounter additional difficulties. This is the problem of **moral hazard**. To illustrate the problem, suppose that an insurance firm believes that the risk is 1 in 2 that any insured individual will be in an accident with losses of $100. The firm comes to this belief by observing that before any insurance is issued, half of the time individuals lose $100 in accidents whereas half of the time they lose nothing and the risks are independent across individuals. After insurance is issued, however, individuals may have an incentive to change the way that they behave. After all, they no longer bear the risk of the bad outcome. For example, individuals may be less cautious as they drive *merely because they know that any losses are insured.* If individuals can change their behavior so that instead of being in an accident half of the time, they are in an accident three-quarters of the time, or instead of losing $100 half of the time, they lose $500 half of the time, a firm that based its insurance premiums on a probability of ½ and potential loss of $100 will be in trouble. Specifically, it will have to pay far more money in settlements than it had anticipated, either because the probability of the bad outcome or the size of the loss associated with the bad outcome has increased.

For example, if a person is fully insured against hospital care of every sickness and injury, he or she may be more likely to be careless, thereby increasing the probability that the insurance company will have to make payments on the insurance contract. Or the person may be more likely to go to the hospital with small problems that would have been taken care of at home if he or she didn't have insurance, which also increases the payments beyond those that the insurance company expected. It is in this sense that there is a moral hazard—individuals

change their behavior, thereby increasing the risks and losses for an insurer, *after* they have purchased the insurance.

Adverse selection. A third problem with insurance markets is **adverse selection**. This can be illustrated by changing the insurance example in the following way. Suppose that of the 20 people in the insurance pool, 10 are clumsy, with a probability of 3 in 4 of losing the $100. The remaining 10, however, are quite nimble, so they only have a probability of 1 in 4 of losing $100. Suppose further that the bad events are independent and that simply because they are insured, no individual can change from being nimble to clumsy or vice versa. That is, assume that there are no highly dependent-risk or moral-hazard problems. Finally, suppose that a firm observes only the average accident probability in the pool.

In this case, the firm will observe bad outcomes happening one-half of the time, with losses each time of $100. (One-half is the average of 3 in 4 and 1 in 4 when there are 10 people in each group). The firm, in response to the law of large numbers, may offer to insure the 20 people based on its understanding of this average probability and loss. For the clumsy people, the insurance will be a bargain. For the nimble, however, the insurance may not be such a good deal because much of their premium will pay for the clumsiness of the other group. If the 10 nimble people *know* that they are less prone to have an accident than are the 10 clumsy people, they will leave the insurance pool. That is, they won't purchase the insurance. When all 10 nimble people leave the pool, the firm will find that the true probability in the pool is ¾ rather than ½. It will be in financial trouble since its announced premium was based on the average probability of ½ for the pool of 20 people. It is in this sense that there is adverse selection—lower-risk persons leave insurance pools after the premium has been set, leaving higher-risk persons in the pool.

Market innovation in response to moral hazard and adverse selection problems. A detailed analysis of how people behave when there is risk, as well as the technical aspects of the law of large numbers, the supply of insurance, and the operation of insurance-type markets is beyond the scope of this book. The important point of our discussion is that markets may not always exist, *even though everyone* *would prefer that they did*, because of public-goods, dependent-risk, moral-hazard, or adverse-selection problems. Can these problems be overcome? In some circumstances, the answer is "yes."

Deductibles and coinsurance. To protect against moral hazard, insurance companies need to create incentives for people not to change either the probability or the cost of the bad event. One way to do this is to make sure that any change in behavior by an insured person is costly *to that person*. Insurance contracts frequently do not pay the full cost of the accident. As a consequence, an individual has less incentive to increase the probability that the bad event will happen because, if it happens, he or she will have to pay something. These kinds of arrangements are referred to as **deductibles** or **coinsurance**. If you have a $100-deductible automobile-accident insurance policy and get in a wreck that costs $500 to repair, for example, you pay $100 of the bill and your insurance company pays $400.

To see the effect of a deductible or coinsurance, note that in the case of medical care, individuals can determine how frequently they go to the doctor and how much care they take of themselves. When people are fully insured, they may be a bit less careful or tend to go to the doctor more frequently. Both of these are examples of moral hazard. Insurance companies discourage this kind of moral-hazard behavior by not insuring the risk fully. Then, if individuals are less careful or go to the doctor more frequently, it costs them directly. For example, each time a person goes to the doctor there is a deductible, say of $20 per visit. The insurance company pays the rest of the bill. Or the insurance company may offset moral hazard by paying only a share of the medical expenses, say, 80 percent. The remaining 20 percent is paid by the insured person. Clearly, if a person has to pay $20 per visit or 20 percent of all medical bills, he or she is likely to be more careful and go to the doctor less frequently.

Compulsory pooling. Insurance companies can protect against adverse selection by offering insurance either to *everyone* in a pool or to *no one* in a pool. For example, insurance companies sometimes will offer to insure a group of individuals, but only as long as everyone in the group purchases the insurance. Firms often form these kinds of pools on

behalf of their employees, so a person can only exit the insurance pool by leaving his or her job. Because the pool is either all or nothing, the insurance company is protected against adverse selection by those in the pool who are lower risks.

▶ Summary

The public-good problem. Too little of a commodity will be provided by a market if it is not possible to exclude those who do not pay for it from using the commodity, or if consumption of the commodity by one person does not affect the consumption of the commodity by someone else. Commodities with these characteristics are *public goods*. From an efficiency perspective, a market economy will fail to produce enough public goods. Unfortunately, determining how much is enough is a particularly difficult problem because the information necessary to make this judgment is not readily available.

Information as a public good. Information is a particularly important public good. Because of its public good characteristics, certain kinds of information will be underproduced in a market economy. Sometimes the government solves this problem by providing the information. At other times, individuals overcome the problem by producing information themselves through search. If enough people search over service and quality, the information on each will be reflected in the market price. When information is reflected in the market price, markets are, in a sense, collecting the information and conveying it, via prices, to all market participants.

Ideas as public goods. Ideas and innovations are also important public goods. As a consequence, in certain circumstances, they will be underproduced by markets. Patents, copyrights, and registered trademarks are important ways of protecting investments in the development of ideas and, therefore, provide incentives for individuals to be innovative and creative. Each may also create market power, however. When they do, public policy confronts a trade-off of the gains from stimulating innovation and creative activity against the deadweight loss of monopoly.

Uncertainty. When information is imperfect, either inherently or because searching is too costly, decisions will be made in partial ignorance. This creates uncertainty or risk. The degree to which individuals prefer less risk will be reflected by a demand for insurance against the risk. A supply of insurance is possible if some people are tolerant of risks and become speculators who are willing to assume risks for some payment. A supply of insurance is also possible if risks can be pooled so that firms can take advantage of the law of large numbers. However, certain kinds of risks, notably those that are not independent, and certain kinds of behavior, notably moral-hazard or adverse-selection, make it more difficult to supply insurance. In some cases, these difficulties can be overcome by selecting risk pools carefully, by offering contracts with deductibles, by requiring coinsurance, or by all-or-nothing insurance pools.

Chapter 17 ▶▶
Economic Growth, Stagnation and Fluctuations

For one group of graduating seniors, jobs may be relatively easy to find because the unemployment rate is low; for another, jobs may be much more difficult to find because the unemployment rate is high. Sometimes individuals find that purchasing a car or a home is relatively more difficult and more costly because interest rates are high; at other times, similar purchases are easier and less costly because interest rates are low. More generally, an economy's total output increases at some times and decreases at other times. During downturns, resources are idle. During upturns, resources are employed once again. You can see these relationships in graphical terms in Figure 1. When resources are idle or unemployed, an economy produces in the *interior* of its production possibilities frontier at point *A* instead of *on* its frontier at point *B*. But producing at this point imposes costs on a society. The economy is not producing to full capacity and, as a consequence, scarce and otherwise productive resources are wasted. (Remember that a production possibilities frontier represents the *maximum* output an economy can produce when it fully and efficiently uses its scarce resources.) A direct effect of this waste of productive resources is a decrease in individual income as compared to individual incomes in an economy that is producing at full capacity. Unfortunately, these effects—the loss in output, waste of productive inputs, and lower individual incomes—are almost always distributed unequally across the population. In particular, during downturns some individuals are laid off and cannot find other work while others' jobs are unaffected.

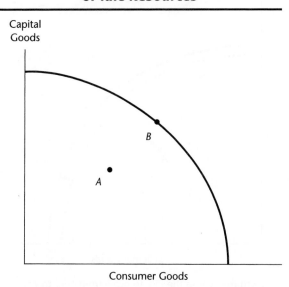

Figure 1
Loss of Output as a Result of Idle Resources

If some, but not all, resources are employed, an economy produces at a point like *A*, to the interior of its production possibilities frontier. When all resources are utilized fully, an economy produces at its full capability, such as at point *B* on its production possibilities frontier.

Even as an economy cycles, however, more slowly evolving trends such as population growth, technological change, organizational innovation, and capital accumulation lead to changes in the output an economy can produce. When either resources are increasing or technological changes are making resource use more effective, an economy's *potential to produce* increases. A way of visualizing this is to note that when an economy moves from *B* to *A* and then back toward the production possibilities frontier, the frontier itself may change position, as illustrated in Figure 2. As a consequence of economic growth, individuals will, on average, find their incomes increasing.

If resources are idle for short periods of time, the economic costs associated with unemployed resources are modest. In this case, an economy might temporarily produce at a point like *A*, but move rapidly toward the frontier and toward the full utilization of its productive resources. If resources are idle for extended periods of time, however, the costs associated with unemployment are substantial and are borne disproportionately by the unemployed and their families.

If an economy's potential output increases more slowly over time than it otherwise might (or doesn't increase at all), individuals will find their incomes grow slowly, if at all. Thus, if an economy does not foster economic growth, individual incomes will also be less, on average, than in a faster growing economy. Even though effects of economic cycles are distributed unevenly across an economy, the effects of changes in the rate of economic growth are distributed widely across the economy. That is, slow economic growth or economic stagnation adversely affects almost everyone. As a consequence, when economic growth rates differ—between different economies or at different times for the same economy—people living in one time or place may find their economic prospects noticeably improving, while those living at another time or place may find that their economic prospects are faltering.

This raises a number of perplexing questions:

1. Why does an economy sometimes produce less, in aggregate, than it is capable of producing? Or, in slightly different terms: Why does an economy sometimes produce off its production possibilities frontier rather than on its frontier, that is, at point *A* rather than at point *B*?

2. When an economy is producing at less than its full capability, will it move *on its own* toward the full employment of all of its resources? That is, if an economy is producing at some point in the interior of its production possibilities frontier, are there forces within the economy that push it to a position where its resources are fully employed (moving from *A* to *B* or *B′*, in Figure 2), or will unemployment persist (as at point *A*)?

3. If an economy does move toward full employment on its own—from *A* to *B* or *B′*, for example—is this movement *rapid or slow*? That is, are the overall social costs of unemployment modest or substantial?

4. If the movement toward full employment is slow and the costs of unemployment substantial, are there public policies that can

Figure 2
The Effect of Economic Growth on an Economy's Potential Output

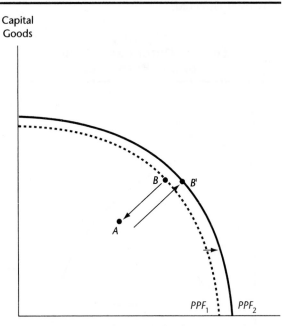

Growth may cause the PPF to grow from *PPF₁* to *PPF₂*. Indeed, an economy may slowly increase its potential output even as it cycles. Thus, instead of moving from *B* to *A* and back to *B*, the economy might move from *B* to *A* and then to *B′*. Because of economic growth, the economy can produce more at *B′*.

minimize these losses by moving the economy toward full employment more rapidly than it would move on its own?

5. What determines the changes in an economy's capacity to produce? What determines the rate at which an economy's production possibilities frontier moves outward, for example, from *PPF₁* to *PPF₂*?

In short: Why is there unemployment? Is it permanent or temporary? If temporary, is "temporary" a short period or a long period? If it is a long period, are there public policies that work to reduce unemployment? And: What determines whether there is long-term economic growth or stagnation?[1]

▶ Business Cycles

You can see the cycling of market economies, with their periods of full employment followed by periods of unemployment or underemployment by examining the pattern of production for the entire economy over time and then comparing the actual output with the output that the economy might have been able to produce. Aggregate output for the United States, as measured by *real GDP*, is illustrated in Figure 3. Figure 3 also shows the aggregate output that the US economy is capable of producing if it fully and effectively utilizes its resources—potential real output as measured by *potential real GDP*. Part (a) shows the *levels* of GDP and potential real GDP; part (b) illustrates the *differences* between real GDP and potential real GDP.

During the 20th century, the rate of growth of real GDP averaged 3.5 percent. It should be clear from Figure 3 that the growth has not been steady, however. Indeed, there have been times when real output has actually fallen. During the Great Depression beginning in 1929, real GDP fell by at least 8 percent each year between 1930 and 1932. As a consequence, the economy was 30 percent smaller in 1933 than it was in 1929. It was not until 1939 that the real output of the economy again reached its 1929 level. Similar but generally less dramatic declines and increases occur periodically; these fluc-

tuations taken together are known as the **business cycle**.

A Stylized Business Cycle

Formally, a business cycle consists of a period of expansion in economic activity followed by a period of contraction in economic activity, followed once again by an expansion then a contraction, and so forth. Figure 4 provides a *stylized* view of a business cycle; *actual* cycles are not as smooth and regular as the one shown here.

A **contraction** is a period when real output either falls or increases at a rate below its long-run trend; an **expansion** is a period when output increases faster than its long-run trend. The point at which an economy moves from a contraction to an expansion is the **trough** of the cycle; the point at which an economy moves from an expansion to a contraction is the **peak** of the cycle. Periods of declining real output (contractions) are generally referred to as **recessions**. During a recession, unemployment increases. A particularly severe and lengthy recession is often called a **depression**. Periods of increasing real output (expansions) are also called **recoveries**. Even as an economy cycles, the level of real output around which the fluctuations occur slowly changes. This change in the average level of real output is the **trend growth path** of the economy. Finally, there are nonbusiness-cycle fluctuations in real output that occur on a regular basis throughout the year called **seasonal variations**. Examples include the increases in economic activity that typically occur each year prior to Christmas and the beginning of school in September.

Table 1 summarizes the economic cycles for the United States as defined by the National Bureau of Economic Research, a private research organization that has studied business cycles extensively and, by tradition, determines the beginning and end of each economic cycle. Glance quickly down the third, fourth, and fifth columns to notice that, unlike the stylized business cycle in Figure 4, cycles in the US economy have been irregular in length.

Potential Real Output

Figure 3 illustrates the business cycle by comparing an economy's gross domestic product ("actual GDP") with its potential gross domestic product ("potential GDP"). **Gross domestic product (GDP)**

---

[1] The study of these and related questions is called **macroeconomics**. "Macro" because of the focus on the overall performance of an economy rather than on the behavior of individual consumers, firms or markets.

Figure 3
Potential and Actual Real GDP, 1930–2009

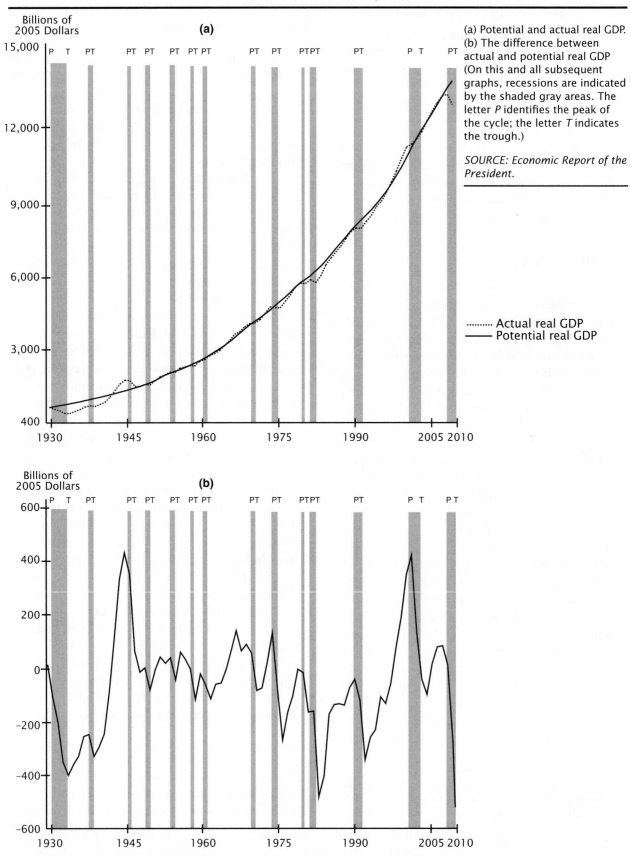

(a) Potential and actual real GDP.
(b) The difference between actual and potential real GDP (On this and all subsequent graphs, recessions are indicated by the shaded gray areas. The letter *P* identifies the peak of the cycle; the letter *T* indicates the trough.)

SOURCE: *Economic Report of the President.*

.... Actual real GDP
—— Potential real GDP

Table 1
Business Cycles in the United States

Table 1
Business Cycles in the United States

Trough	Peak	Length of upturn (months)	Length of downturn (months)	Length of cycle* (months)
December 1854	June 1857	30	18	
December 1858	October 1860	22	8	40
June 1861	April 1865	46	32	54
December 1867	June 1869	18	18	50
December 1870	October 1873	34	65	52
March 1879	March 1882	36	38	101
May 1885	March 1887	22	13	60
May 1891	January 1893	20	17	40
June 1894	December 1895	18	18	33
June 1897	June 1899	24	18	42
December 1900	September 1902	21	23	39
August 1904	May 1907	33	13	56
June 1908	January 1910	19	24	32
January 1912	January 1913	12	23	36
December 1914	August 1918	44	7	67
March 1919	January 1920	10	18	17
July 1921	May 1923	22	14	40
July 1924	October 1926	27	13	41
November 1927	August 1929	21	43	34
March 1933	May 1937	50	13	93
June 1938	February 1945	80	8	45
October 1945	November 1948	37	11	45
October 1949	July 1953	45	10	56
May 1954	August 1957	39	8	49
April 1958	April 1960	24	10	32
February 1961	December 1969	106	11	116
November 1970	November 1973	36	16	47
March 1975	January 1980	58	6	74
July 1980	July 1981	12	16	18
November 1982	July 1990	92	19	108
March 1991	March 2001	120	8	128
November 2001	December 2007	73	at least 20	81
Late summer 2009 (probably*)	n/a	n/a	n/a	n/a

SOURCE: NBER; the U.S. Dept. of Commerce, *Survey of Current Business*, October 1994, Table C-51.

*Precise date unknown at time data were gathered in fall of 2009.

Figure 4
A Stylized Business Cycle

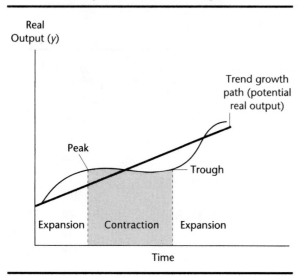

What about potential real GDP? **Potential real GDP** is a constant-dollar measure of the output an economy *could produce if its resources were employed fully.* That is, potential real GDP is the output that would be produced if an economy produced on its production possibilities frontier. (Potential real GDP is defined more carefully in Chapter 19.)

Unemployment

During a period when real output is less than potential real output, resources are **unemployed**. There is a tendency to think of unemployment only in terms of labor resources—more people are out of work and jobs are harder to find during downturns; fewer people are out of work and jobs are easier to find during upturns. Other resources, including capital, also stand idle when real output falls short of potential real output, however. Indeed, during downturns, economic difficulties are not restricted to certain parts of the economy but are generally pervasive.

is a dollar measure of the aggregate output produced by an economy. **Real GDP** is a constant-dollar measure of aggregate output. Differences between the two measures are due to inflation or deflation. (Both measures of the performance of an economy are described more fully in the appendix to this chapter.)

Capital. Figure 5 illustrates this point by considering the employment of capital as measured by the **capital utilization rate**, which is the fraction of the capital stock that is currently being used. If

Figure 5
Capital Utilization Rate, 1950–2009

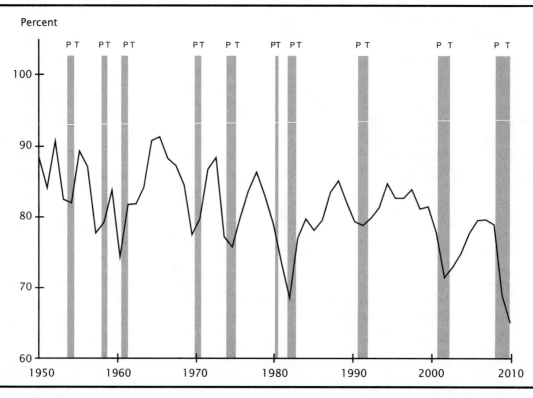

Figure 6
Civilian Unemployment Rate, 1950–2009

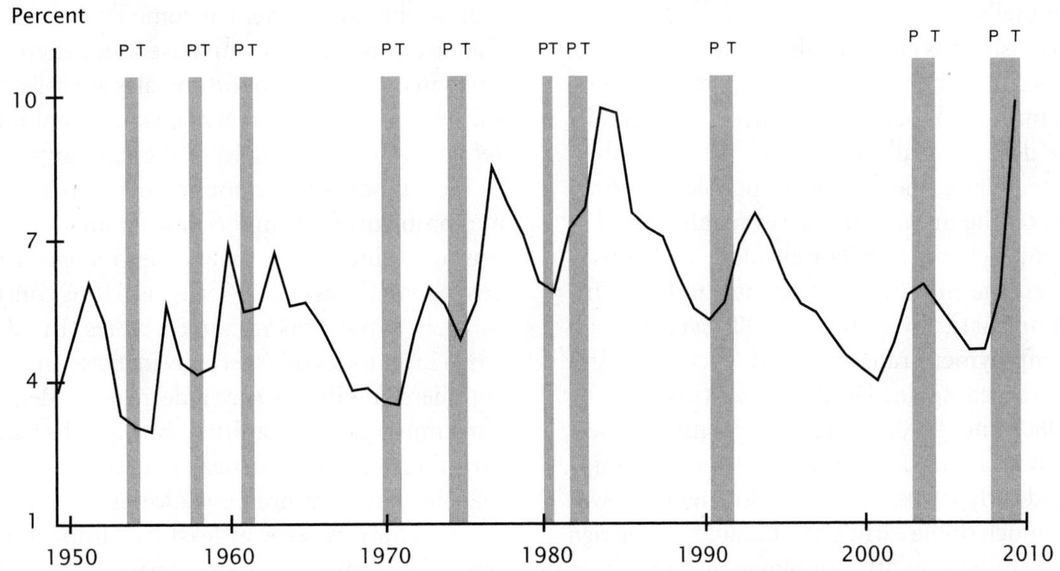

all productive machines, factories, and other kinds of capital were in use, the capital utilization rate would be 100 percent. This rate is never actually achieved. Because of regular maintenance requirements, some of an economy's capital will be idle even when the economy is employing its resources fully. Hence, full employment of capital occurs at something less than a 100-percent capital utilization. For this reason, it is more useful to look at *changes* in the capital utilization rate. When the capital utilization rate falls, some capital that would have been used becomes unemployed. As a consequence, an economy produces in the interior of its production possibilities frontier. In the recession of 1982, for example, the capital utilization rate fell to 70 percent. This decline meant that 30 percent of the productive capital in the United States was unemployed. This increase in the unemployment of capital from the previous year roughly coincided with the decline in real GDP during the same period, as illustrated in Figure 3.

Labor. Figure 6 provides a picture of the US **unemployment rate** across time.[2] Note that periods of

declining real GDP are also periods of high or increasing unemployment of labor. For instance, in the downturn of the early part of the 1980s, the unemployment rate reached almost 10 percent. That is, during that recession, roughly 10 percent of the available productive workers in the United States were not being employed to produce goods and services. During the Great Depression, the unemployment rate was as high as 25 percent; during the downturn in the early 1990s, the unemployment rate was near 7 percent. When the unemployment rate falls, *ceteris paribus*, more labor resources are employed and real output increases. When the unemployment rate increases, however, some of the productive labor resources in the economy are idle.

Zero unemployment, like 100-percent utilization of capital, is not really possible. Just as capital can be considered fully utilized even if the measured utilization rate is less than 100 percent, however, for reasons discussed at some length in Chapter 23 ("More on Unemployment"), labor can be considered fully employed even if the unemployment rate is greater than zero. The unemployment rate consistent with potential GDP in Figure 3 is called the **natural rate of unemployment**. What determines the natural rate of unemployment and its relationship to the actual unemployment rate are also discussed in detail in Chapter 23. For now it is sufficient

---

[2] The unemployment rate is the fraction of unemployed workers compared to the total labor force. This rate will be discussed more fully in Chapter 23.

to note that as real output falls below potential real output, unemployment increases, and as real output increases beyond potential real output, unemployment falls.

Curiously, jobs are generally being created even during periods when there is rising unemployment and the number of persons employed may actually increase despite small increases in the unemployment rate. That is, the number of people employed depends on the number of jobs available as well as the unemployment rate. For example, as Figure 7 illustrates, the number of persons employed increased dramatically over the 1980s even though the unemployment rate increased, decreased, and then increased again. Despite downturns in the early 1980s and 1990s, there were 30 million new jobs created in the US economy between the mid-1970s and early 1990s. The unemployment rate was high for much of the early 1990s because *not enough jobs* were available to offer employment to all those who wanted to work, even after this dramatic increase in the number of jobs in the economy was taken into account. This also means that despite the creation of new jobs, the economy did not produce what it otherwise might have if all resources had been fully utilized.

Inventory Fluctuations

Firms purchase goods with the expectation that they will be able to sell them at some later time. Goods that are produced or purchased and then held by firms in anticipation of future sales are called **inventories**. The aggregate level of inventory holdings also reflects the cyclical activity of the economy—it tends to increase during economic downturns. This creates problems for firms because an unanticipated or unwanted increase in inventories increases a firm's costs, sometimes dramatically, and thus contributes to cyclical patterns in bankruptcies. In addition, when inventories unexpectedly increase, orders from suppliers fall. In this way, a decrease in demand by consumers gets transmitted through the economy. To understand why, we need to first understand the reasons that firms hold inventories.

Inventories serve at least two important purposes: Consumers have additional choices and deliveries can be made faster. When you shop for jeans, for example, you expect to have a selection you can look through before you make a purchase. You also expect that you will be able to take the jeans you purchase with you, and not have to wait for them to be manufactured and shipped to you at some later

Figure 7
Civilian Employment, 1950–2009

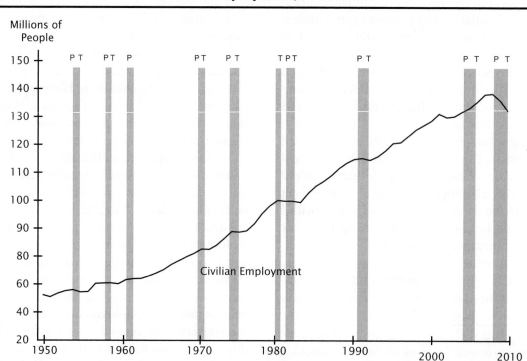

date. To meet these expectations, clothing stores have an inventory of jeans of various sizes and styles.

Holding inventories is costly because the goods held in its inventory tie up some of a firm's money. For example, suppose that over the period of a year a clothing store has an inventory of jeans for which it paid $1,000. The firm's costs have increased by *at least* the interest on $1,000. That is, the firm could have put its $1,000 in a bank account and earned the going rate of interest instead of putting its $1,000 into jeans where it earns no interest. Alternatively, if the firm had to borrow the $1,000 from a bank in order to purchase its inventory, it would have to pay the going rate of interest on the loan. In either case, if the interest rate is 10 percent, for each $1,000 in inventories held for a year, the firm's costs increase by $100.

Firms willingly incur inventory-holding costs because inventories make it possible to better serve consumers. The cost of holding inventories, then, is just another cost of doing business. The problem for a firm is that it is a cost that can change in *unanticipated* ways. Specifically, if a firm's sales do not reach expected levels, its inventories will be *greater than anticipated* and, as a consequence, its costs will be greater than anticipated as well. For example, if a local clothing store expected to sell 30 pairs of jeans in a month, it might have an inventory of 60 pairs at the beginning of the month. If the actual demand was equal to the anticipated demand, the firm would sell 30 pairs during the month and have an inventory of 30 pairs at the end of the month. If the demand for jeans was less than anticipated, however, the owner would have a greater-than-expected inventory at the end of the month (say 50 pairs), and higher than anticipated costs as a consequence. On the other hand, if a firm's sales were greater than expected, its inventories would decrease and there would be less of a selection for new customers. This outcome might also be costly for a firm because some customers might go elsewhere, looking for greater selection or faster delivery. Thus, firms must balance the costs associated with dissatisfied customers against the costs associated with holding money in inventories.

Fluctuations in a firm's inventories reflect fluctuations in the demand for what the firm produces. If demand is less than anticipated, inventories increase; if demand is more than anticipated, inventories decrease. Although the inventories of a single firm may change with its particular fortunes, **aggregate inventories** will not fluctuate much unless there are economy-wide changes in demand. That is, at any moment, some firms find their inventories falling because of an increase in market demand while other firms find their inventories increasing because of a decrease in market demand. If the demand for output across most markets fell at about the same time, however, inventories would, on average, unexpectedly increase. Therefore, fluctuations in **aggregate inventories** are indicative of coordination problems and adjustment difficulties across the entire economy. Moreover, when aggregate inventories unexpectedly increase, firms will cut back on orders from suppliers and an economy-wide change in demand at one level will ripple through the economy. Figure 8 illustrates fluctuations in aggregate inventories.

Changes in Fixed Investment

Economic cycles and their costs can be seen in yet another way. We can look at the additions that *all* firms and households make to the capital stock that they use (**aggregate fixed investment**). Fluctuations in aggregate fixed investment by firms (**aggregate business fixed investment**) and aggregate residential housing by households (**aggregate residential fixed investment**), two important forms of private fixed investment in an economy, are illustrated in Figure 9. These data indicate that there are dramatic *cyclical* changes in aggregate fixed investment, which increases over some periods and then declines, only to increase once again. Investment by one group of firms represents the purchase of output from other firms. Hence, the fortunes of firms producing new capital are directly affected by these cycles.

Price-Level Changes

In addition to cyclical patterns in the use of labor, capital and other scarce resources and the accompanying fluctuations in the real output, there are often changes in an economy's price level. The most common measure of the price level is the Consumer Price Index (CPI). (The appendix to this chapter discusses how the CPI and other price indexes are created.) As we noted in Chapter 3, an increase in the price level (as measured, say, by the CPI) means that there has been **inflation**. Fluctuations in the price level are illustrated in Figure 10 (part b is a graph of the *percentage changes* in the price level illustrated in part a—a positive percentage change, corresponding to an increase in the price level, is an **inflation** and a

Figure 8
Changes in Private Inventories, 1930–2009

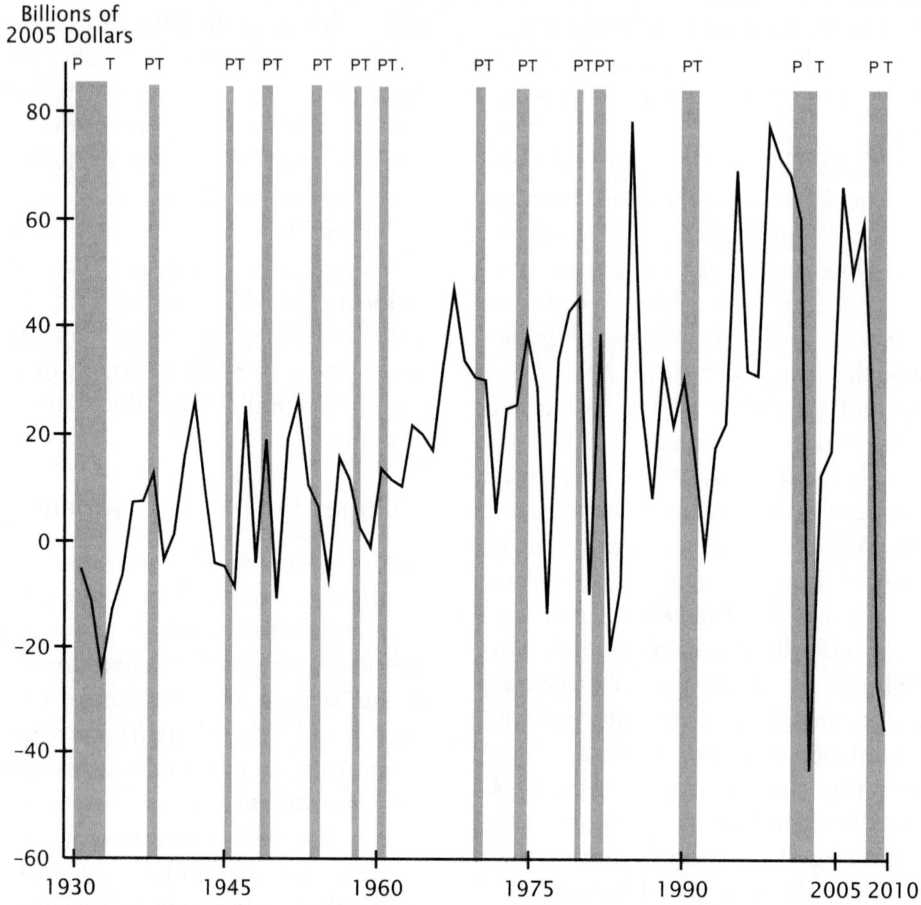

negative percentage of change, corresponding to a decrease in the price level, is a **deflation**).[3]

Figure 10 illustrates something interesting. While the price level has at times increased and at other times decreased, it has *not* done so in a cyclical fashion in quite the same way as changes in real output, capital utilization, labor unemployment, inventories, and real investment. Moreover, recent year-by-year inflation (something less than 4 percent) is a continuation of a *sustained* inflation that begins following World War II. (Indeed, the price level has actually fallen in only one year since 1950.) This sustained inflation over your lifetime might suggest that market economies always have inflation. This isn't so—there have been periods in US history with a gradual decline in the price level (for example, from the end of the Civil War up to the early twentieth century) as well as periods

of sharp declines (as, for example, in the years immediately following World War I and during the Great Depression). There have also been short periods of substantial inflation followed by short periods of deflation or stable prices (for example, the years immediately following the Revolutionary and Civil Wars).

Inflation rates over the last 40 years in the United States, even considering the peak rates in the 1970s, have been modest when compared to inflations occurring elsewhere in the world, either now or in the past. For example, in Hungary following World War II, the inflation rate *per hour* exceeded the highest inflation rate *per year* in the United States in the last 50 years. An inflation comparable to the one in Hungary occurred in the Balkans in the early 1990s. In our own history, the inflations that occurred during both the Revolutionary and Civil Wars make the inflation of the past 20 years appear very modest. Each of these inflations tended to be of a fairly short duration, however. One of the puzzles about the US economy is that, although there have been periods of inflations and deflation

---

[3] The inflation or deflation rate is calculated as price level this year minus the price level for the year earlier divided by the price level for the year earlier, that is, the rate of inflation is defined as $(P-P_{-1})/P_{-1}$.

Figure 9
Percentage Changes in Business and Residential Fixed Investment, 1930–2010

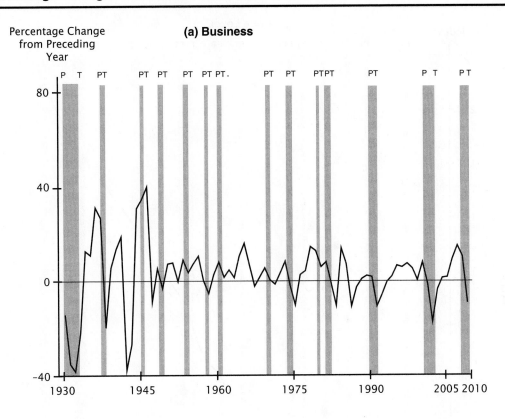

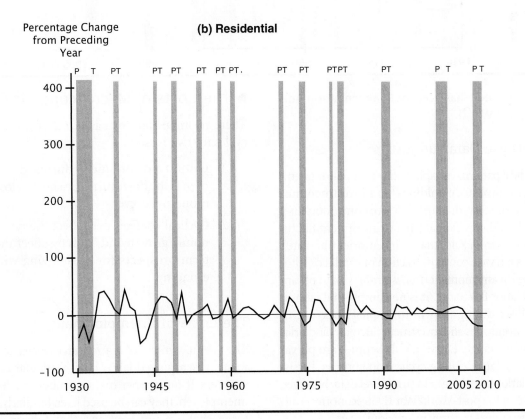

Figure 10a
Price Level and Inflation Rates, 1930–2010

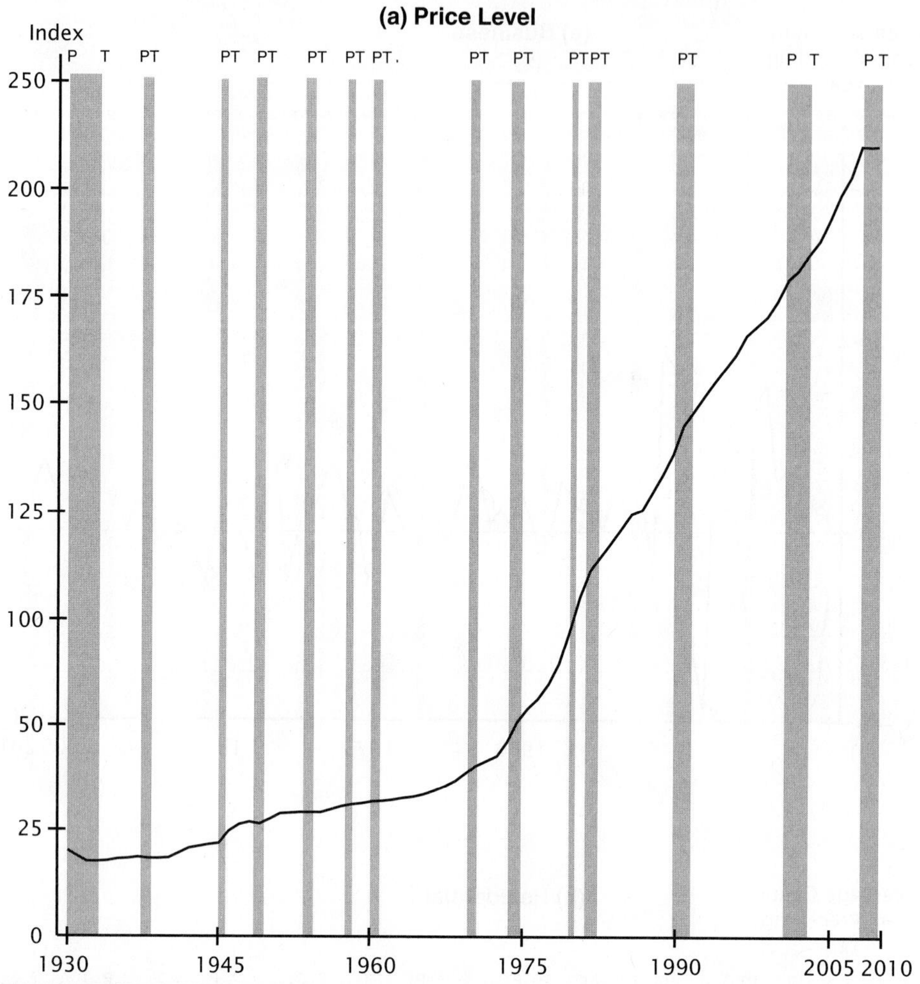

(a) Price Level

in the past, there has been *sustained* inflation only since World War II.

What These Data Suggest

The cyclical patterns of capital utilization, labor unemployment, inventory holdings, and investment just outlined suggest that the US economy does not smoothly add new capital (that is, investment fluctuates) or goods for sale (that is, inventories fluctuate), nor does it have a constant fraction of capital or labor employed at any moment (that is, employment of capital and labor fluctuate). It is not simply that labor is unemployed during a downturn; capital is also unemployed, inventories and investment fluctuate, and price levels may change. Economic difficulties are pervasive, not isolated, during cyclical downturns. Persistent inflation as evidence in price level data, however, suggest that the post-World War II US economy is different from the economy in previous years.

▶ The Costs of Macroeconomic Cycles

There are important costs associated with economic cycles for two reasons.

1. Output not produced during downturns, even if the downturns are short, is lost to the economy forever.

2. Cyclical changes may affect the rate of economic growth and, thereby affect the long-term prospects for those living within an economy.

The Costs of Unemployment

The unemployment of *any* resource creates economic waste. Unemployed labor is of particular concern, however. If oil, copper ore, or timber are currently unemployed, they can be used later. Similarly, inventories that are not sold and that remain unused

Figure 10b

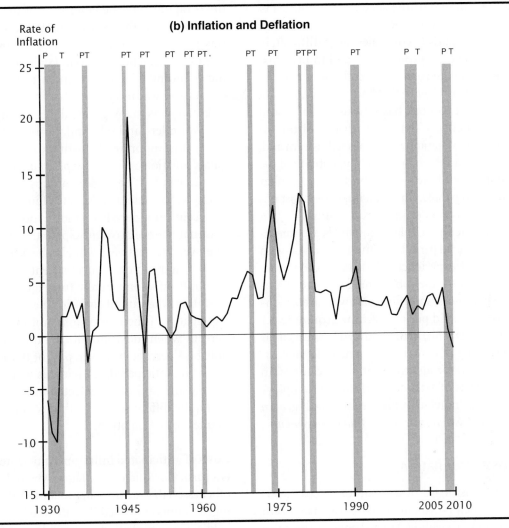

because of a change in demand can usually be stored (at some cost) for sale and consumption later. Even unemployed capital is available for use at some point in the future, although it will generally have depreciated somewhat over time. Labor, however, is *perishable*—it cannot be stored for future use. If you are unemployed today, the output that you would have produced is forever lost to the economy. You may go back to work tomorrow, but it is not possible for the economy to recover and use the hours that you did *not* work today. For this reason, unemployed labor imposes large efficiency losses on an economy.

The losses associated with unemployed labor resources are not limited to the decline in economic output. Unemployment of labor also creates serious social problems. Persons who are unemployed have low incomes and must sustain consumption either out of their savings or from private or public support. By contrast, those who remain employed

during a period of high unemployment are mostly unaffected by the cyclical downturn. This difference in the burden of economic cycles between the employed and the unemployed creates dramatic short-term changes in the distribution of income. It is difficult for a political system to be widely supported by those who live and work within it when such adverse distributional consequences persist for long periods or when the costs of economic cycles fall disproportionately on a particular group of individuals. In the 1930s, for example, a large fraction of the workforce was unemployed and the adverse distributional effects were dramatic and evident. These were years of great pessimism about the future of market economies and the US political system itself. During periods such as these, not surprisingly, alternative economic and political systems seem more attractive. Hitler came to power, in part, because of the economic turmoil in Germany following World

War I. More recently, high unemployment rates following the collapse of the socialist economies in Eastern Europe and the Soviet Union have made movements to market economies more difficult, in part because certain groups have had to bear disproportionately the costs of the collapse.

There is also evidence that being unable to work when you want to work has serious personal and psychological effects. Extended periods of unemployment undermine an individual's self-esteem and, often, corrode family stability and the stability of the communities that have a disproportionate number of unemployed people. This is an important cost not easily measured by a decline in real output.

Finally, when particular individuals are unemployed for extended periods of time, they end up with less job market experience. Workers become more skilled through on-the-job training and other job-related experiences, so individuals who are unemployed for extended periods of time acquire fewer job-related skills. This, in turn, adversely affects their lifetime earning potential and, if unemployment is widespread, the productivity of the economy. In short, the effects of extended periods of unemployment for some individuals may be long-lasting, *even when these individuals eventually find employment.*

The Costs of Inflation

Whereas it is easy to feel or see many of the costs associated with unemployment, the costs associated with inflation are more subtle. Fluctuations in the price level, although not necessarily associated with changes in real income, nevertheless appear to affect our well-being. The adverse social and political responses to higher rates of inflation in the United States in the 1970s clearly indicate that individuals dislike inflation and that *changes* in the rate of inflation are particularly troublesome. Early in that decade, political pressure pushed President Richard Nixon to impose controls on wages and prices to control a relatively modest inflation. The controls were ineffective; after they were lifted, inflation increased. Two large increases in oil prices during the decade further fueled inflationary pressures. By the end of the decade, both inflation and interest rates were high. Two presidents, Gerald Ford and Jimmy Carter, were unable to win reelection, in part because of the dismal performance of the economy during the decade.

Our apparent dislike of inflation might suggest that the opposite, deflation, would be attractive.

However, when the price level was falling—sometimes rapidly—in the latter part of the nineteenth century and in the 1920s and 1930s, the economy was also in distress. Indeed, in the 1890s, there was intense political pressure to *inflate* so as to invigorate the economy. (This in contrast to the late 1970s when there was intense political pressure to *reduce* inflation so as to invigorate the economy!)

To understand why inflation (or deflation) is costly, it is important to distinguish between *anticipated* inflation and *unanticipated* inflation. The difference can best be understood by considering an example. Suppose that the rate of inflation has been 4 percent for a decade or more. Individuals might reasonably expect or anticipate that the inflation rate over the next year will also be 4 percent. They will adjust their behavior consistent with this expectation. If inflation actually turned out to be 4 percent, then the rate of inflation has been correctly anticipated. If the rate of inflation increased to 10 percent when most individuals thought it would only be 4 percent, however, part of the actual inflation is unanticipated. Individuals will find certain costs as they adjust to expected inflation; they will find quite different costs as they scramble to adjust to unexpected inflation.

Costs of anticipated inflation. Anticipated inflation is a particular kind of tax. Those who hold money or other assets that are fixed in money terms such as savings accounts are "taxed" by inflation because money held during an inflationary period purchases less the longer its held. As we learned in Chapter 12, a tax on the use of an item provides an incentive to use it less. It is difficult, however, to hold less money because money is used in transactions. Indeed, the only way to hold less money is to transact more frequently by getting paid and shopping more often. However, transacting more frequently is costly (it takes more time). Thus, even when it is fully anticipated, inflation imposes a cost on individuals because it undermines the important role that money plays in reducing transaction costs. In extreme cases (called **hyperinflations**), people may abandon the use of money altogether. When they do, the time spent transacting increases very dramatically and, as a consequence, the time spent producing goods and services often decreases and real output falls.

Since anticipated inflation is a kind of tax on holding money, individuals will also use scarce resources in efforts to avoid paying the inflation tax.

For example, during an inflation, firms expend resources just to change prices on products already stocked on their shelves, and individuals take time to manage their cash, checking, and savings accounts more carefully. Resources—time or other productive energies—are pulled away from productive activities and are used in inflation-avoidance activities. In this way, inflation further distorts resource use.

Costs of unanticipated inflation. When inflation is not anticipated, it redistributes wealth from those who lend to those who borrow. This redistribution may also impose costs on an economy. Suppose you made a one-year loan of $1,000 to a friend assuming that the rate of inflation would be 4 percent over the year. If the inflation rate turned out to be 20 percent rather than 4 percent, the $1,000 your friend returns to you at the end of the year will purchase only $833 in goods. Clearly, the unanticipated inflation has made you worse off and your friend better off. The risk that this might happen makes it harder to get loans during periods when the rate of inflation bounces around.

The unanticipated redistribution of wealth can also create other costs. In the 1960s, for example, many savings and loan associations made 30-year mortgage loans with interest rates between 4 and 6 percent. It was thought at the time that these interest rates would compensate lenders for making the loans. When inflation unexpectedly increased in the late 1960s and 1970s, however, lenders found that the interest rates on the mortgages they held were lower than the rate of inflation. Persons who borrowed before the unanticipated increase in inflation were delighted—their mortgages rates were low relative to the rates they could earn on savings, and they were also able to make payment on their mortgages with dollars that purchased less than those they borrowed. However, lenders lost and when inflation increased almost all of them eventually went bankrupt. One reason (but not the only one) for the S&L crisis in the 1980s was this unanticipated transfer from lenders to earlier borrowers.

By contrast, an unanticipated deflation redistributes wealth from borrowers to lenders. In this case, borrowers have to make payments with dollars that are worth *more* than those they borrowed. For example, during the Great Depression, the price level declined substantially and unexpectedly and, as a consequence, a large proportion of homeowners in the United States who had mortgage debt found themselves in default because of the dramatic redistribu-tion from them to their creditors—the payments that were owed were increasing in value because of the deflation. That is, they had to pay back more, in terms of what dollars purchased, than they borrowed. These defaults on home mortgages exacerbated the effects of the already very serious economic downturn that started in 1929.

Even when prices do not actually fall, if the rate of inflation decreases *unexpectedly*, redistributions will occur. (A fall in the rate of inflation is called a **disinflation**.) For example, during the early part of the 1980s, the inflation rate unexpectedly declined from 10 percent to 4 percent. Even though there was still inflation, many farmers who had mortgage debt on their farms found themselves in default. They had borrowed when interest rates were high, expecting prices to continue to increase at a much higher rate than they actually did. Then they found that they had to make payments on high-interest loans even though the prices at which they sold their output did not increase as rapidly as they had anticipated. Bankruptcy followed.

Erratic or changing inflation rates impose yet another cost on an economy: Unexpected changes in the rate of inflation create uncertainty about the future course of prices. When the rate of inflation is variable—5 percent one year, 10 percent the next, 6 percent the next, and so on—it is difficult for individuals and firms to negotiate long-term contracts or do long-term planning. Economic growth may be adversely affected because long-term contracting and planning are important for the efficient allocation of certain resources, particularly fixed investment. Countries with wildly gyrating rates of inflation almost always face economic stagnation as a consequence.

Finally, unanticipated inflation undermines the ability of the price system to convey the information necessary for the efficient allocation of commodities by making it difficult for individuals to know exactly what is happening to relative prices. During an inflationary period, for example, it is difficult for a farmer to know whether an increase in the price of a head of lettuce from $.30 to $.60 is a consequence of the inflation or the result of an increase in demand for lettuce. In general, if the price of lettuce doubles because of inflation, the farmer won't want to grow more lettuce because the prices of most inputs will also have doubled. If the price doubles because of an increase in demand, however, the farmer will want to grow more lettuce. This confusion about what is happening to relative prices means that individuals will

Figure 11
Real Per Capita GDP (in 2005 dollars)

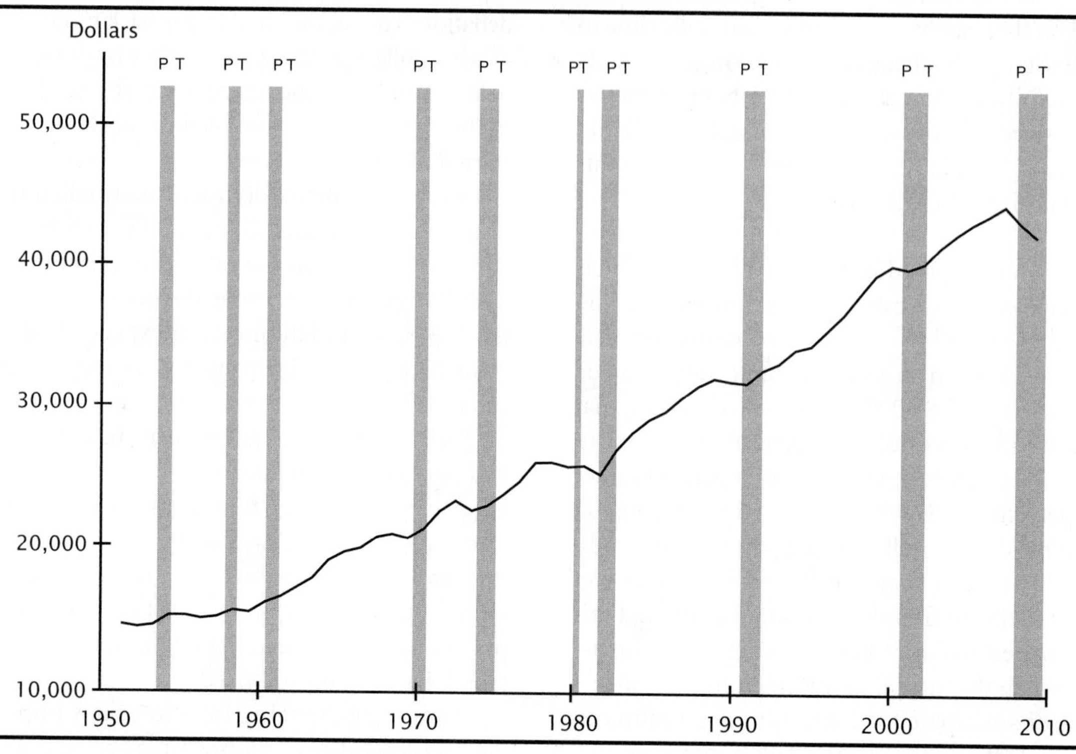

find it difficult to decide which goods to produce or purchase. As a consequence, the economy will coordinate activities less effectively. When this happens, the economy will grow less rapidly or stagnate.

▶ US Economic Growth

Business cycles are the stuff of high drama or, at the very least, they are of sufficient drama that they are followed with great interest by the news media and politicians. Newspaper headlines frequently call attention to unemployment, inflation, a rise in interest rates, or a drop in the value of the dollar. Longer-term changes in potential real output attract far less attention. Although the differences in income levels and consumption opportunities between ourselves and our grandparents may be easy to see, they are easy to see only across a generation or more. If real output is increasing at a rate of 1 percent per year, for example, real output will double in 70 years. When the growth rate is between 2 and 3 percent, as has been typical over much of US history, real output will double about every 25 years. Just prior to the Great Depression, real GDP per person living in the United States was about $6,800. In 2002, real GDP per person living in the United States was about $35,000. (Both in 1996 dollars.)

A more complete historical record of GDP per person from 1950 to 2000 is illustrated in Figure 11. Even though there have been periods when real per capita GDP fell, as for example in the early 1980s, the trend has been upward.

The long-term sustained changes illustrated in Figure 11 are often overshadowed by short-term concerns with cyclical unemployment and inflation. Small changes in the long-term growth rate matter a lot, however. The differences between your economic circumstances and those of your grandparents came about because of changes that were small, slow, and much less remarkable at any given moment of time than were the larger, cyclical movements. Small changes from one month to another or from one year to another, even though they are not very noticeable at the time, result in long-term changes in well-being that are almost always more significant than the effects of cyclical movements. As a consequence, these small changes are enormously important. It is because of small but fairly consistent increases in the productive capacity of the economy that, on average, we are better off than our grandparents. If these changes continue to occur, our children and their children will be better off than we are. This point is best illustrated by considering the long-term changes in the United States over its economic history.[4]

Historical Perspective

In May 1607, a small group of English settlers established a colony, which they called Jamestown, on the James River in Virginia. More than a year had passed since they had left England; over one-quarter of the original group had died of starvation and disease as they crossed the Atlantic Ocean. When relief arrived in January 1608, only 38 of the original 144 colonists were still alive. The settlement by the Pilgrims at Plymouth, Massachusetts, in 1620 was equally difficult. Despite this inauspicious beginning, it is generally believed that, by the early part of the eighteenth century, real wages in the American colonies were higher than those in England, where wages were high in comparison to those in the rest of Europe.[5]

Many immigrants did not work for wages, however. They were either servants (sometimes bound for life or as slaves) or small farmers and fishermen whose incomes fluctuated with the whims of the weather—a good harvest meant a high income, a poor harvest meant a low income. Even so, the best estimates suggest that the standard of living in the colonies by 1710, on average, was not dramatically different from that of England. Thus, very early in the history of the New World, the colonies appeared to be prosperous, at least by the standards of the day. It has been estimated that annual per capita output by 1710 was probably between $450 and $600 (in 1982 dollars). Even though this amount may seem extraordinarily low, the 1990 per capita income in Nepal was less than one half the 1710 per capita income in the United States.

By 1840 when the first reliable economic census was completed, aggregate real output appears to have increased by $75 to $100 *for each dollar of real output in 1710.* If these numbers are accurate, this is one of the highest sustained rates of growth known, anywhere or anytime. However, the population also grew rapidly, probably by somewhat more than 3 percent per year. Thus, real *per capita* output increased, but the changes were much less dramatic than those in aggregate real output. Real per capita output probably doubled over the 130-year period to about $900 (1982 dollars), an average gain of about 0.5 percent per year. To put this in perspective, in modern times, per capita growth rates of from 3 to 5 times this amount have been common. Thus, from 1710 to 1840 there was very rapid growth in *aggregate* real output, but only modest growth in *per capita* real output.

Growth did not occur at these rates every year, but instead fluctuated from year to year and decade to decade. The nature of these fluctuations prior to the Revolutionary War is not known. Following the war, however, the American economy expanded rapidly as the European states were either at war with one another or in domestic turmoil almost constantly until the end of the Napoleonic Wars in 1815. These economic disruptions in Europe provided substantial opportunities for US producers, both of exports and commodities for the domestic market that in times of peace encountered competition from European goods. The end of the Napoleonic Wars, however, brought almost a decade of economic stagnation to the United States. Beginning in the mid-1820s, the American economy began to grow rapidly once again. Real per capita output was probably increasing and doing so at an increasing rate. This rapid growth continued through 1840.

Although the US economy in 1840 was at least 75 times larger than it had been in 1710, it was still small by modern standards. The entire US economy in 1840 was probably about the size of the economy of Iowa today. Despite this modest size, the 1840 economy has been estimated to have been about two-thirds as large as the economies of either Britain or France, the two dominant economies of the world at that time.

Between 1840 and 1960, aggregate real output in the United States increased by about $60 *for each dollar produced in 1840.* This is an average growth rate of about 3.6 percent, an average annual growth rate just a little bit higher than that for the US economy between 1710 and 1840. Again, by standards of economic change elsewhere in the world, the economy's growth over this period was very dramatic. For example, in 1840 the US economy was two-thirds as large as the economies of either France or England while in

---

[4] Not all of the data on which the following discussion is based are equally reliable. Prior to 1840, information about the U.S. economy is incomplete, so discussions of economic growth during that time are necessarily speculative. Between 1840 and 1929, the data are incomplete, but a more confident picture of changes in real output can be drawn. Since 1929, we have a quite detailed picture of changes in the U.S. economy. For other countries, particularly less-developed ones, however, even recent data are incomplete and interpretations based on these data continue to have serious problems.

[5] The real wage is the amount of commodities a person could purchase if he or she were paid the prevailing wage for one hour's work.

1960 the US economy was almost five times larger than the British economy and almost eight times larger than the French economy. This change in relative size occurred even though during the same interval both the French and British economies were growing at rates that were high by the standards of virtually all other countries *except* the United States.

Once again, population growth made growth rates in per capita real output less impressive. There were important changes in per capita output, nonetheless. Indeed, between 1840 and 1960, per capita real output increased at an average annual rate of just over 1.5 percent, a substantially higher rate than that enjoyed by the economy between 1710 and 1840. Many countries, including Japan and Sweden had higher growth rates over part of this period, but very few had comparable *sustained* growth rates in per capita real output for a comparable length of time. Thus, even though the US growth rate in per capita real output was not extraordinarily high, the growth in the economy persisted for an extraordinarily long time. As a consequence, by 1960 the US economy produced about one-third of the total output of the world, even though the US population was only about 6 percent of the population of the world. In per capita terms, real income increased sixfold between 1840 and 1960.

Changes in Aggregate Real Output and Changes in per Capita Real Output

In this discussion of the historical record, we have bounced back and forth between two different measures of economic growth: growth in *aggregate real output* (measured by real GDP) and growth in *per capita real output* (per capita real GDP). Each is a useful measure of a different aspect of economic growth. Growth in aggregate real output measures the increase in the overall size of the economy and what it might mean for the use of scarce resources; growth in per capita real output measures the increase in the size of economy in terms of what it might mean to the average person living within the economy. (In each case, the changes are calculated as annual percentage differences.)

The overall size of the economy is important when we consider the pressures placed on scarce resources or the environment or employment opportunities. It is possible for the economy to increase in size without any increase in per capita real output. This might happen if the population grew as rapidly or more rapidly than aggregate real output did. In these cases, even though per capita real output may not change, an economy that is growing in aggregate real output terms uses more resources. It also provides more jobs.

An economy doesn't have to be large (in terms of aggregate real output) in order for per capita real output to be high. The economy of Switzerland is small, but per capita GDP is high and, hence, the standard of living in Switzerland is high. By contrast, the economy of China is enormous, but so is the population and per capita GDP is low as is the standard of living.

It is also possible for per capita real output to grow but for the increases to be distributed in such a way that many people within the economy do not benefit. Thus, even when measured in per capita terms, economic growth is not necessarily linked to an increase in individual well-being *for everyone* living in an economy. On the other hand, it is difficult to increase individual well-being for all or a large number of individuals within an economy without growth in per capita real output.

Finally, you should not infer from this discussion that the growth rate for the United States, in either per capita or aggregate output terms, *ought* to be either high or low. Rather, the important point is that macroeconomic difficulties that lower growth rates, even by modest amounts, can make a substantial difference in the long-run well-being of individuals. As a consequence, it is important to evaluate macroeconomic policies not just in terms of what happens to the business cycle or price level, but also in terms of their effects on economic growth.

Sources of Growth

The tale of dramatic US economic development sketched above has a simple explanation, at least on the surface. Potential real output depends on the resources available to an economy, so it changes under two conditions: when resources change or when existing resources are used more effectively. This means that there are two sources of economic growth. First, if productive inputs such as labor and capital available to an economy increase, there will be economic growth. Second, if the productivity of these inputs increases, the economy will grow. That is, if we wish to increase the rate of economic growth in the United States, we must either increase the productive inputs available to the economy or increase the productivity of the inputs currently available to the economy.

Table 2
Productive Inputs and Economic Growth, 1840–1960

Input	Estimated percentage contribution to growth rate		
	1840–1900	1900–1960	1840–1960
Labor	47.2%	34.8%	42.7%
Land	9.6	2.5	5.9
Capital	25.9	18.6	22.8
Growth rate in aggregate real output	3.98%	3.12%	3.56%

SOURCE: Robert Gallman, "The Pace and Pattern of Economic Growth," unpublished paper, p. 39.

On the other hand, if the productivity of inputs declines, so will the growth rate of the economy. Some economies remain poor because they are unable to increase the supply of productive inputs or to increase the productivity of the inputs currently available. At the same time, population may continue to increase. As a consequence, real per capita output remains low and changes little.

Increases in productive inputs. In general, available resources have increased over the past century or more of American history. We have more capital, more labor, and more productive land, although we have used up some of our depletable natural resources. It would be straight-forward to estimate the contributions of each input to economic growth if each grew by the same amount. For example, if the economy grew by 7 percent per year and capital, labor, and natural resources each grew by 2 percent per year, then it would seem that each contributed equally to the overall growth rate, 2 percentage points in this example. Thus, of the 7-percent growth rate, increases in inputs would have accounted for 6 percent. The remaining 1 percent could be attributed to a general increase in productivity.

Data show that actual inputs do not have equal rates of growth, however. Between 1840 and 1960, real output grew by a factor of 60 and per capita real output by a factor of about 6. Over this period, the labor force increased by about 13 times, the supply of land by about 12 times, and the stock of capital by 105 times. As a consequence of the vastly different growth rates in inputs, it is difficult to estimate the contributions of different resources to economic growth in the United States. For this reason, the esti-

mates summarized in Table 2 should be thought of as rough approximations only.

As Table 2 shows, nearly half of the growth rate in real output between 1840 and 1900 can be attributed to increases in labor and a little over a quarter of the growth rate can be attributed to increases in capital. Note that although increases in both capital and labor are major contributors to economic growth over this period, the contribution of each declined over time. In addition, note the sharp decline in the importance of increases in land to economic growth.

The economic well-being of individuals in the economy depends upon whether per capita real output changes. Additional workers lead to additional aggregate output *but not necessarily* to additional output per person living in the economy. By contrast, while additional capital leads to additional aggregate output, *changes in the amount of capital available to each worker* can change per capita real output. In the past two centuries, the increase in capital has been much greater than the increase in labor—capital per worker has increased. This increase has made labor *more* productive (essentially, each US worker has more machines to work with than did his or her grandparents), and the fraction of the nation's income paid to workers increased dramatically. [6]

Increases in the amount of capital per worker in the United States have been important to economic growth, but further increases in the capital

---

[6] The additional output produced when additional labor is employed is the marginal product of labor.

Table 3
Productivity and Economic Growth, 1840–1960

Input	Estimated percentage contribution to growth rate		
	1840–1900	1900–1960	1840–1960
Labor	47.2%	34.8%	42.7%
Land	9.6	2.5	5.9
Capital	25.9	18.6	22.8
Productivity	17.3	44.1	28.6
Growth rate in aggregate real output	3.98%	3.12%	3.56%

SOURCE: Robert Gallman, "The Pace and Pattern of Economic Growth," unpublished paper, p. 39.

stock relative to labor are unlikely to be large enough to maintain the economic growth rate at previous levels. For example, an extra percentage point in the capital stock growth rate will add about 0.3 percentage points to the growth in potential real output. Thus, an increase in the growth rate of 1 percentage point per year would require a 3.3 percent increase in the rate of capital accumulation. The capital stock is about $3 trillion in 1982 dollars, so the additional net investment that would be required would be about $99 billion. Total investment has been a little over $300 billion in recent years. As a consequence, investment would have to increase by almost 30 percent to increase the growth rate by 1 percent. Although this very large increase in investment is possible, it is unlikely to be sustainable. Thus, something else will be needed if we are to achieve economic growth comparable to that of the past century or two. Fortunately, there is something else: growth in the productivity of inputs.

Increases in productivity. A second way that economic growth can be sustained or increased is through growth in productivity. **Productivity** is the level of output that can be produced for a specified level of inputs. **Productivity growth** is the *rate of change* in the level of productivity. For example, if output per worker is 100 units in one year and 103 the next, productivity is 103 in the second year and productivity growth is 3 percent.

About 40 percent of the growth in aggregate real output between 1840 to 1960 can be attributed to the growth in labor supply, about 6 percent to increases in land, and about 22 percent to increases

in the stock of capital, as shown in Table 2. The remaining 29 percent is due to increases in productivity. From 1929 through 1948, output per capita grew at a rate of 2.57 percent per year. Of this rate of increase, it is estimated that the growth in inputs contributed 1.56 percentage points, while productivity changes contributed 1.01 percentage points. That is, during this period, growth in productivity alone explains almost 40 percent of the total growth rate. There is evidence that productivity growth has become even more important to economic growth in more recent times, as indicated in Table 3.

Note that after 1900, while the growth rate in aggregate real output fell from 3.98 percent per year to 3.12 percent per year, the contribution of productivity changes to the growth rate increased from 17 to 44 percent. In short, most of the growth in the eighteenth and nineteenth centuries resulted from an increase in the inputs available within the United States—more capital, more labor and more natural resources. But in the twentieth century, nearly one-half of the increase in output was from an increase in the productivity of already available resources.

The effects on per capita real output are even more dramatic. Increased productivity accounted for about one-half of the gain in per capita real output in the nineteenth century. But increased productivity accounted for about 80 percent of the growth in per capita real output in the twentieth century. Hence, any change in productivity growth is certain to affect the future growth rate of the US economy in a very substantial way.

Earlier, we described sustained growth in the United States for more than two centuries from

problematic for the US economy. Between 1973 and 1979, the economic growth rate fell. A further decline occurred after 1979 and growth did not pick up again until the mid-1990s. Thus, for at least two decades there was little economic growth. Why? The persistent increase in productivity, so important in determining the rate of economic growth during the twentieth century, came to a virtual standstill between 1973 and 1979 and then fell between 1979 and 1983. Economists estimate that this change in productivity accounts for more than 80 percent of the slowdown in growth from 1973 through 1982. Because of this slowdown, real output grew by 3.7 percent per year between 1948 and 1973, by 2.61 percent from 1973 to 1979, and by only 0.41 percent from 1979 through 1983. Per capita real output grew by 2.21, 1.59, and −0.62 percent, respectively, for each of these periods. In the late 1980s, potential real output probably started to grow again, but only by 2.3 percent per year, on average. It was not until the mid-1990s that productivity growth rates picked up. Just as increases in productivity during earlier periods fostered relatively robust growth, declines in productivity growth account for much of a slowdown in the overall growth rate in the 1970s and 1980s. The remarkable spurt of growth in the 1990s

occurred only when productivity increased once again. There is an important lesson here: it appears that the economic prospects for the economy during your life will, in large part, be determined by productivity growth rather than an increase in the inputs available to the US economy.

Figure 12 provides a more complete look at changes in productivity since 1950. Note the apparent downward trend in productivity growth over the past three decades. Workers are not becoming less productive. Rather, the *increase* in productivity is falling. Since the mid-1970s, productivity growth has averaged somewhere between 0 and 0.1 percent annually, and for short periods, the growth rate has been negative. Thus, whereas productivity growth averaged 2.4 percent between 1948 and 1973, it averaged less than 1 percent from 1974 until now.

In addition to the dramatic decline in productivity growth for much of the 1970–1995 period, the proportion of resources available for production that were actually employed also decreased. From 1948 through 1969, real output averaged about 99.1 percent of potential real output. From 1970 to 1973, real output fell to 95.1 percent of potential real output, from 1974 through 1979, to 94.5 percent, and from 1979 to 1983, to 90.2 percent. It remained at roughly

Figure 12
Changes in Output Per Hour, Non Farm Business Sector

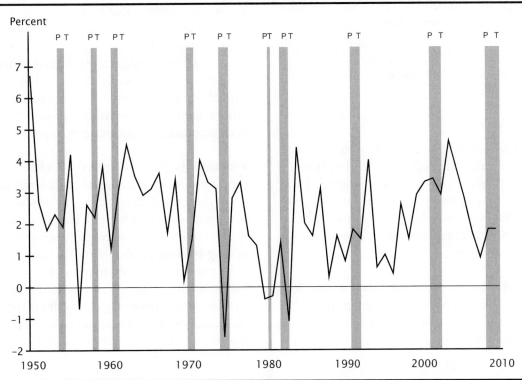

this level through the mid-1990s. This means that in addition to the decline in the growth rate in per capita real output just noted, the US economy was producing less with what resources were available to it. Thus, there were two gaps between where the economy was and where it might have been. One was the gap between what the economy might have been able to produce had it continued along its historic growth path, and the other was between what the economy might have been able to produce, given its lower growth rate, and what it actually did produce. While the 1970s and 1980s are now ancient history, they provide a lesson in the problems that occur when productivity growth is not maintained and resources not fully utilized.

In terms of the broad perspective, it will be useful to keep in mind as we work through the materials in the next several chapters, this discussion of the nature of economic growth suggests two questions in addition to those posed earlier.

- Can the rate of economic growth be influenced by public policy? If so, what policies promote growth and which policies dampen or undermine growth?
- What is the relationship, if any, between policies designed to offset cycles—such as the movement from *B* to *A* in Figure 1—and policies designed to foster changes in the capacity of an economy to produce—such a the movement from *B* to *B'* in Figure 2? Or, put more bluntly, were the problems of the 1970s and 1980s created by misguided or conflicting public policies?

▶ Summary

Cycles. Economies have cycles. As a consequence, at times real output is less than potential real output. When it is, labor resources are unemployed. These fluctuations in employment and real output—commonly called business cycles—are also accompanied by fluctuations in capital utilization, inventory holdings, and investment.

Price-level changes. Economies also have periods when price levels are not stable. When the price level increases, there is inflation; when it decreases, there is deflation. When the rate of inflation falls, there is disinflation. The U.S. has had, over its history, periods of stable prices, inflation *and* deflation. Since World War II, however, there has been a sustained inflation—the rate of inflation has changed with the business cycle, but with exception of one or two very short periods, the price level has not fallen during downturns in nearly 60 years since the war.

Costs. Business cycles impose costs on society. Unemployment lowers the incomes of the unemployed, redistributes income, and creates a loss of labor resources that can never be recovered. Price level changes redistribute incomes, increase transactions costs, divert resources away from productive activities, and create uncertainties that adversely affect the decisions of households and firms.

Growth. Economic growth is defined in two quite different ways. It can be thought of as changes over time in aggregate or total real output an economy produces or it can be thought of in terms of a change over time in per capita real output. Even seemingly small rates of growth lead to substantial effects on the level of GDP when the growth rates are compounded over a number of years. It is these small, but persistent, rates of economic growth that have allowed the industrialized countries of the world to achieve their present economic positions. Similarly, it is the small, but persistent, growth rates in per capita income that have created the high standard of living enjoyed, on average, by people living within these economies.

Several factors determine the rate of growth in an economy. Historically, the growth of inputs—capital, land, and labor—have been quite important. More recently, economic growth has largely been accounted for by increases in productivity.

Productivity. Productivity is the level of output that can be produced by a specified set of inputs. Workers in the United States are highly productive (that is, output per worker is high). *Increases* in per capita income when there is a growing population depend upon *growth* in productivity. The rate of productivity growth was low for much of the last quarter of the twentieth century. With this decline in productivity growth, economic growth rates fell off as well. As a consequence, per capita income increased by less in the 1970s and 1980s than it had in earlier decades—indeed, there was little change in per capita income between the early 1970s and the mid-1990s. Beginning in the mid-1990s, the economic growth rate picked up once again.

▶ APPENDIX: Measuring Aggregate Economic Activity

Measures of **market prices** are easy to understand—$1.59 per pound for hamburger or $3.25 per box of cereal, for example. At a particular price per pound or per box, we decide how much to buy given other, competing uses for our income. Measures of the **price level** may be less easy to understand because they are less commonly used in everyday activities. How are we to understand, for example, a news report that indicates that the CPI is now 280 or that it increased by 1.5 percent over the last three months? What, if anything, does it mean about choices that we might make? What does it imply about the performance of the economy?

Measures of the aggregate or total output produced within an economy are also less grounded in our everyday experiences. Thus, although it is easy to imagine the sale of 1,000 bushels of apples, it is not altogether clear what it means (or what difference it makes) if a news report indicates that GDP is now $9.46 trillion or that real GDP is now $6.42 trillion in 1982 dollars. Yet, being able to measure aggregate economic activity is important in helping to gauge how an economy performs. This is important, in turn, because public policies dealing with inflation, recession, unemployment and other consequences of macroeconomic cycles are almost always responses to measures of changes in the CPI, GDP, the unemployment rate, and other indicators of *aggregate* economic activity.

The general idea of using money to measure economic activity was introduced in Chapter 2. This appendix takes a further look at commonly used measures of aggregate economic activity. At the outset, it is important to note that the word *aggregate* means total, overall, or across most or all of the economy.

Price Indices

An index indicates the value of a given amount of something in terms of its relationship to a base level or amount. For example, the Fahrenheit scale is an index where "32 degrees" is the base freezing point of water. The Celsius scale or index of temperature uses "0 degrees" for the base freezing point of water. Both, obviously, measure exactly the same thing—temperature—but with different bases and index scales. A **price index** is created by considering the ratio of one or more prices in one period to one or more prices in a base period. Creating a price index for a single price is straightforward. Creating an index for a large number of prices is more challenging, since the index uses a single number to summarize many prices.

A price index for a single good. Suppose that in 1990 shirts were priced at $12 and jeans at $24, but that in 2000 the prices were $24 and $48, respectively. While the *relative price* has not changed—a pair of jeans still "costs" two shirts—it must be obvious that *something* has changed: prices in money terms have increased. As a consequence, a given amount of money now purchases fewer shirts and jeans or, put differently, the purchasing power of money has decreased. A price index is one way of measuring the *size* of this particular kind of change.

In order to measure price changes over time, we start with an initial or **base period** price and then obtain subsequent observations on the price *of the same item* through time. If in 1990 jeans were priced at $24 each and in 2000 the same jeans were priced at $48 each, the price of a pair of jeans has doubled, or increased by a factor of two. A price index that reflects this change is constructed in the following way: Divide the price in any year by the base period price. Multiply by 100. That is,

$$I_t = (p_t/p_b) \times 100$$

where I_t denotes the price index for period t, p_t is the price in period t, and p_b is the price in the **base year**. Any year can be selected as a base. If, in this case, we use 1990 as the base year, the index for 1990 is 100 because $I = (\$24/\$24) \times 100 = 100$. Given this base year, the index is 200 for 2000 ($48/$24 × 100). A price index that increases from 100 to 200 conveys the same information as knowing that the dollar price of jeans doubled over that same ten-year interval.

We could have added observations on the price of jeans at any time between 1990 and 2000 or beyond 2000 and created a more complete price index. If jeans cost $36 in 1995, for example, the index value is 150 in that year (obtained by dividing the price in 1995, $36, by the base price, $24, and then multiplying by 100).

After an index is created, it is not possible to tell what the original dollar price actually was, but, in general, we can easily tell what has happened to the price of the good covered by the index. If a price index increased from 100 to 150, the price covered by the index increased by 50 percent (150 − 100 = 50; 50/100 = 0.5); 100 to 185, by 85 percent; 100 to 300, by 200 percent and so forth. Or, if an index increased from 200 to 220, we could easily calculate that, in general, the prices covered by the index increased by 10 percent (220 − 200 = 20; 20/200 = 0.10); 220 to 240 by about 9 percent; and so forth.[7]

A price index for many goods. While an index can be created for a single good, there is not much to be gained by doing so. If we want to trace the pattern of price changes of a single good, the index is no easier to use than changes in the price of the good itself. Price indices become useful when there are a large number of goods and services being sold and we want to trace what is happening, on average, to all of their prices. Suppose, for example, that you purchased one of each of the goods listed below in 1990 and again in 2000 and wished to know what had happened to the prices of the goods, in general, over this ten-year interval.

	Price in 1990	Price in 2000
Shirt	$24.00	$48.00
Haircut	9.50	15.00
Hamburger	1.25	1.50
Paperback book	3.95	5.95
Candy bar	.40	.45

[7] The percentage change in a price index between two time periods is calculated by dividing the change in the index between the two periods by the value of the index in the original period. That is, %Δ = *(index at time 2 − index at time 1)* × 100 divided by *(index at time 1)*

For example, if a price index is 140 this year and was 120 last year, then % Δ = (140 − 120)/120 × 100 =16.7%.

You can easily determine what has happened to the price of each item, but it is more difficult to know what has happened to "all prices taken together." One approach is to consider how the cost of purchasing all of the goods in each year has changed. Purchasing one of each of the goods in 1990 costs $39.10. Ten years later, purchasing the same set of goods (called a **market basket**) costs $70.90. Using these expenditures, we can create a price index with 1990 as the base year: For the base year, the index is 100 (39.10/39.10 = 1.0; 1.0 × 100 = 100); for 2000, the index is 181 (70.90/39.10 = 1.81; 1.81 × 100 = 181). In this example, the cost of buying one of each of these goods increased by 81 percent from 1980 to 1990 [(181 − 100/100) × 100 = 81%]. That is, on average, the prices increased by 81 percent between 1990 and 2000. Generalizing, a price index in period t is

$$I_t = \frac{\text{cost of market basket for period } t}{\text{cost of market basket for base year } b} \times 100$$

where the cost of the market basket is determined by multiplying the *quantity* of each item in the market basket by the *market price* of each item, and then adding up the total amount spent.

Measuring inflation and deflation. Since a price index measures what is happening, on average, to lots of dollar prices, when the price index increases, prices are generally increasing. Increases in a price index are called **inflation**; decreases, **deflation**. Thus, if a price index increased from 200 to 350 over a one-year interval, the **rate of inflation** must have been 75 percent (350 − 200 = 150; 150/200 × 100 = 75%). Alternatively, if an index decreased from 350 to 336, the **rate of deflation** must have been 4 percent (336 − 350 = −14; −14/350 × 100 = −4%).

In interpreting an estimated inflation rate, the period of measurement must be clearly understood. Inflation is usually measured on an *annual* basis. For example, if we speak of the inflation rate as being 8 percent, we usually mean that prices, as measured by a particular price index, have increased by 8 percent over the course of a year. The government, however, publishes some price indices monthly. Thus, if the index changes from 300 to 303 in a single month, the *monthly* inflation rate is 1 percent [(303 − 300)/300) × 100], but the *annual* inflation rate is somewhat greater than 12 percent. That is, *if* the current monthly rate continued for a year, the index would be somewhat more than 336 at the end of the year. Conversely, if the annual inflation rate is announced to be 12 percent, then during the month, prices increased by about 1 percent on average, *not* by 12 percent.

The base period. To create a price index, a base period must be chosen. The selection of a particular base year is arbitrary, but it must be maintained long enough to generate a series of index numbers that will be useful in comparison to the base year index number. That is, it would make little sense to change the base year each year because then there would be no basis for making comparisons. (Incidentally, the first known price index, developed in 1764, covered a 250-year period; it used 1500 as its base year.)

For reasons we will discuss in more detail later—including changes in consumption patterns and changes in the quality of what is purchased—the base period is changed periodically in order to adjust the market basket on which the index is based. Adjusting the market basket allows comparisons to be more meaningful in terms of the prices of goods that individuals actually purchase. That is, what we buy changes over time, so what is included in a price index ought to change as well.

Common price indices. The most commonly cited price index, the **consumer price index (CPI)**, is created in essentially the manner just outlined. The government selects a base year, and, for that year, determines what kinds of goods (for example, food, clothing, housing, transportation, and medical services) an average household consumes and in what quantities. The market basket consists of the mix of goods purchased by an "average" household *and* the number of each good or service purchased over a specified period of time. In the United States, the mix and quantity purchased for an "average" household are determined from periodic surveys of buying patterns conducted by the Federal government. The goods in the market basket are priced at current market prices, weighted by the number of each good typically purchased. That is, the quantity of each good purchased over a year *weights* its contri-

bution to the price index.[8] The index is adjusted, or normalized, to 100 for the base year. The same goods are then priced at various intervals through time (such as monthly, yearly, and so on), and the index is created by dividing the *current* cost of the market basket by its cost *in the base period*.

A similar index, called the **producer price index (PPI)**, is created for the prices of inputs that businesses are likely to purchase. A third price index, the **GDP deflator**, in a sense combines the PPI and CPI in an effort to measure what is happening to the prices of all commodities produced in or provided to the economy. You can access current and historical values of these indicies at *http://stats.bls.gov/*.

The purchasing power of money. The quantity of goods and services that a dollar will buy depends upon the price level. The higher the price level, the higher most prices will be and the fewer goods and services a dollar can purchase. Hence, changes in a price index also indicate changes in the purchasing power of money. If the CPI increases from 200 to 240 in a one-year period, for example, the rate of inflation is 20 percent ($240 - 200 = 40$; $40/200 \times 100 = 20\%$), which means that a dollar now purchases 20 percent less than it could have purchased a year ago. Or, put in a slightly different way, it takes $240 to purchase exactly the same thing this year as $200 would have purchased a year ago.

Problems with price indices. Price indices are useful, but only when they are used appropriately and cautiously. In this regard, several problems merit discussion.

• *A price index does not accurately reflect what happens to the price of any particular good.* For the five goods used above to build a price index, for example, prices increased in general by about 81 percent, but the price of shirts doubled (a 100 percent increase); the price of a hamburger increased by 20 percent; a haircut by 58 percent; a paperback book by 51 percent; and a candy bar by a little less than 13 percent. Obviously, the price index does not reflect the wide

---

[8] To see the importance of weights, note that in creating the price index above, we assumed that one of each of the items was purchased. If, instead, 10 hamburgers were purchased, then the price of a hamburger ($1.25 in 1980, $1.50 in 1990) would be multiplied (weighted) by 10 when calculating the cost of the market basket.

range of changes in individual prices. Nor does the index provide information about what has happened to any particular dollar price. Indeed, no single price in this market basket increased by 81 percent. Because of the differing individual price changes, *relative prices* changed over the decade interval—some relative prices decreased, others increased (e.g., the relative price of shirts in terms of hamburgers changed from 19.2 ($24/$1.25) to 32 ($48/$1.50)). Price indices mask these relative price changes—there is nothing in a price index or in changes in a price index that allows us to understand what the relative prices are or how they might be changing.

• ***Not every household consumes the same mix of goods as those households that were sampled for the index's market basket.*** This means that what happens to the purchasing power of money for any particular household may differ substantially from that indicated by the price index. If, for example, your household spends a higher percentage of its income on food than does the sample used to create the market basket, and food prices increase faster than other prices, then the purchasing power of money for your household will fall by more than the price index would suggest. This is a particularly serious problem when particular groups of individuals rely on an index that is based on a market basket quite different from their actual purchases. The elderly, for example, spend far more on medical care than the "average" household does and, as a consequence, the CPI does not accurately reflect changes in the purchasing power of money for them.

• ***The mix of goods that households purchase changes over time.*** Changes in consumption patterns are of two kinds. In one type, the *quantity* of particular goods purchased changes over time, so individuals end up purchasing a mix of goods that differs from the market basket used to create the index. In the second type, the *kinds of goods* purchased changes over time and individuals end up purchasing different goods and services than those used to create the index.

The problem in both cases is that the market basket used to create the index does not change year by year as consumption patterns change. Thus, as time goes by, the base-year market basket reflects the current-year consumption pattern of households less accurately. For example, if the CPI market basket were

created when most households owned one car, but over time most households came to own two cars, the CPI would not give appropriate weight to changes in the price of automobiles. As a second example, personal computers weren't purchased 20 years ago because they weren't available. Today, of course, many households have one sitting on a desk. Thus, a price index based on two-decade-old consumption patterns simply does not reflect the changing prices of personal computers. A third example: Very few people had cell phones ten years ago; now a large fraction of US households have one or more cell phones. Changes in the quality, use and price of cell phones and cell phone services will not, as a consequence, be reflected in the CPI until a new base-year market basket is created.

• ***The quality of the goods purchased also changes with time.*** For example, washing machines cost more today than they did 50 years ago, but today's machines are of significantly higher quality than the old washers of another era. Similarly, television sets may cost more today than they did 40 years ago, but today's TVs provide color pictures on large screens whereas the earlier ones had black-and-white pictures on small screens. In each case, an increase in the current price compared to the old price reflects something more than just inflation. When appropriately adjusted for quality changes, did the price really increase? A price index cannot answer this question.

As you might guess, these problems are less serious over short periods of time because both consumption patterns and the quality of goods change relatively slowly. When prices are compared over an extended period of time, however, consumption patterns and the quality of goods purchased do change, often substantially. And, importantly, they don't change arbitrarily, but in response to the very price changes that are being measured. Thus, individuals purchase more of those commodities whose relative prices have declined and less of those commodities whose relative prices have increased. As a consequence of this induced change in consumption patterns, a price index tends to overstate cost-of-living changes. That is, the amount actually purchased of items whose prices have increased is less than the calculated weight in the market basket because of choices that individuals make. Likewise, if both quality and prices increase, in a sense the index which picks up only the price increases, overstates the inflation rate.

Because consumption patterns and the quality of goods change over time, the government periodically adjusts the price index by redefining the market basket to be more consistent with then-current consumption patterns. Although this solves some problems, it creates others, because longer-term price-level comparisons then become more difficult.

• **Prices for the same goods differ in different areas of the country.** This poses a problem in creating an economy-wide index because it is not clear which of several possible prices *for the same good* should be used. Moreover, because of discounts, sales, and the like, list prices often differ from actual prices at which goods are sold. Finally, prices change in systematic, seasonally related ways. (For example, fresh fruit prices tend to be higher in the winter and lower in the summer.) In each case, the government solves the problem in a sensible way: It attempts to get the actual transaction price rather than the announced or posted price. It averages across all prices in the economy for an economy-wide index, but it also creates separate versions of the index for various regions and selected cities. It adjusts for seasonal changes by relying on the historical pattern of these changes. (This procedure is called **seasonal adjustment**).

• **The determination of the market basket, its weights, and its pricing are done by statistical sampling, so there are sampling errors associated with any price index.** In this case, the size of this sampling error can be estimated by statistical techniques that estimate how far the measured index is from the "true" index with some degree of confidence.

Measuring Aggregate Output

Despite the old cliché warning about adding apples and oranges, apples and oranges (and everything else an economy produces) can be added by using money as a common unit of account. That is, we can add the *dollar value* of apples produced and the *dollar value* of oranges produced as well as the *dollar value* of all other goods and services an economy produces to obtain a *dollar measure* of the output of the economy. This dollar measure of the aggregate or total output is **gross domestic product (GDP)**.

By convention, aggregate output is measured over a one-year interval. That is, GDP is the dollar market value of all goods and services produced in the US economy within a year. It is a measure of the *rate of production*, not the dollar value of goods and services available at any single moment in time. That is, GDP is a measure of the *flow* of goods and services produced within the economy and not a measure of the *stock* of goods and services available at the moment you're reading this paragraph.[9] Only the production of final goods and services is included in GDP—commodities produced, but only used in the production of yet other commodities (called **intermediate goods**), are not counted in GDP (but the final commodity that incorporates the intermediate goods is).

The Federal government publishes quarterly and annual estimates of GDP (you can find them at *http://www.bea.gov* or *http://www.whitehouse.gov/news/fsbr.html*). When these estimates are reported or discussed by the media, it is important to know whether the estimated changes are being annualized or if they represent the actual change over the preceding quarter. That is, a quarterly change may be quoted in annual terms ("GDP grew last quarter at a 4-percent annual rate") or in quarterly terms ("GDP grew last quarter by 1 percent").

Problems with GDP as a measure of aggregate output. A money measure of aggregate output such as GDP is useful for some purposes, but it also has some problems. As with price indices, the GDP must be used with caution and understanding.

• **GDP may change because of price changes even if the rate of production in an economy doesn't change.** That is, any change in a dollar measure of aggregate output will reflect changes in *both* the number of goods produced in an economy and the price level. To see why, consider a simple economy based on our earlier price index example expanded to include levels of aggregate (that is, economy-wide) production:

---

[9] More generally, a flow is a measure of what is available *over time* whereas a stock is the amount of something available at a particular moment. A flow is measured in units *per time period*; a stock is measured in terms of units only. To see the difference, think of water that is constantly circulated in a fountain. When the pump is on, there is a flow of water through the fountain. The faster the pump works, the greater the flow. If the pump is shut off, the flow stops. The stock of water in the fountain pool remains the same, however.

	Price in 1990	1990 Aggregate Production	Price in 2000	2000 Aggregate Production
Shirt	$24.00	1,000	$48.00	1,100
Haircut	9.50	5,000	15.00	5,500
Hamburger	1.25	50,000	1.50	55,000
Paperback book	3.95	30,000	5.95	33,000
Candy bar	.40	100,000	.45	110,000

At 1990 prices, the GDP for this economy would be $292,500:

	1,000 shirts x $24.00	$ 24,000
+	5,000 haircuts x $9.50	47,500
+	50,000 hamburgers x $1.25	62,500
+	30,000 paperback books x $3.95	118,500
+	100,000 candy bars x $.40	40,000
		$292,500

In 2000, aggregate output measured in dollars would be $463,650 when calculated the same way—an increase of 59 percent. The problem? If you look carefully at the actual physical output you will note that for each good, output increased by only 10 percent, not by 59 percent. The number of haircuts increased from 5,000 to 5,500; the number of hamburgers produced increased from 50,000 to 55,000; and so on. The difference—10 percent versus 59 percent—is important. The reason for this difference is that the change in output measured at *current* market prices *also* reflects the *change in prices from 1990 to 2000*. The change in physical output is, in one sense, a **real change**, whereas the change in the dollar value of output is a mixture of both a real change and a **nominal change**. When the effect of inflation is factored out, a real change is also referred to as a **constant dollar** change.

A price index measured over the same period of time can be used to account for the effects of price changes. For example, if 1990's production numbers are used as for the market basket weights, a price index beginning at 100 in 1990 would be 144 in 2000.[10] That is, in general, prices have increased by 44 percent using this production-weighted index. This price index can now be used to create a measure of the production in 2000 in terms of the price

level in 1990 by *deflating* the 2000 *nominal* aggregate output to create a measure of 2000 *real* aggregate output. That is, because the price index accounts for changes in prices over the decade interval, dividing by the price index in each year tends to neutralize the effect of price changes on a dollar-measure of aggregate output. Thus, we have

$$\text{Real 2000 GDP} = \frac{\$463,650}{144} \times 100$$
$$= \$321,979 \text{ (measured in 1990 dollars)}$$

The increase in *real* output over the decade measured this way is $29,479 ($321,979 − $292,500), which is about a 10 percent increase. That is, this increase in **real GDP** corresponds to the observed 10 percent increase in the actual physical output that actually occurred in the economy.

This is, of course, only an illustration of the method by which real GDP for an economy can be obtained from nominal GDP. The Federal government uses **nominal GDP** and the **GDP deflator** to measure changes in real GDP. For example, if nominal GDP for the United States increases from $8 trillion to $11 trillion and the GDP deflator also increases over the same time period from 100 to 125, then

Real GDP in the base year is: $\frac{\$8 \text{ trillion}}{100} \times 100 = \$8 \text{ trillion}$
and
Real GDP in the second year is: $\frac{\$11 \text{ trillion}}{125} \times 100 = \$8.8 \text{ trillion}$

[10] The production-weighted market basket costs $292,500 in 1990. In 2000, base-year basket's cost is 1,000 x $48.00 + 5,000 × $15.00 + 50,000 × $1.50 + 30,000 × $5.95 + 100,000 × $.45 = $421,500. Therefore, the 2000 value of the index is
$$\frac{\$421,500 \times 100}{\$292,500} = 144$$

Current and historical real GDP are available at the same web sites noted above for nominal GDP. When you compare real and nominal GDP, you will see a substantial difference. The difference is due to inflation in the United States.

• *In general, GDP measures only those activities that occur in markets and ignores non-market activities.* GDP, for example, does not account for production activities that occur within a home. This means that doing your own plumbing does not add to the GDP because it is not an activity purchased in a market; if, however, you hire someone else to do your plumbing, it is counted in GDP because it is a service purchased in a market. Much more significantly, if one spouse provides services at home—cooks, washes, cleans, takes care of children—this contribution is not measured by GDP because these activities are not purchased in a market. For this reason, the value of goods and services that are actually produced in an economy is much greater than those measured by GDP.[11]

• *GDP does not include the value of leisure.* This is a particularly serious problem in measuring "output" for a wealthy economy like our own. Much of the increase in individual well-being in the United States over the past century is reflected in the decline in hours worked and the corresponding increase in leisure. However, this increase in leisure time is not measured in GDP, which only measures market production. Thus, the actual growth of the US economy is significantly underestimated when the growth in GDP is the measure.[12]

• *GDP does not include underground economy or illegal market transactions.* Changing the definition of what is legal and illegal can, therefore, change

GDP without anything really changing in the economy. Far more importantly, higher tax rates often drive some perfectly legal activities underground (to avoid paying taxes). Because of these prohibited and unreported activities, measured GDP underestimates the value of the output of an economy. In some economies where tax avoidance is pervasive, GDP significantly underestimates aggregate output.

• *GDP does not include financial and second-hand transactions.* GDP is a measure of the annual *output* of an economy. Consequently, transactions in which there is no production such as financial transactions and second-hand sales are excluded from GDP.

Excluded financial transactions include transfer payments from one individual to another (such as your parents sending you money to support your education) or from the government to individuals (such as Social Security payments) as well as the buying and selling of securities. The value of stock market transactions, for example, is not part of GDP.

Excluded second-hand sales include market transactions for used goods. These are excluded because the good was included in GDP when it was new and first sold. Any subsequent sale that merely changes ownership does not reflect additional production or output of an economy. If these sales were included in GDP, there would be double counting—a good would be counted when first produced and sold, and then again whenever it was resold.

Both financial transactions and second-hand sales are enormously important in allocating and reallocating goods, but neither is considered as part of GDP. This means that GDP is a measure of an economy's output, but it is not a measure of *all* economic activity occurring within the economy.

• *GDP does not include intermediate goods.* A fundamental rule is that repeated counting of the same thing is to be avoided. This means that GDP is generally restricted to measuring the output of end-use products. If steel and automobiles that incorporate steel were both counted in GDP, for example, steel production would be counted twice—once as steel, once embedded in cars. To avoid this type of double counting, steel production is not counted in GDP except where it is a final product. The value of steel produced is not overlooked, it is just counted as part of the value of finished or end-use products—automobiles, refrigerators, filing cabinets, and so on.

---

[11] Several studies have attempted to quantify the value of household work in the economy and generally indicate that it is equal to about one-third of GDP. This means that traditional measures of real output only account for three-quarters of what is actually produced in the economy. For more detail, see Oli Hawrylyshyn, "The Value of Household Services: A Survey of Empirical Estimates," *The Review of Income and Wealth*, 22, June 1976, pp. 101–130.

[12] Differences in the amount of leisure taken between countries makes GDP comparisons between countries difficult. Thus, for example, GDP per person is about the same in Japan and the United States. The Japanese, however, work more hours per week and, as a consequence, have less leisure.

• **GDP does not account for the size of the population of an economy, nor do changes in GDP account for population growth.** This means that changes in GDP by themselves do not indicate whether there are more or fewer goods and services for each person when compared to other times in the same economy or other economies. For example, China has a large GDP, but it also has a very large population. In fact, **per capita GDP** in China is quite low when compared with countries that have equivalent or smaller aggregate output but have substantially smaller populations. Because GDP does not account for changes in population, two countries that have equivalent growth rates in real GDP may have substantially different measures of the amount of additional goods and services per capita. It is easy to construct a per capita or per person measure of aggregate output by dividing GDP by the population. You can find population data for the U.S. at *http://www.census.gov/epcd/www/recent.htm* to go with the GDP data you've already found.

• **GDP is not a measure of individual well-being.** While GDP is useful for some purposes, there is no reason that a dollar measure of output is supposed to be a measure of how well-off the people living in an economy really are. Per capita GDP is not a measure of well-being either. Per capita real GDP does not indicate how an economy's output is distributed across its population, for example. Nor does it measure how individuals value leisure or how much leisure is available to them. It also omits other activities, including home production, that do not occur in markets. And, it fails to take into account other important factors that determine well-being such as pollution and congestion ("bads"), and increases in life expectancy ("goods") that have a material effect on your well-being.

Production and the Circular Flow of Income

Because GDP is produced using inputs, and inputs are owned by individuals, the value of what is produced within an economy (GDP) will also be equal to the sum of the incomes that individuals living within the economy receive as they supply labor, natural resources, and capital, and provide entrepre-neurial services and other resources to firms they own. This means that corresponding to **aggregate domestic product** is **aggregate domestic income**. As we have seen, domestic product is the market value of all goods and services produced within an economy. Domestic income is the total or aggregate income earned by households, including wages, rents, interest payments, and profits. The two are *equivalent* because when there is a flow of inputs to firms from households, there *must be* a corresponding flow of payments from firms to households for the inputs used, as illustrated in Figure A1.

Since money is used to measure the output the economy produces, GDP can be thought of as a measure of the flow of dollars in an economy. The value of this flow of dollars can then be computed in terms of either the *total income* that individuals who own resources receive in payment for the inputs they provide to the economy or the *total expenditures* individuals pay to purchase goods and services. The equality of aggregate income and aggregate expenditure results from a simple accounting rule: *Every expenditure by one person or firm must be income for some other person or firm.*

This idea—that measuring aggregate output in terms of expenditures is identical to measuring aggregate output in terms of income—is important. It implies that *the only way to increase aggregate income is to increase aggregate output.* If a policy change does not affect aggregate output, it cannot affect aggregate income.

National income accounts. Even though the value of aggregate output is equal to the value of aggregate income, for a variety of reasons, the aggregate income that individuals *actually control* is less than the value of aggregate output an economy produces. The government provides estimates of personal income available to US citizens by working through a system of accounts known as the **National Income Accounts.**

The accounting starts by adding the income earned by US citizens living abroad to GDP and subtracting the income of foreigners living within the United States from GDP. This adjustment results in a measure known as **gross national product (GNP).** The following illustrates the adjustment from GDP to GNP using actual 1990 data.

Figure A.1

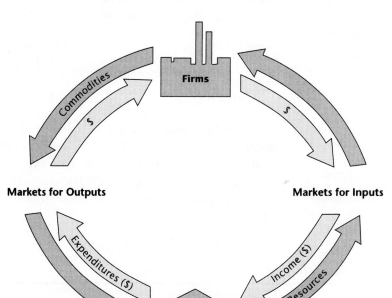

Firms

Commodities $

$

Markets for Outputs

Markets for Inputs

Expenditures ($)

Income ($)

Resources

Households

There are two ways of looking at GDP. Households pay firms for goods and services—expenditures; firms pay wages, rents, interest, or profits to households for resources—income.

Gross domestic product (GDP)	$5,514 billion
+ Receipts from rest of world	+ 148 billion
–Payments to rest of world	–137 billion
Gross national product (GNP)	$5,525 billion

Some of the aggregate output that an economy produces is used to replace and repair buildings, machines, and other capital goods. When buildings, machines, and other capital goods wear out, they are said to **depreciate**. Deducting the dollar value of **aggregate depreciation** from GNP yields **net national product, NNP**:

Gross national product (GNP)	$5,525 billion
–Depreciation	–595 billion
Net national product (NNP)	$4,930 billion

Net national product is still not a measure of the aggregate output available to individuals or households because some of the real output of an economy is claimed by the government through **taxation** and some is held by corporations as **retained earnings**. For example, the government imposes indirect taxes on individuals, such as sales taxes, that are collected by firms. The government also subsidizes businesses and, in some cases, runs its own businesses. Indirect taxes are subtracted at this point.

For example, if a good sells for $20, but a firm must pay $1 in taxes, only $19 is available as income for owners of inputs. The effect of a subsidy is just the opposite: the amount available as income for owners of inputs is greater than the market price. Indirect taxes are subtracted from, and subsidies are added to, NNP to obtain **national income, NI**:[13]

Net national product (NNP)	$4,930 billion
– Indirect business taxes	– 439 billion
– Subsidies to businesses	– 31 billion
National income (NI)	$4,460 billion

---

[13] National income can be divided into five components that are defined by the way the income is earned:
   1. Compensation of employees (73% of NI)—the income of labor in the form of wages and fringe benefits.
   2. Proprietors' income (7%)—the income of nonincorporated businesses.
   3. Corporate profits (11%)—the income of corporations after payments to employees, other resource suppliers, and creditors.
   4. Rental income (2%)—the income that individuals earn as landlords after payments for inputs used.
   5. Net interest (7%)—the interest domestic firms pay, less the interest that they receive, plus interest paid to those in the United States by foreigners.

By subtracting corporate profits, corporate taxes, earnings retained by corporations, and Social Security taxes, and then adding governmental payments to individuals (**transfer payments**), we obtain **personal income** or **PI**:

National income (NI)	$4,460 billion
− Social security contributions + Corporate income taxes + Undistributed corporate profits	−1,311 billion
+ Interest, dividend, and transfer payments	+ 1,531 billion
Personal income (PI)	$4,680 billion

But, of course, individuals have to pay taxes. Subtracting **personal income taxes** from personal income yields **disposable personal income, DPI**:

Personal income (PI)	$4,680 billion
− Personal taxes	− 621 billion
Disposable personal income (DPI)	$4,059 billion

Disposable personal income is a measure of the aggregate production of goods and services that individuals actually can consume or use in other ways. Figure A2 illustrates the relationships between these measures. Notice that to move from national income

Figure A.2

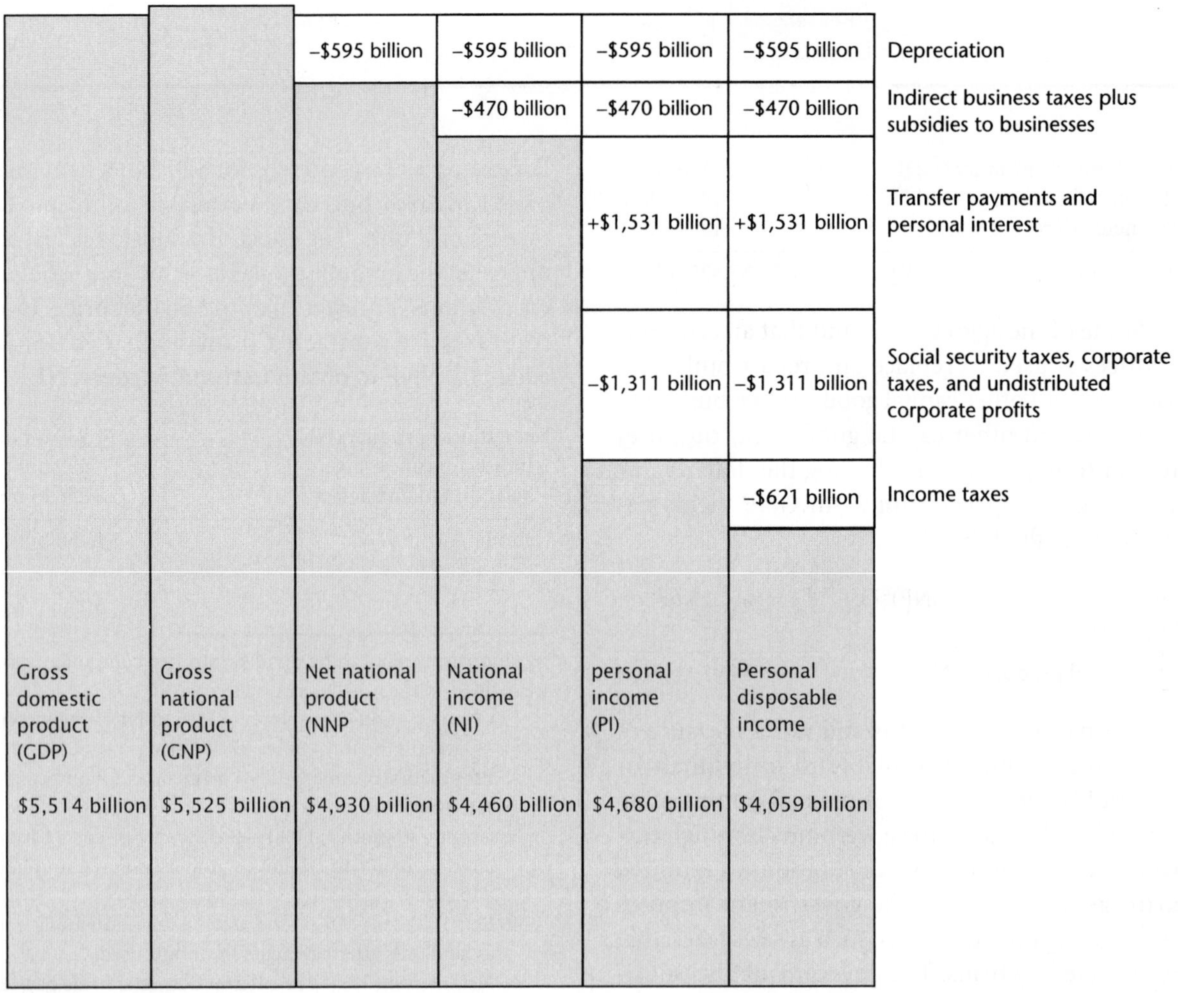

Gross domestic product (GDP)	Gross national product (GNP)	Net national product (NNP	National income (NI)	personal income (PI)	Personal disposable income	
		−$595 billion	−$595 billion	−$595 billion	−$595 billion	Depreciation
			−$470 billion	−$470 billion	−$470 billion	Indirect business taxes plus subsidies to businesses
				+$1,531 billion	+$1,531 billion	Transfer payments and personal interest
				−$1,311 billion	−$1,311 billion	Social security taxes, corporate taxes, and undistributed corporate profits
					−$621 billion	Income taxes
$5,514 billion	$5,525 billion	$4,930 billion	$4,460 billion	$4,680 billion	$4,059 billion	

SOURCE: *Survey of Current Business*, January 1992.

to personal income, some things are added (for example, transfer payments) and others are subtracted (for example, social security taxes). Those that are added reflect income that individuals received even though they did not provide productive resources to the economy; those that are subtracted reflect output that individuals generated by providing productive resources to the economy, but they did not receive the associated income because it was retained in one way or another by business firms or governments.

The Disposition of Disposable Personal Income

What do individuals do with the income they finally receive? Since World War II approximately 90 percent of individual income has been spent on consumption. The rest has been saved. In 1990, for example,

$$\underset{\substack{DPI}}{\$4,059 \text{ billion}} = \underset{\substack{Consumption \\ (92.2\%)}}{\$3,743 \text{ billion}} + \underset{\substack{Saving \\ (7.8\%)}}{\$316 \text{ billion}}$$

Aggregate expenditure categories. For reasons that will become clear when we discuss Aggregate Demand, the spending side of GDP is often broken down into four areas: consumption, investment, government, and net exports. Table A1 illustrates this division of GDP for the U.S. economy in 1990. You can see current and historical breakdowns in the "National Income and Product Account Tables" at *http://www.bea.gov*.

Table A.1

Entity	Purpose	Dollar amount	Percentage of GDP
Households	Consumption	$3,743 billion	67.9%
Firms and households	Investment	803 billion	14.5
Government	Public purposes	1,043 billion	18.9
Exports		550 billion	10.0
Imports		625 billion	11.3
Net exports		− 75 billion	− 1.3

Chapter 18 ▶ ▶

Aggregate Demand and Aggregate Supply: An Overview

Given the sometimes sizeable costs of unemployment, price level instability and economic stagnation, it is important to understand why market economies cycle and why, in particular, resources are not always fully employed. As we will see, this is a challenging task.

At an individual market level, unemployed resources can be thought of in terms of excess supply. If adjustments to changes in market supply and demand are slow, for example, there will be excess supply or excess demand during the period of adjustment, as illustrated in Figures 1 and 2.

If these adjustment problems are isolated to a single market, they create temporary rationing problems when there is excess demand or temporary surplus disposal problems when there is excess supply. However, if slow adjustment and coordination difficulties are widespread across an economy, spilling over from market to market, many resources may become unemployed simultaneously. However, even though market supply and demand analysis hints at possible reasons for unemployment, because there are tens of thousands of goods produced in an economy, trying to understand the effects of possible adjustment and coordination problems by focusing on each of the countless individual markets would be hopeless. We need a way of aggregating across

the millions of markets and market transactions within the economy if we are to have any hope of understanding economy-wide adjustment and coordination problems.

One way both to organize the data presented in Chapter 17 and to approach the questions of why there is unemployment and economic instability is to focus on the **aggregate demand** for and **aggregate supply** of *all* commodities produced within an economy. In aggregating in this way, as will become apparent, we will abstract and simplify considerably. The purpose of the chapter is to provide a broad outline of an aggregate demand/aggregate supply approach so that you have a sense of where the details developed in the subsequent chapters fit and why they are important. In these follow-on chapters, we will use an aggregate demand/aggregate supply approach to explain unemployment, inflation, economic growth, domestic budget and trade deficits, and the important public policy debates in each of these areas.

▶ Aggregate Demand

Aggregate demand describes the relationship between the amount of an economy's aggregate real output that is demanded and the economy's price

Figure 1
Persistent Excess Demand

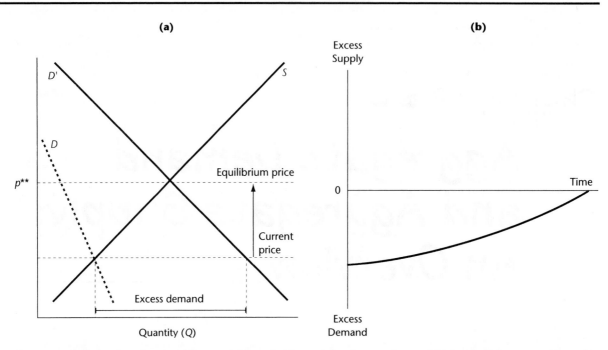

If market prices do not adjust quickly to an increase in demand (or decrease in supply), there will be excess demand for an extended period of time.

Figure 2
Persistent Excess Supply

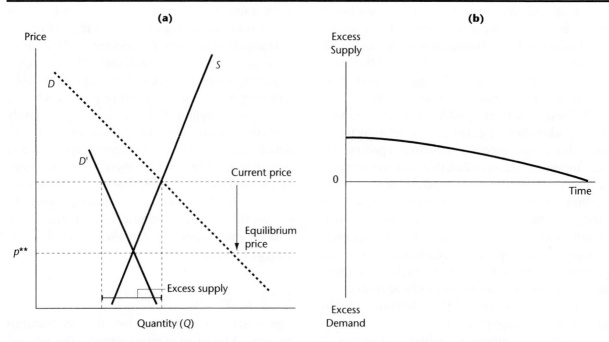

If market prices do not adjust quickly to a decrease in demand (or increase in supply), there will be excess supply in the market for an extended period of time.

level. At each price level, aggregate demand[1] is determined by the demand by consumers for consumption, firms for investment, foreigners for imports, and governments for the use of resources in pursuit of their purposes. We will refer to these four different uses for the output that an economy produces as **consumption**, **investment**, **net exports**, and **government**, respectively. The distinction between them depends on who it is that buys the output an economy produces and their motives or reasons for doing so:

1. *Consumption.* Resources can be used to produce commodities that households and individuals consume. Examples include food, clothing, gasoline, entertainment, and medical services. The sum of *all* such uses across *all* individuals within an economy is referred to as **aggregate consumption (c)**.

2. *Investment.* Resources can be used to increase the amount of capital available to firms and households. That is, part of the economy's output can be used to produce productive inputs that are used to produce output *at some future time.* Examples include new housing, new factories, new trucks and new machines. The sum of *all* such uses across *all* firms and households within an economy is referred to as **aggregate investment (i)**.

3. *Net exports.* Resources within the US economy are used to produce goods and services that are exported. Resources in other economies are used to produce goods and services that are imported. Because we are interested in the demand for all the output produced *within* the United States, we must add the foreign demand for US-produced commodities (exports, denoted by x) to

aggregate demand. Since, however, US households can use part of their income to purchase commodities produced abroad, we must subtract the value of foreign-produced commodities that are imported (imports are denoted by m). If exports were always equal to imports, the effect would cancel: foreigners would use some of our resources, but we would use an equivalent amount of their resources. If exports are not always equal to imports, however, there is a foreign trade effect on the domestic economy. This effect can be measured by considering the *difference* between what is exported and imported—**net exports (ne)**, where $ne = x - m$.

4. *Government.* Resources can be used by the government to provide its citizens with goods and services such as highways, postal service, ships, missiles, and national parks. The sum of *all* such uses is categorized as **government spending (g)**.

The aggregate quantity of real output demanded equals the aggregate quantity demanded by individuals for consumption, *c*, *plus* the demand for output by firms and households for investment, *i*, *plus* the demand for exports less the amount imported, *(x − m)*, *plus* the demand by the government for resources to provide goods and services, *g*, *at each possible price level*. We will refer to this demand for real output as **aggregate demand (AD)**. In symbols, aggregate demand is expressed as

$$AD = c + i + (x - m) + g \qquad (1)$$

Notice that in this "aggregate" approach we are not concerned with the particular types of goods or services consumed, or the particular mix of capital goods produced, or the kinds of things that are imported and exported, or even what goods, services, and resources are used by the government. That is, in considering aggregate demand, we will not be concerned with whether the resources used to satisfy consumers are used to produce televisions, books, clothing, or food. Similarly, we will not be concerned about whether resources are used to produce machines, trucks, or buildings. We will not be concerned with the mix of goods that the government is using and, as a consequence, we will ignore differences between expenditures for roads, welfare

---

[1] This is a little sloppy. You will recall that in the analysis of individual markets, the distinction between "quantity demanded (at a particular price)" and "demand" was important. The analogous distinction here is between "aggregate real output demanded (at a given price level)" and "aggregate demand." The phrase "aggregate real output demanded at a given price level" is awkward and the discussion from this point forward uses only the term "aggregate demand." The context will, in every case, make it clear whether the discussion is about a *point* on an aggregate demand curve or the *entire* aggregate demand curve and you should make certain that you keep the distinction between the two firmly in mind.

services, and defense, for example. Rather, we will focus only on the *total value* of the output of an economy used for *all* consumption purposes, the total value of aggregate output used for *all* investment purposes, and so on.

Figure 3 illustrates how the real output in 2002 was apportioned among the categories of consumption, investment, net exports and government expenditures. Note that about 65 percent of real output is consumed by individuals. Another 19 percent or so is used by the government. Firms and households use the remaining 17 percent for investment (that is, remember, to create new capital). Net exports are negative, which means that we are purchasing more from foreigners than they are purchasing from us, and so these percentages add up to 104. Over time, the shares change somewhat. Figure 4 shows the trend for each component over the period from 1950 to 2000. (You can find current and historical data at *http://www.bea.gov* or selected data conveniently graphed at *http://www.whitehouse.gov/news/fsbr.html*).

The consumption, investment and net export components of aggregate demand are considered more fully Chapter 20. ("Aggregate Demand"). The effects of government spending on aggregate demand are explored in Chapter 21 ("Fiscal Policy: A First Approach").

▶ Aggregate Supply

Aggregate supply (*AS*) relates aggregate output produced to the price level. If resources are fully employed, the aggregate output supplied equals an economy's **potential real output**. In equilibrium, it equals the aggregate output demanded as well. When resources are fully and efficiently employed, aggregate supply is simply a way of looking at the output produced along the economy's production possibilities frontier. On the other hand, if an economy has idle or unemployed resources, it will produce less than its potential.

To make sense of this approach, you might imagine the economy producing, in aggregate, a large "pie." The pie—whose size can vary—represents real output. In the long run, resources *alone* determine the potential size of the pie and aggregate demand determines the division of the pie into different slices—some going to consumers, some to governments, and so on. Over shorter periods of

**Figure 3
Division of Real Output, 2008**

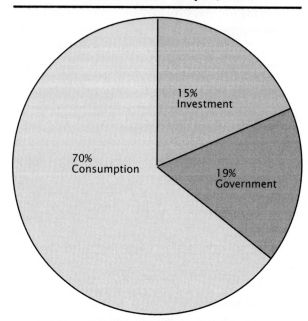

SOURCE: U.S. Bureau of Economic Analysis

Note that the percentages total more than 100% because net exports are negative (imports exceed exports).

time, aggregate demand and aggregate supply *together* determine the actual amount of the pie that is produced, while aggregate demand *alone* determines the division of whatever is produced among its different, and in a sense, competing users— households, firms, government, and foreigners. Although this may be obvious, *what* determines an economy's potential real output is not. And *why* an economy might leave resources idle or unemployed, thereby producing at less than its potential, is not straightforward, either. Chapter 19 ("Aggregate Supply") deals with these questions.

▶ Coordination

If the economy is producing on its production possibilities frontier, the bigger the slice of the pie that goes to households for consumption, the *less* real output there is available for use by firms to build new capital or by the government for its activities. Conversely, if more of the pie is used by firms for new capital, less real output is available for household consumption and government use. This means that there is a tradeoff between the use of real resources for consumption, for investment, for

Figure 4
Consumption, Investment, Net Exports, and Government Spending

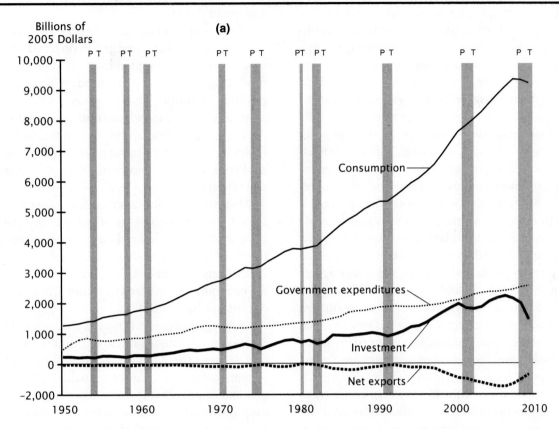

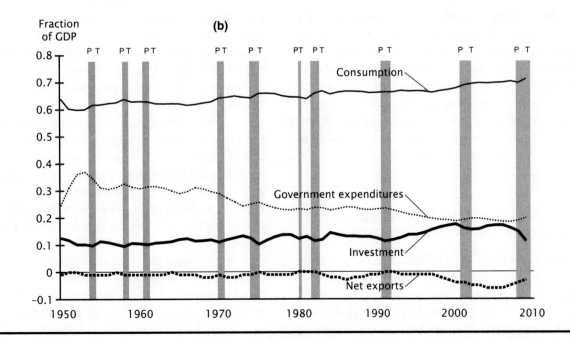

export, and for government purposes. The interests of households, firms, foreigners, and the government may not coincide—they may in fact conflict or, at the very least, compete. *An important coordination problem for an economy is determining the division of real output among consumption, investment, exports and government uses when the interests of individuals, firms, foreigners and the government differ.*

If an economy is employing its resources fully and firms decide they want to invest more in order to increase their stock of capital, individuals must be persuaded to consume less or the government must use fewer resources. This kind of tradeoff should be obvious to you by now. The converse is sometimes less obvious, however. If firms decide that they want to invest less, then households *must* consume more or the government *must* increase its spending on goods and services. Otherwise aggregate demand will fall and resources will be unemployed. From another viewpoint, if the government cuts back on its purchase of goods and services, then either firms *must* increase their investment, or households *must* increase their consumption, or foreigners *must* increase their purchase of exports (or some combination of the three) for an economy to remain on its production possibilities frontier. *A second important coordination problem for an economy is to accommodate changes in the division of real output, without adversely affecting the overall level of output or price level stability when the interests of households, firms, or the government change.*

An economy will only employ its resources fully and efficiently if aggregate quantity demanded is equal to potential real output. *This poses a third coordination problem for an economy. At the current price level, the sum of consumption, investment, net exports, and government spending must be equal to the aggregate real output an economy has the ability to produce. Otherwise, resources will be unemployed or, as we will see, inflation will ensue.*

▶ Using Aggregate Supply and Aggregate Demand Concepts

Figure 5 provides a way of illustrating the aggregate supply of and the aggregate demand for real output. (The next several chapters develop this model more fully.) In this diagram, the **price level**, denoted by *P*, is measured along the vertical axis. Measures of the price level are indices like the CPI, PPI, or GDP deflator, so *P* is measured from a base of 100 and *not* in dollars.

Real output produced, denoted by *y*, is measured along the horizontal axis in dollars. **Potential real output** is represented by y^*. If an economy is producing at its potential it will be on its production possibilities frontier. Thus y^* represents the real dollar value of an economy's real output when it is producing along its production possibilities frontier. It follows that y^* is the output of an economy associated with the full employment of all of its productive resources.

Potential real output is shown as being perfectly inelastic with respect to the price level. This is a way of saying that *potential* real output *is not* affected by the price level. That is, the price level can be 100, 200, or any level in-between, and in the model of the economy summarized in Figure 5, *potential* real output will be unaffected.

Aggregate demand, however, is shown in Figure 5 as sloping downward and to the right. This implies that aggregate demand *is* affected by the price level. In particular, this way of visualizing aggregate demand implies that the quantity of aggregate real output demanded will be higher at a price level of 100 than at a price level of 200, ceteris paribus.

A Caution

Figure 5 looks like the supply-demand model for an individual market that we considered in earlier chapters. Don't let looks deceive you. The aggregate supply-aggregate demand model illustrated in Figure 5 is conceptually quite different from the typical representation of supply and demand in a specific market.

In a *market* supply-demand model such as Figure 1 or 2, the *market price per unit, measured in dollars*, is on the vertical axis—for example, $.50 per pound or $20.00 per shirt. By contrast, in the *aggregate* supply-*aggregate* demand model illustrated in Figure 5, an *index of the price level measured from a base of 100* is on the vertical axis. As a consequence, an interpretation of a movement along the vertical axis in the aggregate demand-aggregate supply model is very different from that in a market demand-supply model. Specifically, an upward movement along the vertical axis indicates an increase in the *price level*, which means that, on aver-

Figure 5
Aggregate Supply and Demand

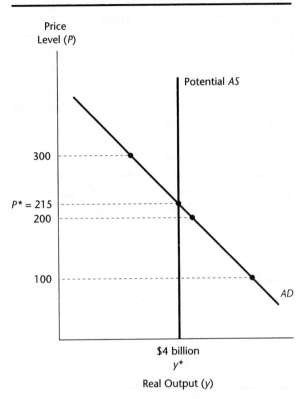

In the aggregate supply–aggregate demand model, real output in the economy, y, lies along the horizontal axis and is measured in dollars, whereas the price level, P, lies along the vertical axis and is measured as an index. For the economy represented in this figure, aggregate demand is equal to a potential real output of $4 billion at a price level of 215.

age, the dollar prices of all goods have increased. By contrast, an upward movement along the vertical axis in the market supply-demand model is interpreted as a change in the *dollar price of a specific commodity* when no other prices are changing and, hence, a change in the relative price of that particular commodity. Understanding this difference in interpretations is important because the price level can change without any change in relative prices. Conversely, the dollar price of a specific commodity can change, thereby changing relative prices, without any change in the price level. Hence, movements in the price level—that is, movements along the vertical axis in Figure 5—tell us nothing at all about changes in the price of any particular product.

In the *market* supply-demand model, the *quantity bought or sold* is measured along the horizontal axis: so many apples, oranges, shirts, and so on. By contrast, in the *aggregate* supply-*aggregate* demand model of an entire economy, the *aggregate real output* of an economy is measured *in dollars* along the horizontal axis. Thus, a movement to the right in a market supply-demand model would correspond to an increase in the number of apples, oranges, or shirts produced, whereas a similar movement in the aggregate supply-aggregate demand model corresponds to an increase in the real dollar value of *all* goods and services produced—apples, oranges, *and* shirts—within an economy.

Coordination and Price-Level Changes

Figure 5 can be used to illustrate some of the ways by which the coordination problems noted earlier can be worked out. For example, suppose that, at price level P^* the government wants to increase its spending on goods and services (increase g). If consumption (c) and investment (i) do not change initially, this increase in government spending will increase aggregate demand as illustrated in Figure 6 by a movement from AD to AD'. But because government spending does not affect the position of the production possibilities frontier, that is, it doesn't affect the real resources available to the economy, *potential* real output is unaffected by this change in government expenditures. Thus, an increase in the government's demand for real output leads to an *excess* overall or aggregate demand for real output at the existing price level, P^*. The higher level of aggregate demand, AD', will be equal to the *potential* real output the economy can produce only if the price level is P^{**}. Therefore, this simple model of the economy suggests that the problem of coordinating the various competing claims on real output can be resolved when two conditions hold:

1. The price level increases when excess aggregate demand occurs.

2. The aggregate quantity demanded decreases, without affecting potential real output, when the price level increases.

The second condition means that when the price level increases, the amount that individuals want to consume in aggregate *or* the amount that firms want to invest in aggregate *or* the amount that foreigners want to purchase from this economy must decrease. It turns out that a higher price level will reduce the value of certain assets in an economy. For example, the value of a $1 bill is lower when the price level increases because it purchases less. When individuals find that the value of the assets they are holding decreases, they will consume less, ceteris paribus. Moreover, as the value of certain assets decreases, firms may find the acquisition of new capital less profitable and want to invest less. Finally, as the price level in the U.S. increases, foreigners will find US goods more costly than goods produced elsewhere and US exports will fall. In these ways, an increase in the price level reduces desired consumption, desired investment and net exports: aggregate real output demanded falls (that is, the economy moves back along the new aggregate demand toward a new equilibrium at which the price level is higher). Note that *potential* real output is unchanged by any of these changes. Note also, that a *movement* of the price level from P^* to P^{**} means that there is *inflation*.

This same argument could be pursued to illustrate an economy's response to changes in other components of aggregate demand—desired investment might increase, for example, or foreigners might suddenly wish to purchase more goods from the U.S. In each case, aggregate demand and potential real output can be reconciled only if the economy adjusts from the initial price level to a higher price level. As the *increase* in the price level *decreases* the aggregate real output demanded (illustrated by a movement back along AD' in Figure 6), the economy will move to a new equilibrium at P^{**} and y^*.

Figure 7 illustrates the inflationary effects associated with an adjustment to an increase in aggregate demand. Inflation occurs as the price level moves from P^* to P^{**}. When the economy achieves its new equilibrium, however, aggregate demand will be *equal* to *potential* real output and there will be no further upward pressures on the price level. That is, once the price level reaches P^{**}, there will be no

**Figure 6
The Effect of an Increase
in Government Spending**

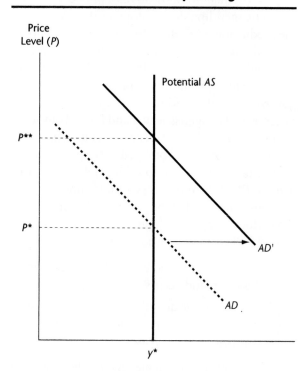

Real Output (*y*)

An increase in desired government spending will shift the aggregate demand curve from *AD* to *AD'*. Aggregate real output demanded will equal potential output when the price level increases from *P** to *P***.

**Figure 7
Changes in the Price Level After an
Increase in Aggregate Demand**

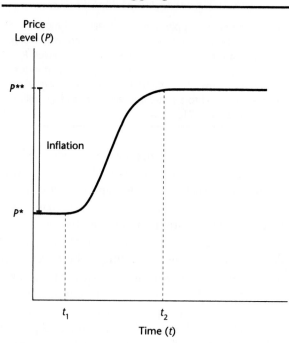

The increase in aggregate demand pictured in Figure 6 will cause the price level to increase from *P** to *P***. This movement is an inflation. However, after the economy reaches *P***, there is no further pressure for prices to increase and there will be no additional inflation.

inflation, *as long as there are no further changes in aggregate demand.*

Suppose that instead of the increase in government spending illustrated in Figures 6 and 7, *all or nearly all* firms decide they want to invest less. If household consumption and government demands for real output are unaffected by this change in the interests of firms, aggregate demand will fall. This is illustrated in Figure 8 by the movement from *AD* to *AD'*. *Potential* real output now exceeds aggregate demand at the initial price level P^*. Clearly, only when the price level is P^{**} will aggregate demand equal *potential* real output. We can conclude that when aggregate demand falls, the price level must also fall if the economy is to move toward full employment. That is, the economy must *deflate*. If the aggregate real output demanded increases as the price level decreases (that is, if the economy moves downward along *AD'*), the economy will once again reach a point at which the actual output coincides

with potential real output. When it does there will be no further changes in the price level, and actual output will equal potential output. Figure 9 shows how the price level changes with time when there is a period of deflation.

In sum, the problem of coordinating the competing and changing claims on real output with an economy's ability to produce real output can be resolved when two conditions hold true:

1. The price level decreases when aggregate demand falls.

2. The aggregate quantity demanded increases, without affecting the ability of an economy to produce real output, when the price level decreases.

Increases in desired consumption, desired investment, net exports, or government expenditures will increase aggregate demand; decreases in desired consumption, desired investment, net exports, or

Figure 8
The Effect of a Decrease in Desired Investment

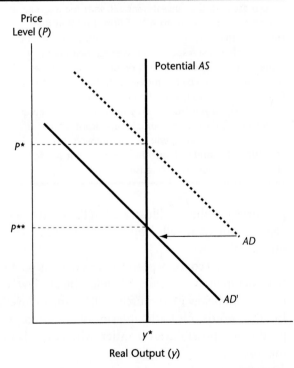

A decrease in desired investment will shift the aggregate demand curve from *AD* to *AD'*. Aggregate real output demanded will equal potential real output only if the price level falls from P^* to P^{**}.

Figure 9
Changes in the Price Level After a Decrease in Aggregate Demand

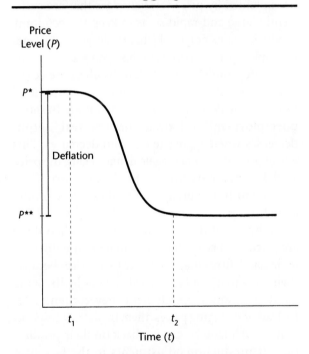

The decrease in aggregate demand pictured in Figure 8 will cause the price level to fall from P^* to P^{**}. This movement is a deflation. However, after the economy reaches P^{**}, prices will stabilize and there will be no pressure for prices to continue to fall.

government expenditures will decrease aggregate demand. Clearly, then, those things that affect desired consumption, desired investment, net exports, or government expenditures will also affect aggregate demand.

Nothing in this discussion suggests *what* things might lead to an initial change in desired consumption, desired investment, net exports, or government spending. Rather, we have considered only the *effects* on aggregate demand and the price level that will follow if one or more changes occur. We will investigate what things might initiate changes in aggregate demand in Chapter 20.

Unemployment and Short-Run Aggregate Supply

For each of the aggregate demand shifts noted above, we focused only on those changes in the price level that would have to occur *if the economy continued to produce at its potential* (that is, at y^*). As was noted in Chapter 17, however, *fluctuations* in unemployment are associated with *fluctuations* in real output. It follows that unemployment cannot be explained by price-level changes that are sufficiently large and rapid so as to keep the economy producing at its potential (that is, along y^*). Instead, unemployment can occur in this aggregate demand–aggregate supply framework only when the economy fails to adjust from one equilibrium price level to another without a change in real output. In short, unemployment will occur only if real output decreases when aggregate demand decreases. This will happen if, after aggregate demand falls, the price level does not move from P^* to P^{**} quickly or if *any* movement in the price level pushes the economy away from y.*

Why might there be output effects when there are price-level adjustments? When faced with a fall in demand, firms may not lower their prices because their costs may not fall immediately or by the same amount as any price changes they contemplate. Instead of changing prices, then, firms may respond to lower demand by cutting back on their production. If production adjustments in the face of a decrease in aggregate demand are widespread, there will be a **short-run aggregate supply curve**, as illustrated in Figure 10, that differs from the economy's potential real output curve (y^*) and has a negative slope. If an economy has a short-run aggregate sup-

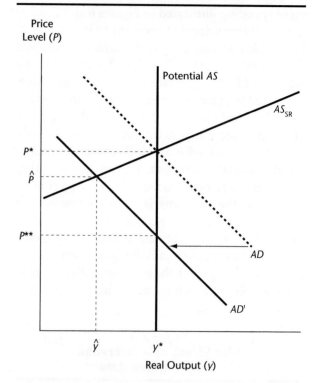

Figure 10
Unemployment in an Aggregate Supply–Aggregate Demand Model

A decrease in desired investment will shift the aggregate demand curve from *AD* to *AD'*. If firms find that their costs remain unchanged when faced with a decrease in demand, they will respond by lowering their prices somewhat and by cutting back on production. This effect is summarized by the movement not from P* to P**, but from P* to P̂, with the accompanying movement in real output from y* to ŷ. However, when actual production, ŷ is below potential real output, y*, resources, including labor, will be unemployed. Thus, if aggregate demand suddenly falls, real output will fall and unemployment will increase.

ply curve like the one illustrated in Figure 10, when aggregate demand falls, *both* the price level and real output fall.

When an economy produces less than its potential, unemployment occurs. Therefore, at any level of real output below y^*, resources will be unemployed. In other words, $\hat{y}$ is to the interior of an economy's production possibilities frontier, whereas y^* is on the frontier.

Stabilization Policy

Unplanned changes in either aggregate demand or aggregate supply are called **shocks**. Aggregate demand shocks create problems because they move the economy away from full employment and stable prices. For instance, if the economy has the short-run aggregate response indicated in Figure 10, an adverse shock to aggregate demand moves output to $\hat{y}$. Policies designed to offset shocks of this sort are called **stabilization** or **countercyclical policies**. The purpose of a stabilization policy is to keep the economy at or near full employment with stable prices. An **expansionary countercycle policy** tries to stimulate aggregate demand; a **contractionary countercycle policy** tries to dampen aggregate demand. (As we will see either approach can also affect aggregate supply and, in particular, long-term economic growth.)

Figure 11
Characterizing Stabilization Policy in an Aggregate Supply— Aggregate Demand Model

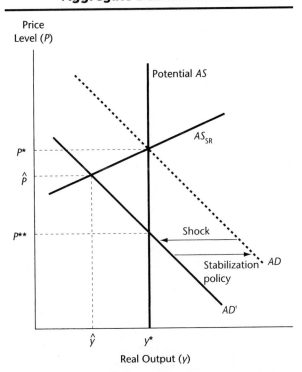

Stabilization policy is a government plan designed to offset an aggregate demand shock that might otherwise result in fluctuations in output. In the situation illustrated in this figure, an aggregate demand shock has reduced the demand for real output. Left alone, output in the economy would fall from y^* to $\hat{y}$ and there would be unemployment. An appropriate countercyclical policy would aim to increase aggregate demand. Such a policy would keep output at or near y^*, if it were effective.

An aggregate demand shock like that illustrated in Figure 11 would affect both the price level and real output—both would fall. This adverse effect on real output would lead to unemployment—real output would fall; unemployment would increase. A stabilization policy would attempt to offset the shock in aggregate demand so as to minimize the price level and real output effects and thereby minimize the adverse effects on unemployment.

Nothing in this discussion suggests *what* policy options the government might actually pursue or, for that matter, why the short-run response might be like that suggested in Figures 10 and 11. Over the next several chapters, we will focus on theories that explain short-run aggregate supply and consider a number of different policy options. You should know that both the theories and the policy options are matters of vigorous debate among economists and policy makers.

▶ A Look Ahead

The preceding discussion leaves many questions unanswered. The purpose of this chapter was to provide an overview and a framework within which to work toward answers. Using the framework sketched out in this chapter, we will organize the data presented in Chapter 17 and systematically approach the questions that were raised and left unanswered, particularly the seven questions posed earlier:

- Why does an economy sometimes produce less, in aggregate, than it is capable of producing so that, as a consequence, the employment of resources fluctuates?

- When an economy finds itself producing less than it is capable of producing, will it move *on its own*, without policy intervention, toward the full employment of all of its resources?

- If an economy moves toward full employment on its own, is this movement rapid or slow?

- If the movement is slow and the costs substantial, can public policies minimize the losses associated with unemployment by moving the economy toward full employment more rapidly than it might move on its own?

- What determines changes in an economy's capacity to produce—that is, its rate of economic growth?

- If the rate of economic growth is less than desired, can it be influenced by public policy?

- What is the relationship, if any, between policies designed to offset cycles and policies designed to foster economic growth?

In the language of a much-used metaphor, this chapter provides a picture of the forest; the next several chapters will look more carefully at the trees.

Chapter 19 ▶▶
Aggregate Supply _____

There is abundant evidence that the use of resources fluctuates through time. More resources are used during some periods, while during other periods, resources are unemployed. These fluctuations impose substantial costs on an economy and on the individuals living within it. Hence there is an urgent need to understand and not just describe these fluctuations. In the previous chapter, we suggested that output fluctuations can be thought of as a combination of two effects: First, events in the economy lead to price-level changes. Second, price-level changes lead to changes in the aggregate real output actually produced—real output actually produced (but not potential real output) increases with increases in the price level and decreases with decreases in the price level. This chapter focuses on the second of these effects. In particular, we look for answers to the question: Why does real output change with changes in the price level?

We begin, however, by focusing on *potential* real output. We will find that an economy's potential real output is *not* affected by its price level or by changes in its price level.

We then consider reasons why an economy may actually produce at a level different from its potential. We will find that *if input price changes lag behind output price changes,* aggregate real output will increase when the price level rises and decrease when it falls. That is, we will find that if input prices do not change in the same proportion and at the same time as output prices change, there will be a short-run aggregate supply curve that slopes upward and to the right—an increase in the price level will lead to an increase in real output, while a decrease in the price level will lead to a decrease in real output. This seems simple enough. However, as we will see, the reasons why aggregate real output changes with changes in the price level are complex and not fully understood.

▶ Potential Real Output

An economy's potential real output is determined by the natural resources available to it, the technologies that it has developed or acquired, the amount of capital that it has accumulated, and the amount of productive labor that it has available. If these productive inputs are employed fully and efficiently, the maximum amount that the economy can produce is its **potential real output** (denoted by y^*). Thus, y^* in Figure 1 corresponds to some point *along* an economy's production possibilities frontier. Because real gross domestic product (**real GDP**) is a measure of real output, we can think of potential real gross domestic product as a way of measuring potential output.

As the resources available to an economy change, so too will *potential* real output. For example, if new natural resources are discovered and used together with existing capital, labor, and technology, *potential* real output will increase. This effect is illustrated by the shift from y^* to y^{***} in Figure 1. Technological innovations that make existing resources more productive will also increase *potential* real output; so

Figure 1
Potential Real Output

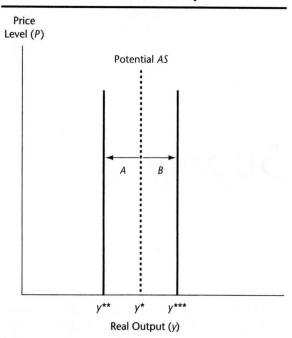

When an economy's resources are fully employed, aggregate supply is equal to potential real output. Potential real output increases from y^* to y^{***} with changes such as technological advances and capital accumulation (shift B). Potential real output decreases from y^* to y^{**} when there are wars or natural disasters that destroy productive resources or when resources are depleted in other ways (shift A).

Figure 2
Economic Growth

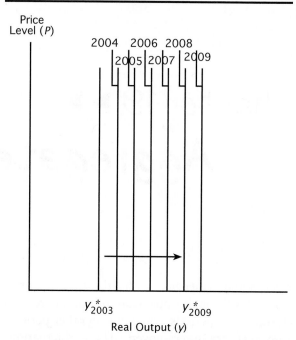

Sustained increases in an economy's ability to produce real output over time is represented by continual rightward shifts in potential aggregate supply.

will the accumulation of capital or a permanent increase in the amount of labor available to the economy. Continuous technological innovation or sustained increases in the amount of capital or other resources will lead to economic growth, which is represented by continual rightward shifts of the *potential real* output curve in Figure 2.

On the other hand, if there is little technological innovation as natural resources are depleted, *potential* real output will decline, from y^* to y^{**} in Figure 1, for example. Similarly, if an economy does not continually invest, the capital stock will slowly decrease as it depreciates with use. The consequence? *Potential* real output will fall.

Generally, these kinds of changes are very slow, with *potential* real output changing by only a few percentage points each year, either up or down. The accumulation of new capital in the US economy, for example, increases potential real output by at most

1 or 2 percent each year. However, during periods of severe distress (generally during wars or natural disasters such as drought), the resources available to an economy may change much more rapidly. For example, during the fourteenth and fifteenth centuries, the bubonic plague killed somewhere between 30 and 50 percent of the population throughout Europe. *Potential* real output declined dramatically as a consequence. That is, when the plague was over, the economy of Europe was able to produce substantially less than it could 50 years earlier. Or, for a more contemporary example, periodic drought in sub-Saharan Africa has led to increased desertification. As a consequence, millions have starved as *potential* real output of the economies in the region has fallen. Dramatic changes in *potential* real output of this sort are the exception. Generally, changes in *potential* real output are small relative to the current level of real output over short periods of time, even over a year or more. As a consequence, we will treat potential real output as if it were *fixed* or *unchanging* when we discuss short-term issues.

Available Resources and the Price Level

In Figures 1 and 2, *potential* real output is represented by a vertical line. This characterization implies that potential real output is not affected by changes in the price level. That is, for the economies these figures represent, it doesn't matter whether the price level is 100, 200, or 800—*potential* real output remains unchanged. This characterization of *potential* real output reflects the fact that *neither the price level, nor price-level changes, change the resources available to an economy.* Increasing the price level, for example, neither increases nor decreases the amount of farmland available or the number of machines and factories within the United States. And, as we will see, after an economy has fully adjusted to any change in the price level, the change in the price level also leave incentives for employees and employers unaffected. If the resources available to an economy are unaffected by the price level, or after suitable adjustment to changes in the price level, an economy's *potential* to produce cannot be affected. Therefore *potential* real output is independent of the price level.

Potential Real Output and the Labor Market

Much of the productive capacity of an economy is embodied in its population. As a consequence, the available labor resources in an economy are an important determinant of its *potential* real output. The relationship between available labor resources and the number of individuals living within an economy is subtle, however. The term *available labor resources* describes the productive effort provided by individuals when labor and other resources are fully employed. But *full employment* does not mean that everyone is working:

1. Even when jobs are available, some individuals will be searching for jobs, and while they are searching for available jobs, will be unemployed. This kind of unemployment is called *natural unemployment*. We will ignore this complication for now, but will return to it in Chapter 23 ("More on Unemployment"). You should keep in mind, however, that full employment means that all those who wish to work at the prevailing wage are able to do so *or* that there are unfilled jobs available for those currently looking for work. In other words, full employment means that there is a job for each person who wants to work at the prevailing wage, but it does not mean that every job is occupied. In this context, unemployment means that there are individuals who wish to work at the prevailing wage who cannot find jobs—there simply are not as many jobs available as there are persons either currently employed or searching for work.

2. Full employment of labor does not mean that each person works 24 hours per day or the maximum amount that is biologically possible. Nor does full employment necessarily mean that every individual who might be able to work is actually employed. Rather, full employment is determined by the amount of labor time that firms want to employ—labor demand—and the amount of labor time that individuals want to supply to the market, given the other uses to which they can put their time—labor supply. Full employment occurs when there is an *equilibrium* in each labor market within the economy.

This notion of full employment is subtle because at one time or in one place, full employment may mean each adult is working 60 hours per week and at another time or place, full employment may mean each adult is working 40 hours per week. This variation is not merely hypothetical. Indeed, the average number of hours worked per week in the United States has declined substantially over the past century. As a result, the meaning of full employment has changed. In 1880, it meant that there were jobs for all persons who wanted to work 60 hours per week at the prevailing wage. Today, it means that there are jobs for all persons who want to work 40 hours per week at the prevailing wage.

The market for labor illustrated in Figure 3 determines the real wage and the number of hours employed, in aggregate, in the economy. That is, the number of hours worked, N, is shown along the horizontal axis.[1] The **real wage**, W/P, is shown along the vertical axis, where W is the **nominal** or **dollar wage** and P is the price level. Thus, the real wage is

---

[1] The quantity of labor could be measured in terms of hours per day or hours per year, each aggregated over all of the economy.

Figure 3
The Aggregate Labor Market

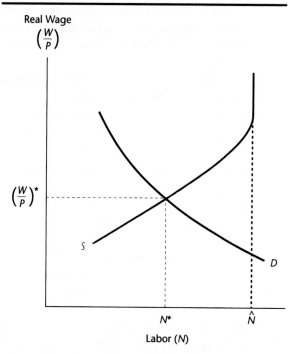

In the labor market, the quantity of labor demanded increases with a decrease in the real wage. The quantity of labor supplied increases with an increase in the real wage. The labor market will be in equilibrium when the real wage is $(W/P)^*$ and N^* hours per week are provided to the economy.

the dollar wage per hour that individuals are paid, measured in terms of the purchasing power of a dollar.

Aggregate demand for labor. Labor is demanded, of course, because it is productive.[2] The productivity of labor depends upon the amount of capital and other resources available to the economy, as well as the education, training, and skills embodied in the workforce. An increase in the overall productivity of labor because of, say, an increase in the capital

stock in an economy or the education level of the workforce would shift the labor demand curve in Figure 3 to the right—employers would be willing to pay more for more productive workers. A decrease in the overall productivity of labor, for example, because of a decrease in the other resources available in the economy would shift the labor demand curve in Figure 3 to the left.

The productivity of labor changes as the amount of labor employed changes. In general, as more labor is employed, given the capital available to the economy, *the additional output produced decreases.* That is, as more labor is employed with a given capital stock, the additional output produced when an additional worker is employed will be less than the additional output produced when the next-to-last worker was employed, which, in turn, will be less than the additional output produced when the third-to-last worker was employed, and so forth. Or, equivalently, as each person currently employed works additional hours, if the capital stock is fixed, the additional output produced when the additional hour is worked will decrease. This effect is called *diminishing marginal returns.* The additional output produced when one additional worker is hired is called the **marginal product of labor.** Thus, beyond some point, as additional labor is employed, the marginal product of labor falls. Or, in more technical terms, there is *diminishing* marginal product of labor.

The demand for labor can be thought of as the highest real wage firms would be willing to pay to attract a given number of workers. As a consequence of diminishing returns, firms will be willing to employ more labor only if the opportunity cost of doing so decreases as successive workers are hired. As a consequence, *there is an inverse relationship between the real wage and the amount of labor that firms wish to employ.* In addition, when the real wage rate increases, firms *substitute other inputs, such as capital, for labor,* if they are given enough time. At higher real wage rates, firms also have an incentive to search out and adopt different technologies that rely less on labor, in this case *substituting technology for labor.* Thus, the aggregate demand curve for labor slopes downward to the right, as indicated in Figure 3.

Why is it that the real wage, rather than the nominal wage, influences firms' demand for labor?

---

[2] Figure 3 is a highly stylized representation of the labor market. There are many labor markets in an economy, not just one, with skill levels as well as wages differing for occupations and for individuals in these different markets. Again, in keeping with our aggregate or *macro*economic approach, these differences are ignored and it is assumed that there is a single, aggregate labor market in the economy.

For a firm, the wage rate is the cost of using labor rather than other productive inputs. Whether a firm cares if it must pay $5 per hour or $50 per hour for workers depends upon how productive those workers are *and* the price at which it sells its output. Firms care about profits, and profits depend upon both costs and revenues. If all output prices are ten times higher when wages are $50 than they are when wages are $5, a wage of $50 per hour won't seem high. Because the price level is a measure of output prices, it follows that firms will respond in *exactly the same way* in terms of the amount of labor they wish to demand if the nominal wage is $10 and the price level is 200 or if the nominal wage is $5 and the price level is 100. In both cases the real wage is the same. From the perspective of firms, the real wage—the nominal wage, W, divided by the price level, P—accounts for both input and output prices.

Aggregate supply of labor. Labor is supplied by individuals. Individuals can choose to work or to use their time for other purposes, including leisure. From the perspective of individuals, the real wage is the opportunity cost of choosing leisure. As the real wages increases, leisure becomes relatively more costly because the income lost for each hour not worked—leisure—has increased. As the real wage increases, individuals have an incentive to substitute goods that can be purchased in markets for leisure—that is, they have an incentive to supply more labor and take less leisure. This effect of an increasing real wage is called a **substitution effect.**

An increase in the real wage also has an **income effect**. If the real wage increases, individuals can earn the same income by working fewer hours, and they may want to work fewer hours in order to take more leisure. The supply of labor increases with the real wage only if the substitution effect outweighs this income effect. In addition, as they choose between leisure and work, some individuals may not choose to participate in the labor market at all at the current real wage. For these individuals, changes in the real wage affect their incentives to participate or not participate in the labor market. These two effects—a change in the number of hours provided by those working and a change in the participation rate by those not currently working—increase the quantity of labor supplied as the real wage increases. This relationship is described in the upward-sloping aggregate labor supply curve in Figure 3. The labor supply curve can also be thought of as representing the highest real wage firms would have to pay to attract a given number of workers.[3]

Changes in the real wage. Because the real wage is a ratio of the nominal wage to the price level, it can change when either changes. That is, the real wage can change because the *nominal wage* increases or decreases with little or no change in the price level or because the *price level* decreases or increases with little or no change in the nominal wage. The nominal wage is the amount that a person is paid per hour or per month, for example $5.50 per hour or $2,500 per month. The price level is a measure of the purchasing power of the dollars earned. Thus, for example, if your hourly wage remains at $5.00 when the price level increases form 100 to 200, your *real* wage decreases by 50 percent. That is, each dollar you earn purchases less. If the nominal wage and the price level both double (from $5.00 to $10.00 and from 100 to 200), however, the real wage does not change. In this case, each dollar you earn purchases less but you are paid more dollars, so the two effects offset each other. More generally, an equivalent percentage change in both the nominal wage and the price level will leave the real wage unchanged.

Full employment. Equilibrium in the labor market occurs when the number of hours individuals are willing to provide to the market is equal to the number of hours firms are willing to employ. Alternatively, equilibrium occurs when the real wage that must be offered to attract a given number of workers is exactly equal to the real wage that firms are willing to offer for that number of workers. In Figure 3, N^* is supplied and demanded at the equilibrium real wage $(W/P)^*$.

If each person works about the same number of hours (say 40 hours per week), N^* can also be thought of as the number of individuals employed. Interpreting Figure 3 this way makes it clear that *not everyone in the economy is employed*

---

[3] As a consequence of the income and substitution effects, the aggregate supply of labor in the United States is quite inelastic with respect to changes in the real wage.

at the equilibrium or prevailing real wage. It is in this sense, that "full employment" is a subtle concept. For example, Figure 3 shows that $\hat{N}$ is the maximum number of people willing to work 40 hours per week *at some wage*. Many of these people are willing to work *only* at a substantially wage higher than $(W/P)^*$, however. This can be seen by noting that there are individuals, illustrated by the distance $(\hat{N} - N^*)$, who are not working because they *choose* not to work at the equilibrium market wage, $(W/P)^*$. These individuals are not considered unemployed. *Unemployment only occurs when individuals who wish to work at the market wage cannot find jobs.*

Changes in the Equilibrium Level of Employment

Potential real output, y^*, is determined by full employment of all resources, including labor. Thus, y^* corresponds to N^*. As a consequence of this relationship between the employment of labor and potential real output, anything that *permanently* affects the labor market equilibrium will affect *potential* real output. For example, suppose there is an increase in the supply of labor (such as happened during the 1960s and 1970s when a larger fraction of married women chose to participate in the labor market). The real wage will fall and more people will be employed, as illustrated in Figure 4.[4] *Potential* real output will increase, as indicated by Figure 5.

On the other hand, if something occurs that makes individuals want more leisure at each real wage, the supply of labor will decrease (the supply curve will shift leftward) and *potential* real output will be lower. It has been argued, for example, that income taxes make working less desirable and leisure more desirable. If this is true, higher income tax rates will adversely affect *potential* real output because the labor supply will fall and *potential* real output will fall as well.

As we have emphasized, not everyone living within an economy who might be able to work will be employed when there is "full employment" in the

---

[4] The substantial migration of workers from Europe to the United States in the nineteenth century also increased the supply of labor and, as a consequence, the potential real output for the economy. A comparable migration, mostly from Asia and South and Central America between 1970 and 2000 increased the potential real output of the US economy in the latter part of the twentieth century.

Figure 4
The Effect of an Increase in the Supply of Labor

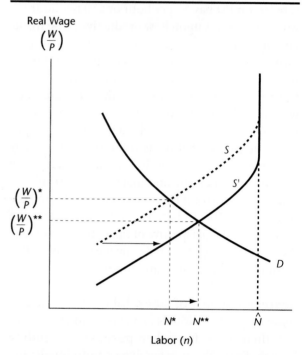

An increase in the supply of labor from S to S' (perhaps because of an increased participation in the labor force by married women) will lower the equilibrium real wage from $(W/P)^*$ to $(W/P)^{**}$ and increase the number of persons employed from N^* to N^{**}.

labor market. Instead, only those willing to work at the market equilibrium wage will be employed. This means that *different equilibrium wages correspond to different levels of full employment*. In Figure 4, for example, both N^* and N^{**} represent *full employment* of labor resources even though there are different numbers of persons actually working in each case. *Potential* real output will be greater when N^{**} persons are employed than it is when N^* are employed, as illustrated in Figure 5.

Economic Growth and Labor Productivity

Compare Figure 4 with Figure 6. In both cases, the equilibrium amount of labor employed has increased. Therefore, in both cases, *potential* real output will increase as well. In Figure 4, the real wage has decreased. In Figure 6, by contrast, the real wage has increased. Individuals would be better off in the latter, rather than the former, case since the amount they are paid per hour worked is increasing rather than decreasing.

Figure 5
The Effect of an Increase in Labor Supply on Potential Real Output

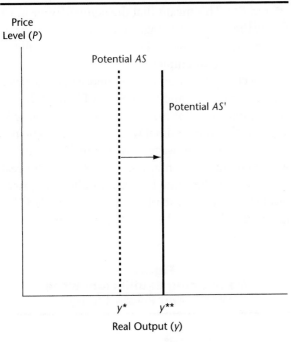

When the supply of labor increases as in Figure 4, potential real output of the economy increases from y^* to y^{**}.

Figure 6

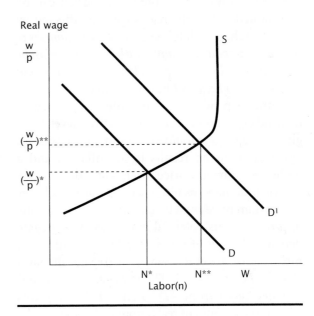

What is the difference between the two figures? In Figure 4, the supply of labor increases. This might occur, for example, because of an increase in the adult-age population. Or it might occur because married women, who a one time did not work outside of the home, entered the work force; or because workers decide to retire at a later age; or because of an immigration of foreign workers. The economy absorbs these additional workers in each case, but only at a lower real wage. Since there is more labor employed, however, *potential* real output increases.

In Figure 6, the demand for labor increases. This can only occur if the amount of money that firms are willing to pay to attract a given number of workers increases. What could lead to such a change? If workers became more productive so that the amount that each worker produced per hour worked increased, the maximum amount that firms are willing to pay increases. Competition among firms for more productive workers increases the real wage toward this maximum. Higher real wages induce more workers into the labor market and *potential* real output increases.

We learned in Chapter 17 that the US economy has had sustained growth in *potential* real output for a long time. Is this growth best understood by Figure 6 or Figure 4? If you take a long-term perspective, the real wage in the United States has increased. Indeed, it has increased substantially. The supply of labor has also increased, but the increases in real wages means that increases in the demand for labor have outstripped these supply changes. As a consequence, there has been economic growth in the sense that *potential (and actual) real output have increased, and* there has also been economic growth in the sense that *per capita income has increased*. Put differently, the US economy produces more than it did a decade or two or three decades ago *and* households, on average, consume more goods and services than they have in the past.

That these per capita gains occur only if there are increases in the maximum amount that firms are willing to pay workers underscores the importance of increases in the productivity of labor. This underscores, in turn, the important role of education, training, and technological innovation in improving the well-being of individuals living within an economy.

Flexible Wages and Potential Real Output

Because equilibrium in the labor market can be maintained *only if* the *real* wage is unaffected by price level changes, it follows that *if an economy is to produce at its potential, any price level change must be accompanied by a comparable change in nominal wages so as to keep real wages unchanged.* When an economy is producing at its potential, aggregate demand determines the economy's price level. For a given level of *potential* real output, an increase in aggregate demand results in an inflation and a higher equilibrium price level; and a decrease in aggregate demand results in a deflation and a lower equilibrium price level. If an economy is to continue to produce at its potential in the face of aggregate demand changes of this sort, *all* prices and wages must move together when aggregate demand changes. For example, in Figure 7 aggregate demand had decreased from *AD* to *AD'*. Following this change, the amount of real output demanded will be

equal to y^* only if the price level falls from P^* to P^{**}. But the aggregate real output produced will equal y^* only if the same amount of labor is employed at P^* and P^{**}. This means that the *nominal* wage must fall by the same percentage as the price level does. If it does, the real wage will be unchanged, as will the amount of labor employed.

To clarify this argument, suppose that the price index is 100 at P^* and 50 at P^{**} in Figure 7. In the corresponding labor market illustrated in Figure 8, suppose that the nominal wage is initially $5.00 per hour. The nominal wage must fall to $2.50 for full employment to be maintained. That is, the real wage will be the same before and after the price-level change only when the nominal wage is $5.00 before the change and $2.50 after the change. *At any*

Figure 8
Maintaining Equilibrium When Wages and Prices Change

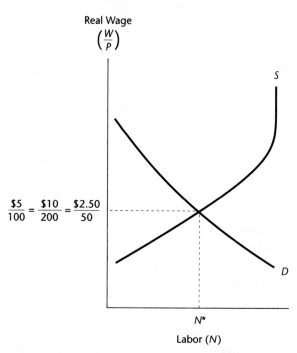

Figure 7
Adjustment with Flexible Wages and Prices

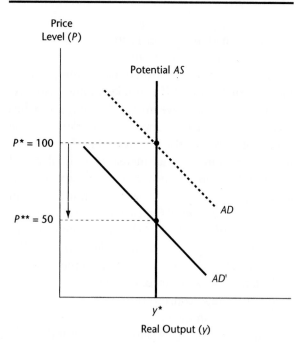

If aggregate demand falls from *AD* to *AD'*, the price level must fall from P^* to P^{**} in order for the amount demanded to be equal to potential real output. If the price level falls, however, nominal wages must also fall by the same proportion in order for the economy to continue to produce y^*.

Suppose the labor market is initially at an equilibrium, with N^* workers employed and a wage of $5.00 when the price level is 100. This equilibrium can only be maintained if the real wage does not change. Thus, if the price level increases to 200, adjustments in the labor market must increase nominal wages to $10.00 to keep the real wage constant. If the price level falls to 50, adjustments in the labor market must decrease the nominal wage to $2.50 to keep the real wage constant.

other real wage, a different number of persons will be employed and real output produced will differ from *y**.

To summarize: In the face of aggregate demand shocks, an economy will produce at its potential, thereby maintaining full employment, *only if* prices *and* nominal wages change easily *and*, in addition, move together. Because of the importance of price and wage flexibility in continuously maintaining output at an economy's potential, the model of the economy illustrated in Figures 7 and 8 is sometimes referred to as a **flexible price model of aggregate output**. The term *flexible price* is used to mean that the price level *and* nominal wages adjust sufficiently to keep the economy producing at its potential. *In the flexible price model, aggregate demand shocks affect only the price level. They do not affect real output.*

▶ Short-Run Aggregate Supply

If follows from this discussion of the flexible price model that *actual* real output can deviate from *potential* real output only if, for some reason, *nominal wages do not move with changes in the price level*. Nominal wages that do not adjust in equal proportion with changes in the price level are said to be **sticky**.

If nominal wages are sticky, real wages will change whenever there are changes in the price level. For example, if the nominal wage remains at $5.00 when the price level increases from 100 to 200, the real wage falls from $5.00 to $2.50. At this lower real wage, firms will want to employ more people. On the other hand, if the nominal wage remains at $5.00 when the price level decreases from 100 to 50, the real wage increases from $5.00 to $10.00. At this higher real wage, firms will want to employ fewer people. Figure 9 illustrates the general relationship between different price levels and the demand for labor. Given this relationship, if the nominal wage does not change, that is, is *sticky*, firms will want to employ fewer workers whenever the price level falls from *P** and more workers whenever the price level increases from *P**.

When fewer workers are employed, real output falls. When more workers are employed, real output increases. Because these changes in employment are a consequence of price-level-induced changes in the real wage, however, they *do not* correspond to changes in *potential* real output. That is, the

Figure 9
The Effect of Price-Level Changes on the Demand for Labor

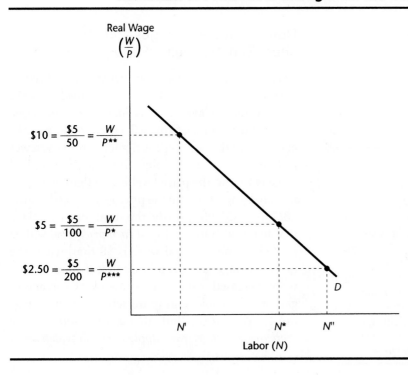

If the nominal wage does not change, then changes in the price level will also affect real wages. If the nominal wage is $5.00 and the price level increases from 100 to 200, real wages will fall from $5.00 to $2.50 and firms will want to increase their employment from *N** to *N''*. Conversely, if the price level falls from 100 to 50, the real wage will increase from $5.00 to $10.00 and firms will want to decrease the number of workers they employ from *N** to *N'*. (Note that the real wage, for example, $2.50 = $5.00/200, has been normalized by implicitly multiplying by 100. That is, $5.00/200 = $0.025 × 100 = $2.50.)

number of individuals that firms would employ at the equilibrium real wage has not changed, so *potential* real output cannot have changed. Instead, when wages are sticky, the real output actually produced differs from *potential* real output. These differences are represented by movements along the **short-run aggregate supply** curve illustrated in Figure 10. *If wages are sticky, real output will increase when the price level increases (because the amount of labor employed increase) and decrease when the price level decreases (because the amount of labor employed decreases).*

Because the real wage falls with an increase in the price level when wages are sticky, it becomes more profitable for firms to increase the amount of labor they use. To see this in a slightly different way,

note that for a firm, profits per unit of output sold are equal to the price at which it sells its output minus the per unit or average production costs:

$$\text{per unit profits} = \text{output price} - \text{per unit or average costs}$$

For example, if your costs are \$.80 per unit produced and you can sell each unit for \$1.00, you make \$.20 in profits for each unit sold. Suppose that, in the short run, your costs are mostly fixed because nominal wages do not change. Then changes in the price of your product will lead to changes in profits. An increase in the price will lead to an increase in profits. That is, if the price at which you can sell your output increases to \$1.10 and costs remain at \$.80, your per unit profits increase to \$.30. On the other hand, if the output price falls to \$.90 and costs do not change, your per unit profits decrease to \$.10.

When profits increase, firms will want to increase the amount that they produce. To do so, they must employ additional resources. By contrast, when profits decrease, firms will want to decrease the amount they produce and, as a consequence, will want to employ fewer resources. This means that if nominal wages are sticky and costs are relatively insensitive to price-level changes, real output will change with changes in the price level.

Nominal Wage Changes and Shifts in Short-Run Aggregate Supply

There is a different short-run aggregate supply curve for each nominal wage. To see why, consider Figure 11. If, when the price level is 50, the nominal wage is \$8 rather than \$5, firms will employ fewer workers because the real wage is higher. Similarly, fewer individuals will be employed when the nominal wage is \$8 and the price level is 200 than when the nominal wage is \$5 and the price level is 200 because \$8/200 > \$5/200. Clearly, the number of workers that firms wish to employ *at each price level* will be less when the nominal wage is \$8 than when the nominal wage is \$5. It follows that if the nominal wage increased from \$5 to \$8, the short-run aggregate supply would shift to the left as shown in Figure 12. We can conclude that *as the nominal wage increases, the short-run supply curve shifts leftward,* ceteris paribus.

**Figure 10
Short-Run Aggregate Supply**

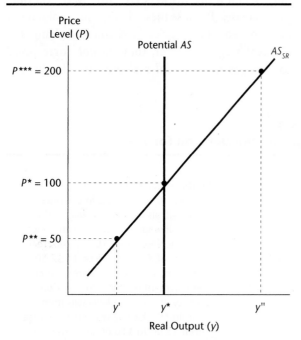

If nominal wages are sticky, as in Figure 9, firms will change the amount of labor that they employ when the price level changes. Then the real ouput that is supplied to the economy will also change. For example, in Figure 9, firms will hire less labor (a decrease from N^* to N') when the price level falls from 100 to 50 and real output will fall from y^* to y'; firms will hire more labor (an increase from N^* to N'') when the price level increases and real output will increase from y^* to y''. The aggregate output that firms supply at various price levels is the economy's *short-run aggregate supply curve.*

Figure 11
The Effect of Different Nominal Wages on the Demand for Labor

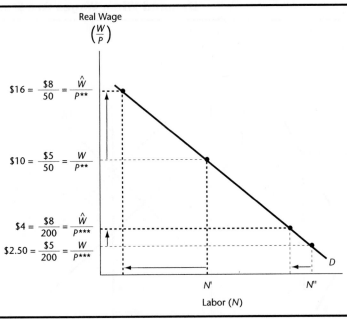

At each price level, a higher nominal wage means a higher real wage. Hence, at each price level, firms will want to employ less labor when the nominal wage increases.

Figure 12
Short-Run Aggregate Supply When the Nominal Wage Increases

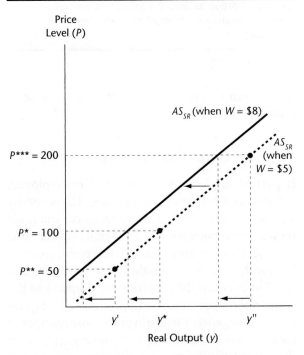

Because firms wish to employ fewer workers at each price level as the nominal wage increases (see Figure 11), the aggregate amount produced will be lower at each price level. This effect is summarized in a leftward shift in the short-run aggregate supply curve

The Real Output Effects of Aggregate Demand Shocks

Sticky nominal wages create unemployment. To see this, note that in Figure 13, the equilibrium real wage is $5 when the price level is 100. If, following an aggregate demand shock, the price level falls to 50 but the nominal wage doesn't change, the real wage increases to $10. At this real wage, firms will want to employ N' workers. But N'' individuals will want to work at this wage. Hence, $(N'' - N')$ will be unemployed. Why? Because a lower price level makes the use of labor less profitable when nominal wages do not change and firms will cut production.[5] The economy will produce at less than its potential. That is, when aggregate demand falls, the prices (and hence, the price level) fall because firms can't sell all that they produce. But when wages are sticky, firms find that when prices fall, profits fall. They respond by cutting output and laying off workers. In Figure 14, for example, real output falls from y^* to y_1 when there is a drop in aggregate demand. In this case,

---

[5] Nominal wages need not be completely sticky for this to occur. For example, if the price level begins to decrease because of a decrease in aggregate demand, say, from 100 to 75, but the nominal wage falls only from $5.00 to $4.50, real wages will increase from $5 ($5.00/100 × 100) to $6 ($4.50/75 × 100) and firms will use less labor.

Figure 13
Price Level Changes, Sticky Wages, and Unemployment

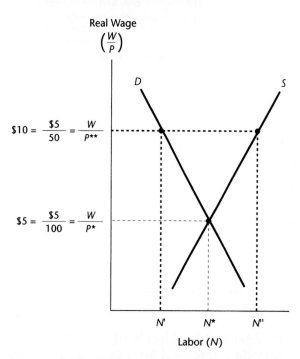

If the nominal wage does not change with changes in the price level, aggregate demand shocks will affect real wages. When real wages increase as the price level falls, firms employ fewer individuals (N') and unemployment ($N'' - N'$) will result.

Figure 14
The Effect of an Decrease in Aggregate Demand When Wages Are Sticky

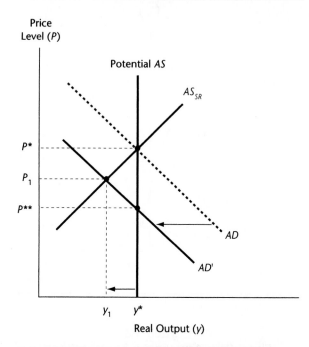

If there is a decrease in aggregate demand from AD to AD' and nominal wages do not quickly decrease by the same proportion as does the price level, real output in the economy will fall from y^* to y_1 and there will be unemployment.

sticky nominal wages lead to **unemployment**, and unemployment results in less real output.

On the other hand, if the labor market does not quickly or readily adjust to a higher price level with higher *nominal* wages when aggregate demand increases, the economy may produce at more than its potential or full employment level. In Figure 15, output will increase from y^* to y_2 when there is an increase in aggregate demand. In this case, sticky nominal wages lead to **overemployment**, and overemployment results in more real output.

Thus, if as aggregate demand changes, nominal wages are sticky, the economy will produce along a short-run aggregate supply curve (AS_{SR}) rather than at its potential real output (y^*). That is, aggregate demand shocks affect real output in the short run: an increase in aggregate demand will be accompanied by an increase in real output, but not an increase in potential real output, whereas a decrease in aggregate demand will be accompanied by a

decrease in real output, but not by a decrease in potential real output.

Potential Output and Unemployment

If part of the labor force becomes unemployed, *potential* real output does not change. The economy still has the same available labor resources and *could* produce at its potential, but it does not because some of these resources are unused. At this point, you may be wondering: "Why should I care about the distinction between the *potential* real output and the *actual* real output an economy produces?" Fair question. It is important to distinguish those changes in the economy that have long-term consequences from those that have shorter-term consequences because each may require quite different kinds of public policy responses. Changes in the labor market equilibrium caused by long-term changes in labor supply or labor demand have long-term consequences. They

Figure 15
The Effect of an Increase in Aggregate Demand When Wages Are Sticky

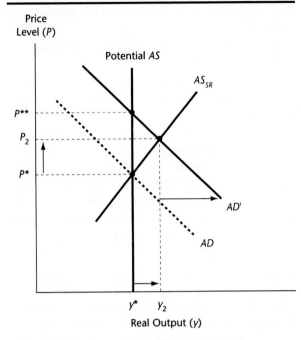

If there is an increase in aggregate demand from *AD* to *AD'* and nominal wages do not quickly increase by the same proportion as does the price level, the real output of the economy will increase from y^* to y_2 and there will be overemployment.

affect economic growth. Whereas slow adjustment of dollar wages in the labor market have shorter-term consequences. They affect economic cycles and instability. Policies that foster economic growth and overcome economic stagnation may be quite different from policies that dampen or offset the effects of business cycles and instability.

▶ Sticky Wages

We now have an explanation for why the actual output an economy produces changes with price-level changes—wages are sticky. Indeed, except for price-level changes, aggregate demand shocks would be completely irrelevant if nominal wages and the price level moved in tandem. While the effects of sticky wages are now clear, nothing to this point in our discussion suggest *why* wages are sticky. There is another problem that has been glossed over as well: The explanation of the relationship between changes in the price level, changes in employment, and changes in real output explains why firms want to

hire more workers when the price level rises. But it does not explain why individuals would be willing to work more. Since there are always two sides to a market, firms would only be able to actually hire more workers if more workers were willing to work.

There are several different approaches to these problems. Each assumes that there is some kind of market imperfection or lack of accurate information that prevents nominal wages or prices from full and rapid adjustment. No single explanation appears to be convincing in every situation—it may be that the different explanations may apply to different workers in different labor markets. Of these approaches, two are considered in the following discussion. The first focuses on *labor contracts and contracting;* the second on *expectations.*

The Fixed Nominal Long-Term Contract Approach

Most jobs are long-term commitments for both the employer and the employee. From the firm's perspective, it is expensive to hire and lay off workers. When workers are laid off, a firm may have to pay severance, pensions, and higher unemployment insurance premiums. In addition, the firm loses the special expertise and training that the laid-off workers have developed. When new workers are hired, a firm also encounters costs. Hiring involves advertising expenses, search time and costs, training costs, and the uncertainty associated with whether the new employee will be as productive as expected. From the worker's perspective, moving from one job to another is often costly because of family ties to a particular community, the time it takes to search for better alternatives, and skills that are specific to his or her current place of employment.

Both workers and firms have incentives to reach agreements about a longer-term employment relationship to minimize these costs. For some firms and workers, notably those in unionized industries, the longer-term employment relationship is formalized by a written or explicit contract. For other firms and workers, an informal or implicit contract often suffices. These explicit and implicit agreements cover matters such as the wage to be paid, how work assignments will be made over time, how wage adjustment will be made, the role of seniority, and how fluctuations in demand for the firm's product will be accommodated. Each of these aspects of the relationship between firms and workers may be influenced, in turn, by social norms that change only slowly over time.

There are two important aspects of explicit or implicit labor contracts. First, both workers and firms find it too costly to adjust the nominal wage *continuously* in response to ever-changing labor market conditions. This gives rise to sticky nominal wages. Second, both workers and firms agree to leave it to the discretion of the firm to hire as many or as few units of labor as it desires at the (perhaps contractually) rigid nominal wage. This means that when the real wages change because the price-level changes, the demand for labor determines the level of employment. Specifically, when the real wage increases, firms will employ less labor and aggregate real output will fall, but when the real wage decreases, firms will employ more labor. Therefore, *as long as workers have agreed ahead of time to provide whatever level of labor the firm wishes at the negotiated nominal wage, the amount of labor employed will change with changes in the real wage and, as a consequence, aggregate real output will change with changes in the price level.*

Firms also have longer-term contracts for other kinds of resources. It would not be unusual for a steel mill to have a long-term contract with a coal supplier that specified the price at which coal would be shipped to the mill. Similar agreements generally exist with suppliers of ore, power, shipping services, kiln refractories, and so forth. Such contracts are not limited to firms that make steel, of course, but are common across the economy. Retail stores almost always have long-term rental contracts on the space they occupy, milk distributors have long-term contracts with dairies for the delivery of milk, and supermarkets have long-term contracts with suppliers for store-brand products, and so forth. Because many of a firm's costs are tied to contracts to extend into the future, *output prices are likely to increase more rapidly than these input prices when there is an increase in the demand for a firm's output.* Both sticky wages and slow-to-adjust costs for other inputs mean that, in the short run, profits for most firms will increase with an increase in the price level and decrease with a decrease in the price level.

Firms benefit from long-term relationships when prices begin to increase; suppliers of inputs appear to lose. Although this may seem one-sided, workers and other suppliers of inputs agree to such contracts because the contracts also work the other way: During a downturn, prices fall more rapidly than input costs which are sticky because of the long-term contracts. When they do, suppliers of inputs benefit and firms appear to lose. If both firms and workers might expect the gains and losses to even out, they will be willing to abide by long-term agreements, whether formal or informal even when they are occasionally disadvantaged by the contract.

In sum, when nominal wages and other input prices are fixed by implicit or explicit contracts, increases in the price level will lead to an increase in the employment of labor and a corresponding increase in aggregate real output. Decreases in the price level will lead to a decrease in employment of labor and a decrease in aggregate real output.

The Price-Level Misperception Approach

The real wage can be affected by changes in the price level *if price-level changes are misperceived.* Suppose, for example, that workers do not immediately notice widespread increases in prices, but that firms promptly perceive that prices have increased. Suppose, further, that workers make their labor supply decisions based on what they *expect* to be the real wage (that is, the **expected real wage**, which is the nominal wage divided by the price level that is expected to prevail over the near future, say, the next few months or even the next year). Suppose, by contrast, that firms make their demand decisions based on the **actual real wage**. For example, a firm might be able to hire the workers it needs for $8 per hour when both it and its employees expect the price level to be 100. In this case, the real wage is also $8 per hour. If the price level increases beyond its expected level, say from 100 to 150, firms immediately notice that the real wage has decreased ($8/100>$8/150). As firms see the real wage fall, they will want to hire more units of labor. Individuals, who are less well informed, still believe the price level to be 100, so they still think that the real wage is $8.

As firms offer higher nominal wages in an effort to get more labor supplied to them, workers, not knowing that prices have increased, see the higher nominal wages as an increase in real wages and accept the firms' offers. For example, if the nominal wage increases from $8 to $10, workers mistakenly think that the real wage has increased (from $8/100 to $10/100). They supply more labor. Firms are delighted to use the additional labor supplied because the real wage has actually *fallen* (from $8/100 to $10/150).

Unexpected increases in the price level relative to the *expected* price level lead to increases in the employment of labor and, hence, increases in aggregate real output. Similarly, *unexpected decreases* in the price level relative to the *expected* price level lead to decreases in employment and a corresponding decrease in aggregate real output.

The key assumption in this approach is that firms and workers differ in their expectations about the price level—firms are assumed to have better information than workers and base their decisions on the *actual* real wage. Workers, less well informed, base their decisions on the *expected* real wage and only slowly adjust their expectations to actual changes in the price level.

A slightly different approach that also relies on price-level misperceptions assumes that firms and employees are equally well informed, but only about certain things. Individuals are assumed to be well informed about the prices of the goods that they produce, either as employers or employees, but less well informed about the prices of other goods and services.

One of the reasons for this lack of information about prices in general is that information is costly to obtain. Many kinds of price information can be obtained only be searching, for example, a process that is costly because it takes time. When the price observed by an individual begins to change, the nature of the change is not immediately evident. To see why this might be a plausible assumption, suppose that the amount you paid for groceries this week increased over last week's bill. Does knowing this provide you any information about whether there is an economy-wide inflation? Not necessarily. It could be that only the prices of the vegetables you bought increased, perhaps because of a frost in the growing areas of California. Or, of course, the increase could have occurred because of a general inflation in which all prices increased. How would you determine whether the change in the amount you paid was due to a general increase in all prices— a change in the price level—or to a large change in the relative price of a few things, that is, a relative price change? This is not a simple question to answer. Changes in prices in particular markets are

relatively easy to observe. Changes in the price level cannot be observed, however, but must be inferred from price changes across lots of different markets. Thus, deciding what a particular market price change means in terms of price-level changes is a difficult problem. When you shop one week, chicken is $1.30 per pound; the next week it could be $.95 per pound. Beef may be $1.79 the first week and $1.89 the next. Week to week, some prices go up, other prices go down. *Most of these are relative price changes that occur in response to changes in market supply and market demand and have nothing to do with an economy-wide inflation or deflation.* During an inflation, however, most prices will creep up; during a deflation, most prices will creep down. There is no easy or quick way to tell if easily observed price changes are part of a more widespread pattern of price changes.

This confusion of relative price changes and price-level changes will affect decisions about how much firms and individuals should supply. If most individuals don't understand that an increase in the price of the output that they produce is really just an increase in the overall price level, they will supply more labor. Aggregate real output will increase. That is, aggregate real output will be greater than *potential* real output when the price level is unexpectedly higher than anticipated and less than potential real output when the price level is unexpectedly lower than anticipated.

How Long Is the Long Run?

No contract lasts forever. Misperceptions cannot last forever either. As explicit contracts are renegotiated, implicit contracts change, or individuals gather better information, nominal wages will adjust to changes in the price level. As nominal wages adjust to changes in the price level so too will the short-run real output curve. More precisely, *as price-level expectations and input prices increase, the short-run aggregate supply curve will shift to the left; as price-level expectations and input prices decrease, the short-run aggregate supply curve will shift to the right.* The effect can be seen by bringing together the analysis summarized in Figure 12 with the short-run effect of an aggregate demand shock illustrated in Figure 15. Consider, then, Figure 16.

In the short run, if nominal wages are sticky, an increase in aggregate demand will increase real

Figure 16
Macroeconomic Adjustment When Nominal Wages Increase Slowly with Increases in the Price Level

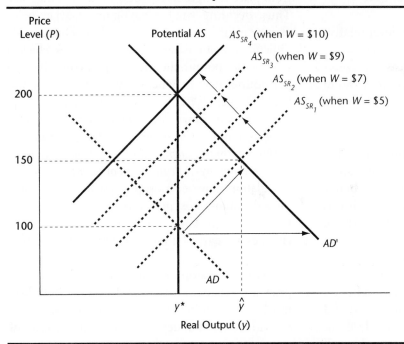

In the sticky-wage model, a shock that increases aggregate demand will increase output along the short-run aggregate supply curve. Aggregate real output in the economy will increase beyond y^*. As nominal wages slowly adjust, however, the short-run aggregate supply curve will shift back and aggregate real output will decrease. Eventually, nominal wages will have increased by the same proportion as the increase in the price level and the real wage will return to its original level. At that point, the economy will be producing at its potential, y^*.

output as the economy moves along AS_{SR_1}. The economy settles at $\hat{y}$ and $P = 150$. Eventually nominal wages will begin to increase in response to the higher price level—as individuals find that prices have gone up (and their real wages have *really* gone down), they will demand higher nominal wages. As a consequence, short-run aggregate supply shifts left and real output decreases. This process continues until, finally, the nominal wage has increased by the same proportion as the price level. When it has, the real wage will be the same as it was prior to the aggregate demand shock and the economy will be producing at its potential, y^*. Note that real output will change with an aggregate demand shock, but not permanently. (This conclusion stands in contrast with the flexible wages approach outlined earlier, where changes in aggregate demand did *not* affect real output.)

Abraham Lincoln is reported to have said that you could fool all of the people some of the time, some of the people all of the time, but not all of the people all of the time. If unemployment is, in part, a consequence of people being fooled, either because they have long-term contracts or because they have imperfect information, it is likely that both firms and individuals will eventually come to have simi-

lar expectations. As time passes, people obtain better information about the price level and the real wage and, as a result, they renegotiate contracts. Hence, unemployment is a *short-run* problem. That is, *over the long run, an economy will adjust so as to fully employ all of its productive resources, including labor.* Since there will always be pressures for prices or wages to change when the economy is producing at a level different than its potential, this suggests that *an economy is in long-run macroeconomic equilibrium only when it is fully employing its resources.*

Much of the debate about stabilization policies among economists and those who design such policies is about the length of time over which these adjustments in prices and nominal wages occur. If adjustments take several years, the economy will have unemployment for extended periods of time following an adverse aggregate demand shock. If adjustments occur in a matter of weeks or months, however, the economy will have unemployment for a much shorter period of time. Of course, it is small comfort to someone who is unemployed to be told that the economy will move toward full employment on its own. It's particularly discomforting if it takes several years rather than several months. On the other hand, *if* the economy moves toward full employment more rapidly than public policies can be implemented, it may make more sense to live with the discomfort of unemployment for brief periods of time.

There are quite different views among economists and policy makers about how long these adjustments actually take "in the real world." An economist who believes that differences between firms' and workers' expectations are eliminated quite quickly or that long-term explicit or implicit contracts are relatively unimportant will have a fundamentally different approach to macroeconomic policy issues than will an economist who believes that differing expectations or the effects of long-term contracting can persist for some time. John Maynard Keynes, perhaps the best-known economist of the period prior to World War II and the person most responsible for a great deal of modern macroeconomics, drew this famous distinction between those who focus on the short run and those who focus on the long run: "In the long run, we're all dead." Keynes was suggesting, of course, that arguments that the economy returns to full-employment "in the long run" aren't much good if the long run is indeed a long time.

Okun's Law

Changes in real output and changes in employment are closely related. When real output increases, the unemployment rate falls, and vice versa. The late Arthur Okun studied this relationship carefully and found that even though the unemployment rate cannot be predicted perfectly by knowing how far real output is from potential real output, there is a close relationship between the two that is reasonably stable. The empirical relationship he estimated now bears his name, **Okun's law**. Okun and subsequent researchers found that for every 2 to 3 percent that actual real output falls relative to potential real output, the unemployment rate increases by 1 percentage point. For example, if the natural rate of unemployment is 6 percent and actual output falls to 98 percent of potential output, then unemployment will increase from 6 to 7 percent. Okun's law doesn't explain why the empirical regularity holds, but it is a useful rule-of-thumb for relating changes in unemployment to the percentage drop in real output relative to an economy's potential real output.

▶ Supply-Side Effects

We conclude this chapter by considering two important effects on aggregate supply: supply shocks and the effects of public policy on incentives.

Supply Shocks

Changes in actual output, unemployment, and the price level can occur because of erratic changes in either aggregate demand *or* aggregate supply. An **aggregate supply shock** occurs when there is a dramatic change in production costs across the economy. The use of oil, for example, is widespread across the US economy and restrictions on the flow of oil by OPEC in 1973 and again in 1979 resulted in supply shocks in each year. A widespread drought that reduces agricultural production across an economy might also lead to a supply shock, as would an economy-wide labor agreement that increases wages for a large fraction of the labor force. Technological innovations that suddenly lower production costs for most of the industries in an economy would also be a supply shock, although in this case, it would be favorable rather than adverse.

When a firm's costs increase without any increase in the price at which it sells its output, its profits fall. It will cut production and lay off workers. If this effect is widespread across the economy, aggregate real output will fall and unemployment will increase. In terms of the aggregate demand-aggregate supply diagram, the short-run aggregate supply curve shifts to the left, as indicated in Figure 17.

As a consequence of an adverse supply shock, the price level increases. At the same time, real output falls and unemployment increases. For example, the price of oil in the United States increased 68 percent in 1974. In the 12 to 24 months that followed, unemployment and inflation both increased. Oil prices increased again in both 1979 and 1980. Inflation and unemployment increased in each of these years as well.

Even though prices increase, with a *temporary* adverse supply shock, since there is unemployment and output is below y*, there will eventually be downward pressure on nominal wages and prices. As nominal wages fall, short-run aggregate supply will increase, as indicated in Figure 18. In the long run, once again, the economy will move toward its potential. If the supply shock is due to a *permanent*

Figure 17
An Adverse Supply Shock

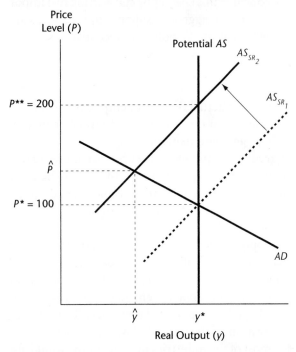

An adverse supply shock decreases aggregate real output below potential output, y^*. Note that unemployment will increase (because $\hat{y}$ is less than y^*) and that there will be inflation (because $\hat{P}$ is above P^*).

Figure 18
The Aftermath of an Adverse Supply Shock

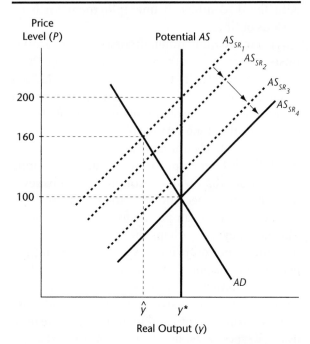

Because real output is below potential real output, there will be downward pressure on prices and nominal wages. As nominal wages adjust, short-run aggregate supply will shift and output will move toward potential output. Note that if the supply shock permanently reduced the resources available to the economy, potential real output would fall along with the decrease in the short-run aggregate supply.

reduction in the amount of a resource available to the U.S. economy, however, both actual real output and *potential* real output will be adversely affected and the price level will remain higher permanently.

Public Policy, Incentives and Potential Real Output

Public policies that change the incentives for individuals to supply labor or firms to demand labor will affect labor markets and will, thereby, change potential real output. For example, if individuals must pay taxes on the wages they earn, labor supply will decrease. This supply shift occurs because with a tax, individuals get to keep only a fraction of each dollar earned—if the tax rate is 20-percent, then for each dollar earned, individuals get to keep $.80. When the tax rate increases to 30 percent, individuals get to keep only $.70. This change in the amount that individuals actually get to keep lessens their incentive to work. (Your wage, net-of-tax-payments, is the opportunity cost of leisure, so an increase in the tax rate lowers the opportunity cost

of leisure. You will, as a consequence, choose to take more leisure. Put slightly differently, if your take-home pay falls because you have to pay higher income taxes, the benefit of working (the quantity of goodies that can be purchased for each hour worked) has fallen. This adverse incentive effect is illustrated by a leftward shift in the supply curve from S to S' in Figure 19(a). The federal income tax might have such an effect, for example.

On the other hand, if the employment of labor is taxed, the demand for labor will fall. This demand shift occurs because firms must pay workers an agreed-upon wage and then pay the government a tax based on this wage. For example, if workers and firms agree on a wage of $8.00 per hour and a tax of 10 percent is imposed on firms based on wages they pay, then the firm must pay $.80 per hour worked to the government. From the firm's perspective, the cost of employing a person for one hour has increased from $8.00 to $8.80. If firms must pay

Figure 19
The Effect of a Tax on Labor on the Labor Market

(a) Tax on Labor Levied on Individuals

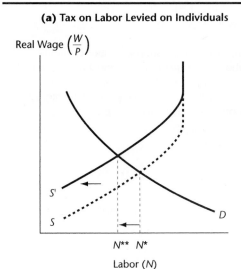

(b) Tax on Labor Levied on Firms

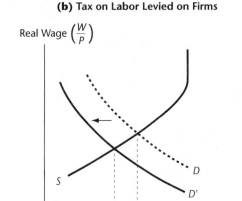

(a) A tax on labor levied on individuals, such as an income tax, will decrease the supply of labor. Consequently, the equilibrium amount of labor employed will fall from N^* to N^{**}. This will decrease the potential real output of the economy. (b) A tax on labor levied upon firms, such as the social security tax, will decrease the demand for labor. Consequently, the equilibrium amount of labor employed will fall from N^* to N^{**}. Because less labor is employed, the potential real output of the economy will also decline.

10 percent tax at every wage level, the demand for labor will fall, as illustrated by the leftward shift from D to D' in Figure 19(b). The social security tax might have such an effect, for example.

As a result of either an income tax imposed on workers or a social security tax imposed on firms, the equilibrium level of employment decreases from N^* to N^{**}. Because *potential* real output is determined in part by the amount of labor employed, tax policies that reduce the *equilibrium* level of employment in the labor market reduce *potential* real output. That is, since each of these taxes illustrated in Figure 19 affects the equilibrium in the labor market, each will affect *potential* real output as illustrated by the movement from y^* to y^{**} in Figure 20.

Part of the idea behind what has been called **supply-side economics** is that government tax policies have created serious distortions of the labor market of the kind just illustrated. This idea is the basis for a sometimes vigorous and long running public policy debate about whether to reduce the *marginal* federal income tax rate. Those in favor, view such reductions as a stimulus to economic growth. Those opposed believe that either the incentive effects are nonexistent or very small. Recognizing the possibilities of supply-side incentive effects,

however, forces policy makers to think carefully about what would otherwise be unintended consequences (that is, lower growth) of policies pursued for purposes that, at least on the surface, have nothing to do with the macroeconomic performance of an economy.

Another supply-side effect occurs when public policies, by design or otherwise, either speed adjustment in the labor market or make adjustments more difficult. For example, a minimum wage law that is set in dollar terms makes labor market adjustments more difficult during periods when the price level is decreasing (if W is fixed, then W/P will increase when P decreases). Or, for example, unemployment compensation makes unemployment less costly. This will mean that individuals search for new job opportunities with less intensity than they otherwise would. Because of unemployment compensation, measured unemployment will remain higher as labor market adjustments are spread over a longer period of time. Neither of these examples is an argument for or against the policies involved. They may have other purposes that warrant their use. Each has a supply-side effect, however, in that they extend the short-run adjustment time and thus the time over which the economy is not fully utilizing its resources.

Figure 20
The Effect of a Tax on Labor on Potential Real Output

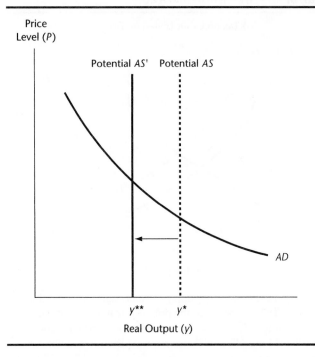

Taxes that affect either the supply of labor or the demand for labor will decrease the potential real output of the economy from y^* to y^{**}. In the long run, real output will be lower and the price level will be higher than would otherwise have been the case.

▶ Summary

Potential real output. Potential real output is determined by the resources available to an economy. Changes in these resources will change the potential real output of an economy. Thus, increases or improvements in natural resources, the capital stock, the labor supply, or in the technologies that combine these inputs in productive ways will increase potential real output.

The effect of labor on potential real output is both straightforward and subtle. Any change in the number of people actually employed will change the amount the economy actually produces. However, the number of people actually employed will be determined by the demand for labor, the supply of labor, expectations that demanders and suppliers have about price levels and real wages, and contracts between suppliers and demanders. When households and firms have the same expectations and contracts have fully adjusted to market conditions, the labor market will be in equilibrium. The amount of labor provided to the economy when this amount of labor is employed will determine the potential real output for the economy. Changes in the equilibrium level of employment in the labor market will lead to changes in potential real output. Not all persons will be employed when the labor market is in equilibrium, only those willing to work at the equilibrium real wage. When the labor market is in equilibrium, however, actual output and potential real output coincide.

Short-run aggregate supply. If nominal wages and prices do not adjust quickly or do not adjust in tandem in response to changes in the economy that push the price level up or down, such changes will create cycles in the economy. Unemployment and a decrease in real output below potential real output, or overemployment and an increase in real output above potential real output, can result fro sticky wages and prices. Thus, changes in aggregate demand affect real output only if prices do not adjust quickly to changes in aggregate demand or wages do not move with changes in price levels.

Long-run effects. Unemployment is a short-run phenomenon. Whatever the reasons for stickiness in prices and nominal wages, price and wage adjustment over time will move an economy toward its potential real output. Economists disagree on how long it takes for an economy to adjust back to full employment and stable prices after an adverse shock. Just because an economy is stable in the sense that it moves toward full employment does not mean that it does so quickly.

Difference between short-run and long-run effects. The important difference between an economy's response in the short run and the long run is that, in the long run, wages and prices are flexible and can respond to changes in market supplies and demands as well as to changes in the overall price level. In the short run, wages are sticky and cannot adjust fully to changes in supply and demand or to changes in the overall price level. The failure of prices and wages to adjust immediately in the short run means that adjustments occur in the actual output produced and, hence, in the employment of labor and other resources. At times, therefore, *actual* real output will deviate from *potential* real output. Hence, both changes in output as well as changes in prices are an important part of the macroeconomic adjustment process.

Supply shocks. An adverse supply shock occurs when resources that are widely used suddenly become less available or increase dramatically in price. This shock causes a shift of the short-run aggregate supply curve to the left. Unemployment and the price level both increase at the same time.

Supply-side policy effects. When public policies reduce the amount of labor employed, they also lower the potential real output for an economy. Moreover, when policies make adjustments longer or more difficult, the adjustment of short-run aggregate supply to long-run aggregate supply will be slower. Supply-side economic policies are advocated as an effort to lessen or minimize such distortions and to increase the potential output from an economy, given its resources, or to hasten adjustment to demand shocks.

Chapter 20 ▶ ▶
Aggregate Demand_____

Two important aspects of an economy's macroeconomic performance were emphasized in the previous chapter: First, an economy's price level changes with aggregate demand shocks. Second, changes in the price level change employment opportunities if nominal wage adjustments are slow—that is, sticky—relative to price level changes. Taken together, these mean that aggregate demand shocks are likely to be an important cause of price-level instability, unemployment and changes in real output. Clearly, if we are to understand macroeconomic cycles, we need to understand aggregate demand and, in particular, the possible sources of aggregate demand shocks.

The discussion that follows is a kind of "whodunit." The unknown culprit in this mystery is the underlying cause of aggregate demand shocks. The search may not be as exciting as an Agatha Christie mystery, but its consequences are far more important. As we proceed, however, it is important not to lose sight of the larger issues. Aggregate demand and aggregate supply are useful concepts only if they help us understand why an economy may not always employ its productive resources fully, have price stability, or grow at an acceptable rate.

▶ The Nature of Aggregate Demand

As we noted in Chapter 18, there are four general kinds of uses for aggregate real output, and hence, for the productive resources available to an economy. Most of an economy's productive resources are used to produce goods and services that are consumed (**consumption, c**). Some of an economy's resources are used to produce commodities that are used, in turn, to produce other commodities (**investment, i**). Some resources are used to produce goods and services for the government (**government, g**). Finally, some resources are used to produce things that are purchased by foreigners (exports, x), but these exports are fully or partially offset by the fact that resources in other economies are used to produce things that we purchase (imports, m) and it is the net effect that matters (**net exports, x-m**). The sum of these at a given price level is the **aggregate real output demanded. Aggregate demand** is the aggregate real output demanded at all possible price levels, *ceteris paribus*.[1]

When net exports are zero, aggregate demand for real output is equal to an economy's potential real output only if desired consumption *plus* desired investment *plus* government spending is at precisely the right level. This point is illustrated in Figure 1. For example, potential output might be $5.5 trillion; consumption, $3.6 trillion; investment $800 billion; and government $1.1 trillion. Aggregate demand would then be $5.5 trillion, equal to potential output.

---

[1] For reasons suggested in Chapter 11, if exchange rates are flexible, net exports (x–m) are for most economies over longer periods of time equal to zero. To make the exposition a little simpler and consistent with this, unless otherwise specified, we will assume that (x–m)=0 and focus on the consumption, investment and government components of aggregate demand.

Figure 1
Aggregate Demand

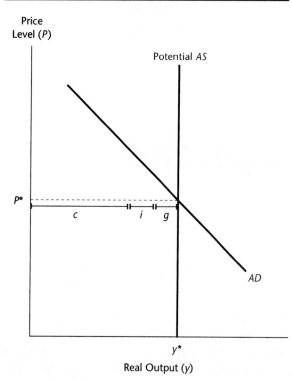

When the price level is equal to P*, the economy will be in equilibrium only if consumption (c) plus investment (i) plus government spending (g) equals potential real output (y*).

Figure 2
Aggregate Demand and a Decrease in Consumption

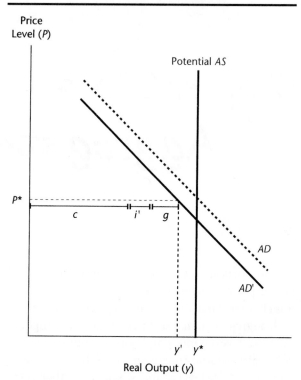

If desired investment falls from the level shown in Figure 1, consumption plus investment plus government spending will no longer equal y* when the price level is P*. As a consequence, at that price level, aggregate demand will be less than potential real output.

If at the current price level, desired consumption falls, say, to $3.0 trillion from $3.6 trillion, and there is no change in either investment or government spending, the aggregate real output demanded will be too low to maintain full employment as is illustrated in Figure 2. That is, at price level P*, the sum of the various components of aggregate demand is less than the *potential* output of the economy. By contrast, if desired consumption and government spending remain the same at the current price level and desired investment increases, say, to $1 trillion from $800 billion, then aggregate real output demanded will be too high as illustrated in Figure 3.

Aggregate demand can change only if desired consumption, desired investment, net exports, or desired government spending change. Therefore, if we are to find the source of aggregate demand shocks, we need to consider the determinants of each more carefully. We begin by considering an economy in which there are only firms and house-

holds who either invest or consume, and focus our attention on these two components of aggregate demand. We then look more closely at the determinants of net exports. The effects of government on aggregate demand will be considered in the next chapter.

▶ Consumption

GDP measures *both* the aggregate income accruing to individuals and the real output the economy produces.[2] Individuals can do three things with their income: consume it by purchasing goods and services, save it, or pay taxes—an option that we will ignore for now but will consider in the next chapter. **Aggregate consumption** is the individual con-

---

[2] See the Appendix to Chapter 17 for a discussion of the reasons why.

Figure 3
Aggregate Demand and a
Increase in Investment

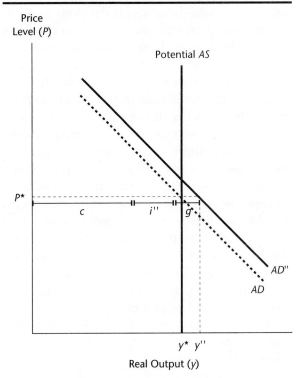

If desired investment increases from the level shown in Figure 1, consumption plus investment plus government spending will exceed potential real output, y^*, when the price level equals P^*. In this case, aggregate demand at P^* will be greater than potential real output.

sumption expenditures summed over all households in an economy; **aggregate saving** is the sum of the saving of all households in an economy. For the economy as a whole, aggregate consumption, c, plus aggregate saving, s, must equal aggregate income, y. In symbols.

$$y = c + s$$

Forward-Looking Consumers

That is, if there are no taxes, then individuals have only two choices, to consume or to save. Not surprisingly, then, when we look at the economy in aggregate, consumption is a large part of aggregate demand. Moreover, as our incomes increase, we consume more. Therefore, when aggregate income increases (because aggregate output increases), aggregate consumption tends to increase as well. (Its use-

ful to think of this as an "income-induced consumption effect.") None of this is particularly surprising and it's clear enough why we consume: we want goods and services because they increase our well-being.

A more interesting question is: Why do we save? That is, why don't we simply consume all of our income? The reason we don't is that human beings are forward-looking. As a consequence, current consumption decisions depend on both *present* and *expected future* circumstances. To see why, think about how you might respond if you expected that your income would vary over time, or that your income would fall at retirement, or that your future income was uncertain, or that the opportunity cost of consuming now rather than at some later date changed.

Responding to transitory income fluctuations. If a farmer has a high income in the autumn but a very low income in winter and early spring, you wouldn't expect her to consume a lot during the harvest season and almost nothing later in the year. Instead, you might expect the farmer to *save* during the times of plenty and draw from what she has saved (*dissave*) during those times when there is less to sell. A farmer saves by forgoing consumption today, thereby consuming less than her current income. Doing so allows the farmer to consume more than her monthly income at some future time. That is, **saving** is forgone consumption. When individuals save, they will generally be able to consume more in the future than their future income would otherwise allow because they can use the saved income to supplement their future income.

To illustrate this point, suppose Table 1 provides the month-by-month pattern for the income received by a farmer, a teacher, and a bank officer.

Despite the fact that these three people have very different incomes in any given month, each has the same annual income, $32,520. As a consequence, each individual has the same *average* monthly income, $2,710. Would you expect consumption expenditures to differ among these three individuals as greatly as their monthly incomes do? Probably not. It would be impossible for the teacher to consume *nothing* from June through August even though his income is zero for those months. Similarly, we would not expect the farmer to fast during the winter and spend only $100 each month, but to live the life of plenty from July to October.

Table 1
Month-by-Month Incomes

	Farmer	Teacher	Bank officer
January	$ 100	$3,613.33	$2,710
February	100	3,613.33	2,710
March	100	3,613.33	2,710
April	100	3,613.33	2,710
May	500	3,613.33	2,710
June	1,000	0	2,710
July	5,000	0	2,710
August	5,000	0	2,710
September	10,000	3,613.33	2,710
October	10,000	3,613.33	2,710
November	500	3,613.33	2,710
December	120	3,613.33	2,710

Instead of monthly consumption being directly determined by monthly income, each individual could save and dissave in order to consume about the same amount each month throughout the year. Indeed, because the three individuals have the same annual incomes, the teacher and the farmer might have quite similar consumption expenditures to those of the banker (and hence to each other). If each person consumed his or her exact income over the year, for example, the farmer, teacher, and banker

might have the consumption and saving patterns illustrated in Table 2.

In the face of fluctuating income, individuals are likely to make consumption decisions based on *expected* or *average* income rather than on *actual* income. That is, individuals are likely to *smooth* consumption relative to income by saving and dissaving or borrowing. Figure 4 illustrates this point.

Although your income may not fluctuate from month to month like that of a farmer or a teacher, virtually everyone engages in this kind of consumption smoothing because most of us get paid once or twice a month rather than every day. When we are paid only on the first day of the month, for example, we save a large fraction of our income on that day and then dissave throughout the month so that our daily consumption doesn't depend upon our daily income. If we didn't do this, we would consume a lot on the day we are paid and then go without for the rest of the month when our income is zero. This does not happen, of course. Why? Because we have followed a pattern of saving on payday (*"now"*) and then dissaving over the rest of the month (*"the future"*).

Responding to life-cycle income. Table 2 suggests that over the course of a year, each person's consumption equals his or her annual income. Current incomes can fluctuate in other ways, however. In

Table 2
Saving and Consumption Patterns

	Farmer		Teacher		Bank officer	
	Saving	Consumption	Saving	Consumption	Saving	Consumption
January	−$2,610	$2,710	$903.33	$2,710	$0	$2,710
February	−2,610	2,710	903.33	2,710	0	2,710
March	−2,610	2,710	903.33	2,710	0	2,710
April	−2,610	2,710	903.33	2,710	0	2,710
May	−2,210	2,710	903.33	2,710	0	2,710
June	−1,710	2,710	−2,710.00	2,710	0	2,710
July	2,290	2,710	−2,710.00	2,710	0	2,710
August	2,290	2,710	−2,710.00	2,710	0	2,710
September	7,290	2,710	903.33	2,710	0	2,710
October	7,290	2,710	903.33	2,710	0	2,710
November	−2,210	2,710	903.33	2,710	0	2,710
December	−2,590	2,710	903.33	2,710	0	2,710

Figure 4
When Consumption Doesn't Equal Income

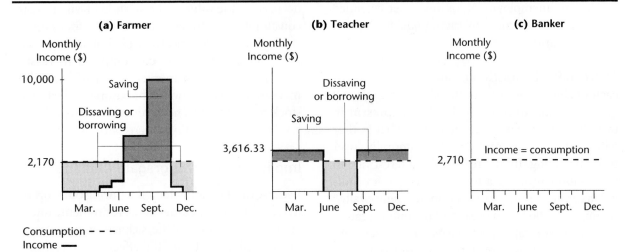

When income fluctuates from month to month, individuals will try to smoothe their consumption by saving during those months when their income is high (that is, they consume less than they earn) and dissaving or borrowing in months when their income is low (that is, they consume more than they earn).

particular, people retire and when they do, their incomes fall dramatically. Our consumption need not fall when our income does, however, because we can finance consumption at retirement by saving during our working years and then dissaving after retirement. By saving during the years when we work, we transfer income earned *now* into consumption *after retirement*. It follows that for most individuals who have not yet retired, their current consumption will be less than their current income. Figure 5 illustrates typical life-cycle income, consumption, and saving patterns.[3]

Responding to uncertainty. We also save because of uncertainties—we cannot know what might happen to our income or how long we might live past retirement. We may become sick or in some other way become incapacitated. Or, we may become unemployed. If these bad events occur, our incomes will fall, perhaps dramatically. We can prevent an equally dramatic decline in our consumption if we have savings that we can draw from during periods of sickness, incapacitation, or unemployment. These possibilities and the corresponding uncertainty about future income provide an incentive for most

---

[3] It is assumed for purposes of illustration that retirement occurs at age 65.

Figure 5
Life-Cycle Consumption Pattern

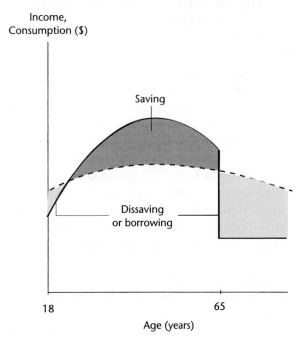

Consumption – – –
Income ——

Individuals also engage in consumption smoothing over their lifetimes, borrowing in their early years (perhaps to finance an education or purchase a home), saving during their peak earning years, and then living off of their savings after retirement.

people to consume less than their current income. That is, we can cushion the effects of sickness, incapacitation, unemployment, or any other extended period without income by saving *now* for a rainy day *in the future*.

Intertemporal substitution and interest rates. For each of the reasons just outlined, individuals will generally want to consume less in the present in order to consume more in the future. That is, they will substitute consumption intertemporally (over time) by saving. In this regard, the interest rate in an economy provides a further incentive for individuals to substitute consumption intertemporally.[4] If you save $100 for one year and the interest rate is 10 percent, you can expect to have $110 a year from now. Thus, there is an opportunity cost to consuming today rather than a year from now—the forgone interest income. If the interest rate increases, consuming today becomes more costly. Why? Because instead of spending $100 today on consumption, you could purchase $120 worth of goods and services a year from now if the interest rate is 20 percent, but only $105 a year from now if the interest rate is 5 percent. Hence, higher interest rates provide greater incentives for individuals to consider reducing their consumption today and instead to consume in the future.

Wealth. As individuals save, they accumulate **assets**. That is, instead of purchasing goods or services, individuals purchase things such as corporate stock or land, or they put money in a savings account. Each of these is an asset. An asset is anything that can be used to transfer current income, via saving, into the future. The sum of the value of all assets that an individual holds is his or her **wealth**. Wealth changes as individuals save and dissave. Wealth also changes, however, as the assets that individuals acquired in the past change in value. For example, prices in the stock market increase or decrease day by day.

Individuals accumulate wealth in order to finance consumption at a later date, so, as wealth changes, consumption will also. In general, an increase in wealth because of an increase in the value of the assets held will increase consumption, and a decrease in the value of the assets held will decrease consumption. Between 1982 and 1987, for example, stock market prices nearly tripled on average. As a consequence, aggregate consumption increased. Similarly, the stock market boom of the 1990s increased consumption. The dramatic decline of stock prices in 2002, however, reduced wealth and, it follows, consumption, *ceteris paribus*.

Implications for Aggregate Demand

Because of fluctuating incomes during our working lives, declining incomes with retirement, uncertainties about length of life, sickness, incapacitation, or unemployment, and the effect of interest rates on the opportunity cost of consuming today rather than in the future, consumption *today* will not be based solely on current income but will instead be determined by *expectations* about *future* income, *future* obligations, *future* uncertainties, *future* consumption opportunities, as well as interest rates and individual wealth. In short, current consumption will differ from current income. This discussion suggests important conclusions about aggregate consumption, and hence about aggregate demand:

1. Aggregate consumption changes with changes in aggregate income, but the changes in aggregate consumption may be smaller than changes in aggregate income. In general, however, as aggregate income increases, so does aggregate consumption.

2. Aggregate consumption changes with changes in expectations. This means that anything that changes *expected future income* for most individuals in an economy will also change aggregate consumption. It also means that developments in the business cycle or public policy that do not change expected future income will have little effect on current consumption.

3. Aggregate consumption changes with changes in interest rates. Specifically, aggregate consumption will decrease when interest rates increase.

4. Aggregate consumption changes with changes in aggregate wealth that result from changes in the value of the assets that indi-

---

[4] There are many interest rates in an economy, not just a single rate. For expositional convenience we will speak of *the* interest rate; you might think of it as the average of the many interest rates.

viduals hold. When wealth increases, aggregate consumption will also increase.

5. Aggregate consumption is smooth relative to aggregate income. This means that temporary or transitory changes in income will have little effect on consumption.

What saving means for the economy. When aggregate consumption is less than aggregate real income, some of what is produced within the economy will not be sold to individuals for consumption purposes. Ignoring the government sector and net exports, that part of real output not used for consumption purposes is, by *definition*, aggregate saving. We know that aggregate individual income is either consumed or saved,

$$y = c + s$$

so by using simple algebra,

$$s = y - c$$

and it follows that *what has not been consumed must have been saved.*

Even though individuals may think of saving in terms of that part of their monthly income that they put in their bank account or in some other asset, from the economy's perspective, **aggregate saving** is that part of real output that is produced, but not sold to consumers. Consumption might be $3.6 trillion, for example, and real output $5.5 trillion. In this case, aggregate saving is $1.9 trillion.

Saving is a two-edged sword for an economy. Saving frees up resources for other, non-consumption, uses. For example, it provides resources that can be used to build new capital or maintain existing capital. Capital formation, in turn, increases the *potential* real output of an economy. New capital will be built, however, only if firms wish to use resources that have been made available for investment projects. This means that an *increase* in desired saving *reduces* aggregate demand *unless it is accompanied by an equal increase in desired investment.* If desired investment does not increase, the decrease in aggregate demand will trigger the set of adjustments in output, prices, and employment described in earlier chapters. Thus, aggregate saving is important if an economy is to grow, but it must be balanced with

desired aggregate investment if an economy is to produce at its potential.

▶ Investment

Investment occurs when a firm uses real output to increase its existing capital stock or to offset depreciation.[5] For example, a firm invests when it uses steel and other materials to build a new warehouse or when it purchases a new machine. Steel, new machines, and similar capital goods are part of the real output of an economy. **Aggregate investment** is the sum of all such uses of real resources, including fixed investment in plant and equipment, and inventory investment by firms.[6]

Expectations and Interest-Rate Effects

From a firm's perspective, using real resources to produce new capital makes sense if the new capital adds to its profits. But investment is something of a gamble: a firm must acquire the new capital before it can be used to produce additional output and, hence, before the firm will see any change in its profits. Put in the simplest terms: a firm acquires new capital *now* but realizes additional profits, if any, only in the *future*. This means that, like individuals making consumption decisions, firms making investment decisions will be forward-looking and, for an investment project to make sense, the *expected returns* must be greater than the *expected costs*.

Expectations about future profits may change for many reasons:

- Firms may become more pessimistic (or optimistic) about the future course of the

---

[5] There is often confusion about the use of the terms *investment* and *saving*. For economists, *investment* is the real output that is used by firms to increase their capital stock and *saving* is that part of real output that is not consumed. However, people commonly speak of a person "investing" in the stock market or in real estate, or having savings accounts or stocks as "investments." In none of these instances is *investment* occurring. Rather, individuals are *saving* by purchasing a stock or real estate, or by putting part of their income in a savings account rather than consuming it. *Investment* occurs only when households or firms use resources to build new physical capital.

[6] In order to keep the exposition simple, we will speak of firms making investment decisions, but it is important to remember that individuals and households make investment decisions as they build new homes or acquire education and other kinds of training.

economy and the demand for real output. For example, if firms think a recession is likely in the near future, acquiring new capital will be less attractive because the firm may not be able to sell the additional output that it could produce.

- Taxes imposed on businesses may change or be expected to change. Changes in the taxation of corporate earnings, tax allowances for the depreciation tax or tax credits allowed for certain kinds of investment will each affect, sometimes dramatically, expected net-of-tax profits and, hence, the incentive to invest.

- Prices of important inputs may change or be expected to change. For example, an increase in the price of oil may lower the expected future profits from many kinds of capital that use oil intensively, thereby affecting desired investment. Or widespread changes in wages may decrease the profitability of capital for firms that also employ a large amount of labor but, at the same time, may increase the expected profitability of new capital that requires less labor. Or a change in the exchange rate may change the expected profits for domestic firms by changing the prices of imported inputs, by affecting the prospects for competition from imports, or by affecting the prospects for exporting goods and services.

- Prices for the output that might be produced with any new capital may change or be expected to change. For example, the post-September 11, 2001 decline in air travel put downward pressure on airfares and, hence, made the purchase of new airplanes less attractive. Or, for example, a firm might expect increased (or decreased) price competition in the future because of entry (or exit).

- Finally, the interest rate may change or be expected to change.

The interest-rate effect on desired investment is particularly important. Firms and households often finance the acquisition of new capital by borrowing, and so when interest rates increase, investment projects become less attractive, *ceteris paribus*. For example, a new factory costing $10 million might promise a return of $800,000 each year. Even though

the new factory is expected to create profits for the firm, if it had to pay more than 8 percent on a $10 million loan, the investment project would not be worth undertaking. Why? The firm's interest payments would be greater than $800,000 and, hence, greater than the return expected from the factory. The investment project would be viable, however, if the interest rate was less than 8 percent because then the interest payments would be less than the expected return. In general, the higher the interest rate, the higher the cost of carrying loans, and the less attractive some investment projects will be.

Even if a firm does not need to borrow money to finance an investment project but is prepared to use funds already at its disposal, its decision would be the same. That is, the firm that already had $10 million could put it in the project and earn $800,000 per year or, if the interest rate was greater than 8 percent, it could put the $10 million in a bank instead and earn more than $800,000 in interest income each year. Clearly, the firm would find it profitable to invest only if the interest income forgone on its $10 million was less than $800,000 per year, in other words, if the interest rate was less than 8 percent.

Thus, an investment project that requires a $10 million outlay *now* with only a *promised* return of $800,000 per year certainly will not be undertaken if the interest rate is greater than 8 percent. When the interest rate is below 8 percent, however, this and other similar investment projects will be undertaken. Because firms will find a greater number of investment projects profitable when interest rates are lower, there is an inverse relationship between desired aggregate investment and the interest rate, as illustrated in Figure 6.

Changes in expected future production costs and expected future revenues also affect investment decisions. For example, if future production costs are expected to increase without a corresponding change in future revenues, then a particular investment will become less attractive because it is likely to be less profitable. Alternatively, if future revenues are expected to increase without a corresponding increase in future costs, a particular investment project will become more attractive because it is likely to be more profitable. These kinds of changes in expectations change aggregate desired investment, as illustrated in Figure 7. In Figure 7, at any interest rate when costs are expected to be higher, firms will choose to acquire less capital and the desired invest-

Figure 6
Aggregate Investment and the Interest Rate

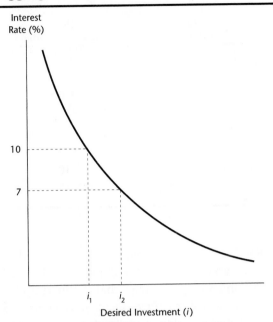

Higher interest rates make investment projects less attractive because, when everything else is equal, they lower the projects' profitability. Hence, there will be less aggregate investment when the interest rate is high and more aggregate investment when the interest rate is low.

Figure 7
Aggregate Investment and Expectations

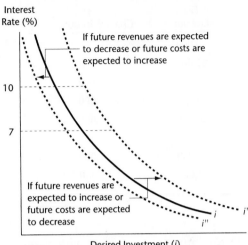

If investment projects are expected to have higher revenues or lower costs, desired investment will increase, *ceteris paribus*. Conversely, if investment projects are expected to have lower revenues or higher costs, desired investment will decrease, *ceteris paribus*.

ment curve shifts to the left; when revenues are expected to be higher, by contrast, firms will choose to acquire more capital and the desired investment curve shifts to the right.

Depreciation

Capital depreciates. Sometimes it simply wears out; at other times it becomes obsolete with technological innovation; at still other times, governmental regulations and tax policies make future use of current capital unprofitable. In each of these cases, the capital stock can be maintained only be investing, in order to offset depreciation. In fact, much of the investment that occurs in any economy is of this sort.

The Accelerator Effect

Desired investment may also be affected by the *rate of change* in real output. To see why, we begin with the assumption that firms want to obtain the stock of capital that makes their operations the most profitable. Once a firm is satisfied with the amount of capital it has, it will acquire more capital only if it

expects its future sales to increase. If the aggregate real output is increasing, of course, producers in aggregate must be selling more. This implies that aggregate net investment is likely to be affected by the expected *growth rate* of aggregate real output, not simply by the *level* of real output. To see why, consider the firm whose output decisions are illustrated in Table 3. To make matters as simple as possible, we have assumed that the firm attempts to maintain a fixed one-to-one hundred ratio between its capital and its production (compare columns 2 and 4).

Because the firm acquires additional capital only when it believes that sales will increase, desired investment increases when output is expected to increase but falls when output no longer increases at the same rate, *even if output still increases!* To see this, compare investment in year 4 with investment in year 5. This simple example suggests that substantial fluctuations in desired aggregate investment can result from modest changes in the rate of increase in real output. This is known as the **accelerator effect**.

Implications for Aggregate Demand

The discussion thus far points to several important things about desired investment that are important in terms of their effects on aggregate demand:

Table 3
A Firm's Output and Desired Capital (in dollars)

(1) Year	(2) Output	(3) Change in output	(4) Desired capital	(5) Investment	(6) Change in investment
1995	20,000	—	$200	—	—
1996	21,000	1,000	210	$10	—
1997	22,000	1,000	220	10	$ 0
1998	25,000	3,000	250	30	20
1999	26,000	1,000	260	10	−20
2000	26,000	0	260	0	−10
2001	27,000	1,000	270	10	10
2002	27,000	0	270	0	−10

1. *Desired investment changes with changes in interest rates.* Specifically, desired investment increases when interest rates decrease and decreases when interest rates increase.

2. *Desired investment changes with changes in the tax treatment of capital or investment.* Changes in corporate income taxes, depreciation allowances for tax purposes, investment tax credits, the tax treatment of interest expenses, etc. will change desired investment.

3. *Desired investment changes as expectations about the future profitability of new capital change.* Investment is a gamble: the cost of acquiring new capital is certain and must, in a sense, be incurred up front; the benefit of the new capital—additional profits—comes only in the future and is, as a consequence, inherently uncertain. This means that when future operating costs are expected to increase or future revenues are expected to decrease, desired investment will decrease. It also means that if firms become pessimistic about future sales, desired investment will decrease. Optimism or confidence will boost desired investment, however. More generally, anything that creates greater uncertainty will adversely affect desired investment but a more stable, predictable environment will stimulate investment.

4. *Because of the accelerator effect,* small *changes* in the rate of growth of real output may lead to substantial changes in desired investment. *In particular, if the growth rate slows, desired investment may fall, even though the growth rate remains positive.*

For these reasons, aggregate investment tends to be highly variable. This point is illustrated in Figure 8, which compares percentage changes in real consumption and real gross investment. As a consequence of this relative volatility, changes in aggregate desired investment are an important—perhaps the most important—component of aggregate demand shocks.

▶ Price-Level Effects

Both desired consumption and desired investment are lower when the price level is higher, *ceteris paribus.* The reasons why will be detailed more fully in subsequent chapters. For now, note that desired current consumption is affected, in part, by saving that occurred in the past. (For example, think of the farmer whose consumption depends upon his savings from the previous October or the retiree whose consumption at age 70 depends upon her savings throughout her working life.) In certain circumstances (to be discussed more fully in subsequent chapters) changes in the price level will affect the purchasing power of these savings. When the price level increases, for example, individuals who have saved by putting money in a savings account will find that the money they later withdraw will purchase fewer goods and services. As a consequence, aggregate consumption will be less at the higher price level.

In certain circumstances that will also be discussed more fully in subsequent chapters, interest rates will be higher when the price level increases. Hence, firms must borrow more money to finance their investment projects. Desired investment will decrease as a consequence.

In Figure 9 we can see a consequence of these price-level effects. When the price level is P^*, con-

Figure 8
Relative Volatility of Investment and Consumption

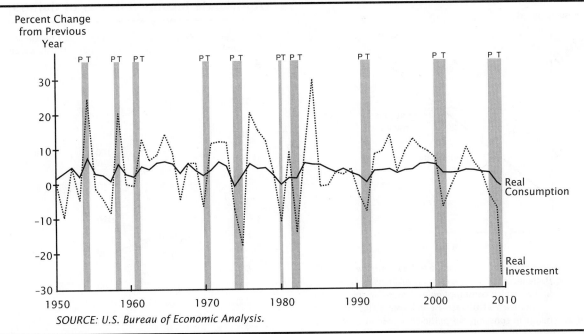

SOURCE: U.S. Bureau of Economic Analysis.

sumption plus investment equals $y^\star$. At a higher price level, such as P_1, *both* desired consumption and desired investment will be less. Aggregate real output demanded at that price level will be less as well. Hence, *aggregate real output demanded is inversely related to the price level.*

▶ Induced Consumption, Coordination Problems, and Adjustment

When desired investment changes, aggregate demand changes. Unless prices and nominal wages are completely flexible, when aggregate demand changes, real output will change. Because desired aggregate consumption is determined in part by current aggregate income, this change in real output will *induce* a change in consumption. Thus, *a change in desired investment will lead to a change in consumption through a change in aggregate income.* This particular interaction makes the determination of aggregate output demanded at any particular price level more complex than is suggested by considering desired consumption and desired investment separately, as we have done to this point.

The interaction can be most easily illustrated by ignoring the effect of expectations on consumption. So, we will assume for purposes of discussion that desired aggregate consumption is a function of *current* aggregate income only and ignore the fact that

Figure 9
Consumption, Investment, and the Price Level

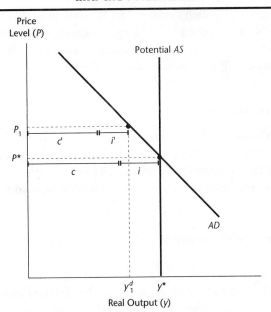

A higher price level reduces consumption because it reduces the value of certain assets that households may hold. A higher price level also reduces desired investment because, in certain circumstances, it results in a higher interest rate.

individuals and firms are forward-looking. Specifically, we assume that aggregate consumption increases in a constant proportion to any increase in aggregate income and, further, that desired aggregate

Figure 10
An Aggregate-Consumption Function

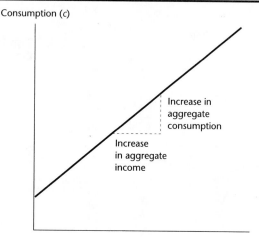

Consumption (c)

Increase in aggregate consumption

Increase in aggregate income

Real Output Demanded (y^d)

Aggregate consumption is assumed to be determined by aggregate income. The slope of this relationship is the amount by which consumption increases—in this case $.80—for each $1.00 increase in income. This ratio of the change in consumption to the change in income is the marginal propensity to consume (MPC).

Table 4
Aggregate Consumption as a Function of Aggregate Income (billions of dollars)

Aggregate income	Aggregate consumption	Change in income	Change in consumption
$ 0	$ 100		
			—
100	180		
		$100	$80
200	260		
		100	80
300	340		
		100	80
400	420		
		100	80
500	500		
		100	80
600	580		
		100	80
700	660		
		100	80
800	740		
		100	80
900	820		
		100	80
1,000	900		
		100	80
1,100	980		
		100	80
1,200	1,060		
		100	80
1,300	1,140		

investment is unaffected by aggregate income as per Figure 10, which could reflect the data provided in Table 4, for example. In Figure 10, aggregate income is measured along the horizontal axis and desired consumption is measured along the vertical axis.

The Marginal Propensity to Consume

In Table 4, individuals increase their consumption by $.80 for each additional $1.00 in income. The graph of this relationship in Figure 10 has a slope of 0.8[7] and can be described by a **consumption function**:

$$C = 100 + 0.80y$$

Or, more generally, by

$$C = a + by \qquad (1)$$

Where *a* can be thought of as that part of consumption that is independent of income (**autonomous consumption**) and *b* as the amount by which consumption increases when income increases by $1.00 (**income-induced consumption**).

The amount by which desired consumption increases when aggregate income increases by one dollar is called the **marginal propensity to consume (MPC)**. In Equation (1), *b* is the marginal propensity to consume. For the consumption function illustrated in Figure 10, the MPC is 0.8. Why? Suppose that income is $600 billion and consumption is $580 billion. Now suppose that income increases to $700 billion. Consumption increases to $660 billion. Thus, a $100 billion increase in income leads to an $80 billion increase in consumption. Given the definition of the marginal propensity to consume,

$$MPC = \Delta c / \Delta y = \$80/\$100 = 0.80$$

Since aggregate saving is, by definition, the aggregate income that is not consumed, the **mar-**

---

[7] Remember, the slope of a graph between two points is the change in the vertical distance between the points divided by the horizontal distance between the points—rise over run.

ginal propensity to save (MPS) is equal to $(1.0 - MPC)$. If the *MPC* is 0.8, for example, the *MPS* would be 0.2. That is, if \$.80 of each additional dollar in income is consumed, \$.20 of each additional dollar in income is saved.

The important aspect of consumption that Equation 1, Figure 10, and Table 4 all illustrate is that *consumption increases when income increases* and, conversely, *decreases when income decreases*. Similarly, because saving is just that part of aggregate income that is not consumed, Equation 1, Figure 10, and Table 4 indirectly illustrate that saving also increases when income increases, and decreases when income decreases.

Income-induced consumption is of particular importance because it creates an interaction between consumption and other components of aggregate demand. For example, if firms decide to increase investment then some group of individual incomes will increase—new capital, like any other good, is produced using resources, and resources are owned by individuals. The same holds for any increase in the government's use of real output or exports—in both cases, the goods demanded by the government or foreigners are produced using resources that are owned by individuals within the economy. Hence, an increase in *i* or *g* or *x* will lead to an increase in income. But as we have just learned, an increase in income will, because of the income-induced part of consumption, lead to an increase in consumption. This consumption is, of course, also a component of aggregate demand.

The Investment Multiplier

This interaction between a change in desired *i* and income-induced *c* amplifies the effect of the initial change in *i* (and, as we will see later, *g* and *x*) on aggregate demand. Indeed, the marginal propensity to consume plays a pivotal role in determining what happens to aggregate demand when desired investment changes. It turns out that the change in aggregate demand that follows from a change in desired investment is much larger than the change in desired investment itself. To see why and by how much, let's explore what happens when desired investment decreases by \$50 million and MPC is 0.8.

If desired investment decreases by \$50 billion, aggregate demand will initially decrease by \$50 billion. Firms that specialize in producing new capital will find that they sell less. Aggregate output will fall. When aggregate output falls, aggregate income for those individuals supplying resources to the firms producing new capital will fall by a like amount. Consumption will decrease with this fall in aggregate income.[8] In fact, when the *MPC* is 0.8, consumption expenditures will decrease initially by \$40 billion (0.8 x \$50 billion). This means that aggregate demand will decrease by an *additional* \$40 billion beyond the initial \$50 billion decrease in desired investment. This decrease is the result of an *induced* decrease in desired consumption, however, whereas the initial decrease occurred because firms wanted to decrease investment.

When aggregate real output decreases by the additional \$40 billion, aggregate income will decrease by an *additional* \$40 billion. That is, if someone consumes less, someone else's income decreases. Because the marginal propensity to consume is 0.8, desired consumption will decrease by an additional \$32 billion. This will lead to a further decrease in aggregate demand of \$32 billion. When firms respond to this decrease in demand, they will buy fewer resources and aggregate income will decrease by \$32 billion. Aggregate real output demanded will decrease in turn by 0.8 × \$32 billion. The results of this process are summarized in Table 5.

The decrease in aggregate demand resulting from the initial \$50 billion decrease in desired investment is equal to the sum of the first column, which can be rewritten as:

$$\text{Total change in } AD = -\$50 \text{ billion} \times (1 + 0.8 + 0.64 + 0.512 + 0.41 + 0.328 + \ldots)$$

which is equivalent to:

$$\text{Total change in } AD = -\$50 \text{ billion} \times (1 + 0.8^1 + 0.8^2 + 0.8^3 + 0.8^4 + 0.8^5 + \ldots)$$

---

[8] The important thing to keep in mind in this discussion is that "investment" is the purchase of new capital from *someone*. If I purchase a machine from you, I think of this as "investment." You, however, think of the payment for investment as "income." Therefore, your income changes whenever I change my investment decisions. Since your consumption is determined by your income, when your income changes so too will your consumption. But "consumption" is the purchase of something from *someone*. You think of this as "consumption." However, the person from whom you buy things, thinks of the payment for consumption as "income." Therefore, when you change your consumption, someone else's income changes. And so on.

Table 5
The Effects of a Decrease in Desired Investment of $50 Billion on
Aggregate Real Output Demanded (billions of dollars)

(1) Change in aggregate demand	(2) Change in income	(3) Change in consumption	(4) Cumulative change in aggregate demand
$50.00	$50.00	$40.00	$ 50.00
40.00	40.00	32.00	90.00
32.00	32.00	25.60	122.00
25.60	25.60	20.48	147.60
20.48	20.48	16.38	168.08
16.38	16.38	13.11	184.46
.	.	.	.
.	.	.	.
.	.	.	.

The sequence of numbers in the parentheses is a **convergent geometric series**. Even though a decrease in aggregate demand is followed by a decrease in consumption (which is followed by a decrease in aggregate demand, which is followed by a decrease in consumption, and so forth), the decreases in aggregate demand as we move from stage to stage in the process become *smaller and smaller* because the effect on consumption in each case is only a fraction of the decrease in aggregate individual income. It turns out that the convergent series equals

$$\frac{1}{1-0.8}$$

Thus, the change in aggregate real output demanded in this particular example can be written as

$$\text{Total change in } AD = -\$50 \text{ billion} \times \frac{1}{1-0.8} = -\$250 \text{ billion}$$

In other words, a decrease in desired investment of $50 billion leads to a decrease in the aggregate real output demanded of $250 billion, at each price level. Of this $250 billion change, $50 billion is the change in investment and $200 billion is the *induced* change in consumption that follows.

Notice that within the expression $1/(1-0.8)$, the marginal propensity to consume, 0.8, appears. The importance of the *MPC* in determining the ultimate size of the aggregate demand shift can be seen

more clearly by rewriting Table 5 slightly, as illustrated in Table 6.

For any *MPC*, the sequence of induced increases in consumption—and hence in aggregate demand—converges to

$$\frac{1}{1-MPC} \times -\$50$$

This expression $1/(1-MPC)$ is called the **investment multiplier**. It is the amount by which aggregate demand changes when desired investment changes by $1. Thus, if the marginal propensity to consume is 0.9, the investment multiplier will be 10, which means that a $1 change in desired investment would change aggregate demand by $10; a marginal propensity to consume of 0.8 has a multiplier of 5; a marginal propensity to consume of 0.5 has a multiplier of 2, and so on. The *larger* the marginal propensity to consume, the *larger* will be the effect of a *change* in desired investment on aggregate demand. To summarize, a change in desired investment [Δi Figure 11], changes aggregate demand by a multiple [$1/(1-MPC)$] of the change [Δy in Figure 11].

Desired Saving, Desired Investment, and Aggregate Demand

Since aggregate saving is equal to aggregate income *not* consumed, if both aggregate consumption and aggregate income change, so will aggregate saving. Another way of looking at the interaction between

Table 6
Relationship of the *MPC* and the Investment Multiplier at a Given Price Level

Change in consumption	Cumulative change in aggregate demand
	$50 Initial change in desired investment
$MPC \times \$50$	$\$50 + MPC \times \$50$
$MPC (MPC \times \$50)$	$\$50 + MPC \times \$50 + MPC (MPC \times \$50)$
$MPC [MPC (MPC \times \$50)]$	$\$50 + MPC \times \$50 + MPC (MPC \times \$50) + MPC [MPC (MPC \times \$50)]$
.	
.	.
.	.
.	$\$50 (1 + MPC + MPC^2 + MPC^3 + MPC^4 + \ldots)$

changes in desired investment and *changes* in aggregate demand is to note that if desired investment increases, in the end, resources to produce the new capital will be available *only if* aggregate saving increases by the *same* amount as aggregate investment does. That is, aggregate demand will be equal to potential real output only if *desired saving at full employment is equal to desired investment,*

$$\text{desired s} = \text{desired i}$$

Thus, if desired investment increases by $50 billion, aggregate real output must increase by enough for desired saving to increase by $50 billion. If the marginal propensity to save is 0.2 (1.0 – 0.8, where 0.8 is the *MPC*), desired saving will increase by $50 billion only if aggregate income increases by $250 billion (since 0.2 x $250 billion = $50 billion), *ceteris paribus*. That is, if aggregate income increases by $250 billion and the marginal propensity to consume is 0.8, desired consumption will increase by $200 billion and desired saving will increase by $50 billion. Only then will the increase in desired saving be equal to the increase in desired investment.

Looking at macroeconomic behavior in terms of saving and investment provides insight into the reasons why the aggregate real output demanded may not always be equal to potential real output at the current price level: In general, savings decisions are made by individuals. At times, individuals will want to save. At other times, they will want to draw down their savings or borrow. How much individuals want to save or dissave depends upon their expectations about future income, future good and bad events, and how much they want to smooth consumption. By contrast, investment decisions are made by firms. Firms want to use real resources in

the form of new capital to increase their productive capacity. How much firms want to invest depends upon their expectations about the profitability of the additional capital. Because saving and investment decisions are made by *different* economic agents with *very different* motives, there is no reason why *desired* saving should always be exactly equal to *desired* investment. This poses a delicate coordination problem: The amount of real output that individuals do not wish to consume—desired saving—must be equal to the amount that firms wish to invest—desired investment—or else the economy cannot sustain a level of aggregate demand consistent with full employment.

▶ Net Exports

The US economy does not stand alone; rather, it is integrated in important ways in a larger worldwide economy. Individuals and firms in other countries purchase some of what we produce, and we in turn consume goods and services that are produced abroad. In addition, foreigners purchase US assets (IBM stock in New York Stock Market, for example) and US citizens purchase foreign assets (a factory in Singapore, for example). Gains from international trade allow economies to specialize and to have a wider array of goods, services, and resources than would otherwise be available. In addition to allowing for further specialization and increased consumption, however, foreign trade exerts an important influence on aggregate demand.[9]

---

[9] A good source of data on the major industrialized economies is the OECD: *http://www.oecd.org*. The World Bank at *http://www.worldbank.org* and International Monetary Fund at *http://www.imf.org* also provide data on the performance of various countries.

Figure 11
The Investment Multiplier

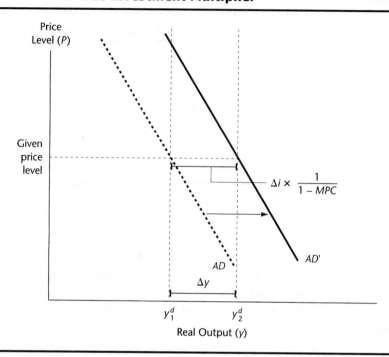

Price Level (P)

Given price level

$\Delta i \times \dfrac{1}{1 - MPC}$

AD

AD'

Δy

y_1^d y_2^d

Real Output (y)

Imports, Exports, and Real Output

When a country imports it has, a sense, additional real output available for domestic uses. This would be analogous to an increase in aggregate supply, as illustrated by the augmented short run aggregate supply ($y^* + m$) curve in Figure 12.

By contrast, if a country exports, then the real output produced within the economy would be divided between domestic and foreign uses. Some of the real output produced within the exporting country would not be available for domestic use but would instead by sold to foreigners. Thus, aggregate demand would be greater than otherwise might be the case, as illustrated in Figure 13. In symbols,

$$y^* = c + i + g + x.$$

In general, of course, economies both import and export. Thus, combining these two effects we have,

$$y^* + m = c + i + g + x$$

or, rearranging,

$$y^* = c + i + g + (x - m) \qquad (2)$$

Figure 12
The Effect of Imports

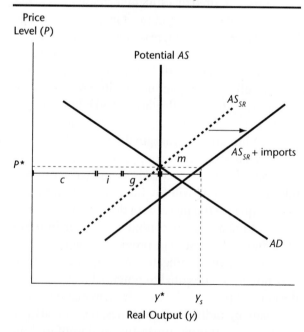

Price Level (P)

Potential AS

AS_{SR}

AS_{SR} + imports

P^*

c   i   g   m

AD

y^* y_s

Real Output (y)

Imports represent an addition to the real output available for domestic consumption, investment, or government uses. Hence, imports (represented by distance m) can be viewed as increasing the aggregate supply available to the economy. For example, at P^*, aggregate real output available in the economy equals y_s—domestic production (y^*) plus foreign production (m).

Figure 13
The Effect of Exports

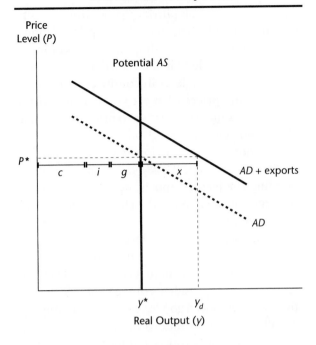

Exports represent an additional demand for the real output available in an economy. They can be viewed as increasing the aggregate demand for real output. Hence, at P^*, aggregate real output demanded equals y_d—domestic demand ($c + i + g$) plus foreign demand (x).

This does not mean that exports create jobs or that imports destroy jobs. An economy moves toward full employment consistent with a stable level of aggregate demand *whatever the level of net exports*. (The United States has been at full employment during periods when imports have been much greater than exports as well as during periods when net exports have been near zero or when exports have been greater than imports.) It does mean that *changes* in net exports *change* aggregate demand, with the possibility of short-run employment and price-level effects. As a consequence, imports and exports provide another avenue through which aggregate demand shocks might come, and another way by which aggregate-demand shocks might be offset.

The trade deficit. The difference between exports and imports is referred to as a **trade deficit** if imports exceed exports or a **trade surplus** if exports exceed imports. A common measure of a country's trade balance is called the **current account**.

Net exports affect aggregate demand, so it follows that a current account surplus ($x > m$) is

where ($x - m$) is referred to as **net exports**. Notice that net exports can be negative (if imports exceed exports), positive (if exports exceed imports), or zero (if imports equal exports).

Equation (2) suggest that net exports are an additional element of aggregate demand. When net exports increase (that is, when exports increase relative to imports), the overall demand for real output produced within the United States will be greater than would otherwise be the case. Put simply, aggregate demand will increase. When net exports decrease (that is, when imports increase relative to exports), the overall demand for real output produced within the United States will be less than would otherwise be the case. If US consumers decide to purchase Japanese, German, or Korean cars rather than US-made cars, for example, aggregate demand will be less than it would otherwise be (unless these imports are offset by US exports of other goods and services to Japan, Germany, or Korea).

Figure 14
Positive Net Exports

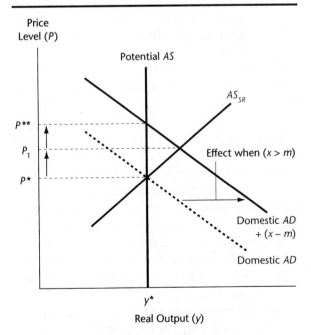

When exports exceed imports, there will be upward pressure on the price level. More generally, when exports increase relative to imports, at whatever the level of net exports, aggregate demand will increase.

Figure 15
Negative Net Exports

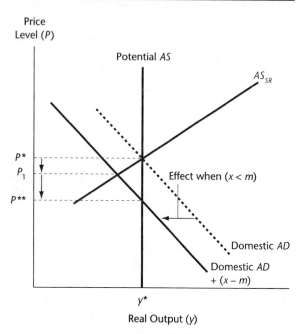

When imports exceed exports, there will be downward pressure on the price level. More generally, when imports increase relative to exports, aggregate demand will decrease.

associated with a greater demand for domestically produced real output than is a current account deficit $(x < m)$. If the current account balance is zero (the value of exports equals the value of imports), then there is no *direct* macroeconomic effect from international trade. Even so, the volume of trade is important because of the gains from specialization and exchange. That is, for reasons noted in Chapters 1 and 11, the *size* of x and m will matter to an economy, even if x equals m.

Net exports change with changes in the price level in one country *relative to* changes in the price level in a second country. Net exports also change with changes in real output in one country *relative to* changes in real output in a second country. Net exports change with financial capital flows and, as a consequence, with changes in interest rates in one country relative to interest rates in other countries. Finally, as we learned in Chapter 11, net exports change with changes in the exchange rate.

Price-Level Effects on Net Exports

In general, individuals purchase goods from the suppliers that provide them at the lowest price. National boundaries do not limit shopping around for low prices. If the price level in the United States increases relative to the price level in countries with whom we trade, the prices of most goods made in the United States increase relative to prices for comparable goods elsewhere—goods made in the U.S. become more expensive to foreigners, *ceteris paribus*. US exports will fall. If they fall without a corresponding change in imports, net exports will also fall. Aggregate demand in the United States will fall as a consequence.

Conversely, if the price level in a country with whom we trade increases relative to the US price level, then goods made in that country will become more expensive to residents of the United States relative to US-produced goods, *ceteris paribus*. Imports will fall. If they fall without a corresponding change in US exports, net exports will increase. Aggregate demand in the United States will increase as a consequence.

At least in the short term, then, differences in the rates of inflation between two economies will affect each economy's aggregate demand through this price-level effect on net exports if the exchange rate does not change by an offsetting amount. In particular, if a country has a *higher* rate of inflation than its trading partners do, its *net exports will fall*, ceteris paribus.

Aggregate-Income Effects on Net Exports

An increase in aggregate income abroad almost always increases US exports, whereas an increase in aggregate income in the United States almost always increases the demand for imports from abroad. Net exports need not change, however, if the growth of income in the U.S. is the same as the growth of income abroad—exports increase, and so do imports. If the rate of growth of income in the U.S. is greater than it is abroad, however, US imports will increase more rapidly than will US exports, and US net exports will fall. When that happens, aggregate demand in the United States decreases. Conversely, if incomes are growing abroad faster than they are in the U.S., US exports will increase more rapidly than will its imports and US net exports will increase. In this case, aggregate demand in the United States increases. Thus, the difference in real output growth rates between two economies affects *each* economy's aggregate demand.

The more rapid growth of the US economy in the 1990s relative to our important trading partners contributed to the very high current account deficit over that period. A similar pattern occurred in the 1980s. In fact, in the 1980s US policy makers put substantial pressure on Japan and Germany to stimulate aggregate demand in their economies so as to increase the demand for US exports, reduce the huge US current account deficit, and stimulate aggregate demand in the United States.

Capital Flows and Interest Rate Effects on Net Exports

If the dollar value of exports does not equal the dollar value of imports, there is a flow of financial capital corresponding to the difference. The flow of capital may take many forms, but it is simplest to imagine that if the United States is running a current account deficit (that is, the dollar value of imports is greater than the dollar value of exports), foreigners are accumulating US dollars, and if the United States is running a trade surplus, US residents are accumulating foreign currencies. Viewed in this way, an immediate consequence of a trade imbalance is that a trade deficit leads to the export of dollars, whereas a trade surplus leads to the import of foreign currencies.

The accumulation of dollars by foreigners poses a problem for them: what should be done with the dollars they are now holding? Similarly, since foreign currencies cannot be used in transactions within the US economy, an accumulation of foreign currencies by US residents poses a similar problem: what should be done with the foreign currencies? The answer to these questions is threefold:

1. Foreigners can use the dollars to purchase goods and services produced in the U.S. and we can use foreign currencies to purchase goods and services from abroad.

2. Foreigners can use the dollars to purchase other currencies and we can use our foreign currency to purchase currencies of still other countries.

3. Foreigners can use the dollars to purchase US-dollar assets and we can use foreign currencies to purchase foreign-currency assets. (A US-dollar asset is any asset that can be purchased only with US dollars. Examples include US Treasury bills and bonds, IBM stock, US corporate bonds, land and buildings in the United States, and so forth. A foreign-currency asset is any asset that can be purchased only with a specific foreign currency. Examples include Euro bonds, Mitsubishi stock, land and buildings in France, and so forth.)

If foreigners use dollars to purchase US goods when the US has a trade deficit, the adjustment to the trade deficit is straightforward: Exports increase and the trade deficit disappears. In this case, there is no aggregate-demand effect, that is, x–m = 0.

A US trade deficit can persist, then, only if foreigners do not wish to purchase US goods with the dollars earned by selling their goods to US residents. In this case the deficit is offset by capital flows and there is a **capital account** surplus that equals the **current account** deficit and there is an aggregate demand effect since x–m<0 as long as foreigners are content to hold US-dollar assets. If they aren't, then the dollars will be dumped onto foreign exchange markets and the exchange rate will change.

Exchange Rate Effect on Net Exports

An decrease in the value of the dollar in foreign exchange markets will, as we learned in Chapter 11, make foreign goods more expensive to US consumers and US goods less expensive to foreigners. As a consequence, a depreciation of the dollar will, *ceteris paribus*, reduce net exports (x will increase; m will decrease; (x–m) will move toward 0). This will increase aggregate demand in the United States. It will also reduce aggregate demand in countries whose currencies are appreciating relative to the US dollar.

This aggregate demand effect is one reason why countries sometimes try to manipulate the foreign exchange value of their currency (rather than allowing private supply and demand to determine the exchange rate). For example, Japan has been in an economic slump since the early 1990s. On occasion during that period, the value of the yen has increased relative to the dollar. The effect of this appreciation of the yen (or depreciation of the dollar) is to make Japanese goods more expensive to US consumers. This reduces aggregate demand in Japan, thereby further depressing an already struggling economy. As a consequence, during those periods when the yen has appreciated, policy makers in Japan have tried to drive the foreign exchange value of the yen back down in an effort to stimulate Japanese net exports and aggregate demand.

Or, for another example, on occasion, a country that has "fixed" its exchange rate to the US dollar has been forced by large current account deficits to allow its exchange rate to find a new equilibrium level. Virtually always, the new exchange rate is a substantial depreciation of the foreign exchange value of the country's currency. One of the effects of this kind of substantial depreciation is inflation since following a depreciation, the domestic currency is cheaper in terms of dollars, the demand for the country's exports increases, and its aggregate demand increases as a consequence. At the same time, since the US dollar is more costly in terms of this currency, the demand for US exports decreases (*m* from the foreign country's perspective). Net exports *increase* in the country with the depreciating currency. This pushes aggregate demand outward and puts upward pressure on the domestic price level. In short, substantial depreciations often result in inflationary pressures.

So long as governments do not intervene to manipulate the foreign exchange value of their currencies, exchange rates will tend to change in such a way as to eliminate a trade deficit or trade surplus. A trade deficit will put downward pressure on the value of a country's currency in foreign exchange markets. As the exchange rate depreciates, its exports become cheaper to foreigners and its imports become more expensive to its citizens. Exports will increase; imports will fall; net exports will tend toward 0. That is, with freely floating exchange rates, if net exports increase, they will tend to return to 0 and if net exports decrease, they will also tend to return to 0.

Net export multiplier. The effect of a change in net exports, *ceteris paribus*, will be exactly the same as a change in desired investment. That is, from an economy's perspective, it doesn't matter whether an increase in aggregate demand comes because of a $1 increase in desired investment or a $1 increase in net exports—in both cases, the economy finds that the initial effect is a $1 increase in aggregate demand followed by an income-induced change in consumption. It follows, then, that there will be a **net export multiplier** that is identical in size to the investment multiplier, $1/(1-MPC)$.[10]

▶ Aggregate Demand Shocks

The search for the source of aggregate demand shocks has not resolved itself quite as neatly as an Agatha Christie mystery does. But we have learned some things about the relationship of consumption, investment, net exports and aggregate demand that hint at possible reasons for aggregate demand shocks. Indeed, we have found that, because aggregate demand is determined in part by consumption, investment and net exports, aggregate demand will be affected by:

- Changes in interest rates. *Higher interest rates reduce desired investment and desired consumption,* ceteris paribus, *thereby reducing the aggregate real output demanded at each price level. This effect is summarized by a shift of the aggregate demand curve to the left. It follows that if interest rates fall,* ceteris paribus, *the aggregate demand curve will shift to the right.*

- *Changes in expectations.* Desired investment falls if future costs are expected to increase. The aggregate demand curve will shift to the left. Desired investment increases if future prices are expected to increase. The aggregate demand curve will shift to the right. More generally, aggregate demand will shift to the right if firms are optimistic about future profits, and to the left if they are pessimistic. Desired consumption falls if aggregate real income is expected to be lower in the future. Aggregate demand will shift to the left as a consequence.

- *Changes in wealth.* Desired consumption increases if wealth increases. The aggregate demand curve will shift to the right as a consequence.

---

[10] Since the investment and net export multipliers are identical, they can be lumped together and thought of as an **aggregate demand multiplier**.

- *Changes in the expected rate of growth of aggregate real output.* Changes in the expected rate of growth in aggregate income will lead to changes in desired investment through an accelerator effect. In this case, a reduction in the expected rate of growth of aggregate real output will reduce desired investment. The aggregate demand curve will shift to the left as a consequence.

- *Change in prices abroad relative to changes in prices within the US economy.* If the inflation rate is higher in the United States than inflation rates abroad, US citizens will want to purchase more seemingly less expensive foreign goods (i.e., imports will increase) and foreigners will want to purchase fewer seemingly more expensive US goods (i.e., exports will fall). *Ceteris paribus*, this effect will reduce aggregate demand in the U.S.

- *Changes in economic growth rates abroad relative to changes in economic growth rates within the US economy.* If economies abroad are growing faster than is the US economy, net exports will increase (US exports will increase faster than will US imports, *ceteris paribus*). This means that more rapid economic growth abroad than in the U.S. will shift the US aggregate demand curve to the right; more rapid economic growth in the U.S. than abroad will shift the US aggregate demand curve to the left.

- *Changes in interest rates abroad relative to changes in interest rates within the US economy.* If interest rates in the U.S. increase relative to interest rates abroad, foreigners will want to hold more US assets and US citizens will want to hold fewer foreign assets. This will increase the demand for dollars and reduce the demand for foreign currencies. The resulting change in exchange rates will reduce net exports. This will shift the US aggregate demand curve to the left.

- *Changes in exchange rates.* A fall in the foreign exchange value of the US dollar will, *ceteris paribus*, increase net exports (x–m will become positive if there had been balanced trade; x–m will become less negative if there had been a trade deficit). This will shift US aggregate demand to the right.

- *The investment or net export multiplier.* Each of these changes will be amplified by a multiplier. This means that small changes in expectations about incomes, prices, costs, profits, or the growth rate of aggregate income itself will be amplified and produce much larger changes in aggregate demand. Thus, for example, a small change in the rate of growth of real output will lead to a larger change in desired investment (the accelerator) and this change in desired investment will lead to an even larger change in aggregate demand (the investment multiplier).

Keynesian and Classical Adjustments

If short-run aggregate supply is such that the price level does not change with changes in aggregate demand, then any change in aggregate demand will lead to a change of the *same size* in real output. This change, illustrated in Figure 16, is called a **Keynesian adjustment**. In this case, an aggregate demand shock will change real output, but will not affect prices in the economy. By contrast, if prices and nominal wages are perfectly flexible and adjust quickly, then any change in aggregate demand will have *no effect* on real output, but will affect only the price level. This change, also illustrated in Figure 16, is called a **classical adjustment**.

The Keynesian adjustment dominates only when nominal wages are very sticky. The classical adjustment dominates only when nominal wages are perfectly flexible. In general, nominal wages are neither perfectly flexible nor completely rigid. Hence, as shown in Figure 17, the effects of an aggregate demand shock are *divided* between price effects and real-output effects over short periods of time.

▶ Summary

Consumption. The largest component of aggregate demand is consumption. Consumption expenditures are relatively stable: individuals tend to smooth consumption over time, drawing from savings if they experience a sudden decrease in income or adding to their savings when their income unexpectedly increases. Aggregate consumption depends on aggregate real income, interest rates, wealth, and

Figure 16
Keynesian Versus Classical Adjustment

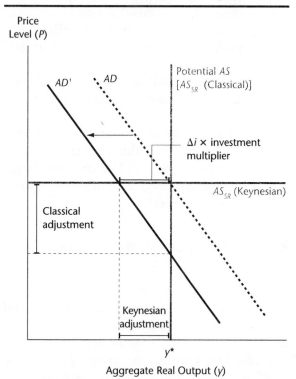

Aggregate demand shifts by the investment multiplier times a change in desired investment. If prices and nominal wages are fixed, then aggregate real output will fall by the full amount of the change in aggregate demand. Thus, the Keynesian short-run aggregate supply curve will be flat. If prices and nominal wages are perfectly flexible, however, then aggregate real output won't change, but the price level will. Thus, the classical short-run aggregate supply curve will be vertical and coincide with potential AS.

Figure 17
Adjustment When the Price Level and Nominal Wages Are Sticky but Not Fixed

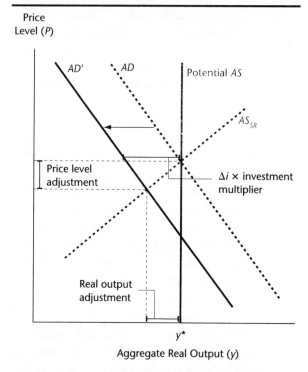

Aggregate demand shifts by the investment multiplier times a change in desired investment. If prices and nominal wages are sticky, both the output and the price level are affected.

expectations about future changes in income, wealth, and interest rates.

Investment. Investment is highly variable because it is sensitive to expectations about the profitability of new capital. These expectations will change as expectations regarding future revenues and future costs change. Aggregate investment also depends upon the interest rate. When the interest rate increase, investment projects become less attractive. Finally, aggregate investment depends upon the *rate of change* of aggregate real output. Thus, small changes in the rate of growth of real output lead to larger changes in desired investment. Indeed, it is possible that desired investment may decrease, even

when real output itself does not decrease, but instead increases at a reduced rate.

Net exports. The demand for exports increases aggregate demand; the demand for imports reduces aggregate demand. Whether there is an effect on aggregate demand depends upon the relationship of exports to imports. If exports increase relative to imports, aggregate demand will increase; if imports increase relative to exports, aggregate demand will decrease. If no one wants to hold either the currency or foreign assets, then exports will equal imports (net exports will equal 0). Foreigners may want to hold US dollars or US dollar assets, however, in which case the US will have a trade deficit and will import financial capital and have a capital account surplus.

Aggregate demand. If desired consumption or desired investment or net exports (or some combination of the three) increases, aggregate demand increases. Hence, *anything* that affects desired consumption or desired investment or net exports will also affect aggregate demand.

Induced changes in consumption. Because consumption is determined in part by real income, changes in income (such as those that follow changes in desired investment) will *induce* changes in desired consumption. As a consequence, small changes in desired investment can sometimes lead to large changes in aggregate real output demanded.

Marginal propensity to consume and the aggregate demand multiplier. The marginal propensity to consume is the amount by which consumption changes when income changes by $1. The investment multiplier is the amount by which aggregate demand changes when desired investment changes. Since a dollar spent within the economy increases the demand for the output an economy produces regardless of whether it's a dollar increase in desired investment or a dollar increase in net exports, the net export multiplier is the same as the investment multiplier. Both the investment multiplier and the net export multiplier are, in their simplest form, equal to $1.0 / (1.0 - MPC)$. Since they are identical, $(1/1-MPC)$ is generally referred to as the aggregate-demand multiplier.

Chapter 21 ▶ ▶
Fiscal Policy: A First Approach

Aggregate demand shocks create problems, including unemployment and price instability. Obviously, public policies that either prevent or ameliorate aggregate demand shocks can, in principle, make the economy function better. There are two broad sets of *countercyclical* policies: fiscal policy, which is introduced in this chapter, and monetary policy, which is introduced in the next chapter.

▶ Government Fiscal Activity

Governments determine how much they will spend and how they will finance their activities. In the United States, these decisions are made at local, state, and federal levels. In analyzing the effects of government spending on the overall performance of the economy, however, we aggregate over all levels of government and speak as a whole of *government spending* and *taxation*.

Decisions to spend or tax affect the aggregate activity of the economy in one of three ways.

1. Government spending directly affects aggregate demand.

2. Taxes and subsidies affect desired consumption or investment, thereby indirectly affecting aggregate demand.

3. Taxes (and occasionally, government expenditures) affect incentives to work, save, or invest and, thereby affect *potential* real output and economic growth.

Government actions to spend, tax, and subsidize are referred to as **fiscal activities** of government. **Fiscal policy** is the use of taxes and expenditures to stabilize the economy or promote economic growth.

Expenditures

Government spending on goods and services is one component of aggregate demand. For example, potential output might be $5.5 trillion; consumption, $3.6 trillion; investment, $800 billion; and government spending, $1.1 trillion. Aggregate demand would then be $5.5 trillion and would equal potential output. Clearly, because government spending is a component of aggregate demand, *an increase in government spending increases aggregate demand and a decrease in government spending decreases aggregate demand.*

Multiplier effect. Because of the income-induced effect on consumption, the effect of a change in government spending on aggregate demand will be greater than a change in government spending alone might suggest.[1] That is, there will be a multiplier

---

[1] The government must fund its spending either by taxing or borrowing or, as we will see later, by printing money, so the full effect of a change in government spending cannot be evaluated without considering the effects of changes in these funding alternatives. When thinking about the full effect, however, it is useful to isolate the spending effect outlined here from the funding effect. Keep in mind, however, that we are working toward an understanding of the full effect.

effect of any change in government spending comparable to the multiplier effect of a change in investment or net exports discussed in the previous chapter. In fact, the **government-spending multiplier** is the same size as the investment multiplier. The reason why is that from an aggregate perspective, the source of a change in aggregate demand makes no difference—$1 in additional spending for goods and services by the government is no different than $1 in additional spending for new capital by firms or $1 of addition spending on exports. In each case, the real output demanded increases initially by $1. As real output increases, aggregate income increases and there is an induced increase in consumption. This kicks off the sequence of increases in real output, real income and consumption traced explicitly in the last chapter.

Thus, in its simplest form,

$$\text{Government - spending multiplier} = \frac{1}{1 - MPC}$$

That is, a $1 change in government spending has a *direct effect* on aggregate demand. This is followed by an *induced consumption effect* that occurs as real output changes in response to the direct effect. If the marginal propensity to consume is 0.9, for example, a $50 billion increase in government purchases will lead to an increase in aggregate demand of $500 billion [$1/(1 − MPC) × $50 billion]. The direct effect in this case is $50 billion; the indirect effect is $450 billion.[2]

The nature and size of this government-spending effect can also be understood by noting that the amount of resources actually available for the government's use will increase by $50 billion only if desired saving increases by $50 billion, that is, only if individuals do not consume all of the real output the economy produces. But desired saving will only increase by $50 billion if real output increases by $500 billion. If real output increased by $500 billion, consumption would increase by $450 million (0.9 × $500), leaving $50 billion in saving that could be used to provide additional real resources for the government. At any increase in output below

$500 billion, the real output available to the government will be less than what the government wants to spend. If aggregate income increases by $400 billion and the marginal propensity to consume is 0.9, for example, consumption will increase by $360 billion, but the additional output available for governmental uses will be only $40 billion. On the other hand, if aggregate output were to increase by $600 billion, consumption expenditures would increase by $540 billion, and $60 billion would be available for other uses. The government wants to increase its expenditures by just $50 billion, so a real output of $600 billion cannot be sustained. Only when real output increases by precisely $500 billion will there be an equilibrium division of output between consumption, investment, and government expenditures.

Taxes

Governments tax as well as spend. When the government levies an income tax, the amount that individuals can actually spend, their **disposable income**, will be less than the amount they earn. Consumption will be less as a consequence. When government taxes business, it also taxes investment indirectly and generally, investment will be less as a consequence. Thus, although taxes are not themselves a component of aggregate demand, they affect either consumption or investment, both of which are components of aggregate demand. The consequence? *A tax increase decreases aggregate demand and a tax decrease increases aggregate demand.*

Tax multiplier. The effect of a tax change on aggregate demand will be smaller than the effect of an equivalent change in government spending. Put simply, a tax increase of $50 billion will have a smaller effect than a $50 billion decrease in government spending. To see why, assume that consumption is determined only by current *disposable* income. Assume, further, that taxes are taken from each individual in a lump sum that does not depend upon income. (Taxes based on income change with changes in income. This introduces another element into the analysis that we will consider later.) Given these assumptions, the consumption function introduced in Chapter 20 is

$$c = a + b\,(y - t). \tag{1}$$

---

[2] As noted in Chapter 20, because the investment, net export and government spending multipliers are identical, we will refer to them collective as the **aggregate-demand multiplier**.

Where t represents the tax and $(y - t)$ is disposable income.

Equation (1) says that if lump-sum taxes increase by $1.00, disposable income decreases by $1.00. Furthermore, it implies that if disposable income decreases by $1.00, consumption falls by $b \times \$1.00$, where b is the marginal propensity to consume. Thus, for example, if the *MPC* is 0.8, a $1.00 increase in taxes will *initially* decrease desired consumption by $.80. This is the initial aggregate-demand effect of a tax increase. Notice that an increase in taxes *does not* reduce consumption by the full $1.00 change in taxes. This is because when disposable income decreases, *both* consumption and saving decrease—individuals pay their taxes partially by reducing consumption and partially by saving less. The $1.00 decrease in disposable income in this example leads to an initial decrease in desired saving of $.20 and an initial decrease in desired consumption of $.80. A decrease in taxes has the opposite effect: A $1.00 decrease increases disposable income by $1.00, but consumption initially increases by only $.80.

This initial effect will be followed by a multiplier effect because of the induced change in consumption that follows the initial change in consumption. That is, when a tax is increased by $1.00, consumption initially falls by $.80. But, remember, consumption is just the purchase of goods and services from firms. A change in consumption leads to a change in the incomes of those supplying resources to these firms by exactly the same amount. Therefore, the initial change in consumption reduces aggregate income by $.80. The story of what happens next should be familiar by now: the decrease in income induces a decrease in consumption, etc. We know that the ultimate size of the change in aggregate real output demanded will be $1/(1 - MPC)$ multiplied by the initial change in aggregate demand. In this case, however, the initial change in aggregate demand is $MPC \times$ tax change and therefore

change in aggregate demand =

$$\left(MPC \times \text{tax change}\right) \times \frac{1}{1 - MPC}$$

Initial change in   *Aggregate demand*
aggregate demand   *multiplier*

or, rearranging,

change in aggregate demand =

$$\frac{MPC}{1 - MPC} \times \text{tax change}$$

Thus, for each $1.00 of taxes that are increased, aggregate real output demanded will *decrease* by

$$\frac{MPC}{1 - MPC} \qquad (2)$$

This expression is called the **tax multiplier** for a lump-sum tax. The marginal propensity to consume is less than 1, so expression (2) will always be less than the investment/government spending multiplier. For example, if the marginal propensity to consume is 0.8, the government spending multiplier will be 5 ($1/[1 - 0.8]$). However, the lump-sum tax multiplier will be 4 ($0.8/[1 - 0.8]$). The reason for the difference in the two multipliers is that a $1.00 increase in government spending initially increases aggregate income by $1.00. A $1.00 tax cut initially increases aggregate income by *less than $1.00*, however, because individuals respond to the increase in disposable income by consuming only a fraction of the dollar—$MPC \times \$1.00$—and saving more ($MPS \times \$1.00$). The initial increase in aggregate income is less for a tax cut, so the final change in aggregate demand will also be less.

The aggregate-demand multiplier and real output. The multiplier measures the size of the shift of the aggregate demand curve due to a change in investment, net exports or government spending. It does not measure *actual* changes in real output. The effect of a change in i, $(x–m)$, or g on aggregate real output actually produced depends on two things: the size of the shift in aggregate demand as measured by the multiplier, and the price adjustment that begins to occur when aggregate demand changes. In the two parts of Figure 1, for example, identical shifts in aggregate demand, from *AD* to *AD'* (where the multiplier is the same in both cases), lead to quite different effects on real output in the short run. When the price level doesn't respond very much to an aggregate demand change, as in part (b), a change in desired investment or government spending will

Figure 1
Real Output Effects Depend on Both the Multiplier and Short-Run Aggregate Supply

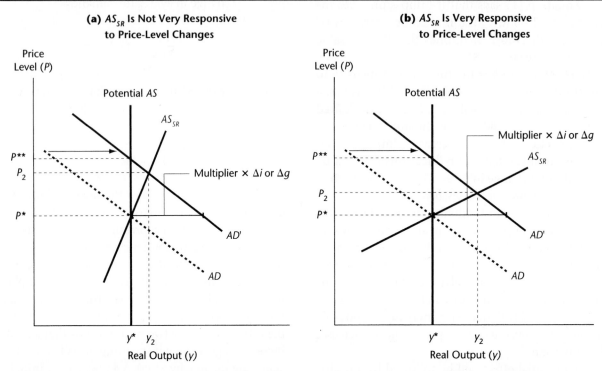

(a) When short-run aggregate supply is not very sensitive to price-level changes, an increase in aggregate demand will have a relatively large effect on the price level and a relatively small effect on real output. (b) When short-run aggregate supply is more sensitive to price-level changes, however, an increase in aggregate demand will have a relatively large effect on real output and a relatively small effect on price level.

lead to a relatively large effect on real output. If the price level and nominal wages respond quickly, however, the same change in desired investment or government expenditures, with the same multiplier effect on aggregate demand, will lead to a relatively small effect on real output, as in part (a).[3]

In either case, the long-run effect of an increase in government spending *on real output* is zero, whatever the multiplier, because a change in government expenditures does not change the real resources currently available to an economy. As a consequence, in the long run, the economy cannot produce more than its potential.

Balanced-Budget Effects

It isn't possible simply to increase government spending and do nothing else—government spend-

ing must be financed in some way. When spending increases, taxes must increase, the government must borrow, or, as we will see later, the government must print money. As a consequence of this funding constraint, it doesn't make much sense to think of a government-spending effect on aggregate demand independent of the possible effects that financing will also have on aggregate demand. Put differently, government spending will affect aggregate demand in the ways discussed earlier only when financing the government's activities does not itself affect aggregate demand. But we have just learned that financing government expenditures with taxes *does* affect aggregate demand. Thus, to fully analyze fiscal policy, we need to consider the effects of both a change in government spending and a consistent change in government financing that funds the spending. We consider the joint effects of spending and taxing here. The effects of spending and borrowing or spending and printing money will be considered in subsequent chapters.

---

[3] Figure 1(a) is closer to the Classical Adjustment introduced at the end of Chapter 20; Figure 1(b) is closer to the Keynesian Adjustment.

Suppose that the government increases g and, at the same time, funds the increase by increasing lump-sum taxes. Your initial response might be that if g and t increase by the same amount, there can't be an aggregate-demand effect—the spending and tax effects would appear to cancel each other. What might seem intuitive, however, is wrong. To see why, remember that a $1 increase in g will *increase* aggregate demand by

$$\frac{1}{1-MPC}$$

A $1 increase in lump-sum taxes, t, will *decrease* aggregate demand by

$$\frac{MPC}{1-MPC}$$

The overall effect will be the sum of these two effects:

$$\text{Net effect} = \underbrace{\frac{1}{1-MCP}}_{\substack{Government \\ spending \\ effect}} - \underbrace{\frac{MCP}{1-MCP}}_{\substack{Taxation \\ effect}}$$

Rearranging, the net effect on aggregate demand, called the **balanced-budget multiplier,** will be

$$\frac{1-MPC}{1-MPC} = 1.0$$

Thus, an increase in government spending of $1 and a simultaneous increase in taxes of $1 will *increase* aggregate demand by $1. Put differently, balanced-budget changes in the fiscal position of the government are not neutral relative to the macroeconomic performance of the economy. *A tax-funded increase in expenditures will increase aggregate demand; a tax-cut and corresponding decrease in expenditures will decrease aggregate demand.*

▶ Countercyclical Fiscal Policy: A First Look

Because aggregate demand is affected by government expenditures on goods and services and by taxes on consumption, saving, or investment, in principle the government can pursue fiscal policies that are *purposefully designed* to offset aggregate demand shocks.

Shocks and Adjustment

Suppose that desired investment falls as indicated in Figure 2. If left alone, aggregate demand will fall as indicated by the shift from in *AD* to *AD'* in Figure 3. At the current price level, P^*, there will be excess aggregate supply—potential real output will exceed the output that individuals, firms and the government are willing to purchase. Prices will begin to fall, but because of sticky nominal wages, real output will fall as well.

Why does this adjustment occur? Because aggregate demand has decreased, firms find that they cannot sell the output they produce. Unwanted inventories accumulate. Prices fall, but firms find that nominal wages do not fall as quickly as prices do, and, as a consequence, their labor costs increase. Workers are laid off as firms try to cut costs in the face of decreasing demand and higher real wages. Fewer goods and services will be produced as a

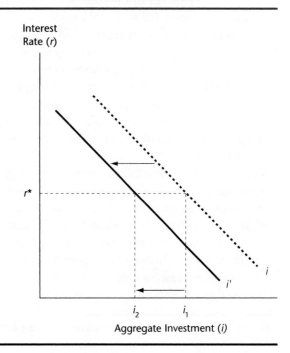

Figure 2
The Effect of a Decrease in Desired Investment

Figure 3
The Short-Run Effect of an Adverse Aggregate Demand Shock

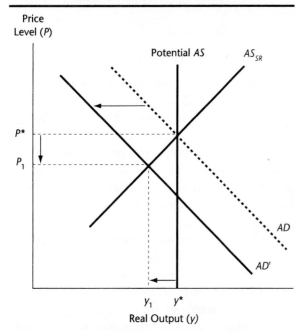

A decrease in investment (see Figure 2) decreases aggregate demand, and real output falls, *ceteris paribus.*

Figure 4
The Long-Run Effect of an Adverse Aggregate Demand Shock

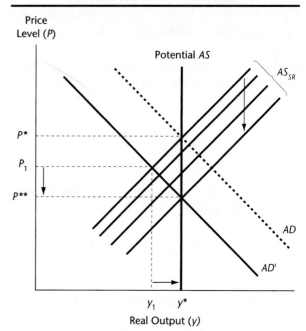

As labor contracts expire or are renegotiated, and as individuals and firms gather better information about changes in the price level, the nominal wage falls. As it does, the real wage falls toward its original equilibrium level. Real output increases and the economy moves toward full employment at a lower price level.

consequence. This outcome is represented in Figure 3 by the short-run equilibrium at P_1 and y_1.[4]

As long-term contracts expire or are renegotiated, and as workers and firms gather better information about changes in the price level, nominal wages will eventually fall even as the price level continues to fall. This effect is represented in Figure 4 by downward shifts in the short-run aggregate supply curve. As the real wage falls toward the equilibrium real wage, the number of individuals employed increases and, as a consequence, real output will increase as well. Eventually the economy will be producing at its potential of y^*, but with a permanently lower price level, P^{**}. Thus, the economy tends toward full employment following an adverse aggregate demand shock. To get there, however, the economy has to endure a period of unemployment and deflation in which it produces less than its potential.

On the other hand, suppose that desired investment increases, as illustrated in Figure 5. Aggregate demand will increase, as indicated by the shift from AD to AD'' in Figure 6. At the current price level, P^*,

there will now be excess aggregate demand—the output that individuals, firms, and the government are now willing to purchase exceeds potential real output. Prices will begin to increase. Because of sticky nominal wages, real output will increase as well.

Why? As prices begin to increase, if nominal wages are sticky, the real wage falls. Firms find it profitable to increase the use of labor. Indeed, they might offer slightly higher nominal wages in order to attract additional workers. As long as workers are not fully aware of the changes that have occurred in the price level, these increases in nominal wage will appear to be an increase in the real wage. The amount of labor supplied to the economy will increase as a consequence. Real output will increase because more resources are now being used. This outcome is represented in Figure 6 as the short-run equilibrium at P_2 and y_2.[5]

---

[4] The difference between y^* and y_1 is sometimes called a **deflationary gap.**

[5] The difference between y^* and y_2 is sometimes called an **inflationary gap.**

Figure 5
The Effect of an Increase in Desired Investment

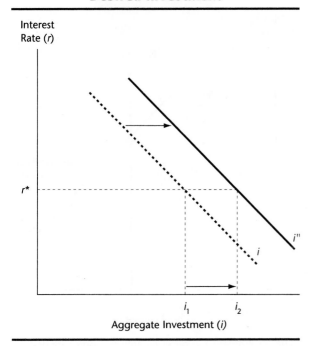

Figure 6
The Short-Run Effect of an Inflationary Aggregate Demand Shock

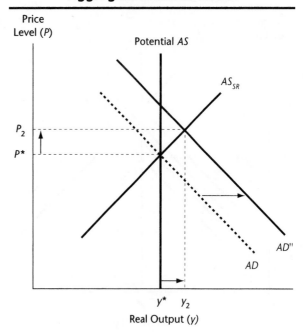

An increase in desired investment (see Figure 5) will shift aggregate demand so that actual output is greater than potential output ($y*$). As a result, prices will increase. Sticky nominal wages will lead to an increase in output as resources become overemployed. As a consequence, the economy will move to a short-run equilibrium at P_2 and y_2.

As long-term contracts expire or are renegotiated, and as workers and firms gather better information about changes in the price level, the nominal wage will begin to increase even as the price level continues to increase. This effect is represented in Figure 7 by upward shifts in the short-run aggregate supply curve. As the real wage increase toward the equilibrium real wage, the number of individuals employed will decrease and, as a consequence, real output will decrease as well. Eventually, the economy will be producing at its potential of $y*$ but with a permanently higher price level P^{**}. Thus, the economy will tend toward full employment. To get to this position, however, the economy has to endure a period of inflation in which output is somewhat greater than it would otherwise be.

Offsetting Anticipated Aggregate Demand Shocks

If the government increases expenditures on real output *in anticipation of the adverse aggregate demand shock* such as the one illustrated in Figure 3, the output effect would be partially or fully offset. The government's action would, in this case, offset the decrease in desired investment. That is, if the gov-

ernment could predict the change in desired investment and *precisely* offset it by changing its expenditures, aggregate demand would be unaffected by an adverse aggregate demand shock as illustrated in Figure 8. This action by the government is called an **expansionary countercyclical fiscal policy**.

Similarly, if the government decreased expenditures in anticipation of an inflationary aggregate demand shock such as the one illustrated in Figure 7, the inflationary output effect would be partially or fully offset. The purpose of the government's action in these circumstances is to offset the increase in desired investment that otherwise would cause an aggregate demand shift. If the government can predict the change in desired investment and *precisely* offset it by decreasing its expenditures, aggregate demand would be unaffected by the inflationary aggregate demand shock as illustrated in Figure 9. This action by the government is called a **contractionary countercyclical fiscal policy**.

Figure 7
The Long-Run Effect of an Inflationary Aggregate Demand Shock

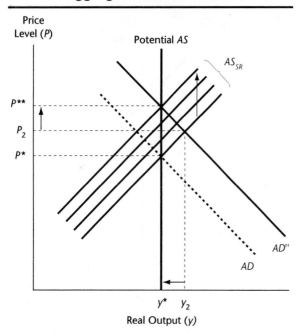

As labor contracts expire or are renegotiated, and as individuals and firms gather better information about changes in the price level, the nominal wage increases. As it does, the real wage increases toward its original equilibrium level. Real output decreases and the economy moves toward full employment at a higher price level.

Figure 8
An Expansionary Countercyclical Fiscal Action

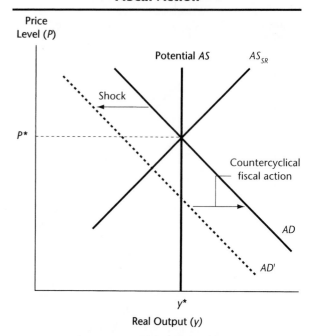

The government can offset an adverse aggregate demand shock that would otherwise lead to unemployment by increasing government expenditures or decreasing taxes, thus increasing aggregate demand.

The government would not necessarily need to increase its expenditures to stabilize the economy when investment or consumption was expected to fall or decrease its expenditures when investment or consumption was expected to increase. It could instead cut taxes on personal income, thus offsetting an adverse aggregate demand shock by stimulating consumption. Or the government could also lower taxes on capital, thereby making investment more attractive and in this way offset an adverse shift in aggregate demand. In the face of an inflationary aggregate demand shock, the government could increase taxes on personal income thereby reducing consumption. Or it could increase taxes on capital, making investment less attractive.

This seductive little exercise is the basis of countercyclical fiscal policy. It appears that with appropriate fiscal policy, the economy can be insulated from the consequences of aggregate demand shocks. That is, countercyclical fiscal policy can move against the business cycle in order to keep output near its potential. Using these policies stabilizes the price level and minimizes unemployment.

Moderating the Effects of Aggregate Demand Shocks

It's hard to imagine that those responsible for fiscal policy can anticipate correctly every movement in aggregate demand. But even when they cannot do so, countercyclical fiscal policy can be useful *if it changes aggregate demand more quickly than the economy can adjust to a demand shock on its own.* In Figure 10, for example, the economy begins at y^* and P^*, but an adverse aggregate demand shock caused by the fall in desired investment illustrated in Figure 3 has not been anticipated by the government. As a consequence, aggregate real output falls to y_1. Once the economy is a y_1, if it were left alone it would reach a new equilibrium at y^* and P^{**}, but only after some period of time. An expansionary fiscal policy implemented when the economy is already at y_1 would, of course, move the economy

Figure 9
A Restrictive Countercyclical Fiscal Action

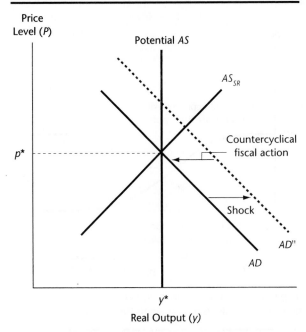

The government can offset an inflationary aggregate demand shock by reducing government expenditures or increasing taxes, thus reducing aggregate demand.

Figure 10
A Stimulative Countercyclical Fiscal Action After an Adverse Aggregate Demand Shock

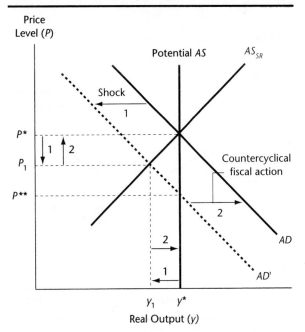

Even if the government cannot accurately predict an aggregate demand shock, countercyclical fiscal policy will be useful if fiscal policy can move aggregate demand back to its original level faster than the economy can move to full employment at P^{**} on its own.

toward the initial equilibrium at y^* and P^*. The important question for policy makers is whether it makes sense to pursue this policy. If the short-run adjustments toward full employment take many months, or perhaps several years, then in principle fiscal policy could move the economy toward full employment *more rapidly* than the economy would move toward it on its own. Figure 11(a) illustrates the gain to the economy of doing so.

While those responsible for fiscal policy may not be able to anticipate adverse aggregate demand shocks, once the economy is headed down, fiscal policy could, in principle, be implemented which stopped the downward slide. Figure 11(b) illustrates the gain to the economy of acting quickly once a downturn is understood to be underway.

A similar situation faces policy makers when responding to an inflationary aggregate demand shock like that illustrated in Figures 5 and 6. If they do not anticipate the shock, then prices will already have begun to increase. If the period of inflation is likely to be a lengthy one and a contractionary fiscal policy can be effectively implemented in a shorter period of time, then fiscal policy could sta-

bilize prices faster than the economy could on its own.

Inflexible Fiscal Changes and Inadvertent Fiscal Effects

There is no single correct countercyclical fiscal policy. That is, during a recession, increasing government spending is not better than decreasing taxes; during an inflation, decreasing government is not better than increasing taxes. Furthermore, because of the difference between the government spending and tax multipliers, an appropriate mix of changes in government spending and taxation can have countercyclical effects. Thus, countercyclical fiscal policy is not intrinsically liberal or conservative. During downswings, one group may lean toward relying on increases in government spending and the other toward relying on cuts in taxes, but nothing in our analysis of fiscal policy options suggests that one approach is more effective than the other. In fact, each is equally effective in changing aggregate

Figure 11
The Effect of Appropriate Expansionary Fiscal Policy

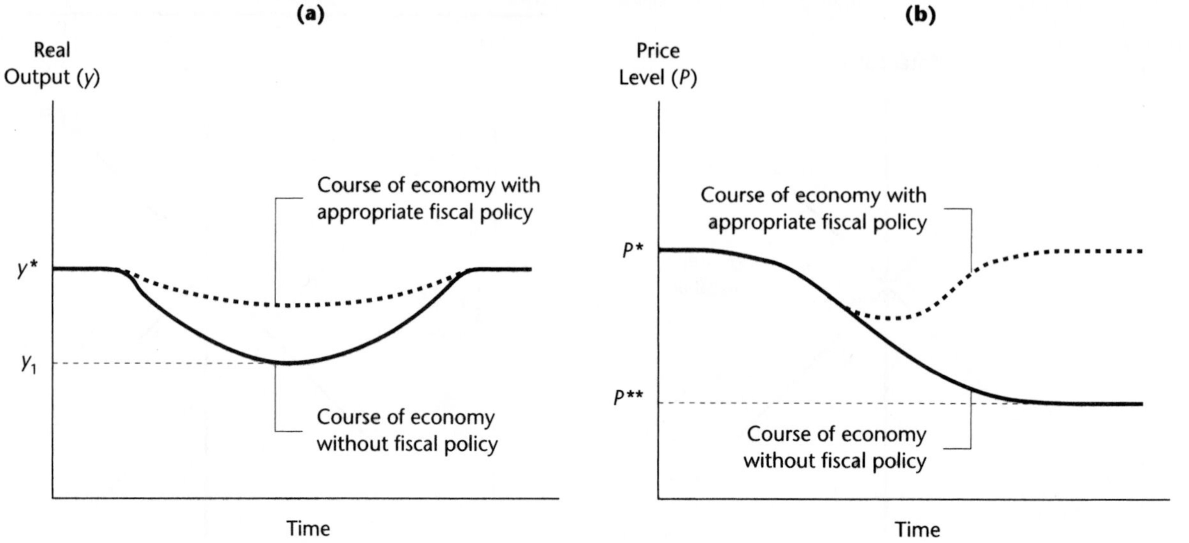

(a)

(b)

If the government either lowers taxes or increases government spending after a decline in aggregate demand, then the output and price-level effects can be moderated so that the economy follows a path along the dotted lines.

demand, although different-sized policy responses may be required to achieve the same effect because of differences in multipliers.

Countercyclical policy must be reversible. If desired investment falls, for example, an appropriate fiscal policy would be either an increase in government spending or a cut in taxes or even balanced-budget increases in government spending and taxes. Desired investment is unlikely to be lower permanently, however. Unless government spending decreases, taxes increase, or there is a balanced-budget reduction in government spending when desired investment bounces back, aggregate demand at the current price level will exceed potential real output. In this case, the initial fiscal policy action if not reversed will create price-level instability. This suggests, of course, that *countercyclical* fiscal policy ought to rely on government expenditures and taxes that can be reversed easily.

A government taxes and spends for many purposes other than to offset cycles in the economy. However, increasing government spending and/or decreasing taxes for *any* reason will increase aggregate demand. Conversely, decreasing government spending and/or increasing taxes will decrease aggregate demand. Clearly, the fiscal activities of the government—pursued for reasons other than macroeconomic stability—may *create* cycles. That

is, changes in government spending and taxation can be another source of aggregate demand shocks and not just a policy method of offsetting or ameliorating adverse shocks. If the resources of the economy are fully employed and, by increasing its expenditures on real output, the government runs a budget deficit without changing its taxes on consumption or investment, for example, aggregate demand will increase. Output may increase in the short run, but the government's increased demand for real output will also lead to an inflation. In this case, the fiscal activities of the government will have induced an economic cycle rather than being countercyclical. It is generally thought that the government's refusal to increase taxes as the expenditures for the war in Vietnam increased triggered an inflation, the effects of which extended into the 1970s for example.

Countercyclical fiscal policy requires that government spending go up at times and down at other times or that taxes go down at times and up at other times. But spending increases, it seldom decreases. And, it is always politically appealing to decrease taxes, but politically difficult to increase them. This means that as a practical matter, pursuing countercyclical fiscal policy is politically difficult. Indeed, it is an open question as to whether the fiscal activities of the government actually dampen or amplify aggregate demand shocks. Certainly, the notion that the government waits to observe a demand shock before it engages in new fiscal activities is naïve.

Deficits

The government's budget position is its tax revenues, t, minus its expenditures, g,

$$budget\ position = t - g$$

The government will have a deficit whenever g is greater than t and a surplus whenever g is less than t. It would appear that appropriate countercyclical fiscal policy would be to run a **federal deficit** (where government expenditures are greater than taxes ($g > t$)) when aggregate demand shifts to the left and a **federal surplus** (where government expenditures are less than taxes ($g < t$)) when aggregate demand shifts to the right.[6]

Does such a policy make sense? It depends. The government is not free to simply spend. It must also decide how it will fund its spending. If is chooses *not* to do so by taxing, then it must borrow. If when it borrows the government competes with firms or households for savings, however, and its deficit will affect other markets in the economy. In particular, interest rates may increase and investment or consumption decrease. Because investment is particularly sensitive to interest rates, a stimulative fiscal policy that is funded by borrowing that pushes interest rates up will reduce investment. Or, if forward-looking individuals consume less in anticipation of a decrease in future income, a stimulative fiscal policy funded by borrowing may reduce consumption as individuals anticipate higher taxes and, hence, lower disposable incomes, in the future. To the degree that either of these effects occur, a fiscal policy that appears to be stimulative but that increases the deficit may not have much effect on aggregate demand. Thus, the ability of fiscal policy to affect real output may very well be limited by the effects that follow from funding the deficit. This conclusion is a bit premature because we have not yet discussed interest-rate determination in the economy. We turn to this issue in the next two chapters. We will then reconsider countercyclical fiscal policy in Chapter 25.

▶ Summary

Fiscal activities. Government expenditures directly affect aggregate demand; tax policies indirectly affect aggregate demand because they change either desired investment or desired consumption. A budget deficit occurs when expenditures exceed tax revenues.

Government-spending and tax multipliers. Taken by itself, an increase in government spending increases aggregate demand by the change in government-spending multiplied by the government-spending multiplier. The government-spending multiplier is the same as the investment multiplier and, in its simplest form, is equal to

$$\frac{1}{1 - MPC}$$

Taken by itself, an increase in taxes decreases aggregate real output demanded at a given price level by the change in taxes multiplied by the tax multiplier. The tax multiplier is smaller than the government-spending multiplier because of the indirect effect of changes in taxes on aggregate demand. The tax multiplier, in its simplest form, is equal to

$$\frac{MPC}{1 - MPC}$$

Stimulative countercyclical fiscal policy. An increase in government spending and/or a decrease in taxes increases aggregate demand. As a consequence of this effect, fiscal policy, in principle, can be used to offset adverse aggregate demand shocks that would otherwise lead to a decrease in real output and an increase in unemployment.

Restrictive countercyclical fiscal policy. A decrease in government spending and/or an increase in taxes decreases aggregate demand. Because of this effect, fiscal policy can be used to offset aggregate demand shocks that would otherwise lead to an inflation and a short-term increase in real output.

---

[6] The national debt is the accumulation of previous deficits less repayments. Thus, it is the *stock* of outstanding U.S. government debt. The deficit is the *flow* of new debt.

Balanced-budget effects. An increase in government spending matched by an increase in tax revenues increases aggregate demand. A decrease in government spending matched by a decrease in tax revenues decreases aggregate demand. Thus, a balanced-budget *change* in fiscal activities will affect aggregate demand. This means that balanced-budget changes can be used for countercyclical policy.

Chapter 22 ▶▶

Money, Interest Rates, and Aggregate Demand __

We have learned three important things about economic cycles:

1. Real output will change with changes in aggregate demand if nominal wages are sticky.

2. Aggregate demand will change with changes in its components—desired investment, desired consumption, net exports or government spending—if a change in one component is not offset by an opposite change of the same magnitude in another component.

3. Changes in one or more components of aggregate demand that would otherwise lead to undesirable fluctuations in real output and the price level can, in principle, be offset by appropriate, well-timed countercyclical fiscal policies.

Pursuing appropriate fiscal policies that counter the adverse effects of aggregate demand shocks is not the only policy option available to the government, however. Because certain components of aggregate demand are sensitive to changes in interest rates and the mix of assets in an economy, policies that influence interest rates or that change the mix of assets will also affect aggregate demand. These policies are called **monetary policies** because they affect aggregate demand by changing the supply of money in the economy.

The avenues by which monetary policy affects aggregate demand are less direct than those for fis-

cal policies. As a consequence, our analysis of these policies will be somewhat less direct as well. We first summarize the relationships between interest rates, aggregate demand, and real output suggested in earlier chapters. We next examine possible relationships between the supply of money and interest rates. We then consider the relationship between monetary policy and the supply of money. This leads, finally, to a consideration of the link between monetary policy and aggregate demand.

▶ Interest Rates, Aggregate Demand, and Macroeconomic Policy

Some components of aggregate demand—desired investment, in particular—are sensitive to interest-rate changes. In addition, interest-rate changes may induce individuals to adjust consumption patterns and, therefore, saving. Finally, interest-rate changes can affect the willingness of foreigners to hold US assets and, by doing so, affect the exchange rate and net exports.

Interest Rates and Desired Investment

When the interest rate increases, firms expect new capital to be less profitable and invest less, *ceteris paribus*. There is substantial evidence that the acquisition of new plant and equipment is highly sensitive to interest-rate changes. Similarly, when the interest rate is higher, households find the acquisition of certain kinds of household capital less attractive, *ceteris paribus.* In this regard, there is substantial evidence that the purchase of new homes is also highly sensitive to interest-rate changes. As a consequence, new housing construction—an important form of investment in an economy—decreases when the interest rate increases. Household demands for durable commodities, such as automobiles, are also sensitive to interest-rate changes. In particular, higher interest rates make the purchase of new cars less attractive.[1] The effects of higher interest rates are particularly evident if you borrow to purchase a home or buy a car because their full cost includes the purchase price and the amount of interest that will be paid over the life of the loan. As the interest rate increases, the amount of interest paid and the full cost increases. Even if you don't borrow to finance the purchase, however, changes in the interest rate change the opportunity cost of your purchases. If you have enough money currently in hand to purchase a new car and use it for that purpose rather than putting it in the bank, you forgo the interest income you could have earned on your deposit. When the interest rate is higher, the amount that you have to forgo if you purchase a new car increases. Hence, the opportunity cost of buying a new car or new home changes with the interest rate.

In sum, for both firms and households, desired investment increases when the interest rate decreases and decreases when the interest rate increases. As a consequence, aggregate investment is inversely related to the interest rate, as is illustrated in Figure 1.[2]

Consumption and Saving

The consumption of goods and services (excluding consumer durables in this case), and therefore saving, may also be affected by interest-rate changes.

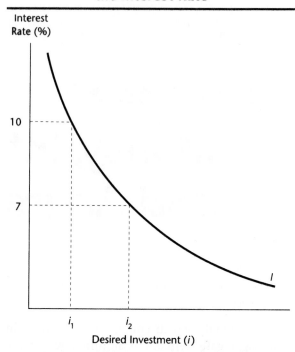

Figure 1
Aggregate Investment and the Interest Rate

For firms, higher interest rates make investment in plant and equipment less attractive because, everything else being equal, higher interest rates lower the profitability of new capital. For households, higher interest rates make the purchase of housing and consumer durables less attractive because higher interest rates increase borrowing costs. Hence, there will be less aggregate investment when the interest rate is high and more aggregate investment when the interest rate is low.

Remember that individuals save in order to smooth consumption relative to possible future income changes. Individuals can choose to save more today and consume more in the future if their income suddenly falls. (Saving, remember, is a way of transferring current income into future consumption.)

The choice to consume more today, like all choices, has an opportunity cost. If an individual is trying to decide whether to consume an additional dollar's worth of goods now or to save the dollar and consume at some point in the future instead, the amount that could be purchased in the future will affect this decision. If the interest rate is 10 percent, consuming a dollar's worth of goods today has an opportunity cost of $1.10's worth of goods that could be consumed a year from now. If the interest rate is 5 percent, the cost of consuming today is less in terms of future consumption—$1.05's worth of

[1] Automobiles are part of a category of goods that households purchase called **consumer durables**. Other consumer durables include common electronic items such as TV's, VCRs, and stereos, as well as kitchen and utility equipment such as refrigerators, stoves, ovens, dishwashers, clothes washers, and driers. The purchase of many of these items is interest-rate sensitive because their purchase prices represent a large fraction of average monthly household incomes. That purchases of these kinds of goods are interest-sensitive is perhaps best seen by noting that advertisements often focus on low-interest financing.

[2] Although it is not strictly accurate to speak of investment as being determined only by firms, for expository purposes we will continue this usage. You should keep in mind, however, there are other kinds of investments that occur within an economy.

goods. Hence, changes in the interest rate change the opportunity cost of consuming *today* rather than *in the future.*

As the opportunity cost of consuming changes—that is, as the reward for saving changes—the mix of consumption and saving will change as well. Higher interest rates will lead to less consumption and more saving today; lower interest rates will lead to more consumption and less saving today. The relationship between interest rates and consumption reinforces the effect of interest rates on aggregate demand through desired investment—an increase in interest rates will reduce aggregate demand by reducing desired investment *and* desired consumption.

Investment has been found to be sensitive to interest-rate changes, but the empirical evidence suggests that consumption and saving are not much affected by changes in the interest rate. Put differently, interest-rate changes appear to lead to large changes in desired investment, but only to small changes in desired saving.

Net Exports

The effects of interest rates on net exports are somewhat more indirect. When people around the world save, they have to decide which kinds of assets to hold—savings accounts, corporate bonds, government bonds, corporate stock, etc. To make matters more complex, they also have to decide whether to hold assets within their own economy or in another economy. A US citizen can, for example, purchase corporate stock in foreign stock markets. Similarly, a Japanese citizen (or corporate or government entity) can choose to hold Japanese government bonds or US government bonds. Indeed, virtually anyone in the world can buy stocks and corporate or government bonds in the New York financial markets. Likewise, virtually anyone in the world can hold US dollars if they wish, and many can open savings accounts in US or other banks denominated in dollars.

Since there are choices, there must be opportunity costs. The opportunity cost for Japanese residents of holding Japanese-yen assets is the return they could get if they purchased US-dollar assets instead. (Examples include US Treasury bills or bonds.) When the interest rates on US-dollar assets increases *relative* to interest rates in Japan, the opportunity cost of holding yen assets increases.

This means that an increase in US interest rates will reduce the demand for Japanese-yen assets and increase the demand for US-dollar assets. But to purchase US-dollar assets, Japanese residents must purchase US dollars (the US Treasury or IBM, for examples, don't accept Japanese yen as payment for their bonds or stock). Hence, an *increase* in interest rates in the United States *relative* to interest rates elsewhere in the world, will *increase* the demand for US dollars in foreign exchange markets, *ceteris paribus.* This will cause the US dollar to appreciate, *ceteris paribus.*

When the dollar appreciates, US goods and services become more expensive *from the perspective of foreigners* even though prices within the U.S. haven't changed—foreigners have to pay more for the dollars used to purchase US goods. US exports will fall as a consequence.

For the US dollar to appreciate, other currencies must depreciate and become cheaper on foreign exchange markets for anyone who has dollars. This means that *from the perspective of US residents,* foreign goods are less expensive even if prices abroad haven't changed. US imports will increase.

Therefore, an increase in interest rates in the US *relative to interest rates abroad* will reduce net exports. An analogous argument to that presented above suggests that net exports will increase when interest rates within a country decrease relative to interest rates abroad.

In Sum

Each of the components of aggregate demand except government spending—*c, i,* and *(x–m)*—is sensitive, to some degree, to interest rates: when interest rates increase, aggregate demand decreases; when interest rates fall, aggregate demand increases. The interest sensitivity of investment is of particular interest and for this reason, and expositional convenience, the discussion from this point focuses on investment. You should keep in mind, however, that there are other avenues by which interest rates, and changes in interest rates, affect aggregate demand.

Macroeconomic Policy

The sensitivity of desired investment to interest-rate changes provides another possible way by which public policies might affect aggregate demand. If the government can *purposefully* change interest rates,

Figure 2
The Effect of a Purposeful Change in Interest Rates on Aggregate Demand

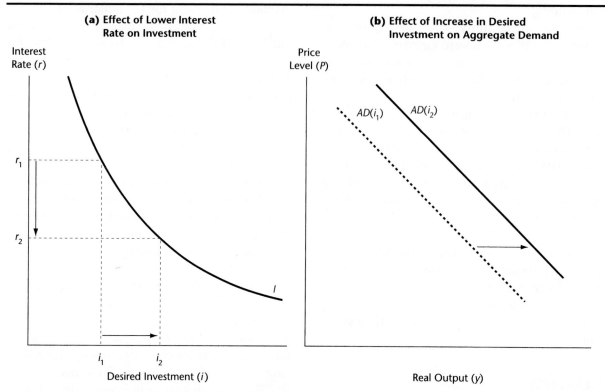

(a) Effect of Lower Interest Rate on Investment

Interest Rate (r)

r_1

r_2

I

i_1 i_2

Desired Investment (i)

(b) Effect of Increase in Desired Investment on Aggregate Demand

Price Level (P)

$AD(i_1)$ $AD(i_2)$

Real Output (y)

If the government can lower the interest rate (from r_1 to r_2), the amount of investment that firms wish to undertake will increase. As a consequence, the aggregate real output demanded at any price level will increase. Aggregate demand will shift rightward from $AD(i_1)$ to $AD(i_2)$.

it can offset aggregate-demand shocks. For example, if the government could pursue policies that purposefully lowered interest rates, firms would want to invest more, as illustrated in Figure 2(a). Aggregate demand would increase, as illustrated by the movement from $AD(i_1)$ to $AD(i_2)$ in Figure 2(b).

As a consequence of this interest sensitivity, appropriately designed policies can offset changes in desired investment that would otherwise adversely affect aggregate demand. To see why, suppose that, at every interest rate, firms become more pessimistic and want to invest less. The aggregate effect of this pessimism is illustrated by the shift from I to I' in Figure 3(a). If interest rates do not change, the change in the desired level of investment will cause aggregate demand to fall, as illustrated in Figure 3(b). Deflation and unemployment will follow if wages or prices are sticky. Real output will fall to y'. If the government can pursue policies that lower the interest rate, however, it can stimulate a greater quantity of investment. Properly pursued,

such policies would offset the effect of the shift in the demand for investment.

The effect of this policy is illustrated by the movement from r_1 to r_2 in Figure 4(a). At the lower interest rate, the desired level of investment increases from i_2 to i_1. Because the desired level of investment increases, aggregate demand increases from its otherwise low level. As a consequence, aggregate demand shifts from AD' back to its original level, as illustrated in Figure 4(b). The interest rate is lower, however. Indeed, given the change in expected returns from new capital reflected by the initial shift in the investment demand function, only a lower interest rate will induce those who are making investment decisions to purchase the amount of new capital necessary to maintain the economy at its full employment position. In a sense, the lower interest rate overcomes the pessimism about the economy and makes the acquisition of new capital profitable, in spite of the change in expectations.

Figure 3
The Effect of Pessimistic Expectations on Desired Investment and Aggregate Demand

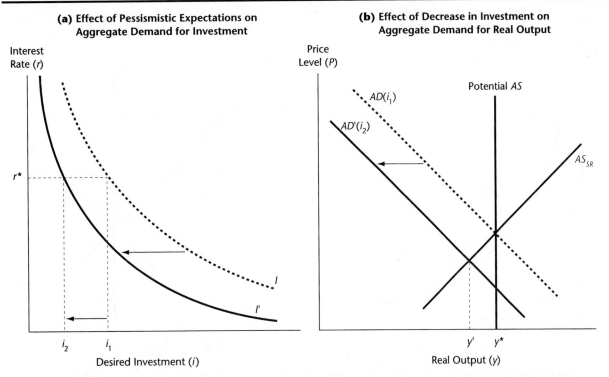

(a) Effect of Pessismistic Expectations on Aggregate Demand for Investment

(b) Effect of Decrease in Investment on Aggregate Demand for Real Output

At a given interest rate, the amount of investment that firms wish to undertake falls with pessimistic expectations. As a consequence, aggregate demand falls and, without countercyclical policy of one sort or another, real output in the economy will move toward y'. Because y' (actual output) is less than y^* (potential real output), unemployment will result.

Inadvertent interest-rate effects. Sometimes governments pursue actions that incidentally change interest rates. These actions will have unintended consequences because if they increase interest rates, they will decrease desired investment and shift aggregate demand. These policy-induced aggregate demand shocks will be followed by adjustments in real output, price levels, and employment. Activities that incidentally decrease interest rates will increase desired investment and aggregate demand, *ceteris paribus*, setting off adjustments in the opposite direction.

The interest-sensitivity of investment, then, is a two-edged sword. It may allow for purposeful public policy designed to offset aggregate-demand shocks, but it may also lead to aggregate-demand shocks when public policies inadvertently affect interest rates. In other words, because aggregate demand is sensitive to interest-rate changes, *any* public policy that affects interest rates will also affect desired investment and aggregate demand, even if it was not meant to do so.

▶ Money and Interest Rates

It should be clear that policies that are intended to purposefully change interest rates make sense in terms of macroeconomic stabilization. In order to know how to design sensible policies, however, we need to know a good deal more about how interest rates are determined in an economy. We begin with the market for money.

Money

As was indicated in Chapter 3, money evolves as a mechanism for lowering transaction costs. That is, money is a *medium of exchange.* Something that we would call money has evolved in virtually every economy, whether developed or primitive. An

Figure 4
The Effect of a Policy That Reduces Interest Rates When There Are Pessimistic Expectations

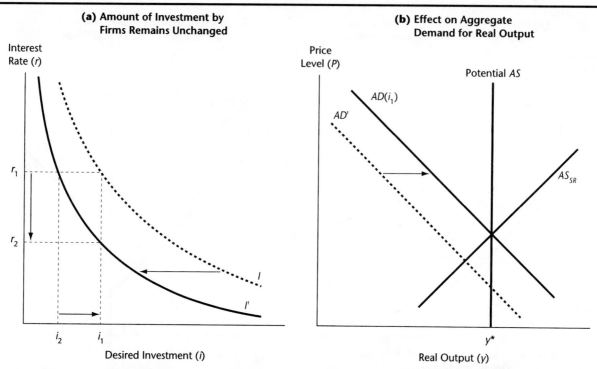

(a) Amount of Investment by Firms Remains Unchanged

(b) Effect on Aggregate Demand for Real Output

A government policy that reduces the interest rate from r_1 to r_2 will provide an incentive for firms to continue to invest at the same level, even though they are more pessimistic about the future. Essentially, because the lower interest rate makes investment more profitable, it offsets firms' pessimism. Done correctly, the policy will keep aggregate demand at a level consistent with full employment, that is, it will keep real output at its potential. Note that in part (b), AD' is the aggregate demand that would result from investment of i_2 at interest rate r_1, while $AD(i_1)$ is the level of aggregate demand consistent with an investment of i_1.

extraordinary variety of things are used as money. Cattle were apparently important in exchange throughout early recorded history. In fact, the word *pecuniary* is derived from the Latin word for cattle, and the Indian monetary unit, the rupee, is derived from the Sanskrit word for cattle. Small clam shells (*wampum*) were used by the American Indians as money; cowerie shells have been used throughout the South Pacific. Bronze was used as money in ancient Egypt, Babylon, and China. That the weight of metals was used to determine monetary value is evidenced today by the British *pound*, a word derived from the Latin *pondus*, meaning weight, and the Italian *lira*, derived from the word *libra*, meaning balance and weight.

Coinage first appeared with the Aegean civilization of the eastern Mediterranean. The Aegeans marked metal to indicate weight and purity. Soon, the marked pieces began to be used in transactions. The Greek civilization refined this effort, establishing a system of coinage that was used throughout the eastern Mediterranean and Mideast, particularly following the conquests of Alexander the Great. Greek trade through Italy brought the custom to the western part of the Mediterranean and Europe. The use of coins was picked up by the Gauls and then by the Britons. Charlemagne imposed a monetary reform in coins during the eighth century: 1 pound equaled 20 shillings, which, in turn, equaled 240 pennies. This reformed monetary system lasted in France until the French Revolution and in Britain until the 1960s.

Paper money begins in China. It was light and easy to carry; it was also easy to divide into units ($1s, $5s, $10s, etc) that were convenient for transacting. As a consequence, over time, it came to dominate other forms of money.

Monetary aggregates. In a modern economy, currency and checking accounts are most often used in transactions.[3] Both are considered part of the money supply. Beyond that, determining what money is gets a little tricky. In particular, through financial institutions and brokerage firms, individuals can hold any of a large number of different kinds of deposits or accounts that can be drawn on with a check and used in transactions. In addition, it is relatively easy to shift a deposit from a savings account to a checking account. The Federal Reserve Board of the Federal Reserve System (which we will call from now on the Federal Reserve, or the Fed), an agency of the U.S. government, provides several measures of **monetary aggregates** that are estimates of what individuals and firms actually use in transactions. The narrowest monetary aggregate, **M1** (pronounced "*m*-one"), includes currency and checkable accounts as well as traveler's checks. Another measure, **M2** ("*m*-two"), is a slightly broader aggregate that includes everything in M1 plus small savings accounts (less than $100,000), accounts held by individuals with brokers that are backed by short-term securities known as money market accounts, dollar accounts held abroad (called Eurodollars), and financial contracts known as overnight repurchase agreements. A third monetary aggregate, **M3** ("*m*-three"), includes everything in M2 plus large savings accounts, accounts held by firms with brokers, and certain deposits that are made for longer periods of time. (Data on money aggregates and interest rates are available at *http://www.federalreserve.gov/rnd.htm*.)

There is no consensus about which measure best represents what is "money" in the US economy. Indeed, some disagreements about the direction for monetary policy occur because, at times, the different aggregates tell different stories about changes in the amount of money in the economy. Generally, however, these different measures move together so when we use the term *money* from now on, you should think of M1.

The Demand for Money

Money can also used to transfer income from the present to the future—all you have to do is hold a dollar earned today for a year and then spend it. Thus, money is both a medium of exchange and a *store of value*[4] or, as we have learned, since it can be used to transfer current income into the future, an **asset**. Money is nearly unique as a medium of exchange, but it is only one of many possible assets available in an economy.

In some ways money is inferior to other assets because the future purchasing power of money changes with changes in the price level. In addition, other assets generally earn higher rates of return. When there is inflation, for example, money that has been held for a rainy day purchases less. If you choose to hold a $1,000 bill for a year, at the end of the year you have a $1,000 bill whose purchasing power has changed with changes in the price level. (Because of this property, money is referred to as a **money-fixed** or **nominal asset**.) Most kinds of money-fixed assets pay interest which compensates the holder of the asset for his or her sacrifice of current consumption and for the loss in purchasing power due to *expected* inflation. If you deposit $1,000 in a bank account paying 8 percent interest, for example, if will yield $1,080 a year from now. However, money either pays *no* interest (currency) or *very little* interest (checking accounts). Holding a $1,000 bill for a year yields only the $1,000 bill. The interest rates on checking accounts are lower than on other assets.

Individuals do not need to hold money-fixed assets. Instead, they may choose to hold real assets. (A **real asset** is any asset whose purchasing power does not *necessarily* change with changes in the price level. Examples include real estate, corporate stocks, and gold.) Although the return on real assets fluctuates, over longer periods of time, they virtually always provide a greater rate of return than money-fixed assets do.

Then why hold money? The important advantage of money is that it can be used directly for transactions without any intermediate transactions. Indeed, money can be thought of as the one asset which is used directly in transactions. If individuals hold assets other than money, at some point these non-money assets must be sold for money in order to

---

[3] Of course, coins are also used. To keep the exposition simple, we will use *currency* to mean both paper money and coins.

[4] We discussed a third traditional use of money, as a *unit of account*, when we discussed using money as a measuring device for market or aggregate activity in the appendix to Chapter 17.

make purchases. If you own IBM stock, for example, it must be sold for money before you can purchase your groceries or pay your tuition. Or, if you have a savings account deposit or a bond, you must *liquidate* it, that is, sell it for money, in order to purchase other things.

Interest rates and the opportunity cost of holding money. The interest rate is the opportunity cost of holding money rather than other kinds of assets.

Figure 5
The Demand for Money

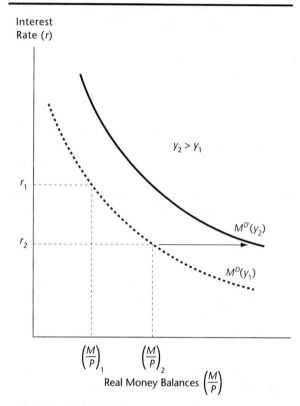

The interest rate is the opportunity cost of holding money as an asset rather than holding other assets that earn interest. The interest rate is shown along the vertical axis; real money balances are measured along the horizontal axis. That is, the quantity of money in the economy, *M*, is measured in terms of its purchasing power, *P*, where *P* is the price level. Because the interest rate is the opportunity cost of holding money, the quantity of money demanded increases as the interest rate falls from $(M/P)_1$ to $(M/P)_2$. In addition, because individuals use money in transactions, the demand for money increases from $M^D(y_1)$ to $M^{D'}(y_2)$ as aggregate real income increases, *ceteris paribus*, because, as aggregate income increases, so do the number of transactions.

Individuals will want to economize on money holdings when the interest rates (or other returns on non-money assets) are high relative to the rate earned (if any) on money. When they do, individuals will end up holding *more* non-money assets and *less* money. When interest rates or yields on other non-money assets are low relative to the interest earned (if any) on money, individuals will be willing to hold *more* money rather than transfer it into and then out of non-money assets.

For example, if a non-money asset is paying a return of 10 percent, then holding a dollar bill for one year has an opportunity cost of $.10. If the return on the asset increases to 15 percent, then the opportunity cost of holding a dollar bill for one year increases from $.10 to $.15. As the opportunity cost of holding money increases, individuals will want to hold less money. It follows that the **demand for money** is *inversely related to the interest rate*. More precisely, when the interest rate is higher, the quantity of money demanded is lower, *ceteris paribus*. Figure 5 illustrates this relationship.

A downward sloping market demand curve reflects *substitution*, remember. One asset, money, substitutes for other money-fixed or real assets that are not money. Because no other asset is a perfect substitute for money as a medium of exchange, the demand for money is not horizontal, but slopes downward in much the same manner as the demand for any other commodity for which there are no perfect substitutes.

Real money balances. The interest rate, which reflects the opportunity cost of holding money, is shown along the vertical axis in Figure 5. The quantity of money measured in terms of what a dollar will purchase, is shown along the horizontal axis. This measure, *M/P*, is called **real money balances**. Thus, Figure 5 indicates that the *demand for real money balances* is inversely related to the interest rate.

Note that real money balances can change either because the stock of money (*M*) changes, or because the price level (*P*) changes. For example, if the stock of money is $500 billion and the price level 100, an increase in the stock of money from $500 to $600 billion will increase real balances as long as the price level doesn't change. On the other hand, if the stock of money is $500 billion and the price level increases from 100 to 200, real balances fall, even though the stock of money hasn't changed.

Changes in output, transactions, and money demand. Since the principal reason that people hold money is to transact, the demand for money increases when the number of transactions in an economy increases. An economy with greater real output has more transactions. Therefore the demand for money is positively related to real output. That is, when real output increases, the quantity of money demanded at any given interest rate increases. This means that an increase in real output shifts the money demand curve to the right as illustrated in Figure 5.[5]

There is evidence that over longer periods of time, the demand for money increases *proportionally* with nominal aggregate output. To see why, we begin with an accounting relationship,

$$MV = Py \qquad (1)$$

Equation (1) is an identity that says that the dollar value of all transactions in the economy in a year (P times y) must equal the stock of money in the economy (M) multiplied by the number of times the stock of money circulates through the economy in a year, a number called **velocity (V).** To be concrete, suppose that nominal GDP is $10 trillion ($P \times$ real GDP) and the money stock (M) is $2 trillion. Because nominal GDP of $10 trillion measures the dollar value of market transactions in the economy in a given year and the amount of money used in those transactions is only $2 trillion, each dollar has to circulate five times through the economy over the course of the year on average. That is, each dollar bill buys five dollars of output over the course of a year and V equals 5.

Determinants of velocity. Anything that encourages individuals to economize on money holdings will increase the velocity. As a consequence, how many times an average dollar circulates depends in part on the frequency of wage payments and the efficiency of the payment mechanisms. The more frequently that wage payments are made, the more that individuals can economize on money holdings (that is, the more that individuals can hold other assets that pay higher rates of return) and the greater the velocity will be. To see this, suppose that you are

paid $3,000 per month and spend $100 per day. If you are paid on the first day of the month, then you need to hold money balances in order to make purchases on the last day of the month. If you keep your entire salary payment as money, your average holdings of money over the month would be $1,500. If you were paid each day, however, you wouldn't need to worry much about holding money balances because your employer gives you $100 each day. In this case, your money holdings would average only $100. It follows that velocity will decrease if people get paid less frequently and the same number of dollars circulates fewer times. Similarly, the more efficient the payment mechanisms in an economy, the more that individuals can economize on money holdings and the greater will be velocity.

Over shorter periods of time, velocity also depends upon the interest rate. This is just another way of saying that the quantity of money demanded depends upon the opportunity cost of holding money. In this case, Equation (1) is just a compact way of expressing the demand for money illustrated in Figure 5. Given a level of real output (y), the quantity of real balances demanded is inversely related to the interest rate. Given an interest rate (say, r_2 in Figure 5), the demand for real balances is positively related to the level of real output—the position of the money demand curve in Figure 5 will depend upon the number of transactions that individuals make in aggregate. The position of the curve will shift with changes in the number of transactions, including those associated with changes in real output. The elasticity of money demand with respect to the interest rate depends upon how well money substitutes for other assets as a store of value.

The interest rate, aggregate income, the price level, and the demand for money. Pulling the various components of the demand for money together, we have:

1. Individuals will want to hold less money when the interest rate is higher and more money when the interest rate is lower.

2. Individuals will want to hold more money when aggregate income is higher and less money when aggregate income is lower.

3. Individuals will want to hold more money when the price level is higher and less money when price level is lower. In other words,

when the price level changes, individuals will want to hold the same real balances, *ceteris paribus*, and, as a consequence, nominal money holdings will change with changes in the price level.

4. Individuals will want to hold more money when the average payment period is longer or when the payment system isn't very efficient.

The Supply of Money

Some history: During the Middle Ages, goldsmiths found they could earn a living by safeguarding the precious metals of the wealthy. Owners of gold who entrusted it to goldsmiths for safekeeping were given a certificate or receipt indicating their ownership of gold in the goldsmith's vault. Rather than returning to the goldsmiths to pick up their gold, the owners began to use the certificates to make payments as they purchased commodities. Hence, the receipts rather than the gold began to circulate. (Because the receipts rather than the gold itself were used in transactions, the receipts became money.)

Soon goldsmiths realized that because much of the gold was never withdrawn, they could earn an even better living by making loans in the form of additional receipts against the gold they were holding, thereby maintaining only a *fraction* of the total value of the receipts as gold in their vaults to cover actual withdrawals. At this point, of course, the gold certificates in circulation had only fractional backing by gold. With only fractional backing, a goldsmith would not be able to honor all outstanding gold certificates he had issued, but, because most individuals preferred to transact using gold certificates rather than redeeming them for gold, it really wasn't as risky as it might seem as long as the goldsmith's reputation for honoring gold certificates with gold was good.

Now back to the main story: The U.S. government has a legal monopoly on minting coins and printing currency. However, most of what we use as money is created by banks, not by the Federal Reserve. For example, at the end of 2001, M1 was $1.2 trillion, but the amount of currency in circulation was only $580 billion. Why the difference? The short answer is that banks issue checking accounts and people use checks as money in many circumstances. This reliance on checks means that *if banks*

hold reserves against only a fraction of the checking deposits they issue, then most of the money in the US economy is created by private banks, not by the Federal Reserve.

Suppose, for example, that the Federal Reserve prints a $1,000 bill and gives it to you. The money supply has certainly increased by at least $1,000. If you deposit the $1000 bill in your checking account, the money supply will increase further, for the following reason:

When you deposit the $1,000 in your bank, you now have a demand deposit (that is, checking account) with a $1,000 balance. That is, your bank owes you $1,000 on demand. Your bank has $1,000 in currency in its vault. The table below illustrates this transaction using a **T-account**.[6]

Your Bank

Assets	Liabilities
$1,000 currency in vault	$1,000 checking account

Because you use your checking account in much the same way that you use currency, from your perspective, you still have an additional $1,000 in money—you're simply holding it as a checking account rather than as a $1,000 bill. Long ago, banks learned something from goldsmiths: Individuals are unlikely to write checks for the full balance in their checking accounts immediately after making a deposit or, in fact, on any single banking day. Therefore, your bank need only keep a *fraction* of your $1,000 on reserve in its vault in order to honor checks you might write in the immediate future. Based on experience, for example, your bank might have found that individuals draw no more than $200 for each $1,000 deposited on any given day. As a consequence, your bank will keep only $200 on reserve against your account and will lend the remaining $800 to someone seeking to borrow money. The following table illustrates your bank's financial position after it loaned this money.

---

[6] A T-account is a simplified way of looking at the holdings of a financial institution such as a bank. The T-account compares claims against the bank, called *liabilities*, and bank claims against others, called *assets*. Rather than listing *all* assets and liabilities (a **balance sheet**), a T-account includes only assets and liabilities *that change*.

Your Bank

Assets	Liabilities
$200 currency in vault $800 loan	$1,000 checking account

If the $800 borrowed from your bank—this discussion assumes that the loan was made in the form of currency—is spent immediately, it generally ends up in someone else's checking account. The borrower might pay tuition, for example, and upon receipt of the payment, the university might deposit the $800 in its checking account. Or, if the borrower doesn't spend the $800 immediately, he or she is likely to deposit it in a checking account so that it can be used when needed. In either event, when the $800 is deposited in another checking account, the money supply increases by an additional $800. Why? The answer is straightforward: People use checks to transact and someone else's checking account now shows an additional $800 on deposit. That is, someone else's bank is in the following position:

Someone Else's Bank

Assets	Liabilities
$800 currency in vault	$800 checking account

At this point, the story repeats itself: Based on experience, the bank where the $800 was deposited, finds that it needs to keep only a fraction of the deposit in its vault in order to honor checks drawn on the account. Hence, it will not keep the $800 on deposit but will keep only a fraction. The rest of the $800 will be lent to someone who has come to this bank to borrow money. If someone else's bank, like your bank, keeps 20 percent on deposit, it will put $160 in its vault and loan out $640. Someone else's bank is now in the following position:

Someone Else's Bank

Assets	Liabilities
$160 currency in vault $640 loan	$800 checking account

When the second borrower purchases something with the $640 loan and the seller deposits the $640 in his or her checking account, checking account deposits once again increase, this time by $640, illustrated as follows:

Third Person's Bank

Assets	Liabilities
$640 currency in vault	$640 checking account

Where are we now? Add up the changes in the checking account balances in the economy that result from the Fed's $1,000 gift to you. You have an additional $1,000 in your checking account; someone else has an additional $800 in his or her checking account; a third person has an additional $640 in his or her checking account. Thus, at this point, the money supply has increased not by $1,000 but by $2,440 ($1,000 + $800 + $640). *And* the story hasn't ended. If, *in each case,* the borrower or anyone who sells something to the borrower deposits the *full* amount borrowed in his or her checking account and each bank holds 20 percent of the amount deposited in reserve, the money supply will increase in the manner illustrated in Table 1.

The money multiplier. Because of the Fed's action, the money supply increases by the total of the second column in Table 1:

$1,000 + $800 + $640 + $512 + $409.60 + \ldots,$

**Table 1
Bank Creation of Money**

	Checking account deposit	Increase in bank reserves	Cumulative increase in money supply
Person 1	$1,000.00	$200.00	$1,000.00
Person 2	800.00	160.00	1,800.00
Person 3	640.00	128.00	2,440.00
Person 4	512.00	102.40	2,952.00
Person 5	409.60	81.92	3,361.60
.	.	.	.
.	.	.	.
.	.	.	.

or, factoring out $1,000, we have

$$\$1,000\ (1 + 0.8 + 0.8^2 + 0.8^3 + \\ 0.8^4 + 0.8^5 + 0.8^6 + \ldots).$$

The numbers inside of the parentheses form a geometric series that, for a long series—that is, for repeated loans and subsequent deposits in checking accounts

$$1+0.8+0.8^2+0.8^3+0.8^4+0.8^5+0.8^6+\ldots = \frac{1}{1-0.8} = 5.0$$

The result? The increase of $1,000 in currency leads to an increase in the money supply of

$$\$1,000 \times \frac{1}{1-0.8} = \$1,000 \times 5 = \$5,000$$

if individuals *always* deposit *all* currency in their checking accounts. Note that $(1 - 0.8)$ is equal to the fraction of each dollar deposited that each bank holds in reserve, that is, 20 percent or 0.2.

More generally, the change in the nominal money supply, ΔMs, caused by a change in currency is:

$$\Delta M^s = \Delta \text{currency} \times \\ \frac{1}{\text{fraction held as reserves by banks}} \quad (2)$$

if the fraction of each checking account deposit held in reserve is the same for all banks. In Equation (2), "1/fraction held as reserves" is called the **potential money multiplier**.

A caution. The algebraic mechanics for the money multiplier are the same as those for the aggregate-demand multipliers developed in Chapters 20 and 21, but it is important not to confuse the money multiplier with these aggregate demand multipliers. The money multiplier indicates the *maximum amount* by which the *money supply* can increase when additional currency is introduced into the economy by the Federal Reserve. The aggregate-demand multipliers are the *maximum amount* by which *aggregate demand* shifts when desired investment, net exports, government spending, or government taxation changes.

Bank reserves and the money multiplier. If each person uses only checks for transactions, the $1,000 in currency printed by the government and put into circulation must end up as bank reserves against

checking accounts. That is, if everyone uses checks, all loans are either immediately deposited in the borrowers' checking accounts or else they are spent and deposited in sellers' checking accounts. Then if each bank holds reserves equal to 20 percent of the new checking account deposits, the $1,000 in currency the Fed introduced will serve as reserves for $5,000 in *new* checking accounts across the entire banking system (because 0.2 x $5,000 in checking accounts equals $1,000 in reserves). The consolidated T-account for change in assets and liabilities for the banking system as a whole is as follows:

Consolidated Accounting for the Banking System

Assets	Liabilities
$1,000 currency on reserve $4,000 loans	$5,000 demand deposits

Because of fractional-reserve banking, most of what we think of as money is created not by the Fed, but by banks. The extent to which the economy relies on checking account balances as money can be understood easily by imagining what would happen if *every* person in the U.S. simultaneously decided that the banking system was in trouble and tried to withdraw *all* funds from his or her checking account. Because no bank actually has enough currency on reserve to simultaneously honor every checking account claim, the banking system would collapse. The banking system creates money because at any moment, only a *small* fraction of all checking account deposits is used by individuals to make payments. Put differently, a large fraction of all deposits is held as a asset, transferring current income and the ability to consume into the future, be it tomorrow, next week, or next month.

Incentives to make loans. Why do banks lend money that has been deposited in checking accounts? The answer: To earn interest income, and thus profits. While currency sitting in a vault provides reserves against withdrawals, it does not earn any interest income for a bank. Loans do. Consequently, banks have an incentive to move currency out of their vaults and into loans. However, the incentives for banks to make loans from deposits will be affected by the interest rate they can earn on loans, among other things. That is, holding an extra

Figure 6
The Supply of Money

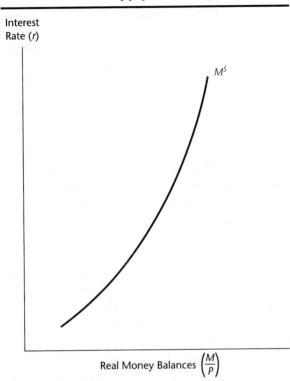

The supply of money in the economy will increase as interest rates increase. Banks create most of the money in the economy by offering checking accounts, but they hold only a fraction of the amount deposited in reserve and lend the remainder. Banks have a greater incentive to make loans when interest rates are high, so the supply of money in the economy will increase somewhat as interest rates rise.

dollar in the vault is less costly to a bank when the interest rate on loans is 3 percent than it is when the interest rate on loans is 15 percent. As a consequence, the willingness of banks to make loans will depend upon the interest income that they expect to receive from loans. As the interest rates on loans increase, banks hold fewer reserves and the money supply increases. Figure 6 illustrates a possible supply curve for money consistent with this discussion.

The money multiplier as a practical matter. Equation (2) is called the *potential* money multiplier because it gives the *maximum* possible increase in the money supply. The actual money multiplier for the US economy depends on three things.

1. How much currency individuals hold. In the above example, if any person fails to deposit

the currency in a checking account, the sequence stops.[7] If the government gave you the $1,000 bill and you put it under your mattress, the money supply would increase by only $1,000, not by $5,000. Or, if you made a deposit of only $800 and kept $200 in your pocket, the money supply would increase by less than $5,000 because less is available to be loaned.

2. How much "excess" reserves banks hold. If any bank fails to loan out 80 percent of its deposits, the amount of checking accounts given the $1,000 increase in currency will be smaller and, hence, the money supply will be smaller as well even if everyone always deposits all money in their checking accounts.

3. The demand for and supply of loans.

For a number of years, the actual money multiplier for M1 has been somewhat above 3.0.

► Federal Reserve Control of the Money Supply

In the United States, the Federal Reserve controls the creation of money by banks in three different ways:

1. The Federal Reserve sets the *minimum* legal reserve requirement.

2. The Federal Reserve stands willing to loan reserves to banks, but it alone determines the interest rates that banks must pay if they borrow reserves from it. That is, the Fed sets the discount rate.

3. The Federal Reserve engages in open market operations, thereby affecting the amount of currency in the economy.

The Reserve Requirement

Consider once again the fate of the $1,000 bill we assumed the Fed gave you. If banks held 25 percent rather than 20 percent of the deposits that individuals made to their checking accounts in reserve, a $1,000 bill added to the economy would lead to a

---

[7] Holding currency rather than depositing it in a checking account is referred to as a **leakage**.

maximum increase in the money supply of $4,000 rather than $5,000 ($1,000 × 1/0.25 versus $1,000 × 1/0.2). Or, if banks held 10 percent, a $1,000 bill added to the economy would lead to a maximum increase in the money supply of $10,000 ($1,000 × 1/0.1). Clearly, the Fed can regulate the money supply if it regulates the fraction of checking account deposits that banks are required to hold as reserves. And it does. The Fed has been given the legal power to regulate the *minimum* fraction of deposits that banks must hold. This regulation is called the **reserve requirement (RR)**. Banks are free to hold more reserves against each deposit than required by the Fed if they choose, but they cannot legally hold fewer than those required by the Fed. (**Excess reserves**, that is, reserves in excess of the legal requirement are actually very small.)

Using the potential money multiplier formula, it should be clear that when the Fed prints and puts into circulation an additional $1,000 bill, the maximum amount the money supply can increase is 1/*RR*. Most recently, the reserve requirement on demand deposits has been 10 percent. Since the 1960s, it has generally been between 10 and 18 percent, as indicated in Figure 7. (You can find current and historical data on reserve requirements, M1 and related measures of money at *http://www.federalreserve.gov/rnd.htm* .)

Until now, you may have assumed that the government could only create money by printing it. However, we have just learned that the Fed can increase the money supply by simply *decreasing the reserve requirement* or it can decrease the money supply by *increasing the reserve requirement*. Changing the reserve requirement changes the money supply *without the government having to print a thing.* Suppose, for example, that the banking system has $10 million in currency held as reserves and checking accounts equal to $50 million (in other words, the banking system is holding 20 percent reserves against the checking accounts). If the Fed lowers the reserve requirement from 20 percent to 15 percent, banks in the system would be required to hold only $7.5 million in reserves against $50 million in checking accounts. As a consequence, of this change in the legal reserve requirement, that banking system now has $2.5 million in excess, noninterest-earning reserves that can be loaned out in order to generate

Figure 7
Bank Reserve Requirements

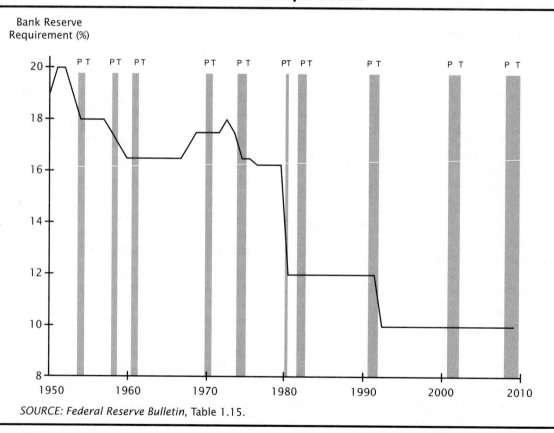

SOURCE: *Federal Reserve Bulletin*, Table 1.15.

additional interest income. Banks are not required to make loans, but profit incentives will generally lead them to loan all or part of their excess reserves. As they do, deposits in checking accounts will increase. In the end, as long as there is no leakage and banks hold only 15 percent against demand deposits, the banking system would end up with the same $10 million in reserves, but checking accounts would total $67 million. That is, with a reserve requirement of 0.15, the banking system could have $67 million in checking accounts if it had $10 million in reserves, in contrast with $50 million in allowable checking accounts when the reserve requirement is 0.20. Notice that the money supply increases by about $17 million, or $2.5 × 1/RR—the excess reserves multiplied by the money multiplier. Notice also that the Fed hasn't printed a single new dollar.

On the other hand, if the bank had $10 million in reserves and the Fed increased the reserve requirement from 0.20 to 0.25, the legal reserves would have to be $12.5 million against the $50 million in checking accounts (0.25 x $50 million). Total reserves in the banking system are only $10 million, so some (or perhaps all) banks would be short of the legal requirement. Banks who find themselves short on reserves under the new regulations would have to call in some loans, limit the number of new loans made, and use payments on current loans and any additional deposits to checking accounts to build up their reserves to meet the legal requirement. As banks make fewer loans, checking accounts across the banking system would decrease and the money supply would decrease as a consequence. What would happen after the banking system had fully adjusted to the Fed's change in the legal reserve requirement? Checking account balances would have fallen from $50 million to $40 million because the $10 million in currency can serve as reserves for only $40 million in checking accounts when the reserve requirement is 0.25.

What is the effect of these changes in the Fed's reserve requirement? As Figure 8 illustrates, an increase in the reserve requirement decreases the money supply, thereby increasing the interest rates, *ceteris paribus*. That is, because real balances have fallen, the interest rate in the economy must increase in order to induce individuals to hold more non-money assets—a movement back along the demand for money curve. Conversely, a decrease in the

Figure 8
Changes in the Reserve Requirement

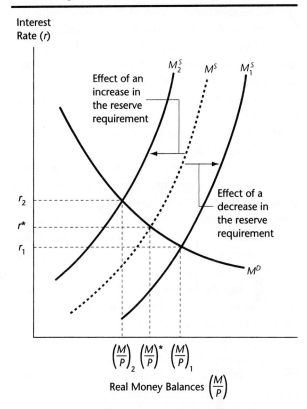

An increase in the reserve requirement will decrease the money supply from M^S to M_2^S and consequently increase interest rates. A decrease in the reserve requirement will have the opposite effect, increasing the money supply from M^S to M_1^S and lowering interest rates.

reserve requirement increases the money supply; interest rates will fall as a consequence as individuals hold fewer nonmoney assets and more money—a movement down along the demand for money curve.

Reserve Loans and the Discount Rate

The revenues and profitability of banks depend upon loaning deposited money to borrowers. As a consequence, most banks have reserves quite close to the Fed's legal reserve requirement. The number of checks a bank receives each day is not under its control, however. You, your friends, and others who have checking accounts with your bank determine how many checks the bank must honor each day, not the bank. Hence, as you might guess, the number of checks drawn on accounts at a bank will fluctuate day by day. This means that the *actual* reserves a bank has against its checking accounts will also fluctuate day by day. Banks that are close to the legal reserve requirement may find themselves with too few reserves if more checks than expected are written on a particular day, or they may find themselves with excess reserves if fewer checks than expected are written on a particular day. If a bank is short of reserves, it can borrow from the Fed to remain in compliance with the legal requirement. A bank borrowing from the Fed must pay interest on the Fed's loan of reserves, however.

In addition to setting the legal reserve requirement, the Fed attempts to control the money supply be setting the cost to banks of borrowing reserves. The interest rate that the Fed charges on loans to cover reserve shortfalls by banks is called the **rediscount interest rate** or, more commonly, the **discount rate (r_d)**.

By changing the discount rate, the Fed provides incentives for banks to be more cautious or less cautious in meeting the legal reserve requirement. If the Fed wants to encourage a small increase in the money supply but does not want to change the reserve requirement, for example, it can charge a low discount rate. If the interest rates at which banks can make loans are high, a low discount rate may make it attractive for them to make additional loans and cover reserve shortages by borrowing from the Fed. That is, banks would be less cautious about meeting the reserve requirement because they would be more willing to borrow reserves from the Fed to meet any shortfall since the costs of doing so are low. On the other hand, if the Fed wants to decrease the money supply by a small amount, it can charge a high discount rate. Banks then have an incentive to keep extra reserves to meet the legal requirement so that they do not have to borrow from the Fed if the number of checks written on a particular day is larger than they expected. That is, banks will want to minimize their exposure when the cost of reserve loans is high relative to the earnings on any loans that they might make to individuals.

If excess reserves are close to or even below zero—that is, banks are close to or below the legal reserve requirement—the money supply is larger than it would be if they held larger excess reserves. For example, suppose that banks have $80 million in reserves and the legal reserve requirement is 0.2. If all banks were holding only the legal minimum, the money supply would be $400 million. If banks were holding only 18 percent of their deposits in reserves

and borrowing from the Fed to cover the shortfall because the discount rate was low relative to interest rates on loans, the money supply would be about $444 million ($80 million/0.18). Or if, because of a high discount rate relative to the interest rates on loans, banks held 21 percent of their deposits in reserves, the money supply would be about $381 million ($80 million/0.21). Hence, the Fed can affect the money supply by making it either more costly or less costly for banks to be slightly above or below the reserve requirement.

As with changes in the reserve requirement, changing the discount rate also changes money supply without actually changing the amount of coins or currency in circulation. Instead, the Fed's discount rate policy changes the amount of demand deposits, *given* a particular level of currency in the economy.

The recent history of discount-rate changes is provided in Figure 9a. Not surprisingly, changing the discount rate on the money market has an effect similar to that of changing the reserve requirement. When the money supply decreases, for example, the interest rate in the economy will increase in order to bring the quantity of real balances demanded into line with the quantity of real balances available in the economy. Figure 10 illustrates these effects.

The federal funds market. Banks are not limited to borrowing from the Fed when they fall short of reserves. They can also borrow from other banks that happen to have excess reserves. Because the amount deposited, and the number of checks drawn on a bank, will fluctuate from day to day, on any given day some banks will find that their reserves are short of the legal requirement, while other banks find that they have money in their vaults in excess of their reserve requirement that is earning no interest income. These day-by-day outcomes create a large, active *private* market for reserve loans among banks market called the **federal funds market**.

The federal funds market is a little unusual in that most of the loans are for a very short period of time, frequently extending for only one night. By borrowing overnight, a bank ends one banking day and begins a new banking day with the legally required reserves. For example, suppose that your local bank finds itself $1 million short of reserves after it locks up this afternoon. If it can find another bank that has at least $1 million in excess reserves, it can negotiate an overnight loan. After the loan has

Figure 9a
Federal Reserve Discount Rate

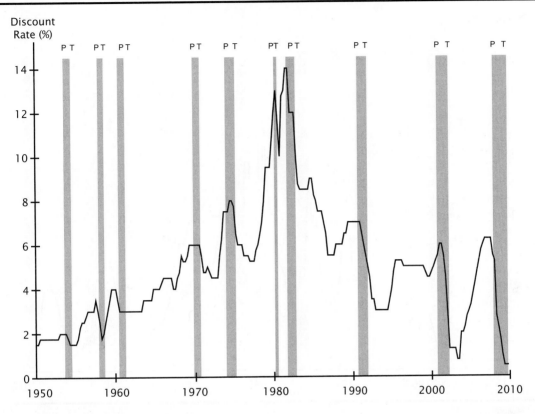

SOURCE: Federal Reserve Bulletin, Table 1.14.

been made, both banks meet the legal requirement for that day. On the next day, the loan is repaid.

The market for federal funds is just like any other market. There are demanders who wish to purchase something (in this case borrow) and suppliers who wish to provide something (in this case lend). Moreover, just as in any market, there is a market equilibrium price. For the federal funds market, the market price for overnight loans is the **federal funds interest rate** or **federal funds rate**, for short. This interest rate changes each day because each day different banks find that have excess reserves while other banks find that they are short of the legally required reserves and, hence, the excess reserves and reserve shortfalls across the banking system vary from day to day. Figure 9b illustrates these movements in the Federal Funds rate.

Because of this private market for reserves, demanders (banks that are short of reserves) no longer have to go to the Fed, and suppliers (banks with excess reserves) no longer have to sit with non-interest earning reserves. As a consequence, banks

usually borrow from the Fed only as a last resort. That is, most reserve shortfalls are met in the federal funds market and not by banks borrowing from the Fed.

Since a bank always has the option of borrowing from the Fed at the specified discount rate, the federal funds rate tends to fluctuate near the level of the discount rate. That is, borrowing from the Fed is a very good substitute for borrowing from banks and, therefore, the federal funds rate cannot differ much from the discount rate. Borrowing in the federal funds market and borrowing from the Fed are not perfect substitutes, however. The Fed looks at borrowing as a privilege, not a right, and banks are not allowed to borrow from the Fed continually. (You can get current and historical federal funds market data at *http://www.federalreserve.gov/rnd.htm* .)

Open Market Operations

The third policy option for the Fed should be obvious: the Fed can change the money supply by changing the amount of currency in circulation. The Fed changes the amount of currency in circulation

Figure 9b
Effective Federal Funds Rate

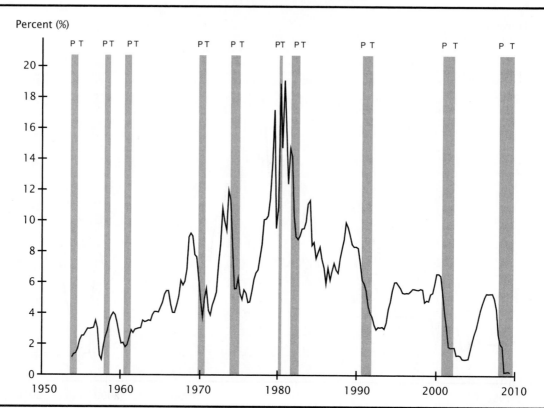

through an **open market operation**, its most frequently used method for changing the money supply.

In an open market operation, the Fed buys or sells U.S. government bonds. These obligations, called Treasury bills (T-bills) or Treasury bonds (T-bonds), are issued by the U.S. Treasury in order to fund federal government deficits—a matter that we explore in Chapter 25. T-bills and T-bonds trade actively. Anyone is free to buy or sell T-bills and T-bonds through a broker, hence the name, *open market*.

An open market purchases. When the Fed wants to increase the amount of currency in circulation, it takes currency from its vault and purchases T-bills from private agents in the open market. (The currency is in the vault because the Fed prints it.) These agents now have currency instead of bonds. For example, if you owned a $1,000 T-bill and sold it to the Fed, after the sale you would have $1,000 in currency. The Fed, on the other hand, would have an additional bond in its vault and $1,000 less currency. Immediately following the Fed's purchase, the money supply increases by $1,000.[8] The following tables summarize this transaction from the perspectives of the Fed, you, and your bank.

Federal Reserve

Assets	Liabilities
+ $1,000 T-bill	+ $1,000 currency

You

Assets	Liabilities
+ $1,000 currency − 1,000 T-bill	

Your Bank

Assets	Liabilities
+ $1,000 currency in vault	+ $1,000 checking account deposit

---

[8] Actually the Fed pays by check and then credits the bank where you make your deposit with $1,000 in additional reserves when the check is presented for payment. Because of this, it may be that all that changes are the account balances at banks. From your perspective, and that of your bank, however, it is as if the Fed paid with $1,000 in currency. As a consequence, the technical details of the payment mechanism are not important.

Figure 10
Changes in the Discount Rate

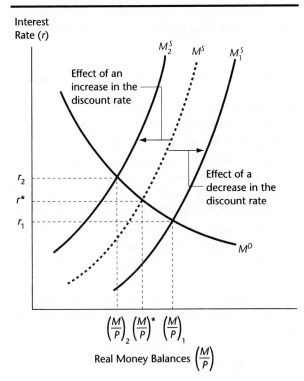

An increase in the discount rate will decrease the money supply from M^S to M_2^S and consequently increase interest rates. A decrease in the discount rate will have the opposite effect, increasing the money supply from M^S to M_1^S and lowering interest rates.

Figure 11
Open Market Operations and the Money Supply

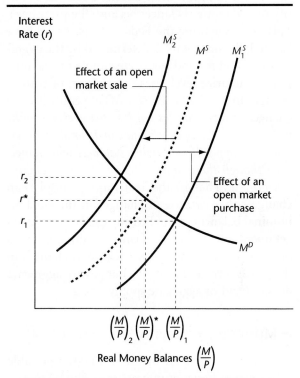

An open market sale will decrease the money supply from M^S to M_2^S and consequently increase interest rates. An open market purchase will have the opposite effect, increasing the money supply from M^S to M_1^S and lowering interest rates.

When you deposit the $1,000 in your checking account, banks begin the process of creating money by making loans, as described earlier. The money supply will increase by some multiple of the $1,000. For example, if the reserve requirement is 0.2, the $1,000 T-bill purchase by the Fed could result in as much as a $5,000 increase in the money supply after the banking system had fully adjusted. Thus, *a purchase of bonds in the open market by the Fed increases the money supply, generally by some multiple of the dollar value of the bonds purchased.*

An open market sale. If the Fed wants to decrease the money supply, it takes a $1,000 T-bill from its vault and sells it on the open market. (The T-bill is in the vault because the Fed purchased it at some earlier date—the Fed does *not* print T-bills.) A person who purchases the T-bill has to pay with either $1,000 in currency or a $1,000 check. If the payment is made with a check, the reserves of some bank fall by $1,000.

That is, the banking system loses $1,000 in reserves. If the reserve requirement is 0.2, the $1,000 decrease in reserves leads to a decrease in the money supply of as much as $5,000 as banks make fewer loans in order to increase their reserves by $1,000. As a consequence, *a sale of bonds in the open market by the Fed decreases the money supply, generally by some multiple of the dollar value of the bonds sold.* The effects of open market operations are illustrated in Figure 11.

Nominal Versus Real Money Balances

This discussion of money creation has been a bit ambiguous in its use of the term *money supply.* Each of the graphical representations of the money market implies that the important elements are the demand and supply for *real money balances* (M/P). However, our discussion of the money supply has only focused on changes in nominal money balances, M, not on real money balances, M/P. This is because the Fed can directly affect only the quantity of *nominal* money balances, or stock of money, in the economy. It cannot directly affect the quantity of *real* money balances because the price level, P, is not something the Fed controls. As we have learned, the price level is determined by the aggregate demand for and aggregate supply of real output. If the price level does not change, of course, changes in nominal balances (M) are equivalent to changes in real balances (M/P). However, *when the price level changes, either because of deflation or inflation, the supply of real money balances will change, even though the nominal stock of money remains unchanged.* That is, the real money supply can change either because of changes in the stock of nominal balances as the Fed engages in open market operations (or makes changes in discount rates or reserve requirements) *or* because of changes in the price level because of changes in aggregate demand and/or aggregate supply.

▶ Monetary Policy: A First Look

We began this chapter by examining the possible relationships between interest rates and aggregate demand. We noted that changes in interest rates affect aggregate demand primarily through changes in desired investment—as interest rates fall, desired investment increases and, therefore, aggregate demand increases. (Remember, however, that interest rates may also affect desired consumption and net exports.) We next examined the relationship between the demand for money and interest rates and found that the demand for money was inversely related to the interest rate—as returns on non-money assets increase, the quantity of real balances demanded decreases. We then examined the relationship between three policy instruments under control of the Federal Reserve and the nominal money supply and found that the Fed can affect the money supply in one of three ways: (1) by engaging in open market operations, (2) by changing the discount rate on reserve loans, or (3) by changing the reserve requirement.

It should be clear where this argument is heading: *The Fed can affect aggregate demand and hence real output by changing the amount of money in the economy.* As the Fed changes the nominal money supply, *ceteris paribus*, interest rates will change. When interest rates change, desired investment and other interest sensitive components of aggregate demand change. When desired investment changes, aggregate demand changes. When aggregate demand changes, real output changes in the short run, and the price level changes in both the short and long run.

The Effect of an Open Market Purchase

If the Fed purchases bonds on the open market, for example, the money supply increases by a multiple of the size of the purchase (because of the money multiplier), as shown in Figure 12.

The increase in the money supply reduces the interest rate from r_1 to r_2, as indicated in part (a). The lower interest rate stimulates investment and the rate at which new capital is acquired increases, as illustrated by the movement from i_1 to i_2 in part (b). An increased level of investment shifts aggregate demand by some multiple of the change in desired investment (because of the investment multiplier), as illustrated by the shift from AD_1 to AD_2 in part (c).

As the price level begins to increase, real output also increases if nominal wages are sticky. That is, as the price level begins to increase, employment increases, and consequently, real output increase from y^* to y_1. As nominal wages adjust fully to the price-level changes, however, employment declines toward its previous equilibrium level and real output declines from y_1 toward *potential* or *full employment* real output, y^*. When the economy has completely adjusted, the price level will have increased from P^* to P^{**}, but real output will be unaffected by the increase in the money supply. Nominal wages will have increased by the same proportion as the price level, and the real wage will be the same as it was prior to the change in the price level. Labor resources will be fully employed.

A decrease in the discount rate or reserve requirement leads to similar adjustments. Thus, *an open market purchase, a decrease in the discount rate, or a decrease in the reserve requirement will each increase the money supply, thereby decreasing interest rates, thereby increasing aggregate demand.*

The Effect of an Open Market Sale

If the Fed decreases the money supply by selling T-bills in the open market, the nominal money supply will decline. This effect is illustrated in Figure 13. Interest rates will increase. As a consequence of the increase in interest rates [from r_1 to r_2 in part (a)],

Figure 12
Effect of an Open Market Purchase

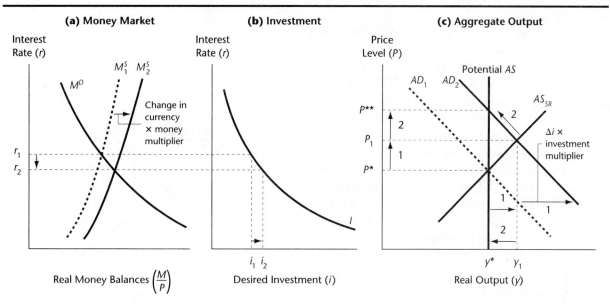

An open market purchase increases the currency in circulation. If there is no leakage, the supply of nominal balances will increase by the change in currency multiplied by the money multiplier ($1/RR$). Interest rates will decrease as a consequence, making investment more profitable. The amount of investment that firms, in aggregate, wish to make then increases. An increase in aggregate investment increases aggregate demand by the change in investment multiplied by the investment multiplier [$1/(1-MPC)$ in the simplest case]. As a consequence, the price level begins to increase and real output increases in the short term. Note that the change from i_1 to i_2 in part (b) is equal to Δi in part (c).

Figure 13
Effect of an Open Market Sale

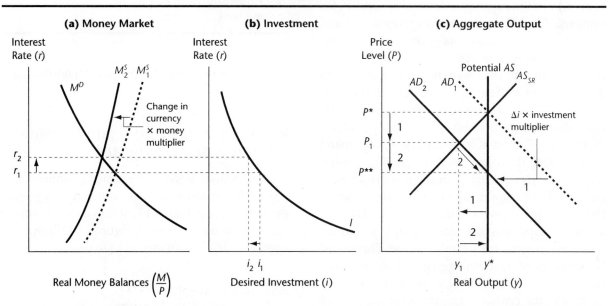

An open market sale decreased the currency in circulation. The supply of nominal balances will decrease by the change in currency multiplied by the money multiplier ($1/RR$). Interest rates will increase as a consequence, making investment less profitable. The amount of investment that firms, in aggregate, wish to make then decreases. A decrease in aggregate investment decreases aggregate demand by the change in investment multiplied by the investment multiplier [$1/(1-MPC)$ in the simplest case]. As a consequence, the price level begins to decrease and real output decreases somewhat in the short term. Note that the change from i_1 to i_2 in part (b) is equal to Δi in part (c).

investment will decreases [from i_1 to i_2 in part (b)]. Aggregate demand will fall from AD_1 to AD_2 [as indicated in part (c)].

If nominal wages or prices are sticky, the decrease in aggregate demand will lead to a short-run increase in unemployment. With fewer persons employed, real output must decline. This effect is illustrated by the movement from y^* to y_1 in part (c). Because resources are unemployed, however, adjustment in the economy will continue. In the long run, nominal wages will fall and the employment of labor will increase. At the new long-run equilibrium, the price level will have declined from P^* to P^{**} and the economy will be producing at its potential, y^*, with full employment in the labor market. Nominal wages will have fallen by the same proportion as the price level declined, of course, and the real wage will be the same as it was prior to the change in the money supply.

To recap, *an open market sale, an increase in the discount rate, or an increase in the reserve requirement will each decrease the money supply, causing the interest rates to rise, thereby leading to a decrease in aggregate demand.*

Countercyclical or Stabilization Policies

It would be silly, of course, for the government to willy-nilly bounce aggregate demand around. If, for some reason there was an adverse aggregate demand shock, however, monetary policy could, in principle, be used to move the economy back toward full employment instead of waiting for the economy to adjust on its own. If aggregate demand fell from AD to AD' in Figure 14 because of a change in expectations about the profitability of new investment, for example, the Fed could stimulate aggregate demand by increasing the money supply. Specifically what might it do? It could engage in an open market purchase of T-bills, lower the discount rate, or lower the reserve requirement. If the Fed pursued any (or all) of these policies, the money supply would increase and interest rates would decline. This would stimulate investment, and aggregate demand would increase. (See Figure 12.) As aggregate demand increased, the economy would adjust toward full employment, moving toward y^* in Figure 14, but at price level P^*. Because the price level does not fall following the aggregate demand shock, nominal wages would not have to adjust (it won't matter if wages are sticky), and the labor market can move

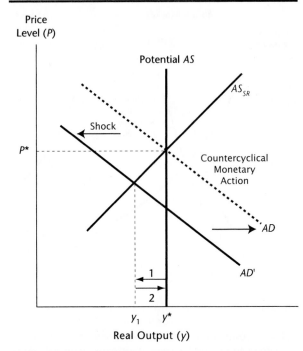

Figure 14
Effective Countercyclical Monetary Policy

If aggregate demand falls either because firms want to invest less or because individuals want to save more, the government can pursue monetary policies that will reduce interest rates (by an open market purchase, lowering the discount rate, or lowering the reserve requirement). This policy will increase investment, causing aggregate demand to increase and thus return to its original level.

toward full employment at the original nominal and real wages.

▶ Why Does the Aggregate Demand Curve Slope Downward?

The phenomenon we are interested in understanding is the movement back along the aggregate demand curve in Figure 12, or downward along the aggregate demand curve in Figure 13, following an aggregate-demand change in each case.

Assets and Wealth

If an individual purchases a bond for $1,000, that person gives up $1,000 in current consumption for the additional future consumption provided by the interest payments from the bond, and the repayment of the $1,000 when the bond is redeemed.

Similarly, if a piece of land sells for $1,000, an individual purchasing it would give up $1,000 in current consumption for the additional future consumption associated with the price at which he or she could sell it at some future date. The important difference between these two kinds of assets is that a bond is a money-fixed asset whereas the land is a real asset. That is, owning the bond means that the individual will receive a payment of a *fixed amount* of money at some point in the future, but owning the land means that the individual will receive whatever the land sells for when he or she chooses to sell. With money-fixed assets, how much you can consume a year from now depends upon the purchasing power of the dollar. If the price level has increased substantially, you will be able to purchase far fewer goods than you gave up. If the price level doubles, for example, a $1,000 bill will purchase half as much a year from now as it would purchase today. But if you purchase a piece of land for $1,000, its value a year from now is not fixed in dollar terms. If the price level doubles the price of land may very well double, from $1,000 to $2,000, in which case the $1,000 in income you gave up this year would grow in nominal value so that it would have the same purchasing power a year from now. Of course, the price of land may also decrease, or increase but not by as much as the price-level changes. In either of these events, your sacrifice of $1,000 in consumption today would lead to less than $1,000 of consumption when you sell the land in the future. *Real assets do not guarantee constant purchasing power through time, but the purchasing power of the asset does not necessarily decline as the price level increases (or increase as the price level decreases).*

The total value of all assets that an individual holds constitutes his or her **wealth**. The amount of wealth changes as individuals save, thereby accumulating assets, or as they dissave, thereby selling assets. It also changes, as we have just seen, when the price level changes because some of the assets are fixed in money terms.

Wealth, Consumption, and Induced Price-Level Effects

Individuals with more wealth generally consume more. To make this example more concrete, suppose that each of two individuals had an annual income of $25,000, but one individual had no wealth whereas the second had assets worth $500,000; we would expect the second person to consume more than the first.

Real wealth changes when the price level changes. Indeed, because of the enormous value of money-fixed assets in the US economy (around $8 trillion), a small change in the price level will change real wealth by a substantial amount. For example, a 1 percent decrease in the price level will increase aggregate wealth by $80 billion. By contrast, when the price level increases, the value of money-fixed assets decreases, making individuals poorer. Consumption decreases as a consequence. A change in consumption, of course, changes aggregate demand. Because the change in consumption is *induced by a change in the price level,* the change in real output demanded corresponds to a movement *along* a given aggregate demand curve. We have learned, then, that the aggregate demand curve slopes downward and to the right, in part because of changes in consumption that occur because of change in wealth that, in turn, occur because of price-level changes. Put differently:

↑ price level
  leads to a ↓ wealth
    which leads to a ↓ consumption
      which leads to a ↓ aggregate real output demanded

Real Balances, Interest Rates, Investment, and Induced Price-Level Effects

Real balances (M/P) are also affected by changes in the price level. The Fed does not control the *real* money stock, remember, but only the nominal money stock, M. If the nominal money stock does not change, but the price level increases, the real money stock (real money balances) decreases. In Figure 15, for example, an increase in the price level from 100 to 130 decreases the real money supply from M^s to $M^{s'}$ even though the Fed did not take action to change the money stock. Changes in real money balances of this sort can be substantial. In the United States, the nominal money stock (measured by M1) is about $1.3 trillion. Hence, a 1 percent increase in the price level decreases the *real* money stock by about $13 billion.

When the real money stock decreases because of an increase in the price level, interest rates will increase, and desired investment will decrease. A change in desired investment changes aggregate

Figure 15
Effect of an Increase in the Price Level on the Real Money Supply

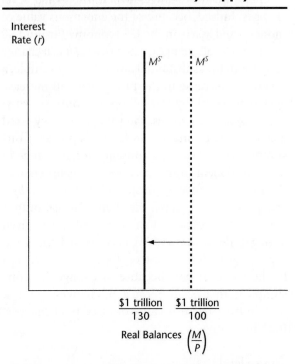

An increase in the price level will reduce the real money supply when the stock of money doesn't change.

Figure 16
Price Level Effects

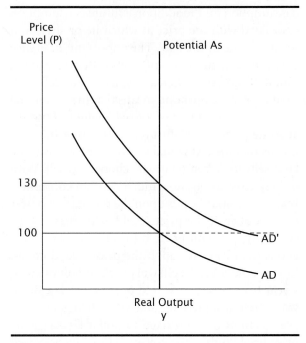

demand. Because the change in desired investment *is induced by a change in the price level,* the change in real output demanded corresponds to a movement *along* a given aggregate demand curve. That is, *the aggregate demand curve slopes downward and to the right, in part because of changes in desired investment that occur because of changes in real money balances that, in turn, occur because of price-level changes.* Or,

↑ price level
→↓ real balances
→↑ interest rate
→↓ investment
→↓aggregate real output demanded

Net Exports and Induced Price-Level Effects

Changes in the price level also influence net exports. When the price level increases in the U.S. relative to

the price levels in our trading partners, US goods and services cost foreigners more. US exports will fall. The opposite occurs when the price levels of our trading partners increase and ours does not—foreign goods and services cost those living in the U.S. more and US imports will fall. Thus, net exports increase as the price level decreases (exports increase relative to imports) and decrease as the price level increases (exports decrease relative to imports). Once again, because net exports are a component of aggregate demand, the change in net exports *induced by a change in the price level* is reflected in a movement *along* the aggregate demand curve. In this case

↑ price level
→↓ net exports
→↓ aggregate real output demanded

The Overall Effect

An increase in aggregate demand—either because of an aggregate demand shock or stimulative fiscal or money actions—puts pressure on the price level to increase as illustrated in Figure 16. As it increases, four things happen:

1. The higher price level decreases consumption because money-fixed assets decline in value. With less wealth, consumption declines.

2. The higher price level decreases investment because the real money supply decreases when the price level increases, causing interest rates to increase. When interest rates increase, desired investment decreases.

3. Consumption decreases because the increase in interest rates makes current consumption more costly relative to future consumption, thereby increasing savings.

4. Net exports decline.

Each of these effects causes a movement *along* the new aggregate demand curve toward the new long-run equilibrium. By contrast, changes in desired investment or desired consumption or net exports that occur for any reason *other than a change in the price level* will shift the aggregate demand curve.

▶ Summary

Interest-sensitive components of aggregate demand. Investment by firms in new plant and equipment and by households in housing as well as household expenditures on consumer durables are sensitive to interest-rate changes to varying degrees. Lower interest rates increase desired investment by both firms and households, *ceteris paribus;* higher interest rates decrease desired investment.

Money market. Although individuals and firms demand money for use in transactions, there is an opportunity cost of holding money, namely, the interest that could be earned by holding another asset such as a savings account or a bond. At a higher interest rate, individuals will economize on money holdings; at a lower interest rate, they will hold relatively more of their savings as money and less in other nonmoney assets. As a consequence, there is an inverse relationship between the demand for money and the interest rate.

The reserve requirement and fractional reserve banking. The supply of money is determined in part by the Fed and in part by banks, who play an important role in money creation by holding only a frac-

tion of the deposits made to checking accounts as reserves (a system called *fractional reserve banking*). The maximum amount of money that the banking system can create is determined by the money multiplier, $1/RR$.

Federal reserve control of the nominal money supply. The Fed has significant control over the money supply because it can change the amount of currency in circulation through open market operations, or it can change the reserve requirement (the legal limit on the fraction of deposits that banks can lend out), or it can change the discount rate at which firms can borrow reserves.

Open market operations. The Fed's most common method of monetary control is an open market operation in which it purchases or sells U.S. government bonds in the open financial market. A purchase of bonds (**an open market purchase**) increases the amount of currency in circulation and increases bank reserves. Hence, an open market purchase increases the money supply. By contrast, a sale of bonds (**an open market sale**) decreases the amount of currency in circulation and eventually decreases bank reserves. As a consequence, the money supply decreases.

Discount-rate changes. A change in the discount rate will also change the money supply, but without any change in the amount of currency in circulation. A decrease in the discount rate makes it more attractive for banks to lend, thereby increasing the money supply; an increase in the discount rate makes it less attractive for banks to lend, thereby decreasing the money supply.

Federal funds market. Banks generally do not borrow from the Fed but from each other in the federal funds market. Banks who happen to have excess reserves at the close of the day are suppliers; banks who happen to be short of reserves at the close of the day are demanders. The interaction of supply and demand determines the federal funds rate, which fluctuates day-by-day.

Reserve-requirement changes. An increase in the reserve requirement decreases the money supply; a decrease in the reserve requirement increase the money supply.

Table 2

	Effect on currency or reserves	Effect on effective money multiplier	Effect on money supply
Open market purchase	Increase	None	Increase
Open market sale	Decrease	None	Decrease
Increase in discount rate	Increase	Decrease	Decrease
Decrease in discount rate	Decrease	Increase	Increase
Increase in reserve requirement	Increase	Decrease	Decrease
Decrease in reserve requirement	Decrease	Increase	Increase

Monetary policy. Table 2 provides a summary of possible Fed actions and the effects on either the money supply or the money multiplier.

Monetary policy path. The path by which monetary policy affects the economy can be summarized as follows:

ΔM^s
  $\to \Delta r$
    $\to \Delta i$ *(and other interest-sensitive spending)*
      $\to \Delta$ *aggregate demand*
        $\to \Delta y$ *and ΔP (in the short run)*

The price level and aggregate real output demanded. Because individuals hold money-fixed assets, wealth will change with changes in the price level. Consumption will change as a consequence. In addition, the real money supply will change with changes in the price level. Changes in the real money supply will lead to changes in interest rates. Two aggregate-demand effects follow: First, desired investment will change with price-level induced changes in interest rates. Second, consumption with price-level induced changes with changes in interest rates. Finally, changes in the price level affect net exports. Thus, aggregate real output *demanded* will change with changes in the price level. Because the changes are caused by changes in the price level rather than by changes in desired investment or consumption or net exports that are *independent* of price-level changes, however, these price-level-induced changes determine the slope of the aggregate demand curve.

Chapter 23 ▶▶
More on Unemployment___

The United States has committed itself as a matter of national policy to provide "useful employment opportunities . . . for those able, willing, and seeking work" (The Employment Act of 1946). Unemployment is, however, a curious problem. On the one hand, it represents an enormous waste of resources and, when prolonged, a source of human despair and misery. To be unable to find work when you are quite willing and able to do so may be personally devastating and the output that you would have produced is lost to the economy forever. On the other hand, unemployment also reflects the changes that occur in a dynamic economy as businesses come and go and as individuals look for jobs on entering (or reentering) the workforce or as they look for better jobs. Taking time to search for a job that best fits with one's skills is important, but it also means that individuals may be unemployed as they search. Unemployment is not a single problem with a single consequence, then, but a set of problems and possibilities with quite different consequences.

▶ Measuring Unemployment

Each month 1,700 Census Bureau workers conduct a telephone survey of about 60,000 randomly selected households. The person who answers the phone is asked if he or she worked at any time during the week preceding the phone call. If the person worked, he or she is considered part of the labor force and employed. If the person responds that he or she has not worked in the last week, however, the interviewer then asks if the person was available for work during the past four weeks and whether the person actively looked for a job at any time during that time period. If the answer is yes, the person is considered part of the labor force but unemployed. If the answer is no, the person is not considered to be in the labor force and is not considered unemployed. That is, to be part of the **labor force** a person must either be currently working, or must be not working, but looking for a job.[1]

In terms of measuring unemployment, a person is considered unemployed if he or she did not work in the last week, but did look for work at some point during the past four weeks. That is, to be **unemployed**, a person must be part of the labor force, but out of work. People with jobs are employed. People without jobs who are looking for work are unemployed. People without jobs who are not looking for work are not in the labor force.

Using the data gathered in this way, the government estimates the size of the labor force, the labor force participation rate, and the unemployment rate. The **labor force participation rate** is the fraction of the working-age population that is in the labor force. The **unemployment rate** is the percent of those sampled who are in the labor force and currently looking for work. Figure 1 provides a picture of changes in the unemployment rate from 1900 through 1991.

---

[1] The interviewer actually asks questions about each household member who is 16 or older, not in the military or in a prison or other institution.

Figure 1
Civilian Unemployment Rate, 1950–2010

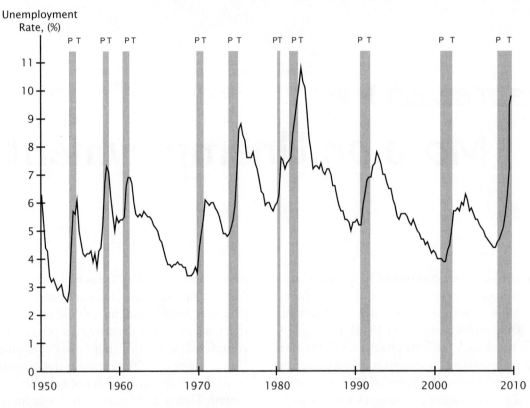

SOURCE: *Economic Report of the President.*

The high unemployment rates during the Great Depression of the 1930s are particularly noticeable. (There has been some dispute about the exact numbers because some individuals who were employed in government jobs programs were counted among the unemployed. Excluding these workers lowers the unemployment rate by 4 to 7 percentage points during each year of the Great Depression.) Less noticeable perhaps are two important changes in unemployment rates:

1. The unemployment rate, averaged over decade intervals, has increased from around 4.5 percent in the decade prior to World War I and in the 1950s, to 4.8 percent for the 1960s, to 6.2 percent for the 1970s and to 7.3 percent for the 1980s. But it has fallen dramatically in the 1990s.

2. Year-by-year fluctuations in the unemployment rate are smaller today than they were prior to World War II.

Thus, the labor market appears to be more stable today than in earlier years, but it also seems—

unless the 1990s are the beginning of something different—to operate with a higher fraction of the workforce unemployed, on average.

Biases

Important biases in the unemployment data published by the government make them only an approximation of the economy's "true" unemployment at best.

1. Out of frustration individuals who have been unemployed for a long time may quit searching for a job. Because they are no longer actively looking for a job, these **discouraged workers** are not considered to be part of the labor force and, hence, are not considered unemployed. As a consequence of this phenomenon, the published unemployment statistics underestimate the true unemployment rate.

2. Anyone working during the week preceding the interview is considered employed. The survey does not distinguish between part-time and full-time workers, which means that unemployment statistics fail to account for

those who are **involuntarily part-time workers**. That is, people are considered employed even if they are working part-time but actually want full-time work. This is an important source of bias because during a recession, firms may ask workers previously employed full-time to accept part-time employment rather than be laid off. As a consequence of this phenomenon, the published unemployment statistics underestimate the full effect of a recession on employment opportunities. (The U.S. Bureau of Labor Statistics publishes statistics on part-time employment. For example, in 1990, about one-quarter of those who worked part-time were doing so for "economic reasons" and the remaining three-quarters were employed part-time by choice.)

3. Individuals may not be working at the current wage rate, but may want to work if only they can get a job with a sufficiently high wage. Because the survey does not ask whether people would be willing to work at the *current or prevailing* wage rate—a very difficult question to formulate in an economy with hundreds of different wage rates corresponding to hundreds of different skill levels—individuals may tell the interviewer that they are looking for work even though they would *not* accept a job at the current market wage. That is, they may be holding out for a job that pays $20,000 per year, even though their last one paid $14,500. In this case, the published unemployment statistics overestimate the true unemployment rate.

4. Unemployment data tell us little about the fraction of the population that participates in the labor market or about the ability of the economy to provide for changes in desired labor force participation. To see why this matters, consider some data. The unemployment rate increased from 3.8 to 6.8 percent between 1948 and 1958 and the overall *employment rate* (the fraction of the population holding a job) decreased slightly. The unemployment rate increased from 3.6 to 6.1 percent between 1968 and 1978 but, by contrast with the earlier decade, the overall employment rate increased over this decade (see Table 1). Thus, although the unemployment rates were similar in 1948 and 1968 and again in 1958 and

Table 1
Employment and Unemployment Rates

Year	Employment Rate	Unemployment Rate
1948	58.8%	3.8%
1958	59.5	6.8
1968	59.6	3.6
1978	63.1	6.1
1988	65.9	5.5
1998	67.0	4.5
2008	66.0	5.8

SOURCE: U.S. Bureau of Labor Statistics.

1978, the unemployment rates masked substantial difference in the labor markets between the two decades. Put directly, the unemployment rate provides little information about changes in employment opportunities. Thus, between 1978 and 1985, both the unemployment and employment rates increased—a larger fraction of the population found jobs, but of those wishing to work, a larger fraction was also unemployed.

The differences between the interval in the 1950s and the intervals in the 1970s and 1980s are important. The expanding economy in the latter periods provided for more employment opportunities, even as the unemployment rate was increasing. As a consequence, even though the decade-by-decade unemployment rates rose somewhat, the number of persons actually employed increased rather dramatically during the 1970s and 1980s. This rise can be seen in the steep climb of the chart in Figure 2.

Duration

Unfortunately, the unemployment statistics do not tell us whether unemployment is a consequence of a large fraction of the labor force being unemployed for a short period of time or a small fraction of the labor force being unemployed for a long period of time. To see why this is important, consider two extremes. First, think of an economy where everyone is out of work 5 percent of the work year. Then imagine a different economy where 95 percent of the workforce is always employed, but 5 percent is out of work for the entire year. The measured unemployment rates would be 5 percent in both cases. However, in the first case, the **duration of unemployment** would be about

Figure 2
Number of People Age 16 and over Who are Working

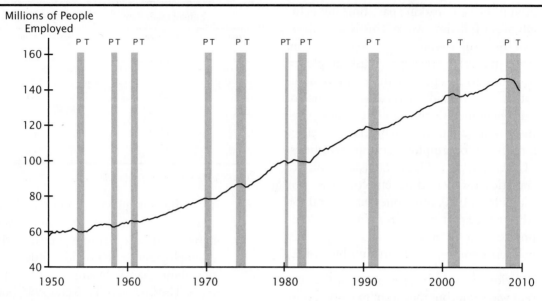

SOURCE: U.S. Bureau of of Labor Statistics.

2.5 weeks, with the costs more or less evenly spread across the population. In the second, the duration of unemployment would be one year, with the cost concentrated on 5 percent of the population. Clearly, it makes a difference how the duration of unemployment is distributed across the population.

Studies indicate that the duration of unemployment is distributed unequally across the population: for the U.S., the unemployment rate reflects a smaller number of people being unemployed for longer periods of time rather than a larger number of people being unemployed for very short periods of time. For example, a careful study of unemployment in 1974 (when the unemployment rate was 5.6 percent) indicated that 60 percent of all periods of unemployment lasted less than one month. Sixty-nine percent of the weeks of unemployment, however, were experienced by individuals whose un- employment lasted more than three months. How can this be? Suppose that 20 people are unemployed, but 15 of them are unemployed for one month while the remaining five are unemployed for 12 months. The total number of months of unemployment is 75 [(5 people × 12 months) + (15 people × 1 month)]. Seventy-five percent of the unemployment (measured in terms of individuals affected) is due to short-term spells (15/20 = 75%). However, eighty percent of the unemployment (measured in terms of weeks) is due to long-term periods of unemployment (60/75 = 80%).

Empirical evidence and common sense suggest that the unemployed are not a homogeneous group. Thus, unemployment rates will be different depending on a person's education, the kinds of occupations for which the individual is prepared, and will differ also by race, by age, and by sex, as indicated in Table 2. Moreover, the duration of unemployment differs for different groups of individuals.

Duration of unemployment also differs by age. Teenagers, who have a high unemployment rate, tend to be unemployed for short durations as they move in and out of jobs and in and out of the labor force. By contrast, older workers who lose their jobs tend to have longer periods of unemployment. What accounts for the differences? Teenagers tend to have high unemployment rates because they are searching for jobs that interest them and fit with their abilities and skills. They also move between work and schooling more frequently than other workers. (Full-time students are not considered unemployed.) By contrast older persons have often been in particular jobs for some time, and when they become unemployed they are less mobile. Their periods of unemployment last longer, even though their risks of becoming unemployed are lower.

The risks of becoming unemployed differ across different sectors or industries within the economy. Thus, for example, blacks have higher unemploy-

Table 2
Unemployment Rates for Various Groups

Group	1981	1983	1991	2000	2007	2009
overall	7.6%	10.1%	6.9%	4.0%	4.6%	9.8%
males, 16–19 years old	20.6	24.0	19.9	14.1	17.6	29.8
males, 20 years and older	6.2	9.1	6.5	3.3	4.2	10.3
females, 16–19 years old	18.9	24.0	17.0	12.0	13.8	22.0
females, 20 years and older	6.7	8.7	5.8	3.9	4.0	7.8
whites	6.5	8.7	6.2	2.6	4.1	9.0
blacks	15.6	19.5	12.5	7.6	8.3	15.7
hispanic and latino	10.4	13.7	10.0	5.7	5.2	12.7
males, married	4.3	4.5	6.6	2.6	2.5	7.4
OVER 25 with:						
no high school diploma			11.9	6.4	7.1	15.0
HS diploma			6.8	3.5	4.4	10.8
some college			5.6	2.8	3.5	8.5
college degree			3.1	1.6	2.0	4.7

NOTE: *1983 was in the middle of a recession; 2000 was at the end of a long expansion; 2007 was at the end of the recovery from the 2001 recession; 2009 is during a recession.*

ment rates in part because they tend to occupy blue-collar jobs disproportionately, and blue-collar jobs are more susceptible to unemployment.

Short-term or Long-term Problem?

Is unemployment a short-term or long-term problem? Although the answer depends upon which data are considered, in an important sense, the answer is that it is both. That duration and incidence differ across the population means, to put it bluntly, that the costs of unemployment are unevenly distributed across the population. A 7 percent unemployment rate does not imply that everyone will be unemployed for three to four weeks during the year, but rather that a much smaller number of individuals will be unemployed for a much longer period. Nor does a 7 percent unemployment rate imply that everyone is at equal risk to be unemployed, but rather that some groups within the population—the young, the lower-skilled, single-parent households, blacks—have higher probabilities of being unemployed in general and of becoming unemployed during a downturn in particular.

► The Varied Nature of Unemployment

For some of those who are unemployed, there are jobs available. In this case, there is a person without work, but there is also a job vacancy somewhere in the economy, offering exactly the wage for which the person is willing to work. That is, both unemployment *and* job vacancies exist at the same time. If the unemployment rate were exactly the same as the job-vacancy rate and the unemployed had the skills necessary to fill the vacant jobs, unemployment would be a consequence of the frictions associated with finding open positions. In this case, solving the unemployment problem would just be a matter of waiting for individuals to find the vacancies. If the unemployment rate exceeds the job-vacancy rate, however, some of those looking for jobs will not be able to find them because there are fewer jobs available than the number of persons looking for work. In this case, solving the unemployment problem would require the creation of jobs either through wage adjustments, aggregate demand changes, or economic growth. Finally, if the skills of the unemployed and the skills required in the jobs available do not match, then some of those looking for jobs will find that jobs requiring their skills are simply unavailable in the economy. In this case, solving the unemployment problem may require retraining individuals or restructuring the economy.

To understand these differences, consider a frequently encountered problem: finding a parking place on campus or at the local shopping center or mall. If a large parking lot that is mostly full, you will most likely have to drive up and down the aisles looking for a vacant space. Suppose that there are 20 vacancies in the parking lot and 1,000 parking places. If there are five cars looking for a vacancy, then the lot is not full, even though the drivers of the five cars may not have found an open space. Since finding a parking space may take a while, not every car is parked. Moreover, people frequently drive past open spaces that are further away from their destination in order to see if there isn't an open space closer.

On the other hand, if there are 100 cars looking for a place to park, only 20 will be able to do so. It follows that for some drivers, finding a parking space will be impossible. The parking lot is full, even though there may be 20 vacant spots at a particular moment. The excess number of cars in this case is 80, not 100, however, even though 100 cars do not have parking places at any one time.

You can also imagine that some of the 980 parked cars will leave while people are searching for a parking place, so new vacancies are created as the old vacancies are filled. And, as parked cars leave, new cars will pull into the lot and join those searching for parking places.

The labor market is much like this: Some people are looking for jobs and there are job openings—the person and the opening just haven't been matched yet. Other people are looking for jobs, but there are not enough job openings for each person to find one. Hence, for some, no match is available. Still others are currently employed, but are also looking for a new job, others are leaving jobs hoping to find something better, some are being laid off as the fortunes of a firm or industry change, recent graduates are looking for a job for the first time, and some workers are retiring. Thus some of the unemployment is merely **frictional**, where there are openings waiting for the unemployed to find them, and some of the unemployment is **cyclical** or **structural**, where there are no jobs for those without work. The important thing to understand in this respect is that the labor market is *dynamic*—unemployment is like a pool with small streams flowing in and out. Not all of the water in the pool gets there in the same way; analogously, not all of the unemployed get there in the same way.

Flows *into* unemployment include:

1. Those previously employed who lose their jobs involuntarily.

2. Those previously employed who leave their jobs voluntarily in order to look for work.

3. Those previously out of the labor force who decide to reenter and look for work.

4. Those who are new entrants to the labor force.

A breakdown of these categories for 2009 appears in Figure 3.

Flows *out of* unemployment include:

1. Those who find jobs
2. Those who leave the labor force.

Recent data suggest that about 68 percent of the unemployed lost their jobs (job losers) while about another 2 percent left their jobs (quitters). A little over 7 percent of the unemployed are looking for their first job (new entrants). The remaining 23 percent are people who are reentering the labor force (reentrants), but have not found a job. This pattern is unusual because of the 2007–2009 recession. In more typical periods, about one-half of the unemployed are job losers; about 13 percent are job quitters; about the same number are new entrants and the remaining quarter are reentrants. For example, consider the changes in flows in and out of unemployment illustrated in Table 3. Both 1983 and 1991

Figure 3
Categories of Unemployment, 2009

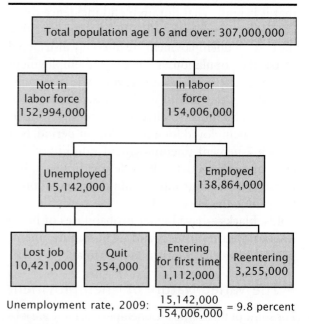

Unemployment rate, 2009: $\dfrac{15,142,000}{154,006,000} = 9.8$ percent

Table 3
The Pattern of Unemployment

	1978	1983	1991	2001
Job losers	41.7%	58.4%	54.7	50.8%
Job leavers	14.0	7.7	11.6	12.3
Reentrants	31.7	22.5	24.8	30.0
New entrants	15.4	11.4	9.0	6.7
Total	6.2 million	10.7 million	8.43 million	6.74 million
Unemployment rate	6.1	9.7	7.1	4.8

SOURCE: *Economic Report of the President.*

were in the middle of serious recessions, although not as serious as the 2007–2009 recession. 1978 was at the end of a decade of so-so economic performance; 2001 was at the end of a long recovery.

Frictional Unemployment

As we have just seen, part of the measured unemployment rate is **frictional**. Even though workers are unemployed, job openings for which they are qualified are available. Frictional unemployment results when individuals leaving one job (or looking for a first job) do not find a new job *immediately,* even though there are vacancies in the economy. In this case, unemployment for a particular individual is temporary. For the economy as a whole, the frictional rate may not change much because as some individuals find jobs, others quit to look for new jobs and still others enter the labor force.

Cyclical Unemployment

Cyclical unemployment occurs when, because of a decrease in aggregate demand or aggregate supply, the number of jobs available declines relative to the number of qualified persons looking for jobs. During a downturn in the economy, five things happen in the labor market:

1. People are laid off and, as a consequence, the unemployment rate rises.

2. There is less demand for labor overall and, as a consequence, the level of employment falls or its rate of increase drops.

3. Jobs are more difficult to find and unemployed individuals looking for jobs become discouraged and drop out of the labor market. (The **discouraged worker effect**.)

4. Firms offer workers only part-time employment opportunities. (The **involuntary part-time employment effect.**)

5. The duration of unemployment increases. (The **duration effect.**)

During a boom, the opposite occurs: unemployment falls, growth of employment increases, the labor force participation rate increase as individuals return to the labor market, there are more full-time employment opportunities, and unemployment duration falls. Cyclical unemployment is the kind of unemployment that is associated with sticky nominal wages and aggregate demand shocks explored in previous chapters.

Why temporary layoffs rather than wage cuts? A puzzle that is not well understood is why some individuals are laid off during a recession rather than being offered continued employment but at a lower wage. That is, during a recession, when demand is weak, a firm can cut labor costs *either* by laying off some workers or by offering lower wages to some or all. Why do we see layoffs rather than widespread wage cuts? This question is related to the question about why wages are sticky and the explanations are pretty much the same.

Employers may have better information about the level of aggregate demand than workers do. If firms ask workers to take wage cuts, workers may not understand that aggregate demand has declined and refuse, noting that the employer (as contrasted with the employees) loses nothing with a wage cut. If a firm temporarily lays off workers, however, it loses the output these workers would have produced and workers may more readily understand and accept this action—it is clear that the firm is making a decision that hurts it, as well as those who are laid off. According to this explanation, the asymmetry of information between employees and employers forces layoffs rather than wage cuts.

It also appears that workers often acquire skills that are specific to a particular firm (called **firm-specific human capital**). As a consequence, employers have an incentive to minimize turnover (the number of workers coming and going) because turnover increases training costs. Widespread wage cuts might provide an incentive for employees to quit, to shirk, or in other ways to reduce work effort and productivity. In contrast, layoffs can be targeted at the least-experienced workers in whom the firm has invested the least in training costs. This explanation suggests that firms will find layoffs more profitable than wage cuts and so will more experienced workers who continue to work at their unchanged (higher) wages.

If the norm is to lay off some workers rather than make nominal wage cuts for some or all, then workers may be willing to work for lower wages, on average. The argument goes as follows. If workers are averse to risk, they will prefer the certainty of a constant earnings stream to the uncertainty of one that bounces around because of nominal wage cuts even if the fluctuation income stream provides higher wages on average. As long as firms adopt rules that lay off the most recently hired employees first, experienced workers have a kind of implicit contract that guarantees that their incomes will be unaffected by aggregated demand changes except in the most serious recessions. If workers prefer this pattern of lifetime stable earnings, then they should be willing, on average, to accept slightly lower wages than they would otherwise, *and firms will have lower costs as a consequence.* Thus, by this argument, both firms and workers prefer layoffs to wage reductions in response to aggregate demand shifts. Firms have lower wage payments; most workers have a more steady income stream.

Structural Unemployment

With cyclical employment, jobs for individuals with particular skills are not currently available, but will become available as the economy's actual output moves toward its potential real output. Sometimes, however, long-term changes in the economy leave persons who lack certain skills or training without job opportunities, even when the economy's output

nears its potential. For example, someone who doesn't have a high-school education may be willing to work, but will have fewer job-related skills and, thus, fewer employment opportunities than those with a high-school education. Thus, each Sunday, your local paper is filled with hundreds and frequently thousands of job listings. Your locality also has individuals who are unemployed. If the job openings and the job qualifications of persons looking for work do not match, however, these individuals will have great difficulty finding jobs. Unemployment of this sort is called **structural unemployment.**

Structural unemployment occurs because of changing patterns in the demands for labor with *particular* skills. When it is difficult for those who are currently employed in industries where demand is falling to move to other industries, either because of high costs of retraining or because of high costs of moving from one place to another, structural unemployment results. In a sense, changes in the structure of the economy place some individuals with limited abilities or skills outside of the labor market. Some reasons for structural unemployment are fairly easy to identify and, in some cases, the government has responded by trying to minimize the amount of structural unemployment.

▶ The Natural Rate of Unemployment

At any moment, it is impossible to know exactly what part of unemployment is frictional, what part is cyclical, and what part is structural. Economists who study labor markets guess that between 5 and 6 percent of the labor force in the United States is unemployed for frictional and structural reasons. This means that in the long run, the unemployment rate will average between 5 and 6 percent. Hence full employment is obtained when the unemployment rate is around 5 or 6 percent, not when it is 0 percent. For this reason, the frictional rate of unemployment is also referred to as the **natural rate of unemployment.** When the unemployment rate is above this level, the additional unemployment is mostly cyclical.[2] Thus, if the reported unemployment rate is 8 percent, an additional 2 or 3 percent of workers are unemployed than would be if the econ-

---

[2] Different countries that have smaller (or larger) labor markets as well as different institutional arrangements within their labor markets have different frictional unemployment rates.

Figure 4
Actual Versus Natural Unemployment Rates (1950–1991)

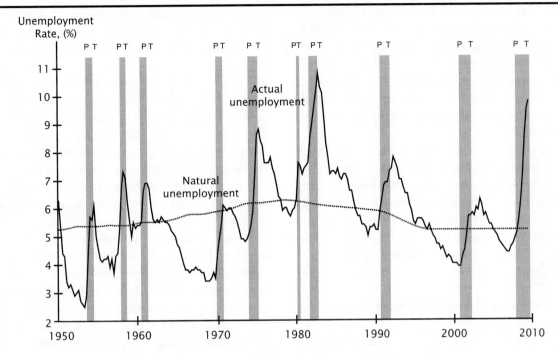

SOURCE: U.S. Bureau of Labor Statistics and Congressional Budget Office.

omy were producing at its potential. Figure 4 contrasts the actual unemployment rate with an estimate of the natural, or frictional, rate of unemployment.

Changes in the Natural Rate

The natural or frictional unemployment rate isn't natural in the sense that it is constant at all times and all places. Indeed, in the United States, the natural rate increased between 1970 and 1990 by as much as 2 percentage points. It may have fallen in the 1990s. Thus, full employment in the 1960s probably meant that 3 to 4 percent of the labor force was unemployed, but in the 1980s, it meant that 5 to 6 percent of the labor force was unemployed and in the 1990s, it meant that 4½ to 5 percent of the labor force was unemployed. Why was the natural rate apparently changing?

The frictional or natural unemployment rate is determined, in part, by the composition of the labor force. Those who have completed formal schooling have historically had a lower unemployment rate than have those who left school before completing a degree. Younger workers have historically had the highest unemployment rate and women have had a slightly higher unemployment rate than men have had. These differences imply that a change in the

demographic composition of the population changes the natural unemployment rate.

The composition of the labor force changed between 1970 and 1990. Data indicate that the fraction of males who have completed formal schooling fell. In addition, as Table 4 illustrates, the percentage of women in the labor force increased from about 33 percent in 1960 to more than 45 percent by 1990 and the percentage of younger workers (between the ages of 25 and 34) increased from

Table 4
Labor Force Shares

Group	1960*	1990*	2007
Men	66.6%	54.8%	53.6%
Women	33.4	45.2	46.4
Men and Women, 16–24	16.6	17.6	14.5
Men and Women, 25–34	20.7	29.1	21.6
Men and Women, 35–44	23.4	24.7	23.2
Men and Women, 45–54	21.3	16.2	23.3
Men and Women, 55–64	13.5	9.6	13.5

SOURCE: Statistical Abstract of the United States, 2008.

* Percentages may not add up to 100 because of workers under age 16 or over age 64.

about 21 percent to somewhat more than 29 percent. By the 1990s, the fraction of women working was no longer increasing and the population was aging a little rather than getting younger. The changing composition of the workforce combined with these differences in unemployment rates for the different groups have each contributed to an increase in the frictional unemployment rate and then, perhaps, an decrease in the natural unemployment rate in the 1990s.

The empirical evidence suggest that changes in the composition of the labor force and changes in the costs of looking for a job a little longer *cannot* fully explain the changes in the natural rate of unemployment. Part of the explanation appears to be tied to changes in incentives that affect how individuals search for jobs and employers search for employees.

The importance of search in the labor market. A person who is currently employed must decide whether to stay in his or her job or look for another job. A person without a job must decide what kind of job to seek, how to gather information about the nature of job opportunities, and how intensively to look for a job.

A firm currently employing a person must decide whether to continue or terminate the employment relationship. A firm intending to expand must decide what kind of workers to seek, how to gather information about the nature of prospective employees, and how intensively to look for new workers.

If an unemployed individual takes a job offer, he or she passes up the possibility of finding a better job. The better job might have had a more attractive work environment, been more consistent with the worker's skills, or offered a higher salary. Similarly, if a firm offers a position to an individual, it passes up the possibility of finding a more capable, more productive employee.

What is the optimal search time or search strategy? An individual should continue to search as long as the expected gain from looking a little longer is greater than the expected costs of being out of work a little longer. Suppose, for example, that the expected gain can be measured in terms of finding a higher starting salary. If an individual believes that by searching a little longer she might find a job that pays more, she should continue to search as long as

the difference between the salary offers that she currently has and those that she might expect in the future is greater than the lost income and other out-of-pocket costs from being unemployed another day. To make the point more concrete, suppose that out-of-pocket costs are $50 a day to search for a job and that you currently have an offer that would pay $200 per day. It makes sense to continue to search, at least for a little while, if you expect to be able to find a job that pays $400 per day; it doesn't make sense to continue to search, however, if you expect that your current offer is the best you will get.

The costs of searching a little longer probably increase with the length of time a person has been unemployed. Savings are being depleted and unemployment compensation benefits, if any, are being used up. The benefits of additional searching, by contrast, probably decrease with the length of time that a person searches. In this case, the longer a person has looked for a job, the more information he or she will already have and the less useful any *additional* information is likely to be. For example, if one half of the employers pay $25,000 and the other half pay $20,000, the chances of getting the highest paying job are fifty-fifty if you interview with only one firm. If you interview with two firms, however, the chances are three in four (75 percent) that you will find the highest paying job. If you continue your search and interview with three firms, the chances are 88 percent that you will find the highest paying job. And if you interview with a fourth firm, the chances are 90 percent that you will find the highest paying job. Note that the improvement in the odds of finding the highest paying job is getting smaller and smaller with additional searching. That is, additional searching has a lower and lower expected payoff because it is increasingly likely you have already found a high-paying job.

If the costs of additional searching increase with the length of search, and if the expected benefits of additional searching decrease, then individuals should continue job searching until the point where the expected gain from an additional interview or another day's search is just equal to the cost of spending another day searching rather than employed. When this point is realized, they will take the best job offered up to that point.

Now consider the situation from a firm's perspective. Firms want to fill job openings with the most productive person possible. They do not have perfect information about the productivity of those individuals currently searching for work, however. Thus, firms must also search. In doing so, they encounter direct costs such as advertising, employing search agencies, placing ads in newspapers, using employees who could be doing other things within the firm to screen and interview prospective candidates, and so on. Firms will benefit from their search, however, because, if they screen job applicants more carefully, they should be able to hire more productive workers. Thus, if a firm takes a little longer to look for new employees, it will be able to increase the probability of having a high-quality workforce. Like an individual, a firm must balance the additional costs and benefits from continuing to interview for employees.

If the labor market works this way, what affects the duration of unemployment? Duration falls when individuals and firms reduce the amount of time they search. *It follows that anything that lowers the benefits or raises the costs of searching further will reduce the duration of unemployment. Conversely, anything that raises the benefits or lowers the costs of searching further will increase the duration of unemployment.*

When workers search, they often begin with a **reservation wage**: "I will not work for less than specified dollar amount per hour." Firms may begin their search with maximum wage offers.[3] The first firm that offers a worker his or her reservation wage will be able to hire that person. Unemployment duration will increase when the spread between the reservation wages that individuals expect and wage offers that firms make increases; duration will decrease when the spread decreases. That is, if individuals choose slightly higher reservation wages, they will reject a greater number of lower-wage job offers because their reservation wage leads them to search for longer period of time. This will lower the probability of finding work in a given period of time, thereby increasing unemployment duration. During a recession, firms may lower their wage offers to new employees by more than individuals who are looking for jobs lower their reservation wages. Unemployment duration will increase as a consequence. Therefore, not only are there fewer jobs available at a given reservation wage during a recession, but individuals find that if they do become unemployed, the period of their unemployment lasts longer.

The effects of unemployment compensation and multiple wage-earners in a household. In this context, changing the cost of being unemployed affects the natural rate of unemployment. Thus, just as you might pass up an open parking spot hoping for a better one, people sometimes pass up job offers as they search for more information about the job market. If the costs of passing up a job are reduced, more people will pass up the first employment opportunity, and the frictional unemployment rate will increase. Two changes over the past several decades are thought to have affected the cost of passing up the first job offer: changes in unemployment compensation and changes in the number of individuals within a household who are working.

One of the important legacies of the Great Depression was the creation of an unemployment insurance system. In common jargon, this system provides a "safety net" for those who become unemployed by preventing the complete loss of income during the unemployment spell as long as the unemployment spell is less than six months. (Benefits are limited to six months unless the eligibility period is extended by Congress.) Viewing the labor market in terms of information and search suggest that unemployment compensation has a second effect. Unemployment compensation makes search less costly for individuals in that it makes passing up job offers less costly. As unemployment compensation has become more widely available and the amount has increased, individuals have been more willing to pass up the first job offered. Hence, lowering the cost of additional searching increases the amount of time that individuals search for the best job offer. As a consequence, the duration of unemployment also increases. This is not necessarily bad, because taking longer to find a job may mean that an individual can obtain a better job match and be more productive as a consequence. Unemployment compensation is likely to increase the frictional or natural rate of unemployment, however.

---

[3] Instead of assuming that firms have wage offers that don't change, a more sophisticated version of the search argument allows firms to have reservation offers ("We will not offer a position for more than a specified dollar amount per hour") that they change as they gather information about prospective employees by interviewing and in other ways searching over the pool of individuals looking for jobs.

Because unemployment benefits do not fluctuate much, the existence of a benefit program cannot contribute to a *continual* increase in the unemployment rate. But increased benefits probably have contributed to the higher natural unemployment rate that exists now as compared with several decades ago, when both unemployment compensation and the natural unemployment rate were lower.[4]

Having more than one wage earner in a household also reduces the costs to a household of having one of those workers unemployed. When there is only one wage earner, unemployment leaves the household without income; with a two-earner household, the unemployment of one member creates a partial but not complete cut in the household's income. Again, it is argued, the frictional unemployment rate has likely increased as a consequence.

Searching and the Short-Run Aggregate Supply Curve

Understanding the role of search in labor markets helps explain why real output varies in the short run with price level changes. To see why, suppose that the price level begins to increase because of an increase in aggregate demand. Suppose, further, that workers do not immediately perceive this increase in prices. Firms will find that, because of long-term contracts with their workers, some of their costs are fixed. They will renegotiate some contracts that have expired and start looking for new employees in order to increase their output. As additional firms enter the labor market, the unemployment rate will begin to decrease and wage rates will begin to increase. Individuals looking for work who have not yet perceived price increases will find offers above their reservation wage more quickly. Hence, duration will fall. Thus, with an aggregate demand shock that creates unanticipated inflation, some people will be fooled in the sense that they will find that wage offers are increasing and believe that the real

wage has increased. They will accept an offer that *appears* higher than expected, but that is, in reality, lower when adjusted for the actual rate of inflation. As a consequence, unemployment will decrease and real output will increase.

By contrast, if the price level falls unexpectedly because of a decrease in aggregate demand, firms will perceive that their profitability is falling. Some of their workers have contracts that require fixed or perhaps increasing nominal wage payments. Firms may have other long-term contracts for resources that fix input prices. As a consequence, the price at which firms can sell their output will fall more rapidly than their costs will. Firms will be less concerned with turnover and, when workers leave, will tend to look longer for replacements. As a consequence, those who are currently unemployed will find that offers are lower or harder to get than expected. They will search for a longer period of time and unemployment duration will increase. This means that output and employment will fall.

In this framework, unanticipated inflation can also shorten the duration of unemployment. Why? If workers expect prices to remain at a particular level (or that inflation will increase at a particular rate), they will set their reservation wages consistent with these expectations. An unanticipated inflation will lead to higher wage offers by firms if firms perceive the change in the price level more quickly than workers do. Then a greater number of offers will equal or exceed the reservation wage of job applicants. Therefore, each worker will find a job sooner. This sequence of events occurs because the increase in nominal wages (when inflation is expected to be zero) appears to the worker as an increase in real wages. The worker's reservation wage is more likely to be met or exceeded, and so the duration of search falls. As inflation rises unexpectedly, the benefits to firms for extending searches fall. (Firms will want to hire workers and produce in order to take advantage of the higher prices.) Firms therefore fill positions faster.

The Natural Rate Hypothesis

Even at full employment, there is some frictional unemployment. This helps explain the kinds of macroeconomic adjustments that we have been exploring in the past several chapters. Indeed, these adjustments are known more formally as the **nat-**

---

[4] If the principal purpose of unemployment compensation is to allow individuals to search more carefully and find a better job match, then its success ought to be measured against post-unemployment wages. The evidence on post-unemployment wages is mixed, however. For older workers, there is some evidence that post-unemployment wages are slightly higher when they search somewhat longer, but for young workers, particularly teenagers, there is little evidence of a wage effect.

Figure 5
When Real Output Exceeds
Potential Real Output

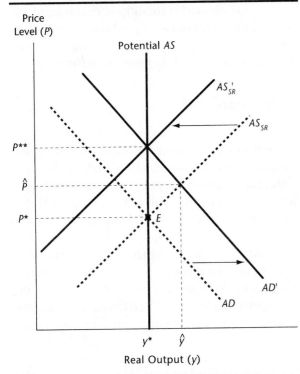

If there is a shock to the economy that increases aggregate demand from *AD* to *AD'*, prices will begin to increase from *P** to *P***. Real output in the economy will exceed potential real output, *y**, only when prices are higher than individuals had expected. In this case, the unemployment rate falls below the natural rate. As soon as individuals expect the price level to be *P***, the unemployment rate will return to the natural rate and real output will once again equal *y**.

ural rate hypothesis: *potential* real output is determined when the economy has unemployment that is equal to its frictional or natural rate.

Adjustments when the unemployment rate is greater than the natural rate. When the actual unemployment rate is *greater* than the natural rate of unemployment, *actual* increases in the price level will begin to fall short of *anticipated* price increases. For example, individuals might expect the price level to be 10 percent higher, but perhaps it is only 6 percent higher. This means, in turn, that as old wage bargains expire, firms will be able to pay workers lower wages, or at least reduce the rate of increase of wages. Either action will lower costs. As a consequence, the short-run aggregate supply curve will

shift downward as the expected price level or expected rate of inflation decreases. In addition, as prices fall, real money balances will increase, and when they do, additional consumption and investment will result. The economy will move down its aggregate demand curve. These adjustments will continue until the real output reaches its potential and unemployment returns to its natural level. No active monetary or fiscal policy need be pursued to move the economy back to its natural rate.

Adjustments when the unemployment rate is less than the natural rate. When the unemployment rate is *less* than the natural rate of unemployment, *actual* price increases will exceed *anticipated* price increases. In this case, individuals might expect the price level to increase by 5 percent, but find that it actually increases by 8 percent. As old wage bargains expire, wages will begin to increase. Anticipated inflation will adjust upward and, as a consequence, the short-run aggregate supply curve will shift upward. As the price level increases, the value of real balances will fall. Consumption and investment will decrease as a consequence. The economy will, as a consequence, move along its aggregate demand curve. These adjustments will continue until real output reaches it potential and unemployment returns to its natural level. Once again, this adjustment process does not require active monetary or fiscal policy.

Evidence. Is there any evidence that an economy works this way? Even though the data are somewhat sketchy, from the middle of the nineteenth century until the Great Depression, there was relatively little purposeful countercyclical monetary or fiscal policy. There were a large number of aggregate demand shocks, however. From the mid-nineteenth century until the Great Depression, the economies in the United States and Europe returned to a fairly stable rate of unemployment following these shocks. That is, an adverse aggregate demand shock would create high levels of unemployment but, over time, the level of unemployment would fall back to the earlier levels. There is no evidence that the unemployment rate increased over this period. Of course, during the Great Depression the unemployment rate did increase very rapidly. It did not remain high, but instead eventually fell to prior levels. Thus, instead of increasing through time, the unemployment rate increased and decreased throughout the nineteenth century and into the middle of the twentieth, with, on average, around 5 percent of the work force unemployed. The evidence appears to be consistent with the natural rate hypothesis.

▶ Is Unemployment Always Bad?

An economy must move resources from areas of declining economic importance to areas of increasing economic importance. The computer industry expanded beginning in the 1980s and the typewriter industry declined, for example. The decline created unemployment. Taken by itself, this appears to be a "bad." But additional resources cannot be made available to growing areas of the economy unless they are shifted from declining areas. In this sense, unemployment is a "good" because it represents the movement of resources from lower-valued to higher-valued activities. Openings are being created even as jobs are being lost, and the accompanying frictional unemployment that results as workers in declining sectors search for jobs in expanding sectors is an important aspect of a dynamic economy.

With structural and cyclical unemployment, however, labor resources cannot move to higher-valued activities because sufficient job opportunities do not exist. This suggests that a society ought to pursue policies that minimize these kinds of unemployment. Although fiscal and monetary policies may, in principle, be able to minimize cyclical unemployment, they are ineffective ways of solving structural unemployment problems. Structural unemployment requires a more concentrated effort on job retraining, education, and developing job opportunities for those who may be less skilled.

Monetary and fiscal policies also cannot lower frictional unemployment. Nor is frictional unemployment affected by job retraining, education, and other such programs directed at structural unemployment. It represents instead the search process of individuals. Many of these workers are in fact moving for reasons that are important to the growth and vitality of an economy. If we could change the frictional or natural unemployment rate, however, real output would increase. Thus, even though much attention is focused on eliminating cyclical and structural unemployment, it may also make sense to pursue public policies that minimize the time required to make matches between vacancies and

job seekers. For example, the frictional unemployment rate would be considerably higher if there were no efforts to provide information about job opportunities and job market conditions. In this sense, job agencies that serve essentially as brokers or middlemen to facilitate and speed up the job-matching process in fact attempt to lower the natural rate.

▶ Summary

Cyclical unemployment. Cyclical unemployment is a consequence of coordination problems between aggregate supply and aggregate demand. During a downturn, there are fewer job openings available relative to the number of people searching for work. Both the number of people looking for work and the duration of unemployment increases. However, focusing only on reported unemployment numbers is somewhat misleading. Even though much of the unemployment will be cyclical during an economic downturn, unemployment occurs for reasons other than just an adverse aggregate demand shock.

Frictional unemployment. Unemployment also occurs because people are entering or reentering the labor market or because some individuals are dissatisfied with their jobs and quit to find better ones. This kind of unemployment is independent of aggregate demand shocks and occurs because finding jobs (and finding employees) even when they are available takes time.

Countercyclical policies will not affect the frictional rate of unemployment. Frictional unemployment will be affected, however, by anything—including public policies—that change the costs and benefits of searching for either individuals or firms.

Structural unemployment. Unemployment also occurs because some individuals do not have the skills necessary to fill available job openings.

Countercyclical policies will not affect structural unemployment. Structural unemployment can be affected by training and (re)educational programs that help individuals acquire the skills necessary to quality for jobs.

Natural rate of unemployment. The frictional rate of unemployment represents a kind of natural rate to which the economy returns. It appears, however, that the natural unemployment rate increased from 1970 to 1990, and then, perhaps, decreased. Several reasons have been suggested for these changes: First, the composition of the labor force has shifted in the 1970s and 1980s toward younger workers and more women; both groups have traditionally had higher unemployment rates. Second, unemployment compensation has increased over time, thereby reducing the costs of being unemployed somewhat and increasing the rate of frictional unemployment as a consequence. Third, the increase in dual-income households has reduced the costs for one of the income earners to be unemployed. As a consequence, the frictional unemployment rate increased. Its apparent decline in the 1990s is more puzzling.

Chapter 24 ▶▶

More on Inflation _____

Unlike other periods in U.S. history when inflations were often followed by deflations, since World War II, there has been persistent inflation in the United States. That is, rate of inflation has increased and decreased over the past 50 years, but with very few exceptions, the rate of inflation has been positive year in and year out. As Table 1 indicates, over the past 40 years, the price level in the United States has increased by a factor of a little over 6. By contrast, the price level hadn't changed much in the 100 years between the end of the eighteenth and nineteenth centuries.

The relationship between the price level and the rate of inflation is straightforward. The inflation rate is defined as:

$$\frac{P_2 - P_1}{P_1} \times 100$$

where P_2 and P_1 are the price levels in time periods 2 and 1, respectively, and the inflation rate is measured as a percentage. Thus, inflation is simply the percentage rate of change in the price level.

It is important not to confuse high prices with inflation. Prices are higher today than they were when your parents were young; so are wages and salaries. The price level is higher because there has been inflation since your parents were young, of course. But a high price level today does not necessarily mean that the inflation rate is high today. The price level can be high with little inflation or low with substantial inflation (although, obviously, if there is substantial inflation, a low price level will become high). In the long run, the price level, high

Table 1
The Price Level in the United States

Year	CPI*	Year	CPI*
1950	24.1	1977	60.6
1951	26.0	1978	65.2
1952	26.5	1979	72.6
1953	26.7	1980	82.4
1954	26.9	1981	90.0
1955	26.8	1982	96.5
1956	27.2	1983	99.6
1957	28.1	1984	103.9
1958	28.9	1985	107.6
1959	29.1	1986	109.6
1960	29.6	1987	113.6
1961	29.9	1988	118.3
1962	30.2	1989	124.0
1963	30.6	1990	130.7
1964	31.0	1991	136.2
1965	31.5	1992	140.5
1966	32.4	1993	144.5
1967	33.4	1994	148.4
1968	34.8	1995	152.6
1969	36.7	1996	157.0
1970	38.8	1997	160.4
1971	40.5	1998	163.1
1972	41.8	1999	166.6
1973	44.4	2000	172.6
1974	49.3	2001	177.6
1975	53.8	2002	179.9
1976	56.9		

SOURCE: *Economic Report of the President.*
* Base period is 1982–1984.

or low, is largely irrelevant to the economy. That is, economic decisions and the allocation of resources

Figure 1
Annual Inflation and Monetary Growth for 16 Latin American Countries (various years)

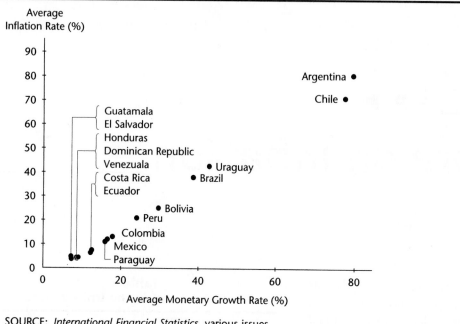

SOURCE: *International Financial Statistics,* various issues.

are unaffected by the dollar level of prices. But economic decisions and the allocation of resources are affected by inflation or deflation, especially if the rate of change in the price level (inflation or deflation) varies in unanticipated ways.

It is difficult to point to specific costs associated with inflation that are comparable to those associated with unemployment. From the choices that individuals make and the political pressures that governments feel, however, it is clear that inflation, like unemployment, is considered undesirable. Yet inflation persists. This chapter explores the reasons why.

▶ Persistent Inflation

Milton Friedman, recipient of the 1976 Nobel Prize in economics, argued that inflation "is always and everywhere a monetary phenomenon." One interpretation of this assertion is that *any* inflation is monetary phenomenon. A second is that a *sustained* inflation is always the consequence of an increase in the money supply at a rate that exceeds the rate of growth of the economy. As we have learned, both aggregate demand and aggregate shocks will, at times, push the price level upward. Not all changes in aggregate demand or aggregate are a consequence of changes in the money supply, however, so the first

interpretation of Friedman's claim is not consistent with what we have learned about how an economy functions at the macroeconomic level. The second interpretation, that *sustained* inflation is always a monetary phenomenon, requires a more careful look.

Some Provocative Data

Figure 1 plots the average rate of inflation against the average growth rate of money for 16 Latin American countries. Some Latin American countries (such as Honduras and Venezuela) had modest inflation rates, while inflation in others countries (such as Chile, Brazil, and Argentina) was substantially higher. It is clear that those countries with higher rates of inflation also had higher rates of money growth.

Figure 2 plots the average annual inflation rate against the average annual money-growth rate for a single country, Israel, during a period when inflation took off. In this case, it is clear that during periods of higher money-growth rates, Israel also had a higher rate of inflation.

Finally, Table 2 provides data on seven major hyperinflations. (A **hyperinflation** is a period in which the rate of inflation is *very* high.) Germany was required to make reparations payments follow-

Figure 2
Inflation and Money Growth in Israel, 1975–1985

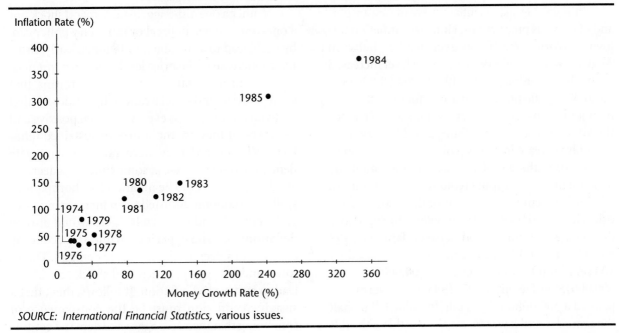

SOURCE: *International Financial Statistics*, various issues.

ing World War I. After struggling with budget deficits and an inability to raise the necessary revenues through taxation or borrowing, the government began printing money. In 1921 the money supply began to grow rapidly. So did the price level. In 1923 when units of the French army occupied the industrial sites of the Ruhr valley because Germany had failed to make its payments, the German government printed money at an even faster rate

and used it to encourage workers in the Ruhr to resist the French occupation with a general strike. As a consequence, a newspaper that cost .30 marks in January 1921 cost 1 mark in May 1922. By October 1922, the price had increased to 8 marks and by February of the following year to 100 marks. Seven months later, in September 1923, a newspaper sold for 1,000 marks; by October 1, 2,000 marks; by October 15, 20,000 marks; just two weeks after that

Table 2
Characteristics of Seven Hyperinflations

(1) Country	(2) Beginning month	(3) Final month	(4) Average monthly price increase	(5) Month of maximum price increase	(6) Maximum monthly price increase	(7) Average increase in quantity of curency	(8) Change in quantity of currency*
Austria	Oct. 1921	Aug. 1922	47.1%	Aug. 1922	134.0%	30.9%	72.0%
Germany	Aug. 1922	Nov. 1923	322.0	Oct. 1923	32.4×10^3	314.0	1.3×10^3
Greece	Nov. 1943	Nov. 1944	365.0	Nov. 1944	85.5×10^6	220.0	73.9×10^3
Hungary	Mar. 1923	Feb. 1924	46.0	July 1923	98.0	32.7	46.0
	Aug. 1945	July 1946	19,800.0	July 1946	41.9×10^{15}	12,200.0	1.03×10^{15}
Poland	Jan. 1923	Jan. 1924	81.4	Oct. 1923	275.0	72.2	106.0
Soviet Union	Dec. 1921	Jan. 1924	57.0	Jan. 1924	213.0	49.3	87.0

* In month of greatest increase in prices.

on November 9, 1923, 15 million marks. Eight days later, a newspaper was priced at 70 million marks.

Although Germany's inflation was of catastrophic and of ruinous proportions, Hungary's inflation following World War II was even wilder: Between August 1945 and July 1946, the price level increased by an almost unimaginable 1,000,000,000,000,000, 000,000,000,000 times! Notice that for both the German and Hungarian hyperinflations as well as for the other illustrated in Table 2, a large average monthly increase in prices (column 4 or column 6) occurs when there is also a large average monthly increase in money supply (column 7 or column 8).

More recently, over a six-month period in 1985 prices increased by 38,000% in Bolivia. In Yugoslavia during a 24-month period between January 1992 and December 1993, the price level increased by 100 septillion times (100,000,000,000,000,000,000, 000,000). On December 23, 1993, the government printed a 500 billion dinar bill. Its value fell by half the same day and it was essentially worthless the following morning.

Figures 1 and 2 and Table 2 are highly suggestive that *money growth* and *inflation* are correlated. Finding a correlation, however, is not the same as producing an explanation that links the two phenomena. Does money growth *cause* inflation? If so, how?

Monetary Policy and Sustained Price-Level Increases

A one-time change in aggregate demand (due to a single demand shock or a one-time change in fiscal or monetary policy) or a one-time change in aggregate supply (a single supply shock) kicks off an adjustment process that may include inflation or deflation, and over-employment or unemployment. Once the economy has adjusted to the one-time change in aggregate demand or aggregate supply, however, resources are fully employed and the price level no longer changes. This means that inflations and deflations associated with one-time aggregate demand or supply shocks are relatively short-lived. To see this, suppose the Fed engaged in a single, large open market purchase when the economy was at full employment. After the economy adjusts fully, as illustrated in Figure 3(a), the economy will have a *stable* price level, P^{**}. (A picture of this adjustment through time is provided in parts (b) and (c).) A similar argument holds for any other policy whose

initial effect is a *one-time* increase in aggregate demand.

Neither a one-time aggregate demand shock nor a one-time change in fiscal or monetary policy can, by itself, lead to a sustained inflation. Clearly, a *sustained* increase in the price level requires a *sustained* increase in aggregate demand. This means that aggregate demand shocks cannot be random—that is, divided more or less evenly between positive and negative—if they are the source of sustained inflation. Why not? If they were random, aggregate demand would increase at some times and decrease at others; there would be inflation for short periods while the economy adjusted to an increase in aggregate demand, and conversely, there would also be deflations for short periods while the economy adjusted to a decrease in aggregate demand. Therefore, random aggregate demand shocks could not lead to a sustained inflation. It follows, then, that a sustained inflation must be the consequence of something that increases aggregate demand continually and predictably.

Could the sustained inflation in the U.S. since World War II be a consequence of the steady *increase* in government spending? The short answer: No. As an empirical matter, government expenditures as a fraction of GDP has been relatively constant over this period, whereas inflation has varied a good deal. In addition, there is an absolute upper limit (100 percent of GDP) to ever-increasing government expenditures as a fraction of GDP that are funded by taxes. The practical or political limits are likely to be well below that level. It follows that although the government can create temporary inflations by increasing expenditures in times of full employment, it cannot sustain a policy of ever-increasing government spending relative to GDP.

Similarly, even though tax cuts stimulate aggregate demand and may in certain circumstances lead to a short-term inflation, tax cuts cannot lead to a *persistent* inflation. There is a limit to how often and how far taxes can be cut—once the government's tax rates are zero, no further cuts are possible. Again, as an empirical matter, taxes as a fraction of GDP have been roughly constant, even as the inflation rate has increased and decreased.

Are supply shocks capable of creating a sustained inflation? That is, can an increase in the price of oil or another important input sustain an inflation? What about higher wage demands by workers

Figure 3
Inflation After a Stimulative Monetary Policy

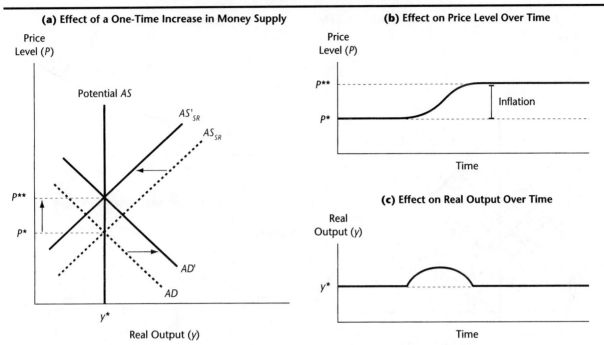

(a) Effect of a One-Time Increase in Money Supply

(b) Effect on Price Level Over Time

(c) Effect on Real Output Over Time

If the Fed conducts an open market purchase to increase the money supply, aggregate demand will increase from *AD* to *AD'* and prices will increase from *P** to *P***. Output will increase in the short run, but will fall back to *y** in the long run.

or higher price demands by firms? Again, the short answer is: No. If workers demand higher nominal wages, or input prices change dramatically, or even if somehow *all* firms demand higher prices for their output, short-run aggregate supply will fall. The price level will increase, but so will unemployment. Unemployed resources put *downward, not upward,* pressure on wages and prices. Over short periods of time, supply shocks may lead to temporary price-level changes, but the accompanying inflation cannot persist.

By a process of elimination we are left with Friedman's proposition that *persistent* inflation must be driven by *sustained* increases in the money supply. Nothing else appears to have the capability of continually increasing aggregate demand. Unlike other things that can affect aggregate demand that are limited in some way, there is no limit to the amount of money that can be printed (or, more precisely, to the number of zeros that can be printed on a piece of currency) and sustained increases in the money supply *can* continually push aggregate demand upward, as illustrated in Figure 4.

Banks create money, but their ability to do so is limited by existing reserves in the banking system. Reserves, essentially currency, are supplied solely by the Fed or central bank. Thus, the banking system, even though it creates money, cannot on its own continually create additional money so as to sustain inflation. In the end, then, an economy cannot have sustained inflation without the government continually increasing the monetary reserves available to banks.

The relationship between sustained changes in the money supply and sustained inflation can be seen by considering a relationship first introduced in Chapter 22

$$MV = Py \qquad (1)$$

which says that the money stock (M) multiplied by the number of times a dollar, on average, circulates in a year (the velocity of circulation (V)) must equal nominal aggregate output ($P \times y$). Equation (1) becomes something more than an accounting identity if velocity is assumed to be constant over time.

Figure 4
A Sustained Inflation

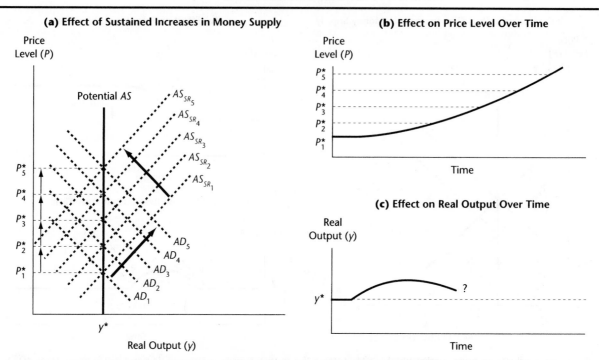

(a) Effect of Sustained Increases in Money Supply

(b) Effect on Price Level Over Time

(c) Effect on Real Output Over Time

A sustained inflation can occur only if there are sustained increases in aggregate demand caused by a continually increasing money supply. When the inflation first begins, real output will increase.

To see why, note that the percentage change in the product of two numbers is approximately equal to the sum of the percentage change in each of the numbers and we can rewrite (1) as

$$\text{\% change in } M + \text{\% change in } V = \\ \text{\% change in } P + \text{\% change in } y$$

If the economy is producing at its potential the percentage change in y is 0. If velocity is constant, the percentage change in V is 0. It follows that in these circumstances, (1) becomes

$$\text{\% change in } M = \text{\% change in } P \qquad (2)$$

and sustained or long run inflation is driven by sustained increases in the money supply.

Sustained Inflation and Real Output

None of the reasons for wage stickiness that we considered when discussing short-run aggregate supply seem likely to hold when inflation is sustained and *fully* anticipated. Will individuals *continually* under-

estimate the true rate of inflation when there is an ongoing inflation? Will contractually determined nominal wages *continually* lag behind inflation? Both seem unlikely. It is therefore also unlikely that continual increases in aggregate demand will lead to output levels much different from the potential real output of an economy. That is, if there is a sustained inflation, individuals and firms will accommodate it by making adjustments in nominal wages (and other nominal contracts) to be consistent with an *expected* rate of inflation.[1] When they do, nominal wages and prices will rise at the same rate and the real wage will be unaffected. If the rate of inflation has been and continues to be 10 percent per

---

[1] In the theories about short-run aggregate supply developed to this point, individuals have expectations about the overall *level* of prices. Here we have introduced a different idea—that individuals have expectations about the *rate of change* of prices, or, equivalently, about the rate of inflation or deflation. That is, we assume that individuals are likely to form expectations about what they believe the inflation rate will be over the next period. For example, if inflation has been a steady 6 percent per year for several years, it is reasonable that individuals will expect inflation to be 6 percent over the next year.

year, for example, workers will adjust their wage demands, insisting on nominal wage increases of at least 10 percent per year. If it then turns out that both nominal wages and the priced level increase by the same amount—10 percent—the *real* wage will be unaffected.

As long as expectations about inflation are consistent with the actual inflation, the economy should have full employment and produce at its potential even though the price level is increasing. That is, if all prices are increasing at the rate of inflation, firms and individuals should willingly agree to increases in wage rates at precisely the rate of inflation, thus preserving the real wage at a stable level consistent with full employment. The economy would then produce at its potential; only the price level would change with the ever upward shifts in aggregate demand, as illustrated in Figure 5.

Accelerating Inflation

If the actual rate of inflation exceeds the expected rate of inflation (is greater than 10 percent, say, when

it is expected to be 10 percent), the effect on real output would be analogous to an unexpected change in the price level explored in Chapter 19. That is, if the price level increases by more than expected because inflation is greater than anticipated, per unit profits will increase. Firms will attempt to increase their output and unemployment will fall. Aggregate real output will increase as a consequence. But only if the actual inflation rate exceeds expected inflation (10 percent in this example) will the real wage rate be affected by the rate of inflation. What difference does this make? Remember that if the real wage is unaffected by a change in the price level, the labor market will be in equilibrium and the economy will produce at its potential. As Figure 6 illustrates, this implies that if the economy is to sustain production at a level *above* potential real output, the inflation rate must *increase* unexpectedly. Hence, a government that tries to permanently hold unemployment below the natural rate, will have to *accelerate* inflation.

Figure 5
A Sustained and Expected Inflation

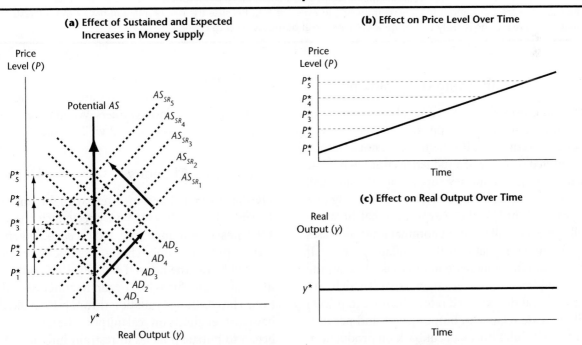

When there is sustained inflation and individuals come to expect that it will continue at the same rate, the short-run aggregate supply curve will shift leftward as aggregate demand increases because individuals will demand higher nominal wages to offset the effect of higher prices. As a consequence, even though there is inflation and the price level increases continuously, real output will not deviate from potential real output.

Figure 6
Accelerating Inflation

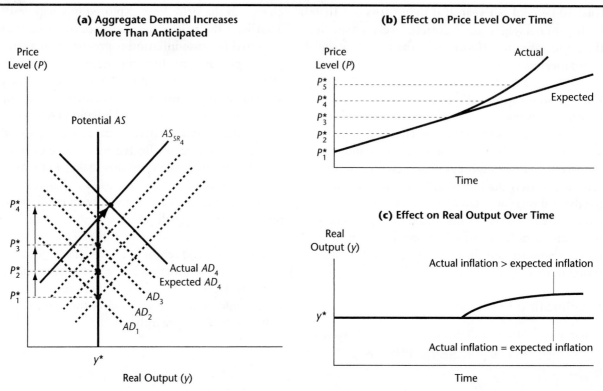

(a) Aggregate Demand Increases More Than Anticipated

(b) Effect on Price Level Over Time

(c) Effect on Real Output Over Time

Production will only exceed potential real output during a sustained inflation if inflation accelerates when individuals do not expect it to do so. This would happen if aggregate demand increased from AD_3 to *actual* AD_4 when individuals were expecting it to increase from AD_3 to *expected* AD_4. Because the rate of inflation has been underestimated, the real wage is likely to change and, hence, real output is likely to change.

Disinflation and Rising Unemployment

Once an economy has sustained, but stable, inflation, it is reasonable to suppose that everyone will expect it to continue. If inflation does not continue as expected (because of a sudden decrease in the rate of increase in the money supply), a recession will occur even though the price level is increasing (see Figure 7). Why? Workers, expecting that inflation will continue, will insist on nominal wage increases consistent with what they think inflation will be. If the actual rate of increase in prices is less than the expected rate, however, then costs (which are increasing at the expected rate of increase in prices) will increase relative to output prices and per unit profits will fall. Firms will cut back on production. Unemployment will increase and output will fall, *even though there is inflation.* Indeed, there will be a recession and inflation at the same time. Put somewhat differently, when inflation turns out to be less

than expected, the real wage will *increase* even though both prices and wages are increasing, and firms will employ fewer workers. When fewer workers are employed, real output will decline.

Real Output Changes

The data in Table 1 are consistent with this analysis. The inflation rate began to unexpectedly increase in 1964. Real output increased and exceeded potential real output for a time. That is, the unemployment rate fell below the natural rate. By 1966, however, individuals and firms had begun to anticipate inflation. The continued inflation through 1966 did not have further effects on real output. The government began to pursue policies to restrain inflation. As a consequence of these policies and the supply shock in 1973, real output began to fall even though the inflation rate continued to increase. By the mid 1970s, however, the Fed was increasing the money

Figure 7
Stagflation

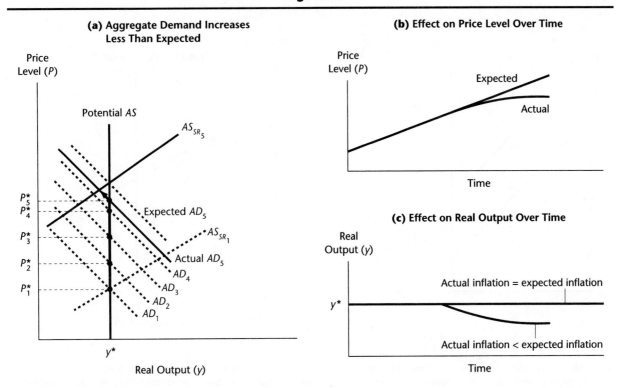

(a) Aggregate Demand Increases Less Than Expected

Price Level (*P*)

Potential *AS*

AS_{SR_5}

Expected AD_5

AS_{SR_1}

Actual AD_5

AD_4

AD_3

AD_2

AD_1

P^*_5
P^*_4
P^*_3
P^*_2
P^*_1

y^*

Real Output (*y*)

(b) Effect on Price Level Over Time

Price Level (*P*)

Expected

Actual

Time

(c) Effect on Real Output Over Time

Real Output (*y*)

Actual inflation = expected inflation

y^*

Actual inflation < expected inflation

Time

An economy may experience both inflation and unemployment if aggregate demand increases less than expected. For example, if individuals expect aggregate demand to increase from AD_4 to *expected* AD_5, but it only increases to *actual* AD_5, the price level will still increase from P^*_4, but not by as much as was expected, and real output will fall.

supply at a rapid clip and there was persistent inflation of about the same magnitude as the money growth rate (boosted by two adverse supply shocks in 1973 and 1979). There were no additional increases in real output beyond potential real output.

Between 1979 and 1981, the inflationary process of the 1960s repeated itself in reverse. The Fed pursued very tight monetary policies and the rate of money growth fell; aggregate demand fell; the rate of inflation fell, that is, there was disinflation; unemployment increased dramatically and real output fell. This fall in real output continued from 1981 through the beginning of 1983. At this point, real output began to increase even as the rate of inflation continued to decrease.

Accommodating economic growth. Even though it may appear that stable prices require a stable money supply, remember that the demand for money is closely related to the number of transac-

tions that occur in an economy. Because it increases the number of transactions, economic growth increases the demand for money. If the Fed does not accommodate economic growth with increases in the money supply, interest rates will increase and there will be macroeconomic difficulties. Put differently, to support a given growth rate in potential real output without inflation or deflation, the Fed must increase the money supply with the growth in transactions (see Figure 8). If the Fed increases the money supply too rapidly relative to the rate of growth of the economy, however, inflation will ensue, as illustrated in Figure 9(a). Or, if the Fed increases the money supply too slowly relative to the rate of growth of the economy, there will be a deflation, as illustrated in Figure 9(b).

Empirical evidence suggests that, in the long run, a 1 percent increase in real output or aggregate real income increases the demand for real money balances by about 0.68 percent. That is, the increase

Figure 8
Accommodating Economic Growth

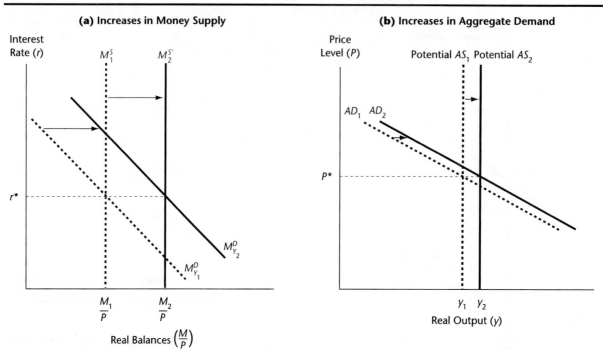

When there is economic growth, the demand for money increases. If the money supply also increases, there will be no effect on interest rates and, hence, no interest-rate effect on aggregate demand. Instead, aggregate demand will increase with the rate of economic growth, and the price level will be constant.

in demand for real money balances is less than proportional to the increase in real output. However, empirical evidence also suggests that the demand for nominal money balances increases at a rate proportional to the rate of increase in nominal output—that is, $MV = Py$, describes the long-term relationship between *nominal* money balances and nominal GDP.

The relationship between an increase in real output and the demand for real money balances (in other words, the elasticity of demand for real money balances with respect to real output) is important to the conduct of monetary policy. If real output is growing at a rate of 6 percent and inflation is 4 percent, for example, then the Fed must increase the money supply by about 8 percent per year in order to support both the rate of growth of the economy and keep inflation constant: The demand for nominal money balances increases proportionally with the rate of inflation, in this case by at 4 percent. A 6-percent rate of growth in real output would

increase the demand for money by about another 4 percent (0.68×6 percent).

▶ Inflation and Interest Rates

Persistent inflation is not just evidenced in escalating prices. *Expected* persistent inflation also affects nominal interest rates. Indeed, the simple model of macroeconomic behavior presented thus far misses some of the subtle connections between real output, investment, savings, employment, and money markets because it ignores the relationship between inflation and market interest rates.

The variety of interest rates in an economy has a simple explanation. In the absence of inflation, different risks are associated with different investments. A lender will take this into account. The effects of differences in risks are illustrated in Figure 10. Notice, for example, the differences between the government's borrowing rate (virtually risk-free), the rate at which AAA firms borrow, (rela-

Figure 9
When Money Growth Rates Differ from Real Output Growth Rates

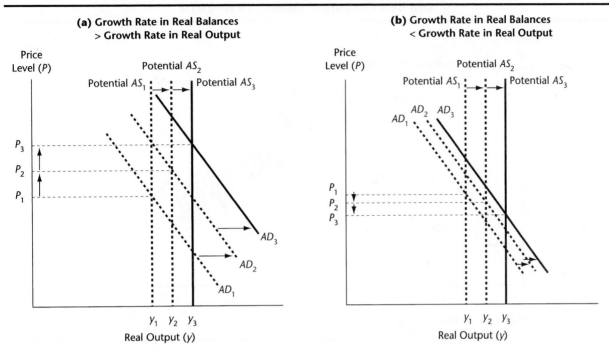

(a) If the growth rate of real money balances is greater than that of the economy (represented by the movement from AS_1 to AS_2 to AS_3), aggregate demand will increase by more than the increase in real output and there will be an inflation. (b) By contrast, if real money balances grow at a slower rate than that of the economy, aggregate demand will increase by less than the increase in real output and there will be a deflation.

tively risk-free), and the rate at which BBB firms can borrow (relatively risky).[2]

Interest rates are not affected by risk differences alone, however. Thus, all interest rates drifted upward until the late 1980s, as shown in Figure 10. Risk difference cannot explain this drift, but inflation can. Inflation erodes the purchasing power of money. In an inflationary environment, a lender will demand a premium associated with the declining purchasing power of dollars that will be repaid in the future. For example, if you lend to a firm by purchasing a $1,000 one-year bond with an interest payment of $60 and there is no inflation, at the end of the year your purchasing power is $1,060—$1,000 from the bond redemption and $60 from the interest payment. If the inflation rate is 10 percent, however, the $1,060 will have purchasing power of only $964 ($1,060/110 × 100). In this case, even though

you have 60 additional dollars, you actually *lose* real purchasing power. Knowing this, it is unlikely that you would willingly make such a loan.

To maintain purchasing power in the face of a 10-percent inflation and to provide a payment to compensate you for sacrificing current consumption equivalent to the 6 percent payment when there was no inflation, the interest payment would have to increase to about $166. That is, the **nominal interest rate** would have to increase from 6 percent without inflation to 16 percent with an inflation rate of 10 percent. Of the $166 payment, $60 compensates you for your sacrifice and $106 compensates you for the loss of purchasing power of the dollars the firm will pay you a year from now. Hence, there is a relationship between observed market ("nominal") interest rates and the sustained or expected rate of inflation. This relationship for one interest rate, the three-month Treasury bill rate, is illustrated in Figure 11. Although the two curves do not move in tandem, the interest rate tends to increase when inflation increases and decrease when inflation decreases.

---

[2] A private firm rates firms from AAA to AA to A and so forth, relative to the risks of default. (A has a higher risk than AA; AA has a higher risk than AAA; and so forth.)

Figure 10
Interest Rates for 10-Year Treasury Bonds, Corporate Bonds, and BBB Corporate Bonds, 1950–2010

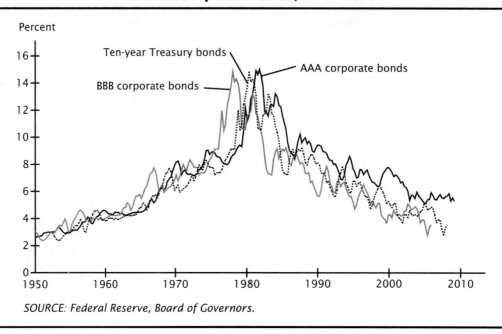

SOURCE: Federal Reserve, Board of Governors.

The relationship between market or **nominal interest rates** and the interest rates that would have prevailed if there was no inflation (the **real interest rate**) can be represented by:

$$R \quad = \quad r \quad + \quad I^e \qquad (3)$$

| Nominal interest rate | Real interest rate | Expected rate of inflation |

Note that it is the *expected* rate of inflation that affects the nominal interest rate. Herein is a problem. We only observe the *actual*, not the *anticipated*, rate of inflation. That is, both r and I^e are unobserved.

Investment

Investment is affected by the interest rate. Which matters, the *real* interest rate or the *nominal* interest rate? Investment decisions *should* be based on the real interest rate. But as was just noted, the real interest rate isn't easy to observe. Nevertheless, because of inflation the additional output that can be produced with any new capital that is acquired should sell at higher prices. So the increasing dollar

revenue stream in the future (due to the effect of inflation on the prices at which output can be sold *in the future*) should offset the higher nominal interest rate that the firm must pay on any loans needed to acquire additional capital. In short, the nominal interest rates may be high because of inflation without causing desired investment to decrease if the real interest rate is unaffected.

That is, suppose that the market interest rate is 4 percent and there is no inflation. Suppose further that the inflation rate increases to 20 percent and, for whatever reason, the nominal interest rate increases to only 22 percent. If inflation is expected to continue at a 20-percent rate, the real rate of interest would have fallen to 2 percent and desired investment will increase even though market interest rates are higher. By contrast, in the mid-1980s nominal interest rates decreased from the 20-percent range to the 10-percent range. Inflation fell much faster than interest rates did, however. As a consequence, the real interest rate increased, even as nominal interest rates declined. We should have expected investment to decrease even though nominal interest rates were lower, because the real interest rate had increased. It did.

Figure 11
A Comparison of the Rate of Inflation and the 10-year Treasury Bond Interest Rate

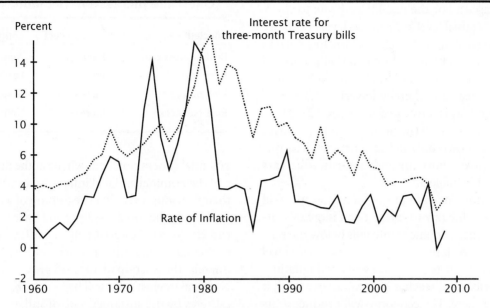

SOURCE: U.S. Bureau of Labor Statistics and Federal Reserve, Board of Governors.

Obviously, there is considerable uncertainty during a period of inflation what about the real interest rate really is because it is not a market rate and, therefore, cannot be easily observed. Indeed, one of the costs of inflation is that it makes it more difficult to borrow and lend, precisely because it makes it more difficult for borrowers and lenders to know what the purchasing power of money will be in the future. Similarly, inflation makes it more difficult to make sensible investment decisions because it is more difficult for firms to know what the real interest rate really is.

A Dilemma for Monetary Policy

Equation (3) implies that the nominal interest rate is affected by two things: the real interest rate and the anticipated inflation rate. Since in the long run, the inflation rate is approximately the same rate as the rate of increase in the money supply, nominal interest rates will increase over the real interest rate by about the rate of increase of the money supply. This appears to contradict our earlier discussion of monetary policy where we argued that an increase in the money supply *decreases* interest rates. Indeed,

this apparent contradiction poses a serious problem for monetary policy.

Countercyclical monetary policy works in part because as the money supply increases, interest rates fall and investment and other interest-sensitive spending increases. We now know, however, that *sustained* stimulative monetary policies create *sustained* inflation. Sustained inflation, in turn, increases nominal interest rates. Because there is a strong correlation between persistent inflation and persistent increases in the money supply, as well as a strong correlation between sustained inflation and high nominal interest rates, it may not be possible to push interest rates down for extended periods of time by increasing the money supply.

Suppose, for example, that the Fed unexpectedly increases the rate of growth of the money supply. The real money supply, M/P, increases (M goes up; P doesn't immediately change). Real interest rates initially decrease as a consequence, stimulating consumption and investment. The price level will increase because of this increase in aggregate demand; real output will also increase and unemployment will fall below the natural rate. In the long run, however, when all prices and wages fully adjust, the output and employment effects will disappear. Only the price effect will remain (the price level will have increased). For the real interest rate to move back to its original level as the price-level effects are fully felt, the real money stock will have to return to its original level. (That is, the original policy increases M, thus increasing M/P, but the subsequent inflation increases P, thereby lowering M/P to its previous level, as is illustrated in Figure 12.) Thus, a persistent increase in the money supply can drive interest rates down only in the short run. The differences between short-run and long-run effects are summarized in Table 3.

A one-time increase in the money supply will initially lower the rate of interest and increase output (as the unemployment rate falls below the natural rate). In the long run, however, the price level will change, but there won't be a sustained inflation: after the price level reaches its new, higher level, it will remain there. The economy will produce at its

Figure 12
The Effect of an Inflation on Real Balances and the Real Interest Rate

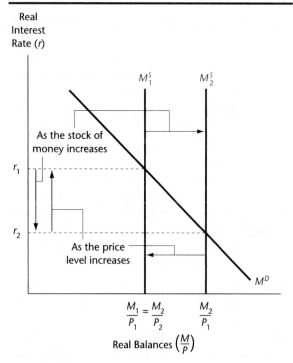

An increase in the money supply (from M_1^s to M_2^s) initially lowers the nominal interest rate. If a higher rate of inflation follows, the price level will increase (to P_2 rather than P_1) and real money balances will fall from M_2/P_1 to M_2/P_2. The interest rate will increase as a consequence.

Table 3
Short-Run and Long-Run Effects of a One-Time Increase in the Money Stock

Affected area	Short-run effect	Long-run effect
Real interest rate	Decrease	None
Price level	Increase	Larger increase
Real output	Increase	None
Real balances	Increase	None

potential (unemployment will be at the natural rate) and the nominal and real interest rates will return to their previous levels. The beginning of a *continuous* increase in the money supply will have these short-run effects. The long-run effects differ, however. In particular, the inflation rate will increase at approximately the sustained rate of growth of money. Nominal interest rates will be higher than real interest rates by the sustained rate of inflation. Because the money supply increases at the same rate as the price level, however, real balances will be at their pre-inflation level (that is, both M and P will be increasing at the same rate and so M/P won't change) Real interest rates will return to their levels prior to the beginning of the inflation.[3] These effects are summarized in Table 4.

This interest-rate effect can be seen in the data in Figure 13(a) and (b). Part (a) illustrates that changes in the money supply appear to lead to changes in the opposite direction in the three-month T-bill interest rate. That is, as the money stock increases, T-bill interest rates initially fall. Part (b) indicates that changes in the money supply do not appear to have much *immediate effect* on longer term mortgage

---

[3] It turns out that, *when there is an ongoing inflation*, a given increase in the money supply will actually have a larger and larger effect on the price level because, when the price level is expected to increase at a certain rate, the rate at which money circulates in the economy (*velocity*) also increases. In the long run, the quantity equation, $MV = Py$, appears to describe the relationship between money and nominal income as velocity increases. Therefore prices must increase more rapidly than the rate of increase in M. Hence the *greater the expected rate of inflation*, the *greater the impact* of a given increase in the money supply on prices. This explains the rapid inflation in the 1970s and also the rapid drop in the inflation rate in the 1980s (where both the interest rate and the rate of circulation of money in the economy fell, and a given increase in the money supply produced less upward pressure on prices).

Figure 13
Some Short-Run and Long-Run Effects of an Increase in the Money Stock

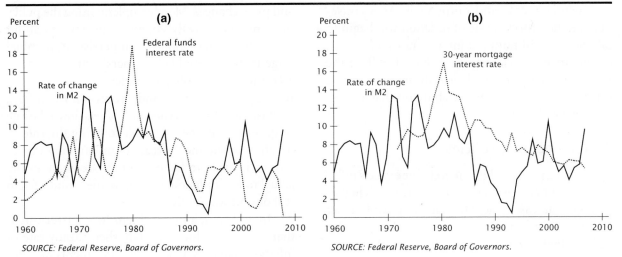

SOURCE: Federal Reserve, Board of Governors.

SOURCE: Federal Reserve, Board of Governors.

(a) A comparison of the rate of change in money and the three-month interest rate. (b) A comparison of the rate of change in money and the mortgage interest rate.

interest rates; as the rate of increase in the money supply increases over a period of several years, however, the mortgage interest rate increases, and as the rate of increase in the money supply decreases over a comparable period, the mortgage interest rate decreases. For example, the rate of increase in the money supply averaged around 6 percent from 1965 until 1983, increased very dramatically in the mid-1980s, and then fell below 6 percent in the late 1980s. The mortgage interest rate, which started at just about 6 percent in 1965, increased to somewhat over 12 percent from 1965 to 1983, and then began to fall in the late 1980s.

These data hint that changes in longer-term interest rates are driven more by expectations about inflation, and that these expectations, in turn, are determined by the long-term sustained rate of growth of the money stock, not by shorter-term changes in monetary policy. In the 1990s, for example, the Fed increased the money supply in the middle of the recession and short-term interest rates fell very dramatically, to 4 percent or so. Mortgage and other longer-term interest rates fell by much less and tended to level off at or above 8 percent, a rate consistent with the longer-term inflation and the underlying real interest rate. These long-term interest rates did fall through the 1990s, however, as the longer-term rate of inflation continued to decrease. The same pattern appeared in the early part of this century: the Fed increased the money supply in the face of a recession and short term interest rates fell to historic lows. Long-term interest rates, however, did not change much from their level in the late 1990s.

► Dealing with Persistent Inflation

If the Fed wants to lower nominal interest rates, it must squeeze some of the inflationary expectations out of the economy (look at equation (3) again). It can only do this by lowering the rate of increase in

Table 4
Short-Run and Long-Run Effects of a Continuous Increase in the Money Stock

Affected area	Short-run effect	Long-run effect
Real interest rate	Decrease	None*
Nominal interest rate	Decrease	Increase
Price level	Increase	Larger increase
Real output	Increase	None*
Real balances	Increase	None*

* When actual inflation equals expected inflation.

the money supply, thereby reducing aggregate demand. Interest rates will initially increase, unemployment increase and output fall. As a consequence, the expected rate of inflation will begin to fall. So too will nominal interest rates. Once full employment is achieved, real output will be the same as it was before the change, the unemployment rate will be at its natural level, but nominal interest rates will be lower.

Accommodating Policies

It is sometimes argued that if everyone expects inflation to occur and, as a consequence, demands higher wages or increases prices then inflation will in fact occur. The argument is incorrect. If everyone believes that public policies will *not* be accommodating to demands for higher wages or prices, then inflation in the long run cannot be created *on demand*. However, if everyone believes that public policies generally will be *accommodating* to widespread demands for higher wages or other supply shocks, *and the policies actually are*, then persistent inflation can be created. But the persistent inflation rests on the central bank accommodating the inflationary pressures. Thus, to prevent inflation, a government must be *non*-accommodating, or at least be widely perceived to be so. Mere pronouncements will not matter, however—the government's actions must be credible.

Note that this means that the government cannot announce policies that are inconsistent. If it announces employment targets that differ from the natural rate and, at the same time, announces inflation targets that are low or even zero, its policies are inconsistent. That is, its employment policy is not consistent with an announced policy of price stability. People will expect inflation and demand higher wages. This has led some economists to suggest that the only way to avoid inflationary expectations and pressures is for the government to adopt non-activist rule-based policies.

Other Approaches

A good deal of attention has been attached to developing credible and sensible anti-inflation policies. One obvious policy is to limit the rate of growth of the money supply. But this policy may not be as simple to implement as it first seems. Moreover, pursuing such a policy may be very painful to initiate once an inflation is underway because wage changes generally depend upon the momentum of *past* wage and price changes. Merely implementing the policy need not necessarily change expectations about inflation. If inflation has been persistent, nominal wage increases are likely to persist after the non-accommodating policy is implemented. If they do, real wages will increase and a recession will follow. That is, when the government ratchets down the rate of growth of money in order to bring the rate of inflation down, the decrease in inflationary expectations is likely to lag behind the decrease in the actual rate of inflation. Unemployment and a fall in real output will result

In addition, a big problem for a government that wants to reduce an established, steady rate of inflation is that its policy pronouncements may not be credible. After all, when there is persistent inflation, as we have just learned, it is the same government's policies that sustained the inflation, even if they did not originally trigger it. If individuals do not believe that the government will do what it says it will do, any decrease in expectations will lag behind adjustments in prices. The problems with credibility have led some economists to argue that discretionary countercyclical monetary policy should be abandoned and be replaced by a rule-based policy regime. In this regime, the money supply would increase at a steady rate consistent with a steady rate of growth of the real output.

Monetary reform. Governments have often been able to signal a commitment to greater discipline through what is called **monetary reform**. For example, after World War I, Germany eliminated its hyperinflation by creating a new money. The commitment of the government to be more disciplined in controlling the new money was believable; the inflation was eliminated without sending the economy into a deep recession. A similar policy was pursued by Taiwan and Israel in the mid-1980s with comparable results. The governments introduced a new Taiwan dollar in the former and the new shekel in the latter and persuaded individuals that it would be disciplined in its monetary policy. Inflation fell quickly as a consequence, without a deep and serious decline in real output. On the other hand, Brazil has gone through at least four currency reforms in the past 20 years, and continues to struggle with inflationary pressures.

A related policy is to abandon internal monetary policy altogether. This can be done by using some other country's currency as money. Yugoslavia ended its hyperinflation in 1994 by adopting the German mark as its currency. Ecuador ended a period of price instability by adopting the US dollar as its currency in the late 1990s. Note that having done so, German monetary policy became, essentially, the monetary policy for Yugoslavia and Alan Greenspan became the central banker for Ecuador. Argentina linked its currency to the US dollar in the early 1990s to end a long period of inflation; for a variety of mostly political reasons, it was de-linked in 2001 and inflation began once again.

Living with inflation. Another option, of course, is to simply live with inflation but get the government to pursue policies that hold it at a constant rate. Even though the U.S. has a modest inflation today (around 2 percent), there isn't any great pressure to reduce the inflation rate to 1 or 0 percent. Unlike the 1970s when the inflation rate bounced around a good deal, the recent US inflation rate has been *both* low *and* relatively stable. No one seems particularly concerned that the inflation rate isn't zero.

Wage and price controls. Yet another option that always seems attractive to politicians, is to impose legal limits—called **wage and price controls**—on how high wages and prices can be or, alternatively, on the rate of increase in wages and prices.

Wage and price controls virtually always create enormous problems. If the legally controlled wages and prices are actually below current wages or prices, they will create widespread rationing and inefficiency problems of the sort described for particular markets in Chapter 12. Indeed, if a price is below the market equilibrium, firms will produce less, consumers will demand more, and a shortage will be created. Moreover, because output generally decreases when there is a price ceiling, the amount that demanders are willing to pay is *greater* than the original market equilibrium price and, in a real sense, the price and wage controls create *hidden inflation*.

Moreover, wage and price controls often lead to transactions that are hidden from the government (black market transactions). As more and more transactions occur outside of the view of the government, the wage and price controls become less and less effective. With widespread price controls, if P is not allowed to increase but M continues to increase, M/P increases. This will put additional pressures on prices. As soon as the wage and price controls are relaxed, the increase in demand rekindles the explicit inflation that had been hidden in the official statistics by the legal ceilings on wages and prices.

This problem is of more than academic interest. Wage and price controls were imposed in the U.S. in the early 1970's. During that period, the money supply continued to grow at a rapid rate. The price controls failed because the shortages and side deals they fostered put increasing political pressure on the government to back away from controls. When it did, the US economy emerged with a higher, not lower, rate of inflation. Similar difficulties occurred in Brazil in the 1980's when wage and price controls were accompanied by rapid increases in the money growth rate, fueling rather than dampening the inflation that the wage and price controls were put in place to control.

As a consequence of the distortions created in an economy and of the effects of "suppressed inflation," economists have generally opposed wage and price controls as an approach to controlling inflation. If the government has the will and power to enforce the controls, it ought to have the will and power to limit the rate of growth of the money supply directly.

▶ Is There a Tradeoff Between Unemployment and Inflation?

In 1958, A. W. Phillips published a paper in which he had plotted rates of unemployment against inflation for the United Kingdom in the period 1861-1957. (Phillips actually used rates of change in wages, but comparable pictures emerged when other researchers picked up his ideas and used rates of change in the price level instead.) Phillips' data showed an apparent tradeoff between unemployment and inflation. As illustrated in Figure 14, periods of higher inflation coincided with lower unemployment and periods of lower unemployment and periods of lower inflation experienced higher unemployment.

This tradeoff was first viewed as a menu of choices: a society could choose a rate of inflation

Figure 14
The Phillips Curve for the United States, 1950–1970

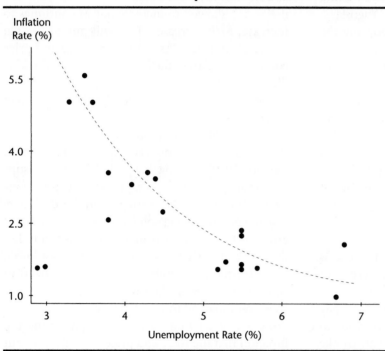

The Phillips curve shows the relationship between unemployment and inflation.

SOURCE: *Economic Report of the President*, 1992.

consistent with its desired rate of unemployment. For example, it might opt for low unemployment as long as it was willing to tolerate a higher rate of inflation. That is, it was assumed that an economy had an inflation-unemployment choice locus like that illustrate in Figure 15.

Although the possibilities appeared attractive, the tradeoff proved illusory. With high inflation accompanying high unemployment, the performance of the economy in the 1970's proved quite different than any of the tradeoffs predicted by the Phillips curves. The economy produced a 5.5 percent unemployment rate and 1.6 percent inflation rate in 1963, but it produced a 5.5 percent unemployment rate and from 5 to 9 percent inflation in the 1970s. As Figure 16 illustrates, the assumed policy choice menu fell apart in the 1970s and 1980s—there is no easily discernable inflation unemployment tradeoff in these data.

The inflation and unemployment problems of the 1970s generated a vigorous debate among economists about the nature of the possible inflation-unemployment tradeoff. One view of the problems of the 1970s was that policy makers had tried to achieve an inflation-unemployment mix in which

Figure 15
A Hypothetical Inflation–Unemployment Choice Locus

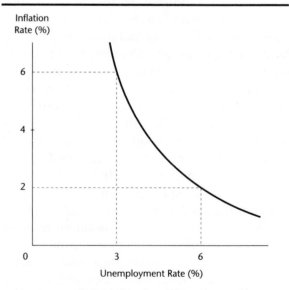

It was assumed at one time that policy makers could choose a particular combination of inflation and unemployment. For example, they might choose a combination of 6 percent inflation and 3 percent unemployment. Or, alternatively, they might choose a lower rate of inflation (2 percent), but at the cost of higher unemployment (6 percent).

Figure 16
The Phillips Curve, 1970–1990

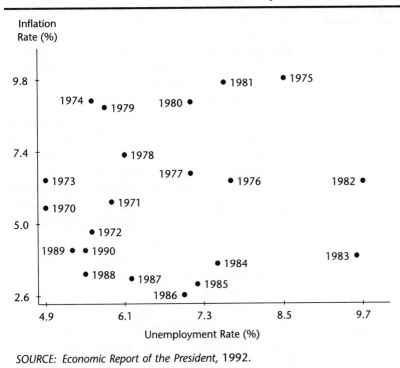

SOURCE: *Economic Report of the President,* 1992.

the level of inflation was simply inconsistent with the chosen level of unemployment. A second view was that although there was a stable tradeoff *at a point in time,* that tradeoff shifted and moved toward a higher level of unemployment for any given level of inflation because of underlying structural changes in the economy. (This shift was reflected in the higher natural rate of unemployment.) A third view was that there was no choice to be made. Even though the data might well show that lower inflation coincided with higher unemployment (and vice versa), no tradeoff could actually be exploited.

Over the long term, the third view is consistent with much of what we have discussed to this point. We know from our earlier discussion that the economy moves toward an equilibrium with full employment (that is, toward unemployment at the natural rate) and price stability. We also know that if there are repeated aggregate demand shocks from continual increases in the money supply, there will be inflation. Once inflation is correctly anticipated, unemployment cannot be maintained below the natural rate. Put differently, unemployment can only be maintained below the natural rate if wages are

sticky in the face of *known* increases in the price level, which is highly unlikely. It is far more likely that nominal wages will change with expected inflation and that the real output of the economy will be unaffected by fully anticipated inflation. Moreover, the natural rate of unemployment is determined by the composition of the labor force and the costs of searching for jobs and employees. These are *unlikely* to be affected by monetary policy. Thus, in the long run, the economy moves to the natural rate of unemployment, whatever the rate of change in prices or nominal wages.

For a short period of time, policy makers may be able to use sticky wages or the confusion created by changing inflation rates to coax additional output from the economy, but producing beyond the economy's potential cannot persist because individuals have strong incentives to gather the kinds of information needed to understand changes in their real wages and to adjust nominal wages accordingly. As they do, unemployment will return to the natural rate, whatever the level of inflation, as long as the inflation rate is understood. That is, the actual long-run policy tradeoff is closer to the one illustrated in Figure 17.

Figure 17
A National Rate Long-Run Inflation–Unemployment Choice Locus

Perhaps the inflation rate can be varied in order to fool individuals for a longer period of time. But this won't work either. If the government chooses to lower the rate of inflation (*disinflate*), unemployment will *increase* when the rate of inflation is less than what individuals expect it to be (even if it is still positive) because individuals will have made their nominal wage adjustments too high and firms will find that real wages are increasing. Thus, if the government wants to reduce unemployment below the natural rate, it can only do so by increasing the rate of inflation in unexpected ways. In this case, unemployment will *decrease* when the rate of inflation is greater than what individuals expect it to be, *but only over the short-run*. Therefore, the only way to continually entice individuals into providing more labor than they wish is to *continually increase the rate of inflation* so they are always underestimating the rate of inflation when they agree to nominal wage changes.

This would lead to an *acceleration* in the rate of inflation—10 percent now, 15 percent a year from now, 25 percent the next year, and so on (leading, in the end, to very high rates of inflation). If these continual changes in the rate of inflation follow a pattern, of course, individuals will come to expect inflation to increase by a certain percentage each year.

That is, they will build expectations abut the future price level, not on the basis of expectations about the rate of inflation, but on the basis of expectations about the *rate of increase of the rate of inflation*. For example, if the inflation rate increases by 3 percent each year, then it is not reasonable to believe that individuals will expect that the inflation will not change from year to year. Instead individuals will expect inflation to increase by 3 percent (that is, if the inflation rate was 10 percent this year, individuals will expect it to be 13 percent next year). In this case, individuals could be fooled only if the inflation rate increases at an increasing but *uncertain* rate. A policy that increases inflation each year but at an uncertain rate would quickly lead to very rapid rates of inflation.

The conclusion? There is no long-run tradeoff between inflation and unemployment *that can be exploited by public policy* in order to permanently increase the real output of an economy beyond its full employment level. The economy's tendency to move toward full employment will return the economy to the natural rate of unemployment, whatever happens to aggregate demand and neither over-employment nor under-employment is sustainable in the long run. This means that, in the long run, aggregate demand determines the price level (or that persistent increases in aggregate demand determine the rate of inflation), while the real resources available to the economy—including the choices that individuals make about how much labor to supply—determine the economy's real output. In a sense, this shouldn't be surprising. We ought to expect that, except for short deviations, what an economy can produce will be determined by the resources it has available, not by other, unrelated things.

Is a Short-Run Tradeoff Possible?

Suppose that unemployment exceeds the natural rate during a period of inflation. This means that there must have been an unanticipated disinflation (where the actual inflation rate was less than the anticipated one). To reduce unemployment in this situation requires either (a) that the actual inflation rate increase to become consistent with expectations or (b) that the anticipated inflation rate decrease to become consistent with the economy's actual inflation rate. Thus, in this situation, it may be possible to increase the inflation rate and lower unemployment and there is a short-run inflation-unemployment tradeoff. This is just another way of looking at the short-run aggregate supply curve. Along that curve, real output increases with aggregate demand as the price level increases, and real output decreases with aggregate demand as the price level decreases. But, of course, increases in the price level occur when there is inflation, and decreases in the price level occur when there is deflation.

As individuals and firms catch on to the price level changes that accompany an aggregate demand shift, however, they revise expectations and contracts. Short-run aggregate supply shifts back. Thus, as we have noted a number of times now, in the long run, an aggregate demand shift leads to an increase in the price level, but not to a permanent increase in real output and, hence, not to permanent decrease in unemployment. Thus, there is a short-run Phillips curve, but it can be exploited only once, because expectations about the rate of inflation that make it impossible to exploit it further will soon form. Indeed, it is important to remember that the short-run Phillips curve is just another way of looking at the now familiar short run supply curve that shifts leftward with expected inflation, thereby pushing the economy toward production at its potential, with unemployment at the natural rate.

▶ Summary

Inflation and money. There is overwhelming evidence that *sustained* inflation is created by *sustained* growth in the money supply, growth that is under almost direct control of the government or central bank. Tax cuts, government spending increases, supply shocks, and the like can cause a one-time increase in the price level, but *only an expanding money supply can create persistent and sustained inflation.* This conclusion is in accord with the empirical evidence from many countries and times.

Sustained inflation and real output. Once an economy has become accustomed to continual inflation, actual changes in the price level will not affect real output if they are anticipated because individuals will plan for them. For example, if inflation has been 5 percent every year for the last five years and is 5 percent again this year, real output will not increase. Only when the inflation rate unexpectedly exceeds 5 percent will unemployment be less than the natural rate. It was once believed that there was a tradeoff between inflation and unemployment (an economy could have high inflation and low unemployment or low inflation and high unemployment, but not low inflation *and* low unemployment). However, any tradeoff appears to hold only in the short run. In the long run, the economy will produce at its potential with any rate of inflation, if inflation is anticipated and modest.

Nominal and real interest rates. Sustained inflation will increase the nominal interest rate but it will not necessarily affect the real interest rate. Indeed, nominal interest rates will equal the real interest rate plus the rate of inflation.

Chapter 25 ▶ ▶

Macroeconomic Policy: A Second Look_____

Aggregate shocks pose serious problems for an economy—they lead to changes in unemployment rates and employment opportunities, cyclical changes in real output, and inflation or deflation. There are four possible sources of shocks.

1. Desired spending may unexpectedly change. For example, desired investment may increase or decrease without a corresponding change in desired saving.

2. Money demand may unexpectedly change. For example, an increase in the demand for money will increase interest rates and lead to a fall in the quantity of desired investment.

3. One or more prices of widely used inputs or widely consumed outputs may unexpectedly change. For example, the price of oil or agricultural products may suddenly increase because of an action taken by OPEC or because of a widespread drought.

4. There may be unexpected fiscal or monetary policy changes that are unrelated to counter-cyclical purposes. For example, government spending may increase dramatically because of a war or natural disaster.

The problems that follow these shocks do not persist forever. Rather, as we have seen, market economies move toward the full employment of their productive resources. If this adjustment toward potential real output takes a substantial period of time, however, the unemployment or price instabil-

ity experienced in the interim will impose substantial costs on an economy. It is little solace to an unemployed person to learn that the economy will move toward full employment in a year or two or three. Nor does it help a retired person living on a fixed income to know that inflation related to a one-time aggregate demand or aggregate supply shock cannot persist forever. The very real human costs associated with unemployment and unanticipated inflation, together with the substantial costs that lost output imposes on the economy as a whole, make the use of counter-cyclical fiscal and monetary policy tools attractive.

Obviously, the objective of counter-cyclical fiscal or monetary policy is to reduce the size of fluctuations in output, employment, and prices and to speed the economy along its path toward full employment. For example, Figure 1 shows a highly stylized economy that cycles (path *A*) around a growth path (path *C*). The purpose of stabilization policy is either to eliminate the cycles completely (that is, move the economy along path *C*), or to moderate the cycles (that is, move the economy along path *B*). Whether it is possible for public policy to move the economy along path *C*, or along path *B*, is the central issue in macroeconomic policy.

▶ Fiscal and Monetary Policies

To investigate this central issue, we begin by pulling together our work to this point on appropriate policy responses to macroeconomic shocks that would

Figure 1
The Goal of Stabilization Policy

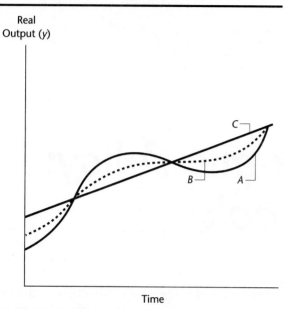

The U.S. economy tends to cycle (path *A*) around a growth (path *C*). The goal of stabilization policy is either to eliminate cycles completely so that the economy moves along path *C*, or to moderate the cycles so that the economy follows a path like *B*.

Figure 2
A Deflationary Aggregate Demand Shock

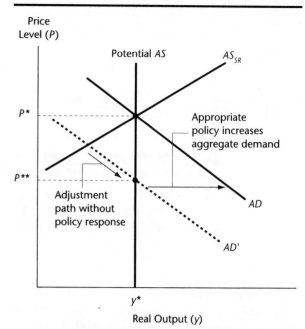

If ignored, an aggregate demand shock that reduces aggregate demand from *AD* to *AD'* will create unemployment followed by a deflation. Appropriate fiscal and monetary policies will increase aggregate demand from *AD'* to *AD*, moving the real output of the economy back to *y** and avoiding a deflation.

lead, in the short run, to cyclical movements in output, employment, and prices.

Appropriate Policy Responses to Deflationary Aggregate Demand Shocks

If aggregate demand unexpectedly declines, as illustrated by the movement from AD to AD' in Figure 2, deflation and unemployment will follow. A goal of stabilizing macroeconomic policies is to offset such a change in aggregate demand and keep the economy as close as possible to its potential output.

Appropriate fiscal policy responses include an increase in government expenditures and/or a decrease in taxes on income, consumption, or investment. Increases in government expenditures increase aggregate demand directly, whereas lower taxes increase desired investment or consumption, indirectly affecting aggregate demand.

Appropriate monetary policy responses include an open market purchase of bonds, a decrease in the reserve requirement, and/or a decrease in the discount rate. Each of these changes increases the money supply, lowers interest rates (at least in the

short run), and stimulates desired investment and net exports, thereby increasing aggregate demand.

Appropriate stimulative fiscal or monetary policies increase aggregate demand, moving the aggregate demand curve back to *AD* and the economy back toward potential output (*y**). The effect of these policies is to prevent or offset a deflation in the economy and keep the price level close to where it was before the demand shock occurred (that is, at *P**).

Appropriate Policy Responses to Inflationary Aggregate Demand Shocks

An unexpected increase in aggregate demand creates inflationary pressures, as illustrated by the movement from *AD* to *AD''* in Figure 3.

Appropriate fiscal policy responses include a decrease in government expenditures and/or an increase in taxes on income, consumption, or investment. Decreases in government expenditures decrease aggregate demand directly, whereas higher

Figure 3
A Inflationary Aggregate Demand Shock

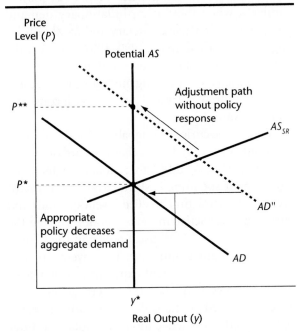

If ignored, an aggregate demand shock that increases aggregate demand from *AD* to *AD''* will result in temporary overemployment and will create inflation. Appropriate fiscal and monetary policies will decrease aggregate demand back to *AD,* moving the real output of the economy back to *y** and avoiding inflation.

Figure 4
A Price Shock

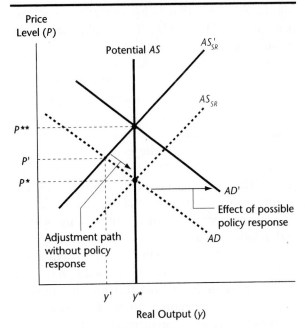

When there is a price shock in the economy that unexpectedly pushed the price level above *P**, short-run aggregate supply will shift leftward from *AS_{SR}* to *AS'_{SR}*. Unemployment will result and, if the economy is left alone, eventually there will be a deflation. The government can avert unemployment by pursuing policies that will increase aggregate demand from *AD* to *AD'*; if it does, the price level will not return to *P** but, rather, will increase to *P***. Therefore, a policy that reduces unemployment will be inflationary.

taxes affect aggregate demand by decreasing desired consumption and desired investment.

Appropriate monetary policy responses include an open market sale of bonds, an increase in the reserve requirement, and/or an increase in the discount rate. One or a combination of these actions will decrease the money supply, increase interest rates and dampen investment and net exports, thereby lowering aggregate demand and moving the economy back toward potential output (y^*). Appropriately pursued, such policies will prevent inflation and keep the price level close to its original level (P^*).

Appropriate Policy Responses to a Price or Supply Shock

Appropriate responses to a supply or price shock are problematic. Suppose that a worldwide increase in agricultural or oil prices occurs. Firms find that important input costs increase, so they reduce supply. That is, firms will be unwilling to provide the

same amount to the market unless the price at which they sell their output increases. The effect of this unwillingness is to shift the short-run aggregate supply curve leftward, as illustrated in Figure 4. The price level increases. As the price level increases, however, real money balances decrease and interest rates increase. Aggregate real output *demanded* decreases as a consequence—there is a movement back along the aggregate demand curve, as illustrated in Figure 4, and real output falls from y^* to y'. Unemployment will increase as a consequence.

If left alone, the economy will eventually return to full employment, but only with a deflation. However, during the period of adjustment, unemployment will be above the natural rate. Rather than waiting for the economy to adjust by itself, the government can move it toward full employment by pursuing appropriate macroeconomic policies, although such policies can only work by *further* inflating the economy, that is, by increasing aggregate demand from *AD to AD'*. If unemployment is the primary concern of policy makers, appropriate fiscal policies include an increase in government expenditures and/or a decrease in taxes; appropriate monetary policies include an open market purchase and/or a decrease in the discount rate or reserve requirement. Each of these policies increases aggregate demand, moving the economy toward its potential real output (y^*), but with *higher* price level (P^{**}). That is, these stimulative policies reduce unemployment, but at the cost of higher inflation. As a consequence, there will be both unemployment and inflation for a period of time.

If inflation rather than unemployment is the primary concern, then the only option is to tolerate unemployment. Traditional anti-inflation policies (a reduction in the money supply, a cut in government spending, and/or an increase in taxes) will shift aggregate demand leftward, increasing unemployment. Alternatively, the government might do nothing and allow the price level and unemployment to increase with the initial shock and then, on their own, fall.

Which countercyclical policies, if any, ought to be pursued depends upon how a society weighs the costs of unemployment against the costs of inflation. A supply shock forces a society to make this uncomfortable choice.

It is generally thought that the 1973–1974 and 1979–1980 downturns were consequences of supply shocks. In both cases, largely unexpected increases in oil prices increased inflationary expectations, shifting the short-run aggregate supply curve to the left. The opposite occurred in the 1985–1986 expansion when oil prices dropped unexpectedly, decreasing inflationary expectations and shifting the short-run aggregate supply curve to the right. In 1973–1974 and 1979–1980, unemployment and inflation both increased; in 1985–1986, unemployment and inflation both decreased.

Mixing Fiscal and Monetary Policies

The government does not need to choose only fiscal policy or only monetary policy responses to aggregate demand or aggregate supply shocks—both types of policies can be combined. For example, when there is a deflationary demand shock, *both* stimulative monetary and fiscal policies might be employed. Similarly, when there is an inflationary demand shock, *both* restrictive monetary and fiscal policies might be employed. In the 1990–1992 recession, the Fed pushed interest rates down and the Federal government increased spending modestly by increasing the budget for highway and public-transit construction, for example.

One of the curious things about fiscal and monetary policies in the U.S. is that they are often not coordinated but at odds. A fiscal policy that increases government spending is stimulative, but it might occur at the same time the Fed is selling bonds and pursuing a restrictive monetary policy. During the early part of the 1980s, fiscal policy in the United States was highly stimulative. Taxes were cut substantially and government expenditures increased slightly. As a consequence, the Federal government deficit increased dramatically. At the same time, the Fed pursued a restrictive monetary policy in order to bring the rate of inflation down. Hence, fiscal policy was stimulative while monetary policy was restrictive. Two policies that push in opposite direction could either tip the balance toward lower inflation with movement toward full employment or lower inflation and higher unemployment, as is illustrated in Figure 5. In the early 1980s, the policy mix led to a rapid fall in the rate of inflation. In this instance, restrictive monetary policy overwhelmed stimulative fiscal policy.

Different real output mixes. The mix of monetary and fiscal policies affects the division of aggregate real output among consumption, investment, net exports and government uses of resources. For example, some economists argued that when, in the early 1980s the policy mix was restrictive monetary policy and the large borrowings by the Treasury to fund the Federal deficit, real interest rates increased, thereby depressing investment *relative to what it otherwise would have been*. Concerned about long-term capital formation (and, hence, investment), these economists urged a quite different policy mix—a more restrictive fiscal policy and a less restrictive monetary policy—that would have dampened aggregate demand to bring down inflation without driving up interest rates so much and depressing investment. A more restrictive fiscal policy and less restrictive monetary policy, even if it had had the

Figure 5
Possible Effects of Pursuing Both a Stimulative
Fiscal Policy and a Restrictive Monetary Policy

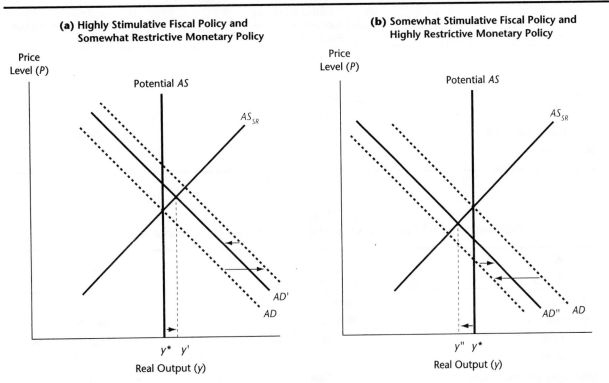

(a) The stimulative fiscal-policy effect is larger than the restrictive monetary-policy effect and real output increases from y* to y'. (b) The simulative fiscal-policy effect is smaller than the restrictive monetary-policy effect, and real output decreases from y to y".

same effect on real output and inflation as did the opposite policy mix that was pursued during the early 1980s, would have resulted in a different mix of consumption, investment, and government spending when the economy obtained a full-employment, low-inflation equilibrium. Table 1 summarizes the different outcomes associated with different policy mixes.

The output mix effect of different policies can also be seen by noting that either a tax cut, or an increase in government spending will increase aggregate demand. The effect on real output and the price level will be the same in both cases: real output will increase and, generally, so will the price level. A tax cut, however, leads to a proportionately larger private sector (aggregate demand increases because of an increase in consumption or investment spending) and a proportionately smaller public sector. By contrast, an increase in government spending leads to a proportionately larger public sector because, obviously, aggregate demand in-

creases with an increase in government spending. Table 2 summarizes these different possibilities.

There is yet another output mix possibility: decreases in either taxes on personal income or on investment will stimulate aggregate demand. A decrease in taxes on personal income will produce a different output mix at full employment than will a decrease in taxes on investment, however. The former will lead to more consumption relative to investment; the latter will do the opposite.

Finally, either countercyclical fiscal or monetary policy can increase aggregate demand, but an increase in government spending will lead to a different output mix than a stimulative monetary policy will. In this case, an increase in government spending increases the share of output going to the public sector whereas an open market purchase of bonds by the Fed will lower interest rates and stimulate investment, thereby increasing the share of real output devoted to investment.

Table 1
Different Mixes of Monetary and Fiscal Policies with the Same Aggregate Demand Effect

Affected area	More restrictive monetary policy and less restrictive fiscal policy	Less restrictive monetary policy and more restrictive fiscal policy
GDP	?	?
Price level	?	?
Money supply	Decrease	Increase
Interest rate	Increase	Decrease
Government spending	Increase	Decrease
Investment	Decrease	Increase

Table 2
Different Fiscal Policies with the Same Aggregate Demand Effect

Affected area	Tax cut	Increase in government spending
GDP	Increase	Increase
Price level	Increase	Increase
Interest rate	Possible increase	Possible increase
Consumption	Increase	Increase
Government spending	No effect	Increase
Investment	Possible decrease	Possible decrease

Clearly, the choice of particular macroeconomic policies whose aggregate countercyclical effects may be the same is also a choice about how the output of an economy will be divided among competing uses. Do we need more and better consumer goods and private investment or do we need more and better schools, roads, parks, and national defense? Obviously, those who prefer the latter would prefer stimulative macroeconomic policy in the form of increased government spending, whereas those who prefer the former would opt for stimulative macroeconomic policy in the form of tax cuts. Different individuals will evaluate these options differently. This means that a particular macroeconomic policy mix is likely to be much debated *even when everyone agrees on the overall counter-cyclical objective.*

Growth effects. When the economy is fully employing its resources, the division of real output among consumption, government spending, net exports, and investment may also affect the long-term

prospects for the economy. An increase in government spending has the same macroeconomic effects on GDP and the price level as does an appropriately sized tax cut, but an economy's output mix will differ. A tax cut that provides incentives to invest and save will lead to capital accumulation and, over time, greater potential real output, in other words, to economic growth. Pursuing policies that discourage either investment or saving will lead to less economic growth, even though they may be equally effective in moving the economy to full employment. Thus, the macroeconomic policy mix has political consequences because it has short-term consequences for employment and price level stability and longer-term consequences for economic growth. Or, in more technical language, aggregate demand-side policies may also have aggregate supply-side effects. Here too, different individuals will prefer different output mixes, *even when everyone agrees on the overall counter-cyclical objective.*

Supply-side effects. Tax policies change the relative prices of work and leisure or of consumption and saving. For example, an income tax makes working somewhat more costly (by reducing net pay), thereby making leisure somewhat less costly. A tax on interest earned on saving lowers the return on saving (by reducing the net return), thereby motivating people to save less and consume more. Saving less, when the economy is at full employment, will result in less capital formation. These supply-side effects are not limited to fiscal policy. Monetary policy affects interest rates, investment, and, as a consequence, capital accumulation. When the rate of capital accumulation changes over time, the growth rate in potential real output also changes. Thus, stimulative spending, tax, and monetary policies may have the same effect on aggregate demand, but they will generally have different long-term effects on aggregate supply because they provide different incentives to work, save, or acquire additional capital. (Similarly, restrictive spending, tax, and monetary policies may have the same effect on aggregate demand, but they will have quite different long-term effects on aggregate supply.)

Much of the debate about supply-side effects has centered on tax policies that stimulate or discourage investment or saving. Changes in tax policy that may have supply-side effects include:

- Reducing taxes on capital gains. Financial assets increase and decrease in price. If a financial asset increases in price, when its owner sells it, he or she obtains a *capital gain*. Prior to 1986 capital gains were treated differently from income from wages or interest for tax purposes. Preferential tax treatment for capital gains makes the purchase of assets more attractive, increasing the demand for financial assets. This, in turn, increases saving and moves resources to firms for investment purposes.

- Reducing taxes on the income from savings. Taxes on savings or on the interest income from savings make saving less attractive and consumption more attractive. Preferential tax treatment for saving or for its interest income makes saving more attractive and hence increases the resources available to firms for investment purposes.

- Reducing taxes on corporate income. Taxes on corporate income reduce incentives to

investment because they make investment less profitable.

- Reducing corporate tax liability by increasing capital depreciation allowances. When a corporation acquires new capital, it is not allowed to deduct the full cost of the new capital against its taxes in the year in which it acquired the new capital. Instead, tax laws force the corporation to spread the cost over a number of years. The amount that can be deducted each year is called a *depreciation allowance*.[1] Allowing for more depreciation each year for a fewer number of years following an investment lowers taxes immediately after capital is acquired and, as a consequence, makes acquiring new capital more attractive.

In each case, taxes are reduced, so aggregate demand will increase. But the reduction in taxes will also affect incentives to accumulate capital. Because the accumulation of capital is important for the long-term prospects of an economy, the effects of a particular counter-cyclical policy mix chosen may extend well beyond the immediate effects on unemployment and prices.

In general, the immediate effects of fiscal and monetary policies on *potential* real output appear to be small relative to the effects on aggregate demand. In principle, this means that by pursuing appropriate counter-cyclical policies, a society might be able to obtain more than it loses because of distortions that reduce *potential* real output. This does not imply that a society ought to ignore supply-side effects. Over longer periods of time, small changes in growth rates make a substantial difference. Indeed, in the long run, changes in the growth rate of an economy may be much more important to individual well-being than the amelioration of economic fluctuations.

▶ Difficulties with Policy Implementation

Devising appropriate countercyclical policies may look simple, but actually implementing countercyclical in a dynamic economy with powerful

---

[1] The number of years covered by the depreciation allowance is generally not related to the actual life of the newly acquired capital. Hence, changing the depreciation allowable for tax purposes is simply a way of changing a corporation's tax liability based on the amount of its capital.

political forces that influence policy formulation is difficult.

The Goals of Macroeconomic Policy

There is general agreement that full employment is better than unemployment, stable prices are preferable to inflation or deflation, and economic growth is better than stagnation. As a consequence, the goals for macroeconomic policy are often stated as

1. full employment
2. stable prices (or, at least, low and stable inflation)
3. sustained economic growth

There is less agreement about exchange rate stability and balanced trade. US policies in these areas, for example, are passive: the dollar is more or less free to fluctuate and little effort has been made to eliminate the now long-running trade deficit. At various times and in different countries, however, it is clear that maintaining the exchange rate at a particular level has also been a goal of macroeconomic policy and, at times, a balanced trade or even trade surpluses has been a policy goal as well. Thus, the following might be added to the list:

4. stable exchange rate (possibly)
5. balanced trade or, perhaps, a trade surplus (possibly)

There is less agreement about how best to obtain full employment, stable prices, and robust growth, and even less agreement about the relative importance of these goals. Disagreements about goals, and particularly, about their relative importance have to be sorted out in a political process.

Timing (Is Almost Everything)

Even if the goals of macroeconomic policy were clear, implementing effective countercyclical policies poses challenges. Has there been an aggregate demand shock? If so, by how much has aggregate demand changed? Does the shock require a policy change? If so, when and by how much? Answers to these questions require fairly detailed information about the economy. Effective countercyclical policies cannot be pursued without knowing whether aggregate demand or aggregate supply shocks have *actually* occurred or are *highly likely* to occur. Nor

can effective countercyclical policies be pursued without knowing the size of the aggregate demand shock. Put somewhat differently, effective countercyclical policy requires that policymakers recognize adverse changes in the economy soon enough to be able to make a difference, and that they understand enough about the adverse shock, and about the economy itself, to be able to know how large an appropriate countercyclical response should be.

The only data readily available are those on the recent performance of some parts of the economy. This may or may not be useful for understanding future movements of key components of the economy, however. Aggregate demand depends upon *desired* consumption, *desired* investment, *changes* abroad and *projected* government expenditure and tax patterns, not on the history of past consumption, investment, net exports or government expenditures.

The US economy is very large, with millions of transactions and tens of thousands of different markets and activities. As a consequence, gathering the information necessary to make forecasts takes time. Often by the time information about macroeconomic performance has been gathered and analyzed, aggregate demand shifts have already occurred and the economy has slipped into a recession or inflation has become substantial. Thus, macroeconomic policy begins with an inherent limitation because there are inherent limitations on the available data.

One approach to these limitations is to use the readily available historical data to try to *forecast* the future course of the economy. In the late 1960s and early 1970s, for example, large computer models of aggregate supply and aggregate demand were developed that relied on historical data to forecast desired consumption, desired investment, and net exports and thus future macroeconomic changes. Despite intensive work, the resulting computer models have not been very good forecasters of upcoming shocks, in large part, because modeling the expectations of individuals and firms has proven to be an extraordinarily complex problem. Put simply, the dynamic nature of economic behavior makes future actions difficult to predict. In addition, of course, shocks can come from unanticipated changes in the activities of the government and from economic and political circumstances abroad. Both are even more difficult to predict.

A second, simpler approach has been to rely on key *indicators* of economic behavior that provide some sense of the direction of the economy. Extensive study of economic data has shown that changes in the following data (called **leading indicators**) often precede changes in real output:

Average weekly hours worked

Average weekly claims for unemployment insurance

New orders for consumer goods

Vendor performance (rate of delivery)

New orders for plant and equipment

Building permits for new private housing units

Changes in unfilled orders for durable goods

Changes in producer prices

Stock price changes for 500 common stocks

Changes in real money balances (M2/P)

Index of consumer expectations

Figure 6 shows how an index of these leading indicators moves with cycles in GDP. Notice that the index often, *but not always*, leads a downturn or

upturn in GDP. (You can find the **index of leading indicators** at *http://www.conference-board.org/ products/frames.cfm?main=lei1.cfm*.)

Computer models are not reliable forecasters of aggregate demand shocks. Similarly, leading indicators do not *always* lead to, but sometimes falsely signal, an upcoming aggregate demand shock. As a consequence, neither computer models nor leading indicators reliably predict coming changes in the economy.

Size, Not Just Direction, Matters

This brings us to a second problem. How large should a particular policy change be? Even if policy makers know that there has been an adverse aggregate demand shock, should taxes be cut by $1 billion or $5 billion? Should government expenditures be increased by $1 billion or $5 billion? Should the Fed purchase $5 million or $10 million in government bonds? Answers to these questions depend in part upon precise estimates of aggregate-demand and money multipliers. Answers also depend upon knowing *where* the economy actually is relative to its potential real output,

Figure 6
Composite Index of Leading Indicators

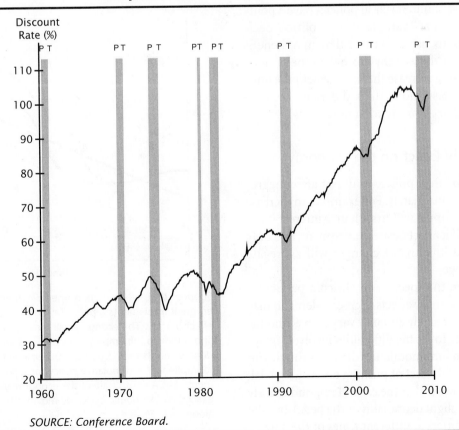

SOURCE: Conference Board.

which, in turn, requires a good deal of specific information. Hence, determining the size of a policy action is not a trivial matter. Size matters, however. If the government chooses a policy that is too stimulative when there is a deflationary demand shock, or too restrictive when there is an inflationary demand shock, the policy can itself create a shock (in the opposite direction). And, a policy that is too timid may not have much effect on real output or the price level.

Implementation Also Takes Time

There are great advantages in being able to anticipate aggregate demand or supply shocks so that appropriate policies can be implemented before the adverse economic changes occur. However, the inability to forecast such changes does *not* mean that there is no role for countercyclical fiscal and monetary policies. Appropriate policies can be used to dampen the business cycle even after the effects of aggregate demand shocks are clearly visible. Notice that any policy response now lags the aggregate demand shock, however. But even when the direction of the economy is known it takes time to implement appropriate policies. In part this time lag occurs because countercyclical policies have a political dimension. For example, it is a political decision whether to use a tax cut that may benefit corporations or the wealthy more than the poor or to use a spending increase that may benefit the poor and middle class more than the rich. Political processes and decisions tend to move slowly.

So Does Any Effect on the Economy

Once implemented, policies will not affect aggregate demand immediately. For example, an increase in the money supply will first change interest rates. Only then will it affect desired investment, and only when desired investment changes will aggregate demand change.

Moreover, the speed with which a particular countercyclical policy affects aggregate demand may not be known precisely and may vary with economic circumstances. To see the difficulties involved, imagine driving an automobile in which, although you know the general effect of pushing on the gas pedal, you don't know whether the car will respond quickly or slowly to a slight depression of the pedal and the actual effect differs at different times of the day.

Recap: Implementation Difficulties

In summary, it takes time to gather information about changes in the economy (a **recognition lag**), to determine the appropriate size of the policy response (a **sizing lag**), to implement the appropriate policy (an **implementation lag**), and for the policy to fully affect the economy (an **effect lag**). The sum of these lags matters a lot—countercyclical policy is effective only if its effects on aggregate demand occur *more rapidly* than the unaided adjustments of the economy would without policy responses. Clearly, if the economy will return to full employment and a stable price level more quickly than policies can be implemented and become effective, stabilization policy is of little value. Worse, in such circumstances, it may be that stabilization policies actually destabilize the economy.

The importance of timing is illustrated in Figure 7. Suppose that there is an adverse aggregate demand shock and real output begins to fall. Policies implemented soon after the demand shock is discovered

Figure 7
Timing Policies to Offset Unemployment

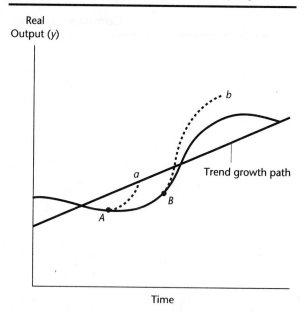

Suppose that, when there is unemployment, the government implements a policy (at point A) that takes effect quickly. The economy will move along path Aa and return to full employment before it would have done so on its own. But if the government waits until B to implement a stimulative policy (or a policy implemented at A doesn't affect the economy until B), it may exacerbate economic cycles by moving the economy along path Bb.

(at point A) and that rapidly affect the economy may move it along path Aa. If so, the economy benefits substantially because this path returns it to its potential (full employment) output more quickly than does the path it would follow if left alone.

If the same policy cannot be implemented until time B or can be implemented at time A but isn't really effective until time B, the stimulus to aggregate demand coincides with increases in real output that are already occurring within the economy. The stimulus may shift aggregate demand beyond the full employment position, moving the economy along path Bb. In this case, the policy does not become effective until the economy has essentially solved its problems and it *amplifies rather than dampens* the economic cycle.

In short, if aggregate demand can be shifted more rapidly by appropriately sized policies than adjustments can occur naturally in labor and output markets, then the economy will move toward its long-run growth path and the policy will be stabilizing. However, if labor and output market adjustments occur more rapidly than policy effects, the economy will move to the growth path *on its own before any policy could be fully effective* and, as a consequence, the economy will be buffeted, rather than benefited, by demand-side policies.

Timing Differences Between Monetary and Fiscal Policy

Most evidence suggests that monetary and fiscal policies are quite different in the time it takes to implement each and the time each takes to affect the economy once implemented.

Monetary policy. Monetary policy can be implemented rapidly. The Fed must simply decide to engage in an open market operation and buy or sell T-bills (or announce changes in the reserve ratio or discount rate). This can be done in a matter of days or even hours. The effects of monetary policy take a relatively long time to work their way through the economy, however. Open market operations change the asset mix in the economy, which then change interest rates, which in turn affect desired investment. Changes in the asset mix and interest rates will also change savings and desired consumption. Only when desired investment and desired consumption change will monetary policy affect aggregate demand. The lag between

implementation of the policy change and its effect on aggregate demand may be several months. To make matters more difficult, there is evidence that the lag varies depending upon conditions in the economy. For example, housing construction takes from six months to a year to respond fully to a change in interest rates. As a consequence, an economy may not feel the full effect of a change in monetary policy for some time and no one can know precisely when the full effect will be felt. In fact, it is generally believed that the full effect of monetary policy is not felt until about two years after the policy change.

Fiscal policy. By contrast, government expenditures on real output affect aggregate demand directly and immediately. Changes in taxes are somewhat less direct. However, they affect disposable income or the profitability of capital immediately, leading to rapid changes in desired consumption or desired investment. Fiscal policy is implemented in the United States by the Congress, however, and the Congress is a deliberative body with rules, traditions, and constitutional constraints that are designed to make public policies change very slowly. For example, the budget for the next fiscal year (beginning for the federal government on October 1) is typically developed by the president the previous summer (more than 15 months before the fiscal year begins) and submitted to Congress in January, some nine months before the fiscal year begins. Following the passage of a budget resolution that guides overall appropriation and revenue activities in April, the Congress debates specific appropriation and revenue bills until the first of October. Frequently the Congress does not have a complete set of appropriation and revenue bills completed by October. If it does, then and only then do the Federal departments and agencies begin to spend the money or prepare to collect the taxes. In short, changes in fiscal policy almost always take a long time to implement, although ever-popular tax cuts seem to move through the budgetary process more quickly. In the most recent downturn, it was widely recognized by March 2001 that the economy was in a recession, but a fiscal policy response did not make it through Congress until April 2002!

Consequences. These differences between monetary and fiscal policies leave us with a curious irony. Monetary policy, which can be implemented rapidly, affects the economy indirectly and slowly over time.

Fiscal policy, which is usually difficult to change rapidly, affects the economy directly and quickly once implemented. It follows that, for either economic or political reasons, neither monetary nor fiscal policy appears able to respond quickly to changes in aggregate demand.

▶ Fiscal Policy, Deficits, and Crowding Out

At first blush, fiscal policy appears to be straightforward: increase government spending or decrease taxes during a recession; decrease government spending or increase taxes during an inflation. Aside from the implementation problems, however, fiscal policy is more subtle than this simple characterization suggests because the government must fund its activities, and an increase in government expenditures without a corresponding increase in taxes or a tax cut without an equal reduction in government spending creates a deficit (or reduces a surplus).

In certain circumstances, funding a Federal government budget deficit increases interest rates. In addition, if the stimulative fiscal policy pushes the price level up, real money balances will fall, and, as a consequence, interest rates will increase. Higher interest rates from either source decrease desired investment. Clearly, the direct effect on aggregate demand of an increase in government spending that increases the deficit, and the indirect effect on aggregate demand of the increase in interest rates on desired investment push in opposite directions. Thus, whether an apparently stimulative fiscal policy will *actually* increase aggregate demand depends upon whether the interest-rate effect on investment is less than the effect of the increase in government spending. Put simply: An important issue for understanding fiscal policy is whether deficits **crowd out** investment and other kinds of private expenditures. Crowding out occurs when an increase in government spending or cut in taxes triggers one or more of the following effects:

$\uparrow$ Deficit   (1)
  $\rightarrow \uparrow$ GDP $\rightarrow \uparrow$ demand for money
      $\rightarrow \uparrow$ interest rates $\rightarrow \downarrow$ investment

$\uparrow$ Deficit   (2)
  $\rightarrow \uparrow$ price level $\rightarrow \downarrow$ real balances
      $\rightarrow \uparrow$ interest rates $\rightarrow \downarrow$ investment

$\uparrow$ Deficit   (3)
  $\rightarrow \uparrow$ government borrowing in competition with private borrowing
      $\rightarrow \uparrow$ interest rates $\rightarrow \downarrow$ investment

Deficits and the National Debt

The government's deficit is the difference between government spending (g) and tax revenues (t). Persistent deficits in turn create a national debt. The **national debt** is the total value of outstanding government obligations; the **deficit** is the increase in the national debt in a particular year. Thus, the national debt is the accumulated value of *all* deficits and surpluses. The deficit is determined by the difference between government *outlays* or *expenditures* and government *receipts* or *revenues* in a single year, as is illustrated in Table 3.

For a variety of reasons, most unrelated to countercyclical fiscal policy, tax policy and expenditure policy have been at odds over much of the past two decades. Thus, federal expenditures have exceeded federal taxes through periods of unemployment *and* through periods of full employment. Through the late 1990s we had (and had had for some time) large and sustained federal deficits, whatever real output, aggregate demand, inflation,

Table 3
The 2008 Federal Budget
(in billions of dollars)

Receipts	$2,521.2
Individual income taxes	$1,219.7
Corporate income taxes	$345.3
Social security taxes	$910.1
Other taxes	$46.0
Outlays	
National defense	$607.3
Transfer payments to individuals	$1,796.1
Grants to state and local governments	$162.2
Administration, investment	$209.4
Interest on national debt	$243.9
Other (undispersed receipts)	−$87.7
Deficit	−$410.0

SOURCE: *U.S. Office of Management and Budget, FY 2009 Budget.*

or unemployment have been. Beginning in the late 1990s, the federal government began to run surpluses. The recession that began in 2000 and the post-September 11, 2001 increase in expenditures quickly erased these surpluses. In 2002 the federal government was once again running a deficit. The large deficits over the past two decades (with only a couple of surpluses) created a very large national debt. Figure 8 provides a historical perspective. Part (a) provides data for the nominal or dollar value of the deficit, and part (b) illustrates the deficit as a percentage of real GDP.

Before the 1980s, most of the outstanding federal debt had been accumulated during World War II. Wars are always periods of serious economic distress. Nations struggle against their production possibilities frontiers to increase output in order to fight the war; governments struggle to move resources from the private sphere to public control in order to direct their use in the war effort. Almost always, taxes do not increase sufficiently to fund the entire mobilization effort, and governments must finance part of the war with a deficit. Thus, even though the U.S. government ran a small deficit each year for most of the period form 1950 to 1980, the size of each deficit was small compared to the very large deficits during World War II.

Beginning in the 1980s, the size of the annual deficit increased very dramatically. Indeed, well over two-thirds of the current national debt has been accumulated from deficits funded since 1980. Put in its most dramatic terms: In the first 200 years of US history, the Federal government accumulated about $1 trillion in debt. In the next decade of its history, by contrast, the federal government more than tripled this debt, accumulating another $2 trillion in just ten years. Table 4 provides comparative data on deficits and public debt for seven industrial countries.

Cyclical and structural deficits. It is useful to divide the deficit into two parts: the cyclical deficit and the structural deficit. Fluctuations in real output over time—the economic cycle—are responsible for the **cyclical deficit**. Longer-term and more persistent differences between government spending and government revenues are responsible for the **structural deficit**. The distinction is useful primarily because much of the cyclical deficit occurs automatically with changes in the economy. This type of deficit arises because some government expenditures automatically increase with a downturn in the economy when tax revenues generally fall. For example, unemployment compensation increases during a recession, and because aggregate income falls, income tax revenues decrease. In addition, during a recession there is almost always explicit countercyclical fiscal activity by the government—President Bush and the Congress agreed on a countercyclical fiscal stimulus package in April 2002 that increased government spending (taxes had been cut earlier in the Bush administration).

The other part of the deficit is a consequence of explicit decisions by the Congress and president about expenditure and tax policies that are *unrelated* to counter-cyclical or stabilization policies. For example,

Table 4
Deficits and Debt, Cross Country Comparisons

Country	National debt, % GDP			Deficit, % GDP	
	2000	2005	2009 est	2000	2009 est
Canada	46.2	30.6	32.6	2.9	−5.9
France	35.1	43.2	57.0	−1.5	−7.9
Germany	34.4	49.8	56.9	1.3	−6.2
Japan	60.4	84.6	106.6	−7.6	−8.7
United Kingdom	26.8	27.2	61.0	3.7	−14.0
United States	36.0	43.2	69.3	−0.4	−11.2

NOTE: 2000 was at the end of a long expansion; 2009 was at the end of a long recession.

Figure 8
Federal Government Surplus or Deficit, 1950–2010

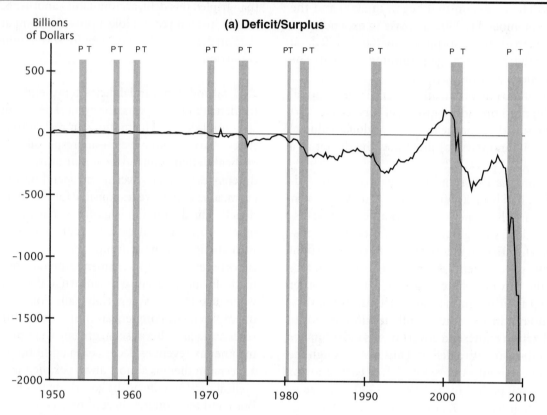

SOURCE: Federal Reserve Bank of St. Louis.

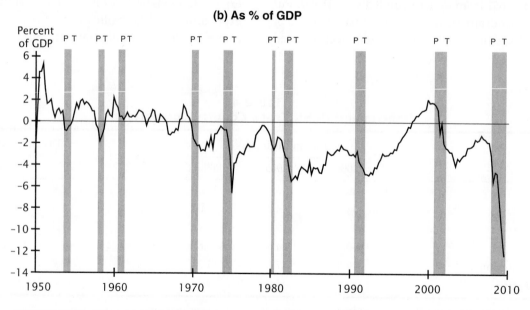

SOURCE: Federal Reserve Bank of St. Louis.

decisions to increase defense spending in the early 1980s were not accompanied by increased tax revenues; these decisions were not related to aggregate demand shocks, but were in response to perceived national defense needs. Similarly, beginning in the early 1970s, a very substantial expansion in entitlement programs was not fully funded by increases in taxes. President Bush pushed through a tax cut when he first took office for reasons unrelated to the business cycle and then expenditures substantially increased in the post-September 11, 2001 period for national defense and antiterrorism efforts.

Long-Term Consequences of Crowding Out

Crowding out makes fiscal policy less potent, but it also has more serious, longer-term consequences for the economy. To analyze these longer-term consequences, we will assume that the economy is producing at its potential, or, in other words that unemployment is at the frictional rate. We will also assume that the government begins to run a deficit even though the economy is at full employment. Thus, in the following discussion we are interested in the effects of a government deficit when the economy is producing somewhere along the long-run aggregate supply curve, y^*.

Money claims and real output. Suppose that real output, y^*, is 1,000 widgets and that there are 1,000 $1 bills in the economy. Widgets sell for $1 each. All of the productive resources used in widget production are owned by individuals living within the economy, so aggregate household income is $1,000. Suppose, further, that firms wish to invest 200 widgets. (Remember that, in order for new capital to be built, firms must obtain real resources; the 200 widgets represent those resources that are used for investment rather that consumption purposes.) In order to obtain the widgets, firms must persuade individuals to consume only 800 of the 1,000 widgets produced. That is, firms have to persuade individuals to transfer $200 to them, because without dollars, firms will be unable to purchase the resources (widgets in this case) necessary to build new capital.

Transferring money claims to firms. In a market economy, firms cannot coercively transfer dollar claims to real output. That is, the transfer of dollars between individuals and firms must be voluntary. In order to get dollars, firms offer debt (bonds) and/or equity (stocks) to individuals. When they purchase either debt or equity, individuals give up dollars to the firms. To keep things simple, let's suppose that the acquisition of new capital is financed by issuing debt. That is, assume that firms in our simple economy print 200 $1 bonds and sell them to individuals. After the bonds have been sold, the individuals will have $800 with which to purchase widgets and, of course, $200 worth of bonds. Because dollars, not bonds, are used to purchase widgets, individuals can now collectively purchase only 800 widgets. On the other hand, as a consequence of this financial market transaction, firms now have $200 and can purchase 200 widgets. Essentially, firms persuade individuals to consume less than the total amount the economy produces by offering debt (essentially promises of future consumption which from the perspective of an individual is an asset since holding a firm's debt is a way for an individual to transfer current income into the future) in exchange for claims on current output (dollars).

An aside: Firms can pay individuals more dollars over the life of their debt than they borrowed if they use the money to acquire new capital which creates profits in the future, part of which the firms can use to pay the interest on and redeem their debt. If the firm squanders the money or the new capital doesn't create additional profits, then the firm cannot make the payments, in which cases it is **bankrupt**.

Transferring money claims to the government. If the government wants 100 widgets, it must also persuade individuals to consume less than the 1,000 widgets that the economy produces. Like private firms, the government can persuade individuals to do this by offering its debt in exchange for dollars. Suppose, then, that the government prints 100 $1 Treasury bonds and sells them to individuals for $100. Following the sale of the T-bonds, the government has $100 and individuals have $900 plus $100 worth of government bonds. The government can now purchase 100 widgets and the remaining 900 will go to individuals for consumption purposes.

When the government and firms sell bonds to individuals, they become obligated to pay dollars to bondholders at some point in the future because, in each case, an IOU has been created. In order to meet these future obligations, firms must earn profits from the capital they purchase. The government, however, can pay interest and redeem its bonds by taxing individuals at some point in the future as the interest payments or redemption dates become due. For firms and the government, the source of future dollars differs, but the initial effect of a sale of bonds is essentially the same for both: dollars and, hence, claims on real output, are transferred from individuals.

Instead of printing and selling bonds, the government can obtain claims on real output by forcing individuals to cut their consumption by taxing income. If the government wants 100 widgets, for example, it can impose a tax of $100, thereby transferring dollars from individuals to the government. In this case, no IOUs are created, the government has no obligations in the future and individuals *cannot* expect that their consumption will be higher in the future. However, their ability to consume current real output changes because of the tax and they will consume less. Specifically, individuals only have $900 and can purchase only 900 widgets (of the 1000 produced) and the government, which now has $100, can purchase the remaining 100.

The federal government has one additional device for transferring real resources from private individuals. Through the Federal Reserve, it has a monopoly on the production of currency. Thus, in lieu of either borrowing or taxing, the government could print 100 additional $1 bills and use these new dollars to purchase 100 widgets. If it did this, individuals would collectively have more dollars— $1,100 in our simple example—and fewer widgets. Indeed, only 900 widgets of the current production of 1,000 widgets would be available for consumption because the government purchases the other 100 using its newly printed dollars. Clearly, consumption must be reduced from 1,000 widgets to 900 widgets. How does this reduction occur? The number of widgets each dollar purchases must fall. Or, put differently, the purchasing power of each dollar in circulation must fall. As long as the economy produces 1,000 widgets and has $1,000, widgets will have a price of $1. When the economy has $1,100 but only 1,000 widgets, however, the price of widgets must increase from $1 to $1.10. This is equivalent to a 10 percent decrease in the purchasing power of a dollar (and is just another way of looking at the inflationary effects of monetary poli-

cies when the economy is fully employing its resources that we considered in Chapter 24).

The Federal government's budget constraint. The federal government's expenditures (g) *must equal* its revenues from taxation (t) *plus* its revenues from printing and selling new debt (ΔB) *plus* the new currency it creates and uses (ΔM). That is,

$$g = t + \Delta B + \Delta M$$

If tax revenues are not equal to the level of government expenditures, that is, if t < g, the federal government *must* either print money (ΔM) or print and sell bonds (ΔB). *The government has no other choices*—it is *not free* to spend more than its tax revenues unless it either prints bonds (ΔB) or prints money (ΔM). In this sense, the government has a budget constraint.

The true tax on an economy. The total resources used by the government can be thought of as a "tax" in the sense that they are *not* available for private use. For example, a scientist used to research the Strategic Defense Initiative cannot be used to develop lasers for CD players and cement used to build a highway or a dam cannot be used to build homes or factories. Since the level of expenditures, g, represents the resources that the government will use in a given year, it, *not* t, represents the *true tax* on the economy.

For a given level of expenditure, g, the government budget constraint means that the government has to choose how it will obtain the resources it wants to use. It can either reduce consumption below income by taxing *directly,* (t), or it can tax *indirectly* by printing bonds (ΔB) or printing money (ΔM). Congress chooses the mix of explicit or indirect taxes when it determines whether g will be equal to, greater than, or less than *t*. If Congress determines that tax revenues will be less than the government expenditures it mandates, the Treasury has no choice but to print and sell bonds. This choice imposes an indirect tax on the economy because the real output purchased using dollars obtained form the sale of the bonds is not available for private use. Or if Congress determines that tax revenues should be less than government expenditures but the Treasury does not want to print bonds, the Fed must be persuaded to increase the amount of currency in circulation to fund the government's purchases. This option also imposes an indirect tax because after the government purchases goods and services using the new currency, fewer goods and services are available for private use.[2]

The effect of printing bonds. If Congress runs a deficit and the Treasury prints and sells T-bonds in order to gain the additional resources needed, the government competes with firms and households that are attempting to sell their bonds to acquire additional capital[3]. This competition between the government and private entities for resources will generally drive up interest rates—individuals must be persuaded to save more and consume less and, of course, they must be persuaded to purchase T-bonds rather than private bonds. As interest rates increase because of this competition between the government and private entities for resources, private investment will be displaced. That is, higher interest rates make some kinds of investment projects less profitable and some firms that would have been willing to borrow in order to acquire new capital when interest rates were lower will no longer find this worth doing. It is in this way that, unless saving increases by the full amount of government borrowing, government expenditures financed by printing bonds displaces some private investment that is also financed by debt. It follows that **crowding out** begins with a displacement of private borrowing by public borrowing, and, in the end, private investment by government spending.

If this displacement of private investment by public expenditures continues over an extended period of time, capital accumulation will be less that it otherwise would have been, and economic growth will be adversely affected. Therefore, deficits that crowd out investment can be said to "tax" the future in the sense that future *potential* real output will be smaller than it otherwise would have been, *ceteris paribus*. That is, deficits that crowd out private investment impose a tax on future generations because less capital and output are available than there would have been had there been no deficit. (Note that if the government spending financed by the deficit is for public capital, however, crowding out would not *necessarily* lead to slower economic growth.)

It is sometimes argued that because the government must make payments on and eventually redeem its debt, deficits impose a tax burden on the future in that future individual income must be taxed to make these payments. This is true. However, it is not quite the "burden on the future" that it is often suggested to be. It is true that a government bond implies a future tax obligation by the government and hence by its citizens. Each T-bond that pays interest must be owned by someone, however. Likewise, each T-bond that will be redeemed at some point in the future is currently owned by someone. Therefore, if the federal government's debt is sold to US citizens, the government's liabilities become assets for individuals living with the United States who own the bonds. This means that the future tax imposed on one person to make payments on the national debt is simply transferred to another person *within the* economy. In other words, one person pays taxes and another person receives them as interest payments. The first person's disposable income is reduced by the amount paid as taxes, but the second person's disposable income in increased by the same amount. For the economy as a whole, these changes in disposable income cancel out. It follows that, in this sense, there is *no* net tax burden for the economy as a whole. The frequent identification of the cost of deficit financing in terms of taxing for future interest and redemption payments is, therefore, incorrect. *Instead, at full employment, the actual burden of the deficit is that it "taxes" capital formation through crowding out.*

Crowding out of exports rather than investment. Almost anyone—foreigner or US citizen—can purchase T-bonds. When interest rates begin to creep up a little because of the competition between the Treasury and private borrowers, foreigners may choose to purchase the T-bonds. If they do, there will be a flow of capital from abroad to the United States and, obviously, the domestic deficit need not

---

[2] Because the Fed is independent from the Treasury in the United States, this is complex. The Treasury can only print bonds but, as it does so, it may put pressure in one way or another on the Fed to purchase those bonds, thus increasing the money supply. In many other countries, the treasury and central banking functions are handled by the same agency. In this case, the choice between printing bonds and printing money to finance the government's activities is much more direct.

[3] Households issue debt in the form of mortgages, car loans, etc.

crowd out domestic investment. Loosely, US firms continue to sell their debt and some or all of the government debt is sold to foreigners. Something like this appears to have occurred during the mid-1980s—the economy was near full employment, the US government ran a large deficit, yet interest rates did not increase by very much and there was a substantial flow of capital from abroad to the United States. This appears to be the best of all worlds. It's not quite, however. Something is crowded out: US exports rather than domestic investment.

The mechanism is as follows: If foreigners wish to purchase T-bonds, they must have dollars. They can get these dollars by purchasing them in foreign exchange markets. Hence, foreign demand for T-bills, increases the demand for dollars. This increases the value of the dollar (an appreciation) and reduces the value of other currencies (a depreciation). When the dollar costs more, however, so do US goods and US exports fall. When other currencies cost US citizens less, so do foreign goods. US imports increase. Therefore, $(x-m)$ falls. Indeed, in order to import capital, there must be a trade deficit. Clearly, in this case, what is crowded out are US exports. (The reason is simple if you keep in mind that real output of an economy at full employment is like a pie that is fixed in size: when g increases, *something* has to fall. If it's not i, then it must be something else, in this case, x.) In sum, a domestic government deficit produces a trade deficit. (This is sometimes called the **twin deficits problem**.)

Will this always happen? No. Foreigners cannot be forced to purchase another government's debt. In fact, they will do so only if they believe that the debt is a reasonably secure asset. If they believe that the government will inflate its economy and thereby render its debt worthless, they won't buy the debt. Likewise, if they believe that the government will be unable to pay interest or redeem its debt, they won't buy it either. Somalia or Mozambique or Argentina cannot play this game because foreigners are reluctant to purchase the debt of these, and similarly situated economies. For these countries, running a domestic deficit creates, at full employment, either crowding out of investment or inflation. The U.S. is fortunate in that its debt is widely viewed as worth holding. This allows the U.S. government to run a deficit and have someone other than US citizens fund a large part of it.

The effect of printing money. When the economy is producing at its potential, increasing the money supply creates inflation. As we learned in Chapter 24, inflation is a tax on money-fixed assets. Money itself is a money-fixed asset, so inflation is a tax on the holding of money. This can be seen easily by noting that $1.20 held for one year when the inflation rate is 20 percent purchases what $1.00 would purchase today. Thus, a 20 percent inflation is equivalent to a 20 percent tax on money or on any other asset that is fixed in money terms such as a corporate bond or a T-bond.

Choosing a method of taxation. Congress determines government expenditures, explicit taxes, and hence the size of the deficit. That is, Congress chooses to tax current income explicitly through direct and indirect taxes on personal income or to tax future income implicitly through the effect of the deficit on capital formation. The Fed can change the implicit tax on the future by replacing bonds with currency. That is, while if Congress chooses a deficit, the Treasury must print and sell bonds, the Fed can always print currency to purchase these newly-issued bonds. If it does, the Treasury does not have to compete with firms for private savings but the money supply increases instead. At full employment, increases in the money supply lead to inflation.

Thus, when the government chooses expenditures, g, it must also choose a mix of methods by which it will tax its citizens, thereby freeing real resources equal to g. It can tax output directly through taxes on income, consumption, or investment (t), or it can tax capital formation through borrowings that crowd out private capital formation (ΔB), or it can tax the use of money and money-fixed assets by printing money and creating inflation (ΔM). The total resources made available through these three alternative taxes must equal the government's expenditures. What the government *cannot* do is use real resources without transferring them from private households through some form of taxation.

All taxes distort decisions. The government chooses which kinds of distortions it will create as it chooses a mix of explicit taxes (t) and implicit taxes (ΔB, ΔM). There is no particular reason for one of these "taxes" to invariably distort more than another. Explicit taxes on income, consumption, or investment distort either labor-leisure, saving-consumption, or capital accumulation choices. Printing money taxes the use of money and money-fixed assets through inflation, thereby distorting decisions about how much money and other kinds of money-fixed assets to hold. Printing bonds taxes capital formation and distorts the growth rate of the economy. The government must balance or trade off these distortions as it considers how to fund its expenditures.

In the United States, there is almost always widespread public pressure to lower explicit taxes (t) *without* lowering government expenditures (g), that is, to impose implicit rather than explicit taxes. As a consequence, over the past decade or more, politicians who dared to suggest that explicit taxes ought to increase found themselves in serious political trouble, as did those who outlined specific cuts in government expenditures. (The general claim that government spending can be cut by reducing waste, fraud, and abuse is always popular, of course.) There is a curious two-part puzzle here: First, why do we collectively appear to prefer implicit taxes on capital formation or on the use of money over explicit taxes on income, consumption, or investment? That is, why are we unwilling to bring t into line with g? Second, why does the federal government, which mostly limited deficit financing except in times of war for nearly two hundred years, now find it difficult *not* to run a large deficit?

Crowding out and the monetary-fiscal policy mix. Earlier we noted that the government could mix monetary and fiscal policies. Frequently, the government does so in an effort to minimize crowding out. If the Fed increases the money supply when fiscal pol-icy is stimulative, for example, there is less crowding out and the full fiscal effect will be felt through aggregate demand shifts. Why? The stimulative fiscal policy puts upward pressure on interest rates but, at the same time, the stimulative monetary policy puts downward pressure on interest rates, at least in the short term. This is a stimulative monetary policy-stimulative fiscal policy mix. The effects are summarized in the second column of Table 5. If the Fed instead pursued a tight monetary policy when fiscal policy was stimulative, interest rates would increase. Investment would fall as a consequence. These results are summarized in the third column of Table 5.

With a stimulative monetary policy-stimulative fiscal policy mix, investment would be higher than it would be with a tight monetary policy-stimulative fiscal policy mix (see Table 5). This means that growth would likely be higher, but so would the rate of inflation. When a tight monetary policy-very stimulative fiscal policy mix is pursued, by contrast, government purchases will be higher as a fraction of real output. There will be less growth, but also less inflation.

The Effect of a Deficit on Inflation

Can a sustained deficit cause sustained inflation? Probably not. A sustained inflation is created by sustained increases in money beyond that necessary to provide for the growth in the economy. When the government runs a deficit, it prints new bonds, but it does not necessarily print new money. Hence, a deficit does not *necessarily* lead to an increase in the money supply and cannot sustain inflation on its own. A sustained deficit may create an environment

Table 5
The Effects of Different Monetary Policy—Fiscal Policy Mixes

Affected area	Mix of stimulative monetary policy and stimulative fiscal policy	Mix of restrictive monetary policy and stimulative fiscal policy
Government spending	Increase	Increase
Deficit	Increase	Increase
Price level	Increase	?
Money supply	Increase	Decrease
Interest rate	No effect	Increase
Investment	No effect	Decrease
Aggregate demand	Increase	?

where there are *pressures* to print money and inflate the economy, however. In particular, if crowding out occurs because financing the government's deficit increases interest rates, there are likely to be political pressures to pursue policies that would bring interest rates back down. The policy pursued in such a circumstance is an expansion of the money supply, of course. Continued pressures of this sort may lead to continual increases in the money supply, thereby creating a sustained inflation. In other words, if the government chooses not to fund its expenditures through explicit taxes, as we have seen, it must choose to tax *either* through deficits *or* through inflation. Deficits may create pressures to replace the newly printed government bonds with newly printed money in an effort to keep interest rates from rising, however. This action by the Fed, called **monetizing the deficit**, means that the deficit will be accompanied by inflation, even though the deficit does not of itself cause inflation.

Why Tax by Inflation?

One of the important reasons for sustained inflation in many countries appears to be a weak central government. In particular, governments that have neither the ability to tax directly (t cannot increase) nor the ability to resist the pressures from various groups to increase government expenditures (g does increase) will almost always turn to the printing press as a way of responding to the many competing pressures. As a consequence, inflations frequently accompany wars or other periods of social distress when a government is pressed to the limit of its ability to generate revenues through the tax system. Hyperinflations of the sort considered in Chapter 24 almost always occur in countries where the political system—and sometimes the economic system—is in a shambles.

In the United States, inflations have accompanied the Revolutionary War, Civil War, World War I, World War II, and the Vietnam War. The effect is perhaps best seen in recent US history: In 1965, President Lyndon Johnson was told by his economic advisors that if he wished to increases America's military presence in Vietnam he would have to raise taxes or pressure the Fed to print money. Johnson, leading an increasingly unpopular effort to fight in Asia, decided he was not politically strong enough to push a tax increase through Congress and opted

instead to finance much of the build-up with printed money. Hence, the Vietnam War caused inflation.

What Does All This Tell Us About Fiscal Policy?

To the degree that increases in government expenditures crowd out private investment, fiscal policy will be less effective. Increased government expenditures increase aggregate demand, but crowding out of investment decreases aggregate demand. The net or overall effect on aggregate demand then depends upon whether there is a one-for-one dollar decrease in private expenditures with an increase in public expenditures. If there is, fiscal policy will be completely ineffective.[4]

This one-for-one displacement of private expenditures with public ones is *unlikely to occur* when there is *less* than full employment because the economy has excess capacity that can provide the additional resources necessary for both private and public expenditures. (That is, unlike a "full employment" pie where if the size of the slice going to g goes up, *some other share—c, i, x—must go down*, when g increases, the "less than full employment" pie gets *larger*.) Thus, when there is unemployment, fiscal policy may be an effective policy tool.

A caution. If the Treasury sells bonds, the money supply does not change. If the Fed sells bonds, however, the money supply decreases. What accounts for this difference?

When the Fed sells bonds, it takes *previously* issued T-bonds from its vaults and sells them on the open market. The currency obtained form the sale is taken out of circulation—an open market sale decreases bank reserves, thus reducing the money supply.

When Congress creates a deficit through its budgetary process, the Treasury must print *new* T-bonds, which it sells on the open market. The money obtained is used to purchase the goods and services mandated by Congressional decisions. That is, the money is used to cover the deficit created when explicit taxes (*t*) are less than government

---

[4] If saving increases dollar-for-dollar with the deficit (an effect known as **Ricardian equivalence**), c would fall even as g increased and aggregate demand would be also unaffected by the fiscal policy.

expenditures (g). Hence, the money obtained from the sale of bonds is immediately returned to the economy. Bank reserves remain the same and the money supply does not change.

In short, after the Fed conducts an open market sale, there are more bonds and less currency in private circulation. After the Treasure sells bonds, by contrast, there are more bonds and the same amount of currency in circulation.

▶ Technical Constraints on Stabilization Policy

It's not enough, obviously, to know that during a recession that appropriate policy would include an increase in the money supply or fiscal stimulus. Appropriate policy design requires an understanding of the *size* of the increase or stimulus. This, in turn, requires a good deal of technical information about the economy.

Aggregate demand multipliers. A large aggregate-demand multiplier means that fiscal policy of a given size will be more effective. At the same time, a large aggregate-demand multiplier means that fiscal actions taken at the wrong time will be more likely to destabilize the economy. By contrast, the smaller the aggregate-demand multiplier, the larger a change in taxes, government spending, or money-supply induced change in investment must be in order to offset a given macroeconomic shock.

If the size of the aggregate-demand multiplier is unknown or not predictable, the size of a change in g or t needed to offset an aggregate-demand shock cannot be determined. Likewise, if the size of the aggregate-demand multiplier cannot be determined or isn't stable over time, the size of a required change in investment induced by monetary policy cannot be determined either.

What must a policy maker know? Answer: aggregate demand multipliers are determined by the marginal propensity to consume, the nature of the tax system, and marginal tax rates.

The money multiplier. The smaller the money multiplier, the larger a Fed open market operation must be to offset a given adverse aggregate demand shock. Hence, the size of the money multiplier matters in conducting countercyclical monetary policy. (It doesn't really matter whether the money multiplier is small or large, as long as its size can be determined accurately.) If the size of the money multiplier changes over the business cycle or, more generally, over time, discretionary monetary policy becomes more difficult because the effects of an open market operation becomes less predictable.

What must a policy maker know? The money multiplier is determined by the amount of leakage and by the willingness of banks to make loans up to the point of the Fed-established minimum required reserves.

Elasticities. The relative effectiveness of monetary and fiscal policy also depends on the sensitivity of desired investment and money demand to interest-rate changes, or in more technical terms, on the *interest rate elasticities* of investment demand and money demand.

Fiscal policy. The size of the crowding out problem associated with a government deficit depends, in part, on the interest elasticity of demand for investment. If investment demand is highly sensitive to interest rate changes, then small increases in interest rates when new T-bonds are sold in competition with private debt will substantially reduce investment and stimulative fiscal policy will be substantially offset by the fall in other components of aggregate demand. Conversely, if investment isn't very interest sensitive, then it will be less adversely affected by this competition and fiscal policy will have a larger stimulative effect on aggregate demand.

This point is illustrated in Figures 9 and 10 and summarized in Table 6. In Figure 9, a fiscal policy stimulus that increases interest rates crowds out some investment, but the effect is small. In Figure 10, by contrast, a fiscal stimulus of the same size increases interest rates by the same amount but, because investment is sensitive to changes in the interest rate, there is a large, offsetting decrease in desired investment.

Thus, even if the aggregate-demand multiplier is known, large and stable, if desired investment is highly sensitive to interest-rate changes and if fiscal policy affects interest rates, fiscal policy will *not* be particularly effective in stabilizing the economy. Put differently, countercyclical fiscal policy is relatively more effective (1) if stimulative fiscal policies do not affect interest rates by much or (2) if interest rates do not affect desired investment by much.

Figure 9
Fiscal Policy When Investment Demand Is Inelastic

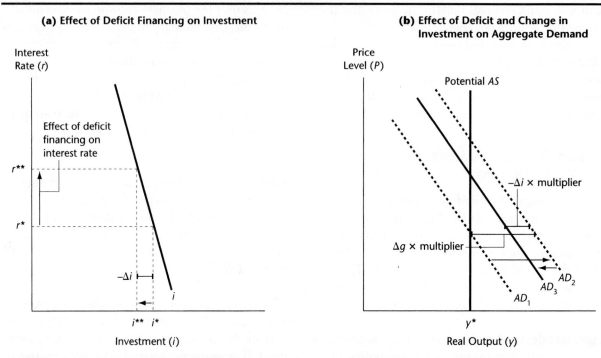

(a) Effect of Deficit Financing on Investment

(b) Effect of Deficit and Change in Investment on Aggregate Demand

When investment is not very sensitive to changes in interest rates, an increase in government spending that shifts aggregate demand from AD_1 to AD_2 [part (b)] and that increases interest rates from r^* to r^{**} will decrease investment by a small amount, from i^* to i^{**} [part (a)]. The crowding out that occurs as investment falls is shown by the movement from AD_2 to AD_3 in part (b).

Monetary policy. A change in the money supply will not affect interest rates by much if the demand for money is highly sensitive to interest-rate changes. Why? If the elasticity of money demand is high, a small drop in interest rates will be sufficient to bring the quantity of money demanded into line with an increased money supply. In this case, for a given change in the money supply, there will be relatively little effect on desired investment.

This point is illustrated in Figure 11 and summarized in Table 7. In Figure 11(a), an increase in the money supply substantially lowers interest rates; in part (b), an increase in the money supply of exactly the same size has a much more modest effect on interest rates. The effects of the *same* Fed policy are quite different in the two cases and the effect on desired investment will be different as well.

A large effect on interest rates of a change in the money supply is not, by itself, enough to stimulate aggregate demand, however. If the demand for money is relatively insensitive to interest-rate changes (so that a given increase in the money supply leads to a large decrease in interest rates), but if investment is itself insensitive to interest rates, then aggregate demand will still be relatively unaffected by monetary policy. This point is illustrated in Figures 12 and 13 and summarized in Table 8. In Figure 12 an increase in the money supply increases

Table 6
Fiscal Policy and the Sensitivity of Investment to Interest-Rate Changes

Area affected by stimulative fiscal policy*	Interest sensitivity of desired investment	
	Low	High
Interest rate	Increase	Increase
Investment	Small decrease or no change	Large decrease
Aggregate demand	Large increase	Small increase

* For example, an increase in government spending.

Figure 10
Fiscal Policy When Investment Demand Is Elastic

(a) Effect of Deficit Financing on Investment

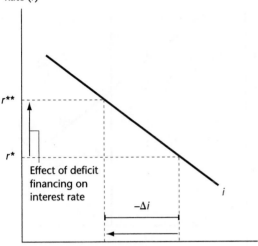

(b) Effect of Deficit and Change in Investment on Aggregate Demand

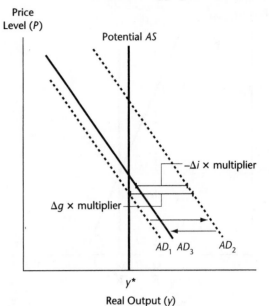

When investment is sensitive to changes in interest rates, an increase in government spending that shifts aggregate demand from AD_1 to AD_2 [part (b)] and that increases interest rates from r^* to r^{**} will decrease investment substantially, from i^* to i^{**} [part (a)]. The crowding out that occurs as investment falls is shown by the movement from AD_2 to AD_3 in part (b). (Note that this shift is substantially greater than that in Figure 1, where investment is not very sensitive to interest rates.)

aggregate demand by more than does an identical increase in the money supply in Figure 13. The difference is that in Figure 12, investment is sensitive to interest-rate changes, but in Figure 13, it is not.

In sum, countercyclical monetary policy will be less effective (1) if interest rates do not fall by very much when the money supply increases or (2) if

interest-rate changes have a small effect on desired investment.

Aggregate-demand multipliers, the money multiplier, the sensitivity of desired investment to interest-rate changes, and the sensitivity of money demand to interest-rate changes all affect the conduct of countercyclical policy. *The size of any policy*

Table 7
Monetary Policy and the Sensitivity of Money Demand to Interest Rates

Area affected by stimulative monetary policy*	Interest sensitivity of money demand	
	Low	High
Interest rate	Large decrease	Small decrease
Investment	Large increase	Small increase
Aggregate demand	Large increase	Small increase

* For example, an increase in the money supply.

Table 8
Monetary Policy and the Sensitivity of Investment to Interest-Rate Changes

Area affected by stimulative monetary policy*	Interest sensitivity of desired investment	
	Low	High
Interest rate	Decrease	Decrease
Investment	Small increase	Large increase
Aggregate demand	Small increase	Large increase

* For example, an increase in the money supply.

Figure 11
The Elasticity of Demand for Money

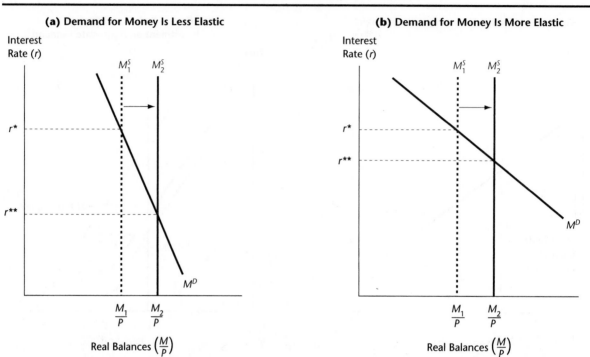

(a) When the demand for money is less elastic, an increase in the money supply leads to a large decline in interest rates. As a result, monetary policy will be more effective.
(b) When the demand for money is more elastic, an increase in the money supply of the same size does not cause interest rates to fall much, so monetary policy will be less effective.

change cannot be determined without knowing these multipliers and elasticities.

Short-run aggregate supply. Whether aggregate demand shocks really matter much as well as the effectiveness of countercyclical policy both depend on the responsiveness of real output to price-level changes. As illustrated in Figure 14(a), if the short-run aggregate supply curve is flat, an aggregate-demand shock will lead to a large change in real output. In this case, expansionary monetary or fiscal policy will greatly increase real output in the short run with relatively little inflation. On the other hand, if there is inflation and the short-run aggregate supply curve is flat, contractionary monetary or fiscal policies won't affect inflation much in the short run, but will substantially decrease output, and hence, employment opportunities. By contrast, if the short-run aggregate supply curve is steep, as illustrated in Figure 14(b), the conclusions are quite different. (You should work through the differences between 14(a) and 14(b)).

Unfortunately, there is little empirical evidence about whether the short-run aggregate supply curve is flat or steep. It may be that if the economy is in a deep recession and there is a good deal of unemployment and excess capacity, *ASsr* will be relatively flat, but as the economy approaches full employment, efforts to increase output may bump into capacity constraints and push prices up. Because there isn't good evidence in this regard, there is substantial debate about whether *ASsr* looks more like Figure 15 (a), (b) or (c). It is generally accepted, however, that the long-run aggregate supply is vertical as is indicated in all three parts of Figure 15.

▶ In Sum

As a practical matter, effective countercyclical policy is difficult. Good information about where the economy actually is and the nature of any shock matters. Timing matters. Technical information about the behavior of economic agents within the economy—multipliers, elasticities, and the like—

Figure 12
When Investment Is More Sensitive to Interest Rates

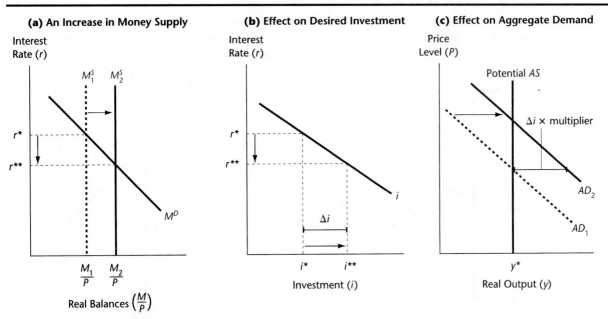

When investment demand is more sensitive to changes in the interest rate, an increase in the money supply that lowers interest rates [part (a)] will increase investment substantially [part (b)] and have a large effect on aggregate demand [part (c)].

Figure 13
When Investment Is Less Sensitive to Interest Rates

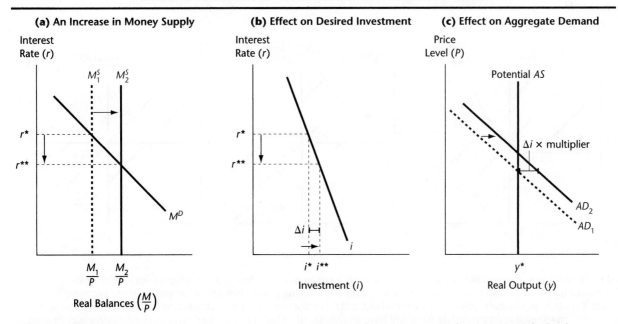

When investment demand is less sensitive to changes in the interest rate, an increase in the money supply that lowers interest rates [part (a)] will not increase investment very much [part (b)] and will not have a very large effect on aggregate demand [part (c)].

Figure 14
Short-Run Aggregate Supply and the Effect of an Aggregate Demand Shock

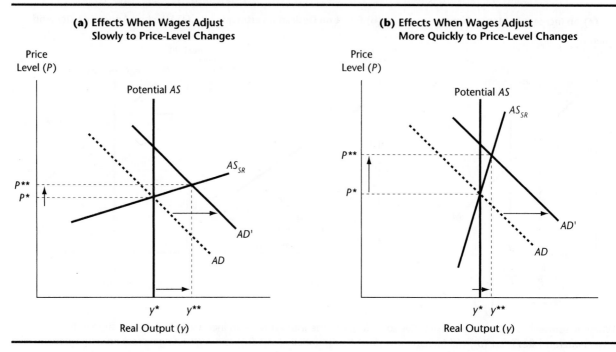

Figure 15
Possible Short-Run Aggregate Supply Effects

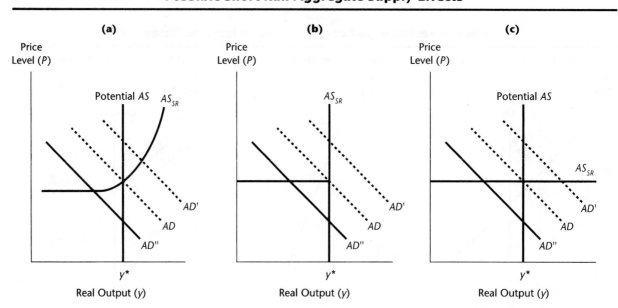

(a) In the short run, an increase in aggregate demand will have an output effect and a small price-level effect if the economy is producing at less than full employment. If the economy is producing at less than full employment. If the economy is producing at its potential, however, there is an output effect, but it is accompanied by a large increase in the price level. (b) In the short-run, an increase in aggregate demand will have an output effect but no price-level effect if the economy is producing at less than full employment. If the economy is producing at its potential, however, there is no output effect and any increase in aggregate demand increases the price level only. (c) In the short run, an increase in aggregate demand has only an output effect and no price-level effect.

matters. And, of course, politics matters. For all of these reasons, it is easy to "get it wrong" and destabilize rather than stabilize the economy. This has led some, but not all, economists to argue that policy makers should *not* actively pursue countercyclical policies. Instead, these economists argue that fiscal and monetary actions should be limited to creating a stable environment within which economic agents make decisions. For example, fiscal actions ought, in the view of these economists and policy makers, to be directed at creating the kinds of incentives that foster efficient uses of resources and economic growth. And monetary actions ought to be directed at creating an environment with very low and stable inflation. Others economists and policy makers are much more willing to employ active countercyclical policies. "Why wait for the economy to, on its own, move toward full employment when countercyclical policies can speed the adjustment?" they ask. While some of the reasons for these different positions are tied to rather arcane technical economic differences, many of the differences have to do with the practical problems outlined in this chapter—different people give different weight to the ease or difficulty of pursuing countercyclical policies that really benefit an economy's aggregate performance. You are now prepared to jump into this ongoing debate. How the debate tips will affect your life enormously.

▶ Summary

Appropriate countercyclical policies. The government can pursue one of two broad types of policy in response to unanticipated shifts in aggregate demand or aggregate supply. The first of these, fiscal policy, affects aggregate demand directly, through the expenditure decisions of the government, and indirectly, through the taxation decisions of the government. Monetary policy, however, only affects aggregate demand indirectly through changes in the interest rate. The appropriate policy response to take depends on the type of shock that occurs.

Appropriate policy responses to a deflationary aggregate demand shock include:

- Fiscal
  Increasing government spending
  Decreasing taxes
- Monetary
  Increasing the money supply by an open market purchase
  Lowering the discount rate
  Lowering the reserve requirement

Appropriate policy responses to an inflationary aggregate demand shock include:

- Fiscal
  Decreasing government spending
  Increasing taxes
- Monetary
  Decreasing the money supply by an open market sale
  Raising the discount rate
  Raising the reserve requirement

Appropriate policy responses to an adverse supply or price shock *if unemployment is the primary concern* are:

- Fiscal
  Increasing government spending
  Decreasing taxes
- Monetary
  Increasing the money supply by an open market purchase
  Lowering the discount rate
  Lowering the reserve requirement

Appropriate policy responses to an adverse supply or price shock *if inflation is the primary concern* are:

- Fiscal
  Holding government spending at its current level
  Holding or increasing taxes
- Monetary
  Holding the money supply at its current level

Effects on the mix of real output produced. The division of output between consumption, investment, and government uses is affected by the mix of fiscal and monetary policies a government chooses, because (in part) the mix affects interest rates. Different macroeconomic stabilization policies directed at aggregate demand also affect potential real output and hence have different effects on the long-term economic growth prospects of an economy. Macroeconomic stabilization policies affect the potential real output of an economy as they affect labor-leisure or saving-consumption choices.

Policy implementation. Although fiscal and monetary policy appear to solve the problems of unemployment and inflation quite nicely, they are not simple to implement.

1. Shocks to the economy are not always easy to predict. As a consequence, it takes time to discover that an aggregate demand or aggregate supply shock has occurred.

2. Designing an appropriate policy requires knowledge of both the size of the shock to the economy *and* the magnitude of the effect on the economy that the policy response will have.

3. Appropriate stabilization policies must affect aggregate demand reasonably quickly and in predictable ways. In this regard, monetary policy, which can be implemented rapidly, affects the economy indirectly and slowly over time. Fiscal policy, which is usually difficult to implement rapidly, affects the economy directly and quickly.

Even if the appropriate responses to an economic shock are understood and are "in principle" possible, they may do little good in practice. The economy may be able to move to full employment more rapidly than a policy can be designed, implemented, and have an effect. Indeed, if the timing of countercyclical monetary and fiscal policy is off, they may actually exacerbate economic cycles.

The government budget constraint. Government spending, that is, government use of real resources, must be funded in some way. For the federal government, the level of expenditures, g, can be funded in one of three ways: direct taxes on income, consumption, or investment (t); or indirect taxes on capital formation through deficits (ΔB); or indirect taxes on money and money-fixed assets through inflation (ΔM).

Deficits and crowding out. In theory, countercyclical fiscal policy calls for running a deficit during an economic downturn and a surplus in an economic boom, but the federal government has consistently run deficits over the past three decades. As explicit taxes have become politically less acceptable as a means of funding government spending, however, deficits have increased and become a persistent fact of economic life.

If the economy is producing at or near its potential, then deficit financing of government expenditures increases interest rates. Interest-sensitive spending, such as investment, will be displaced or **crowded out** by the increased government spending. In this case, the deficit is an implicit tax on the future because the economy accumulates less capital than it otherwise would, thus adversely affecting economic growth.

Deficits and inflation. Alternatively, a deficit can be **monetized**. This occurs when the central bank purchased the newly-issued treasury bonds with currency. If this occurs when the economy is at full employment, inflation will result. A deficit doesn't *cause* inflation, but it may create an environment where there is political pressure to inflate prices.

Multipliers, elasticities, and the effectiveness of countercyclical policy. Fiscal policy is more effective if there is a large aggregate-demand multiplier and if desired investment is inelastic with respect to interest rates. If desired investment is highly sensitive to interest-rate changes, however, countercyclical increases in the deficit tend to crowd out private investment.

Monetary policy is more effective if there is a large aggregate-demand multiplier, the demand for money is not very sensitive to interest rates and desired investment is sensitive to interest rates. By contrast, if the demand for money is highly sensitive to interest rates or desired investment is not very sensitive to interest rates, then countercyclical increases in the money supply must be very large to have even small effects on short run aggregate real output and employment.

Short-run aggregate supply. Whether countercyclical policies have any effect on real output depends on the shape of the short-run aggregate supply curve.

Chapter 25 ▶▶
Appendix: The 2007–2009 Recession

Late in 2007 the US economy entered a recession. This particular downturn in the economy was in many ways to be the worst since the Great Depression of the 1930s, although this was not understood or foreseen in December 2007. Real output fell substantially, particularly in late 2008 and early 2009. The official unemployment rate rose from 5% at the start of the recession in December 2007 to around 10% as a weak recovery started in late 2009. Hidden unemployment due to the discouraged worker and the involuntary part-time effects was much higher than 10%, perhaps as high as 16%. For reasons discussed below, this recession, which started in the US in 2007, spread to the rest of the world in 2008.

The source of the aggregate demand shock triggering the 2007-2009 recession was complex and not well understood until many months after the recession began. Because of its complex origins, the recovery was very slow and the US economy, and its financial system, continue to face challenges. To understand the reasons for the complexity of the causes and the financial challenges facing the economy, we need to consider the way that the purchase of a home has been financed in the U.S., both historically and more recently.

▶ Some History

By the end of World War II, an individual or household generally financed its purchase of a home with a long-term—often 30 year—mortgage. Typically, mortgages were issued by local banks, whose officers sometimes knew the borrower and often knew the particular home or, if the home was to be built, the property where it was to be built and the builder who would construct it. Banks required a down-payment. For example, a person might want to purchase a home costing $200,000. A bank would loan 80% of the purchase price, $160,000; the borrower had to come up with the remaining $40,000—his or her down payment. The bank that issued the mortgage would generally hold it until it was repaid. Mortgages were generally amortized: each monthly payment a person made added something to the amount of money the person had in the home. In the early years most of the monthly payment was interest on the loan. However, slowly the loan would be repaid and as it was, the share of interest in each monthly payment would fall and a larger fraction of each monthly payment would go toward the amount of money the person had in his home. So, for example, the original amount put into the home —$40,000 in our example—would slowly grow to $50,000, then $60,000, then $100,000 and, finally, after 30 years, $200,000. The corresponding loan balance would fall slowly over the same time from $160,000 to $0. These mortgages were "non recourse" loans. This means that the lending bank could repose a home if the borrower defaulted, but could not go after any other assets the borrower might have. Put differently, the mortgage was secured by the home, but nothing else.

In sum, mortgages:

- were long-term, fixed payment, fully amortized loans
- required a down payment
- were generally made, and then held, by a local bank

Generally, an individual would default on his mortgage only if he couldn't make his monthly payments because his income dropped dramatically because he lost his job or was unable to work because of an illness or accident. Even in the face of set backs, however, individuals tried to make their mortgage payments because otherwise they would lose some or all of the down payment that they had made when they first purchased their homes.

In sum, default occurred:

- when a homeowner's income fell because of unemployment
- when a homeowner's income fell because of illness
- when a homeowner's income fell because of an accident

▶ More Recent Events

Over time, this story changes in a number of ways. By the 1970s, for example, a local bank would initiate a mortgage, but once a loan was made, it would often sell the mortgage to a large, national financial institution. The local bank would continue to receive the monthly payments on the mortgage, but would transmit all but a small fraction to the financial institution that now held the mortgage. The small fraction the bank retained compensated the bank for collecting and transmitting the payment.

Two quasi-governmental financial institutions, Fannie Mae and Freddie Mac, played particularly important and large roles in purchasing newly-issued mortgages from banks and other local financial institutions. Initially, they got the money to do so by borrowing in the open credit markets, where their debt carried the implicit guarantee of the Federal Government. Soon, however, Fannie and Freddie started bundling a large number of mortgages they had purchased from banks and issuing an IOU that promised the purchaser of the IOU that it would get the sum of the payments on all of the bundled mortgages as a "pass through" payment. These were called, not surprisingly, "mortgage-backed securities."

Mortgages requiring a down payment that were then amortized over time were viewed as high quality securities because default rates were low—most individuals made their mortgage payments. Indeed, on a pool of, say 1000 mortgages, the law of large numbers made the number of mortgages where borrowers would default predictable. No one knew which households would default, but the fraction of the 1000 mortgages that would go into default was predictable. So, for example, it might be that on a pool of 1000 mortgages "on average" 5 percent would go into default. This means that the mortgage-backed security would "predictably" pass through the payments on 950 mortgages to the holder of the security backed by the 1000-mortgage pool. Because of this, mortgage-backed securities were also viewed as high quality securities. Two firms—Moody's and Standard & Poors—rate the quality of securities. Both routinely gave mortgage-backed securities their highest rating ("AAA"). This meant that lots of US and foreign banks, financial institutions, insurance companies, hedge funds, investment banks, and pension funds bought US mortgage-backed securities. Foreign governments also purchased US-mortgage backed securities, often from Fannie Mae and Freddie Mac.

Somewhat later, mostly after 2000, financial institutions started creating new financial instruments, called derivatives, by taking a fraction of several different mortgage pools and offering the buyer of the derivative the mortgage payments that came from their share of each of these pools. For example, suppose that there are 10 different pools of mortgages, each with 1000 mortgages being held by a financial institution. A derivative could be created by taking 1/10th of the payments of each of the 10 pools. The purchaser of the derivative would then get as a payment on the derivative the payments on each of the 1/10th shares of the 10 mortgage pools—that is, from 100 mortgages in each of the 10 mortgage pools. It was thought at the time that this reduced risk since even if almost all of the mortgages in a particular pool went into default—thought to be an unlikely event—it was thought to be very, very unlikely, that almost all of the mortgages in all 10 of the pools would go into default at the same time.

In the late 1990s and into the early 2000s, house prices were increasing year in and year out in most areas of the US. Often prices were increasing at rapid rates of 10 or more percent each year. Houses and condominiums came to be viewed as a "can't lose" investment—prices were going up and, it was widely assumed, would continue to go up indefinitely.

When house prices are increasing, an individual gets equity—the amount of the value of the home that the individual actually owns, i.e., the difference between the value of the home and the balance of the loan used to finance its purchase—simply by the increase in the house's price. For example, if house prices are increasing at 10% per year, an individual who purchased a $200,000 house, even if he borrowed all $200,000, would have house worth $220,000 after a year and, hence, have at least $20,000 in equity in the house.

Because of this effect, lending rules were loosened beginning in the late 1990s and the required down payment was reduced. By the early 2000s, some mortgages did not require a down payment and the person wanting to purchase a home could borrow the full purchase price. Lending rules were also loosened with regard to the borrower's own financial circumstances. Because the financial institution that made the mortgage got the house back if the homeowner defaulted, if house prices were always increasing, the bank would get something back of greater value than the loan it had made. As a consequence, banks were willing to reduce the required down payment to zero and to allow less credit worthy individuals to get mortgages.

Remember that historically a homeowner would default on his mortgage when his income fell for some reason. However, these new mortgages of the 1990s and 2000s created an additional reason for default: a decrease in the price of a house could lead to default because even small declines in the price of a house when the homeowner had borrowed 100% of its purchase price could create a circumstance where the homeowner owed more on the mortgage than the house was worth. If, for example, a household purchased a home for $200,000 using a no-down-payment mortgage and the price of housing fell by 10% (instead of increasing by 10%), then after a year the homeowner would owe the bank almost $200,000, but have a home worth only $180,000.

In sum, mortgages:

- no longer required down payments in all cases
- were often offered based on the expected increase in house prices rather than on the ability of the borrower to make payments

In these circumstances, the homeowner has an incentive to quit making payments on the mortgage and default. Notice that this incentive doesn't depend upon whether a person can or cannot make his mortgage payments. To give an extreme example, suppose that a person with $5 million in the bank and a $300,000 annual income, borrowed $1,000,000 and bought a house. If, because of a decrease in house prices, a year later the home would sell for only $900,000 but the homeowner owes the bank $1,000,000, then the homeowner has an incentive to default even though he still has a high paying job and plenty of money in the bank.

And, of course, if the homeowner's income falls because of unemployment, illness or accident, then he also has an incentive to default.

In these circumstances, whether the homeowner will or will not make payments may depend upon lots of things: Whether he can get into another home; whether he is concerned about the effect of a default on his credit score and ability to borrow money in the future; the size of the difference between the value of his home and the amount he owes on his mortgage; what is happening to his income, etc. So he may or may not default. But because he has an incentive to default, this creates substantial uncertainty about whether he will make his payments. This creates, in turn, substantial uncertainty about the pass-through income on mortgage-backed securities and the income on derivatives based on pools of mortgages. As a consequence, these securities lose value, often by an uncertain amount (since the income expected on the security has become more uncertain).

They also lose value, of course, if because of a downturn in the economy, some borrowers who have taken on a lot of mortgage debt, cannot make their payments because their incomes fall.

In sum, default now occurred:

- when a homeowner's income fell because of unemployment
- when a homeowner's income fell because of illness
- when a homeowner's income fell because of an accident

AND

- when the price of the home fell below the amount owed on the mortgage (which also increased the risk of default, even if the homeowner/borrower didn't immediately default on his mortgage)

Because house prices were increasing during the late 1990s and early 2000s, securities backed by these new, no-down payment, mortgages and with mortgages made to borrowers who were less credit worthy were still given the highest credit rating ("AAA") by Moody's and Standard and Poors. As a consequence, these kinds of securities and derivatives based on a group of mortgage-backed securities were purchased by large governmental and private financial entities throughout the world.

▶ Five Final Elements to This Long Prologue

First, because house prices were increasing and it was thought that they would continue to increase, households rushed to get into homes, thereby increasing the demand and pushing up prices.

Second, some individuals started purchasing homes and condominiums as investments—they didn't intend to live in them, but, rather, intended to resell them a year or two later at the expected higher price. For example, a person might buy a home at $200,000 with the expectation that it will sell for $220,000 in a year and then, when it does, sell it in a year making $20,000.

Third, some individuals who had been in their homes for some time decided to refinance in order to turn the appreciation in the value of their home into money. For example, someone who had purchase a home for $200,000 ten years earlier in an area with a high rate of increase in house prices, might have a mortgage with a balance of $160,000 on a home that is now worth $400,000. He might get either a new mortgage or a second mortgage and increase his total mortgage debt to $380,000 on a

home worth $400,000. If he could find a lender willing to make this loan, he could stay in his home, but have $120,000 in cash from the refinancing and, of course, he would now have a mortgage debt of $380,000.

Fourth, over this same period of time the Federal Reserve pursued a monetary policy that kept interest rates low, thereby making the kind of borrowing described above attractive for first-time home buyers, people purchasing homes as an investment, and individuals who wanted to refinance their homes. Put differently, the cost of borrowing was low so individuals had an incentive to borrow.

Fifth, several large financial institutions, among them a very large insurance company, AIG, started to insure the pass-through payments on mortgage-backed securities and mortgage derivatives through a complex mechanism known as a "credit default swap." The details of the mechanism aren't important. Essentially what AIG offered was insurance to big institutions purchasing mortgage-backed securities that if the pass-through payments on mortgage-backed securities weren't made, the insurer would make payments of an equal amount to the holder of the security.

▶ Fueling High Housing Prices

The expectation that house prices would always increase, with house price increases fueled by the demand created by new mortgage instruments, loosened lending standards, speculative investment decisions, homeowner refinancing of existing mortgages, and low-interest monetary policy, pushed the price of housing up, thereby fulfilling the expectations that people held that the price of housing would go up. This led to further mortgage lending and additional construction. Looking back, it is now clear that there was a speculative bubble in housing.

▶ The Beginning of the End

Things began to unravel in late 2006 and early 2007 when the prices of homes didn't increase as expected, but began to fall in several areas through the country (primarily in California, Las Vegas, Arizona and Florida). This was a simple supply/demand response: the quantity of housing built became much greater than the quantity demanded and the excess supply of housing pushed prices down, not up.

Home construction activity fell dramatically, thereby leading to rising unemployment in the construction industry. Some mortgage defaults occurred for the traditional reason that some homeowners/borrowers found that they could not make their mortgage payments. But many more defaults occurred because the declining price of homes meant that a growing fraction of homeowners/borrowers owed more on their homes than their homes were worth at current prices. And, as described above, the potential for defaults increased dramatically because some homeowners/borrowers continued to make payments on loans that were larger than the value of their homes, but had an incentive to default.

The rising default rate and the rising level of uncertainty about future defaults spread through the US economy and abroad as financial institutions and governments who thought that they had purchased relatively secure mortgage-backed securities, now found that the value of these securities had decreased dramatically, either because the expected payments were no longer being made or because of the increased riskiness associated with the incentives of individuals to default on their mortgages. These mortgage-backed securities quickly came to be called "toxic assets."

Since these now worth-a-lot-less mortgage-backed securities were assets for these financial institutions, most found themselves with serious financial problems: holding assets that had fallen substantially in value, but with liabilities that hadn't changed much. A large New York brokerage house, Bear Stearns, was essentially bankrupt by March 2008. It was purchased, at the urging of the Federal Reserve, by J P Morgan, another large NY financial firm. By the summer, Fannie Mae and Freddie Mac were bankrupt. They were taken over by the US government in September 2008. In mid-September, 2008, the US government bailed out AIG—which was insolvent because, with mortgage default rates increasing, it did not have the money to pay the "insurance" it had offered on mortgage-backed securities.

The Federal Reserve and US Treasury were sometimes applauded, often criticized, for bailing out failing firms. The concern was often expressed that financial firms—which had paid executives and employees generously during the go-go years as a reward for taking risks—had become too large to fail, but that if they didn't fail, they would have an incentive to take even greater risks in the future. (A type of moral-hazard problem of the sort we discussed in Chapter 16.) As a consequence, when Lehman Brothers neared bankruptcy in late September 2008, neither the Federal Reserve nor the Treasury would step in and Lehman Brothers went into bankruptcy. The effect on credit markets was stunning! Individuals world-wide tried to move out of whatever assets they were holding and into U.S. Treasury bills. Banks, many of which were also in deep financial trouble because they had purchased mortgage-backed securities and were now holding "toxic assets," refused to lend to one another even for short periods of time.

Credit markets froze. Banks reduced their lending and became much less willing to lend. Even well-established, financially healthy firms found it difficult to get credit to finance their operations, acquire inventories or make investments. Individuals wishing to buy homes found that lending standards had increased dramatically. New firms trying to get the financial resources necessary to start or expand could not get loans.

This, along with the earlier collapse of the construction sector of the economy, created a large, adverse aggregate demand shock, both in the US and abroad. Real output began to decline, with a corresponding increase in unemployment.

▶ Policy Responses

Fiscal Policy

In March 2008, the Congress passed legislation authorizing a tax rebate. Rebates were made beginning in May 2008.

As the recession deepened in March 2009, the Congress passed a stimulus package increasing government spending by nearly $800 billion. In this case, however, the increase in spending was spread out over the remainder of 2009 and the next two or three years.

Unfortunately, individual savings, which had been near 0 as a percent of national income through much of the early 2000s, increased substantially in 2008 and 2009. Hence, at the same time as there was a fiscal policy stimulus (part with a tax cut (rebate); part with an expenditure increase), saving increased.

Evidence indicates that the May 2008 rebate had no effect on aggregate demand; evidence regarding the starting-in-May 2009 expenditure increase isn't yet available, in part because the increase in expenditures in the stimulus package built slowly through 2009, with most of the increase not occurring until 2010 or later.

Monetary Policy

As we have discussed, the FED engages in open market purchases of T-bills in order to increase the money supply. It can also reduce the reserve requirement. And it can reduce the discount rate and target Federal Funds rate.

The FED did the first and third of these: It aggressively made massive purchases of T-bills. It also reduced the discount rate and target Federal Funds rates to, essentially, 0—the lowest in US history. It found, however, that these policy tools were too limited and substantially expanded the kinds of securities that it was willing to purchase: commercial paper, mortgages, long-term Treasury notes, etc. Essentially, the FED rushed to increase the amount of money in the economy by purchasing a wide range of public and private securities.

These policies could not erase the shocks to aggregate demand, but they did prevent a complete collapse of the US financial system. Similarly aggressive actions by central bankers in Europe and Asia, which couldn't erase the shocks to their aggregate demands from the US housing-and-mortgage markets problems, likewise prevented a collapse of the world financial system. But in the US and abroad, the aggregate demand shocks rippled through economies and real output fell throughout the world.

Other Policies

The move out of other assets and into T-bills in late September 2008 had the characteristics of an old-fashioned run on banks. (Before deposit insurance, if people thought that a bank might fail, they would rush to withdraw their deposits—a run on the bank—which, for reasons we discussed in Chapter 22, almost always insured that their bank would fail. A policy response coming out of the Great Depression was to insure bank deposits.) To calm the fears of depositors, deposit insurance was increased from $100,000 to $250,000. In addition, deposit insurance was extended to previously uninsured money market funds.

The FED and the Treasury jointly asked the Congress to authorize around $800 billion to deal with the "toxic asset" problem—the TARP legislation. Dealing with the toxic assets problem, however, turned out to be a knotty problem and policy makers went back and forth between (1) buying the toxic assets from banks and other financial institutions or (2) directly capitalizing banks by giving them cash in exchange for partial ownership by the US government. (In a misuse of these funds, the Treasury essentially purchased General Motors in February 2009—GM, of course, had no toxic assets but it was headed for bankruptcy and had political clout.)

The short run versus long run dilemma for policy makers. The economy will recover faster if individuals save less, if the FED keeps interest rates low, if the FED increases the money supply, if the FED and the Treasury stabilize the financial system, if banks and other financial institutions increase lending and, possibly, if the Federal government runs a deficit. The latter policy response is, however, more controversial and there is vigorous debate about whether there is any stimulative effect of a deficit per se or, separately, of increased government spending as one element of the increased deficit or of decreased taxes as the other element of an increased deficit.

However, if the US economy is to be healthy over the long run, individuals have to save more than they have in the recent past, interest rates have to increase, the FED must reduce the money supply or we will face a substantial inflation, the FED and Treasury have to allow banks and financial institutions to thrive or die without intervention, banks and other financial institutions need to have higher lending standards (e.g., no more no-down-payment mortgages), and the Federal government must move toward fiscal balance and eliminate its deficits. Is any of this possible? That is, are the aggressive policies pursued in 2008 and 2009 reversible? As an economic matter, it's important that they be reversed as the economy recovers. As a political matter, it's going to be very difficult.

Workbook

to accompany

Economics and Public Policy
An Analytical Approach

Part A ▶▶
Assignments

Part M ►►
Additional Questions and Problems

1. What is *scarcity*? In what sense does it force you to make *choices*?

2. Why do choices have *costs*? How are these costs measured?

3. In what sense do individuals minimize the costs of their choices?

4. The residents of Happy Land are involved in two primary activities: spreading good cheer and helping others. There are 1,000 hours of time available in Happy Land; it takes 30 minutes to spread one ounce of good cheer, whereas it takes four hours to help someone else. What is the opportunity cost of spreading good cheer in terms of helping others, and vice versa? Construct a production possibilities frontier for Happy Land.

5. a. You buy a Utah Jazz ticket for $50 and drive to Salt Lake City to watch the game. As you are about to enter the Delta Center, a gentleman approaches you and offers you $100 for your ticket. You reject the offer and attend the game. What was your opportunity cost of attending the game?

   b. When Jane graduated high school, she moved in with some roommates in Provo. She was trying to decide whether to accept a full-time secretary position nearby that paid $2000 per semester or to attend BYU for a semester. Her rent was $200 per month and her food bill was $100 per month. Tuition and books would total $2500 for the semester if she chose to attend BYU. As a full-time student taking a heavy class load, she would be unable to hold a job during the semester. Based on this information, what is her opportunity cost of attending BYU for the semester?

6. In what sense does scarcity create *competition* and possible conflict?

7. Air is limited; seawater is limited. Are either of these scarce in an economic sense? What does your answer suggest about the point at which limited resources become considered scarce resources?

8. Are there costs associated with decisions when there are no options? If there are no options, are there decisions to be made?

9. When former President Reagan proposed that the United States study the possibility of a Strategic Defense Initiative (SDI) against missiles; many critics have argued that this effort would be too costly. What are the costs of the Strategic Defense Initiative? In what sense is something considered "too costly"?

10. Are there reasons why a society may choose to save lives by lowering the speed limit to 60 mph, but not choose to save lives by installing smoke detectors in every home or by changing the design of highways?

11. Suppose that individuals interact in the following way (this is a form of what is called a *prisoner's dilemma game*): Individuals A and B tentatively agree to do something that will yield each a gain of $500. After the agreement, however, they are tempted to change their decisions with the following possible outcomes:

	Individual B changes decision	Individual B does not change decision
Individual A changes decision	A loses $1500 B loses $1500	A gains $600 B loses $2000
Individual A does not change decision	A loses $2000 B gains $600	A gains $500 B gains $500

What will be the equilibrium in this game? Why? Is the equilibrium outcome the optimal outcome? If so, why? If not, why not and what would it take to get to the optimal outcome? If the individuals repeatedly interacted with each other and this matrix described the outcome each time they did, would the equilibrium be different Why or why not? Explain.

12. Most urban expressways do not have toll charges. How is the scarce space allocated during rush hours? During non-rush hours?

13. There are far fewer babies available for adoption than couples who would like to adopt. Are babies scarce? How is competition for babies accommodated?

14. Service stations are commonly found in small towns or cities, but they are much more difficult to find in large metropolitan areas. Is this sensible, given the obvious differences in the number of cars in small towns and large cities?

15. Why do you stand and applaud when others stand and applaud? How does a crowd coordinate sitting down after some have stood to applaud?

16. If one person butts in line, does it affect those behind very much? Why do we get so irritated when a person butts in line?

17. Frequently banks offer "free" checking for anyone keeping a minimum deposit of $100. Is it really free?

18. What is *exchange?*

19. In what sense does exchange coordinate competition?

20. What is *specialization?*

21. In what sense does specialization coordinate competition?

22. Why do exchange and specialization increase individual well-being?

23. If everyone specializes according to comparative advantage, do we have the *best* person in each productive activity? (For example, is your doctor the person who, with appropriate training, would be the most adept at medicine?)

24. Working all day, Lucy can produce either 60 lollipops or 150 popsicles. Her husband Ricky can produce either 50 lollipops or 25 popsicles. Who has the absolute advantage in producing lollipops? Popsicles? Who has the comparative advantage in producing lollipops?

25. Evaluate the following statement: "Saudi Arabia can pump all the oil it needs. Therefore, consumption of oil is free in Saudi Arabia."

26. Evaluate the following statement: "A society can always produce more automobiles if it chooses to do so; therefore there can never be any real scarcity."

27. How can the concept of opportunity cost be used to explain why people occasionally buy milk at convenience stores where they buy their gas even though it costs more than at the local grocery store?

28. Suppose that the current price of gold is $400 an ounce. If at some earlier time, A bought gold for $200 an ounce and B bought gold for $1000 an ounce, would you expect A or B to be more likely to sell at the current price if both have the same expectation about the future price of gold?

29. College students are disproportionately young (that is, older people work; younger people go to college or grad school). What must be true about the opportunity cost of schooling for the two groups. Why?

30. How can the concept of opportunity cost be used to explain why college students are mostly younger, not older, people?

31. The following table indicates how many hamburgers and hot dogs each person can cook in one hour. Each person can work 8 hours.

	hamburgers	hot dogs
Ty	10	20
Jon	5	15
Derek	15	15

a. If the relative price is 1 hamburger for 2 hot dogs, who will produce hamburgers?

b. What is the maximum number of hot dogs that could be cooked per day?

c. If all three persons are currently cooking hot dogs and the price of hamburgers increases, who would shift from hot dog cooking first?

d. What does it cost to produce the 1st hot dog?

e. If the relative price of hamburgers decreases, who will benefit the most and who will lose the most?

Chapter 2

1. What, precisely, is an aggregate production possibilities frontier?

2. Why might an economy confront increasing costs as resources are moved from one activity to another?

3. During the fourteenth century, the bubonic plague killed a large portion of the European population. What happened to the production possibilities of the European economies? What might have happened to per person consumption possibilities?

4. Why do changes that increase the overall well-being of an economy also change the distribution of goods and services among individuals and, hence, the distribution of economic well-being?

5. What is economic growth?

6. What choices must an economy make if it wishes to stimulate economic growth through capital formation?

7. If an economy chooses to use some of its resources to build more capital, what will be the consequences? Is the economy necessarily better off as a consequence of this decision? Why or why not?

8. Can things other than new capital stimulate economic growth? Why or why not?

9. Why might economic growth not necessarily be desirable?

10. Why will international trade affect the domestic prices that individuals must respond to as they choose to specialize and exchange? Can international trade increase domestic prices? Can international trade decrease domestic prices? Does it matter?

11. Why might a recession lower the cost to a government of a volunteer army?

12. In what sense is staffing a volunteer army just like staffing a large corporation? In what sense is it different?

13. Recent developments in medical technology, such as CAT scanners, greatly facilitate the diagnosis of certain diseases. This technology is very expensive. Should we put a CAT scanner in each hospital in the country?

14. Suppose that an economy can produce only two goods, A and B.

    a. Draw a PPF if the opportunity cost of each A is 4 B.

    b. Draw a new PPF if an increase in resources doubles the amount of A and B that can be produced. What is the new opportunity cost of A in terms of B?

    c. Draw a new PPF if a technological innovation doubles the amount of A that can be produced but doesn't affect the production of B? What is the new opportunity cost of A in terms of B?

    d. Draw a new PPF if a technological innovation doubles the amount of B that can be produced but doesn't affect the production of A? What is the new opportunity cost of A in terms of B?

15. The following gives the number of pens or pencils each person could produce in 1 day:

	pencils	pens
Candace	4	2
Joce	3	1
Linda	2	2

    a. Who has an absolute advantage at pens? At pencils?

    b. Who has a comparative advantage at pens? At pencils?

    c. What does the aggregate PPF look like for a work week of 5 days?

    d. What is the opportunity cost of the 1st pen produce? The last pen? The first pencil? The last pencil?

Chapter 3

1. What are *transaction costs?*

2. Why are there transaction costs?

3. What is *money?*

4. How does money lower transaction costs?

5. What are *intermediaries?*

6. How do intermediaries lower transaction costs?

7. What expectations are important if an economy is to use its resources in appropriate ways?

8. What are *property rights?*

9. How do property rights, contracts, and other "rules of the game" lower the costs of transacting?

10. Computer software frequently comes packaged with an agreement along the following lines: "The purchaser agrees, upon opening this package, not to copy or to distribute the enclosed materials to anyone else." Why is this kind of notice attached to software boxes but not to boxes of cereal? How effective do you think this type of agreement is? What kinds of arrangements would make it more effective?

11. Does honesty have economic value? Why?

12. At the end of World War II, candy bars and nylons were frequently used as money in occupied Germany. Why?

13. If the development of money is important for exchange within an economy, shouldn't it be important in exchange between economies? Are there any things that serve as international-trade money?

14. During the 19th century, the money for international trade was supposed to be gold (the world was on the gold standard). Nevertheless, most international transactions were not paid for in gold but in the British pound. Why?

15. Mail-order clothing is generally less expensive than clothing you buy at the local store. Why doesn't everyone buy from the mail-order stores?

16. If the government needs to use your property, it may take it under its powers of eminent domain but it must pay you the fair market value for the property. Is the payment important to anyone but the property owner? Why?

17. Who has the rights to the air in an airplane cabin? Does it make a difference whether the rights belong to smokers or nonsmokers? What if they belong to no one?

18. Do zoning laws protect property rights or infringe on property rights?

19. Why are whales in danger of extinction, whereas cattle, whose use for food far exceeds whales, are not in danger of extinction?

20. Middlemen or intermediaries are frequently said to do nothing except contribute to high prices. Are prices higher or lower because of middlemen or intermediaries? If prices were higher *because* of middlemen, would it still make sense to trade through them rather than engaging in direct trade?

21. What is a *firm?*

22. Why might firms be organized hierarchically?

23. How do firms lower the costs of specializing and producing goods and services?

24. Why is it sometimes advantageous for a firm to internalize some activities rather than rely on the marketplace?

25. Explain why team production occurs. Why might team production create shirking problems? Explain how "firms" solve shirking problems.

26. If the opportunity cost of time increases, would you expect to see more or less reliance on intermediaries. Why? How, specifically, does your answer to this question explain the growth of fast food restaurants?

Chapter 4

1. What is meant by "at the margin"?

2. What are marginal costs?

3. What are marginal benefits?

4. Why does choosing the best option require equating marginal costs with marginal benefits?

5. Why should you ignore sunk costs?

6. Does it make economic sense to continue a public project (like a highway or a dam) because "we have already invested so much in it that we cannot quit now"?

7. Does it make economic sense to continue a public project because "we have so much invested that we have to get all we can out of this"?

8. If the marginal benefit of a decision decreases, and nothing else changes, how would you expect individual behavior to change? Why?

9. Suppose that the benefits of a public project are calculated to be worth $10 million while the costs of the project are calculated to be $8 million. Should the project be started? (Be careful. Have you considered other projects that might be started?)

10. It is sometimes claimed that firms in a market economy will use old, obsolete equipment rather than new, efficient equipment because they have already invested in the old machines and have a lot of money tied up in them. Does this make sense?

11. Suppose that you have the following utility or satisfaction schedule for your consumption of compact discs:

Number of compact discs	Total utility or satisfaction
1	200
2	350
3	450
4	500
5	525
6	540
7	550

What is the marginal utility that you receive from each compact disc? If a CD costs $15, how many CDs will you buy? What if the price increases to $25? $30? If CDs are $15, how many will you buy if you first have to pay $150 for a compact disc player? What if the CD player costs $300?

12. The following table shows the total benefit from having various amounts of a good:

units	benefit	marginal benefit
0	0	
1	20	
2	38	
3	54	
4	68	
5	80	
6	90	

a. Calculate marginal benefit and then graph the MB curve

b. If MC=14, graph the MC curve

c. How much should be purchased

d. What is the total benefit of the best choice (show that this is the same as the sum of the benefits of all of the units purchased

e. What is the total cost of the best choice

f. What is the net benefit

g. If MC=10, graph the new MC curve

h. How much should be purchased?

i. What is the net benefit of the optimal choice?

13. The following table represents the relationship between the amounts of K and L and total output Q

L	K	Q	L	K	Q
1	2	10	1	3	12
2	2	18	2	3	20
3	2	24	3	3	27
4	2	28	4	3	33
5	2	30	5	3	38

a. If L = 2 and K = 2, what are the marginal products of L and K? (Hint: look at various levels of L holding K constant; then look at various levels of K holding L constant.)

b. What is the marginal product of L when K=2?

c. Does the law of diminishing returns apply to labor (L)?

d. If L,K increases from 2,2 to 3,3, what happens to Q; By what percentage have L and K increased? By what percentage has Q increased?

14. Explain the difference between a total quantity, an average quantity and a marginal quantity.

15. If a student has $120 per month that can be spent on CDs, which cost $6 each, and paperback books, which cost $8 each, graph her budget line. (Hint: put the quantity of CDs on one axis and the quantity of books on the other axis and then graph the combinations of CDs and books could be purchased for $120 per month.)

a. Describe in words what the budget line means.

b. What happens to the budget line if the price of a CD increases to $10?

c. Describe in words what has happened to the student.

d. If, at the original prices, MU/p = 5 for CDs and MU/p = 4 for books, is she maximizing her utility?

e. If not, should she consume more CDs and fewer books, or more books and fewer CDs? Explain why?

16. Another student consumes only pizza and CocaCola. He gets the following utility or satisfaction as follows:

Pizza		CocaCola	
Quantity	Utility	Quantity	Utility
4 slices	115	5 cans	63
5	135	6	75
6	154	7	86
7	171	8	96

If CocaCola costs $.50 per can and pizza, $1 per slice and the student has $9 to spend, what combination of pizza and CocaCola will maximize his utility or satisfaction? Explain why other combinations do not maximize utility?

17. The Smiths have $10,000 to spend on food and shelter. Food costs $2 per unit; shelter costs $1 per square foot. They currently spend the same amount ($5000) on each.

    a. Derive a budget line for the Smiths.

    b. Suppose that shelter increases in price to $2 per square foot. What happens to the Smiths possible choices?

    c. Suppose that the government makes a special $5000 grant available that must be spent on food or shelter. What does the post-grant budget line look like?

    d. Show that the Smiths could now purchase the same amount of food and shelter as they did before the price of shelter increased. Will they? Explain why or why not.

18. Suppose that Sarah's utility schedules for chocolate bars and cookies are as follows:

# of bars	Tot. Utility (Chocolate)	# of Cookies	Tot. Utility (Cookies)
0	0	0	0
1	150	1	50
2	200	2	90
3	240	3	120
4	260	4	140
5	275	5	155
6	280	6	165

    a. If Chocolate bars are $3 each and cookies are $2 each, and if Sarah has $15 to spend, how many chocolate bars and how many cookies will she buy in order to maximize her utility?

    b. If the price of cookies were to decrease to $1.50, and if Sarah's income remained at $15, how many chocolate bars and cookies would she buy?

    c. What two effects, resulting from a decrease in the price of cookies, caused Sarah to alter her purchasing decision in part (b)?

    d. Suppose that the prices of the two goods were the same as in part (a), but that Sarah received an extra $5 to spend. How many chocolate bars and how many cookies would she buy?

    e. Which one effect, resulting from an increase in Sarah's income, caused Sarah to alter her purchasing decision?

19. Dave's preferences for ice cream obey the Law of Diminishing Marginal Utility. Suppose that Dave's total utility from eating 1 scoop of ice cream is 5.

    a. Would you expect Dave's total utility to be higher or lower than 5 if he were to eat 2 scoops of ice cream?

    b. Would you expect Dave's marginal utility from eating a 2nd scoop of ice cream to be greater than 5 or less than 5?

    c. Suppose that Dave's total utility from eating 2 scoops is 9. What was the marginal utility he obtained from eating the 2nd scoop?

20. In the 1984 Orange Bowl game, the undefeated Nebraska Cornhuskers faced the once-beaten Miami Hurricanes. Nebraska needed only a tie to secure a national championship but Nebraska fell behind by 31-17 in the fourth quarter only to come back to make the score 31-23. Tom Osborne, the Nebraska coach, went for a single point after the touchdown rather than for two points. Nebraska then scored again just as time was running out. The score was now 31-30. Instead of going for the tie, Osborn elected to go for two points. The attempt failed. Given that Osborne wanted to win rather than tie, did he make a rational choice by going for one point when the score was 31-23? That is, is there a decision or sequence of decisions that dominated the one Osborne made?

21. Complete: marginal is to maximization as _____ is to _____.

22. Complete: marginal is to total as _____ is to _____.

23. Buffets are typically a fixed price for a "seat at the table" but then "all you can eat" after that. Are people likely to eat more or less at a buffet than at a restaurant where dishes are ordered ala carte? Explain why. Describe the equilibrium for a demander in an all-you-can-eat buffet and its implications.

24. Is the optimal amount of something that is "bad" (e.g. pollution or crime) likely to be zero? Explain why or why not? Under precisely what circumstances would the optimal amount of the "bad" be zero?

25. If you are maximizing, can one good or service be more valuable to you than another? Explain.

Chapter 5

1. Suppose that a gallon of milk costs $2 and a loaf of bread costs $1.

   a. What is the relative price of bread in terms of milk?

   b. Now suppose that the money price of both goods increased by the same percentage. What is the relative price of milk in terms of bread?

   c. If the money price of milk were to increase and the money price of bread were to decrease, would the relative price of bread in terms of milk *increase, decrease,* or *stay the same?*

   d. Would the relative price of milk in terms of bread *increase, decrease,* or *stay the same?*

2. Why might a demand curve slope downward? (What does it mean to say that there is an inverse relationship between relative price and the quantity demanded?)

3. Why might a supply curve slope upward? (What does it mean to say that there is a positive relationship between relative price and the quantity supplied?)

4. Why does a market adjust toward an equilibrium? If markets did not adjust toward an equilibrium, what behavior would you observe?

5. Do you suppose that a market ever reaches equilibrium? Why is the concept of equilibrium useful?

6. Making aluminum requires a great deal of electricity. Why do you suppose that most aluminum is manufactured in the northwest part of the United States?

7. Should the quantity of housing demanded have increased or decreased if housing prices increased by 100 percent when the price level increased by 130 percent?

8. In some societies there is the concept of "just price" (this was widespread in medieval Europe). Is it immoral for someone to increase the price simply because there is an increase in demand?

9. When the Chernobyl nuclear power plant accident occurred, there was widespread fear in Europe that fresh vegetables and milk would be contaminated. What would you guess would happen to the price of these commodities? Did demand change or was there a change in the quantity demanded? Did supply change or was there a change in the quantity supplied?

10. What would you expect the demand curve for an appendectomy to look like? Would it differ from the demand curve for gasoline at a local station? Why or why not?

11. Suppose that a local bus company is losing money and driving half-empty buses. Should fares be increased or decreased to cut the losses?

12. Technological innovations led to a dramatic decrease in the price for facsimile machines that allow one to send documents by telephone lines in a few seconds. What do you think happened to overnight document delivery services?

13. In the fourteenth century, the bubonic plague ("black death") killed a large fraction of the population. What would you expect to have happened to wage rates?

14. What are the characteristics of a market equilibrium? Describe a market equilibrium from the perspective of demanders. Describe it from the perspective of suppliers. Describe if from the perspective of someone interested in analyzing the properties of markets.

Chapter 6

1. Are the following pairs of goods substitutes, complements, or neither?

   a. ice cream and frozen yogurt

   b. salad and salad dressing

   c. bicycles and roller skates

   d. shoes and leather

   e. airplane tickets and luggage

   f. trees and shade

2. Suppose two commodities are nearly perfect substitutes for each other. Is it useful to think of two separate markets for the commodities or is there only one market?

3. Why might higher market incomes for women decrease the number of children that a couple might have?

4. In 1978, dentists in the United States used about 706,000 ounces of gold. In 1980, they used 341,000 ounces. What probably happened?

5. A bottle of Pepsi sells for about the same price everywhere in the United States, but apartment rents differ dramatically from one location to another. Why?

6. If cholesterol is linked to heart disease, what will happen in the market for eggs (eggs have cholesterol)? What about the market for butter (so does butter)? What about the market for no-cholesterol margarine?

7. Part of the price of wrecking your car is the higher insurance premium you will have to pay. Is it likely that higher premiums will cause drivers to be more careful? Will it cause them to drive less?

8. If you consume only two goods, can both be inferior?

9. "Seconds" (products with defects) are generally sold at factory outlets near where they were produced rather than being shipped across the country. Why?

10. Foreigners frequently import expensive cars from abroad but not inexpensive cars. Why?

11. "There is an inverse relationship between price and quantity demanded, *ceteris paribus*." What does *ceteris paribus* mean in this context? Is it useful when, in fact, may things are changing at the same time?

12. In a November 1977 editorial, *The Wall Street Journal* argued that "The coffee market is behaving the way the basic textbooks say a market behaves: Prices go up, demand falls, and prices come down." Is this the way *this* basic textbook explains market behavior?

13. We have represented a demand schedule with numbers. Does this mean that individuals have numerical schedules in their minds as they make decisions? What do these numerical schedules illustrate about an individual's behavior?

14. If couples with small children must hire baby-sitters when they spend an evening out, would you expect that they would be more likely to go to expensive restaurants and theaters than couples who do not have to hire a baby-sitter? Who would you expect to go out most often?

15. Why might the market demand differ from individual demands?

16. What can be learned about individuals from the market demand?

17. Given the following information, what will be the individual demand curve:

q	total satisfaction
0	0
1	40
2	75
3	105
4	130
5	150

18. Air fares are higher for travel during certain days of the week and at certain times of the year. Why?

19. Explain why an increase (or reduction) in the demand for a commodity tends to increase (reduce) the price of a commodity if supply does not change. At the same time, the quantity bought and sold tends to increase.

20. Three people have the following individual demand schedules for Jamba Juice's Orange Berry Crush:

price	person 1	person 2	person 3
$5.00	0	1	2
$4.50	0	2	3
$4.00	0	3	4
$3.50	1	3	5

   a. What is the market demand schedule?

   b. What does the market demand curve look like?

21. Complete: *Substitution* is to *demand* as _____ is to _____.

22. Evaluate the often heard complaint that "the university simply doesn't have enough parking."

23. Draw a demand curve when:

   a. there are *many* good substitutes at the current price
   b. there are *few* good substitutes at the current price

24. Explain why "being able to substitute" implies a downward sloping demand curve. Then explain why "a downward sloping demand curve" implies substitution.

25. Is there a relative price reason why you might expect lines to be of different length, ceteris paribus, at a McDonalds in the suburbs versus a McDonalds in a poorer area of the city? If so, where would you expect lines to be the longest?

Chapter 7

1. Is the elasticity of demand likely to be higher or lower for Cheerios than for all cereals? Why?

2. Would the elasticity of demand for soft drinks on your campus be affected by the number of drinking fountains around the campus? Why?

3. The overall demand for farm commodities has a lower elasticity than does the overall demand for industrial commodities. Why might this be so? If farm and industrial output both increase by 10 percent, what will happen to the price of farm commodities relative to the price of industrial commodities?

4. Would the elasticity of demand for electricity be greater for homeowners or for large industrial users? Why?

5. If the demand for some commodity is inelastic, what will happen to the amount that individuals spend on the commodity when the price increases? Why?

6. If the demand for some commodity is elastic, what will happen to the amount that individuals spend o the commodity when the price decreases? Why?

7. How might ignorance affect the elasticity of demand?

8. If few people are riding trains and the demand for train travel is inelastic, should ticket prices be increased or decreased if the train company wishes to increase revenues?

9. If your income increases from $5,000 per year to $10,000 and your consumption of candy bars increases from 100 to 150 per year, what is your income elasticity for candy bars? Are candy bars a normal or an inferior good? Are they a luxury item?

10. Suppose you consume only two goods and your income suddenly doubles. If the first good has a negative income elasticity, what do you know about the elasticity of the second good? What if the first one has a positive elasticity which is less than one?

11. During the 1980's, the Reagan administration provided humanitarian aid to the Contras fighting the government in Nicaragua. Congress did not want the aid used for military purposes. Did it matter?

12. What do you suppose is the elasticity of substitution of dimes for nickels?

13. The elasticity of demand for x has been estimated to be .80. If the price falls by 10%, what will happen to the quantity demanded? What will happen to total expenditures for this good?

14. Do you suppose that the price elasticity for cocaine is greater than or less than 1.0? Given what you think the elasticity is, will expenditures for cocaine increase or decrease when the price of cocaine increases? What would you expect to happen to the drug-related crime rate?

15. Draw a demand curve that is perfectly inelastic. Is a demand curve of this sort consistent with the principle of substitution and the ideas developed in Chapter 6? What does your answer suggest about the figure that you've drawn? (HINT: Is it useful to think about polar cases even if they do not actually exist? If this seems odd, think of the use of the idea of a "frictionless pendulum" in physics.)

16. Given the following demand schedule, calculate the price elasticities between each price indicated in a) through d). Indicate whether demand between each price is elastic, unitary elastic or inelastic.

P	q
$5	50
10	40
15	30
20	20
25	10

a) Price increases from $5 to $10.

b) Price falls from $20 to $10.

c) Price increases from $15 to $20.

d) Price falls from $25 to $15.

17. Indicate whether the resulting percentage change in quantity demanded will be less than, equal to or greater than the percentage change in price, given the indicated price elasticity.

a) The demand for ping pong balls is elastic, and the price of ping pong balls falls by 10%.

b) The price elasticity of gasoline is less than one, and its price increases 6%.

18. Answer the following questions in reference to good X:

a) Income increases by 10%, and X is income inferior. Will the demand for X increase, remain the same or decrease?

b) Income falls and the demand for good X falls. Is X income normal or income inferior?

c) The price of good Y falls, and the demand for X increases. Are goods X and Y complements or substitutes?

d) Good Y is a substitute for good X, and the price of Y falls. Will the demand for X increase, remain the same or decrease?

19. a) If a product did not have any close substitutes, would its demand likely be elastic or inelastic? If it had many substitutes would this change your answer? Why or why not?

b) If the supply decreases for a product with an inelastic demand, will the price rise by a large or small percentage as a result? If demand were elastic would this change your answer? Why or why not?

c) If the demand decreases for a product with an inelastic supply, will the price fall by a large or small percentage as a result? If supply were elastic would this change your answer? Why or why not?

20. Indicate whether the following are elastic, unitary elastic or inelastic:

a) An increase in price has no effect on total revenue.

b) An increase in price leads to a decrease in total revenue.

c) Total revenue increases when price is decreased.

d) Total revenue increases when price is increased.

21. What is wrong with the following statement: "When the demand for a product increases, the market price will rise. As the market increases the demand for the product will fall back down again. As a result, nothing will happen to demand."

22. In 1978 it rained during the harvest of lettuce and destroyed half of the crop. As a consequence, the price of a carton with 24 heads of lettuce was $18 on May 1, 1978. However, on June 29, 1978 a new crop of lettuce had been picked and the market price was $2.75. Make a rough estimate of the elasticity of demand for lettuce.

23. In 1977 a devastating frost destroyed about 75 percent of Brazil's coffee crop. At that time, Brazil supplied about one third of the world's coffee exports. Following the freeze, the price of unroasted coffee beans rose about 400 percent. Make a rough estimate of the elasticity of demand for coffee.

24. Suppose a firm projects a 20% price reduction will increase sales volume by 40%

a. What is the elasticity of demand?

b. What will happen to sales revenue?

25. Suppose a firm projects a 20% price reduction will increase sales volume by 10%

a. What is the elasticity of demand?

b. What will happen to sale revenue?

26. Assume that demand is linear (i.e., a straight line).

    a. Will demand be elastic or inelastic for changes near the price axis? Why?

    b. Will demand be elastic or inelastic for changes near the quantity axis? Why?

    c. What is the relationship between elasticity and slope?

27. Suppose that your landlord increased your rent today. How would you respond:

    a. now

    b. over the next month

    c. over the next six months

    d. over the next year

    What do your answers to these questions imply about your elasticity of demand?

28. Complete: *Time* is to *substitution* as _____ is to _____.

29. If a firm found that its market demand was perfectly inelastic and cut its production, would its revenues from supplying goods increase or decrease?

30. If a firm found that its market demand was perfectly elastic and cut its production, would its revenues from supplying goods increase or decrease?

31. What kinds of things do you suppose affect the elasticity of demand? Why might the elasticity of demand for commodity be high? Why might the elasticity of demand for a different commodity be low?

32. "People won't buy much more even if we cut the price." What does a demand curve consistent with this view look like? What is the elasticity of demand in this case?

33. "Our industry is so competitive that if we increase our price by only 5 percent we will lose more than half of our customers." What does a demand curve consistent with this view look like? Is demand elastic or inelastic?

1. Suppose that there are 30 grocery stores in your city: 10 had no debts, another 10 recently borrowed money to open, and the remaining 10 received subsidies from the government sufficient to open. Would the prices on the typical grocery items differ from store to store?

2. Frequently, when a firm goes bankrupt, another firm purchases its capital and opens for business. If the first firm couldn't make it, why does the second firm believe that it can? (*Hint:* Consider what might happen to the price at which the capital was sold from the first firm to the second firm.)

3. Why does a competitive firm respond to relative price changes by employing more or fewer workers?

4. If all firms in an industry borrowed money to acquire capital and then the interest rate increased, would these firms make different decisions about how much to produce?

5. In what way is short-run supply affected by diminishing marginal returns?

6. How is marginal cost linked to diminishing marginal returns?

7. Why might a firm continue to produce even though it was losing money? How long would this continue?

8. Why might marginal costs increase when all firms in an industry increase their production?

9. If a firm finds that its fixed costs suddenly increase, will it change its production decision?

10. Would you close your firm if it were making zero economic profits?

11. The price of a railroad stock is $3. If the railroad had not made a profit for three years, why shouldn't its stock price be $0?

12. If a firm must pay $6 per hour to hire workers, what does the payment represent? To whom?

13. Quantity per time period is measured along the horizontal axis of a supply-demand graph. Therefore, what does a typical short-run supply curve suggest about costs and the rate of output?

14. If a person from a planned economy asked you who told firms how much to produce, what would your reply be?

15. If this person then told you that in a planned economy, profits and losses had been eliminated, what would your reply be?

16. Is incurring a cost the same as sacrificing an opportunity?

17. Is it cheaper to rent than to buy? (Or is it cheaper to buy than to rent?)

18. Frequently it is argued that the market price bears no relationship to the actual cost of producing something. Is this true in competitive markets?

19. "In the short run there is a positive relationship between price and quantity supplied, *ceteris paribus*." What does *ceteris paribus* mean in this context? Is it a useful idea when, in fact, many things are changing at the same time?

20. Does a firm in a competitive market set its price?

21. What is a *competitive* market?

22. Why might the market supply differ from the amount that a single firm would like to provide to a market?

23. For each of the following market characteristics, state whether or not the characteristic is typically found in perfectly competitive markets.

    a. Marginal Revenue from sales of the good is never negative.

    b. The price of the good is constant.

    c. The demand for the good is perfectly inelastic.

    d. A firm in the market can sell as much of the good as it wants at the market price.

    e. Only a few suppliers manufacture the good.

    f. The good is homogeneous (it is the essentially the same product regardless of which firm in the market produces it)

    g. The demand curve for the good is a horizontal line.

24. What can be learned about firms from the market supply?

25. Suppose that the marginal product (MP) of labor is 1/4 units per day

    a. If the wage is $50 per day, what is the marginal cost (MC)?

    b. If the price is $150, is it profitable to produce an unit?

    c. If the MP was 1/2 units per day, what would MC be?

    d. Would it be profitable to produce an extra unit

26. Suppose that you own an airplane. The market value is $6,000,000. You make 2 round trips per day. The fare is $150. You expected to fill 100 seats. Your cost is $14,500, including fuel and landing fees. You turned down a job of $3000 per month to fly for another airline. A normal rate of profit is 12% or 1% per month

    a. What is the total revenue in a 30 day month

    b. What is the total cost

    c. What is the accounting profit; what is the economic profit

    d. Should you shutdown or continue to operate

27. Explain why an increase (or reduction) in the supply of a commodity tends to lower (raise) the price of that commodity if demand does not change. At the same time, the quantity bought and sold usually increases.

28. The 1990-91 orange crop in Florida was forecasted to be 165 million 90 pound boxes. This would almost a 50% increase over the prior year (when frost damaged the crop) and the largest since 1980 when 146.6 million boxes were harvested. (The record was 206.7 million boxes harvested in 1979–80.) How did growers feel about this? A spokesman for the largest growers association in Florida commented: "There is a lot of concern about the pricing structure and the total juice supply worldwide in the years ahead." The Associated Press then noted that "industry leaders believe that they will have a major challenge ahead in selling all of the processed juice that will be squeezed from bumper crops foreseen in the coming years." Does this make sense? What must the AP have meant?

29. Let demand be given by Qd = 500 − 50 p and supply by Qs = 50 + 25 p. What will be the equilibrium price and quantity? What is the elasticity of demand at the market equilibrium price?

30. Given the following demand and supply schedules, graph the demand and supply curves. Use the original numbers to answer each question.

price	quantity demanded	quantity supplied
$12.00	300	1500
10.00	600	1200
8.00	700	1000
6.00	800	800
3.00	900	600
2.00	1000	500
1.00	1200	200

    a. What is the original price and quantity?

    b. Suppose something happens which causes the suppliers to supply half of the original quantity. Indicate the new equilibrium.

    c. Assume that at every price level consumers demand two-thirds of their original quantity. Indicate the new equilibrium level.

    d. Suppose that at every price level the quantity supplied doubled. What is the new equilibrium?

    e. Suppose that at every price level the quantity demanded increases by 3 times the original level. What is the new equilibrium? (You may have to make an educated guess.)

    f. Suppose that the relative price level of all goods increases by one hundred percent. Indicate the equilibrium price and quantity level.

31. Both demand and supply curves can be represented in simple algebraic terms. Consider, for example, the following:

    supply: $p = 4 + .6\,Q^s$

    demand: $p = 20 - .2\,Q^d$

Note that the price that individuals are willing to pay is inversely related to the amount that they are willing to purchase (hence the negative sign in front of Q^d) and that a higher price encourages firms to provide more to the market (the positive sign in from of Q^s). (If this isn't clear, rearrange the demand function so that Q^d is on the left hand side, $Q^d = 100 - 5\,p$.) What will be the market equilibrium price and quantity?

32. What will be the equilibrium price and quantity for the following supply and demand schedules?

	P	Q
S:	$5	90
	4	80
	3	70
	2	60
	1	50

D:	$5	60
	4	70
	3	80
	2	90
	1	100

a. What will happen to the market equilibrium if, at each price, demand increases by 10 percent?

b. What will happen to the market equilibrium if, at each price, supply decreased by 10 percent?

33. The price of a basic VCR has dropped from over $1000 to under $250. Describe in supply and demand terms what must have happened in this market?

34. Consider following:

	p	Q
D:	$20	40
	12	60
	4	80

S:	$ 8	40
	12	60
	16	80
	20	100

a. What will happen if the price is $16?

b. What will happen if the price is $8?

c. What is the equilibrium price and quantity?

d. What is the price elasticity of supply at the equilibrium?

35. What are the constraints on a competitive firm's ability to earn profit? How does each constraint arise?

36. You used to work for a software development firm at an annual salary of $35,000. But you decided to be your own boss, quit your job, withdrew $10,000 from your savings (which paid 5% interest), and started your own software firm. You also converted the basement of your home, which you had been rending for $250 per month, into an office. To get started, you sign a one-year lease on hardware for $3,600 and hire two part-time programmers for $12,500 each per year. It costs you about $50 per month to provide electricity and heat to your office.

a. what are your total annual explicit costs

b. what are your total annual implicit or opportunity costs

c. at the end of the first year, your accountant tells you that your total sales were $55,000 and congratulates you on a profitable year. Did you deserve to be congratulated?

37. The following data are price/quantity/cost combinations for firm A:

quantity	price per unit	total cost of production
0	above $225,000	$200,000
1	$225,000	$250,000
2	$175,000	$275,000
3	$150,000	$325,000
4	$125,000	$400,000
5	$90,000	$500,000

a. What is the marginal revenue for each level of sales (e.g., the marginal revenue of going from 2 to 3)?

b. What quantity should the firm produce to maximize profits?

c. Is this the same quantity that maximizes revenue? Explain why or why not?

d. What are A's fixed cost?

e. What is the marginal cost for each level of production?

f. How does marginal cost behave as output increases? What kind of firm might have this kind of marginal cost behavior?

38. The following gives cost/price data for firms B and C:

quantity	price	total cost of production
0	above $125	$250
1	$125	$400
2	$100	$500
3	$75	$550
4	$50	$600
5	$25	$700
0	above $500	$500
1	$500	$700
2	$400	$900
3	$300	$1,100
4	$200	$1,300
5	$100	$1,500

In the short run, how much should each firm produce?

39. Graph the marginal cost and marginal revenue curves for a representative competitive firm.

a. Suppose that the wage rate the firm pays its workers increases. What happens in your diagram? How will the profit-maximizing level of output change?

b. What happens to employment opportunities at this firm when the wage increases? Why?

c. If every firm responds in the same way as the representative firm, what will happen in the labor market? (Hint: draw a second diagram with the wage on one axis and the amount of labor on the other. Who are the demanders of labor? Who are the suppliers?)

40. Suppose that you are the manager of a large barber shop. Of course, you seek to maximize the profit of your shop. Having a limited amount of space and equipment, you have changed the number of haircutters you employ many times while trying to find the number that will be most profitable for you. Your observations have been as follows:

# of Barbers	# of Haircuts given per day
1	30
2	70
3	100
4	125
5	145
6	160
7	170
8	175

You rent your shop and equipment for $100 per day and pay each haircutter a wage of $100 per day. The price of a haircut in your shop is $10.

a. How many haircutters should you employ in order to maximize profit?

b. How many haircuts will be performed per day at your shop, and what will your profit per day be?

c. The marginal cost of hiring an additional worker is that worker's wage. The marginal benefit of hiring an additional worker is the extra revenue that worker earns. At the profit maximizing decision (derived above), what is true about marginal cost and marginal revenue?

1. Do you suppose an industry ever actually reaches a long-run equilibrium? If it does not, is the concept useful? Why or why not?

2. If an industry has many firms, some small and some large, and neither exit nor entry is occurring, what does this suggest about its long-run costs (or its technology)?

3. Why should anyone invest in a firm making zero economic profits?

4. Why don't firms immediately close if they incur losses?

5. Controls on entry are much more frequent than controls on exit. Why?

6. In what sense does a long-run competitive equilibrium benefit consumers?

7. Why are long-run adjustments different from short-run adjustments?

8. In what ways do profits affect competitive markets in the short run? Do the long-run effects of profits on competitive markets differ from the short-run effects? Why?

9. What is a rent? In what ways do rents differ from profits?

10. What is the process by which rents go to the scarce factor? What is meant by "scarce factor" in this case?

11. Suppose that development costs for a new textbook are $1,000,000 and that production costs are $20 per book. What does the marginal cost curve look like?

12. Sony Walkmans were priced at $300 in 1979 ($500 in current dollars). In 1992, the price was about $30. VCRs were priced at about $2,000 in 1976 ($4,000 in current dollars). In 1992, the price was about $200. Do these changes make sense?

13. Which would be fixed and variable over a time horizon of one month? Of six months?

    a. ovens in a Nabisco bakery

    b. wood to a La-Z-Boy Chair company

    c. oranges to Minute Maid Juice company

    d. buns to a McDonald's hamburger franchise

    e. cars to Hertz Car Rental company

    f. steel to General Motors

    g. flour to Pillsbury

    h. tenured professors to Brigham Young University

    i. newsprint to the Wall Street Journal

14. Explain one possible reason for a merger between firms that make completely unrelated and different products.

15. Why don't firms always get larger over time?

16. The following table gives the short and long run costs for firm A:

quantity	long run cost	short run cost
0	0	350
1	300	400
2	400	435
3	465	465
4	495	505
5	560	560
6	600	635
7	700	735

    a. Why is the third column "short run cost" (and not "long run cost")?

    b. For each quantity, find the TFC, TVC, AVC, and MC.

    c. At what output levels would the firm's short-run and long-run input mixes be the same?

    d. Over what ranges do you see economies of scale? Diseconomies of scales? Constant returns to scale?

    e. If the firm is currently producing 2 units of output, and want to double its production, should it double all of its inputs (in the long run)?

17. To calculate the profit or loss for a competitive firm, a firm would look at the difference between p and ATC, but to determine the profit-maximizing (or loss-minimizing) level of production, a firm would focus only on p and MC. Explain why.

18. What distinguishes the short run from the long run? Will the short run (or long run) be the same for all industries? Explain why or why not.

19. What is the difference between economic and accounting profits? Why is the distinction important? True, False, Uncertain (discuss): "In a perfectly competitive market, output will only increase in the short run if price increases, but this isn't true in the long run."

Chapter 10

1. What would be the effects of a freeze that destroys all or part of the apple crop in Washington on the apple, banana, orange, and other fruit markets?

2. What would be the effects of a hurricane that destroys the sugar cane crop in the Caribbean on beet sugar producers, the corn syrup market, the market for other uses of corn, the market for crops that can be planted where corn or beets are planted and so forth?

3. Between 1980 and 1986, the number of 16-to-25-year olds fell by 2 million. At the same time, there was boom in the fast-food industry. Discuss what happened in the market for fast food.

4. Speculators are important in arbitraging prices *through time*. What would happen to market prices through time if a speculator bought when the price was high and sold when the price was low? Would it make sense for the speculator to do this?

5. Utilities (power, gas, water companies) frequently charge higher prices during periods of peak demand. Similarly, hotels frequently charge higher prices during the peak tourist season. These firms undoubtedly do this to increase their profits. Are there any social advantages to higher prices during periods of peak demand?

6. During peak periods there is congestion and delay for planes landing at major airports. Rationing, in part, is by waiting. Could a market allocate landing slots? How?

7. Why are the following inefficient?

    a) Producing a lot of butter and very little margarine when people would prefer a lot of margarine and very little butter, assuming that butter and margarine cost about the same to produce.

    b) Providing a lot of butter to margarine-lovers and lot of margarine to butter-lovers.

    c) Producing butter with resources that are better used in margarine production and producing margarine with resources that are better used in butter production.

8. What might create the inefficiencies listed in Problem 7?

9. How would a market economy in which prices were free to change deal with each of the inefficiencies in Problem 7?

10. In 1982, tuna fisherman complained that the low price of chicken was hurting their incomes. Does their complaint make any sense?

11. When a crop is partially destroyed by bad weather, the price often increases substantially. Does the higher price induce more to be available? Does it matter? Wouldn't it be more efficient to have a lower price if the price did not affect availability?

12. Respond to the following:

    a) "It is more efficient to use computers than faculty members in teaching algebra."

    b) "It is more efficient to harvest watermelons by hand than with a machine."

    c) "It is less efficient to use college graduates than high school graduates as secretaries."

    d) "It is more efficient to use water than airplanes to transport goods."

13. Seeking profits is often considered to be an unsavory and socially irresponsible activity. If many of the firms in an industry decided not to maximize profits (so that marginal costs were less than the market price), would we be better off or worse off?

14. If we have a great demand for diamonds, will diamond sellers earn substantial profits?

15. The government has the right to condemn property for public use, but it must pay the market value of the property it obtains in this way. Frequently, however, those who are forced to sell to the government believe that they have not bee adequately compensated. Can you explain why this might be?

16. Can you think of ways that a firm might be able to capture part of the consumer surplus? (We will return to this question when we discuss monopolistic markets.)

17. How might it be possible for consumers to capture part of the producer surplus?

18. Why do competitive markets maximize the sum of consumer and producer surpluses?

1. In what sense do specialization and exchange make an economy better off? Are the benefits from international trade spread evenly across the economy? Explain.

2. Why will international trade affect the domestic prices that individuals must respond to as they choose to specialize and exchange? Can international trade increase domestic prices? Can international trade decrease domestic prices? Does it matter? Explain.

3. Suppose that the Japanese or Koreans have both lower wages and more technically advanced production facilities than does the United States. Does it make sense for the US to trade with either country? Does it make sense for Japan or Korea to trade with the US? Explain.

4. Suppose that a foreign government subsidized domestic industries that exported goods to the United States. How would this affect specialization according to comparative advantage?

5. If another country refuses to allow U.S. goods to be imported but wants to export to the US, should this matter?

6. If the world price of rice increases, is a country exporting rice likely to be hurt or helped? What about a country that imports rice? Why? Will everyone within the economy be affected in the same way? Why?

7. In the United States, dams are built with lots of machinery and few people. In China, dams are built with lots of people and few machines. Is China using its resources foolishly?

8. In what sense is an exchange between two persons within an economy just like an exchange between two economies? In what sense is exchange between two persons within an economy different from an exchange between two economies?

9. If foreigners want to accumulate U.S. assets, what does this imply about U.S. net exports? Explain.

10. If a government uses its own currency (say, the government of Japan uses yen) to purchase a foreign currency (say, dollars), will the value of the domestic currency appreciate or depreciate? What about the value of the foreign currency?

11. Why should a government care about the foreign exchange value of its currency? (In other words, why not let the currency value float?)

12. Can a country simply choose to run a balance of trade surplus or deficit? (Hint: If a country runs a surplus, what must be happening elsewhere in the world?)

13. If all exchange rates are free to move and no one wants to hold another country's currency or assets, can a country run a persistent trade surplus or trade deficit?

14. In 1992, the U.S. dollar fell to its lowest level in many years in foreign exchange markets. Who benefited from this change? Who was hurt? In what ways might a depreciation of the dollar affect the average American? What does your answer suggest about possible responses to a depreciation by Americans?

15. Suppose the U.S. and Saudi Arabia produced only two commodities, wheat and oil.

	Wheat	Oil
Saudi Arabia	10	30
United States	20	20

Saudi Arabia can produce either 10 bushels of wheat or 30 barrels of oil or some combination of the two. The United States can produce 20 bushels of wheat or 20 barrels of oil or some combination.

a. Draw the Aggregate Production Possibilities Frontier each for the U.S. and Saudi Arabia.

b. What are the opportunity costs of producing these commodities for each nation?

c. Who has the absolute advantage in producing wheat? Oil?

Who has the comparative advantage in producing wheat? Oil?

d. Suppose the U.S. and Saudi Arabia decide to specialize and trade with each other. At most, how much oil would be traded for one bushel of wheat? At least?

e. Before trade, each country used half of its resources producing wheat and half producing oil. What will be the total wheat and oil produced for each country before and after trade? Indicate the net gains from specialization and trade.

Before Trade	Wheat	Oil
S.A.		
U.S		
Total		
After Trade		
S.A.		
U.S.		
Total		
Net Trade Gains		

f. Have the U.S. and Saudi Arabia benefited from trade? How?

g. Now suppose that the Aggregate Production Possibilities Frontier for the United States changes so that the U.S. can produce either 40 bushels of wheat or 40 barrels of oil. The Production Possibilities Frontier for Saudi Arabia remains unchanged. Answer questions a-f for this new data.

16. Suppose that the United States and Korea had the following production possibilities for Television Sets and Rice:

	Korea	U.S.
Television Sets	25	50
Kilos of Rice	50	200

Answer the following questions given the information above. Assume that it is possible to trade fractions of television sets or fractions of kilos of rice.

a. What is the opportunity cost (in terms of kilos of rice) of producing one television set in the United States? What is it in Korea?

b. What is the opportunity cost (in terms of television sets) of producing one kilo of rice in the United States? What is it in Korea?

c. If the two countries engage in trade, who should specialize in rice production? Who should specialize in television set production?

d. What is the maximum number of kilos of rice that the United States would be willing to give to Korea in exchange for one television set?

e. What is the minimum number of kilos of rice that the Korea would accept from the United States in exchange for one television set?

f. If Korea had substantially more bargaining power than the United States, the price of one television set, agreed upon by the two nations, would likely be (circle one)

a. less than 2 kilos of rice

b. between 2 and 3 kilos of rice

c. between 3 and 4 kilos of rice

d. greater than 4 kilos of rice

e. none of the above

g. Draw and fully label the PPF for the United States and Korea combined, without specialization. Then on the same graph, draw the combined PPF with specialization. Is specialization and trade good for the US? Is it good for Korea? Why?

17. Suppose that the current world price for wheat is $6 per bushel. A government tariff of $2 per bushel on imported wheat was passed by the federal legislature several years ago, and the current domestic price of wheat is $8.00 per bushel. Assume that the domestic market for wheat is perfectly competitive.

a. Is the current tariff benefiting domestic consumers or domestic producers? Why?

b. What is the current marginal cost (MC) of wheat for domestic producers?

c. If the government tariff were lifted, would the amount of wheat purchased domestically increase, decrease, or stay the same? Why?

d. If the government tariff were lifted, would the amount of wheat produced domestically increase, decrease, or stay the same? Why?

e. Who is more likely to be in favor of free trade, domestic producers or domestic consumer groups? Why?

18. Suppose that, because of the uncertainty of many investors about the long-term political stability of country Z, the country's currency lost value on foreign exchange markets.

a. All else equal, what will happen to the amount of exports from country Z demanded on the world market? (Will they increase or decrease?)

b. What will happen to the relative price of foreign goods for citizens of country Z? (Will they increase or decrease?)

c. What is likely to happen to net exports for country Z?

1. Why are rationing problems created by price ceilings but not by price floors or restrictions on entry?

2. Price floors and price ceilings require the government to do something with the excess supply or excess demand but restrictions on entry do not. Does this explain the pervasive nature of restrictions on entry? Why?

3. If you want to enter a profession would you favor restrictions on entry? If you are already *in* a profession would you favor restrictions on entry? If your answers were different, what was the source of the difference? If your answers were the same, why?

4. Why does excess demand that is not allowed to be eliminated by price increases create potential political power?

5. As we have seen, both price ceilings and price floors reduce the quantity that consumers actually purchase in the market. Why?

6. The price of natural gas has been regulated with a price ceiling for many years. In 1981, Congressman Jack Kemp made the following argument: "We need to decontrol natural gas [lift the price ceiling] and get production of natural gas up to a higher level so we can bring down the price." Does this make sense?

7. In 1983, the Reagan administration proposed the PIK (Payments-in-Kind) program to help agriculture. Farmers who agreed to withdraw land from cultivation were compensated by the government for the lost earnings with surplus grain. The farmers could either hold or sell this grain at the open market price. How does this program differ from a simple price floor?

8. Are there legitimate public policy reasons for certain kinds of licenses? If so, how would you distinguish between licenses used for these purposes from those used only to limit entry?

9. We have seen that a tax on profits is usually passed on to consumers in the form of higher long-run prices. Suppose a government could devise a tax on economic rents. Would prices be affected by such a tax?

10. The social security tax is collected from both employers and employees. Each must pay a percentage of the employee's earnings to the government. Might social security taxes affect the demand for labor? In what ways? Could social security payments affect the supply of labor? Explain.

11. It has been argued that unemployment compensation is a subsidy to unemployment. Does this make sense? Explain. Even if it were a subsidy, are there good economic reasons why a society might want to provide unemployment benefits?

12. If we are to subsidize consumption by the poor, would it be better to give them food stamps that effectively reduce the price of food or simply give them the equivalent amount of money with which they can buy anything? (*Hint:* Would you prefer $100 in cash or $100 in food? Why?)

13. Many farms remain in business even though the support price does not cover their average costs. Why? Is this a short-run situation or a long-run situation?

14. What long-run message does the market send to farmers and the agricultural sector of the economy?

15. Public colleges and universities frequently set their tuition low. How do they ration their scarce services? Who gains from such a system?

16. Parking spaces on many university campuses are provided free. How are they rationed? Who gains by this system of rationing?

17. The American Medical Association and the American Bar Association both recently warned about surpluses of doctors and lawyers. What exactly does this mean? What does it imply about incomes for these professions? When does such a surplus persist? When does it end?

18. In 1974, the price of sugar rose by about 600 percent per pound. In 1977, the price of coffee rose about 400 percent, and in 1978 the price of lettuce rose by about 400 percent as well. What would have happened in each case if price ceilings had been imposed? Did the higher prices mean that more sugar was available in 1974, more coffee in 1977, and more lettuce in 1978?

19. How should adoptive children be rationed among the many parents who want to adopt? How should organs available for transplant be rationed among those who need them?

20. Utah sells 27 licenses each year to hunt buffalo. The fee is $200 for residents and $1,000 for nonresidents. The state receives more than a thousand applications each year, after which it holds a lottery to decide who gets to hunt. Why does the state allocate with a lottery rather than increasing the price? Should lucky recipients of licenses be allowed to sell them to someone else?

21. In 1979, in response to a second oil-price shock and an oil shortage, President Carter declared that the problem was the "moral equivalent of war" and encouraged people to voluntarily conserve oil. Do you suppose that voluntary conservation is an effective rationing device? Why?

22. Why did the U.S. government choose to set the speed limit on highways at 55 mph during the 1970s rather than simply relying on higher gasoline prices to ration scarce gasoline?

23. In this chapter we discussed subsidies initially paid to consumers and subsidies initially paid to producers. If the subsidy is the same size in either case, will a market outcome differ if the subsidy is paid to one or the other?

24. The hot-lunch program provides subsidized lunches to schoolchildren. Should farmers be in favor of such a program? Why?

25. Is the effect of a tax likely to be different in the long run than it is in the short run? Why?

26. Instead of distorting agricultural prices, some people have proposed giving farmers a cash subsidy equal to the difference between the market equilibrium price (which farmers would receive) and some target price. What would be the advantages and disadvantages of such a policy?

27. Does it matter (for demanders or suppliers) if a commodity tax is collected directly from consumers based on their purchases rather than from firms as described in the text?

28. Is an effective price ceiling above or below the equilibrium price? Why? Will it create an excess supply or an excess demand? Why? What about an effective price floor?

29. The supply and demand curves for this question are below. A sales tax of $2.00 per unit is imposed by the government.

   a) If consumers are responsible for paying the sales tax to the government, show the new market price and quantity. How much is paid by consumers, suppliers? (Show in dollars or on the graph.)

   b) If firms are responsible for paying the tax to the government, show the new market price and quantity. How much is paid by consumers, suppliers? (Show in dollars or on the graph.)

   c) How much revenue will the government collect? What will happen to tax revenue if the tax per unit is doubled?

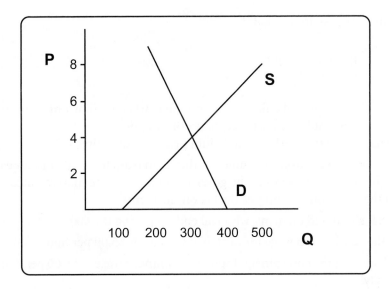

30. In the market described by the above graph:
    a) Find the cost to the government of establishing a price floor at $6.00 per unit by (1) buying the surplus and (2) subsidizing consumption.
    b) If the profit per unit of sales was $0.50, how much would it cost to pay enough firms not to produce to keep the price at $6.00?
    c) At the price floor output, what is the marginal cost of producing additional output?
    d) At the price floor output, what is the maximum amount individuals are willing to pay for additional output?
    e) Why is the market output inefficient?
31. For this same market:
    a) What would the output be if there was a price ceiling at $2.00?
    b) At the price ceiling output, what is the marginal cost of producing additional output?
    c) At the price floor output, what is the maximum amount individuals are willing to pay for additional output?
    d) Why is the market output inefficient?

32. In an earlier problem, we found that if

supply: $p = 4 + .6\,Q^s$ and
demand: $p = 20 - .2\,Q^d$,

the market equilibrium price would be $16 and the market equilibrium quantity would be 20. Suppose that the government levies a $4 specific tax on suppliers.

a. What will happen to the market equilibrium price and quantity?

b. If a tax of $4 is collected from consumers rather than from firms (that is, for each unit a consumer purchases, he or she must send to the government $4) will the market outcome be different from that when the government imposes the tax on the firm?

c. If a tax of $4 is imposed on firms, who will end up paying the tax?

33. Assume that the equilibrium wage for unskilled workers is $5.00 per hour.

a. What will happen if the government imposes a minimum wage of $6.00 per hour? Show your analysis graphically.

b. Advocates of the minimum wage typically argue that the employment effects will be minimal and that the total amount paid to all unskilled workers will increase. What must they be assuming about the market for unskilled workers? Show your analysis graphically.

34. Imagine that the current price for a bushel of wheat in Harvestland is $8. To aid the farmers, Harvestland's Congress passes a law stating that no wheat may be bought or sold within the country's borders for less than $10 per bushel.

a. Does the new law create a *price floor* or a *price ceiling*?

b. Will the law create a *shortage* of wheat, create a *surplus* of wheat, or have *no effect*?

c. Below is a graph representing the wheat market in Harvestland prior to the new law. At the equilibrium price of $8 per bushel, the equilibrium quantity is 3,500 bushels. Given this information, label the x-axis and the Supply and Demand curves on the graph. Then, draw in the price floor/ceiling.

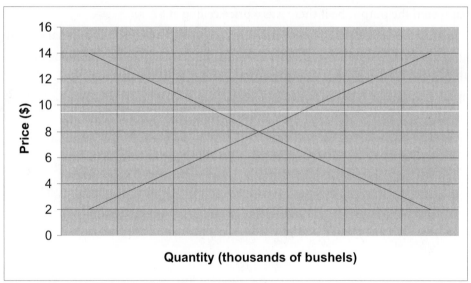

d. How many bushels of wheat will be demanded in the market after the new law?

e. How many bushels of wheat will the market be willing to supply in the market after the new law?

f. Which of your answers in (d) and (e) will be the *actual* amount of wheat that will be bought and sold under the new law, assuming no government intervention?

g. Suppose that the government in Harvestland decided to intervene in the wheat market in an effort to correct for the distortion it created. If the government wanted to purchase enough wheat to eliminate the excess supply in the market that it created by passing its new law, how many bushels would it have to purchase?

h. How much money would the government have to spend to purchase the extra wheat described in (g)?

i. Is Harvestland's new law economically efficient? Why or why not?

j. How much consumer surplus (in dollars) is lost with passage of the new law?

35. The city council in Big Buck City decided that apartment rent prices in the city were too high. To fix the problem, the city passed a new ordinance making it illegal for owners to charge more than $1400 per month for rent on a two-bedroom unfurnished apartment inside the city limits.

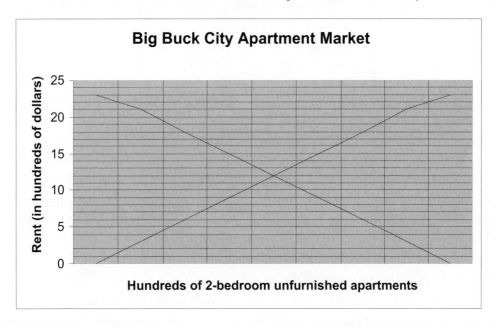

a. Given that the equilibrium number of 2-bedroom apartments bought and sold in Big Buck City prior to rent controls was 450 apartments, label the x-axis and the Supply and Demand Curves on the graph above.

b. What will be the number of 2-bedroom apartments bought and sold in Big Buck City after the rent control is implemented?

c. Will the rent control create a *surplus*, create a *shortage*, or have *no effect* on the market for 2-bedroom apartments in Big Buck City?

d. Why does your answer in (c) differ from the answer you obtained in Question 34(b)?

36. The market for packages of cigarettes is described below (quantity figures are in millions).

Price	Q Demanded	Q Supplied
$0.00	50	0
$0.50	40	10
$1.00	30	20
$1.50	20	30
$2.00	10	40
$2.50	0	50

a. Draw and label the market for cigarettes on the diagram below.

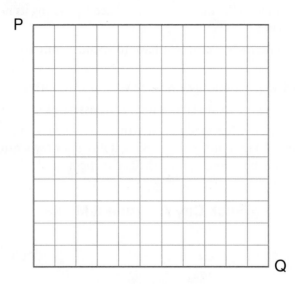

b. What is the equilibrium quantity and price for cigarettes in the market?

c. How much total consumer surplus is obtained at the equilibrium price and quantity?

d. How much producer surplus is obtained at the equilibrium price and quantity?

e. Suppose that, to curb smoking, the government set a production quota that stated that no more than 15 million packages of cigarettes could be produced. Draw this quota as a dotted vertical line at Q=15 on the diagram.

f. With the quota in (e), what is the new market price of cigarettes?

g. What is the producer surplus with the quota?

h. Now, suppose that, instead of a quota, the government implements a tax

of $1.00 per package of cigarettes produced. Draw the new supply curve created by the tax on the graph above. (Hint: The supply curve shifts upward by $1.00)

i. With the tax in (h), what is the new market price of cigarettes?

j. What is producer surplus with the tax?

k. If the government was determined to pass a law that had the effect of reducing smoking, which would tobacco producers prefer, a *tax* on cigarettes or a *quota* that limited the number of cigarettes that could be produced and sold? Why?

l. Is there a difference between the deadweight loss created by a quota and

the deadweight loss created by a tax? Why or why not?

37. Evaluate: "NAFTA (the North American Free Trade Area) is a swindle—we can't compete with the Mexicans because they have lower wages than we do and can always produce goods cheaper than we can."

Chapter 13

1. In what sense does a monopoly create an inefficiency?

2. Would the only supplier of gasoline in a town halfway across the desert between Los Angeles and Las Vegas be a monopolist? What about the only supplier of Exxon gasoline in any town?

3. In what sense might a monopolist earn an "excess" profit?

4. Why is price discrimination a clear indication that firms act as if demand curves slope downward?

5. Suppose that parking lots in a downtown area are owned by many different people and that all of the slots in the lots have been leased to persons commuting to the area. A new commuter complains that the parking-lot owners have a monopoly because there are no slots that can be leased, except at a much higher price. Is there a monopoly in this instance?

6. It has been argued that the development of low-cost transportation (such as railroads) lowered the market power of manufacturers. Why might this have been so?

7. Suppose that a college bookstore charges faculty members 10 percent less for books than it does students. Are students being exploited? Are faculty members getting a discount? Are the being subsidized by the students?

8. If 7-Eleven prices are always greater than the local supermarket, why does anyone shop at 7-Eleven? Do 7-Eleven stores have a monopoly? Do they have market power?

9. Is a monopolist subject to competitive pressures?

10. Can imports limit the power of a monopolist? Why?

11. Why is price discrimination more common in the markets for services than in the markets for goods?

12. Doctors sometimes charge poorer patients lower prices. This might be considered a charitable decision, but are there other reasons for charging these patients lower prices?

13. If the government auctioned off the right to exclude others from entering a market, thereby creating a monopoly, what is the maximum amount that would be paid for this right? Explain.

14. If a single firm produced the entire supply of some commodity, but there were no barriers to entry, should policy-makers be concerned?

15. If a university charges a high tuition but offers everyone a different scholarship based on need, is it price discriminating?

16. Why are coupons for purchasing groceries a form of price discrimination? What about the following kinds of offers: (a) "The first candy bar sells for $.50; the second for $.25." (b) "A single candy bar sells for $.50, but two sell for $.75."

17. Why might a restaurant have the same item at a lower price on its luncheon menu than on its dinner menu?

18. Hardback books sell for a good deal more than paperback books. The former cost more to produce than the latter. Are there other reasons why the prices may differ?

19. For two decades, railroads have successfully blocked legislation in the U.S. Congress that would allow coal to be transported in large pipes by a method known as "slurry piping." Why?

20. Can a small firm be a monopolist? Explain.

21. Why might a higher elasticity of market demand make it more difficult for firms to form a cartel?

22. Prices are generally higher for purchasing magazines at a newsstand than for subscribing for some period of time. Is this price discrimination? Why?

23. Gold Cross pens sell at one price, silver Cross pens at a somewhat lower price, black or gray at a still lower price, and stainless steel at the lowest price. Might this be price discrimination? Why?

24. Given the following marginal cost and demand curves, find monopoly and competitive price and quantity. How large a subsidy would be needed to induce the monopolist to produce the competitive output?

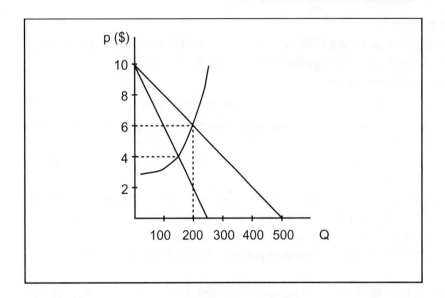

25. Given the demand schedule in the following table, calculate and graph total revenue and marginal revenue. If the marginal cost for the firm is constant at $10.00, what is the profit-maximizing quantity? Show this in a marginal revenue-marginal cost graph. Calculate and graph the firm's profits (assume that average fixed costs are $5 per unit produced). Compare the profit graph with the marginal revenue-marginal cost graph.

price	quantity
$50	1
45	2
40	3
35	4
30	5
25	6
20	7
15	8

26. Suppose the firms in a market collude, reducing their output to the monopoly level and raising the market price. All firms reduce their output by the same percentage under collusion.

a. Compare the competitive and collusive price.

b. Show the profits for the typical firm at the competitive price.

c. Show the profits for the typical firm at the collusive price.

d. Show the profits for the same firm at the collusive price if it increases its output to maximize its own profits, assuming that the other firms continue to keep output low to keep the price high.

27. Under what conditions could a monopoly earn economic profits in the long run? Draw a demand, MR and ATC curve that illustrates this case.

    a. Draw the same curves for a monopoly that is just breaking even.

    b. Draw the same curves for a monopoly that is losing money, but continues to operate in the short run.

    c. Draw the same curves for a monopoly that is losing money and will shut down, even in the short run.

28. The following represents demand in a market that has a single supplier protected by a patent:

quantity	price	ATC
100,000	$100	$20
200,000	$80	$15
300,000	$60	$16.66
400,000	$40	$22.50
500,000	$20	$31

    a. Determine the monopolist's optimal quantity and price.

    b. Calculate the firm's profits and show that these are the highest profits the firm can make.

    c. Suppose that someone else holds the patent and negotiates a $1,000,000 use fee (this cost was not included in the ATC calculations above). What is the firm's optimal quantity and price?

    d. Calculate the firm's profits.

29. Are there any circumstances when a monopolist would choose the same price as a perfectly competitive firm selling the same product? Explain.

30. The demand curve for a monopolist is given by $p = 20-4Q$. Marginal revenue is $MR = 20-8Q$. Marginal cost is Q^2.

    a. How much will the firm choose to produce?

    b. What will be the market price?

31. A monopoly supplier of electricity faces a demand curve given by $p = 15 - Q$, where p is the price in cents per kilowatt-hour of electricity and Q is thousands of kilowatt-hours. The marginal revenue is $MR = 15 - 2Q$. The marginal cost of producing electricity is constant at $MC = 5$ (i.e., $. 05 per kilowatt-hour).

    a. What are the equilibrium price and quantity?

    b. Suppose the government wants to negotiate a special price at which an additional 2000 kilowatt-hours of electricity will be sold to low income households. What is the maximum price per kilowatt-hour the supplier can charge and still expect to sell the extra electricity? What is the minimum price it would be willing to accept?

    c. Would moving to a two-price system increase efficiency? Explain why or why not? Show who would be the winners and losers (and their gains and losses) from such a system.

32. A maker of computer software has a monopoly on a new data processing program. The company spent $20 million to develop the new software, but its variable costs of producing copies of the program are only $0.50 per copy. The company is trying to decide how many copies it should sell given the information about the market for their product described in the table on the next page:

#Units Sold(Millions)	Price	TR(millions)	MR	TVC(millions)	TC(millions)	π (millions)
1	$50	$50	$50	$0.50	$20.50	$29.50
2	$45	$90	$40	$1	$21	$69
3	$40	$120				
4	$35	$140				
5	$30	$150	$10			
6	$25	$150				
7	$20	$140				
8	$15	$120			$24	
9	$10	$90				
10	$5	$50				

TR=Total Revenue, MR=Marginal Revenue, π=Profit, TVC=Total Variable Cost, TC=Total Cost

a. Complete the table above.

b. At what price does the Marginal Revenue become 0?

c. Which of the prices listed in the table allows the monopolist to maximize its profit?

d. Notice that even though the company can produce the last 10 million units for only $0.50 each and sell them for $5 each, it maximizes profit when NOT producing these units. Why does producing the last 10 million units actually *reduce* the company's profit?

33. The following is a hypothetical market demand schedule for good X. Assume that there are no fixed costs.

Price($)	Q Demanded
2	150
4	120
6	90
8	60
10	30
12	0

a. First assume that this market is perfectly competitive and that the marginal cost of production (MC) is constant at $4.

   i. How many units will be produced and sold and at what price?

   ii. What will be total profit generated in the market?

b. Now, assume that the market is monopolistic, meaning that only one company supplies product X to the market and there are high barriers to entry.

   i. If the MC is still constant at $4, how many units will be produced and sold and at what price? (Hint: Use the MR=MC rule or simply calculate profit at each level of production.)

   ii. What will be the profit to the monopoly?

c. The quantity produced in your answer to part (b) should have been less than in part (a). Why was the monopolist able to generate a profit even though it sold fewer units than would have been sold in a perfectly competitive market?

d. Which type of suppliers would consumers typically prefer, a monopoly or a perfectly competitive supply? (Hint: consider the market price of the good in each case.)

34. Acme Widget Company has a monopoly in widgets and has perfect information about all 6 existing widget consumers, which allows the company to *perfectly price discriminate*. The Marginal Cost to Acme of producing an additional widget is constant at MC=$5. The market for widgets is described in the table on the next page:

Price	#Widgets Demanded
$30	1
$25	2
$20	3
$15	4
$10	5
$5	6

a. How many widgets will Acme produce and sell?

b. How much total consumer surplus will there be in the market?

c. Assuming no fixed costs, what will be Acme's profit from widget sales?

d. If this market were perfectly competitive, how many units would be produced and sold in the market?

e. Compare your answer in (a) to your answer in (d). Explain why your answers are the same (or why they are different).

1. Should activities that are unambiguously beneficial be considered *per se* legal?

2. Under the Robinson-Patman amendments to the Clayton Act, price discrimination is illegal, except in certain circumstances. One such circumstance is when costs differ for different customers. If costs differed by 10% in servicing two customers, but prices differed by 20%, is price discrimination occurring? How does your answer explain the difference in prices between paperback and hardback books.

3. If you were to develop legal rules dealing with price discrimination, would they be *per se* or rule-of-reason rules?

4. Why might the courts want to scrutinize carefully vertical price restraints? (Are there harms?)

5. In what sense is service a benefit in the sale of a commodity? Can you give examples of commodities for which service is important? How does resale price maintenance encourage service?

6. How would you determine the appropriate definition of a market within which a particular farmer sells apples? Should the definition be based on geography? Should it be based on similarities between commodities (such as type of apple, apples and other fruit, food in general)?

7. How do markets undermine monopoly power?

8. What is the difference between *per se* rules and a rule-of-reason approach to monopoly power?

9. Why is a cartel unambiguously harmful whereas a merger has ambiguous effects?

10. What kinds of information does a regulatory body need if it is to successfully overcome the natural monopoly problem?

11. What kinds of information does a regulatory body need to know in order to successfully regulate a monopolist that is not a natural monopolist?

12. Why might regulation of a monopolist's price lead to changes in the quality of the commodity the monopolist produces?

13. Why might limiting the rate of return to a fair rate influence a firm to acquire more capital than it otherwise would?

Chapter 15

1. In what sense do markets fail when there is a negative externality?

2. In what sense do markets fail when there is a positive externality?

3. Can you think of situations in which one person may think that the externality being produced is negative while another person may think that is it positive?

4. Why are whales, which few people actually eat, becoming extinct, whereas no one is concerned about the extinction of beef cattle, which are slaughtered by the thousands each day?

5. What differences would you expect to see between homes that were rented and homes that were owned by their occupants? Why?

6. In what sense is there an optimal amount of pollution?

7. If many people commute and there are several different roads that they can use, why might the commuting time on each road be about the same, even if one of the roads is an urban expressway?

8. If tolls were charged on an expressway, why might it make sense to charge more during rush hour than during other times of the day?

9. Will markets be efficient if no one defines who has what rights? What does your answer suggest about:

   a) the right of landowners to do what they wish with their own land?

   b) the right of automobile owners to improve the performance of their cars by removing pollution-control devices?

   c) the right of someone to smoke in an enclosed space?

   d) the right of someone to insist that no one smoke in an enclosed space?

   e) the right of someone to put a satellite reception dish on their property to watch cable TV?

10. When radio firms developed, access to broadcast frequencies was not regulated. Anyone who wanted to broadcast a message could do so if he or she had the appropriate equipment. What do you think the result was?

11. The Federal Communications Commission (FCC) was established to regulate access to broadcast frequencies. Today you must obtain a license to broadcast on a particular frequency. How does this solve any externality problems you identified in Problem 10? Should stations be able to sell their licenses? If they cannot (because of FCC regulations), what will happen?

12. Assuming that property rights are defined, if transaction costs are low, will there be any externality problems?

13. Why might high transaction costs create externalities?

14. Public transportation (bus, train, and subway service) is frequently subsidized. What externality arguments might be used to support this public policy?

15. Should all externalities be eliminated?

16. There are severe restrictions on markets for untested drugs, marijuana, cocaine, heroin, body organs for transplant, and even donated blood. Are there externality reasons for these markets to be regulated? Are there other reasons?

17. Explain the difference between determining an efficient allocation of a specified amount of pollution (or pollution reduction) and determining the efficient overall amount of pollution reduction.

18. The social and private marginal cost and benefit (demand) curves are given below.

    a) Compare the efficient output, the competitive output and the monopoly output (label on the graph).

    b) Indicate whether a tax or subsidy would correct the externality in a competitive market and show this on the graph.

c) Indicate whether a tax or subsidy would correct the externality in a monopoly market, and show this on the graph.

monopolized market   competitive market

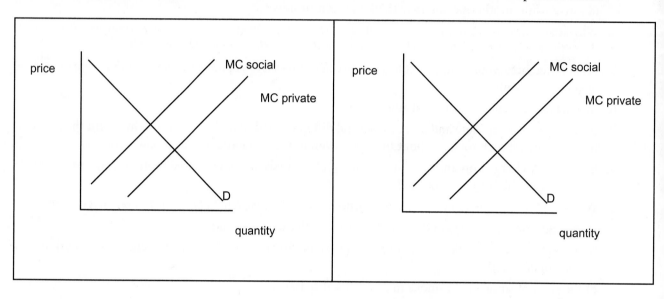

19. Elementary and secondary school children are often required to have immunizations to prevent major communicable diseases. These immunizations are almost always subsidized by the government.

a) In what sense in an immunization an externality?

b) In what sense is an immunization a public good?

20. Education has often been referred to as having an externality.

a) In what sense does education create externalities? Are the externalities positive or negative? Why?

b) Graphically illustrate the external effects of education. Illustrate the socially optimal solution as well as the market solution (without the imposition of a tax or subsidy). Indicate whether a tax or subsidy would be appropriate. Graphically indicate what the amount of tax or subsidy is that the government should provide.

21. Positive externalities and monopolies have which of the following in common?

   a. They are both characterized by too much pricing power.

   b. They are both characterized by barriers to entry.

   c. Their existence implies too little production and consumption.

   d. They cannot be compared.

22. It has been suggested that a market for pollution should be created. If a firm wanted to pollute air or water, they would have to purchase the right to do so from the owner of the "property".

   a. What will happen to the amount of pollution created?

   b. What will this do to the prices of goods whose production creates large amounts of pollution?

   c. What incentive will this create for consumers?

   d. What should the government do with the money it collects?

23. Most universities subsidize football. That is, ticket sales and related revenues are not sufficient to cover the cost of the football program and the university makes up the difference. Are there positive externalities that justify such a subsidy? If so, what *specifically* are they? Who are the third parties that benefit from a football program?

24. Complete: A *negative externality* is to an *efficient market outcome* as _____ is to _____

Chapter 16 ▶

1. In what sense is there a market failure when there are public goods?

2. Why is information a public good?

3. How does searching for information solve the public-good problem?

4. Mail-order catalogues often offer clothing and other goods at lower prices than local stores. Why doesn't everyone purchase these goods by mail?

5. What kinds of advertising provide no economically useful information? What kinds of advertising are likely to provide more useful information?

6. To repeat a question posed in an earlier chapter, if 7-Eleven prices are always above those of the local supermarket, why does anybody shop at 7-Eleven?

7. Suppose someone offers you a Rolex watch (that sells in a jewelry store for $800) for $50. Would you buy it? Why or why not?

8. Students usually complain about the low prices that the college bookstore pays for their used texts, yet they sell them to the bookstore. Why?

9. In what ways is charitable giving a public good? (Is there free riding?) What does this suggest about private charities? How would you use your understanding of ways in which public goods might be provided to organize a charitable-giving campaign?

10. Assume you are in poor health. If the uncertainty about whether you would live another year increased substantially, would you increase or decrease your savings?

11. Why is it difficult to purchase earthquake insurance?

12. In what ways might middlemen or intermediaries lower search costs?

13. What kinds of advertising lower search costs? What kinds of advertising don't lower search costs? Should advertising that doesn't lower search costs be prohibited?

14. Would a non-market economy have public-good problems?

15. Do risks disappear just because they are insured?

16. Sometimes public policies are directed toward reducing the risks that individuals must confront. Should risks be reduced to zero where possible?

17. Would you prefer a lower-paying job with more security or a higher-paying job with less security? Why?

18. Why is more spent on advertising for soft drinks than for diesel trucks?

19. What problems would you expect a public TV station to encounter in trying to fund its costly operations?

20. In what sense could education be considered a public good? In what sense is it a private good? What does your analysis suggest about the provision of education by a market?

21. For each of the following, discuss whether the good/service is more likely to be a *public good* or a *private good* and explain why.

    a. A large clock located on a tower in the center of a town

    b. An apple sliced into several pieces

    c. An aerial fireworks display

    d. A formula for calculating equal payments of interest over a time period

    e. A city bus

    f. A municipal office building

    g. Electricity

    h. Books at the public library

1. What is the difference between real and nominal GDP?

2. What determines potential GDP?

3. If the price level was 178 in 1980, 196 in 1981, and 207 in 1982, what is the rate of inflation? What characteristics of an economy does the rate of inflation describe?

4. Why should unemployment of labor (or any other resource) fall when real output increases?

5. In your opinion, what should the goals for macroeconomic policy be? Why?

6. If there are tradeoffs between price stability and unemployment or between price stability and economic growth, would your goals remain the same?

7. If inflation redistributes wealth, who is likely to gain? Who is likely to lose? Is such a redistribution a cost associated with inflation?

8. Would economic growth increase or decrease with a decrease in the birth rate? With a change in the rate of immigration?

Chapter 17, Appendix ▶

1. Why can money be used to measure economic activity?

2. Why is it useful to be able to measure economic activity?

3. When can changes in dollar prices be used as indicators of changes in *relative* prices?

4. Are there some goods or services that are unlikely to change in price when there is an inflation (or deflation)?

5. In what sense does the growth in real per capita GDP discussed in Chapter 17 *underestimate* the increase in individual well-being over the past century?

6. In what sense might the growth in real per capita GDP discussed in Chapter 17 *overestimate* the increase in individual well-being over the past century?

7. Automobiles are different now than they were 20 years ago. How does this create problems for the CPI?

8. What problems do comparisons of an economy's aggregate output over time create?

9. What problems do comparisons of aggregate output between economies create?

10. Is it possible for real GDP to decrease even though nominal GDP increases? Why?

11. What does it mean to deflate GDP by a price index? What is being measured?

12. What are the National Income Accounts?

13. Why is there a difference between gross domestic product and the disposable income that individuals really have to spend? Be specific.

Chapter 18

1. What is aggregate demand?

2. What is aggregate supply?

3. What is aggregate consumption?

4. What is aggregate investment?

5. What is aggregate government spending?

6. In Questions 1-5, what does *aggregate* mean?

7. What are aggregate net exports?

8. In Question 7, what does *net* mean?

9. What is the difference between *aggregate supply* and *aggregate quantity supplied?* (Hint: Review the distinction between *market supply* and *market quantity supplied* outlined in Chapter 3 and then extend the distinction by analogy.)

10. If the price level doesn't respond when aggregate demand decreases, what are some possible consequences?

11. In what specific ways is the aggregate model of an economy presented in this chapter different from the market supply-demand model used in earlier chapters?

12. How does the price level differ from the price of a Big Mac or a CD?

Chapter 19

1. What criteria determine the potential real output of an economy?

2. How do changes in the price level affect potential real output?

3. What determines full employment of labor? When will an economy have full employment?

4. "If all prices and wages are flexible, aggregate demand changes will not affect real output." Comment.

5. Why does the labor demand curve slope downward and to the right?

6. Why should a market economy move toward full employment in the long run?

7. Is it possible for real output to be falling even while there is an inflation? Is it possible for real output to be increasing even while there is a deflation? Why?

8. If the population in a country increases at a moderate rate through time, what will happen to potential real output?

9. If potential real output increases because of an increase in the capital stock, natural resources, or because of technological developments, but there is no change in the population, does this necessarily mean that per capita real income increases?

10. If all prices and wages are completely flexible, will there be unemployment in the economy? What if wages are not flexible, but are sticky?

11. If both firms and individuals have the same expectations, can there be unemployment? Why or why not?

12. Why does the short-run aggregate supply curve slope upward to the right whereas the long-run aggregate supply curve (potential real output) is vertical?

13. Why might the movements in nominal wages differ from changes in the price level?

14. What evidence is there that changes in output and unemployment usually result from changes in aggregate demand rather than from aggregate supply shocks?

15. Why is the long run aggregate supply curve drawn vertical?

16. Why is the short run aggregate supply curve drawn with an upward (to the right) slope?

17. Suppose the economy starts in long run equilibrium, and aggregate demand decreases.

    a. Show the change in the price level, real output, the real wage rate, and unemployment in the short run.

    b. Show the change in the price level, real output, the real wage rate, and unemployment in the long run.

18. If wages and prices are *completely* sticky, what will happen to employment and real output when aggregate demand increases?

19. If wages and prices are *completely* flexible, what will happen to employment and real output when aggregate demand increases?

20. What happens to short run aggregate supply as the nominal wage increases? Decreases?

21. What happens to long run aggregate supply as the nominal wage increases? Decreases?

22. What happens to long run aggregate supply when labor productivity increases over time?

23. What are the ways that an economy can increase its potential real output? If its potential real output is increasing, is the standard of living also increasing? Explain.

24. Suppose that wages are sticky downward but not sticky upward (i.e., they are slow to adjust down, but fast to adjust up). What would the ASsr curve look like? How would this affect an economy's adjustment to aggregate demand shocks compared to the analysis provided in the text?

25. How would you explain to someone who had not had any economics the intuitive meaning of W/P?

1. What will happen to aggregate demand if firms become more pessimistic about the future? Why? What might make firms more pessimistic about the future?

2. What will happen to aggregate demand if firms become more optimistic about the future? Why? What might make firms more optimistic about the future?

3. In the absence of fiscal activities by the government, are changes in aggregate demand caused primarily by changes in investment or by changes in consumption? Why?

4. Do we understand why desired investment changes? (Is it really helpful to know that desired investment decreases when firms become pessimistic or that it increases when firms become optimistic?)

5. Under precisely what conditions will aggregate-demand changes be primarily responsible for fluctuations in real output?

6. What precisely is the marginal propensity to consume? Why might it be important?

7. Is it possible for actual investment to always equal actual saving, even though desired investment differs from desired saving? (Hint: Consider the role of inventories.)

8. Suppose we all suddenly want to save more. Is it possible that as a consequence, we might actually save less in aggregate? (Hint: Consider what would happen to real output if everyone decided to save more. Then consider what might happen to aggregate saving as a consequence of the change in real output.)

9. Why do individuals save part of their income rather than consuming it all?

10. Why does investment add to the instability created by changes in aggregate demand? Does consumption have the same effect?

11. What determines the change in real output when prices are flexible? When prices are sticky?

12. Suppose the economy starts in long run equilibrium.
    a. Graph the effect of an increase in government spending.
    b. Graph the effect of a decrease in the income tax rate.

13. Suppose that consumption at potential output (y^*) increases by $100.
    a. Will y be greater or less than c+i?
    b. What will happen to inventories?
    c. What will happen to real output?

14. Show the first four rounds of spending caused by a decrease in investment of $400 million if the MPC equals .75. What is the total of the first four rounds? What is the total of all rounds (using the multiplier)?

15. For each of the following explain why each option is correct or incorrect:

    If saving is less than desired investment at potential income (y^*), then

    a. y>c+i at y^*, so that y will increase.

    b. y<c+i at y^*, so that y will increase.

    c. y>c+i at y^*, so that y will decrease.

    d. y<c+i at y^*, so that y will decrease.

    If saving is greater than desired investment at y^*, then inventories will

    a. decrease, causing y to increase.

    b. increase, causing y to increase.

    c. decrease, causing y to decrease.

    d. increase, causing y to decrease.

16. The first column of the following table indicates a series of changes that might affect the economy. Indicate in the second column the component of aggregate demand most likely to be affected and indicate in the third column the direction of the effect

change	agg D component affected	direction of effect
increase in population		
reduced money supply		
increased income taxes		
recession abroad		
expected domestic recession		
rapid escalation in house prices		
stock market crash		
cut in defense expenditures		
higher prices abroad		

17. Consider the following:

GDP	c	i	g	t	x	m
900	340	200	500	500	250	90
950	370	200	500	500	250	90
1000	400	200	500	500	250	100
1050	430	200	500	500	250	115
1100	460	200	500	500	250	110
1150	490	200	500	500	250	115
1200	520	200	500	500	250	120
1250	550	200	500	500	250	125
1300	580	200	500	500	250	130
1350	610	200	500	500	250	135
1400	640	200	500	500	250	140
1450	670	200	500	500	250	145,
1500	700	200	500	500	250	150
1550	730	200	500	500	250	155
1600	760	200	500	500	250	160
1650	790	200	500	500	250	165
1700	820	200	500	500	250	170
1750	850	200	500	500	250	175
1800	880	200	500	500	250	180
1850	910	200	500	500	250	185
1900	940	200	500	500	250	190
1950	970	200	500	500	250	195
2000	1000	200	500	500	250	200
2050	1030	200	500	500	250	205

a. What is the equilibrium level of aggregate demand?

b. At that level, what would be i, s, g-t, m-x?

c. If the economy were closed, what would be the equilibrium level of aggregate demand?

d. Opening the economy increases, decreases or leaves unchanged aggregate demand?

e. What is the MPC?

f. What is the multiplier?

g. If investment increased by $250, what would happen to AD if the economy were closed?

h. If the economy were open, AD would increase by how much?

i. Verify your approach by determining GDP, i, s, g-t, m-x?

h. Suppose x falls to 0, would AD increase/decrease/remain the same? By how much?

i. Suppose x increases by 100 and imports decrease by 30, what has happened to the currency?

j. The new equilibrium would be?

18. Okun's law says that for each 2% decrease in GDP, unemployment increases by 1%. Given the following information, complete the column for the predicted unemployment rate.

starting year	ending year	pot GDP%	act GDP%	initial UE % predicted UE %
1960	1961	3.3	2.2	5.5
1965	1969	3.3	6.0	4.8
1970	1971	3.3	-.2	3.5
1975	1976	3.3	-1.1	5.6
1981	1982	2.7	-1.3	7.5

19. Suppose that firms become pessimistic. Describe the short-run effects on real GDP and the price level. Suppose that the price level doesn't change, how does your answer change?

Chapter 21

1. Will government fiscal policy *always* stabilize the economy? Why?

2. Will countercyclical fiscal policy affect both aggregate demand and aggregate supply? Why?

3. Fiscal policy is usually conducted by changing taxes and expenditures. Could it be conducted by changing subsidies and expenditures just as easily?

4. What are "sensible" fiscal policy responses to unemployment? To inflation?

5. What difficulties might arise in actually implementing "sensible" fiscal policies?

6. What effects does fiscal policy have on the division of the real-output "pie"? Do the effects on the division matter in evaluation the overall effects of fiscal policy?

7. Are there fiscal policies that might simultaneously increase aggregate demand and decrease aggregate supply? What would the consequences of such policies be?

8. Are there fiscal policies that might simultaneously increase aggregate demand and increase aggregate supply? What would the consequences of such policies be?

9. Is there a difference between the amount the government spends and the amount of goods and services the government purchases? (Hint: Consider redistributive transfers from one household to another.)

10. Does the active use of fiscal policy imply that the government must be large and growing?

11. Fiscal policy stimulates the economy by increasing aggregate demand. Does this cause inflation? If so, are there policies that stimulate the economy but that are not inflationary?

12. For stabilization policy, what is the difference between a change in government spending on goods and services and a change in government transfer payments?

13. What is the government-spending multiplier?

14. How do taxes affect the investment or government-spending multipliers?

1. Why does the interest sensitivity of investment provide another avenue for the government to make policy?

2. Why is the demand for money inversely related to the interest rate?

3. In what sense does money have backing? Does this mean that it is not useful? What does this suggest about the intrinsic value of money?

4. What is the money multiplier? What determines the multiplier in practice?

5. If all banks were required to keep 100 percent of the deposits in checking account on reserve, what would happen in the economy if a $1,000 note dropped from a helicopter?

6. What reasons can you think of for the money supply to increase somewhat with interest rates?

7. Discuss the effects of the following on the money market:

   a. An open market sale of U.S. Treasure bonds by the Fed

   b. An increase in the discount rate

   c. An increase in the reserve requirement

8. Discuss the effects of the following on aggregate demand:

   a. An open market purchase of U.S. Treasure bonds by the Fed

   b. A decrease in the discount rate

   c. A decrease in the reserve requirement

9. If the Fed decreases the reserve requirement, *must* the supply of money increase? Would your answer be any different for a decrease in the discount rate? What about an open market purchase?

10. In what sense do banks "create" money?

11. Precisely what is fractional reserve banking? What kinds of vulnerabilities does it create for an economy? Would banks prefer to have fractional reserves or 100 percent reserves against checking accounts?

12. If individuals and firms wanted to increase the amount of currency they hold at Christmas every year, what would happen in the money market?

13. What is the difference between the aggregate demand multiplier and the money multiplier?

14. If the Fed wants to change the money supply, what factors do you think will influence its choice to do so by open market operations, by changing the discount rate, or by setting a new reserve requirement?

15. Why does the aggregate demand curve slope downward?

16. What would happen to the level of wealth in an economy if the price level increased? What effect would this have on the demand for real output?

17. Suppose that the money supply is $1 trillion. The Fed decides that it wishes to reduce the money supply by $100 billion. If the required reserve ratio is .05, what does the Fed have to do to carry out its wishes?

18. In July 1989, the Fed began purchasing government bonds and the interest rate fell.

   a. How did the Fed's purchase of bonds issued by the Treasury lead to a lower interest rate?

   b. Suppose that the Fed hadn't purchased the T-bonds, would the Treasury have issued fewer (or more) of them?

   c. What would have happened to the interest rate in this case?

19. Suppose that the required reserve ratio is .2.

   a. If the Fed purchases $20 billion in bonds, how much can demand deposits increase?

   b. Is your answer different if the required reserve ratio is .1?

   c. Why or why not?

20. Suppose that bank reserves are $100 billion, the required reserve ratio is .2 and banks are fully loaned up.

   a. What is the total number of deposits in the economy?

    b. Suppose the reserve ratio is reduced to .1 and banks are once gain fully loaned up with no excess reserves.

    c. What is the new level of demand deposits?

21. For each of the following determine whether the money supply will increase, decrease, or stay the same:

    a. Depositors become concerned about the safety of banks and begin withdrawing cash.

    b. The Fed lowers the required reserve ratio.

    c. The economy enters a recession and banks have a hard time finding credit-worthy borrowers.

    d. The Fed sells $100 million in bonds to a bank in Utah.

22. A bond promises to pay $500 one year from now. Given the following:

bond price	amount paid in one year	interest payment	interest rate
$375	$500		
$425	$500		
$450	$500		
$500	$500		

    a. What are the corresponding interest payments and interest rates that the bond offers at each price.

    b. As the price of the bond rises, what happens to the bond's interest rate?

    c. Explain why.

23. Assume that the Fed's goal is to stabilize GDP. How should it respond in the following cases:

    a. Everyone believes that interest rates will fall in the near future and money demand falls.

    b. Many credible financial advisors recommend buying bonds.

    c. Tired of credit card debt, everyone begins to use credit cards less frequently.

    d. How will the interest rate be affected by the Fed's actions in each case?

    e. How will real GDP be affected by the Fed's actions in each case?

24. Suppose that the Federal Reserve buys several million dollars in bonds on the open market. Assume that wages are sticky.

    a. Will the money supply *increase* or *decrease*? Explain your answer.

    b. Will the real interest rate *increase* or *decrease*? Explain your answer.

    c. Will investment in the economy *increase* or *decrease*? Explain your answer.

    d. Will short-run real output (assuming a closed economy) *increase* or *decrease*? Explain your answer.

25. Suppose that a tax cut is given to every taxpayer in a country. Assume that wages are sticky.

    a. Will disposable income for the nation's taxpayers *increase* or *decrease*? Explain your answer.

    b. Will consumption *increase* or *decrease*? Explain your answer.

    c. Will the Aggregate Demand Curve shift *in* or shift *out*? Explain your answer.

    d. Will the price level *increase* or *decrease*? Explain your answer.

    e. Will unemployment *increase* or *decrease*? Explain your answer.

26. How would you explain to someone who had not taken economics the intuitive meaning of M/P?

27. Explain:

    a. why the amount of money in circulation is a multiple of the amount of currency the Fed prints and puts into circulation.

    b. how the Fed measures the amount of money in circulation and why the Fed employs several different measures.

    c. the difference between the discount rate and the federal funds rate.

    d. how the Fed can increase the amount of money in the economy without actually printing a thing.

Chapter 23

1. What is frictional unemployment?

2. What is the difference between the measured unemployment rate and the real unemployment rate?

3. Is it possible to eliminate frictional unemployment?

4. What determines full employment of labor?

5. Would the costs associated with unemployment be the same for a teenager as for a head of a household? Do the unemployment statistics treat these two persons differently? Should they?

6. To what extent is unemployment voluntary?

7. Economists have suggested that the frictional rate of unemployment has increased during the past two decades. Why might this have occurred?

8. Is it difficult to define *full employment*? Why?

9. Is unemployment unambiguously bad, or does it serve some useful purpose in the economy?

10. In what ways are government unemployment statistics biased?

11. What policies can the government pursue to reduce cyclical unemployment? Structural unemployment? Frictional unemployment?

12. How does the government define and calculate unemployment?

13. Why might firms and workers prefer temporary layoffs to wage cuts when aggregate demand falls?

14. What is the natural rate hypothesis?

15. Frictional unemployment occurs when:

    a. there is friction between management and unions.

    b. changes in the economy mean that some skills are no longer demanded.

    c. the economy may move more slowly to full employment.

    d. firms and workers have incomplete information.

16. Structural unemployment occurs when

    a. there is friction between management and unions.

    b. changes in the economy mean that some skills are no longer demanded.

    c. the economy may move more slowly to full employment.

    d. firms and workers have incomplete information.

17. Cyclical unemployment occurs when

    a. there is friction between management and unions

    b. changes in the economy mean that some skills are no longer demanded.

    c. the economy may move more slowly to full employment.

    d. firms and workers have incomplete information.

1. Can fiscal policy (spending increase or tax cuts) create inflation? Can they create sustained inflation?

2. What appears to be the primary cause of sustained inflation?

3. How does a constant, sustained rate of inflation affect real output?

4. How does inflation affect interest rates?

5. In order for the economy to constantly produce more than potential real output, what must happen to the price level?

6. What is a cost-push inflation? A demand-pull inflation?

7. Can there be sustained cost-push or demand-pull inflations?

8. Several countries have imposed wage and price controls to lower inflation. Under what circumstances can these policies control inflation successfully?

9. Can tax incentives to not raise prices, control inflation successfully?

10. Is there a short-run tradeoff between inflation and unemployment? Why or why not?

11. Is there a long-run tradeoff between inflation and unemployment? Why or why not?

12. Can the inflation rate be decreasing at the same time that the price level is increasing? Can the inflation rate be increasing at the same time the price level is decreasing? Explain.

13. If there is a 5% inflation for 8 years, what is the total amount of inflation (that is, how much has the price level changed in the 8 years)? (Hint: the answer is not 40%.)

14. Inflation is a tax on holding money. If you hold a $100 bill and the price level increases by 10%, the purchasing power of money falls by 10%. Who benefits?

15. Your friend comes to you and asks to borrow $2000 from you to be repaid in exactly 1 year. He agrees to pay you interest equal to the expected inflation rate over the next year, which is 4%. You agree to loan him the money.

    a. How much will your friend pay you in 1 year?

    b. Suppose that inflation turns out to be 8% over the next year.

        i. If you had invested your $2000 in an account earning 8% interest and made no withdrawals, how much money would be in your account after 1 year?

        ii. Who benefited from the unanticipated increase in inflation, *you*, or *your friend*?

        iii. How much money did your friend save on the $2000 loan because of the difference in expected and actual inflation rates?

16. The Fisher Equation states that the nominal interest rate is the sum of the real interest rate and expected inflation over a period.

    a. If inflation is expected to be 3% over the next year and the current annual nominal interest rate is 7%, what is the real interest rate?

    b. Suppose that the real interest rate hasn't changed but the nominal interest rate has increased by 2%. Explain how this could happen.

1. Nominal interest rates have declined since about 1983. What information would you need to know to find out if real interest rates have also declined?

2. We have emphasized the effects of monetary policy on interest rates and, by way of interest rates, its effects on private investment. What else might be affected when the money supply increases?

3. Why might it be highly likely that stabilization.policies will overshoot, as some economists have argued?

4. What kinds of policies should be pursued if there is a supply or price shock and the government wants to foster economic growth?

5. Why does it take a long time to implement fiscal policy? Do you suppose fiscal policy is ever implemented only for the purposes of stabilization? What other purposes might fiscal policy serve?

6. Why does it take a much shorter time to implement monetary policy than fiscal policy?

7. What are some of the reasons for the lag between the time that a demand (or supply) shock occurs and the time that we come to realize it?

8. Is it likely that stabilization policies will ever completely eliminate the cycles in an economy? Under what conditions would such policies completely eliminate the cycles?

9. Why might it take longer for monetary policy than fiscal policy to affect the economy?

10. Usury laws place ceilings on interest rates in particular loan markets. How might usury laws create difficulties during periods of inflation?

11. How did the United States accumulate its national debt? To whom is it owed?

12. In what sense is the deficit a burden on future generations?

13. How might a large national debt limit the ability of the government to pursue fiscal or other domestic policies? (*Hint:* consider the interest payments on the debt.)

14. Is it possible for market interest rates to decrease when the government has increased the deficit?

15. What is the "true tax" created by the government deficit?

16. How might financing a deficit affect the economy?

17. Suppose that the government has decided to decrease aggregate demand by $400 million to reduce inflation. The MPC = .75, the RR= .10 and every $1 decrease in the money supply will raise the interest rate enough to reduce desired investment by $2.

    a. How many dollar's worth of bonds should the Fed buy or sell?

    b. If the government wanted to use fiscal policy instead, by how much should they increase or reduce government spending?

18. Suppose you are president of the U.S. and are faced with the following situation: output is too low and the price level is increasing (relative to a beginning position of full employment). What sort of fiscal and/or monetary policy would you consider appropriate to move the economy back to full employment? Be as complete as possible, outlining what the effects of your policy decision will be, using graphs, explanations, etc.

19. Given the following data, calculate the real interest rate for years 2, 3, and 4.

year	CPI	nominal interest rate	real interest rate
1	100		
2	110	15%	
3	120	13%	
4	115	8%	

If you loaned $1000 to a friend at the beginning of year 2 at an interest rate of 15% and your friend repaid the loan at the end of year 2, plus interest, did you benefit or lose from the deal?

20. Suppose that net taxes depend upon income, specifically, each time household income increases by $100, the government's net tax revenue increases by $25. What happens to the multiplier? (Hint: Construct a table where you look at each round of induced consumption following a $1 increase in investment that incorporates taxes and the fact that in each round, the increase in disposable income will equal the increase in income minus any increase in taxes.)

21. Describe how an increase in taxes affects both aggregate demand and long-run aggregate supply.

Part S ▶▶
Sample Problems

Learning by doing is important. The following materials contain sample problems, where I have worked out in some detail an approach to the question.

Chapter 1

Opportunity Costs and Pricing

Consider the pricing problem of a jeweler when the price of gold fluctuates. Suppose, to simplify matters, that a jeweler has an inventory of rings, each weighing one ounce, each made of pure gold, and each purchased at a time when the price of gold was $350 per ounce. What will happen to the price of rings if the price of gold increases from $350 per ounce to $700 per ounce?

In approaching this kind of question, you should focus on opportunity costs. To do so, you need to first determine what opportunities are available to the jeweler. Specifically, what choices does the jeweler have? Answer: The jeweler can sell the rings as jewelry or the rings could be melted and sold for their gold content. If the jeweler sells rings to persons wanting jewelry, the jeweler gives up the opportunity of selling the gold in the ring on the world market at $700. Therefore, the opportunity cost of selling a ring for jewelry is $700, not $350. Even though the jeweler has not had to pay any additional amount of money for her inventory of rings, when the world price of gold increases, the jeweler's costs of operating the jewelry store increase, in this case quite substantially, and the price of rings should increase commensurate with the increase in cost.

Even though the jeweler might have an invoice indicating that the cost per ring is $350, this invoice "cost" is not the opportunity cost of selling a ring. Costs are determined by *current* opportunities, not opportunities that were once available but which no longer can be chosen. If the current price of gold is $700 per ounce, then the jeweler cannot buy gold rings at $350 per ounce. Put differently, *opportunity costs are determined only by choices that can actually be made.* Things that cannot actually be chosen cannot affect opportunity costs. The only opportunities currently facing the jeweler are 1) to sell rings or 2) to sell the gold in the rings. Hence, the cost of selling rings is the best-forgone opportunity, which is selling gold at $700.

The price of gold may, of course, decrease instead of increase. For instance, consider the jeweler's costs when the world price of gold declines to $200 per ounce. Once again, she can either sell the rings as gold in the world gold market *or* as jewelry. The cost of choosing to sell rings as jewelry is now $200. The jeweler's opportunity cost has declined. The price of the rings will also decline.

Won't the jeweler lose money in this case? Yes, but this does not affect the opportunity cost of selling rings. For example, if the jeweler tries to sell rings for $350, she will be undersold by rival jewelers because they can stock their inventories at $200 per ring. Therefore, the jeweler will confront the choice of selling no (or very few) rings for $350 each, or selling her inventory of rings priced at $200, either as jewelry or as gold. Hence, less money will be lost by selling rings at $200 per ounce than if the jeweler tried to sell rings for something greater than $200.

Chapter 2

The Costs of a Volunteer Army

Does it cost more to have a volunteer, rather than a conscript or draft, army? This question can be answered by a straightforward application of the ideas represented by an aggregate PPF. You should begin your analysis of any question about "costs" by asking "costs to whom?"

Consider first the costs to the government. With a volunteer army, the government must pay a wage rate sufficient to attract the number and quality of personnel it requires to maintain its desired military force. Suppose that this wage is $10 per hour. (It is often helpful in thinking through problems to put numbers with the ideas.) With a draft army, where individuals are forced into service on threat of jail, the government could set this wage much lower, say $4 per hour. Note that if the government could get all the volunteers it needed at $4 per hour, then even if it had a draft, it would not need to actually draft anyone. Thus, it appears that if the government actually uses the draft, the cost to the government of a volunteer army is likely to be higher than the cost of a draft army.

Now consider the costs to society as a whole. With a volunteer army, the wage rate would have to be at least as great as the opportunity cost of those entering the military. That is, in terms of our example, all those who actually volunteer at a wage of $10 per hour, must have alternatives with wages at or below $10 per hour or they wouldn't enlist. This opportunity cost is the value of output lost elsewhere in the economy. (Resources are being used for military purpose instead of being used to produce goods and services.) Therefore, even though a draft army costs the *government* less than a volunteer army of the same size, the draft army costs *society at least as much* as the volunteer army in that in both cases an equal number of resources are moved from elsewhere in the economy to the military.

Who pays the difference between the cost to the government and the cost to society? The difference is paid by the draftees, who are paid less than their opportunity costs (otherwise they would have volunteered). Thus, a draft army is paid for by a large, hidden tax on those who are drafted, whereas a volunteer army is paid for by a large, visible tax on the citizens who are being defended.

Are there other possible costs? With a draft, individuals with opportunity costs above and below the volunteer army wage would be forced to serve because the draft takes individuals without regard to opportunity cost. For example, it might be that someone with an opportunity cost of $20 per hour was drafted as well as someone with an opportunity cost of $5 per hour. With a volunteer army, however, only individuals with opportunity costs below $10 per hour will join the army because joining a volunteer army where the pay was $10 per hour would not be attractive to someone with options that would pay $20 per hour. If the opportunity costs for individuals represent their contributions to the economy (that is, if a person being paid $20 per hour produces goods and services worth $20 and a person being paid $5 per hour produces goods and services worth $5), the draft army will probably be more costly than a volunteer army since it will take more valuable resources from the economy than will a volunteer army. That is, the draft will occasionally take a person with opportunity costs of, say, $20 per hour, whereas only those with opportunity costs below $10 per hour will volunteer. When this happens, the economy as a whole will lose $20 of output per hour when the same sized army could be created with a loss of no more than $10 of output per hour.

Chapter 4

Should the Reclamation Project Be Completed?

Suppose that the initial cost of a large system of dams and canals to capture water from melting snow in the mountains and move it closer to a population center was estimated to be $10 billion. Because the benefits, say $15 billion, were thought to be greater than this amount, the project was started. After spending $5 billion, the project comes to the Congress for the appropriation necessary to finish it. Members of Congress from the state where the project is being built provide the following data:

Money already spent	$5 billion
Benefits already obtained	$12 billion
Total benefits to be obtained if project is finished	$15 billion

Would you vote to approve the expenditure (assuming there were no competing uses for the money)? How would you evaluate the argument that "having invested $5 billion in the project with the aim of getting $15 billion in benefits, we can't waste the $5 billion already spent but must push on and complete the project since by spending $10 billion overall, $15 billion in benefits can be obtained."

Suppose, instead, these data were presented:

Money already spent	$5 billion
Benefits already obtained	$5 billion
Total benefits to be obtained if project is finished	$9 billion

Would you vote to approve the expenditure? How would you evaluate an argument that "the overall benefits are now only $9 billion and spending $10 billion to get $9 billion in benefits is foolish."

Finally, suppose that instead of either of the above, the following data were presented:

Money already spent	$5 billion
Benefits already obtained	$2 billion
Total benefits to be obtained if project is finished	$9 billion

Would you vote to approve the expenditure? How would you evaluate an argument that "the overall benefits are now only $9 billion and spending $10 billion to get $9 billion in benefits is foolish."

In each case, you should begin by asking what *additional* benefit can be obtained from *additional* spending—that is, you should find the marginal benefit and the marginal cost and apply the principles of marginal analysis since we know that doing so leads to the best or optimal outcome. In the first case, the expenditure of an additional $5 billion results in only an additional $3 billion in benefits. In the second case, spending an additional $5 billion results in an additional $4 billion in benefits. In the third case, spending an additional $5 billion results in an additional $7 billion in benefits. Marginal benefits exceed marginal costs only in the last case. Hence, it only makes sense to spend additional money in this case but not in the first two cases.

Given you analysis to this point, how should you respond to the arguments that were advanced, namely:

a. "We don't want to waste the $5 billion already spent."
b. "Overall, we would be spending $10 billion to get only $9 billion in benefits."
c. "Overall, we would be spending only $10 billion to get $15 billion in benefits."

The answer is that sunk costs are irrelevant! In the first case, the net benefit if no additional money is spent is $12 billion minus the $5 billion already spent or $7 billion. Completing the project, however, *reduces* the net benefit from $7 to $5 billion. In the second case, the net benefit if the project is not funded further is $0 ($5 billion minus $5 billion). Completing the project *reduces* the net benefits to -$1 billion. In the third case, by contrast, the net benefits of the presently uncompleted project are -$3 billion, but if the project is completed, the losses will only be -$1 billion. Therefore, completing the project *increases* net benefit by $2 billion.

Chapter 4

The Diamond/Water Paradox

There is a famous puzzle in the history of economics that goes as follows: Diamonds, which are not essential to survival, are expensive, whereas water, which is essential to survival, is cheap. Why?

In approaching any problem where individuals are making decisions, it is important to distinguish marginal benefits and marginal costs from overall or total benefits and total costs. In this case you might ask yourself: "For an individual, what are the *marginal* benefits and *marginal* costs of obtaining a diamond?" and "For the same individual, what are the marginal benefits and marginal costs of obtaining a glass of water?" Since water is generally abundant, the principle of diminishing returns suggests that drinking one additional glass of water contributes very little to a person's well-being. That is, total satisfaction doesn't increase by much by drinking one additional glass of water. Therefore, the marginal benefit of an additional glass of water is likely to be near zero. As a consequence, individuals will not be willing to pay much for any additional water.

Diamonds are attractive and are an important part of our culture in marriage engagements. Diamonds, however, are relatively scarce and few individuals have more than one or two. The principle of diminishing returns suggests that, given the small number of diamonds an individual is likely to have, one additional diamond is likely to contribute a good deal to a person's well-being even though it is not essential to life. Therefore, the marginal benefit of an additional (which may be the first) diamond is high and individuals will be willing to pay a good deal for it.

Hence, water is of little value in terms of the amount individuals are willing to pay for *additional* water, whereas diamonds are valued highly in terms of the amount that individuals are willing to pay for an *additional* diamond. The overall benefits from water can be, and undoubtedly are, greater than the overall benefits of diamonds. In marginal analysis, however, overall benefits don't matter—it's marginal benefits that affect the value in the market. With this, the paradox is resolved.

Chapter 5

Determining the Market Equilibrium 1

Suppose that you were able to identify the demand and supply relationships shown in the following table. To find the market equilibrium, pick a price, say $.60. At this price, the quantity demanded is 17,000 units and the quantity supplied is 11,000 units. There is excess demand at this price. What happens when there is excess demand? Answer: The market price will increase. Thus, we know that the equilibrium price must be greater than $.60. Pick another price consistent with what we have just learned, say $.75. In this case, quantity demanded is 15,500 units and quantity supplied is 12,500 units. Hence, there is still excess demand and the market equilibrium price must be above $.75. Next, guess $1.00. At this price, the quantity demanded is 13,000 units and the quantity supplied is 15,000 units—there is an excess supply of 2,000 units. The equilibrium market price must therefore lie between $1.00 and $.75. Clearly, the equilibrium price is $.90. At this price the quantity demanded, 14,000 units, is equal to the quantity supplied, 14,000.

Price per unit	Quantity demanded	Quantity supplied
$ .50	18,000	10,000
.55	17,500	10,500
.60	17,000	11,000
.65	16,500	11,500
.70	16,000	12,000
.75	15,500	12,500
.80	15,000	13,000
.85	14,500	13,500
.90	14,000	14,000
.95	13,500	14,500
1.00	13,000	15,000
1.05	12,500	15,500
1.10	12,000	16,000

Now suppose that market supply increases by 1,000 units at each possible market price. The new market supply is as shown in the following table. At $.90, the original equilibrium price, there is now excess supply, because the quantity supplied is 15,000, but the quantity demanded is 14,000. If you follow the procedure outline above, you should find that the new equilibrium market price must therefore be below $.90. The new equilibrium price is $.85.

Price per unit	Quantity supplied	Price per unit	Quantity supplied
$.50	11,000	$ .90	15,000
.55	11,500	.95	15,500
.60	12,000	1.00	16,000
.65	12,500	1.05	16,500
.70	13,000	1.10	17,000
.75	13,500		
.80	14,000		
.85	14,500		

Chapter 5

Determining the Market Equilibrium 2

Suppose that instead of the demand and supply schedules just given, you were told that demand and supply could be described by the following:

    Quantity supplied   = 5,000 + (10,000 x price per unit)
    Quantity demanded   = 23,000 – (10,000 x price per unit)

To find the equilibrium, recall that at the equilibrium price, the *quantity supplied* must equal the *quantity demanded*. Therefore, at equilibrium,

$$5,000 + 10,000p = 23,000 – 10,000p$$

where p is the price per unit. Rearranging,

$$20,000p = 18,000$$

and

$$p = \frac{18,000}{20,000} = .90$$

When the price is $.90, the amount that demanders wish to purchase

    Quantity demanded   = 23,000 – 10,000(.90) = 14,000

while suppliers *independently* wish to sell

    Quantity supplied   = 5,000 + 10,000(.90) = 14,000

Thus, the independent interests of demanders and suppliers happen to coincide when the price is $.90, which is, therefore, the equilibrium price.

Chapter 5

Determining Market Outcomes When Both Supply and Demand Change

Suppose that individuals become ecologically more conscious and make every effort to conserve paper and, at the same time, the price of wood pulp decreases because of an innovation that allows logging firms to use previously discarded lumber for pulp. What will happen in the market for paper?

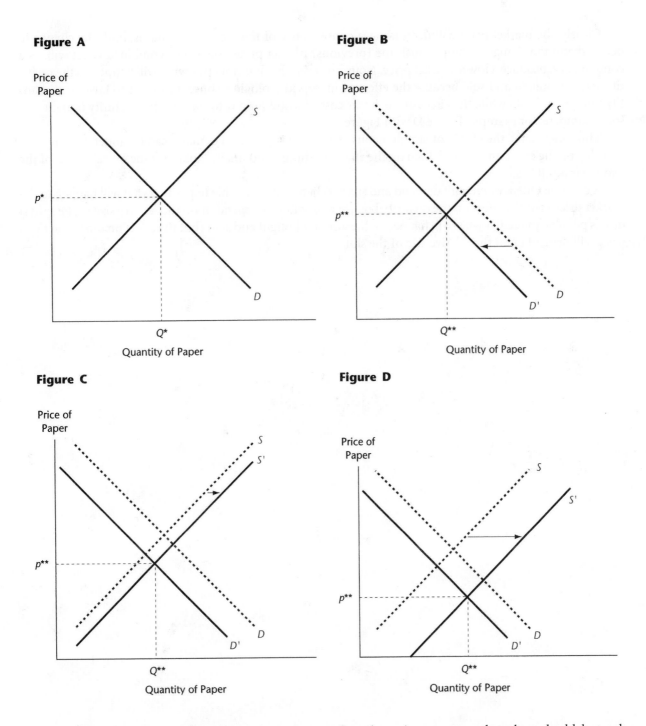

Figure A

Price of
Paper

p*

S

D

Q*

Quantity of Paper

Figure B

Price of
Paper

p**

S

D'

D

Q**

Quantity of Paper

Figure C

Price of
Paper

p**

S
S'

D

D'

Q**

Quantity of Paper

Figure D

Price of
Paper

p**

S
S'

D

D'

Q**

Quantity of Paper

Since this question is not concerned about the actual market price or amount bought and sold, but only with the general direction of effects, it is easiest to approach this question with a simple supply-demand diagram where the market for paper is initially in equilibrium. For example, Figure A might be a picture of the market for paper.

With this diagram in mind, consider what is likely to happen to demand when individuals become ecologically more conscious. Demand, in this case, will decrease. That is, *at every price,* individuals will wish to purchase less paper. This change is illustrated in Figure B.

Next, consider what is likely to happen to the supply when firms find that they now pay less for wood pulp suitable for making paper. In this case, supply will increase, as seen in Figure C.

Clearly, the market price will decrease as a consequence of these changes. That is, both the change in demand and the change in supply push the (previous) market price down. The combined effect will, as a consequence, produce a lower market price. Note, however, that it is not clear what will happen to the quantity actually bought and sold because the effect of increased ecological consciousness is to lower the quantity bought and sold while the effect of the lower cost of wood pulp is to increase the quantity bought and sold. Compare, for example, Figure D with Figure C.

Thus, in general, the effects of simultaneous changes to supply and demand can be understood by first focusing on the effect on demand, then on the effect on supply, and finally looking at the overall result of the two separate effects.

A caution: Often, when both demand and supply change, it is possible to predict what will happen to the market price (but the effect on the quantity bought and sold will depend upon the relative size of the shifts) or it is possible to predict what will happen to the amount bought and sold (but the effect on the market will price will depend upon the relative size of the shifts).

Chapter 6

Analyzing Exceptions to the First Law of Demand

Frequently, it is alleged that in particular markets there is an exception to the inverse relationship between quantity demanded and market price because (a) "when the price increases, people want to stock up before it increases again" or (b) "some things have prestige only if the price is high" or (c) "demand increases with the price because quality increases." Let's examine each of these more closely.

"When the price increases, people want to stock up before it increases again; therefore a higher price is accompanied by greater demand." Clearly, the issue in this claimed exception to the First Law of Demand has to do with expected future prices and whether to purchase today or wait until some time in the future. It is useful in analyzing this claim to think of two markets for the same good, a market "today" and a "future" market. The cost of choosing to purchase in the future market is the *expected* higher price that you will have to pay. The claimed exception suggests that the price today (even though it is increasing) is lower than the expected future price. The First Law of Demand suggests that individuals will want to buy more when the relative price is low (and less when it is high). Hence, if prices are really expected to be higher in the future, individuals will increase their purchases today. (Indeed, if everyone expects prices to be higher, the price today will increase because of the increase in demand in today's market. In this case the result will be a rightward shift in the demand curve, not a movement along a fixed demand curve.) Buying more today, when the price is *relatively* lower (even if it has increased), is a confirmation not a refutation of the First Law of Demand.

"Some things have prestige only if the price is high; therefore individuals will demand more at a higher price than they would at a lower price." One way to evaluate this apparent inconsistency is to ask what would be implied if the statement were true. That is, suppose that you were running a firm selling the "prestige" good, what could you do if the statement were true? Clearly, if you increased your price, you would increase your revenues (and profits) because you would be selling more. Therefore, if quantity demanded increases when the price increases, as suggested in the quote, we ought to see prices of "prestige" goods *continually* increasing—every price increase should make the good more valuable, leading to greater demand, leading to a further price increase, etc. We don't see this, of course. Instead, we see "prestige" goods—like Mercedes' and BMW's and Air Jordan's—selling at prices that are high, to be sure, but the prices don't change much from day to day, and certainly do not continually increase. Why doesn't the supplier of prestige goods increase its price in order to make its good "more prestigious"? It must be that believe that if it did, it would lose sales (and hence revenues). That is, firms are behaving as if the quantity demanded would decrease if the price increased.

"Demand increases with price because quality increases." You might approach this alleged inconsistency of "the facts" with the notion of demand by asking whether you would be willing to pay more for a good demonstrably higher in quality. The answer is, undoubtedly, yes. But to see whether this is inconsistent with the first law of demand, you need to ask what is being compared. Two things, in fact, are changing: the price and the quality. What does the First Law of Demand actually say? It says that there is an inverse relationship between price and quantity demanded, *ceteris paribus*. That is, when the relative price *alone* changes, the quantity demanded should change in the opposite direction. Thus, goods of different quality ought to be thought of as separate goods (even though they might be very close substitutes) and, hence, in this case there are two demand curves, not one: one for lower quality goods and one for higher quality goods. *Ceteris paribus* means, in this case, "for goods of equal quality" (among other things). For each good, there should be an inverse relationship between price and quantity demanded, but individuals will, not surprisingly, be willing to pay higher prices for commodities of higher quality. You may respond that this argument about quality misses the point. If quality is unknown, sometimes individuals will infer quality from price. This is, in fact, an important property of prices.

Chapter 6

Explaining the Seasonal Variation in Prices

The use of beach cottages is higher during the summer months than at other times of the year. Similarly, the consumption of fresh fruit is also highest during the summer months. Whereas the lease price for cottages is higher in the summer than in the winter, however, the price of fresh fruit is almost always lower in the summer than in the winter. What accounts for this seeming contradiction?

In approaching this question, you ought to ask yourself what is likely to happen to the supply of cottages, the demand for cottages, the supply of fresh fruit, and the demand for fresh fruit between winter and summer.

First, the supply of cottages. It probably doesn't change much from season to season unless there is a natural disaster that destroys beach-front property. The demand for cottages? Most people don't like to spend cold winter evenings on the beach, but prefer to spend warm sunny days there, so demand is undoubtedly greater in the summer than in the winter. Thus, the change in the market for beach cottages from winter to summer probably looks something like the market pictured in Figure A.

Next, the demand for fresh fruit. It probably doesn't change very much from winter to summer. The supply of fresh fruit? It clearly is greater in late summer than it is at other times of the year. Hence, the change in the market for fresh fruit from winter to summer is probably something like that shown in Figure B.

Even though the demand for fresh fruit may not change much from season to season, the quantity actually consumed increases in the summer because of the lower market price. Similarly, even though the supply of cottages doesn't change from winter to summer, the quantity actually occupied increases in the summer, and the market price is higher.

Figure A

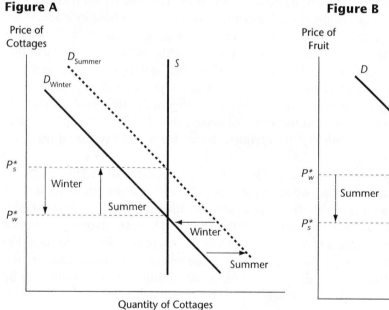

Figure B

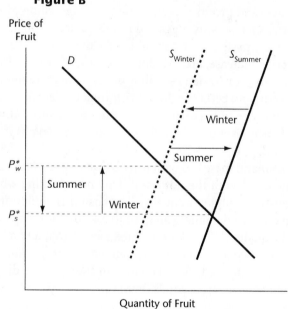

Chapter 6

Changing Air Fares

Air fares are higher for travel during certain days of the week and at certain times of the year. Why? The maximum number of seats on any particular day, or even over a year, is determined by the number of planes an airline owns. New planes take time to build and are large and expensive pieces of capital. The number of planes, therefore, doesn't change from day to day and changes little over the course of a year. This means that supply is likely to be quite unresponsive to price. When supply is not very responsive to price, any price change would have to be explained by changes in demand. That is, prices are changing, but supply isn't so the explanation for the price changes must lie in changes in demand. Thus, as illustrated in Figure C, it must be that on certain days of the week, demand is lower than on other days. Fares fall as a consequence. If they didn't, airlines would have a large number of planes on the ground or would be flying planes with a large number of empty seats. A similar shift in demand between peak (Christmas, Thanksgiving, summer) and off-peak seasons would explain why fares are lower during these periods as well.

Figure C

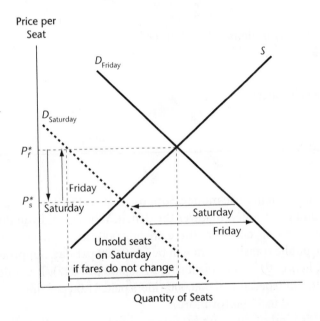

Chapter 7

Estimating the Elasticity of Demand for Lettuce

In 1978 rainfall during the harvest of lettuce destroyed half of the crop. As a consequence, the price of a car-ton of 24 heads of lettuce was $18 on May 1, 1978. However, by June 29, 1978 a new crop of lettuce had been raised and picked and the market price fell to $2.75. Is the demand for lettuce elastic or inelastic?

You should approach this kind of problem by reminding yourself of the definition of elasticity of demand:

$$e_d = \frac{\text{percentage change in quantity}}{\text{percentage change in price.}}$$

For the lettuce crop described above, the percentage change in quantity of lettuce delivered to the market is 50 percent ("half the crop was destroyed"). Calculating the percentage change in the market price of lettuce is a bit more difficult. Should we measure the percentage change from the original price ($18) or the new price ($2.75) or somewhere in between? By convention, economists measure the percentage change half-way between $18 and $2.75. Thus,

percentage change in the market price of lettuce

$$= \frac{(\$18 - \$2.75)}{\$10.38} \times 100 = 147\%$$

An approximation of the elasticity of demand for lettuce is,

$$\frac{50}{147} = 0.34$$

and the demand for lettuce is inelastic.

Chapter 7

Pricing to Eliminate Losses

Most public transportation systems lose money. Suppose that you were making the pricing decisions for one of these systems and you wanted to lower the deficit. What would you do?

Suppose, to make the example specific, that there are 500,000 riders each day, each of whom pays $.50. The current revenue for the public transit system will be $250,000 per day. Supposed, further, that expenses are $500,000 per day (and, hence, the system is losing $250,000 per day). It would be tempting to simply increase the fare from $.50 to $1.00 because, if 500,000 riders paid $1.00 per ride, the expenses would be cov-ered. Should the fare be increased to $1.00 (or more)?

You should approach this kind of question by first noting that when the price increases, there will be fewer riders. Some individuals will substitute other forms of transportation for public transportation. Oth-ers will simply commute less often. Thus, even if the correct thing to do is raise fares, the new fare will cer-tainly have to be greater than $1.00 if its to generate the target revenue.

Next, understanding that individuals will always substitute, you should ask whether they are likely to sub-stitute a lot or a little. That is, is demand price elastic or inelastic? Whether fares should be increased or decreased depends on the answer to this question. Hence, knowing the elasticity of demand is important! If you found that demand was inelastic, for example, then a price increase would, in fact, increase revenues and you could select a new fare of something greater than $1.00 that would cover the deficit, even with the decline in commuters. If, however, demand was elastic, then increasing fares would reduce revenues and the public transit deficit would increase, not decrease and the appropriate policy would be to *lower* fares and increase ridership sufficiently to increase revenues. Clearly, it is important in approaching problems of this sort, to have a good estimate of the price elasticity of demand and increasing prices is not necessarily the way to increase revenues.

Chapter 7

Can Bad Weather Be Good for Farmers?

If bad weather reduces the output of all farmers (for example, a drought throughout the corn-growing area of the United States), market supply will fall, as illustrated in Figure A. The market price always increases as a consequence. Is this good or bad for farmers? It depends. A farmer's revenues will depend upon both market price and the quantity sold. When the amount harvested and provided to the market falls, the price goes up and the quantity sold goes down. If the percentage increase in the price is greater than the percentage

Figure A

Price (*p*)

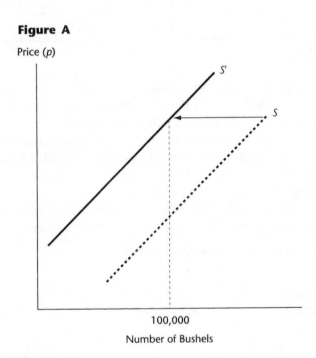

Number of Bushels

Figure B

Price ($)

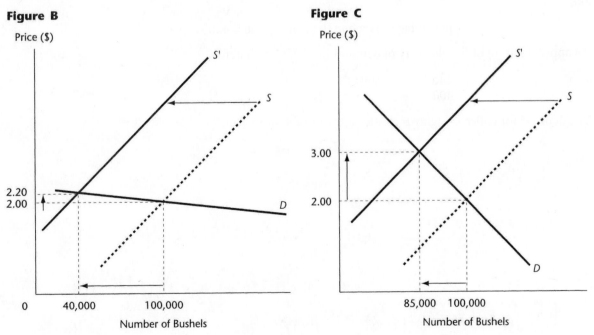

Number of Bushels

Figure C

Price ($)

Number of Bushels

decline in the amount sold, a farmer's income will increase because of the bad weather. If, however, the percentage increase in the market price is less than the percentage decrease in quantity sold a farmer's income will decrease. These two possible outcomes are illustrated in Figures B and C.

The differences between these outcomes can be described technically in terms of the elasticity of demand. If demand is inelastic, a higher price will increase market expenditures and hence farmers' incomes. If demand is elastic, a higher price will decrease market expenditures and farmers' incomes. A more intuitive description would be that, at the current market price, substitution is easier in Figure B than in C and hence, that, as the quantity provided to the market decreases, the price can't increase by as much without pushing consumers to substitute goods.

Chapter 7

Estimating the elasticity of Demand for Coffee

In 1977 a devastating frost destroyed about 75 percent of Brazil's coffee crop. At that time, Brazil supplied about one-third of the world's coffee exports. Following the freeze, the price of unroasted coffee beans rose about 400 percent. Can you make a rough estimate of the elasticity of demand for coffee?

First, make a guess: Is it likely to be high or low? The much larger price change (when compared to the quantity change suggests that demand is likely to be quite inelastic (in other words, quantity demanded is quite unresponsive to changes in the price). The reason for this is that the price appears to have changed significantly in order to bring the quantity demanded down by the amount lost to the frost.

You can confirm this by calculating a rough estimate of the elasticity. Remember, elasticity of demand is determined by measuring the percentage changes in quantity and in price when something happens. Thus,

percentage change in the quantity supplied to the world

$$= \quad 0.75 \times \quad 0.33$$
Brazil's   Brazil's share
loss   of world supply

$$= \quad 0.25 \text{ or} \quad 25\%$$

and

percentage change in the world price $= 400\%$

An approximation of the elasticity of demand for coffee is, therefore

$$\frac{25}{400} \quad = \quad 0.06$$

The demand for coffee is highly inelastic, at least in the short run.

Chapter 8

Determining the Equilibrium Price and Quantity

Both demand and supply curves can be represented in simple algebraic terms. Consider, for example, the following:

Supply: $p = 4 + 0.6 Q_5$

(or, $Q_5 = -40/6 + 10/6p$)

Demand: $p = 20 - 0.2 Q_d$

(or, $Q_d = 100 - 5 p$)

Note that the price that individuals are willing to pay is inversely related to the amount that they are willing to purchase (when Q_d increases by 1, p decreases by 0.2) and that a higher price encourages firms to provide more to the market (when Q_5 increases by 1, p increases by 0.6). (If this isn't clear, rearrange the demand function so that Q_d is on the left-hand side: $Q_d = 100 - 5p$.)

What will the market equilibrium price and quantity be? In approaching this question, remember that at equilibrium, the price consumer pay is equal to the price firms receive. Hence, at market equilibrium,

$$4 + 0.6 Q = 20 - 0.2 Q$$

where the subscript on Q has been removed because the quantity demanded will also equal the quantity supplied at the market equilibrium. A little rearranging yields

$$0.8 Q = 16$$

and, hence

$$Q^* = 20$$

If the quantity supplied and demanded is 20, the market price must be

$$p = 4 + 0.6(20)$$

or

$$p^* = \$16$$

Chapter 8

Evaluating the Effect of and Increase in Supply

The 1990-1991 orange crop in Florida was forecast to be 165 million ninety-pound boxes; almost a 50 percent increase over the prior year (when frost damaged the crop), and the largest since 1980 when 146.6 million boxes were harvested. (The record was 206.7 million boxes harvested in 1979-1980.) How did growers feel about this? A spokesman for the largest growers' association in Florida commented, "There is a lot of concern about the pricing structure and the total juice supply worldwide in the years ahead." The Associated Press then noted, "Industry leaders believe that they will have a major challenge ahead in selling all of the processed juice that will be squeezed from bumper crops foreseen in the coming years." Does this make sense? What must the AP have meant?

In approaching this question you ought to ask yourself under what circumstances a firm or group of firms would have difficulty selling all that produced. The answer is if it priced above the market equilibrium price. What must the AP have meant, then? That growers were fearful not of not being able to sell all of the processed juice, but of not being able to do so at the current market price.

SOURCE: "Florida Orange Growers Fear . . ." Deseret News, January 14, 1991, p.A4

Chapter 8

Why Are Football Ticket Prices Higher Than Baseball Ticket Prices?

Ticket prices for most regular season NFL games are three for four times as costly as ticket prices for regular season baseball games in cities where there are teams from both sports. Why might this be?

You might argue that football is just a better game to watch than baseball and that the difference in ticket prices supports your argument. Although this is a possibility, economists are loath to rely on taste differences to explain different outcomes. Besides, there is no obvious reason why people would prefer football to baseball. Setting aside possible taste differences, how can this price difference be explained?

One approach to questions of this sort is to consider possible difference in supply and in the elasticity of demand. Suppose, for example, that fans had identical preferences for the two sports (or that a group of individuals enjoyed both equally). First note that there is a substantial difference in supply. There are about 10 times as many baseball games as football games (162 per season versus 16 per season). This means that if you wanted to attend all home games, you could easily spend more on baseball than on football. For example, suppose that ticket prices were $40 for football and $10 for baseball. Your total expenditures for football would be $320, but your total expenditures for baseball would be $810. Elasticity of demand, remember, is determined, in part, by the fraction of typical consumer's budget spent. Attending all home baseball games would absorb a larger share of your budget than attending all home football games would. Therefore, if football and baseball ticket prices were priced about the same, the elasticity of demand for baseball would be greater than for football. Given this difference, baseball teams find it more profitable to have lower ticket prices so that individuals attend games rather than find substitutes.

Chapter 8

Supply in Agricultural Markets

Sometimes it is tempting to think of supply as being quite inelastic because there is some maximum output possible for any particular firm. For example, after a field is planted it might seem that the supply available form that field is perfectly inelastic because crops planted later in the season will not mature in time for the harvest and the number of acres with crops growing is, therefore, essentially fixed after the planting season ends. Is it possible for farmers to vary output in response to price once they have planted their crops?

You ought to approach this question not by asking whether the number of acres planted is fixed, but by asking what actually gets to the market. It is this latter quantity, not the amount planted, that determines market supply. Consider first, what might happen if farmers believed that the market price was going to be very low. They might choose not to harvest anything that they have planted. In this case, the quantity supplied would be low even if the acres planted was high. On the other hand, what might happen if the market price was expected to be very high? The farmers might harvest very carefully to reduce spoilage and damage that would make part of the crop unmarketable. In both cases, the quantity supplied would respond to the anticipated market price. Thus, even though a particular good appears to be in fixed supply, the delivery of that good to the market may be sensitive to the market price and hence supply might be price-elastic.

For example, watermelons are planted as a second or third crop in a number of agricultural areas. After being planted, the maximum amount of watermelons that can be produced is roughly fixed. However, if the market price is low, farmers will often plow part or all of the watermelons into the ground thus delivering a smaller number to the market. As the price increases, it becomes more profitable to harvest them, but they might be handled roughly, since it is costly to harvest with great care. Rough handling means that a number of the watermelons will be damaged or destroyed before they can be delivered to the market. On the other hand, if the market price is very high, it will pay the farmer to employ extra workers and handle the watermelons with great care in order to get almost all of those available in the field for harvest to the market. Thus, even though the acreage of watermelons planted may be fixed, the quantity supplied to the market may be quite responsive to the market price.

The story doesn't end here, however, because watermelons delivered to a store still aren't in the retail market where you are a demander. Thus, once watermelons are delivered to a local grocery store, if the price is low, it will not be worthwhile for the store to refrigerate the watermelons in order to extend the period over which they can be sold. Instead, the store might simply sell all that it can before they spoil and then throw the remainder away. However, if the price of watermelons is very high, the store will probably be willing to pay for careful handling and refrigeration in order to increase the number of watermelons available for purchase. Thus, even though the number of watermelons available for market seems fixed, the number that actually get to the retail market will change with the price.

This analysis suggests that the retail market supply of almost all agricultural commodities has some elasticity even though there are, in any given year, a given number of acres of land in cultivation and, after planting season, a given number of acres of land devoted to each crop.

Chapter 9

Explaining Computer Prices

The first commercial delivery of a computer occurred in 1954. Between then and 1985, computer prices fell an average of 19 percent each year. The price of PCs declined even faster—by about 25 percent per year from 1982 through 1986. The first commercial computer had 20 kilobytes of memory with a machine cycle time of 2,400 microseconds. Its cost? $192,000. In 1986, however, a PC or its clone had 640 kilobytes of memory, a machine cycle time of 0.2 microseconds, and cost around $1,000. Can you make sense of these changes?

First, it should be clear that the demand for computers has increased very substantially. Few people had personal computers as recently as a decade ago and the uses were quite limited. The uses and users have expanded enormously since then. Shouldn't this have led to an increase in price? Yes, but only if there was no change in supply. Supply, therefore, must have increased much faster than demand. If this is true, wouldn't firms find that they incurred losses at the lower market price? Yes, but only if there was no change in long-run production costs. So it must be that average costs have fallen even as the market has expanded in size.

In terms of long-run production costs, there are two possible sources: scale economies and technological innovations. The number of computer manufacturers has increased dramatically. Therefore the explanation for the changes must lie in the technological innovations that lowered production costs, even as these innovations increased the capacity of computers.

Chapter 9

The Farm Problem

A segment of the American farm population is in serious economic difficulty. Part of the difficulty stems from decisions made during the relatively prosperous period (for farmers) of the 1970s when exports and prices increased and farmland became more valuable. During this time, many farmers expanded production with new land purchased using loans. It was expected that land prices and agricultural demand would continue to be robust. The downturn in international demand in the 1980s and the increased supply from U.S. farmers lowered food prices and the value of land, however, making payments on loans difficult. Moreover, farm incomes—without governmental intervention—appear to be falling, at least in real terms. What is happening in this market? You might approach this problem by first considering what might be happening to demand and then to supply.

Farm incomes tend to fall, *ceteris paribus*, if the demand for agricultural commodities is inelastic and supply increases. To see why, take the extreme case where demand is perfectly inelastic and draw a demand curve. Now impose a supply curve on the diagram and shift the supply curve to the right. Note what happens to the market price and to the total amount spent (the area of the rectangle defined by the intersection of the supply curve and the demand curve). Both fall. We noted in earlier chapters that the demand for food is inelastic. Thus, relatively small changes in total farm output will result in relatively large changes in market prices. It follows that relatively small increases in supply will lead to large decreases in agricultural prices.

With regard to supply, there has been a tremendous increase in farm productivity over the past century. Output per unit of input almost doubled between 1950 and 1985, for example, even though the number of farms and farmers decreased. Output increased dramatically as a consequence. Combining this increased output with the inelastic demand, however, led to lower prices for agricultural products and, in general, to lower farm incomes. In fact, net farm income fell from about $20 billion in 1951 to about $8 billion in 1985 despite a very substantial increase in the population of the United States.

When incomes fall, at some point resources will have a higher return in other activities. Thus, the market appears to be signaling to farmers to exit.

Chapter 9

The Effect of Inventories on Price Changes

Demand and supply are unlikely to be the same from day to day. More people probably shop on weekends than during weekdays, for example. If markets respond to changes in demand and supply, why don't prices change from day to day?

It turns out that inventories (goods that a firm holds for future sale) can be used to minimize day-by-day fluctuations in prices, if the average price is expected to remain more or less the same. If, for example, demand falls but is expected to increase, firms can purchase and hold inventories, thus keeping the price from falling, as illustrated in Figure A. These inventories can then be used to keep prices from increasing when demand temporarily increases (see Figure A). Or if supply increases but is expected to fall, firms can purchase excess supply at the current price for inventory and then, when supply decreases but is expected to increase, they can sell from inventories and offset the excess demand at the expected price, as illustrated in Figure B.

Figure A   **Figure B**

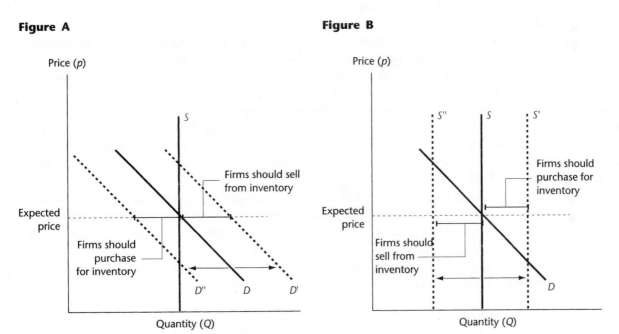

This argument seems to imply that firms need a lot of information about demand and supply and the changes in each. Note, however, that in both Figures A and B, firms purchase for inventory whenever the price begins to decrease from its expected level and then sell from inventory whenever the price begins to increase from its expected level. Thus, firms need not guess whether the price change is caused by a change in demand or a change in supply. If they purchase for inventory when prices begin to fall and sell from inventory when prices begin to increase, prices will fluctuate less in response to temporary day-by-day changes in demand and supply than they otherwise would.

Chapter 9

Rents in Agriculture

It is sometimes argued that the price of food is high because the price of farmland is high. For example, the price of farmland increased dramatically in the later 1970s. Did this contribute to an increase in the price of agricultural products during this period?

First note that it is true that if input prices increase, production costs increase as a consequence and, in general, will be reflected in higher market prices. This effect can be understood by shifting the supply curve to the left and then examining what happens to market price. Thus, an increase in the price of farmland could have pushed up the price of agricultural products.

It is possible, however, that the price of farmland increased because the price of agricultural products increased. To see why this might this have happened consider again the relationship between Koby Bryant's salary and the demand by fans to see him play discussed earlier in this chapter. As long as the supply of the unique input is inelastic, an increase in demand will increase the rent the unique input creates. Competition for this rent will transfer most of it to the unique input.

Does this argument work in the case of farmland? The amount of highly productive farmland is essentially fixed. Thus, supply is inelastic. An increase in demand for agricultural products leads to an increase in agricultural commodity prices. Higher prices provide an incentive for farmers to expand output. Expanding output, however, often requires additional land. Since most of the productive land is already being cultivated, a higher price for agricultural commodities leads to increased competition among farmers for the most productive land. This creates an economic rent for the most productive land because its supply is essentially unchanged. Current landowners can capture the rent by selling their land to others. The new owners now have a high-priced input and it appears that since their costs have gone up, the price at which they sell their output must go up. But, of course, the causality runs the other way—the price of land is high because it produces high-priced output.

Given this argument, what would you expect to happen if the price of agricultural commodities decreases? Farmers who borrowed money to purchase land because they thought that the prices would remain high will have lower incomes than they expected and might not be able to make payments on their loans. Bankruptcy and default will increase. The high price of farmland will not prevent food prices from declining (as they did in the 1980s). Instead, declining food prices lead to declining land values, much to the misfortune of those farmers who purchased expensive land earlier (in the late 1970s).

Chapter 10

Adopting New Technologies

What happens to old capital when technological change is persistent and new firms or firms that upgrade and purchase new capital have lower costs than firms using old capital?

In approaching this question, it is helpful to think of two kinds of firms: old firms (with old capital) and new firms (with new capital). If new firms have lower costs than old firms, does it make sense for old firms to continue to operate? Yes—old firms or firms with antiquated equipment and factories will continue to operate in some circumstances.

Once the capital has been built and a production facility organized with an existing technology, it makes sense to operate it as long as the market price covers variable costs. In the figure below, the first plant will be shut down, but the second will continue to operate even when the newest plant comes on line. That is, the long-run market price will be determined by the minimum average cost of the most cost-effective plant. After the market price has fallen below the average variable cost for the least cost-effective firm, this firm will be shut down or abandoned. However, the losses are lower if the second plant continues to operate. Notice that the lower-cost technology will eventually displace the older, higher-cost, technology. But the displacement occurs only slowly. As a consequence, plants of differing efficiencies and ages frequently exist at the same time in the industry. An example is jet planes. Boeing's newest 737, 757 and 767 are far more cost-effective to fly than its older 727. Likewise, its newest 777 is more cost-effective than is its older 747. Having already purchased lots of 727s and 747s, however, airlines continue to fly them, although they are slowly being phased out. But it wasn't true, of course, that all 727s and 747s were grounded the day after a more efficient, newer plane, rolled off Boeing's assembly line.

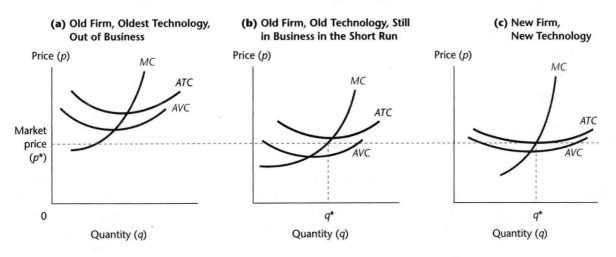

Chapter 10

The Diamond/Water Paradox Revisited

Earlier we posed what has become known as the diamond/water paradox. Diamonds, which are not particularly essential for survival, are expensive, whereas water, which is absolutely essential for survival, is generally inexpensive. We resolved the paradox, remember, by comparing the difference between the willingness to pay for an additional glass of water and the willingness to pay for an additional diamond. Can you resolve the paradox using the concept of consumer surplus?

You might begin with two demand curves, one for diamonds and one for water. Draw the graphs so that the supply of diamonds is low and, hence, the price of diamonds is high, whereas the supply of water is high and the price of water is low. Now, measure the consumer surplus on each graph. In the market for diamonds, where the price is high, consumer surplus will be small; in the market for water, where the price is low, consumer surplus is large. Hence, in a real sense water is far more valuable than diamonds. However, since price is determined by the marginal use and since water is abundant, the marginal use has low value. This difference in consumer surplus and price is illustrated in the following figure.

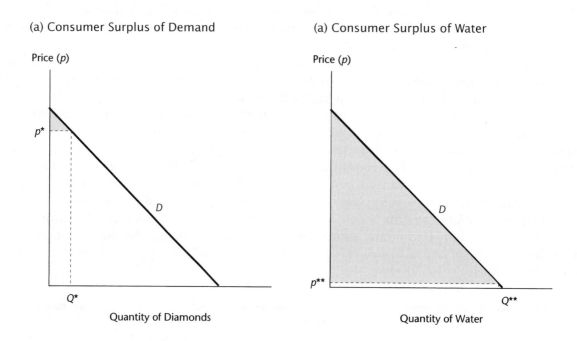

Chapter 10

Can Everyone Know That a Price Will Increase (or Decrease)?

Sometimes it is said that "Everyone knows that the price of x is going to increase." In the 1970s, for example, it was common for forecasters to claim that the price of oil would only increase through time. Predictions that the price of oil would increase to $80 or $100 per barrel were common. In fact, oil prices got as high as $35 per barrel and then came down, instead of continuing to rise. Similarly, it is frequently alleged that the price of some stock, say, IBM, is "too low and everyone expects that it will increase" or "too high and everyone expects that it will fall." Is it possible for everyone to know that a price will increase *before* it actually increases?

To approach this problem, it is useful to think of two markets; the market for a particular commodity *today* and the market for the same commodity at some point in the future ("*tomorrow*"). Claims that "everyone knows that price of x is going to increase" can be analyzed by considering what they imply about supply and demand in today's market and about supply and demand in the future market. Setting the problem up this way, it is easy to show that if *all* suppliers or *all* demanders *knew* that the price would change in the future, it would, instead, change today.

For example, suppose that *all* owners of IBM stock believed that the price would be higher tomorrow than it is today. What would result from this widely held belief? Almost no one would sell IBM stock today. Instead, those who wanted to sell would wait one more day so that they could sell at the expected higher price. As a consequence, the amount of IBM stock supplied to the market today would fall and the amount supplied to the market tomorrow would increase. This would mean that today's price would increase (the supply curve would shift to the left) and the expected price tomorrow would decline (the supply curve tomorrow would shift to the right). Put simply, today's price would increase relative to tomorrow's price *because* everyone believed that tomorrow's price would be higher.

When will this movement of IBM stock from today's market to tomorrow's market stop? Clearly, individuals would only be willing to sell today if they believed that the price today would be roughly the same as the price tomorrow. Thus, this adjustment would continue until those who bought stock today *expected the price to be higher* tomorrow and those who sold stock today *expected the price to be the same or lower* tomorrow. Only then would the market be in equilibrium.

Similarly, if everyone *knew* that the price of oil would be higher a year from now than it is now, suppliers would pump less oil now with the intention of pumping more oil later, when the market price was expected to increase. When suppliers respond this way, however, the price today will increase because today's supply will decrease. That is, the actions of suppliers in response to their expectations about profitable opportunities later will drive up prices *now*. And, if less oil is pumped today, there will also be greater reserves for delivery a year from now. With greater reserves, the expected price a year from now will be lower. Hence, there is a market equilibrium only when the price expected a year from now is just a bit above the current price.

In a market, for every buyer there has to be a seller. When will buyers purchase today rather than tomorrow? Answer: When they believe that the price tomorrow won't be lower than the price today. When will sellers sell today rather than tomorrow? Answer: When they believe that the price tomorrow won't be higher than the price today. Loosely, at the market *equilibrium* price half the market (buyers) have to believe that prices will be going up, and half the market (sellers) have to believe that prices will be going down. Hence, it cannot be true that "everyone believes the price of x is going to increase."

Chapter 12

Determining the Equilibrium Price and Quantity When There Is a Commodity Tax

In an earlier chapter's sample problem, we found that if the supply function is

$$p = 4 + 0.6Q_s$$

and the demand function is

$$p = 20 - 0.2Q_d$$

the market equilibrium price is $16 and the market equilibrium quantity is 20. Suppose that the government levies a $4 specific tax on suppliers. What happens to the market equilibrium price and to the quantity?

Whatever price suppliers receive, they have to pay $4 to the government. However, the supply function noted above indicates the price that the firms in the market must receive if they are to provide the corresponding quantity. Hence, for firms, the price net-of-tax is $(p - 4)$ and the quantity supplied to the market is unchanged only if

$$p - 4 = 4 + 0.6Q_s$$

or

$$p = 8 + 0.6Q_s$$

In words, this relationship states that firms supply only the same quantity they were willing to prior to the imposition of the tax if the price increases by $4.

Despite the tax, a single price is observed in the market. Therefore,

$$8 + 0.6Q = 20 - 0.2Q$$

and

$$Q^\star = 15$$

The market equilibrium price is, therefore,

$$p = 20 - 0.2(15)$$

and

$$p = \$17$$

This is the price that consumers pay and suppliers receive. Suppliers, however, must pay $4 for each unit sold to the government; thus, the price net-of-tax that suppliers receive is $13. (The government's tax revenue is $4 x 15 = $60.)

By comparing the new equilibrium quantity and price we can see that the tax results in a market outcome in which the quantity bought and sold decreases (from 20 to 15).

Chapter 12

Does it Matter from Whom a Sales Tax is Collected?

We found that the supply function is

$$p = 4 + 0.6Q_s$$

and the demand function is

$$p = 20 - 0.2Q_d$$

when a tax of \$4 is collected from firms for each unit sold, the market equilibrium price is \$17 and the among bought and sold is 15. Firms receive only \$13 per unit sold, however.

Suppose that the government collects the tax from consumers rather than from the firm. That is, for each unit a consumer purchases, he or she must send the government \$4. Will the market outcome be different from that when the government imposes the tax on the firm?

In this case, the price net-of-taxes that consumers pay is

$$p + 4 = 20 - 0.2Q_d$$

or

$$p = 16 - 0.2Q_d$$

In words, this relationship states that individuals only want to purchase the same quantity they did prior to the imposition of the tax if the price falls by \$4.

Thus, at market equilibrium,

$$16 - 0.2Q = 4 + 0.6Q$$

or

$$Q^* = 15$$

which is exactly the same amount that is bought and sold when the tax is imposed on suppliers rather than demanders. The market price is

$$p = 16 - 0.2(15)$$

or

$$p^* = \$13$$

This is the price that individuals pay and firms receive in the market. Individuals, however, must add the \$4 that they are required to send to the government. Hence, the price including tax is \$17. From both the suppliers' and demanders' perspectives, this is exactly the same outcome that occurred when the tax was collected from firms rather than from demanders. The only difference is that when the tax is collected from firms, the market price that individuals pay is \$17 and the net-of-tax amount that firms receive is \$13, whereas, when the tax is collected from individuals, the market price that firms receive is \$13 and the price-plus-tax that individuals pay is \$17. (Notice that the government's revenue is \$4 x 15 = \$60—the same in either case.)

The conclusion? It doesn't matter on whom the government levies the tax. That is, the government can't protect demanders from the tax by collecting it from firms nor can the government impose the tax on individuals and protect suppliers from the tax by collecting it from individuals. The market, not the government, determines what happens to suppliers and demanders when the government imposes a tax.

Chapter 12

Tax Incidence of Specific and ad Valorem Taxes

Does it make any difference if the government imposes an excise tax that is a fixed dollar amount (*specific*) or fixed in terms of a percentage of the sales price (*ad valorem*)? One way to approach this kind of question is to assume that marginal costs are constant and then consider the effects of the two different kinds of excise taxes on market demand. The vertical axis is measured in dollar terms, so a specific tax shifts demand by an equal amount at every price. An ad valorem tax, however, shifts demand more when the price is higher because a fixed percentage of a higher price is a larger dollar amount (for example, 10 percent of \$1.00 is \$.10 whereas 10 percent of \$5.00 is \$.50). Figure A indicates that the tax incidence is exactly the same in a competitive market.

For a monopoly, however, the effects of the two kinds of excise taxes differ. This difference is illustrated in Figure B. Part (a) illustrates the effect of a specific tax collected from consumers. The amount that individuals are willing to pay in the market decreases by the amount of the tax. Because that amount is the same at any price, the effect is equivalent to a parallel downward shift in the demand curve. The marginal revenue curve for the monopolist shifts down by a fixed amount as a consequence. Part (b) illustrates the effect of an ad valorem tax, also collected from consumers. In this case, the demand curve shifts, but because the dollar value of the ad valorem percentage is larger for higher prices than for lower prices, the demand curve rotates, as illustrated. The outcome: For any given level of output, the tax revenue generated from an ad valorem tax will be greater than that from a specific tax. Thought of another way, for any given amount of tax revenue, output in a monopoly market will be higher with an ad valorem tax than with a specific tax.

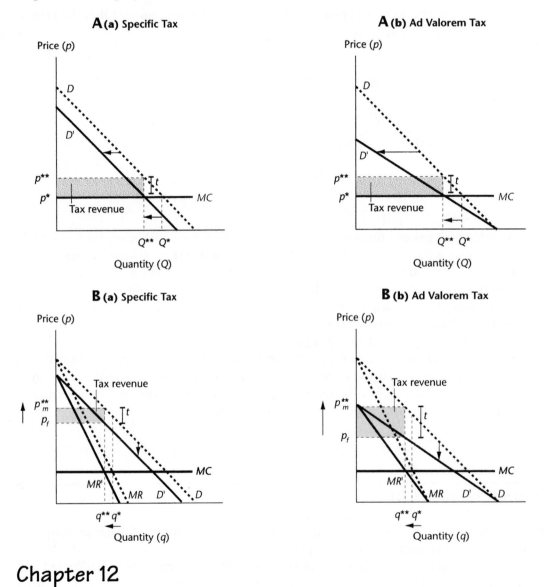

Chapter 12

Expenditure Incidence

Even though the discussion in this chapter has focused on taxes, a comparable incidence analysis can be made for subsidies. How would you determine who really received a subsidy? Begin by carefully reviewing the method for analyzing tax incidence. Note that we considered the effect when a tax was collected from suppliers when demand was perfectly inelastic and then when it was perfectly elastic. We did so because the tax incidence depends upon the change in the market price when the supply curve shifts. We then considered the effect when supply was relatively less elastic at the initial equilibrium and then relatively less elastic at the initial equilibrium. Suppose then, that a subsidy is provided to demanders. In this case, demand will shift. Hence, by analogy, you ought to consider what happens to the market price when supply is perfectly inelastic and then when it is perfectly elastic. Remember that demanders always receive the per-unit subsidy for each unit purchased. They have to pay the market price, however. The analysis is illustrated in parts (a) and (b) of the figure.

What can you conclude? Clearly, when supply is perfectly inelastic, a subsidy provided to demanders will increase the market price by the full amount of the subsidy. Hence, suppliers, not demanders, receive the subsidy. When supply is perfectly elastic, a subsidy provided to demanders will not affect the market price; the demanders receive the full amount of the subsidy. (Note that the suppliers sell more, however.)

To explore for possible effects of differing elasticities of demand, consider parts (c) and (d), which both show a similarly sloped supply curve. At the initial equilibrium, a steeper demand curve is less elastic (or more inelastic) than a demand curve that is flatter—but remember that elasticity itself cannot be determined by the slope of the demand curve. What can you conclude in this case? When demand is more elastic (or less inelastic), a subsidy provided to demanders will increase the market price by more, and more of that subsidy will be transferred to suppliers. Thus, the government can determine to whom it provides the subsidy initially, but

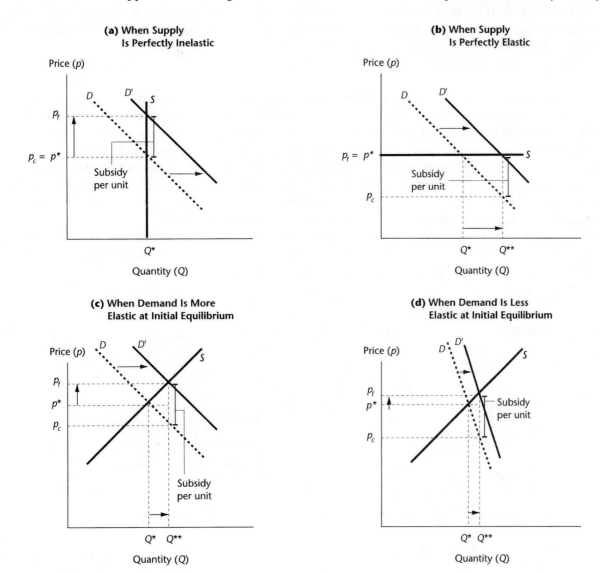

it cannot determine who actually gets the subsidy. For example, a rent subsidy to the poor may simply increase incomes for landlords rather than benefit the poor—it all depends upon market elasticities, not on the government.

Chapter 12

Evaluating an Excess Profits Tax

Although an excess profits tax is not currently part of the U.S. tax system, when prices increase dramatically, there is often a flurry of activity exploring the possibilities of instituting one. During the 1970s, when the price of oil increased, for example, there was an excess profits tax on oil. How would you evaluate the effects of an excess profits tax?

The first problem is defining "excess profits." This definition, of course, depends on the definition of *excess*. Market adjustments often lead to *economic profits* for firms who happen to be in a market where demand has increased. For example, if demand increases, from D to D' in the figure, each firm currently in the market will make profits. Generally, these profits do not disappear immediately, but are only reduced as entry occurs. Entry may take time. Suppose that in response to the "evils" of profits, an excess profits tax is imposed on each firm. If the tax is crafted so that it does not depend upon production, marginal costs will not change. Average costs, however, will increase. Why? The reason is that firms must now pay the government a tax that does not change with changes in production (except, of course, with the decision to not produce). This effect can be illustrated by the shift from ATC to ATC' (average total costs change with the tax) in the figure.

If the government has taxed all of the economic profits successfully, what was a short-run equilibrium now becomes a long-run equilibrium. (If, however, the government taxes more than the economic profits, then the rate of return in this market will be less than in other markets, giving firms incentives to exit.) That is, because there are *no economic profits* to be earned after the tax has been imposed, there are no incentives to enter or expand. As a consequence, what was the short-run equilibrium price, p^{**}, now becomes the long-run equilibrium price. In this case, the tax has distorted the movement of capital, even though it has not driven a wedge between the price that consumers pay and the marginal costs to firms for producing the good. And, as a consequence, the market price will not decrease from its short-run level.

Because "excess profit" is difficult to define for tax purposes, what are often called excess profits taxes are really something else. The excess profits tax on oil noted above, for example, was really a complicated sales tax. Unlike a true tax on profits, the tax affected production incentives.

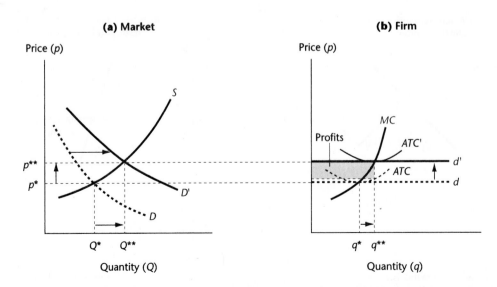

(a) Market

Price (p)

p^{**}
p^*

Q^* Q^{**}

Quantity (Q)

(b) Firm

Price (p)

Profits

MC
ATC'
ATC
d'
d

q^* q^{**}

Quantity (q)

Chapter 12

Analyzing the Likely Effects of Rent Control

Rent controls have become common in major cities in the United States. What are the likely consequences?

To analyze this issue, first you should recognize the kind of distortion (a price ceiling) the rent-control policy creates. Then you might consider two questions: (1) Is supply likely to be relatively elastic or inelastic in the short run? (2) How is the rationing problem solved?

In the case of housing, supply is likely to be very inelastic in the short run and, in general, those already occupying the housing available when the rent control law is passed stay in the dwellings.

Is reallocation likely? What would you expect to happen, for example, if current renters could sublet their apartments? What would the sublease rent be? Unless that was also controlled, of course, you would expect it to be above the ceiling rental. If sublets are not allowed or sublet rents are also controlled, you would expect to see some kind of queue for available apartments and perhaps rationing by who knows who.

You might then ask if tied sales are possible. One way to get around the rent ceiling, for example, might be to rent only furnished apartments. The furnishings could then be rented for an amount greater than their purchase price, essentially increasing the rent above the ceiling. ("This apartment only rents furnished. The rent-control price is $200 per month; the furniture rents for $800 per month.")

What if a city allowed a landlord to increase the rent to a new tenant but not to the current tenant? In such cases an elaborate and extensive system of sublets may emerge in which the original renter offers a contract to a new renter instead of the new renter contracting with the owner of the apartment. This arrangement would tend to occur because the original renter has an incentive to try to get part of the difference between what would be the market rental and the rent-control rental. You might then expect to see landlords trying to limit sublets in some way.

You ought to decide whether exit from the housing market is likely. If so, how might it occur in a market where rent controls are effective? For example, if rental apartments can be sold as condominium without any price controls, then exit can quickly occur. Exit might, however, be much more subtle if you also take into account what happens to the buildings and the services previously provided. Buildings would probably be allowed to run down the little or no maintenance provided; services, if provided at the option of the landlord, would likely not be provided. (A study of rent controls in New York City found that repair expenditures on rent-controlled apartments were about one-half the repair expenditures on other apartments.) Clearly, you would not expect new apartments to be constructed. (This slow movement of capital implies that current renters often benefit from rent controls but that the next generation of renters, who inherit a smaller stock of lower-quality housing as a consequence of the rent control, are harmed.)

Finally, as a consequence of these kinds of adjustments, each of which tends to subvert the intention of the law, what would you expect in terms of governmental policies? Rent control often spawns a series of laws and regulations: rent-control boards to oversee allocations an rent adjustments; laws controlling sublets; laws allowing different rents for new units and old units in an effort to encourage construction; laws limiting or regulating tied sales; maintenance codes and inspections; laws regulating the services that must be provided with the apartment; laws limiting conversion to condominiums, and so on. Such laws tend not to increase the amount of rental housing available. In fact, the more restrictive the controls are, the more the housing stock deteriorates.

SOURCE: G. Sternlief, *The Urban Housing Dilemma* (New York: City of New York Housing and Development Administration), 1972.

Chapter 12

The Effect of an Increase in Domestic Demand on International Trade

By now you should be thoroughly familiar with the effects of changes in market demand and supply—when demand increases, for example, the market price will increase, at least in the short run. Suppose that imports are available and that the domestic market is small relative to world-wide production. What will happen if domestic demand increases?

In approaching this question, you should consider three things: domestic demand, domestic supply, and the supply of imports. If the domestic market is small relative to the world-wide market, the supply of imports will be perfectly elastic at the world price. This is illustrated in (a). With this set up, allow demand to increase as illustrated in (b). Because imports are readily available at the world price, the supply of imports determines the price within the domestic economy both before and after the demand change. Thus, with free trade, an increase in domestic demand need not increase to an increase in the market price but, instead, only to an increase in the amount that consumers purchase. Can you show that consumers are better off? (Hint: What happens to consumer surplus?)

Note that domestic firms are unaffected by the increase in demand in the sense that the amount they produce and sell doesn't change. Their share of the domestic market falls, however, because the domestic market is now larger but more of it is supplied by foreign firms. Often, changes in domestic market shares are used in trade-policy debates. For example, there was concern in the early 1980s because of an increase in the share of the domestic steel market was supplied by foreigners. Note that your solution to the question posed earlier shows that domestic steel producers need not necessarily have been harmed just because they were losing market share. Can you illustrate a change in which domestic firms are adversely affected when the market share supplied by foreign firms increases?

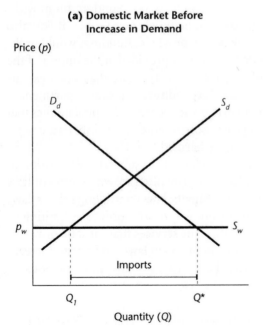

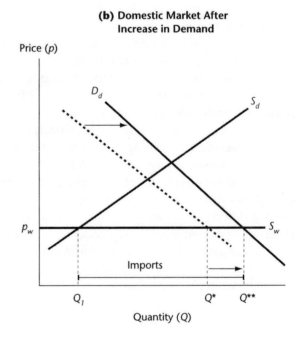

Chapter 13

The Effect on a Monopolist of a Demand Shift

What happens when market demand decreases in a monopolistic market? To answer this question, begin with the usual monopolistic market outcome in which the monopolist chooses a level of output such that its marginal cost of production is equal to its marginal revenue. The market demand then determines the selling price for the monopolist's output, as indicated in part (a) of the figure. Now shift demand down. Because the monopolist's marginal revenue is less than the market price at every level of production, marginal revenue falls as well. This shift is illustrated in part (b) of the figure. Now find the level of production at which marginal cost is equal to marginal revenue. In part (b), both the amount the firm produces and the selling price have decreased because of the decrease in demand. Thus, it appears that a monopolist's response to a demand shift is the same as a competitive firm's. Appearances are deceiving in this case. To see why, experiment with several different kinds of demand shifts where demand rotates instead of shifting down in

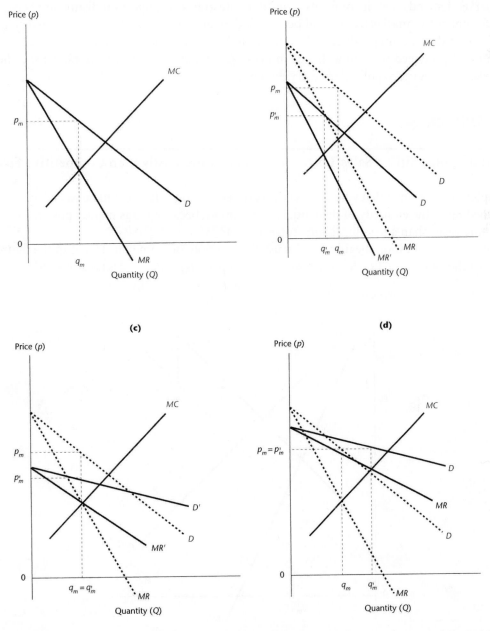

a parallel fashion as in part (b). Remember, the monopolist does not make its production decisions based on the price at which it can sell its output. Instead, its production decisions are based on marginal revenue.

If you experiment a bit, you might come up with something like the situation pictured in part (c). In this case, the new marginal revenue curve intersects the marginal cost curve in exactly the same place that the old marginal revenue curve did, as indicated in part (a). The firm maximizes profits by choosing the level of output where marginal cost is equal to marginal revenue; clearly, it will not change the amount that it produces, even though the demand for its output has decreased. Because demand has fallen, the market price decreases, however.

Experiment some more. You might come up with something like the shift in part (d). In this case, because marginal revenue is equal to marginal cost only when the firm increases its output, the firm will, in fact, choose to produce more. Note that if the demand curve shifts as indicated, the monopolist will produce more, even though the selling price for its output doesn't change.

In competitive markets, there is a clear relationship between the market price and supply. Indeed, the supply curve represents the marginal cost of production for the industry as a whole. A monopolistic market has no supply curve, however, because a monopolist's output decision depends upon marginal cost an the shape of the market demand curve it confronts. The figure illustrates an important distinction between monopolistic and competitive markets: as should be clear, a demand change can lead to (1) a change in price without a change in the amount produced, (2) a change in both price and the amount produced, or (3) a change in the amount produced without a change in price. A competitive industry supplies a specific quantity at each market price. A monopolized industry does not.

Chapter 13

Can a Monopolist Shift a Sales Tax to Consumers More Easily than Competitive Firms?

In Chapter 12 we learned that whether a sales tax collected from a firm could be passed along to consumers depended upon the elasticity of demand. Is a monopoly, because it has market power, able to pass along the tax more easily than a firm in a competitive market?

To answer this question, begin with the usual monopoly outcome illustrated in the figure (where the monopolist chooses production level q_m and the market price is p_m). The sales tax shifts the monopolist's mar-

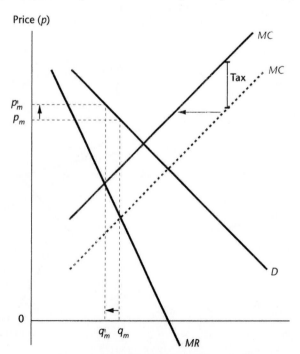

ginal cost curve from *MC* to *MC'*. (The vertical distance between the two curves represents the amount of the tax in dollars.) What happens to the production level? The monopolist chooses to produce where marginal revenue equals marginal cost, including the amount that it must collect from its customers to pay to the government. Hence, the monopolist will reduce its output from q_m to q'_m. As a consequence, the market price will increase from p_m to p'_m. This answers the question: the monopolist is unable to pass along the full amount of the sales tax.

Chapter 13

The Use of Grocery Coupons

Providing coupons to potential customers might be considered another way of price discriminating. Why? You might approach this question by first asking if everyone uses coupons. If so, then they are merely a way of discounting. If some people use coupons and others do not, however, clearly the same goods are being sold at different prices. Whether this constitutes price discrimination depends, however, on whether the two groups of individuals are systematically different. That is, are those who pay lower prices (use coupons) also those who would be unwilling to purchase either the kind or quantity of goods that they do *except for the coupon?*

To analyze this question, you might try to determine the differences between the two groups of individuals. One difference, for example, is that it takes time to clip and gather coupons. Therefore, those who do are willing to spend more time shopping than those who do not (because anyone is free to clip and gather coupons if they wish to). If firms believe that those willing to take the time are also those with higher elasticities of demand, then using coupons as a way of discriminating makes sense.

In an interesting variant, firms often include a coupon packaged with a product. What might be the economic reason for this? To approach this problem, consider what you would pay for the first purchase, and then for any subsequent purchases. Clearly, the first unit you buy costs the full marked price. The second, however, costs you less. Because you have bought the same commodity for different prices, this must be a form of price discrimination. In this case, the producer has assumed that some consumers will only purchase additional amounts if the price is lowered somewhat.

It's worth noting that the possibilities for price discrimination in supermarkets appear almost boundless. The same products are almost always packaged in different sizes (small, medium, and family size) and sold at different prices per equivalent units. For example, the price per ounce of cereal differs depending upon whether you purchase a large or small box. Is this price discrimination? You ought to first ask whether the price differences reflect differences in costs, say, of packaging and handling. Some of the price difference obviously does result from cost differences. Without actual cost data it would be difficult to know for sure, but you can imagine that a firm could use different packages as a way of price discriminating. Those wishing to purchase large packages (perhaps those with large families or those with greater storage room) might have a greater elasticity of demand than do those purchasing in smaller quantities (buyers with smaller families or smaller storage areas).

Chapter 13

The Incidence of an Excise Tax on a Monopolist

Recall that a monopolist chooses to produce so as to make marginal cost equal to marginal revenue, but for a monopolist, marginal revenue is not equal to the market price. This difference between competitive and monopolistic markets can make a difference in the incidence of an excise tax.

An excise tax collected from a monopolist can be thought of as an increase in the cost of providing output to the market. This relationship is illustrated by the shift from *MC* to *MC'* in *Figure A*. We noted earlier that when a tax is imposed on sales in a competitive market, the increase in the price is generally less than the amount of the tax because demand is generally less than perfectly inelastic. As *Figure A* indicates, the same is true for a monopolist *if a monopolist's marginal costs increase as its rate of production increases*. Because

Figure A

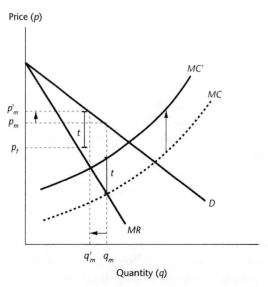

When demand is neither perfectly elastic nor perfectly inelastic, a tax in a monopolized market will have much the same effect as that in a competitive market. The price that consumers pay will increase, although by less than the full amount of the tax (from p_m to p'_m), while the price that the monopolist receives will fall (to $p_f = p'_m - t$).

Figure B

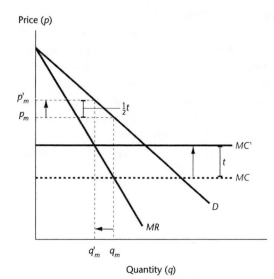

When demand is linear and marginal costs are constant, a tax on a monopolist will cause the market price to increase by exactly one-half the amount of the tax. However, the government collects the full tax, t, on each unit sold. This means that the tax burden is shared equally between consumers and the monopolist.

Figure C

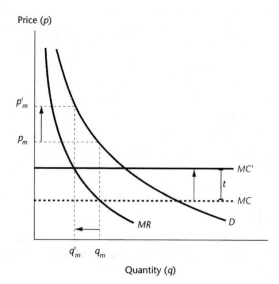

When a commodity tax is imposed on a monopoly with constant marginal costs and a demand curve with a constant elasticity throughout, the market price will increase by more than the amount of the tax. Clearly, in this case, the burden of the tax falls completely on consumers.

Workbook pages may not be reproduced in any form without the written permission of the publisher.

the increase in price is less than the tax, the net-of-tax price for the monopolist will be lower than the original monopoly price. This means that a monopolist is worse off when a tax is imposed because it cannot pass along the full amount of the tax, even though it has market power.

If a monopolist's marginal costs are constant, the incidence of a tax will differ between competitive and monopolistic markets, however. To see this, note first that in a competitive market with constant marginal costs—that is, one with perfectly elastic market supply—the tax burden falls completely on consumers. In a monopolized market with constant marginal costs, however, the incidence of the tax depends upon the shape of the demand curve. With a linear demand curve, for example, the market price will increase by exactly one-half the tax rate, as illustrated in Figure B. This means that consumers and the monopolist share the tax burden equally. If, however, the elasticity of demand is constant throughout, so the market demand curve looks like those illustrated in Figure C, the market price will increase by *more* than the tax. This is a curious outcome: consumers pay not only the full tax, but then some!

Chapter 14

Deciding Whether a Merger Will Be Challenged

Suppose that you work for one of 20 firms in an industry, each of which has an equal share of the market. Suppose also that the firm you work for wants to explore the possibilities of merging with another firm in the same market. What is the DOJ likely to say about the proposed merger?

When there are 20 firms in a market, each with an equal share, the Herfindahl index is 500. To calculate this number, first note that each firm has 5 percent of the market. The Herfindahl index is calculated by squaring each firm's market share and summing over all firms:

$$20 \times 0.05^2 = 0.0500$$

and then multiplying by 10,000,

$$0.0500 \times 10,000 = 500$$

If two firms merged, there would be 19 firms; 18 with a 5 percent share of the market each, and one with a 10 percent share of the market. Thus,

$$18 \times 0.05^2 + 1 \times 0.1^2 = 0.0550$$

Multiplying by 10,000 gives

$$0.0550 \times 10,000 = 550$$

Because this is below the index level at which the DOJ will challenge a merger, your firm would probably not encounter legal difficulties if the merger occurred.

Chapter 15

Who Pays Effluent Charges?

If the government charges an effluent fee, who pays, consumers or firms? In approaching particular questions it is often useful to ask whether the problem is analogous to something you know well. In this case, you might want to think of the effluent charge as something like a sales tax because, as the firm changes its level of output, its level of emissions will change as well. Figure A illustrates the effect for a competitive industry and a monopoly. In both cases, in the short run, firms pay part of the fee and the rest is passed along to consumers in the form of higher prices. However, if the market demand is the same for both the competitive market and the monopoly, the effect on output is smaller in the case of the monopoly, as is the effect on the price. This means that, in the short run, a larger fraction of the tax is paid by the monopolist.

What about the long run? To answer this question, you need to know if the monopoly will survive in the long run. It will, remember, if there are barriers to entry. Suppose, then, that there are barriers to entry. For the competitive industry, by contrast, entry won't be an issue. If the firms were making zero economic profits prior to the imposition of the fee, they will make losses afterward and may exit the market. This means that, in the long run, the outcomes will be those in Figure B.

Because monopolists persist in the long run when there are barriers to entry, there will be no change for the monopolist. That is, the monopolist will pay part of the fee and pass along the rest. For the competitive industry, however, exit means that supply will decrease until there are zero profits for the firms remaining in the industry. Thus the fee will have a larger effect on output in a competitive market and, if costs are essentially constant, the full amount of the emission fee will be passed along to consumers in the long run.

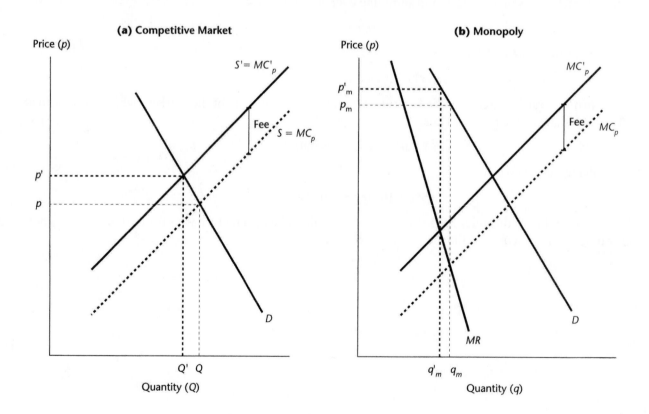

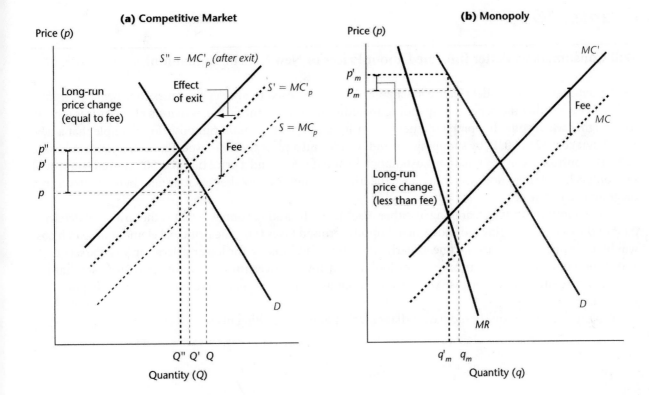

(a) Competitive Market

Price (p)

$S'' = MC'_p$ (after exit)

Effect of exit

$S' = MC'_p$

Long-run price change (equal to fee)

$S = MC_p$

Fee

p''
p'
p

D

Q" Q' Q

Quantity (Q)

(b) Monopoly

Price (p)

MC'

p'_m
p_m

Fee

MC

Long-run price change (less than fee)

D

MR

q'_m q_m

Quantity (q)

Chapter 16

Will Consumers be Better Informed about Prices of New Cars or Cinnamon?

The optimal search model (Figure 4, Chapter 16) can be used to answer this question. Begin by asking yourself whether the benefits of spending an additional hour gathering information about prices is likely to be higher when your shopping for a new car or for a can of cinnamon? Suppose, for example that a new VW Passat cost $25,000. If, by shopping around, you found a price that was even 1% lower, you would save $250. By contrast, a can of cinnamon costs about $5 and if you found a price that was 50% lower, you would save only $2.50. Where does searching have the highest benefit? Draw the two marginal benefit curves in a diagram like Figure 4.

What about the cost of searching in either case? Begin by asking yourself what is the principal determinant of the cost of shopping around? Since shopping around takes time, the principal element of search cost will be the opportunity cost of time. Clearly, an hour spent looking for lower prices for VW Passats costs about the same amount as an hour spent looking for lower prices for cinnamon. This suggests that the marginal cost curves in either case will be similar. Draw a marginal cost curve for search in a diagram like Figure 4.

Having done this, you should have a diagram that looks something like:

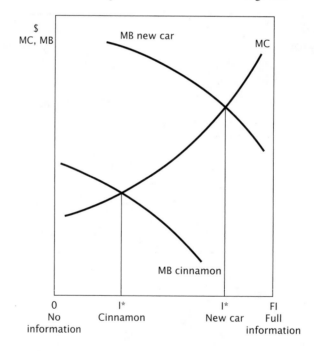

The answer to the question should be evident from the diagram you've drawn: Search costs are likely to be about the same in either case because the principle cost of searching is the opportunity cost of time and, hence, $MC_{VW} = MC_{cinnamon}$. However, the marginal benefits of finding a VW Passat at a 1% lower price are much higher than the marginal benefits of finding cinnamon at even a 50% lower price. Therefore, MB_{VW} will be well above $MB_{cinnamon}$ and, it follows, that I* associated with information on Passats will be closer FI than will the I* associated with information on cinnamon.

What can you generalize from this example? The optimal search model as you have developed it in this figure helps explain why consumers search more for "big ticket" items. That is, you are likely to spend far more time searching for the lowest price for a new home or new car or refrigerator, etc than for the lowest price for cinnamon or soda pop or burritos, etc.

Chapter 16

Who Will Spend the Most Time Looking for Lower Food Prices, Students or Lawyers?

For both groups searching takes time. Searching takes time. It probably takes a lawyer about the same amount of time to go from one super market to another super market in search of the lowest prices as the time it takes a college student. If it takes about the same amount of time for lawyers and students to gather information about which super market in town is selling groceries, on average, at the lowest price, then what will the marginal search cost curve for a lawyer look like *relative* to the marginal search cost curve for a student? The opportunity cost of searching is likely to be much higher for lawyers (with high hourly rates) than for students (with low hourly earnings). Draw a MC_{lawyer} curve in a diagram like Figure 4. Now draw a $MC_{student}$ curve consistent with your sense of the differences in opportunity costs.

The marginal benefit of searching is the lower prices that might be found. These benefits are likely to be pretty much the same for both lawyers and students. That is, finding a store that sells groceries for, on average, 5% below other stores in the area reduces the lawyer's expenditures and the student's expenditures for food by roughly the same amount. (Unless, of course, you believe that lawyers each a lot more than students do.)

If you draw these different *MC* curves as below, it should be clear that there will be predictably different I^*'s. This application of the optimal search model suggests that college students might spend a lot more time searching for the lower food prices than lawyers.

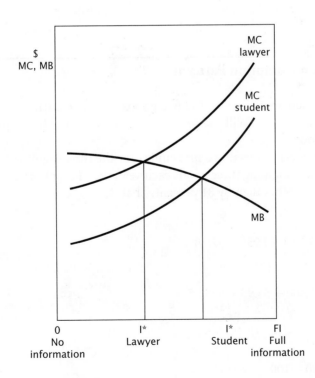

Chapter 17

Price Level Versus Relative Price Changes

Suppose that the 1990 prices for the commodities listed in Table 1 were as shown in the table below. What would the price index be for 1990 if one of each commodity is purchased? To calculate this, weight each price by the amount purchased (1 unit) and calculate the cost of purchasing the market basket.

$$\$40.00 + \$18.85 + \$3.75 + \$7.95 + \$.35 = \$70.90$$

In 1980, the market basket could be purchased for $39.10, therefore,

$$70.90 = 1.81; \quad 1.81 \times 100 = 181$$

and the price index is about 181.

Note that this is exactly the same as the price index calculated in the text. Now compare the prices in 1990 in Table 1 with the prices listed here. The price of a shirt is $40 rather than $48; the price of a haircut, $18.85 rather than $15.00; the price of a hamburger, $3.75 rather than $1.50; the price of a paperback book $7.97 rather than $5.95; and the price of a candy bar $.35 rather than $.45.

This illustrates an important distinction. The *change* in the *price index* from 1980 to 1990 is the same in both cases, but the *changes* in *relative prices* are very different. One dollar price, the price of a candy bar, has fallen over the decade interval and another dollar price, the price of a shirt, has increased by a more modest amount. All of the other prices have increased by much more than in Table 1. Yet the price index is the same in both cases. The important point is that the price index a d relative prices are different concepts.

Chapter 17

Dealing with Different Consumption Patterns

Suppose that the average person consumed the five goods indicated in Table 1 but that you never consumed hamburgers or candy bars. Will the price index indicate what has happened to prices of those goods that are relevant to you?

You can answer this question by creating a price index for the three goods that you do consume. If you consumed one of each of the remaining three goods each year, the relevant prices would have increased for you by 84 percent on average, rather than by 81 percent. That is,

Your 1980 market-basket cost:

$$\$24.00 + \$9.50 + \$3.95 = \$37.45$$

Your 1990 market-basket cost:

$$\$48.00 + \$15.00 + \$5.95 = \$68.95$$

and

Index in base year:

$$\frac{\$37.45}{\$37.45} \times 100 = 100$$

Index in 1990:

$$\frac{\$68.95}{\$37.45} \times 100 = 184$$

On the other hand, suppose that you did not purchase shirts but did purchase hamburgers, haircuts, paperbacks and candy bars. Then,

Your 1980 market-basket cost:

$$\$9.50 + \$1.25 + \$3.95 + \$.40 = \$15.10$$

Your 1990 market-basket cost:

$$\$15.00 + \$1.50 + \$5.95 + \$.45 = \$22.90$$

and

Index in base year:

$$\frac{\$15.10}{\$15.10} \times 100 = 100$$

Index in 1990:

$$\frac{\$22.90}{\$15.10} \times 100 = 152$$

Over the decade covered by the index, the prices you care about increased by only 52 percent in general. Thus, the index based on the average market basket does not accurately reflect what is happening to those particular prices you care about.

There is also a more general problem about how to weight the various items in the index market basket. In the examples we have been using, each item is purchased once. If your consumption pattern differs from that index market basket, however, you would give different weights to the various items. For example, if you don't eat hamburgers or candy bars, then the appropriate weight would be 0 for those two items.

To illustrate the importance of the weights, suppose that the market basket for the index included one each of shirts, hamburgers, paperback books, and candy bars, but included five haircuts per year. In this case, between 1980 and 1990, the index would change from 100 ($77.10/$77.10 = 1.0; 1.0 x 100 = 100) to 170 ($130.90/$77.10 = 1.70; 1.70 x 100 = 170). This is a considerably different index from the one we created earlier in which each good had equal weight and the index changed from 100 to 181. It is easy to see why the weights have such an effect. With equal weights, the large item that doubled in price, a shirt, heavily influences the index. With different weights, it is the haircuts, for which prices did not change by as much, that now influence the index more heavily.

Chapter 17

Analyzing the Effects of Changes in the Consumption Pattern Over Time

Suppose that a good was not available in 1980, but in 1990 almost everyone buys it and its price is changing. Would this change be reflected in the price index? To answer this question, ask yourself what the weight of the good would have been in the market basket for 1980 if it had been purchased in 1990 but not in 1980. The answer: zero. Thus, its price cannot affect the index based on a 1980 market basket, even though it is now commonly consumed. Of course, this poses a problem for the use of price indices. If this change in available goods were an unusual or rare occurrence, it wouldn't much matter; however, it is a fairly common situation. People did not purchase personal computers in 1960 or 1970 but did purchase them in 1980. Thus a price index created on the basis of consumption patterns in 1960 or 1970 did not accurately reflect what happened to personal computer prices in the years since the mid-1970s. Similarly, few people flew on airplanes in the 1950s but travel by air is now common. A market basket based on consumption patterns in the 1950s will not reflect changes in the prices of air transportation in the 1970s.

There is a more subtle aspect to this particular problem with price indices. Suppose that you did purchase shirts in 1980 and again in 1990 but that the *quality* changed substantially over the decade. For example, suppose that a shirt purchased in 1980 lasted one year, but that a shirt purchased in 1990 lasted two years. The change in price from $24 to $48 would now have a quite different interpretation. You are really not purchasing quite the same good even though you are purchasing "a shirt." Or, for example, consider the changes in automobiles between 1950 and 1990. Standard equipment on many cars may now include air conditioning, tape decks, cruise control, power steering, and digital displays, none of which were common features in 1950. Or, consider the changes in the television from 1960 to 1990 with the introduction of large screens, color, and VCR capabilities. Changes in the prices of automobiles or television sets between 1950 and 1990 may reflect more than merely an increase or decrease in prices. In an important sense we are now purchasing different goods even if we call them by the same name.

Chapter 20

The Effects of a Change in the Aggregate Marginal Propensity to Consume

What happens to aggregate demand if the marginal propensity to consume decreases? It is easiest to approach this kind of question by starting with a particular *MPC*, say 0.7, and assuming that there is a simple linear relationship between income and consumption. You can then determine the level of aggregate demand consistent with desired consumption and desired investment for this *MPC* by determining the level of aggregate income such that $(c + I = y)$, as shown in Figure A. Remember that y^d corresponds to a point along an aggregate demand curve, as shown in the bottom part of the figure.

Now choose a lower *MPC*, say 0.5. The *MPC* is the slope of the consumption function so a lower *MPC* is equivalent to a flatter consumption function, as indicated. If desired investment doesn't change, the level of income consistent with desired investment plus desired consumption will be $y^d{}_2$. Note that $y^d{}_2$ is less than $y^d{}_1$. Along the function that shows desired consumption plus desired investment the price level is assumed to be unchanging. Thus, at that price level, real output demanded is less than it would be at a higher *MPC*. This same effect would be true for any other price level. Thus, a decrease in the *MPC* shifts aggregate demand to the left.

What happens to the investment multiplier as a consequence?

First, recall the definition of the investment multiplier. It is the amount by which aggregate real output demanded changes at a given price level, when aggregate investment changes. Next, recall that if the investment increases by $1 at a given price level, income must increase until there is an induced increase in desired saving equal to $1. But, if the *MPC* is 0.7, this means that income will have to increase by $3.33 for each $1 increase in desired investment. The reason is that desired saving will increase by the marginal propensity to save, *MPS*, for each $1 increase in income. The *MPS* is 0.3 $(1.0 - MPC = 1.0 - 0.7)$, so

0.3 x change in income = desired change in saving

0.3 x change in income = $1

Change in income = $\dfrac{\$1}{0.3}$

Following the same argument when the *MPC* is 0.5, the investment multiplier will be 2. That is, if desired investment increases by $1, income must increase by $2 in order to induce an increase in desired saving equal to $1, it $.50 of each $1.00 is saved.

You can also answer this question using Figure A—just look at the size of the effect on aggregate real output demanded for the same change in investment before and after the change in the marginal propensity to consume. Suppose, for example, that desired investment increased. The effects on aggregate real output demanded are illustrated in Figure B.

The investment multiplier is the change in aggregate real output demanded (at a given price level) divided by the change in investment. Therefore, it should be clear that when the marginal propensity to consume is smaller, the multiplier is smaller as well. This means that small changes in desired investment will be amplified less—that is, the aggregate-demand effect will be smaller.

Chapter 20

The Paradox of Thrift

In the preceding problem, notice that when individuals want to save more, the demand for real output actually falls, *ceteris paribus*. As a consequence, it is possible that if everyone wants to save more, everyone may actually end up saving less. This apparently curious outcome is known as the "Paradox of Thrift."

This paradox can be understood by noting that, for example, 50 percent of $8 ($4) is less than 30 percent of $15 ($4.50). Thus, if real output actually falls by enough when the marginal propensity to consume decreases, aggregate saving may fail. This result occurs because a decrease in the marginal propensity to consume is equal to an increase in the marginal propensity to save.

Under what conditions will real output decrease when the marginal propensity to consume decreases? Or, equivalently, under what conditions will real output decrease when the marginal propensity to save increases? We have already found that when the marginal propensity to save increases from 0.3 to 0.5, the aggregate demand curve shifts to the left, as long as there is no corresponding change in desired investment. Real output will fall, for example, if the short-run aggregate supply curve is flat, as pictured in the figure. In this case, the full adjustment to a change in desired consumption occurs in real output. But of course, if real output is lower than before, individual incomes will also be lower, and both consumption and saving will fail. This relationship can be seen in the bottom part of the figure where, clearly, a larger fraction (0.5) of a smaller income (y^d_2) may be smaller than a smaller fraction (0.3) of a larger income (y^d_1). Hence, *wanting to save more induces changes that lead to less actual saving, unless desired investment increases by the increase in desired savings.* Wanting to save more creates an outcome where it is impossible to save more.

Chapter 20

Possible Interest-Rate Effects

In the discussion in the first part of this chapter, we noted that both investment and saving were influenced by changes in the interest rate. In particular, investment is inversely related to the interest rate. On the other hand, saving is positively related to the interest rate, because an increase in the interest rate increases the opportunity cost of consuming now, rather than in the future. What are the possible effects of the interest rate on the macroeconomic adjustments outlined in this chapter in terms of real output and/or the price level?

To answer this question, recall that the decrease in aggregate demand illustrated in the figures in the previous two sample problems occurs because desired saving increases *with no change in desired investment.* Suppose, however, that when desired saving increases, the interest rate falls. (This would be possible because the supply of funds for investment purposes will increase if everyone saves more of each dollar in income.) There is an inverse relationship between desired investment and the interest rate so when the interest rate falls, desired investment will increase. This increase in desired investment will move aggregate real output demanded $(c + i)$ upward, as illustrated in the figure below. Thus, on the one hand, $(c + i)$ falls because desired saving, s, increases and, as a consequence, desired consumption, c, falls. On the other hand, $(c + i)$ increase because as s increases, interest rates fall, and i increases. Clearly, it is possible for the interest-rate effect on investment to offset the effect on aggregate demand that would have resulted form an increase in s. (This adjustment, sometimes called the *classical adjustment,* occurs when prices are flexible. In this case, the "price" is the interest rate in the market for funds that are saved and invested.)

Chapter 21

Determining a Level of Real Output Demanded That Is Consistent with Desired Investment and Government Spending

Suppose that you were a member of the President's Council of Economic Advisors and were provided with the data in the table (in billions of dollars). What level of real output if produced will be consistent with aggregate real output demanded?

In approaching this question, recall that real output demanded is the sum of consumption plus investment plus government purchases. Thus, to answer the question, you need to find the level of real output that would be equal to the sum of the second, third, and fourth columns of the table. For example, in the first row, real output demanded would be $2,450 + $550 + $1,100 = $4,100. But this is greater than the level of real output in the first column. That is, if real output were $3,500, real output demanded would be $4,100; there is an inconsistency between the two. In the last row, by contrast, real output demanded would be $4,900 + $550 + $1,100 = $6,550, which is less than the level of real output in the first column.

If you go row by row and sum the last three columns, you will find that only when real output is $5,500 is it consistent with the components of aggregate demand—$3,850 + $550 + $1,100 = $5,500.

Now suppose that investment increases from $550 billion to $850 billion. What happens? Clearly, $5,500 is no longer consistent with the sum of the components of aggregate demand ($3,850 + $850 + $1,100 = $5,800). If you step back for a moment from the numbers, it should be clear why this is so: when desired investment increases, aggregate demand increases and the level of real output that must be produced to accommodate the higher level of desired investment must increase as well.

Once again, if you go row by row and sum consumption and government purchases with the higher level of desired investment, $850, you will find that, if real output is $6,500, then consumption is $4,550 and the components of aggregate demand are consistent with what the economy is actually producing ($,550 + $850 + $1,100).

What is the investment multiplier in this case? To answer this question, note that when desired investment is $550, aggregate real output demanded is $5,500 but when desired investment is $850, aggregate real output demanded is $6,500. Therefore, a $300 change in desired investment ($850 – $550) leads to a $1,000 change in aggregate real output demanded. Hence, the multiplier is 3.33 ($1,000/$300).

Is this actual multiplier consistent with what we might predict using the marginal propensity to consume? To answer this question, we need an estimate of the marginal propensity to consume. Begin with its definition: the amount that consumption changes when income changes by $1. An estimate can be obtained by dividing the difference between consumption as income increases by the change in income. For example, in the second row, income is $4,000 and consumption is $2,800, whereas in the third row, income is $4,500 and consumption is $3,150. Therefore, when income increase by $500, desired consumption increases by $350. Thus, from these data we would estimate the MPC to be $350/$500 = 0.7.

Using the formula for the simple multiplier, we have

$$\text{Investment multiplier} = \frac{1}{1 - 0.7}$$

$$= \frac{1}{0.3} = 3.33$$

which is consistent with our other calculation.

Chapter 21

Calculating an Investment Multiplier

Suppose that everyone pays a tax of 20 percent and that individuals spend $.90 of each additional dollar in disposable income. What will the investment multiplier be?

In this case, the marginal propensity to consume out of disposable income is 0.9. However, the multiplier is determined by the amount spent from *each dollar of aggregate income*. When aggregate income increases by $1.00, disposable income increases by $.80, so consumption will increase by

$$0.9 \times \$.80 = \$.72$$

Therefore, for each dollar increase in aggregate income, consumption increase by $.72. The multiplier will be

$$\frac{1}{1 - 0.72} = 3.57$$

What would the multiplier be if taxes were not determined as a fraction of income? In this case, each time aggregate income increases by $1.00, disposable income would increase by $1.00. Therefore, consumption would increase by

$$0.9 \times \$1.00 = \$.90$$

and the multiplier would be

$$\frac{1}{1 - 0.9} = 10$$

Notice that even though the marginal propensity to consume is the same in either case, the multiplier is much larger when the tax rate is lower.

What does this mean for the economy in terms of random aggregate demand shocks? Clearly, a random increase in investment will cause a greater shift in aggregate demand when the tax rate is lower. That is, a $1 increase in investment will increase aggregate real output demanded by $3.57 when the tax rate is 0.2 and by $10 when the tax rate is 0.0.

Chapter 21

The Effect of an Income Tax on the Multiplier

Suppose the government relies on a proportional income tax, rather than a lump sum tax, to fund its activities. What will happen to the multiplier?

To answer this question, you need to think about how a tax that is proportional to income affects disposable income. If t_r is the tax rate, then

disposable income= income x (1.0 – the tax rate)

For example, if income is $1,000 and the tax rate is 30 percent, then disposable income is $700. That is, 1.0 – 0.3 = 0.7; 0.7 x $1,000 = $700. Since consumption is determined by disposable income, we have

$$c = a + b(1 - t_r)y$$

Note that the consumption function is flatter. That is, the consumption function without an income tax has a slope of b; now it has a slope of $b \times (1 - t_r)$. Figure 1 illustrates this difference between the effect of a lump-sum tax and an income tax on disposable income, which is most clearly seen by comparing the effects of a change in a lump-sum tax (t) with a change in an income tax rate (t_r).

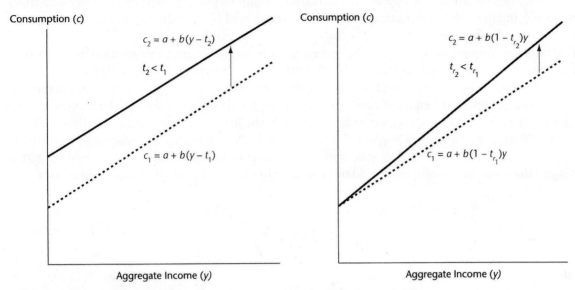

(a) Effect of a Cut in a Lump-Sum Tax

Consumption (c)

$c_2 = a + b(y - t_2)$

$t_2 < t_1$

$c_1 = a + b(y - t_1)$

Aggregate Income (y)

(b) Effect of a Cut in the Income-Tax Rate

Consumption (c)

$c_2 = a + b(1 - t_{r_2})y$

$t_{r_2} < t_{r_1}$

$c_1 = a + b(1 - t_{r_1})y$

Aggregate Income (y)

A lump-sum tax cut shifts the consumption function upward; an income tax cut rotates the consumption function.

The effect on the multipliers can be found by noting that because the tax rate is less than 1.0, a proportional income tax lowers the effective or net-of-tax marginal propensity to consume to

$$b' = b\,(1 - t_r)$$

For example, if the *MPC* is 0.8 and there is no tax, then when income is $1,000, consumption will be $800. If there is a 30 percent proportional tax, however, disposable income will be $700 and consumption will be $560. In this case, consumption changes by $560 for each $1,000 change in income and the effective or net-of-tax marginal propensity to consume is 0.56 [$560/$1,000 or 0.8 x (1.0 – 0.3)]. Thus, you could think of aggregate consumption decisions being made using a new consumption function,

$$c = a + b'y$$

We know that the aggregate-demand multiplier is 1/(1-*MPC*). Therefore, by substituting *b'* for the marginal propensity to consume we have

$$\text{multiplier} = \frac{1}{1 - b'}$$

$$= \frac{1}{1 - b(1 - t_r)}$$

Thus, if *b* equals 0.8 and t_r equals 0.3, the aggregate demand multiplier will be 2.27 [1/(1 – 0.8 x 0.7]. That is, an increase in desired investment of $1 will increase aggregate demand by $2.27. If income had not been taxed, the aggregate-demand multiplier would have been 5 [that is, 1/(1 – 0.8)] and the same $1 increase in desired investment would have increased aggregate demand by $5.00.

What are we to make of this? Tax policy affects not just aggregate demand but the size of the aggregate-demand multiplier. In particular, taxing income reduces the size of the multiplier. This means fluctuations in investment or net exports will lead to smaller aggregate demand shifts than would occur if income were not taxed.

What happens when the tax rate increases? If you work through the preceding with a higher tax rate, you'll find that the multiplier is smaller. In a sense, income taxes are a shock-absorber—an aggregate demand shock changes income, but the induced-consumption effects are dampened because disposable income changes by $(1 - t_r) \times \Delta y$ rather than by Δy.

The marginal propensity to consume in the United States is quite high, probably around 0.9. This would suggest a simple multiplier of around 10.0 ($1/(1-.9)$). Best estimates place the aggregate-demand multiplier in the 2.0 to 4.0 range, however. We now know one of the reasons for the discrepancy. Our simple formula overstates the multiplier effect because it does not account for the dampening effect of the income tax system. Indeed, if the average tax rate on income is 0.2 (roughly the federal tax income as a fraction of GDP), the aggregate demand multiplier will be about 3.5 rather than 10.0, even though the marginal propensity to consume by individuals is unchanged. If state and local income taxes are included, the average tax rate is about 0.3 and the theoretical multiplier would then be close to the actual multiplier found in the data.

Chapter 23

Calculating the Effects of an Open Market Purchase

Suppose that the Fed purchases T-bills for $10 million. How much will the money supply increase? To answer this question, note first that individuals who once held $10 million in T-bills would now have $10 million in currency. Thus, the money supply has increased by at least $10 million. At this point, however, you ought to wonder what the money multiplier is. Clearly, not enough information has been provided to allow you to calculate the potential increase in the money supply. You need to know what the reserve requirement is.

Suppose, then, that the reserve requirement is 0.12. In this case, the money multiplier is

$$\frac{1}{0.12} = 8.33$$

and a $10 million increase in currency in circulation could increase the money supply by as much as $80.33 million.

What would the increase be if the Fed sets the reserve requirement at 0.15 instead? In this case, the money multiplier would be

$$\frac{1}{0.15} = 6.67$$

and a $10 million increase in currency in circulation could increase the money supply by as much as $66.67 million.

Why is the generality "as much as" included in each of these conclusions? To answer this question, think of why there is a money multiplier. The reason is that banks hold only a fraction of a checking account deposit as vault cash and in this way, they create money. Thus the money supply increases by $80.33 million only if $10 million in currency ends up as reserves in banks. If individuals hold some of the currency in their wallets or purses, the money supply will increase by less because bank reserves will increase by less. More precisely, the money supply will increase $80.33 million only if the $10 million ends up as reserves *and* banks loan out all reserves in excess of those that they are required to hold. Thus, the actual increase in the money supply depends only upon the willingness of banks to make loans.

Chapter 25

Is "Crowding In" Possible?

The discussion in the text focuses on a government deficit and crowding out. Would *crowding in* occur if the government ran a sustained surplus? More generally, what happens when the government runs a surplus?

In this case, the government would be contributing to the pool of savings available in the economy. It would do so by redeeming more debt than it issued. As a consequence, interest rates would decrease. The decrease in interest rates would stimulate investment, providing a partial offset to the effect of the decrease in government spending. Because the initial effect of a decrease in government spending is a decrease in aggregate demand, at first unemployment would be likely to increase. As a result, nominal wages would also begin to fall. Output and employment would increase. This process would continue until wages and prices had declined enough to bring the labor market into equilibrium and until the interest rate had declined enough to equate aggregate demand with potential output. At this point, of course, the decline in government spending would be completely offset by an increase in private spending.

Therefore, an increase in government spending leads to crowding out, and just the opposite—crowding in—occurs when government spending decreases. In the long run, when government spending increases, there is full displacement of private spending. When government spending decreases, there is full replacement of government spending by private spending. Thus, in the long run, fiscal policy affects the division of the real output pie, but dos not affect its size. (However, if investment is lowered for a sustained period of time, the economy's growth rate may drop and, in this way, fiscal policy may affect the long-run size of the pie.) In the short run, aggregate demand shifts resulting from changes in fiscal policy will affect real output. Because consumption spending depends primarily on income and, in the long run, income is unchanged (because it is equal to potential output), after the full adjustment has occurred, most of the change in private spending will occur in investment.

Glossary _____

A

An individual has an **absolute advantage** in production of a good if he or she can produce more of it than can someone with whom the individual might trade. Absolute advantage is irrelevant in determining what choices individuals will make—all that matters is comparative advantage. A nation has an **absolute advantage** if the cost of producing a commodity that can be traded internationally is less than the cost for other nations of producing the same commodity. Absolute advantage is, however, irrelevant because *relative costs for different commodities within an economy create a comparative advantage* not cost differences for the same commodity between economies.

The **accelerator effect** is the fluctuation in desired investment that occurs when there are changes in the *rate of increase* in real output. If firms attempt to keep a relatively constant relationship between their production and their capital stock, real output must grow at a constant rate to keep investment stable.

Accounting costs are the direct or explicit costs of an activity measured in monetary terms, usually in the form of payments that a firm actually makes in response to bills or invoices.

Adverse selection occurs when individuals with lower risks leave an insurance pool, thereby increasing the average risk in the pool.

An **ad valorem commodity tax** is a tax on the sale of a commodity that is set as a percentage of the purchase price.

Aggregate demand (*AD*) is the sum of the amount that agents in an economy are prepared to purchase for *consumption, investment, net exports,* and *government spending* purposes at different price levels.

Aggregate depreciation is the dollar value of depreciation across the entire economy.

Aggregate fixed investment is the value of investment in buildings (also called *plant*) and equipment by all firms (**aggregate business fixed investment**) and of the value of new housing, housing remodels, and housing repairs by all households (**aggregate residential fixed investment**).

Aggregate inventory is the dollar value of inventories aggregated or summed over *all* firms and industries in an economy.

Aggregate investment is the sum of investment in plant, equipment, and inventory holdings by firms, and new housing construction by households.

Aggregate saving is equal to the dollar amount of real output that is produced but not used for consumption purposes.

An **aggregate supply shock** is a dramatic change in the productive resources available to an economy that changes the amount that firms are willing to produce at a given price level.

An **aggregate production possibilities frontier** is the boundary between what an economy can produce and what it is unable to produce because of resource and technological constraints. That is, an aggregate PPF shows all possible combinations of output that an economy might produce if its resources were used in the best possible way.

Aggregate supply (*AS*) is the aggregate or total output an economy produces at different price levels.

A market outcome is **allocatively efficient** if it is not possible to reallocate some resources, goods, or services to make at least one individual better off without, at the same time, making someone else worse off. This concept of efficiency is called *Pareto efficiency*.

Antitrust policy is the collection of legal rules, court interpretations, and enforcement efforts directed at firms and market structures where exploiting market power is possible. (Trusts were legal organizations that facilitated coordination among firms that would have been rivals.)

An **appreciation of a currency** is an increase in the value of a currency in a foreign exchange market. Following an appreciation, it takes less of a currency to buy a unit of foreign currency.

Arbitrage is the activity of buying a commodity where the price is low and selling the commodity where the price is high in order to make a profit on the difference between the two prices.

Arc elasticity is an estimate of the elasticity between two points on a demand or supply curve. That is, arc elasticity of demand (or supply) = [(q1–q2)/ (q1+q2)/2]/[(p1-p2)/(p1+p2)/2]

An **asset** is something held through time in order to transfer current or past income into future consumption. A **money-fixed** or **nominal** asset is one whose future payoff is a fixed amount of money and hence whose purchasing power necessarily changes with changes in the price level. A **real** asset is one whose future payoff depends on market conditions on the day the asset is sold for money and, hence, whose purchasing power does *not* necessarily change with changes in the price level. An asset is a *store of value*.

A firm's **average revenue** (*AR*) is equal to its total revenue divided by its output, but this is always equal to the market price at which it sells its output, that is, $AR = TR/q = (p \times q)/q = p$.

Average total cost is the total cost per unit of output produced, **average variable cost** is the total variable cost per unit of output produced, and **average fixed cost** is the total fixed cost per unit of output produced. That is, *ATC = TC/q, AVC = VC/q, and AFC = FC/q.*

B

The **balanced-budget multiplier** is the change in aggregate demand that occurs when government sending increases by $1 and tax revenues increase by $1 or when government spending decreases by $1 and tax revenues decrease by $1. In its simplest form, the balanced budget multiplier is 1.0. That is, a $1 increase in government spending funded by a $1 increase in taxes increases aggregate real output demanded at a given price level by $1.

A **barrier to entry** is a condition that disadvantages new firms and prevents or delays their entering a market in response to the economic profits of existing firms.

Barter is the direct trade of one commodity for another commodity without using money.

The **base year** or **base period** is the year or period from which a price index is measured.

Illegal market transactions are frequently referred to as occurring on the **black market**.

A **budget deficit** is the shortfall between a government's expenditures and its tax revenues during a specified period of time, usually one year.

C

Capital is anything that is produced and then used to produce other things. Capital in the form of tools is called **physical capital**; and capital in the form of individuals with developed skills is called **human capital**.

The **capital utilization rate** is the ratio of capital stock currently being used in an economy, compared to the total available capital stock. When the rate increases, more capital is employed; when the rate decreases, less capital is employed and some of the economy's productive capital is left idle.

A **cartel** is a group of otherwise competing firms that collude. They make joint decisions about how much to produce, thereby jointly acting like a monopolist.

Ceteris paribus. A Latin phrase meaning "all else equal" or in many economic contexts, "all other things held constant."

A **change in the quantity demanded** or **supplied** corresponds to a movement along a demand or supply curve.

A **classical adjustment** is one in which the price level and interest rates adjust sufficiently to bring aggregate demand into line with potential real output *without any effect on real output over the period of adjustment.*

An individual has a **comparative advantage** in the production of a good if his or her relative production costs are lower for that good than are the relative production costs for someone with whom the individual might trade. An economy has a **comparative advantage** if the *relative cost* of producing a commodity that can be traded internationally is less than the *relative cost* for another economy of producing the same commodity. *Relative cost* is the amount of one good that must be given up if resources are shifted to the production of a single unit of another good *within an economy*. That is, *relative cost* refers to costs within an economy, not any "cost" differences between two economies.

The **Coase theorem** states: "Under perfect competition, once government has assigned clearly defined property rights in contested resources and as long as transactions costs are negligible, private parties that generate or are affected by externalities will negotiate voluntary agreements that lead to the socially optimal resource allocation and output mix regardless of how the property rights are assigned."

Coinsurance is the sharing of risk in an insurance contract that occurs when those who are insured pay a portion of any loss (the **deductible** or **co-payment**).

Collusion is an explicit or implicit agreement among otherwise competitive firms to coordinate their decisions so as to reduce competition.

A **common market** is an agreement to have common tariffs against the rest of the world but no tariffs within the common market.

The **common property problem** is the problem of overuse of a resource that occurs when additional users of that resource cannot be excluded, either because the costs of doing so are high or because ownership rights are not clearly specified.

Comparable options are choices A and B for which an individual can state a preference. He or she may prefer A to B, or B to A, or may state that A and B are equally good.

Complements are goods that tend to be consumed jointly or together. If two commodities are complements and the price of one increases, the demand for the other will decrease. However, if two commodities are complements and the price of one decreases, the demand for the other commodity will increase.

Consistent or **transitive choices** are those that are "predictable" in that if an individual prefers A over B, and B over C, the individual also prefers A over C.

A firm encounters **constant returns to scale** if, when it increases all inputs, the increase in output is proportional to the increase in inputs. In this case, minimum average cost for an optimal choice of inputs will be the same for a larger new firm or an expanding existing firm. In either case, the firm has **constant long-run average costs**.

Consumer surplus is the difference between what individuals would be willing to pay for what they are currently consuming and the amount they actually have to pay.

The **consumer price index (CPI)** is a measure of what is happening, in general, to the prices of a market basket of goods and services commonly purchased by households.

Consumption (*c*) is that part of aggregate real output, purchased by households and individuals, which is used to increase their material well-being.

A **contract** is an agreement, frequently written, that can be enforced through a legal system.

A **contraction** is a period when aggregate real output either falls or increases at a rate well below its long-run trend. A period of falling real output is a **recession**. A particularly severe recession is sometimes called a **depression**.

A **contractionary countercyclical fiscal policy** is one that decreases aggregate demand by either decreasing government expenditures or by increasing taxes when inflation is increasing.

The **cross-price elasticity of demand** is the percentage change in quantity demand when the price of another commodity changes by 1 percent.

Crowding out is the displacement by government borrowing of private borrowing and, eventually, of private investment and capital formation.

A **customs union** is an agreement among a group of nations to have common tariffs against the rest of the world but lower tariffs within the union.

Cyclical unemployment occurs when changes in aggregate demand or aggregate supply create fewer job vacancies than the number of individuals who would be willing to work.

D

A **deadweight loss** or **deadweight burden** is the loss in consumer and producer surpluses associated with a government policy that is not offset by any revenue the government receives from pursuing the policy.

Declining block pricing is a form of price discrimination in which the same consumer is charged a lower price for consumption beyond a specified amount.

A firm encounters **decreasing returns to scale** or **diseconomies of scale** if, when it increases all inputs, the increase in output is proportionally less than the increase in inputs. In this case, minimum average costs for an optimal choice of inputs for a large new firm (or an expanding existing firm) will be higher, and the firm will have **increasing long-run average costs**.

A **deductible** or **coinsurance** is a cost-sharing insurance arrangement in which a person who is insured has to pay part of the cost when a bad event occurs. Instead of the insurance company assuming full payment for the loss, it pays the full payment less the deductible, or it pays a certain fraction of the loss, with the remaining fraction, or coinsurance, remaining the responsibility of the individual.

Deflation is a decrease in the price level, that is, a general decrease in the average of all prices. It is measured by a negative *percentage* change in a measure of the price level like the CPI. With deflation, the purchasing power of money increases. a **deflation** is a *general* decrease in dollar prices (*most* prices are decreasing).

A **deflationary gap** occurs when real output is less than potential real output, causing a downward pressure on prices.

A **demand schedule** is a list of the maximum amount demanders are willing to purchase from a market at each market price over a particular time period. Alternatively, a demand schedule can be thought of as the maximum that individuals are willing to pay for a given amount purchased.

A **demand curve** is a graph of a demand schedule in which, by convention, the relative price is measured along the vertical axis and the quantity provided to the market at each market price is measured along the horizontal axis.

The set of all combinations of price and quantity that individuals desire to purchase are referred to as **demand**. Demand refers to the *entire* demand schedule or demand curve. **Quantity demanded** refers to the amount demanded at a single point on the demand schedule or demand curve, that is, to a particular price-quantity combination. A change in the quantity demanded is a movement along the demand curve.

Depreciation is the decrease in the value of capital that occurs as it wears out while being used to produce outputs.

A decrease in the value of a currency in a foreign exchange market is called a **depreciation of a currency**. Following a depreciation, it takes more of a currency to buy a unit of foreign currency.

A particularly severe and lengthy recession is a **depression**.

Diminishing marginal returns is an effect that occurs when, as the *amount* of a chosen item increases and nothing else changes, the *value* of the additional (marginal) unit decreases.

A **disincentive** is a penalty that discourages an activity or choice.

Disinflation occurs when the *rate* of inflation declines. For example, when the inflation rate falls from 10 percent to 4 percent, a disinflation is occurring. Notice that the price level may still continue to rise, but it does so at a slower rate. That is, the *rate* of inflation is lower.

Disposable personal income (DPI) is equal to PI minus personal taxes.

Disposable aggregate income is equal to aggregate real income less taxes, plus transfers.

Dissaving occurs when an individual draws down savings or borrows in order to consume more than can be purchased with current income.

The **distribution of individual income** is the division of the output an economy produces among those living within the economy.

Division of labor is the breaking up of a task into smaller, more specialized tasks so that each worker becomes more proficient.

Dumping is the sale of a product in a foreign market at a price lower than that at which the same commodity is sold in its domestic market.

The **duration of unemployment** is the period of time a person remains unemployed.

E

Economic growth is the sustained increase in real GDP or real GDP per capita over time.

Economic profits are equal to the difference between a firm's total revenue (TR) and its total economic cost (TC), which includes both explicit costs and implicit or opportunity costs and a normal rate of return for the owners of the firm.

Economics is the study of how individuals and groups of individuals respond to and deal with scarcity.

Economics of scale are present when average total costs decrease as the volume of output of a single firm increases.

Economies of scope occur when average total costs decrease because the number of different goods produced by a single firm increases.

An economy's organization of production is **efficient** if it is not possible to increase the production of one thing without decreasing the production of something else.

An **effluent tax** is a levy on those who produce pollution.

An **emission fee** is a charge imposed on each unit of a polluter's emissions.

Demand is **price elastic** or **elastic** if the quantity demanded is sensitive to relative price changes. Conversely, demand is **price inelastic** or **inelastic** if the quantity demanded is not sensitive to relative price changes. The **price elasticity of demand** is the percentage change in the quantity demand when the market price changes by one percent. It is also called the **own-price elasticity of demand** or simply the **elasticity of demand.** Quantitatively, elasticity of demand = %Δ qty demanded/ % Δ p. Demand is said to be **elastic** if the absolute value of the measured elasticity of demand is greater than 1; demand is **inelastic** if the absolute value of the measure elasticity of demand is less than 1. If the absolute value of the measured elasticity of demand is equal to 1.0, demand is said to have **unitary elasticity.**

Elasticity of supply is the percentage change in quantity supplied when the market price changes by a small percentage amount. Quantitatively, elasticity of supply = %Δ qty supplied/ % Δ p. Supply is **elastic** if the measured elasticity of supply is greater than 1. If the measured elasticity of supply is less than 1, supply is **inelastic**. If the measured elasticity of supply is just equal to 1, supply is said to have **unitary elasticity.**

An **emissions standard** is a specific legal limit on the quantity of pollution that an individual activity is allowed to dump into the environment.

Entry occurs when new firms enter a market; **expansion** occurs when existing firms increase their capacity or scale of activity.

A market is in **equilibrium** when the quantity that suppliers are willing to provide to the market at a specific market price is exactly equal to the quantity that demanders desire to purchase in the market at the same market price. More generally, there is equilibrium when there is no tendency for change and a particular market situation is self-perpetuating.

The **equi-marginal principle** is a rule for choosing the best mix when there are many different possible things from which to choose. The best or optimal mix is obtained when the marginal benefit per additional dollar cost is the same for each thing chosen.

Excess demand occurs when, at a particular market price, the quantity that suppliers want to provide to the market is less than the quantity that demanders want to purchase.

Excess demand is the difference between quantity demanded and quantity supplied at that price.

Excess supply occurs when, at a specific market price, the quantity that suppliers want to provide to the market exceeds the quantity that demanders want to purchase. The excess supply is the difference between quantity supplied and quantity demanded at that price.

The price of one currency in terms of a second currency is the **exchange rate**. That is, the exchange rate is the purchase price of a unit of foreign exchange when a foreign currency is thought of as a commodity just like any other commodity (apples, for example).

An **exclusive territory** is an area that is designated by an agreement between a manufacturer or wholesaler and a retailer. The agreement limits the area where a particular retailer can market a particular good purchased from the manufacturer or wholesaler.

Exit occurs when firms leave a market; firms may, in difficult circumstances, also **contract** by reducing their capacity or scale.

An **expansion** is a period when output increases faster than its long-run trend.

A **expansionary countercyclical fiscal policy** is one that increases aggregate demand either by increasing government expenditures or by cutting taxes when unemployment is increasing and real output is falling.

Explicit collusion is an agreement among a group of otherwise competitive firms to coordinate production decisions.

An **export** is a good or service produced in a domestic market that is sold in a foreign market.

An **externality** is a side-effect, either bad or good, that results whenever a person or firm making a decision does not consider costs or benefits of the particular decision, and, as a consequence, directly affects the utility or profits of other consumers or producers.

F

A **factor of production** is a resource that is used as an input to produce goods or services: land, capital, labor, entrepreneurship, etc.

A **federal deficit** is a shortfall in the government's budget that occurs when the federal expenditures are greater than federal revenues; a **federal surplus** occurs when federal revenues are greater than federal taxes.

The **federal funds market** is a market for bank reserves. Banks with excess reserves are suppliers and lend overnight to demanders—banks who are short of the legally required minimum reserve. The price in the federal funds market is known as the **federal funds interest rate** or, more commonly, the **federal funds rate**.

A **firm** is an entity that organizes production so as to take advantage of the gains from team activity and minimizes the shirking that accompanies team activity.

The inverse relationship between market price and the quantity demanded—as the price increases relative to other prices, the quantity demanded decreases—is such a pervasive and important regularity that it has come to be known as the **first law of demand**. The **first law of demand** is that, everything else equal, there is an inverse relationship between the relative price of something and the quantity that is demanded. Put simply, when the relative price increases, the quantity demanded decreases, *ceteris paribus*.

Fiscal activities are the expenditures, taxes, and subsidies of government.

Fiscal policy is the use of taxes and expenditures to stabilize the economy and promote economic growth.

Costs that are independent of changes in a firm's output are **fixed costs**.

In the **flexible price model of aggregate output**, changes in aggregate demand affect only the price level and the nominal wage level. They do not affect real output because nominal wages move in equal proportion to price-level changes; as a consequence, the real wage is unaffected by changes in aggregate demand.

A **flow** is something that can only be meaningfully measured over time.

A **foreign exchange market** is a market in which one kind of money is traded for a different kind of money, that is where the currency of a foreign country can be purchased or sold.

Fractional reserve banking occurs when banks keep only a fraction of the money deposited and, more precisely, have only a fraction of their outstanding liabilities in money.

Free riding occurs when a person benefits from or uses a valuable good or service without having to pay for it.

A **free-trade area** is an agreement among a group of nations to eliminate tariffs within the group but to allow each nation to set whatever tariffs it wishes for trade with the rest of the world.

Frictional unemployment occurs when, in a dynamic economy, individuals entering the labor force or changing jobs do not immediately find a job even though there are jobs available.

Full employment occurs when all workers who desire employment at current wages are employed or, if unemployed, there are unfilled jobs available for them.

A **futures market** is a market where contracts for some future performance, usually the delivery of a good, are bought and sold now. The price of delivery of a commodity at some date in the future is the **futures price.**

G

Government spending (**g**) is that part of the aggregate real output of an economy that is purchased by the government and used to provide goods and services to its citizens.

The **government-spending multiplier** is the change in aggregate demand that occurs when government spending changes by $1.00. In its simplest form, it is equal to $1/(1 - MPC)$.

Gross domestic produce (**GDP**), is the money value of the aggregate or total output that an economy *actually* produces measured over a given period of time (such as one year), with output valued using prices prevailing during that period.

H

A **hedger** is a person or firm who wishes to minimize risks by selling a futures contract.

If two or more firms selling in the same market merge, there has been a **horizontal integration**.

Horizontal price fixing is an agreement among otherwise competitive firms that supply the same commodity to set the price at which each will sell its output.

Human capital includes the acquired skill, education, and experience that markets a person more productive. Typically, human capital takes time and other resources to acquire and cannot be easily transferred to another person.

Hyperinflation is a very high and often accelerating rate of inflation.

I

An **implementation lag** is the time between when a policy maker recognizes that there has been an aggregate shock and when an appropriate policy is implemented.

Implicit cost is a cost incurred when an alternative is sacrificed, but not actual payment is made.

Imports are commodities produced in other economies, but sold in domestic markets.

An **incentive** is anything that provides an inducement to make a particular choice.

The **incidence of a tax**, or **tax incidence**, is a determination of who actually pays a tax.

When the relative price of a good decreases, it takes less income to purchase exactly the same amount of the good, hence it is possible to purchase more because of this change in purchasing power. This effect is called the **income effect** of a price change. For example, an **income effect** occurs in the labor market when, as the wage increases, a person can earn more by working the same amount or less, and thereby chooses to take more leisure.

The **income elasticity of demand** is the percentage change in quantity demanded when income changes by 1 percent. Quantitatively, income elasticity = = %Δ demand / % Δ income. A good or service is said to be **normal** is the income elasticity is greater than 1.0 and **inferior** if the income elasticity is less than 1.0.

An **increase** or **decrease in demand** corresponds to a shift in the demand curve. Similarly, an **increase** or **decrease in supply** corresponds to a shift in the supply curve.

Increasing relative costs describes the change in relative costs as an economy shifts production from one commodity to other commodities. The amount of one commodity that must be given up in order to free resources to produce other commodities *increase* because resources are not equally productive in all activities.

A firm encounters **increasing returns to scale** or **scale economies** if, when it increases all inputs, the increase in output is proportionally greater than the increase in inputs. In this case, minimum average costs for an optimal input mix will be lower when a new firm is large or an existing firm expands. The firm will have **decreasing long-run average costs**.

Independent risks occur when a bad outcome for one person does not affect the probability that the bad outcome will happen to another person.

A person is **indifferent** between A and B if he or she feels that A and B are equally good choices.

An **individual demand schedule** or **individual demand curve** represents (1) the maximum quantity that an individual wishes to purchase at each price offered, and (2) the maximum price that an individual would be willing to pay for an additional unit of a commodity, given his or her current level of purchases of that commodity.

If, when individual incomes increase, the market demand for a commodity decreases, then the commodity is an **inferior commodity**. The effect of an increase in income on an inferior commodity is represented by a leftward shift in the demand curve; the effect of a decrease in income on an inferior commodity is represented by a rightward shift in the demand curve.

Inflation is an increase in the price level, as measured by the increase in a price index such as the CPI. With inflation, the purchasing power of money decreases. **Inflation** is a general increase in the average of all prices and is measured by a positive *percentage* change in some measure of the price level. An **inflation** is a *general* increase in dollar prices (*most* prices are increasing); The **rate of inflation** or **rate of deflation** is measured by the percentage change in a price index.

An **inflationary gap** occurs when real output is greater than potential real output, causing an upward pressure on prices.

An resource that is used to produce goods or services is an **input**.

An **insurance market** is one where an individual facing risks pays a firm to, in turn, pay them money should a bad event happen. The amount the individual pays for insurance is the **premium**.

An **intermediary** is a person or organization that specializes in trading rather than producing goods.

Investment is the production of new capital. Aggregate investment (i) is the use of aggregate real output to produce capital. **Investment (*i*)** is that part of aggregate real output purchased by firms in the form of capital goods.

The **investment multiplier** is the change in aggregate demand that occurs when investment changes by $1.00. In its simplest form, it is equal to $1/(1-MPC)$.

Inventories are those goods produced or purchased and then held by firms in anticipation of future sales. Inventories can consist of materials, supplies, work in progress, and finished goods.

The **invisible hand** is a concept first invoked by Adam Smith in *The Wealth of Nations* to describe the unintended beneficial consequences that follow from the pursuit of self-interest in certain circumstances.

K

A **Keynesian adjustment** to a change in aggregate demand is one in which real income adjust sufficiently to bring saving into line with desired investment, *but the price level is constant over the period of adjustment.*

L

The **labor force** is the part of the population that is either currently employed or looking for a job. The **unemployed** are that part of the labor force that is currently looking for a job. In the U.S., the labor force is measured as all persons 16 years of age or older who are (1) employed, or (2) actively looking for work, or (3) waiting to be recalled from a layoff.

The **labor force participation rate** is the percentage of the working-age population that is in the labor force.

Leading indicators are economic data that have historically changed before changes in real output have occurred.

Leakage is the amount of currency deposited in banks that is not deposited in checking accounts.

Legal reserves are reserves (vault cash and deposits in the Federal Reserve system) that can be used to meet Fed reserve requirements.

Leisure is time spent in any activity other than working.

Limit pricing is a business practice that occurs when a monopolist adjusts its production away from the short-run profit-maximizing position in order to lower the market price and discourage entry by competing firms.

A **logical model** is an abstraction that shows the most important elements of a complex situation in which many things interact and change, by focusing attention on a simplified version, in which only a few important things interact and change.

Long-run average cost is the minimum average cost of producing each level of output when all inputs can vary, that is, when a firm is free to substitute one input for another in organizing and making production decisions.

Long-run competitive supply describes the response of quantity supplied to changes in the market price when firms can enter or exit freely and all possible technological adjustments have been made.

A market is in **long-run equilibrium** when the economic profit that entering firms expect to earn is zero.

An economy is in **long-run equilibrium** when aggregate demand equals long run aggregate supply (potential real output).

M

Macroeconomics is the study of the overall performance of an economy.

In economics, **marginal** always refers to the last or additional or incremental unit.

Marginal cost is the *change* in the firm's costs that occurs when there is a small change in the amount of a commodity that a firm produces and sells in the market. Formally, MC (marginal cost) $= \Delta TC/\Delta q$

Marginal cost can also be the *change* in total cost when a person's consumption of something increases or decreases by a small amount.

Marginal utility or **marginal satisfaction** is the additional utility or satisfaction obtained when the consumption of one item increases but nothing else changes.

Marginal product is the additional output produced when a firm increases or decreases the use of a particular input by a small amount. Formally, MP (marginal product) $= \Delta TP$ (q)$/\Delta$quantity of an input. For example, the **marginal product of labor** is the additional output produced when an additional unit of labor is employed. The marginal product of labor will decrease as additional labor is employed if the amount of capital does not change, an effect called *diminishing marginal returns*.

The **marginal product of capital** is the amount by which the output of a firm changes when the firm changes its capital by a small amount. The **marginal product of labor** is the amount by which the output of a firm changes when the firm changes the amount of labor it employs by a small amount.

The **marginal propensity to consume** (MPC) is the amount by which consumption changes when income changes by a small amount. Formally, $MPC = \Delta c/\Delta income$ (y).

The **marginal rate of substitution in consumption** is the amount of one good that must be obtained when one unit of another good is taken away in order to make an individual indifferent between the two different allocations.

The **marginal rate of transformation** is the amount of one good that can be obtained when one fewer unit of another good is produced and resources are transferred from the second productive activity to the first.

The **marginal propensity to consume** (MPC) is the *change* in consumption per dollar *change* in income.

The **marginal propensity to save** (MPS) is defined as the *change* in saving per dollar *change* in income. When there are no taxes, the *MPS* is equal to $(1.0 - MPC)$.

Marginal revenue is the *change* in the firm's revenue that occurs when there is a small change in the amount of a commodity that a firm produces and sells in a market. Thus, MR (marginal revenue) $= \Delta TR/\Delta q$.

Marginal social benefit is the sum of marginal private benefits and marginal external benefits (if any) from increasing the level of activity (such as from consuming additional goods or services).

Marginal social cost is the sum of private marginal costs and marginal external costs (if any) associated with an increase in the level of activity (such as producing additional goods or services).

Marginal utility or **marginal satisfaction** is the amount by which utility or satisfaction changes when the amount purchased changes a small amount: MU (or MS) $=\Delta$utility (or satisfaction)$/\Delta q$

A **market** is a set of related transactions for a particular good, service, or resource, usually with money as the medium of exchange.

The **market basket** is the set of commodities whose prices are included when creating a price index.

In a market, the quantity demanded at a particular price is the sum of the desired purchases of all individuals at that price. The **market demand** for a commodity is, hence, the sum of the quantities demanded by individuals at each possible price.

A **market equilibrium** occurs when, *at a given price*, the amount that demanders wish to purchase coincides with the amount that suppliers wish to sell. At a market equilibrium, there is no excess supply or excess demand and all profitable arbitrage opportunities have been fully exploited.

A firm has **market power** if, acting on its own, it can affect the market price for the output that it produces.

Market share is the fraction of the market output produced by a single firm.

A **market subsidy** is an amount of money paid by the government either to demanders when they purchase or to suppliers when they produce a particular commodity.

Anything that is commonly used in transactions is a **medium of exchange**. Hence one of the properties of money is that it is a medium of exchange.

Microeconomics is the branch of economics concerned with the decisions of groups of individuals and firms that buy and sell in a market and with the way that individual markets work, including the effects of governmental policies and actions on specific markets.

Minimum efficient scale is the smallest output that a firm can produce and attain minimum average cost.

Money is anything commonly used in virtually all transactions to trade for goods, services, or resources. Consequently, it is frequently referred to as a **medium of exchange**. Money can be used as **unit of account**, that is, as a way of measuring economic activity in the economy.

Money aggregates as defined by the Federal Reserve Board include **M1** (currency, checking account deposits, and traveler's checks); **M2** (M1 plus money-market deposit accounts and money-market mutual-fund shares, savings accounts under $100,000 held by individuals, dollar accounts held in foreign banks (Eurodollars), and overnight repurchase agreements); **M3** (M2 plus large-denomination time deposits such as certificates of deposit or CDs, long-term repurchase agreements, and institutional money-market mutual-fund shares).

A **money-fixed** or **nominal asset** is an asset whose future payoff is a fixed amount of money; hence, its purchasing power *necessarily* changes with changes in the price level.

If there is a single producer in a market, it has market power and is called a **monopolist** or a **monopoly**. The market structure is called **monopolistic**.

Moral hazard is the ability of an individual to change either the probability or the size of the loss associated with a risk *after* purchasing insurance against the risk.

N

National income (NI) is equal to NNP minus indirect business taxes, plus subsidies to businesses.

The **national debt** is the total value of outstanding government obligations. The **deficit** is the increase in the national debt in a particular year and is equal to the shortfall between government expenditures and government revenues (g–t).

A **natural monopoly** is a business organization that arises when a single firm can produce all of the output for the market at a cost lower than a group of smaller competitive firms can.

The **natural rate of unemployment** is that rate of unemployment equal to the frictional rate of unemployment, that is, where the number of job vacancies is equal to the number of individuals with the right skills who are looking for jobs.

The **natural rate hypothesis** states that the economy deviates from the natural frictional rate of unemployment only when wages are sticky, and hence, in the long run (when wages and prices can adjust fully), the economy will have unemployment equal to the natural frictional rate.

A **negative externality** is a side-effect that exists whenever the costs associated with a particular decision are not fully borne by the person or firm making the decision but are instead imposed on third parties who are not directly involved.

Net exports (*ne*) is that part of the domestic aggregate real output used to produce commodities purchased by foreigners *less* that part of the aggregate real output of other countries used to produce commodities purchased by individuals and firms resident within the economy. When the dollar value of exports is greater than the dollar value of imports, net exports are positive. Net exports are negative when the dollar value of imports is greater than the dollar value of exports, however. If exports are equal to imports, the claim on domestic real resources for foreign uses is offset, one for one, by the claim on foreign real resources for domestic uses.

The **net export multiplier** is the change in aggregate demand that occurs when net exports change by $1.00. In its simplest form, it is the same as the investment multiplier: 1/(1–MPC).

Net national product (**NNP**) is equal to GNP minus aggregate depreciation.

Nominal refers to a measure in current dollars, whatever the purchasing power of the dollar;

The **nominal wage** is the dollar wage individuals are paid per hour or per month of work.

The **nominal interest rate** is the money obtained when $1.00 is saved for one year. Nominal interest rates increase with expected inflation, so lenders can be compensated for the diminished purchasing power of the money they lend.

If, when individual incomes increase, the market demand for a commodity increases, then the commodity is a **normal commodity**. The effect of an increase in income on a normal commodity is represented by a rightward shift in the demand curve; the effect of a decrease in income on a normal commodity is represented by a leftward shift in the demand curve.

Consumption is **noncompetitive** or **nonexhaustive** if the consumption of a good by one person does not affect another person's ability to consume the same good.

Consumption is **nonexclusive** if one person cannot easily prevent a second person from consuming what he or she has purchased.

Nonprice competition is competition between firms based on aspects other than price. When firms change the quality of what is sold or include extras like service in order to attract customers rather than changing the price they are competing on terms other than price.

Normal rate of return occurs when the owner of a firm or asset receives what he or she could expect to earn, on average, in the best alternative elsewhere in the economy.

O

Okun's law (or rule-of-thumb): For every 2 to 3 percent that actual output falls below potential real output, unemployment will increase by 1 percentage point.

Opportunistic behavior is the taking advantage of a commitment made by a person so as to benefit oneself and disadvantage the person making the commitment.

The **opportunity cost** of a choice is the value to an individual of the *best alternative* that the individual could have chosen but did not. Put slightly differently, the opportunity cost of a choice is the value of the best-forgone opportunity.

An **open market operation** is a purchase or sale of U.S. government securities by the Fed. When the Fed purchases government securities, the money supply increases; when it sells government securities, the money supply decreases.

Overemployment occurs whenever the amount of labor employed by firms exceeds that which individuals would be willing to provide, compared with a period when the nominal wage changes in the same proportion as the increase in the price level.

P

The point at which an economy moves from an expansion to a contraction is the **peak** (highest point) of the business cycle.

Per capita GDP is GDP divided by the number of persons in the economy.

A *per se* approach to a particular action or activity determines its legality or illegality solely on the basis of a general legal rule.

Perfect competition is a market structure where no single decision maker (either demander or seller) can influence the market price. In perfect competition, decision makers are *price takers*, that is, they make decisions based on the observed or expected market price.

Personal income (PI) is equal to NI minus the total of social security contributions and corporate income taxes and undistributed corporate profits, plus transfer payments.

Point elasticity is the ratio of the price and quantity demanded multiplied by the inverse of the slope of the demand curve at that quantity and price. That is, point elasticity of demand $=p/q \times 1/\text{slope}$

Portfolio diversification is a way of lowering risks in which an individual divides his or her wealth among a number of different assets (such as different stocks, different bonds, real estate, bank accounts) rather than holding all wealth in a single asset.

A **positive externality** is a side-effect that exists whenever the benefits associated with a particular decision are not fully considered by, and do not accrue to, the person or firm making the decision.

The **potential money multiplier** is equal to 1/RR, where RR is the required reserve ratio or fraction of demand deposits that banks must hold as reserves. It is the maximum amount by which the money supply can increase if the Federal Reserve increases the currency in circulation by $1.00.

Potential real GDP is a measure of the aggregate or total real output that an economy *could* produce if it used its scarce resources fully and efficiently, that is, it is a measure of potential real output.

Potential real output is that output an economy can produce when it employs its resources fully and efficiently. Thus, an economy's potential real output is determined by its natural resources available, the technologies that it has developed or acquired, the amount of capital that it has accumulated, and the amount of labor that individuals are willing to provide. If an economy fully and efficiently employs its scarce resources, the aggregate output supplied to the economy will be equal to the economy's **potential real output**.

Predatory pricing is a business practice that occurs when a firm prices below its costs in order to drive a competing firm from the market.

The **present value** is the value today of a specified sum or money to be received in the future. It is equal to the amount of money that one would have to have today which would, with compound interest, grow to be equal to the specified future sum. The **present discounted value** is the sum of the present value of a stream of payments made in the future.

A **price ceiling** is a legal limit on how high the market price of a commodity may be. To be effective, the price ceiling must be below the current equilibrium market price and must be enforced by the government.

Price discrimination is a pricing behavior in which a firm charges different customers different prices for the same commodity or when it charges the same customer different prices for the same commodity when consumption of the commodity increase.

A **price floor** is a legal limit on how low the market price of a commodity may be. To be effective, the price floor must be above the current equilibrium market price and must be enforced by the government.

A **price index** in period t is

$$I_t = \frac{p_t}{p_b} \times 100$$

where b is the base year, p_b is the price of a market basket in the base year, and p_t is the price of a market basket in period t. A **price index** is a measure of the overall price level in an economy. Commonly used price indices for the U.S. economy include the *consumer price index (CPI)* and the *producer price index (PPI)*.

The **price level** is the average of prices which are measured in dollar terms or, more generally, in money terms.

An individual who delegates or engages someone else (an **agent**) to make certain decisions is a **principal**. A principle-agent problem occurs when the principal and the agent have different goals or objectives and hence when the agent doesn't act in the interest of the principle. As a consequence, principals have to design, where possible, arrangements that create incentives for their agents to act in ways consistent with the interests of the principal.

The **producer price index (PPI)** is a measure of what is happening, in general, to the prices of a market basket of inputs commonly purchased by firms.

A **production possibilities frontier (PPF)** is the boundary between the output mixes that can be produced and those that, given scarce resources and available technologies, cannot.

Producer surplus is the difference between what firms receive for producing a certain output and what they would have been willing to receive and still make the same production decision.

Productivity is the level of output that can be produced by a specified level of inputs. Productivity is usually measured by the output per hour worked by nonfarm labor.

Productivity growth is the rate of change in the level of productivity. Productivity growth is most often measured by the percentage change in an index of output per hour worked by nonfarm labor.

Profits are the difference between revenues and costs, where costs include explicit or accounting costs and implicit or opportunity costs and normal rate of return for the owner of the firm. Profits defined this way are zero when the owner is just earning a normal rate of return. Economic profits are being earned if the owner is earning more than a normal rate of return. Economic profits are negative (that is, there are economic losses), if the owner is earning less than a normal rate of return *even if* accounting profits are positive.

Property rights are the legal and social arrangements that allow a person owning a resource to exclude others from using the resource, now and in the future.

A **public good** is any good or service whose consumption by one person is *not* affected by the simultaneous consumption of the *same* good or service by someone else.

Purchasing power is the amount of goods and services a dollar will buy. Purchasing power changes with changes in the price level.

Q

Quantity demanded refers to the amount demanded at a *single point* along a demand curve. That is, the quantity demanded is the amount of a commodity that demanders are willing to purchase from a market at a specific market price.

Any specific price-quantity combination—for example, a single point on a supply curve—is referred to as the **quantity supplied.** Thus, the quantity supplied is the amount of a commodity that suppliers are willing to provide to a market at a specific market price.

The **quantity theory of money** suggests that the demand for money is *proportional* to nominal aggregate income or that the demand for real money balances is *proportional* to real output.

A **quota** is a quantitative limit on the number or amount of imports allowed into a country that is set by the importing country. It has the same effect on the domestic price as a tariff that leads to an equivalent level of imports.

A **quota rent** is the revenue obtained by purchasing at the world price and selling within an economy at a higher domestic price when imports are limited by a quota.

R

The **rate of return** is the explicit or implicit payment that the owners of capital get each year as a fraction of the amount of financial resources they have provided to the firm. The **normal rate of return**, also called **normal profits**, is the amount the owner could expect to warn, on average, elsewhere in the economy.

Rational behavior occurs when individuals can compare among options, are consistent in their comparisons, and choose those options they prefer.

Rational expectations are the best guesses or forecasts that are made using all the relevant information available.

Real refers to a dollar measure, but one that also takes into account any changes in the purchasing power of the dollar. (Measures in real terms are sometimes called **constant-dollar** measures.)

A **real asset** is one whose purchasing power does not *necessarily* change with changes in the price level. The price of the real asset may increase as the price level increases (or decrease as the price level decreases), although it does not necessarily do so.

Real aggregate output, or **real GDP,** can be measured by dividing the dollar value of aggregate output measured using current market prices (**nominal GDP**) by a suitable price index. **Real GDP** is the real value of aggregate or total output that an economy *actually* produces, with output valued using a base-period price level to eliminate the effects of inflation or deflation.

The **real interest rate** is the amount of additional goods that can be purchases when $1.00 is saved for one year.

The stock of money (M) available in an economy at any given time, measured in terms of the purchasing power of a dollar (P), is called **real money balances**.

The **real wage** is the purchasing power of the dollar wage payment.

Periods of declining real output (contractions) are referred to as **recessions**.

Periods of increasing real output (expansions) are called **recoveries**.

A **recognition lag** is the delay between the time at which a macroeconomic shock occurs and when it is understood to have occurred. A **sizing lag** is the delay between the time a macroeconomic shock occurs, is recognized and when the size of the shock is known. An **implementation lag** is the delay between the time at which a macroeconomic shock is recognized and appropriate policies are implemented. An **effect lag** is the delay between the time at which a policy is implemented and its effect is fully felt in the economy.

The **rediscount interest rate** or **discount rate** (r_d) is the interest rate the Fed charges for loans made to banks to meet reserve requirements.

Relative production cost is the amount of one commodity that must be given up to produce one additional unit of a second commodity.

A **relative price** is the amount of some good that must be given up to get one additional unit of some other good.

Rents, also called **economic rents**, are economic profits or returns greater than normal that do not disappear with the entry of new firms.

Rent seeking is the unproductive use of resources which are devoted to getting rents.

Reputation is the perception that individuals have of a commodity's or other individual's attributes.

The **required reserve ratio** (**RR**) is the minimum fraction of checking account deposits that the Fed determines a bank must hold in the form of reserves.

Resale price maintenance, sometimes called **vertical price fixing**, is a practice in which a minimum price level is set and maintained through an agreement between a manufacturer or wholesaler and a retailer. The retailer can sell the product that is purchased from the wholesaler or producer only at or above the specified price.

A **restriction on entry** is a legal limitation on who can sell in a particular market.

Restrictive covenants are private agreements among a group of landowners about how each owner can use his or her land.

Resources are the available inputs with which an economy can produce outputs. Important categories of resources include **labor**, the effort and ability that humans put into producing output; **capital**, the production inputs that are produced and then used to produce other commodities; and **natural resources**, the inputs that nature provides. **Technology** is the method by which the resources are combined to produce outputs.

A **risk-averse** person prefers secure outcomes to risky ones and, for this reason, is willing to pay some amount of money to be insured against possible risky outcomes.

A **rule-of-reason approach** to a particular action or activity considers potential benefits as well as potential harm with determining its legality. That is, legality is determined by particular circumstances, not by a general legal rule.

S

Saving is forgone consumption. Essentially, saving allows individuals to transfer income from today to the future. **Aggregate Saving** occurs when individuals choose to consume less than the economy produces.

Something is **scarce** if we want more than is available.

Nonbusiness cycle fluctuations in real output that occur on a regular basis throughout the year are called **seasonal variations**.

The **second law of demand** is the observation that it is easier to find substitutes over a longer period of time than it is to immediately respond to a price change. As a consequence, the elasticity of demand increases with time.

Self-interest is the pursuit of options, consideration of choices, and response to particular circumstances in terms of how those options, choices, and responses affect the individual making the choices, and not how they affect others.

When individuals avoid work or work less intensively than is expected of them, they are said to be **shirking**. Shirking may undermine the productivity of a firm, particularly when output is produced by teams and shirking is difficult to easily detect.

Shocks are unplanned changes in either aggregate demand or aggregate supply.

The **short run** is that period of time over which a firm's capital stock is fixed. Or, in slightly different terms, the short run is that period of time over which a firm can increase its output only by employing more labor and other resources together with the same amount of capital.

Short-run aggregate supply is the actual real output produced when the employment of resources changes as the price level changes.

The **shut down rule** is that a firm should stop production if its revenues at current market prices are less than variable costs.

The **social structure** is the collection of formal and informal rules, norms, expectations and constraints that create incentives and thereby determine the way that individuals interact or compete with one another.

A **specific commodity tax** is a tax on the sale of a commodity that is fixed in dollar terms and, hence, does not depend upon the price at which the taxed commodity sells.

A **speculator** is a person or firm who buys with the intention to sell the commodity at some future date.

Sticky wages are nominal wage payments that do not change immediately in equal proportion to changes in the price level.

Stabilization or **countercyclical policy** is a government plan designed to minimize the adverse effects of shocks on employment and/or the price level. An **expansionary policy** attempts to stimulate aggregate demand; a **contractionary policy** attempts to dampen aggregate demand.

Stagflation is a term that was coined to describe the condition of the economy when both inflation and rising unemployment occur at the same time.

Structural unemployment occurs when there are individuals who would be willing to work but who do not have the skills, training, or education necessary to fill available job vacancies.

A **subsidy** is a sum of money paid to a supplier or demander.

Two commodities are **substitutes** if, when the price of one increases, the demand for the other commodity increases. Conversely, if the price of a commodity decreases, the demand for the substitute commodity decreases.

When the relative price of a good decreases, the good becomes relatively less expensive than other goods and an individual will substitute this good for other goods. This effect is called the **substitution effect** of a price change. For example, in the labor market, a **substitution effect** occurs when, as the wage increases, a person substitutes work for leisure, thereby working more.

Sunk costs are those expenditures that have already been made or, more precisely, those costs that were incurred before a current choice is made, and that, as a consequence, are not affected by the current choice.

Supply-side economics is an economic perspective that is concerned with the effects of government policies on incentives and, thus, on the level and growth rate of potential real output.

Supply (also called **market supply**) is the maximum quantity that suppliers would be willing to provide to the market over a particular period of time for all possible market prices. That is, supply refers to the entire supply schedule or supply curve.

A **supply curve** is a graph of a supply schedule where, by convention, price is measured along the vertical axis and the quantity supplied is measured along the horizontal axis.

A **supply schedule** is a list of the *maximum* amount that suppliers are willing to provide to a market at each market price over a specified period of time.

T

Tacit collusion occurs when firms independently choose actions that create and exploit collective market power, but don't explicitly agree.

A **tariff** or **duty** is a tax imposed on a foreign-produced good, but not on the same good when it is produced domestically. A **specific tariff** is fixed in terms of dollars per unit imported; an **ad valorem tariff** is set as a percentage of the per unit import price.

The **tax multiplier** for a lump-sum tax is the change in aggregate demand that follows a $1 change in lump-sum taxes. In its simplest form, this multiplier is equal to $MPC/(1 - MPC)$.

Technology is the particular method by which tools and work effort are combined to produce goods and services. Technology is often embodied in the tools themselves. For example, a computer chip is a capital good; it is also a tool that embodies a technology that increases production when applied to particular activities.

A **tied sale** or **tie-in sale** occurs when, in order to purchase one commodity, a person must also purchase a second commodity.

Total cost can be divided into **variable costs**, which change when output changes, and **fixed costs**, which do not vary with changes in output.

Total product is the output a firm produces in a given period of time.

Total Revenue is equal to the output (q) a firm sells multiplied by the price (p) at which the output is sold. If there are no commodity taxes, the **total revenue** for suppliers is equal to **total expenditure**.

The **total revenue test for elasticity** is if total revenue increases when market price increases, demand is inelastic, while if total revenue decreases when market price increases, demand is elastic.

Transaction costs are the opportunity costs of using productive resources, including time and effort, in making trades rather than in producing goods and services for consumption or other purposes.

The point at which an economy moves from a contraction to an expansion is the **trough** (lowest point) of the business cycle.

A **transferable emission permit** is the legal right, which can be traded among potential polluters, to dump a specified amount of pollutants into the environment.

A change in the average level of real output over time is the **trend growth path** of the economy.

Transfer payments are money taken through taxation from one individual and provided to another individual. Social security payments, for example, are transfer payments.

U

Unemployed resources are productive resources that are idle or unused.

The **unemployment rate** is the percentage of the labor force that is unemployed.

Unitization is the creation of single ownership and control of resources whose uses might conflict to create an externality.

Money is a **unit of account** when it is used as a common way of measuring relative prices, the value of production, etc.

V

Costs that change with changes in a firm's level of production are called **variable costs**. Costs that are independent of the level of production are **fixed costs**.

Velocity (V) is a measure of the number of times an average dollar circulates during a one-year period.

Vertical integration occurs when several steps in a production and marketing process are consolidated within a single firm. Mergers between firms at different levels in a production process are called **vertical mergers**.

A **voluntary export restraint** (**VER**) is a quantitative limit on the number or amount of exports shipped to another country that is set by the exporting country.

W

Wealth is the sum of all of an individual's assets net of any liabilities. Wealth changes as individuals save or dissave and as the value of assets held increases or decreases.

Work is an activity an individual engages in that increases the amount of goods and services the individual can consume.

Index